Manual of Curatorship

A Guide to Museum Practice

Manual of Curatorship

A Guide to Museum Practice

Butterworths
London · Boston · Durban · Singapore · Sydney · Toronto · Wellington

First published, 1984
© Museums Association 1984

British Library Cataloguing in Publication Data
Manual of curatorship.
  1. Museum techniques
  I. Thompson, John M. A.   II. Prince, David R.
  069   AM111

  ISBN 0–408–01411–3

Library of Congress Cataloging in Publication Data
Main entry under title:

Manual of curatorship.

  Includes index.
  1. Museum techniques—Handbooks, manuals, etc.
  2. Museums—Administration—Handbooks, manuals, etc.
  I. Thompson, John M. A.   II. Prince, David R.
  AM151.M32   1984   069.5   84–4965
  ISBN 0–408–01411–3

Printed in Great Britain by
Hartnoll Print, Bodmin, Cornwall

Typeset by Phoenix Photosetting, Chatham

Foreword

We are confident that this book will satisfy a long-felt need within the museums profession for an authoritative work covering all aspects of museum skills for the practising curator.

Its multi-disciplinary approach and emphasis on the state and status of contemporary curatorship has been designed to enhance the understanding of recent advances and techniques required in the collection, conservation, management and presentation of objects from both the natural and cultural heritage.

There is growing awareness of the role which museums play in the educational and leisure activities of society, and of the increasing pressures to provide a cost-effective and improved service, which calls for the greatest expertise in all who care for the nation's heritage. This *Manual* will, it is hoped, contribute to the achievement of this aim.

The Association would like to record its appreciation of the grant from the Office of Arts and Libraries, H.M. Government, for the period 1981–1983, which enabled this project to come to fruition.

The Lord Montagu of Beaulieu
President, The Museums Association

Sir Arthur Drew, KCB, JP
Chairman, The Museums and Galleries Comission

Acknowledgements

On behalf of the Editorial Board, I wish to thank the many members of the museum profession who have assisted in the project, beginning with the original working party comprising: Mr D. Addison, Mr R. Foster, Mr G. Stansfield, and Mr M. Watkins, as well as all contributors to the *Manual*, including representatives of the various specialist groups, related organizations, and interested parties who have submitted comments. I am grateful to Mr H. Coutts for his advice on those aspects of the text which have reference to the particular conditions in Scotland. On the legal aspects of the *Manual*, the Editorial Board has benefitted from the assistance of Dr J. Phillips, Department of Law, University of Durham, and from Mr D. J. Chapman, formerly Deputy County Solicitor, Tyne and Wear County Council, with the latter contributing a note on interpretation of the law relating to museums.

The Editorial Board is grateful for the help given to Dr David R. Prince by the staff of the UNESCO–ICOM Documentation Centre, Paris, and in particular the Head, Snr Louis Monreal, for access to material in the library, and to Mme Suzanne Pommellette for translation services.

The work for the *Manual* has been funded entirely by a research grant awarded by the Department of Education and Science, Office of Arts and Libraries, H.M. Government, and I wish to record the thanks of the Board for the services given by the staff of the Office both prior to, and during the currency of, the research project, especially Mr M. Hodges, Miss G. Dishart, and Mr V. Westlake.

As well as overseeing the details of the project, members of the Editorial Board have in a number of instances prepared their own specialist contributions and have in addition edited sections of the *Manual* and written supporting commentaries. The contribution of two members of the Editorial Board, Mr G. D. Lewis and Dr A. J. Duggan has been herculean, as illustrated by the size and complexity of their work, and to both, as well as to the other members, my personal thanks are recorded. The task of the Editorial Board has been lightened considerably by the work of Dr D. R. Prince who has been responsible for compiling the *Manual*, and co-ordinating the research programme within a strict timetable. It has been largely due to Dr Prince's careful attention to the many details of the project and his ability to communicate with all individuals and organizations concerned that the project has come so successfully to fruition. Thanks are also due to Bernadette Higgins-McLoughlin for the secretarial assistance given to Dr Prince in the day-to-day administration of the project.

Finally, I wish to express the thanks of the Editorial Board to Mr M. Ware and Mr R. Cole, of Butterworth Scientific Limited, for their skill in handling the publication arrangements, and to Ms A. McDermid of Curtis Brown for advice on the publishing contract.

John M. A. Thompson
Project Director and Chairman, Editorial Board

Contributors

Rosemary E. Allen, BA, AMA, Keeper of Social History, Beamish North of England Open Air Museum, Beamish

Michael B. Alt, BSC, PhD, FSS, M. B. Alt & Associates, London (formerly Head of Visitor Resources Group, The Britsh Museum (Natural History), London)

Frank Atkinson, OBE, MA, BSC, FSA, FMA, Director, Beamish North of England Open Air Museum, Beamish

Donald M. Bailey, FSA, FMA, Curator, Department of Greek and Roman Antiquities, The British Museum, London

Iain Bain, Publications Manager, The Tate Gallery, London

Douglas A. Bassett, BSC PhD, FGS, FMA, Director, The National Museum of Wales, Cardiff

Michael Belcher, NDD, MPhil, FSIAD, FBIM, FBDS, FRSA, FMA, Head of School of Art and Design, The Polytechnic, Huddersfield

Roger Bland, BA, Curator, Department of Coins and Medals, The British Museum, London

David Bomford, BSC, MSC, Restorer, Department of Conservation. The National Gallery, London

P. Michael Bottomley, BA, DAA, Assistant Archivist, The West Yorkshire Archive Service, Wakefield

Alan Bowness, CBE, MA, Director, The Tate Gallery, London

Robert Bracegirdle, BSC, ASDC, CCol, AMA, Keeper of Technology, The Leicestershire Museum of Technology, Leicester

Peter C. D. Brears, DipAD, FSA, FMA, Director, Leeds City Museums, Leeds

Roy D. Brigden, BA, FMA, Keeper, The Museum of English Rural Life, The University of Reading, Reading

Peter Cannon–Brookes, MA, PhD, FRSA, FMA, FIIC, Keeper, Department of Art, The National Museum of Wales, Cardiff

P. Graham Carter, MIBiol, Head of Interpretation and Education, The National Motor Museum, Beaulieu

David J. Chapman, LLB, formerly, Deputy County Solicitor, Tyne and Wear Metropolitan County Council, Newcastle upon Tyne

Francis Cheetham, OBE, BA, FMA, Director, Norfolk Museums Service, Norwich

David T–D Clarke, MA, FSA, FRNS, FMA, Curator, Colchester and Essex Museum, Colchester

Michael Compton, BA, Keeper of Museum Services, The Tate Gallery, London

Neil Cossons, OBE, DSOCSC, MA, FSA, FMA, Director, The National Maritime Museum, London (formerly Director, Ironbridge Gorge Museum Trust, Ironbridge)

D. Gareth Davies, BA, FSA, FMA, Director, St Albans Museums, St Albans

Geoffrey T. Denford, MA, AMA, Keeper of Archaeology, Winchester City Museums, Winchester

P. Michael Diamond, MA, FMA, Director, Birmingham Museums and Art Gallery, Birmingham

Philip S. Doughty, BSC, MSC, FGS, FMA, Keeper of Geology, The Ulster Museum, Belfast

Antony J. Duggan, MD, BS, FRCP, FIBiol, DTM, FMA, Director, The Wellcome Museum of Medical Science, London

Dennis Farr, MA, DLitt, FRSA, FMA, Director of Courtauld Institute of Galleries, University of London, London

Alexander Fenton, MA, BA, DLitt, FSA, FSA SCOT, Director, The National Museum of Antiquities of Scotland, Edinburgh

Anne E. Fleming, MA, Keeper, Department of Film, The Imperial War Museum, London

Richard A. Foster, MA, BSCEcon, FSA, FMA, Director, Merseyside County Museums, Liverpool

Jean M. Glover, CertEd, ConCert, FIIC, FMA, Senior Textile Conservation Officer, North Western Museum and Art Gallery Service, Blackburn

Frank Greenaway, MA, MSC, PhD, CChem, FRC, FSA, FMA, formerly Keeper, Department of Chemistry, The Science Museum, London

Steven A. Griggs, BSC, PhD, Steven Griggs & Associates, London (formerly Evaluation Coordinator, Visitor Resources Section, The British Museum (Natural History), London)

John C. Hallam, AMA, Group Museum Officer (Science and Engineering), Museum of Science and Engineering Newcastle upon Tyne

Max Hebditch, MA, FSA, FMA, Director, The Museum of London, London

C. Velson Horie, BSC, Dipcons, Keeper of Conservation, The Manchester Museum, The University of Manchester, Manchester

Michael V. Hounsome, BSC, PhD, MIBiol, MBOU, Keeper of Zoology, The Manchester Museum, The University of Manchester, Manchester

Francis M. P. Howie, BSC, Senior Scientific Officer, The British Museum (Natural History), London

John P. C. Kent, BA, PhD, FSA, Keeper, Department of Coins and Medals, The British Museum, London

Hannah P. Lane, FIIC, Conservator, Department of Scientific Research and Conservation, The British Museum, London

Elizabeth R. Lewis, BA, FMA, Curator, Winchester City Museums, Winchester

Geoffrey D. Lewis, MA, FSA, FMA, Director, Department of Museum Studies, The University of Leicester, Leicester

Stephen Locke, BSC, FGS, FMA, Director, The Area Museum Council for the South West, Buckland Abbey, Devon

Jane McAusland, FIIC, Independent Conservator and Restorer of Works of Art on Paper, Suffolk

George Y. McInnes, concert, techcon, Senior Technician (Taxidermy), Merseyside County Museums, Liverpool

Keith B. Priestman, FIIC, Keeper of Conservation, Merseyside County Museums, Liverpool

David R. Prince, BEd, PhD, FRGS, Prince Research Consultants, London

Elizabeth Pye, MA, FIIC, Lecturer in Conservation, Department of Archaeological Conservation and Materials Science, The Institute of Archaeology, The University of London, London

D. Andrew Roberts, MSC, MIInfsc, Secretary, The Museum Documentation Association, Duxford

Sarah Staniforth, BA, Dipcons, Higher Scientific Officer, Scientific Department, The National Gallery, London

Geoffrey Stansfield, BSC, FMA, Lecturer, Department of Museum Studies, The University of Leicester, Leicester

Sheila M. Stone, MA, AMA, Keeper of Archaeology, The Verulamium Museum, St Albans

Patrick V. Sudbury, MSC, PhD, AMA, Deputy Director, Merseyside County Museums, Liverpool

John M. A. Thompson, BA, MA, FMA, Director of Museums and Galleries, Tyne and Wear County Council Museums, Newcastle upon Tyne

Giles Velarde, FSIAD, Exhibitions Officer, The Geological Museum, London

David J. Viner, BA, FSA, FMA, Curator, The Corinium Museum, Cirencester

Alan Warhurst, MA, FSA, FMA, Director, The Manchester Museum, The University of Manchester, Manchester

Christopher J. Wheatley, Dipcons, Conservator, The National Maritime Museum, London

Sir David M. Wilson, Kt, MA, DrFil, PhilDr, LittD, FBA, MRIA, FSA, Director, The British Museum, London

Contents

Section III: Visitor Services
Section Editors
*Douglas A. Bassett and
David R. Prince*

Section IV: Management and Administration
Section Editor
John M. A. Thompson

Introduction

John M. A. Thompson and David R. Prince

The Manual of Curatorship: A Guide to Museum Practice has been compiled to be of use to all those concerned with the management, administration, and professional care of museum collections. It fulfills a long-expressed requirement for a comprehensive reference work on museum practice by those involved in the diversity of activities which characterise museums in the present times. Although its value will lie primarily in its usefulness for the professional museum officer and the student preparing for a career in museums, it will also be of relevance for those who form the governing bodies responsible for museums whether local authority, governmental or independent. The work of the growing number of supportive bodies, such as friends of museums and associations of volunteers, as well as related organisations which make regular use of the services that museums provide, should benefit from the information it contains.

This *Manual* has evolved from the findings of a working partly established by the Education Committee of the Museums Association and was guided by a synopsis for a Manual prepared by Dr. A. J. Duggan which had been previously issued to assist in the Association's training programme for museum curators. After consulting widely with representatives of the museum profession, and with the Department of Museum Studies, University of Leicester, the working party recommended that a period of research was required to establish in detail the scope of the work, the contents, and the form in which it should be published. As a result of a two-year research grant awarded by the Office of Arts and Libraries this work was able to proceed under the aegis of an Editorial Board, with Dr. D. R. Prince appointed as the full-time research co-ordinator responsible for the compilation of the *Manual*.

At an early meeting, the Board determined that the *Manual* would be an edited work based on original contributions from museum professionals arising from their own experience. The overall aim of the *Manual* was to present the current issues involved in curatorship and, where appropriate, to suggest future trends and directions. As a standard work of reference, it would consist of practical material based on a firm theoretical foundation. It was established in the early meetings of the Editorial Board that it would be a fundamental policy that the arrangement of the *Manual* should reflect the multi-disciplinary nature of curatorship and that it was therefore not necessary, or indeed at all practical, to incorporate detailed material of a specialist nature if this could be found in other existing published sources available to the curator. It was therefore agreed that the requirement for specialist information could best be met by the References being as extensive and up to date as possible, with annotations where necessary, thus serving as a primary bibliographical source.

The *Manual* is arranged in four sections and examines the key functions of museums, namely the management of, and research into the collections they maintain, and the presentation of the collections to, and their use by, the visiting public. The role of the museum as a social institution and the way its philosophical and ethical foundations have developed is examined, as well as the issues involved in the administration and management of resources other than the collections, including finance, buildings and personnel.

Although the major emphasis in the *Manual* is placed on the experience of the museum profession in the United Kingdom, account has been taken of the institutions and wider social forces that have affected the development of museums both in the past as well as in the present. Due to the wide-spread differences between countries, and as a matter of editorial policy, specific references to the legislative

1

implications of curatorship have been made in notes within the relevant articles, with an interpretation of the law affecting museums provided in Appendix I. With the application of scientific and technological advances to the key functions of museums, and as museums continue to evolve in response to changing social and economic factors, there are new and exciting opportunities both now and in the future for meeting the needs of the museum user. In turn, the role of the curator and other museum professionals, in all departments, is changing as improved or new skills are required in the face of these developments. It is therefore inevitable that parts of the *Manual* will become out of date within a relatively brief period. In order that the *Manual* should continue to reflect the current state of museum practice, the Editorial Board has made provision for it to be revised at regular intervals, by commissioning new material, and for this to be incorporated into future editions.

SECTION ONE

THE MUSEUM CONTEXT

Section Editor

Geoffrey D. Lewis

1

Introduction

Geoffrey D. Lewis

The story of the development of museums is still largely unwritten. For this reason, more attention has been paid to setting the scene in this section than might otherwise have been necessary. But even so there are many gaps in the narrative. When it comes to grouping museums in the essays that follow, it is readily apparent that even a traditional approach does not accommodate them successfully. Indeed, the museums of Britain represent a diversity of institutions, unequalled elsewhere in the world. From the British Museum, maintaining its universal and encyclopaedic stance (albeit now within the humanities) to the smallest museum catering for the interests of its community, all contribute to the fascinatingly variegated, some would say idiosyncratic, museum scene in Britain.

Closer examination of Britain's museums reveals that the early global, encyclopaedic concept is also present in some of the larger provincial museums – Birmingham, Glasgow and Liverpool, for example, or, in the University sector at Cambridge and Oxford. Most of these are on a scale and with a quality to their collections which stand the closest comparison with the principal museums of many nations. Britain's museums are a product of their country's history. The influence of a colonial power with wide trade connections not only carried the museum idea out of Europe, but had its impact on collections at home and, indeed, on the concept of the nation's heritage. It is no accident that England contains no national museum of antiquities, history or natural history in the continental European style. It is this lack of a nationalistic expression nationally that provides such strength to the predominantly regional museums centred on and financed by major urban centres such as Bristol, Leicester and Sheffield. Much of the country's national heritage is to be found in such centres and accounts for their richness.

But if museums are the primary vehicle for housing and preserving the nation's heritage, it does not follow that the major conurbations and their museums necessarily coincide with areas of rich heritage. And so it is that the museums of, say, Chester, Chichester, Colchester, St Albans or York, all in their way equally bear a vital role in relation to the archaeological and historic heritage. Smaller museums, with resources even more slender, are also contributing to the same goal for their immediate locality. To the older, established museums have been added in recent years new varieties, the idea of the 'museum service' and the so-called 'independent museums', still with similar goals but often different emphases. Like some of their public-sector counterparts, a few of the independent museums can also be regarded as national in their approach and importance.

If the history of museums reveals that Britain was in the vanguard of public museum provision, it also shows that the art of collection, conserving, inventorying, displaying and interpreting cultural property is of far greater antiquity. Despite this, the theory of museums and their practice, unlike many more recent professions, remains under-developed. Curators throughout the ages have sometimes been persuaded to commit to paper what they are doing, but very rarely to explain why they are doing it, except in the most general terms. The satisfaction derived from technical accomplishment and identification with contributions to one of the many disciplines represented in museum collections, have tended to eclipse thought on the *raison d'etre* of museums themselves. As a result, museums have been followers rather than innovators of change. This ought not to be so. Nevertheless, museums have survived massive social change and today, in a smaller world of mass travel, greater leisure, better education, increased environmental awareness, and more conscious economic goals, museums play an increasingly important role in society. To achieve this there has been a marked shift of emphasis towards improved public facilities, reflected particularly, but by no means exclusively, in the new types of museum. This has brought with it vastly improved technical competence in display and exhibition, educational work and other visitor facilities. Apart from better public service, this has resulted in awards for the 'museum of the year' and good museum guides, lay concepts based on criteria to assess a museum's visible public facade. Welcome though these may be in the promotion of the museum idea, those within the profession are equally concerned with well-kept and accessible collections, their supporting records and all that goes with museum work.

A balanced approach to the standards of museum provision and curatorial practice is necessary. Training, in which Britain has been at the forefront, codes of ethics and the accreditation of museums are all contributing to this. But despite recommendations by both government bodies and the profession to achieve some semblance of structure, order and co-ordination to museums in Britain, which would bring recognized standards, these have so far not been implemented. Nor is there a mandatory requirement to preserve the nation's cultural heritage in museums. It is against this background that curatorial practice has developed in Britain, borrowing heavily in many areas from a variety of disciplines.

Bibliography

BAZIN, G. (1967) *The Museum Age,* Dessor, Brussels

BRITISH ASSOCIATION FOR THE ADVANCEMENT OF SCIENCE REPORT OF THE COMMITTEE ON THE PROVINCIAL MUSEUMS OF THE UNITED KINGDOM, *Report of the British Association for the Advancement of Science 1887,* 97–130, London. Also 1888, 124–132.

COMMITTEE ON NATIONAL MUSEUMS AND GALLERIES IN SCOTLAND (1981) *A Heritage for Scotland,* HMSO, Glasgow

DEPARTMENT OF EDUCATION AND SCIENCE (1973). *Provincial Museums and Galleries,* HMSO, London

DEPARTMENT OF EDUCATION FOR NORTHERN IRELAND (1978), *Regional Museums in Northern Ireland,* HMSO, Belfast

DUGGAN, A. J. (1982), 'Professional ethics: introduction of working party report', *Museums J.* **82**(3), supplement, 10–11

FLOWER, SIR W. H. (1898), *Essays on Museums and Other Subjects,* MacMillan, London

GREENWOOD, T. (1888), *Museums and Art Galleries,* Simpkin Marshall, London

INTERNATIONAL COUNCIL OF MUSEUMS, *Treatise on Museology,* Volume 1, Paris (forthcoming)

MACGREGOR, A. (1983), *Tradescant's Rarities,* Oxford University Press, Oxford

MARKHAM, S. F. (1938), *The Museums and Art Galleries of the British Isles,* CUKT, T. & A. Constable, Edinburgh

MIERS, SIR H. A. (1938), *A Report on the Public Museums of the British Isles,* CUKT, T. & A. Constable, Edinburgh

MILLER, E. (1973), *That Noble Cabinet,* Andre Deutsch, London

MURRAY, D. (1904), *Museums: Their History and Their Use,* J. MacLehose and Sons, Glasgow

ROYAL COMMISSION ON NATIONAL MUSEUMS AND GALLERIES, (1928 and 1929), *Interim Report: Final Report,* parts 1 and 2, HMSO, London

STANDING COMMISSION ON MUSEUMS AND GALLERIES (1963), *Survey of Provincial Museums and Galleries* (The Rosse Report), HMSO, London

STANDING COMMISSION ON MUSEUMS AND GALLERIES (1967), *Area Museum Services, 1963–66,* HMSO, London

STANDING COMMISSION ON MUSEUMS AND GALLERIES (1977), *Report on University Museums,* HMSO, London

STANDING COMMISSION ON MUSEUMS AND GALLERIES (1981), *Report on Museums in Wales,* HMSO, London

TAYLOR, F. H. (1948), *The Taste of Angels,* Little, Brown & Co., Boston, USA

THOMPSON, J. (1982), 'The accreditation scheme of the Museums Association 1974–82', *Museums J.* **82**(2), 67–69

WITTLIN, A. (1970), *Museums: In Search of a Usable Future,* MIT Press, Cambridge, Massachusetts, USA

2

Collections, collectors and museums: a brief world survey

Geoffrey D. Lewis

If the term museum[1] is taken to mean a 'non-profit-making, permanent institution, in the service of society and of its development and open to the public' (ICOM, 1974) then the phenomenon of the museum is of comparatively recent origin. The derivation of the word, however, is of far greater antiquity. To the Greeks a *mouseion* was a place of contemplation, a philosophical institution or a temple of the Muses, while the Romans seem to have restricted their use of the word *museum* to places of philosophical discussion. It was not until the fifteenth century that the term was used to describe a collection in Renaissance Florence and then it carried with it connotations of comprehensiveness and encyclopedic knowledge[2]. However, since the late eighteenth century a museum has been, by popular usage, a building used for the storage and exhibition of historic and natural objects.

The classical associations of the term with the Muses and contemplation, together with a strong tendancy to collect, preserve and exhibit only 'high' art and the exotic rather than representative assemblages of our heritage has had a marked influence on the public perception of museums and their role in society. However the museum today is in no sense maintaining a latter-day classical tradition. Rather, at a general level, it seems to be a reflection of an inherent human propensity towards inquisitiveness and acquisitiveness combined with a wish to communicate to others; it also attempts to respond to present day social needs[3]. The motivation for acquisition may vary[4] but is to be found from earliest times in the grave goods accompanying Palaeolithic burials, a characteristic by no means peculiar to prehistoric societies. The earliest evidence of communication through another medium is also of Palaeolithic origin, occurring in the cave and mobiliary art of the latter part of this period. In due course came the

development of writing in Sumerian Mesopotamia and by the third millennium BC the formation of remarkable state archives of which that at Ebla is the earliest known. But while such a collection of documents provides evidence of a wish to record, to communicate and of an inquisitiveness about the past, the museum idea goes further. This requires the *original* material to communicate and not some secondary source. It is, therefore, to the earliest manifestations of this that we should look in tracing the history of the museum concept. The story is far from complete and in all probability not an evolving continuum until the European middle ages.

The earliest recorded instance of the use of historical material to communicate information dates from the beginning of the second millenium BC, when earlier inscriptions in Larsa, albeit copies, were being used in the schools of that Mesopotamian city (Woolley and Mallowen, 1962 p. 17). This spirit of enquiry into historic objects also appears during the time of the Babylonian empire. Certainly during the sixth century BC, Nebuchadrezzar[5] and Nabonidus collected antiquities and even excavated and restored parts of their city, Ur 'of the Chaldees'. But it is probably to Nabonidus' daughter, En-nigaldi-Nanna, that credit for creating what was almost certainly a school museum must be given. In Woolley's excavation of the temple at Ur (*op. cit*) he discovered evidence of a boys' school and, in two connecting room, a number of antiquities pre-dating it by up to sixteen hundred years. Fascinatingly, what appears to have been a museum label was also found; this included copies of brick inscriptions of Amar-Suena (nineteenth century BC) which the label[6] described, and had been found by the Temple a hundred years earlier. The scribe wrote the inscriptions out for 'the marvel of the beholders'.

Classical collecting[7]

To this strong evidence of the educational use of historical material for teaching must be added the reasonable supposition that Aristotle (fourth century BC) used his natural history collection similarly at the Lyceum in Athens. That most celebrated museum, founded by Ptolemy Sotor at Alexandria about 290 BC, is attributed to Aristotlian influence and it is likely that one of Aristotle's followers, Demetrius Phalereus, was involved in its creation.

There is little doubt that this Alexandrian museum contained some objects and it was associated with a botanical and zoological park. But the emphasis was not here. It was a philosophical institution, a college of scholars, a prototype university with a large library and facilities for the state-supported philosophers to engage in their studies. Such scholars as Euclid and Archimedes worked here. It was not a museum in the contemporary sense of the word.

For the preservation of works of art there is some evidence in the second millenium BC from the Minoan temples of Crete (Chadwick, 1958). In classical Greece many collections of works of art were formed from votive offerings to the particular deity concerned and could be viewed by visitors on payment of a small charge. This was not just for the devout but for the tourist as well. The administration of these treasuries included many familiar features: the offerings were inventoried in some detail and active conservation measures taken to preserve them; many of the objects were on open display but others were displayed in cases. The fifth century BC saw the earliest of the *pinakothekai* in the Acropolis of Athens to house examples of paintings of different artists; the paintings were provided with protective shutters (Bazin, 1967 p 14). Extensive collecting of works of art by the Greek aristocracy, however, does not seem to have been in vogue before Hellenistic times.

The fall of the Greek empire in the second century BC saw the conquering Romans removing many of these works of art as spoils of war; these reappeared in their own temples and also formed the basis of many private collections. Indeed the Romans became avid collectors which in turn gave rise to an antique trade and also to the copying of many of the Greek masterpieces. The Emperor Hadrian, at his villa near Tivoli the grounds of which covered some 7 square miles (18 km²), erected copies of some of the structures he had visited during his tours of the empire to form a precursor of the idea of an open-air 'museum'. For paintings special galleries were sometimes built, due attention being paid to their siting and the desirability of orientating them to receive a north light.

The Roman temples contained more than works of art among their exhibits. They were also places where the unusual and the curious were displayed, often brought back by travellers or soldiers from the far-flung provinces. Thus at Hierapolis, Indian jewels, the jaw of a snake and elephant tusks were among the items shown in the temple of the Syrian goddess; the temple of Hercules at Rome contained a number of animal hides while rare plants, foreign weapons, and an obsolete flute were amongst the collections at Carthage.

Ignoring the etymological difficulties that arise, it is necessary to ask whether this great awareness of art in classical Rome led to the formation of museums as we known them today. Certainly there was considerable public exhibition of art and the curious, and on a number of occasions public opinion took issue with the aristocracy for keeping works of art for their own enjoyment. Julius Caesar actually dedicated his own collection to temples while Agrippa, who avowed that the best art should belong to the people, opened his collections to the public. But few followed his example and no organized structure existed for the administration and upkeep of these collections, responsibility being left to whoever held them. As Bazin (1967, p. 23) states: 'Rome had no museum *per se* but all Rome was a museum'.

Early Islamic collecting

With the rise of Islam in the sixth century AD and the spread of its culture and learning in the succeeding centuries across the southern mediterranean lands and as far east as Indonesia, there is abundant evidence of fine art, expressed mainly in three-dimensional objects. There is considerable evidence of collecting at this time, but not in furtherance of the museum idea. Rather it arises mainly from religious motives and takes the form of treasuries associated with the tombs of Muslim martyrs. The best known of these is at Meshed in north-east Iran containing the body of the eighth-century Iman-Reza. The subject of pilgrimage to this day, many fine gifts were made which came to be venerated as sacred relics; they are now housed in a museum adjacent to the tomb. An important factor which contributed to the preservation of cultural property was the idea of *al-waqf*[8]. This involved giving, in perpetuity, property for the public good and religious benefit and was formalized as a concept by Mohammad himself. In this way collections were formed and, where appropriate and they have survived, many have been incorporated into museum collections today.

Collections were also formed from the spoils of war, and after the defeat of the Umayyads in the middle of the eighth century, the Abbasid caliphs and princes are recorded as having amassed works of art such as textiles, weapons and glass as trophies of their victory. The Fatimids (AD 909–1160) who reigned in Egypt and founded an academy at Cairo in the eleventh century also collected, housing their *Khanzaneh* in certain of their palaces for the pleasure of their caliphs and princes but this material was destroyed at the end of the dynasty.

Early oriental collecting

It has been a characteristic of the Chinese peoples from antiquity to look to the past for guidance, and this has expressed itself in collecting from very early times. Hoards of fine gold and bronze artefacts dating from the Shang dynasty (*c.* 1600–1027 BC) have been found during excavations in Honan Province[9]. Collecting was almost certainly the prerogative of the rich and, by the time of the Empire, an activity of the Emperors who also acted as patrons to calligraphers and painters. The Emperor Hien-ti (AD 190–220) established a room devoted to portraits of his ministers while Wu (AD 229–280) amassed paintings and calligraphs in an imperial academy and this tradition appears to have continued in China over a very long period.

In Japan the past and its personalities were also venerated and collections gathered by the aristocracy often found their way to a temple. One such offering, to the Buddha Vairochana, was made by the widow of Emperor Shomu (AD 724–756) to the Todaiji temple at Nara where a special building, the Shoso-in, was constructed for it. This building and its fine contents still exist today.

Medieval Europe

The destruction of Roman civilization in Western Europe in the fifth and sixth centuries AD brought to an end many of its customs and institutions, not least the mass appreciation and display of art. The main preoccupation now was economic and social self-sufficiency. Communities concerned with a primitive economy were more likely to find satisfaction from the talisman, and their ruling families from easily realizable precious metal and stones. But a further factor was to emerge in the form of the reintroduction and spread of Christianity. For those under the influence of Augustinian teaching, the collection of things relating to the pagan classical world would have been unacceptable. However with the rise of Christianity and of princely families it became commonplace for both to have treasuries associated with their institutions and these were to become the main source of collections throughout medieval Europe.

For the church, some of the collections were of a religious nature, embracing much sought-after relics of Christendom. Many of these allegedly unique items were duplicated in different churches in Europe[10]. Because of their reputed therapeutic qualities they were the subject of pilgrimage and therefore of gifts. As the church assumed greater power, so its holdings increased, sometimes in close collaboration with the ruling families of the time. The majority of the treasures of Charlemagne at Aix-la-Chapelle, for example, were divided among some twenty-four religious houses early in the ninth century AD. But on a number of occasions sovereigns made demands on ecclesiastical treasuries to assist in financing wars and other state expenses, a fate which periodically affected French collections as late as the eighteenth century. Thus, while the motivation for establishing both ecclesiastical and secular treasuries at this time served cultural purposes, there can be little doubt of their economic significance as well.

By the twelfth century Europe was more stable and evidence of private collections and of pilgrims visiting the ancient monuments of Rome can be found. Indeed, in 1162 Trajan's column was effectively the subject of a preservation order as a monument in honour of the Roman people. Nowhere was the prosperity more apparent than in Venice which maintained maritime supremacy in the Mediterranean at this time. Although normally strictly neutral in their dealings, at the beginning of the thirteenth century the Venetians joined the Fourth Crusade and captured Constantinople and among other things brought back the bronze horses of Nero to grace the outside of the Cathedral of St Mark. The latin occupation of Constantinople also saw the beginning of the decline in Byzantine art which had flourished for over half a millennium.

The Renaissance

The awakening of interest in classical material and in the new learning developed and, for example, some extant fourteenth-century accounts refer to the purchase of a cabinet of antiquities by a private collector in Trevisio. By the following century a number of fine collections had been established, particularly by the great bourgeois families of Florence.

Outstanding among these was that assembled by Cosimo (the Elder) Medici (1389–1464) and developed by members of the family. By the time of his grandson, Lorenzo the Magnificent (1449–1492), the collection ranged from books, intaglios, precious stones, medals, tapestries, Byzantine icons, Flemish and other contemporary paintings and sculpture, a number of which had been specially commissioned. The fact the Jan van Eyck's 'St Jerome' was purchased for thirty florins and 'the horn of a unicorn' for six thousand florins gives an insight into the relative value of the pieces in the Medici collection. The vicissitudes that affected the Medicis after Lorenzo's death were responsible for the pillaging of the collections on at least three occasions until Cosimo I (1519–1574) began to reassemble it; he also added to it, including artefacts from Etruscan sites and a fine collection of natural history specimens. To house the collections, additions to palaces and new ones were constructed by the Medicis. Francis I (1541–1587) however was responsible for converting the upper floor of the Uffizi into a picture gallery which was completed in 1582. The Medici collection continued to flourish until it was bequeathed to the state in 1743 on condition that it remained accessible in Florence to the people of Tuscany and to all nations.

Many other collections formed by the ruling houses and the rich existed in fifteenth-century Italy. Further, many of the collections were available to visitors, often on payment of a small fee, and they were popular enough to be listed in the tourist guides of the period. Among them was the now increasing Vatican collection, towards which considerable resources were being devoted. The forming of collections was not restricted to Italy from whence there was an active trade in antiquities and art; indeed in 1534, the Pope attempted to ban this export trade, but without much effect. One of the principal recipient countries was France. There the royal collections were kept at Fontainebleau to which were added curiosities brought to France by merchants and explorers.

In Central Europe, the Dukes of Bavaria, Wilhelm IV and Albrect V both established collections in Munich, the latter erecting a gallery to hold the paintings, between 1563 and 1567. This building, now the Mint, is probably the oldest-surviving purpose-built 'museum'. Albrect also built a long-vaulted Antiquarium at the Munich Residenz for his collection of antiquities between 1569 and 1571. Vespasiano Ganzaga, Duke of Sabbioneta, similarly built an Antiquarium for his Roman collection, between 1580 and 1584, as an annexe to the Casino del Giardino near Mantua, Italy. At Ambras Castle, near Innsbruck, Ferdinand of Tyrol established a number of different types of collection; included in them were two Chinese Ming paintings, German mechanical clocks and ivory spoons from Benin.

The spirit of the Renaissance, with its emphasis on experiment and observation, led to the formation of scientific collections. Collections of natural history material were particularly common in sixteenth-century Italy, over two hundred and fifty being recorded there alone. Perhaps the first herbarium collected for scientific purposes was that of Luca Ghini (1490–1556) at Padua.

Konrad von Gesner (1516–1565)[11], whose *Historiae animalium* was an outstanding contribution to the natural history of his time, also gathered an important collection. This was acquired by Felix Platter (1536–1614), another notable naturalist, part of

whose collection is held in the Natural History Museum at Basle. Ulisse Aldrovandi (1527–1603), whose large collection of plant, animal and mineral illustrations, prepared for his encyclopaedic work on natural history, found its way into the University of Bologna's museum in 1743. Another important Italian collection was that of Ferrante and Francesco Imperali at Naples. Of particular interest during the sixteenth century was the exotic natural history introduced to Europe as a result of exploration and trading, but the indigenous fauna and flora were not ignored[12].

The first recorded instance of the use of the word *museum* to describe a collection related to the Medici material at the time of Lorenzo the Magnificent. Other terms used more frequently were, from the sixteenth century, *gallery* to denote a place where paintings and sculpture were exhibited while, later, a *cabinet* was used to describe either a collection of curiosities or the place where decorative art material was housed. Both terms were used in English and French. In German, *Kabinett* or *Kammer* was used, normally prefixed to give it greater precision for example *Naturalienkabinett, Wunderkammer* (normally a natural science collection), *Kunstkammer,* etc.

The sixteenth century saw many changes in Europe, not least the changing balance of sea power. Throughout medieval times the principal route from Africa and the Orient to Central and Northern Europe had been through the ports of Genoa and Venice. Thus the influence of the Italian Renaissance had spread through Europe and there the trade in antiquities, classical and exotic, had centred.

This now changed as Spain and Portugal, France, the Netherlands and also Britain commenced trans-ocean exploration, trade and eventually colonization. Among the well-known private collections in Northern Europe were those of Olaf Worm (1588–1654) in Copenhagen and Bernardus Paludarius (1550–1633). Both of these followed the cabinet of curiosities pattern, and visitors were admitted to them. In due course they became part of public museum collections. Taylor (1948) noted that only one painting was to be found in the palace of Gustavus Adolphus in Stockholm although it should be recorded that this King was responsible for the appointment of a *Riksantikvarie* in 1630 to look after Sweden's national antiquities. His daughter Christina, however, set out to improve the country's holdings of foreign culture and, when her troops occupied Prague, much of the fine collection of Rudolph II was transferred to Stockholm. When she abdicated and left the country in 1654 many of the works of art went with her but she left behind a number of Dutch and German paintings which contributed to the formation of the National Museum in Stockholm.

The Enlightenment

By this time the age of applying system and scientific method to an understanding of humankind and nature was already underway. A century earlier Nicolas Copernicus had led the way for a revolution in astronomy; Francis Bacon had propounded the need to establish an inductive empiricism and expressed the need for useful knowledge to be catalogued, while René Descartes, who ended his days at Christiana of Sweden's court, was seeking mathematical solutions to rationalize religion and science. Moreover, many of the collections were already more than just an assemblage of curiosities; they were well ordered. As early as 1565, Samuel van Quiecheberg, a Flemish doctor, had written that ideally collections should represent a systematic classification of all materials in the universe and this work undoubtedly influenced the Tradescants of England in ordering their collection. Indeed such general guidance was readily available in published form by 1727 for the amateur collector; it dealt with the problems of classification, collection care and sources to supplement collections and was to be found in Casper F. Neickel's *Museographia*, published in Leipzig. But the naturalists and antiquarians had still to await Linneas and Thomsen, both Scandinavians who, in 1735 and 1836 respectively, provided the beginning of modern classification for their material. These frameworks, necessary to bring better order and understanding to the natural and prehistoric worlds, were constructed and developed from collections. An important part of Linneas' collection is now housed at the Linnean Society in London, while Thomsen used the collections of the Danish National Museum of Antiquities, of which he was the first curator, for his work.

This was the age of the development of learned societies of which many also formed collections. In Florence the *Accademia del Cimento* was founded by the Medicis in 1650, by no means the first such society in Italy; another, the Etruscan Academy founded in 1726, arranged excavations and in due course opened its *Galleria del publico* to show archaeological and art objects in its collection. At Haarlem the natural history cabinet of the *Hollandsche Maatschappij der Wetenschappen* was opened in 1778 as a result of Pieter Teyler van der Hulst's benefaction. The development of the collection thereafter changed direction towards natural philosophy and as a result Teyler's Museum today holds an important collection of eighteenth-century scientific instruments (Turner, 1973). There is no doubt that this society and the *Accademia* in Florence became centres for scientific experimentation for their members (Bedini, 1965). Many other countries in Europe had similar societies, their collections being formed primarily for the benefit of their own members, but often, in later years, contributing to the foundation of public museums.

The first public museums

The development of collections and their public availability was gradual and much influenced by prevailing social and philosophical considerations. The point in time when a corporate body acquired or formed a collection with the clear intention of making it available for the public benefit must be regarded as a watershed in the history of museums and an important step nearer the institution as it is known today. The Venetian Republic appears to have been one of the earliest public bodies to receive collections, bequeathed by the Grimani family in 1523 and 1583; these collections went to form the basis of the present archaeological museum in Venice. Sixteenth-century Switzerland saw many paintings, antiquities and manuscripts taken over by a number of the municipalities as a result of the Reformation and these were in due course to contribute to some of its leading museums, for example, the National Swiss Museum in Zurich and the Historical Museum, Berne. Another Swiss city, Basel, purchased the important Amerbach collection in 1662 to prevent it leaving the country and this was installed in the new university library building to which there was public access in 1671 (Lapaire, 1980 p. 24). The first museum specifically for the public benefit in France was in the Abbey of St Vincent at Besançon as a result of the head abbot's bequest of his personal collection of books, paintings and medallions in 1694. In England the first public museum was the Ashmolean at Oxford, opened in 1683, to be followed by the British Museum in 1759.

The French capital had to wait rather longer for its first truly public museum, the Louvre, to which visitors were admitted in 1793, based on the magnificent royal collection. The inaccessibility of this had been the subject of public disquiet for at least fifty years and to appease this Louis XV exhibited about a hundred of the paintings at Palais Luxembourg in 1750. However, the campaign continued. When Diderot published the ninth volume of his *Encyclopaedie* in 1765 he included a detailed scheme for a national museum in the Louvre which would also accommodate the Academies; in this the proposals suggested a latter-day Alexandrian *mouseion*.

In fact proposals were already afoot to use the *Grande Galerie* of the Louvre as a museum, and in 1784 a Conservateur was appointed to prepare it. But in the event it was not to be a museum of the royal collection, but of the nationalized collections following the creation of the French Republic in 1792 and therefore a public museum in the true sense of the phrase. The *Museum Central des Arts* was created by decree the following year and opened to the public in August. However, because of the condition of the gallery it was open only for a short time, not fully re-opening until 1801. The museum collection, however, grew rapidly. The *Convention Nationale* instructed Napoleon to appropriate works of art dur-ing his European campaigns and as a result many looted collections found their way to the Louvre. It was no accident that for about a decade from 1803 the institution was known as the *Musée Napoléon* and during this period undoubtedly contained the finest collection in Europe. Following the Congress of Vienna in 1815 much of the material was returned to its owners, this constituting the first major example of the restitution of cultural property[13].

The latter years of the eighteenth century and the beginning of the nineteenth century saw the opening of a number of collections to the public in different parts of Europe. Many of these resulted from royal favour rather than public benefaction. Thus the opening of the Schloss Belvedere in Vienna as an art gallery around 1784 was the direct result of Joseph II's wish for some of the royal paintings to be displayed for the public benefit. Chretian de Mechel who was responsible for the collection, arranged it by schools because a great public collection of this type, he said, should be 'more for one's instruction than delight'. This approach was controversial, if not novel, but it marked an important move in the ordered presentation of paintings for the public benefit (Bazin 1967). Admission to the Schloss was possible on three days a week.

In Spain the royal collections at the Escorial Palace were certainly available to visitors on request from the seventeenth century but it was not until the reign of Charles III that this was taken a stage further.

In 1774 he brought together in the reconstructed Goyeneche Palace some of his works of art and natu-ral history collections with the idea that the St Fern-dinand Royal Academy of Fine Art should be based there and that an Academy of Science should also be created. In 1785, however, the King directed that a new building should be erected to serve as a Museum of Natural Science. The premises were completed about twenty years later and, but for the Spanish War of Independence, the original intention might have been realized in 1808. The usurper, Joseph Bonaparte, proposed the establishment of a public museum of paintings in the Buenavista Palace and also the transfer of fifty pictures to the *Musée Napo-léon* in Paris; only the latter was effected. The new museum building however was requisitioned and damaged during these troubles and it was not until 1818 that the reinstated Ferdinand VII ordered its repair and preparation to display some of the royal pictures. And so the Prado Museum eventually opened its doors to the public of Madrid on 19 November 1819. Today one of the world's great art galleries, there is some evidence (Sanchez, 1973 pp. 68–70) that it also displayed natural specimens in its early days. The collections were nationalized after the Revolution of 1868 and, since 1870, have been administered by the State.

Another country occupied by the French was the Netherlands. Here the collecting tradition did not rest with royal families but with official bodies, par-ticularly the municipalities. Notwithstanding this, some of the art treasures were seized and dispatched to Paris as war trophies. Perhaps as an indirect result of this, the idea of a national art gallery was mooted for some of the remaining paintings in Haarlem and these were transferred to the Huis den Bosch which opened in 1800; for a small fee the public could visit the museum for a guided tour. This museum, however, was short-lived, being transferred to Amsterdam in 1808 by Louis Bonaparte to become the Koninklijk Museum to which several paintings were loaned by the city of Amsterdam. In 1815 it was renamed the Rijksmuseum. This museum suf-fered severe accommodation problems and the mod-ern paintings were transferred to Haarlem. It was not until 1885 that the present purpose-built Rijksmuseum was opened in Amsterdam by which time the collections had expanded considerably, drawing on the many private art collections that had been built up in this international trading nation.

It was the return of the looted royal works of art from France to Berlin and their public exhibition in the Unter den Linden Academy that gave the impetus to the erection of the Altes Museum by Frederick William III and the acquisition of a large number of paintings by the State to supplement the royal collection. It was not opened to the public, however, until 1830. The Altes Museum was the first building in what was to become a major planned museum development over the next century on the peninsula formed by the rivers Spree and Kupfer-graben, later known as the Museum-insel; first the Neues Museum (1855), linked by bridge with the earlier museum, followed by the National Gallery (1875), the Kaiser Friedrich Museum (1904) and finally as one complex in the renaissance tradition, the Deutsches Museum, the Pergamon Museum and the Vorderasiastisches Museum, completed in 1930.

Thus, while most of the early museums of Europe came into existence by the accident of circumstances with collections available at the time and often housed in a building redundant from some other purpose, the Berlin development from the outset was based on a clear plan. The Altes Museum was in fact conceived by art historians and directed by one, unlike its counterparts in Britain and France where artists seem to have been preferred to head their art museums. As Wilhelm von Hulboldt, Chairman of the Commission for the establishment of the Altes Museum reported to the king in 1830: 'the Royal gallery here is different in that it covers systematically all periods of painting and provides a visual history of art from its beginnings' (quoted in Klessmann, 1971, p. 40); other galleries at Dusseldorf and Vienna had followed this approach in 1756 and 1784 respectively. The subsequent development of the site extends this philosophy of the scientific approach to collections, with division into different subjects.

The collections of the Alte Pinakothek, opened in Munich in 1836, were also displayed chronologically by schools; as Leo von Klenze, the architect, explained: the gallery 'was intended for the whole nation, not just to artists who will be favourably disposed to their nature' (quoted in Dube, 1970, p. 8). The architect required the building to be situated in an open space, protected from fire, dust and vibration, and that internally the rooms should be separately accessible, lit by skylights or north-facing windows and moderately heated both for the conservation of the pictures and the comfort of the visitors. Thus were displayed the finest pictures of the Dukes of Wittelsbach.

The last of the important major royal collections to be displayed to the public was that of the Russian Tsars. Remarkable for the fact that it was built up over the relatively short period of about 150 years and that the fine art collection was entirely of non-Russian work – a feature which it still retains – it also included the fine picture collection of Sir Robert Walpole whose heirs sold it to Catherine the Great in 1778 for £30,000. The Tsars' collection was the subject of a Napoleonic request in 1812 and certain of the works were dispatched to Paris but returned the following year. As the collection continued to grow it spread from the Winter Palace at what is now Leningrad into the adjacent Hermitage. Following a severe fire in the Winter Palace, Leo von Klenze, who designed the Alte Pinakothek in Munich, was commissioned to plan new adjacent premises to house the collection, known as the New Hermitage. The building and collection were opened by Nicholas I in 1852 and the public allowed to enter on presentation of an admission ticket and provided they wore full regimental uniform or tail coats (Piotrovsky, 1978, p. 10). These regulations were rescinded in the following decade and the Hermitage took on the role of a public museum although still nominally under royal administration until the revolution of 1917.

It is at the beginning of the nineteenth century that the first realization of the role of the museum in contributing to national consciousness arose in Europe. With it came the recognition that the museum was the appropriate institution for the preservation of a nation's historic heritage. In Budapest the national museum, which originated in 1802, was built from money raised from voluntary taxes and was to figure prominently later in the fight for Hungarian independence. In Prague a revival in nationalism led to the founding of a museum in 1818 specifically to foster cultural identity and the study of the Czech and Slovak peoples. The Danish government, responding to a suggestion that it should collect and preserve the nation's early archaeological heritage, established the National Museum of Antiquities in Copenhagen in 1819. The Swedish state, which had been collecting national antiquities since the seventeenth century, did not make them available to the public until the Statens Historiska Museum was opened in Stockholm in 1847. In a sense the *Musée des Monuments Français,* created in Paris in 1795, served a similar purpose until its dissolution in 1816 to be followed by the *Musée de Cluny* and eventually the *Musée des Antiquités Nationales* at Saint-Germain-en-Laye in 1862.

Museum development outside Europe

The concept of the public museum as defined here is essentially European in origin and the idea seems to have been transmitted to other parts of the world through trading and colonialism. As far as Britain is concerned there is no evidence of Government policy to establish museums in the colonies; rather it was left for those in the colonies to take the initiative. In consequence museum development, as in Britain itself, was haphazard.

The American Continent

The earliest recorded museum outside Europe was in the American English Colonies. In 1773 the Charleston Library Society of South Carolina announced its intention of forming a collection of the 'natural productions, either animal vegetable or mineral' with a view to displaying the practical and commercial aspects of agriculture and medicine in the province. The resulting museum, although its activities were interrupted by the War of Independence and not revived until 1785, reflected two features which were to characterize museum development in the United States: an overtly educational role and an origin resulting from the initiative of a local society.

Another eighteenth-century American institution was Mr Peale's Museum in Philadelphia. Opened in his home in 1785, this was rather more European in concept but, in advance of its time, with the clear intention of the instruction and entertainment of all classes. It soon outgrew its accommodation and moved a number of times to larger premises. As a private museum it went through a number of economic vicissitudes and after being declined both by the city and the nation, finally became incorporated in 1821 as the Philadelphia Museum Company. This enterprise was known on both sides of the Atlantic. In 1840 James Silk Buckingham, a protagonist for municipal museums in Britain, visited it and he describes the collection in his book *The Eastern and Western States of America;* he was responsible for arranging for an exhibition of the Museum's fine Chinese collection in London. However, the Museum waned and the dispersal of its collections commenced in 1845, to be completed nine years later (Sellars, 1980).

The national museum for the United States cannot be really considered as established until 1858 after a long gestation period (Oehser, 1970). Collections had been forming for some time, however, and there had been a keeper of the Cabinet since 1850. Its origins lie in the remarkable bequest of James Macie Smithson (1765–1829), a son of Hugh Smithson, first Duke of Northumberland, and Elizabeth Macie. The first beneficiaries under James Smithson's will having died, the alternative provisions became operative:

> to the United States of America, to be founded at Washington, under the name Smithsonian Institution, an Establishment for the increase and diffusion of knowledge among men.

And so in 1838 just over £100 000 (about half a million US dollars) was shipped across the Atlantic. It was not until 1846, however, that the US Senate approved an Act establishing the Smithsonian Institution which *inter alia* provided for the creation of a building to house 'all objects of art and curious research, and all objects of natural history, plants and geological and mineralogical specimens' belonging to the United States, together with the Smithson material. The objects were to 'be arranged in such an order . . . as best facilitate the examination and study of them'; additions to the collection were authorized which 'may be obtained . . . by exchanges of duplicate specimens . . . by donation . . . or otherwise'.

The first Secretary of the Smithsonian Institution, Joseph Henry, laid the foundations on which the Institution, including its museum, would develop. In his view 'Smithson was well aware that knowledge should not be viewed as existing in isolated parts'; and this approach has been an important factor in its development. In one respect Henry's view was not accepted in that he would have preferred the museum to be separate from the main Institution. When Spencer Baird was appointed Keeper of the Cabinet in 1850, however, the museum side of the enterprise developed, eventually to dominate it, though even as late as the 1930s there was still an official view that the Smithsonian was not a museum.

The US National Museum, as it was then known, opened in 1858 under Baird who eventually succeeded Henry. Another Assistant Secretary, George Brown Goode, joined the staff in 1877 having already been an honorary curator of the Museum, and continued the work, becoming one of the leading curators of his time in the United States. Today, the Smithsonian complex, once described as 'the octopus on the Mall' includes the National Museum of Natural History, the National Museum of History and Technology, the National Air and Space Museum, the National Gallery of Art, the Freer Gallery, the National Portrait Gallery, the Museum of African Art and the Hirshorn Museum and Sculpture garden. A zoo and the Anacostia Neighbourhood Museum also form part of the Institution.

The first art museum of any standing in the United States was the Wadsworth Atheneum, founded at Hartford in 1842. It was not until 1870 that the Metropolitan Museum of Art was established in New York; the Museum of Fine Arts in Boston was founded in the same year. Another of the well-known United States institutions, the American Museum of Natural History, was founded in 1869. Both of these New York institutions established an important precedent, to be followed subsequently by a number of other museums in the United States, whereby the city authorities agreed to provide and maintain the buildings while the Trustees accepted responsibility for the collections and professional staff.

The predominance of history museums, particularly the historic house museum, in the United States is due largely to the work of the historical societies of which the earliest was the Massachusetts Historical Society, founded in Boston in 1791. The first historic house to be preserved as a museum was Hasbronck House, Newburgh – George Washington's headquarters – but this was purchased by the State of New York in 1850. The second, purchased through private initiative three years later, was Mount Vernon, Virginia, also with Washington connexions. Both were established in a period of civil unrest and can be regarded as patriotic gestures.

The earliest museum collection in Canada seems to have been in the eastern Maritime Provinces. Key (1973) records that the Picton Academy of Nova Scotia had a museum, probably by 1822; certainly it was described some seven years later as having 'the most extensive collection of zoology in the country'. He also attributes the development of many of the community museums there to the Mechanics' Institute movement, the earliest of which appears to be that founded at Halifax, Nova Scotia in 1831. The natural history collections of this Museum, by now defunct, were transferred to the new Provincial Museum in Halifax about thirty-five years later.

Montreal also had some early collections. *Le Musée del Vecchio* was operated for a short time from 1824 by an Italian entrepreneur. The Natural History Society of Montreal certainly had a fine collection by 1826 (Murray, 1904, **3**, p. 131), part of which was transferred to the Redpath Museum at McGill University, as also had the Literary and Historical Society of Quebec. In Quebec City a museum was opened by a sculptor and gilder, Pierre Chasseur, in the same year, and this collection was purchased by the Government of Quebec in 1836 to become the first public museum in Canada; it was destroyed by fire in 1854.

The National Museum commenced as an adjunct of the Geological Survey of Canada in 1843 at Montreal and although it was transferred to Ottawa in 1880 it remained part of the survey until a separate Director of the museum was appointed in 1920 and later separated administratively. In this it was unlike the National Gallery of Canada, which had a common founding with the Royal Canadian Academy of Arts in 1880, and operated under an Advisory Council until this was replaced with a board of trustees in 1951. Under the *National Museums Act, 1967* the Canadian national museum scene was rationalized and today four national museums operate under its remit: the National Gallery and the national museums of man, natural sciences and technology. This statute, an important landmark in Canadian museum history, owes much to the interest generated in museums both national, provincial and local, in the run-up to Canada's centennial year.

Further west in Toronto the Ontario Provincial Museum was founded in 1855; it appears to have been predominantly anthropological in character. The University of Toronto also developed a number of teaching collections but the oldest of these were destroyed in a fire in 1890. These two institutions, together with a museum at Victoria College, combined to form the Royal Ontario Museum, a purpose-built museum completed in 1912. The Art Gallery of Toronto was opened the following year. A feature of the Canadian scene is the number of historical society museums that exist, particularly in Ontario. These appear to have commenced in the last decade of the nineteenth century and have continued to increase ever since (Miers and Markham, 1932). The appearance of museums in British Colombia and the Prairie Provinces also dates to the end of the last century.

The earliest museums in South America were also the result of colonial influence. The first, at Rio de Janeiro, was formed from a collection of paintings given by the King of Portugal and opened in 1815 (Coleman, 1939); it is now the national museum. Another early museum was the National Museum in Buenos Aires, Argentina which was founded shortly after independence in 1823 (Wittlin, 1970).

Australasia

Australia's first collection dates to 1821 and was established in Sydney by the Philosophical Society of Australasia. The Society appears to have continued for only a year but the collections probably remained

in the Colonial Secretary's office until a new incumbent, Alexander Macleay, a Fellow and past Honorary Secretary of the Linnean Society in London, arrived in 1826. He brought with him a fine collection of European insects which eventually formed the basis of the University of Sydney's Macleay Museum founded, in 1874, through a legacy from a descendant of the family.

However the shipment of specimens at the beginning of the nineteenth-century was in both directions. The Governor of New South Wales was a member of the Newcastle-upon-Tyne Literary and Philosophical Society and sent material to them, as he did also to Sir Joseph Banks (see Chapter 3). There were also close links with the Hunterian Museum in London (Strahan, 1979). It is thought likely that Alexander Macleay was responsible for the establishment of what was to become the Australian Museum. Certainly representations were made to the Colonial Office in 1827 but the appointment of a zoologist to run the Museum did not occur until 1829[14]. The following year, the local newspaper refers to 'a beautiful collection of Australian curiosities, the property of the Government' which Mr Holmes (the zoologist), 'between the hours of ten and three politely shows . . . to any respectable individuals who may think fit to call'. The Museum remained in temporary quarters for over twenty-five years, purpose-built premises, although commenced in 1846, not being opened to the public until 1857. In the meantime the *Australian Museum Trust Act 1853* had given the Museum corporate status under the administration of trustees.

The National Art Gallery of New South Wales in Sydney was much later and a permanent gallery was not opened until 1897. The National Gallery of Victoria commenced as the Museum of Art in part of the Public Library in Melbourne in 1861 but did not have its own trustees until after the second world war or a separate building until the present fine gallery was opened in 1968 (Cox, 1970). The National Museum of Victoria commenced as an independent institution in 1854 (Prescott, 1954) to be followed in 1870 by what was to become known as the Science Museum of Victoria (Perry, 1970). By this time the library, museums and art gallery had been incorporated under one body of trustees. These were national institutions in the sense that they were financed by the Government of a Crown State Colony.

The Ancanthe Museum to the north of Hobart was probably the earliest purpose-built museum structure in Australia, having been built in 1842. Although a private museum, it was subsequently merged with the collections of the Royal Society of Tasmania. Other museums founded during the mid-nineteenth century were the Queensland Museum, Brisbane (1855), the Museum of the Swan River Mechanics' Institute in Perth (1860) and the Adelaide

Museum (1861). Most of the major art galleries in Australia opened later the same century.

In New Zealand the initiative of the Mechanics' Institute at Taranaki led to the formation of a collection of ethnographic material and curiosities in the late 1840s which survived for about half a century. The earliest museum, however, is the Nelson Provincial Museum at Stoke, dating to about 1841, to be followed by the Dominion Museum at Auckland (now the Auckland Institute and Museum) eleven years later. The Christchurch Museum, opened in 1861, was supported financially by the Provincial Government until it was abolished in 1875 (Markham and Richards, 1933). The National Museum in Wellington did not open until 1865 and was the result of a jointly sponsored venture by the Government and the New Zealand Geological Society (Thomson, 1981). The present building, opened in 1936, was also a joint enterprise in which the Government provides a matching contribution to funds raised in Wellington, and brought together the National Museum and National Art Gallery in one building; the latter was first opened as the Wellington Public Gallery in 1906.

Asia

Perhaps the earliest museum on the Asian continent was that of the Asiatic Society of Bengal which, although conceived eighteen years previously, eventually opened in 1814. The Society maintained the Museum in Calcutta for a number of years, considerably adding to its predominantly geological and natural history collections; in 1875 the collection was vested in trustees in a new building provided by the Indian Government. The Prince of Wales Museum of Western India, Bombay also had an early foundation.

In Japan a Government Order protecting old wares and objects was made in 1871 and the following year a museum to encourage industry and the development of natural resources was opened. These collections formed the basis of the museums known as the Tokyo National Museum and the National Science Museum (Tsuruta, 1960). The latter Museum had a strong educational bias when it opened to the public in 1877 and included aids for scientific teaching school appliances as well as a natural science collection (Greenwood, 1888).

Shanghai in China witnessed the establishment of the Sikowei Museum in 1868 and a further museum four years later under the aegis of the Royal Asiatic Society; both museums appear to have been intended for a restricted, mainly overseas audience[15]. The Museums Department of the State Administrative Bureau of Museums and Archaeological Data (1980) records the first museum of modern type as being the

Nantung Centre of Natural History, founded in 1905.

Africa

Early museum development in Africa was in either the South or the North. The South African Museum in Cape Town is the earliest of these, having been founded in 1825 by the 'father of South African zoology', Dr Andrew Smith (Barry, 1975). In the north, perhaps to be expected, it was in Egypt that the first museum was established in Cairo in 1858. Much of the remainder of North Africa was at this time under Ottoman rule and there is some evidence that antiquities were sent from these countries to the museum at Constantinople (Istanbul). Some further museums appeared in Africa at the beginning of the twentieth century, including Bulawayo (1901), Salisbury (1902) and Nairobi (1909).

The twentieth century

By the beginning of the twentieth century the world museum scene had changed significantly. With the population movement in the industrialized nations to urban centres many of these communities developed their own museums either through their local authorities, particularly in Europe, or as a result of individual patronage or the initiative of local groups of citizens as in the United States. In certain countries a more centralized State museum system developed, for example in France and in the Soviet Union, the latter much encouraged by the Leninist philosophy to protect the cultural heritage and make it available to the people; elsewhere museum development was less controlled.

New types of museum also emerged. While many of the earliest museums were encyclopedic in character, reflecting the spirit of their age, now more specialized museums appear. One such important development was the proliferation of 'folk museums'. The idea originated in Sweden where Artur Hazelius opened his museum of Scandinavian folklore (now the *Nordiska Museet*) at Stockholm in 1873. Before long, however, his work had extended beyond easily transportable artefacts to buildings and, in 1891, the first open air museum was opened at Skansen.

Such a conscious attempt to preserve and display a nation's more recent past, or aspects of it, was increasingly to characterize much museum activity as the century progressed. In certain cases such museums were exploited for propaganda purposes. This was a feature of post-First World War Germany when over two thousand *Heimatmuseen* were created (Bazin, 1967) and of post-revolution Russia where, for example, the opening of the new Central Lenin

Museum, Moscow in 1936 prompted the newspaper *Pravda* to report that it was 'a new powerful propaganda weapon for Leninism'.

Science Museums were much earlier in origin. Collections of scientific instruments could be found in the Dutch museum of Pieter Teyler and in the *Conservatoire National des Arts at Metiers* in Paris towards the end of the eighteenth century. The application of science to industry was reflected during the following century at the *Conservatoire* and in London's embyonic Science Museum at South Kensington, both institutions benefiting considerably from material received from the international exhibitions in their respective countries. But the Deutches Museum in Munich, when it was finally transferred from its temporary home in 1925, set the pace in interpreting science and technology to a lay audience. Following the Second World War rapid technological change brought a concern not only to preserve and interpret industrial artifacts but also to recreate industrial environments, their impact on communities and the rapidly disappearing processes involved. Important catalysts to these developments were an increasing public interest in the past and developing tourism. In the United Kingdom the North of England Open Air Museum at Beamish and the Ironbridge Gorge Museum, which commenced with corporate identity in 1970, typify this movement (Cossons, 1980). A similar project but with closer involvement of the indiginous community developed in France in 1972 at the Museum of Man and Industry at Le Creusot-Montceau-les-Mines to the south-west of Dijon (de Varine-Bohan, 1973; Evrard, 1980). Related to these developments but involving a mainly simulated location and resited buildings is the Sovereign Hill Goldmining Township and Historical Park at Ballarat, Victoria in Australia which also opened in 1970.

On-site preservation of historic environments for museum purposes has also become an increasing trend. Perhaps the best known is Colonial Williamsburg, the restored capital of eighteenth-century Virginia in the USA. This project was founded in 1926 (Kocher *et al*, 1961). More recent examples include the restoration of the walled medieval cities of Suzdal and Vladimir in the Soviet Union (Aksenova, 1978) and the rehabilitation of the buildings of the small island of Gorée, off the west coast of Senegal, in Africa, with its slave trade associations (Thiam and Thilmans, 1980).

The changing philosophy towards museums in the second half of the twentieth century, however, has by no means been exclusively European in origin. In Latin America, Asia and Africa there have been strong moves to integrate the museum more fully with the community it serves. At a meeting of curators from Latin American countries held in Santiago, 1972 the museum was recognized as a medium of life-long education through which an awareness of the social, economic and political aspects of scientific, technological and environmental development could be created (UNESCO, 1973).

Nations newly gaining their independence also closely examined the role of museums and their contribution in a developing State. This was particularly marked in Africa and where a country had inherited a colonial museum this, according to Diop (1973), 'like most European museums . . . was rather a sort of warehouse in which exhibits were deprived of their true essence in a totally inanimate setting'. For the Nigerians, the museum became an important means through which their heritage could be preserved and national cultural unity promoted and for which a network of national museums was created. At Jos a representative series of traditional buildings were created to form a museum of Nigerian architecture – it is not feasible to resite traditional buildings – while other museums developed workshops where traditional crafts could be demonstrated and the products sold. In the National Museum in Niamey, Niger there are two craft workshops, one worked by professional craft-workers and the other specially provided to train the blind and physically handicapped in craft work in order that they can take their place in the community. The products are sold in the museum shop and exported to Europe and North America (Saley, 1976).

A rigorous examination of the role of museums has not been peculiar to new and developing States. In certain countries detailed studies have been made into the theory underlying museums, of which the work in the Museology Department of the J. E. Purkyně University at Brno, Czechoslovakia is particularly well known. In Canada, a survey of the population has been used to provide evidence of the public perception of the museums' role (Dixon, 1974). Action to relate museums more closely to the community they serve can be seen in the displays on contemporary social problems provided by the Anacostia Neighbourhood Museum, Washington DC, a branch of the Smithsonian Institution, (Kinard and Nighbert, 1972) while a detailed study has been undertaken by Toronto's Royal Ontario Museum (1976) to develop techniques of communicating with their visitors. Also in Toronto, the Art Gallery of Ontario's seminar 'Are art galleries obsolete?' examined some of the pressing issues with this type of institution. As the keynote speaker there said:

> To some, the art gallery has become a sanctuary of scholarship with aesthetic selectivity. To others it is a club and fashionable warehouse for the wealthy. In such institutions, art, at best, is seen as a cultural artifact and rarely as an instrument of illuminating the human perception and visual awareness of the public. (Cameron, 1969).

Experimentation with art museums has taken place elsewhere particularly in associating them with other forms of art provision. In Australia the Art Gallery of Victoria, Melbourne, although a separate building, forms part of an arts centre complex, while Georges Pompidou National Centre for Art and Culture in Paris combines a gallery of modern art and special exhibition galleries with other cultural activities (Fradier, 1978). The temporary exhibition programme and in the largest art museums the 'block-buster', almost became the measure of success in the search for wider audiences to the extent that Bazin (1967, p. 276) comments 'of all the visitors, the connoisseur is the one who is short-changed'.

That museum visiting has much increased is amply borne out by such national statistics as are available. For example, in the United States a survey of some 1800 museums suggests that in the early 1970s they were attracting over 300 million visits a year (National Endowment for the Arts, 1974) while in the Soviet Union the State museums alone record an annual attendance of some 140 million (USSR Ministry of Culture, 1980). Museums are a matter of public interest and, together with the increasing significance of cultural property, have been the subject of reports by a number of governments: in Britain, the Rosse (1963), Wright (1973), Malcolm (1978) and Williams (1981) reports; in the United States the Belmont report (American Association of Museums, 1969); in Canada the Massey (1951) report and more recently the report of the Federal Cultural Policy Review Committee (1982a, b); in Australia the Piggot (1975) report, while the Netherlands Government has issued a memorandum 'Towards a new museum policy' (Spaandonk, 1977). The incidence of government action in promoting legislation concerning museums and cultural property has also increased not least, as might be expected, among the newly-independent States where, quite often, movable and immovable cultural property is treated together (Burnham, 1974; UNESCO 1979, 1981).

Cultural action on the scale now being witnessed could only take place through the development of a professional and governmental consciousness, both national and international. At first this expressed itself through the formation of professional associations such as the Museums Association (1889), the American Association of Museums (1906), the all Russia Museums Conference (1919) and the Japanese Museums Association (1928). Following the First World War, the League of Nations was founded to promote international peace and security and developed a Committee of Intellectual Co-operation. From this the International Museums Office originated, publishing a journal *Mouseion* and a number of books on museum matters. It continued to be active during the Second World War and one of its last acts was the publication of *Cultural reconstruction* in 1945.

The United Nations Educational, Scientific and Cultural Organization (UNESCO) was formed as an agency of the United Nations in 1946. Most of its member states have a UNESCO National Commission in their countries – it is operated through the Government's Overseas Development Administration in the United Kingdom – and a permanent delegation at the UNESCO headquarters in Paris. UNESCO's Division of Cultural Heritage is responsible for museums, monuments and sites. The Organization has been involved much in museum and related matters, believing that greater cultural understanding between nations promotes peace; it also publishes the quarterly journal *Museum*. As newly independent states have become members, so it has turned its attention increasingly to the problems of developing countries. Among its many Conventions and Recommendations are those concerned with prohibiting and preventing the illicit export, import and transfer of ownership of cultural property (1970), the protection of both the world and national cultural and natural heritage (1972), the international exchange of cultural property (1976) and the protection of movable cultural property (1978). It has also been actively promoting the return of cultural property to its country or origin, particularly material which may have been removed during colonial occupation or through commercial exploitation. Five member states of UNESCO were responsible for establishing the International Centre for the Study and Preservation and Restoration of Cultural Property in Rome (ICCROM) as an intergovernmental agency to provide training and conservation facilities; there are now about seventy participating countries.

The International Council of Museums (ICOM) was also formed in 1946 as a professional non-governmental organization. Based on national committees comprising a maximum of fifteen members to represent as widely as possible the museum interests of their country, some sixteen nations, including Great Britain, were present at the first interim conference held in Mexico in 1947; twelve months later it was reported that some fifty-three nations had organized national committees. Following a major reform in 1974 membership of ICOM was changed so that all museum staff could participate fully in their national committee. ICOM also operates a number of international committees which provide a forum for the discussion of specialist matters and assist in formulating international policy. ICOM is officially recognized as the international non-governmental organization for museum affairs by UNESCO to which it provides professional advice, aided by a jointly operated Documentation Centre at its headquarters in Paris. Recently ICOM has become more involved in the implementation of UNESCO projects.

At a governmental level, a number of supra-national organizations in many parts of the World impinge on museum affairs. In Western Europe these include the Council of Europe, founded in 1949 with its headquarters in Strasbourg and the European Communities based in Brussels. Britain is a member of both organizations. The Council of Europe created a Council for Cultural Co-operation in 1962 and since then has been involved in a number of activities concerning museums. For example, it was responsible for the European Convention on the protection of the archaeological heritage, ratified by Britain in 1973, for various studies on museums (e.g. Rebetez, 1970; Gilman, 1977), for promoting a Council of Europe museum prize and in supporting the European Museum of the Year Award (von Bieberstein, 1979).

The European Communities organization had its origin in economic co-operation between certain European nations in 1950 and has since evolved into its present form, commencing work in the cultural field following a resolution of the European Parlia-ment in 1974. In this it co-operates with the Council of Europe which has a liaison office in Brussels, and with UNESCO. Its work has included the introduction of regulations to ease customs procedures and grant relief from duty on goods in transit for exhibition purposes, and encouraging the development of 'European Rooms' in museums, as at Norwich (Cheetham, 1981), to present a public view of the European heritage[16]. The Community fund for regional development has also provided capital funds for museum development where the scheme involves the up-grading of urban areas, as on Merseyside and elsewhere. The European Communities (1978) issued a general statement about its action in the cultural sector in which it particularly encourages exchanges between museums. The structural relationship between these various governmental and non-governmental organizations is shown in *Figure 2.1*.

As the 1980s developed in a deep economic recession, with consequential severe restraints on museum provision and development in many coun-

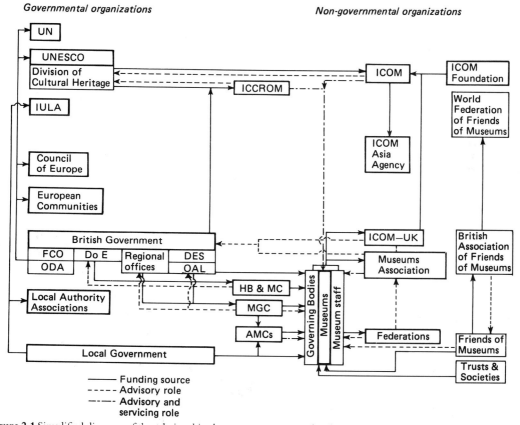

Figure 2.1 Simplified diagram of the relationships between governmental and non-governmental organizations as they relate to museums in Britain (British governmental organizations are treated in more detail in *Figure 4.1* which should be used to interpret the abbreviations.)

tries, the world community's attention, however, was directed at a very different financial matter: the unequal distribution of wealth in the world. This 'North–South debate' related to museum affairs as much as any other. In a recent study undertaken by ICOM on the financing of museums (de la Torre & Monreal, 1982) it has been shown that two-thirds of the world's 26 700 museums – a conservative estimate – are in the industrialized countries. Thus while in Africa there was an average of one museum for every 1.3 million inhabitants; in Europe the ratio was 1:43 000[17].

As the study pointed out there is a need to search for new and innovative solutions to finance museums in both developing and industrialized countries, but potential funding agencies should take into account not only the ratio of museums to population, but other factors such as population distribution, the extent of a country's heritage and the adult literary rate, the latter in view of the contribution that museums can make to this area.

In many countries of the world museums have been undergoing a 'democratization' process at a national level during the second half of the twentieth century and may now find an increasing emphasis on 'democratization' on an international level.[18] This is no more than a continuation of UNESCO's present policies of funding cultural development in the non-industrialized nations and seeking to ensure that such countries have a representative selection of their own heritage through the return of cultural property where necessary. In the words of paragraph 18 in the Mexico City Declaration, following the UNESCO world conference on cultural policies in 1982:

> Culture springs from the community as a whole and should return to it; neither the production of culture nor the enjoyment of its benefits should be the privilege of *elites*. Cultural democracy is based on the broadest possible participation by the individual and society in the creation of cultural goods, in decision-making concerning cultural life and in the dissemination and enjoyment of culture.'

While different nations will interpret such doctrine in their own individualistic way, one thing is abundantly clear. Cultural affairs, and museums among them, are now a significant factor in national and world politics.

Notes

[1] This term is used to mean a museum or art gallery in Chapters 1–4.
[2] In this sense the term museum has been used to describe compilations, not necessarily of objects, for example, see *A Poetical Museum* (1784) or *Museum of Dramatists* (1906), both books claiming to cover their topics comprehensively.

[3] For a hypothesis that the museum is the product of a specific social system, *see* Taborsky (1982).
[4] Wittlin (1970, pp. 4–60) discusses the motivation for forming collections.
[5] von Holst (1967), p. 21) suggests that Nebuchadrezzar's collecting had religious and political motives.
[6] Kenyon (1927) questioned the interpretation of the evidence but no alternative hypothesis has since been offered. Woolley and Moorey, (1982, pp. 231, 252) continue to refer to it as a 'museum label'.
[7] Taylor (1948) and Bazin (1967) have been used as a base for the period to the mid-eighteenth century.
[8] This section owes much to the work of H. Akerba-Abaza, *Legislation relating to the protection of cultural property with particular reference to the Arab States.* MA dissertation, University of Leicester, 1981. See also the same author in the forthcoming ICOM *Treatise of Museology,* Vol. 1.
[9] Based on Ho, C-H. (1978) *The growth and use of collections before the advent of modern museums in the 20th century,* MA dissertation, University of Leicester.
[10] The catacombs of the Pechersky monastery at Kiev are reputed to have been the source of a substantial trade in 'saints' bones' in medieval times. I am grateful to Raymond Singleton for this information.
[11] Gesner published a catalogue of Johann Kentmann's collection at Dresden in 1565; other early catalogues of collections include those of Olaf Worm in Copenhagen (1655), John Tredescant in London (1656), the Gottorffische Kunstkammer (1666), Ferdinando Cospi in Bologna (1677), the Royal Society in London (1681) and of King Christian V of Denmark at Copenhagen (1696) (*see* Newton, 1891).
[12] For a more detailed survey of the early naturalists' collections see Whitehead (1970, 1971).
[13] For a detailed study see Quynn (1945) and an excellent summary, Taylor (1948, Chapter 5).
[14] Although the Australian Museum celebrated its centenary and sesquicentenary in 1927 and 1977 respectively, new evidence (Strahan, *et al* 1979, p. 10) suggests that these events were two years premature.
[15] Based on Ho, C-H. *The Growth and Use of Collections in China before the Advent of Modern Museums in the Twentieth Century,* MA dissertation, University of Leicester, 1978.
[16] For a fuller discussion on 'the Common Market and the Art Market' see *Int. J. Museum Management and Curatorship,* **1** (4), 303–338 (1982) and **2** (1), 11–26 (1983).
[17] According to the study the ratio in the following selected countries is: Australia 1:14 000; Canada 1:23 000; France 1:43 000; India 1:1 831 000; Japan 1:77 000; New Zealand 1:27 000; Nigeria 1:3 177 000; USSR 1:189 000; UK 1:55 000; USA 1:41 000.
[18] On cultural democracy see, for example, Key (1973, 234–5) concerning Canadian national museum policy, Simpson (1976) and UNESCO (1982), pp 25–7, 43.

References

AKSENOVA, A. I. (1978), 'Vladimir and Suzdal, museum cities', *Museum,* **30**(2), 116–121
AMERICAN ASSOCIATION OF MUSEUMS (1969), *America's Museums; The Belmont Report,* AAM, Washington DC

BARRY, T. H. (1975), '150 years – an assessment', *South African Museums Association Bulletin,* **11**(7), 249–260

BAZIN, G. (1967), *The Museum Age,* Desoer, Brussels

BAZIN, G. (1979), *The Louvre,* Thames & Hudson, London

BEDINI, S. A. (1965), 'The evolution of science museums', *Technology and Culture,* **6**, 1–29

BURNHAM, B. (1974), *The Protection of Cultural Property; Handbook of National Legislations,* ICOM, Paris

CAMERON, D. R. (1969), *Are Art Galleries Obsolete?,* Peter Martin Associates, Toronto, Canada

CHADWICK, J. (1958), *The Decipherment of Linear B,* Cambridge University Press, England

CHEETHAM, F. (1981), 'Norfolk in Europe', *Museums J.,* **80**(4), 183–5

COLEMAN, L. V. (1939), *The Museum in America 1–3,* American Association of Museums; Washington DC

COSSONS, N. (1980), 'The museum in the valley, Ironbridge Gorge', *Museum,* **32**(3), 138–53

COX, L. B. (1970), *The National Gallery of Victoria 1861–1968: A Search for a Collection,* National Gallery of Victoria, Melbourne, Australia

DE LA TORRE, M. AND MONREAL, L. (1982), *Museums: An Investment for Development,* ICOM, Paris, 1982

DE VARINE-BOHAN, H. (1973), 'A fragmented museum: the Museum of Man and Industry, Le Creusot-Montceaules-Mines', *Museum,* **25**(4), 242–249

DIOP, A. S. G. (1973), 'Museological activity in African countries: its role and purpose', *Museum,* **25**(4), 250–6

DIXON, B. *et al* (1974), *The Museum and the Canadian Public,* Arts & Culture Branch, Department of the Secretary of State, Toronto

DUBE, W. (1970), *The Munich Gallery, Alte Pinakothek,* Thames & Hudson, London

EUROPEAN COMMUNITIES, (1978), *Community Action in the Cultural Sector,* Bulletin of the European Communities, supplement 6/77, Commission of the European Communities, Belgium

EVRARD, M. (1980), 'Le Creusot-Montceau-les-Mines: the life of an ecomuseum, assessment of ten years', *Museum,* **32**(4), 226–234

FEDERAL CULTURAL POLICY REVIEW COMMITTEE (1982a), 'Heritage' in *Report,* chapter 4, Information Services, Department of Communications, Government of Canada, Ottawa

FEDERAL CULTURAL POLICY REVIEW COMMITTEE (1982b), 'Heritage' in *Summary of Briefs and Hearings,* Chapter 3, Information Services, Department of Communications, Government of Canada, Ottawa

FRADIER, G. (1978), 'The Georges Pompidou National Centre for Art and Culture, Paris', *Museum,* **30**(2), 77–87

GILMAN, B. (1977), *Le Musee: Agent d'Innovation Culturelle,* Council of Europe, Strasbourg

GREENWOOD, T. (1888), *Museums and Art Galleries,* Simpkin Marshall, London

ICOM (1974), *ICOM Statutes,* Paris

KENYON, (1927), *Museums and National Life,* Clarendon Press, Oxford

KEY, A. F. (1973), *Beyond Four Walls: the Origins and Development of Canadian Museums,* McClelland & Stewart, Toronto

KINARD, J. AND NIGHBERT, E. (1972), 'The Anacostia Neighbourhood Museum, Smithsonian Institution, Washington, DC', *Museum,* **24**(12), 103–109

KLESSMANN, R. (1971), *The Berlin Gallery,* Thames & Hudson, London

KOCHER, A. *et al* (1961), *Colonial Williamsburg: its Buildings and Gardens,* Holt, Rinehart and Winston, New York

LAPAIRE, C. (1980), *Schweizen Museum Führer/Guide des Musées Suisses,* Paul Haupt, Bern

MALCOLM, W. G. (1978), *Regional Museums in Northern Ireland,* Department of Education for Northern Ireland, HMSO, Belfast

MARKHAM, S. F. and OLIVER, W. R. B. (1933), *A Report on the Museums and Art Galleries of New Zealand,* Museums Association, London

MARKHAM, S. F. and RICHARDS, H. C. (1933), *A Report on the Museums and Art Galleries of Australia,* Museums Association, London

MASSEY, V. (1951), 'Canadian museums and art galleries' in *Report of the Royal Commission on Arts, Letters and Sciences,* the King's Printer, Ottawa

MIERS, SIR H.A. AND MARKHAM, S. F. (1932), *The Museums of Canada,* Museums Association, London

MURRAY, D. (1904), *Museums: Their History and their Use, 1–3,* J. MacLehose & Sons, Glasgow

MUSEUMS DEPARTMENT OF THE STATE, ADMINISTRATIVE BUREAU OF MUSEUMS AND ARCHAEOLOGICAL DATA (1980), 'Museums in China Today', *Museum,* **32**(4), 170–182

NATIONAL ENDOWMENT FOR THE ARTS (1974), *Museums USA,* US Government Printing Office, Washington, DC

NEICKEL, F. (1727), *Museographia,* Michael Hubert, Leipzig

NEWTON, A. (1891), 'Notes on some old museums', *Report of proceedings . . . at the Annual General Meeting held at Cambridge . . . 1891,* 28–48, Museums Association

OEHSER, P. H. (1970), *The Smithsonian Institution,* Praeger, New York

PERRY, W. (1972), *The Science Museum of Victoria: A History of its First Hundred Years,* Science Museum of Victoria, Melbourne, Australia

PIOTROVSKY, B. (1978), 'Introduction' in *Western European painting in the Hermitage,* Aurora, Leningrad

[PIGGOT, P. H.] (1975), *Museums in Australia,* Australian Government Publishing Service, Canberra

PRESCOTT, R. I. M. (1954), *Collections of a Century: The History of the First Hundred Years of the National Museum of Victoria,* National Museum of Victoria, Melbourne, Australia

QUYNN, D. M. (1945), 'The art confiscations of Napoleonic wars', *American History Review,* **1**(3)

REBETEZ, P. (1970), *How to visit a Museum,* Council for Cultural Co-operation of the Council of Europe, Strasbourg

[ROSSE, EARL OF] (1963), *Survey of Provincial Museums and Galleries* Standing Commission on Museums and Galleries, HMSO, London

ROYAL ONTARIO MUSEUM (1976), *Communicating with the Museum Visitor – Guidelines for Planning,* Royal Ontario Museum, Toronto, Canada

SALEY, M. (1976), 'Action to help the blind and physically handicapped, Niger National Museum, Niamey', *Museum,* **28**(4), 210–211

SANCHEZ CANTON, F. J. (1973), *The Prado,* Thames and Hudson, London

SELLARS, C. C. (1980), *Mr Peale's Museum,* Norton, New York

SIMPSON, J. A. (1976), *Towards Cultural Democracy,* Council of Europe, Strasbourg

SPAANDONK, J. W. M. (1977), *Towards a New Museums Policy*, (English Summary of Government memorandum), Ministry of Cultural Affairs, Recreation and Social Welfare, Netherlands Government Printing Office, The Hague

STRAHAN, R. *et al* (1979), *Rare and Curious Specimens – an Illustrated History of the Australia Museum*, The Australian Museum, Sydney, NSW

TABORSKY, E. (1982), 'The Sociostructural role of the museum', *The International J. of Museum Management and Curatorship*, **1**(4), 339–345

TAYLOR, F. H. (1948), *The Taste of Angels*, Little, Brown and Co., Boston, USA

THIAM, A. and THILMANS, G. (1980), 'Gorée – the museum island', *Museum*, **32**(3), 119–29

THOMSON, K. W. (1981), *Art Galleries and Museums in New Zealand*, A. H. and A. W. Reed, Wellington, NZ

TSURUTA, S. (1960), 'Museum administration in Japan' in *Museums in Japan*, 1–34, Japanese National Commission for Unesco, Kasal, Tokyo

TURNER, G. L'. E. (1973), 'A very scientific century' in Lefebvre, E. and de Bruijn, J. G. (Eds) *Martinus van Marum: Life and Work*, Volume IV, Noordhoff, Leyden

UNESCO (1973), 'The role of museums in today's Latin America', *Museum*, **25**(3), 128–202

UNESCO (1979), *La Protection du Patrimoine Cultural Mobilier I*, UNESCO, Paris

UNESCO (1981), *La Protection du Patrimoine Cultural Mobilier II*, UNESCO, Paris

UNESCO (1982), *World Conference on Cultural Policies, Final Report*, UNESCO, Paris

USSR MINISTRY OF CULTURE (1980), *Museums in the USSR*, Moscow

VON BIEBERSTEIN, M. M. (1979), 'Museums in Britain and the Council of Europe', *Museums J.*, **79**(3). 124–125

VON HOLST, N. (1967), *Creators, Collectors and Connoisseurs*, Thames and Hudson, London

[WILLIAMS, A.] (1981), *A Heritage for Scotland – Scotland's National Museums and Galleries: The Next 25 Years*, HMSO, Glasgow

WITTLIN, A. (1970), *Museums: In Search of a Usable Future*, MIT Press, Cambridge, Massachusettes, USA

WHITEHEAD, P. J. P. (1970), 'Museums in the history of zoology' (Part 1) *Museums J.*, **70**(2), 50–57

WHITEHEAD, P. J. P. (1971), 'Museums in the history of zoology' (Part 2), *Museums J.*, **70**(4), 155–160

WOOLLEY, SIR L. AND MOOREY, P. R. (1982), *Ur 'of the Chaldees'*, Herbert Press Ltd., London

WRIGHT, C. W. (1973), *Provincial Museums and Galleries*, Department of Education and Science, HMSO, London

3

Collections, collectors and museums in Britain to 1920

Geoffrey D. Lewis

There is little evidence of collecting antiquities in pre-historic times in Britain and little can be inferred from the occasional discovery of chronologically alien artefacts in archaeological levels. One possible exception, however, is the modified Bronze Age pal-stave associated with the rich Iron Age burial in the Lexden Tumulus, Essex, dating to the late first century BC. By Roman times, prehistoric stone axes seem to have assumed some importance at certain temple sites – perhaps those associated with Jupiter; a palaeolithic hand axe was present in a pit near the second-century AD probable temple at Kelvedon, Essex, while the Ivy Chimneys Romano-British temple complex at Witham contained two depressions filled with votive offerings which had been lined with at least thirty-two palaeolithic hand axes. Stone axes have also been found on temple sites in France[1].

For Britain, at the farthest limits of the Roman Empire, there is no evidence of the public exhibition of art either, on the scale that was prevalent in Rome. Nor has excavation produced evidence of displays of exotica from distant parts in Britain's Roman temples; this would have more point in the homeland. But there is no doubt that the temples, as well as public buildings, were places where collections of sculpture, figurines and other objects could be seen. Suetonius, for example, records that many busts of Titus were to be seen in Britain. Salway (1981), drawing on archaeological evidence, imagines even the rural shrines to have been 'decked with votive offerings'. Certainly classical art was already entering Britain in small quantities by Claudian times; by the end of the second century AD it was common-place, and much of it was being executed by native craftsmen (Frere, 1978). The collection of fine objects seems also to have been a feature of the early Christian church in Britain. The Water Newton trea-sure, for example, certainly had Christian conne-

xions as did the finds at the Roman villa site at Lul-lingstone in Kent with its remarkable fourth-century wall paintings.

The evidence of collecting and collections becomes scarcer as Britain enters Medieval times and the pat-tern is no doubt similar to that of mainland Europe. Documentary evidence supports the view that a number of ecclesiastical establishments and royal households held rich treasuries. The seventh-century boat burial at Sutton Hoo with its fine jewellery (Bruce-Mitford, 1975, 1978) and the St Ninian's treasure (Small et al, 1973) of the late eighth or early ninth century add weight to this evidence of such secular collections. But if the writings of Bede show some evidence of historical enquiry, these collections do not; nor is there any evidence that they were dis-played for the public benefit. Nevertheless antiqua-rian studies, albeit of varying validity, continued throughout the period leading up to the Renaissance, drawing mainly on documentary material. Matthew Paris writing in the twelfth century, however, used the antiquities of St Albans as his source while, for example, a later tract describing the pictures and other contents of the abbey church of that city was probably written, as Gransden (1980) suggests, at least partly for the benefit of visitors.

There is some evidence of contact between Britain and Italy although the influence of the Renaissance on the former country was slow. As early as the twelfth century Taylor (1948) records Bishop Henry of Winchester bringing back a collection of anti-quities from Rome while Humphrey, Duke of Gloucester, a patron of the new learning, amassed a library which was to found the Bodleian Library of the University of Oxford in the fourteenth century. However it does not appear to have had any impact on teaching at the University before the latter part of the fifteenth century. The Kings of England were not great art collectors, although the new learning did affect them in other ways, Henry VIII acting as patron to poetry and music which flourished in his court. In 1533, he appointed the country's only King's Antiquary, John Leland, to describe and list material of antiquarian interest in England and Wales. Later in the century a society for the preservation of national antiquities was formed and by 1586 William Camden's guide to British antiquities, *Britannia,* had been published. The sixteenth century saw many changes, some of which have a direct bearing on collecting and the eventual emergence of museums in Britain. One of them was, of course, the dissolution of the monasteries and their collections; another, increasingly to have a profound effect on the nature of the country's major cultural collections, was the changing balance of sea power as trans-ocean exploration, trade and eventually colonization by Britain took place.

The first royal collection of significance in England was that formed by Charles I. He inherited a small collection of paintings and other *objects d'art* at the palaces of Whitehall, Windsor and Hampton to which he added with taste. One of his major acquisitions was the purchase in 1627 of the entire Gonzaga collection from Mantua; another was the purchase of Raphael's original cartoons used for the Papal tapestries, 'The Acts of the Apostles', now in the Victoria and Albert Museum; about 1400 paintings and 400 sculptures were listed in the catalogue of Charles' collection. After his execution, the majority was sold and dispersed to many private collections in Europe. Of those that remained, most were destroyed in a disastrous fire at the Whitehall Palace in 1697 and it was not until the later eighteenth century, during the reign of George III, that royal patronage of art re-emerges in Britain.

It was the private, mainly aristocratic collectors who were to contribute their collections to the first public museums. A number of them were operating during the first half of the seventeenth century, amongst them Thomas Howard, 21st Earl of Arundel (1586–1646), Sir Dudley Carleton (1573–1632), Sir Robert Cotton (1571–1631), John Tradescant (1587–1638) and his son of the same name (1608–1662). Another collector, whose cabinet and specimens have recently been rediscovered by Mr David Sturdy, was John Bargrave (1610–1680) who became Canon at Canterbury and whose travels contributed much to his collection. The Earl of Arundel was one of the first to appreciate the importance of Asia Minor and Greece as a source of antiquities. For over thirty years he travelled to bring together a superb collection of classical marble statues and inscriptions, pottery, gems, pictures and manuscripts. They were exhibited in London's Strand in a gallery at Arundel House, modelled on the Uffizi Gallery, and undoubtedly were available to the scholars of the time. Amongst them was Francis Bacon who, in

1594, had suggested to Elizabeth I that a cabinet of man-made products, a library, botanical and zoological garden should be provided to further scientific work. Much of the Arundel collection became dispersed but the library was given to the Royal Society, and many of the inscribed marbles to the University of Oxford, now to be seen in the Ashmolean Museum. Sir Dudley Carleton (later Viscount Dorchester) formed his collection not only for pleasure but profit. As a British ambassador, his duties enabled him to create a network of agents in different parts of the world to acquire antiquities and paintings. Many of these he sent to England and elsewhere where there was a ready market. Rubens was among his customers and exchanged some of his paintings for antiquities to improve his cabinet at Antwerp.

The original impetus for Sir Robert Cotton's collection probably came while he was at school; William Camden, who was second master at Westminster School, no doubt encouraged him in antiquarian matters. His interests related not to the classical world but to Britain which he toured to collect manuscripts, particularly those concerned with the suppressed monasteries, together with coins and antiquities to form one of the fine founding collections of the British Museum.

John Tradescant's collection and background was of a humbler nature. Probably of yeoman farming stock he spent his working life as a skilful gardener on four country estates. That the last two were owned by George Villiers, Duke of Buckingham, and Charles I, both avid collectors, may be significant but he was certainly collecting exotic plants and other material before these appointments. He visited many places in Europe, including Archangel and the Isle of Rhe, as well as North Africa and also enjoyed a number of contacts elsewhere overseas. In 1625 he leased a house in Lambeth where he assembled his collections and created a garden for his foreign plants. His house was opened to the public and, Tradescant's Ark as it was known, became a well-known London sight. From contemporary descriptions it contained stuffed birds and animals and a wide variety of artefacts from many parts of the world. There was certainly a printed guide to the garden and its plants, but a catalogue of the whole collection was published after Tradescant's death under the title *Musæum Tradescantianum* in 1656; this appears to have been the first use of the term 'museum' in England in its currently understood form. His son, also John Tradescant, continued to maintain and supplement the collection which eventually became the major founding collection for the Ashmolean Museum at Oxford (MacGregor, 1983). At least one other collection in London was opened to visitors at this time: this was the Tower where, apart from the armoury and the Crown Jewels, a

Zoo and other objects, including the horn of a 'unicorn', could be seen.

From the mid-seventeenth century a new scientific movement developed in England. This led, in 1660, to the establishment of the oldest extant learned society in the country, the Royal Society. Charles II granted it a charter two years later; in the same year one of the subjects under discussion was the preservative qualities of spirits of wine in keeping animal material. Strong antiquarian interests in England led to the formation of a club in 1707 primarily concerned with the history and antiquities of Great Britain. The members met regularly at two London taverns and in 1718 formed the Society of Antiquaries of London, which received its Royal Charter in 1751. Coffee houses were also places of popular resort. One of these, run by 'Don Saltero' in Chelsea, fulfilled a 'museum' role throughout the eighteenth century, even though its collections boasted such things as 'Pontius Pilate's wife's chambermaid's sister's sister's hat' and other equally improbable curiosities. Another coffee house, Rawthmell's, was the venue for the inaugural meeting in 1754 of a society for the encouragement of arts, manufactures and commerce, now better known as the Royal Society of Arts. All three maintained collections for the interest of their members although some have now passed them to museums. The Linnaean Society was established in 1788.

Interest in the classical world continued. Excavations at Herculaneum in 1709 saw the beginning of a new wave of intensive exploration in Italy and Greece. This in turn was to affect taste and design in Europe generally during the eighteenth century and it became an important feature in the cultural education of the English gentleman to undertake the 'grand tour' of the classical world. A group of these formed the Society of Dilettanti in 1732 to encourage 'a taste for those objects which had contributed so much to their entertainment abroad'. Increasingly at this time we find galleries being established at the great English country houses, often to display classical sculpture[2].

London was not, however, the only centre where learned societies were formed. The Spalding Gentlemen's Society, founded in 1710 by Maurice Johnson, one of the leading members of the embryonic Society of Antiquaries of London, was seen as 'a cell' to that Society in its earlier days. The Society maintained a library and museum for its members in Spalding and it remains the oldest society museum in Britain. Other later eighteenth-century societies, which included the formation of a museum collection among their aims were the Newcastle-upon-Tyne Literary and Philosophical Society (1770); the Society of Antiquaries of Scotland (1781); the Manchester Literary and Philosophical Society (1781) and the Perth Literary and Antiquarian Society (1784).

Their number was to increase considerably in the following century.

The first public museums

The first public museum in England was the Ashmolean at Oxford. Based on the Tradescants' collection which Elias Ashmole acquired, with additions from his own material, he gave the collection to the University of Oxford on condition that a room was built to house it. The University seems readily to have accepted the gift and incorporated it on the upper floor of a new Chemistry laboratory built in Broad Street (now the Museum of the History of Science). Known initially as Ashmole's Repository, this was soon changed to the Ashmolean Museum, the name now borne by the successor institution in Beaumont Street. The Museum was opened by James, Duke of York, in May 1683 and admission, on payment of a small fee for a guided tour, was open to anyone. The first Keeper was Dr Robert Plot, author of a natural history of two counties (Oxfordshire and Staffordshire), who gave lectures on chemistry in the museum three times a week. The stimulus that the collection gave to the study of natural history in Oxford seems to have been limited. Plot resigned in 1691 and in a letter to his successor deplored the lack of interest taken by both the Royal Society of London and the local Philosophical Society. Nevertheless it remained the centre of scientific work in Oxford for over 150 years. With the subsequent development of specialist museums in Oxford, different parts of the founding collection were passed to them (MacGregor, 1983).

The Act of Parliament to facilitate the creation of the British Museum was passed in 1753. In describing the founding collection of Sir Hans Sloane it meticulously qualified the use of the word 'museum' with 'collection'; the Harley and Cotton material, however, was described as the collection of manuscripts and the library respectively. This was the first occasion the word had been used in an Act of Parliament, the term repository was used for the building to house it. The Act describes the purpose and role of the collection:

> Whereas all arts and sciences have a connexion with each other, and discoveries in natural philosophy and other branches of speculative knowledge, for the advancement and improvement whereof the said Museum or collection was intended, do and may, in many instances, give help and success to the most useful experiments and inventions; . . . [and that] the said Museum or collection may be preserved and maintained, not only for the inspection and entertainment of the learned and the curious, but for the general use and benefit of the public.

This is a commentary on the encyclopaedic philosophy of the time and the role envisaged for the museum in this context. The Act also makes it clear that there should be free public access to view and peruse the collection 'at all stated and convenient seasons'.

The interpretation of free public access considerably exercised the minds of the Trustees (Miller, 1973, pp 61–63) and as a result strict rules governing admissions to the Museum were drawn up when it opened in 1759. With the exception of holy days it opened from Monday to Friday each week during the winter from 9 am to 3 pm; the daytime opening was restricted to three days during the Summer but on the other two days it opened from 4 pm to 8 pm for the benefit of those unable to come at the normal times. To gain admission it was necessary to apply for a ticket, return to collect it and then come again to visit the collection on the day and time authorized. Only ten tickets were issued for each hour and visitors were conducted round the Museum in parties of five. Despite this, François de la Rochefoucauld noted with approval in 1784 that the Museum was expressly 'for the instruction and gratification of the public', no doubt reflecting in part the prevailing conditions in France and also the different approaches of the two countries, perhaps expressed best in Bazin's words (1967): 'The institution's approach to art is from the standpoint of archaeology'. In its early years the British Museum attracted about 10 000 visitors annually.

The major founding collection of the British Museum was that of Sir Hans Sloane (1660–1753) to which were added those of Robert Harley, first Earl of Oxford (1661–1724) and Sir Robert Cotton, already discussed. The latter's grandson was responsible for giving the collection, supplemented by his father and himself, to the nation; despite Acts of 1700 and 1707 it remained in temporary quarters and was subjected to a disastrous fire before the 1753 Act secured its permanent home. The Harley library had been sold after the death of Edward, the second Earl, in 1741 but the manuscripts remained and these were offered to the government by Lady Oxford and her daughter, Margaret, Duchess of Portland, for £10 000 on hearing of the proposals for the Sloane and Cotton collections.

The Sloane collection originated from a natural history collection made during his stay in Jamaica as personal physician to the Governor, the Duke of Albermarle. To this he added further specimens, classical antiquities, ethnographical material and paintings which were supplemented in 1702 by William Couten's fine personal collection. Contemporary accounts of the collection[3] give some idea of its size and splendour. In his Will he directed his trustees to offer the collection to the nation in return for £20 000. The money for this, the Harley collection and the acquisition of Montagu House, Bloomsbury to house them came from a public lottery which raised £95 000.

Reference has already been made to the collections of the aristocracy. Particularly well known in the second half of the eighteenth century were the collections of Charles Lennox, Duke of Richmond (1735–1806) and the second Duchess of Portland (1715–1785). Both collections could be viewed by friends and scholars. After Lennox's visit to Italy in 1758 where he had observed that art students were given access to collections, he adopted a similar practice with his paintings, classical sculpture and casts. The Duchess of Portland's fine collection, which included the 'Berberini' or 'Portland' vase eventually found its way into the British Museum in 1810.

Although in the tradition of Tradescant's Ark of more than a century earlier, the London exhibitions of Sir Ashton Lever (1729–1788) and William Bullock had an entrepreneurial character not revealed earlier (for these and others see Altrick, 1978). They became prominent features of the London scene in their time but both had their origins in the industrial north midlands of England. Lever's collection of natural history specimens (particularly birds) and ethnographic material was first opened to the public at Alkringham Hall to the north of Manchester. Judging from a press advertisement issued in 1773 he became 'tired out of the insolence of the common people' visiting his museum and resolved that in future he would refuse admittance 'to the lower class except that they come provided with a ticket from some Gentleman or Lady of my acquaintance' (Mullens, 1915, p. 125). In the event, the size of his collection forced him to find other accommodation and about 1774 he transferred much of it to London, where he opened his 'Holophusikon' in Leicester Square. The admission fee was reputed to have been half a guinea. This show, however, waned in popularity early in the 1780s and was eventually acquired by a Mr Parkinson who exhibited it at the Rotunda on the south side of Blackfriars Bridge until its dispersal in 1806 (Mullens, 1915).

Bullock first exhibited his collection about 1795 in Sheffield (in Museum Street in the town centre) from whence he moved to Liverpool in 1801 and then to London where, for ten years from 1809, it was shown in Piccadilly. Housed in two rooms, the 'Pantherion' and the 'London Room' for which separate admission fees of one shilling for each were charged, the former contained dramatic habitat groups of many of the quadrupeds which were clearly one of its major attractions. The collection had a natural history bias and was arranged in Linnaean order, but also included art and armour, natural freaks, and other historical and ethnographical material (Mullens, 1917). There is no doubt that these two entrepreneurs helped to popularize the museum idea, at least among those who could afford to pay for the privilege.

At the other end of the spectrum scientists and antiquarians maintained private collections which were made available to their peers, if not the public at large. One of these collections housed in Leicester Square, London was the systematically arranged physiological specimens of John Hunter (1728–1793), younger brother of William Hunter whose collection formed the Hunterian Museum at Glasgow University. This eventually became the Museum of the Royal College of Surgeons in Lincoln's Inn Fields. Another was Sir Joseph Banks (1743–1820) whose eclectic collection at Soho was freely available to scholars, the botanical section of which is now in the British Museum (Natural History). Banks, who was with James Cook on his first voyage to the Pacific, employed Daniel Solander (1733–1782) as an assistant. A pupil of Linnaeus in Sweden, Solander was also on the staff of the British Museum; his name is perpetuated in the Solander box.

The early nineteenth century

The turn of the century, therefore, saw a number of agencies making collections for a variety of reasons: the government, universities, schools and other educational establishments, learned societies, scholars and scientists, the entrepreneur and certain trading companies.

Foremost among the trading enterprise collections was that of the East India Company whose employees were encouraged to contribute specimens to it. Founded in 1801 with the serious intention of promoting Asian studies, it was opened to the public who gained admission by ticket; it was no doubt seen principally as a cabinet of curiosities but was an acknowledged public attraction in London. Its collections played an important role in the Indian pavilion of the Great Exhibition of 1851 and when they were transferred to the Government in 1857 they became known as the India Museum. After a separate existence for seventy-seven years its collections were dispersed, many of them going to the South Kensington Museum (Desmond, 1982).

In 1799 a new Principal Librarian was appointed to oversee the British Museum. He had to face considerable problems, not least a building too small to hold its collections – the Egyptian material including the Rosetta Stone, had to be stored in wooden sheds in the garden when it arrived early in 1802 – and in a very poor state of repair for lack of funds. The latter situation was eventually alleviated when, in 1815, building maintenance became the responsibility of a government department rather than the Trustees, a situation prevailing to the present day. The conges-

tion was relieved when the Townley Gallery was opened in 1808, to house the Museum's rapidly expanding antiquities collection. The library also increased considerably in size and when the King's Library was also offered to the Museum in 1823 a master plan was drawn up to rebuild the British Museum completely. Designed by Sir Robert Smirke this took place in stages over a period of nearly half-a-century. The King's Library came first with a picture gallery to house the national collection above it. In the event the gallery was not needed for this purpose.

The creation of a national public art gallery in Britain came late, compared with many other European countries. This, Bazin (1967) argues, was because the English conceived the museum to have a predominantly scientific role. Certainly an important opportunity was lost in 1778 when the British government declined to build an art gallery to house the Walpole collection but the Royal Academy of Arts, established in 1768, partially fulfilled this role. John Constable criticized the idea of a national gallery although he hardly invoked the 'scientific' argument: he feared that its influence would bring 'an end of the art in poor old England'. But the prospect of the loss of the fine Angerstein collection abroad precipitated the issue and in 1824 Parliament voted the necessary funds to buy it and form a National Gallery in the owner's house at 100 Pall Mall. Other collections followed and the gallery moved into its purposebuilt premises in Trafalgar Square in 1838.

The University of Oxford's Ashmolean Museum saw little change during the eighteenth century but shortly after 1823 displays were rearranged systematically and much of the founding collection relegated to stores (MacGregor, 1983). By this time, however, collections in other universities were being maintained for teaching purposes. The Woodward geological collection had been acquired by the University of Cambridge in 1727 but when Sedgwick was appointed to the Chair of Geology in 1818 this was considerably expanded to form the basis of the Museum now named after him. Similarly, the bequest of Viscount Fitzwilliam (1745–1816) founded the well-known museum of that name at Cambridge although it did not move into the present purposebuilt premises until 1848; it is worthy of note that Lord Fitzwilliam had been deterred from giving his collection to the British Museum because of the Trustees' powers to dispose of duplicate specimens. Glasgow University's museum was opened in 1804 following the bequest, some twenty years previously, of Dr William Hunter.

A few other educational institutions also formed museums during this period. Stonyhurst College, near Blackburn, formed a museum in 1794 while another school, Ampleforth College, is reputed to have had a museum in 1802. At Liverpool the Royal

Institution, founded in 1814, housed a natural history museum as well as a picture gallery and continued to fulfill this function long after the Town Council established their museum. The Royal Institution of Cornwall started its museum in Truro in 1818 where it remains the country's principal museum.

This was the period when a number of other learned societies were established, many of them forming collections for the benefit of their members and friends. Some dating to the eighteenth century have already been listed, but others included the Society of Antiquaries of Newcastle-upon-Tyne (1813), the Royal Geological Society of Cornwall in Penzance (1814), the Belfast Natural History Society (1821) now part of the Ulster Museum (Nisbett, 1979), the Leeds Philosophical and Literary Society (1821), the Manchester Natural History Society (1821) and the Sheffield Literary and Philosophical Society (1822). Like the Belfast Society, the collections of these also found their way into the public museums later established in these cities. The Yorkshire Philosophical Society was responsible for establishing the Yorkshire Museum at York in 1823 (Orange, 1973) while the Scarborough Philosophical Society built their museum in 1829 in the form of a rotunda at the suggestion of William Smith so that the geological collections could be displayed in stratigraphic sequence.

Private collections were also being formed of Britain's natural and antiquarian heritage. A tradition of antiquarian field exploration dates from John Leland's day. For some, like William Borlase (1754), this was a substitute for classical travel which they could not afford. During the eighteenth century these interests developed into the digging of sites, mainly burial mounds, particularly by the landed gentry and clergy, and thousands were explored during the next hundred-and-fifty years. This antiquarian movement, which during the 1840s formed two rival national organizations, the British Archaeological Association and the Royal Archaeological Institute of Great Britain and Ireland, became concerned that unlike many other European countries there was no national museum of antiquities in Britain. In answer to this criticism the British Museum opened two small rooms for British antiquities by 1850 but another sixteen years elapsed before a Department of British and Medieval Antiquities was formed (Kendrick, 1951).

In the absence of a national lead, many of the important discoveries remained outside of London, eventually to find their way into provincial museums. Among these were the collection of the Rev. Bryan Faussett (1720–1776) purchased by Joseph Mayer – after they had been declined by the British Museum – and through whose generosity they were given later to the Liverpool Museum; those of Sir Richard Colt Hoare (1758–1838) and

William Cunningham (1754–1810) from Wessex now form an important part of the Devizes Museum. Another collection, not only of local antiquities, was made by William Bateman (1787–1835) and his son Thomas (1821–1861); housed at Lomberdale House, Derbyshire and the subject of a published catalogue (Bateman, 1855), it now forms the core of the archaeological collection at the Sheffield City Museum.

But the doyen of nineteenth-century private collectors in this field was Lieut-General A. H. Lane-Fox Pitt-Rivers (1827–1900). Initially he amassed a world-wide collection of ethnographical and prehistoric material and, following his detailed study of the history of British firearms, came to the conclusion that artefacts generally should be arranged typologically rather than geographically, to demonstrate their development. His collection was lent for a time to the Bethnal Green Museum in 1874 but was given to the University of Oxford in 1883 where it is housed in the Pitt Rivers Museum. He also founded the Farnham Museum in Dorset to house the finds from his excavations, particularly on Cranborne Chase, which formed part of the Rivers estate he inherited in 1880.

The municipal museum movement in Britain

The origins of municipal museums in mid-nineteenth century Britain stem from the social and political influences of the previous forty years. This was an age of reform with the Government attempting to respond to the effects of the industrial revolution which, over a relatively short period, had created major population centres outside the metropolis, bringing with it the need for massive social reform. There was a concern that those in manufacturing industry, including the working classes, should have opportunities to extend their knowledge, particularly in the arts and principles of design; in this the Society for the Encouragement of Arts, Manufactures and Commerce had played a prominent part since its foundation (Hudson and Lockhurst, 1954).

The learned societies and the museums, in their way, were contributing to the needs and the spirit of the age but only for those with the means to support them. For the operatives of the new industrial society experimental classes were organized in Glasgow, Edinburgh and London which led to the formation of a Mechanics' Institution in the latter city in 1824. The idea spread rapidly in Britain and by 1860 there were 610 institutes with over a hundred thousand members (Woodward, 1979); as has already been seen its influence also spread to the colonies. Although primarily intended to provide formal educational opportunities, the Institutes soon found themselves organizing excursions to places of interest, including country houses, and arranging exhibitions, the latter often to raise funds.

The London Mechanics' Institution was responsible for the development of the 'National Repository' of new inventions and improved productions acquired, to be shown at the annual exhibition of the Institution; by 1835 this collection was open daily to the public as the Museum of National Manufactures and of the Mechanical Arts in Leicester Square (Kusamitsu, 1980). Other Institutes also formed museums, among them Keighley and Bradford; Keighley specialized in fossils and minerals but also had a technical section; Bradford attempted to develop on local lines but was less successful (Tylecote, 1957). Manchester started a natural history class in 1836 and acquired an extensive herbarium and a collection of British insects which formed the basis of a museum, for which there was a salaried curator for a time. There can be little doubt that these enterprises and the great success of the Mechanics' Institution exhibitions were an important contribution in developing public opinion towards local museums. Indeed letters to the *Manchester Guardian* in January 1838 expressed the hope that the success of the Manchester Institute's recent exhibition would add support to the idea of opening museums and galleries to the general public.

In the meantime government was grappling with its social problems. Not surprisingly the main protagonists were from the industrial constituencies of whom, in the context of museums and galleries, James Silk Buckingham (MP for Sheffield 1832–1837) and William Ewart (MP for Liverpool 1830–1837), and Dumfries 1840–1868) were particularly prominent. Another, Benjamin Hawes (MP for Lambeth) was responsible for a report on foreign museums and libraries in 1834. He was a member of a parliamentary committee, of which Buckingham was Chairman, to consider possible remedies to the 'vices of intoxication amongst the labouring classes' which recommended *inter alia* that through the joint aid of government, local authorities and residents, open spaces, libraries, museums and reading rooms should be provided (Select Committee, 1834). The following year he was a member of a parliamentary committee investigating allegations that the management of the British Museum was bad and its staff were living in indolence and affluence (Hawes, 1835). As a result of the report on drunkeness, Buckingham sought to introduce the necessary legislation which would have empowered local authorities to have provided at least the capital expenditure for museums, the running costs to be met from low charges and local benevolence. Despite three attempts, he failed.

By this time the *Municipal Corporation Act 1835* had

come into force which provided a more appropriate organizational base for local government, at the same time retaining central government control over its activities. In the same year another Parliamentary Select Committee was set up on the proposal of Ewart to enquire into existing institutions concerned with the arts and ways of extending a knowledge of the arts and principles of design among the people. It recommended that museums and galleries should be formed, sculpture and painting should be introduced to public buildings and a school of design be created in London (Select Committee, 1849); only the latter was implemented. It was not until 1844 that a public meeting in Manchester suggested that local authorities should be empowered to establish and run museums from the rates.

The *Museums Act 1845* followed authorizing the expenditure of a half-penny rate for the purpose, in places with a population of more than 10 000. Introduced by Ewart, it was intended to promote 'the instruction and amusement' of the public. There is little doubt, though, that its easy passage through Parliament was because museums were seen as a moral benefit to society and that their collections would be a means of contributing to better industrial design. Known popularly as the 'Beetle Act' it permitted an admission charge not exceeding one penny and vested the specimens acquired to be held in trust for ever by the Corporation. Parliament saw fit also to bring into effect the same day the *Protection of Works of Art and Scientific and Literary Collections Act 1845,* which did not extend to Scotland, introducing penalties for malicious damage to such material. One of the arguments against providing general public access to museums had been the fear of damage to the specimens, a factor dispelled to a considerable extent in the behaviour of visitors to the Mechanics' Institution exhibitions.

Six towns adopted the Museums Act in the next four years: Sunderland (1846), Canterbury (1847), Warrington (1848) and Dover, Leicester and Salford (1849). With the exception of Salford, the local authorities took over the collections of the local Literary and Philosophical Societies (in the case of Warrington, the Natural History Society) to provide these museums. At Canterbury, Salford and Warrington a library was also provided under the Act, probably illegally. In justification of this, the Town Clerk of Warrington explained (Select Committee, 1849) that they employed 'a skilled naturalist who is competent to stuff and prepare specimens and he and his family act also as librarians'. Public Library legislation was much more difficult to achieve and a Bill introduced by Ewart in 1850 brought considerable opposition; such provision was thought better provided by the Mechanics' Institutes and similar organizations and was considered likely to cause civil agitation rather than promote public morals. As a result when the *Public Libraries and Museums Act 1850* reached the statute book, it had been modified. This Act was a retrograde step for museums in that it repealed the 1845 Act as far as future museums were concerned, necessitated a two-thirds majority of voting ratepayers before the new Act could be adopted, made no additional provision to the half-penny rate authorized for museum expenditure in 1845 and removed the power to purchase specimens. It did, however, require all museums to be free of an admission charge.

Winchester opened its library and museum in 1851 but here, as at Canterbury and Warrington, and later Ipswich (1853) and Maidstone (1855), the library formed a small adjunct to the museum. In these early days of joint libraries and museums only Salford seems to have given its library priority in space, the museum being housed in one small room, perhaps for lack of specimens.

This legislation was extended to the remainder of Britain, through the *Public Libraries (Ireland and Scotland) Act 1853* but its severe limitations resulted in further legislation, the *Public Libraries (Scotland) Act 1854,* which empowered certain local authorities to raise a one-penny rate which could also be used to purchase specimens. England and Wales received similar provision in the *Public Libraries and Museums Act 1855.*

Not all of the mid-century municipal museums, however, were provided under this general legislation. An example of this was Liverpool.[4] In 1850 there was a move to establish a library, museum and art gallery in the Royal Institution there, based on its collections, and by December of that year an Association of Citizens had been formed to promote the idea and solicit subscriptions, specimens, etc. The negotiations with the Royal Institution, however, came to no avail, but about the same time the thirteenth Earl of Derby[5] died expressing the wish in his will that his collection of stuffed birds and animals should be made available in Liverpool or its environs and administered by trustees, preferably in a building administered by the public authorities. Accordingly, the Liverpool Town Council obtained special local legislation, the *Liverpool Public Library, Museum and Gallery of Art Act 1852* which, as far as the museum was concerned, permitted it to be run by trustees and allowed the Corporation to levy a one penny rate to establish and maintain it, with the library; an art gallery was not provided until 1877. The museum and reference library were opened late in 1852, the former containing Lord Derby's natural history collection, a model of Liverpool and a case of imports which had been shown at the Great Exhibition the previous year. It was reported to have attracted 150 000 visitors in the first seven weeks and maintained an average attendance of over 500 people a day during the next six years until it moved to new pre-

mises. Among the visitors recorded were the King of Portugal and Prince Bonaparte and particular mention is made of the number of 'excursionists' who came by railway to see it.

The first Curator of the Liverpool Museum, Thomas Moore, set to work naming some 12 000 specimens from the Derby collection, establishing contacts with shipowners, the East India Company, the Zoological Society of London and with private visitors abroad to increase the collections, as well as exchanging specimens with Norwich and other museums. The resulting cramped conditions of the Museum were eventually relieved through the benefaction of William Brown, MP, who purchased a site and erected a new building in Shaw's Brow (now William Brown Street). This building was opened in 1860 and the event occasioned a general holiday in Liverpool. About 350 000 people visited the Museum each year at this time and the annual revenue expenditure was in the order of £3 300.

Additional national museums

The story of the Great Exhibition of the Works of Industry of all Nations held in Paxton's 'Crystal Palace' at Hyde Park in 1851 has been told many times (for a recent description see Allwood, 1977). Apart from the museum involvement in it, for example that of the East India Company's Museum (Desmond, 1982), the influence of such exhibitions on the public expectation of museums (Wittlin, 1970, p. 133) and as a stimulation generally for museum development (Burcaw, 1975, p. 20; Key, 1973, pp. 204–206), our concern here is with the contribution it made in the formation of the South Kensington Museum opened in 1857, eventually to become the Victoria and Albert Museum and Science Museum. Unlike the first two national museums in Britain, which were precipitated into existence by the sudden availability of major collections, the South Kensington Museum was planned. Initially a Museum of Manufactures was established in Marlborough House in 1852 which included some material bought from the Great Exhibition. According to Greenwood (1888) over 90 000 people visited it in that year. During its five-year sojourn there (it also went under the name Art Museum and Museum of Ornamental Art) it was the scene of a number of important museum developments introduced by Henry Cole (1808–1882), a joint secretary in the Government's Department of Science and Art of which the Museum was a part. These included the evening opening of the Museum and the provision of museum lectures.

A site for this new museum was purchased at South Kensington out of the profits of the Great Exhibition and in 1857 it moved into temporary corrugated iron buildings which became known as the Crompton Boilers. Bazin (1967) argues that there was a certain confusion about the role of this museum, instancing the changes of name in the first few years and, from 1857, the title South Kensington Museum, which avoided precision as to its aims. There was nothing imprecise about Henry Cole's oversight of this pioneering operation. He saw it as 'a national centre for consulting the best works of science and art and as a storehouse for circulating objects of science and art throughout the Kingdom' (Cole, 1884). It was an integral part of a much larger scheme to improve taste and knowledge among those concerned with the manufactures of Britain.

In 1864 this Museum's loans scheme was inaugurated to promote good taste and design in recognized schools of art. The scheme was extended to municipal museums in 1886 but certain museums were benefiting from it earlier than this; the loans scheme continued until 1977. Contrary to the spirit of the age, and to one of the purposes that the earlier reformers saw in museums, was the establishment of a refreshment room in the Museum where wine, beer and spirits were sold. Despite Cole's clear vision however, the scientific aspects of the collection were not developed in the same way as the decorative arts.

The encouragement of an interest in industry and industrial design was also one of the main motivating forces in the establishment of the Industrial Museum of Scotland in 1854. Like its English counterpart it was formed as part of the British Government's Science and Art Department. The intended role of the museum concerned the industry of the world in special relation to Scotland rather than Scottish industry alone. The necessary finance was voted for the purchase of a site, the acquisition of specimens and the employment of staff. In 1855 a Director was appointed and in the same year the Natural History Museum of the University of Edinburgh was transferred to the Department of Science and Art. This collection which commenced in 1812 and included some ethnological material, remained in the University open to the public until it was merged in a new building. The new displays included small natural groups on brackets and printed labels. By this time the museum had been renamed the Edinburgh Museum of Science and Art, a move away from its original aim, to take account of the nature of the two collections; it became the Royal Scottish Museum in 1904. For a period it organized lecture courses for artisans and in 1875 a refreshment room was opened; this lost its licence to sell alcoholic drinks through the temperance movement in 1891. It also had a loan collection, provided guidance to several local authorities in Scotland on setting up their own museums and, certainly in the later 1870s staged loan exhibitions (Allen, 1954).

The mid-nineteenth century also saw two other significant developments in public museum provision in Scotland. In 1851 the Museum of the Society of Antiquaries of Scotland, which commenced in 1781, was given to the Board of Trustees for Manufactures in Scotland for the benefit of the nation on the understanding that a public building would be provided to house it. This was done in 1859 although the custody of the Museum remained with the Society (Bell, 1981). The other development was the establishment of the National Gallery of Scotland in 1858 at the Mound where it is still housed. The Scottish National Portrait Gallery was opened in 1889 in a building shared with the Antiquities Museum.

In Ireland a different situation prevailed. The Royal Dublin Society (founded 1731) and the Royal Irish Academy (incorporated 1786) maintained collections of art and science, and antiquities respectively. The Government, which had assisted both bodies in purchasing collections, proposed that the two collections be merged to form a national museum and the *Dublin Science and Art Museum Act 1878* was passed to effect this. The resulting building to house the rich archaeological collections was opened in 1889 next to the Natural History Museum which had been built for the Royal Dublin Society in 1857.

In London, despite its rebuilt and much enlarged premises, the British Museum was suffering from severe space problems. As early as 1859 the Trustees had received a report suggesting that the natural history collections should be moved to other premises. A Government Committee looked into the matter but decided that these collections should stay at Bloomsbury. However, the natural history section was moved eventually to Alfred Waterhouse's new building at South Kensington. The British Museum (Natural History) was opened to the public in 1881 but remained under the control of the Trustees at Bloomsbury until 1963 (Miller, 1973). Thus the eighteenth-century encyclopaedic concept that all knowledge might be stored in one place finally came to an end, although the first erosion of the idea had occurred with the founding of the National Gallery in 1824.

Museum development 1860–1920

By 1860 there were about ninety museums in Britain (based on the British Association 1887 list). At least twenty of these had been founded in the previous decade but not all of them were the result of the new municipal museum legislation. The Curtis Museum, Alton (1855) was a product of the Mechanics' Institute; the Devizes Museum (1854) was established by one of the new breed of county archaeological societies, the earliest of which, in Sussex and Essex, had formed museums at Lewes and Colchester respectively at their inception in 1846; the Gloucester Museum (1859) was the collection of the local history and scientific association, while the museums at Berwick-on-Tweed (1857) and Salisbury (1860) were based on private collections. However, Glasgow's town council acquired its first picture collection in 1856 while Lichfield (1859) and Stockport (1860) invoked the legislation for museum purposes, the latter, like Leicester, not providing a public library until some years later.

Northampton opened its museum in 1865 while Birmingham, although it adopted the 1850 Act in 1860, did not open a museum until 1867 in a small room in its library building. This housed a collection of paintings and a large Buddha all of which had been given to the Corporation over the previous three years. The donors of one painting expressed the wish that it 'may be the means of educating the tastes of those upon whom the reputation of Birmingham manufacturers chiefly depends' (Davis, 1981). This museum also exhibited a loan collection from South Kensington in its early days which led to a demand for a Museum of Industrial and Decorative Arts, for which some of its early acquisitions were drawn from the International Exhibition of 1871. Space soon became a problem and the collections were transferred to Aston Hall, now a branch museum, until the present building was opened in 1885.

Indeed it was not until the 1870s that the municipal museum movement gathered momentum. *The Public Libraries (England and Scotland) Amendment Act 1866* eased the way for the adoption of the legislation and the *Public Libraries (Scotland) Act 1867* identified the local authorities eligible to provide libraries and museums in Scotland. There Paisley (1870) and Dundee (1873) formed museums, the latter based on the collections of the Watt Institution (Blair, 1973). In England, Nottingham opened a museum formed from the local natural history society's collections in 1872 and Sheffield followed three years later. The first curator of the Sheffield Museum, Elijah Howarth, came from Liverpool Museum where he started as an office boy in 1868; he played an important role in provincial museum development. Excluding the national institutions and the provincial art galleries, some 217 museums were recorded by 1887. But of these only 47 were rate-supported, three being in Scotland and three in Wales; another nine were being assisted from municipal funds (British Association, 1887 and 1888).

A national climate of increasing professionalism – for example, the Civil Service had introduced promotion examinations in 1855 – eventually led to the suggestion that there should be a professional body for museums. The initial initiative came from Elijah Howarth at Sheffield, who in 1877 called attention in *Nature* to the need for such a body. The matter went into abeyance, however, because of 'the absence of any co-operation whatever among museums' (Museums Association, 1890). But a number of issues of mutual concern were already exercising the minds of curators at this time.

One of these was the circulation of material between museums. The Royal Society of Arts was particularly active in promoting this and it found expression in the development of the Bethnal Green Museum as a branch of the South Kensington institution from collections moved there in 1866. This Society made a considerable grant to the Museum but its intentions were far wider: to lobby Government to develop museums as a matter of policy. This was not successful and in consequence they formed a standing committee in 1873 to look into the question of establishing a national scheme for museums under the control of a Minister of State and of giving increased museum powers to local authorities. The resolutions of this Committee went to the House of Commons, but even today not all of them have been implemented (Hudson and Luckhurst, 1954).

Another matter of concern was the opening hours of museums. Most opened on three or four weekdays, with at least one other day being reserved for student access. The most common opening hours were from 10 am until dusk but with the increased availability of gas for lighting, a demand arose for a year-round evening opening. The British Museum Trustees reviewed the question with expert advice on the fire hazards involved, and were unanimous that the dangers were sufficient not to open at any hour that would require gaslight (Parliamentary Papers, 1861). The Trustees of the National Gallery, however, having received a report from a committee of scientists (which included Michael Faraday) agreed to introduce it and as a consequence the Vernon and Turner galleries at South Kensington were opened on three evenings a week. The South Kensington Museum had been lit since it was opened. At Liverpool electric lighting had been installed in the Library next door in 1881 (the first municipal library to do so) but it was gas lighting that first lit the Museum, and then only in 1888. As a result it was opened on eleven occasions that winter, bringing an average of 343 visitors each time; the following year it was reported that the evening attendance included 'all ages and classes, operatives largely predominating'. The museum at Canterbury probably had the longest opening hours, from 9 am to 10 pm (British Association, 1887).

There was also a demand in 1889 for more weekday opening at Liverpool and as a consequence the opening was extended to five days a week, Monday to Thursday, and Saturday. The British Museum had been open each week-day for the previous ten years, although all galleries were not available every day. Sunday opening was a controversial issue on religious grounds for many years. By the time Greenwood (1888) was writing on the subject, the Natural History Museum and some of the other London museums were opening together with those in some ten provincial cities including Birmingham, Manchester, Salford and Newcastle-upon-Tyne. It was not until 1896, however, that the House of Commons approved a motion that the national museums and galleries, including the British Museum, should open on Sunday afternoons.

Charging for museum admission also had its protagonists. The *British Museum Act 1753* had specified free entry although there had been an unsuccessful attempt to make a charge in 1784. The *Museum Act 1845,* however, had permitted it and an atttempt was made to amend the *Public Libraries Act 1866* to this end. The Bill failed. In the private sector museums a charge was common but varied from a penny to one shilling, although there were normally reductions for parties and children. The Yorkshire Philosophical Society's museum, which charged a shilling (although this included admission to the gardens as well) probably raised over £500 in this way each year.

Following the report of the British Association's Committee on Provincial Museums in 1887, which contains considerable information on contemporary curatorial practice, the Committee reported again the following year (British Association, 1888) on their concept of an 'ideal' rate-supported museum. They were particularly concerned that provincial museums collected in a very unsystematic manner and pointed out:

> To represent the history of the entire inorganic world and of the development and present condition of its vegetable and animal life, as far as these things are known to science, is an object worthy of a great State department but impracticable in any ordinary provincial town.

The role of the rate-supported provincial museum was seen, therefore, as collecting and preserving specimens of the natural and artificial productions of its area and local collections of scientific value. The latter, together with specimens to illustrate the general principles of science and the locality in relation to the rest of the world, could be arranged and displayed for popular instruction in a way consistent with their preservation. Special assistance to local students and science teachers was also recommended.

The educational aspects of museums for child and adult alike, received particular attention by the Committee and generally at this period. This was due at least partly to the work of Sir Henry Cole in advocating their use to develop taste, and the Royal Society of Arts and Mechanics Institute's desire to promote a better understanding of industrial design,

together with the free education movement which culminated in the *Education Act 1870.* Thus in the second half of the century, 'the educated youth ought, in a well-arranged Museum to be able to instruct himself', as Professor Edward Forbes said in 1853 (quoted in Greenwood, 1888).

Certainly at Leicester models were used to aid interpretation, while at Liverpool habitat groups were in use in the galleries as early as 1865. The Chairman of the latter Museum, however, accepted that the labelling of the exhibits could be improved in 1884, commenting that 'it is admitted that a public museum should as far as possible to be self-explanatory without the aid of a guidebook'. The British Association Committee (1887) preferred clear advice on labelling:

> Effective labelling is an art to be studied; it is like style in literature. A good writer conveys his meaning clearly, tersely, artistically. The reader grasps the thought with the least possible effort and with a pleasing sense of elegance and harmony. A good labeller produces the same effect.

But as Flower (1893) pointed out 'the majority of museums – especially of natural history – . . . nearly always confound together the two distinct objects . . . research and instruction'.

Although loans of specimens to recognized schools of art had been made by the South Kensington Museum since 1864, this does not seem to have been the practice of provincial museums until the early 1880s. By then the Liverpool Museum was certainly providing specimens to assist teaching at the University College there and to local societies for their soirées. In 1884 the same museum introduced its 'circulating school museum' which can be regarded as the beginning of school loans services in Britain. The object of this innovation, was 'not so much teaching as training: not so much the inculcation of facts as the illustration of the happiness to be obtained through habits of observation' (quoted in Chard, 1890). This scheme attracted considerable attention and the cabinets were exhibited at one of the Paris exhibitions and used by other museums, including South Kensington and Sheffield. The British Association (1887) found little evidence of organized school class work in museums although it was clear that schools were visiting museums. An exception to this was the Ancoats Hall Museum (Horsfall Museum), Manchester. This Art Museum was established with a strong educational bias in 1877 and certainly ten years later school parties were being taught by a museum teacher (Horsfall, 1892; Hindshaw, 1941). This museum also operated a loans service to schools. The first real impetus for school visits came in 1894 when the Day School Code was revised to allow instruction in a museum to be reckoned as school attendance.

In 1877 the Library Association was formed. Having had little response to his earlier overture to form an association for museums, Elijah Howarth approached them in 1884, at the request of others, to see whether they would be willing to include museums within their remit. This may be regarded as surprising for, as the British Association reported three years later 'the two offices of librarian and curator are frequently combined . . . but it is rarely satisfactory for the museum', but it went on to suggest that 'there was a considerable advantage in having the two institutions under the same roof'. But the Council of the Library Association did not wish to extend their area of influence and the proposal was dropped. It fell to the Yorkshire Philosophical Society to test reaction and call a meeting on the matter; eleven provincial curators met in 1888 at York and agreed that a Museums Association should be formed. The Association was inaugurated on 20 June 1889 at York. From the outset, membership specifically included curators and 'representatives of the Committees and Councils of management' of their museums. In the first ten years the membership rose from 30 to 64 and included five overseas members. There were in addition a similar number of associated museums.

The Municipal reforms of 1835 had affected only a small number of urban centres and the time was overdue for similar treatment to be given to the rural areas. The *Local Government Act 1888* provided this for England and Wales, creating elected County Councils, County Boroughs, Boroughs and, in further legislation in 1894, Urban and Rural District Councils. In Scotland a similar reorganization followed legislation in 1889 with only the largest burghs being kept free of some control by the new counties.

New statutes followed affecting the provision and maintenance of museums by local authorities: the *Museums and Gymnasiums Act 1891* and the *Public Libraries Act 1892*. The former enabled urban authorities to provide and maintain museums in England, Wales and Ireland, but excluded London until 1901. The latter Act repealed all previous Libraries Acts and transferred museums so provided to the new library authorities in England and Wales and permitted the provision and maintenance of new museums by these authorities; the new administrative counties were not involved. Whereas the 1891 Act required museums to be opened to the public free of charge on not less than three days a week, admission fees were permitted on other days and charges could be made for the use of their facilities, the 1892 Act required that no charge be made for admission to museums established under this legislation. This libraries legislation also made no provision for the sale of a museum, although it was permissible under the 1891 Act provided the museum had been established for

not less than seven years, and was either to expensive to run or unnecessary; the proceeds from such a sale were to be treated as capital money and to be disposed in a way approved by the Local Government Board (later the Minister for Education).

The Museums and Gymnasiums Act permitted the levying of a separate half-penny rate for museum purposes but this was no more than had been authorized in 1845. Under the 1892 provisions museums and libraries had to be funded by a penny rate, little enough to run a library on, and if the local authority provided both, one or other was likely to suffer particularly in authorities with a low rateable value. More often the museum suffered; its role was never defined in this library-dominated legislation. Nor was the 1891 provision much better: a museum was a place 'for the reception of local antiquities or other objects of interest'. As far as England and Wales were concerned the 1891 Act was effectively repealed in 1919 by which time most municipal museums were provided by library authorities anyway but it remained in force until 1981 in Northern Ireland. The consolidation of library legislation in 1892 also meant that local authorities operating these services under special Acts could now adopt this general enabling legislation. Liverpool was a case in point and as a result Lord Derby's collection, ceased to be administered by trustees on behalf of the local authority in 1893.

Scottish local authorities have never had separate museum legislation. Previous library statutes, enabling the provision of museums were repealed by the *Public Libraries Consolidation (Scotland) Act 1887* which remains the principal Act in force today. This permits local authority museums to sell or exchange duplicate works of art and other property provided the ensuing monies or objects are applied for the purposes of the Act – which, of course, includes the provision and maintenance of libraries. Thus there was no consistency in the museum legislation of Britain although it all passed through Parliament within the space of six years.

Most of the museums founded during the period under review were started as the result of a gift of collections, often to the local authority. But it was also a time of considerable benevolence in the form of offers or bequests of money for the erection of museum buildings or adapting existing buildings for museum purposes. Unlike libraries, there was no Andrew Carnegie to provide museum buildings although sometimes his initiative acted as a catalyst in bringing forward a benefactor to build a museum as an addition to a Carnegie library; for example, at Worthing the Museum and Art Gallery was built integrally with the Public Library in 1908 at the expense of Alfred Cortis. Nor was the Cornishman, John Passmore Edwards, who built twenty-four libraries in London and the West Country, to contribute significantly to museum provision, although his libraries at Whitechapel (1892), Bodmin (1897) and Camberwell (1898) included museums or galleries, while the museum at New Ham (1898) occupied a Passmore Edwards building and now bears his name.

Of the less-known benefactors, only a few can be mentioned. To Liverpool, already given a museum building, came the gift of its art gallery by Sir Andrew Barclay Walker in 1877 and extended at his expense seven years later; Sheffield's first art gallery was built in 1887 in accordance with the Will of John Newton Mappin and the city was later to receive the buildings for its second art gallery (1934) and its museum (1937) from Alderman Dr J. G. Graves; at Preston, the museum and art gallery were erected in 1895 as part of the bequest of Edmond Robert Harris to the town; in Bradford, Lord Masham, wishing to create a memorial to Dr Edmond Cartwright (the inventor of the power-loom and woolcombing machine), offered a sum of money in 1898 for the erection of the Cartwright Hall Museum, while Bolling Hall, dating to the fourteenth century, was given to the same city by G. A. Paley in 1912. Also the site for St Alban's City Museum was given by Earl Spencer enabling it to be build and opened in 1899; Canterbury's present museum, opened in 1900, resulted from the legacy of Dr J. G. Beaney; both a new building and the founding collections of the Horniman Museum were given to the London County Council by the Mr F. J. Horniman while the Art Gallery in Blackpool was built at the expense of J. R. G. and C. C. Grundy in 1911.

Local authorities were not the only recipients of private benefaction for museum purposes. The cost of the new building for the National Portrait Gallery in London, which had been founded in 1856, was borne almost entirely by William Henry Alexander forty years later. The following year, 1897, saw the opening of the National Gallery of British Art, built by Sir Henry Tate who also gave his collection of contemporary art to the nation. Now known as the Tate Gallery, this fulfilled the need for a gallery of modern art in Britain which many of its European counterparts had enjoyed for some years. Another bequest to the nation was that of Lady Wallace in 1897. This comprised both the house and art collection of the Hertford family and was opened to the public as the Wallace Collection in 1900 under the administration of trustees appointed by the Prime Minister.

Sir Henry Tate's offer to build a national art gallery led to a stormy debate among the scientific community in the 1890s because the Government considered a site for the new gallery at South Kensington which had long been regarded as for the National Science Museum. Indeed, the story of the Science Museum is one of the anachronisms of the period. Henry Cole's wish to create a national centre for 'the best works of science' clearly took second place to the decorative arts at South Kensington. In the mid 1860s the science collection was moved to temporary quarters in Exhibition Road. Acquisitions were being made, but it was not until 1874 that the first recommendation was made for a permanent building; then the Government declined to act. Further committees were set up, each strongly supporting the development of the Museum, but by 1888 some of the collections were being dispersed because of increasing congestion. It was not until 1913 that work began on the erection of a building. In the event the war intervened, temporary Government usage followed and the Museum only began to move into a section of its new premises in 1919 as soon as parts were either released from occupation or completed. The official opening did not take place until 1928 although the public had been admitted some years earlier; they totalled a million visitors in the year following the opening (Follett, 1978).

One of the reasons for the long delay in achieving proper premises for the Science Museum was undoubtedly the pressing space needs of its decorative art partner in the South Kensington Museum. Its collections had vastly increased, not least from the international exhibitions. Eventually new premises were planned and in 1898 Queen Victoria laid the foundation stone, renaming it the Victoria and Albert Museum in memory of her consort. The building was completed and opened to the public in 1909. The displays, which previously had been arranged geographically, were now ordered largely by the materials from which the objects had been made. When the new building opened a separate administration was created for the Science Museum although it had been under separate direction since 1893; both insitutions, however, continued under the control of successive education departments rather than independently under trustees, until the National Heritage Act 1983 gave them trustee status with effect from April 1984. Thus, like the British Museum before it, the old South Kensington Museum divided, amoeba-like, to produce two more institutions of world renown in London.

At the British Museum collecting continued. The results of Museum-sponsored excavations, particularly in the Middle East, were again causing severe congestion in the antiquities departments. This was relieved to some extent by the building of the King Edward VII galleries although it took ten years from their inception to completion in 1913. The salaries paid to staff at the British Museum had been a matter of discussion for many years and on one occasion Gladstone stated that he would never be a party to increasing their salaries as he could imagine no more delightful an existence (quoted in Kenyon, 1927). However a Treasury Committee, having looked at the intellectual and scientific output of the Museum in 1898, supported the Director's contention that there should be considerable increases and these were implemented, particularly for the lower-paid staff.

On the provincial scene collections were also being amassed, the largest museums, like their national counterparts, organizing collecting expeditions abroad. The first Keeper of the Birmingham Museum did so to supplement the industrial and decorative arts collections while the Liverpool Museum's expedition to Sokotra in 1899 was for natural history and ethnological material. New museums continued to be opened at the rate of about six a year, mainly in the public sector, until the First World War reduced the rate. By 1920 there were about four hundred museums in Britain.

However, public concern about museums and their role in society was beginning to be heard. This related to both national and provincial museums. One powerful group, led by Lord Sudeley (1840–1922) lobbied considerably on the public utility of museums. Others argued for closer links with the education authorities. The British Association for the Advancement of Science, having heard papers from Dr Joseph Clubb and Mr A. R. Horwood on the educational use of museums in 1913, set up a Committee on Museums in relation to education the same year. Because of the war, it did not complete its report for seven years but it provided useful data on the position during this decade (British Association, 1920).

There is no doubt that the Committee was influenced considerably by the educational work being undertaken in the United States and also by the scheme developed by the Manchester Museum, in common with other educational institutions in that city, whereby classes from elementary schools attended the museum for instruction. This commenced in 1915 with the secondment of trained teachers from the Manchester Education Committees who provided classes in natural history and Egyptology. By 1919–1920 some 2500 children were being taught at the Museum each week by six teachers.

Apart from recommendations for the development of schools work both in the museum and through special loan collections to schools, the Committee took a much wider view. Museums should be developed into research centres; interpretive work should be improved by better labels, the provision of temporary exhibitions, published guides, conducted tours and public lectures; better facilities should be provided for the advanced student. The resources available to the provincial museum were also the subject of particular comment as well as the lack of any general principles of government and administration for museums and therefore the need for common standards to be defined. The Committee deplored the fact that there was no means of influencing museums outside the public sector which would

continue 'to be governed more in the interest of the Societies that ran them than in that of the general public'. On museum staff it suggested a minimum salary for curators and stressed the need for a sound university training and the teaching of museum technique in which the role of the national museums was emphasized.

While the British Association's committee had been deliberating, the Ministry of Reconstruction had created its Committee on Adult Education which issued a series of reports in 1918 and 1919. Amongst its many recommendations it proposed that museums and art galleries be transferred to the local education authority. This view, which has been the subject of periodic debate in the profession over the ensuing years, was contested by the Museums Association at the time on the grounds that the Board of Education already had the means of assisting local museum authorities (Lowe, 1919). The report also recommended that the limiting halfpenny rate for museum expenditure imposed by the *Museums and Gymnasiums Act 1891* should be removed, that museums should be eligible for grants from the Board of Education and that co-operative schemes be developed by museums to meet rural needs.

New legislation for museums and galleries in England and Wales made it possible for local authorities to implement all of these proposals if they so wished. The *Education Act 1918* permitted the local education authorities to grant-aid a museum and school visits for instructional purposes. The *Public Libraries Act 1919* amended previous library legislation, enabling county councils to provide museums for the first time and also to aid a town museum, allowing for the voluntary delegation of a library authority's powers to the education authority and removing the limit on rate-borne expenditure. Despite the possibility of the transfer of museums to the education authority, the legislation was welcomed, Lowe (1919) considering that 'museums and art galleries had received their charter'. Some statutory modifications were also introduced for Scotland under the *Education (Scotland) Act 1918* and the *Public Libraries (Scotland) Act 1920*. Variations from the English and Welsh legislation still remained: in Scotland the rate for museum purposes was limited to threepence in the pound while in Northern Ireland the maximum expenditure in urban districts and county boroughs was twopence and sixpence respectively.

Notes

[1] I am most grateful to Paul Sealy of the Colchester and Essex Museum for drawing my attention to the Lexden, Kelvedon and Ivy Chimneys discoveries.

[2] Galleries were built at Chatsworth (1696), Chiswick House (1725), Castle Howard (1759), Holkham Hall, Norfolk (1759), Townley's villa, Park Street,

Westminster (1772), Somerset House (1780) and Petworth (1780).

[3] *See*, for example, *Gentleman's Magazine,* 18 July 1748, reproduced in Wittlin (1970, p. 249).

[4] Unless otherwise stated references to Liverpool have been obtained from the minute books at the Merseyside County Museum.

[5] The thirteenth Earl of Derby (1775–1851) spent much of his life collecting and had been President of both the Linnaean and Zoological societies of London.

References

ALLAN, D. A. (1954), 'The Royal Scottish Museum: general survey' in *The Royal Scottish Museum 1854–1954,* Oliver and Boyd, Edinburgh

ALLWOOD, J. (1977), *The Great Exhibitions,* Studio Vista, London

ALTRICK, R. D. (1978), *The Shows of London,* Harvard UP, Cambridge, Massachusettes and London

BATEMAN, T. (1855), *A Descriptive Catalogue of the Antiquities and Miscellaneous Objects Preserved in the Museum of Thomas Bateman at Lomberdale House, Derbyshire,* Gratton, Bakewell

BAZIN, G. (1967), *The Museum Age,* Desocr SA, Brussels

BELL, A. S. (1981), *The Scottish Antiquarian Tradition,* J. Donald, Edinburgh

BLAIR, J. A. (Ed.) (1973), *100 Years of Dundee Museums and Art Galleries, 1873–1973,* Dundee Museums and Art Galleries

BORLASE, W. (1754), *Antiquities of Cornwall,* Clarendon Press, Oxford

BRITISH ASSOCIATION (1887), 'Report of the Committee on the provincial museums of the United Kingdom', *Report of the British Association for the Advancement of Science 1887,* 97–130, London

BRITISH ASSOCIATION (1888), 'A further report of the Committee on the provincial museums of the United Kingdom', *Report of the British Association for the Advancement of Science,* 1888, 124–132, London

BRITISH ASSOCIATION (1920), 'Final Report of the Committee on museums in relation to education', *Report of the British Association for the Advancement of Science, 1920,* 267–280, London

BRUCE-MITFORD, R. (1975), *The Sutton Hoo Ship-burial,* Vol. 1, British Museum, London

BRUCE-MITFORD, R. (1978), *The Sutton Hoo Ship-burial,* Vol. 2, British Museum, London

BURCAW, G. E. (1975), *Introduction to Museum Work,* AASLH, Nashville, USA

CHARD, J. (1890), 'On circulating museum cabinets for schools and other educational purposes', *Report of Proceedings, . . . at the First General Meeting held at Liverpool,* 54–68, Museums Association, London

COLE, SIR H. (1884), *Fifty Years of Public Work,* Bell, London

DAVIES, S. (1981), *Birmingham Museum and Art Gallery,* Department of Local History Information Sheet No. 9, Birmingham Museum and Art Gallery

DESMOND, R. (1982), *The India Museum, 1801–1879,* HMSO, London

FLOWER, SIR, W. H. (1898), *Essays on Museums and Other Subjects,* MacMillan, London

FOLLETT, D. (1978), *The Rise of the Science Museum under Henry Lyons,* Science Museum, London

FRERE, S. (1978), *Britannia: A History of Roman Britain,* Routledge & Kegan Paul, London (revised edition)

GRANSDEN, A. (1980), 'Antiquarian studies in fifteenth century England', *Antiquaries J,* **110**(1), 75–97

GREENWOOD, T. (1888), *Museums and Art Galleries,* Simpkin Marshall, London

HAWES, B. (1835), *Hansard,* **35**, 20, c 617

HINDSHAW, B. (1941), 'The museums and the child: pioneer work at the Horsfall Museum, Manchester', *Museums J,* **40**(12), 325

HORSFALL, T. C. (1892), 'The Manchester Art Museum', *Report of Proceedings . . . at the Third Annual General Meeting held at Manchester,* 51–65, Museums Association

HOWARTH E. AND PLATNAUER, H. H. (1911), *Directory of Museums in Great Britain and Ireland . . . with a Section on Indian and Colonial Museums,* Museums Association, London

HUDSON, D. AND LUCKHURST, K. W. (1954), *The Royal Society of Arts, 1754–1954,* Murray, London

KENDRICK, T. D. (1951), 'The British Museum and British Antiquities', *Museum J,* **51**(6), 139–149

KENYON, SIR F. G. (1927), *Musuems and National Life,* Oxford

KEY, A. (1973), *Beyond Four Walls,* McClelland & Stewart, Toronto

KUSAMITSU, T. (1980), 'Great exhibitions before 1851', *History Workshop Journal,* **9**, 70–87

LOWE, E. (1919), 'The question of transferring the control of museums to the Education Authority', *Museums J,* **19**(3), 36–37

MACGREGOR, A. (1983), (Ed.), *Tradescant's Rarities,* Oxford University Press

MILLER, E. (1973), *That Noble Cabinet,* Andre Deutsch, London

MULLENS, W. H. (1915), 'Some museums of old London – 1 The Leverian Museum', *Museums J,* **15**(4), 123–129 and **15**(5), 162–173

MULLENS, W. H. (1917), 'Some museums of old London – II William Bullock's London Museum', *Museums J,* **17**(4), 51–56; **17**(9), 132–137 and **17**(12), 180–187

MUSEUMS ASSOCIATION (1890), *Report of the Proceedings . . . at the First Annual General Meeting held at Liverpool,* Museums Association, London

PARLIAMENTARY PAPERS, (1861), *British Museum: Lighting by Gas,* House of Commons, **34**, 224

ORANGE, A. D. (1973), *Philosophers and Provincials,* Yorkshire Philosophical Society, York

SALWAY, P. (1981), *Roman Britain,* Clarendon Press, Oxford

SELECT COMMITTEE ON INQUIRY INTO DRUNKENNESS, (1834), *Report,* p. viii

SELECT COMMITTEE ON PUBLIC LIBRARIES (1849), *Report,* pp. 107–111

SMALL, A., THOMAS, C. AND WILSON, D. M. (1973), *St Ninian's Isle and its Treasure,* Vols 1 & 2, University of Aberdeen

TAYLOR, F. H. (1948), *The Taste of Angels,* Little, Brown and Co., Boston, USA

TYLECOTE, M. (1957), *The Mechanics Institutes' of Lancashire and Yorkshire before 1851,* Manchester University Press

WITTLIN, A. (1970), *Museums: in search of a usable future,* MIT Press, Cambridge, Massachusettes

WOODWARD, SIR L. (1979), *The Age of Reform, 1815–1870,* 2nd edition, Oxford University Press

4

Museums in Britain: 1920 to the present day

Geoffrey D. Lewis

New legislation, an awakening interest in museums, combined with the profound social consequences of the First World War on a universal scale laid the foundation for a new era which continues to the present day. At a national level two new museums appeared on the scene during the period between the two wars. Perhaps not surprisingly, both have strong connexions with the armed forces while at a provincial level regimental museums began to proliferate.

Towards the end of the First World War, the War Cabinet had ordered the formation of a national war museum, and the *Imperial War Museum Act 1920* put this into effect. The Museum was first opened at the Crystal Palace but transferred to the Imperial Institute at South Kensington where it remained for eleven years before being housed in its present building at Lambeth in 1935. Although the role of this Museum was not clearly defined in the legislation, it originally housed only 1914–1918 war material and acted as a memorial for that war (Royal Commission on National Museums and Galleries, 1929c, p. 94). This was extended later to include material from the Second World War.

The other national museum formed during this period was the National Maritime Museum, established by Act of Parliament in 1934. Its role was defined as illustrating the maritime history of Britain. The Museum was established in the Queen's House and Royal Hospital School at Greenwich, based on collections by the Royal Naval Museum and Sir James Caird. While the Science Museum had by this time already amassed a fine collection of ship models, as indeed had a few provincial museums, notably Liverpool, and while there was some overlap on naval matters with the Imperial War Museum, nevertheless this now became the centre for naval and mercantile material.

Although the Royal Artillery Institution's museum at the Rotunda, Woolwich had existed as a collection since 1778 and the Royal Engineer's Museum was formed in 1875, the idea of a museum associated with regimental headquarters and their recruiting areas only began to appear in the 1920s. The earliest of these seems to have been at the School of Infantry at Hythe, (1920) followed by the Royal Armoured Corps Museum at Wareham (1923), the Royal Corps of Signals and Blackwatch museums (1924) at Catterick and Perth respectively. By the end of the decade there were fourteen such museums and their number had reached forty by the outbreak of the Second World War. Another impetus to the formation of military museums was the creation of a Committee on Military Museums by the War Office in 1913 which in its early days was concerned more with rationalizing the collections in the Tower; as a result the Greek and Oriental armour collections were passed to the British Museum. Another of its recommendations was to provide a central London base for the fine arms collection based at Woolwich; in 1927 a representative collection of arms was transferred to the Tower.

Lord Sudeley, who had campaigned for improved museums for many years, died in 1922. Two years later, however, a Sudeley Committee was formed to continue his work in promoting better public access to museums both in London and the provinces and making them more intelligible to visitors. Both Lord Sudeley and the Committee had been particularly concerned with the status and funding of the provincial museums and, had it not been for the intervention of another body, the Committee had planned to look at the issues in some depth. In the event the Carnegie United Kingdom Trust (CUKT) commissioned a survey of the public museums in the provinces with special reference to their services and potential in education, culture and learning. The Museums Association assisted in the formative stages of the proposal in 1925 and the CUKT eventually appointed Sir Henry Miers, lately Vice-Chancellor of the University of Manchester and a trustee of the British Museum, to undertake the work. His report was published in 1928.

In his recommendations Sir Henry (1928) stated that the time was ripe for a movement that would sweep away the conventional attitude towards museums and arouse widespread enthusiasm for them. He went on to say:

> . . . most peoples in this country do not really care for museums or believe in them; they have not hitherto played a sufficiently important part in the life of the community to make ordinary folk realize what they can do. . . . how dull many of them have become and how low the worst of them have sunk.

His main conclusions were that museums should be formed in every town with sufficient population, that there should be clearly defined collecting policies with one museum in each county being reorganized to arrange exchanges, loans, circulating exhibitions for educational purposes and travelling exhibitions for rural areas. He saw the need for the national museums to institute an advisory board to promote relations with local museums, assist in establishing the travelling educational museums and new types of museum to cover such fields as agriculture, applied arts, a folk museum and nautical history. On staffing, there was a need for museums to be under a full-time qualified curator rather than a librarian as was in many instances the case – a point echoed by Librarians some twenty years later (McColvin, 1942) – and that their status and salaries should be improved; he saw the Museums Association as the vehicle to assist in implementing the recommendations and in particular instituting a scheme of museum education. The educational and research role of museums was also stressed in this report.

At least partly concurrent with the CUKT study, a rigorous examination of the national museums was being undertaken by the Royal Commission on National Museums and Galleries of which Sir Henry Miers was also a member. Appointed in 1927, their terms of reference were aimed mainly at the financial and congestion problems of the national institutions. The Commission however dealt exhaustively with far wider issues, seeking evidence from many overseas museums as well as enquiring into the British provincial scene. The evidence received (Royal Commission on National Museums and Galleries, 1928b, 1929c) provides a particularly important commentary on the situation prevailing at that time.

The evidence of the Museums Association indicated a deep concern for closer links between national and local museums particularly in the matter of loans of reserve collections from the national institutions and urged that powers should be given

for the disposal of surplus material to local museums either by gift or sale. It also sought that the range of objects available from the Circulation Department of the Victoria and Albert Museum should be extended to include archaeology, the fine arts, the physical and natural sciences and so on. On the grant-in-aid for purchases in the provincial museums, which commenced before 1896 and was administered by the same Department for the Board of Education, the Association sought improved conditions and a review in order that small museums might also benefit. Although the issue of extending grant-aid to other museum purposes, such as display, was raised in discussion, they saw considerable danger in this. On the question of free entry to museums, the Association was unanimous that this practice should continue. The report of Miers (1928) for the CUKT and of the Royal Commission on the National Museums and Galleries (1929a, b) set the scene for museum development in the ensuing years. Common to both reports was the need for far closer collaboration between national and provincial museums and as a result of the Commissioners' recommendations, an advisory body was established to consider issues concerned with the development of the national institutions, co-operation between them and the provincial institutions and the stimulation of benefactions to museums. Thus the Standing Commission on Museums and Galleries was founded in 1931; it retained its title and terms of reference for the next fifty years. Other recommendations from the Royal Commission included the need for the national museums to show a far greater awareness of their visitors, to differentiate between the requirements of the general public and students, to improve their displays and extend their contact with schools. They also recommended that the Circulation Department of the Victoria and Albert Museum be enlarged, that other national institutions should come within the system as well and that a National Folk and Open Air Museum should be created. One indirect outcome of the report was the formation of the Conference of Directors of National Institutions to assist co-ordination at that level.

Major reports recommending the development of museums have a propensity for appearing just before a down-turn in the British economy or other national emergency. The Royal Commission and Carnegie reports were no exception and many of their recommendations, although still valid, remain unimplemented to this day. But if anything the Carnegie report was to have the greatest impact on the museums of Britain, more particularly in the provinces. From this the CUKT developed a policy of aiding museums which was to last for fifty years. Its first act enabled the Museums Association to set up a permanent office and appoint its first paid Secretary in 1929. Indeed, with Sir Henry Miers now as President of the Association and Frank Markham, MP as its Secretary, the organization moved forward. The following year it became incorporated under the Companies Act, ran its first training course for curators and increased its membership to five hundred.

The problem of curatorial training had been under discussion for some time. A paper on the desirability of a Diploma for museum curators had been prepared for the annual conference of the Museums Association in 1919, but in the event was delayed to the following year (Hoyle, 1920). The British Association for the Advancement of Science (1920) had drawn attention to the high specialism of national museum staff and the self-taught, unsystematically trained provincial personnel; future curators, it added, would need a sound training at a University and in museum technique. Miers (1928) had underlined the problem in his report while the Royal Commission (1929b), as with the others, saw an important role for national museum staff in providing initial training, anticipating that curatorial training would lead to a Diploma from the Museums Association in due course and 'ultimately perhaps . . . to a University diploma'. In fact the National Museum of Wales, which commenced an affiliation scheme with other museums in the Principality in 1922, introduced a training summer school in 1925 (Lee, 1928) which became an annual event for some years. Like these, the teaching on the Museums Association's first course was undertaken mainly by national museum staff; it was based at the Science Museum. One of the speakers, Dr F. A. Bather who lectured on first principles of museum work, had earlier in the year been elected President of the new *section de muséologie de l'Association Française pour l'avancement des sciences* where he must have greatly surprised his colleagues by denying the existence of a science that could be termed museology (Bather, 1930).

In 1932 a diploma and degree course intended to train art museum curators was introduced at the University of London's Courtauld Institute (Constable, 1933) and five years' later its new Institute of Archaeology commenced courses concerned with archaeological material and its preservation. By October 1932, however, the Museums Association had published regulations governing the award of its in-service Diploma, and courses followed on museum administration, methods and techniques. Candidates were required to have worked in a recognized museum or art gallery and assessment was based on a thesis on museum work and an example of their curatorial skill.

This Diploma scheme received financial assistance from the CUKT as part of their five-year experimental funding for museums which also included grants for development in small town museums, stringent conditions relating to finance

and the employment of staff having to be met. A system for assisting museum services to rural areas was also introduced. In 1936 grant-aid for museum reorganization was introduced by the Trustees and for many years a number of small museums received an expert report and subsequent financial assistance to improve their displays under this scheme. At the same time they announced that they wished to establish experimental circulating exhibit schemes to rural and other country areas; as a result two schemes were started in Leicester and Derbyshire. The Derbyshire School Museum Service was based not on a museum but a local education authority. This service was stocked with material 'based on the requirements of the school curriculum' (Winstanley, 1967) rather than such specimens as might have been made available in an existing museum. The Trustees also offered travel grants to enable museum staff to visit other museums at home and abroad.

Another innovation of this period was the founding of the Lancashire and Cheshire Federation of Museums in 1927[1]. Intended to promote closer cooperation between museums in the two counties, particularly in encouraging the exchange of surplus specimens and sharing professional advice and facilities, the Editor of the *Museums Journal* felt constrained to comment[2]: 'this is just the kind of cooperation for which the Museums Association was founded. Why has it not met with better success?' Notwithstanding this, other areas of the country soon followed the example and so eventually provided a country-wide network of regional organizations which, at minimum, provided a forum for members of a region to discuss common problems. Markham (1938) usefully devotes a chapter to their progress by the mid-thirties and they continue to operate, although now partially eclipsed by the Area Museum Services.

Although the depression of the early 1930s had a major impact on many museum revenue budgets, it does not seem to have materially affected the growth of a number of new museums. According to the list in Rosse (1963) no less than sixty-three museums appeared on the scene between 1931 and 1935. In fact there are likely to have been more, judging from the regimental museums listed by Cowper (1935), for at least twenty-two of these were formed during this period although not all of them opened to the public. The Royal Scottish Museum was able to build a new central staircase in 1932 but other schemes were deferred and the grant-in-aid of purchases was reduced (Allen, 1954). In London, however, the British Museum found £100 000 to buy one of its most valuable manuscripts in 1933, the *Codex Sinaiticus* and the following year, jointly with the Victoria and Albert Museum, a further £100 000 for the Eumorfopoulos collection of oriental antiquities. These purchases were achieved through remarkably successful fund-raising and short-term borrowing (Miller, 1973). But the depression had a far greater impact on the provincial museums. Markham (1938) records that while national museum budgets had increased by about 20 per cent over the previous ten years, provincial budgets were very little different from those of ten years ago and that from 1931–1934 many salaries were severely cut. At Liverpool Museum increases in attendance figures were attributed to the extent of unemployment in that city in 1931–1932 but a drop the following year, particularly during the Easter and Summer holidays, was considered to result from the reduction in day trips now being made by railway. This Museum's committee proposed that special tours of the museum be arranged for the unemployed, but the evidence is sparse for any major response from museums generally to the social conditions of the time.

The issue of local collecting policies for local museums had long been a matter of debate (e.g. British Association, 1888; Miers, 1928) but had by no means been generally adopted. The South-Western Group of Museums and Art Galleries, however, did draw up guidelines for its members in 1938 but had to admit that the chief issue, that of delimiting the collecting area for each museum, appeared insurmountable, 'natural and cultural areas being exceedingly difficult actually to fix on a map by a line' (Wallis, 1938). The issue was also stressed by Markham (1938) who pointed out that miscellaneous collections of objects had little educational usefulness.

The report by Markham (1938) was undertaken on behalf of the Carnegie United Kingdom Trust to review progress since Miers' study published ten years previously and assist the Trustees in continuing to grant-aid museum development. Major museum defects listed in the report include inadequate finance, lack of space, untrained, part-time and ill-paid curators, the absence of any national subject-index of collections. He concludes the list with:

> the lack of sufficient drive and energy in the museum movement itself. Much of the slowness of development is due to the fact that the very qualities that go to make up a good curator are often opposed to those that make good reformers. Many curators are so close to their problems that they tend to lose sight of the fact that they are part of a national service that needs adequate publicity.

But at the root of the matter, Markham saw the absence of any authorative central body with the oversight of all public museums. There was only one body in the country capable of doing this, the Government, and he recommended the establishment of a Commission to consider the whole question of the provincial museums. Without authorative oversight he believed that his other recommendations would not bring museums generally up to the level of the best overseas examples.

These recommendations went far beyond the purview of the Carnegie Trustees and were under consideration by the Board of Education when the Second World War broke out in 1939; thereafter they became submerged by more pressing matters. In preparation for the war many museums packed and transported their major holdings to safer locations, a precaution fully justified in the light of events published in war-time issues of the *Museums Journal;* even so some valuable collections were lost. Other museum buildings were requisitioned for war purposes. Staff, too, were depleted as they left for war service or were dismissed for economic reasons. An indication of the impact of the war on the museum service can be seen from Markham's (1948) survey. Although he records that 160 museums had closed since 1938, nevertheless there appears to have been a greater effort than in the 1914–1918 war to maintain a museum service. Indeed museums played a more active role in the community and involved themselves in the war effort by providing special classes for children evacuated to their area (e.g. Stevens, 1940), arranging lunch-time concerts and holding such Ministry of Information exhibitions as 'Dig for Victory', 'Anti-gossip' and 'Buy a Spitfire'. The journal *Nature* (7 July 1945) acknowledged particularly the role and achievements of the larger museums and galleries during the war and expressed the hope that smaller institutions would now emulate them. Although Rosse (1963) records the foundation of about ten museums during the war it is unlikely that many of them were opened to the public on a regular basis. An exception to this was Leicester's Newarke Houses Museum which, although taken into trusteeship by the Corporation in 1936, was first opened to the public in July 1940.

The post-war years

During the lean war years, the Museums Association had been looking to the period when hostilities ceased. A memorandum on museums and reconstruction was published (Museums Association, 1942) and formed the basis for discussion between the Association and the Ministry of Reconstruction in 1943.

An extended version appeared at the close of the war (Museums Association, 1945) to act as a blueprint for the years ahead. Finance figured high in the list of priorities and Markham's recommendation for a national body concerned with all museums was developed in the form of a Museum and Art Gallery Grants Board, modelled on the University Grants Committee (UGC), which would assess new schemes, allocate grants, define standards and ensure they were maintained through a system of inspection. The report envisaged finance being available for capital schemes involving new buildings and reconstructing old ones; providing sufficient trained and adequately paid staff to maintain the museum service, increase circulating exhibitions, provide for certain museums and galleries to act as centres for a region to advise and assist smaller museums and develop educational services, purchase and hire exhibits and generally improve museum amenities.

The proposed Grants Board was seen to have two complementary sections, one concerned with museums and the other with art galleries. The latter would also be concerned with developing a loan pool of works of art, taking over the responsibilities of the Council for the Encouragement of Music and the Arts (CEMA), initiating art appreciation education based on galleries and arts centres, acting as a central publication agency for reproductions and catalogues and advising galleries on disposal policies; the influence of a discussion document issued in 1944 by the Art Enquiry and published two years later under the title *The Visual Arts* can be seen in this. In the event, the Arts Council of Great Britain was established in 1946, taking over responsibility for a number of these art functions. However, no similar body was created to help co-ordinate, finance and assist museums and galleries in their established role.

By 1946 most of the damaged national museums were reopened, partly or fully, the British Museum being amongst the last, although not all of the important items that had been removed from their premises were yet reinstated. The Museums Association held its first conference outside of London since the war commenced and among the items reported was the resumption of training courses for the diploma and special refresher provisions for those involved in war service. Its continuing concern for training was also reflected in the publication of a series of notes for students in its Journal from 1948–1950 which were also reprinted as separate booklets. With a medium-term aim for achieving chartered status for its diploma holders, the Association changed its Articles of Association in 1951. The new Articles provided for certain professional members to qualify for election to Associateship and Fellowship of the Museums Association; today Associateship is restricted to holders of the Association's diploma.

The Festival of Britain, held to commemorate the centenary of the Great Exhibition of 1851, involved many museums and galleries both in the preparation of the main exhibition and in special events in the institutions themselves. Some of them benefited from new galleries to commemorate the occasion, as with the Cotman collection at Norwich Castle, or as recipients, in due course, of displays from the main London exhibition, for example, Jewry Wall, Leices-

ter and Worthing Museum which both received archaeological models for their displays. The Festival was responsible, indirectly, in fostering better display design in museums, for in 1951 Leicester Museum became the first provincial institution to employ a qualified designer for its exhibition work.

Indeed the 1950s saw the beginning of an awareness of the need for many specialized non-curatorial skills, in the manifold functions of museums. The Museums Association introduced a Technical Certificate in 1953. This awareness was also reflected in the formation of the first specialist groups, separate from the Museums Association. These included the foundation in London of the International Institute of Conservation (IIC) in 1950 and the reconstruction of the Childrens' Activities Group in 1951 to become the Group for Childrens' Activities in Museums, later the Group for Educational Services in Museums and now the Group for Education in Museums (GEM). In 1955 the Military Museums Federation was formed, to be followed the next year by the Ogilby Trust which has contributed much to advising and making grants to the regimental museums. There had, however, already been in existence for some years another organization for curatorial and technical staff other than those in charge of a museum. Formed in 1938 from diploma course members, the Junior Officials Group of the Museums Association was revived after the War to become the Museum Assistants Group. It was renamed the Museum Professionals Group (MPG) in 1979.

But if the Festival of Britain had given an impression of prosperity in the early 1950s, the reality was a period of severe financial restraint. In 1952 economies of £30 000 had to be made by the national museums, and the Museums Association, in annual conference at Oxford, passed a resolution condemning the Government's action. On the same occasion a further resolution sought the rehabilitation of those provincial museums still incapacitated by war damage. But despite this, public interest in museums was increasing, fostered without doubt by television. For six years during the 1950s the BBC screened its highly successful quiz programme *Animal, Vegetable or Mineral?* In which different museums challenged a panel of experts to identify objects from their collections. The entertainment value of the programme was high, resulting in increased visitors to museums generally and museum objects took on a new interest and museum people were perceived in a new light. Indeed, the chief panellist was a past-president of the Museums Association, the distinguished archaeologist Sir Mortimer Wheeler.

This was clearly the time for the Association to renew its attempts to gain State aid for provincial museums. Discussions immediately following the War had reached the stage by 1949 when steps were being taken to provide a central fund of £250 000. An election, a static economy and dissention from a minority of local authorities conspired to prevent further progress. In 1955 a memorandum on the subject was prepared by a joint committee involving the Carnegie United Kingdom Trust, the Arts Council and the Association and presented to the Chancellor of the Exchequer. By 1958 a new factor had entered the arena, regionalization, and an experimental scheme of mutual co-operation between museums had been established in south-west England. In the belief that Government might be more willing to finance regional organizations of museums rather than individual museums, the Association proposed a scheme based on Regional Museums Services. A weakness in the Association's case was a lack of detailed information about provincial museum services and it sought to rectify this. Lord Bridges, who had called for a UGC-type body to fund the arts in his 1958 Romaines lecture, came to a similar conclusion in his report following an enquiry into the arts for the Gulbenkian Foundation and called for a general survey to be made of material in museum collections.

In the event neither of these surveys took place. In 1960 the Standing Commission on Museums and Art Galleries was asked to undertake a review of the provincial museums and galleries with the following terms of reference:

> To ascertain the scope, nature and significance of the local collections, the manner in which they are organized, the resources available to them and the possibilities of their further development on a basis of regional co-operation.

The Commission's report *Survey of provincial museums and galleries,* prepared under the chairmanship of the Earl of Rosse, was published in 1963. The survey listed some eight hundred and seventy-six provincial museums and galleries with a permanent collection and open to the public. A number of its recommendations echo those of earlier reports: that there should be an increase in the Victoria and Albert Museum grant to aid purchases in provincial museums and its travelling exhibitions, and that these should be extended to involve material from the British Museum, the Science Museum and other national institutions; that curators should be paid an adequate salary, have adequate qualifications and not generally be subordinated to a librarian; that school museum services should be established throughout the country and particularly loan services for rural areas. In addition the continuing financial condition of the Museums Association received attention with particular recommendations for Government grant to enable it to set up a training institute to develop its work and appoint an education officer of senior status.

The requirement that the report should cover problems relating to the provincial collections led to a number of topical recommendations as they related to different types of collection. The need for one museum to provide the facilities necessary to deal with the increasing archaeological discoveries in each area is reminscent of the more general recommendations of earlier reports, as was the idea for central stores of ethnographical material in the provinces. Despite its provincial terms of reference, however, the report also recommended that a National Museum of Ethnography should be built as soon as possible drawing attention to the earlier aborted attempt at this in 1938; that the National Army Museum should be established in central London and that type specimens should normally be housed at the British Museum (Natural History). The suggestion that museum buildings should be adapted to further their use for social purposes and staff provided for this, was a clear acknowledgement of the now widely-recognized role of the museum in its own community. Impetus for this no doubt commenced as a result of the extended use of museums during the war, as well as a recognition of success of such work in the United States.

The Commission had been asked particularly to look at regional co-operation. By the time its report was published in 1963 the South-West and the Midlands had Area Museum Services for their regions and north-west England was actively considering one. The report recommended that all local authorities should prepare a co-ordinated scheme for museum improvement and development in their areas; further, that the Government should help financially in setting up the schemes, and in the costs of providing services, including capital schemes, to the museums on the basis of the equivalent of the amount subscribed locally. The Government responded with a revenue grant of £10 000 to assist local museums. The inadequacy of such a sum produced an immediate reaction and agreement was reached that the grant should in future be calculated on the basis of half of the net expenditure of the Councils; this base was changed to half of the gross expenditure in 1966. The services provided by the Area Councils concentrated mainly in the areas of conservation and exhibition and were intended primarily for the smaller, poorer museums (Harrison, 1971). Many of these services were provided by agencies based on existing museums but certain of the Area Services established their own facilities in a headquarters building. The development of these services can be traced in the various reports of the Standing Commission on Museums and Galleries (1965, 1967, 1973a, b, 1978).

New legislation

A series of reports on local authority library matters led to the *Public Libraries and Museums Act 1964* which came into force on 1 April 1965. This repealed all previous library and museum legislation for England and Wales. Henceforward it became a duty of every library authority to provide an efficient library service; the provision of museums by these authorities, however, was not mandatory. For museums, the legislation was general allowing a local authority to provide and maintain museums anywhere in England and Wales or to transfer a museum or gallery and its collections to another local authority. The only specific provisions related to the authorization of admission charges, provided the interests of students and children were taken into account and the museum or gallery was playing its full part in promoting education in its area (the 1892 and 1919 legislation had prohibited charging although Hewitt (1947, p. 34) argued that it was admissable for art galleries to make a charge); to the contribution towards the expenses of any person providing a museum or art gallery or advisory or other services related to them in England and Wales (this particularly concerned contributing to Area Museum Service schemes); and to the establishment of a cumulative purchase fund (as recommended by the Standing Commission, 1963). Schedule 2 of the act also allowed for the proceeds of the sale of objects to be credited to this fund. Powers to use premises for educational or cultural events, also recommended by the Standing Commission (1963), were given to both libraries and museums.

Legislative change also came to the British Museum. After two hundred and ten years, the original Act was repealed by the *British Museum Act 1963* thereby abolishing the old *ex-officio* and family trustees and replacing them with two separate boards of Trustees, one for the Bloomsbury institution and the other for the British Museum (Natural History) at South Kensington. Another important change under the Act was the authorization of the Trustees to lend objects to other institutions. The next decade was to see the development of plans which would eventually move two important collections at the British Museum to other locations. The recommendations of the Royal Commission (1929b), reiterated by the Standing Commission (1963), to set up a national museum of ethnography came to fruition, albeit in temporary quarters, when the Museum of Mankind was opened in Burlington Gardens in December 1970 (Fagg, 1972). The other move proposed involved the British Museum Library. After considerable controversy, particularly concerning the library's location, it was eventually determined that this should be amalgamated with other national libraries, including the Science Museum Library, to form the British Library under an Act of that name in 1972. The severance of a museum from its library had its precedents in the provinces; many of the Liverpool Museum's book holdings were transferred to the Central Library in the 1930s while in 1892 the Bristol Museum library was taken over to form the substantial part of the Reference Library there.

A matter of recurring debate during these postwar years was the responsibility of museum governing bodies towards their collections. The issue was the subject of considerable discussion and press comment during the passage of the *National Gallery and Tate Gallery Act 1954* through Parliament. This statute, *inter alia,* removed at the Trustees request, their power to sell items from their collections and permitted the transfer of material only to certain other national institutions listed in the Act. The decision of the Royal Academy to sell its Leonardo cartoon in the early 1960s also gave rise to public concern, and a Committee of Enquiry appointed to examine the issue drew attention to the special position of property given for the public benefit (Cottesloe, 1964). The debate continued within the Museums Association (Jacob, 1971) and at a Government level, the Minister with Special Responsibility for the Arts called for a report on the sale and gift of surplus objects in the national collections and the possibility of circulating and loaning such objects to the regions. The report, by the Standing Commission (1973b), usefully lists the legal position and the views of Trustees of the national institutions on the matter. For local authority museums considerable variations in their powers of disposal remain in the current legislation[3].

Expansion and diversification

The ten years 1965–1974 represented an important period in the development of museums in Britain. Not only did the number of new museums increase rapidly but new types of museum appeared and existing museums responded to changing social and cultural conditions. This expressed itself in a number of ways, including the increase in the number of appointments to posts concerned with the public face of museums, particularly educationists and designers; a wish to know more about museum visitors and their attitude through visitors surveys of which that in Ulster (Doughty, 1968) was the first of a number to be published at this time; an increasing involvement with the natural and human heritage outside the museum; greater activity at a community level, particularly under the Government's urban aid programme for the declining industrial cities (Thompson, 1980) and to a lesser extent with minority groups (Thompson, 1972). Some of this work had an art bias, at least partly attributable to the formation during this period of a country-wide network of Regional Arts Associations established on a basis similar to the Area Museum Councils with government funding through the Arts Council.

Awareness of the archaeological heritage was forced on museums as a result of post-war building and road development by the mid 1950s. Faced with increasing numbers of discoveries, archaeological staff in the provincial museums mounted rescue operations, often in collaboration with local societies, to salvage what they could. The incidence of archaeological sites does not necessarily coincide with major museum provision and many small museums, for example Chester, Winchester and Worthing, found themselves preoccupied with these problems with minimal staff resources.

But with one or two notable exceptions a decade passed before museums were able to recruit additional staff, particularly at a county level, to cope with the work (Barton, 1974). Government grants became available to assist excavation work and major rescue operations took place in many parts of the country; Government aid, however, rarely extended to the long-term storage and use of the resulting finds and it devolved on museums to meet these continuing costs (Thomas, 1976).

In the wake of this intense activity came a growing interest in industrial archaeology in which museums were also closely involved. Perhaps the earliest excavation of an industrial site was that at the Abraham Darby furnace, Ironbridge in 1959; another, involving Sheffield City Museums, was at the Catcliffe glassworks in 1961. This Museum also opened the Abbeydale Industrial Hamlet, an eighteenth-century steel and scythe works, as a site museum in 1970 (Greenaway, 1970). But the major industrial site development of this period for museum purposes was at Ironbridge. Here a charitable trust was established to restore, preserve and develop as a museum, various industrial and related monuments *in situ* in what is regarded by many as the cradle of the industrial revolution (Cossons, 1973). Funded through a charitable trust under the *Charities Act 1960,* it has become the archetype of the so-called Independent Museums, large numbers of which, particularly associated with preservation projects, were to appear on the museum scene in the 1970s. At Torfaen, the local authority transferred their museum to a charitable trust in 1974 and Oxfordshire's Cogges Farm was similarly transferred in 1983, but these were exceptions rather than the rule. This movement gave rise to the formation of the Association of Independent Museums (AIM) in 1977.

Museums also became involved with the interpretation of the countryside, a response to an increasing public awareness of the need to use our natural heritage wisely. This movement, which received some impetus in the early 1960s manifested itself through the involvement of museums in providing nature trails and interpretative centres and, for example, the creation of the CUKT Field Study Unit based at Leicester Museums. Some of these develop-

ments have been summarized by Stansfield (1967, 1969). Conservation awareness has influenced natural history displays considerably since that time.

Expansion and diversification brought with it the need for new skills and the development of old ones, for improved standards among museum staff and for a better understanding of the purpose of museums and their role in society. As the result of a three-year grant from the Calouste Gulbenkian Foundation, the University of Leicester established a full Department of Museum Studies (Singleton, 1966). This development took place in close collaboration with the Museums Association and for the first decade concerned itself primarily with training graduates intending to make a career in the museum profession; holders of its Graduate Certificate in Museum Studies were accorded considerable exemptions in the examinations for the Museums Association Diploma. A similar course, with specialization in the fine and decorative arts, was commenced in the Department of the History of Art at the University of Manchester in 1971 (Smith, 1971). Thus the development of university-based curatorial training, foreshadowed in more than one report of the 1920s, came to fruition.

Like the Museums Association Diploma these training facilities attracted overseas participation. At Leicester, the introduction of an additional taught course leading to a Master's degree in 1975 and opportunities to undertake research into the museum function to doctoral level, accentuated this. After fifteen years of operation, some 14 per cent of the 287 Leicester graduates held museum appointments abroad. Of those employed in the United Kingdom, about half served in local authority museums and the remainder were fairly evenly spread among the national, university and independent museums. From 1980, the Department of Museum Studies at Leicester commenced providing all the compulsory course requirements for the in-service Museums Association Diploma[4].

The early 1970s saw the opening of two new purpose-built national museums: the National Army Museum at Chelsea in 1971 (Reid, 1971, 1973), the realization of the Standing Commission's (1963) recommendation that the Museum should be moved from Sandhurst to London; and the Royal Air Force Museum at Hendon in 1972 (Tanner, 1973) based on a collection which had been amassed by the Ministry of Defence. In the same year a much-enlarged Ulster Museum was opened to the public (Warhurst, 1973). As part of its regional policy, the Science Museum opened its National Railway Museum at York in 1975 incorporating collections originally held by British Rail at York and Clapham; its National Museum of Photography, Film and Television opened in 1983 at Bradford. In 1976 another purpose-built museum opened in London. Conceived as an amalgamation of the London Museum and the Guildhall Museum in the late 1950s, the Museum of London was established by the Government, the Greater London Council and the City of London under the *Museum of London Act 1965* to preserve and interpret the history of the capital from earliest times to the present day (Simmons, 1977).

The beginning of the 1970s also saw the foundation of the first lay organization to support museums nationally. Known as National Heritage and subtitled the museum action group, its genesis can be attributed to a concern that museums were approaching a 'crisis' situation and to the lack of any national policy for museums (Letts, 1970, 1971). With associated sponsorship, this organization was responsible for introducing the Museum of the Year Award in 1973; it also publishes a bulletin, *Museum News*. Also created about the same time was the British Association of Friends of Museums, concerned with co-ordinating and advising 'Friends' of various museums throughout Britain (Muirhead, 1974). Another organization, the National Association of Decorative and Fine Arts Societies (NADFAS), was inaugurated in 1968 to co-ordinate a growing number of societies formed to stimulate interest in the national heritage and assist in its care (Fay, 1974).

The proliferation of organizations concerned with museums was not restricted to museum users. The Museums Association's increasing professional membership, resulting from the relative affluence of the mid-1960s, was growing more restive about the state of the nation's collections. In 1967 a group of curators, concerned about the inadequacies of museum documentation, formed the Information Retrieval Group of the Museums Association (IRGMA) and continued to work on the problems for the next nine years (IRGMA Standards Sub-Committee, 1977). By the mid-1970s a number of new professional groups concerned with different types of collections and different aspects of the museum function had been created. Among the first of these specialist organizations were the Geological Curators' Group (GCG), Museum Ethnographer's Group (MEG), and the Group for Regional Studies in Museums (GRSM), now the Social History Curators Group. The Museums Association actively supported this move but when some of the groups failed to seek affiliation, expressed concern at the potentially divisive situation within its ranks at a time when it was trying to achieve greater cohesion in the profession generally.

Another issue arose at this time, by no means new to the museum movement. There had been an unprecedented growth in Britain's educational provision during the 1960s. This had included the establishment of school resource centres, seen by some as a threat to the concept of museum school loans services, and the creation of community schools with the opportunities these presented for extending the museum services to a wider audience. The profession's educationists, led by the then Group for Educational Services in Museums, sought a far more overtly educational role for museums. A number of reports ensued, published by the Council for Museums and Galleries in Scotland (1970), the Department of Education and Science (1971), and the Schools Council (1972). A Working Party on Museums in Education also examined the issue for the Museums Association, its report being accepted at the 1970 Annual Conference and published the following year (Museums Association, 1971a).

But the Museums Association was mainly preoccupied with attempting to achieve some semblance of structural and strategic sense to the museum service nationally. Its latest proposals saw the designation of certain museums with collections of international importance as 'national museums in the provinces' and a larger group with specialized collections of national, or considerable regional importance as 'regional museums', both aided by central government funds. The supporting paper (Museums Association, 1971b) drew attention to the fact that, in their primary concern for small museums, the Area Councils were not contributing to the major problems confronting museums: the important holdings of the larger museums. By the time these proposals had been approved in principle by the Association's conference in 1971, two new factors had emerged: the Government had announced its intention to reorganize local government and the Paymaster General, who also had special responsibility for the arts, appointed a committee to review the provincial museums and galleries.

This committee was chaired by C. W. Wright and had terms of reference to examine particularly the conservation and display needs of the principal local museums and galleries in England and improve relationships between them and the national institutions. It reported two years later (Department of Education and Science, 1973). Drawing attention to the number of recommendations made on the needs of museums in previous reports over the last fifty years which had never been implemented, many of its conclusions and recommendations make familiar reading. On the organization of museums, the need for a new central body reappears. This it was envisaged, would advise central and local government on provincial museums and galleries, channel funds to them according to a considered plan, and be supported by both professional and administrative staff. To co-ordinate this at a regional level, provincial museum councils were proposed to continue and expand the existing work of the area museum councils. As far as the museums were concerned the Committee made proposals similar to those of the Museums Association two years previously: that a limited number of museums, or groups of museums, should become 'provincial centres of excellence' which by their own performance and services to other museums would improve standards throughout the country.

Local government reorganization

By the time this report appeared, planning for the reorganization of local government in England and Wales (except London) was already well underway. The principal legislation, the *Local Government Act 1972*, provided for a two-tier system of government, County and District, and, on the basis that 'bigger is more efficient', amalgamated many of the old local authority administrative units within this framework. Six areas of the country, involving the major conurbations, were given 'metropolitan' status, tthe Districts in these areas being responsible for the library service, whereas elsewhere this function is undertaken by the 'Shire' counties. Although not the unanimous view of its members, the Museums Association lobbied strongly that museums should be a mandatory first-tier function and this was debated during the passage of the Bill through Parliament; in the event museums became a concurrent function which could be exercised by both counties and districts. In this it was similar to the *London Government Act 1963* which had reorganized local government in the capital ten years earlier and given powers to both the Greater London Council and the London Boroughs to provide museums.

Apart from restricting the provision of museums to the two types of authority, the 1972 Act also amended other aspects of the *Libraries and Museums Act 1964*. Among these, it became no longer necessary to obtain the consent of the Secretary of State for Education and Science to provide a museum or transfer a museum or its collections to another local authority. In addition the provision was repealed whereby a non-county authority providing a museum could be exempt from paying the rate precept for its county museum services. Under the 1972 Act successor authorities were premitted to retain powers given under local acts for a time[5].

In Scotland, local government reorganization was effected in 1975, under the provisions of the *Local Government (Scotland) Act 1973*. As in England and Wales, a two-tier structure was introduced involving Regions (with Islands Councils to meet the special needs of Orkney, Shetland and the Western Isles) and Districts and each was given museum powers; in contrast, however, the Regions had 'mandatory' duties to ensure in consultation with District Councils within their Region adequate provision of such facilities within their area[6]. At the time of reorganization the provision and maintenance of museums could be under either the *Public Libraries Consolidation (Scotland) Act 1887* or the *Education (Scotland) Act 1969*[7]. Under the 1887 Act museums must be opened to the public free of charge but the education legislation allows admission fees to be charged, subject to certain conditions; there are other variations, particularly regarding the disposal of collections.

The reorganization of local government in Northern Ireland took place in 1974 as a result of the *Local Government Act (Northern Ireland) 1972*. Museum powers continued to be available under the *Public Libraries Acts (Northern Ireland) 1855 to 1924* or the *Museums and Gymnasiums Act 1891*, but there were no local authority museums in Northern Ireland in 1974, the Belfast Museum and Art Gallery having been transferred to trustees under the *Ulster Museum Act 1961* with the Armagh County Museum subsequently coming within its purview[8].

Local government reorganization had a profound effect on local services, not least museums. The amalgamation of old authorities brought together a number of museums under one administration for the first time. Certain of the old County Borough museums were transferred to the new County Councils, notably Liverpool to Merseyside and Leicester and Norwich to their respective counties. While the former involved only Liverpool's museums and gallery but included all assets, in Norfolk buildings and collections remained with the successor district councils while the Museum Service was provided by a Joint Committee of the County Council which included district representation. In Tyne and Wear a County Museum Service was created shortly after reorganization to become responsible for ten museums in four of its constituent districts. Elsewhere some county councils commenced museum services from scratch even where, for example in the case of South Yorkshire and Humberside, existing district museums were already providing a regional service. Because the majority of the local authority museums services were still small departments by local authority standards, many of them found themselves amalgamated with other Departments – Education, Recreation and Leisure particularly – while ironically the two metropolitan county services each became one of the larger departments of their authorities. At a committee level there was also considerable diversity. Hopes for greater structural cohesion, so long sought, faded and as Cheetham (1974) stated 'the "unique opportunity" has largely been allowed . . . to slip away' (see also Loughbrough, 1978).

Despite this, and a deteriorating economy, it was a period of expansion for museums. New posts were created to meet the needs of new services and lacunae were filled in existing establishments particularly in providing staff to improve public services. There was also some improvement in the level of museum staff remuneration, either because of increased responsibilities or in providing parity with other similar officers in larger composite departments. But this was short-lived as financial stringency increasingly gripped the local authorities for the next decade.

Recent developments

The economic situation was also to affect the national museums. In 1975. by agreement with the Department of Education and Science and the Treasury, certain of the national museums administered by trustees were devolved giving their governing bodies far greater autonomy. This, in a sense, anticipated a recommendation made by Lord Redcliffe-Maud (1976) in a report to the Calouste Gulbenkian Foundation, that the administration of the arts in provincial England and Wales would best be achieved on the 'arms-length prinicple'. The Victoria and Albert Museum, however, did not have such delegated powers and in 1977, when required by Government to reduce its staff, found no alternative but to discontinue its circulating exhibition programme. The cessation of this service after some 113 years of operation was a severe blow to many provincial museums.

But some important developments still took place. One of these was the creation of the Museums Documentation Association (MDA) to advise museums on documentation procedures and to seek to achieve minimum data standards in this work. The MDA took over the work of the Information Retrieval Group of the Museums Association (IRGMA) and was financed by an additional subvention in the Government's Area Museum Council grant and individual subscriptions from most of the national museums (Roberts *et al*, 1980). The establishment of a national specialized unit in one aspect of the museum function to establish standards, advise and service museums, irrespective of their funding source, was an important professional and organizational development.

Besides the documentation of specimen data, many museums were by now maintaining environmental records (Stewart, 1980) and this was given further impetus through a Museums Association resolution of 1977 supporting the idea of county-based centres for this purpose, located wherever possible at museums. Knowledge of the natural science holdings of museums at a collection level was also the subject of attention, initially through the formation of a voluntary body, the North West Collection Research Unit (Hancock and Pettit, 1980), an example soon followed in other parts of the country. These joined forces in 1981 (Pettit and Hancock, 1981) in a co-ordinating body, the Federation for Natural Sciences Collection Research (FENSCORE).

These developments, together with the availability of documentation advice and the IRGMA/MDA record cards, coincided with the establishment of Government-financed job creation schemes to relieve unemployment. A number of museums took advantage of these and subsequent schemes to provide work in a variety of areas. One of its most common applications was in improving museum documentation and Atkinson (1978) records that a quarter of the four hundred temporary posts thus created in museums during the first two years of operation were concerned with cataloguing and related work.

The physical state of the nation's collections was also a matter of increasing concern. The paucity of conservators and conservation facilities was the subject of a survey by the UK Group of the International Institute for Conservation (1974); the Standing Commission on Museums and Galleries (1980) also reported on conservation needs in the various museum and gallery disciplines. One discipline, geology, was the subject of a detailed survey, conducted by the Geological Curators' Group, which provided lists of named collections and their locations and an alarming picture of the current state of collection management in this field, some two-thirds of the geological collections in the UK having no formal curatorial arrangements of any kind (Doughty n.d.).

Meanwhile, the public services of one museum came under closer examination. The British Museum (Natural History), about to embark on a thirty-year display renewal programme, brought together a team to develop a new exhibition scheme (Miles and Alt, 1979). The first of the resulting experimental exhibitions, the Hall of Human Biology, was heavily criticized by the profession (e.g. Duggan, 1978) as it incorporated new educational technology, communication and evaluation techniques but few specimens. Subsequent displays redressed the balance. This work represents the first serious attempt to apply modern educational strategies to the museum situation. Other major display work took place in national museums, including the Geological Museum's 'Story of the earth' gallery, and the new Greek and Egyptian galleries at the British Museum. But this was also the age of the 'block-buster' exhibition the first of which, 'Treasures of Tutankhamun' shown at the British Museum in 1972, attracted some 1 600 000 visitors.

In the provinces the housing of the magnificent Burrell collection, given to Glasgow in 1944 with an endowment for a building, began slowly to move forward (Wells *et al*, 1972). An architectural competition was held in 1972 but work on the building with a Government contribution towards half the net cost, did not commence until 1978 and was completed in 1983. Following the gift of the Sainsbury art collection to the University of East Anglia and monies for the construction of an art gallery in 1973, the Sainsbury Centre for Visual Arts was opened at Norwich four years later (Borg, 1979). On the local authority scene, the opening of the new purpose-built Stoke-on-Trent City Museum and Art Gallery in 1981 (Mountford, 1982) represented a major event in a bleak economic climate. Although both the Glasgow and Stoke projects received grants from the Government towards their realization, these were one-off awards. The long sought-after regular allocation of government money for museum capital development followed in 1981 albeit on a small scale. Another major project was the raising of the Tudor Ship 'Mary Rose' from the Solent in 1983 for public display.

Inevitably in a period of severe recession the issue of free admission to museums arose again. The Government introduced charges to the national museums in 1974 through the *Museums and Galleries Admission Charges Act 1972* but this lasted only three months, a period which saw a dramatic fall in attendances. This legislation remained on the statute book. Towards the end of the decade many local authorities considered the introduction of entrance fees. Some effected them but in terms of a revenue source they were not, generally, a success; at least one authority discontinued the practice (Besterman and Bott, 1982). The position of the independent museums, however, appeared to be different with a public willing to pay, particularly for an open-air experience.

One of the over-riding themes of the 1970s and early 1980s was the definition of professional standards. For institutions the Museums Association introduced its accreditation scheme in 1974, similar to the United States model, to encourage museums to achieve recognized acceptable professional standards (Cubbon, 1973, 1975). The scheme has had limited success to date (Thomson, 1982). In 1977 the Association's conference adopted a *Code of Practice for Museum Authorities* and *Guidelines for Professional Conduct* (Boylan, 1977). The latter has been the subject of major revision (see Appendix 2). The former embodied a number of the Association's policy statements including matters concerning the acquisition of objects arising from international sources. Among these were the Council of Europe's *Convention on the Protection of the Archaeological Heritage,* ratified by the British Government in 1973 and the UNESCO *Convention on the Means of Prohibiting and Preventing the Illicit Import, Export and Transfer of Ownership of Cultural Property 1970*. The Code of Practice supports the principle of the UNESCO Convention although it has not been ratified in Britain. The more recent promotion by UNESCO of the return of cultural property to its country of origin is not covered, nor is there a British policy statement on the matter. Certain Museums have adopted the Code of Practice and at least one Area Museum Council

requires this as a pre-requisite to giving grant aid. This has encouraged the Association to revive the idea of a register of museums, discussed originally in the late 1960s (Clarke, 1969), which conform to certain minimum standards for the purpose of grant aid.

Increasing concern among the international community about the preservation of the human and natural heritage has also been reflected in recent British legislation, including the *Ancient Monuments and Archaeological Areas Act 1979,* and the *Wildlife and Countryside Act 1981*. Both of these statutes have implications for museum-collecting policies. Other recent legislation suggests that there may be a trend to bring some of the many agencies concerned with museums and related institutions together. The *National Heritage Act 1980,* which *inter alia* provides purchase grants for heritage material, operates under the Secretaries of State for Education and Science, the Environment, Scotland, and Northern Ireland. The *National Heritage Act 1983* granted trustee status to the Science Museum and Victoria and Albert Museum, previously part of the Department of Education and Science, to bring them into line with other major national institutions; this followed a recommendation of the Rayner Scrutiny involving a detailed management study of these two museums (Burrett, 1982). This Act also made certain provisions for armed forces museums, currently under the Ministry of Defence, as well as for historic monuments and buildings; however, a complex structure of museum provision in Britain still remains (*Figure 4.1*).

The Standing Commission on Museums and Galleries (1979) published its report *Framework for a System for Museums* and developed certain of the proposals contained in the 1973 report of the Department of Education and Science and again proposing that a central policy-making body should be established. In 1981 the Standing Commission became the Museums and Galleries Commission with revised terms of reference and increased responsibilities (Drew, 1981); although not a policy-making body its additional powers give it greater strength towards a pivotal place in museum affairs.[9] Reports on museums in Wales (Standing Commission, 1981), the need for regional museums in Northern Ireland (Malcolm, 1978)[8] and the national collections in Scotland (Williams, 1981) drew attention to problems in these regions of the United Kingdom, the latter including the recommendation to appoint a Scottish Museums Commission. A further report (Museums & Galleries Commission, 1982) encouraged counties to set up consultative committees to co-ordinate museum activities at that level, as suggested in its 1979 report.

Support for the designation of certain of the most important provincial museums to receive direct

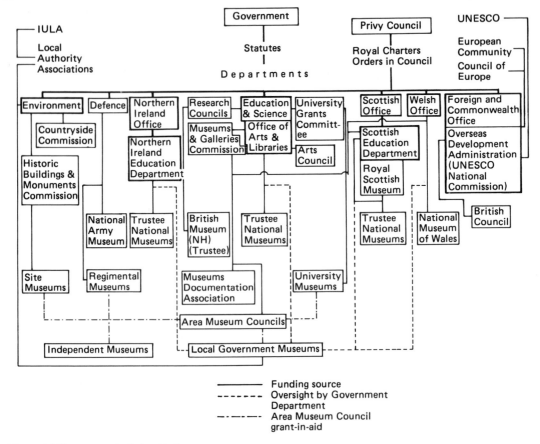

Funding source

------- Oversight by Government
          Department

—·—·— Area Museum Council
          grant-in-aid

Figure 4.1 The structural relationship between
government and museums in Britain

government funding, first raised in a report from the Department of Education and Science (1973) and elaborated by the Standing Commission on Museums and Galleries (1979), has come from an all-party committee of the House of Commons (1982). The Government's response to this has been cautious, but they have acknowledged the principle in proposals to abolish the Greater London Council and Metropolitan County Councils which, if implemented, will have major consequences for some of the outstanding institutions of this country.

Currently the museums of Britain are in a paradoxical situation: a period of increasing financial stringency during which a plethora of Government reports have appeared recommending additional funding and better organization. There can be no doubt that the last twenty years have seen a consciousness and responsibility to the public not witnessed to the same extent during this century. This has led to national recognition of the important role played by museums not only in preserving key aspects of the nation's heritage but as a public ser-

vice, as a contribution to the quality of life and as an influence in economy of the country through tourism. Such recognition augers well for the future.

Acknowledgements

My thanks are due to Raymond Singleton who painstakingly read Chapters 2–4 and made a number of helpful comments. Dr Tony Duggan and Alan Warhurst read the post-war section of Chapter 3 and I am grateful for their constructive comments.

Notes

[1] *Museums J,* **27**(5), 141–142. Subsequently known as the North Western Federation of Museums and Art Galleries
[2] *Museums J,* **28**(1), 1–5
[3] cf. *Public Libraries & Museums Act 1964; Public Libraries (Scotland) Act 1887; Education (Scotland) Act 1980; Museums (Northern Ireland) Order 1981*
[4] For a fuller statement on the history and development of

the training of museum personnel in the United Kingdom, see Lewis (1983)

[5] Where such provisions exist for museums these normally relate to the sale of collections, the accumulation of a purchase fund (now provided under the 1964 Act) and the disposal of uncollected specimens left for an opinion (now permitted under the *Local Government (Miscellaneous Provisions Act 1982*).

[6] All museum duties given to the Regions were repealed by the *Local Government and Planning (Scotland) Act 1982* which are now the responsibility of District Councils. Regions, however, may still make grants towards the costs of museums if they so wish.

[7] Now repealed by the *Education (Scotland) Act 1980* although the museum provisions remain the same.

[8] Although the Malcolm (1978) report recommended specific legislation for the establishment of regional museums in Northern Ireland, this was not implemented. Instead museum powers under these and subsequent Acts were repealed by the *Museums (Northern Ireland) Order 1981* which now provides for the two national museums in the Province and for District Councils to create and maintain museums.

[9] The terms of reference of the Museums and Galleries Commission are:

(1) To advise generally on the most effective development of museums and galleries and to advise and take action as appropriate, on any specific matters which may be referred to them from time to time.

(2) To promote co-operation between museums and galleries and particularly between national and provincial institutions.

(3) To stimulate the generosity and direct the efforts of those who aspire to become public benefactors.

References

ALLAN, D. A. (1954), 'The Royal Scottish Museum: general survey' in *The Royal Scottish Museum 1854–1954*, Oliver and Boyd, Edinburgh

ATKINSON, F. (1978), 'A report on job creation in museums, 1976–8', *Museums J.*, **77**(4), 158–160

BARTON, K. (1974), 'Rescuing museums', in Rahtz, P. A. (Ed), *Rescue Archaeology*, Penguin Books, Harmondsworth

BATHER, F. A. (1930), 'British Association: conference of delegates from corresponding societies', *Museums J.*, **30**(1), 2–5

BESTERMAN, T. AND BOTT, V. (1982), 'To pay or not to pay', *Museums J*, **82**(2), 118–119

BORG, A. (1979), 'The Sainsbury Centre for Visual Arts', *Museums J*, **78**(4), 167–169

BOYLAN, P J. (1977), 'Museum ethics: Museums Association policies', *Museums J*, **77**(3), 106–111

BRITISH ASSOCIATION (1887), – 'Report of the Committee on the provincial museums of the United Kingdom' in *Report of the British Association for the Advancement of Science 1887*, 97–130, London

BRITISH ASSOCIATION (1888), 'A further report of the Committee on the provincial museums of the United Kingdom' in *Report of the British Association for the Advancement of Science 1888*, 124–132, London

BRITISH ASSOCIATION (1920), 'Final report of the Committee on museums in relation to education' in *Report of British Association for the Advancement of Science 1920*, 267–280, London

BURRETT, F. G. (1982), *Rayner Scrutiny of the Departmental Museums: Science Museum and Victoria and Albert Museum*, Office of Arts and Libraries, DES, London

CHEETHAM, F. W. (1974), 'Local government reorganization and the Norfolk Museums Service', *Museums J.*, **74**(1), 27–28

CLARKE, D. T–D. (1969), 'Register of museums', *Museums J.*, **69**(3), 141

CONSTABLE, W. G. (1933), 'Training for museum work: a year's experience at the Courtauld Institute', *Museums J.*, **33**(8), 273–279

COSSONS, N. (1973), 'The Ironbridge project', *Museums J.*, **72**(4) 135–139

COTTESLOE, LORD (1964), *Report of the Committee of Enquiry into the sale of works of art by public bodies*, HMSO, London

COUNCIL FOR MUSEUMS AND GALLERIES IN SCOTLAND (1970), *Report on Museums and Education*, CMGS

COWPER, L. I. (1935), 'British military museums', *Museums J.*, **35**(2), 40–49

CUBBON, A. (1973), 'Accreditation', *Museums J.*, **73**(3), 97–98

CUBBON, A. (1975), 'Accreditation: the position to date', *Museums J.*, **75**(3), supplement, xx–xxi

DEPARTMENT OF EDUCATION AND SCIENCE (1971), *Museums in Education*, Education Survey 12, DES, HMSO, London

DEPARTMENT OF EDUCATION AND SCIENCE (1973), *Provincial Museums and Galleries*, a report of a Committee appointed by the Paymaster General, DES, HMSO, London

DOUGHTY, P. S. (1968), 'The public of the Ulster Museum: a statistical survey', *Museums J.*, **68**(1), 19–25 and **68**(2), 47–53

DOUGHTY, P. S. (n.d.), *The State and Status of Geology in UK Museums*, Geological Society, London

DREW, SIR A. (1981), 'The government and museums', *Museums J.*, **81**(3) (supplement), 3–5

DUGGAN, T. (1978), 'The shape of things to come? Reflections on a visit to the Hall of Human Biology, South Kensington', *Museums J.*, **78**(1), 5–6

FAGG, W. (1972) 'The Museum of Mankind: ethnography in Burlington Gardens', *Museums J.*, **71**(4), 149–152

FAY, P. (1974), 'Why NADFAS? The work of the National Association of Decorative and Fine Arts Societies', *Museums J.*, **73**(4), 164

GREENAWAY, F. (1970), 'Abbeydale Industrial Hamlet', *Museums J.*, **70**(2), 78

HANCOCK, E. G. and PETTITT, C. W. (1980), 'A register of collections and collectors in North-West England (Botany, Geology and Zoology): the first edition, March 1979', *Museums J.*, **79**(4), 185–187

HARRISON, R. F. (1971), 'The first seven years 1963–70; reflections on the work of the Area Councils', *Museums J.*, **71**(1), 20–84

HEWITT, A. R. (1947), *The Law Relating to Public Libraries, Museums and Art Galleries*, London

HOUSE OF COMMONS (1982a), *Public and Private Funding of the Arts*, Eighth report from the Education, Science and Arts Committee, session 1981–82, Volume 1 – report, HMSO, London

HOUSE OF COMMONS (1982b), *Public and Private Funding of the Arts*, Volume 2 – memoranda HMSO, London

HOUSE OF COMMONS (1982c), *Public and Private Funding of the Arts,* Volume 3 – memorandum and appendices, HMSO, London

HOYLE, W. E. (1920), 'The Museums Association Winchester Conference [a Diploma for Museum Curators]', *Museums J.,* **20**(3), 55–56

INTERNATIONAL INSTITUTE FOR CONSERVATION (1974), *Conservation in Museums and Galleries: a Survey of Facilities in the United Kingdom,* IIC UK Group

IRGMA STANDARDS SUB-COMMITTEE (1977), 'Ten years of IRGMA, 1967–1977', *Museums J.,* **77**(1), 11–14

JACOB, J. (1971), 'The sale or disposal of museum objects: the principles involved and an account of some cases in point', *Museums J.,* **71**(3), 112–115

LEE, A. H. (1928), 'A museum summer school', *Museums J.,* **28**(2), 50–52

LETTS, J. (1970), 'A national organization for museum support', *Museums J.,* **70**(3), 117–118

LETTS, J. (1971), 'National Heritage', *Museums J.,* **71**(3), 110–112

LEWIS, G. D. (1983), 'The training of museum personnel in the United Kingdom', *Museums J.,* **83**(1), 65–71

LOUGHBROUGH, B. (1978), 'The effects of local government reorganization', *Museums J.,* **77**(4), 165–166

MCCOLVIN, L. R. (1942), *The Public Library System of Great Britain,* Library Association, London

MALCOLM, W. G. (1978), *Regional Museums in Northern Ireland,* Department of Education for Northern Ireland, HMSO, Belfast

MARKHAM, S. F. (1938), *The Museums and Art Galleries of the British Isles,* CUKT, T. & A. Constable, Edinburgh

MARKHAM, S. F. (1948), *Directory of Museums and Art Galleries in the British Isles,* Museums Association, London

MIERS, SIR H. A. (1928), *A Report on the Public Museums of the British Isles (other than the National Museums),* T. & A. Constable, Edinburgh

MILES, R. S. AND ALT, M. B. (1979), 'British Museum (Natural History): a new approach to the visiting public', *Museums J.,* **78**(4), 158–162

MILLER, E. (1973), *That Noble Cabinet,* Andre Deutsch, London

MOUNTFORD, A. (1982), 'The City Museum and Art Gallery, Stoke-on-Trent', *Museums J.,* **81**(4), 210–220

MUIRHEAD, D. (1974), 'The British Association of Friends of Museums: its formation and first conference', *Museums J.,* **73**(4), 165

MUSEUMS AND GALLERIES COMMISSION (1982), *Countywide Consultative Committees for Museums,* HMSO, London

MUSEUMS ASSOCIATION (1942), 'Memorandum on museums and reconstruction', *Museums J.,* **42**(4), 78–80

MUSEUMS ASSOCIATION (1945), Museums and art galleries – a national service, *Museums J.,* **45**(3), 33–45

MUSEUMS ASSOCIATION (1971a), *Museums in Education,* report of a working party, Museums Association, London

MUSEUMS ASSOCIATION (1971b), *A Museum Service for the Nation,* proposals submitted to the 1971 Conference by the Council of the Museums Assocation, London

PETTITT, C. W. AND HANCOCK, E. G. (1981), 'Natural science collection research units, their origin, aims and current status', *Museums J.,* **81**(2), 73–74

REDCLIFFE-MAUD, LORD (1976), *Support for the Arts in England and Wales,* Calouste Gulbenkian Foundation, UK and Commonwealth Branch, London

REID, W. (1971), 'The new National Army Museum', *Museums J.,* **71**(2), 63–66

REID, W. (1973), 'The National Army Museum', *Museums J.,* **73**(3), 114–116

ROBERTS, D. A. *et al* (1980), 'The Museum Documentation Association', *Museums J.,* **80**(2), 81–85

ROSSE, EARL OF (1963), *Survey of Provincial Museums and Galleries,* Standing Commission on Museums and Galleries, HMSO, London

ROYAL COMMISSION ON NATIONAL MUSEUMS AND GALLERIES (1928a), *Interim Report,* HMSO, London

ROYAL COMMISSION ON NATIONAL MUSEUMS AND GALLERIES (1928b), *Oral Evidence, Memorandum and Appendices to the Interim Report,* HMSO, London

ROYAL COMMISSION ON NATIONAL MUSEUMS AND GALLERIES (1929a), *Final Report, part 1,* HMSO, London

ROYAL COMMISSION ON NATIONAL MUSEUMS AND GALLERIES (1929b), *Final Report, part 2,* HMSO, London

ROYAL COMMISSION ON NATIONAL MUSEUMS AND GALLERIES (1929c), *Oral Evidence, Memorandum and Appendices to the Final Report,* HMSO, London

SCHOOLS COUNCIL (1972), *Pterodactyls and Old Lace,* Evans and Methuen Educational, London

SIMMONS, J. (1977), 'The Museum of London', *Museums J.,* **77**(1), 15–18

SINGLETON, H. R. (1966), 'The Leicester course', *Museums J.,***66**(3), 135–138

SMITH, A. (1971), 'The Postgraduate Course in Gallery and Musuems Studies, Department of Art History, University of Manchester', *Museums J.,* **71**(3), 100–101

STANDING COMMISSION ON MUSEUMS AND GALLERIES (1963), *Survey of Provincial Museums and Galleries,* HMSO, London (The Rosse Report)

STANDING COMMISSION ON MUSEUMS AND GALLERIES (1965), *Seventh Report, 1961–1964,* HMSO, London

STANDING COMMISSION ON MUSEUMS AND GALLERIES (1967), *Area Museum Services, 1963–1966,* HMSO, London

STANDING COMMISSION ON MUSEUMS AND GALLERIES (1968), *Universities and Museums,* HMSO, London

STANDING COMMISSION ON MUSEUMS AND GALLERIES (1970), *Eighth Report, 1965–1969,* HMSO, London

STANDING COMMISSION ON MUSEUMS AND GALLERIES (1971), *Report and Recommendations on the Preservation of Technological Material,* HMSO, London

STANDING COMMISSION ON MUSEUMS AND GALLERIES (1973a), *Ninth Report, 1969–1973,* HMSO, London

STANDING COMMISSION ON MUSEUMS AND GALLERIES (1973b), 'Loans from national institutions to provincial museums' in *Ninth Report, 1969–1973,* HMSO, London

STANDING COMMISSION ON MUSEUMS AND GALLERIES (1977), *Report on University Museums,* HMSO, London

STANDING COMMISSION ON MUSEUMS AND GALLERIES (1978), *Tenth Report, 1973–1977,* HMSO, london

STANDING COMMISSION ON MUSEUMS AND GALLERIES (1979), *Framework for a System for Museums,* HMSO, London (Drew Report)

STANDING COMMISSION ON MUSEUMS AND GALLERIES (1980), *Conservation,* HMSO, London

STANDING COMMISSION ON MUSEUMS AND GALLERIES (1981), *Report on Museums in Wales,* HMSO, London

STANSFIELD, G. (1967), 'Museums in the countryside', *Museums J.,* **67**(3), 212–218

STANSFIELD, G. (1969), (Ed.), 'Conference on countryside centres', *Museums J.,* **69**(2), 63–73

STEVENS, F. (1940), 'Salisbury and South Wilts Museum:

special war-time classes for evacuees and Salisbury children', *Museums J.*, **40**(1), 9–10

STEWART, J. D. (1980), 'A summary of local environmental record centres in Britain', *Museums J.*, **80**(3), 161–164

TANNER, J. (1973), 'The Royal Air Force Museum', *Museums J.*, **73**(3), 116–118

THOMAS, N. (1976), 'Museums and rescue archaeology', *Museums J.*, **76**(3), 106–109

THOMPSON, J. (1972), 'A Bradford project in community involvement', *Museums J.*, **71**(4), 161–163

THOMPSON, J. (1980), 'Cities in decline: museums and the urban programmes 1969–79', *Museums J.*, **79**(4), 188–190

THOMPSON, J. (1982), 'The accreditation scheme of the Museums Association 1974–82: a review', *Museums J.*, **82**(2), 67–69

WALLIS, F. S. (1938), 'Delimitation of museum areas', *Museums J.*, **38**(4), 182–183

WARHURST, A. (1973), 'The new Ulster Museum', *Museums J.*, **73**(1), 3–6

WELLS, W. *et al* (1972), 'The Burrell collection – five years on', *Museums J.*, **72**(3), 101–106

WILLIAMS, A. (1981), *A heritage for Scotland, Scotland's National Museums and Galleries: the Next 25 Years* Report of a Committee appointed by the Secretary of State for Scotland, HMSO, Glasgow

WINSTANLEY, B. (1967), *Children and Museums*, Blackwell, London

5

National museums

David M. Wilson

To compare the form, function, philosophy and policies of institutions as vital and as different as the Smithsonian Institution, the National Museum of Bulgaria, the Louvre, the Imperial War Museum and the National Anthropological Museum of Mexico is as useless as to generalize about museums in any fashion. Each museum fulfils its own function, ill or well. Each museum exists for conservation, collection and display as primary objectives, but to compare the grand panorama of the Victoria and Albert Museum with the intimacy of the Kunstindustri Museum in Copenhagen is as useless as comparing a Jaguar car with an Austin Seven. In what follows I shall attempt to discuss national museums under three heads:

(1) Monolithic institutions[1].
(2) State museums of national culture.
(3) Specialist national institutions.

Less attention will be given to the third of these categories as their functions and philosophies are often clearly perceived in their title. It is obvious, for example, that the National Portrait Gallery in London is just that; similarly the Greek National Archaeological Museum in Athens or the Historical Folk Museum of the Land of Israel in Tel Aviv are also clearly described in the titles.

Monolithic museums

The great public collections which were created as national museums (like the British Museum) or became national museums (like the State Hermitage Museum in Leningrad) comprise the elite of the world's museums, not merely because their collections are so rich and varied but because they also represent a vast reservoir of scholarship and expertise.

The philosophies which lie behind the great monolithic museums vary, but all work towards a universal view of man's achievement or knowledge. The first major, truly universal museum was the British Museum, which split into its component parts with the departure of the natural history collections in the 1880s and of the library departments in 1973. It was founded in 1753 on the principles of the French encyclopaedists as a kind of collegiate expression of universal knowledge and curiosity: in a period when the universities were at their nadir in England, the collections of books and manuscripts formed by Sloane, Cotton, Harley and others[2], together with antiquities and natural history specimens, provided hope for the young scholars of the day. Scholars like the poet Thomas Gray who wrote in 1759 (Toynbee and Whibley, 1971):

> The musæum is my favourite Domain, where I often pass four hours in the day in the stillness and solitude of the reading room.

Here also studied Blackstone, Hume and Stukeley, the latter at least interested in objects. The Museum also provided, for the respectably dressed, stimulus to their natural curiosity.

The public function of the Museum was still secondary to the learned, collecting aspects of the Museum's services. But the most extraordinary fact is that the Museum was founded at all. In a period not renowned for public support for learning, the British Government was able to move expeditiously not only to buy annuities for Sir Hans Sloane's heirs, but was also able to provide a building to house the collections and open it to the public within six years.

The Museum prospered and collected widely although often in the face of considerable financial opposition. The result is seen today – a collection of millions of items from all over the world illustrating the history of the world as expressed in artefacts.

The National Gallery in London, however, has an entirely different *raison d'etre*. It is a national collection of great works of art – unlike practically every European gallery it was not founded from a royal or princely nucleus. In the words of the present Director (Ragghianti, 1973):

> It has operated on the principle that it is a gallery of art – not a mere collection of historical objects. One masterpiece is worth more in aesthetic significance than twenty minor pictures, all with some historical interest.

These two examples illustrate the difficulty of classifying great national collections and if we were to look at the stated philosophy and aims of, say, the Victoria and Albert Museum, the British Museum (Natural History) and the Science Museum many further different judgements could be made.

Among the great monolithic museums of the world the State Hermitage Museum in Leningrad is one of the most remarkable and yet, in some ways, typical. Its history is different from that of the British Museum in that until the Revolution it was hardly a public museum (rather a private palace museum of the Tzars), although from 1852 when the 'New Hermitage' was inaugurated it fulfilled many of the functions of a national museum (even though ethnography, ethnology and much of the archaeological material was located elsewhere) (Persianoya, 1975). Strangely enough, Russian painting went to the Russian Museum which was not opened until 1898 in the Mikhailovsky Palace (in its first year 100 000 people visited it) (Novouspensky, 1979).

In many ways the Louvre (Ragghianti, 1968) is a similar institution to the Hermitage: it emerged after a revolution as a purely public institution, and hived off part of its collection, the ethnographical and oriental collections, for example. But housing as it does the offices of the Director General of the French museums it has a more central role than practically any national museum in the world. Only the massive Smithsonian Institution, with its semi-autonomous sections (for example, the National Gallery of Art, National Air and Space Museum, National Museum of Natural History) and the *Staatliche Museen Preussischer Kulturbesitz* (with its collections of paintings, antiquities and oriental art) supported federally and locally, come anywhere near the centralized control of the French collections.

To most of the general public, however, it is the great picture galleries which are the national museums of the world, the *Prado* in Madrid, the *Kunsthistorisches Museum* in Vienna or the *Rijksmuseum* in Amsterdam. The reason for this is probably that these are the museums which show above everything else the highest visible form of human endeavour in the arts, painting. But perhaps a

contributory factor is that these museums are international. They demonstrate the breadth of man's interest more completely than state museums of national culture. Is it not perhaps significant that the *Nasjonalgalleriet* in Oslo is described as 'national' whereas the great museums of national culture: *Universitetets Oldsaksamling* and *Norsk Folkemuseum* are not distinguished in this manner?' Is it possible that universality is an element of importance of museums, or is it simply an index of size?

One great museum of monolithic structure must at least be mentioned here – The Metropolitan Museum of Art in New York (Tomkins, 1970). In many ways the variety of its collections and its very size have given it, to many people, a position equivalent to the Louvre or the Hermitage. Few non-national museums have this stature, (perhaps the Uffizi is another example, but this is a state-funded museum). The Metropolitan is a private foundation, aided by city and federal money, but largely financed from outside sources. Its collections are also universal and indeed unlike many of the great monolithic museums it has even an interest in ethnography (although largely of 'artistic' quality). Here surely is a museum which has achieved a national character.

State museums of national culture

The existence of national museums of avowedly chauvinistic purpose throughout the world has considerable impact and influence. One of the most remarkable examples of these which illustrates many of the reasons for the existence of such institutions is the Hungarian National Museum (Fülep, 1978a). 'It was founded', according to its present Director, 'in the first half of the nineteenth century as part of a movement to preserve Hungarian historic traditions and to instill greater appreciation of the Hungarian language and culture. The movement was influenced by the ideals of the Enlightenment and the National Museum was one of its first fruits.' Its symbolic place in the history of Hungary is illustrated by the part the Museum's new building played in the Revolution of 1848 (Fülep, 1978b):

> It was on the steps of the museum that Sandor Petöfi's *National Song* was first recited; the Upper House of the National Assembly met in the museum's state apartment; exhibitions on industrial and agricultural production, designed to rouse the whole country were held in its galleries. The most important of the gatherings of the unions and associations, formed for the promotion of public education, were also held within its walls.

Later, in 1956, it was a rallying point for Hungarian nationalism during the Russian invasion, an incident also reflected in Prague in 1968 when the front of the Bohemian National Museum was damaged by Russian gunfire.

The propaganda and political value of a museum in such circumstances should not be underestimated. Exhibitions like *'Das politische Deutschland'*, *'Nürnberg, die deutsche Stadt'* in 1936 and 1937 or perhaps even more poignantly *'700 Jahre im Weichselbogen'* in 1939 (Deneke and Kahsnitz, 1978), which were held in the Germanisches National Museum in Nuremburg, show that propaganda and political pressure can rally a country in difficult times, in a fashion rather different from the wartime concerts in the National Gallery in London.

Patriotism, chauvinism, struggling nationalism all blend imperceptibly together to produce the national museum a country needs. In the period of the Russian control of Finland the National Museum in Helsinki was built in the national architectural style of the beginning of the century by one of Finland's greatest architects, perhaps to emphasize the autonomy of a country under foreign domination. In other cases, as with the Indian National Museum in Calcutta, enlightened colonialists emphasised the culture of the land they controlled. Founded by the Asiatic Society of Bengal in 1814 and encouraged by disinterested benefaction, this museum has grown into one of the finest national and scientific collections in the world, interestingly enough not in the capital although it is not strictly speaking nowadays the National Museum (Markham and Hargreaves, 1936).

The function of such museums is clear; they express the history and aspirations of the country in which they are placed. They are sometimes, but rarely, used for jingoistic purposes and often (as with the National Museum of Ireland) enshrine an exhibition (sometimes rather badly displayed) of the struggle to freedom with personalia of heroes of revolutions, risings or rebellions.

Such museums are largely, if not completely, run on scholarly lines for a curious public and only occasionally do circumstances push them into excess with overweighted displays. The best such museums have produced some of the most original scholarship: the National Museum of Denmark, for example, was the source of the archaeological division of prehistory into the three Ages (Stone, Bronze and Iron Age). Others have set new standards in architecture and display, as witness the National Museum of Anthropology in Mexico City – the masterpiece of Pedro Ramirez Vazquez – which is one of the wonders of the modern world (Ragghianti, 1970). Others have influenced the economic development of a country, the Geological Museum and Survey in London, for example; while some have concentrated on small, specialized facets of history or culture, as for example, the National Portrait Gallery in London. The latter comes into my third class of National museums.

Specialist national institutions

The specialist national institutions speak for themselves. The *Musée de l'Horologie* in Geneva needs no explanation, nor does the *Mineralogisches Museum* in Berlin. The *Musée de l'Homme* in Paris – ancient and out-moded in its displays although only built in the 1930s – is another type of specialist museum; dealing universally with human anthropology it is a major force in French academic life. Museums like this, the Imperial War Museum in England (or indeed any national army museum in any country in the world), the great museum of modern art in Mexico City or the Tate Gallery in London, the Ethnographical Museum in Belgrade or the National Archaeological Museum in Athens have a function which is probably more important than their displays in that they provide high level academic and technical support for a super-structure of scholarship which serves both the national and international academic community. This is the main function of such specialist museums, national or private, although a nation which celebrates its naval achievements or its great generals, its main industry or its great painters through a specialist museum is putting a lot of scholarly eggs into one academic basket.

The danger with such museums is that they can fossilize through lack of sensitive national support. Sometimes it is simply their display which suffers. The recent extended refurbishing of that great scholarly institution, the Wallace Collection in London, will be a salutary reminder to an English audience that neglect (although curable) can happen under the most enlightened government. As director of a monolithic museum I feel that the German or American experience shows that such institutions are often better served under a large umbrella. At the same time the idea of the *Direction des Musées de France*, although helpful in some cases, does not serve the nation well: the small museums suffer.

The Collections

But basic to all museums are the collections, and it is here that the policy of a national museum is supremely important. A national museum's relationship to the provincial museums is often fraught with jealousies on both sides. In some cases, Sweden or Denmark for example, the disposal of all archaeological material lies in the hands of the central archaeological service which works cheek by jowl with the national museum (*Statens Historiska Museum* or *Nationalmuseet*). Only now – and reluctantly – are the national museums yielding finds to the provincial museums as these become more expert in their curatorial abilities. In England there is no such central system; in fact it is often difficult for the relevant part of the British Museum, which embodies a national function, to acquire objects to bring its British collections up-to-date – although the power of the purse sometimes helps. In France the excavator has the right to say where finds go, with the result that the *Musée des Antiquités Nationales* at St-Germain-en-Laye, has made hardly any acquisitions in the last fifty years. These statements are to a lesser degree true of the fine and decorative arts, but here it is usually the financial capabilities of the museum which secure an object.

Only an ostrich would deny national/provincial competitiveness. In England the system seems to work reasonably well, in some other countries it does not and bad-will is easily engendered. It is however, one of the most difficult areas of museum relations, capable of much strain and bad feeling. Only constant attention and contact can heal such breaches.

The collecting problems of monolithic museums of universal content are full of pitfalls. In such a museum 'bigger is generally better'. There is, however, a very good case for the purely aesthetic museum, the picture galleries, to collect only the highest quality (as anyone would agree who has looked at the secondary collections in the National Gallery in London). But more generalist museums covering decorative arts, science, history and natural history are clearly at their best when they collect over a wide area. Few museums start with a *tabula rasa*, so the first imperative is to build on strengths. Thus a print room with a good collection of French Impressionists will attempt to purchase individual items so that unrepresented periods, schools or artists may be represented in the collections. On the other hand, poorly represented schools must also be acquired if possible. Thus, for example, the British Museum recently started an aggressive policy of acquiring modern prints, the first fruits of which was the highly successful American exhibition in 1980 (Carey and Griffiths, 1980).

It is now impossible – legally – to import major pieces of art from certain countries. The campaign for the return of cultural objects, fuelled by Third World members of UNESCO, rightly makes most curators realize that they cannot buy smuggled objects or objects without a proper pedigree. But much can be done to bring international collections up to date. Many countries allow *partage* after excavation, some will donate type series. The international art market flourishes and it is still possible – and always should be possible – to buy a Poussin from an English collection and export it (HMSO, 1981). Further collections of ethnographic material can – and should – continue to be made to supplement old, tired and ill-documented collections. A fresh collection was recently made *de novo*

by the British Museum in India and formed the basis of the Vasna exhibition (Durrans and Knox, 1982), but this is but one of many such brought together in the last few years without offending the laws or the susceptibilities of the countries from which objects have been brought.

A museum which does not collect is a dead museum. This is particularly true of all national museums. When one source dries up another must be found; some of the greatest collections have been built up by acquiring the unfashionable. This is still the best way to increase a museum's stock.

National museums and their public

The role of national museums in education, publicity, exhibition and information services varies widely, and should do so. The monolithic museum, possibly with a tendency towards a very high foreign tourist input, has and must have a different approach to a state museum of national culture. Large museums can often more easily afford large exhibitions: on the other hand they cannot afford to give much individual attention to children.

To a certain extent it is the duty of the large museum to make its own and other museums' collections available to a wide public through special exhibitions. Such exhibitions need not be blockbusters, like Tutankhamun which beat every record everywhere in terms of attendance and profit, but can initiate, explain, educate and entertain in a fashion, and with a frequency often difficult for smaller museums – no matter how prestigious – to emulate. In recent years the British Museum, for example, has staged major exhibitions in large provincial centres as a matter of policy – in Norwich, Manchester, Glasgow, Cambridge, Leeds and so on.

The educational role of the great national museum is difficult to evaluate. For the monolithic museum it almost certainly lies in educating the teacher, providing teaching notes and facilities for school classes. Only rarely can direct contact with children be catered for (the American volunteer docent system is rarely used outside that country for a number of reasons, among them union objections). But tertiary education must be provided for, partly by educational specialists and partly by the curatorial staff. Post-graduate and specialist seminars are also a *sine qua non* in such institutions. National museums in my other two classes will find it easier to provide such services although the problems of such an institution as the Science Museum in London with its vast number of visitors[3] will surely be similar to those of the monolithic institution.

The primary duty of museums – it must be emphasized – is not didactic. This is even more true of national museums. The public must have an experience, aesthetic, cultural, emotional or one of half a hundred exclamatory sensations, ranging from the spiritual to the curious, when they visit the museum. The visitor must not be pandered to by labels in Noddy language, by coloured flashing lights or any of these caricatures and gimmicks beloved of the educational administrator venturing into the museum field. The museums' client is generally intelligent and able to read or use libraries to look up background. He must be led to this process. The national museum director generally – unless using his museum for political purposes – is usually catering for the intelligent child or the intelligent adult. Imagination must be stirred, but tiresome rhetoric, fussy comparisons and gimmicky flourishes are to be avoided at all costs. Good taste and restraint are vital. It is the objects which are important: they must speak for themselves.

Notes

[1] A term borrowed from Finlay, I. (1977) *Priceless heritage, the future of museums,* Faber and Faber, London.
[2] For the history of the British Museum, cf Caygill, M. L. (1981). *The story of the British Museum,* British Museum Publications, London and the sources cited there.
[3] Such figures are difficult to attain, but cf. Alt, M. B. (1980) *Four Years of Visitor Surveys at the British Museum (Natural History) 1976–79, Museums J.* **80**(1) 10–25.

References

CAREY, F. AND GRIFFITHS, A. (1980) *American Prints 1879–1979,* British Museum Publications, London

DENEKE, B. AND KAHSNITZ, R. (1978), *Das Germanische Nationalmuseum. Nürnberg 1852–1977,* Deutscher Kunstverlag, Berlin, 1146

DURRANS, B. AND KNOX, R. (1982), *India: Past into Present,* British Museum Publications, London

FÜLEP, F. (1978) (Ed.), *The Hungarian National Museum,* Corvina Press, Budapest

HMSO (1981), Export of works of art 1980–81, *27th Report of the Reviewing Committee appointed by the Chancellor of the Exchequer in December 1952,* HMSO, London

MARKHAM, S. F. AND HARGREAVES, H. (1936), *The Museums of India,* Museums Assocation, London

NOVOUSPENSKY, N. (1979), *The Russian Museum, Leningrad,* Aurora Art Publishers, Leningrad

PERSIANOVA, O. (1975), *L'Ermitage, Guide,* Editions d'art Aurore, Leningrad

RAGGHIANTI, C. L. (1968) (Ed.), *Great Museums of the World: Louvre, Paris,* Newsweek and Mondadori, New York

RAGGHIANTI, C. L. (1970) (Ed), *Great Museums of the World: National Museum of Anthropology, Mexico City,* Newsweek and Mondadori, New York

RAGGHIANTI, C. L. (1973) (Ed.)., 'Introduction' in *Great Museums of the world: National Gallery, London,* Newsweek and Mondadori, New York

TOMKINS, C. (1970), *Merchants and Masterpieces; the Story of the Metropolitan Museum of Art,* Longmans, London

TOYNBEE, P. AND WHIBLEY, L. (1971), (Eds.), *Correspondence of Thomas Gray . . .,* **11** 632, Clarendon Press, Oxford

6

The national galleries

Michael Compton

The idea of a national gallery of paintings depends upon the view that there is something distinctive about paintings which separates them from other man-made objects, however fine. It is a view that is implicit in writings upon art from early times although not always by any means absolute. At any rate it existed well before the foundation of the National Gallery in London in 1824. It was embodied in the Louvre, part of which was opened to the public as a national gallery following the Revolution in 1793, as well as in the proposals for a national gallery in London made by the dealer, Noel Desenfans, in 1799. The German romantic poet Wackenroder had written in 1797:

> Picture halls . . . ought to be temples where in subdued and silent humility we may admire the great artists. . . . Works of art, in their essence, fit as little into the common flow of life as the thoughts of God.

The National Gallery in London represents almost the extreme position in respect of the distinctiveness of the medium of painting. Not only is painting set apart from other visual arts as a category, but it is housed a mile or more from the closely related arts of sculpture, drawing and print making in the British Museum and the Victoria and Albert Museum. It is even set apart from modern painting, but more of this distinction later on. The present function of the National Gallery, defined in the Act of 1954, is to collect works of art of acknowledged excellence just as it was at the start. The Gallery exhibits virtually all of its possessions continuously, making the minimum distinction between the great and not so great. Its layout is by 'schools', that is, generally, the countries in which the works were created. Chronology, whether the association of what is contemporary, or the sequence of what is not, is given relatively little importance, although the over-all tendency is a chronological drift beginning with the early Italians on the left of the main entrance and continuing clockwise to the post-Impressionists at the right, just before you leave or go to the restaurant.

In this circuit, if you have taken in the lower galleries as well as all those on the main floor, you will have looked at, or passed by, some 2,000 paintings. The character of the entrance to the building is that of a temple, as recommended by Wackenroder, up to which you have to climb, both approaching the door itself, and again inside, to reach the pictures. The galleries are literally elevated. The detail of the recent competition for an extension building on the Hampton site to the left of the National Gallery confirms the quasi-religious concept in asking for a gallery resembling a Basilica.

The present arrangement of the pictures on the walls is also more aesthetic than historical. You will often see a large, vertical picture in the middle of a wall flanked by two smaller paintings and then two more on either side rather larger. The symmetry may be emphasised by the relative placement of dominant colours or other internal characteristics of the pictures. This sort of arrangement is not altogether innocent of historical association however, since it can be related to the way an altarpiece may be featured in a church or any great painting in the grand rooms of a palace or country house. It is not surprising that studies have shown that most public attention is drawn to the picture in the centre of a wall, especially if that is large, so that the display is, to this extent, hierarchical, emphasizing certain works at the expense of others.

The attempt to place paintings in any other context than their school is limited (apart from special exhibitions) to the choice of room size and shape, the choice of wall-covering, occasional pieces of furniture and statuary, an exceptional placement on the wall and, above all, the actual frame of the painting. The scholarly catalogues of the collection, certainly among the very best in the world, are primarily concerned with the identity, authorship and provenance of the work itself. Apart from identifying the iconography or subject matter, there is almost no attempt to elucidate the picture, least of all by placing it in a wide cultural ambience. This is evidently a policy, in my opinion a good one, and one that is consistent with the display policy – that is, with the view that paintings are essentially apodictic. As Michael Wilson (1977) writes:

> Some people criticise the clinical aspect of the modern gallery . . . But such criticism seems sometimes to betray a lack of feeling for the pictures themselves. In the attempt to recreate the period setting of a particular picture, there is a danger of giving too great an importance to historical authenticity. A painting can thus be reduced to the status of an archaeological specimen. The process becomes self-defeating . . . Originally designed to fulfill a very limited function . . . a painting may offer very much more for the imagination, and this quality places it apart from the vast majority of works of its kind. It has meaning outside its original circumstances and for people living perhaps centuries later. It is this factor which distinguishes an art gallery from an historical museum. The exhibits are there for people to find present pleasure in them. [However]: 'Paintings are not always self-explanatory, and for the visitor confronted with examples of Western art from the 13th century to the 19th, some guidance is desirable. The gallery provides "bats" with printed information that the visitor can carry around with him.

In any case, the Gallery rejects the theory of Alfred Doerner, which would have placed every picture in a period setting approaching those of the period rooms of the Victoria and Albert Museum.

In this, the National Gallery resembles all of its near equivalents. The specialized art museum follows quite closely the doctrine affirmed by Sir John Fosdyke, Director of the British Museum (RSA, 1949):

> The essential element is the material document, and I mean this in the physical sense of the actual object, not pictorial reproductions of it, still less artistic or literary illustration. The photographs, lantern slides, film strips, microfilms, cinematograph films, dioramas and diagrams which are so largely used in what is called "visual instruction" are books adapted for community reading . . . I can imagine an extremely useful institution containing nothing but this apparatus of visual instruction but I would not call it a museum.

Certainly the architecture of the National Gallery, internal as well as external, by poor as well as by distinguished architects, expresses the same understanding. It would be impossible to create within it the period rooms that Doerner called for since it is an excellent example of what he was against (Cauman, 1958):

> The pared down nineteenth century version of the palace – a conventional building on the outside, on the

inside a succession of bare rooms serving as a "neutral" background for a variety of equally varied styles.

It is likewise impossible without setting up intrusive barriers to create a single, let alone simple, circuit that the visitor might follow in a manner predetermined by the curators. That this way of articulating a building is still current is demonstrated by the design of the 1975 extension and the brief for the Hampton site, although the former can be considered as virtually a single loop from the point of view of the visitor going from rooms 15 to 25.

The function of the present building is to protect and make visible the pictures. This accounts for the blind windows on the facade that are impregnable and do not admit side-light to dazzle the eye, reflect on surfaces or irradiate the pictures too strongly. The light is, according to the still unsurpassed nineteenth century formulation, top-light, but in many rooms it is controlled by louvres which can reduce the amount of light on the walls and paintings to determine maxima and annual totals. The Gallery's scientists have been among the leaders of those who have studied the effects of light on the substances that paintings comprise, including pigments, media and even supports (such as paper, canvas and so on) and who have shown that it is damaging in proportion to time, intensity, and the vulnerability of materials. Levels are therefore kept down to the minimum compatible with the adequate perception of the works of art. At any such level the pictures themselves will appear more brightly lit if the ambience is at a lower luminosity. This is not possible in all circumstances, for example in galleries where a diffusing ceiling is certain to be brighter than anything on the walls. However the darkened and low hung ceilings of the 1975 extension rooms make them appear oppressive.

In general it is very difficult to reconcile the demands of conservation and perception with the powerful feeling that the gallery should be a 'real' space, not too distinct from that of other types of building. The National Gallery has made a variety of attempts to do this.

Consciousness of the need to preserve works of art and the development of appropriate technology has led to the progressive, but still incomplete, programme of installing air-conditioning. There is almost no incompatibility of the demands of pictures and viewers in respect of the most important factors – especially overall levels and rapid changes of relative humidity. The massive architecture of the older parts of the building, the linings of the walls, timber floors and the large volumes, all help to stabilize the atmosphere. However, there is a conflict in the matter of glazing pictures. Air-conditioning may permit the removal of glass, but glazing may still be necessary for vulnerable works and to prevent possible accidents or vandalism. At the same time, even the most carefully adjusted lighting cannot altogether eliminate the barrier between painting and person that glass represents. The decision to glaze or not to glaze, remains an awkward one for conservators and curators when full air-conditioning is installed. Where there is no air-conditioning, glass frame and backboard will limit and slow down changes of humidity and ward off pollution.

The high value given to conservation by the National Gallery is reflected in the establishment of scientists of high rank as well as conservators (restorers). Two handbooks to the Gallery published recently, as well as exhibitions, have drawn attention to the physical make up of pictures as well as to the rewards and problems of dealing with them. Cleaning, however, has almost always been controversial. No matter how conclusive the evidence supplied by the gallery that pictures have not been flayed, doubts have been entertained quite often by the well informed, while the wide public has been more frequently outraged. As more and more of the paintings have been cleaned and restored so as to reveal what has survived – never identical to what was painted – and as people have become used to the bright colours that artists often used rather than to yellowing varnish, complaints have begun to die down. Certainly the policy maintained by the Gallery of revealing the pictures as they are and not attempting either to accommodate them to what people may expect, or to restore them to what they might have been, is one which is consistent both with the general attitude of the Gallery, described above, but also with the archaeological truth of the object as a document comprising its history in itself. The requirements of conservation and delectation also determine to some extent what is collected. The Gallery would not acquire what it could not keep and what no one could enjoy. But these factors are by no means sufficient to explain either the original or the accumulated purchasing policy of the Gallery.

In its early days the gallery 'built on strength'. That is, having acquired works by the most highly estimated artists of the day, they looked for more, instead of filling the gaps. Lord Farnborough, said that the main objectives should be limited: 'to the works of Raphael, Correggio and Titian . . . which . . . must be obtained whenever the opportunity presents itself'. The Gallery did for a time continue this policy which included also the works of Rubens and Rembrandt and other seventeenth-century painters. However, following an enquiry by a Select Committee in the 1850s and the appointment of a Director with power to purchase (1855), the policy switched to one of collecting all major schools. The primitives (roughly thirteenth to fifteenth century) were strongly favoured. The shape of the National Gallery's collection, has come to correspond remarkably closely to the generally estimated 'map' of painterly creativity. The biggest weaknesses are in Central and Eastern European painting and generally in the eighteenth and first half of the nineteenth century. The current Director, however, has been as keen as any more historically-minded one, to remedy this imbalance. Of course, such a policy may result simply from the ambition to satisfy all educated tastes, but its effect is to make possible the greater understanding of any painting by showing characteristic examples of what went before. Nevertheless, the hang does not make the most of this potential. For example, the close connections between Italy and Flanders in the mid-fifteenth century are not highlighted by placing works in reasonable propinquity.

In Britain the National Gallery of Scotland, founded in 1858, follows the London model closely. With its shorter history and relative lack of purchase funds (which are, however, slightly weighted in its favour as a ratio of population), it can never equal the strength of the prototype. Its 'balance' is, nevertheless, fairly impartial as between the 'schools'.

However, the National Gallery of Scotland differs from the London Gallery in one major respect, for not far away in the same country there is another very fine collection – the municipal collection of Glasgow, including the Burrell Bequest. Glasgow is richer in its collections than any other British municipality. But the London National Gallery is far, far richer and more complete than any city art gallery. Only the old universities and the Royal collections compare with the 'provincial' collections of, say, Switzerland, Germany and the USA. Yet the National collections are perhaps worth 10 to 100 of these and are proportionately more copiously endowed with purchase funds. Without trying to make the complex and academic calculations necessary, very few of the 'developed countries' have a similar proportion of wealth at the centre.

The only remaining point to make about the National Gallery is that it gives little or no favour to the National School. It has almost no British art of the sixteenth, seventeenth and late-nineteenth centuries. It is not the kind of national museum, described in UNESCO documents, in which the inhabitants of a country can find their own cultural identity celebrated. Or, rather, it is as if the cultural identity of Britain is sought mainly in the works of art created in other countries, but admired and collected here. The 'national heritage' is in other words, not essentially what we have made, but what we have loved and learned from. Sir Charles Eastlake, the first director (1855–1865), was a strong importer of works, and one who, in this sense, added greatly to our heritage.

The history and disposition of the Tate Gallery have been, from the start, very different. First it began, in 1893, precisely as a shrine for contemporary national talent, a collection of British art for the British. It was in fact a patchwork of three relatively large gifts, or bequests from Tate, Vernon and Chantrey. Historically this was at the time of the country's period of greatest relative cultural, political and economic power. Why should our art not be equally great? It was also a period when certain painters achieved a peak of social status (from which they have declined perceptibly since) and one in which exhibitions and galleries attracted very large crowds. They were a public entertainment of the type, more or less, of the medium of the film which supplanted them. This, however, did not prevent the National Gallery using the Tate, which was its satellite, as a depot, not only for lesser British works, but for those of the later foreign works which it did not wish to hang.

In due course (1916) when the Lane bequest, mainly of the then relatively unappreciated Impressionist paintings, came to the nation, these were also sent to the Tate. Galleries for modern foreign art were eventually added and paid for by Sir Joseph Duveen. In the same period most of the paintings of the Turner Bequest (too large to be housed at the National, and out of balance) passed to the Tate, and galleries for it were likewise provided by Duveen. The Tate's role was extended backwards in time to include British art from the sixteenth century and modern, British and foreign sculpture (galleries again by gift of Lord Duveen).

The Tate became, then, a national gallery of the sort which does offer precisely to the public an image of their identity. Of course the British collections serve other purposes: to show off that national identity to tourists, to act as a promotional showcase for national talent, and to be a resource of reference for British artists where one may expect to find typical works of all those above a certain level of quality. It serves as an institution which preserves and exhibits the representation that it has collected, which continues to collect and which studies British art and publishes the results. It is, moreover, a visible sign of the State's respect for art, as declared by its architecture, just as temple-like as that of the National Gallery.

British art includes truly contemporary art and the Tate may buy work by quite young artists, sometimes in their twenties. Generally it does not acquire works by foreign artists when they are so young, both out of policy, and because staff and Trustees cannot be so instantly and comprehensively well-informed about foreign artists. It does buy British paintings or sculpture at a time when the reputation of artists may be changing quite rapidly, both because their own performance may be variable, and because the activities of galleries, museums and critics, not to mention the flow of word-of-mouth

appreciation, have their effect. The reputation of artists and the respect given to varieties of artistic practice, may spread slowly and irregularly to a wider public and even more slowly to the public at large. There exist, moreover, many kinds and qualities of imagery which may be collected and appreciated by distinct or dispersed sections of this wider public, which are not recognized or are rejected by those who advise on, or decide what is collected by the Tate.

The contentiousness of contemporary art remains a constant in the judgement of a large proportion of the public. Nobody concerned is surprised that contemporary art should be shocking and yet, looked at in one way, it is indeed surprising. For, since the art is produced by people who inhabit the same culture as ourselves, and who have had broadly the same experiences, one might think that we should be able readily to perceive and respond to it. That is, the modern collection should be a shrine of 'our century' just as the British collection is of 'our country'. If anything, it should seem so natural to us – as our clothes and hairstyles do – that it would appear rather banal. Of course, it is true that certain contemporary clothes and hairstyles do seem shocking. These are often worn precisely in order to shock others, while, at the same time acting as a sign of membership of an in-group. There is a sense in which contemporary art functions in the same way, but it is not the whole story.

Modern art was clearly distinguished from other art by Sir Joshua Reynolds (Wark 1975). His fear, however, was that contemporary art was too popular:

> The works of those that have stood the test of ages, have a claim to that respect and veneration to which no modern can pretend. The duration and stability of their fame is sufficient to evince that it has not been suspended upon the slender thread of fashion and caprice, but bound to the human heart by every tie of sympathetic approbation.

Of course many people think the same – that is, that contemporary art, if it is not a conspiracy, 'is suspended on a slender thread of caprice'. Meanwhile those within the art world are convinced that what they admire will eventually be admired by a very much larger audience. The Impressionists and post-Impressionists have often been cited as the example. There is point to this for it is enshrined in the history of the great French collections.

Just as the Louvre, established after the French Revolution, was the first 'national gallery of art', so the Luxembourg in Paris was the first 'museum of modern art'. This time it was the restored monarchy that brought it into being. The idea was that contemporary French art should be exhibited there until five (at other times ten) years after the death of the artist, when it could be dispassionately decided whether it reached the high standard that would allow it to be transferred to the Louvre. The official *Moniteur Universelle* of 1818, said, at its foundation, that the Luxembourg was 'to form an intermediary between the salon, where the pupil is placed next to the master, and the Royal Museum (the Louvre) where France gathers together the masterpieces of the whole world when, after their death, universal opinion has established their glory.'

In practice, pressure of public or critical opinion canonized certain artists in their life-time and the 'after death plus five or plus ten years' rule was never strictly applied. Jacques Louis David, the regicide, was admitted (since art was already to a great extent kept insulated from politics) but it was in part the purely aesthetic problem of the Impressionists that broke the system. Very few of their works even entered the Luxembourg. Such had been the scorn with which they had been received that the Louvre could not bring itself to admit even Manet until long after his death. In due course a special museum had to be set up for the Impressionists between the Louvre and the Museum of Modern Art (which succeeded the Luxembourg in 1947) when public detestation of Impressionism *en bloc* turned to adulation and when the quantity of works was too much for the Louvre itself. Only now is it become possible to put the Impressionists and post-Impressionists in the same buildings and galleries as the other forms of painting nearly contemporary with them. So it was precisely the existence of museums of art that forced the necessity for the judgement of contemporary art and brought about the separation which was in turn institutionalized by the creation of museums, or at least departments of Modern art.

However, most of the phases of modern art, subsequent to Impressionism, have not found a ready and ever-growing public acceptance. The taste for Cubism and De Stijl, for example, is still a very rare one. It is as if the eventual acceptance of Impressionism has led to a third phase, what may be a virtually perpetual contemporary (that is, not yet understood) art, to be for ever contested between the friends and enemies of modernism.

Contemporary art is actually understood by very many people, but the meanings and values they see in it are simply rejected as alien. Their demand to be told what works of contemporary art mean is merely the traditional expression of hostility, so an explanation of the meaning, to the limited degree to which this is possible for any work of art, does not usually satisfy them. Accordingly, the role of the very active education department of the Tate is not so much to explain contemporary art, as to introduce and to confront people with it, so that they are induced to see it as it is, and to experience an understanding of it. In short it is no more than an intensification of the role of the collection of modern art as a whole which

is primarily to manifest modern art to the public. Just as the building expresses the state's commitment to art, lecturers must, first of all, express intense interest, enthusiasm and respect for art.

The function of exhibitions is very similar. The catalogue, which may contain both information and interpretation, is read by a relatively small proportion of the visitors, five to ten per cent, and of course, quite rightly, few of these read much while going round. They look at the works of art using the catalogue and labels mainly to identify what they are seeing. Unlike the National Gallery, most of whose exhibitions comprise mainly works from the collections, the Tate has a considerable programme of loan exhibitions. One of the reasons for this difference is that the problems and expense of gathering works comparable to its own, are simply too onerous for the intensely select National Gallery. For the Tate, they are less severe, since British and modern art do not yet command the very high prices and the very highest degree of conservationist concern that the best-known of the old masters do.

Moreover, both in relation to British and to modern art, there is felt to be a much greater necessity both for education and proselytization. The gathering together of a large proportion of the work of a modern master can do much more to promote understanding, through the perception and development of the range of variety possible for that artist, than any verbal account alone. That is, by considering the transformations available to him or her, one may learn in effect the 'language' of the artist. Of course it is helpful to have in mind both the historical context and the art practice or culture from which the work came. The former must be brought in the heads of the visitors, it cannot really be exhibited, and this may be why the visitors to museums of modern art tend to be highly educated. The 'art' context is manifested by the surrounding permanent collections. Accordingly, they need to be fairly complete or well-balanced. As a matter of policy, the Tate's exhibitions are almost always a presentation in depth, whether of an artist, or of a type of art, that is represented necessarily more sketchily in the permanent collections.

The mutual support of collections and exhibitions is not, of course, the essential reason for the former to be balanced and, within reason, comprehensive. This derives directly from the concept of the museum of modern art itself. In so far as it is a museum, and not an arbitrary assembly of objects for delectation and excitement – a museum collection is one whose elements are themselves mutually supporting. That is, you may discern the distinctive character of an artist's work or even of an individual painting, sculpture and so on, by comparison with others contemporary with, earlier than, or indeed later than it. New art derives its power to express partly from the way it varies and transforms the tradition it inherits. Conversely, it gives new meanings to the manifestations of that older tradition.

The practical problem that arises is that the attempt to collect fairly rapidly the range of objects that can make really contemporary art 'meaningful' by such a means, results in the Gallery collecting a larger number of works that it can easily conserve and display later on. The ever-increasing diversity of twentieth century art, the rising numbers of artists and the spread of the practice of making art in the western European tradition, have made it necessary, on this assumption, to collect faster and faster. The Tate's British (sixteenth to nineteenth century) and its modern (twentieth century) collections (excluding prints and drawings) are each of about the same number as that of the National Gallery, covering, as it does, Europe for seven centuries. The Tate's twentieth century foreign collection alone is already half that of the National Gallery.

In spite of the argument above, it has become increasingly clear that galleries like the Tate should not all try to collect something of everything (down to a given level) but that, like the National Gallery in its early days, each should also build on strength. The Tate has in Turner an exceptional strength that cannot possibly be copied elsewhere. It has, in the British collection, other strengths: for example, Constable (shared anomalously with the Victoria and Albert Museum) and William Blake. In the twentieth century there are groups by some of the great British artists, such as Henry Moore and Stanley Spencer, and even some quite young artists, like Richard Long. You may find unique groups of work, too, by Giacometti, Gabo and Rothko. Nevertheless the Tate bears a distinct responsibility because it is the only substantial museum of modern international art in England. It is the nation's unique collection of such art and has a duty to represent a balanced range so that domestic visitors can see what is being created.

The present director, Alan Bowness, has recently added one really original concept to what has become a tradition, existing with variations, throughout the developed world. This is the Gallery of New Art. The strategy is that the Tate, having already budded the Clore Galleries for Turner on the adjacent site, should eventually develop three more institutions there, having a core of services in common. The Tate would revert to its original role as the national gallery of British art. There would then be a museum of modern international art (exhibiting a due proportion of British art), a gallery of new art and a centre for documentation, including probably a library, an archive, a print room and access to reserves and education facilities. The library would be used by the staff of the Gallery as a means by which they may advise the Trustees as competently

as possible, and would also be a final resource for other users in respect of its many items unique in this country. It should become generally accessible. The archive is growing as a means of conserving and making accessible, in due course, the whole range of documentation that may render art and the lives and practices of artists, accessible in ways that the painting alone may not.

However it is the gallery of new art that is the truly novel concept, though it is, in essence, a more radical version of the founding concept of the Luxembourg. This gallery will acquire, by purchase or loan, a continuous representation of the new in art, work, that is, by young artists – up to about 40 – and that is itself less than about ten years old. It will be considered to be all in the present, so that no chronological or other historical concepts need determine its arrangement. It will not have to compete so closely for interest with the classical moderns. It will be a celebration of, and commitment to, that which is most specifically of our time. The Tate has formed, within the association of the Friends of the Tate, who support the whole range of the Tate's functions, a special group of Patrons of New Art. They will support the art by their subscriptions and interest and will act as a pressure group to encourage the Tate itself and the higher authority – the state (which supplies overwhelmingly the great part of the funds both for activities and for purchases of the Tate Gallery and National Gallery), to remain always aware of the need to examine constantly the newest creations of art and to represent them in the Gallery. The group also aims to foster the spirit of collecting new art. The paucity of private collections in this country compared with many European and North American countries, is probably both a cause and the effect of the loneliness of the Tate as a public institution collecting contemporary international art.

It should be acknowledged here that governments of both parties, since the 1960s, have voted the National Gallery and the Tate considerable sums for purchase – currently more than three and two million pounds a year respectively. However, while the price of great paintings of, say, the sixteenth century, may be as high as five or more million pounds, many British and twentieth-century works are also priced above the level of the whole annual grant. In the case of the Tate this is spent in practice on one or two first-class and expensive works and quite a large number of lesser or cheaper ones. The annual growth rate of the collections of the Tate is perhaps twenty or more times that of the National Gallery so it cannot hope to show all that it owns. Every new work acquired must displace another to the depot.

It becomes ever more necessary, therefore, that the Tate should achieve the building programme outlined above, which will not only allow visitors to see a just proportion of the national heritage in the fields where the Tate is the national gallery, but will also allow ready and convenient access to nearly all those works which cannot at present be shown.

References

CAUMAN, S. (1958), *The Living Museum, experiences of an art historian and museum director*, Alexander Dorner, New York University Press, New York

GOULD, C. (19??)

LYNES, R. (1973), *Good old Modern: an Intimate Portrait of the Museum of Modern art*, Athenaeum, New York

POTTERTON, H. (1977), *The National Gallery, London*, Thames and Hudson, London

ROTHENSTEIN, J. (1962), *The Tate Gallery*, Thames and Hudson, London

ROYAL COMMISSION ON NATIONAL MUSEUMS AND GALLERIES (1928), *Interim Report: 1 September 1928*, HMSO, London

RSA, (1949), *Museums in Modern Life*, Royal Society of Arts, London

WACKENRODER, W. H. AND TIECK, J. L. (1797) *Herzensergeiszungen eines Kunstbliebenden Klasterbruders*, 61–62, Gillies (Ed.), 1948

WARK, R. R. (1975) (Ed.) 'Discourses on Art' Chapter 6: Reynolds, J. 'Second Discourse', Yale University Press

WILSON, M. (1977), *The National Gallery, London*, Orbis Publishing, London

7

The larger provincial museums and art galleries

Richard A. Foster

By 1851, the year of the Great Exhibition at Crystal Palace, Britain had emerged from the uncertainties of the first half of the century as a strong, imperial power. Her prosperity derived chiefly from the application of steam power to manufacturing industry and the ready-made markets of the Empire. Production was based on the larger provincial towns, all of which in this period experienced a dramatic increase in population. In Manchester for example, between 1801 and 1851, the population grew from 100 000 to 367 000. Although Disreali refers in the novel *Coningsby* to Manchester as a 'city of illuminated factories with more windows than Italian palaces and smoking chimneys taller than Egyptian obelisks' both he and other visitors were profoundly aware of the other side of the picture, the horrific conditions in which the cotton-mills operatives lived and the environmental and social price of this unprecedented economic growth. Despite the prevailing attitudes of *laissez-faire* however the 1840s saw a response to these conditions in a number of important enquiries into the plight of factory workers and the conditions in which they lived, including a Royal Commission into the 'State of Large Towns'. One of the most important conclusions of these investigations was the importance of the role to be played by the local authorities in this new situation.

In the 1840s there began a period of reform in which the town council became a major instrument in meeting the challenge of urban problems. Before the *Municipal Corporation Act 1835* the functions of local authorities were restricted, but faced with the threat of social disorder, the responsibilities and activities of local authorities had developed very substantially by the time Victoria came to the throne. As the local authorities grappled with the consequences of boom conditions, a familiar theme of more recent times, the need to improve the 'quality of life' was

frequently proclaimed. As one commentator put it (Davies, 1981a):

> Towards the end of the 1860s a few Birmingham men made the discovery that perhaps a strong and able Town Council might do almost as much to improve the conditions of life in the town as Parliament itself. They spoke of . . . providing gardens and parks and music, of erecting baths and free libraries, an art gallery and a museum.

These expressions of corporate opinion and the organized lobbying of town councils to adopt powers available to them for introducing cultural and recreational amenities sprang chiefly from the liberal sentiments of a growing middle class. The changes brought about by industrial growth were accompanied by a fundamental shift in the country's social structure. While the power and influence of the aristocracy remained, the long, slow ascent of the middle classes to positions of social and political influence had made substantial progress. Nowhere is this more evident than in the social and political life of the large Victorian cities where the middle-class occupants of the suburban villas, sought to invest their surroundings with the style and taste of a capital city, and to improve the conditions for those on whom their prosperity depended. Strangely enough, legislation for establishing public museums preceded that for public libraries in this anxious search for a stable metropolitan life-style. What then were the sources from which it sprang? In some cases the new local authority museums were presented with, or purchased, the objects and specimens collected by private individuals which had sometimes been made available to the public in privately-run museums. Liverpool provides a good example of these forces at work. In 1800 William Bullock, a goldsmith, opened the 'Liverpool Royal Museum' in Church Street, where by 1807 he had accumulated over 4000 zoological specimens, 'Indian war weapons', 'ancient armour' and 'works of art'. The Museum was open from 9 am to dusk with an admission fee of one shilling. Bullock's marketing style is to be admired for he could offer season and family tickets to his patrons. Significantly, the guidebook to the Museum, published in 1808, pays a generous tribute to a long list of Liverpool citizens, many of them sea captains who 'have presented curiosities to the Liverpool Museum' (Bullock, 1808).

Bullock's Museum was removed to London in 1809 and auctioned in 1819 from which some of the ethnographical material found its way back to the Royal Liverpool Institution established by the city's merchant class in 1817 for the promotion of literature, science and the arts. Throughout its existence of 70 years the Institution maintained a museum but eventually its ethnographical collections passed to the Corporation's City Museum (now Merseyside County Museums).

Private collecting of a more scientific and distinguished kind is represented in Liverpool by the activities of the thirteenth Earl of Derby, whose Will, on his death in 1851, expressed the wish that his fine collection of birds and animals should be made available in Liverpool or its environs and administered by Trustees preferably in a building managed by public authorities. Another private museum in Liverpool was that of Joseph Mayer, a Fellow of the Society of Antiquaries. Like William Bullock he was also a goldsmith. He established a private museum to show his remarkable collection of antiquities and ethnography, all of which he presented to the Liverpool Museum in 1867 (Nicholson and Warhurst, 1982).

A second, and perhaps more significant, influence in the development of the Victorian public museum service was that of the business and professional men who established and subscribed to the Literary and Philosophical Societies and the Institutions for the Arts and Sciences in several large cities in the mid-nineteenth century. Many of these institutions shared the prime objective of establishing a museum collection or of mounting an annual exhibition, initially for the benefit of the proprietors or subscribers.

The Bristol Institution for the Advancement of Science Literature and the Arts opened a museum in 1823 'for objects of natural history, including zoology, comparative anatomy, botany and geology'. Provision was also made for an 'exhibition of pictures, statues, casts and other objects of the fine arts and antiquities' (Walton, 1980). In Leeds, in 1821, the Philosophical and Literary Society opened a private museum chiefly to display specimens which formed the basis of the members' deliberations. After a time the museum was opened to the public on payment of a one-penny admission charge. The present City Art Gallery at Manchester occupies the former headquarters of the Royal Manchester

Institution for the promotion of Literature, Science and the Arts, opened in 1829 and which during the next half-century provided a setting for art exhibitions, lectures and an early home for the Manchester Academy of Fine Arts and School of Art. In Leicester the Literary and Philosophical Society founded in 1835 established a museum of natural history and, in 1841, this was opened in a small room in the Mechanics' Institute, the public being admitted free of charge on Mondays, Wednesdays and Saturdays with the rest of the week being reserved for members of the Society (Boylan, to be published).

The contribution made by these institutions to the evolution of the public museum service was reinforced by the success of a movement rooted more deeply in the aspirations of working-class people. The newly-established Mechanics' Institutes, like the societies and institutions, established their own museum collections, annual exhibitions, lecture programmes, excursions and field trips. It was the confluence of pressure from the members of these societies and the institutes, each convinced of the value of museums as a source of information and inspiration for the knowledgeable and curious alike, that led to pressure for legislation by Parliament. Parliament obliged by approving the *Museums Act 1845*, which authorized the expenditure of a half-penny rate on the maintenance of a museum in places where the population exceeded 10 000. Nowhere was the combination of middle-class and working-class enthusiasm in the promotion of a public museum service better demonstrated than in Leicester. As early as 1846 the Leicester Literary and Philosophical Society, acting jointly with the Mechanics' Institute and the Athenaeum Society, presented a Memorial to the Town Council petitioning the Corporation to accept responsibility for the management and development of the Society's museum which had been opened at the Mechanics' Institute in 1841. The Society's Memorial stated:

> that the formation of a Public Town Museum is highly desirable it being an important means of refining the public taste, of yielding amusement and instruction to all Orders of Society and especially of inducing habits of thought and study amongst the working classes.

There was an expression later in the petition of a fundamental principle for the establishment of a public museum:

> . . . many individuals having objects of interest in their possession, would be glad to present them to the Town, although unwilling to place them in the keeping of a private society which might otherwise fail to preserve them.

The Mechanics' Institution in its memorial stressed the appeal to all classes which the museum, hitherto operated by the Literary and Philosophical Society, had demonstrated and expressed the hope that the provision of a public museum would (Boylan, 1982):

> . . . raise the intellectual standard of the [town's] inhabitants . . . and prove highly useful to all engaged in the Trade and Manufacture of their district by affording opportunities for deposition and exhibition of improved machinery, new patterns etc.

Despite legislation being available from 1845 for local authorities to maintain museum and art gallery services, there was, in general, a cautious response by the town councils. Where the private societies and institutions were financially secure and could continue to maintain and open their museums to the public there was no need for the councils to intervene, but where the institutions faced financial problems, the town councils came under increasing pressure to take over. In certain cases however the local authorities became directly involved by choice at an earlier date. Leicester and Liverpool took prompt action to adopt museum powers, Leicester providing one of the first local authority museums in 1849, although the Literary and Philosophical Society retained ownership of their collections, vested in a Trust, and provided a curator until 1872. Liverpool, encouraged by the availability of private finance for a museum building and the gift of the Derby zoological collection, obtained its own Act of Parliament, the *Liverpool Public Library, Museum and Gallery of Art Act 1852*. In Birmingham matters took a little longer, the Corporation adopting museum powers in 1860 but only responding to public pressure by providing a small gallery in the Library in 1867. The Corporation in Bristol seems to have relied on the 'arms length' principle by making a regular subscription to the Bristol Institution and its museum from 1835. It was not until 1891 that the Corporation adopted museum powers and took over the collection and the building of the Institution's impecunious successor, the Bristol Museum and Library Association. At Sheffield, the local authority opened its museum in 1875, and the Mappin Art Gallery in 1887 while in Newcastle, the city's involvement in art gallery provision did not begin until 1903 when the Laing Art Gallery was opened. The Norfolk and Norwich Museum, a private institution founded in 1824, remained an independent institution until the Norwich Corporation purchased the Castle, previously a prison, and re-opened it as a civic museum in 1894. In Leeds the Philosophical and Literary Society retained their museum for a hundred years before lack of funds forced them to sell the museum and collection to the Corporation in 1921 for a nominal sum. Despite the fact that some of the formative arguments for museum legislation had been made in Manchester the city did not involve itself directly until 1882 when the Manchester Institution transferred its collection and building to the City.

In general the museums created by the societies and institutions concentrated on the natural sciences or the 'useful arts'. Art gallery provision stimulated by annual exhibitions took longer to develop in Manchester, Bristol and Liverpool. While Liverpool's City Museum was opened in a new building in 1861, the addition of the Walker Art Gallery to that impressive line of civic buildings in William Brown Street did not take place until 1877. Although Bristol's museum was managed by the Corporation in 1893, the art gallery did not appear until 1905.

Private benefaction also played an important part in the large provincial museums. Liverpool had good reason to thank Mr (later Sir) William Brown, MP for providing its museum and Mr (later Sir) Andrew Barclay Walker for the Walker Art Gallery, and more recently in 1978 the trustees of Lord Leverhulme presented the Lady Lever Art Gallery to Merseyside County Council as a branch museum for the Walker Art Gallery. The Wills family figure substantially in the building of the Bristol Art Gallery, while Birmingham is indebted to John Feeney for the gift of its art galleries. In Newcastle it was Andrew Laing, a wine merchant, who provided a substantial sum for the construction of the Laing Art Gallery. In Sheffield the Mappin Art Gallery opened with a bequest from John Newton Mappin, a local brewer. The words on the memorial stone in the entrance hall to Birmingham Museum and Art Gallery echo the sentiments of the day: 'By the gains of industry we promote Art'.

In this brief survey of the origins of some of the great provincial museums and galleries the factors motiving the creation of a public museum service have been identified: first the existence of collections available to the public authorities by gift or purchase from private collectors, societies or institutes. Secondly the need to provide educational and recreational facilities for the expanding urban population. Lastly, the crucial and often deciding factor in the successful establishment of the local authority museum service was the gift of funds for the building of the museums and galleries by wealthy benefactors.

Early development and the growth of branch museums and galleries

We have seen the varying circumstances in which some of the large provincial museums and galleries became established. It was not long before their success in attracting bequests and donations of objects and specimens for their permanent collections began to outstrip the accommodation in the central institutions. In some cases this seems decidedly to have stimulated the growth of branch museums and galleries. Certainly the convenience of having older buildings, owned by or presented to the Council, transferred to and administered by the city museum or art gallery was seized very early on. By the early years of the twentieth century some of these larger museums had acquired a relatively sophisticated staffing and departmental structure and in most of the institutions a strong emphasis was placed on service to the public and in particular to schools. The following examples show how these trends developed in the case of four institutions at Birmingham, Liverpool, Bristol and Manchester. In Birmingham, by 1919, the Central Museum and Art Gallery had developed to much the same size as today but the pressure on space was unrelenting, giving rise to serious concern about the conditions in which the collection were displayed and stored. This pressure on the museum and art gallery service was reflected in the development of branch museums throughout Birmingham. The first of these was Aston Hall acquired by the city in the mid-nineteenth century. Aston Hall is a fine seventeenth century brick house and in recent years has been restored to display furniture and decoration of the seventeenth and eighteenth centuries. In 1932 Blakesley Hall was opened as a branch museum of manorial history. Weoley Castle, the remnants of a stone-built manor house was purchased in 1930 and brought under museum administration in 1956, Sarehole Mill, acquired by the city in 1946, was transferred to the Museum in 1967 and perhaps the best-known branch museum, the Science and Industry Museum was opened in 1950. With the increasing size of the collections at Birmingham it was inevitable that specialist departments should be formed to care for them. The Department of Natural History was established in 1950, the Education Department in 1963, Conservation in 1971, Applied Art in 1979 and Local History in 1980.

In Liverpool the City Museum did not spawn branch museums to the same extent as in other large museums. The first fifty years of its existence did however see the establishment of a strong sense of service to the public and particularly to schools. The Reverend Henry Higgins, Chairman of the Museums Committee and first president of the Museums Association introduced a highly-successful loan service to schools in 1884 in which teachers were able to borrow travelling cases of exhibits drawn from the natural science collections. By 1937 the rich collections of Liverpool Museum had justified the creation of a relatively sophisticated structure with the Museum Director presiding over six keepers in charge of departments covering invertebrate zoology, geology, botany, ethnology and archaeology. There were in addition two sub-departments of shipping and ceramics. The Museum had well-equipped workshops, taxidermist rooms and a photographic studio.

In May 1941 an incendiary bomb destroyed a substantial part of the Museum and it was not until the 1960s that the process of reconstruction began. The drive to rebuild the museum produced new departments to service this activity and a design and production department and a technical services department were established. At this time the Museum took over responsibility for Speke Hall, a sixteenth century Tudor house owned by the National Trust.

Bristol Museum and Art Gallery was regarded in 1913 as a model of its kind and it was reported that the new Belfast Museum and Art Gallery would be designed along the same lines. However the Annual Report of 1920 reflected some of the frustrations felt also by Birmingham and Manchester, namely an acute shortage of space in which to accommodate the growing permanent collections particularly where the Art Gallery was concerned. Fortunately space was available for an extension to the rear of the Art Gallery at Bristol and with generous assistance from the Wills family it was built on this site and officially opened in 1930. Like Liverpool, war-time brought catastrophe to the Museum and Art Gallery. In November 1940 the Museum building was almost totally gutted by an incendiary bomb. It was decided that as a temporary measure the Museum should move into the Art Gallery, the latter taking the upper floor to benefit from top lighting. Until 1940 both Museum and Art Gallery were administered under one director. Now, although occupying the same building, there are separate directors of the Art Gallery and of the Museum.

Perhaps the shortage of accommodation in the central institution gave impetus to the acquisition of branch museums of which both Bristol Museum and Art Gallery have quite a number. In 1920, the Red Lodge, a late sixteenth-century house was presented to the Council and in 1937 the Georgian House built in 1790 for a wealthy sugar merchant was presented to the city and came under the Museum and Art Gallery's administration. In 1949 the Museum opened Blaise Castle House as a museum of folk life and since then St Nicholas Church Museum and the Bristol Industrial Museum have been added.

Acute shortage of space seems to have been experienced in Manchester City Art Gallery very shortly after it was opened in 1880 in the former Royal Manchester Institution building. Complaints grew that the annual exhibitions of old master paintings were vying for space with the growing permanent collections. Many options for extending the Gallery were examined but it was not until 1938 that the Athenaeum Club (first contemplated as an extension in the 1890s) was acquired and the central institution provided with adequate space. But if frustration over the inadequacies of the central City Art Gallery predominated it did not stop; indeed it may have stimulated a burgeoning branch gallery network. In 1902 part of Heaton Hall was acquired, in 1906 Queens Park Art Gallery was opened, in 1923 the Old Parsonage in Didsbury and in 1925 Platt Hall, later to become the Department of Costume's main centre in 1947, were acquired. In 1930 Wythenshaw Hall was added.

Collections

It is the importance of their collections that distinguish the large provincial museums and art galleries. The Standing Commission on Museums and Galleries (1979) report *Framework for a System of Museums* drew attention to the need for special provision for these museums and galleries. This report recommended that museums having responsibility for collections of national significance and serving a wider area than that of their local authority, should be entitled to special help. It recommended that museums and galleries in this position should be able to apply for 'designation' which, on acceptance by the government of a development plan drawn up by the applicant museum authority, would attract a high level of government grant towards both capital and revenue expenditure on selected improvements. All the museums mentioned in this paper, and several more including some of the university museums, would meet this preliminary classification, for it is the quality and range of collections that would form any criteria for 'designation'. The following brief assessment of the strengths in this area of some of the larger provincial museums and galleries bears out their claim for special treatment. Birmingham City Museum and Art Gallery has a fine collection of old master paintings including works by Simone Martini, Botticelli, Claude and Guardi. However, the collection is known particularly for its outstanding group of pre-Raphaelite pictures with masterpieces by Rossetti, Holman Hunt, Ford Madox Brown, Millais and Edward Burne-Jones.

In Birmingham the Museum from its inception expressed an interest in and sought to encourage the 'useful arts'. The city is world-famous for the manufacture of coins, commemorative medals, trade tokens and cheques and the Museum collections amply reflect this. Its collections of applied art are wide and include a collection of silver by Mathew Boulton illustrating Birmingham's importance in this field. For the citizens of Birmingham, as elsewhere in the large Victorian cities, the Museum provided a window on the world, a glimpse of the vast British Empire of which most knew very little. One of the earliest acquisitions was the copper Buddha from Bengal a classic example of early Gupta work. The Gandhara and Hadda sculptures, Japanese sword furniture, Chinese tomb figures, Peruvian textiles and Egyptian antiquities further illustrate the range and diversity of the Museum's international collections.

The Midlands is the centre of the engineering industry and in 1950 the Birmingham Science Museum, a branch of the main Museum and Art Gallery was established to record and interpret this. The collections include a variety of heavy engineering exhibits, steam turbines, hot air engines, electrical generators and machine tools. However there is little to illustrate the traditional craft industries. Much of the evidence for a 'town of a thousand trades' was lost in the redevelopment of the city in the 1950s and 1960s. Recently, however, a local history gallery has been opened in an attempt to concentrate attention on the life and traditions of this great provincial city (Davies, 1981b; Gunstone, 1982).

Bristol Museum and Art Gallery, like Leeds and Liverpool, suffered badly from war-time bombing. After several 'false dawns' plans for a new city museum were abandoned. The Museum continues to share premises with the Art Gallery but despite being thrown together, both institutions have achieved much in their post-war history and made exemplary use of their fine collections. The antiquities collection reflects the intense public interest in the early years of the twentieth century in the activities of British archaeological expeditions then working in the Near and Middle East. Through subscription to excavation funds the Museum acquired several important groups but pride of place must go to the carved gypsum reliefs from the Palace of Ashurnasipal II at Nimrud (884–859 BC) purchased in 1905. The decorative art collections include the Bamford collection of ancient glass, British silver, European ceramics, glass, silver and textiles, metalwork and furniture from the seventeenth century to the present day. The Bristol area is of special geological interest, the pioneer geologist William Smith basing his theories on work in the area. It is not surprising that the Museum has an excellent collection of fossils and minerals. Bristol Art Gallery possesses internationally significant holdings of Oriental Art in the Schiller collection which covers the whole range of Chinese art including what is believed to be the world's largest collection of Chinese glass. Bristol Museum has for a long time acted as a major regional centre for south-west England and recently a new gallery of natural history in south-west Britain has been opened exhibiting animals of coastal and freshwater habitats against backdrops of seaside and country. Foreign animals are exhibited on a mainly geographical basis with mammals from Africa, Australia and South America well represented.

The Art Gallery has a marvellous collection including French paintings by Delocroix, Renoir and Seurat together with Italian panel paintings of the fourteenth and fifteenth centuries and sixteenth and seventeenth-century Dutch, German and Flemish works. Of particular interest is an altarpiece by the

Venetian artist, Antonio da Solario, commissioned by a wealthy Bristol merchant in 1514.

At Leicester, where the founding collections were those of the Literary and Philosophical Society's Museum, the emphasis initially was on the acquisition of zoological, botanical and geological material. In 1864, a collection of lepidoptera was purchased from Henry Walter Bates, a distinguished naturalist and explorer born in Leicester. During the 1870s and 1880s the Museum even maintained a department of meteorology with an observatory. The Museum's interest in the archaeology of Leicester was a significant early development with important evidence of the Roman town being acquired as early as 1853 when the Museum purchased the Roman pavement in Jewry Wall Street. In 1880, as elsewhere at this time, interest in the town turned to the fine arts with a project to establish an art gallery with the creation of a purchase fund to buy pictures. However, the development of the art gallery was slow and it was not until 1944 when, following an exhibition of mid-European art at New Walk, the art gallery achieved prominence with the purchase of a number of notable German expressionist pictures. Like Birmingham, Leicester Museum developed an interest in the applied arts, with the purchase in 1919 in the first examples furniture and crafts by Ernest Gimson. In 1925 the Museum began to acquire examples of machines used in the Leicester hosiery trade which by the 1980s was to become one of the most comprehensive collections of knitting machines in the world.

Liverpool City Museums' (now Merseyside County Museums) collections are based on the thirteenth Earl of Derby's zoological specimens and the rich Joseph Mayer bequest. The Mayer collection includes important Anglo-Saxon finds, classical archaeology and an internationally-significant collection of ivories. The first Curator, Thomas Moore, was extremely energetic in establishing contact with Liverpool's seafarers, who in the course of the second half of the nineteenth century brought back many items of interest from the remoter parts of the world. Occasionally the Museum took the initiative for, during the last quarter of the nineteenth century, its staff participated in collecting both locally and overseas, adding some of the most important specimens to the Museum's collections, especially in invertebrate and vertebrate zoology. In 1909 a further important section was added to the Museum's collections when the herbarium of the Liverpool Botanic Gardens was transferred to the Museum. It was not until 1931 that the systematic collection of maritime history really began but these collections are now so extensive that a large new museum is being established for them in the Liverpool South Docks. Merseyside County Museum's collections also include highly important Liverpool

delftware and porcelain, costume silver and glass. From very early in its history the Museum has maintained an aquarium and in 1969 it was the first institution outside London to open a planetarium. The development of a public art gallery in Liverpool in 1877 followed some years after the establishment of the Museum and Library. Long before this, however, in 1810 the Liverpool Academy had been formed to run an art school and mount an annual exhibition. As in Bristol the Liverpool Corporation supported the Academy's work with grant-aid and a tradition of highly successful annual exhibitions was established, responsibility for which was taken over by the Corporation in 1871 after disagreements with the Academy. The Liverpool Autumn Exhibitions were held by the Corporation from 1873 until the last war. When Andrew Barclay Walker offered to present the Gallery to the city in 1873 his intention was to provide galleries for this popular autumn series. His gift, however, led to the creation of one of the finest public picture collections in this country. The Italian paintings, which include Simone Martini's 'The Finding of Christ in the Temple', came from the collection of William Roscoe, a Liverpool banker and poet, whose paintings eventually came to the Walker in 1893, after being with the Liverpool Royal Institution for 77 years. In general, however, the aim of the committee in charge of the Walker Art Gallery was to acquire contemporary British pictures of 'popular character . . . appealing to common feelings and sentiments of our daily life and which have afforded . . . a fine moral lesson and given great pleasure to the numerous visitors to the Gallery who are uninitiated in the higher form of life' (Walker Art Gallery, 1970). An indication of what the committee had in mind is illustrated by one of the earliest purchases, W. Yeames *And when did you last see your Father?* Most of The Walker's purchases initially were from the Annual Exhibitions and this was seen as an inducement to the leading artists of the day to continue to contribute. The Walker's tradition of encouraging living artists continuing today in the holding of the biennial John Moores Exhibition. Just over a century after its foundation the Walker's collection includes pictures by many famous painters including Rembrandt, Salomon Ruysdael and Stubbs while its most recent purchase of the outstanding 'Ashes of Phocion' by Nicholas Poussin will ensure that the Walker maintains its position as one of the finest art galleries in Europe. In 1978 the Walker acquired the Lady Lever Art Gallery in Port Sunlight, the personal collection built up by the first Lord Leverhulme which includes superb collections of Chinese ceramics, furniture and paintings.

In Newcastle, the Laing Art Gallery (now part of the Tyne and Wear County Museums) has one of the finest art collections in the north of England. The 1 500 works include works by Richard Wilson,

Reynolds, Constable, Landseer, Holman Hunt, Lowry and Spencer. Of particular importance is the large collection of British watercolours representative of all the leading artists. The collection is rich in silver and metal work from the seventeenth century onwards and in English pottery, furniture, arms and armour, Egyptian, Greek and Roman pottery and a substantial representation of Newcastle glass.

The present Tyne and Wear County Museum Service has brought together under one administration museums and galleries in Newcastle, Gateshead and Sunderland. Sunderland Museum and Art Gallery was one of the earliest local authority museums in the country when in 1846 Sunderland Corporation took over the collections of a local Natural History and Antiquarian Society. Sunderland has particularly fine ceramics collections, British oils and watercolours and many fine topographical and marine paintings. The Shipley Art Gallery was opened in 1917 with funds provided by Mr Joseph Shipley, a Newcastle solicitor who had acquired a large collection of pictures and who wanted to create a building to house his lifetime's interest. The strength of the collection lies in a number of works by Flemish, Dutch and Italian artists together with a substantial collection of the British school. Like Birmingham, Tyne and Wear County Museum Service has a large and interesting science collection, the majority of the exhibits illustrating the achievements of scientists and engineers in the north east. This collection was formerly housed in an exhibition building opened in 1934 but has recently been moved to the centre of Newcastle where 80 full-sized engines and models are on show. The collection contains the yacht 'Turbinia', of 1897 the first vessel in the world to be powered by steam turbines.

In 1894 Norwich Castle was opened as a civic museum, the new Museum attracting a number of striking gifts including pictures by Norwich School artists from the East Anglian Art Society and a large and valuable collection of antiquities bequeathed by Robert Fitch in 1892. Most of the collections acquired by the Norwich Castle Museum have been donated, but like other museums described here, it has entered the sale room with increasing frequency. The Friends of Norwich Museums, one of the first organizations of its kind in the country (formed in 1921) have assisted with substantial grant-aid. The collections range from local natural and human history, the rich natural history of the Broads, and important archaeological finds of particular significance to pre-conquest studies. There is a considerable collection of objects presented by private collectors including Egyptian mummies, seventeenth-century Japanese armour and mounted specimens from East Africa and other parts of the former British Empire. The Museum's collection of silverware, hall-marked in Norwich between 1565 and 1702 and

its Lowestoft porcelain are like the Norwich School pictures of more than regional interest.

Local government reorganization in England and Wales 1974

All the large provincial museums have in the course of their history acquired branch museums, but most of these are situated within the boundary of the city in which the main museum is situated. In the case of four museums in this survey, however, local government reorganization in England and Wales 1974 placed them at the centre of a county-wide service. In Leicester it was decided that the Leicester Museum and Art Gallery should be managed by the County Council and the Leicestershire Art Gallery, Museums and Records Service with its headquarters in New Walk now administers six museums in the city together with a local history museum in Oakham, and newly opened museums in Melton Mowbray, (Boylan, 1981) and Market Harborough.

In Newcastle it was decided that all the museums within the new Metropolitan County of Tyne and Wear should be administered by the County Council. The main institutions brought together in the new service being the Laing Art Gallery, the Science Museum and John Joicey Museum in Newcastle, the Shipley Art Gallery, and the Sunderland Museum and Art Gallery. On Merseyside the situation is less clear-cut. It was decided at the time of reorganisation that the City Museum and Walker Art Gallery should be administered by the new Metropolitan Merseyside County Council to ensure that these two large institutions could be more adequately cared for by the broader rate-base, Liverpool Corporation ceding its powers accordingly. However the four other metropolitan district councils decided to operate concurrent powers and thus museums in Birkenhead, St Helens and Southport are not administered by the County Museum Service.

It was in Norfolk however that perhaps the most thorough-going changes in museum provision were made at the time of reorganization of local government, providing Norwich Castle Museum with an unparalleled opportunity among English provincial museums to assume a regional role. As part of an agreement with the District Councils, the new Norfolk County Council took over responsibility for the funding and operation of the Norwich Castle Museum and its branches together with museums in Great Yarmouth, Kings Lynn, Thetford and Cromer, to establish the largest and best example in England of an integrated county museum. The administration of this large museum service, comprising fourteen museums, is overseen by a joint committee on which representatives not only of the controlling County Council sit but also those of all the District Councils. However, both the museum buildings and the museum collections (acquired prior to 1974) remain in the ownership of the District Councils represented on the joint committee. All alterations or improvements to the fabric of buildings required for museum purposes are borne by the County Council. Unless a District Council wishes to retain control of access to the museum building, the cost of maintenance is borne by the County Council through the joint committee. All the staff in every part of the service are on the payroll of the County Council. The Norfolk Museum Service, as it is now called, also administers the Norfolk Archaeological Unit which organizes surveys and conducts rescue excavations on the threatened archaeological sites in Norfolk (Cheetham, 1974).

Services

A large number of people visit our larger provincial museums. In 1980–1981 a total of 7.3 million visitors were received by sixteen of our larger provincial museums and galleries. The total net cost of operating these museums in 1980–1981 was £17.7 million while the total capital expenditure was of the order of £6.2 million (Foster, 1982). Nearly all these museums have in recent years experienced retrenchment in their operating budgets and the low level of capital expenditure reinforces the comments in the Drew Report about the need for special assistance to museums in this category.

Despite these difficulties there is still a refreshing attitude towards the provision of public services in most of the large provincial museums which contradicts their characterization as 'muscle-bound dinosaurs.' A good example is the association in the public gallery of the collections on show with the skills of the craftsman. In Norfolk the Norwich Castle Museum has linked artist–craftsmen at work in a series of week-long demonstrations with temporary exhibitions of the relevant collections. Participants have included a weaver, a toymaker, a jeweller and a potter. The craftsmen have provided lunchtime talks about their work as part of the programme. Tyne and Wear County Museums, at its Shipley Art Gallery, is at present experimenting with a new crafts gallery and craft information centre while at the same time building up a collection of high quality craft objects. The momentum behind the promotion and presentation of the crafts illustrates the mutually beneficial relationship nutured by the Crafts Council acting in conjunction with provincial museums, the regional arts associations. The demonstration of traditional crafts has also found an effective platform in the larger museums and galleries. This is the hallmark of Sheffield Museums where, at Abbeydale, the industrial hamlet rings to the sound of hammers and is lit by the glow of the hearth. At Kelham Island Industrial Museum, Sheffield Museums are provid-

ing a number of permanent work places for traditional Sheffield craftsmen.

The same principle of the museum providing the environment within which a craftsmen or an artist can practise his art and at the same time make contact with the public has been followed by the Walker Art Gallery in Liverpool. The result of the artist-in-residence scheme has not only been exhibitions of the artist's work but also the opportunity for visitors to watch the artist at work and to talk to him about his own paintings and those of other artists represented in the Gallery. Manchester City Art Gallery has made a determined attempt to broaden the appeal of its collections by re-creating a period setting in which potted palms, and double-banked hanging, places pictures and cases within the context of the Gallery's architecture. The Gallery has also attempted to say more about the pictures it shows with informative labels intended to remove the barriers between art and the public, reinforced in some institutions by the apparent reluctance of the staff to share their knowledge with the visitor.

The activity at Manchester City Art Gallery also illustrates a revival of confidence in the architectural qualities of museum and gallery buildings. In attempts over the last twenty years to banish the fusty image of museums, plywood panels and bland decoration have often screened the Georgian, Victorian or Edwardian setting. Occasionally this may be preferred; but where collections can be returned to an earlier context we can rediscover and appreciate the intention of the founders to make the museum architecture itself one of the most striking exhibits. At Birmingham Museum and Art Gallery the spectacular construction of cast-iron roofs and balconies of the 1885 Industrial Gallery once again forms the backdrop to the exhibition of glass, ceramics, stained glass, costume, metalwork, sculpture and coins. At Port Sunlight on the Wirral the Walker Art Gallery is now restoring and revealing the original features of the remarkable Lady Lever Art Gallery. In spite of their 'municipal' image there is plenty of evidence to show that our larger provincial museums and galleries have responded significantly to what might loosely be called the 'environmental movement' of the 1970s. Most of the museums operate record centres of archaeological or natural history data, providing information to planning authorities and conservation groups. Where the collections are concerned, new ideas such as the Environment Gallery and the Botany Plant Room at Merseyside County Museums illustrate another aspect of this approach. Merseyside's plans to preserve an area of historic dockland on Liverpool's waterfront and to operate its collections within their historical environment is another aspect of this philosophy. Leeds City Museums are using Armley Mills, once Yorkshire's largest woollen mill, for a new museum of science and industry, while a different but equally appropriate environment has been chosen for the development of the international sculpture study centre in a new extension to Leeds City Art Gallery, funded by the Henry Moore Foundation.

Most of the large provincial museums and galleries would place considerable importance on their temporary exhibition programmes as an important method of expression for institutions holding so much material in reserve. Birmingham City Museums and Art Gallery staged an important exhibition of William Morris's textiles and embroideries accompanied by a catalogue of a standard equal to anything produced by a national museum. Four years ago Merseyside County Museums mounted an exhibition entitled *Historic Glass from North West England* which provided an opportunity to compare for the first time glasses from several North-West museums. The catalogue provided a scholarly reference work and achieved world-wide sales.

The temporary exhibition not only provides a changing face for the museum, important in terms of maintaining visitor numbers, but it can also provide an important stimulus for the museum or gallery to re-examine its collections and to interpret and publish its research. Through its temporary exhibition programme the museum or gallery can be informative, entertaining and make a significant contribution to knowledge. Certain temporary exhibitions have revealed the attraction of undertaking museum-based research in front of the public. At Bristol City Museum, the unwrapping of one of the Museum's Egyptian mummies in the University Medical School was relayed by closed-circuit television to the Museum where a total of over 11 000 people watched the examination, queues forming every day.

It is hardly surprising that given their location, for the most part in cities, the larger provincial museums and galleries should, early in their history, have encountered demands for 'out-reach' services. Sheffield City Museums has for over twelve years mounted travelling exhibitions in showcases located in branch libraries and hospitals. Tyne and Wear County Museum, through its urban programme staff, provides exhibitions to pubs and clubs, while Leicestershire Museums wisely make sure that police stations are included in their travelling exhibition venues. Several museums and galleries operate picture-lending schemes to private companies and individual borrowers. Leeds City Art Galleries established a picture loan scheme in 1961 based on its Print Room and Art Library in which over 95 per cent of the works are originals rather than reproductions. Manchester City Art Gallery has its patrons scheme whereby in return for financial support the Gallery will lend pictures from its reserve collection.

On Merseyside the Walker Art Gallery and Merseyside County Museums are considering the extension of a successful mobile exhibition service introduced four years ago with a teaching team of four to operate a programme to serve inner city schools in Liverpool. Perhaps the extended service, hopefully to be financed under the government's Inner City Partnership Scheme, might concentrate on running activities in the evenings using the exhibition trailer and the objects and pictures as an introduction to a programme of activities which relies also on the use of school or community centre premises.

So far the discussion about the use of collections has concentrated on the services in the public galleries and in outreach programmes. What of the situation in the provision of services for specialists and the museums' and galleries' activity in the documentation, research and publication of their collections? Consideration of these responsibilities immediately brings one face to face with the supreme dilemma of deciding how to accord priorities among the bewildering and burgeoning duties that museums and galleries have attracted or have had imposed upon them in recent years. Dr John Eames of Liverpool University, addressing the Annual Conference on this subject in Leicester in 1969, drew attention to the minimum obligation of a museum or gallery to make known information about what it holds, in other words the cataloguing of its collections as the prime and immediate need in the field of scholarship (Eames, 1969). Fourteen years later there are signs that at long last museums and galleries may be starting to make significant progress in this vital area, and that the standard of performance is steadily improving. Birmingham is engaged in the cataloguing of its natural history collections, storing the information on an IBM information processor. Bristol, using the GOS package, has the computerization of its archaeological, ethnographical, natural history and geological collections under way. Leeds City Museums have begun the computerization of their natural history collections while at Leicestershire Museums and Art Galleries a major computerization project is in progress using the County Council's Sperry-Univac 1100/10 main-frame computer operated through the Museums' own terminal network.

Manchester City Art Gallery is also using a Manpower Services Commission (MSC) team to compile a basic inventory of certain parts of the collection. Merseyside County Museums, Sheffield City Museums and Tyne and Wear County Museum Service are also heavily involved in catching up on massive backlogs in the documentation of their collections. As far as the research and publication of collections is concerned, Leeds City Art Galleries have established an exemplary record with the publication of comprehensive catalogues of the English pottery collection (1976) and furniture (1978), financed under a guarantor system. Similar catalogues of the silver, paintings, oriental ceramics and costume collections will follow.

If the present activity with documentation and computerization is sustained, however, museums and galleries may, by the end of the decade, be able to contemplate a greater commitment to research and publication.

Turning to the vexed question of accommodation for reserve collections, the picture is still fairly grim in the larger provincial museums and galleries. Few could match Bristol City Museum's achievements over the past twelve years in modernizing their storage areas, although Leeds City Museums have now centralized the storage of their collections and Leicestershire Museums have unified sections of their holdings. Leeds City Art Galleries, on the other hand, are trying to abolish the concept of storage by making available their entire collections in a series of storage on-display galleries. It may not be entirely coincidental that they have one of the best working relationships of a local authority with its university where undergraduates of Leeds University, taking the special decorative arts honours degree option, use the collections and are taught by the curatorial team. It is possible that with improved relations between museums, galleries and universities a similar definitive purpose could be found for some of our vast natural history collections, some of which seem to be in search of a useable future. There is no doubt, however, that the preference of local authority committees for resources to be directed towards the public service and the near impossibility of attracting capital grants either to extend or to improve physical space and environmental control ensure that many directors and their curatorial colleagues remain frustrated caretakers.

Most of the large museums and galleries regard this as their major problem and the Museums and Galleries Commission must look urgently at the capital needs of the larger provincial museums in order to prepare a case for a 'housing-the-museums fund'. Present government policy of severe controls on capital and revenue expenditure of local authorities threatens to erase even this inadequate provision.

In general, collections are often regarded as being mainly of interest and value to specialists from other museums, universities and research institutions. Is it reasonable however to tie up so much space, equipment and staff for use by as little as three per cent or four per cent of the museum's clients? Do we simply 'sit on too much stuff'? It may well be, if we wish to encourage it, that museums and galleries could bcome a new kind of centre for 'continuing education', particularly at the weekends and in the evenings. Many people, stimulated by what they see on television, are now, in their mature years, undergoing a second informal education and developing a deep interest in subjects such as zoology, archaeology or maritime history. With their interest reinforced by the collections displayed in the public gallery they seek a deeper involvement with the museum's store of knowledge, objects, pictures, specimens and data held in reserve. The effect of promoting schemes to make reserve collections more available to the public should help to attract funding for the improvement of storage and work areas from committees who at present tend to rate these as low priorities.

Bearing that in mind, these words of John Cotton Dana, the founder of the Newark Museum, New Jersey, seem as relevant today as they did in 1909:

> a good museum attracts, entertains, arouses curiosity, leads to questioning and this promotes learning. It is an educational institution that is set up and kept in motion that it may help the members of the community to become happier, wiser and more effective human beings. The Museum can help people only if they use it, they will use it only if they know about it and only if attention is given to the interpretation of its possessions in terms they, the people, will understand.

References

BOYLAN, P. J. (1981), 'The developing role of a County Museum, Art Galleries and Records Service in England', *Museumleven* **7–8** 132–138

BOYLAN, P. J. (1982), 'Why museums?' *Transactions of the Leicester Literary and Philosophical Society*, **76**, 4–7

BOYLAN, P. J. (to be published) 'Leicester Museums 1835–1974', *Leicestershire Museums Record*

BULLOCK, W. (1808), *A Companion to the Liverpool Museum*, privately printed, Hull

CHEETHAM, F. W. (1974), 'Local Government Reorganisation and the Norfolk Museums Service', *Museums J.* **74**(1) 27–28

DAVIES, S. (1981a), (Ed.), *Birmingham Museum and Art Gallery*, Department of Local History, Information Sheet 9

DAVIES, S. (1981b), 'Birmingham's Local History Gallery', *Museums J.* **81**(3), 159–163

EAMES, J. (1969), 'Museums and Scholarship', *Museums J.*, **69**(3), 103–105

FOSTER, R. A. (1982), 'Standards of Performance – the Larger Provincial Museums and Galleries', *Museums J.*, **81**(3), Supplement, 7–9

GUNSTONE, A. (1982), 'Local History in Birmingham: Review and Reminiscence', *Museums J.*, **82**(3), 180–182

NICHOLSON, S. AND WARHURST, M. (1982), The Mayer Collection, *The Museum Archaeologist* No. 8

STANDING COMMISSION ON MUSEUMS AND GALLERIES (1979), *Framework for a System of Museums*, HMSO, London, 1979

WALKER ART GALLERY (1970), *Guide to the Walker Art Gallery and its Collections'* published for Museums Association Conference, Liverpool

WALTON, K. M. (1980), *75 Years of Bristol Aart Gallery*, City of Bristol Museum and Art Gallery

8

University museums

Alan Warhurst

There is no single type of university museum in the United Kingdom. What may appear from the title of this chapter to be a homogeneous group of museums, contains a variety of institutions whose origins, purposes and collections vary greatly. The only common strands running through them are that their administration and finance are provided, although not always exclusively, by a parent university; that their collections and buildings are generally owned by a university; and that, in one way or another, they make a contribution to the purpose of that university.

At one end of the scale, many of the fifty museums attached to British universities are little more than aggregations of specimens which are, or have been useful to the research and teaching functions of a university department. Some of these, particularly a number of geological museums, are orderly collections. At the other end of the scale are several institutions containing collections which in quantity and quality far exceed what is needed for the university's teaching and research purposes. The latter museums, of which the Ashmolean Museum at Oxford and the Fitzwilliam Museum at Cambridge are the best known, form one of the most important elements in the framework of museum provision in this country. As well as these types of university museums there are several museum collections, some of considerable antiquity, which for different reasons have been adopted or fostered by universities. Altogether, the collections of university museums are a significant part of the nation's cultural, historical and scientific heritage.

History

If the functions of a university are considered to be teaching and research, along with a wish to stimulate

and fulfil the wider intellectual, cultural, artistic and scientific aspirations of its students, staff and non-university public in the neighbourhood, then it need occasion no surprise that universities have been regarded as suitable locations for museums from early times. The earliest public museum in Britain is generally accepted to be the Ashmolean Museum which was opened in 1683 after Elias Ashmole donated his inherited Tradescant Collection to the University of Oxford in 1677. Although at its inception the museum was primarily for scholars of the university, the public were admitted albeit after payment for admission. The Sedgwick Museum owes its origins to the bequest of Dr John Woodward of his collection of fossils to Cambridge University in 1727. Dr William Hunter bequeathed his private collection to the University of Glasgow in 1783 and the Hunterian Museum was opened in 1804. The Fitzwilliam Museum was established at Cambridge in 1816 following a bequest to the university. In 1868 the collections of the Manchester Society of Natural History were accepted by Owen's College (later the Victoria University of Manchester) after having been rejected by the City of Manchester, and the Manchester Museum was opened to the public free of charge in 1888. Oxford, Cambridge, Glasgow and Manchester Universities all provided splendid new buildings by distinguished architects for their collections, an indication of their enthusiasm for their museums.

These museums were undoubtedly institutionalized manifestations of the spirit of scientific curiosity and academic inquiry which was such a feature of eighteenth and nineteenth century intellectual life. Nonetheless, their collections, particularly those of the natural sciences, formed an important university teaching resource by the end of the nineteenth century and by this time archaeological and ethnological collections became important in the same way. University museums at Cambridge, Oxford, Glasgow, London and Manchester came to hold some of the most significant collections of botany, entomology, zoology and geology in the country, together with important collections of fine and applied art, British, classical and Egyptian antiquities, ethnology and numismatics. Their collections were of the greatest importance to the pursuit of research both internally within the university and to international scholarship. Elsewhere, university departments concerned with taxonomic studies or with teaching from artefacts and original works of art accumulated collections of appropriate material. Teaching by handling specimens or observing them at close quarters was considered more beneficial than looking at the encased objects during a visit to a national or local municipal museum. Some of these collections, like their more illustrious early-nineteenth century predecessors, became of national importance in addition to providing an essential resource for teaching and research purposes of a highly specialized kind[1].

At the same time it came to be recognized that possession of a valuable art or museum collection endowed a university with a prestigious asset: useful for teaching purposes but also giving the university a sense of patronage of the arts and sciences for the intellectual benefit of its students and staff as well as the general public. When university finance was readily available in the 1960s it seemed natural enough that universities should take over responsibility for private society museums which were falling on hard times, in just the same way that local authorities had rescued the same sort of museum a hundred years earlier. Particularly important examples of this process were at Bath, Manchester, Newcastle and Swansea where potentially impoverished museums[2] with significant collections were given, as it was then thought, secure financial footing backed by government funds channelled through the University Grants Committee and the university system. Other universities acquired or formed collections by negotiations with discerning patrons as at London, Birmingham, Sussex and East Anglia[3] or formed useful art collections such as those at Nottingham, Hull and Liverpool.[4]

In the late 1970s and early 1980s British universities have been subjected to severe financial constriction and the ability of the university system to support museums on the same scale as hitherto must be in question.

Buildings

That universities in the nineteenth century valued their museums greatly is shown by the relatively generous and liberal-minded provision made for some museum buildings. Oxford and Cambridge Universities in the 1840s both employed C. R. Museums (although the design of the latter was actually by G. Basevi). These buildings are of high architectural quality in the classical style of the early-nineteenth century. Equally interesting are the University Museum of Natural Science (1855–1860) at Oxford by Benjamin Woodward and the Manchester Museum (1888) by Alfred J. Waterhouse, which together with the Hunterian Museum (1870) by Giles Gilbert Scott are distinguished and highly individual essays in the Gothic style of the late-nineteenth century.

The latest example of this tradition of employing eminent architects for university museum buildings is at the University of East Anglia at Norwich where the firm of Norman Foster Associates was commissioned to produce a gallery to house the Sainsbury Collection. The resulting Sainsbury Centre for Visual Arts is a building of distinctive design and has received many accolades including a Royal Institute of British Architects (RIBA) award in 1978. More recently the new Hunterian Art Gallery by William Whitfield set a high standard of art gallery design in 1981.

Although there are some architecturally interesting university museum buildings, the majority are now generally inadequate for their purpose. The fundamental problem is financial, for the system of university funding through the University Grants Committee makes it extremely unlikely, even in good times, that funds can be provided from that source for new museum buildings or even the rehabilitation of old ones (Standing Commission, 1977a). Consequently, new buildings have been extremely rare, and where they have arisen finance has come substantially from sources other than the University Grants Committee. At Manchester, for example, a new extension opened in 1977 at a cost of £250 000 was financed by equal grants from the University and the Greater Manchester Council with a relatively small grant from the University Grants Committee for furniture and fittings.

As far as the provision of new buildings is concerned the funding of university museums through the University Grants Committee has been unsatisfactory despite the heroic and expensive efforts of some universities to maintain buildings of considerable historical and architectural merit. The Standing Commission report of 1977 lists a catalogue of inadequacies in both the quantity and quality of university museum buildings. Collections both in store and on display are over-crowded and environmental control in any sophisticated form is rare outside a handful of the larger art galleries.

Administration

The administration of university museums varies greatly. Those which are primarily study collections for the teaching or research needs of a university department are usually administered as an element in that department, which in turn will be part of a faculty of the university. In such a case the administration will probably be under the nominal control of the head of the department, perhaps with the aid of a small committee of his staff. One or more members of the staff, probably with teaching or research interests in taxonomy or in artefacts, will carry out the actual curating. In the majority of such cases the museum as such will probably never report to the governing body of the university and the financial and other needs of the museum will not be identified separately other than within the department concerned.

Most of the larger university museums have boards or committees which report directly or indirectly to the governing body of the university. This is a procedure much favoured by the Museums and Galleries Commission, which as the Standing Commission in its Report on University Museums (1977b) stated:

> A Museums Board should be formally established in each university with museums with the task of identifying clearly the essential needs of university museums in terms of staff, accommodation and facilities, generally, and the best ways of meeting them. Although the precise composition and terms of reference of each Board would depend on the administrative structure of the university concerned, there should as a general rule be local authority representation.

A recent survey by the author has shown that nearly all the university museums which the Standing Commission (1977) identified as having public responsibilities, have boards or committees to manage their affairs. Their construction varies greatly. Frequently, there is a substantial lay element in the committee, derived either from the lay members of the governing body of the university, or from local authorities, learned societies or other museum bodies. The latter is particularly the case, as one would expect, where the university has taken over the responsibilities for running the museum from a private society or as part of a trust to administer the affairs of a benefaction which forms the basis of the museum. In Manchester there is an exceptional situation due to the heavy involvment financially of the Greater Manchester Council (before 1974 the City of Manchester) in the affairs of the Manchester Museum, the Whitworth Art Gallery and the former North Western Museum of Science and Industry.[5] Substantial numbers of local authority elected representatives sit on the committees of these museums but the university retains majority voting rights.

In the majority of university museums administrative, financial and building maintenance services are provided centrally. On any university campus there is much extremely helpful academic and technical advice which a university museum can draw upon both formally and informally. This, together with the excellent library facilities available, can be of the greatest assistance in the running of the museum and in the pursuit of research and interpretative projects.

A survey undertaken for this purpose shows that 20 university museums are members of the Museums Association (although some of these may have membership derived from a common university membership; 22 are members of area museum councils, whereas only 10 are members of regional federations; 7 are members of the International Council of Museums (ICOM) although some of these are probably through personal membership. The relatively high membership of area museum councils, as opposed to regional federations, probably reflects the very reasonable membership terms and an appreciation of the usefulness of area museum council services, particularly in conservation and agency grants, to university museums.

Finance

Generally speaking, a university museum's finance will come from the university, which receives a block grant from the government through the University Grants Committee. The amount of money to be spent on a university museum is not identified in this block grant; indeed, it will probably only be identified within the university accounting system in those cases where the museum has a board or committee responsible to the governing body for estimates and accounts. Even then, some or all of the staff costs may be concealed within the university staff budget, as may also the cost of the administrative, financial and maintenance services provided by the university generally. Some university museums have access to trust funds which may have been provided by benefactors of the university for the benefit of the museum. University museums may also have an easier access to sponsorship funds than their national or local authority colleagues. Commercial and industrial support for both equipment and even staff in universities has long been a perfectly acceptable practice. University museums also have access to the kind of funds available to other museums, such as agency granting through the area museum councils, Victoria and Albert Museum and Science Museum grant-in-aid for specimen purchase and the National Arts Collections Fund. The university financial year runs from August to July inclusive. Because of this discrepancy between the financial year of universities and area museum councils, it is often possible for university museums, if they have any funds at all, to take up agency grant monies unallocated at the end of the local authority financial year. Few university museums charge for admission, notable exceptions being at Bath, Newcastle and Swansea where former private society museums have been taken over by the universities.

The actual costs of running university museums are very difficult to ascertain for much of their financial support is concealed within the general financing of the university. No university museum can be regarded as adequately financed, even by the standards prevailing elsewhere in other types of museums in Britain.

The Museums and Galleries Commission has identified two ways in which the chronic underfunding of university museums might be alleviated. The Commission (1977c) favoured the indication of grants for museums by the University Grants Committee, although the difficulties were recognized. It is easy to understand why the University Grants Committee has resolutely set its face against such a course of action in that it does not wish to interfere with a university's freedom of academic decision as to how it applies its funds. Although in good times it is probably difficult to see how identification of funds could be more beneficial than the university's own benevolent control, the recent cuts in university expenditure have given a new sense of urgency to this problem.

At such a time there is a strong case for the selective implementation of that part of the Drew Report, which suggested that certain university museums should be among those designated as eligible for direct government grant-aid on account of the quality, depth and quantity of their collections and the extent of the areas which they serve (Standing Commission, 1978).

The other course of action advocated by the Commission (1977d) is that there should be local authority financial contributions to university museums which are providing a public service. As has been seen, the only instance of such support on a substantial scale is at Manchester where there is a very significant contribution by the Greater Manchester Council to the running of the Manchester Museum, the Whitworth Art Gallery. In addition, the City of Manchester Education Authority finances the employment of teachers in the Manchester Museum.

Staff

Relatively few university museums have a structured staff system such as might be found in a national or local authority museum. More frequently, curation is the responsibility of one of the academic teaching staff of the department to which the museum is attached. Only the larger institutions have staff occupying posts dignified with the titles of Director, Keeper, Assistant Keeper and so on. Whichever is the case, curatorial staff are most likely to be employed on university grades and conditions of service. Where these posts are regarded as truly academic, staff will be graded in the non-clinical academic teaching grades of Professor, Senior Lecturer or Lecturer (the term Reader implies an academic status between the first two of these and carries no financial implications). Alternatively, other university categories for research and analogous staff, administrative or other related staff may be used; the various grades within these are related to the academic teaching grades and carry the same conditions of service. There is often an unusually long probationary period of up to four years for these posts. University museum technicians will probably be employed on one of the eight technical grades, although one would expect most of the technical work being done in museums to be remunerated in the higher of these eight grades. There are also university grades for secretarial and clerical staff and a structure for porter (attendant) and cleaning staff on the campus.

In general, university museum curatorial staff are highly qualified academically and in some instances the Director holds a professorial chair. Consequently, academic research probably occupies a proportion of the time of staff in university museums which is nearer to that of their colleagues in the national museums than to those in local authority or other museums. This means that only relatively rarely are display and educational work for schools given the prominence they would receive in other museums. Qualified exhibition officers or design and education staff are, therefore, rare.

As one would expect from the underfunding of university museums, staffing at every level of museum activity is generally inadequate to fulfill the museums' functions properly. The Standing Commission report (1977) reveals a catalogue of staffing inadequacies. One can only fear that the recent university cuts will have the effect of reducing staff still further.

Function

If the functions of a museum are to collect and care for collections, to research, interpret and educate, then university museums do not, in essence, differ from other museums. They may, however, be expected to place a different emphasis on these functions; indeed, even among university museums themselves this emphasis differs greatly.

University museum collections form an important part of the nation's museum resources. A brief summary of the more important of these is contained in the Standing Commission report (1977e).[11] Most of the great university natural science collections at Oxford, Cambridge, Manchester and Glasgow were formed during the nineteenth century at the height of the period of taxonomic and systematic collecting. At this time the teaching of the subject was also taxonomic and systematic and these large collections were directly useful within the university for undergraduate teaching and post-graduate research. In the latter half of the twentieth century, teaching in the biological sciences is now dominated more by chemistry, biochemistry, mathematics and statistics. Huge collections of skeletal material, bird skins, insects and herbarium sheets are no longer regarded as absolutely essential to undergraduate teaching although they are useful in certain aspects of that teaching and in giving students the feel of real things. This does not mean that university museum collections have become redundant any more than similar collections existing in national and local authority museums. Large collections of this kind invariably contain substantial numbers of type specimens and these, together with the sheer volume of other specimens, make the collections important for research by museum staff and visiting scholars. They also form the core from which specimens may be selected and displayed in temporary or permanent exhibitions, where the university museum has such a positive public display policy. In such cases it is wrong to speak of 'reserve collections'; there is only one 'collection', some of the specimens from which may be on display. The large natural science collections in university museums do pose huge curatorial problems because of severe understaffing. Some of these museums, notably at Glasgow, Cambridge and Manchester have embraced computerized cataloguing in an attempt to cope with the logistics of information handling arising from the large number of specimens in their collections.

Some university art collections, particularly those of long-standing at Oxford and Cambridge, are important national resources, comparing in quality with the collections in the national institutions, in addition to their use for undergraduate teaching. Art collections such as those at Liverpool, Nottingham and Hull may be used for teaching purposes, but principally supply a cultural and aesthetic quality to university life. Collections of oriental art at Durham and London are an integral part of specific teaching and research schools, as is also the case with the Petrie Collection of Egyptology at University College, London. The Courtauld and Barber Institutes at London and Birmingham respectively have collections of the highest quality which make a significant contribution to the study of fine art and art history in the universities.

Rich archaeological and numismatic collections are contained in the museums at Oxford, Cambridge, Manchester, Glasgow, Newcastle and Bangor. In all these places the collections form an important part of the national resource. In some universities small, but

choice, collections of classical archaeology perform the same teaching and research functions as the art collections mentioned above.

There are highly specialized museum collections in science and technology at Oxford, Cambridge and Manchester, in agriculture at Reading and in musical instruments at Edinburgh.

In many cases university museums will have access to laboratory and workshop facilities in the university to assist in the conservation of their collections. In the case of the natural sciences, such laboratories are likely to be as good, if not better than any museum conservation laboratories and workshops. At Oxford, Cambridge, London, Cardiff, Durham and Bradford the universities support conservation laboratories in art and archaeology for research and teaching purposes. Otherwise only a small number of university museums have specialized conservation facilities and staff, and appreciable use is made of the area museum service for this purpose.

Purchase funds for the acquisition of new exhibits may be found at 13 university museums, although all are of extremely modest amounts in relation to the quality of the collections. All these museums take advantage of grant-aid for specimen purchase, usually from the Victoria and Albert Museum (Royal Scottish Museum in Scotland). An equal number undertake field-work, excavation or natural science collecting for the purpose of adding to the collections. Museums at Oxford, Cambridge, Glasgow, London and Manchester make contributions to such field-work by other bodies, both at home and abroad. Such contributions, in addition to supporting the essential research purpose of the project, also help to assure a controlled influx of documented specimens.

The quality and quantity of research undertaken in university museums is high. The survey of university museums undertaken for this paper shows research to occupy a high priority. In those museums with collections which do nothing more than fulfil basic teaching needs, such research is more likely to be concerned with some aspect of the discipline rather than with the actual specimens in the museum. All academic staff in a university have a responsibility to undertake research and this would apply just as much to full-time curatorial staff in a university museum as to those whose museum duties are more incidental.

All the large, older university museums at Oxford, Cambridge, Glasgow and Manchester have considerable numbers of research projects by the staff under way. One example of this is the Egyptian mummy research programme at the Manchester Museum where the mummified remains of humans and animals in the museum collection have been subjected to exhaustive examination by a team of scientists on the university campus led by the Assistant

Keeper of Archaeology. Up-to-date medical, chemical and physical techniques have been brought to bear upon the specimens and the results have been published (David, 1979). Such a research project could probably only be carried out on a university campus, utilizing the combined knowledge and expertise of a number of university and hospital staff.

Although most university museums assist undergraduates or post-graduate research workers in their tasks, only the Hunterian Museum, the Percival David Foundation of Chinese Art and the Sainsbury Centre for Visual Arts have post-graduate research studentships attached to the museum. It is perhaps a little disappointing to find that more such posts do not seem to be attached to university museums.

Curators in the larger university museum collections play a full part in the wider field of academic research. It is a truism that highly specialized collections such as those in Chinese ceramics at Brighton or London, or in entomology at Oxford or Manchester, are more likely to be used for research by the international scholar than by their local communities. That this is so is supported by the very large numbers of loans despatched to specialized research workers or institutions elsewhere in the UK and abroad recorded at the Hunterian and Manchester Museums.

Some difficulty exists in deciding how far university museums should be the natural resting place for specimens and information gathered by students and staff in the course of the pursuit of higher degrees. Logically there can be little doubt that this ought to be the case, particularly with type or figured specimens, but a lot of material is involved and it is often very difficult to recover it once the thesis has been presented. Many museum workers feel that the accession of such specimens and information, to a museum collection should be an integral part of thesis requirements (Strachan, 1979).

One of the original functions of a university museum was to assist in the teaching of undergraduates. Despite the change of emphasis in university teaching, particularly in the biological sciences, most university museums feel that there is still an important role for them to play in this field. Although the large systematic collections which the older university museums have amassed no longer contribute so significantly to this particular purpose, sections of the collections are still used heavily for teaching purposes. The connection between the departmental geological museum and undergraduate teaching still seems to be strong and the highly specialized collections of Egyptology or oriental art at the University of London or of oriental art at Durham form the basis of academic teaching and research departments. At Manchester University, the Whitworth Art Gallery is used annually for students of the post-graduate Art Gallery and Museum Studies diploma

course for learning the process of mounting a major art exhibition in co-operation with the staff of the gallery and a professional designer. At Manchester also there are instances where university museum staff, who are fully engaged in a curatorial role, lecture to students as part of the curriculum of academic courses. The Pitt Rivers Museum at Oxford is actually a university teaching department as well as a museum, and its staff, together with university lecturers in the museum, provide teaching in ethnology and pre-history for undergraduate courses.

Although most university museums would not refuse organized visits by school children, few provide anything that can be called an educational service for this purpose. The Manchester Museum is exceptional in providing such services which are staffed by qualified teachers, resulting from the long-standing local authority involvement in financing the museum. Together with another education unit at the Manchester City Art Gallery, these services financed by the City of Manchester represent in total one of the largest museum educational projects in this country. The Manchester arrangements may be regarded as the logical outcome of substantial local authority involvement with university museums.

The Hunterian Museum has used a team of three teachers funded by the Manpower Services Commission, and the Ashmolean Museum has recently established a voluntary guide scheme which provides teaching for children of all ages in the galleries and occasionally undertakes some visits to schools.

All museums need to identify the audience with which they are communicating. University museums face the same problem but will have different approaches. Those which are strictly departmental teaching museums will clearly aim their arrangements at the undergraduate student in the department. University museums with a wider brief may not be able to do this. Even where a museum is primarily for the benefit of a campus population, probably running into several thousands of staff and students, the great majority of its visitors will inevitably be non-specialists in any particular part of the museum collection. Where a museum has to fulfil a public role as well, the relative number of non-specialist vistors will be greater still. In these cases it would not be justifiable for, say, undergraduate level zoology displays to be provided for the benefit of, at most a few hundred zoology students, when these could not be comprehended by undergraduates in other subjects, let alone the general public. Galleries of fine art may not feel the dilemma to the same extent.

Nonetheless university museums have a duty to provide for the teaching of students. One solution proposed for doing this in their displays involves two levels of presentation, one for the general public and one for the undergraduate (Seyd, 1970). This has much merit, particularly if the physical arrangements are designed to keep the displays separate but capable of easy cross-reference within the same gallery or even within the same case. It is a solution, however, which demands fairly expensive and resourceful design if it is to be done well. Otherwise an essentially public display might be preferred leaving any undergraduate teaching arrangements to be negotiated specifically between the curator, the lecturer and the students to take place in study rooms or parts of stores made over for this purpose.

Whatever may be the preferred solution, university museum displays are more likely to contain larger numbers of objects and larger amounts of information than those of most other types of museum and this is probably useful in counteracting different trends in other kinds of museum. Only the Manchester Museum and the Hunterian Museum have design officers. The Whitworth Art Gallery and the Sainsbury Centre for Visual Arts have exhibition officers.

A surprisingly high number of university museums have temporary exhibition programmes, most of which are achieved on very small budgets. A small number of university museums provide material for other bodies such as the Arts Council or the Area Museum Councils to circulate. At the Manchester Museum exhibitions are produced specifically to circulate to institutions in Greater Manchester and this scheme, together with one for the circulation of about fifty single case exhibits, is financed by the Metropolitan County. Some of the Manchester exhibitions have been shown beyond the region not only in the UK but also overseas.

Most university museums welcoming public visits provide a point of sale for museum publications, but only at the Fitzwilliam Museum is this done by an independent company. Many universities have a University Press and the expertise and facilities, particularly in dealing with printers and marketing, may be helpful to university museums in their more scholarly publications. About twenty university museums organize lectures, thus fulfilling an important role for campus staff and students as well as for the general public. Eight university museums, mostly art galleries, have Friends' organizations and that at the Fitzwilliam Museum is the oldest in the country.

Conclusion

This brief survey of university museums presents both a heartening and disturbing picture. We may marvel that a small number of Britain's universities has successfully nurtured some of the country's most significant collections and enabled them to survive intact into the last quarter of the twentieth century.

This is an act of dedicated responsibility to academic scholarship and to the public of this country. Around the 1960s universities came to the rescue of several museums which were in straitened circumstances. Several distinguished collections might well have suffered seriously at this time but for the responsibility shown by the British university system. Many universities have recognized that an art gallery or museum can be a civilizing influence on the university campus and have formed discreet collections for the benefit of the cultural life of the considerable campus population of staff and students. And all the time universities have provided, where appropriate, collections to be used for undergraduate teaching and post-graduate research. All this has been done from the money allocated to the universities' main functions of teaching and research.

The Museums and Galleries Commission has repeatedly warned that all is not well with the mechanics of providing for the welfare of this particular part of the national heritage. While universities were expanding and financial problems seemed hardly to exist, university museums fared not too badly. Now that the financial screw has been vigorously tightened, university museums find themselves competing for funds in a contracting financial situation. No university administration can protect its museum from the same sort of financial cuts which the teaching and research departments of that university are currently bearing. As a result university museum provision is now being cut back at a harsher rate than any other form of museum service.

The money for national museums and university museums is provided directly or indirectly by government. There would seem, therefore, to be a strong case for making arrangements that at least the larger university museums with wide public obligations should be the direct financial responsibility of government. Probably only in this way will university museums be able to continue their contribution to the framework for the system of museums in this country.

Notes

[1] Other university museums founded in the nineteenth or early-twentieth centuries include: the Pitt Rivers Museum (1883), and the University Museum (1853) at Oxford; the Museum of Archaeology and Ethnology (1883), the Museum of Classical Archaeology (1884) at Cambridge; the Anthropological Museum, Marischal College, Aberdeen (1907); the Department of Geological Sciences Museum. Birmingham (1906); the Cockburn Museum, Department of Geology, Edinburgh (1908, with earlier ancestors); Kings College Geology Department Museum (1830); University College Museum of Egyptology (the Petrie Collection), London (1913); University College of Wales, Museum and Art Collections, Aberystwyth

(1872); School of Animal Biology, University College of North Wales, Bangor (1900).

2 The Holburne of Menstrie Museum, Bath University (1973); the Whitworth Art Gallery, Manchester University (1958); The Hancock Museum and the Museum of the Society of Antiquaries of Newcastle-upon-Tyne, Newcastle University (1958 and 1960 respectively); the Royal Institution of South Wales Museum, University College of Swansea (1973).

3 The Courtauld Institute of Art (1931) and the Percival David Foundation of Chinese Art, London University, (1951); the Barber Institute of Fine Arts, Birmingham University (1939); the Barlow Collection of Chinese Ceramics, Bronzes and Jades, Sussex University (1974); the Sainsbury Centre for Visual Arts, University of East Anglia (1978).

4 University Art Gallery, Nottingham University (1936); Hull University Art Collection, Hull University (1963); University Art Gallery, Liverpool University (1977).

5 In 1983 the North Western Museum of Science and Industry became the Greater Manchester Museum of Science and Industry. The Museum is now managed by an independent Trust on which the Greater Manchester Council has substantial representation. It is no longer a university museum, but the Trustees include representation of the University of Manchester and Salford and the University of Manchester Institute of Science and Technology.

References

DAVID, A. R. (1979) (Ed), *The Manchester Museum mummy research project,* Manchester Museum

SEYD, E. L. (1970), A university museum and the general public, *Museums J.,* **70**(4), 180–182

STANDING COMMISSION ON MUSEUMS AND GALLERIES (1977a), *Report on university museums,* para 12, HMSO, London

STANDING COMMISSION ON MUSEUMS AND GALLERIES (1977b), *Report on university museums,* paras 24–29 and 127(c), HMSO, London

STANDING COMMISSION ON MUSEUMS AND GALLERIES (1977c), *Report on university museums,* para 23, HMSO, London

STANDING COMMISSION ON MUSEUMS AND GALLERIES (1977d), *Report on university museums,* para 109, HMSO, London

STANDING COMMISSION ON MUSEUMS AND GALLERIES (1977e), *Report on university museums,* pp. 31–39, HMSO, London

STANDING COMMISSION ON MUSEUMS AND GALLERIES (1978), *Framework for a system for museums,* paras, 6.1 and 6.5, HMSO, London

STRACHAN, I. (1979), 'Palaeontological collections and the role of university museums' in Bassett, M. G. (Ed.), 'Curation of Palaeontological collections', *Special papers in Palaeontology,* **22**, 70 and 73–74, The Palaeontological Association

9

Independent museums

Neil Cossons

There are, and always have been, a substantial number of museums in Britain outside the established pattern of funding and management which for many years has consisted of two main groups, both financed almost entirely from public funds. The national museums derive their income in the main from central government, although it reaches them through a variety of channels. Local authority museums are run and funded by local government, usually through committees of district or county councils. Outside these two major groups are, for example, university museums, most regimental museums, and what in recent years have come to be called independent museums. This last group are considered in this chapter. There are thought to be about 1500 independent museums in Britain.

A crude definition of independent museums might be those which are not administered directly by any central or local government agency or authority. Within this group there is a wide variety of constitutional framework ranging from unincorporated societies and associations to charitable companies, and from those which have significant public authority financial support to others which receive little or none.

Although since the mid-1960s there has been a rapid growth in the number of independent museums, the concept of a museum run by a society, club or other group of interested people dates back many years. Indeed, many of the great collections now held by public authorities, and some of the buildings that house them, have their origins in the activities of literary and philosophical societies, scientific, archaeological or natural history societies and gentlemen's clubs which, if they were still being run in this way today, would certainly place them in the category of independent museums. Similarly, the basic curatorial divisions which characterize so many multi-disciplinary museums, derive from the nature

of the collections formed by these societies and the interests of the gifted amateurs who so frequently made up their membership. In short, the familiar pattern of public authority museums in Britain owes much to the way in which this first generation of 'independent' museums grew up, reflecting as they did the needs of contemporary society for popular learning and for a point of contact with the new discoveries of science and exploration. The history of many of these societies is well documented (Lowe, 1923; Walden, 1960; Boylan, 1982). A few still exist in more or less their original form – for example, the Museum of Sussex Archaeology at Lewes set up in the 1840s by the Sussex Archaeological Society – although more frequently their collections and buildings have become wholly integrated into local authority museum services. A few still retain an independent identity with a governing body consisting of representatives of the society and elected member nominees of the local authority.

In many cases a large part of the funding comes from the local authority. For example, the Torquay Natural History Society's Museum was established in 1844 and is still run by the Society in the museum which it built in 1874. Torbay Borough Council is represented on the Executive Committee and makes a substantial contribution towards operating costs. Similarly, the Devizes Museum run by the Wiltshire Archaeological & Natural History Society and the Salisbury & South Wiltshire Museum run by its own independent Council of Management (set up with charitable status in 1969 to replace the original governing body of 1860) both receive grants from Wiltshire County Council that are related in general terms to their curatorial and administrative salary costs. In the case of Salisbury the district council also makes an *ad hoc* contribution while the Kennet District Council supports Devizes. The Dorset County Museum, run by the Dorset Natural History and

84

Archaeological Society is still almost wholly independent although it enjoys a grant from the county council more or less equivalent to salary costs. The Yorkshire Museum on the other hand, set up by the Yorkshire Philosophical Society in 1825 passed to the local authority in 1960 and is now wholly run by the North Yorkshire Councy Council although the Society still has three members on the museum committee and makes a nominal contribution towards costs.

The reasons for the demise of these society museums in their original forms are not hard to see. Dedicated, sometimes as a matter of principle, to the concept of free admission, they were largely dependent on the subscriptions of their membership, sometimes supported by endowments. Neither source of income proved sufficient to sustain them for long after the first generation of members and, with increasing costs of maintaining collections and more particularly their museum buildings, the only solution was for them to be taken over by the local authority or form a partnership with it. It is not insignificant that all the examples cited above charge admission to their visitors.

In the early 1960s it would have been reasonable to assume that these early society museums formed part of the transitional, formative phase of museum development in this country; a phase that had been superseded by a more formalized local authority-based structure of museums providing a service to the population of their respective localities. In the long term this assumption may still prove to be correct. However, the last twenty years have seen sharp changes in attitude on the part of the public towards the sort of material for which museums have traditionally cared. Rapid changes in the landscape as the result of urban and industrial renewal and new farming technology, increased wealth, leisure and mobility, the impact of good quality documentary television with good coverage of archaeology and natural history, are just some of the factors that have combined to create an attitude of awareness and a sensitivity towards environment and place which had not previously existed at a popular level. Many of the new museums of the last 20 years are part of the response to this awareness; but while some have grown out of existing local authority museum organizations others are completely new, founded in the main by groups of people whose interest and enthusiasm has led them to form new independent bodies specifically to create and run museums. In this last respect they differ from most of their nineteenth-century predecessors, for in these earlier examples the museum often represented only one of a number of activities which they had been set up to pursue and today, free of their museum responsibilities, many of these societies successfully continue their programmes of lectures and visits and the publication of their transactions.

It is also important to appreciate that this new museum movement is only one facet of the broader-based environmental conservation interests that have developed so actively in the same period. A strong desire to participate, by active engagement in the processes of environmental conservation, or more passively by joining a conservation organization, has led to a rapid expansion in many membership-based conservation bodies at both national and regional level. The National Trust, with over one million members, is now one of the largest conservation bodies in the world, while on a smaller scale innumerable voluntary preservation groups, civic societies, nature conservation trusts and museums have sprung up anxious to protect historic town centres or endangered species, excavate archaeological sites in advance of motorway construction, revive derelict canals or save steam pumping stations from destruction.

The larger, new independent museums that have grown out of this broader environmental conservation movement have a number of characteristics in common:

(1) They frequently reflect new popular interests of people in subject areas that have not, generally speaking, been covered by traditional museums or for which no existing museum could or would assume responsibility. Industrial archaeology, transport history, vernacular architecture and building preservation – often *in-situ* – are some of the themes they embrace. Most of them are in fact thematic rather than multi-disciplinary museums.
(2) These people have the motivation and enthusiasm to set up and in many cases run a museum themselves, although almost invariably there is a nucleus of paid professional staff.
(3) Most of these museums are charitable trusts and many are non-profit companies, that is, companies limited by guarantee and not having a share capital.
(4) They raise their capital by fund-raising aimed at both public and private sector sources.
(5) They are substantially or, in some cases, completely self-supporting on their revenue accounts. This is achieved in the main by charging the visitor for admission.
(6) They tend, of necessity, to be strongly market-oriented.
(7) They are often outside large urban areas with existing mueums services.

Many of these new museums have developed what might be called their product around a readily identifiable market of relatively affluent and mobile people. Significant reductions in the real cost of petrol have contributed towards this (Shell UK, 1981). Numbers of visitors to all types of attractions – museums represent about a third of the visitor market in Britain – have risen spectacularly since 1955, reaching a peak in 1978. Since then there has been something of a reduction to both free and charge-admission museums.[1] Over the same quarter century or so the number of cars on the roads grew from three million to fifteen million. In other words, a new type of museum has become possible which could not have readily existed before. Independent museums are in part a product of this new museum-going public – there are some 60 million visits to museums in Britain each year. Their influence however, particularly on the public conception of what a museum is – or can be – has been out of all proportion to their size, their numbers and their budgets. This has been in part because of the nature of their product and in part because they have needed to market themselves energetically and sometimes quite competitively in order to develop.

It would be wrong, however, to regard these new, market-oriented, charge-admission museums as setting the universal pattern for museums in the future. On the contrary, while one set of social and economic circumstances has created conditions for the growth and development of the independent museums movement, long-established public authority museums, often based in urban areas, have responded to different pressures. Clearly, while public authority and independent sectors have much to learn from each other it is reasonable to assume that they can fulfil a fruitful and complementary relationship in the future.

However, one gap has not been filled adequately by the large, independent museums any more than it has by traditional public authority museums. The need of local communities, often of very small size, to see evidence of their own history collected and preserved in their own local museum has become a strong one. Thus, of the 1495 museums surveyed by the Association of Independent Museums[2] the largest single group – 215 museums – consists of local history museums, most of which are very small, of relatively recent origin, and set up by local history societies or groups of enthusiasts. This desire by local communities to have their own museum which they are prepared to run themselves at little or no cost and usually on an entirely voluntary basis is clearly a strong one and the 'official' museum world has not and perhaps cannot satisfy demand in this area. The people who set up these museums are collecting, primarily for themselves, material which reflects their own need to identify with the place in which they live and the evidence of its history. They are not necessarily interested in visitors as such, and have little interest in the tourist market which sustains larger independent museums. But they must not be dismissed out of hand as they are repeating in their own way the same basic motives which, for more than two hundred years, have led to the establishment of collections and out of which have grown many of the great museums with which we are familiar today. What makes them distinctive,

however, is the fact that they have this extremely local value and meaning, that they involve the participation of a group within the community in the curatorship of its own past, and that they are entirely voluntary in nature. A clear distinction needs to be made between these *voluntary* museums and the bigger independent museums and public authority museums in which *volunteers* often work.

A further and important new strain of museum is a direct product of the rapid changes which are taking place in the industrial landscape. 'Industrial Archaeology' as a term was coined in Britain in the mid-1950s (Rix, 1955) when a few people began to recognize that the replacement of old technologies with new and the desire to sweep away the unattractive remains of past industrial activity was at the same time eliminating the evidence of an important cultural phenomenon of world significance. In the eighteenth century, Britain had become the world's first industrial nation, in the nineteenth the 'workshop of the world'. Some 70 per cent of the built environment of Britain dates from the period of the Industrial Revolution and in the 1950s it was still possible to identify within that environment many of the key monuments of that period. In more recent years, the decline throughout Europe of many of the traditional coal, steam and iron-based industries has had its most dramatic impact in the old industrial heartlands of Britain, presenting a wholly new set of economic circumstances and a rate of social change unknown for nearly two hundred years. An environment within which people can begin to contemplate a 'post-industrial society' has important and fascinating implications for museums and, perhaps more importantly, for the processes of curatorship. Many of the new independent museums are museums of industrial archaeology concerned with the preservation *in-situ* of industrial sites and monuments, and the machinery which they contain, or the preservation of industrial buildings which are being used for more traditional museum purposes. The new farm and rural museum movement, which has emerged still more recently, is again a reflection of the changes which have taken place in the agricultural landscape, not only as the result of new technologies, but in response to a large-scale interest in the countryside and country pursuits on the part of increasingly reluctant urban dwellers.

The scale of this problem of de-industrialization in curatorial terms is enormous, but although industrial archaeology is still in its infancy there is ample evidence to indicate that new, and often ingenious, solutions are being found to cope with sites and artefacts of great scale and complexity. Some museums, such as Ironbridge, have set out to preserve whole areas of past industrial activity, others have developed along the lines of more traditional open-air museums in which industrial buildings and artefacts have been reconstructed in special sites laid aside for them. The Black Country Museum in the West Midlands is an example. More frequently, however, industrial archaeological conservation has centred around the preservation *in-situ* of specific industrial sites, on many of which working activity and in some cases manufacturing is an important part of the conservation, interpretation and marketing formula. Working wind and water-mills abound, beam pumping engines have been preserved at, for example, Crofton in Wiltshire, Kew Bridge in London and Ryhope, Sunderland, a water-powered scythe works is regularly demonstrated at Sticklepath in Devon, Styal Mill in Cheshire is being developed as a textile museum while at Chatterley Whitfield near Stoke-on-Trent, the first mine in Britain to produce a million tons of coal a year, which closed in 1976, has been opened to the public who can descend below ground in the cage and walk through the preserved workings. It would be wrong to assume that these new industrial archaeological museums have been confined to the independent sector; rather an independent body, purpose-built for the project and adapted specifically to its funding and management requirements, has in many cases been the best means of achieving the objective.

The constitutional framework within which any museum operates must ensure that its collections are, as far as possible, safeguarded. In this respect, many small, independent museums have unsatisfactory constitutions as they are unincorporated societies which do not have charitable status. Thus the fate of the collections is entirely in the hands of those individuals who form the membership or governing body. The best form of protection that an independent museum can afford its collection is through the medium of charitable status. A charity, for the purposes of the *Charities Act 1960*, means any institution which is established exclusively for charitable purposes and these must satisfy the essential tests of altruism and public benefit required of all charities. There is no statutory definition or test by which it can be decided if any particular purpose is charitable in law, but the provision of a museum has been held to be a charitable purpose, constituting a public amenity with an associated educational advantage to the public to be derived from it. In England and Wales, each museum must satisfy the Charity Commission[3] that its particular purpose is charitable and details of each scheme are considered in detail by the Charity Commissioners and a decision is made on the merits of each case. The Commissioners liase with the Inland Revenue in considering an application for charitable status. In Scotland, where there are no Charity Commissioners, a test of charitable status must satisfy the Inland Revenue.

A museum must make an application for charitable status whether it is a trust or any other undertaking and whether it is corporate or not. If a corporate structure is used, the company will usually be one limited by guarantee not having a share capital, rather than a company limited by shares. Alternatively, the institution in question may be a trust formed by a Declaration of Trust or it may be an unincorporated association. Often it is useful for an unincorporated association to provide in its constitution for a trust to hold its property, and equally it may be useful to graft a set of rules or constitution for the running of the trust on to the basic Declaration of Trust. There is great flexibility available in the variety of structures which can be developed and it is advisable therefore to obtain professional advice in order to achieve the most advantageous form. The Association of Independent Museums have published a Guideline, *Charitable Status for Museums*[4], which outlines the advantages and disadvantages of various types of structure and provides a model Declaration of Trust for a charity and model Memorandum and Articles of Association for a company limited by guarantee and not having a share capital. These models have been approved as drafts by the Charity Commission.

The essential pre-requisite of a museum which has any serious intent is that it should have charitable status in order to protect as far as possible the inalienability of its collections. Typically, a Declaration of Trust ensures that the collections can only be disposed of under such terms as the trustees may think fit, provided that any such disposal shall be made only for the purposes of improving, enhancing or extending the quality of the collection and in furtherance of the objects of the charity, and providing that any such item is offered first to another charitable institution, museum, school, college or university or other appropriate body by gift, exchange or private sale before it is offered to the public at large. This gives some flexibility to the trustees in order to enable them to dispose of items in appropriate circumstances although strictly speaking it runs contrary to the object of preserving the collection. However, by defining the Trust Fund – that is the collections and all other assets held by the trustees – as a variable fund some discretion can be afforded to the trustees. Without this the specific authority of the Charity Commission would be required for any disposal.

Even this may have its weaknesses, however, in the event of the museum, whether an unincorporated charity or a charitable company, being wound up through insolvency, as one of the duties of the liquidator would be to meet the debts of the institution and the collections, unless specifically protected, may be liable to be disposed of in the same way as any other assets. This can be avoided by ensuring that the collections are held under a separate Declaration of Trust from the other assets of the institution

and that the trustees have the power to loan the collections to the 'parent' institution. The loan arrangements must be set out in an agreement between the
two bodies in order to regulate responsibilities for
maintenance, conservation, insurance and inspection
and to specify the events giving rise to termination of
the loan through receivership or liquidation. Thus,
the parent institution can hold land, property and
other assets and, provided that these are not held in
pursuance of any charitable objectives, they are available for securing mortgages, debentures and other
charges. In the case of, for example, a site museum
or open-air museum where the land and buildings on
it may form a part of the collections then these too
would need to be held under the separate Declaration
of Trust outlined above.

Charitable status, although without the necessity
for a separate Declaration of Trust, is a pre-requisite
for independent museum membership of the area
museums councils and for receipt of grant-in-aid
funds from the Science Museum or Victoria and
Albert Museum. In the case of the Association of
Independent Museums, the main category of membership is for museums which are controlled by or
registered as charitable trusts or satisfy other acceptable tests of charitable status. Although the Association accepts non-charitable independent museums as
category B members it offers strong encouragement
to them to gain charitable status.

In all but the smallest museums it is usually advantageous to be incorporated as a limited company,
although whether or not the body is incorporated,
the persons responsible for the administration and
management of the charity will have the duties and
liabilities of charity trustees. The main advantages of
incorporation are that the company will have a legal
entity separate from its members, may hold assets in
its corporate name and enter into contracts in its own
name. Liability of members is limited in the event of
winding up to their guarantee sum which is usually
£1. The overall structure of a company limited by
guarantee is the same as that of a company limited by
shares and it is a generally convenient way of allowing members to participate in a venture with ultimate
responsiblity while leaving day-to-day management
in the hands of a board of directors. The disadvantages of incorporation are that registration and
annual running costs are involved and that the terms
of the Companies Acts must be complied with in
respect, for example, of keeping annual returns and
accounts.

The format of a company limited by guarantee not
having a share capital and registered as a charitable
trust has thus become the most popular for all but the
smallest independent museums. In fact, many of
these companies have opted for charitable status for
reasons other than the degree of protection that may
be afforded to their collections. Charities have a

number of fiscal privileges, one of the most important being the almost complete exemption from
income and corporation tax provided the funds are
applied for charitable purposes only and, usually
more importantly, they may in appropriate circumstances reclaim tax against gifts from individuals
and companies providing a binding agreement – a
covenant – has been attached to that gift. There are
important advantages too in relation to capital gains
tax and capital transfer tax; charities are statutorily
eligible for 50 per cent rate relief (the other 50 per
cent is at the discretion of the local authority) and
there are numerous other minor benefits. Where a
charity's trading activities, as is often the case with a
museum shop for example, cannot be classed as
'occasional fund-raising through trading' and would
therefore be free of tax on the profits, the tax may be
reduced by forming a special trading company,
usually as a wholly-owned share-capital subsidiary
which covenants its profits back to the parent
charity.

Most of the new independent museums find charitable company status an admirable framework for
their management, fund-raising and trading activities. An independent museum constituted in this
manner lies within the public domain to the extent
that it must control its affairs in a responsible manner
and that its activities are for the public good. The
term 'private museum' is thus an inappropriate one.
At the same time, its independent status can prove
attractive to a potential donor, trustee, or other participant in its affairs who can readily identify with its
objectives and perhaps have some active involvement in its work. Indeed, a number of charitable
company museums have set up parallel 'development trusts' not only as a convenient management
framework within which to raise capital or other
funds for the museum but as a mechanism for providing involvement in and identity with the affairs of
the institution as a whole. The first process, therefore, of a development trust is the enlistment of support which in due course may be translated into a
continuing flow of donations usually and preferably
in the form of convenanted gifts. One of the claimed
responsibilities of development trusts is that they
protect the interests of the donors by ensuring that
their gifts are spent on the projects for which they
were intended. It must be pointed out, however, that
the development trust formula, which may or may
not have advantages, represents only one point of
view in the complex world of fund-raising, and any
museum contemplating a major capital-raising programme is well advised to examine as many techniques as possible, and consult several professional
fund-raising organizations before embarking on a
particular course of action.

The charitable company museum structure can
have a number of attractions to public bodies and

what might be called a second generation of new independent museums have been set up by local authorities. The Black Country Museum, for example, has been detached from the departmental responsibilities of the Metropolitan District Council of Dudley and set up as a charitable company. Similarly, in 1978 Torfaen Borough Council in Gwent transferred its museum and heritage functions to the then newly-incorporated Torfaen Museum Trust Ltd[5] including the existing Pontypool Museum Project. Again, the benefits to a public authority of quasi-independent status require careful analysis but they may be summarized as follows:

(1) The active participation and commitment of a broad spectrum of the local community in the running of the museum can be generated through the membership of the governing body. For example, whereas elected councillors normally form the sole membership of a local authority committee, in a charitable company museum trustees can be drawn from academic, industrial, business or trade union circles.

(2) Fund raising in the private sector may be easier when the museum is seen not to be a department of a local authority.

(3) Where a partnership of several disparate authorities – for example, a district and county council, university or learned society – needs some formal organization in order to participate together in the running of a museum, then the charitable company may be a convenient format for funding, management and employment of staff, (The trust formed in 1982 to administer the Greater Manchester Museum of Science and Industry is an example of this).

Whether or not there are operational advantages in a public authority placing its museum responsibilities in the hands of a 'quango' (Cossons, 1976) is, of course, open to debate and it may be many decades before a clear picture emerges. While some would argue that the structure of government or local government is inappropriate to run museums (the same argument applies to the performing arts) and that museums need their own governing bodies of highly committed people drawn from all walks of life, others would say that to separate museums from the seat of political power and source of funding will in the long term be disadvantageous. What is undoubtedly true, however, is that independent museums have blossomed in the last twenty years as a reflection of a wide variety of needs within society. They have emerged spontaneously, without prompting by any of the governmental or other agencies who would seek to regulate museums on a national or regional basis, and they have, by virtue of the nature of their product and market awareness, had a significant impact on the public's interpretation of the word 'museum'. There is little doubt that the best can and indeed do achieve standards of scholarship and curatorship at least as good as those of more conventional museums; by the same token the

not-so-good, as in the public sector, can fall far short of the desirable standard but in so doing are much more vulnerable to closure as a result of loosing their markets.

Trends for the future are difficult to detect but radical rethinking of capital funding of independent museums will undoubtedly take place, with new relationships between trusts and their trading companies being devised so that loan capital can be more effectively injected. Similarly, the strong market orientation of independent museums will push them further in the direction of providing facilities for the family unit – as opposed to the individual member of a family – with increased opportunity for participation in the work of the museum. Membership may become the most important growth point for some of them and it is by no means far-fetched to envisage a museum in which the largest single element of revenue income is made up of the annual subscriptions of its members with visitor admission charges forming a secondary source. Although those members may not be motivated by the same enthusiasms as their predecessors of two centuries ago their will and ability to participate will be equally important. Above all, museums will stand or fall not only by their competence to manage collections but their ability to care for people.

Notes

[1] The best statistical survey for England is the *English Heritage Monitor* published annually by the English Tourist Board, 4 Grosvenor Gardens, London SW1N 0DU.

[2] The Association of Independent Museums (AIM) was established in 1978 to represent the interests of independent museums in the United Kingdom and the Republic of Ireland. It publishes a quarterly *Bulletin* and a series of *Guidelines* on topics particularly relevant to independent museums and holds seminars on aspects of museum management.

[3] The address of the Charity Commission is 14 Ryder Street, St James, London SW1Y 6AH.

[4] Association of Independent Museums, 1981, Guideline No. 3 *Charitable Status for Museums*. This covers England and Wales and contains comments relating to the Isle of Man, the Channel Islands and Northern Ireland. A separate AIM publication, *Charitable Status for Museums/Scotland* offers guidance to museums seeking charitable status in Scotland. Advice is also available from the Council for Museums and Galleries in Scotland, County House, 20–22 Torphicen Street, Edinburgh, EH3 8JB. It offers guidance for museums seeking charitable status.

[5] For those finding use of the term 'limited' distasteful in relationship to a charitable company, under Section 25 of the *Companies Act 1981* there is provision for it to be omitted, where a statutory declaration has been filed with the Registrar of Companies stating that this company is one operating in conformity with the provision of that Section.

References

BOYLAN, P. J. (1982), 'Why Museums?', *Transactions of the Leicester Literary and Philosophical Society*, **76**, 1–24

COSSONS, N. (1976), 'The Case for the Cultural Quango', *Museums Association Conference Proceedings, 1976*, 26–27, The Museums Assocation, London

LOWE, E. E. (1923), 'The Society and the Museum', *Transactions of the Leicester Literary and Philosophical Society*, **24** 5–20

SHELL UK (1981), *Report on Shell Shareholders' Meeting*, Shell UK, 4–6

RIX, M. M. (1955), 'Industrial Archaeology', *Amateur Historian*, **2**, 225–229

WALDEN, T. A. (1960), 'Address by the President', *Transactions of the Leicester Literary and Philosophical Society*, **54**, 5–13

10

Small museums

Geoffrey T. Denford, Elizabeth R. Lewis, David J. Viner

There is no easy definition of a small museum, although no one studying the pages of *Museums Year-book* would be in any doubt that a great many – and a wide variety – of museums exist which might be classified in this way. Furthermore, there exist a large number of small museums which are not listed in the *Yearbook*. Many of these museums have no professional staff and, thus, a major difficulty in undertaking a study of such museums lies in obtaining relevant data. Such establishments (*Figure 10.1*) highlight the disparity between the professional's use of the word 'museum' (see, e.g. ICOM, 1974 or the Museums Association, 1983) and its more common usage.

A number of points of definition arise. The first must be the physical size of the building housing a museum and the floor areas available for display, storage and the preservation of the collections. This is, of course, a widely varying factor, from a few hundred square feet housing all the museum's actual functions in the building, as at Hythe in Kent, where 87m² (940 square feet) constitutes the Local History Room's displays and storage areas (Millard and Kent, 1980), through to rather larger areas, for example, 372m² (4000 square feet) at the Street Shoe Museum (Dyer, 1974), up to perhaps 929m² (10 000 square feet) as a working maximum figure for a small museum.

Other significant factors in definition include the staffing and budget levels applicable to a small museum, whatever its framework of operation and organization. Variations will, thus, be considerable and an analysis of these form part of the discussions advanced elsewhere in this manual. Although Doughty (1970, p. 19) suggested that a small museum is one employing fewer than four professional staff, there might be endless debate as to the point in staffing levels beyond which a museum ceases to be 'small' and a figure of even three or four

permanent, full-time staff would probably grossly over-balance the averages which typify the majority of small museums. Thus a curator at, for example, the Shirehall Museum at Little Walsingham in Norfolk (a small museum by any standards) has other duties within the county's museum service to which his museum belongs and it is arguable that a full-time post might not otherwise be possible at such a venue. Accepting this point, it should be noted that the 1982 *Yearbook* lists about 220 museums with full-time curatorial staff of no more than two, and that this forms 18 per cent of the total individual museum entries listed.

Equally significant are budget levels – which vary widely and require a more detailed assessment than is possible here – and the associated study of the range and nature of the controlling authorities. The latter would offer variations almost as wide as the types of museums themselves and it would be noted how significant is the balance between local authority museums and those in the private sector.

As a group, small museums might be regarded as essentially a small-town phenomenon; the gathering together of the local history of a community in a predominantly parochial way, without regard to the wider view. This is a narrow view which disregards the many small specialized museums (see Doughty, 1970, p. 20) as well as much of the strength of character of smaller museums and the developments in them which have been such a feature in recent years.

Growth

Correspondence between the Museums Assocation or, for example, the Area Museum Service for South-East England (AMSSEE), and individuals and groups seeking to establish their own museums indicates that their numbers are mushrooming. That there has been a rapid growth in numbers of

Figure 10.1 Potter's Museum of Curiosity, Arundel, West Sussex

museums, particularly in post-war years, can easily be demonstrated: in 1955 the *Museums Calendar* records 837 museums in Britain while, by 1982, 1330 are listed in the *Museums Yearbook*. These figures do not include the small, independent museums, data on which is difficult to gather: as Norgate (1980, p. 104) has pointed out, 'there is no reliable list of museums in the United Kingdom and there are more small private museums than some of us imagine or would admit to.' The Association of Independent Museums (AIM) estimates that there are about 1300 independent museums in Britain (personal communication to G.T.D.). Many of these are small museums by any standard.

What are the reasons for this growth? One factor must be the accelerating rate of change in society generally (Singleton, 1979, p. 11; Thompson, 1970, pp. 25–29) and, in particular, technological change (Foster, 1979, pp. 54–55). This has led to a search for 'roots'; a search for identity that has become manifest in the growing interest for and concern in the local environment (Bott, 1979, p. 1)[1]. Atkinson and Holton (1973, p. 140) note a recent rash of plans to set up a wide variety of open-air and folk museums and

comment on how 'such museums have caught the interest and imagination of a wide cross-section of the ordinary people of this country, who perhaps have a greater latent interest in how their own forbears lived and worked than in the tribes of distant lands'.

Types of small museums

There are many different kinds of small museum. Numerous examples of local societies, with their own small museums, could be quoted. The Frome Society for Local Study is one such example. Founded in 1958, it covers local history, archaeology, architecture, natural history and geology and, since 1966, has run Frome Museum with collections that reflect the aims of the Society (Biannual *Bulletin of the Wiltshire Archaeological and Natural History Society*, No. 13, September 1972). Another, the Bishop's Waltham Museum Society, which has yet to open its museum, nevertheless has clear aims[2]. Many small museums, however, are long-established. Various factors have compelled them to re-examine and redefine their role and many have formulated collecting policies which concentrate on the local area. This aspect of museums – their changing role – is crucial to any consideration of the development of small museums, for as their role changes, so does their philosophy (Foster, 1979, pp. 54–57; Singleton, 1979, pp. 11–12). One example is provided by Bott (1979): the Bruce Castle Museum, Tottenham. Established in 1906, it originally attempted to cover the entire history of the world in its displays. Today it concentrates on the history of the area covered by the London Borough of Haringey. Increased interest in, and concern for, the environment has been fostered in recent years by the popularization of subjects like natural history and archaeology. Television is held to have had a considerable effect here (Wright, 1973, p. 6).

For other museums, the preservation of a specific purpose and locally oriented collection is a prime concern, as at the company-formed and owned Street Shoe Museum in Somerset. Its collection is unique to its specific environment and is, therefore, highly significant to the history of the particular community in which it is displayed. The problems of volume in relation to display area (Dyer, 1974) are relatively minor in comparison with the difficulties which many smaller local history museums face when attempting to cater for the whole gamut of social history material. There are few better published examples of this than the history and development of the Tiverton Museum in Devon (Authers, 1976 and Jenkins, 1976). In little more than two decades, a virtual torrent of material has been gathered by a small, voluntary group of local enthusiasts, creating immediate problems of storage and display and the greater, and arguably more significant problem, of long-term care and conservation of the collected material. Early weaknesses in the approach to collecting are acknowledged, to which the purist response might well be one of criticism of aims as well as methods. However, without doubt the difficulties faced at Tiverton, and which have not yet been overcome, are those which have confronted a great many smaller museums over the years as the role of the museum and its ability to cope have been critically examined. There are also an unknown number of small museums which belong to and are run by individuals, for example, the Heathcote Museum at Birchover or the Military Heritage Museum at Lewes, where 'Butler has gone on collecting . . . to the point where he has attained the sub-species ideal – his own museum' (Ritchie, 1982). Lambie (1970, pp. 15–17) gives an interesting account of setting up a very small 'amateur' museum. Other groups of small museums are those concerned with the armed services and with historic sites and monuments.

Many small museums are, in fact, part of larger organizations. The county museum service in Oxfordshire, for example, encompasses museums at Banbury and at Wantage, each admittedly serving the district area in which it is placed as well as the immediate town locality. They remain, nevertheless, examples of smaller collections, albeit supported by a larger network of staff and resources, and are able, for example, to develop their display themes into literature of some considerable local value (Stebbing, 1978). Local government reorganization brought together a number of small museums under single district authorities, for example, in North Hertfordshire, while in other cases it provided an opportunity to develop further small museums, as with the Cotswold District Council. Here the Corinium Museum at Cirencester, founded in 1856 (Viner, 1976), was the subject of capital development (Hebditch, 1976), with the result that it become a joint runner-up in the 1976 Museum of the Year Award,[3] while at Northleach the Cotswold Countryside Collection has been opened (Viner and Harwood, 1981; Brigden, 1982).

Nor is the small, local museum peculiar to the provinces. In many ways the Livesey Museum in the London Borough of Southwark (Slaney, 1976) is an archetypal local museum, existing 'primarily for local residents' and providing, in the Keeper's eyes, a 'small, informal and local' centre for cultural activities. Livesey might well be a special case because of the nature of the area of deprivation which it serves and because of its own response to such challenges, but much is clearly expected from an institution with only a recent history and few permanent collections. But as Bott (1980) has shown there are many other small, local museums in London.

Many of the museums quoted here are in South-West England and it is likely that the incidence of small museums in this region is higher than elsewhere. A recent assessment (Viner, November 1982, unpublished), based on the institutional membership of the South-Western Federation of Museums and Art Galleries has shown that over 80 member museums can be defined as being small, using the definitions suggested earlier in this paper. To this should be added a similar number of institutions that are not members of the Federation. This assessment has indicated just how extensive and varied the range seems to be: everything from the Fire Defence Collection at Potterne in Wiltshire to the Philpot Museum at Lyme Regis in Dorset. Hudson (1982) lists no fewer than 63 museums within this region as worthy of inclusion as 'good museums'; a total more or less equally divided between local authority and private/trustee museums, and including no less than four of the 'Top Twenty' from all over Britain.

Aims and Objectives

As already discussed, many small museums have assumed an essentially local role, for the preservation of local material – or at least locally *donated* material – though not all such museums need necessarily be regarded as locally-based in terms of collections. This point leads into other areas of collection management. Contrast, for example, the firmly-based local collections at Hythe in Kent, which include a significant civic content in the displays, with the more general challenge facing the staff at St Helens on Merseyside (Lloyd, 1977, 1981; Burgoyne, 1981). Here a significant part of the collections – and hence the displays – are not primarily of local source material.

A more studied approach can be seen in one example of the many single-purpose museums to develop in recent years. At Lacock, Wiltshire, the Fox-Talbot Museum was seen by Ball (1976) to have eleven, clearly defined objectives and was regarded by the reviewer as living up to those aims and aspirations. This latter point is the subject of a recent article (Schadla-Hall and Davidson, 1982) and there is much of interest here with particular reference to museums within this category. The isolation of a specific group of material in what otherwise might be an unremarkable collection is often the occasion for comment; witness the discussion of the Tiffany glass collection – about 130 items altogether housed in the Haworth Art Gallery in Accrington, Lancashire (Smith, 1977). This is, incidentally, a good example of benefaction to the museum by a local individual of material which would not otherwise be associated with the collections housed there.

Use by visitors

Published visitor statistics must be viewed with some caution in this sphere and balanced against, for example, the method of recording used and the imposition, or otherwise, of admission charges. However, it is clear that in general terms, many small museums attract no more than 20 000 visitors per annum, even in a full year. Others will attract far in excess of this figure; for example, Corinium Museum records about 75 000 visitors of which approximately one-third are school groups. The Roman Baths Museum and Pump Room at Bath, however, recorded 704 100 visitors in 1980 (British Tourist Authority, 1981) and with an admission fee of £1.10. Many small, private museums have been established as commercial propositions with the tourist in mind. The Poldark Mining and Wendron Forge Museum in Cornwall is financed entirely from income, closes for five months of the year and is totally dependent on its summer visitors: some seventy per cent of its 250 000 visitors appear in the twelve weeks of mid-summer. Nor is the density of urban population a guarantee of exclusion from the category of 'small' in museum terms. For example,

the 8 500 visitors to the Cookworthy Museum in Kingsbridge, Devon with a local population base of only 4 142 has a high seasonal throughput of visitors during the summer months, while the Powell Museum in Wigan recorded only 9 984 visitors in a full year of opening, and this against a population base of 307 700.

Improved Provision

Many of the small museums lack adequate finance and expertise and as one American curator observed: 'A proliferation of unattractive, poorly designed and inadequately staffed museums can seriously endanger the public image of all museums' (Randel, 1971, pp. 21–22). In Britain, the Association of Independent Museums (AIM) has as one of its aims the raising of standards throughout its membership. To achieve this, it organizes seminars and publishes guidelines[4] which seek to assist museums in securing a firm financial base on which acceptable curatorial standards can be founded.

Finance is a crucial constraint on the activities of many local museums. The financial insecurity of many local society museums is a fact of history (Markham, 1938, pp. 19–20). Many such museums, founded in the eighteenth and nineteenth centuries, have been transferred to local authorities – some as early as the middle of the last century (for example at Warrington in 1848). The old society museums are a rarity today. In the past they have had access to large gifts of capital and bequests of material and buildings from their membership, but find increasingly that their sources of revenue – derived from admission charges and invested capital but unsupported by local government grants – are insufficient to maintain their buildings, or adequately finance trained curatorial staff. Financial problems also beset many of the new, small museums founded in recent years.

Despite this difficult financial background, it seems clear that considerable attempts have been made by smaller museums to take stock of the contents of their collections, their state of preservation and the services offered to visitors. A glimpse at the pages of *The Good Museums Guide* (Hudson, 1982) makes the last point particularly well: the quality of presentation and improvements in concept and layout, for example, are welcomed at Avebury and at Budleigh Salterton, as are detailed improvements in labelling, exemplified in two recent developments in Bath. The creation of a suitable atmosphere is also part of the same challenge and the same *Guide* commends the Newlyn Orion Galleries, Penzance for this and, as a direct response to the material displayed, the Barbara Hepworth Museum in St Ives. The vague, but nonetheless discernable, attraction of an 'old fashioned' approach can be seen at the Cornwall County Museum in Truro. Nor is Hudson (1982) merely being polite in ascribing a refreshing, homespun quality to the displays at the small Shaftesbury and District Museum in Dorset, a quality which characterizes many successful presentations to the public, which are neither intimidating in scale nor poor in style.

Success within the physical limitations of the space available and the nature of the museum buildings themselves can also be recognized as at Lyme Regis, commended for 'ingenious adaptation and skilful design'. Thus at Dawlish in Devon, the society-run museum reflects the general nature of the town over two centuries, with little regard for the tourist industry and has created, for the same critic, 'a pleasant monument to respectability'. Omissions can, however, create an obvious gap and the need for a greater emphasis at Bridport on the significance of seafaring in the history of the town is only one such example.

There is no doubt that improved facilities in many of the smaller museums has resulted from outside financial assistance. There is a long history of such aid. In 1930 the Carnegie United Kingdom Trust (CUKT) began its policy of direct financial assistance to the provincial museum services (Markham, 1938, pp. 155–164; and Appendix II). This took the form of development grants, based on expert reports, with the object of establishing better standards of exhibition and curatorship and of arousing local interest and raising local money. This assistance continued until the early 1970s. The scale of expenditure by the CUKT on museums and museum services from 1931–1970 is summarized neatly in its Annual Report for 1970 (para. 35, p. 15). Many small museums benefitted from this support, although it should be noted that the CUKT did not grant-aid museums without competent curatorship.

Today, an important source of capital work for museums in tourist areas are the grants administered by the English Tourist Board (ETB) under Section 4 of the *Development of Tourism Act 1969,* and many small museums have benefitted from these. For example, the Wheal Martin Museum at St Austell, Cornwall, an open-air museum of the china clay industry which opened in 1975, has received grants for various capital projects, including the restoration of buildings and the establishment of permanent displays. The ETB believes that museums should seek to be 'essentially regional or even local in character' (Mills, 1976, p. 31), and guidelines have been formulated for awarding these grants after it was realized that many projects suffered from a lack of specialist expertise and finance.

The Area Museum Services have been a vital source of revenue aid for small museums (Thompson, 1760, pp. 25–29), and this has been particularly so in South-West England. An examination of the nature of the projects approved for grant-aid by the Area Museum Council for the South West shows that, of a total of some 56 and 64 projects approved for each of the financial years 1981/82 and 1982/83, approximately 35 and 54 per cent respectively might be regarded as for display improvements only; the remainder being concerned with other aspects of the conservation of collections, the buildings themselves and environmental control. Much activity classified under 'display', however, includes important aspects of conservation and environmental control, but recent policy decisions taken by the same Council[5] have rationalized an already well-established sequence of priorities under which grant-aid applications in future years will be considered. The priorities are, primarily, the care and conservation of the collections, their adequate housing, control and documentation and, secondly, the display and interpretation of the collections, together with the associated museum service. The Drew Report recommended the establishment of Countywide Consultative Committees (CCCs) to represent all museums, irrespective of size and organization, and a more recent report elaborates on this recommendation (Morris, 1982). Such CCCs, if established – and one of the conclusions drawn by Morris in his survey is that very few counties have as yet taken any action towards this end – could be of great benefit to small museums.

On the problem of the lack of professional guidance for voluntary museums, one solution is seen in the appointment of peripatetic curators, in the knowledge that travelling curators have provided valuable assistance to many local museums. The experience of both Chaplin (1978) and Norgate (1980) has led to the suggestion that such a curator's skill should be directed primarily towards the solution of fundamental problems – environment, documentation – rather than on elaborate or expensive display schemes. It is a fact that in many small, amateur museums storage and documentation do not attract 'the enthusiastic involvement of the amateur' (Norgate, 1980; p. 105), while display does, and thus many opt for 'showmanship'.

Successful museums rely as much on the involvement and support of their visitors as from the commitment of their staff. There is much that a small museum serving a fairly well-defined local community can achieve in this respect. The sympathetic support of the Area Museum Council, especially in the constant battle against problems of conservation, provides an essential base from which local resources can develop. Constant vigilance concerning the welfare of the collections has not always been apparent in museums of all sizes and there remain many which have yet to tackle this problem effectively. Yet recent trends are encouraging. Improvements in display techniques and services to both the visitor and the wider community are indications of a changing philosophy and of the essential need to involve museums in the life of that community.

Notes

[1] This can also be charted, perhaps, by examining National Trust Membership figures:

1945	7 850
1955	55 658
1965	157 581
1975	539 285
1981	1 046 864

[2] The constitution of the Bishop's Waltham Museum Society states that its objects are:

(a) To promote the permanent preservation for the benefit of the public generally and especially the inhabitants of the Parish of Bishop's Waltham in the county of Hampshire of lands, buildings or objects of beauty or historical interest, and, as regards lands, of historical or archaeological importance, within the said parish, and generally to protect and preserve the character and amenities of the said parish, and for the attainment of the foregoing to consider, and if it shall seem necessary or desirable, to promote, assist or oppose proposals for the use or development of land within the said parish.
(b) To establish and manage a museum to display objects of historical or archaeological interest relating to the said parish or information relating to objects, lands or buildings of beauty or historic interest found or relating to the said parish and to act as a centre to encourage the study of such objects, lands or buildings within the said parish.

[3] BTA 'Come to Britain' award special commendation 1975; Central Council for the Disabled 'Building for the Disabled' award 1976; European Architectural Heritage guide book award 1975.
[4] For example, *Setting Up and Running a New Museum*, AIM Guideline, no. 2.
[5] Approved 21 October 1982: details from Director, Area Museum Council for South West, Buckland Abbey, Yelverton, Devon, PL20 6EY.

References

ANNABLE, F. K. (1971), 'Museum News', *Bi-Annual bulletin of the Wiltshire Archaeological and Natural History Society*, **11**, 14–15

AUTHERS, W. P. (1976), 'The Tiverton Museum', *Museums J.*, **76**(3), 111–112

ATKINSON, F. AND HOLTON, M. (1973), 'Open air and folk museums', *Museums J.*, **72**(4), 140–142

BALL, L. C. (1976), 'Fox Talbot Museum: a new museum of photography', *Museums J.*, **75**(4), 163–164

BOTT, V. (1979), *Local Museum Collections in Greater London*, MA Thesis, University of Leicester, Department of Museum Studies

BOTT, V. (1980), 'Local collections in Greater London', *Museums Association 1980 Conference Proceedings*, 17–20

BRIGDEN, R. (1982), 'Where will it all end?', *Museums J.*, **81** (4), 199–203

BRITISH TOURIST AUTHORITY (1981), *Visits to Historic Properties/Museums and Galleries in Britain in 1980*, BTA, London

BURGOYNE, I. (1981), 'A Visit to the new St. Helens Museum', *Museums J.*, **81** (1), 21–22

CHAPLIN,.R. E. (1978), 'The travelling curator service in Scotland', *Museums J.*, **78** (4), 177–180

DOUGHTY, P. S. (1970), 'The small museum – the size of the problem and its implications', *Museums Assistants' Group Transactions*, **9**, 18–24

DYER, E. (1974), 'The Street Shoe Museum, Street, Somerset', *Museums J.*, **74** (1), 17–19

FOSTER, R. (1979), 'The changing philosophy of museums', *Museums J.*, **79**, 54–57

HEBDITCH, M. (1976), 'The Corinium Museum at Cirencester: an appraisal', *Museums J.*, **76** (1), 7–8

HUDSON, K. (1982), *The Good Museum Guide*, Macmillan, London

ICOM (1974), 'Statutes', in *ICOM News*, **27** (3/4), insert, ICOM, Paris

JENKINS, J. G. (1976), 'The Tiverton Museum – a review', *Museums J.*, **76** (3), 113–114

LAMBIE, B. (1970), 'Setting up a small museum', *Museum Assistants' Group Transactions* **9**, 15–17

LLOYD, E. (1977), 'St. Helens: the main gallery redesigned', *Museums J.*, **77** (2), 63–64

LLOYD, E. (1981), 'A new Museum for St. Helens', *Museums J.*, **81** (1), 19–20

MARKHAM, S. F. (1938), *The museums and art galleries of the British Isles*, Carnegie United Kingdom Trust, T. & A. Constable, Edinburgh

MILLARD, L. AND LENT, C. (1980), 'Hythe Local History Room: the reorganisation of a small town museum', *Museums J.*, **80** (1), 33–35

MILLS, S. (1976), *Museums Association 1976 Conference Proceedings*, 30–32

MUSEUMS ASSOCIATION (1982), *Museums Yearbook 1982*, Museums Association, London

MORRIS, B. (1982), *Countrywide Consultative Committees for Museums*, Report by a Working Party, HMSO, London

NORGATE, M. (1980), 'Pastoral care of museums', *Museums J.*, **80** (2), 104–106

RANDEL, J. S. (1971), 'When starting a small museum', *Museum News*, **49** (7), 22, Washington DC

RITCHIE, B. (1982), 'A Soldier of Fortune', *Sunday Times*, 21 March 1982

SCHADLA-HALL, T. AND DAVIDSON, J. (1982), 'It's very grand but who's it for?', *Museums J.*, **82** (3), 171–175

SINGLETON, R. (1979), 'Museums in a changing world', *Museums J.*, **79** (1), 11–12

SLANEY, J. (1976), 'Livesey: a new museum for Southwark', *Museums J.*, **75** (4), 167–169

SMITH, A. (1977), 'Tiffany "Favrile" glass at Accrington a new display by the North West Area Service', *Museums J.*, **76** (4), 155–156

STEBBING, N. (1978), *The Vale of White Horse: Land and People*, Oxfordshire County Council Dept. of Museum Services publication no. 9, 32 pp

THOMPSON J. (1970), 'Area councils and the small museums', *Museum Assistants' Group Transactions*, **9**, 25–29

VINER, D. (1976), 'The Corinium Museum at Cirencester: redevelopment and conservation', *Museums J.*, **76** (1), 5–6

VINER, D. AND HARWOOD, A. R. (1981), 'New home at last for the Lloyd-Baker Collection', *Gloucester and Avon Life,* July 1981, 56–60

WRIGHT, C. W. (1973), *Provincial Museums and Galleries,* Department of Education and Science, HMSO, London

11

Ethics and the curator

Antony J. Duggan

Only in the applied sense can ethics be usefully discussed by those who lack a formal training in philosophy. Most standard definitions of ethics introduce moral considerations which are linked to a sense of duty in the discharge of social obligations. Such definitions are unsatisfactory for the present purpose, as they employ concepts which are difficult to define and are open to varying interpretation. However, when the field of discussion is narrowed, as in this case, to rules of conduct which are accepted by persons in limited spheres of human activity, the subject becomes more amenable and less abstract, and its difficult aspects, of which there are many, become easier to dissect.

Development

At some time during the evolution of a science or art, those who pursue it to the point at which the exercise of their pertinent knowledge and skill is rewarded by the community, become 'professionals' and begin to combine as integral components of a 'profession' which provides a unique service to society. The evolution of the profession of curatorship, still far from complete, is described elsewhere in this book, and the contemporary effort being made to formulate rules of conduct is but one testimony to the ongoing construction of an organized professional body.

During such an evolution it becomes everywhere apparent that the members of a 'profession' enjoy privileges that are denied to the community at large. In the case of a curator these include:

(1) Free access to rare and precious objects which are not his or her own. (2) The use of paid time for research. (3) The status of advisor to the community, individually and collectively, on matters relating to the nation's heritage. (4) The right to contend against social developments which may be damaging to his professional ideals. (5) Freedom to set standards for others, including those who aspire to become curators. (6) The opportunity to be selected as an expert witness in matters of legal contention.

There are other, social, advantages, which are less easy to define. The successful curator attracts a local, or even widespread, respect, born either of gratitude, admiration or curiosity. His daily life is eased by unconscious touches of deference invited by the apparent mystery of his unusual vocation. His friendship may be sought by some of those about him, although not always for disinterested reasons. And, perhaps most importantly of all, he is trusted.

The unspoken convention of give-and-take in human relationships must, at some point, be acknowledged along the path which a young 'profession' treads in establishing itself. It must eventually declare its privileged position, for otherwise it cannot retain the public confidence upon which it has to depend. Obscurantism can carry it no further. Its house-rules have to be plainly stated, for all to understand, and a code of ethics has to be formulated and published.

It follows immediately that the stimulus for constructing such a code must come from within the 'profession'. There is no Law which demands a code; there is no political faction or united body of public opinion which seeks powers of compulsion in that respect. It is a tribute to the integrity of curators past and present that the option remains in curatorial hands. The option must be taken while those circumstances still prevail.

The construction of a code is a matter of great difficulty, largely because of the heterogeneous interests of curators and the variety of their terms of employment in the institutions which they serve. It is one thing for a body of well-educated people united by an ideal but by not much else to agree upon the need for a code, but an entirely different thing for them to agree upon what the code should contain. That agreement can be reached only after intensive self-examination and the exposure of ingrained mental attitudes in debate, sacrifices which even the most dedicated curators do not readily bring upon themselves.

Much of the impetus which provoked the current attempts to construct a curatorial code was supplied by the Museums Assistants Group (MAG) (now Museums Professionals' Group) who, in January 1974, published the report of its working party under the title 'Towards a Code of Conduct for the Museum Profession'. The events which followed the appearance of that seminal paper have been described in detail by Patrick Boylan (1977). The subject was referred by the Conference of the Museums Asssocation to its Council, who placed matters in the hands of its Information, Membership and Publications Committee. Those parts of the paper concerned with the responsibilities of governing bodies were identified and made the basis for the existing *Code of Practice for Museum Authorities,* which was formally adopted in July 1977 at The Museum Assocation's Conference in Bradford.

Not surprisingly, progress towards a code of professional ethics was less dramatic, notwithstanding the labours of Kay Staniland, who had already made a signal contribution to the original MAG report. In due course, her efforts and those of a subcommittee chaired by Kenneth Barton produced the current *Guidelines for Professional Conduct* which were adopted at the Bradford Conference in 1977.

Although the *Guidelines* contain much that is derived from sound ethical principles, there remained a conviction that those principles needed to be stated with greater firmness and clarity in the form of rules, to which guidelines should be appended. The Museum Professionals' Group held a symposium in London in April 1981, later published as *MPG Transactions No. 16,* entitled 'Towards a Code of Ethics in Museums'. In responding to this fresh stimulus, the Council of the Museums Association set up a working party to devise a Code of Conduct for Museum Curators containing both rules and guidelines as proposed by Graeme Cruickshank at the London Symposium. A draft of that code was presented at the Museum Association Conference in Nottingham in 1982.[1]

In the preamble to that draft, the working party stated that a code of ethics for curators was necessary 'primarily in the interests of the society which they serve, and secondly to establish themselves as a specialized and reputable group of practitioners whose standards of work were open to judgement'.

Museum collections
Ethics of collecting

It is clearly understood by curators that the exercise of their service to their governing bodies and their public depends upon the acquisition, study and preservation of museum items in an orderly and retrievable form. The first of these activities must be governed by ethical principles if the other two are to be carried out satisfactorily. The consequences of indiscriminate collecting are described elsewhere in this book, and are wholly undesirable; it follows that a curator must submit to the necessary restrictions by adhering to a scheme known as an acquisition policy which is devised by the governing body of his museum, not only with his consent, but often at his instigation. The acquisition policy is central to practical considerations such as finance, accommodation, equipment and available expertise *(Figure 11.1).* As these resources change with time, and they inevitably do, the policy must be modified, but never in such a way as to jeopardize the items already acquired.

The curator's ethical problems begin with the actual act of acquiring material for his museum or gallery. It goes without saying that items should never be obtained from illegal sources and the Guidelines include here consideration of items whose owners contravene the UNESCO Convention[2]. A curator

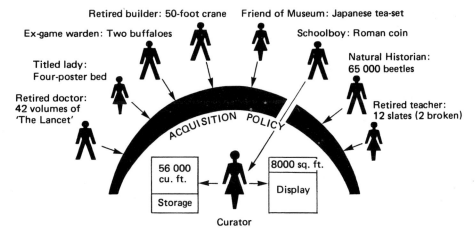

Figure 11.1 An acquisition policy is an essential instrument for the control of collections and the best use of resources

would be open to criticism for obtaining items from a source which was unidentifiable, particularly if they were discovered to be spurious or obtained by stealth or fraud.

No items should ever be collected by taking advantage of others, and this caveat applies to many kinds of circumstances, including the out-bidding of more deserving institutions in the auction room, and using persuasion to obtain material from members of the public who have no special knowledge of the worth or cultural value of what they offer. The curator, moreover, must not acquire material at the cost of depriving the nation of a part of its heritage. This can come about in subtle ways, such as spoiling an ecological niche by the removal of a critical specimen, or by acquiring one item from a collection, thus removing the item from its historical or scientific framework.

The acquisition of objects by collection in the field is often fraught with ethical problems. *Figure 11.2* illustrates a hypothesis in which the curator at Museum A finds himself at a complete disadvantage in terms of reconnaisance and collection in adjacent territories in the ambience of other curators outside his discipline working under different governing bodies. The temptation of forthright action in such a case must be resisted, and the question of right to the natural collecting area must be negotiated with professional diplomacy.

The current *Guidelines* and the draft *Code of Conduct* expound the obligations of a curator in respect of items acquired not only by him but by his predecessors. There is nowadays little excuse for permitting the forces of attrition to work unchecked on museum items. Deliberate neglect of such material and of the opportunities that abound in connection with its pre-servation must be regarded as unethical conduct by default. Losses have been incurred through the alternation of specialists from one generation of curators to another in museums whose collections range over different academic disciplines. The resolution, for example, of an archaeologist to put away, not to say put out of his mind, the natural history material accumulated by his predecessors, must not prevail in such a way that previously-acquired collections deteriorate or lose their value.

A most difficult ethical matter arises in the case of the disposal of museum material. The draft *Code* takes a realistic view of the situation in museums which suffer financial stress. There must always be a strong presumption against disposing of material, and certain safeguards must be adopted by the curator before an irrevocable course of action is taken.

Ethics of research

One reason for collecting like material is to enable the curator or his staff or qualified members of the public to use it for academic research purposes. This apparently simple objective is heavily overlain with problems of space, conservation and personnel management. In large museums, the situation is clear because staff of high academic standing undertake research into the collections as their main professional activity, and are expected to contribute publications of a high order to the artistic, historical or scientific literature. In such cases, few ethical problems arise, but in many museums the time spent on research has to be balanced against the needs for attention to other areas of curatorial activity. It is unethical to pursue research at the cost of the deterioration of collections in which the research worker has no interest.

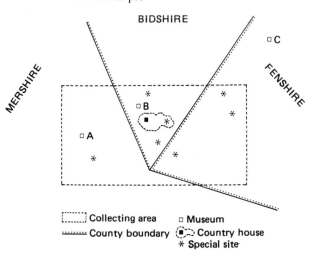

Figure 11.2 A natural or historic collecting area relates to the speciality of the curator at Museum A. At least six sites of particular interest fall within other administrative localities, including the grounds of a country house. The solution of problems of investigation and collection in the area must begin with an ethical agreement between the curators involved

One of the most difficult aspects of this problem is to define at what point a research project ceases to be relevant to the museum's cultural and academic objectives. Serious questions are sometimes posed as to whether museum research is worthwhile at all, being as it is, mostly of a demonstrative rather than an experimental nature. As to whether the research is relevant or worthwhile depends, as in most research, upon the worker himself. Curatorial managers of museums sometimes find it difficult to control a research project once it has been authorized, for often the nature of the programme itself is open-ended, and the most important results may be derived from the most unexpected and apparently irrelevant departures. The ethical problem, therefore, is real, although difficult to define. A sound guideline is to examine carefully the effects of continuous research preoccupation upon the museum's aims and other activities, and to decide accordingly.

Another ethical problem arises when curatorial staff withdraw material from circulation during the course of a research programme. The question may have to be answered as to whether that material should be made available, on request, to research workers outside the museum. It is clearly unethical for a curator to impede the legitimate research of others during the course of his own investigations. Common sense suggests that in such cases the interested parties should join forces with the intention of publishing a joint communication.

Ethics of private collecting

One of the most difficult and contentious issues hinges upon the right of curators to collect museum material for themselves. The views of curators of great experience are polarized on this issue. Some maintain that personal collecting is to be commended as showing a curator's dedication to his discipline and his willingness to immerse himself in learning outside working hours. Others see great danger in private collecting, particularly when the curator's collection is of the same nature as that which he curates in the museum which employs him. The present draft *Code*, in attempting to compromise between these views, insists that if a curator collects privately he must agree with his governing body the various terms under which he is permitted to do so, and the governing body should be informed of any change which might alter that understanding. In some countries private collecting by curators is banned altogether, but it is doubtful whether such a radical departure would be acceptable to curators in the United Kingdom at present.

An argument, seen by the author as too simplistic, is that a curator, being an alert and conscientious individual, is capable of defining for himself the border line between his own interests and those of his governing body, and that no conflict will arise. Were this argument valid, there would be no reason to codify an ethical system for curators at all. One purpose of a code is to assist them with guidance rather than compunction in defining correct professional behaviour.

The chief practical difficulty arising from personal collecting is that it will almost inevitably lead to dealing, and this is clearly a field in which it may become impossible for the curator to avoid a charge of putting his interests before those of his employer and his public (*Figures 11.3* and *11.4*).

Ethics of publication

Difficulties may arise when curators advance upon the matter of private publication. It can be argued that much of the scholarship put into works on which royalties are collected is derived from the experience gained in the service of an employer. Hence the curator owes reimbursement to his employer for the professional opportunities which made his publication possible. However, the nub of the problem depends upon the time and place in which the work of private publication occurs. Although the physical fact of his employment is regulated by his terms of service, his intellectual activities are at his disposal outside working hours. Hence the view is taken by the author that he may, without ethical offence, publish privately work that he performs in his own time. However, paragraph 71 of the National Joint Council for Local Authorities A.P.T. and C. Services Scheme of Conditions of Service Handbook (the *Purple Book*)[3] makes it clear that above the service grade of AP5, the curator is, in fact, the servant of his employing authority for 24 hours every day. When that undertaking applies, it is urged that a curator will obtain the express consent of his employers before proceeding with private publication on the basis of his professional experience. Indeed, it would be a wise precaution for any member of staff who is considering publishing privately any of his work to enquire first into the authority's policy regarding private publication.

Ethics of expertise

Delicate situations arise when a curator undertakes identification, authentication or valuation for personal gain, and in some countries this practice is prohibited. The exercise of expertise in such matters is not the main consideration but, as in the case of private collecting, it brings the curator close to dealing which is again emphasized as best avoided if a curator is to maintain an unimpeachable image. The type of situation which may arise in relation to dealers of perfect credentials, is shown in *Figure 11.3*, in which the curator is seen to be a link in a chain which involves profit-making at the expense of his own museum. The fact that he does not directly

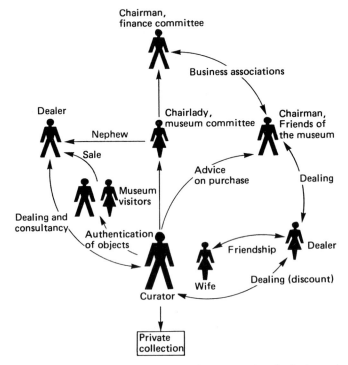

Figure 11.3 Hypothetical case of a curator who collects and authenticates privately. Such practices are 'vulnerable to abuse'. (Draft *Code*, Part 2, 4.4/5, Duggan *et al* (1982)

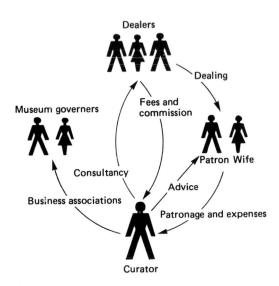

Figure 11.4 A difficult ethical position arising from the practice of consultantship by a curator (based on a published case)

participate in the profits does little to modify the ambiguity of his position.

There is always a need for communities to seek consultation with the staff of museums in their specialized capacities, and the fulfilment of such requests is an important contribution to society. Consultancy fees are attractive and the service reflects well upon the institution which the curator serves. Provided he informs his governing body of the work which he does in this respect no ethical problems arise, although some governing bodies question the right of the curator to retain his fee when the consultation is conducted in museum time.

Nevertheless, scrupulous care must be taken, particularly in the sphere of art, that consultancy fees are on no account confused with commission on the sales which result from the consultant's advice, and if the consultant's appraisal is related to his museum, it is strongly advisable to reject the consultancy. *Figure 11.4* shows an example which, after action in open Court, was to the detriment of the curator's career.

Museum services

Ethics and the public

The curator's responsibilities are varied, and his contact with the public must be conducted with courtesy and fairness. He should regard information imparted to him as confidential, particularly when disclosure could set at risk valuable objects in private possession or material of importance to the national heritage located in the countryside.

A curator is often asked to identify objects brought to his museum, and in general he is expected to do so when his knowledge is adequate. Curators are strongly advised against making valuations. If the enquirer asks for the name of an outside expert in this respect, the curator should give several names rather than hold to one who values objects for a fee.

Curators have an ethical responsibility to the public in presenting museum displays. These should be balanced, and must never deliberately mislead. Every care must be taken to avoid giving offence, particularly in regard to the display of human remains or objects associated with religious beliefs and ceremonies. The public reaction to art forms varies from one community to another and from one period to another. Even the most impeccable academic and cultural reason for their exhibition may be judged as insufficient justification for the expenditure of public money.

The management of museum shops involves ethical considerations. The articles on sale and the nature of their promotion should always be in good taste and be consistent with the museum's academic standpoint. Rare objects should not be offered for sale, and indeed the merchandise should never be of a nature which could be interpreted as the wherewithal of a genuine antique dealer.

Ethics and commerce

At one time or another curators conduct negotiations with suppliers of goods, auctioneers, dealers and others, and all such transactions must be carried out with complete integrity. The curator must not accept inducements to trade, or place himself in a position of obligation to one firm rather than another. He should not accept from them gifts or gratuities of any kind.

The sponsorship of a display or other public museum activity by a commercial firm can create problems. The curator may find himself under subtle pressure to orient his exhibition with partiality towards the interest of the sponsoring company. Although adequate acknowledgement of any assistance from commercial sources must always be made, this should never be done in such a way as to suggest that the museum is being used as a vehicle of promotion. In the kind of situation illustrated in *Figure 11.5* which also involves the media, the curator must ensure that the information provided is impartial and factually correct.

Non-professionals, including volunteers, are playing an increasingly important part in museum work. The curator should at all times satisfy himself of the integrity of part-time and short-time workers, and ensure that they are not permitted to undertake tasks which normally require a trained curator on the permanent staff. Similar considerations apply to curatorial trainees during their practical sessions.

Ethics and professional colleagues

It goes without saying that curators should treat their colleagues with deference and courtesy. When there is dispute, care should be taken to avoid bringing it to public notice in such a way as to bring a discredit on either of the persons concerned. Disputes over collecting areas should be quickly resolved, if necessary by independent arbitration. In particular, the dispute should not be conducted so as to place a

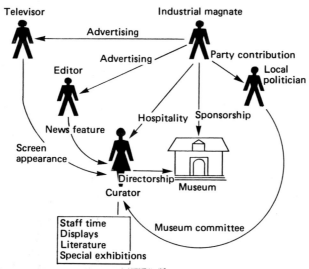

Figure 11.5 Sponsorship may give rise to ethical problems of publicity and advertising

benefactor or land-owner in an invidious position (*Figure 11.2*).

The curator should be careful not to use his museum for self-advertisement, and this is particularly important in communicating with newspaper reporters and television interviewers. It is, of course, impossible to divorce his office and his personality from his institution, but he should never use the media to give him advantage over his colleagues.

A curator should ensure that all his activities are consistent with the *Code of Practice for Museum Authorities*. Curators must familiarize themselves with the procedures that operate within their governing bodies and must clearly understand the powers and responsibilities which are delegated to them.

Legal aspects

All curators are bound by the Law and should be thoroughly acquainted with legislation which particularly affects their professional activities. Much subsidiary legislation also impinges upon museum activity and includes Acts related to malicious damage, copyright, firearms, field work and health and safety at work.

Numerous legal obligations are placed upon a curator by virtue of his employment, and these include Acts concerning contractual obligations on the employer and employee. The so-called *Purple Book*[3] (*Blue Book* in Scotland) lays down the contractual conditions of service relating to county, (region in Scotland) and district councils. In addition, the Book includes important guidelines to an employee's rights and restrictions in various fields, including the assurance that he may distance himself from the political activities of his governing body.

While transgression of the Law invites various forms of penalty, there is at the present time no machinery for enforcing a code of curatorial ethics. Under Article 11 of its Constitution, the Museums Association reserves the power to expel members who give rise to conduct which places the reputation of the profession in jeopardy, but this provision is far from applicable to all curators in the United Kingdom. At present, therefore, it is better to regard a code as essentially preventative, and as a guide to which curators can refer when faced with difficult ethical situations.

Conclusion

Any code of ethics is almost certain to be incomplete as social conventions continually change and new patterns of practice bring novel opportunities for professional misconduct.

In this brief chapter the author has attempted to be comprehensible rather than comprehensive, but even the most detailed code can never supply clear-cut answers to every problem. No two curators will ever see an ethical dilemma in exactly the same way or have recourse to the same solution.

The student who wishes further to acquaint himself with this difficult subject is referred to the bibliography. However, no amount of reading can make an ethical curator or a curator ethical. The preamble to the present draft code ends with the words of David Clarke, '. . . no code can be a substitute for the highest personal standards of integrity and dedication . . .' The author can come to no better conclusion than that.

Notes

[1] This text is based on the 1982 draft code. The *Code of Conduct for Museum Curators* was adopted by the Annual General Meeting of the Museums Association at Swansea in 1983 (see Appendix 2).
[2] UNESCO Convention on the Means of Prohibiting and Preventing the Illicit Import, Export and Transfer of Ownership of Cultural Property, 1970.
[3] Scheme of Conditions of Service of the National Joint Council for Local Authorities' Administrative, Professional and Technical and Clerical Services, *Purple Book*, (*Blue Book* in Scotland).

Bibliography

AMERICAN ASSOCIATION OF MUSEUMS (1978), *Museum Ethics*, AAM, New York, 31 pp
BOYLAN, P. J. (1976), 'The ethics of acquisition: the Leicester code'. *Museums J.*, **75**, 169–170
BOYLAN, P. J. (1977), 'Museum ethics: Museum Association Policies', *Museums J.*, **77**, 106–111, (29 refs)
COLBERT, E. H. (1958), 'On being a curator'. *Curator*, **1**, 7–12
DUGGAN, A. J. *et al* (1982), Draft *Code of Conduct for Museum Curators*. Museums Association, London, 8 pp
GIBBS-SMITH, C. H. (1974), *Copyright Law concerning Works of Art, photographs and the written and spoken word, Information Sheet no. 7*, Museums Association, 14 pp
KING, M. E. (1980), 'Curators: Ethics and Obligations'. *Curator*, **23**, 10–18, (84 refs.)
MUSEUMS ASSOCIATION (1982), 'Code of Practice for Museum Authorities, 1977' in *Museums Yearbook 1983*, 5–7, Museums Association, London, (8 refs)
MUSEUMS ASSOCIATION (1982), Guidelines for Professional Conduct 1977' in *Museums Yearbook 1983*, 8–9, Museums Association, London
MUSEUMS ASSOCIATION OF AUSTRALIA INC. (1982), *Museum Ethics and Practice* (Interim Document), 22 pp, (cyclostyled)
MUSEUM PROFESSIONALS GROUP (1981), 'Towards a code of ethics in museums', *Museums Professionals' Transactions*, No. 16, Museum Professionals' Group, London
PARR, A. E. (1960), 'Is there a museum profession?' *Curator*, **3**, 101–106
ROYAL ONTARIO MUSEUM (1981), *Statement of Principles and Policies on Ethics and Conduct Royal Ontario Museum*, Ontario 102 pp
TEASDILL, G. (1970), *An Introduction to the Law Relating to Museums, Information Sheet no. 5*, Museums Association, 5 pp, (9 refs)
WALKER, B. W. (1953), 'The Curator as a custodian of collections', *Curator*, **6**, 292–295

12

Accreditation

John M. A. Thompson

The search for standards applicable to every aspect of professional work in museums has long been a serious concern. The wide variety of museums and their staffing arrangements, the differing responsibilities of their governing bodies and the separate methods of funding have clearly justified the quest; although the application of standards will demand a major exercise in co-operation by the museum profession as well as museum committees/trustees and the controlling authorities if it is to be achieved. In this country, standards have now been set for controlling authorities and for professional conduct (see Chapter 11). At the same time, in order to evaluate and assess the standard of work and the day-to-day operation of a museum, a scheme of accreditation has been developed in the USA and in more recent years, in the UK.

The application of standards may be said to have arisen from the 'coming of age' of the museum profession and is one of a number of features which defines the profession. These include a formal and regulated training programme leading to approved qualifications, a common body of knowledge and information, and agreed practices over many technical matters and curatorial issues.

The emergence of the museum has also been stimulated by factors which have impinged on museum work in recent years. These have included the growth of independent and private museums, and the curatorial and administrative and technical departments whether, for example, conservation, design and display, or shop management and publishing; the reorganization of the controlling authorities resulting in the formation of large departments of leisure, recreation or cultural services and so on, where museums may be only one of a number of related services. At the same time, the demand from an increasingly sophisticated and educated public for an improved and more relevant service of their needs, and the desire for greater accessibility to museums by interest-groups, including those representing the disabled and disadvantaged, have hastened far-reaching developments.

The argument that this increase in professionalism is also a form of self-defence must be countered, at a time of financial pressures and uncertainty, in an attempt to defeat a real or imagined threat by corporate action. Neither is it a move towards uniformity or standardization which would be completely impracticable given the variety of museums and their purposes. Rather, professionalism is a desire to improve museum services for the public and, as Reger (1982) has suggested, to raise the *quality* of the experience for the visitor. The best way to improve museums is to examine thoroughly all that a particular museum stands for and does and relate these to agreed practices. This process of evaluation leads to accreditation.

The aim is to ensure that the museum user should not only derive maximum enjoyment and value from the use of the museum but also be assured that all the services that are required both directly and indirectly are provided on a permanent and consistent basis.

The original momentum for accreditation was given by the *Belmont Report* (1968) on museums in the USA as a response to the unprecedented growth in the number of museums during the 1960s. Many of these had inadequate funding, an uncertain institutional basis and had often been established for reasons other than pure scholarship and public service. At the same time, as in the UK, museum standards of performance varied widely and, while uniformity was neither possible nor desirable, there was a widespread need among the museum profession to provide guidelines and to define professional standards of service to which museums should aspire, and by which they would wish to be judged. It was agreed that the evaluation should be carried out by the museum community itself rather than by government officials or lay representatives.

At the time the scheme was under discussion, it was felt very strongly by all concerned that if the museum profession in the USA could not develop and apply such standards, other bodies and interest groups would and the effect would be haphazard and unsatisfactory. The scheme was initiated by the American Association of Museums with a grant from the Federal Government. By October 1982, 511 museums had been accredited by the Assocation and 97 applications were being considered. Fifteen museums have been re-accredited, the mandatory procedure which all accredited museums undergo every five to ten years following initial accreditation. Like the UK scheme, the applicant pays a fee and meets the expenses of a visiting panel, but, unlike the UK scheme, the fee has not had a depressing effect upon the number of applicants. The success of the scheme so far had led L. C. Jones, Director of the New York State Historical Association, to claim that for the first time many of the long-standing problems of the nation's museums are close to being solved.

L. L. Reger (1982), Director of the American Association of Museums, in his keynote address to The Museums Association Conference (UK) in September 1982 summarized accreditation in the USA in the following way:

> By helping a museum assure that it has certain qualities or characteristics the AAM accreditation programme helps the museum work towards becoming an institution of quality.

Reger insists that the accreditation programme, far from being a form of protectionism for museum professionals, is a major force in the raising of standards and, above all, the quality of the experience gained by museum visitors. Accreditation can be the culmination of an overall assessment of the workings of a museum commencing with the separate Museum Assessment Programme which, based on a questionnaire and an on-site visit by an experienced fellow professional, can indicate to a museum where it stands regarding professional standards and practices.

Reger stresses both the continual process of assessment and the time involved before accreditation can be achieved. The preparatory moves in the accreditation process, as described by Reger, are perhaps the key to the successful application of accreditation in other countries, including the UK, where there has been some resistance by museum professionals and others to embark upon the scheme.

The accreditation office of the American Association of Museums has issued an informative chart

(*Figure 12.1*) illustrating the sequence of accreditation.

In the early stages it was agreed that the evaluation should be carried out by the museum community itself. The practical benefits of accreditation emphasized by the American Association of Museums include the development of public confidence in museums by certifying that they meet professional standards and levels of service, the promotion of institutional self confidence and pride, the strengthening of respect and co-operation among accredited museums generally, and as a basis for qualitative judgements about the institution for the benefit of private and governmental agencies considering grant applications. The success of the scheme has, however, raised some fears that if a majority of the museums in the USA are accredited, foundations and government-funding agencies may insist that only museums that have been accredited will receive grant-aid. This would be contrary to the spirit of accreditation which is entered into on a voluntary basis for the overall benefit of the institution; not as prerequisite for Federal funding. However, there is a growing feeling in the UK that only those museums able to demonstrate minimum standards should receive grant-aid through the Area Museums Councils.

The accreditation scheme in the UK has been available since 1974, and although the scheme is maintained on the basis of the full recovery of costs from applying museums – unlike the US scheme which had the benefit of Federal Funding – it has made some progress, with six museum services being accredited.

Over the years, the Accreditation Committee has made a number of amendments to the original scheme in the light of experience and from the constructive comments of applicants, and closer links have been forged in the working of the scheme both with Area Councils and the Museums and Galleries Commission. There is no doubt that the closer association of the Commission with the Accreditation Scheme since 1980 has provided a welcome boost and has assisted in the arrangements for the nomination of independent chairmen of assessing panels and, in general, the joint reviewing of the scheme with the Association. At the same time, the Committee has been encouraged by the support of the Area Councils especially in giving preliminary advice to potential applicants about accreditation, and the steps that may need to be taken to give an applicant a fair chance of success. The Council for Museums in Wales, in recognizing the value of the scheme to its members, decided some time ago to offer grant-aid towards the Accreditation fees.

The Committee has responded to some criticism of the procedural aspects of the scheme from museums that have undergone the accreditation pro-

Figure 12.1 The steps in the accreditation process in the USA

Initial application (Step 1)	The Museum reviews the basic definition of a museum.	The Museum completes the application forms, and it is signed by the Museum Director and the head of its governing body.	The Museum forwards the application fee to the accreditation office.
Questionnaire (Step 2)	The accreditation questionnaire is sent to the Museum upon the receipt of the application and fee.	The questionnaire requests information on all aspects of the Museum's operations: its purpose, resources, plans and performance.	Museum staff are encouraged to use this time for comprehensive self-examination.	One year is allowed for reflection and revision before the questionnaire, supporting documents and final registration fee are due in the accreditation office.
Initial review (Step 3)	At its next meeting, the Accreditation Commission determines if the materials submitted by the Museum indicate that that it fulfils accreditation criteria.	The commission may: grant interim approval; table application for additional information or specific improvements;★ deny interim approval.	This decision is relayed promptly to the Museum.
On-site evaluation (Step 4)	Museums granted interim approval are given several months to prepare for an on-site evaluation.	The visiting committee seeks in a one- or two-day visit to verify the presence of minimum standards through the examination of the Museum's facilities, operations, and activities.	The committee submits a narrative report, evaluation checklists and recommendations to the accreditation office.
Final review (Step 5)	At its next meeting the Accreditation Commission determines if the narrative report and checklists indicate that the Museum meets accreditation standards.	The commission may: grant accreditation; table application for further improvements;★ deny accreditation.	The Museum receives notification of the commission's decision along with copies of the narrative report and checklist.	Accredited museums receive a formal certificate for public display.

★ Applications tabled at either the initial or final review will be considered at a time specified by the Commission.

cess and, following an evaluation of the procedure, has agreed on a number of points which will remove some misunderstandings about the scheme at the beginning of the process rather than later when the report of the assessors has been made. The amendments are as follows:

(1) That a much more rigorous screening of applications be made at the preliminary stage, if information suggests that the application may be premature.

(2) That the panel should ensure that a preliminary discussion be held with the museum director so that confidential issues or matters of political sensitivity may be aired.

(3) That a code of ethics for visiting panels be introduced along the lines of the American model.

(4) That the Committee accept applications only when they carry the signature both of the professional and appropriate officer of the governing body.

(5) The Committee will continue to select panels to show a balance of views and wherever possible include an experienced assessor to ensure continuity of criteria.

(6) Where an Area Council subsidizes an application it should agree with the museum what access it will have to the resulting report.

The operation of the scheme is described in The Museum Assocation's *Yearbook 1982,* and can be summarized as follows: The museum authority wishing to apply either on behalf of an individual institution or all the museums it administers pays a small registration fee and completes the detailed questionnaire. On the return of the questionnaire, the Accreditation Committee decides what further evidence is required and appoints a panel of assessors to visit the applicant museum. The chairman of the visiting panel is normally a member or nominee of the Museums and Galleries Commission, which collaborates in the scheme. An applicant museum has the right to query or reject names from a list of suggested members. The panel prepares a report for submission to the Accreditation Committee and this is forwarded to the applicant museum, omitting such sections as have been written for the confidential information of the Committee, with its decision whether the museum should be accredited or not. A museum failing to obtain accreditation has an opportunity to correct deficiencies and to request a review within two years. Accredited status is subject to a periodic review (initially 10 years), although the Committee reserves the right to review the award of accreditation should there be a major change in the museum's circumstances. A plaque and certificate are presented for display at a successful museum and accreditated institutions are designated by a symbol in the *Museums Yearbook*. To cover the costs of the accreditation exercise, a sliding scale of fees is payable by applicant museums, together with the expense of the visiting panel of assessors. The review fee is negotiable.

While the Accreditation Committee can continue to review and evaluate its procedures there is the continuing difficulty that, with some distinguished and notable exceptions, the profession as a whole has taken little serious interest in the scheme, especially when it is remembered that the original concept was that half of the museums in the UK should be accredited within the early years of the scheme. There is also the prevailing misunderstanding that the scheme is an award for excellence, rather than for an all-round, basic competence and institutional and financial stability, related to the declared aims and policies of the museum.

As serious a problem, at least in terms of public relations, is the view expressed that the accreditation award is a test of professional respectability only, failing to give proper weight to other attributes such as flair, showmanship, and concern for the needs of the museum visitor. This view has led the distinguished historian and museum commentator, Kenneth Hudson (1980), to remark that:

> It would be quite possible for a dull, little visited museum to receive this honour and for a lively, attractive establishment to be turned down.

Hudson also contrasts the scheme with the Museum of the Year Award, which emphasizes the needs of visitors. This view is unfortunate and could lead to a schism represented on the one hand by the professional policies of the Association, and on the other by the pragmatic approach of the Museum of the Year award. Although it is clearly recognized that the two awards are quite different in purpose, there is an opportunity for the two bodies to explore common ground and to see if their efforts could be coordinated.

The confidentiality of the accreditation scheme does not easily engender publicity, although the Committee has often been made aware of the value of the assessors report for bringing about essential and far-reaching improvements, and occasionally for discovering deficiencies in the operation of the museum. At the same time, the publicity value of the award is becoming more widely recognized and the Committee has been able to organize a number of official presentations which have been appreciated by the recipient museums. The American Association of Museums has always emphasized the positive benefits of the scheme, most of which are applicable to the UK, and from which clear lessons can be drawn. Museums that have been accredited in the USA have been prepared to report on their experience and testify to the value of the scheme. In many cases, an application for accreditation has heralded a new sense of purpose and the beginnings of a comprehensive development plan for the institution.

Another difficulty in the UK is that the scheme has not thus far been taken up by the national museums. This would have helped to set an example for others to follow. It is felt in some quarters that a definition of acceptable standards of performance and provision is neither possible nor desirable. This view should not be accepted, especially when the accreditation scheme is available. The present scheme has been designed carefully as the only machinery presently available to the museum for an objective, nationally-recognized assessment of standards in every department of the institution. As the American Association of Museums has warned, if the profession is not prepared to undertake the formal evaluation of standards, others may begin to do so, with results that may be unfortunate.

In the UK, the size of the accreditation fee has been

often quoted as a reason for a museum not applying, and it must be recognized that during the annual preparation of estimates at a time when other schemes and services are at risk, it may seem a luxury to maintain. A sum of between £500 and £1000 for a detailed assessment is at the present time, only a fraction of the cost of a professional consultant's report and, as can be illustrated with examples from both this country and the USA, may be of considerable long-term benefit to the institution in realizing improvements and development plans. The deferment of a small display scheme, a reduction in the number of exhibitions in one year, or the foregoing of an exhibit purchase could put the fee within the reach of most museums and provide them with something which may in turn generate a level of resource investment for which the fee and associated costs are modest prices to pay.

Although in 1968 the Annual General Meeting of The Museums Association adopted a resolution to institute assessment of museums, another three years were to elapse before Conference accepted the two-part statement of policy which resulted in the establishment of the Accreditation Committee to organize the form of the scheme and its implementation. After the success of the pilot scheme, and the recommendation of the Wright Committee that accreditation be further investigated by a Central Museums Council, the scheme was introduced by the Museums Association in 1974. An early difficulty was that two of the Local Authority Associations, namely the Association of District Councils and the Association of County Councils, had commended the scheme, but the Association of Metropolitan Authorities had objected on the grounds that it was not for a professional body to approve or disapprove of the services provided by Local Authorities. This objection was overcome partly by the suggestion that the scheme be operated under the aegis of the Standing Commission, and subsequently a formula was established whereby the Commission could participate by providing general support for the scheme and latterly by providing chairmen for visiting panels from among its own membership.

When the scheme was introduced the effect of local government reorganization was becoming clear, but with no uniform pattern of museum services emerging from the new structure. Responsibilities for museums continued to be vested in different types of authorities, and within these exercised by different committees such as Leisure, Education, Amenity or Recreation. Some county museum services were established to include all museums in a county area, for example Norfolk and Tyne and Wear. Other county services included some, but not all, local authority museums, for instance Merseyside, and some were established with no museums at all, for example, West Yorkshire. The

Museums Association was prepared to offer advice to authorities at the time of reorganization, but generally the concurrent arrangements within the Local Government Bill meant little or no standardization and museums were often the last services to be re-formed by the new authorities. Museum directors had to face these challenges alone. Some were able to take advantage of the situation and to lay the foundation of first-class museum services, others were allowed less opportunity to participate in the corporate planning of their authorities and here the results were sometimes less than satisfactory.

At a time of constraint in Local Authority expenditure, and when resources were allocated strictly in accordance with proven needs, the value of the accreditation scheme in the 1980s can be demonstrated clearly. It may be argued that it is as valuable for a museum to fail as to pass; the report of an external authority being a useful, objective assessment in helping to bring about the necessary improvements to the museum service. The visit and report can also bring fresh thoughts and ideas to the museum, often enabling the curator and governing body to consider long-standing problems in a new light. It has often been remarked that one of the major problems facing the museums profession is the relatively isolated position of the curator from other professionals who might be grappling with similar difficulties, coupled with a reluctance to share and discuss their problems openly. Fellow professionals of distinction serving as members of the assessment panel can often see the problems in a new perspective which can result in positive benefits.

With the reorganization of the Standing Commission into the Museum and Galleries Commission with additional responsibilities for the purchase grant arrangements from the national museum, together with the continuing oversight of the grant-aid arrangements to the Area Museum Councils, the central body which has so often been demanded by the museums profession is within sight. It might now be an appropriate time for the profession to discuss with the Commission how the accreditation scheme could be of value in fostering a planned nation-wide museum service whereby the available grant-in-aid to museums would be used to encourage them to raise standards in accordance with an overall strategy.

In the UK the general reluctance of museums to apply for accreditation has led to the idea that some preliminary assessment is necessary, which may lead in due course to a formal application for accreditation. The way forward may be found in making parts of the *Code of Practice* mandatory within certain essential areas such as constitutional basis, acquisition policy, de-accessioning procedures, security and documentation, as well as discretionary clauses to deal with levels of performance.

A register of museums which have achieved minimum standards in the essential areas is now being actively investigated by the Museums Association. A proposed system of registration might work as follows:

(1) Basic registration of those museums and galleries which have achieved minimum standards.
(2) A review of the registered museums possibly in conjunction and consultation with the Area Councils as to whether a full accreditation application would be appropriate.
(3) Accreditation.
(4) A periodic consideration and evaluation of the accreditation report examining the various courses of action which the museum has taken to achieve higher standards.
(5) Supplementary reviews of those museums to ensure that standards are being maintained and that new developments and changes are of an agreed standard.

In time, the profession may come to share the confidence of our colleagues in the USA that the accreditation scheme is the basis for defining museum standards and needs and therefore is a solution to one of the critical problems facing the profession. It will then no longer be necessary to be reminded of the statement made by Marshall Cubbon (1975), who played a major part in pioneering the scheme in the United Kingdom:

If museums do not seize on this opportunity to have their standards impartially assessed with a view to effecting improvement, the fault does not lie with the Association but with the individual museums.

The accreditation scheme is an important service offered by the Museums Association to member museums. While the decision to apply rests with the Director and governing body, it is hoped that staffs at all levels will inform themselves of the scheme, and recognize its value not only for the institution but also in relation to their professional responsibilities.

As Professor Brian Morris, a member of the Museums and Galleries Commission and chairman of an Accreditation Panel, has said:

The future of the scheme depends on the courage of museums to come forward and take the test.

and he has remarked that in the words of Plato:

An unexamined life isn't worth anything.

Bibliography

AAM (1970), *Museums Accreditation, A report to the Profession,* American Association of Museums, Washington DC

AAM (1973), *Professional Standards,* American Association of Museums, Washington DC

AAM (1978), 'Professional Standards for Museums Accreditation' in Swinney, H. J. (Ed.), *The Handbook of the Accreditation Programme of the American Association of Museums,* American Association of Museums, Washington DC

ALEXANDER, E. P. (1979), *Museums in Motion,* American Association for State and Local History, Nashville

CUBBON, A. M. (1975) 'Accreditation: the position to date', *Museums J.,* **75**(3) Conference report, xx–xxi

HADWIN, M. (1980), 'The Ella Sharp Museums', *Museums News,* **59**(3), 54–59, AAM, Washington DC

HOLT R. J. (1980), 'Small Museums and Accreditation. Chesapecke Bay, Maritime Museum', *Museums News,* **58**(5), 60–62, AAM, Washington DC

HUDSON, K. (1980), *The Good Museums Guide,* Macmillan, London

LOUGHBOROUGH, B. (1982) 'Professional standards and Accreditation *(1)' Museums J.,* **82**(3) Supplement, 5–7

MUSEUMS ASSOCIATION (1982), 'Policy Statements of the Museums Association: Museum Accreditation', *Museums Yearbook 1982* Museum Association, London

OTT. W. (1980), 'Small Museums and Accreditation. *The Rosewell Museum and Art Center', Museums News,* **58**(4), 46–49, AAM, Washington DC

REGER, L. L. (1982), 'Professional Standards', *Museums J.,* **82**(3) Supplement, 2–5

SWINNEY, H. J. (1976), 'Looking at Accreditation', *Museums News,* **55**(2), 15–17, AAM, Washington DC

THOMPSON, J. M. A. (1980), 'Getting the Strength', *Museums Bulletin,* **20** (1)

THOMPSON, J. M. A. (1982), 'The Accreditation Scheme of the Museums Association 1974–1982: a Review' *Museums J.,* **82**(2)

TIMMS, P. (1980) 'Small museums and accreditation: Fitchburg Art Museum', *Museums News* **58**(6), 54–57, AAM, Washington DC

SECTION TWO

COLLECTION MANAGEMENT

Section Editor

Antony J Duggan

13

Introduction

Antony J. Duggan

The acquisition of objects and their subsequent maintenance and use is so much a part of human everyday experience on personal and domestic levels that it is difficult for lay people to grasp the idea that such an activity could demand the existence of paid professionals to do it. The concealed distinction lies in the fact that the professional, in this case the curator, is responsible for looking after things that are not his own, and from this all else is derived.

Even curators themselves have come to realize only in comparatively recent times that the key to their operations is an acquisition policy and that unregulated collection ultimately leads to the deterioration and loss of the very material which it is their duty to conserve. Many curators are surrounded by the forlorn evidence of the lack of such a policy in times gone by. It is now accepted as misguided, even unethical, to acquire what cannot be given a reasonable chance of survival for posterity, but who, it may be asked, is posterity? The creations of nature are cyclical and those of man are finite, but the resulting timelessness of the curatorial struggle against the forces of change and attrition provides no excuse for failing to use such weaponry as exists in a competent and rational way to preserve for as long as possible the best of what has already been handed down.

Although the heritage is primarily that of the society proximate to the area in which the curator works, his collections, if they have merit at all, have wide implications for the nation, and in many cases, the international community as well. In theory, at least, whatever lies in his custody is for the use of everyone. Much skill and administrative ability may be needed to reduce or allay the hazards of such use which conflict with the obligation to preserve everything at all costs.

The problem is compounded by the immense diversity of artefacts by which a curator may be confronted, and such is the span of human creativeness that the curator of a local museum is just as, or even more, likely to be taxed by this than his colleagues in larger but more specialized institutions.

It would be wrong to pretend that solutions exist to all the practical and philosophical problems which are posed by the management of collections. In the chapters which follow, many of those problems are defined and authors of knowledge and experience furnish advice and guidance as to the paths which should be followed in pursuing this fundamental aspect of curatorship.

Further reading

AMERICAN ASSOCIATION OF MUSEUMS (1978), Museum ethics: a report to the profession, *Museum News*, 56(4), 21–30

ART GALLERY AND MUSEUMS ASSOCIATION OF NEW ZEALAND (1978), Art gallery and museum officers' code of ethics, *AGMANZ News*, 9(3)

BOYLAN, P. J. (1977), Museum ethics: Museums Association policies, *Museums J.*, 77(3), 106–111

BOYLAN, P. J. (1981), Towards a code, in *Towards a Code of Ethics in Museums, Museum Professionals Group Trans.*, 16, 9–21

CANADIAN MUSEUMS ASSOCIATION (1979), *A Guide to Museum Positions Including a Statement on the Ethical Behaviour of Museum Professionals*, Ottawa

COLBERT, E. H. 'On being a curator', *Curator*, 1(1), 7–12, New York, 1958

CRUICKSHANK, G. D. R. (1981), A future code, in *Towards a Code of Ethics in Museums', Museum Professionals Group Trans.*, 16, 38–47

GROVE, R. (1974), You don't need a weatherman to tell you which way the wind's blowing, *Museum News*, 52(9), 33–34, AAM, Washington, DC, USA

HILL, C. (1981), Towards an international code of ethics, in *Towards a Code of Ethics in Museums, Museum Professionals Group Trans.*, 16 4–8

INTERNATIONAL COUNCIL OF MUSEUMS (1971), *Ethics of Acquisition*, Paris

INTERNATIONAL COUNCIL OF MUSEUMS (1972), Ethics of Acquisition, *ICOM News,* **26**(2), 77–80

MADISON, H. L. (1925), Tentative code of museum ethics published for the 20th annual meeting of the American Association of Museums, *Museums J.,* **25**, 19–23

MUSEUM ASSISTANTS GROUP (1973), Professional ethics, *Museum Assistants Group News,* 5–9, November

MUSEUM ASSISTANTS GROUP (1974), Professional ethics, *Museum Assistants Group News,* 16–17, January

MUSEUM ASSISTANTS GROUP (1974), Towards a code of conduct for the museum profession, *Museum Assistants Group News,* 13–16, January

MUSEUM ASSISTANTS GROUP 'Museum ethics', *Museum Assistants Group News,* 10 October, 1874

MUSEUMS ASSOCIATION (1982), Code of practice for museum authorities, *Museums Yearbook 1982,* pp. 4–7, Museums Association, London

MUSEUMS ASSOCIATION (1967), Editorial, *Museums J.,* **66**(4), 245–246

MUSEUMS ASSOCIATION (1982), Guidelines for professional conduct, *Museums Yearbook 1982,* pp. 7–9, Museums Association, London

PARR, A. E. (1960, Is there a museums profession?, *Curator,* **3**(2), 101–106

ROYAL ONTARIO MUSEUM (1982), *Statement of Principles and Policies on Ethics and Conduct,* ROM, Canada

SOUTHERN AFRICAN MUSEUMS ASSOCIATION (1979), *Code of Ethics of the Southern African Museums Association,* Capetown

ULLBERG, A. D. (1981), Recent developments in ethical codes and practices among museum staff in the United States, in *Towards a Code of Ethics in Museums, Museum Professionals Group Trans.,* **16**, 57–69

14

The nature of museum collections

Peter Cannon-Brookes

Collecting is a very basic activity, in that food-gathering is a characteristic of all animals, but, setting aside the activities of certain species of birds, the systematic collecting of objects which fulfil a cerebral, as against bodily, function is confined to a limited number of cultures and societies of man. In the evolution of this phenomenon certain, but not all, societies in Western Europe, together with those springing from them, have played a crucial role. However, the identifying characteristics of museum collections – objects assembled and maintained within a specific intellectual environment – separate them from accumulations of household objects, no matter how princely, originally brought together under different criteria, or collections of votive objects given in response to favours sought or received from a deity, church or temple treasuries etc., though by means of a subsequent conscious decision, such accumulations may be converted into museum collections. The intellectual environment which has provided the essential framework for the assembly of museum collections is Renaissaince Humanism and although the first systematic collections would appear to have been formed in the Greek and Roman world, the fundamental Humanist concept that Man could be understood through his creations and Nature through the systematic study of Her manifestations, positively demanded, for the first time, the formation of collections for study purposes.

For the fifteenth-century Humanist the collecting of the surviving remains of Classical antiquity – sculpture, coins, architectural fragments and so on, as well as the texts of the ancient authors – fulfilled an important function and these objects provided a potent insight into the vanished civilization which they sought to emulate and became a powerful stimulus to scholars and creative artists alike. Thus, the formation of collections for study purposes was a concomitant of both the rebirth of Classical rationalism and of experimental science, after the arid philosophical speculations of the Middle Ages, and it is only too easy to underestimate the intellectual basis of the formation of the Renaissance *Kunst – und Wunderkammern* which are the immediate forerunners of modern museum collections. Consequently, the process of collecting cannot be considered separately from the cultural characteristics of the society undertaking it and the widely differing pattern of distribution of museum collections world wide is by no means accidental.

Seen in a historical context, the vast majority of societies, past and present, are 'concept-centred' and for these the individual object is of very limited significance. For these societies the process of collecting/preserving objects is limited to fetishes, totems and so on which perform an ongoing functional role and the transmission of cultural traditions is overwhelmingly oral. However, for the minority – the 'object-centred' societies – the accumulation of objects is of crucial importance in the transmission of the cultural traditions, and the curiosity manifested by them in the artefacts created by the 'concept-centred' societies is not reciprocated. Consequently, the relevance today of museum collections to any particular society, and the significance accorded by it to them, varies widely and although museum collections are relevant to most Western societies, they are not equally important and may indeed be irrelevant to many other societies in the world. Unfortunately, within the 'object-centred' societies the possession of great collections of artefacts and natural history specimens became, during the nineteenth century, a manifestation of nationalism and the concept of the *Musée Napoleon* ultimately reached an apogee of megalomania in Hitler's plans for Linz. On the other hand certain societies, such as the Australian aboriginals and Bushmen, are fundamentally opposed to the collecting of objects because of the danger of interfering with the spiritual dimensions of all objects, and thus the concept of the museum collection is totally unacceptable to them.

Consequently, the process of collecting not only cannot be considered separately from the cultural characteristics of the society undertaking it, but also must take into account the cultural characteristics of the society being collected. Mercifully, the impact of collecting on 'concept-centred' societies has generally been relatively limited, as might be expected from their characteristics, and much less than is sometimes claimed for them today. But the historical consequence has been that for many living societies the only artefacts of any age to survive are those which have been collected by the 'object-centred' societies. This state of affairs remained acceptable to all the parties concerned until the materialistic values of the 'object-centred' societies began to be adopted by all other societies, more as a political manifestation of national cultural identity, cast in an alien mould, than as a newly-developed fundamental need, and the growing demands of previously 'concept-centred' societies for the outward trappings represented by museum collections present formidable problems. Indeed, one of the major museum problems in the last decades of the twentieth century is that posed by the ambitions of societies which were 'concept-centred' and have subsequently adopted the priorities of an 'object-centred' society, and their rights as against those of the long-term 'object-centred' societies through whose collecting activities the artefacts of the former have survived.

Collecting policy

The fundamental role of the museum in assembling objects and maintaining them within a specific intellectual environment emphasizes that museums are storehouses of knowledge as well as store-houses of objects, and that the whole exercise is liable to be futile unless the accumulation of objects is strictly rational. The process of selection is dependent upon the knowledge which has been accumulated and new acquisitions cast new light on previous acquisitions leading to a constant revision of ideas. This feedback process is not only the intellectual lifeblood of the institution, it is also one of the basic elements in the formulation and evolution of an institution's collecting policy. For static collections, such as the Wallace Collection, London, or the Isabella Stewart Gardner Museum, Boston, the processes of selection have been undertaken initially by the private collector who formed them, but these processes have been confirmed by the community in accepting responsibility for those collections as entities, in perpetuity.

For collecting museums there are as many collecting policies as there are museums, but within the general parameters already established by the terms of reference of the institution *per se,* the collecting policy adopted will almost invariably be a matter of reducing rather than increasing the collecting options (that is, a natural history museum is unlikely to consider the acquisition of a Raphael altarpiece as central to its collecting policy, notwithstanding the considerable botanical interest of the plants depicted around the feet of the Virgin!). Collecting policy will be, in most institutions, heavily circumscribed if not dictated by much more mundane considerations, such as financial constraints and limitations on space, before the strategic plan for the future development of the collections can be formulated.

Given those constraints, and the legal and moral limitations imposed upon the freedom of action of the institution in its collecting activities, the main questions in formulating a collecting policy will revolve around the present and future balance of the collections and the services which are to be based on them. In evolving that policy within the resources available the first strategic objective to be clarified is whether the collection is intended to be representative of a broad spectrum of possible material, or comprehensive within a much narrower field, or what compromise between the two; although the desirability of concentrating a high proportion of rare or unique material into relatively few collections is hotly disputed. The advantages for scholars and scientists of such concentrations are self-evident, but by their very nature they increase the risks of catastrophic loss in the event of a disaster and they tend to negate the fundamental strategy of museum collections in providing comparative material on a geographically wide spread. The same arguments can also be put forward in respect of temporary concentrations, as represented by temporary exhibitions, but an important factor in the formulation of collecting policy all too often neglected is the capacity of the institution to curate and conserve both its existing collections and the objects it is seeking to acquire.

The formulation of collecting policy and its operation are likely to be two different matters since it can be justly argued that a too tightly defined and operated collecting policy ignores the realities of collecting and may bar the institution from benefitting from the unexpected. On the other hand, windfalls accepted more out of opportunism than as the product of a rational analysis can be extremely detrimental to the future development of the institution. Nevertheless, the fundamental function of museums is the acquisition of objects (a museum without a permanent collection of objects is a misnomer) and in this process there is the act of deliberate selection. The exercise of judgement can only be undertaken on the basis of a sound knowledge of the object, the group to which it belongs and its interrelationships; the geologist taking a specimen from one bed in a cliff face is as much exercising a process of rational selection as an art gallery director bidding for a Rembrandt at an auction. Furthermore, apart from being able to obtain good title for any new acquisition and to conserve it, the museum should be able to preserve it under conditions which will ensure its availability for museum purposes and should make the acquisition with the intention of retaining it within the collection in perpetuity. If there is any doubt about the latter it should be clearly stated in the documents recording the decision to acquire it.

Perpetuity is not accepted by a number of museums, such as the Metropolitan Museum, New York, which as early as 1885 decided that 'the Museum could in all propriety exchange duplicates of which it had no use, for others which would prove important and valuable additions to the collection'. In the Metropolitan Museums *Annual Report*, published in October 1970, the Trustees announced formally the renewed emphasis on the upgrading of its holdings, rather than on simple accumulation, with the statement that;

> The Metropolitan has begun a determined effort to refine the quality of its numerous collections. From now on the various funds restricted for the purchase of works of art given to the Museum will be utilised to pursue the rare masterpiece of the highest quality. It is an important part of our policy to reach out for the few works of art of exceptional importance and to reject the temptation to purchase large numbers of objects of secondary or tertiary significance. Refinement of the collections also involves the disposal, whenever legally and professionally permissable, of those objects that for any one of a variety of reasons are no longer appropriate for the Museum. Objects selected for deaccessioning are examined with care every bit as stringent as that brought to bear upon a work of art proposed for addition to the collections.
>
> The provisions for exhibition and storage space in the Comprehensive Architectural Plan were based on this stabilisation of the extent of the collections; indeed, the Museum's firmly stated commitment to stay within the boundaries provided in the Plan was a major reason that the Plan was approved.

Thomas P. F. Hoving, the then Director of the Metropolitan Museum, reissued the relevant sections of the Annual Report in a statement made in 1973 (*Museums News,* May 1973) and added 'It is important to emphasize that it is aesthetic gain, not financial gain, that ultimately determines the Metropolitan Museum's program of deaccessioning and acquisition. In such transactions, the aesthetic factor must be weighed as well as economic ones. But the economic factors concerning works of art are extremely complex and open to many interpretations.' The evolution of the Metropolitan Museum's collecting policy illustrates excellently the pitfalls as well as the advantages of accepting disposals deacces-

sioning as an integral part of a museum's collecting policy, and no hard and fast rules can be proposed. On the other hand the culling of natural history collections, for example, fortunately does not often have the same economic overtones and can be undertaken that much more dispassionately.

More than any other great museum, the Metropolitan Museum has been in recent years prepared to explain both its philosophy and its techniques of collection in great detail, and in *The Chase, the Capture* (1975) a wide range of collecting activity has been discussed by the then Director, Thomas Hoving, and his staff. In that account there is an exhaustive description of the processes leading to an acquisition, and although other museums have been less willing to make public their own processes of acquisition, few will differ greatly in their fundamentals. The Metropolitan Museum 'Recommended Purchase Blank' and 'Recommended Purchase – Curator's Report' are models of their kind.

An additional constraint placed upon the collecting activities of art museums is concerned with the moral and legal rights of the creative artist (the 'Droit Morale'), and this is a particular problem in the acquisition of three-dimensional works of art. Apart from aesthetic objections to the pernicious practice of surmoulage (the casting of bronzes from a finished bronze and not the original plaster prepared by the artist) such casts, when not specifically authorized by the sculptor, should not be acquired by museums, and similarly museums should avoid the acquisition of unauthorized enlargements and unauthorized transfers into new materials (in particular posthumous bronze casts from welded or carved original sculptures) unless they be clearly identified at all times as unauthorized reproductions. However, when a sculptor has created a model with the specific intention of casting it in bronze such casts, be they contemporary or posthumous, are legitimate and it is for the curator to satisfy himself that the aesthetic standard is appropriate to his collection. Further problems are posed by the rights claimed by artists to have their works displayed only in conditions which do not distort their artistic intentions. What constitutes a significant distortion will all too often be the subject of sharp differences of opinion between artists and their heirs or curators, but the museum must consider carefully the implications of acquiring damaged or modified works of art if the intention is to display them to the public, and these constraints are over and above the normal critical judgement exercised by the curator.

Sources of specimens

There are almost as many sources of specimens as there are specimens themselves and in pursing its collecting activities the museum has a very wide range

RECOMMENDED PURCHASE BLANK

TO THE DIRECTOR AND THE ACQUISITIONS COMMITTEE: cc: Vice-Director for Curatorial and Educational Affairs (2 copies of this blank and 2 copies of Curator's Report) Registrar (this blank only) Secretary (this blank only)

I recommend the purchase of the object(s) fully described in the attached report and briefly captioned below.

Classification _____

Artist. title. date:

Vendor: Recommended loan class:

Price:

Additional expenses: Transportation $ _____ Insurance $ _____
                          Sender to pay   Sender to pay
                          M.M.A. to pay   M.M.A. to pay

                     Installation $_____ Restoration $ _____

                     Other $_____

Recommendation approved: Submitted by:

_____   _____

Director: Curator of _____

                                           Date _____

FOR USE OF SECRETARY'S OFFICE ONLY

ACTION BY ACQUISITIONS COMMITTEE To be charged against income from the

        (authorized)   _____ Fund. 19

Purchase (not authorized) _____ Authorized at: $_____

Reported to Board _____   Secured for: $_____

Reported to   Purchase authorization no._____

Acquisitions Committee _____   Accession no. _____

RECOMMENDED PURCHASE – CURATOR'S REPORT

Classification

Attach at least one photograph of the object(s) to the Director's and Vice-Director, copies.

I. Name the title, artist, nationality or school, period, material, dimensions in inches and centimetres.

II. Full description of the object. Provide a complete visual account, including the description of all parts. Transcribe any inscriptions, describe marks and mention any added attachments or missing parts, etc.

III. Describe the condition of the piece, indicating any repairs and attempting a prognosis for future condition. Name the results obtained from scientific investigations, whether of miscroscopy, chemical tests, X-ray, infra-red, ultra-violet, spectrographic analysis, thermo–luminescence, etc.

IV. State the function of the piece, and whether anything about the object indicates its function as part of a greater whole or as an independent work.

V. Describe the iconography of the object. Does it follow traditional iconography, or is there something unusual in its iconography?

VI. Stylistic considerations

   A. State briefly your initial reaction to the object.

   B. Describe the style and relate the style of the piece to the appropriate artist, school, period, etc.

   C. Discuss and illustrate the two or three pieces that make the best stylistic comparisons with this piece. Indicate what distinctive qualities this piece has in relation to them in terms of style, technique, condition, documentation, etc.

   D. Provide a list of all relevant works of art, whether copies, variants or other closely similar compositions, pointing out the relationship to each work named.

VII. State how the work of art complements the existing Museum collections or how it fills a gap.

VIII. Explain your plans for exhibiting and publishing the piece.

IX. Give the history of the piece, all known provenance with traditional documentation, when available. Include any hearsay evidence or traditional provenance, with source.

Recommended Purchase—Curator's Report—*cont.*

X. Give any significant archaeological information.

XI. List all published references, pointing out those of greatest importance. Also include any expert advice sought or volunteered from outside the Museum.

XII. Give a resume of your reasons for deciding to recommend the piece, being candid as to its strengths and weaknesses, its rarity of quality, technique, type, etc. Mention any problem outstanding that could affect the decision to buy.

XIII. Tell how long you have known of the piece and give a history of negotiations.

XIV. If possible give recent market prices for comparable works of art.

XV. Financial considerations

    A. If the object is to be purchased, state the price _____

    B. State the name of the fund if you recommend that a specific fund be used.

    C. If the object is to be acquired by exchange, specify M.M.A. object(s) involved, including accession number(s), valuation and status of de-accessioning.

    D. Specify any anticipated additional expenses:

Transportation $ _____ Insurance $ _____
   Sender to pay _____ Sender to pay _____
   M.M.A. to pay _____ M.M.A. to pay _____

Installation $ _____ Restoration $ _____

Other $ _____
    E. State any conditions attached to the purchase. State chances for bargaining.

of opportunities within its collecting policy. However, the museum is not alone in the world, and in obtaining its specimens, directly or vicariously, it must respect the need to conserve both the world's natural resources and its cultural heritage. Consequently, the deliberate killing of an individual with breeding potential belonging to a threatened species, in order to obtain a specimen, is contrary to the spirit of conserving natural resources and the museum seeking to acquire such a specimen should approach a zoo or obtain a specimen from an earlier collection, which for extinct species, such as the Great Auk, is the only possible course. All collecting activities should seek to inflict a minimum of damage on the ecology of the area in which the collecting takes place and indiscriminate techniques (such as moth lamps) should only be employed when more specific techniques are unavailable. The role of the museum is that of the active conserver and passive connivance at, or financial encouragement of, the flouting of conservation measures is unacceptable. Similarly, the museum must actively discourage illicit excavations and avoid purchasing archaeological and related material which is inadequately documented. Indeed the *sine qua non* of all museum acquisitions is that no laws and regulations have been contravened en route to the museum.

The relationship between museums and ancient monuments is a great deal more fraught and the responsibility of museums to co-operate in the con-

servation of ancient monuments and historic buildings has all too often been ignored. Art museums
are, in a sense, at the top of the art food chain, in as
much as virtually nothing now housed in them was
in fact created specifically for them, and little, once it
has entered, will leave them in the future.

It is convenient to divide the accommodation of
works of art into primary, secondary and tertiary
environments in order to clarify that chain. Primary
environments house works of art specifically created
for them, such as the monumental sculpture and frescoes which form an integral part of the structure of
buildings and also the suites of furnishings, etc., created for a specific room. Unfortunately the scruples
of most museums in not removing the sculpture or
frescoes does not extend to the furnishings or, for
that matter, the framed paintings hanging on the
walls even if they were painted specifically for that
location. This lack of consistency, encouraged by the
fiscal policies of governments, results all too often in
the finest objects being torn from a primary environment and the remainder being broken up on the
grounds that it has been irretrievably compromised.
The museum should only acquire objects from
primary environments as a last resort and only after
every effort has been made to preserve that environment intact. However, with archaeological specimens it is often impossible to conserve them *in situ*
and the removal of them to the museum is the only
means of ensuring their continued survival after
excavation.

Secondary environments are those accommodating works of art created for other locations but
brought together by later collectors exercising discrimination, so that the totality of the assemblages are
more significant than merely the sum totals of their
component parts. In such a secondary environment
there may be major works of art which are less
closely linked to the accommodation than those in
the primary environment, but the totality is worthy
of conservation and, although the removal of specific
items might be marginally less compromising, the
future conservation of the ensemble is likely to be
hazarded. In contrast to the primary and secondary
environment, the tertiary, which includes all
museums and art galleries, is deliberately depersonal-
ized and the context in which the works are displayed is totally artificial. Consequently there are
moral arguments to support the view that, contrary
to the *laissez faire* attitude of allowing museums to
use historic buildings as a convenient source of raw
materials for their displays, the museums should
have a specific responsibility for the conservation of
primary and secondary environments and only
acquire works of art removed from them as a last
resort when it is for their protection. Consequently,
art museums should exercise great discretion as to
their sources of specimens and, like the natural his-

tory and archaeological museums, seek to avoid
hazarding, by their own actions, the conservation of
the resources on which they draw. Similarly, the collecting of technological artefacts should not, where
possible, lead to the destruction of the site and related
material of significance.

Acquisition of specimens

Having formulated its collecting policy and agreed
the acceptable sources of specimens, the next task is
to clarify the means by which the acquisition of
specimens may be achieved. The principal mechanisms by which museums acquire artefacts are gift,
purchase or bequest, while for natural history specimens it is more often by direct or indirect collection.
All can present increasingly formidable legal and
moral problems, but despite the tendency for
UNESCO to include natural history specimens in
the category of cultural property, the problems
posed by them are at present the least intractable.
Indeed, the main difficulties experienced in the collecting of natural history specimens are those concerned with the legitimacy of the authority under
which the collecting is, or was, undertaken. One
view, albeit extreme, is that any specimen collected
during a period of colonial rule has been acquired
illegally and that neither the museum nor a private
collector seeking to sell such a specimen possesses
'good title'. Other problems stem from the
increasingly complex laws intended to conserve
threatened species and the need for the vendor/donor
to prove to the curator that the material offered to
the museum had been obtained before the introduction of the relevant legislation, or had been acquired
legally since then. To take an example, for birds'
eggs this is often well-nigh impossible and the temptation to fence eggs which have been illegally
acquired, by a process of 'topping up' a genuine private collection formed shortly before the regulations
came into force, is self-evident. Indeed the 'topping
up' of ancestral collections of works of art is not
unheard of and provenances cannot always be
accepted at their face value. The museum has to take
all reasonable precautions to ensure that the specimens which it is acquiring have been obtained by the
owner legally, and that its own collecting actitivies
do not contravene either individual property rights
or relevant legislation in the country of origin.

Similarly, the acquisition of 'good title' is of crucial importance in acquiring artefacts and the
museum can only make acquisitions on this basis,
exercising the utmost good faith. Thus the vendor/
donor must himself not only possess good title but
the transfer of ownership must not contravene any
legislation or statutory controls. Both of these factors will vary from country to country, as do the

122 *The nature of museum collections*

limitations on their effective lives, so that materials stolen during the Napoleonic Wars do not present any legal problems today when bought and sold, while the status of material stolen during the Second World War will depend upon which country it was stolen from and the country in which it is located today. It is for the vendor to establish that he has good title before entering into a contract of sale, but *caveat emptor* applies and the wise museum, when making major purchases, will seek specific assurances from the vendor, backed if necessary with documentary evidence, and will enter into a formal contract with him. The moral problems posed by the acquisition of artefacts which have, at some time in their history, been the subjects of illegal acts must be assessed by the museum in accordance with the particular merits of the case in hand if the vendor can nevertheless prove good title. The limitations will depend upon the laws effective at each stage and it can be argued that as the guardian of the public interest the museum must behave strictly in accordance with the law as it is, no more and no less, and not, perhaps, as the over scrupulous curator might wish it to be. The question of balancing legality and morality when the passage of legislation is so much slower than the rate of development of informed opinion remains highly controversial, and it is always essential that governing bodies are fully aware of all contingent facts when deciding upon an acquisition.

The Metropolitan Museum has, in the last decade, become particularly sensitive to the problems posed by illicit exports and when an object is offered to it without a clear provenance or plausible history, a formal letter is sent to the appropriate bodies in the possible country (countries) of origin.

Dear

1. The Metropolitan Museum of Art in New York is considering the purchase of the following work of art which, to the best of our knowledge, is unpublished (photograph attached as Appendix I).

   a) Subject _____

   b) Material _____

   c) Dimensions _____

   d) Condition _____

2. In this form letter we should like to ask whether you, your ministry or service, have any information concerning the provenance or previous ownership of the described work of art.

3. We would appreciate hearing from you at your earliest convenience. If after 45 days we have received no reply from you, we shall assume you have no information concerning the above mentioned work of art.

4. At your early convenience, we would appreciate the return of the enclosed photograph.

Very truly yours,

Ashton Hawkins
Secretary

If no objections are raised, or after at least 45 days, no reply is received, the Metropolitan Museum assumes that all is well and it proceeds with the purchase.

Additional problems are posed by copyright and *droits de suite* which some would wish to be made inalienable. In making an acquisition the museum should always seek to acquire the copyright but if this is not owned by the vendor/donor the governing body should be informed of the limitations placed upon the museum's freedom of action by making such an acquisition. *Droits de suite* (resale royalty rights) are only applicable if a work of art subject to them is deaccessioned/sold in a country or state of the U.S.A. subject to the relevant legislation, and this may influence the place and means of disposal selected. Once again the museum acquiring a work of art subject to this liability should seek either to acquire the rights from the artist or his heirs at the time of acquisition or seek a waver of his rights.

Collection ethics

Collection ethics, as against collecting ethics, have been the subject of much less detailed scrutiny in recent decades although the ethics of conservation have attracted considerable attention and are discussed elsewhere. The holding of a collection is the acceptance of a trust on behalf of mankind, though the more immediate beneficiaries are those defined in legal terms. However, the legal rights of the community with regard to collections held on trust for its benefit vary enormously between different countries and they do not always correspond closely to the moral rights claimed for them. This is again in part due to the more rapid rate at which moral rights become accepted to their becoming enshrined in legislation. Consequently, the legal rights of the community remain often minimal, when sought in respect of specific problems, and its moral rights are closely limited to the extent to which it is prepared to carry out the trust. In other words, the whole community is, through its political representatives, a trustee and it has in this respect no more rights than its degree of commitment allows. On the other hand the legal rights of the object in the museum – not to be hazarded or neglected so as to compromise its survival – are minimal while the moral rights of the object to be the recipient of basic conservation services and security are fundamental to the establishment of a museum. In other words, the community, once it has taken on the responsibility for the housing and maintenance of an object in perpetuity is morally not at liberty to change its priorities and neglect that object at will, and the legal constraints placed upon trustees under British and British-based law are clear, but few legal precedents exist for the courts to enforce them.

Much more controversial are the rights of the creator of the object (*Droit Morale*), notwithstanding its acquisition by the museum, and not only to continue to enjoy the fruits of copyright. The artistic rights of the creator are claimed to be that his creation may not be willfully destroyed, mutilated or exhibited in such a condition or manner as to distort seriously his artistic intentions, without his specific consent, and the constraints which they impose upon the museum's collecting policy have been noted above. However, the ethical problems posed by the display of works of art which have been damaged and/or restored while in the possession of the museum are of great significance, since the maintenance of the integrity of the object is a fundamental objective of all museums. The problem becomes particularly acute with certain types of contemporary art, not least paintings with large areas of undifferentiated colour, when the creator can claim that a single scratch has distorted his artistic intentions beyond redemption. The artist is, unfortunately, not always the most dispassionate and disinterested of judges.

Disposals

Disposals, or deaccessions, from a museum collection require a higher standard of care than that accorded to acquisitions, if for no other reason that whereas the object entering the collection only attains its full potential in relation to the objects which it joins, the removal of an object can damage irreparably a group or sequence of objects in ways not immediately apparent. A school of thought, in opposition to that represented by the Metropolitan Museum, holds that museums must live with their mistakes as well as their successes, and the disposal of objects thought to be mistakes constitutes an attempt to falsify the historical record the museum was set up to document dispassionately. However, setting aside these fundamental objections to disposals, the first question must be whether the museum has the legal right to do so. Many art museums do not have the legal power to dispose of items from their collections, no matter what were the particular conditions under which the individual acquisition was made. Others allow only the disposal of purchases, not gifts or bequests, while others treat their collections as stock with the quality to be upgraded by a balanced programme of acquisitions and disposals as the opportunity arises. The arguments for employing the latter approach are perhaps easier to justify in the field of contemporary art than, for instance, in the Old Master field, and there is justification for the proposal to make such acquisitions into a holding collection for a period of say twenty years and then for the board to reconsider the acquisition before recommending its inclusion in the permanent collection.

If the institution has the legal power to dispose of objects from its permanent collection much will depend upon the precise wording of the decision previously taken to acquire it and any conditions laid down by the vendor/donor. Unless there are overwhelming reasons for acting otherwise, it is always understood that any pecuniary gain stemming from a disposal is reserved for the acquisition of further material and no other purposes. However, the mechanisms which have been evolved to enable disposals vary enormously and can take the form of gifts (appropriate, for example, to natural history and archaeological material of little or no pecuniary value), exchange or part-exchange (particularly useful for study collections, but also used by some museums in the United States of America for the acquisition of works of art from the Fine Art trade) or sale. In any such disposals the residual rights of the donor/vendor/creative artist must be safeguarded, as well as those of the institution as a legally-constituted body and those of the community which it serves. The public scandals which have stemmed from the disposal in the past of individual objects and collections have encouraged museums either to cloak their disposals in great secrecy (an approach likely to increase the risk of abuse, as well as the public outcry if or when they are made public) or to undertake the drafting of detailed policy documents well in advance of any specific disposals. One of the most recent and most thorough documents of this nature is the *Deaccessioning Policy* prepared by the Art Gallery of Ontario and its accompanying *Disposal Policy*, and the separation of deaccessioning (a curatorial decision) from disposal (an administrative function) is particularly valuable and is quoted below.

Deaccessioning policy

Introduction

The Art Gallery of Ontario has disposed of works of art in the past. The most significant recent instances was the sale of Pissarro's *Printemps, Temps Gris, Eragny* (1890) in 1972. Such deaccessioning was done in an orderly and responsible fashion with the full participation of staff, respective Collection Committees and the Board. Nevertheless, practice and procedure for deaccessioning have heretofore not been defined in a formal way as policy.

Deaccessioning

It should be understood that the term 'deaccession' as used by the Gallery does not necessarily mean sale. It does mean that the appropriate persons at the Gallery, that is the relevant collection committee and the Board, have concluded, with the aid of staff recommendations, that a work of art may be removed from the Collection and be further considered for disposal by sale, exchange, etc. Before proceding to deaccession a work of art, the Gallery should consider the alternative of offering the work on extended loan to a sister institution, preferably in Ontario. A work of art may be removed from the Collection for a number of reasons:

(a) The work has no relevant place or useful purpose within the collecting, exhibiting, or research programmes of the Gallery.
(b) The work does not add significantly to the Gallery's holdings in its historical period or in its representation of a specific and could be disposed of in order to acquire another work which would add to the depth or scope of the Collection.
(c) The work is truly a duplicate, as may be possible in the case of prints or so-called multiples.
(d) The work for some reason has deteriorated beyond usefulness.

It is important, however, that procedure for deaccessioning include a system of checks and balances to ensure that a proposal for deaccessioning be discussed from all points of view. While such a system must not be so extensive as to deter proposals, its purpose is to allow a review of all pertinent considerations such as:

(1) *Changing Taste*. Deaccessioning must not be governed by current fashion or the individual taste of curators. Consideration must be given to the temporal nature of aesthetic judgements and changing taste in art historical and aesthetic evaluations.

(2) *Presentation/Installation*. The presence of a pair of, or even several, similar works in the collection may not be a justification for deaccessioning. Such concentration may make not only a stronger statement for the artists, but allow a more handsome and telling installation.

(3) *Research Use*. It is sometimes a rule of thumb referred to by collection committees when considering gifts that if we would exhibit a work of art we should accept it. The reverse – that if we do not use a work of art we should deaccession it – is not so clearly applied. The usefulness of a work may also be gauged in relation to the research function of a museum. While there can be no question regarding the importance of acquiring exhibitable and significant works of art, it would be a mistake to assume that works not on display are not important to the collection. A collection becomes increasingly important to scholars and other museums when it

holds a group of significant works by a given artist, or that are representative of a period school, even if many of these are viewed only in the vaults. Building in depth should never be undermined by a deaccessioning policy which assumes that exhibition is the primary function, and those works which appear to be less important or unexhibitable should be disposed of. Such works might better be sent on loan to sister institutions until they are needed.

(4) *The Fabric of the Collection.* The Collection has a character; it is made up of many separate collections and collection minds, and reflects the changing taste of different periods and individuals. It is, as a whole, an entity reflecting the community, curators, private collectors (Walker, Presgrave, Wood, etc.) and other organizations (the CNE), who have contributed to its growth. The pictures acquired, both 'good' and 'bad', all document the history of collecting in Toronto and the influence of these collections is an important part of the history of the development of art in Canada. The fabric of the Collection should be respected as having integrity and importance in its own right.

(5) *Historical Perspective.* This is not unrelated to the question of taste but is specifically concerned with the problem of how long it takes for a work of art to find its proper place within the history of art. For the gallery this is a consideration which might apply to such modern non-Canadian works which fall outside the Paris-New York mainstream tradition (for example, the English paintings acquired in the 1950s). That such works may currently be little exhibited is in itself not a sufficient criterion for deciding their future.

Steps for deaccessioning

(1) A proposal for deaccessioning can originate only with the curator responsible for the area of the collection in question.

(2) The curator recommends the deaccessioning to the Chief Curator and the Director. If all three decide that the matter should be considered further the following steps are taken:

(a) The Gallery ascertains that there are no legal or time restrictions against disposal of the work and that the disposal will not contravene Cultural Property legislation. Where there are no legal restrictions to deaccessioning, the Gallery will consult with the donor or, if the donor is not living, the donor's heirs or legal representatives.

(b) The recommendations for deaccessioning by the appropriate curator is presented to a committee comprised of the Director, Chief Curator and all curators

(c) Only upon receiving unanimous approval by the above committee is the recommendation for deaccessioning presented to the appropriate Collection Committee.

(d) The curator makes a presentation to the appropriate Collection Committee. The presentation must include an evaluation of the work. If the curator estimates the work to be worth more than $2000.00, two outside appraisals should be presented.

(d) The Collection Committee decides on the basis of the preceding presentation whether to forward the recommendation for approval by the Board.

(f) The Chairman of the Collection Committee, with the participation of the responsible curator, presents the recommendation for deaccessioning to the Board. Approval by the Board requires a two-thirds majority vote of members present.

Disposal policy

Methods of disposal are: outright sale, credit against future purchase, gift and destruction. If disposal is by outright sale, sale by public auction is preferable, but other recipients may be another institution, a private individual or a dealer. If disposal is not by public auction, sister institutions, especially in Canada, should be given preference over private individuals or dealers. Only public institutions may be the recipients of gifts of deaccessioned works. Given the range of options, the responsible curator would seem to be in the best position to explore possibilities and to undertake negotiations.

At no time should a staff member, board member, or anyone connected with the Gallery in any formal way, including membership of a committee or under a contract, etc., be permitted to acquire directly from the Gallery a deaccessioned work of art.

Steps for disposal

(1) In order to protect the Gallery from criticism, authority for the method of disposal of the work of art be granted by the Director, the Chief Curator and the appropriate Collection Committee.

(2) If the method of disposal is other than auction (or destruction) the negotiated terms of disposal (sales, exchange, etc.) must be approved by the Chief Curator and the Director.

(a) If the work of art is valued at less than $25 000 and the negotiated terms fall below the evaluation as determined by the two outside and disinterested appraisals as provided in Step (d) of the Deaccessioning Policy, further approval is required from the appropriate Collection Committee.

(b) If the work of art is appraised above $25 000 and the negotiated terms fall below the appraisal as provided in Step (d) of the Deaccessioning Policy, approval of the Board is required.

(3) After the proposal for disposal has been approved as per the appropriate preceding steps, the Corporate Secretary reviews and approves the exact terms of the sale or exchange, and in the case of a consignment sale such terms are then set forth in a letter of agreement signed by the Corporate Secretary on behalf of the Gallery.

All proceeds realized from an act of deaccessioning and disposal must be credited to the art purchase fund. Prior consideration should be given to allocate such proceeds to the collection area from which the deaccessioning proposal originated.

All acts of deaccessioning and disposal will be reported at the meeting immediately following the General Meeting of the Art Gallery of Ontario.

Bibliography

AAM (1978), *Museum Ethics,* American Assocation of Museums, Washington

ART GALLERY OF ONTARIO (June 1983) Deaccessioning and disposal policies of the art gallery of Ontario, *The International Journal of Museum Management and Curatorship,* **2**(2), pp. 204–208

ASSOCIATION OF ART MUSEUM DIRECTORS, (1981) *Professional Practices in Art Museums – Report of the Ethics and Standards Committee,* AAMD, Savannah

DIA (1979), The Detroit Institute of Arts *Guidelines for Professional Practices,* Detroit

ELSON, A. *et al: Statement on Standards for Sculptural Reproduction and Preventive Measures to Combat Unethical Casting in Bronze*

HOVING, T. P. F. (May 1973), A Policy Statement from the Met *Museum News,* **51**(9), pp. 43–45

HOVING, T. P. F. (1975), *The Chase, the Capture: Collecting at the Metropolitan,* New York, approved by the College Art Association of America 27 April 1974

MERRYMAN, J. H. (1977), *Legal Aspects of Museum Operations: Principles and Code of Curatorial Conduct,* Stanford

TABORSKY, E. (December 1982) The socio-structural role of the museum, *The International Journal of Museum Management and Curatorship,* **1**(4), pp. 339–345

15

Documenting collections

Sheila M. Stone

The museum has a unique role as a repository for three-dimensional objects gathered from both the natural and the man-made environments. The very act of collection removes them from their context and, although many of them are inherently interesting or aesthetically appealing, it is the close interrelationship with their environment which increases their usefulness, and the enjoyment of them by the museum public. Preserving the non-intrinsic information about an object, such as where it comes from, who found or used it, and what it was used for is the responsibility of the institution that keeps it. For that reason the documentation of museum collections is vital.

The function of documentation

Many museums have collections of poorly documented objects which have lost much of their usefulness due to the lack of associated information. Documentation is fundamental to curatorial work, and is used as a basic source of information on the collection. Comprehensive documentation is the pivot on which curatorship depends, and is essential:

(1) For the effective management of collections, encompassing storage, security, auditing and insurance.
(2) To formulate acquisition policies by identifying the scope and limitations of the collection.
(3) To enable the collections to be researched and published. The value of publications and the presentation of the collection through displays and educational work is related to the quality of the documentation.

As stated by the Museum Documentation Association:

With an effective documentation system such activities will still involve a great deal of effort: but they will be possible. Without an effective documentation system many of them will be impossible. (MDA, 1980a)

The development of museum documentation

Since the 1960s, there has been a growing awareness of the need for systematic documentation of collections. The vocational, as well as academic, training of museum personnel has led to an increased professionalism and re-evaluation of the role of museums in society. Before 1960, often the only person likely to come into direct contact with the collection was the curator, but now collections are used by a growing number of people in a variety of ways. Efficient information retrieval is essential if collections are to be utilized to the full and the information contained within them is to be exploited.

Another, less happy, aspect of late-twentieth century society which has emphasized the need for documentation, has been the increasing number of thefts from museums. The security implications of this are detailed in an MA Information Sheet (Museums Association, 1981) and include the inability to trace items at district and internal audits, the apparent difficulty of museums in proving title to stolen objects in the Courts, and an increase in what are euphemistically termed 'internal losses'.

The inaugural meeting of The Museums Association in 1889 considered the possibility of producing a comprehensive index of all provincial museum collections (Plantnauer and Howarth, 1890). Its desirability was reiterated by Lewis (1965) who added a note of urgency:

However intimidating the sheer volume of the work may appear, unless a plan is formulated speedily for the compilation of such an index, national specialist indexes will come to fruition. If, however, a standardized system of indexing museum collections can be agreed by a body of expert opinion, then not only can a national index be started but curators wishing to re-catalogue their collections can do so to the standard.

To promote this objective, the Information Retrieval Group of the Museums Association (IRGMA) was formed in 1967. An account of its progress, and the subsequent formation of the Museum Documentation Association (MDA) is given in the following paper by Roberts, and in a report of the IRGMA Standards Subcommittee (1977). The future development of the MDA, and the current state of documentation in the UK museums has been summarized by the MDA Development Committee (1982). Documentation in other countries has been described by Roberts and Light (1980).

Principles of documentation

Data standards

The standardized system of recording for museums referred to by Lewis (1965) now exists, encapsulated in the Museum Documentation System (MDS). This system, derived from the work of IRGMA and the MDA, defines the standard form for the recording of museum data, known as the *data standard*. Porter (1978) describes it as follows:

> Basically, the standard supplies a format, which is a hierarchical organization of museum data concepts, and a set of recommendations for slotting pieces of museum data into the various concept headings in the format.

The data standard and data definition language is described in detail in an MDA manual (MDA, 1980c). A range of recording media based on the MDS data standard, such as cards, forms and instruction manuals has been published, and the GOS computer package is available for the processing of museum records. A full description of the Museum Documentation System is published in an MDA manual (MDA, 1980b). The MDA cards have proved extremely popular throughout the United Kingdom; over half a million were sold in the two years after publication, and the number sold to date exceeds two and a half million. Any museum setting up a new documentation system, or redesigning an existing one, should ensure that the MDS data standards are followed, even though MDA recording media may not be employed.

Features of a documentation system

The aims of a museum documentation system are to preserve all known information about an object and to help satisfy the needs of the user, whether he be a curator, research worker or member of the public. To achieve these aims a documentation system should possess singular features, and should include three types of documentation which comprise a comprehensive museum record:

(1) *Initial documentation,* on the entry of the object into the museum for loan, identification, acquisition or other purposes.
(2) *Item documentation,* being a full record of all information about the object incorporated in the record, or cross-referenced to other files.
(3) *Control documentation,* which records the movement and location of an object. This is an essential tool for collections management.

The system into which this comprehensive record fits should be capable of including any number of entries, and should not impose a limit on the size of the total record. Examples are given in *Figures 15.1–15.5.*

It is important that the system should allow for the addition of data. It should be able to accept information about a wide range of items, and allow adequate cross-referencing between the different types of record incorporated in it. There should also be safeguards to protect confidential information. It is most important that the system should be easy to use and maintain, and that documentation procedures are set down in a manual. A system that is too complex or cumbersome may serve the collection little better than no system at all.

Documentation practice

Designing the system

When considering documentation, many curators start from the 'hardware', such as cards, registers, sheets and computers, without undertaking a comprehensive analysis of the documentation problems and information retrieval requirements in their museums. Such critical assessment is known as the *systems approach* which, as Orna (Orna and Pettitt, 1980) has pointed out:

> is often thought of as being exclusively a computer technique; it is in fact a straightforward and commonsense way of looking at problems, which pays off whether the end result is computer use or not.

The diversity of documentation systems has been illustrated by Orna and Pettitt (1980), and Roberts *et al.* (1983), and serves to reflect the variety of museums and their collections, and emphasize that no one system can suit all museums.

Those contemplating system design will find useful advice in Orna (1982) on defining information needs and analysing the existing information situation. The analysis should take into account the scope

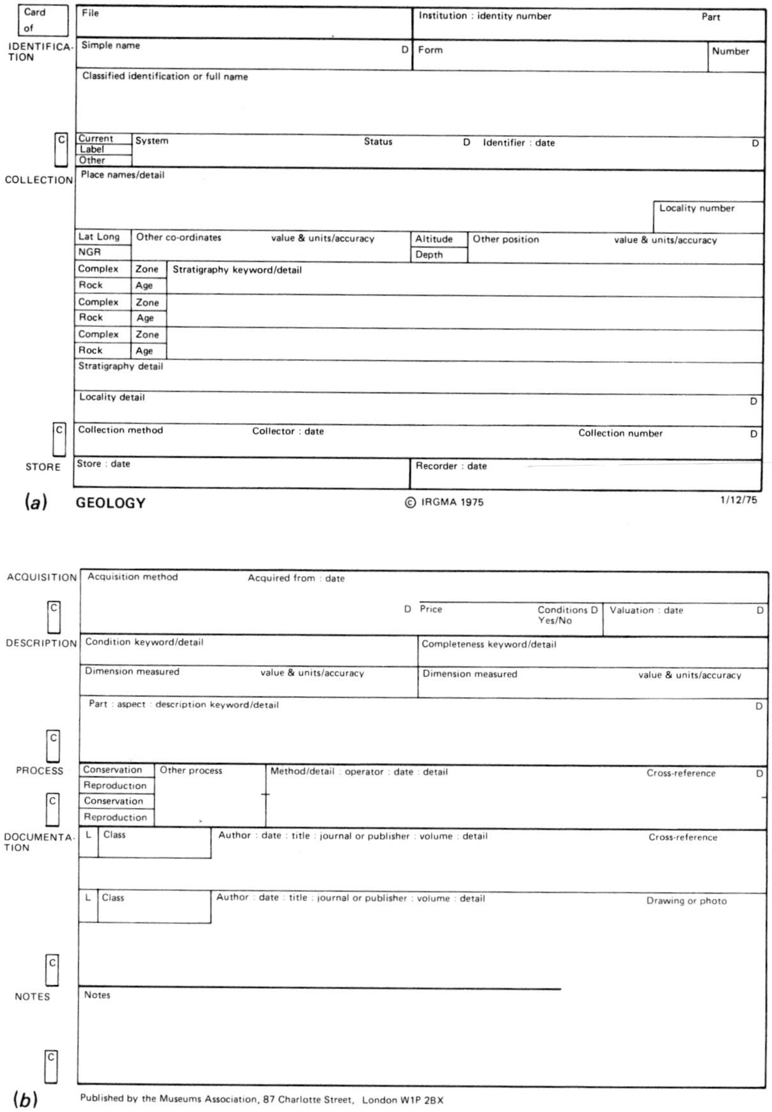

(a) Geology data card front

| Card of | File | | Institution : identity number | Part |

IDENTIFICATION
- Simple name | D | Form | Number
- Classified identification or full name

C
COLLECTION
- Current Label Other | System | Status | D | Identifier : date | D
- Place names/detail | Locality number
- Lat Long NGR | Other co-ordinates | value & units/accuracy | Altitude Depth | Other position | value & units/accuracy
- Complex Rock | Zone Age | Stratigraphy keyword/detail
- Complex Rock | Zone Age
- Complex Rock | Zone Age
- Stratigraphy detail
- Locality detail | D

C
- Collection method | Collector : date | Collection number | D

STORE
- Store : date | Recorder : date

(a) GEOLOGY © IRGMA 1975 1/12/75

(b) Geology data card reverse

ACQUISITION
- Acquisition method | Acquired from : date
- C | D | Price | Conditions D Yes/No | Valuation : date | D

DESCRIPTION
- Condition keyword/detail | Completeness keyword/detail
- Dimension measured | value & units/accuracy | Dimension measured | value & units/accuracy
- C | Part : aspect : description keyword/detail | D

PROCESS
- Conservation Reproduction | Other process | Method/detail : operator : date : detail | Cross-reference | D
- C | Conservation Reproduction

DOCUMENTATION
- L | Class | Author : date : title : journal or publisher : volume : detail | Cross-reference
- L | Class | Author : date : title : journal or publisher : volume : detail | Drawing or photo

C
NOTES
- Notes

C

(b) Published by the Museums Association, 87 Charlotte Street, London W1P 2BX

Figure 15.1 Geology data card, (a) front; (b) reverse

and extent of the collection, the likely demands to be made on it, and the staff, time, and resources available for documentation. Their availability is crucial to the development of an effective system. As an absolute minimum, all non-intrinsic information about each object should be recorded. Intrinsic information may be obtained by examining the object, but for security purposes any lack of description in a record should be made good by a photograph. A new documentation system should relate not only to new acquisitions; a strategy for tackling backlog, or re-cataloguing old collections if necessary, should be incorporated in the system design.

Putting it into effect

The whole process ultimately depends on human resources. Documentation is costly in staff time and money, and effective management is vital if they are to be utilized fully. Ideally, at least one member of staff should be responsible for the co-ordination of documentation. In a small museum the curator is likely to assume this function, but in a large institution it may be necessary to create a separate department, headed by a registrar, for this purpose.

The functions of a registrar include developing the system, writing and updating procedural manuals,

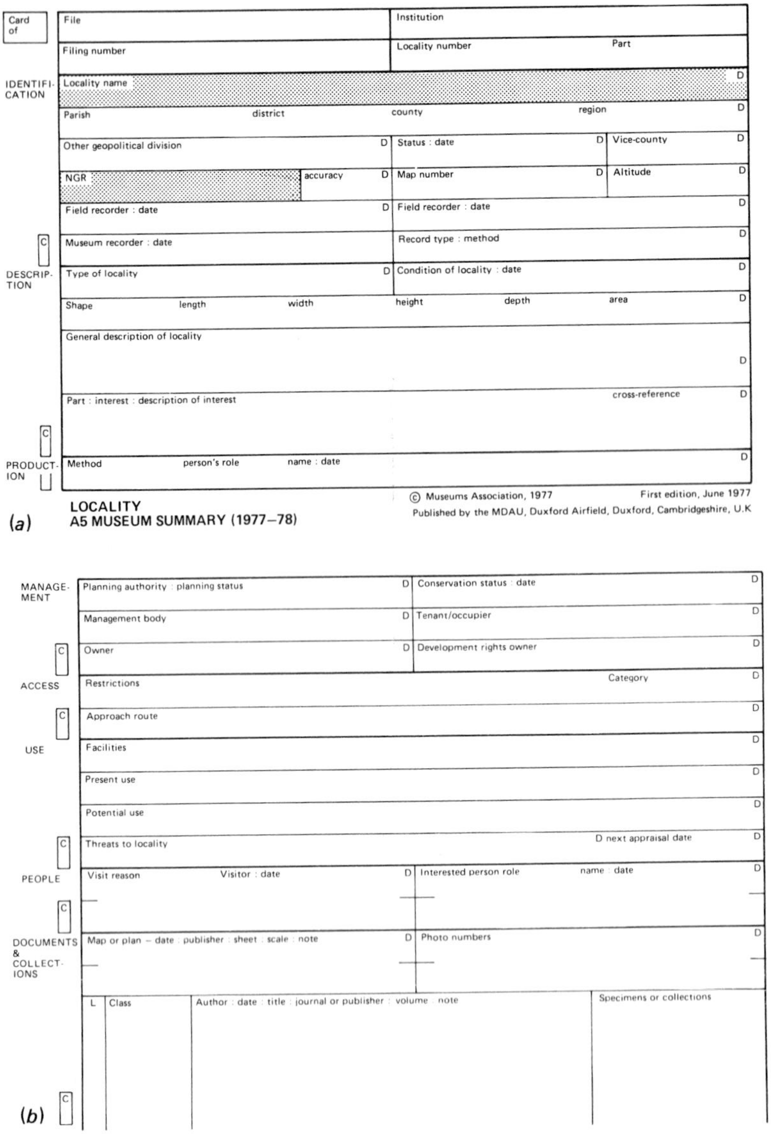

Card of	File		Institution		
	Filing number		Locality number		Part

IDENTIFICATION

Locality name

Parish   district   county   region

Other geopolitical division   Status : date   Vice-county

NGR   accuracy   Map number   Altitude

Field recorder : date   Field recorder : date

DESCRIPTION

Museum recorder : date   Record type : method

Type of locality   Condition of locality : date

Shape   length   width   height   depth   area

General description of locality

Part : interest : description of interest   cross-reference

PRODUCTION

Method   person's role   name : date

© Museums Association, 1977   First edition, June 1977

LOCALITY
A5 MUSEUM SUMMARY (1977–78)
Published by the MDAU, Duxford Airfield, Duxford, Cambridgeshire, U.K

(a)

MANAGEMENT

Planning authority : planning status   Conservation status : date

Management body   Tenant/occupier

Owner   Development rights owner

ACCESS

Restrictions   Category

Approach route

USE

Facilities

Present use

Potential use

Threats to locality   next appraisal date

PEOPLE

Visit reason   Visitor : date   Interested person role   name : date

DOCUMENTS & COLLECTIONS

Map or plan – date : publisher : sheet : scale : note   Photo numbers

Class   Author : date : title : journal or publisher : volume : note   Specimens or collections

(b)

Figure 15.2 Museum summary card of locality, (a) front; (b) reverse

assigning initial and accession numbers to objects entering the museum, monitoring the movement of objects internally and externally, developing standardized terminology for general and discipline-based recording in the museum, ensuring a high standard of accuracy and neatness in documentation, and updating all catalogues and indexes at central and departmental levels. The registrar is also involved in the security of the records of the collections, with auditing and insurance procedures, and is responsible for the training of personnel and the close supervision of the cataloguing team. Orna (Orna and Pettitt, 1980) gives detailed advice on the use of human resources in information management.

Finally, it is important to the success of any documentation system, especially when a large backlog is involved, that curatorial staff responsible for recording realise the direct benefits which accrue. Cataloguing may seem less of an imposition when documentation saves time in dealing with enquiries,

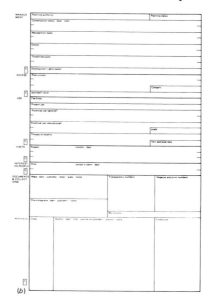

(a)

(b)

Figure 15.3 Summary record card of geology locality, (a) front; (b) reverse

allows research which was previously impossible to be conducted, and removes the frustration which may be experienced when carrying out routine maintenance on the collection.

Safeguarding the information

The establishment and maintenance of an effective documentation system represents a considerable investment, and safeguards must be introduced for the preservation of the records and the information within them. Fire, flood and theft are potential threats to security, and it is important to maintain a duplicate set of records in a separate location. The preservation of paper records depends on the chemical stability of the paper and inks used, the environment in which they are stored and their physical storage conditions and use. Records should be stored in a secure room in lockable, fireproof cabinets, and protected from light, pollution, damp and insect infestation. The confidentiality of data can be assured by screening sensitive information from the general user. This may be achieved by keeping a separate listing of confidential information cross-referenced to the master file, or by maintaining two sets of master records, one of which is for general use and from which all sensitive information has been excluded.

Creating an object record

The essential reference work on object recording is *Practical Museum Documentation* (MDA, 1980a) which also includes a section on non-intrinsic documentation, for example, the locality, bibliographical and biographical records enabling cross-reference with the collection records themselves.

Stage 1: the object enters the museum
Initial documentation is the mechanism used to cope with every object entering the museum, whether temporarily or permanently. It ensures that information is not lost before a full, permanent record is prepared, and it acknowledges the receipt of an item by the museum. Loans, identifications and acquisitions should be assigned an initial serial number which links the object to its associated information.

This initial record should be made in a 'daybook' or initial register, a bound book with column headings for the different types of information to be recorded. Alternatively, a duplicated form such as an MDA Entry Form may be used; if this method is employed, one copy of the form is passed to the depositor as a receipt, one copy remains with the object and the third copy passes to the museum's file. Typical information included in an initial record is: date and method of reception (for example, gift, purchase, loan); from whom received; basic

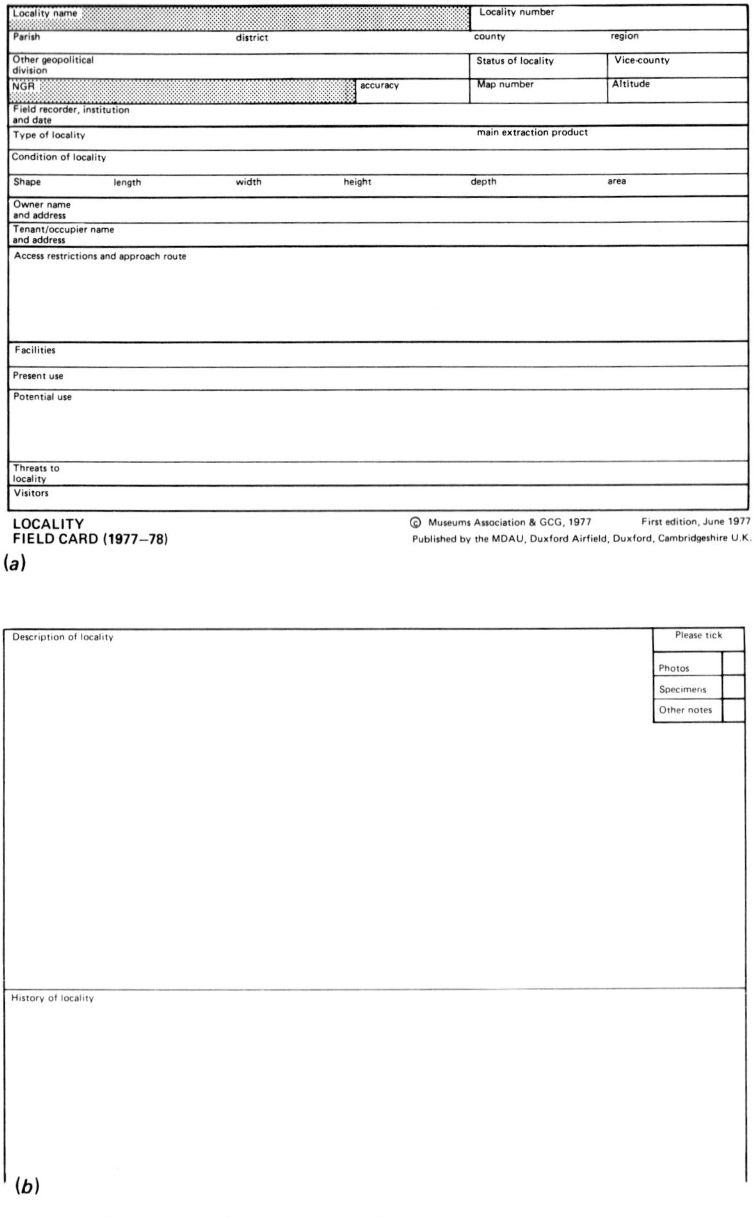

Locality name		Locality number	
Parish	district	county	region
Other geopolitical division		Status of locality	Vice-county
NGR	accuracy	Map number	Altitude
Field recorder, institution and date			
Type of locality		main extraction product	
Condition of locality			
Shape	length	width	height	depth	area
Owner name and address			
Tenant/occupier name and address			
Access restrictions and approach route			
Facilities			
Present use			
Potential use			
Threats to locality			
Visitors			

LOCALITY FIELD CARD (1977–78)

© Museums Association & GCG, 1977   First edition, June 1977
Published by the MDAU, Duxford Airfield, Duxford, Cambridgeshire U.K.

(a)

Description of locality	Please tick
	Photos
	Specimens
	Other notes

History of locality

(b)

Figure 15.4 Locality field card, (a) front; (b) reverse

identification and description (including condition); provenance and method of collection; history of the object; storage location; disposal (including permanent accession number if object is retained); name of staff member who received the object.

Stage 2: the museum acquires title to the object
Once an object has been acquired, an *accession number* should be assigned to it, and marked on it in a permanent manner. (*Practical Museum Documentation*

has a useful appendix on methods of marking the various types of material). An accession number is the unique number assigned to an object or a group of objects added to the permanent collection, and the processing of the acquisition into the collection is known as *accessioning*. Various combinations of numbers are used for accessioning. They are usually based on a serial sequence which may be date-linked, and often, in large museums, prefixed or suffixed by a departmental letter code. An accession number

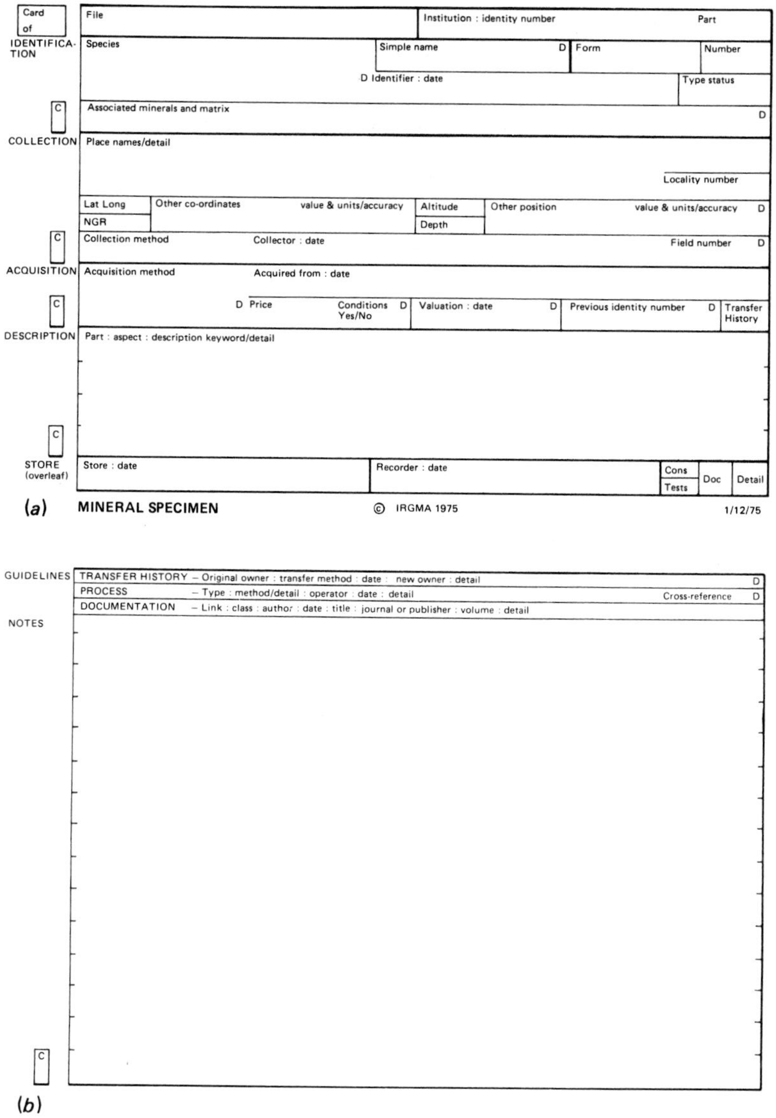

Card of
IDENTIFICA-TION

File | Institution : identity number | Part

Species | Simple name | D | Form | Number

D Identifier : date | Type status

C
COLLECTION

Associated minerals and matrix | D

Place names/detail

Locality number

Lat Long | Other co-ordinates | value & units/accuracy | Altitude | Other position | value & units/accuracy | D
NGR | | | Depth

C
ACQUISITION

Collection method | Collector : date | Field number | D

Acquisition method | Acquired from : date

C
DESCRIPTION

D Price | Conditions D Yes/No | Valuation : date | D | Previous identity number | D | Transfer History

Part : aspect : description keyword/detail

C
STORE
(overleaf)

Store : date | Recorder : date | Cons Tests | Doc | Detail

(*a*)   **MINERAL SPECIMEN**   © IRGMA 1975   1/12/75

GUIDELINES | TRANSFER HISTORY – Original owner : transfer method : date : new owner : detail | D
| PROCESS – Type : method/detail : operator : date : detail | Cross-reference | D
NOTES | DOCUMENTATION – Link : class : author : date : title : journal or publisher : volume : detail

C

(*b*)

Figure 15.5 Mineral specimen card, (a) front; (b) reverse

should be unique and should never be re-used, even if an object is lost or disposed of. In addition to the accession number, the object may be marked with the MDA code for the institution, a five-letter abbreviation of the town and museum name. A full list of MDA codes is published by the MDA (1979) and occasional updates appear in 'MDA Information'. Even if this code is not marked on the object, it should be incorporated in the museum documentation.

At this stage a specimen (or history) file should be opened for each accession. It consists of a folder or envelope into which all supplementary information about an object is placed. *Specimen files* are usually arranged in accession number order. Some museums use bound accessions registers in which brief details about all acquisitions to the permanent collection are recorded for security purposes. The legal obligation to keep such a register to prove ownership of an object is now questioned, and many museums no longer use accession registers but proceed directly to the next stage.

Stage 3: a permanent record of the object is produced
This stage aims to provide, in one source, all the information known about the object, including

cross-references to other files, such as conservation treatment records, photographic negative numbers, and locality files.

From this record, catalogues and indexes may be produced to help staff answer enquiries about the history and contents of the collection. Many museums have adopted MDA cards for recording all or part of their collections. Others prefer to use recording media they have designed for specific collections or, in some cases, to suit the idiosyncrasies of specific curators. If staff time and resources are limited, it may be acceptable to produce a less detailed record as a first step, ensuring that the minimum standard described earlier is attained. This may be added to as further resources become available.

At this stage it is important to ensure that the documentation system of which this record is to form a part possesses the features described earlier, and that the record is completed accurately and neatly, duplicated (some museums produce a typed copy of the hand-written card completed by the curator), and stored with due regard to security and preservation. At least one set of these records should be filed in accession number order.

Stage 4: exploiting the records

As Roberts and Light have stated (1980): 'The need for a wide range of entry points to a single record remains a basic problem of museum documentation.' Indexing is a complex subject, and is discussed fully by Orna (Orna and Pettitt, 1980) and the MDA (1980a). An index is an ordered sequence of entries acting as a directory to one or more aspects of a catalogue. In 1973 the Wright Report on provincial museums (DES, 1973) recommended that a minimum standard for museum cataloguing using traditional manual methods should consist of a numerical catalogue of the collection, and a classified index facilitating access to specimens from the records. The MDA has now expanded these recommendations (1980a) and advises that a museum has one or more fully descriptive catalogues about its collections, and a number of indexes to act as information directories to the catalogues. Using manual methods, the number of indexes a museum can produce is constrained by factors such as staff time, cost and storage space. Few museums have the resources to produce more than five manual indexes, and the ones which should answer most collection enquiries are: an object name index; object period index; collection place name index; donor index; and storage location index.

The hardware for manual indexing, such as plain cards, edge-notched cards and punched feature cards, is described in detail by Orna (Orna and Pettitt, 1980).

One of the commonest problems in indexing, whether manual or computer-based, is the lack of terminology control. This makes indexing less effective by separating objects which have similar characteristics, but have been recorded in different ways. Computer-based documentation exposes inconsistencies in recording and is a salutary experience for all recorders. Guidance on terminology control should be included in the manual describing the documentation system. Aspects of terminology control and thesaurus construction are discussed in *Practical Museum Documentation* (MDA, 1980a) and Orna (Orna and Pettitt, 1980), and a good example of a thesaurus for human history (though with a distinct North-American flavour) may be found in Chenhall (1978).

Stage 5: control procedures

Currently, there are no detailed guidelines in the museum literature on the establishment of *control procedures*, but this situation should be improved if the MDA produces an integrated system for control documentation. This is planned to start in 1983, but until it becomes available museums will have to continue to use *ad hoc* methods already developed for controlling and documenting the movement of objects. Controls and spot-checks are vital to collections management and should be carried out from time to time by staff not involved in documentation. The updating of catalogues and indexes when objects are moved is a vital part of control documentation and, although occasionally onerous, should be carried out methodically to ensure that records remain as up-to-date and as accurate as possible.

Documentation is fundamental to the craft of curatorship, and the welcome increase in awareness and knowledge about documentation should be of immense benefit to museums. It is to be hoped that the next generation of curators will not have to face a legacy of poorly-documented collections, and that those of today will ensure that the objects they collect will be of use and enjoyment in the future.

References

ALLAN, D. A. OWEN, D. E. AND WALLIS, F. S. **(1960)**, *Handbook for museum curators. Part A. Section I. Administration*, Museums Association, London

CHENHALL, R. G. (1978), *Nomenclature for Museum Cataloguing. A System for Classifying Man-made Objects*, American Assocation for State and Local History, Nashville, Tennessee

GREAT BRITAIN, DEPARTMENT OF EDUCATION AND SCIENCE (1973), *Provincial Museums and Galleries. A Report of a Committee Appointed by the Paymaster-General*, HMSO, London

IRGMA STANDARDS SUBCOMMITTEE (1977), Ten years of IRGMA, 1967–1977, *Museums J.*, **65**(1), 11–14

LEWIS, G. D. (1965), Obtaining information from museum collections and thoughts on a national museum index, *Museums J.*, **65**(1), 12–22

MDA DEVELOPMENT COMMITTEE (1982), The future development of the Museum Documentation Assocation, *Museums J.*, **82**(2), 71–76

MDA (1979), *MDA Museum Codes,* Museum Documentation Association, Duxford, Cambridgeshire

MDA (1980a), *Practical Museum Documentation.* Museum Documentation System, Museum Documentation Association, Duxford, Cambridgeshire

MDA (1980b), *Guide to the Museum Documentation System,* Museum Documentation Association, Duxford, Cambridgeshire

MDA (1980c), *Data Definition Language and Data Standard,* Museum Documentation Association, Duxford, Cambridgeshire

MUSEUMS ASSOCIATION (1981), *Museum Security,* (Museums Association Information Sheet IS25), Museums Association, London

ORNA, E. (1982), Information management in museums: there's more to it than documentation and computers, *Museums J.*, **82**(2), 79–82

ORNA, E. and PETTITT, C. (1980), *Information Handling in Museums,* Clive Bingley Ltd, UK

PLANTNAUER, H. M. AND HOWARTH, E. (Eds.) (1890), *Report of Proceedings. Museums Association First Annual Report,* Museums Association, London

PORTER, M. F. (1978), Establishing a museum documentation system in the United Kingdom, *Museum,* XXX (3/4), 169–178

ROBERTS, D. A. AND LIGHT, R. B. (1980), Progress in documentation. Museum documentation, *Journal of Documentation,* **36**(1), 42–84

ROBERTS, D. A., LIGHT, R. B. AND STEWART, J. D. (Eds.) (to be published) *Museum Documentation Systems,* Butterworths London

16

The development of computer-based documentation

D. Andrew Roberts

It is now almost two decades since thought was first given to using computers as an aid to museum documentation. Since then, a number of museums have made impressive strides in adapting the new technology to their problems. In recent years, a growing body of curators has become conscious of the potential of computers, particularly the new generation of microcomputers suitable for local use.

This contribution includes a brief review of the development of computing systems, and the parallel examination of other documentation procedures, by UK museums. It notes the uses that have been made of computers and their potential application in future years. Readers interested in these areas are referred to an examination of the use of information technology for museum documentation, and a review of current practice in museums (Roberts, in press). Aspects of computer use in museums are also considered in recent publications describing documentation procedures in both this country and overseas (MDA, 1981a; Orna and Pettitt, 1980; Light *et al,* in press). Reference should also be made to the general documentation texts cited in the previous contribution by Sheila M. Stone.

The computer concept

At the heart of the computer concept is the ability to store and manipulate large quantities of information. Typically, one can input into the machine a series of records about objects; edit these records until they conform to the intentions of the original recorder; store the corrected records in a form suitable for subsequent use; display a file of such records in a convenient catalogue order; and permutate the information in the records into different sequences to form indexes; search the file selectively; and pass details of the records to another centre for combination with those from other museums.

Once entered, records in the computing system can be re-ordered into any number of different sequences at relatively low cost. They can be updated and others added to the file and can be processed into other guises, such as output suitable for publication. However, before these advantages become apparent, a major investment has to be made in the system itself and in staff with the expertise to use the system effectively. The computers forming the core of these systems can be categorized into three types: *mainframe machines, minicomputers* and *microcomputers.*

Although no museum in Britain currently possesses its own inhouse mainframe facility, a number have made use of such a machine in their umbrella organization or as part of an external bureau service. These systems require major initial and recurrent investments and special environmental conditions, and demand the attention of expert computer scientists, systems managers, and operating staff. In return, they offer considerable processing power and storage capability.

Minicomputers are more appropriate for inhouse use by larger museums (three of which currently have such a system in the UK). They can usually be accommodated within an office environment, after relatively minor physical changes to the room in which they are housed. They tend to require the attention of one or more computer scientists and system managers. Although their power may be less than that of a mainframe system, it can still be more than adequate for museum requirements.

One of the most rapid recent developments has been that of microcomputers: relatively inexpensive machines suitable for use by staff without a formal computer science background in a normal office environment (Light, 1982). In many ways, the unqualified use of the term *microcomputer* can be misleading, since it tends to suggest small, relatively restrictive machines, such as the majority of those used to date. The real situation is already very different, with some 'microcomputer' systems being comparable in scope to the mainframe facilities of the late 1960s. It seems likely that by the 1990s microcomputer hardware will be sufficiently cheap and powerful to allow any museum to consider adopting a sophisticated inhouse system for documentation (MDA Development Committee, 1982).

Development of the use of computers

In the previous contribution, Stone touched on a useful distinction between initial, item and control documentation: initial documentation encompassing the recording of information about all objects entering the museum, whether on loan, as an acquisition and so on; item documentation being the preparation and utilization of a formal detailed record about each object acquired for incorporation into the collection; and control documentation being for operations such as locations management (Roberts, 1983). Until recently, the dominant emphasis of computer use in the UK was as an aid to item documentation.

In the 1960s, the view was that computers offered a means of preparing national catalogues, to which all museums might contribute and themselves have access. In effect, it was being argued that museums should computerize and then pool their item records.

In the UK these ideas were related in a thought-provoking paper which hinted at the value of a computing system and called for the use of the then new technology as the basis for a national index (Lewis, 1965). In the USA, similar considerations led to the establishment of the Museum Computer Network, a co-operative venture by a group of museums (predominantly art museums) from the eastern States. Similarly, in France, Italy and Canada, plans were laid for the development of national computer-based catalogues (Light *et al*, in press).

In the UK and USA, financial and political constraints precluded any significant development of national catalogues. Elsewhere, particularly in Canada and France, the museum structure resulted in work towards national catalogues which were, to a large extent, isolated from the day-to-day problems of the museums themselves.

In the UK, a significant attempt was made instead to encourage the development of computing systems which museums could acquire for independent use on local mainframe computers. These systems placed a considerable emphasis on item documentation.

In the USA, co-operative schemes to develop systems flowered, then faded, to be replaced by the independent application of home-grown or commercial software packages by individual museums (Roberts and Light, 1980). The use of these systems was often initiated by a registrar's department, responsible for initial and control documentation. These were the departments that showed most interest in computing projects and more emphasis was placed upon these aspects of documentation (Dudley and Wilkinson, 1979).

After the mid 1970s, these four disparate threads of initial, item, and control documentation and national catalogues began to coalesce into a more unified approach to the documentation problem. For example, in the UK, greater concern began to be shown towards control documentation and national catalogues. In Canada the National Inventory Programme became more concerned with aiding documentation developments in individual museums, a change emphasized by a revision of name, in 1982, to the Canadian Heritage Information Network. These changes were prompted by a growing curatorial concern for systems that provided effective help with collections management problems and by the more effective computer hardware systems that were becoming available for use.

Co-operative developments: the United Kingdom experience

The new interest in museum documentation shown during the 1960s was discussed at a colloquium held in Sheffield in 1967 (Lewis, 1967). As a result of that meeting, it was agreed to approach the Museums Association with the idea of establishing a small professional group of active curators and computer scientists working in museums: a group which, when formed, soon became known as IRGMA (Information Retrieval Group of The Museums Association). While never including more than a handful of members, this group was the driving force behind the co-operative development of documentation during the next decade (IRGMA Standards Subcommittee, 1977). From the outset, the group was concerned to undertake a rigorous examination of the underlying principles of museum documentation. It initiated a project to examine the form and content of a museum record, identifying the different data categories that together made up a record, and the way in which these categories were logically related (IRGMA, 1969). This careful analytical examination was a revolutionary step that established a firm theoretical background for all subsequent developments of documentation systems. It clearly distinguished work in the UK from the more pragmatic approaches in other countries. However, it also meant that initial progress appeared to be slow, to the understandable dissatisfaction of some museums that decided to take independent action.

With the initial theoretical analysis always in mind, a number of working parties then began to examine specific disciplines, including archaeology, fine art, geology, natural history and social history. These working parties used the basic framework as a guide when developing individual data standards for their discipline, each listing the different categories (object number, name, producer or collector, acquisition date, and so on) appropriate to that discipline. These individual documents were then combined into a unified data standard which was used as a basis when designing record cards and computer systems. The various boxes on the record cards were one reflection of the different data categories that had been identified. The computer storage format used in the computing systems was another reflection of the same list.

However laudable its aims, a voluntary group is often severely handicapped in the amount it can achieve. Fortunately, the part-time effort of the IRGMA members was paralleled by a series of research projects which led to a concentrated attack on the development of computing systems. The majority of these projects were undertaken at the Sedgwick Museum, Cambridge, where teams under the direction of Dr J. L. Cutbill investigated the software and procedural requirements of documentation systems. The last of these grants – from the British Library Research and Development Department – included funds to assist IRGMA with the promotion of its aims (Porter, Light and Roberts, 1977). Another award during the early 1970s enabled IRGMA to evaluate the data standards and recording procedures that it was developing and to demonstrate the computer processing of the accumulated records (Hackmann, 1973). Separate funding at a later stage of the work – 1975 to 1976 – permitted the group to undertake a survey of documentation practice in museums, based on proposals by the Cambridge team (Roberts, 1975). Although unfortunately never published, this survey highlighted the abysmal overall quality of documentation in museums, the genuine willingness of many curatorial staff to improve this position and the significant interest in future computerization projects.

During 1975, IRGMA and the Cambridge team drafted and tested a series of record cards based on the ideas developed in the previous years. These cards were concerned with the item recording stage of museum documentation. They were seen as a means of recording primary information about an object in a collection. It was intended that they be suitable for manual use, but also be amenable to straightforward interpretation for computer processing. IRGMA believed that a number of museums might adopt the cards as an alternative to existing less-adequate recording media.

A number of draft cards and associated instructions were prepared for experimental use by curators in one hundred museums around the country. The completed cards were returned to Cambridge with comments (often critical and always constructive) where they were data-prepared and processed using prototype computing systems (Porter, Light and Roberts, 1977). The resulting unified multidisciplinary catalogues and indexes effectively demonstrated the power of the approach. The exercise enabled the team to revise the drafts cards and instructions and to pursue the development of the computing ideas.

The finished cards were issued by the Museums Association in January 1976. The initial cautious print run of 10 000 cards was over-subscribed long before it was received from the printers. By the end of the first year, some 300 000 cards had been distributed to 80 museums, a number of whom were heavily committed to their continued availability and support. Meanwhile, the Cambridge team had begun to attempt to co-ordinate the use of the cards by arranging seminars and training courses throughout the country (IRGMA Standards Subcommittee, 1977).

The experimental computerization of the draft cards utilized the Cambridge Geological Data System (CGDS) program package developed by the Cambridge team. CGDS was designed originally to process the records of the extensive palaeontolological collection at the Sedgwick Museum, using the IBM 370 computer at the University of Cambridge. It was always recognized as a prototype package, being written by a number of programmers in different styles and different languages, with little or no documentation. As with other packages of its generation, some parts worked brilliantly, exactly to specification, others never worked, for unknown reasons, and some occasionally worked, without anyone really knowing why or how. Rather than attempt to revise the package, it was decided to go back to first principles and develop a new system. The final grant to the Cambridge team included funds to examine the design of such a system.

The design brief called for a program package capable of processing complex museum records which could easily be transferred between different computer installations. This need for 'portability' was an important consideration. It was intended that the system originating from the project would be transferrable to other computers for independent use by local museums. The dominant interest in this option came from a number of the national museums and some major local authority services that were anxious to pursue their own computerization schemes.

By the end of 1976 the two major thrusts of card development and computing system design were at a critical stage. With the end of the last research grant to Cambridge, it was agreed to form a new permanent organization, the Museum Documentation Association, to continue the work (Roberts, Light and Stewart, 1980). The key step in the negotiations to form the Association was the willingness of the Area Museum Councils and the majority of national museums to provide a subscription income to support its work. The strong support of these two groups has continued into the 1980s, although the bulk of funding is now obtained from other sources.

The staffing nucleus of the Association was the research team based at Cambridge. The staffing continuity was paralleled in the development aims, which were initially concentrated on the support of the range of record cards and the implementation of the computing system design brief. Committees were formed to examine those subjects not covered by the original set of eight cards. In this way, the range of item record cards was gradually extended to over twenty, including the major types of interest to curators. Parallel work was undertaken with locality and archaeological excavation recording and with conservation.

Each subject was supported by an instruction book, the content of which was gradually refined as a first attempt to co-ordinate recording conventions and terminology in different museums.

With the active co-operation of each Area Museum Council, seminars and museum visits were arranged on a regular basis in each area to assist curators who were using the cards. The cards themselves were distributed from the new Association by its incipient Publication Service. Annual sales continued at around 300 000 a year, the total exceeding two million by the early 1980s.

Meanwhile, the first part of the computing system design was being implemented, with a new software package called GOS being written and tested. The major evaluation of the new package was the processing of the Sedgwick Museum files, previously managed by CGDS. Smaller, but equally significant, evaluations began with pilot projects on behalf of a number of museums. The majority of the package was written and then documented by Dr M. F. Porter during a concerted effort from 1977 to 1979 (Porter, 1981).

With the completion of the basic card range and the core computer programs, it was possible to consider the overall design of the Museum Documentation System (MDS) discussed in the previous contribution (MDA, 1981). Fundamental to its effectiveness was the data standards work initiated ten years before by IRGMA (MDA, 1980) which acted as a unifying factor underlying the different card designs and procedures. Its computer equivalent was the storage format used to hold data within a computer file. This format was the central feature of the second part of the computing system design, the development of an Object Application Package (OAP) tailoring the general GOS programs to the specific problem of the Museum Documentation System.

The nucleus of the OAP was designed from 1979 to 1982. One emphasis was on input procedures to enable data from any of the record cards to be incorporated into a standard computer file conforming to the storage format. Another was on indexing routines to permutate the information in the files into different sequences conforming to the requirements of users (see, for example, MDA, 1981a). The OAP itself is now extensively applied by a number of museums, particularly those using the MDA Computing Service.

As already indicated, it was originally anticipated that most museums interested in computerization would act as independent agents, perhaps by implementing GOS and the OAP on their local computer and receiving background advice from the Association. However, by the late 1970s it was clear that the managerial and technical cost of running an independent computing system was prohibitive unless the scale of use was considerable or the ease of use was dramatically improved. For many museums, it was more cost-effective to use a bureau service such as that developed by the MDA.

For those who felt justified in undertaking their own work, the Association's Software Service was established to provide copies of GOS and its related procedures. In recent years there have been about ten independent implementations of the package in this country and overseas on both mainframe and minicomputers and, most recently, microcomputers.

The references to ease of use and microcomputers are felt to hold the key to future computing developments by the Association. A major new development programme is now under way to produce effective systems on cheap inhouse microcomputers (MDA Development Committee, 1982). The outcome of this programme should be an important step forward in the acceptability of computing systems. Most significantly, it seems possible that efficient procedures can be developed to aid the initial and control aspects of documentation, which have previously remained almost untouched by computing developments.

The potential expansion of use of inhouse microcomputers has made it even more essential that uniform standards are adopted when recording, structuring, and interchanging information. If the original dream of national catalogues is to be realized, it must be possible for museums to pool their records from their independent systems. The Association will also be concerned with developing procedures to ensure that such interchange is possible (Light, 1982).

Computing systems in action

By 1982, over thirty museums in the UK had begun to computerize some aspect of their documentation, with the majority concentrating on item documentation (Roberts, in press). It is convenient to group these users into three categories: those adopting a bureau service, those with access to a major internal mini- or microcomputer, and those making independent use of an external mainframe computer. These categories are not mutually exclusive.

The majority of users are currently adopting the bureau facilities provided by the MDA Computing Service. This is able to offer a data entry, processing and management service for museums, producing catalogues and indexes. The first approach adopted is to pass source records to the service for data entry and processing. This has the merit of involving the museum in the minimum of staff and capital investment, but the disadvantage of external expenditure. Museums such as St Albans, Kent County Museum Service, Wiltshire Museum Service and the National Army Museum have made extensive use of this approach. The second approach is for the museum to undertake in-house data entry on its own machine, and then pass the data to the service for subsequent processing. This has a number of advantages, including giving the museum a greater degree of control and security over its records; but has the disadvantages of internal staff and financial investments and the difficulty of developing data interchange procedures. The Hunterian Museum, Glasgow, Imperial War Museum, National Army Museum, Tyne and Wear County Museum Service, and others, pass data to the MDA Computing Service in this way.

Most of the museums doing their own data entry have acquired small microcomputers of the type discussed earlier. They have agreed with the Service the procedure whereby data from these machines is transferred to the MDA. In some cases, this involves passing floppy discs to the Service, which are then read on its own microcomputers. In other cases, the data is first sent to a local computing centre where it is transferred onto a magnetic tape which is itself then passed to the MDA.

A small number of museums have now made a far greater internal investment in equipment suitable not only for data entry but also for in-house processing. Nearly all of these museums are currently making independent use of MDA software on either a major microcomputer or a minicomputer. For example, at the MDA itself and the National Maritime Museum, microcomputer-based systems are used for processing. In the British Museum, a minicomputer has been applied in a number of projects, the most significant being that to computerize information about the Museum of Mankind's collections. A major exception is the Science Museum, which has invested in a commercial software system (Adlib) centred on an in-house microcomputer.

The third category of users is those adopting external mainframe computers. These include a number of local authority and university museums whose parent bodies have major computing systems for financial or research use. For example, Leicestershire Museums Service has adopted the computing facilities available within the County Council and has been aided by the development of a locally produced application of an online software package. Derbyshire County Museum Service has also adopted its County Council service, where GOS has been implemented for independent local use. The Sedgwick Museum has built upon early experience and is now applying MDA systems on the University of Cambridge computer, as is the National Maritime Museum and the MDA itself. The Hancock Museum has been a major user of the SPIRES system available at the University of Newcastle's regional computing centre. Similarly, the Manchester Museum has had valuable assistance from the University of Manchester regional computing service on which the FAMULUS package is available.

The latter museums have been particularly fortunate in the degree of assistance they have received from Manpower Services Commission schemes. These have aided the museums with staff and resources and helped them pursue both the recording and computerization of large numbers of records.

Future developments

The future has an embarrassing habit of arriving very quickly within the computing world. Hardware developments take place at an alarming speed, while software and managerial skills lag far behind. The potential use of microcomputers made little impact before 1980, when viable systems began to become available: it now seems to offer an unprecedented opportunity to aid documentation practice (Roberts, in press).

It seems likely that a growing number of museums will acquire in-house machines, initially for local data entry and subsequently for local processing. With local processing power will come the possibility of using computing systems for day-to-day collections management procedures, concentrating on initial documentation (including accessioning) and control documentation (including location and valuation control). With the declining cost of mass storage devices will come the option of having large numbers of records available for local direct online access.

The equipment to satisfy these requirements is already available. What is lacking is suitable software and procedures adequate for use by any museum curator with no computing expertise. It is hoped that it will be possible to develop such facilities on a cooperative basis during future years (MDA Development Committee, 1982).

References

DUDLEY, D. H. AND WILKINSON, I. B. (Eds), (1979), *Museum Registration Methods,* 3rd edn, American Association of Museums, Washington, D.C.

HACKMANN, W. D. (1973), *The Evaluation of a Museum Communication Format. Part 1. Collection of Input Data.* (OSTI Report, no. 5154), Office for Scientific and Technical Information, London

IRGMA Information Retrieval Group, (1969), *Draft Proposals for an Interdisciplinary Museum Cataloguing System,* Imperial War Museum, London

IRGMA STANDARDS SUBCOMMITTEE (1977), Ten Years of IRGMA, 1967–1977. *Museums J.,* **77**(1), 11–14

LEWIS, G. D. (1965), Obtaining information from museum collections and thoughts on a national index, *Museums J.,* **65**(1), 12–22

LEWIS, G. D. (1967), Information retrieval for museums, *Museums J.,* **67**(2), 88–91

LIGHT, R. B. (1982), Today's microcomputers for museum documentation? *Museums J.,* **82**(2), 77–78

LIGHT, R. B., ROBERTS, D. A. AND STEWART, J. D. (in press), *Museum Documentation Systems*

MDA (1980), *Data Definition Language and Data Standard,* Museum Documentation Association, Duxford

MDA (1981a), *Practical Museum Documentation,* 2nd edn, Museum Documentation Association, Duxford

MDA (1981b), *Guide to the Museum Documentation System,* 2nd edn,. Museum Documentation Association, Duxford

MDA DEVELOPMENT COMMITTEE (1982), The future development of the Museum Documentation Association, *Museums J.,* **82**(2), 72–76

ORNA, E. AND PETTITT, C. (1980), *Information Handling in Museums,* Bingley, London

PORTER, M. F. (1981), *GOS Reference Manual,* Museum Documentation Association, Duxford

PORTER, M. F., LIGHT, R. B. AND ROBERTS, D. A. (1977), *A Unified Approach to the Computerisation of Museum Catalogues,* (British Library Research and Development Reports, – Report no. 5338 HC) British Library, London

ROBERTS, D. A. (1975), Proposals for a survey of cataloguing practice in British museums. *Museums J.,* **75**(2), 78–80

ROBERTS, D. A. (in press), *Planning the Documentation of Museum Collections.*

ROBERTS, D. A. AND LIGHT, R. B. (1980), Progress in documentation. Museum documentation, *Journal of Documentation* **36**(1), 42–84

ROBERTS, D. A., LIGHT, R. B. AND STEWART, J. D. (1980), The Museum Documentation Association, *Museums J.,* **80**(2), 81–85

17

Research: science collections

Frank Greenaway

Meaning of research

The word *research* is used here to signify an enquiry of some depth and detail aimed at exposing facts about things or events which have not hitherto been recorded, or aimed at relating observations about things or events in such a way as to form the basis of a connected contribution to knowledge. More particularly, the word is used with reference to material objects which constitute the physical evidence of some activity in the field of human creativity

At the outset it is necessary to distinguish clearly between research and *connoisseurship*. Truly substantial contributions to knowledge are difficult to make and require a particular cast of persistently enquiring mind, able to identify important problems requiring solution. Fewer curators are likely to possess this aptitude than that for connoisseurship, that is, for the mature judgment of the nature, origins, relationships and significance of a wide range of objects of some common character. The connoisseur may be able to undertake research; the researcher may in time develop a lesser or greater degree of connoisseurship, but the two qualities are of equal rank.

Specifically, in the fields of science and technology, the kinds of evidence which come into the care of a curator are so numerous that it is pointless to attempt a list here. However, roughly speaking, he may have to deal with:

(1) The devices used for technical activity in antiquity or in the centuries before the Renaissance.
(2) The apparatus used by investigators in the physical sciences, in geology or in medicine. It will be noted that the reference here is to objects of historical significance. The concern is not, for example, with the research a curator may undertake in current taxonomy, ecology, mineralogy or whatever.

(3) Craft and industrial equipment of any period.
(4). Means of transport of any period.

Although this has an enormous scope, it is still only a fraction of the museological repertoire. Large though it is, it has a uniform character which determines the attitude likely to be adopted by the researcher: every object in any of these groups has at some time been used to alter man's knowledge of, or physical subjection to, his environment.

Objectives of research

Research can be undertaken for many purposes. In the academic world it can be done (although is not always done) solely for the extension of knowledge or for subjective satisfaction. A curator may indeed do this, and he will rightly be encouraged by his colleagues in the academic world. However, it can be expected that research undertaken by a curator will be supported by his superiors, if they are aware of the objective nature of the research. It is possible to identify the principal objectives of research in the principal elements in the curatorial function.

Curatorial functions

The areas of curatorial responsibility are generally taken to be acquisition, conservation, exhibition, academic output, and education (direct or by liaison). In practice, each fertilizes the others, so in any curator's work this sequence is a matter of temperament and training. The order followed above is chosen to draw out the importance of the research outlook.

142

The professional background to research

No research by the curator can be carried out fruitfully without reference to, and the constant use of, the resources built up by previous investigators of his field and by those who are currently active in the same or allied fields. Thus, the researching curator needs contact with books, libraries and their librarians, learned and professional societies and university departments, as well as colleagues in his own and other museums. It is thus a responsibility of directors and of museum trustees to ensure that the curatorial staff of their museums are given time and resources to make these contacts – but that is a matter for discussion elsewhere. It is assumed in this paper that the curator is adequately supported by enlightened superiors and governing authorities.

The main resources available are of the same kinds in every country in which there is a developed museum community. The literature of the history of science and technology is enormous. The primary sources are, of course, the literature of science itself. The secondary material originated in the early histories (which are primary sources for the historiographer) and ranges from, say, the biographical *Eloges of the Académie Royale des Sciences,* to the twentieth century *ISIS, Ambix, Annals of Science, Technology and Culture,* and to the sixteen volumes of the *Dictionary of Scientific Biography.* Many of these are held in university libraries, and in some other major libraries. The curator of a science or technology collection should familiarize himself with the nearest, and also (for UK museums) with the Science Library in South Kensington, the most comprehensive of them all, as well as attempting to extend the relevant holdings in his own museum.

In the past half century, very many specialist societies for the history of science and technology have been formed. Some, with headquarters in the UK, are the *British Society for the History of Science, Newcomer Society* and the *Society for the History of Alchemy and Chemistry.* Many of the professional associations have established historical groups, such as the Historical Group of the *Royal Society of Chemistry.*

Research is co-ordinated in the international field through the *International Union of the History and Philosophy of Science* and its *Scientific Instrument Commission,* and also associated bodies like the *International Committee for Co-operation in the History of Technology* and the *Commission for Historical Metrology.* The curator of a science/technology collection should try to familiarize himself with their work through some colleague already active in one of them, or by direct collaboration.

In all countries, the National Academies play a special role. In the UK the British National Committee for the History of Science, Technology and Medicine, established and managed by the Royal Society and consisting of representatives of bodies like the BSHS, maintains a general review of research on the history of science, and has a small sum of money to distribute as research grants.

The most important stimulus to research comes from like-minded colleagues, and the curator ambitious to carry out research of any quality will get to know them, by direct approach or through the various learned societies. Contacting the GSTMC (Group for Scientific, Technological and Medical Collections) is as good a first step as any.

Physical resources for research

Any curator embarking on object- or collections-based research will need at some point to carry out measurements, make tests or analyses, dismantle or reconstitute objects, or otherwise deal with objects in a manner distinct from their preparation for exhibition. It is desirable that, if resources allow, separate space be allowed for research purposes. Clearly, no specification can be given which would provide equally for research on a group of microscopes or a collection of ploughing engines. What can be said is that in the planning of physical resources (space, equipment, power and water supplies) it should be remembered that the research activity is likely to be intermittent (in the face of other activities) and erratic. Equally clearly, the amount of space which can be allowed for physical investigations varies from museum to museum, but even in a very large museum, pressure on space can be intense. The curator must, therefore, be very clear about his program and proposed method, before submitting an application for space, or even in allocating space over which he has control. Nowhere is a sentimental attitude to research more detrimental than in the allocation of space and equipment. The demands of other duties are heavy, and unused space is a severe reproach.

Training for research

Ideally, training for any responsible curatorial post should equip a student with the skills needed for original investigation. This is, unfortunately, hardly true in practice. An enthusiastic curiosity for historical origins is no substitute for a hard-headed discipline of formulation of problems and criticism of evidence. The curator who thinks it would be pleasant to do research, or that he should research to gain esteem, is doomed to be time-wasting. However, the curator who sees some question which he believes he may one day answer stands a chance of success if he has undergone 'training in research methods'. This phrase, used in most university Ph.D regulations, implies that the would-be researcher is guided in his first efforts by some senior person who will help him to learn how to clarify his concepts, organize his time, examine his evidence, seek support material, criticize his own work, analyse results and, finally, record the course of the investigation and its outcome. In a museum big enough to provide for the training of new curators, a responsibility falls on the heads of departments to give this kind of assistance, or to make sure the curator receives it from someone else with a good enough record in research to be trusted to lead.

Assuming enlightened supervisors, the best guidance is probably to be gained through work for a Ph.D, but it may be difficult to find a university whose regulations allow for a curator's internal work to qualify. The Council for National Academic Awards offers an alternative, but this goes beyond the scope of this article.

The most important factor, other than the logical discipline of investigation, is the development of a habit of mind of enquiry in harness with the ability to decide how far it is worth going. The research worker must know when to stop work and get the results down on paper.

If any recommendation is to be made to a curator about skills he should acquire to equip him as a research worker, one is paramount: a knowledge of languages. For the historian of science this comes hard. He should ideally be able to cope with French, German and Italian, make sense of easy Latin, and be brave enough to tackle the languages of countries which have a place in his speciality.

Research for acquisition

The curator generally has the duty of extending his collection by the acquisition of new material, and the way in which he does so should be determined by his knowledge and judgment of where this material is to be found. Having a desirable acquisition, the decision to acquire may entail a study of the object itself and its associations, over and above what is already available.

The curator aiming at effective research must start from a broad base of subject knowledge. For example, the curator of a collection of microscopes must develop the same general extensive knowledge of the history of science and technology as the curators of collections of marine engines, telephones, or printing presses. The former ought to know the role of metallography in the history of engineering practice; the latter must appreciate the place of his devices on the broad map of the history of communication which includes the printing press. An alert erudition will equip the curator to examine the relations between the objects in his collection against the overall background of the history of all objects of that kind. He will be able to initiate two kinds of enquiry. First, does the general history of the field have any gaps or weaknesses which might be strengthened by the study of some object so far unavailable, and, if so, where can it be found? Second, is some object he can acquire (by purchase, loan, gift), all that it appears to be as regards evidential value? (It is presumed at this stage that there is no immediate question of authenticity.)

It will be seen that these questions are of the same nature as the questions of any scientific enquiry: what additional information will impressively support or falsify an existing hypothesis about some historical pattern or some specific object? Ideally, asking these questions and seeking answers should cause the curator to submit himself to as strict a scientific discipline as if he were at work in a laboratory. In practice, the real laboratory work, although reported as an orderly progression, is usually a hop, skip and jump from one position to another. So it must be with the curator's research into desirable acquisition, but the orderly ideal should be there to aim at in organizing the investigation.

Research for conservation

Once an object has been acquired, it is brought into a potentially hostile environment from which it must be protected. The underlying philosophy of all conservation (that nothing is inert, and that no two things change in the same way) implies that conservation decisions need to be based on enquiries which sometimes rank as original research. Many conservators have built up an impressive corpus of technical knowledge, much of it supported by historical learning, but they will always be grateful for the fullest possible information about the objects put before them. For example, to restore a painted surface (such as coach-work, furniture or interior decoration) it is necessary to know the history of the technique used for the object in question, and also the individual history of the object itself. The general history of types of object may not, in the case of a novel object, be recorded.

The curator and conservator must pursue research in the field until he is reasonably certain that he can place the object in the right context. He must then make sure that the history of the object is known as fully as possible. This enquiry may entail documentary studies or scientific examination of the object itself. These are truisms of the conservator's profession, but it is important that the curator who has to work with a conservator, understands fully the role of his own enquiries in enabling his collaborator to work properly.

Research and exhibition

There are two sides to the relationship between exhibitions and research. On the one hand, a proposal to create an exhibition is a challenge to engage in original research. On the other, fruitful research on some collection or category of object may best be presented in exhibition form.

To put two or more objects together and, *for the first time,* offer an explanation of why it was thought worth while to present them together, needs some degree of original enquiry. Reference was made above to the research needed for acquisition. The concern here is with the enquiries about objects already acquired (perhaps by someone else, or borrowed for a temporary exhibition). One other aspect raises the exhibition enquiry to the level of research, namely, that when the exhibition is over, the body of knowledge is permanently changed. This paper began by painting a distinction between research and connoisseurship, but in the study needed to prepare an exhibition this distinction is blurred, because it is likely that a good deal will be known already about some of the objects to be shown, while others need deeper study, so as to portray all the objects at a common level of communication. The preparation of an exhibition entails, ideally, a preliminary, quantitiative study of how many statements can be made in the space available, how many objects are needed to make each statement, and how many pieces of text can be incorporated. The planning of an exhibition may therefore stimulate enquiries over a wide field, filling in gaps and eliciting connections, so that, in order to give the exhibition uniformity, the general level of knowledge is raised.

The other approach to research for exhibition is that of exhibiting the results of research. This is not the place to lament the fact that too many curators are called upon merely to exhibit illustrations of other people's views. When a curator has made an original study in a historical field, it may have produced results which illuminate theories, social attitudes, professional activities or much else which can only be fully expressed in the written word. However, if the physical objects in his charge have contributed substantially to the results, he has in his care the making of an exhibition. Exhibitions, therefore, may be viewed as a medium of original research publication.

Research and academic relations

The curator belongs to an intellectual community made up of many specialists, operating from bases in many types of institution. The curator who does not work actively with any of these loses much. The value to the curator of these relationships is greatest in the field of research. He may have his own research problems, for which he will seek help; he may share a common problem with another academic; or he may act as an advisor on particular details of someone else's study.

Occupying a special place in the promotion of academic collaboration are the university museums. They may appear to some extent protected from the pressure to display to a large public, but they are still subject to the economic pressures which govern university activities. However, the curator who can create good relations with a curator of a university collection is likely to find the enquiring side of his mind constantly stimulated. He is likely also to find these university curators acting as links with academics in his own field who base their work on library or documentary evidence.

How did it work?

Much of what has been said applies generally to research in many fields, but there is one in which the study of scientific or technological material is distinctive. Consider an astrolobe, a whiskey still, a micrometer, a ploughing engine, an X-ray set and a helicopter. Each of these had to be operated with a purpose. The curator who acquires any one of these must enquire into both operation and purpose. Very often, a talent for manipulation, a sense of mechanical or electrical design, will solve many of the problems of operation, but it needs a gift for identifying a problem beyond the more operational technique, to spark off a research enquiry. The distinction between research and connoisseurship described earlier is useful here. To be in the position of the original user of a piece of apparatus, to be able to follow through the successive acts which made that apparatus useful, is an achievement of very great value, and no curator should be diverted from developing this talent unless he has that gift for imaginative enquiry which energizes research, as the word is used here.

However, there is a connected value in the imaginative enquiry if the curator who has made a thing work can then go on and ask how and why the original user approached the object, and what use he made, or was compelled by social and economic circumstances to make, of the results obtained with it.

An ideal to aim at is the organization by the curator of his overall resources of staff, and of his own time, so as to get the right balance between connoisseurship and research – and this balance is never the same for two individuals or institutions.

Acknowledgements

This paper has been read by Antony J. Duggan and David R. Prince whose comments have been invaluable, but any opinions and errors of judgement remain the author's own.

Bibliography

FERGUSON, E. S. (1968), *Bibliography of the History of Technology*, Society for the History of Technology, Cambridge, Mass. (An excellent guide to the literature of the subject)

JAWAWARDENE, S. A. (1982), *Reference Books for the Historian of Science*, (Science Museum Library Occasional Publication 2), Science Museum, London

KITSON CLARK, G. (1969), *Guide for Research Students Working on Historical Subjects*, 2nd edn, University Press, Cambridge

MCCONNELL, A. (Ed.) (1976), *Preservation of Technological Material Proceedings of a Symposium held at the Science Museum*, Science Musum, London

MCCOY, F. M. (1974), *Researching and Writing history, A Practical Handbook for Students*, University of California Press, Berkeley, California. (A step-by-step guide to the preparation of a research paper)

MULTHAUF, R. P. (1960), The research museum in the physical sciences, *Curator*, **3**, pp. 355–360

PLENDERLEITH, H. J. AND WERNER, A. E. A. (1971), *The Conservation of Antiquities and Works of Art*, 2nd edn, University Press, Oxford

SARTON, G. H. (1952), *A Guide to the History of Science*, Chronica Botanica, Waltham, Mass.

SMART, J. E. (1978), *Museums in Great Britain, with scientific and Technological Collections: a List*, 2nd edn Science Museum, London

18

Research: Technological collections

Robert Bracegirdle

The field of technology is large and a single paper can only hope to offer guidance on its potential for research by curators, other specialists and museum visitors.

Research sources

The object

Objects are necessarily the major resource for museum-based research. Thus it must be part of the curator's role to encourage the use of collections for this purpose. This applies especially to technological material when research into the function and use of particular machines requires the examination of specimens either working or in working order. Although this need may apply to other types of museum collection, it is an obvious requirement in the case of industrial equipment.

The availability of working specimens is often limited to the public galleries, but consideration should also be given to their accessibility in storage areas. For instance, of a collection of textile machines only a small proportion sufficient for the general visitor's needs and interests may be on display. However, the committed researcher may wish to examine an individual machine in store and to compare it with the others on display. If it is not working, inaccessible or dismantled, the central reason for preserving the object may be lost, and the meaning and value of its place in the collection obscured.

The curator may wish to research his own collections only to find that the demands placed on his time prevent him doing so. He must, therefore, encourage other researchers to make their results available both to him and to others who use the collections.

Research on collections in one museum inevitably involves the referencing of material from others, and a two-way flow of information comes about. This implies that the publication of research findings in a specialist magazine or catalogue is of paramount importance and value[1]. Sadly, with restrictions on finance, the production of such catalogues has become less common. If this results in a reduction in those that are mere lists of exhibits then perhaps it will be no bad thing. However, curators should do all they can to produce catalogues that contain the conclusion and implications of research on the collection, summarizing their significance, and mentioning the accuracy of the provenance and the working condition of individual specimens.

Other resources

Archives

The resources of national and local record offices are no doubt familiar, but their use, and potential difficulties, may be less so. A similar lack of information may exist about private archival sources, particularly in commercial organizations.

One of the problems in general archives is that much of the material relating to technology remains uncatalogued. This is partly because of lack of time and also as a result of lack of specialists within the particular fields. Hence, the researcher will have to look hard for his source material and, indeed, may need a degree of prior knowledge to make even an intelligent guess as to where it can be found. In general, the sources can be itemized as:

(a) Individual business records, including catalogues and instruction manuals. Company minutes often give an insight into particular technological processes.

(b) Local Government Records such as Highways or Transport committee minutes. These often provide a wealth of detail about the use of historic equipment.

(c) Quarter sessions records containing plans for industrial buildings and railways.

(d) Maps and plans, including those produced by the Ordnance Survey.

(e) Wills and inventory records often show the values and uses of industrial objects.

(f) Business Directories are a useful source for showing changes in the use of an industrial site.

Other museums

Curators should know the location of other potentially important material. In rare cases, a record office is associated with the museum department, as in Leicester. In other places this is not so, and several major museums of technology house important archives and relative source material.

Major reference libraries

Apart from the multiplicity of secondary sources which these contain, libraries often house a great deal of patent literature. Armed with patent information, the accuracy – or otherwise – of accession records can be determined.

Private records

Most firms retain their own records. Quite apart from documentary files and drawings, employees may be able to provide explanations of the material detailed in such records. In addition, the working environment may still be visible and can be recorded.

Industrial archaeology records

In order to place the material gleaned from such sources into their wider context, evidence from the general field of Industrial Archaeology will be needed. Work in this subject often requires the ancilliary use of museum resources and is often undertaken by one or more members of groups and societies that are involved with this discipline. It is important to foster their activities which can provide not only a record of industrial work within a specific area, but also much additional information.

Oral evidence

Personal reminiscences can provide a wealth of background material about the operation of industrial processes. Although tape-recording is more commonly used within social history, curators of technology should also make such a resource available. Ideally, tapes should be transcribed and indexed immediately after recording.

Pictorial evidence

It is important to support the collections with illustrations. Although the majority will be photographic, paintings and sketches may also show industrial material and, after verification, can be used as visual records[2]. In addition, the curator should be aware of the many illustrative resources in historic books such as Agricola's *De Re Metallica* and various encyclopaedias published in the eighteenth and nineteenth centuries.

Published research

All the research on such resources is worth little until the resulting information is disseminated. Not only does this enlighten the museum visitor, but it also leaves a permanent record of the relationships and meanings extant in the objects within the museum. In addition, scholars and curators can compare results of research and apply them to other collections. This information can be made available in several ways.

Catalogues

Simple lists of exhibits do not develop knowledge to any great extent, and catalogues should be as detailed as possible, not only describing dimensions, materials used in manufacture and provenance, but also details of methods of use and the dates of manufacture and operation. They must also indicate the location and availability of the collection for further research. A more specialized form of catalogue is the kind which is produced in association with a temporary exhibition. Here there is an opportunity to include material from other institutions, and discuss related specimens.

Articles

Occasionally, the results of research may be published in an appropriate journal. In this way a potentially larger audience can be reached than that associated with a catalogue of limited circulation, and others may be encouraged to make further use of museum material. In the field of technology there are many suitable publications; *Textile History, Journal of Transport History, Newcomen Bulletin,* and the *Museums Journal* are examples. Several Industrial Archaeology publications, both national and local, accept museum-researched contributions.

Books

In some cases it is possible to publish research material in conjunction with a publishing house.

However, the material must be well chosen. The most popular technological subject is transport, although this has already been well documented.

Conclusion

Many research problems in technology have a great deal in common with other fields, particularly that of social history. The special problems of technology are associated with the complex issue of how machinery works. In many cases this requires specialist knowledge which may be outside a curator's field and demands more extensive research than is necessary in other museum disciplines.

Notes

[1] See list in Section on Articles.
[2] Particularly good examples are mentioned in *Coal, British Mining in Art 1680–1980,* Exhibition Catalogue published by the Arts Council of Great Britain.

Further Reading

CANTACUZINO, S. (1975), *New Uses for Old Buildings,* London

COSSONS, N. (1974), *Conservation of industrial monuments, Museums Journal,* **74**(2), 62–66

HODGES, H. (1964), *Artefacts,* London

PLENDERLEITH, H. AND WERNER, A. E. (1971), *The Conservation of Antiquities and Works of Art,* 2nd edn, London

MCGOWAN, A. P. (1972), A paddle-tug in a museum: an exercise in patience and imagination, *Museums Journal,* **72**(1), 3–6 (See also ensuing correspondence in *Museums Journal,* **72**(3))

MCCONNELL, A. (1976), *Preservation of Technological Material,* Science Museum, London

SMITH, C. S. (1965), Materials and the development of civilization, *Science,* **148**, 908–917

SMITH, C. S. (1970), Art, technology and science: notes on their historical interaction, *Technology and Culture,* **11**, 493–549

STANDING COMMISSION ON MUSEUMS AND GALLERIES (1971), The preservation of technological material, *Report and Recommendations: Standing Commission on Museums and Galleries,* HMSO, London

TAYLOR, M. C. (1973), *Conservation of Industrial Monuments: a survey of local authorities in England and Wales,* Royal Town Planning Institute, London

19

Research: natural science collections

Michael V. Hounsome

Museums have many functions, but natural history museums, or departments, have one fundamental and necessary imperative which is laid upon them by the scientific community. The absence, or insufficiency, of certain services may render a museum inadequate, but the absence of attention to its fundamental taxonomic function denies it the title 'Museum' and makes it 'an exhibition' or 'an educational centre' or whatever title describes its remaining functions.

The philosophy of the scientific method ensures that it should never be necessary to believe the statements of other scientists; observations by one authority must always be repeatable, or verifiable by others. In practice, it is not possible to verify for oneself every conclusion drawn by every other scientist, so one is obliged to believe an eminent authority. Nevertheless, for observations to be called scientific they should be verifiable. In the physical sciences, this means that experiments must be repeatable before they are accepted. One should understand the difference between observations and the conclusions which may be drawn from them. The same observations may be susceptible to more than one set of conclusions, and it is in this field that debate and logical argument find their place.

In the fields of taxonomy and distributional biology the scientific observations are seldom the result of experimentation, but rather of accurate observation. The only way in which such observations can be rendered scientific is for the material observed by one person to be available for observation by others. The presence of a specimen in a museum is (duplicity excepted) proof of its existence, and its identity can be checked by all subsequent investigators.

Living things are named according to the Linnaean system, as administered by two professional bodies, one botanical and the other zoological. The rules are, for the most part, similar. An organism is identified as belonging to a species which was given a name in a certain year by a certain author. That species is regarded as a member of a group of species, or a genus. Thus the components of the name are: Genus (always with a capital initial letter), species (never with a capital), author, date. Both names must be in latin, or in latinized forms of non-latin words, and they must obey the normal rules of latin grammar. The word after the generic name is termed the 'trivial' name or the 'specific epithet', so that the 'specific' name consists of both the generic and trivial names.

It may be that some populations of a species are distinct, but not distinct enough to be regarded as separate species; in such cases a sub-specific name can be added after the specific name, in which case the author and date refer to the description of the subspecies. For example, in 1758 Linnaeus gave the European sparrowhawk the name *Faloc nisus, i.e.*

Falco	generic name,
nisus	trivial name, or specific epithet,
Falco nisus	specific name.

The tenth edition of Linnaeus' *System Naturae,* dated 1758, is taken as the start of the Linnaean system; names given before this date have no status under the rules of nomenclature. The sparrowhawk has now been taken out of the genus, *Falco* and put into the genus *Accipiter*, and several sub-species are now recognized, two of which are:

Accipiter nisus nisus (L, 1758) – most of the palaearctic,
Accipiter nisus granti Sharpe, 1890 – Madeira and the Canaries.

These two examples illustrate several points:

(1) The use of trinominal names for sub-species.
(2) The abbreviation of well-known authors' names (e.g. L. for Linnaeus).

(3) The use of italics (underlined in typescript) for latin names.

(4) The use of parentheses around authors' names when their species have been taken from the original genus and put into another. Sharpe originally described his bird in the genus *Accipiter,* so his name is not in parentheses, but Linnaeus' species has been transferred, so his name and date (separated by a comma) are enclosed.

(5) The nominate sub-species is that which bears the same sub-specific epithet as its specific epithet; thus the type of the species is also the type of the nominate sub-species.

Sometimes names are abbreviated on museum labels, and it is common to omit the date, and even the author; both practises are to be deprecated for all but the most common species. Abbreviation of the latin names and the authors' names are justifiable where ambiguity can be avoided. Thus '*A.n.nisus*(L)' is acceptable, especially in a collection where one expects to find only European species. Where space permits, and especially with types, abbreviations should be avoided.

Taxonomy is the process, and study, of the giving of names; in biology this involves identifying specimens as to which taxon (or name group) they belong, and devising new names for those which cannot be allocated to any existing taxon. The description and definition of new taxa is the work of the taxonomist. Nomenclature is the branch of taxonomy concerned with the legalistic rules governing the giving of names. Most taxonomists also regard themselves as systematists, as it is not sufficient simply to describe a new taxon, but one must comment on its relationship to other taxa. A systematist is concerned with the arranging of taxa into a classificatory system which illustrates the relationships between them. Systematics has been, therefore, not as precise a science as taxonomy, because supposed relationships are seldom, if ever, scientifically verifiable. In recent years there has been a rise in interest in systematics, especially in phylogenetic systems which illustrate the supposed evolutionary history of taxa.

Central to the international functioning of taxonomy is the *type system.* The word 'type' has been used in more than one context, one of which is synonomous with 'typical', or 'representative'. This is not acceptable in biology, as the type concept is rigidly embodied in the International Codes of Nomenclature. Zoological nomenclature is governed by the International Code of Zoological Nomenclature (Anon, 1964), devised by the International Commission on Zoological Nomenclature. The corresponding botanical code is The International Code of Botanical Nomenclature (Stafleu *et al,* 1972). The nomenclature of cultivated plants is governed by the International Code of Nomenclature of Cultivated Plants (Gilmour *et al*, 1969).

A brief discussion of the zoological type system will serve to illustrate the main points relating to types, which is the area most likely to concern museum curators. The rules governing the naming of animals are couched in a legalistic framework, and can be correspondingly difficult to understand, but the central rule is that of priority. This states that the name of the species shall be the earliest valid name that was used for it; the date of publication (and page number in the same publication) determines which is the earliest description. This appears to be perfectly straightforward, but there may be considerable difficulty with early publications because the descriptions may be so poor as to cast doubt on which taxon is being described. The value of museum specimens, particularly types, in such cases is clear. A type specimen is the actual specimen that the taxonomist described as a new species, and is the ultimate arbiter of the definition of that species. This is true even if, subsequently, that species is deemed to be a synonym of an earlier-described species. Thus it is the duty of every name-giver to ensure that types of his new taxa are deposited in places that, as far as one may tell, are permanent, which will care for them, and make them available to taxonomists throughout the world in perpetuity.

The intricacies of taxonomic argument are sometimes so complex as to baffle the mind, but most changes of name have their origin in one of two situations: synonymy, and homonymy. In the first, an earlier name may be found, or what was thought to be two or more different species is considered to be a single species, which must, therefore, bear the earliest name. In the second, a name is found to refer to more than one species, so that new names must be devised for portions of the orginal taxon. In both these cases examination of the types is necessary, and it is their absence which opens the way to doubt and dissension.

Types come in several guises, from the rigorously defined Holotype, down to the less important Topotype. The more important categories are:

Holotype: A single specimen, chosen by the author to be the physical embodiment of the concept of his species. Once chosen, this specimen takes precedence over any abstract concept of the species, whether the author's or anyone else's. Colonial animals, such as corals, complicate the issue, but generally there is only one holotype.

Paratype: All the remaining specimens in the sample from which a holotype was chosen. There may be many of these, and they are often deposited in several museums

Allotype: for safety and availability for consultation. They will all have been collected at the same place at the same time. New species based upon only one specimen (the holotype) will have no paratypes.

Allotype: A special paratype, in that it is a single specimen chosen from the paratypes, that is of the opposite sex to the holotype. Allotypes have no more status than other paratypes, but it is sometimes useful to designate such specimens.

Syntype: Authors have not always chosen holotypes, and have distributed 'types' to museums or friends; members of such a type series with no holotype are termed 'syntypes'. They are not encouraged in modern taxonomy, but museums may contain specimens labelled as such, or simply as 'type'.

Cotype: An outmoded and imprecise term for either paratype or syntype.

Lectotype: A holotype subsequently chosen from a syntypic series. The remaining syntypes are paralectotypes.

Neotype: A new holotype, usually chosen from a paratype series from which the original type has been lost or destroyed.

Topotype: A specimen collected from the same site as the original types. One of a range of so-called types which have no taxonomic status.

The object of taxonomy is to present the agreed framework of names that is necessary for the unambiguous exchange of information between biologists. Such a framework is essential to all ecological and distributional biology, and responsible museums are a vital part of the system. Type specimens are not the only scientifically important elements of a collection; they are of primary importance, but it is possible to distinguish two further groups of secondary and tertiary status. Specimens which have been figured or described in publications have a special value, particularly if the author was the author of the species or of a major taxonomic review or monograph. Specimens commented upon, in print or otherwise, by eminent specialists are similarly valuable. In the former case, the original description may not be sufficient to settle a particular point, and reference may have to be made to the actual specimens, to examine parts not figured or described, or to dissect the gonads, for example. Specimens authoritatively commented upon can greatly clarify ones view of the attitudes and intentions of such eminent commentators and can, for example, help in the selection of lectotypes.

Museum specimens can also act in confirmation of new or interesting records. New county or national records are put beyond question by the presence of the specimen in a museum, with the reservation that even this will not rule out deliberate deception. Subsequent workers may call into question the identity of a species claimed to have occured for the first time in, say, a county, but a specimen in a museum will allow anyone to confirm its identity for themselves. Whenever it is legal and ethical to do so, such new records should be collected and preserved in a museum as voucher specimens for posterity. It is impossible for future workers to repeat once-and-for-all events, so that first records cannot be regarded as scientific in the absence of specimens. For sensitive groups, such as birds, where it is neither legal nor, most would say, ethical to kill unusual individuals, the acceptance of records is governed by a panel of experts. These experts sometimes have recourse to museum collections to compare written descriptions or photographs with authenticated specimens. Much acrimonious debate would have been avoided if previous generations of biologists had implemented either a voucher or a panel system for the verification of new records.

Of tertiary scientific importance are collections made locally, even of common plants or animals; or collections of single groups made over any area; or collections of unusual forms or aberrations; or, most elementary of all, collections showing as wide a range of specimens as possible. Modern biometrical studies demand large numbers of specimens from which it is possible to determine the range of variation. Indeed, some workers regard the type system as outdated, and prefer to consider populations rather than single representatives. Even within the traditional system it is essential to determine the variability within a species before establishing criteria to distinguish it from others.

There are many other reasons why a collection, or specimens within it, may be considered important, from interest in the taxidermal or preservation technique, to historical associations with people or events. The possibilities are legion; indeed, if no point of interest, actual or potential, can be found in a specimen or collection, then its place in a museum is questionable. The practical problem for curators in deciding what does or does not have a place in their collection is carried by the word 'potential', for they must make decisions based upon what work they *think* future workers will regard as important. Considerable experience in museum work is necessary for the development of a 'feel' for what is potentially important and what is not. It is possible to lay down guidelines for the assessment of the current value of specimens, but inexperienced curators should not be called upon to make, unaided, decisions upon their potential importance.

Most of the research upon a collection will be either taxonomic or distributional. Taxonomic research involves the examination of types or specimens authoritatively commented upon, and the examination of a series of specimens to determine the degree of variation to be found within a single taxon. Distributional research also uses large series of specimens, both to establish the limits of occurrence in time and space, and to assess the degree of geographical variability. Biometrical studies involve the measuring of large numbers of specimens, and researchers may well travel the world to visit several museums in order to measure, or otherwise assess, as large a sample as possible.

Research may not always be directly related to specimens, as bibliographers may want to consult manuscripts, diaries and letter-books pertaining to people who were, perhaps incidentally, collectors. The cost of objects or services, such as taxidermy, can be of interest to historians and bibliographers. The collecting details themselves are proof of a person's presence at a certain place on a certain date, and the course of an expedition can be traced onto a map using the dates and localities on museum labels. Of more biological relevance is the plotting of past avian breeding distributions using museum egg collections. Museum collections are almost never random samples so that research demanding numbers or proportions is ruled out, but the presence of a clutch of eggs in a collection is proof of at least an attempt to breed at the recorded locality. It is thus vital that all documentary evidence should be preserved no less assiduously than the specimens themselves, and that such documentation is effectively related to the material or to the collector. The advice of conservators should be sought for the preservation of documents as well as for the specimens. It is clear that there is little point in keeping specimens, important or otherwise, if they are not stored effectively. This involves the proper initial preservation, careful conservation, and the use of suitable containers. These are discussed elsewhere in this volume.

Just as there is little point in having collections if they are not adequately looked after, they are of little use if nobody knows where they are or what they contain. It is necessary to maintain adequate catalogues, or at a bare minimum, to arrange the collection systematically so that it acts as its own catalogue. Ideally, all collections should be catalogued, and should have cross-referencing facilities from, for example, taxon to locality, and from taxon to collector. Such catalogues should be published so that they are available throughout the world. In practice, no museum does this for all its specimens, although type catalogues have been published for many collections, and many more are likely to be published in the future. The advent of computer cataloguing and the willing hands supplied by the Manpower Services Commission has put many museums on the road leading to this ideal, but it remains to be seen whether it is ever achieved. Certainly, it is within the powers of most museums to make available to scholars a catalogue of their types and specimens of primary importance.

An adequate library is the aid to research which many museums find most difficult to provide. Only very large museums have libraries adequate for all researchers. Others should content themselves with supplying key works which relate to the strengths in their collections. Even this objective may be impossible to achieve within the limited budgets available to many museums. It sometimes happens that a collection comes to the museum complete with the collector's library; in this case it is vital that the library is not split up or irrevocably disassociated from the collection as it is likely to contain all the important references relating to the material. Further value is added to the library if the books are annotated by the collector, or the author.

Both taxonomic and curatorial research involve a considerable amount of detective work, and clues found in manuscripts and annotated books may form vital links in a chain of reasoning. It is also important that original labels, in whatever state, are preserved; apart from explicit information, such as dates and field-book numbers, such labels may contain valuable handwriting clues which the experienced researcher can interpret.

Visiting researchers usually require some kind of work-space in which to lay out their books and equipment, and to examine the specimens. They may need to use the museum's equipment. Most researchers make contact initially by post, and in reply any deficiencies in the available equipment should be made clear, so that alternative arrangements can be made.

The question of who is allowed access to the collection and under what circumstances is a delicate one to be decided by individual curators in the light of local conditions. Clearly, collections should be available for as wide a range of users as possible, but frivolous demands should be rejected and impossible demands on the curator's time should be firmly discouraged. The major problem is that of security; unknown and unvouched for visitors should not be given the run of the collection. Ideally, there should be a visitor's room to which the material is brought, but some people may want to examine a large amount of material, so that is more practical for them to work in the storeroom. If they are unknown to the curator and are unvouched for, then they must be accompanied by a staff member at all times. This can place heavy demands on the staff, and it can be insulting to the visitor.

The circumstances in which loans are made are similarly fraught with problems. Monographs and extensive revisions of the systematics of a group may demand the examination of hundreds of types and authoritatively named specimens from all over the world. It may be impossible to visit all the museums which hold the relevant specimens, so requests are made to borrow material. Museum curators should have a clear policy on the loan of specimens, particularly types. Clearly, it is pointless for a museum to preserve specimens if their use is denied to scholars; on the other hand, holotypes are unique and priceless, and perhaps should not be entrusted to the postal systems of certain parts of the world.

Restrictions on the loan of specimens usually centre around three factors: what can be loaned; the mode of transport of the specimens; and to whom a loan may be made. It may be decided, for example, that anything other than holotypes may be loaned, and that types must be collected by hand but other specimens can be sent by registered post. It is quite usual for loans to be made only to professional biologists at an institutional address, but such restrictions may be waived for certain persons known to the curator. A wide range of conditions may be enforced, and each museum, or museum department, should have a clear policy on these conditions. One is never certain of attaining the correct balance between caution and imprudence, and individual curators' views tend to be determined by whether they have ever lost an important specimen. Curators should be encouraged to be as liberal as their consciences, or their superiors, will allow them; loss is then regarded as a rare occurence to be accepted philosophically.

One of the privileges, and duties, of a museum curator is to carry out research on the collection in his care. Not all museum authorities encourage this activity, but besides bringing a good reputation to the museum, it is one of the best ways of obtaining a thorough knowledge of the collection. Being an active researcher gives greater insight into the needs of visiting scholars, and enables the curator to meet them as equals and to discuss matters relating to the collection with authority. The choice of research topic may be predetermined by the curator's experience, but is often related to a particular strength in the collection. In the course of reorganizing a major collection the curator will become a specialist in the taxonomy of the group, and may feel that he should let others known of his discoveries. This process is a natural one and should be encouraged, even though there may be no immediate and obvious advantage to the museum. The long-term benefit is found in the extra attention the collection receives, the use made of the collection by other experts throughout the world, and the job satisfaction derived by the curator.

Publication of results is an essential part of research, and curators should be encouraged to publish freely. The museum will gain in reputation, and the collections will be publicized and hence more frequently consulted. Some directors or governing bodies reserve the right to approve or disapprove of proposed publications by their staff. This is not an unreasonable restriction, provided it is impartial and the criticisms are fair. Some authorities may restrict curatorial research to topics directly related to the collections, rather than to the wider aspects of taxonomy. In some cases this may be reasonable, but it is usually unjustified and short-sighted. It should always be made clear to visiting researchers and people receiving loans that the museum should be acknowledged in any publications which may result, and that reprints or copies of books should be sent to the museum.

Research in museums is usually specimen-oriented. The fundamental duty of the curator is to safeguard the collection and to make it available to the world's scholars in the most useful manner possible. If resources allow, then the collection should be brought to the attention of potential researchers by the publication of catalogues and research. The role of research in museums is fundamental, and its neglect often results in institutional stagnation.

Bibliography

The following bibliography is intended as a source of further reading largely on the subject of systematics and taxonomic procedure. References to museum procedures and philosophy are given elsewhere in this volume.

ANON (1964), *International Code of Zoological Nomenclature Adopted by the XV International Congress of Zoology, London, July 1958,* International Trust for Zoological Nomenclature, London

BLACKWELDER, R. E. (1967), *Taxonomy* John Wiley and Sons, New York

CROWSON, R. A. (1970), *Classification and Biology,* Heinemann, London

DAVIS, P. H. AND HEYWOOD, V. H. (1963), *Principles of Angiosperm Taxonomy,* Oliver and Boyd, Edinburgh and London

FERNALD, H. T. (1939), 'On type nomenclature, *Ann ent. Soc. America,* **32,** 689–702

FRIZZEL, D. L. (1933), Terminology of type, *Am. midl. Nat.* **14,** 637–638

GILMOUR, J. S. L. *et al* (1969), International code of nomenclature of cultivated plants, *Regnum Vegetabile,* **64,** International Bureau for Plant Taxonomy and Nomenclature, Utrecht

HAWKSWORTH, D. L. (1974), *Mycologists Handbook. An Introduction to the Principles of Taxonomy and Nomenclature in the Fungi and Lichens,* Commonwealth Mycological Institute, Kew

HENNIG, W. (1978 in English, 1966 in German), *Phylogenetic Systematics,* University of Illinois Press, Urbana, Chicago, London

HEYWOOD, V. H. (1976), *Plant Taxonomy,* 2nd edn, Edward Arnold, London

HUXLEY, J. (Ed.) (1940), *The New Systematics,* Clarendon Press, Oxford

INTERNATIONAL COMMITTEE OF MUSEOLOGY (1978), *Possibilities and Limits in Scientific Research Typical for Museums,* ICOM, Brno

JEFFREY, C. (1977), *Biological Nomenclature,* Systematics Association, Edward Arnold, London

JEFFREY, C. (1982), *An Introduction to Plant Taxonomy* 2nd edn, University Press, Cambridge

JONES, S. B. AND LUCHSINGER, A. E. (1979), *Plant Systematics,* McGraw Hill, New York

LEENHOUTS, P. W. (1968), *A Guide to the Practice of Herbarium Taxonony,* International Bureau for Plant Taxonomy and Nomenclature of the International Association for Plant Taxonomy, Utrecht

MAYR, E. (1969), *Principles of Systematic Zoology,* McGraw Hill, New York

NASH, R. AND ROSS, H. (1978), The type method and the species, *Porcupine Newsletter* **1**(5), reprinted in *BCG Newsletter,* **9**, pp. 29–33

PANKHURST, R. J. (1978), *Biological Identification, the Principles and Practice of Identification Methods in Biology,* Edward Arnold, London

PARR, A. E. (1959), *Mostly about Museums,* American Museum of Natural History

SAVORY, T. (1962), *Naming the Living World,* English Universities Press, London

SIMPSON, G. G. (1945), The principles of classification and a classification of mammals, *Bulletin of the American Museum of Natural History,* **85**, pp. 350

SIMPSON, G. G. (1961), *Principles of animal taxonomy,* Colombia University Press, New York

STACE, C. A. (1980), *Plant Taxonomy and Biosystematics,* Contemporary Biology Series, Edward Arnold, London

STAFLEU, F. A. *et al* (Eds.) (1972), International code of botanical nomenclature adopted by the eleventh International Botanical Congress, August 1969 *Regnum Vegetabile* **82**, International Association for Plant Taxonomy, Utrecht

ZUSI, R. L. (1969), 'The role of museum collections in ornithological research' in Cohen, D. M. and Cressey, R. F. (Eds) Natural history collections. Past. Present. Future, *Proc. biol. Soc. Washington,* **82**, 651–661

20

Research: geological collections

Philip S. Doughty

This paper is concerned purely with research related to the curatorial method applied to collections as entities. The legitimate uses of collections as raw materials for academic observations on rocks, fossils and minerals are legion and beyond the scope of these writings. The concern here is chiefly with curatorial procedures practised on collections, ensuring that the view of them is not stilted because the curator has a limited concept of their potential.

Philosophical considerations

It is possible to conceive of a collection in terms of a finite number of specimens, allocated to stated taxa, derived from defined areas, and rocks of given age, collected by a stated collector, at a given time, worth a specified price for insurance or replacement purposes and used by a list of academics to develop geological thinking in a further compilation of academic papers. Such concepts are readily embraced by recording formats (MDA, 1980a, b.) and if meticulously stated can be digested in computing systems and rapidly rendered into invaluable catalogues for the scholar and curator. Such records are basic management tools for museums and if systematically and accurately constructed can be seen as evidence of curatorial competence. Curatorial expertise lies outside these highly structured systems, and relates basically to an entirely different view of collections where hunches, intuition and other supposedly indefinable qualities come into play. The apparent mystique is in reality a synthesis of a large mass of detail, the product of generations of talented geological curators who have developed, tested and refined skills and practices which only now are being recognized as the exploration of the wider scope of curation. The collections they have curated testify to their methods, but the methods themselves have

never been discussed in detail, perhaps because they were considered too specialized a brand of common sense to be worthy of statement.

The difference between the developed curator and the competent practitioner is his concept of collections, the adoption of a more metaphysical approach. Geological specimens are not mere caches of natural objects. They are ideas, concepts, hypotheses, expressions of interest, trophies of the search and reflections of the development of precepts which, at least in part, required material expression. A collection is part of the life of an individual, or a group of like-minded people, an enthusiasm, a passion, an intellectual quest of which objects were an essential part. Collectors prize such specimens in a way that few other things are valued and a good curator will endeavour to discover the nature of that acquisitive compulsion. If a collection is not seen as the product of some process and motivation then much of what it represents is lost or never sought. Whether museums like it or not, their geological collections are more than a source of specimens assisting the advancement of science, they are part of the history of ideas, and the two are inextricably linked (Waterston, 1979; Medawar, 1979, pp. 29–30); one cannot proceed without the other. If a curator fails to recognize this fundamental relationship his concept of the specimen or collection is flawed.

The way in which a collection or specimen is perceived conditions the kind of information gathered about it. A limited perception confines observation, and a restricted view almost always qualifies the future uses of material. Yet no curator can forsee the full potential of his collections into the indefinite future so it is inevitable that concepts crucial to coming generations of users will be missed or imperfectly grasped. All the good curator can do is attempt to minimize such omissions by being constantly aware of cultural and technological developments, and alert to the latent possibilities of a collection, taking time and trouble to gather such further material and information while he can. Museums which have traditionally adopted this approach have strong character, rich collections and real stature.

Receiving the collection

When a collection is accepted by the museum the curator whose charge it will become should take control. He should try to ensure that the collection moves in its original storage furniture with no disturbance. The nature of the furniture could be important. It may have permanent labels on doors, drawers, liners or side panels. It may be of a standard pattern for its period or it may be custom-built. It may represent a considerable investment for the collector or it may be the cheapest possible solution to his storage problems. What appears to be trivial detail may ultimately prove to be important.

Examine the arrangement of the collection carefully and maintain it undisturbed through the initial period of examination. If the arrangement has to be disturbed, as when specimens are in packing cases and cardboard boxes, keep as accurate a record as possible. Even when it is known that someone other than the collector did the packing, follow the same procedure because, almost certainly, the packing will have been systematic and retained elements of a former arrangement. From such information the collector's views on taxonomy and classification may emerge, or his preferred arrangement for his method of working or collection management, useful factors in assessing him. Geographical or stratigraphical arrangements in early collections, particularly if they are unpublished, might indicate pioneering research long pre-dating the first published work. Collectors tend to isolate material of special interest, material on loan, incorporated collections, all revealed in arrangement. The maintenance of duplicate collections suggests exchange arrangements which might be sought in documentation.

If specimens are wrapped, examine the wrappings with care. The nature of many wrappings is important and may help in fixing the earliest date of packing and something of the intellectual and academic environment of the collector. Note the titles of newspapers, but pay particular attention if pages from notebooks, discarded drawings, pages of learned journals, outside correspondence or page proofs are used. Even unpaid bills have turned up in this context. Examine wrappings for notes and markings, and where they are found ensure their elevation to the status of labels. Unwrap carefully so that loose slips enclosed with specimens are kept with them. If they become dissociated it may be difficult or impossible to rematch them with the specimen later. If wrapping has been poor, or disturbed in storage so that labels have become dissociated, identification sometimes allows rematching, as do label shapes and corresponding marks, or the nature of an adhesive and its failure. If there is no immediate relationship store the specimens and labels from the one container together for a time. Information from undisturbed parts of a collection often gives new insight making at least a partial rescue possible.

The specimen

Geological specimens are of a different kind from almost all others in natural history. Unlike biological specimens they are not merely a convenient but poor substitute for the living organism, but the ideal expression of it. Only the context of its finding is absent in the cabinet specimen, and the good collector ensures that those details are known, or the expert geologist can infer them. It might therefore appear that the scope for individuality of specimens in collection terms is limited, but this is rarely true, and the treatment of specimens by some collectors is highly idiosyncratic.

First look for surface data, such as numbers, letter/number combinations, identification labels, paper pointers, colour coded stickers, and even newspaper clippings. The mechanics of data association are important, whether the information is engraved into the specimen, written on its surface, written onto a prepared area such as a ground flat or painted panel, or written onto a label stuck to the specimen. Collectors have strong preferences in these matters and vary them only when the nature of the material is unsuitable for their favoured method. Numbers and letter/number combinations indicate the existence of notebooks, registers, ledgers, catalogues or indexes which must be found to give the specimens meaning and value. Handwriting is treated with labels in the following section. Newspaper cuttings may relate specimens to specific events or at least indicate the breadth of the collector's reading. The complexity of marking is a measure of the degree to which a collection was worked.

The style of preparation of specimens in matrix is useful, sometimes unique. If the matrix has been trimmed, note whether it has been done with hammer and chisel, plyers, vice, saw or some other means. There is often a favoured 'finished' form of a specimen such as a rectangle, a rectangle with rounded corners, a tendency to follow the outline of form, or a preference for total extraction or as near as can be achieved, bearing in mind the nature of the material. Some results are highly distinctive, usually in thoroughly developed specimens with marks such as chisel courses, needle courses, picked surfaces, etched surfaces and those left in deliberate patterns or textures.

Methods and materials of repair are also informative and the adhesive used must be recorded. Brown organic glue, shellac, celluloid, sealing wax of a variety of colours, tallow, paraffin wax, beeswax and even bituminous compounds were used by early collectors as adhesives. Wax, plaster, glue-soaked cotton wadding and other absorbent and pliable materials were, with plaster of Paris, popular fillers. Shields (1984) and Rixon (1976) give information on more recent adhesives.

Since the middle of the present century many of the materials and much of the equipment used in geological technology have become more standardized nationally and to some measure internationally. This has not resulted in standardized presentation because materials science has produced so many new products and advancement is so rapid that the possible variations and permutations are now greater than ever. In any case, laboratories now keep records of treatments so documentation exists to assist the curator, and in the case of amateurs limited access to technical facilities imposes many of the constraints common to the nineteenth and first half of the twentieth century.

Museums are already repositories for other geological media such as microscope thin sections, other microscope mounts, peels, casts, moulds, electron microscopy studs, specimen preparations used in analytical procedures, such as X-ray diffraction and fluorescence, and many more. All these methods lend themselves to variations, and individuality can still emerge when the same principles of examination are applied. Other technical treatments were, and still are, used on a rule-of-thumb basis for want of thorough research into conservation of geological materials (Howie, 1979). In consequence, personal preferences show clearly, particularly in old collections, and most treatment was limited to the consolidation of fragile and friable specimens. The materials were commonly thin solutions of familiar adhesives such as organic glues, gelatin, shellac and size. Waxes (Swinton, 1941) and various varnishes were sometimes used in special circumstances.

There is no formal history of geological techniques, but a growing need for some authoritative statement is emphasizing this gap in the literature. Undoubtedly geological collections will provide much of the material for such a work and the creation of chronologies of materials, processes and methods will in turn be applied to new work on all collections.

The label

Original labels have proved to be the most fruitful single source of information about collections and fortunately most collections in the UK have most data in the form of original labels (Doughty, 1981). Regardless of kind, all labels should be kept.

Label materials, form and presentation should be examined minutely. Pay particular attention to the paper of plain labels noting such matters as type, weight, tint, watermarks, dimensions and any other characteristics that might be useful features of recognition (Higham, 1968; Britt, 1970). Printed labels should be photocopied and a file of types established. Dimensions, the nature of printed lines and decorations, printed titles, and print fount are all important. For large collections, second and subsequent printing of labels are often subtly but recognizably different due to changes of paper, line detail, print weight or slight variations in fount size or face. Often there are several versions of the label for a single specimen, indicating events such as the supplanting of a field label by a cabinet label, and both may be accompanied by display labels. Display labels are a study in themselves (North *et al.* 1941).

Handwriting is of the greatest importance but it is a difficult subject requiring careful analysis and where fine judgements require expert opinion. Nevertheless, most handwriting is sufficiently characteristic to be identifiable (Harrison, 1981; Hilton, 1956; Cleevely, 1982). It should be stressed that the style of most individuals is variable and that the writing on the confined area of a label usually differs significantly from that of the same individual in, say, correspondence. Hand printing on labels is normally very different from the writing of the same individual. Specimens of writing and printing for each collector, preferably dated and showing the range of variation, should be photocopied and a file for individual collectors compiled. The practice must also be followed for unidentified collectors because it is usual that an identity is eventually established and the lead back to the specimens is then secure.

Frequently labels and specimens are related by a system other than the ubiquitous card tray, as when card, glass or wooden tablets are used, or closed boxes of a variety of kinds. Tablets are frequently hand-made by the collector, or for him, and many collectors made their own boxes rendering these presentation devices recognizable as their work. If storage space permits, there is much to be said for retaining specimens and labels on their tablets and for keeping containers.

Labels were primarily used as identification markers and reference to other information was normally slight. Locality is the next commonest item included, followed by period or formation name, and sometimes a date. There is a practice among some modern curators of discounting early identifications which are 'wrong'. If the collection is to be properly appraised it is worth establishing whether a name was wrong by the standards of the day, perhaps indicating a naïve or inexperienced collector, or whether it was accurate or justifiable by contemporary standards. If an experienced collector consistently misnames relatively small numbers of his specimens it is worth while checking his identification media to see whether they were misleading. Frequently it means his judgment was contrary to that of his peers in which case it must be respected and his material examined in this light.

The command of a collector over identification is important. It reveals his concept of names, his access to literature, his association with other collectors and his ability to critically blend opinions. Many early names were drawn from rapidly advancing concepts of classification which served a purpose for a time before being modified or abandoned leaving a wake of debased and deserted terms. The problem of determining an acceptable modern interpretation of these names, *not* merely a modern name of the specimen, is mainly a curatorial preoccupation, and one without a ready solution, although there is a limited literature to help.

(i) Minerals

Many names on minerals in old collections have been abandoned or slipped from usage. The second edition of Hey's *Index* (1962) and its subsequent appendixes (Hey, 1963; Hey and Embrey, 1974) is an invaluable sourcework for obsolete names. Other useful references are Dana's *System of Mineralogy* sixth edition (1892), Chester's dictionary (1896), English's *Descriptive List of the New Minerals 1892–1938* (1939), largely a compilation from other handy sources, and most recently Embrey and Fuller's manual (1980). A convenient, but limited, source of name derivations is Mitchell (1979).

(ii) Rocks

There has been less interest in compilations of rock names, although because there are fewer of them, problems are reduced. The Wernerian system was widely applied in the eighteenth and early nineteenth century. Jameson's account (1808; facsimile, 1976) gives all Werner's German terms and his own English equivalents. Most of the rock names survived into the post-Wernerian age but there is no useful summary. Early primers such as Phillips's *A Guide to Geology* (1834, 2nd edn 1835) give neat outlines of classifications then current, and Jukes's *Students Manual of Geology* (1857, 2nd edn. 1862) gives more names and some insight into development over the intervening quarter century. The failure of petrologists to adopt any single classification provoked Kinahan (1873) into the preparation of his book *A Handy Book of Rock Names,* an invaluable but rare reference not fully indexed. Recent geological dictionaries cover most other names except the

legacy from miners, masons, and quarrymen whose decorative vocabulary, frequently met in collections, is documented by Arkell and Tomkeieff (1953).

(iii) Fossils

According to current literature, there are fifty times more fossil than mineral names and most museum collections are numerically dominated by fossils (Doughty, 1981). Fossil names are therefore an important factor in the lives of most curators. By 1825 fewer than 1000 names were applied to British fossils and by 1850 around 4000 species were described. It follows that all early names applied to fossils collected during or before this time are interesting, and a proportion important. With new names appearing rapidly from about 1840 synonymies could not hope to keep palaeontologists abreast of developments and a number of summaries appeared, now of value to the curator. The most useful are Morris (1845), Sedgwick and M'Coy (1854) and Etheridge (1888). No more were attempted, probably because it was obvious late in the century that the *Zoological Record* (1870 onwards) was meeting the need. The last great summary of genera was Zittel (1895, English revised edn. 1900) before the massive redescription of invertebrates now substantially completed in the various volumes of the *Treatise on Invertebrate Paleontology* (1953 onwards). It remains true that for many taxa the only recourse for the curator is to the systematic study of material and literature.

Important errors can arise from a misinterpretation of some labels, particularly those of the nineteenth and early-twentieth century stating 'type' or 'type specimen', and there are instances of curators publishing specimens to which such labels adhere as having type status. The typology of specimens in the modern sense has been defined by rules only since 1901 when the International Code of Zoological Nomenclature was first adopted. All specimens with such markings should be thoroughly investigated. In this context it is worth mentioning that there are hazards in type recognition as when original drawings or photographs are poor, or poorly reproduced, when text numbers referring to plates are wrongly given, when images are reversed in the engraving process, when artists or photographers idealize drawings or retouch prints to eliminate imperfections in the original material, or when the wrong registration number is quoted for the figured specimen (Edmonds, 1977). Coloured stickers on specimens can also indicate special status and it is worth assembling similarly marked specimens to see if a common factor emerges, and checking literature if the collector has left no notes.

Much of the work on the housing of specimens, their appearance and treatment and their associated labels is an attempt to establish a unique identity for a collection. In combination the kinds of details discussed give a particular quality or character, here addressed as 'style'. Style is often sufficiently distinct for specimens to be recognized outside their usual context and seasoned curators often distinguish elements of collections familiar to them in other museums and normally sufficient further evidence is available to corroborate such judgement. The recognition of collections, collectors, their competence, significance, dates, balances of interest, contacts and publications are the fundamentals of curation, and research based on collections is unsound without this foundation.

Association of collections

Many collectors use only a *stored data* system with *double bonding* (Palmer, 1977), that is a catalogue or register kept remotely from the specimens with a unique notation linking specimens and information. It follows that for the collection to have any scientific worth the catalogue must accompany it. But there may also be notebooks describing the sections from which specimens were collected with dates and further details. Diaries of serious collectors are invaluable, as are their commonplace books. Nebulous verbal geography can become exact landscape features from marked maps, and annotations of books in collectors' working libraries can, in a few pungent comments, assert an attitude otherwise elusive. Inscriptions on papers and books indicate correspondents, associates, collaborators and friends, while sketches, diagrams and correspondence may all relate to collecting activities. Portraits of the collector, and his geological photographs, negatives or transparencies are becoming increasingly important. How far to press for associated material to be included in a donation is a judgment for the curator and undoubtedly there is potential for conflict with archival organizations. Papers which are meaningless without the collection should obviously accompany it. Display potential must also be considered and personalia from working materials and equipment, to items of clothing, suitably presented, can mutely state what a dozen labels never can.

The biography

A rounded view of a collector is a vital ingredient in any measure of his achievements. The basic information on file should include full name; dates of birth and death; names of parents, with dates; full list of brothers and sisters; education, including all schools and other institutions; qualifications; marriage date, full name of partner and offspring; residences, parti-

cularly during the period of active collecting; socio-economic standing; personality, career, institutional and society memberships; honours; lectures and papers given and published; professional associates and friends (geological associates for amateurs); travels, including all formative influences as well as collecting excursions; collections, with the history of dispersals; whereabouts of other material, for example books and manuscripts; eponymy; obituaries, biographies, assessments; portraits. If the collector is alive or recently dead this kind of information is relatively easy to gather but when researching old collections obituaries may have to be sought in appropriate journals, or even newspapers. A useful compilation of information for better-known collectors, including references to obituaries, is Lambrecht and Quenstedt (1938), and for collectors dying between 1850 and 1900 Thackray (1972) is useful. The *World Directory of Mineralogists* (1962) is also a useful source-work and any collectors with botanical interests might be sought in Desmond (1977). Prominent scientists may have entries in the *Dictionary of National Biography* and *Dictionary of Scientific Biography*. Otherwise registry documents are a starting point from which other leads can be pursued. The skills here are more appropriate to genealogists and local historians – who often prove sympathetic and helpful allies – than those of the geologist. Where the collections are those of institutions, histories are much more demanding to compile but sources more plentiful.

Locating collections

Until comparatively recent times the problems of locating collections or elements of dispersed collections have been substantial. Sherborn's (1940) was the only useful compilation, sometimes a little obscure, veiled as it is in the pedant's sophisty and waggishness. Those in the British Museum can be traced through their *History of the Collections* (1904) and subsequent reports mention the most important additions since. A few museums with type material have published catalogues, a few more collections have parts of their transfer histories in Chalmers-Hunt (1976). The North-West Collections Research Unit has published a list of collections (Hancock and Pettitt, 1981), including about 160 of geological interest, in the museums of north-west England, and Doughty (1981) has listed the location and some additional details of around 800 geology collections throughout the UK. In combination these works cover only a fraction of surviving collections. At the time of writing, there is a list of around 5,000 palaeontology collections in press, most of them British, compiled by Cleevely, to be published by the British Museum (Natural History), and the Federation for Natural Science Collection Research is listing all details that curators can provide on collections. On a wider, more general scale the *World Directory of Mineral Collections* (1972) may be worth consulting depending on the nature of the collection. If all else fails, it is well worth placing an enquiry in the *Geological Curator,* a Geological Curators' Group publication.

By far the most useful statement on the principles which underlie research procedures is that of Torrens (1974) which should be read by all interested in this topic.

A final word of warning. Never accept that a collection described in the literature as 'lost' has actually ceased to exist unless its complete destruction was witnessed. Edmond's (1977) cautionary tale of John Phillips's collection and Hill's (1938) account of James Thomson's collection demonstrate the dangers of uninformed judgment. Both collections were described by authors as lost when they had largely survived.

The scope of collection research

The view that curatorial research involves human trivia in the recording of antiquarian trivia, while it is an attractive caricature, is difficult to sustain. The importance of apparent trifles is readily illustrated by Torrens (1979) and Forbes (1979) in a case presented to the International Commission on Zoological Nomenclature in 1974 for the designation of a particular specimen as the lectotype for a species of fossil ammonite. The identification of the original specimen as that seen by an earlier authority, depended on an unbroken chain of evidence involving the recognition and dating of a mounting tablet, the survival of an original label and the verification of the handwriting on it, the survival of a paper note added to the tablet, a note on the reverse of the specimen indicating that it was the specimen seen by the original authority, and an annotation of a printed book by a subsequent owner of the collection whose handwriting was recognized. A knowledge of the transfer history of the specimen and a knowledge of glue patterns was also useful. On the basis of evidence presented by the curator the specimen he identified, and not the one originally proposed for designation, was accepted by the Commission in their ruling. This case is unusual only in the length of the chain of evidence and there are many similar examples involving a wider range of material evidence.

The thorough researching of collections make their academic, cultural and social significance clear, and their importance emerges often quite startlingly. The wealth of the collecting tradition and its contribution to our cultural life is now giving rise to revealing social histories which are still struggling with the generalized view (Allen, 1976; Barber, 1980), but undoubtedly the collecting movement has changed our perception of the world we inhabit in important, sometimes radical, ways. Individual careers of geologist collectors are an established tradition of English literature but they have generally favoured the erudite and great, the Lyells, Darwins and Murchisons. There are now signs that the other ranks are worthy of notice (Fountaine; 1980) and perhaps more attainable by a general public. The missing dimension of almost all these accounts – the collections themselves – is something curators and a very few others appreciate. Some daring authors have discussed the importance of individual specimens in a generally readable form (Colbert, 1968; Desmond, 1975; Stearn, 1981); indeed, in the case of the Piltdown forgery a book was based around a single 'specimen', but these are preliminary explorations only, and a fuller blossoming will emerge as cabinets, stores and catalogues are further explored. Authors treating these themes show little confidence or sureness of touch because there is so small a perspective of comparison.

The academic geologist generally fails to see the collection for the specimens, but a single work has shifted irretrievably the palaeontologist's view of his science and demonstrated the supremacy of collections and individual specimens in the founding of palaeontology and its subsequent development. In *The Meaning of Fossils* Rudwick (1972) wrote a text unashamedly and confidently centred on specimens and their impact on scientific thought. It points many clear paths of research and some of the complexities are now under examination (Porter, 1977). Some realities of collection research can be examined in journals treating the history of science, particularly the *Archives of Natural History,* the *Geological Curator,* and *Annals of Science* and occasional papers in a wide range of other journals.

As more curators pool resources it becomes clear that there were major movements in collecting, reflecting a changing and evolving pattern of specimen use. The curiosity collection was followed by the show collection around which philosophical discussions revolved in the seventeenth and eighteenth centuries. The investigation of variety is reflected in early nineteenth century collections and the relationships and grouping of specimens became a major preoccupation later. The use of fossils for dating rocks is a practice continued to the present time, with emphasis turning from macrofossils to microfossils.

There are collections of all periods that are regionally centred, local responses to national movements; there are teaching collections, investment collections, obsession collections and in the second half of this century collections based around hypotheses of geology, the product of state sponsorship of higher education. Analyses along these lines are rare but should prove rewarding, offering possibilities for research in small and large museums.

For any of this kind of work to proceed confidently, the curator must be more than a ledger clerk and if this paper has indicated some of the possible directions of curatorial development it will have achieved its intention. The watchwords are: observation – hone the faculty finely; common sense – employ liberally; and over confidence and self deception – to be recognized and guarded against.

References

ALLEN, D. E. (1976), *The Naturalist in Britain*, Allen Lane, London

ARKELL, W. J. AND TOMKEIEFF, S. I. (1953), *English Rock Terms*, University Press, Oxford

BARBER, L. (1980), *The Heyday of Natural History 1820–1870*, Jonathan Cape, London

BRITISH MUSEUM (NATURAL HISTORY) (1904), *History of the Collections, contained in the Natural History departments of the British Museum,* Vol. 1. xviii, British Museum, London

BRITT, K. W. (1970), *Handbook of Pulp and Paper Technology*, Van Nostrand Reinhold, Wokingham

CHALMERS-HUNT, J. M. (1976), *Natural History Auctions 1700–1972*, Sotheby Parke Bernet, London

CHESTER, A. H. (1896), *A Dictionary of the Names of Minerals Including their History and Etymology*, John Wiley, Chichester

CLEEVELY, R. J. (1982), 'Some thoughts on methods of classifying and cataloguing hand-writing collections', *The Geological Curator*, **3**(4), pp. 189–194

CLEEVELY, R. J. (1983), *World Palaeontological Collections*, British Museum (Natural History) and Mansell Publishing Ltd, London

COLBERT, E. H. (1968), *Evolution of the Vertebrates*, John Wiley, Chichester

DANA, E. S. (1892), *System of Mineralogy*, (6th edn), John Wiley, Chichester

DESMOND, A. J. (1975), *The Hot-blooded Dinosaurs*, Blond and Briggs, London

DESMOND, R. (1977), *Dictionary of British and Irish Botanists and Horticulturists including Plant Collectors and Botanical artists*, Taylor and Francis Ltd, London

DOUGHTY, P. S. (1981), *The State and Status of Geology in United Kingdom Museums*, Miscellaneous Paper 13, Geological Society, London

EDMONDS, J. M. (1977), 'The legend of John Phillips's "lost fossil collection"'. *J. Soc. Bibl. Nat. Hist.*, **8**, pp. 169–175

EMBREY, P. G. AND FULLER, J. P. (1980), *A Manual of New Mineral Names 1892–1978*, British Museum (Natural History), London, and University Press, Oxford

ENGLISH, G. L. (1939), *Description List of the New Minerals 1892–1938*, McGraw-Hill, Maidenhead

ETHERIDGE, R. (1888), *Fossils of the British Islands Stratigraphically and Zoologically Arranged*, Vol. 1, University Press, Oxford

FORBES, C. L. (1979), 'Credit where it is due', *Newsletter of the Geological Curators' Group*, **2**, p. 404

FOUNTAINE, M. (1980), *Love among the Butterflies*, Collins, Glasgow

HANCOCK, E. G. AND PETTITT, C. W. (Eds), (1981), *Register of*

Natural Science Collections in North West England, 178 pp., Manchester Museum

HEY, M. H. (1962), *An Index of Mineral Species and Varieties Arranged Chemically*, Trustees of the British Museum, London

HEY, M. H. (1963), *Appendix to the Second Edition of an Index of Mineral Species and Varieties arranged Chemically*, xii, Trustees of the British Museum (Natural History), London

HEY, M. H. AND EMBREY, P. G. (1974), *A Second Appendix to the Second Edition of an Index of Mineral Species and Varieties arranged Chemically*, xii, Trustees of the British Museum (Natural History), London

HIGHAM, R. A. (1968), *Handbook of Papermaking*, xvi, Business Books, London

HILL, D., (1938–1941), *A Monograph on the Carboniferous Rugose Corals of Scotland*, Palaeontographical Society, Reprinted, 1966, by Johnson Reprint Corporation, London

HILTON, O. (1956), *Scientific Examination of Questioned Documents*, ix, Callaghan

HOWIE, F. M. P. (1979), 'Museum Climatology and the Conservation of Palaeontological Material', in *Curation of Palaeontological Collections*, M. G. Bassett (Ed), Special Papers in Palaeontology no. 22, pp. 103–125, Palaeontological Association, London

IMA (1977), *World Directory of Mineral Collections*, 2nd edn., International Mineralogical Association, Berlin

IMA (1962), *World Directory of Minerologists*, International Mineralogical Association, Berlin

JAMESON, R. (1808), *System of Mineralogy*, Vol. iii, Blackwood, Edinburgh (Facsimile reprint Hafner Press, (1976)

JUKES, J. B. (1857), *The Student's Manual of Geology*, A. and C. Black 2nd edition (1862) A and C. Black, London

KINAHAN, G. H. (1873), *A Handy Book of Rock Names*, Hardwicke, London

LAMBRECHT, K. AND QUENSTEDT, A. (1938), *Palaeontologi. Fossilium Catalogus. I: Animalia*, Ed Junk, W. (Reprint edition, 1978, Arno Press Inc., New York

MDA (1980a), *Geology Specimen Card Instructions*, Museums Documentation Association, MDA, London

MDA (1980b), *Mineral Specimen Card Instructions*, Museums Documentation Association, MDA, London

MEDAWAR, P. B. (1979), *Advice to a Young Scientist*, Harper and Row Ltd, London

MITCHELL, R. S. (1979), *Mineral Names. What do they Mean?*, Van Nostrand Reinhold, Wokingham

MORRIS, J. (1845), *A Catalogue of British Fossils*, x, J. Van Voorst, London

NORTH, F. J., DAVIDSON, C. F. AND SWINTON, W. E. (1941), *Geology in Museums*, University Press, Oxford

PALMER, C. P. (1977), 'Data security in scientific objects', *Newsletter of the Geological Curators' Group*. **9**, 446–449

PHILLIPS, J. (1834), *A Guide to Geology*, Longman Rees; 2nd edn (1835), Longman Rees, London

PORTER, R. (1977), *The Making of Geology*, University Press, Cambridge

RIXON, A. E. (1976), *Fossil Animal Remains: their Preservation and Conservation*, Athlone Press, London

RUDWICK, M. J. S. (1972), *Meaning of Fossils: Episodes in the History of Palaeontology*, Elsevier, Amsterdam

SEDGWICK, A. AND M'COY, F. (1854), *A Synopsis of Classification of the British Palaeozoic Rocks, with a Systematic Description of the British Palaeozoic Fossils in the Geological*

Museum of the University of Cambridge, University Press, Cambridge

SHERBORN, C. D. (1940), *Where is the . . . Collection?,* University Press, Cambridge

SHIELDS, J. (1984), *Adhesive handbook,* 3rd edition, Butterworths, London

STEARN, W. T. (1981), *The Natural History Museum at South Kensington,* Heinemann, London

SWINTON, W. E. (1941), see North, F. J. *et al.* (1941)

THACKRAY, S. (1972), *A Bio-Bibliography of British Geologists who Died between 1850 and 1900,* Science Museum Library Bibliog., Gen 801, London

TORRENS, H. S. (1974), 'Locating and identifying collections of palaeontological material'. *Newsletter of the Geological Curators' Group,* **1,** 12–17

TORRENS, H. S. (1979), 'Detection at the Sedgwick: an illustration of the importance of data retention.' *Newsletter of the Geological Curators' Group,* **2,** 333–340

WATERSTON, C. D. (1979), 'The unique role of the curator in palaeontology', in *Curation of Palaeontology Collections* M. G. Bassett (Ed), Special Papers in Palaeontology No. 22, pp. 7–15, Palaeontological Association, London

WILSON, R. H. (1981), *Suspect Documents—their scientific examination,* Nelson Hall, London

ZITTELL, K. A. VON (1895), *Grundzuge der Palaeontologie,* vii, R. Oldenbourg,

ZITTELL, K. A. VON (translator and Ed. Eastman, C. R.) (1900 and 1902), *Textbook of Palaeontology,* 2 vols., Macmillan, London

21

Research: archaeological collections

D. Gareth Davies

With archaeology, particularly prehistoric archaeology, becoming increasingly oriented towards an explanation of 'culture change' and with the attendant proliferation of deductive systems backed by borrowed methodology, often mathematically based, it could be assumed that artefact study, if not obsolete, has become secondary to defining 'laws' and delineating 'processes'. However, such an assumption is challengeable, with objects retaining a validity independent of hypothesis, model or paradigm and with the historial landscape, forming the 'reality' of the archaeological past. This is not to deny the so-called *new archaeology*[1], rather, to recognize the status, both philosophical and evidential, of material culture and to reaffirm research based on collections. Morgan (1973) argued that:

> The major goal of scientific endeavour is the acquisition of knowledge about the world. Crudely speaking science seeks to find out what the 'facts' are . . . Explanation is not itself a goal of science but may perhaps be a by-product; rather than an 'end' explanation plays the role of a 'means' in scientific methodology.

Hawkes (1982) puts this succinctly:

> But the primacy, in all our thinking, must be held by *things*. (Biological, geological, and features in the ground, as well as artefacts: they all mean people . . . .). As for models, they're theories for explaining the *systems* which ought to be formed by *things*. The more we learn of things and come to see them in their systems, the better for archaeology – and philosophy.

Material culture (things) and historical landscape (monuments) are elements in a cognition of the past with some basis in objectivity. Thus, research based on museum collections remains essential. The reality of this situation was stressed by Manning (1980):

> . . . a great deal of academic archaeology is dependent on the study of artefacts; indeed for some periods they form almost the only source of information available.

Since the word *research* is arguably overworked and abused – not just in common parlance, for it has been so accused (and defended) in rescue archaeology (Thompson, 1975a, b; Jarrett, 1975) – its usage here is declared imprecise, for it is applied to the collecting and ordering of data as well as sorting it into meaningful conclusions, often to test hypotheses. In a museum context, these activities are closely related: the former a prerequisite of, and having a potential to result in, the latter.

Collection research and collecting policy

Academic research on collections is necessary not simply for itself, but as a basis of other museum activities, particularly the prime duty of collecting. Collecting policy and academic research are inextricably linked. Research requires collections, and collecting policy should grow out of research for either to be effective. A formative museum contribution to academic archaeology, with its attendant research requirements, is the development of an integrated policy in which at each of three levels – local regional, and national – collections attempt to reflect *patterns of the past* rather than current administrative boundaries[2]. Longworth (1980) has gone some way towards defining such a policy for the British Museum and in doing so emphasized the research potential:

> To have . . . a representative series brought together in a single institution is of tremendous assistance to the research worker, and here we have a unique role to play.

Neustupný (1971) has stressed the interrelationship of discipline and museums, across the board:

Museology is closely linked to, and in its entire activity dependent upon the theory and needs of the branches of science represented in the museum.

In archaeology, this is nowhere more true than in building up museum collections based on, and able to stimulate, research.

Existing museum collections (with associated data, such as context information, excavation archives, sites and finds records), are fundamental resources in determining archaeological methodology, particularly in formulating the basis of integrative problem-sampling techniques (Groube, 1978). Saunders (1979) has sought to evaluate the role of museums and has emphasized, rightly, that their involvement in British archaeology must be:

> something more than simple 'collecting policy' and more than a simple contextual locality index; it will provide a set of local archaeologies with their corresponding archives, at one time preserving the past and an intellectual concept of it and allowing for interlocality modelling and synthesis on a larger and wider scale in the future.

As well as this, research can be facilitated by the provision of reference material representing classes of artefacts. Again, such collections may be locally, regionally or nationally oriented. Pottery of all periods lends itself readily to such treatment in which as much attention is paid to fabric, manufacture and distribution as to form, decoration and use (Rhodes, 1977; Cherry, 1980; Green, 1980). Here, the building of type series (especially from closely dated contexts) is a major avenue of data development with research implications and potential, which awaits application to many periods and categories of material, and it has been applied already to a multiperiod study of skeletal material (Kruszynaki, 1978). Such collections would include the results of any scientific analysis, such as thin sectioning, thereby reducing the need for successive researchers to duplicate procedures, although not precluding the use of new techniques as these become available. Most ceramic traditions would benefit from such treatment, particularly those of the Roman period, especially if the earlier imports can be matched with continental material. Allied to representative reference collections is the need for comprehensive corpuses and indexes (Atkinson, 1955; Hawkes, 1955; Renfrew, 1967). The potential here is enormous and should be on a national scale, although regional coverage may be adequate for certain categories of material of limited distribution.

The ability of museums to influence what is collected (and for pragmatic reasons, at what pace) is implicit in the concept of systematic collections and vital for type series. This is not the place for an in-depth analysis of direct museum responsibility for rescue archaeology (see Eames, 1969; Rance, 1975; Thomas, 1976; Davies, 1978), but it must be stressed that if museums regard collections as their major resource, then ideally they should be initiators rather than recipients. Certainly, they should have the capability to mount excavations specifically to complete collections or to recover data to support existing, but inadequately documented, material, thereby increasing its research potential (Clarke, 1976; Longworth, 1980; Mercer *et al*, 1981).

Collection research and museum staff

The use of collections in, and for, research should involve museum staff to a large extent, stimulating colleagues from other backgrounds to widen its scope and synthesize the results. Nicholas Thomas (1976) in his presidential address to the Council for British Archaeology, restated this fundamental:

> Research-orientated curatorship in the same building as the related samples and collections . . . make sense to me.

So it does. The museum's contributions to research should be positive (Davies, 1978) and grown out of the traditional curatorial role defined by Pearce (1974) which is passive rather than active and promotional. It emphasizes curator as scholar without demeaning curator as steward. Eames (1969) commented that:

> The diversity of museums is part of the pleasure of using them, but this diversity is imperilled if standards of scholarship considered applicable in provincial and local museums are different from those prevailing in the metropolis, because, in archaeological material at least, the collections themselves may well be as important.

As a corollary he argued that:

> . . . museums must compete with other academic institutions for persons of comparable calibre.

In recent years there has been an increase in the numbers of young, well-qualified graduates wishing to practice archaeology in museums. Their future job satisfaction must be ensured through encouraging the intensive study of collections.

Collection research and associated data

Besides the major resource of the collection, internal and visiting researchers will use similar methodologies and will require common facilities. The systematic accumulation of all supporting evidence concerning specimens is primary, and from the totality of available data, when properly structured, to assess the current attainable level of knowledge. Encapsulated in this is the need for adequate documentation and storage systems to allow the efficient recall of this 'total data base'. These aspects of collection management are dealt with elsewhere in this manual, yet a short discussion of what has come to be called the *excavation archive* may be profitable, for on it hinges much research potential. This concept grew out of rationalizing the publication of excavation reports (AMB, 1975), thereby producing a synthesis incorporating minimal evidential material commensurate with verification requirements, and leaving the full record, structured as an archive, to accompany the finds as the ultimate reference source. To be an effective research tool, the archive requires mutual structuring by the parties concerned in order to achieve compatibility. This must be given priority – in staff and resources – so that sound foundations are laid, ensuring that in the future the matter is one of standard routine (Stone, 1979; Rhodes, 1980; Stewart, 1980). A major problem is posed by past excavations whose accompanying documentation frequently leaves much to be desired. Many excavations remain unpublished, and even when they have been it is often with scant regard for future needs, especially in terms of archive. Thomas (1976) has wittily criticized this in a barbed adaptation of a Wheeler dictum – 'publish and be dumped'. Many museums are faced now with the dilemma of 'rescuing' past excavations; some may be beyond saving.

Collection research: towards a priority

Resources for documenting collections, updating information retrieval systems, and providing adequate storage, are limited, and although minimum acceptable curatorial levels pertain for all material, some categories and functions may profit from higher standards. Research needs more than the non-intensive cataloguing forced on the bulk of collections by the desperate need to remove the backlog or to keep pace with the arrival of new material from rescue excavations. Most specimens may have a research role, but it is unlikely that all of them will exercise the potential at the same time. Research can be aided by intensive cataloguing and the ready accessibility of certain material. There may thus be a case for dividing collections into research and reserve categories, concentrating attention on the former. However, little, if any, evaluation has been made of this, even at a time when stretched resources make the definition of priorities essential. This begs the question 'How are research collections determined?'. Although difficult, there are pointers which make attempting this task worth while. First, there are internal, inherent attributes – size, comprehensiveness, representative nature and quality of associated information – linked with staff interest and expertise.

Second, experience of its past study and proven contribution to the advancement of knowledge, coupled with the intensity of its more recent usage. Research has fashions, and these may be discerned from current undergraduate and postgraduate theses[3] and the academic literature. Third, there are the research avenues advocated from time to time by the period societies. Such attributes and information may make possible a reasoned division of collections, indicating which may have current research potential. Obviously, the categories will overlap and remain dynamic, with material moving from one to the other.

There is a positive stimulus controlled by museums which can be used to help determine research and so categorize collections. From the base of 'assessed current attainable level of knowledge' museums should be able to advance profitable lines of enquiry as subjects suitable for undergraduate dissertations.

Students reveal another avenue where collections can contribute to academic need – participation in undergraduate teaching and training. For university museums this may be a major *raison d'être*, but it need not be confined to them. Indeed, in some countries, particularly the USA, it is quite developed;

> Many museums essentially independent of universities, however, have become affiliated with them in limited academic programmes, in which members of their curatorial staffs serve as adjunct professors in charge of courses taught within the museum's own collections . . .

(Folds, 1970; Manning, 1980 for British achaeology).

The use of collections for university teaching is likely to stimulate research on collections for academic purposes and may be one way of encouraging joint university/museum research fellowships (Davies, 1978).

Collection research: bibliographic and catalogue back-up

Alongside the facilities outlined already another major requirement of staff (and visiting researchers) is the provision of a good internal library. Often this is the most neglected aspect of research management, and it undermines the ability to use the collection fully, frustrating comparison and synthesis frequently. Most museums spend pitifully small amounts on their libraries, and many are adequate to answer only minor enquiries. Some rely on the curator's personal study, while others are fortunate to house the library of the local or county society. No provincial museum library can be complete and arrangements for recourse to university, national and specialist libraries must exist on an established basis.

The above has assumed that much academic research on collections is undertaken by workers from other institutions. Along with the resources and facilities so far described, a major provision remains to be discussed. Long recognized, poorly met, the need has been stated (Manning, 1980) in bold practical terms:

> a researcher has to know if a visit to a museum will justify the time and cost involved . . . (he) can travel widely providing that his supervisor certifies that such travel is necessary . . . something which cannot be done if the student has not confirmed the value of a visit with the museum in question.

This necessitates the basic duty of staff to produce collection catalogues, (Davies 1978), a responsibility largely abrogated by museum archaeologists.

> one of the most regrettable things about provincial museums is how infrequently their staffs publish papers on the objects under their care" (Manning 1980)
> 'If scholarly work is to be done on museum objects it is at least the fulfilment of such basic requirements as these (catalogues) that museums ought to undertake, rather than thrown the job onto the visiting scholar to whom they are merely the bricks with which to build a fuller structure. (Eames, 1969).

Catalogues need not be prestigious and costly to be effective. Simple catalogues should be within the capability of most museums to produce, for their basic function is to list, describe and illustrate, with no need of lengthy discussion and synthesis. Eames (1969) instanced the *Inventaria Archaeologica (An Illustrated Card-Inventory of Important Associated Finds in Archaeology)* series as an efficient form of catalogue. Based on sets of cards, and contained in a fold-around cover, it made a significant impact on the study of Bronze Age hoards and assemblages both in this country and on the continent. Although no longer available, the basic format is capable of modification for use in more traditional publications, thereby ensuring that museum collections are brought to the attention of researchers (Davies, 1979). It may be profitable for museums to re-evaluate the *Inventaria* concept, for it can be adapted to cover many aspects of the collection. If all else fails, information can be disseminated with an effective documentation system capable of generating computerbased indexes which can be duplicated cheaply and sent to appropriate institutions.

Collection research: routine management

There are mundane, practical requirements which internal and visiting researchers need. Adequate study space, good lighting (some daylight for colour matching), illustrating (drawing board and stand), reprographic and photographic facilities, are all examples. A degree of comfort and convivial surroundings and stimulating company will not go amiss (Manning, 1980). Paramount, however, is an attitude and atmosphere in which it is apparent that the museum takes research on its collections seriously, and welcomes the sharing of that task with others.

Supervision and security – major management problems – need a mention, as both exercise a call on staff time which may often be beyond the capability of the museum. Supervision has a positive and helpful connotation, for it is essential that the visitor is shown the museum resources and facilities and understands fully what is available to him, and where to find them. It is not always possible to bring these to him, not even collections, and he may need to search for material himself. In this case, the museum may be at risk from security requirements, and as much as possible should be done beforehand to minimize this by carefully checking credentials. Many of the researchers will be known personally and undergraduates can be vetted by their supervisors. However, unless a member of staff can be spared for continuous supervision and surveillance, the museum has to rely ultimately on trust. With the more casual visitor, of whom nothing is known, provision must be made to service him in a controlled manner, by preventing free access to security-sensitive areas. This requires a special place to which material is brought and which can be checked as the person leaves. Even greater vigilance is necessary with material of intrinsic monetary value, and where the problem can be aggravated by substitution (Kent, 1981). Exceptional care must be taken when access to such a collection is requested by individuals whose credentials cannot be checked adequately. Sometimes, it is necessary for a member of staff to remain with the researcher for the duration of the visit.[4]

In return for museum facilities and assistance, visiting researchers should be encouraged to help the museum. This may be achieved most readily by the provision of information for incorporation in the museum's catalogues and specimen files. Researchers are useful also in keeping staff abreast of the latest research trends and new methodologies, and time should be set aside for discussion.

Collection research and the visitor

It is necessary and pertinent to relate academic research to the visitors' needs.

> However strong may be his urge to pursue his own researches he (the curator) should remember that he

remains a student rather than a scholar unless he can communicate what he has learned. (O'Dea, 1970)

Many visitor requirements including interpretive display, enquiries, information and publications should have a grounding in an adequate research base. Museums should stimulate visitors to enquire and then assist them in their quest for knowledge.

The casual visitor can be entertained but the serious enquiring minority is the real justification for a science (*all*) museum. (O'Dea, 1970).

There is no better way to end than with the words of John Eames (1969):

I hope you will have read in my words a respectful wish that, among the multifarious duties of museums, scholarship may have a very high priority, not just because scholars elsewhere will benefit, but because museums are one of the most vivid means by which the practice and standards of scholarship may be valued by the world at large.

Notes

[1] Conveniently summarized by Saunders (1979) especially as it affects museums. To his useful bibliography should be added Watson *et al.* 1971).

[2] The term 'region' often does not have the same connotation in disciplinary usage as it does in museological usage. In the latter it tends to be associated with visitor/usage patterns based on existing collections (Owen, 1971; Cheetham, 1971; Museums Association, 1971). The problem of *region* as a meaningful academic entity is not confined to archaeology, occurring in other historical disciplines – 'in the collection of ethnographic material a political unit is not of necessity a cultural unit . . .' (Jenkins, 1974).

[3] Useful, if irregular in its appearance is *Current Research in Archaeology* a duplicated list of undergraduate and post-graduate theses, pioneered by students at the Institute of Archaeology, London University, the latest edition (1984 edited by the Department of Prehistory and Archaeology, University of Sheffield.

[4] Museums should pass information to each other on suspect 'researchers'.

References

ANCIENT MONUMENTS BOARD FOR ENGLAND, (1975), *Principles of Publication in Research Archaeology*, Report of a working party of the Ancient Monument Board for England Committee for Rescue Archaeology, HMSO, London (For DoE)

ATKINSON, R. J. C. (1955), 'A national index of archaeological collections', *Museums J.*, **54**(10), 255–259

CHEETHAM, F. W. (1971), Regionalisation, *Museums J.*, **71**, (3), 98

CHERRY, J. (1980), 'The reference collection of medieval pottery in the British Museum', *The Museum Archaeologist*, **6**, 8–11

CLARKE, D. V. (1976), 'Excavations at Skara Brae: a sum-mary account', in *Settlement and Economy in the Third and Second Millenia BC*, 223–250, C. B. Burgess and R. Miket (Eds) Oxford, BAR 33

DAVIES, D. G. (1978), 'Museums and archaeology – a lost cause?', *Museums J.*, **78**(3), 123–125

DAVIES, D. G. (1979), 'Hatfield Broad Oak, Leigh, Rayne, Southchurch: Late Bronze Age Hoards from Essex', in *Bronze Age Hoards: some Finds Old and New*, 149–172, C. B. Burgess and D. Coombs (Eds) Oxford BAR 67

EAMES, J. V. H. (1969), 'Museums and scholarship', *Museums J.*, **69**(3), 103–105

FOLDS, T. M. (1970), 'Educational personnel in museums', in *Training of Museum Personnel* pp. 48–75, Hugh Evelyn, London (for ICOM)

GREEN, S. J. (1980), 'National reference collection for post-medieval ceramics', Stoke on Trent, *The Museum Archaeologist*, **6** 12–13

GROUBE, L. M. (1978), 'Priorities & Problems in Dorset Archaeology', in Darvill, *et al* (Eds), *New Approaches to our Past (an Archaeological Forum)*. pp. 29–52, University Archaeological Society, Southampton

HAWKES, C. (1955), 'Curatas and Corpuses', *Museums J.*, **55**(7), 178–181

HAWKES, C. (1973), *Rescue News*, **5**, 2–3

HAWKES, C. (1982), 'Archaelogical retrospect 3', *Antiquity*, **LVI** (217), 93–101

JARRETT, M. (1975), 'Rescue archaeology & research', *Antiquity*, **XLIX** (194), 137–139

JENKINS, J. G. (1974), 'The collection of ethnological material', *Museums J.*, **74**(1), 7–11

KENT, J. P. C. (1981), 'Storage of coins', *Archaeological Storage*, p. 20, Society of Museum Archaeologists and Humberside Federation of Museums and Art Galleries, Humberside

KRUSZYNSKI, R. G. (1978), 'New storage facilities for Britain's largest skeletal collection', *Museums J.*, **78**(3), 138–140

LONGWORTH, I. H. (1980), 'The British Museum and British archaeology: an acquisitions policy', *The Museum Archaeologist*, **5**, 3–5

MANNING, W. H. (1980), 'Universities and museums', *The Museum Archaeologist*, **5**, 6–10

MERCER, R. J. (1981), *Grimes Graves, Norfolk Excavations 1971–72*, Vol. 1, Dept of the Environment Archaeological Report 11, HMSO, London

MORGAN, C. G. (1972), Archaeology and explanation, *World Archaeology*, **4**(3), 259–276

MUSEUM ASSOCIATION (1971), 'Minutes of the annual general meeting (a museum service for the nation: paper present by council)', *Museums J.*, **71**(3), 127

NEUSTUPNÝ, J. (1971), 'What is museology?', *Museums J.*, **71**(2), 67

O'DEA, W. T. (1970), 'The training of personnel for science museums', in *Training of Museum Personnel*, pp. 138–154, Hugh Evelyn, London (for ICOM)

OWEN, D. E. (1971), 'Regionalisation of museums: what is a region?', *Museums J.*, **71**(1), 25–26

PEARCE, S. M. (1974), 'The role of the archaeological author in the wider pattern of archaeological research: some suggestions', *Museums J.*, **73**(4), 149–151

RANCE, A. B. (1975), 'Archaeology units and museums', *Museums J.*, **75**(3), iv–vi

RENFREW, C. (1967), 'The requirements of the research worker in archaeology', *Museums J.*, **67**(20), 111–134

RHODES, M. (1977), 'A pottery and fabric type-series for London', *Museums J., ***76**(4), 150–152

RHODES, M. (1980), 'Some thoughts concerning the definition of aims and objectives in the development of excavation archives', *The Museum Archaeologist,* **5**, 28–35

SAUNDERS, C. (1979), 'Archaeology and museums – another view', *The Museum Archaeologist,* **3**, 10–19

STEWART, J. (1980), 'Integrated excavation and museum recording systems: methods, theories and problems', *The Museum Archaeologist,* **5**, 11–27

STONE, S. M. (1978), 'St. Albans museums documentation project', *Museums J., ***78**(3), 117–119

STONE, S. M. (1979), 'Excavation recording at St. Albans', *The Museum Archaeologist,* **2**, 10–15

THOMAS, N. (1976), 'Museums and archaeology', *CBA Archaeology in Britain 1975–76,* **26**, 44–55 (abstracted in the *Museums J., ***76**(3), 106–109)

THOMPSON, F. H. (1975a), 'Rescue archaeology: research or rubbish collection?', *Antiquity,* **XLIX**(1983), 43–45

THOMPSON, F. H. (1975b), rejoiner to Jarrett (1975), pp. 139–140

WATSON, P. J., LEBLANC, S. A. AND REDMAN, C. L. (1971), *Explanation in Archaeology: an Explicitly Scientific Approach,* Columbia University Press, New York and London

22

Research: social history collections

Roy D. Brigden

Social history collections are the residues of previous existence, and, therefore, represent the material remains of life. Artefacts from previous generations have always been the subject of curiosity and, in present society, many possess a financial value far greater than their original. The extent to which these objects can illuminate aspects of the age from which they originated depends primarily upon knowledge resulting from the research input.

Individually, the objects can embody the differences in technology and fashion that separate one social period from another. Collectively, they can indicate patterns of behaviour, social customs, and standards of living, and, by tracing the stages by which man has sought to manipulate his environment, they become a medium for analysing the concept of change. Hence, one of the basic skills of a curator is the ability to interpret the objects within a historical context so that each may be induced to reveal its story.

The means of acquiring this expertise is not immediately obvious. Indeed, in most cases, the accumulation of in-house experience must compensate for the absence of suitable formal training. Little of the social history research currently undertaken in academic institutions is object-based, or makes sufficient use of existing three-dimensional sources. To concentrate research solely on literary and documentary evidence is to ignore this entire dimension of information. Above all, lack of familiarity with the material evidence inevitably reduces the depth of insight and understanding gained to a degree which is impossible to disguize.

Jenkins (1961) commented that:

> folk life study still finds itself in much the same position that archaeology did in the nineteenth century: an attraction for the enthusiastic amateur, but not a serious academic discipline.

After twenty years, it is still left to the curator to develop and maintain his own standards of research. As a professional, he must be in equal command both of detail, (with regard to individual items), and of the broader aspects of collection. The trap of viewing social history material in terms of any aesthetic appeal alone must be avoided if the historical perspective is to remain. At the same time, fixed and narrow-minded concentration on minutiae should be kept at bay, lest all sense of proportion be eroded.

The central idea, and the one that distinguishes the social history museum from just a collection of objects, is that of *context* – historical, geographical and cultural[1]. Once formulated and defined by research, the context can be projected through an exhibition to create a suitable medium of interpretation. The context makes the object speak: characteristics that delineate one period from another emerge together with the threads of continuity that inextricably link our present way of life to its roots.

Within this overall historical framework, the objects possess their own context, for behind each there is a human element. The object itself is the clearest tangible link with the people who made it, the people who used it, and the society to which it belonged. Research brings us closer to an understanding of those people, and separates each item individually; for even with mass-produced goods, the story of ownership and use is different in each case.

Procedures

Most attempts using objects in systematic research depend on locating sufficient examples to provide the data base. Variations between the objects, their manufacture, design and use, can suggest distinct cultural regions whose boundaries encompass common streams of material. This concept is particularly suited to objects that were either home-produced or emanated from local craftsmen in districts where clear expression was given to regional traditions and influences[2].

The plough is a clear example of an implement adapted for use in different parts of the country under the combined pressures of external influences and local agricultural conditions and prejudices. However, during the last century, specialist agricultural engineering firms, by capturing national markets, complicated the picture by sending factory-built versions of traditional plough designs to compete alongside the products of smaller, regional workshops. Consequently, this aspect of farming history presents a number of uncertainties worthy of nation-wide research. By studying in detail the surviving type specimens and adding to that the fruits of field-work and documentary research, it is conceivable that the regional nature of the plough would be perceived with greater clarity.

Where data is plentiful, distribution can be mapped to reveal the extent of the cultural regions. The *Atlas of Swedish Folk Culture,* two volumes of which appeared in 1957 and 1977, assimilates information collected from a network of informants on a range of cultural features, including objects, customs and dialect[3].

Although trends can usefully be established in this way, there are limitations to a method that tends to remove inconsistencies and codify social development into neatly-defined segments. The *Atlas* can identify different regions, but cannot, in isolation, account for the differences between them. As this must be the ultimate objective, the *Atlas* is a means to an end rather than an end in itself.

In Britain, systematic object research is hampered by the absorption of original material into private collections where, in many cases, haphazard restoration and disregard of provenance have undermined its usefulness by destroying the context. Furthermore, the conventions of ethnology are less applicable to the problems of twentieth-century material. In the case of the plough, the last sixty years have seen manufacture concentrated in a small number of national and multi-national organizations. Modern technology produces many different types of plough, and while these have been designed to match varying specifications of tractor, and to cater for different working conditions, the regional element is no longer applicable in the same way.

This principle applies to other goods manufactured in the twentieth century. It is not easy, for example, to think in terms of regional variations in television sets or refrigerators. However, while the technological design features exist at a general level, from the point of view of use in particular, there is a local story to be told. The part played by local distri-

butors and the social impact of such products on a community are but two aspects that the social history museum can profitably investigate[4].

Rather than concentrate on one type of artefact, research projects often seek to analyse the evolution and development of one occupation, industry or aspect of social life[5]. This can proceed naturally from the existence of a particular collection in the museum, and the desire to extend the known background information. Alternatively, the research project can begin with the intention of adding to existing collections. A temporary exhibition, especially when accompanied by a publication is a useful focus for presenting the fruits of such work by promoting a wider understanding of the museum's function and, by arousing public interest, may lead to the discovery of further relevant material[6].

Once the subject has been chosen, the results of preparatory work in libraries and record offices will often suggest the pattern of subsequent field-work[7]. Appeals through the local press may cause people associated with the activity to come forward. The forthcoming clearance of a site, the closure of a business, or the retirement of a traditional craftsman may have been the initial stimulus for the project. In such cases, all the varied sources of information, the building[8], the business records, the tools of the trade and the people concerned – must be fully researched and synthesized[9].

The current methodology for research programmes of this kind has evolved mainly from studies into traditional countryside customs and occupations[10]. They are not, however, confined to these subjects. Recent work has demonstrated the rich and varied patterns of social and commercial behaviour associated with urban areas that are ideal for the attention of the museum[11]; the recent study of fast food outlets in the USA being a good example (Lohof, 1978).

In its other main form, museum-based research is not confined to a single category, but works through a spectrum of social material in order to study a particular community at one or more periods in the past. This, in effect, is the role of the social history museum in creating a sense of local identity by giving the community an insight into its historical development. Here the curator requires the skills of the local historian[12] to correlate the information embodied in his collection with that derived from documentary evidence, buildings and other landscape features, and from the memories of the inhabitants. This type of research establishes and enriches the link between the museum and its environment.

Site and open-air museums (Atkinson and Holton, 1973) extend this concept by arranging their material in order to immerse the visitor in the cultural atmosphere of the past. Authenticity can only be achieved through sustained preparatory research and field-work[13]; research which may also reveal gaps in the collections, to be filled by further field investigations or through public appeals.

Other evidence of value unfolds in the course of creating the museum itself. The work reconstructing or restoring the building implies a mastery of architectural developments and building techniques that in some cases can only be acquired through detailed examination of previously hidden parts of surviving structures (Lowe, 1972). Similarly, the operation of machinery in the museum requires a knowledge of how that machine works, and perhaps an ability to reconstruct missing or broken parts, faculties that may not otherwise have been acquired. Furthermore, by operating the machinery, more can be learned by the curator – as well as the visitor – about the working conditions of the original operators. Hence, research is not only inseparable from the conservation function of a museum, but is closely linked with the display and interpretation function.

All these forms of research depend upon the accurate recording of the information associated with the objects. This is a basic requirement of the accessioning procedure and one aspect of the discipline of research that allows for further work. In many museums, the potential for researching and exhibiting material has suffered because this ground work was not completed at the time of accessioning, resulting in the loss of important background details. No amount of computerization can retrieve what was never recorded.

Levels of information

The information associated with museum collections may be separated into three tiers. The first contains the *physical details* of the object, and includes, for example, the material it is made from, the process of manufacture, and any recognizable period features. This level can reveal clues about its working life: whether the original form has been altered or converted, and whether any repairs that have been made to it are authentic or the result of later restoration. Many agricultural implements bear the marks of clumsy adaptation. It was not uncommon, for example, for old scythe blades to be fashioned into a variety of small edge tools for general purpose use. A mower or binder, initially intended to be horse-drawn, will often have been converted, sometimes crudely, for tractor draught. Careful recording of such characteristics outlines a unique profile for each object and suggests questions for further research.

The second tier covers *oral information* about the object supplied by the donor and his environment. Of particular importance is the personal connection between the two. The donor may have made the object and so be able to describe the techniques of

manufacture. Further probing may reveal the tools and equipment used, and the history of the business. If the firm is still trading, or at least if the premises have survived, then an accompanied tour may result in further material for the note book, tape-recorder and camera. The donor's colleagues and employees may also provide information. By asking them for the names of past and present business associates, before long a research project on a trade or occupation has developed and begun to generate its own momentum.

Oral information does not come solely from donors. A museum may possess an extensive collection of objects, but only a moderate degree of accompanying background material. An appeal through the press, local associations, and other groups, may suggest contacts able to supply a local context for the collection. As Ewart Evans (1976) has quoted:

> What oral history does admirably in this respect is to supplement, supplying extra resources for conventional history by salvaging the sort of material that tends to slip between the meshes of print or documentation.

Context enhances the exhibition potential of museum material as well as increasing understanding and appreciation of the objects. The emergence of oral history as a discipline in its own right has over the last decade served to 'affect the presentation of history in museums, record offices and libraries. These all now have a means of infusing life into their collections, and through this of bringing themselves into a more active relationship with their community' (Thompson, 1978).

Recordings have been incorporated into social history exhibitions, particularly temporary exhibitions, to allow the human voice to heighten the atmosphere and the personal sense of contact with the past[14].

Not all museums are in a position to afford the considerable labour input required for an extensive programme or oral history research. Very often a worthwhile recording is possible only after two or three meetings – when the informant is completely at ease – and the subsequent production of transcriptions may burden secretarial resources. While, therefore, it is important that the curator should take detailed notes of conversations, a tape recorder should also be used[15]. Some curators have overcome manpower limitations by enlisting the help of volunteers, thereby involving other sections of the community in the research work. This has the added advantage of widening the museum's circle of contacts, and, so, of extending the range of potential informants.

The questionnaire is another survey tool that complements the methods already described[16]. When composed around a research theme and actively distributed through local organizations, the net is cast widely in search of otherwise untapped data. The drawbacks of questionnaires include the preconceived and contrived nature of the questions and their tendency to invite short, standard answers, while leaving unsaid much of the more colourful and idiosyncratic details of the informant's experiences. A questionnaire, however, is useful in locating people willing to co-operate with research. They may then be visited, so that the information from the questionnaire is supplemented by that obtained in conversation.

The third tier includes *two-dimensional* background information. Primary sources, contemporary in date with the object, includes manufacturer's catalogues, instruction manuals, advertising material and photographs. The institute of Agricultural History at the University of Reading has extensive collections of trade material, produced by over 2000 manufacturers of agricultral equipment. From these records, machinery can be dated, colour schemes identified, and a great deal learned about operation in the field. A business archive has a serious research function: production figures, with the names and geographical distribution of agents and individual customers, enable theories on the introduction and diffusion of new equipment to be tested. Other papers may show how the business was managed, how many men were employed, what the conditions of work were like, and what form of housing or recreation, if any, was provided. Business records, particularly advertising material, have in addition an immediate visual appeal, with a graphic style evocative of the period concerned, that gives them outstanding exhibition potential. Similarly, contemporary photographs not only supply vital information about how something was used or what a building, since demolished, looked like: they also create an atmosphere, providing the human context that allows associated objects to be viewed sympathetically.

However, danger lies in accepting at face value the visual images that such material provides. Would an early-twentieth century photograph of corn being mown by scythe imply that this method was the norm in the area, or was the photograph taken because hand harvesting was by then a rarity? The print cannot supply the answer, and this example underlines the importance of background research into contemporary agricultural reports, journals, and farm records. Similarly, all may have a mental picture of the furnishings in an eighteenth century cottage, but how much is accurate and how much arises from commonly held romantic notions? The checking of inventories is one way of going back to the basic data upon which to build a more informed and authentic portrait[17].

Historical context depends not only upon the consultation of all these sources but also on a sound environmental awareness. Evidence of the interaction between man and his environment over the centuries is all around in the form of buildings, landscape features and people. It cannot be confined within the walls of a museum. It can, however, be recorded and interpreted so that, in matters of environmental preservation and conservation, the museum becomes a source of informed opinion. Further, the museum may be involved actively in external interpretation by, for example, organizing a town or country trail around features of historic interest. The underlying principle is to harmonize what is inside the museum with what is outside. This link is forged through field-work, the process that takes the curator out to discover and study the raw material of his subject. Knowing where to look, and what to look for, is the basis of successful field-work, and involves extensive preparatory work on the surviving records[18]. For a local project on brickworks, for example, a scan of early editions of six-inch ordnance survey maps (Harley, 1972) will pinpoint some sites while the evidence of names such as 'Kiln Farm' will suggest others. More information about the individual firms on the site will be forthcoming from directories, local histories, and business archives in the record office. In the field, some kilns may still be operating, providing an opportunity to record the process in action, while others will exist only as ruins. The physical remains can be measured and photographed, present or former employees interviewed, and perhaps some material acquired for the museum. As a simultaneous research and public-relations operation, organized field-work utilizes all the curatorial skills in concentrated form. Not surprisingly it is one of the most important and enjoyable activities of the social history museum.

Notes

[1] For example, see Jenkins, J. G. (1969), 'Folk museums – some aims and purposes', *Museums J.*, **69** (1).

[2] Jenkins, J. G. (1961), *The English Farm Wagon*, Oakwood Press, Hinton. Nearly 600 wagons around the country were recorded. For further research into a single category of artefact see Fenton, A. (1974), 'The Cas-chrom. A review of Scottish evidence', *Tools and Tillage*, **11** (3).

[3] An analysis of 'classical' Nordic ethnology is provided by Owen, T. (1977), 'Folk life studies: some problems and perspectives', *Folk Life*, **19**.

[4] For comment on the social history content that should be evident in a motor car, see Green, O. (1981) Museum of British Road Transport: A review, *Museums J.*, **81** (3).

[5] For an example of a survey combining historical material and oral evidence see Porter, E. (1969), 'Fen skating', *Folk Life*, **7**. See also the craft bibliographies in *Newsletters*, Nos 4–9 of the Group for Regional Studies in Museums.

[6] For example, see Caffrey, H. (1979), 'Some craftsmen in the Tame valley', *Folk Life*, **17**, A research project that resulted in an exhibition in 1978.

[7] *See* Jenkins, J. G. (1974), 'The collection of ethnological material', *Museums J.,* **74**(1), a description, with case studies, of how a research project is set in motion.

[8] For information on the recording of buildings see Major, J. K. (1975) *Fieldwork in industrial archaeology,* Batsford, London.

[9] For example, Viner, D. J. (1976), 'The marble quarry, Inner Hebrides', *Industrial Archaeology Review,* **1**(1), which describes how a dossier is compiled for a site from a combination of information sources.

[10] For example, Jenkins, J. G. (1977), 'Cockles and mussels: aspects of shellfish gathering in Wales', *Folk Life,* **15.**

[11] McKelvie, D. (1963), 'Aspects of oral tradition and belief in an industrial region', *Folk Life,* **1,** demonstrates through a study of Bradford that traditions can live on vigorously in an urban community.

[12] Here the works of W. G. Hoskins are inspirational, e.g., Hoskins, W. G. (1967), *Fieldwork in Local History, Faber and Faber,* London.

[13] Brears, P. C. D. (1976), Regionalism in the historical museum, *Museums Association Proceedings,* Describes research undertaken as part of project to furnish Clarke Hall, near Wakefield, as it might have been in the late-seventeenth century.

[14] See *Yorkshire Farming Memories,* a tape cassete compiled by Stephen Harrison and published by the Castle Museum, York, (1981).

[15] For advice on use of tape recorders *see* Winstanley, M. (1977), 'Some practical hints on oral history interviewing', *Oral History,* **5**(1).

[16] For example, *see* Cheape, H. (1978), 'Some technical means for higher quality: recording in oral history', *Oral History,* **6**(1).

[17] For the value of inventories in research *see* Trinder and Cox (1981), *Yeoman to Collier,* Phillimore, Chichester.

[18] For a run through of the sources available *see* Stephens, W. B. (1973), *Sources for English local history,* University Press, Manchester.

References

ATKINSON, F. AND HOLTON, M. (1973), 'Open air and folk museums', *Museums J.,* **72**(4),

EWART EVANS, G. (1976), *From Mouths of Men,* Faber and Faber, London

HARLEY, J. B. (1972), 'Maps for the Local Historian' *Standing Conference for Local History,* National Council of Social Service, London

JENKINS, J. G. (1961), 'Folk life studies and the museum', *Museums J.,* **61**(3),

LOHOF, B. A. (1978) 'Hamburger stand: industrialization and the American fast-food phenomenon', *Industrial Archaeology Review,* **11**(3),

LOWE, J. (1972), 'The Weald and Downland Open Air museum', *Museums J.,* **72**(1),

THOMPSON, P. (1978), 'The voice of the past', *University Press,* Oxford

23

Research: social history sources

Peter C. D. Brears

The documentary research sources for the social historian are extremely rich, ranging from formal archival material to a wealth of oral, literary and pictorial evidence. By using a combination of these, it is possible to establish, with a fair degree of accuracy, the life style, attitudes and working practices of the societies under consideration.

Research sources (documentary)

Standard archival sources

It is assumed that standard archival sources held in national and local record offices are sufficiently well known not to require detailed description. In brief, they include records of land ownership and management (manorial court rolls and custumals, estate papers and lease books, enclosure and tithe awards), maps and plans (including ordnance survey and earlier material), judicial records, (such as those from manorial, quarter-session and ecclesiastical courts), testamentary records (including wills, inventories and administrations), ecclesiastical records (established, and other churches' visitations and parish registers), business records, household accounts, directories, census returns and local government records[1].

Museum records

Every museum should be able to provide documentation of its collections in the form of accession registers, correspondence and information files. It is particularly important that the information gained from such records is verified from external sources wherever possible. The name and address of the donor, as recorded in accession registers, need bear no relationship to the original provenance of a specimen, for example, while the re-accessioning of museum specimens may cause sound provenances to be lost.

When dealing with individual collections, it is important that every effort should be made to trace any notes or catalogues prepared by the collector. Frequently, these have become separated from the collection itself, perhaps remaining in the possession of the collector's family, or passing into the hands of local societies or records offices.

Museum catalogues

Few worthwhile catalogues of social history collections have been published to date, and much remains to be done in this field. In 1903, the Guildhall Museum published its 'Catalogue of London Antiquities' which remains the only published source to that most important of collections. New standards were set by Dr Lorwerth Peate of the National Museum of Wales, in his *Guide to the Collection of Welsh bygones* of 1929 and *Guide to the Collection – Illustrating Welsh Folk Crafts and Industries* of 1935. Since this time, very little activity has taken place in this important field[2].

Collectors' publications

As social history material was already being collected by the late-nineteenth century, a number of important, seminal articles have appeared in a variety of collectors' publications from that time. The pages of periodicals such as *The Reliquary*, *The Connoisseur*, *Country Home*, or *The Bazaar, Exchange and Mart* contain a wealth of relevant information, as do the individual volumes of *Collectors Guides*.

Descriptive sources

One of the most important and easily accessible sources of information for the social historian is provided by the great wealth of both printed and manuscript descriptions of this country, provided over the past three centuries. Works such as Camden's *Britannia* (English edition, 1695) and Plot's histories of Oxfordshire (1677) and of Staffordshire (1686) established a form of topographical writing which combined historical evidence with current accounts of manufactures, domestic and social life, and customs, which has continued unabated to the present day[3]. Most districts possess their sequences of local histories, providing unique evidence of the development of their particular communities.

Further descriptive accounts are given in the travelogues of Celia Feinnes, or Daniel Defoe[4], and in the reports of the Boards of Agriculture, the Factories Inspectorate, or the Sanitary Commissioners. For customs and beliefs, ample material has been published in the pages of the *Gentleman's Magazine,* and in such works as W. Hone's *Everyday Book* (1826).

Evidence of a more personal nature may be gained from diaries, autobiographies, and commonplace books, many works of this type now being available in printed form.

Literary sources

From the early-nineteenth century a number of major novelists and poets have tended to lay claim to different regions and social strata of this county. Thomas Hardy is inseparable from rural Wessex, Jane Austen from middle-class Southern England, the Bronte sisters from the South Pennines, or more recently, James Herriot from the Yorkshire Dales[5]. Although such works were intended to serve literary ends, the contain many unique and illuminating passages referring to most aspects of human activity within their region. Where available, the source notes and manuscripts, biographies, memoirs and personalia of such writers may also provide further information.

The works of other, more general, writers may provide sources of a different kind. Dickens' account of Christmas celebrations, or school life at 'Dotheboys Hall', or Kingsley's description of the life of climbing boys, provide classic examples of this type of source. It should be remembered, however, that these sources are essentially of a secondary nature and should be verified from other primary, contemporary material wherever possible.

Dialect publications

From the late-seventeenth century, poetry, prose and plays have been composed in dialect, and this movement expanded rapidly in the third quarter of the nineteenth century due to the increasing literacy of the working classes and the respectability given to dialect composition by such poets as Robert Burns. These works are often based on early memories, or

on events of local significance, and throw considerable light on the practices and attitudes in the writer's environment. In addition to documenting practical details, they also possess an 'atmospheric' quality, giving a unique impression of 'what it was like'.

Dialect dictionaries and glossaries can provide similar information, but usually of a more practical nature. Here, the main interest lies not only in the derivation or distribution of the word itself, but more particularly in the definition of the operation or artefact described. Joseph Wright's *English Dialect Dictionary*, Oxford (1898) is still the standard work of this type, its bibliography providing sources for further work. It may also be worth while to examine entries in the *Oxford English Dictionary*, drawing on its depth of etymological research in order to obtain the earliest references and quotations to the widest variety of artefacts and practices.

Oral evidence

The personal reminiscences of individuals provide one of the richest primary sources for the social historian, and museums working in this field should undertake tape-recording in the field as a matter of course. The tapes should be transcribed, indexed, and placed in suitable storage conditions as soon as possible, in order to ensure their ready availability and the permanence of their content.

Pictorial evidence

The vast range of pictorial sources available to the social historian includes paintings, sketch books and topographical prints (these frequently being housed in separate art gallery collections, due to their aesthetic quality); photographs (in local collections, newspapers, libraries, and in commercial picture libraries largely serving the publishing trade); illustrated books (including volumes on regional costume, street cries, or various books of trades, such as Pyne's *Microcosm* of 1806) and political, satyrical, and humorous prints, such as those by Hogarth and Rowlandson.

In addition to this original material, much relevant information may be extracted from the reproductions printed in sale catalogues, advertisements and on greetings and postcards.

Comparative studies

As museum studies are primarily concerned with actual specimens, it is important that any research into collections should consider every aspect of their physical qualities. This practice is already well-established in most other disciplines, but is only slowly being adopted by social history departments within museums. It should be recognized that comparative studies of material culture between one region and another is just as valid and important in the post-medieval period, as it is for those earlier periods considered by the archaeologist. Such studies might be based on:

(1) Manufacturing and decorative techniques – on general themes, such as blacksmithing, domestic rug and quilt making, and horse decoration, or on more specialized subjects, such as the use of pewter inlay or coloured wax inlay in aspects of folk art.

(2) Design of tools and working practices – such as the design of hedging implements and their relationship in different landscapes, the distribution of certain culinary artefacts in relation to their local environment and cultural tradition.

(3) Decorative motifs, which may include survivals from the pre-historic periods, such as rosettes, 'x' motifs, or 'celtic' heads, or survivals from more recent political and social events, such as the 'Bonny Bunch of Roses' commemorating the 1801 Act of Union. The use of distinctive decorative motifs may also be used to trace the distribution of products from a particular workshop or craftsman.

Work of this type can be successfully completed only by following detailed surveys of the collections of many museums. Due to the present state of documentation and information retrieval, comparative studies may have to be undertaken by making personal visits to many separate collections. The adoption of common classification systems and the increasing use of computers should enable the scattered knowledge to be brought together and assimilated.

Exposition

All research work undertaken in the museum should be publicized in one form or another, both to disseminate the results, and to leave a permanent record for the use of future scholars and other institutions holding comparable material. In addition, educationalists, academics, designers, and craftsmen, may wish to make use of the knowledge accumulated by the museum.

The dissemination of the results of museum research may be achieved in a number of ways:

Museum catalogues

Catalogues of museum collections, including descriptions of physical characteristics, dimensions and provenance, should be published, line drawings or photographs being used as fully as possible.

Where the details of provenance are weak (this being a common feature of collections acquired from private collectors), comparative studies of soundly provenanced specimens in other collections should be made in order to suggest a region or date of origin. Where such suggestions are made, the catalogue entry must make it clear that they are suggestions, and not documented facts.

It is important that catalogues should not be mere lists of the museum's holdings, but that they should be accompanied by a reasoned introduction, providing details of the background of the collection, relevant details of the subject gathered from documentary and comparative research, and a description of the location and availability of the collection itself.

Exhibition catalogues

Exhibitions featuring particular aspects of social history provide a valuable opportunity for the publication of catalogues, particularly when the specimens are being drawn from a number of separate, and perhaps disparate institutions. The above approach is recommended.

Academic articles

Where museum-based research contributes to the development of fresh concepts, it is often preferable to publish the results in the appropriate academic journal. The *Journal of Folk-Life Studies* serves most aspects of social history in the British Isles, in addition to which there are a large number of more specialized journals dealing with costume, numismatics, agriculture, military history, industrial history and post-medieval archaeology.

For more general distribution, such well-established periodicals as *Country Life* and *The Countryman,* or various county magazines, can provide an excellent avenue of publication.

Books and booklets

Where there is sufficient commercial interest, curatorial staff may be able to work with publishing houses on preparing books and booklets for general sale. Where these publications are based on the museum's collections and on research carried out within the museum, an appropriate financial agreement should be made between the publisher, the author, and the controlling body of the museum concerned. Subject to this condition, this is perhaps the most effective way of making widely available the museum's collections and academic standards, frequently permitting many copies of a good quality production to be printed, while attracting income to the museum concerned.

Notes

[1] For national records, see Guiseppe, M. S., *Guide to the Contents of the Public Record Office,* 3 volumes (1963–1968), HMSO, London

[2] See also Curtis, W. H. and Warner S. A. (1979), *List of Smaller Implements . . . in Use on Farms,* Alton, Hants, and Brears, P. C. D. (1979), *The Kitchen Catalogue,* York.

[3] E.g., Howitt, W. (1840), *The Rural Life of England,* London and the works of Gertrude Jekyll, George Sturt, Flora Thompson, Marie Hartley and Joan Ingilby, George Ewart Evans, etc.

[4] See Feinnes, C. (1888) *Through England on a Side Saddle,* London and Defoe, D. (1748) *A Tour through the Whole Island of Great Britain,* London.

[5] *See Oxford Literary Guide to the British Isles,* Oxford University Press, Oxford (1977).

24

Research: social history – a case study

Rosemary E. Allan

The special task of the museum dealing with social history is to communicate the relationship in society, between needs, resources and traditions, by collecting, preserving and documenting artefacts and, by researching and interpreting them, making them available to the academic scholar and visitor alike. The study of social history is concerned with the whole society (Trevelyan, 1944):

> the daily life of the inhabitants of a land in past ages: this includes the human as well as the economic relation of different classes to one another, the character of family and household life, the conditions of labour and leisure, the attitude of man to nature, the culture of each age as it arose out of these general conditions of life, and took ever-changing forms in religion, literature and music, architecture, learning and thought.

The main purpose of the social history curator is, therefore, to record and interpret the way of life and tradition of a region, whether rural or urban, through its material and non-material culture, both in the present as well as the past (HMSO, 1951).

> History never ceases to be made, we are never at the end of time, but always in the middle of it. With every economic, social or industrial change, there goes an atmosphere, a whole world of habit, incident, thought and terminology, the memory and savour of which can be preserved only if recovered from the lips of those who lived in it and through it.

The mere collection of material objects is only a starting point in the study and research of social history. The student must be prepared to seek the social organization, the economy and the culture associated with the artefact, and to research the characteristics of the individual, his language, dialect, customs, buildings and equipment, in order to portray a complete picture of a region.

Why research?

The museum has two main purposes, one the preservation, use and study of its collections, and the other in making these collections available for use by the scholar or visitor. Inextricably linked with these two functions is the overriding one of research. It is the specimens or artefacts within the museum which make it a unique institution. Its specimens are of primary importance. They must be researched, and careful thought must therefore be given to what is collected and preserved.

Preliminary research for the reconstruction and fitting out of miners' cottages in an open air museum – Beamish 1976

Preliminary research was undertaken to find a row of typical miners' dwellings, built around 1850, in County Durham, which would be suitable for dismantling and re-erection in an open-air museum. Much research was needed to assess what was typical, important and significant within the geographical area specified. The relevant cultural elements in the area were examined to build up an overall picture of its personality and to identify features which typify County Durham.

Background reading

A formal research programme was designed, beginning with a search through the available literature contemporary to the period to put the subject in perspective. Background reading covered the study of locality, population, comparative national and regional history, the coal companies and their mines, studies of pit villages and houses, and work in the house. The background of religion, the Union, the Durham Miners' Association lodges, the WEA, the Co-operative Movement, Institutes and the Big Meeting were all researched to ascertain their influences on the housing of the time. Present-day studies and accounts were also consulted and an outline of research methods formulated.

Written descriptions

Observations of travellers throughout the region provide an insight into contemporary attitudes and impressions. Some nineteenth-century observers doubted that miners lived in houses at all. William Cobbett, describing the coal districts through which he passed during his Northern Tour in 1832, wrote:

> Here is the most surprising thing in the world; thousands of men and thousands of horses continually living underground; children born there, and who sometimes, it is said, seldom see the surface at all though they live to a considerable age.

One witness, writing in about 1840, remarked that he found the houses to contain comparatively showy and costly furniture. Typical items of furniture in the principal room included an eight-day clock, a good chest of drawers and a fine four-poster bedstead with large quilt or coverlet composed of squares of printed calico. The quality of the furnishings often highly contrasted with the quality of housing.

One of the first detailed observations on miners' living conditions was contained in the report of the Commission on Child Employment, published in 1841. A valuable series of articles was produced in the Newcastle Weekly Chronicle from 1872–1874 entitled *Our Colliery Villages*. This series consists of descriptions of mining villages in both Northumberland and Durham, commenting on the provisions of facilities for recreation, learning and worship as well as housing and sanitary conditions. Official reports which deal with conditions in mining villages are rare and the observations of travellers tend to be little more helpful than those of Cobbett.

Later, however, with the establishment of the Local Government Board and other, wider-reaching developments in local administration, documents dealing with housing in both general and specific terms, became more plentiful. There were, for example, reports into local conditions, reports of the Medical Officers of Health, Sanitary Inspectors and the minutes of the committees responsible for employing their new officials.

Plans and documents

Inspectors' reports for the period in question were studied. These described the different types of min-

ers' dwellings in the region as well as giving the first detailed observations on miners' living conditions. *Our Coal and our Coal Pits,* published by the Travellers' Library in 1856, though based on the earlier 1841 Child Employment Commission report, divides miners' dwellings into three categories:

Two-roomed houses	: One ground floor room
	: One upper floor room
Two-roomed houses	: Two ground floor rooms
Three-roomed houses	: Two ground floor rooms
	: One upper floor room

However, it proved most difficult to enlarge upon this very basic classification as very few plans of this period survive. The National Coal Board's Estates Department possessed some modern plans of older houses which were also consulted. There was an almost complete dearth of any plans of the housing erected by the colliery companies which would normally have been deposited with the Coal Board. Local Archive offices had a number of house plans deposited from coal companies and these plans proved to be most valuable. The absence of regulations controlling the submission of building plans earlier in the century meant that local authorities' plan depositories for the earlier period of study were incomplete. However, it was possible to study a number of different types of house plans going back to the 1850s and, from these, to select one which represented a number of typical features.

An important, and obvious, source of information was the housing to be found in the field. Very little pre-1870 colliery housing remains in County Durham and that which has survived has been altered to the point that it was virtually unrecognizable. Early plans, including the first edition and subsequent editions of the Ordnance Survey, were studied to give details of the development of the village and to illustrate the growth of housing.

Photographs and illustrations

Practising artists of the day rarely recorded such aspects of working class life. However a rare example does survive in a little drawing by S. H. Grimm (1734–1794) of pitmen's *Houses on the Road to Newcastle (Figure 24.1)*. Other early illustrations are contained in T. H. Hair's *Sketches of the Coal Mines in Northumberland and Durham,* first published in 1839.

The houses in mining villages did not tend to attract the nineteenth-century photographer, as has Sutcliffe's *Scenes of Whitby.* However, some photographic evidence of the nineteenth- and early-twentieth centuries does exist with housing at least in the background. A number of surveys of houses were carried out in the 1890s, 1920s and 1930s by the Medical Officer of Health, and many of these include photographs taken to illustrate the sanitary condi-

Figure 24.1 Colliers' houses on the road to Newcastle – S. H. Grimm (British Museum)

tions. These photographs are invaluable as they often illustrate interiors of houses, back-yards and lanes (*Figure 24.2*).

The buildings themselves

By using the above criteria, it was possible to select a row of cottages which typified the housing in a number of pit villages of the 1850s and 1860s (*Figure 24.3*). Six houses from one particular row, Francis Street, Hetton-le-Hole, were selected for dismantling and removal, and work began on researching in detail these particular houses (*Figure 24.4*). Work was undertaken to discern the physical material and social background to the houses. The records of the Hetton Coal Company, the original builders, were searched for information. Early maps, including the first-edition Ordnance Survey, were studied to give details of the development of the village as well as to illustrate the growth of housing.

Detailed plans and elevations of the houses were drafted with specifications of the types of building material used, so that defective materials could be replaced if necessary. As many of the original features as possible, such as skirting boards and ceiling mouldings, were removed quickly before they could be vandalized. Photographs were taken not only of the exteriors of the houses but also of the interiors, to illustrate fixtures, fittings and methods of construction.

More photographs were taken and drawings made throughout the whole dismantling procedure. It was often easier to discern what alterations had been made while the building was being dismantled.

Additions, alterations and features which had disappeared leaving some traces were recorded so that they could be incorporated as desired in the final presentation. A number of features such as the gardens, the immediate surroundings of the houses, fence types and walls were photographed and recorded (*Figure 24.5*). Information was filed on the type of flowers and vegetables cultivated. It was often a tradition for pitmen to keep livestock, and pigsties were built for the miners by the coal company. These were examined and recorded along with other features, such as communal brick ovens for baking bread, often to be found as small separate buildings in the back-street (*Figure 24.6*). Water supply to the houses was important, often taking the form of one standpipe to every six houses.

Fittings, furnishings and interior decorations

It was essential to record as much information as possible about the interiors of the houses. Plans were made of each room, including walls, floors and

Figure 24.2 Interior or back-to-back house at Marley Hill, County Durham (Dr L. W. Darra Mair's *Report to the Local Government Board on the Sanitary Circumstances,* 1907)

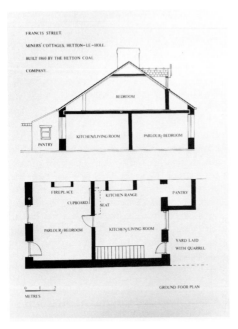

Figure 24.3 Francis Street, Hetton-le-Hole. Pit cottages built between 1850 and 1860 – plan of houses

ceiling, and photographs taken. Walls were checked for nails, screws and hooks. Samples of paint, floor-coverings and soft furnishings were removed for reference purposes. Samples of wallpaper were removed and recorded, and these later proved useful in dating alterations.

Details of timber and plaster mouldings were noted and samples taken. Light fittings, if any, were also recorded. Many of the houses had built-in furniture, for example, settles at the side of fireplaces, cupboards and shelves. These were all recorded.

Much information was gleaned by straightforward observation and recording. In this particular case, however, the museum was fortunate in that a year was allowed in which to carry out essential research work on the buildings while the occupants were still in residence. Many of them were elderly, having been born and brought up in the houses and could provide detailed information on the furniture and interior furnishings over a period of years.

The museum took into account other historical sources such as descriptions of house interiors and furnishings. This information proved invaluable. It was possible to collect the contents of one particular house after the death of the occupant (*Figure 24.7*). With the help of his relatives this house was entirely recreated in the museum.

Figure 24.4 Francis Street pit cottages, Hetton-le-Hole

Figure 24.5 Six houses from Francis Street rebuilt at
BEAMISH: North of England Open Air Museum

Figure 24.6 Communal bread oven at Mickley, near Prudhoe, Northumberland, once a typical feature of many pit villages

The people

Because social history collections are essentially about people, no research would be complete without reference to the occupants of the houses. In this, the use of oral recording cannot be underestimated. A structured interview can often reveal information which could not be obtained in any other way. Oral history is a unique source of information in its own right which often complements the object, photograph or manuscript. It is an important means of collecting information about a specimen and also in preserving evidence of attitudes, opinions, ideas, dialects and working and social conditions.

All the occupants from two long rows of houses, including Francis Street, were interviewed and the following details were recorded: the name and ages of the people; their present occupation and place of work; how long they had worked there; their length of residency in these houses; their father's occupation; their father-in-law's occupation, religion and place of birth. Many of the interviews were tape-recorded with the purpose of preserving anecdotes and reminiscences.

Summary

These data were checked against contemporary accounts and an overall picture formed, from which the rebuilding, refurbishment and display was created (*Figures 24.8–24.10*). This research information proved to be an invaluable source upon which to

Figure 24.7 Joseph Barry in his pit cottage, 1976

Figure 24.8 Kitchen in rebuilt cottage depicting the 1890s period. Note sideboard-bed on left and typical round-ovened range

Figure 24.9 Front parlour/bedroom in rebuilt cottage depicting the 1890s period

Figure 24.10 Bedroom in rebuilt cottage depicting the 1890s period

base interpretation. Research which throws more light on museum objects is a basic interpretative function of a museum and, without it, it is not possible to produce an intelligible, reasoned, historical and accurate display of museum artefacts. A museum of social history must encourage the visitor to think not so much about the facts, but about the meanings, relationships and concepts that derive from these facts.

References

HMSO (1951) *Libraries, Museums and Art Galleries,* A report of the Advisory Council on Education in Scotland, HMSO 91, London

TREVELYAN, G. M. (1944), *Illustrated English Social History,* Vol. 1, Longman, Harlow

25

Research: fine art collections

Dennis Farr

Research on art collections, in this context, includes paintings, sculpture, prints, drawings, watercolours and applied arts – glass, furniture, textiles, ceramics, metalwork; and *objets d'art* – a term used here to describe small items in precious or semi-precious metals, and/or other precious or semi-precious materials (such as snuff boxes, paperweights, and inkstands, or artistic curiosities), which may have no practical use, but are simply beautiful ornaments or ingenious toys (Fabergé mechanical toys are an example).

An implied distinction is made between research on collections which is intended for academic use, and that performed for the benefit of the interested, but non-specialist, visitor. In practice, basic information about a work of art, its physical shape and size, the material(s) from which it is made, its subject-matter or function, and data about the artist or crafts-man who is thought to have made it, are of prime interest to both the scholar and the layman. The next stage for the specialist will be to establish its prove-nance (that is, where it came from, who commis-sioned it, and who has owned it at various times during its existence), its purpose, and its historical significance in relation to what is known about the wider cultural context of the country, or region, or city of origin at the time of its creation.

The knowledge thus accumulated by the specialist historian can then be presented in a variety of ways, depending on the type of public to be catered for. It is essential for art curators, who are now usually by training academic art historians in museum employ-ment, to establish clearly in their own minds for whom the information is intended before deciding on the format to be used for its presentation. It is a truism that it is often more difficult to write an intel-ligible and interesting popular introduction to a spe-cialist subject than to prepare a learned dissertation. If we need proof that an academic historian and a museum curator can write popular introductions to the history of art, we have only to refer to Ernst Gombrich (1950) *The Story of Art,* or Michael Levey (1962) *From Giotto to Cézanne: A Concise History of Painting.*

Both these authors draw on their own very wide knowledge of the subject, and work within a care-fully considered framework, so as to present a cohe-rent, simplified narrative unencumbered by exces-sive detail or too many names and dates. They select the important developments in the evolution of art, and illustrate their story by examples accepted as key works. That is, works which can stand as the epi-tome of an aspect of the civilization which produced them, or which point the way to new developments, either technical, artistic, or both.

These books are general in their scope, and are not directly related to the collections of one museum or gallery. Consideration must now be given to the research that should be undertaken for specific col-lections and an attempt made to categorize the stages by which the basic physical information about a work of art is recorded, the use to which this is put, the problems which may be posed by physical evi-dence, the use and interpretation of data gained from scientific examinations (for example, X-rays, ultra-violet and infra-red photography, pigment analysis, spectrometry), and the retrieval of information.

Having established a dossier of information about the object itself, the task of linking this with known facts about other similar objects or works by the same artist/craftsman, either already in the museum collection or known first-hand or from documents and printed sources, should be begun. The physical evidence can be considered as a *primary* historical source, in the same way as contemporary docu-mentation (contract notes, letters (published or unpublished), and other archive material) can be regarded as primary. *Secondary* sources include accounts written either some years after the work was completed (assuming its approximate date is known), or which have only indirect bearing on the work and its creator. Biographies of artists written by contemporaries, or near-contemporaries, are primary sources, but need to be used with special care, as they may contain legends about the artist's career which he had wished to have perpetuated, or be written by those who were prejudiced against their subject. The same caveat must be entered for tape-recorded interviews with living artists, valuable though these are. *Tertiary* sources would include recent historical research and commentaries about an artist, or craftsman, or a school or movement. This information may be published as a book, monograph, conference paper, or be accessible to scholars as unpublished dissertations held by university libraries. (A regular publication, *Dissertation Abstracts International,* covers universities in North America, with a small selection of European universities; but for more detailed, world-wide coverage, the researcher is advised to look elsewhere. (The University of London Library, Senate House, London, WC1, produces a guide to sources of this kind.)

For the museum curator, there are many ways of presenting the material evidence about his collections, and it is proposed to deal with the principal types of publication by which information may be disseminated, starting with the simplest. For ease of reference, attention is confined to United Kingdom publications, but the reader is reminded of the wealth of publications now available from North-West Europe and North America.

Brief guides

The size of the museum and the variety and range of its collections will determine the scope of a brief guide. As well as essential information (location, opening hours, etc.), the guide should present a concise history of the museum's development and purpose, its principal masterpieces, and so on. Illustrations, with some in colour, will add to the usefulness and enjoyment of the guide. *Labels* to the exhibits should be legible and well-designed, with basic information, supplemented by *information sheets* in each gallery where this is practicable. If some form of house style and typographical linkage between the brief guide and the labels can be achieved, so much the better.

The brief guide which acts as a room-by-room survey of the permanent collections has obvious advantages, but may require constant revision if the permanent displays are altered frequently. *Pre-recorded sound tapes* are another form of guide, providing a form of spoken running commentary for the visitor by means of portable cassettes and head-phones. These recordings, like the printed brief guides, can be provided in different languages, but they too will require updating if the displays are changed frequently.

The character of a museum should be conveyed in the guide, and the *Victoria and Albert Museum: Brief Guide* (c. 1970) serves this purpose. Somewhat more discursive, and more of a concise history, is the *British Museum Guide* (Pope-Hennessy, 1976), which gives a very clear picture of this august institution's history, of its departments, and its principal treasures.

The National Gallery, London, has produced *100 Great Paintings: Duccio to Picasso* (Gordon, 1981) which admirably conveys to the general reader an idea of the range and quality of the collections. Each of the hundred masterpieces is reproduced in colour, with a page of explanatory text, and there is an introduction in which the history of the National Gallery is outlined.

Where a museum authority has charge of a country house it is highly desirable to provide an illustrated guide with an accurate account of the history of the building, and of its previous owners. Original research can be incorporated in such publications, as, for example, in the revised guide to Aston Hall, Birmingham (1981) (Fairclough, 1981).

Handlists

These usually deal with specific collections, and are intended to convey basic information. Those for collections of paintings and drawings will list the artists represented and the individual works by each artist held in the collection. Title, accession number, medium, size and date (also whether and how signed or inscribed, and where) are given, and sometimes, how acquired. All this information can be computer-coded and printed, with updating or corrections incorporated for subsequent editions. An example of this type of publication is *The Collections of the Tate Gallery: British Paintings; Modern Paintings and Sculpture* (Tate Gallery, 1967). Handlists can be illustrated, often by small-scale photographs of each work, which are intended for reference purposes, such as the recent concise catalogues prepared by the Manchester City Art Gallery (Treuherz, 1976).

Summary Catalogues

Similar in format to a handlist, a summary catalogue contains additional information about provenance, previous collections, and essential documentary references (such as oeuvre catalogues), with a brief account of the history of the object and/or any iconographical or stylistic feature of particular significance to an understanding of the content or subject-matter of the work. The catalogue of *Paintings in the Ashmolean Museum,* University of Oxford (1962), the *Katalog der Alten Meister der Hamburger Kunsthalle* (1956), the *Catalogue of 170 paintings and drawings of Vincent Van Gogh belonging to the Collection of the State Museum Kröller-Muller* (1952), and *The Museum of Fine Arts, Houston. A guide to the Collection* (1981) are excellent examples of four different types of summary catalogue (Agee, 1981; Hammacher, 1952; Hentzen, 1956; Parker, 1962).

Catalogues Raisonnés

The catalogue raisonné, as its title implies, is the vehicle for presenting all the relevant data about a work of art, its history, iconography, and where the attribution may be in question, the arguments for and against its authorship by a particular artist. The writer will also be expected to indicate his own view of matters open to discussion. The material to be presented is often complex, and ranges over a wide field of scholarship. The compiler may have to familiarize himself with points of erudition culled from, say, the writings of the Early Fathers of the Church, obscure aspects of Greek mythology, of medieval legend, or of the now vanished topography of a *quartier* in nineteenth-century Paris. In the history of art, new standards of scholarship have been set by the late Sir Martin Davies and his successors in the series of catalogues of the major schools of painting represented in the National Gallery, London.

Davies' *Early Netherlandish School* (1945), was the first of the genre to be published after the war, the format of which has been followed, with typographical improvements introduced to facilitate the cross-referencing within, and legibility of, the individual entries. While Davies did not invent the catalogue raisonné, he introduced new subtleties and refinements, which, like all good scholarship, made his catalogues raisonnés into works of art in their own right. Davies' catalogues of the *French School,* of the *British School* and of the *Earlier Italian Schools,* followed in quick succession, he having had a unique opportunity to examine the paintings closely during their war-time sojourn in the slate quarries of Wales, to which they had been transferred for safekeeping. His catalogues were complemented by those on the German, the seventeenth- and eighteenth-Century Italian, the Spanish, and the Dutch schools, compiled by his colleagues Michael Levey and Neil MacLaren, and further catalogues for other parts of the collection have also now been published (Davies, 1945, 1946, 1951; Levey, 1959; MacLaren, 1952, 1960).

In the highly specialized field of old master drawings, the Department of Prints and Drawings of the British Museum has long been pre-eminent; and

Freeman O'Donogue and Henry M. Hake's six-volume *Catalogue of Engraved British Portraits . . . in the British Museum* (1908–25), is an invaluable source of historical material in this field (O'Donogue and Hake, 1908–1925). Recourse to this compilation has often enabled the historian or interested laymen to identify the sitter, and sometimes, the artist of what might otherwise have been yet another anonymous seventeenth- or eighteenth-century portrait painting. The catalogue raisonné may also be devoted to the work of one artist represented in a collection, such as Johannes Wilde's *Italian drawings in the Department of Prints and Drawings in the British Museum: Michelangelo and his studio* (1953), which while published as one of a series of catalogues under A. E. Popham's editorship, stands as a fundamental and authoritative contribution to our knowledge of Michelangelo, (Wilde, 1953). The catalogues raisonnés of the Royal Collection, which are divided into two series comprising many volumes, *Drawings in the Royal Library at Windsor Castle* and *Pictures in the Collection of her Majesty the Queen,* draw on the expertise of many authors who provide in these catalogues most valuable scholarly contributions on the collections (*see,* for example, Clark and Pedretti, 1969). Another series has been begun to deal with the furniture and *objets d'art* in the Royal Collection.

Sir John Pope-Hennessy's exemplary three-volume Catalogue of *Italian Sculpture in the Victoria and Albert Museum* (1964), published by Her Majesty's Stationery Office for the Victoria and Albert Museum, and his many other publications and catalogues on Italian sculpture, perform the same service for this specialism as the National Gallery catalogues do for old master paintings.

In the field of contemporary art, the catalogues raisonnés of the modern foreign and modern British collections at the Tate Gallery have introduced an interesting principle (Alley, 1959; Chamot Farr and Butlin, 1964). Wherever possible, the artist, or his close relatives and friends, have been approached for first-hand information not only about the works acquired for the collections, but also biographical data not always readily available elsewhere. In this way, unique primary sources have been tapped, and the results edited and published. The *Annual Reports* of the Tate Gallery from 1953–1967, and *Biennial Reports* since 1968, contain detailed information about new acquisitions and provide a running record for the use of the public. The documentation thus acquired is preserved in the Tate Gallery archives, along with much other source material such as dealers' records and annotated exhibition catalogues and press cuttings.

Scholarly research on collections particularly rich in the work of individual artists has also been published as catalogues raisonnés, notably the collections of paintings by J. M. W. Turner and of William

Blake's paintings and drawings at the Tate Gallery, by Martin Butlin, who has subsequently enlarged the scope of his Blake catalogue (first published 1957) of the Tate holdings to provide a catalogue raisonné of the complete works of William Blake (Butlin, 1981). Similarly, the late Professor Andrew McLaren Young's catalogue of the complete works of J. McNeill Whistler, which was completed and edited by three of his former colleagues and published in 1980, had as one of its starting points the rich collections of paintings, drawings, prints and memorabilia at the University of Glasgow (Young *et al*, 1980).

Exhibition catalogues

Much new research on specific aspects of art history or of the work of individual artists is incorporated in the catalogues of major thematic or retrospective loan exhibitions. Such temporary exhibitions may often be related to the permanent collections of the museum and include items from those permanent collections which, because they are seen in a new context, may deepen understanding of their place in the history of art and shed light on the culture of which they are a part. The important series of Council of Europe exhibitions held in various European cities over the past thirty years, fall into this category, examples being *The Age of Humanism* (Palais Royal, Brussels, 1951), *The Age of Rococo* (Residenz, Munich, 1958), *The Romantic Movement* (Tate Gallery and Arts Council of Great Britain, 1959), *Les Sources du XXe Siècle; les Arts en Europe de 1884 à 1914* (Musée Nationale d'art Moderne, Paris, 1960), and *The Age of Neo-Classicism* (Royal Academy of Arts and Victoria and Albert Museum, London 1972). Each of these international exhibitions surveyed a major artistic movement which transcended national frontiers.

There has also been a number of detailed investigations into particular aspects of the modern movement, of which the *Paris–Moscow 1900–1930* exhibition (Centre Georges Pompidou, Paris 1979) and *Art of the Avant-Garde in Russia: Selections from the George Gostakis Collection* The Solomon R. Guggenheim Museum, New York, 1981), are important recent examples (Hulten, 1979; Rudenstein and Rowell, 1981). In this connection, tribute must be paid to the pioneering work of the Museum of Modern Art, New York, which, since 1937, has produced many important exhibitions of the art of our time, the published catalogues for which have often become standard books on the subject (Barr, 1937).

An important new bequest or acquisition may provide an opportunity for publishing a scholarly exhibition catalogue which will serve as a permanent record of the collection. This was done for the Princes Gate Collection, bequeathed to the University of London, Courtland Institute Galleries, and first exhibited to the public in July 1981 (Braham, 1981). The historical growth of a gallery collection, or the pattern of taste and patronage over a given period can also be charted, thus adding to our knowledge in a particularly graphic manner. Two recent exhibitions of this type were Colin Thompson's *Pictures for Scotland: the National Gallery of Scotland and its Collections,* (Edinburgh, 1972), and Allan Braham's *El Greco to Goya: The Taste for Spanish Paintings in Britain and Ireland,* (National Gallery, London 1981).

In recent years, several major commemorative exhibitions for individual artists have been held which have advanced scholarship. A few may be noted here: *Rembrandt* (Rijksmuseum, Amsterdam and Boymans Museum, Rotterdam, 1955), *Poussin* (Musée du Louvre, Paris, 1960), *Dürer* (Germanisches National Museum, Nuremberg, 1971), *Rubens* (Musée Royal des Beaux-Arts, Antwerp, 1977) and *El Greco* (Museo del Prado, Madrid, 1982). In London *Turner* (Royal Academy, 1975), *Constable* (Tate Gallery, 1976); and *Landseer* (Tate Gallery, 1982), have been honoured.

The decorative arts have been well served by the work of specialists at the Victoria and Albert Museum, London, and the staffs of some major British provincial museums. Floud's *Victorian and Edwardian Decorative Arts* (1952) set the standard for the series of major exhibitions which have done much to re-awaken the public's interest in, and knowledge of, this aspect of our heritage (Floud, 1952; Jervis, 1972; Pope-Hennessy, 1971; Wild *et al*, 1973).

References

AGEE, W. C. (1981), (Introduction and Ed.), *The Museum of Fine Arts, Houston. A Guide to the Collection*, The Museum of Fine Arts, Houston, Texas

ALLEY, R. (1959), (2nd edn, revised and enlarged 1981) *Tate Gallery Catalogues: the Foreign Paintings, Drawings and Sculpture*, Tate Gallery, London

BARR, A. H. (1937) (Ed), *Fantastic Art, Dada, Surrealism*, The Museum of Modern Art, New York

BRAHAM, H. (1981), *The Princes Gate Collection*, Courtauld Institute of Art, University of London

BUTLIN, M. (1981), *The Paintings and Drawings of William Blake*, 2 vols, Yale University for The Paul Mellon Centre for Studies in British Art, New Haven and London

CHAMOT, M., FARR, D. AND BUTLIN, M. (1964), *Tate Gallery Catalogues: the Modern British Paintings, Drawings and Sculpture,* 2 vols, Oldbourne Press for Tate Gallery, London

CLARK, K. AND PEDRETTI, C. (1969), (a 2nd edn of 1935 revised and enlarged), *A Catalogue of the Drawings of Leonardo da Vinci in the collection of Her Majesty the Queen at Windsor Castle,* 3 vols, The Phaidon Press, London

DAVIES, M. (1945), *Early Netherlandish Schools* (revised 1955), Publications Dept, National Gallery, London

DAVIES, M. (1946), *French School*, Publications Dept, National Gallery, London

DAVIES, M. (1946) *The British School,* (revised 1959), Publications Dept, National Gallery, London

DAVIES, M. (1951) *The Earlier Italian School,* (revised 1961), Publications Dept, National Gallery, London

FAIRCLOUGH, O. (1981), *Aston Hall. A General Guide,* Publications Unit, Birmingham Museums and Art Gallery, Birmingham

FLOUD, P. (1952) (Ed), *Victorian and Edwardian Decorative Arts,* Victoria and Albert Museum, London

GOMBRICH, E. H. (1950) (and many subsequent edns), *The story of Art,* The Phaidon Press Ltd, London and Oxford

GORDON, D. (1981), *100 Great Paintings: Duccio to Picasso. European Paintings from the 14th to the 20th century,* Publications Dept, National Gallery, London

HAMMACHER, A. M. (1952) (Ed.), *Catalogue of 270 Paintings and Drawings of Vincent van Gogh belonging to the Collection of the State Museum Kröller-Müller,* Rijksmuseum Kröller-Müller, Otterlo-Gelderland

HENTZEN, A. (1956), *Katalog der Alten Meister der Hamburger Kunsthalle,* 4th edn, Kunsthalle, Hamburg

HULTEN, P. (1979) (Ed.), *Paris-Moscou 1900-1930,* Centre Georges Pompidou, Paris

JERVIS, S. (1972) (Ed.), *Victoria and Edwardian Decorative Arts. The Handley Read Collection,* Royal Academy of Arts, in collaboration with the Victoria and Albert Museum, London

LEVEY, M. (1959), *The German School,* Publications Dept, National Gallery, London

LEVEY, M. (1962) (and later edns) *From Giotto to Cézanne. A Concise History of Painting,* Thames and Hudson, London

LEVEY, M. (1971), *The 17th and 18th Century Italian Schools,* Publications Dept, National Gallery, London

MACLAREN, N. (1952), *The Spanish School,* Publications Dept, National Gallery, London

MACLAREN, N. (1960), *The Dutch School,* Publications Dept, National Gallery London

MILLAR, O. (1963), *The Tudor, Stuart, and Early Georgian Pictures in the Collection of Her Majesty the Queen,* 2 vols, Phaidon Press, London

O'DONAGHUE, F. AND HAKE, H. M. (1908-1925), *Catalogue of Engraved British Portraits . . . in the British Museum;* British Museum, London

PARKER, K. T. (1962) (Ed.), *Paintings in the Ashmolean Museum. Illustrated Catalogue,* for the Visitors of the Ashmolean Museum, University Press, Oxford

POPE-HENNESSY, SIR J. (1971), (ed.), *'Victorian church art',* Victorian and Albert Museum, London

POPE-HENNESSY, SIR J. (Ed.), (1976), *British Museum Guide,* British Museum Publications Ltd, London

RUDENSTEIN, A. AND ROWELL, M. (1981), *Art of the Avant-Garde in Russia: Selections from the George Costakis Collection,* The Solomon R. Guggenheim Museum, New York

SELZ, P. AND CONSTANTINE, M. (1963), *Art Nouveau. Art and Design at the Turn of the Century,* Museum of Modern Art, New York

TATE GALLERY (1967), *The Collections of the Tate Gallery: British Paintings; Modern Painting and Sculpture,* Publications Dept, Tate Gallery, London

TREUHERZ, J. (1976) (Ed.), *Concise Catalogue of British Paintings. Artists born before 1850,* City Art Gallery, Manchester

TREUHERZ, J. (1978), *Concise Catalogue of British Paintings. Artists Born in or after 1850,* City Art Gallery, Manchester

TREUHERZ, J. (1980) (Ed) *Concise Catalogue of Foreign Paintings,* City Art Gallery, Manchester

V & A MUSEUM, *Victoria and Albert Museum: Brief Guide* (c. 1970), Victoria and Albert Museum, London

WILD, G., LATTA, C. AND POW, V. (1973), *Gold and Silver 1773-1977. An Exhibition to Celebrate the Bicentenary of the Assay Office,* Birmingham Museum and Art Gallery, Birmingham

WILDE, J. (1953), *Italian Drawings in the Department of Prints and Drawings in the British Museum: Michelangelo and his Studio,* British Museum, London

YOUNG, A. M., MACDONALD, M., SPENCER, R. AND MILES, H. (1980), *The Paintings of James McNeill Whistler,* 2 vols, Yale University Press for the Paul Mellon Centre for Studies in British Art, New Haven and London

26

Environmental conservation

Sarah Staniforth

Introduction

Conservation is now understood to encompass preservation as well as restoration. The majority of works of art are inherently unstable because impermanent materials are used in their making which undergo physical and chemical reactions as they age, resulting in changes of appearance, strength and other physical properties. This deterioration is accelerated by poor environmental conditions, and although changes are inevitable and irreversible they can be slowed by environmental conservation. An understanding of the relationship between a work and its environment is needed and it has been established that works of art are most vulnerable to unsuitable levels of light, relative humidity and air pollution.

This paper will examine how adverse environmental conditions affect works, will recommend the most suitable conditions for collections of various types and will show how the environment can be controlled by measuring conditions and adjusting them to within specified limits. It must be emphasized immediately that environmental considerations apply at all times, regardless of whether a work is on exhibition, in storage, on loan or travelling. All the care that is taken while a work is under the protective wing of its home is undone as soon as its safety is jeopardized by, for example, a journey in an unsuitable packing case to a museum with no environmental controls.

Light

The nature of light

Radiation from the sun, sky and artificial light sources can be divided into three regions according to wavelength. The human eye is sensitive to the visible region (from 400–700 nm) and perceives this part of the electromagnetic spectrum as violet at the short wavelength end changing through the spectral colours blue, green, yellow, orange to red at the long-wavelength end. Infrared (IR) radiation extends from the end of the visible spectrum to longer wavelengths; it may cause heating problems.

Ultra-violet (UV) is to the short-wavelength side of visible light. Electromagnetic radiation is energy and if it is absorbed by a material it may cause photochemical change (chemical change induced by radiation). If absorbed, short wavelengths are more damaging than long wavelengths, since they are of higher energy, so UV is more damaging than an equal amount of blue light, which in its turn is more damaging than an equal amount of yellow light. Red light causes a negligible amount of photochemical change. Most materials will undergo photochemical change and will therefore be damaged by UV and visible light; stone, metals and ceramics are among the few materials that are not affected. However, there is less UV than visible radiation in all light sources, and in a museum with a general collection approximately half the photochemical damage is caused by UV and half by visible light.

Dyes and pigments change colour; cellulosic materials (derived from plants) such as paper, cotton and linen, and proteinaceous materials (derived from animals) such as wool, leather, feathers are discoloured and weakened. Therefore, it is important to limit the exposure of objects that contain these materials as far as possible.

Measurement and control of ultra-violet radiation

Since the eye is not sensitive to UV radiation it can be eliminated without having any effect on the appearance of an object. This can be achieved using a filter that absorbs wavelengths of radiation in the UV but allows visible light to pass through. Of the forms of lighting used in museums, daylight contains the highest proportion of UV but tungsten–halogen and some fluorescent lamps also emit significant amounts. UV is most conveniently measured in units of microwatts/lumen[1] and the proportion emitted by tungsten lamps, approximately 80 microwatts/lumen, is considered the maximum level that is acceptable in a museum; there is a commercially available meter that will measure UV proportion directly when the meter is pointed at the light source[2]. Tungsten–halogen lamps, which are increasingly used because of their high light output, emit a small amount of highly energetic, and therefore dangerous, short-wavelength UV; these lamps should always be used with a piece of glass in front of the bulb since glass absorbs short-wavelength UV.

Ultra-violet filters are available in various forms. Unfortunately, it has not been possible to incorporate one into glass but plastic films containing a UV absorber laminated between two sheets of glass are made and these can be used for glazing windows. Rigid plastic acrylic sheets containing UV absorbers can be used for exhibition cases and glazing in frames. Thin acetate or polyester films and varnishes containing UV absorbers can be applied to windows and these provide a relatively cheap and simple solution. Plastic sleeves are available for slipping around fluorescent tubes. If it can be arranged for all light to be reflected off a painted wall before falling on any work then this will often provide sufficient UV absorption; most modern paints contain the white pigment titanium dioxide, which is a very effective UV absorber.

Ultra-violet filtering is not permanent and should be checked periodically (say every six months). There are no reported instances of the acrylic sheets failing but plastic films and varnishes are usually guaranteed for no more than ten years. This is often because of failure of the film or varnish which results in its mechanical breakdown rather than a reduction of efficiency of the UV absorber. If the windows to which these applications are made suffer from condensation then this will also reduce their life-span. Sleeves for fluorescent tubes last for two or three changes of tubes.

Measurement and control of visible light

The rate of deterioration caused by light is proportional to both the light level and the time that the object is exposed to that level. The damaging exposure experienced by an object illuminated at 400 lux[3] for 1 hour is the same as if it has been illuminated at 100 lux for 4 hours, in both cases the total exposure is 400 lux hours. This is a consequence of the reciprocity law which states that the rate of photochemical

change is proportional to the product of illuminance and the length of exposure. So to reduce the damage inflicted by light it is important to limit the length of time that the works are illuminated as well as the level of illumination.

The recommended levels of illumination are listed in *Table 26.1*. The levels selected are the minimum

Table 26.1 Recommended levels of illuminance which should not be exceeded*,†

Material	Illuminance (lux)
Easel paintings Animal and plant materials where surface colour is important (including undyed leather, wood, bone, ivory)	200
Works of art on paper (including water-colours, drawings, prints, stamps, wallpaper, historical documents, photographs) Textiles (including tapestries, costumes, upholstered furniture, carpets) Miniatures and manuscripts Dyed leather Natural history exhibits	50

* Materials that are not light-sensitive may be lit at higher levels but is unwise to increase the levels to above 300 lux in a museum where there are also light-sensitive exhibits because of problems with adaptation as the visitor moves from room to room.
† For photography, light levels may be increased to 1000 lux for short periods provided there is no significant heating caused by the lights. Restoration may sometimes require 2000 lux.

consistent with satisfactory visual acuity for the viewer. These levels are already a compromise, since all exposure to light will cause deterioration; there is no minimum level below which damage will not occur. A light meter should be used to measure light levels since the eye readily adapts itself to changes in intensity and is therefore very unreliable for estimating levels of illumination. There are various pocket light meters available that are reliable and simple to use[2].

Of the types of lighting that can be used in a museum – daylight, fluorescent lamps, tungsten and tungsten–halogen lamps – daylight is the most difficult to control since it changes through the day and throughout the year. The only satisfactory way of limiting it to within a reasonable range of 200 lux is by using motorized blinds that are controlled by photocells. The photocells sense the light falling on a surface and then open or close the blinds according to whether the surface is under- or over-illuminated.

If the blinds are fully open and there is still too little light then artificial lighting can be switched on. However, this involves the installation of complicated and expensive machinery which may be unsuitable for many collections. Manually-controlled blinds can be used, but there is always the problem of staff not being available to open and close them, and this may result in their being left open the whole time. A third possibility is to apply a solar-control film (either paint or a metallized acetate or polyester sheet) to windows. These can lower the illumination to an acceptable level on the brightest days and artificial lighting can be used to supplement the lighting on duller days. Direct sunlight should never be allowed to fall on any object. In addition to the photochemical damage that it causes it may result in local heating which will affect the relative humidity in the vicinity of the object. Sensitive objects should not be placed near windows where the light is brighter than in the centre of the room.

50 lux of daylight appears gloomy and it is preferable to use artificial lamps at this level. If a light meter is used when the lamps are first installed, this will ensure that no exhibit is over-illuminated. Colour temperature is a measure of the appearance of a light source. A warm or reddish light has a lower colour temperature than a cool or bluish light. There is a choice of colour temperature among fluorescent lamps. However cool lamps require excessive light levels if they are not to appear gloomy. Lamps should also be selected for good colour rendering. The colour rendering index of a lamp is a measure of the distortion of the appearance of objects in that light. A lamp with good colour rendering properties will cause no distortion. The colour rendering indices of lamps are available from manufacturers. Tungsten lamps have good colour rendering properties but some fluorescent lamps can cause considerable distortion, and should not be used. The new triphosphor lamps which emit large amounts of light at three wavelengths in the visible spectrum should be avoided because of their poor colour rendering. Lamps with low colour temperatures (tungsten and warm fluorescent lamps) are more suitable for exhibits to be illuminated at 50 lux because they appear brighter.

The phenomenon of two colours matching in one light source but not in another is called metamerism. This may create problems if, for example, a restoration is carried out in daylight using different dyes or pigments from the original and then exhibited in tungsten lighting. A competent restorer will, in fact, be aware of this difficulty and will choose materials accordingly. A more banal example might be if a carpet and wallpaper match in daylight but not in artificial light. The ability of viewers to discriminate between colours in certain types of lighting at low levels has been questioned. For example, is 50 lux high enough for full colour discrimination and are subtle shades of blue less discernible in tungsten lighting than daylight (tungsten light is low in blue radiation)? Experimental work (see, for example, Crawford, 1973) indicates that colour discrimination is satisfactory for all light sources at the levels recommended in this paper.

It is important when using relatively low light levels to ensure that the viewer's eye remains adapted to those levels. Therefore bright areas in a museum should be avoided and glare from, for example, a spotlight pointing at the viewer or the reflection of lights on glazing, should be eliminated by placing lamps in appropriate positions.

Light should be reduced to a minimum when the museum is not open to the public. Lights should be turned off and blinds drawn to exclude daylight in the early morning and in the evening. For very sensitive materials, exhibition cases can be covered with curtains which are drawn back by the viewer or they can be fitted with lights on timers. Exhibition of these objects can be alternated with periods of storage. As with all environmental control, the same principles apply when works are in store, and therefore lights should not be left on in storage areas.

Another approach to the control of lighting is to set an exposure value for a year; 200 lux of illumination for a museum that is open from 10 am to 6 pm is equivalent to 666,000 lux hours. So light levels may be allowed to rise above 200 lux provided they are compensated with periods of lower illumination or darkness.

Temperature

It is undoubtedly true that of all the environmental conditions that will be mentioned in this paper temperature is the one of which people are most conscious and therefore instinctively consider most important to control. However, as far as collections are concerned, temperature is the factor to which they are least sensitive and it is therefore the least important. If the temperature is high, then the rate of chemical reactions and biological activity will increase, so lower temperatures are preferred. Its relation to relative humidity (RH) is important and this will be discussed in the following section. Direct heating should be avoided since it may cause local drying. For this reason sunlight should not be allowed to fall on exhibits, powerful spotlights should be avoided, lamps should be mounted outside exhibition cases, objects should not be placed above radiators and pictures should not be hung on chimney-breasts above fires.

The levels of temperatures recommended (18–25 °C) are usually governed by the comfort of people in museums where the exhibits are on display. In stores, or in collections that are not open to the public, the temperature may be allowed to fall to a low level provided the RH is such that condensation will not occur on cold surfaces, that precautions are taken to avoid condensation on cold exhibits brought into the warmth and that warm damp air is not allowed to leak into cold areas where it might condense on cold surfaces.

Relative humidity

Definition

All materials that contain water react to the amount of water that is present in the air surrounding them. In 'dry' air they lose water and in 'damp' air they gain water. It is necessary for a scale to be defined that relates the amount of water in the air to its drying or moistening properties. One possibility is to measure the weight of water in a given volume of air (g/m^3); this is called the *absolute humidity* of the air. The weight of water in a given weight of air (kg/kg) or any material is also used and is called the *moisture content*. However, neither of these is suitable since warm air can hold more water than cool air. A scale of relative humidity which relates the amount of water in a given quantity of air to the maximum amount of water that the air can hold at that temperature is the most appropriate scale to use for museum purposes. Relative humidity (RH) is expressed as a percentage and is defined as follows:

$$\text{relative humidity} = \frac{\text{amount of water in a given volume of air}}{\text{maximum amount of water air can hold at that temperature}}$$

The amount of moisture that a material can hold depends approximately on the RH of the air surrounding it. If the RH of the air falls, the material will lose water. Provided the RH of the air surrounding objects is kept constant then the moisture content of the objects will also remain constant.

Damage caused by unsuitable relative humidity levels

High relative humidity can affect objects in three ways: it can encourage biological activity, it can cause changes in physical dimensions, and it can accelerate certain chemical reactions.

Mould growth will occur on most organic materials if the RH is higher than 65–70 per cent. Its growth is also encouraged in stagnant air and warm temperatures.

Materials which can absorb water from the atmosphere swell more across the grain than along it. An apparent contradiction of this is canvas and other twisted threads, which shrink along their length in high RH. This contraction is caused by the fibres swelling across their width, which tightens the twist in the thread. The canvases of some paintings shrink dramatically in damp conditions and since the ground and paint layers cannot shrink by the same amount, cleavage occurs between the canvas and the ground.

The corrosion of metals increases in high RH, particularly if the air is acidic. 'Bronze disease' may occur if the RH is above 70 per cent. Light damage to textiles and dyes is also accelerated by high RH. Some glasses are moisture-sensitive and become opaque and brittle if exposed to high RH.

Water-sensitive materials shrink when the relative humidity is low. Wooden objects are particularly affected and may crack and warp. Some materials become brittle, textile fibres break and adhesives fail. Veneers may lift during periods of low humidity, partly because of adhesive failure, and partly because of dimensional changes in the thin slivers of wood.

Rapidly fluctuating conditions of RH are particularly damaging for composite objects which consist of a number of different materials all of which are affected by water in a different way. As the RH rises each material absorbs water and swells at a different rate, and similarly, as the RH falls the materials shrink at different rates. Repeated cycles of expansion and contraction (such as may occur during the winter in rooms which are centrally heated during the day but not during the night, resulting in dry air during the day alternating with damper air during the night) will cause warping and cleavage. The speed with which objects react to changes depends on the material. Paper and textiles react quickly (in minutes), large pieces of wood slowly (in months).

Recommended levels of relative humidity

The recommended levels of RH will depend on the nature of the collection and its location. These levels are listed in *Table 26.2*.

The humid tropics, which include large parts of the Far East, have an RH of above 65 per cent for most of the year. The major problem in these regions is mould growth. It is usually only feasible to reduce the RH to 65 per cent because the cost of running an air-conditioning plant to reduce the RH further would be high.

The major problem in European and North-American museums comes from excessive dryness during the winter months when heating is used. If no humidification is available the absolute humidity of the air remains constant and the more the air is heated the lower the RH becomes. For example, air from outside at 0°C and 50 per cent RH will have an RH of 13 per cent when heated to 20°C.

The recommended level of 55 per cent for mixed collections may be too high in some cases during the

Table 26.2 Recommended levels of relative humidity★

Materials	Relative humidity (%)
Mixed collections in humid tropics. (Air circulation important to discourage mould growth.) Too high for metals.	65%
Mixed collections in Europe and North America. (May cause frosting and condensation problems in museums where winter temperatures are low.)	55%
Compromise for mixed collections in museums where winter temperatures are low. Textile collections.	45–50%
Metal-only collections. Local material exhibited in museums in arid regions.	40–45%

★ Ideally all levels should be maintained to within ± 5 per cent but at any rate the danger limits of 65 per cent and 40 per cent should not be exceeded.

winter months, since condensation will occur on singly-glazed windows. In temperate climates, 45–50 per cent is an acceptable level in these circumstances.

In extremely severe climates it is possible for frost to form in the walls of the building as the water in the internal conditioned air diffuses out and freezes before it reaches the external surface of the masonry. Repeated freezing and thawing within the wall will eventually crack it. In these circumstances even lower levels of RH are necessary during the winter months. As has been said already, the most important humidity consideration is to avoid setting up daily cycles of high and low RH. For the welfare of the collection at all times, as well as for the comfort of people during the day, all humidity and heating control should operate in all areas of the museum for 24 hours a day.

Measurement of relative humidity

An instrument used to measure relative humidity is called a *hygrometer*. Wet-and-dry bulb hygrometers (also called psychrometers), when used correctly, give accurate results against which all other hygrometers may be calibrated. The sling psychrometer (or whirling psychrometer or sling or whirling hygrometer) is the simplest and least expensive of these instruments. All museums should own and use one. It consists of two thermometers, one of which has a fabric sleeve around its bulb, which is moistened with distilled water. If air is moved past the wet-bulb thermometer by swinging the psychrometer, water will evaporate from the fabric sleeve; this cools the thermometer bulb. The amount of cooling depends on the amount of water that evaporates which in turn depends on the relative humidity of the air. The lower the RH the greater the depression of the wet-bulb temperature will be with respect to the dry-bulb. A scale is provided with the psychrometer which shows the RH for various wet- and dry-bulb temperatures. The RH can also be determined using a psychrometric chart (or hygrometric chart). Accurate results are obtained provided care is taken when the instrument is used.

Wet- and dry-bulb hygrometers are manufactured in which air is drawn past the thermometer bulbs by an electric fan. These are easier to use but more expensive than sling instruments.

Hair and paper hygrometers and the recording hygrograph rely on the expansion and contraction of moisture-sensitive elements with changes in RH. Hair and paper reacts quickly enough and with a large enough change in dimension to be used for this purpose. In a paper hygrometer two strips of paper which respond differently to changes in RH are glued together and coiled so that when the RH changes the coil twists and moves a pointer attached to the end of it. Hair hygrometers are used in the familiar recording thermo-hygrographs. A bundle of hairs is attached by a series of levers to a pen, as the RH changes the hairs expand or contract which makes the pen rise or fall on the chart. The temperature is recorded using a pen that is moved by the twisting of a coiled bi-metallic strip. Neither of these hygrometers is an accurate instrument, and they require frequent calibration, using a wet- and dry-bulb instrument.

There are now electronic instruments available in which a moisture sensitive element undergoes a change in electrical property as the RH varies. Providing they are supplied with a calibration cap (usually saturated solution of a salt which gives known RH at a particular temperature) these hygrometers are as accurate as wet- and dry-bulb instruments. Dew-point hygrometers are made in which a gold mirror is cooled until moisture is deposited on it at the dew-point temperature of the air. The change in reflectance of the metal when condensation occurs is detected and the RH is calculated from tables. These instruments are accurate, but expensive. Humidity-indicating papers which change colour as the RH changes are available and these are useful if a large number of areas are to be monitored.

Humidistats are essential for the automatic operation of RH-controlling equipment. The most common type consists of a bundle of hairs connected to electrical relays which switch the instrument on and off. Humidistats require frequent calibration to ensure that the RH is at the correct level.

Control of relative humidity

Complete control of RH is possible using air-conditioning. However, the installation and running costs of an air-conditioning plant is beyond the means of many museums. RH control may be achieved within a room using free-standing humidifier and dehumidifier units that are automatically controlled by humidistats. For many museums, these units provide an inexpensive and satisfactory method of keeping RH within acceptable limits. They may not allow the fine control that a satisfactorily maintained air-conditioning plant is capable of, but they are quite adequate for avoiding dangerous conditions.

It is extremely unlikely that both humidification and dehumidification will be necessary in one room. Humidifiers will probably be required to combat dryness caused by winter heating and dehumidifiers for damp basements or cellars.

Humidifiers

Humidifiers are designed to add water quickly to the air in a controlled manner. Unfortunately, bowls of water standing around the room and water containers on radiators are quite inadequate because they are unable to evaporate sufficient quantities of water. There are three types of humidifiers that may be used. Atomising humidifiers draw water onto rapidly rotating blades which disperse particles into fine droplets which vapourize near the machine. Unless distilled or de-ionized water is used the minerals that are present in tap water and a film of salts will be deposited on all surfaces. A further problem is that if the humidistat fails and the machine does not switch off, water will continue to be added until the air is saturated and water condenses. Steam humidifiers heat water (like a kettle) so that it evaporates into the air; these are used in air-conditioning plants but usually only in emergencies for rooms. The most suitable humidifier for museum use is the unheated evaporated humidifier. A drum which carries a sponge belt slowly revolves dipping the sponge into a reservoir filled with water. A fan blows room air through the wet sponge. Unlike the atomizing humidifier, if the humidistat fails in the 'on' position the RH will not rise to much above 70 per cent since the damp air can only absorb a certain amount of water from a damp material. The minerals are left behind on the sponge, so tap water may be used in evaporative humidifiers.

Dehumidifiers

There are two types of room dehumidifiers, dessicant and refrigerant. Which is more suitable depends on the climate. In a dessicant dehumidifier room air is passed over a salt which absorbs water from the air. A drum which contains the dessicant slowly rotates passing in turn a region where hot air drives moisture from the dessicant through an exhaust and out of the room, and then a region where room air is passed through the dessicant. Refrigerant dehumidifiers work on a similar principle to a domestic refrigerator. They contain refrigerant gases (usually fluorinated hydrocarbons) which liquify when compressed. This occurs in the 'condensing' coils which are warm because of the heat which is given off when a gas turns into a liquid. In the 'cooling' coils the liquid expands and vaporizes, absorbing heat from its surroundings. Room air is passed over the cooling coils where it is cooled below its dew-point and deposits moisture. It is reheated by passing over the warm condensing coils. Refrigerant dehumidifiers are preferred for warm climates but frost up too readily in very cold conditions. For these regions dessicant dehumidifiers are preferred.

Dehumidification can be achieved by heating alone, and this is a possible solution where the damp air is also cold; however, heating consumes more energy than either of the other dehumidifier types.

Silica gel and other humidity buffers

It is possible to control the relative humidity of small enclosed volumes using materials that are conditioned to maintain the RH at a predetermined level. When the RH drops below that level they will give off water and when it rises they will absorb water. Any moisture-containing material such as wood, paper, natural textile has this property but the amount of water they can hold and the speed with which they react will often not be adequate for conditioning purposes. Silica gel is a suitable buffering agent because it holds sufficient water, responds rapidly to changes in RH and it is chemically inert. Before being used in an exhibition case or packing case, the silica gel is preconditioned to the required RH by allowing it to stand in a room or environmental chamber at this level for at least two weeks. There will be further information on the use of silica gel in the section on exhibition cases and packing cases.

Air circulation and the capacity of humidity controllers

It is important to ensure that once the humidity controllers are installed, the conditioned air that they supply is circulated around the room. A hygrometer should be used to check that there are no pockets of stagnant air in the corners of rooms. Fans can be used to improve air circulation. The size of humidity controllers and the number of units depends on such factors as the size of the room, the speed with which the air changes in the room (this will be determined by the number of doors and windows), the difference between internal and external conditions and the number of people to pass through the room. Manufacturers will be able to help with these calculations.

Air pollution

Nature of air pollution

Museums and galleries in cities and industrial towns are likely to suffer from the damaging effects of pollution since it is a product of the burning of fossil fuels and the exhaust from motor-cars. Unfortunately today there are few pockets of 'clean' air in the world, so no collection can consider itself free from air pollution. Pollutants may be classified into two types; particulate or gaseous.

The diameter of particulates (suspended solid particles) in the air ranges from approximately 0.01 to 100 μm (microns). In some cases up to 30 per cent of the particulate mass has a diameter of less than 1 μm and this will influence the choice of air filters. Particles may be generated by mechanical processes, occur naturally (pollen) or be formed by chemical processes in the air.

There are two main types of gaseous pollutant, acidic and oxidant. Acidic sulphur dioxide is produced in biological processes but it is also a product of the burning of fossil fuels, all of which contain sulphur. Sulphur dioxide reacts with oxygen and water in the air to form sulphuric acid. Sulphuric acid is very involatile so once it is on a surface it will remain there. Ozone is an oxidizing pollutant which is produced naturally in the upper atmosphere. But it is also generated by the action of sunlight on car exhaust fumes and in certain types of electrical equipment (for example, photocopying machines). Nitric oxide and nitrogen dioxide are both produced in car exhaust fumes. Nitrogen dioxide is converted to nitric acid by water. Nitric acid is an oxidizing agent as well as an acid. It is less damaging than sulphuric acid because it is more volatile.

Damaging effects of pollution

Particulates attach themselves to all surfaces in a museum, and will eventually form an unsightly layer, particularly if they contain a high proportion of sooty material from the incomplete burning of fuels. This surface dirt will need removing periodically and the cleaning operation can be dangerous for the objects. In addition the particles are often acidic from adsorbed sulphur dioxide.

Acids attack calcium carbonate. Sulphuric acid will convert calcium carbonate to calcium sulphate. Marble and limestone are both forms of calcium carbonate and buildings or statues made of these materials that are exposed to the acidic rain that results from industrial air pollution are badly affected. The calcium sulphate that is formed is washed away by the rain, thereby exposing a fresh surface of calcium carbonate to be attacked. Frescoes, in which the pigment particles are trapped in a matrix of calcium carbonate crystals, are also vulnerable to sulphuric acid attack. Cellulosic materials (paper, cotton) and protainaceous materials (wool, silk, leather) are embrittled and discoloured after sulphur dioxide attack. The rusting of iron is accelerated in the presence of sulphur dioxide.

Ozone is an extremely powerful oxidizing agent and will react with most organic materials, degrading their chemical structure. It weakens cellulosic materials, discolours dyes and deteriorates varnish and oil-paint films. Because of its extremely high reactivity its concentration by the time it has diffused indoors is likely to be low.

Levels of pollution

The unit commonly used to measure the concentration of pollutants (both particulate and gaseous) in air is micrograms per cubic metre ($\mu g/m^3$), Particulate levels in Western Europe are lower now than they were earlier this century. Sulphur dioxide levels are also improving. Ozone and nitrogen dioxide levels are highest where there are many cars and sunshine. Los Angeles was the first city suffering from dangerous levels of oxidant pollution to be studied. Now there are many such cities throughout the world.

Recommended levels and preventive measures

There is no minimum acceptable level of pollution. As with ultraviolet radiation, it should be eliminated as far as possible. The complete answer for the control of pollution is air-conditioning. Air from outside is drawn into the ducted system through filters. It is circulated around the building several times each. On occasion it passes through further filters to remove any pollutants that may have been introduced. There is a fuller explanation of air-conditioning in the following section. It is impractical to try to eliminate all the particulates in the air using filters since high pressures are necessary to force the air through these Absolute Filters and particulates are introduced into the museum by visitors. 'Viscous' filters which use a liquid such as oil to trap coarse particulates are suitable for rough filters when the air first enters the building. 'Fabric' filters which are bags made of layers of fibres are used for more efficient particle-filtering. Acceptable efficiencies for these filters are shown in *Table 26.3*

The filters must be changed periodically. As they remove particles they become more resistant to the passage of air through them. This results in a pressure difference across the filter and when this reaches a level specified by the manufactuers the filters should be changed. It is possible to remove particulates using electrostatic precipitators. The air passes positively charged wires, the particulates acquire a positive charge and are held on negatively charged

Table 26.3 Acceptable efficiencies for filters used in air-conditioning plants

Filter	Efficiency (%) Eurovent 4/5★
Viscous†	< 20
Fabric	25–90
Absolute‡	99

★ Eurovent 4/5 is a new standard for testing air filters being adopted by all European manufacturers. It replaces the various national standards (until now British Standard 2831 was widely used in the UK).
† Absolute filters are not recommended for use in museums, they are mentioned here for information only.
‡ Viscous filters are suitable for use as pre-filters, they remove coarser particles and extend the life of the main filters which will generally be of the fabric type.

collector plates downstream. As these precipitators produce small quantities of ozone they should *not* be used in museums.

Gaseous pollutants may be removed by water sprays and activated carbon filters. Sulphur dioxide and nitrogen dioxide are soluble in water and they are mostly removed by water sprays. These are not effective against ozone. Activated carbon filters adsorb pollutant gases. As with the particle filters they need periodic replacement. Suggested maximum acceptable levels of pollutant gases are shown in *Table 26.4* and these levels are attainable if air-conditioning with recirculation is used.

The only alternatives to air-conditioning is using exhibition cases and this is discussed in one of the following sections.

Air-conditioning

An air-conditioning installation consists of a central plant which distributes air from which particulates and pollutant gases have been removed at a required RH and temperature. The air is distributed to all parts of the building through a system of ducts. It is the most effective way of controlling environmental

Table 26.4 Maximum acceptable gaseous pollutant levels in a museum using air-conditioning★

Pollutant gas	Concentration (Mg/m^3)
Sulphur dioxide	< 10 μ
Nitrogen dioxide	< 10 μ
Ozone	0–2

★ It is not necessary to monitor the level of pollutants continuously in museums, but there are tests available that can record pollution levels over a period of time.

conditions that is available at the moment. A typical specification for a museum air-conditioning system is:

Temperature: Summer 22 ± 1°C
          Winter   19 ± 1°C

Relative Humidity: 55 ± 5%

Particulates filtered to an efficiency of 85% to Eurovent 4/5

Sulphur dioxide and nitrogen dioxide filtered to reduce the concentration to below 10 μg/m^3.

These requirements to be met 24 hours/day, every day of the year.

(Specification used in competition for Hampton site extension to the National Gallery, 1982).

Its successful operation relies on a competent maintenance team and adequate monitoring. It is vital that the temperature and humidity sensors located in the ducting and near the outlets to the rooms are correctly calibrated and maintained since these sensors control the system. It is also important to monitor the conditions in the exhibition rooms. This can be done by hand (using wet-and-dry-bulb instruments or electronic sensors) or using a data-logging scheme (*see* section on Monitoring).

Exhibition cases and packing cases

The control of the environment in a whole room has been discussed. In circumstances where this is impractical for one reason or another (size of room, impossibility of introducing ducting into a building, expense) conditions can be controlled on a small scale in an exhibition case. The technology of environmental control in exhibition cases applies equally well to packing cases and so they will be discussed together.

Construction

Since the aim of the exhibition case (or the packing case) is to isolate the objects (as far as possible) from external conditions, then the cases should be as efficiently sealed as possible. If the RH outside the case changes then the RH within the case will also change but at a slower rate and to a lesser extent depending on the rate at which air leaks into the case from the outside and the amount of moisture-buffering material within the case. Experiments suggest a typical leak rate of about one air change per day. In a sealed case without buffering, if the temperature changes then this will affect the RH within the case, since (provided the water content remains the same) the RH increases as the temperature falls (and *vice versa*).

These effects can be minimized by using materials with good properties of thermal insulation in the construction of packing cases which may experience extreme temperature conditions in unheated aircraft luggage holds or on loading bays in winter. If a case is likely to travel in these conditions then it should be lined with a highly insulating material like polystyrene or polyethylene foam.

Material

Cases should be constructed using 'safe' materials which do not give off vapours that are likely to damage the objects in them. This is also an important point to consider when objects are stored. In the microclimate within any poorly-ventilated space, pollutants can rapidly accumulate to damaging levels. For example, woods give off acids such as acetic and formic acid, wool releases volatile sulphides, polyvinyl chloride releases hydrogen chloride. These pollutants can have dangerously damaging effects on objects. Lists of 'safe' materials are available (Padfield, *et al.*, 1982) and should be consulted when cases are designed.

Silica gel and humidity buffering

One of the most active fields of development in environmental conservation is the RH control of small areas using materials such as silica gel. This is a particularly popular form of control for temporary exhibitions and for museums where there is no possibility of installing large-scale conditioning schemes. It has already been mentioned that silica gel gives off water when the RH falls and absorbs it when the RH rises in such a way as to maintain the RH at a level to which the silica gel has been previously conditioned. It is recommended that 20 kg of silica gel are used per cubic metre of exhibition case. Depending on the leak rate of the case this amount efficiently buffers RH changes over the yearly cycle. Conditions within the case should be monitored using a hygrometer. Over the year, although stability will be maintained, the RH in the case will drift towards the average room RH. In the temperate climates with winter heating this will be too low. Therefore, either some form of simple humidifier will have to be used in the room or the silica gel will have to be reconditioned if the hygrometer shows too large a drop. One kilogram of silica gel per cubic metre of packing case should be sufficient for the short time that a work is in transit. The case should be constructed in such a way that air can circulate around the case with easy access to the silica gel which should be laid out exposing as great a surface area as possible.

Air-conditioning units for exhibition cases

An ingenious design for a home-made air-conditioning unit to be used to control the environment (RH and pollution) within exhibition cases has been published by Michalski (1982). The prototype supplies pollutant-free air at a specified RH and temperature to a number of exhibition cases. It is not a forced ventilation system, and merely introduces the air at a slight excess pressure. The air is lost through natural leakage from the cases. If a large number of exhibition cases are to be conditioned, then this system has distinct advantages over silica gel buffering because of its low cost. However, it is unable to compensate for RH changes induced by sudden temperature changes. Development of this idea could provide further possibilities for RH and pollution control on a small scale.

Design of packing cases

Packing cases fulfil two functions: to protect their contents from mechanical damage, vibration and shock and to provide a stable environment around the object. A typical specification for a case might consist of a solid outer case made from plywood or aluminium, lined with a foam to provide cushioning and insulation and a sheet of polythene enclosing the object with some silica gel. The case should also be shower-proof, fire-proof, or at least constructed from flame-resistant materials, and, obviously, secure. Any device that increases ease of handling should be used, such as extra handles or light materials. Accidents are more likely to occur if the case is particularly heavy or awkward to lift.

Monitoring

It might be tempting when systems for environmental control have been installed to become complacent and to assume that they are doing their jobs efficiently and maintaining conditions to within specifications. Unfortunately this is seldom the case. No machinery can be immune from malfunction or miscalibration and only constant vigilance can ensure that all is operating well. This responsibility must lie with the museum staff, the curators and conservators. Surveys of conditions within the museum must be performed whether by hand (using hygrometers and light meters) or by datalogger (a central computer linked to a number of environmental sensors around the museum). This check should be made frequently and the results passed on to those responsible for the maintenance of the systems.

Conclusions

The level of environmental control achieved will be governed to a major extent by the resources of the museum. The complete answer would be to install air-conditioning, to use UV screening on all windows and light sources, and to control daylight using automatically controlled motorized blinds. This has been called Class I environmental control. Class II uses free-standing RH-controlling units, UV screening and lighting control with manually operated blinds or only artificial lighting.

There is a developing trend towards control on a smaller scale through the use of exhibition cases, and this has distinct advantages over the complicated and elaborate machinery required for air-conditioning.

Light levels generate far more controversy than RH. Is the 200 Lux level adequate? Is daylight essential for viewing works of art? Surely it loses much of its 'changeable' quality when restricted to 200 Lux in a system using motorized blinds?

Might it be as acceptable to use artificial lights that simulate daylight? But if we wish to retain the 'changeable' quality, then is an annual exposure a possible alternative?

Environmental questions must always be asked when a new museum building is designed or rooms are renovated. The curator and conservator should write a specification for environmental controls to be installed.

This paper has presented the present recommended specifications for environmental control. One or two points may provoke controversy, but hopefully we are beyond the time of, on the one hand, the museum curator and designer exposing collections to high light levels with complete disregard of RH and pollutants for maximum impact in an exhibition, and on the other, the conservator who appears to endeavour to closet objects in poorly-lit exhibition cases. The curator and conservator should be prepared to work together to achieve the far-from-impossible goal of exhibiting collections in an attractive, stimulating and above all safe environment.

Acknowledgements

I am grateful to the National Gallery for allowing me to make this contribution and to several members of the staff for their comments and advice. I would particularly like to thank Garry Thomson for the help that he has given me during the preparation of this paper and for all he has taught me during the last two years.

Notes

[1] Ultra-violet is measured as the amount of UV energy per unit of visible radiation. It should be noted that cutting down the total amount of daylight radiation by, for example, installing blinds will not reduce the proportion of UV. It is still necessary to use UV screening.

[2] There will be no reference to commercially available products in this paper. This is deliberate since there is a tendency for companies to change their products or to go into liquidation, which will render any specific recommendations made here useless in the future. However, The Museums Association publishes Information Sheets which are regularly updated. They contain details of equipment and products with the names and addresses of suppliers. There are two which are particularly relevant for this paper: Thomson, G. and Bullock, L., Museums Association Information Sheet No. 6 (3rd edn revised 1978) *Conservation and Museum Lighting;* Thomson, G. and Bullock, L. (1980), Museums Association Information Sheet No. 24, *Simple Control and Measurement of Relative Humidity in Museums.*

[3] The lux is a unit of illumination. 1 lux equals 1 lumen per square metre and is approximately equal to 0.1 foot candle (the old unit of illumination). It is a measurement of energy that takes into account the spectral sensitivity of the human eye.

References

Lighting

BROMMELLE, N. S. AND HARRIS, J. B. (1961, 1962), Museum Lighting, Parts 1–4, *Museums J.,* **61**, 169–176; **61**, 259–267; **62**, 337–346; **62**, 176–186

CLARKE, J. (1980), Ultraviolet filtering films for museum use, properties and effectiveness, *ICCM Bulletin,* **6**, 3 and 4, 35–40

CRAWFORD, B. H. (1973), Just perceptible colour differences in relation to level of illuminatin, *Studies in Conservation,* **18**, 159–166

FELLER, R. L. (1964), Control of deteriorating effects of light upon museum objects, *Museum,* **XVII**, 57–98

HORIE, C. V. (1980), Solar-control film for reducing light levels in buildings with daylight, *Proc. IIC Vienna conference* Conservation within Historic Buildings, pp. 49–54

LOE, D. L. (1981), *Appropriate Lighting Conditions for Viewing Works of Graphic Art,* M. Phil. thesis, University College, London

THOMSON, G. (1961), A new look at colour rendering, level of illumination and protection from ultraviolet radiation in museum lighting, *Studies in Conservation,* **6**, 49–70

Relative Humidity, Cases and Storage

BLACKSHAW, S. AND DANIELS, V. (1978), Selecting safe materials for use in the display and storage of antiquities, *Proc. 5th Triennial Meeting, Zagreb,* ICOM Committee for Conservation, 78/23/2

BLACKSHAW, S. AND DANIELS, V. (1979), The testing of materials for use in storage and display in museums, *The Conservator,* **3**, 16–19

DE GUICHEN, G. (1981), Pourquoi les conservateurs n'utilisent-ils pas le gel de silice ou les trois usages de gel de silice, *Proc. 6th. Triennial/ICOM Committee for conservation meeting, Ottawa*, 81/18/7

HOLDEN, C. (1979), Notes on the protection of modern art works during handling, packing and storage, *The Conservator*, **3**, 20–24

KENJO, T. (1982), A rapid response humidity buffer composed of nikka pellets and Japanese tissue, *Studies in Conservation*, **27**, 19–24

MICHALSKI, S. (1982), A relative humidity control module for display cases, *Proc. IIC Washington conference*, Science and Technology in the Service of Conservation, 28–31

MIURA, S. (1981), Studies on the behaviour of RH within an exhibition case. Part II: the static and dynamic characteristics of sorbents to control the RH of a showcase, *Proc. 6th. Triennial/ICOM Committee for Conservation meeting, Ottawa*, 81/18/5

PADFIELD, T. *et al* (1982), Trouble in store, *Proc. IIC Washington conference*, (Science and technology in the Service of Conservation) 24–27

RAMER, B. L. (1981), Stabilising relative humidity variations within display cases: The role of silica gel and case design *Proc. 6th Triennial Meeting, Ottawa*, ICOM Committee for Conservation, 81/18/6

THOMSON, G. (1977), Stabilisation of RH in exhibition cases, hygrometric half-time, *Studies in Conservation*, **22**, 85–102

WEINTRAUB, S. (1980), A new design for a low maintenance silica gel system for the control of relative humidity in a sealed case, *Proc. IIC Vienna Conference*, Conservation within Historic Buildings, 55–56

WEINTRAUB, S. (1981), 'Studies on the behaviour of RH within an exhibition case. Part I: Measuring the effectiveness of sorbents for use in an enclosed showcase,' *Proc. 6th Triennial Meeting, Ottawa*, ICOM Committee for Conservation, 81/18/4

Air Pollution

CHASTON, S. H. H. (1977), Pollution and the deterioration of materials, *Conservation in Australia*, 54–59

COOK, I. (1976), Air pollution and aspects of polymer degradation, *ICCM Bulletin 4*, 2, 4–20

MARSH, S. (1976), Air Pollution: A select bibliography, *ICCM Bulletin 4*, 2, 21–24

Monitoring

THOMSON, G. (1981), Control of the environment for good or ill? Monitoring, *National Gallery Technical Bulletin*, **5**, 3–13

Further reading

Brommelle, N. S., Garry Thomson and Smith, P. (1980) (Ed.), *Conservation within Historic Buildings*, IIC, London. The IIC conference of 1980 that was held in Vienna produced a collection of papers of which many relate to environmental conservation.

Thomson, G. (1978), *The Museum Environment*, Butterworths, London. This book is indispensable for curators. It contains sections on light, relative humidity and air pollution. It is written in two parts, the first part at a less technical level than the second. It has an extensive bibliography and I refer readers to this for all articles published before 1977, I have not repeated those references here except for articles or books of great importance.

Thomson, G. (1963) (Ed.), *Recent Advances in Conservation – Contributions to the IIC Rome Conference, 1961*, Butterworths, London. Contains five papers on museum climate.

Thomson, G. (1968) (Ed.), *Contributions to the London Conference on Museum Climatology 18–23 September 1967*, IIC, London. The foundations for the understanding of environmental conservation were laid in the early 1960s. The IIC (International Institute for Conservation of Historic and Artistic Works) conference on museum climatology draws together most of the preliminary work on the subject. Most of the ideas put forward in the papers still hold true today.

27

Conservation and storage: archaeological material

Elizabeth Pye

The adjective 'archaeological' is often used to describe material of early date, but for the purposes of conservation and storage the significant fact is that archaeological material has been buried or entombed at some time. In this sense the word 'archaeological' may be applied to a wide range of artefacts from all cultures and periods up to the quite recent past.

The effects of burial and excavation

In normal burial conditions – in the presence of oxygen, moisture and micro-organisms – all material will deteriorate to some extent and most organic materials will ultimately deteriorate completely. In certain conditions, however (for example where oxygen is excluded, as in waterlogged contexts) material may be well, or even exceptionally well, preserved. During burial, artefacts tend to achieve an equilibrium with their environment and the deterioration rate, which may have been fast at first, may slow down appreciably.

Unfortunately, however, the effect of excavation is to change the environment suddenly and completely, with the result that the deterioration rate speeds up considerably. Not only is the chemical and biological environment changed, but the physical support provided by the surrounding soil is removed. Many objects are too weak to bear their own weight and cannot survive normal handling. Unless proper conservation measures are taken on the site, excavation can be a very damaging process.

Although it is not always possible for a conservator to be present on site at all times, planning and liaison between archaeologist, curator and conservator should ensure that all fragile, fragmentary or particularly sensitive material is prepared correctly for, and given adequate support during excavation. It should then be packed in a way which minimizes the 'shock' caused by excavation and removal from the site. In some cases this may be achieved by packing which simulates the burial environment.

The condition of excavated material

The condition of excavated material is dependent on many factors including handling during and after excavation. Unnecessary touching, and on-site cleaning may be very damaging to artefacts and may result in the loss of valuable evidence. Condition is also dependent on the conservation care the material has received and whether it has been continuous or was undertaken some time after excavation as a 'rescue' measure. Condition also depends on where and when the material was excavated. Archaeological material in British museums comes either from this country or from overseas; for example, Egyptian artefacts are likely to include a high proportion of dry organic materials and exhibit problems unlike those of many British assemblages.

Material excavated in the past
Unconserved, excavated material will eventually achieve some equilibrium with its environment: it may survive reasonably intact or may disintegrate in the process of achieving this equilibrium. Material which has been excavated and treated in the past may be in a worse condition than similar untreated material, since many early conservation treatments involved the use of substances or methods now known to be unsatisfactory.

Recently excavated material
Some recently excavated objects reach the museum after receiving only 'first aid' in the field, and unless promptly treated, they will deteriorate very quickly. If a fragile artefact is encased in plaster of Paris or polyurethane-foam to give it support during excavation and simply left in store, it is likely to disintegrate

inside the jacket. Waterlogged material may reach the museum after temporary wet packing. If it cannot be treated immediately it will need constant monitoring and possibly repacking to ensure that it does not dry out or give rise to the growth of algae or micro-organisms. Untreated material may arrive in unsuitable packaging such as tobacco tins, brown paper envelopes and cotton wool and will need examination and repacking as soon as possible.

Ideally, where liaison between archaeologist, conservator and curator is effective, recently excavated material should have been properly conserved to an agreed level, packed in suitable containers and should arrive with full instructions for storage.

Once a museum accepts a collection of archaeological material, provision must be made for controlled storage and long-term conservation. In whatever condition the objects reach the museum, they should be received, assessed and thereafter monitored by a qualified conservator who will advise on conservation and storage and carry out treatment.

Conservation Part I: aims, records, examination, selection.

Aims of conservation

The aim of conservation is to prolong the life of the material. Two factors are particularly important: first, action at the time of excavation, or as soon as possible afterwards, to counter the likely increase in deterioration, and second, meticulous examination before and during treatment to establish the function of the objects, how they were made, and how they were affected by burial and excavation.

Objects are prepared for handling, drawing, study, publication and display. These different requirements involve different levels of conservation including the removal of accretions and/or chemical and physical stabilization. Correct storage is essential, and is sometimes referred to as 'passive conservation'. This is, in fact, the main type of conservation which much archaeological material receives.

The limitations of conservation treatment

Although methods of treatment are improving all the time, many of the substances employed, such as adhesives and consolidants, do not possess all the properties desirable for conservation use or the ultimate survival of the object. Conservators agree that ideally all treatments should be reversible. This is sometimes difficult to achieve because some substances may not remain reversible, and the artefacts may be endangered by attempts to remove them. Accelerated ageing tests can provide some indication of the likely long-term behaviour of conservation materials, but all treatments need monitoring to assess their effectiveness on the artefacts themselves. Efficiency of treatment is also limited by the efficacy of packaging, and of storage and display conditions, which are often unsatisfactory.

The role of the conservator

On site and in the museum, the informed archaeologist or curator can deal with most preliminary conservation care, and may also undertake first-aid procedures when a conservator is not available or after an emergency such as flood or fire. However, it is essential that a conservator should be consulted, and should undertake any full conservation treatment. Intervention by the more inexperienced in conservation can cause irreparable damage or the loss of valuable information.

Records

Full records are essential. Recording should begin on site and the written record should accompany the object or be readily accessible at all times. All necessary information should accompany the object from site to store or laboratory. The record should provide concise information about the object in the ground, including archaeological context, soil conditions and associated material, its condition when excavated, the method of lifting it, and first-aid procedures. The complete record should include methods and results of examination, reasons for level of treatment chosen, unambiguous information on treatments themselves and recommendations for handling, packaging, storage and display. The written record should be augmented with drawings, photographs, X-radiographs and analytical reports.

Precise details of all substances used must be recorded. These should include both chemical and trade names, and any distinguishing numbers which indicate a particular property such as grade or molecular weight. Other information about solution strengths and duration of treatment should be equally precise.

The use of records
There are two major uses for conservation records. Firstly, the information yielded during microscopic examination and cleaning is vital for the understanding of the artefacts and is therefore of great importance to archaeologists, curators and students. Secondly, the information enables conservators to assess the effectiveness of treatments and provides a basis for the choice of further treatment. Where an early treatment has failed, the record may help to avoid unnecessary investigation before further treatment. Good records are important aids in archaeological and conservation research, and ensure the safety of the object.

Methods of keeping records
Records should be made on a standard card or form designed to cover all aspects of the information (including photographs and X-radiographs which may be stored separately because of size).

Information retrieval
It is desirable to retrieve the information under a number of headings so that the conservator can, for example, find the treatment already given to an object, or its storage conditions. Conservation and curatorial records should be cross-referenced so that *all* the information on an object is accessible to both conservator and curator.

Examination

Examination is part of the care of an object. It is essential in deciding on the level of conservation to employ; and it must take place at every stage of treatment. Much archaeological material is in fact subject to closer scrutiny during conservation than at any other time and this is why the conservation record contains much essential technological and archaeological information.

When dealing with a complex object on site the conservator may use simple visual examination and cautious investigative cleaning to establish its type and condition and to decide on lifting and handling methods. Inspection for shape, size, colour, surface texture and accretions can be useful and, if the object can be handled safely, an estimation of its weight can sometimes give information on its condition. A small magnet may be used to estimate the extent of metallic iron remaining in an object. This type of examination will be repeated during the selection process, but once an object is in the conservation laboratory, more sophisticated examination methods can be used. During examination, handling should be minimized by packaging methods which allow a large part of the object to be seen without touching or removing it from the container.

The binocular microscope
A binocular microscope providing magnifications of ×10 to ×30 allows the conservator to examine in detail the surface of an object and small fragments of associated material, such as textile fibres, which are not clearly distinguishable with the naked eye. The microscope is also used during investigative cleaning, particularly of metal objects. Here, the partial removal of accretions may reveal information not only about the accretions themselves but also about the surface of the object.

X-radiography
In some cases the object, or group of objects, may be an amorphous mass or may reveal insufficient information about its structure and components. X-radiography, may provide some of the answers. Normally, industrial equipment in the 80 to 110 kV range is the most suitable, but medical equipment can give reasonable results if skillfully used. Careful selection of position and exposure will increase the amount of information gained but further cleaning and further use of X-radiography may be necessary before the maximum possible detail is revealed.

X-radiographs of iron objects are essential (they are extremely useful in the case of other metal objects) before selection for treatment. They may reveal the extent of deterioration and clarify the shape of the object (*Figure 27.1*). They may also provide other very important information about metal objects such as the surface detail on coins, evidence of organic materials preserved in corrosion products, and indication of methods of construction or repair. They may be equally useful on non-metallic or composite objects in revealing, for example, structural details of wooden objects, traces of metallic or other ornaments on organic materials and the remains of cores in cast metal objects. X-radiographs have proved to be essential guides for the cleaning and elucidation of intricate objects such as inlaid buckles or strap ornaments.

Chemical and physical analysis
The conservator may employ simple chemical tests to establish for example, the nature of a white metal decoration or of the salts on ceramics or stone, or of pigments or other coloured deposits. Whenever possible the help of the archaeological scientist will be enlisted in the application of X-ray fluorescence or other physical methods to provide further information on corrosion products and similar substances, or to confirm the results of the chemical tests.

Results and limitations of examination
Detailed examination produces useful technological evidence and provides essential information without which it is not safe to start a treatment. There are, however, limitations on the sensitivity of all the examination methods, and interpretation of results relies heavily on the training and experience of the conservator.

Selection and levels of conservation

Many archaeological sites yield large amounts of material from which a selection must be made for treatment. Different objects will receive different levels of conservation. The selection is governed by the needs of the objects themselves and the requirements of the archaeologist, curator and conservator.

In most cases only a small proportion of the objects will be fully treated and only a very few will go on display. However, much of the material will

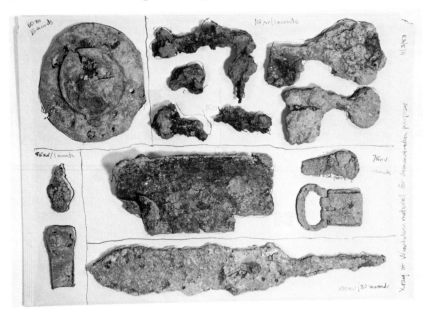

a

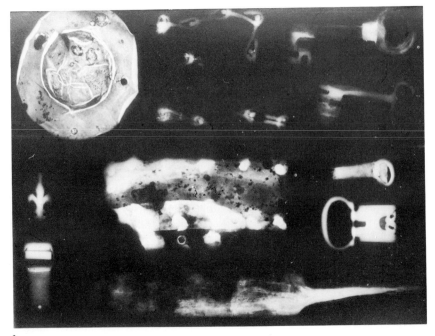

b

Figure 27.1 (a) A group of corroded iron objects laid out in
preparation for routine X-radiography. (b) The
X-radiograph revealing details of form and construction
(By courtesy of the Institute of Archaeology, University of
London)

be studied and drawn for publication and as it will form part of the site archive, it is necessary for each distinguishable item to be given at least the basic conservation care of examination, recording and proper storage.

Criteria used in selection

The criteria used for selection may be archaeological, curatorial or conservation ones. Some objects such as coins are of particular significance to the site, and need prompt attention. Some objects may be needed for immediate display to promote local interest in the site, and others may be so sensitive to environmental change that they must be treated immediately. Large quantities of similar material must be sorted into various categories, and here X-radiography should be routine, particularly for iron.

Levels of conservation

Some material will simply be stored, some will need clarification before drawing, and some will need full treatment possibly including restoration. In *Conservation Guidelines No. 1: Excavated artefacts for publication: UK sites,* the Archaeology Section of the United Kingdom Institute for Conservation distinguishes five possible levels of treatment from *no conservation* (merely involving handling and checking) through *minimal, partial* and *full* conservation to *display-standard conservation* which includes photography, X-radiography, examination, investigation, cleaning, stabilization, reconstruction, restoration and, possibly, cosmetic treatment.

Selection of material excavated in the past

In the case of large amounts of material from past excavations, a similar selection, undertaken by curator and conservator, will be necessary, but may be complicated by the effects of early treatments or the absence of records. Some material will require priority treatment because the earlier treatment has failed or become actively damaging or because storage or display conditions have been unsuitable.

Conservation Part II: handling, packaging and storage

Introduction

The following section deals with the packaging and storage of material from land sites. Material from marine sites is considered to be a separate and special category which is covered in *First Aid for Marine Finds* (Robinson, 1981). Further details on packaging and storage methods can be found in the *Guidelines* (Numbers 2 and 3) prepared by the Archaeology Section of the United Kingdom Institute for Conservation (UKIC, forthcoming).

Handling

Handling during examination, selection and in preparation for packing should be kept to a minimum. Apart from the physical dangers, fingering may deposit moisture and salts which encourage corrosion on metals. Unnecessary exposure to the air and to micro-organisms may lead to degradation of organic materials. The ideal is to pack objects so that they are easily visible without handling.

Small objects are sometimes more safely handled with delicate flexible forceps (or vacuum tweezers) than with the fingers. Large objects should be cradled with both hands, wearing protective cotton or surgical plastic gloves when necessary, and should be carried on a padded tray or trolley after enlisting aid in opening doors. Objects on the conservation bench should not be touched or lifted without first ascertaining from the conservator that it is safe to do so. For a further discussion see the chapter by Horie.

Packaging

Packaging should provide appropriate physical, chemical and biological protection, should allow the object to be examined easily, and should be informative and durable. Packing materials should be, as far as possible, inert and should not cause physical damage.

Containers

Each object should be in a container which provides physical protection and supported by firm shock-absorbing padding. If more than one object are packed together each should be clearly separated from the next, and padding should prevent damage caused by knocking or rolling together. Small objects may be packed in individual boxes or bags which are then grouped in larger boxes.

Padding should be positioned below and around the object and a final pad placed above (*Figure 27.2 (a)–(c)*). This provides complete support while allowing the object(s) to be examined easily by lifting off the final pad. Wrapping or winding in paper is unsuitable as it obscures artefacts and may cause damage or loss during unpacking.

Where necessary a purpose-built container should be used with a well made in the padding of exactly the size and shape to hold the object (*Figure 27.2 (d)* and (*e*)). A large object in a deep container may be provided with a sling which passes underneath it and helps to take its weight when lifting it out. This is safer than grasping part of the object. Otherwise, a container should be designed with one side that folds down or lifts off, exposing the full height of the object.

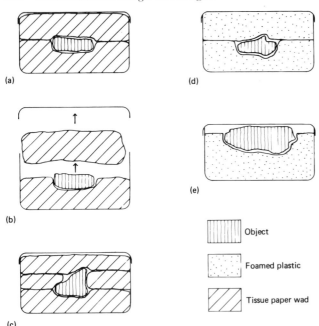

(a)

(d)

(b)

(e)

(c)

	Object
	Foamed plastic
	Tissue paper wad

Figure 27.2 Padding. (a) Use of a tissue paper wad beneath and another above an object. The wads can be 'moulded' into the shape of the object. (b) The wad above can be lifted off, allowing easy access to the object. (c) An awkwardly shaped object can rest on one wad and be surrounded by others with a final wad placed above. (d) A well, made in the padding, of exactly the shape to take the object. In this case, foamed plastic is used, and a second piece, also cut to shape, is used to cover the object. (e) An object resting in a well cut in foamed plastic and held securely in position by the lid of the box. Where a clear plastic box is used, this method allows viewing of the object without opening the box

Packaging materials (see Appendix 27.1 for details of suppliers)

Clear plastic boxes (which are better than even good-quality cardboard boxes) with inert foamed plastic sheet or acid-free tissue paper padding should be used to provide maximum protection. Some foamed plastics degrade easily and may give off undesirable breakdown products. Most low-grade paper, including newspaper, coloured tissue and toilet paper, may give off acids. Cotton wool may catch in, and damage, fragile surfaces. It is safer to use wads made of acid-free tissue paper (*Figure 27.3*) unless a reliable foamed plastic is available.

Boxes, bags

The following could be used:

Small clear polystyrene snap-shut boxes
Polythene boxes with self-seal lids (various sizes)
Polythene bags (self-sealing)

'Tailor-made' bags may be made from Polythene tube or sheet with the aid of a heat sealer.

Padding

Acid-free tissue wads may be used for dry packaging. The following types of inert foamed plastic sheet may be used with both wet and dry material:

Small clear polystyrene snap-shut boxes
Polyethylene (Polythene) foam
Polyester foam
Expanded polystyrene

Labelling

Clear and efficient labelling is necessary. Objects should be labelled with an identifying number. Methods of labelling should be agreed by archaeologist, curator and conservator since they depend on the type and condition of the objects.

Robust objects may have a label attached loosely in an appropriate position, but the knot should be firm. On no account should the string cut into the surface of a fragile object; wide strips of lightweight Polythene sheet may be used as a less damaging alternative. Labels should not be stuck directly onto objects and self-adhesive labels should never be used as the adhesive may stain or damage the object (*Figure 27.4*) and be difficult to remove.

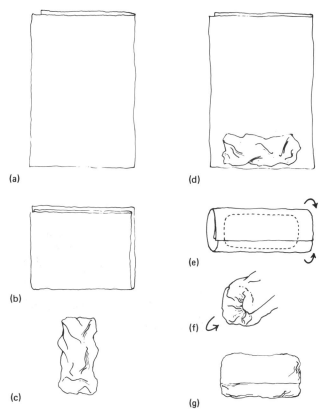

(a)

(d)

(b)

(e)

(c)

(f)

(g)

Figure 27.3 How to make a tissue paper wad. (a) and (b) A sheet of tissue paper of the required size is doubled and then folded again. (c) The folded tissue is rolled and very slightly compressed to form a crumpled pad. (d) and (e) The pad is then rolled in a single or double sheet of tissue. (f) The ends of the outer sheet are tucked in neatly around the pad. (g) A smooth and resilient cushion of tissue paper results

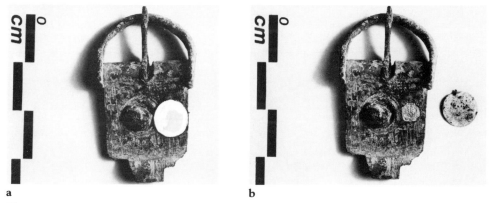

a   b

Figure 27.4 (a) A copper alloy buckle to which a self-adhesive label has been attached. (b) After removal of the label, a patch of corrosion is revealed beneath, indicating that chemical damage has been caused or exacerbated (such labels will also endanger fragile surfaces) (Copyright, Velson Horie)

The best way to guarantee that the label does not become detached is to write the relevant information directly onto the object in Indian ink. This method is suitable only for certain materials and should be fully discussed with the conservator.

Packaging should be labelled durably in and outside giving an identifying number, an indication of which way up the container should be held and stored, the number and description of objects or parts of objects, type of material, instructions for unpacking, and instructions for storage and monitoring of conditions.

Wet material stored in a sealed Polythene bag may have an inert label sealed in with it together with a second label sealed into a separate compartment (*Figure 27.5*).

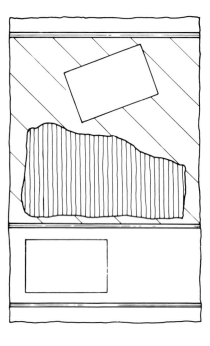

Water

Object

Figure 27.5 A waterlogged object sealed in a Polythene bag. An inert label is sealed in the bag with the object. As a safeguard against water damage a second label is sealed in a separate dry section of the bag (this two-compartment system provides a useful means of holding a label in position on any Polythene packaging; it also protects the label from dirt)

Labelling Materials
All materials used including labels, string and ink should be durable. Labels of spun bonded polyethylene (Polythene) which looks like paper are particularly suitable because they can be used successfully with wet material. Ideally, the label attached in the field should be large enough to allow the later addition of museum and laboratory information. String should be durable (for example made of Terylene, such as blind cord; strips of Polythene sheet are a useful alternative. Ink should be resistant to water and the effects of light. Good quality, spirit-based waterproof permanent markers or good quality ball-point pens should be used.

Packaging to control the environment
If packaging is judiciously chosen it can be used to prevent decay of material. The climate within the package may be dry, desiccated, damp or wet.

Dry or desiccated packaging
Because of the danger of condensation, sealed containers cannot be used for dry packaging unless the object is thoroughly dry before enclosure. Some sensitive materials must be desiccated rather than just dry, and in this case a desiccant such as silica gel must be included in the package. Silica gel absorbs moisture efficiently until it is saturated, after which it is no longer effective and must be dried out (regenerated). Self-indicating silica gel has a colour indicator which shows when the gel is dry (bright blue) and when it is saturated (pink). The gel is regenerated by heating gently at 120–130°C until the blue colour returns.

The amount of silica gel included should equal one fifth to one tenth of the volume of the object(s). It should be placed in the package in a perforated bag or container so that it can be removed easily for regeneration (*Figure 27.6 (a)* and *(b)*): it should never be used loose or in direct contact with objects. If the bag is placed at one end of a Polythene box any colour change should be clearly visible even if several boxes are stacked together (*Figure 27.6 (e)*). Where several Polythene bags containing objects are to be packed inside a large box each bag should be perforated with holes of 2mm or more in diameter and one batch of silica gel placed in the sealed box (*Figure 27.6 (c)* and *(d)*). Alternatively, it is possible to use relative humidity indicator cards or strips in conjunction with non-indicating silica gel, but the strips can be difficult to read accurately.

This type of desiccation is possible for long-term packaging only if it is monitored regularly.

Damp or wet packaging
Different methods must be adopted when storing damp or wet materials. Not only must the damp conditions be maintained, but microbiological

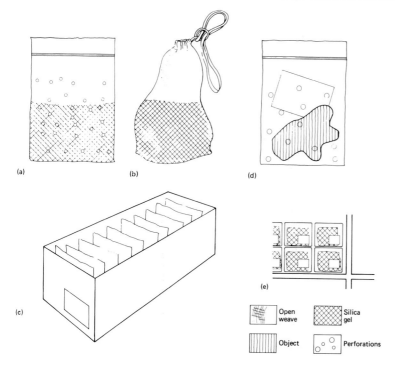

Figure 27.6 The use of silica gel in packaging. (a) A perforated Polythene bag containing silica gel, probably the simplest way to include the gel in a package. (b) An open-weave bag containing silica gel; the weave must be open enough to allow adequate air circulation. If the bag is made of heat-resistant material there is no need to remove the gel from the bag for regeneration. (c) A box containing several objects each in a Polythene bag. A single bag of silica gel may be used, provided that the bags within the main box are perforated (see (d)). (d) An individual object housed in a perforated Polythene bag. To ensure adequate air circulation there should be plenty of large holes, preferably larger than 2 mm diameter. (e) Self-indicating silica gel visible through the ends of plastic boxes stacked in a storage area

growth and other undesirable changes, for example in the degree of acidity or alkalinity of the storage water, must be prevented. This type of packaging is suitable for short-term duration.

Well-sealed Polythene boxes or several layers of sealed Polythene bags will help to maintain wet conditions. Foamed plastic may be used as a 'reservoir' by thoroughly wetting it before including it as padding in the package. The exclusion of oxygen will also reduce the rate of deterioration.

Low temperatures, the exclusion of light and the use of a biocide when absolutely necessary, will deter microbiological growth. As an alternative to the use of biocides, material may be refrigerated (*not* frozen), and this will slow down other changes.

The efficiency of packing methods depends on storage in controlled conditions. This needs constant monitoring by trained personnel.

Storage

The importance of protection from physical, chemical and biological deterioration has been mentioned. Well-designed packaging methods provide a great deal of protection but will fail if storage conditions are unsuitable. One of the difficulties in storing archaeological material is the large volume of space needed, and many museums have been forced to make use of unsuitable areas. Poor storage conditions may cause valuable archaeological evidence to be lost from some objects while others may deteriorate completely.

The storage area

Storage areas should be designed or modified to maintain desired conservation conditions. The room should be structurally sound, dry and clean. Lifts, passages and doors should be of reasonable size and situated so that trolleys and large containers can be brought in easily. It should be possible to restrict access, and the store should not be used as a through-route. It should not be near a heating system since this may bring fluctuating temperatures, undesirable fumes, and flooding. It should also be remote from sources of vibration.

Storage conditions

Well-designed storage areas and good packaging will prolong the life of many objects. The standard store should be used for materials such as ceramics and stone which do not need stringently regulated conditions. Each object is well packed but the climate within the package is not individually controlled. The sensitive store should be used for materials such as certain metals, glass and dry organic material, which require more strictly controlled conditions.

Some materials, such as many metals, and ivory require special microclimates and here the conditions in the individual packages are controlled; for example iron can be kept very dry using silica gel.

Where there are large quantities of material such as iron which need precisely the same special conditions, separate cabinets or sealed tents (or separate storage areas) may be controlled to the right humidity levels using equipment such as dehumidifiers, thus obviating the need for individually controlled packages. In this case the objects must be packed in a way which allows the air to reach them.

The standard store

To attain a suitable climate for general storage, certain factors must be controlled. The factors which are most crucial are relative humidity (RH), temperature, light (considered also as a source of heat), micro-organisms, dust, dirt and pollutant gases.

Relative humidity

Relative humidity levels in the store and in the packages are dependent on temperature and this will be affected not only by the heating but also by the lighting system and the impact of sunlight. Fluctuations and extremes of RH may be damaging, and it should not rise above 70 per cent for more than 10 per cent of the time. A stable level of 65 per cent RH is preferable. Generous amounts of acid-free tissue paper padding helps to buffer objects against rapid fluctuations in RH.

Temperature

Temperature is chiefly important for its effect on the relative humidity and to some extent on micro-organism growth. Again, extremes and fluctuations may be damaging and in the standard store the temperature should never be outside the range 4–30°C and should lie preferably between 10°C and 25°C with no more than a daily movement of ±5°C.

Light

Sunlight should be screened out completely. Visible and ultra-violet light can cause breakdown of organic materials and fading of some paints, dyes and inks. Objects which are covered or enclosed in opaque packing will be protected from light but the packing materials and labels may suffer. Ultra-violet filters should be used on fluorescent lamps.

Insects, fungi, micro-organisms

Air-borne micro-organisms are difficult to control without an efficient filtering system but they (and insects and fungi) will be deterred by clean, dry (below 65 per cent RH), well-ventilated conditions. Where there is a particular danger of algal or fungal growth cool, dark conditions are deterrent. Infestations such as furniture beetle or dry rot affecting the building spread readily to shelving, packing and objects.

Dust, dirt and pollutant gases

Dust and dirt are undesirable because they give rise to, or encourage, deterioration and because the repeated cleaning of objects is damaging. Filtering systems can be used to exclude much such pollution, but proper packaging provides good protection. Pollutant gases are difficult to exclude from storage areas.

The sensitive store

Sensitive material should be stored in more stringently controlled conditions. The relative humidity should lie between 45 and 60 per cent, preferably between 50 and 60 per cent, with very little variation. The temperature should be between 15°C and 25°C with a gradual daily movement of only ±5°C. All daylight should be excluded and ultra-violet filters used on fluorescent lamps. All objects should be boxed; open storage is permissible only if dust filters are in use.

It should be noted that, ideally, the conditions in both the standard store and the sensitive store should be even more closely controlled than is suggested here. The figures given above represent levels and ranges which should be possible to achieve and maintain in museum storage.

Monitoring of storage conditions

The regular monitoring and recording of conditions and the cleaning and inspection of storage areas are essential. The stored objects should be examined regularly by a conservator who can then advise on any necessary changes to the storage arrangements.

Conservation Part III: treatment

Cleaning

Almost all objects will be at least partially cleaned during initial investigation and further cleaning will depend on the level of conservation chosen.

The term 'cleaning' covers a number of different processes including the removal of accretions from corroded metals, the removal of dirt and stains from poorly stored material, the washing of archaeological textiles or of waterlogged wooden artefacts. Cleaning is an essential part of conservation as it can help not only to reveal evidence but also to preserve it.

For example, the removal of salts from some metals or ceramics may halt rapid deterioration, and the removal of dust, dirt and spores from organic objects may minimize the development or spread of mould or fungal attack. On the other hand, cleaning destroys some types of evidence (the nature of corrosion, or adhering soils or organic substances) and all such materials must be thoroughly investigated and fully recorded. Details of the cleaning method used and observations made in the process must be included in the conservation record.

Cleaning is a highly skilled part of the archaeological conservator's job, calling for careful judgement in the selection and manipulation of tools or chemicals. It is not a simple process. Indiscriminate cleaning, or over-cleaning, can result in loss of evidence and in damage to the objects. Part of the skill is knowing when to stop. Sometimes objects which have been cleaned by an experienced conservator may appear 'unfinished' to the lay eye but the conservator has stopped at a certain point, knowing that further cleaning could be damaging. In short, cleaning should *reveal* evidence, not remove it.

Almost all conservation techniques can be harmful if used incorrectly or applied inappropriately. Simple washing may remove slips or paint from pottery or cause low-fired or unfired material to disintegrate. Washing, particularly if it involves the use of unsuitable detergents or other cleaning agents, can remove or obscure evidence of tannins and dyes in leathers and textiles; unskilled mechanical cleaning may remove the surface and detail from a coin. Only a trained, experienced conservator should undertake the cleaning of archaeological material.

Stabilization

The conservator uses particular treatments and makes recommendations in order to keep archaeological material stable. Stabilization is not a 'one-off' process although certain individual treatments may be called stabilization treatments. Correct handling, packaging and storage or display methods are – in general – more important than any other aspect of stabilization and are essential before, during and after laboratory treatment. In most cases, the treatment used by the conservator is not fully effective unless supported by good storage or display conditions.

Most laboratory stabilization can be divided into four categories:

(1) The strengthening of weakened objects, such as the consolidation of fragile ceramics, or the joining and backing of wall-plaster fragments.
(2) Removal of substances or organisms in the objects which cause deterioration. This includes the removal of water-soluble salts from ceramics, or salts causing corrosion of metals or microorganisms in organic materials.

(3) Inhibition or prevention of certain chemical or other reactions by the use of corrosion inhibitors, insect or fungal repellants.
(4) Control of one or more environmental factors such as by lacquering metals to limit access of oxygen, moisture or pollutant gases.

There are considerable variations in the methods used within these categories, and some methods cannot be fitted into them at all. The treatment of waterlogged organic materials such as wood and leather must effect the removal of the water without the structural collapse of the object. It can also involve the introduction of an agent which bonds chemically with the deteriorated structure and gives mechanical strength. The treatment of composite objects is also difficult to categorize. Where both inorganic and organic parts of an object survive it is difficult to choose a suitable treatment.

As far as possible, stabilization treatments should be reversible. Sometimes, however, the condition of the object or the limitations of the treatment mean that a method cannot be considered reversible.

Restoration

Restoration, in the sense of reinstatement, may be considered part of the process of revealing archaeological and technological evidence. Restoration, in the sense of repairing or replacing missing parts in an attempt to regain the original state of an object, may increase its strength but may go further than conservation in the strict sense.

Restoration is often necessary to prepare an object for use in teaching or display. Where the original shape or purpose of an object is not clear, the conservator will discuss the problem with the curator before attempting restoration.

A restored feature should be shaped or modelled as accurately as possible, but a restoration should be neither invisible nor glaringly obvious. Archaeological evidence of use, breakage, repair and burial should not be obscured by producing too perfect a restoration. The colour and texture of restored areas should approximate to those of the original, but not match them. It should be possible for anyone at a distance of 10–15 cm to see which parts are original and which are restored. Yet it should be possible to appreciate the object as a whole at a distance of a metre.

The methods and materials used in restoration must be just as carefully chosen by the conservator as those used in stabilization treatments as they can also be potentially damaging. They should be reversible as far as possible. This is important for the welfare of the object and because the interpretation of shape and form in archaeological objects changes. The methods and materials used and the evidence on which the restoration is based, must be included in the conservation record. Where a large amount of restoration is necessary to make an object 'presentable', it is sometimes preferable to make a facsimile for display rather than to endanger the original.

Display

Archaeological objects which have been conserved, restored and prepared for display must still be considered to be fragile and potentially unstable. The conservator should advise on suitable conditions for displaying archaeological material and should be fully involved at the earliest stages and throughout the process of exhibition design. Failure to make suitable provision for the well-being of the objects from the start may necessitate extensive modification of the exhibition design at a later (and expensive) stage.

Environmental conditions in display cases should be as rigorously controlled as those in storage areas and particular regard should be given to the effects of both light and heat within the display case. Methods of mounting should be carefully chosen so that no stress is placed on potentially fragile objects; for example suspension from nylon thread can be very damaging. Materials used in the construction of display cases such as woods, adhesives and sealing strips and in the display itself, such as textile backings or paints, should be thoroughly tested in order to avoid those which may be chemically harmful. The condition of the object on display should be monitored regularly by the conservator.

The care of archaeological materials

Introduction

The care of archaeological materials falls into four main groups:

1. Porous materials (ceramics, stone, plaster, mosaics).
2. Glass.
3. Metals.
4. Organic materials (wood, leather, bone and ivory, textiles).

Emphasis is placed on monitoring and care of archaeological material in display or in store. Each section concludes with a brief summary of the changes or signs that indicate active deterioration and urgent need for conservation treatment. Although the special problems of marine material are not discussed specifically most of what is said here is applicable. Before conservation treatment, all such material must be stored *wet*. For further information see *First Aid for Marine Finds* (Robinson, 1981).

Porous materials: ceramics

In general, ceramics, including brick and tile, are considered to be reasonably stable and not to need special conditions of storage or display. However, many archaeological ceramics, particularly pots, are highly porous, fragile and affected by burial conditions.

Handling of ceramics
Pots which appear to be whole should be handled carefully using both hands to encircle the body. They should not be picked up by the rim or by a handle as the fabric may be weak or earlier repairs may have failed. Adhesives and gap-filling materials can become brittle and shrink away from the pot. Plaster of Paris, often used as a gap filler can be broken or chipped. When an object is dirty it is often difficult to distinguish areas of weakness or early repairs.

Ceramics after long-term storage or display
Archaeological ceramics which have been stored or exhibited for some time may be badly affected by greasy dirt and dust which are easily absorbed into their porous surfaces. They may even show signs of mould growth (which can cause particularly resistant stains). Ordinary washing is not advisable as it can cause stains to spread and deepen, and water soluble adhesives to dissolve. Adhesives can become unsightly with age and may even be damaging (an unsuitably strong adhesive can cause considerable damage to the edges of porous sherds; *Figure 27.7*).

Figure 27.7 The adhesive applied to these sherds is stronger than the pot itself, the failure of the joins has resulted in thin slivers of ceramic being pulled away from the break-edges (Courtesy of Institute of Archaeology, University of London)

Much early material, for example Neolithic or Bronze Age pots, was fired at low temperatures and is thus likely to be weak, friable and badly affected by water. On material fired at a higher temperature paint slips or glazes may be flaking or coming away from the surface of the ceramic either because of faults in composition or manufacture or because of the effects of burial. In the case of ceramics from marine sites or from arid areas this type of damage is particularly likely to be caused by the presence of water-soluble salts (which may be visible in the form of fine crystals); *Figures 27.8* and *27.9*). Occasionally,

Figure 27.9 Large salt crystals and consequent damage on the inside of a pot (Copyright Kathryn Tubb)

Figure 27.8 Damage in the form of loosened flakes and pitted surface caused by water-soluble salts. The salt crystals are visible only as patches of whitish 'bloom' (approximately ×2 (reduced by ⅗ in reproduction) (Courtesy of Institute of Archaeology, University of London)

apparently similar damage may be caused by an earlier treatment which has failed (*Figure 27.10*). All such material should be handled very carefully, should not be washed and should be conserved as soon as possible. Where water-soluble salts are suspected, carefully controlled storage conditions help to prevent further damage before treatment can be undertaken.

Recently excavated ceramics
Recently excavated ceramics may be sent to the museum after washing, marking and packing on site. It is as well to make sure that the material is properly dry (any further drying should take place in cool,

well-ventilated conditions; heat should never be used) and that the packaging is durable, protective and well-labelled. Paper bags, used for packing loose sherds, are not suitable for long-term storage. Sherds may be packed in linen bags or in well-perforated polythene bags; fragile sherds should be packed between pads of acid-free tissue paper, or foamed plastic sheet, in strong cardboard or Polythene boxes.

If necessary, well-fired, robust sherds can be washed carefully in regular changes of clean tap-water plus one or two drops of non-ionic detergent and using soft brushes (those with nylon bristles should be avoided). Care should be taken not to scrub the surfaces or edges too vigorously; drying should again take place in cool, well-ventilated conditions.

Storage of ceramics
Treated ceramics, and those showing no active deterioration, can be housed in the standard store. Material which is suffering from the effects of water-soluble salts should be conserved as soon as possible; in the mean time it should be maintained at the relative humidity it has become 'used to'. Fluctuations in relative humidity are most likely to cause further damage. Early or low-fired ceramics (normally excavated in a block of surrounding soil) must be kept damp. All such material should be stored only temporarily and conserved as soon as possible, as should any object which has been consolidated in the field or provided with a polyurethane foam or plaster jacket.

Porous materials: stone

Porous stone such as some limestones, sandstone and marbles may exhibit many of the same problems as porous ceramics. The stone may be friable, dirty, affected by water-soluble salts or mould growth and

Figure 27.10 Extensive damage probably caused by a combination of water-soluble salts and the application of a coating. Rather than halting the damage, the coating has made the situation much worse (approximately ×1.5 (reduced by ⅘ in reproduction); (Courtesy of Institute of Archaeology, University of London)

suffering from the effects of earlier treatment. Non-porous stones such as flint or granite develop fewer problems.

Handling
Stone artefacts should be fully supported and handled with care as cracks and weak areas may not be immediately apparent. Large and heavy items may be much weaker than they appear and may be difficult and dangerous to lift without proper equipment and experience. Protective padding (for example foamed plastic sheet) may be necessary when lifting or carrying an awkward-shaped object as may a purpose-built container for transport.

Stone after long-term storage or display
The surface of stone artefacts may be dirty and flaking and such objects should be touched as little as possible (*Figure 27.11*). They should be examined for signs of water-soluble salts, moulds and for traces of paint, gilding and so on. A small soft brush (for example squirrel or sable hair water-colour brush) and a magnifying glass (×10 magnification) can be

useful when examining the surface, but great care must be taken not to dislodge flakes of paint or stone (*Figure 27.12*).

General cleaning should be avoided, particularly if paint or other decoration is visible or if the surface is deteriorating. Stone artefacts should not be wetted or washed. It is particularly important not to wet trans-

Figure 27.11 Dust and dirt on a stone object, which may conceal both traces of paint and a very fragile surface (Courtesy of Institute of Archaeology, University of London)

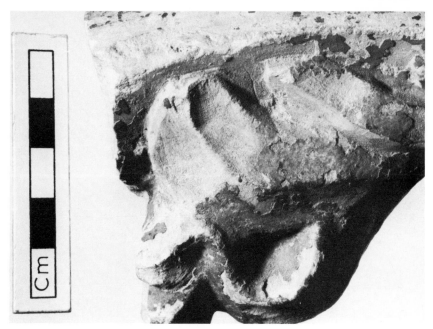

Figure 27.12 Traces of paint on stone, which may be removed all too easily by injudicious handling or treatment (Courtesy of Institute of Archaeology, University of London)

lucent stone as this may be alabaster and slightly water-soluble.

Objects which are displayed in the open gallery, such as statuary, will inevitably become dusty. The best solution is to filter the dust and dirt particles from the museum atmosphere. Where this is not possible, routine cleaning should be carefully controlled. Objects should *not* be rubbed over with cloth dusters (these may drive dirt into the surface of the stone) but gently brushed with a *clean*, very soft brush (the dust being collected with a vacuum cleaner). Where objects are on open display, the conservator's advice should be sought over the suitability of cleaning methods and improvement of display arrangements.

Occasionally, archaeological stonework is displayed in the open air. Moisture and pollutant gases in the atmosphere may cause the formation of a dirty and damaging crust on the surface of the stone, which may come away in flakes or sheets causing much loss of detail. Iron dowels inserted as part of a repair can corrode in these conditions and cause stains and disruption of the stonework. Deterioration will continue unless the objects are removed, fully conserved and housed indoors.

Recently excavated stone
Such stone should be examined carefully for signs of deterioration and for traces of decoration. Shale,

which is normally recognized by its dark colour, fine grain and highly laminated structure, may need special treatment particularly if it comes from a waterlogged site. If it is allowed to dry out the laminae will separate and the object disintegrate (*Figure 27.13*). It must be packed and kept wet until it is conserved.

Storage of stone
Stonework showing no signs of deterioration can be housed in the standard store. It should be covered with light cloth rather than Polythene, or packed in boxes, to exclude dust. Material suffering from the presence of water-soluble salts should be conserved as soon as possible and, in the mean time, housed at a constant level of relative humidity. Wet or waterlogged material should be given special provision in the sensitive store.

Porous materials: painted wall-plaster

This usually consists of lime plaster with a painted surface. It is porous and suffers from problems similar to those of porous ceramics and stone. The paint surface may be relatively strong (in some cases of true *fresco*) or very fragile (where *tempera* has been used). Any unevenness in the surface such as isolated areas of thickly applied pigment may be very vulnerable and liable to flake (*Figure 27.14*).

Figure 27.13 Shale from a waterlogged site, which has
been allowed to dry out causing separation of the laminae
(Courtesy of Institute of Archaeology, University of
London)

Figure 27.14 Two fragments of wall-plaster showing the
fragile painted surface and vulnerable break-edges
(Courtesy of Institute of Archaeology, University of
London)

Handling of Wallplaster

Plaster should always be fully supported when being moved. Suitably-sized padded trays should be used and individual fragments handled as little as possible. Where several fragments are stored together they should be packed so as to prevent shifting or touching.

Wallplaster after long-term storage or display

Material which has been stored or displayed for some years may be adversely affected by water-soluble salts, by early attempts at consolidating the paint layer, by accumulated dirt and by methods of support and display now considered unsuitable. In such cases the painted surface may be very delicate and should not be touched. No attempt should be made to clean untreated, excavated fragments which have been stored for some time; the obscuring dirt may be more firmly attached to the paint than the paint to the plaster and cleaning may simply remove the paint layer. All such material should have specialist conservation treatment.

Recently excavated wallplaster

Freshly excavated fragments which have been packed and brought into the museum damp should be kept damp, because once the surface dries, the adhering soil and dirt may become very difficult to remove. Large sections of plaster which have been removed from a standing wall by means of adhesive and cloth facing should be stored only for a short time in case the adhesive becomes difficult to remove. Both types of recently excavated wallplaster should be conserved as soon as possible.

Storage of wallplaster

Controlled storage is the best care much of this material can be given while awaiting conservation. In general, the same conditions of storage apply as for stone. Freshly excavated plaster which has been deliberately packed damp can be stored only temporarily; it should be inspected regularly and sent for conservation treatment as soon as possible.

Porous materials: mosaics

Mosaics normally consist of predominantly porous tesserae such as stone, ceramic, and occasionally glass set in lime mortar. The mortar may deteriorate and the tesserae become loose; the surface may be dirty and affected by water-soluble salts or by earlier treatment. Sometimes however, the problem is of a different kind. A complete mosaic may have been excavated in the past and placed on the floor or wall of a public building. Such mosaics were often set in concrete which makes them very difficult to reposition or remove.

Mosaics after long-term storage or display

Small mosaics and fragments should be handled, examined and stored in a similar manner to wallplaster or stone. Large areas of mosaic, or complete floors, need specialist advice and treatment. They should not be washed or wetted unnecessarily for example to 'bring up' the colours for photography, and they should be carefully examined for damage which might be caused by water-soluble salts and damp coming through the floor or through the wall. They should also be examined for other signs of deterioration such as the corrosion of iron rods or bolts which may have been inserted when the mosaics were placed in position.

Recently excavated mosaics

Fragments of mosaic recently removed from a site with the use of adhesive and cloth facing should be fully conserved as soon as possible. Although the mosaic is unlikely to be as fragile as painted wallpaper it is advisable not to leave a temporary adhesive on the surface for longer than is absolutely necessary. Ideally, no large area of mosaic floor should be stored for any length of time before treatment. If the decision is taken to lift such a floor from a site, a team of experienced conservators or a specialist firm should be called in and provision should be made for immediate and complete conservation.

Indications of active deterioration on porous materials

When any signs of the presence of water-soluble salts or of flaking and loss of surface are found, the conservator's advice should be sought.

Glass

Depending on the way they were made, some types of glass are more stable than others. The less stable glasses may simply not have survived the effects of burial or occasionally may be discovered in an extremely deteriorated and fragile state. Some Roman glass is in very good condition, much Medieval glass less so. For a discussion of the problems of more recent glass see the chapter by Horie.

Handling of glass

Much archaeological glass consists of small fragments which should be handled with care both because they are fragile and because of their sharp edges. In many cases sherds and vessels are extremely thin. They may also have flaking and vulnerable sufaces which should, as far as possible, not be touched or disturbed. Glass vessels should be handled by cradling them carefully with both hands and carrying them in padded trays or boxes. As it is very difficult to make durable repairs in glass (many adhesives are not effective), all objects which may have been repaired or gap-filled should be handled with particular care.

Glass after long-term storage or display

Glass which has been in a museum for some time may show varying degrees of surface deterioration. There may be a slight iridescence or a series of iridescent skins (*Figure 27.15*), or a thick opaque crust which may be whitish (*Figure 27.16*) or discoloured (often dark). There may be remains of a thick crust which has flaked off in places revealing a pitted glass surface beneath. In all cases, deterioration may continue. Moisture is the chief cause of changes in glass but heat or extreme dryness can also be damaging. When a deteriorated surface dries out it can craze, become opaque and flake off, thus damaging the glass and changing its appearance considerably.

Decorated glass should be handled with great care. The decorative paints or enamels may be thick and can flake easily and gilding can be easily abraded.

Crusts and iridescent flakes must not be cleaned off (*Figure 27.17*) and none of this material should be washed. It should be kept away from direct heat, preferably at a constant relative humidity of 45–55 per cent. Conditions in the sensitive stone (50–60 per cent RH) may be adequate, but the conservator's advice should be sought.

Adhesives and gap-filling materials may not only fail but often become yellow and discoloured through exposure to light. Although some modern adhesives and fillers appear to be more resistant than earlier ones it may be worth using a filter to exclude ultra-violet light when displaying a collection of recently restored glass objects.

Display of glass

When displaying glass, all forms of heat (including lights) should be carefully screened or controlled; the use of filters to exclude ultra-violet light may prolong the life of adhesives and gap-filling materials. For further discussion of conditions suitable for glass see the chapter by Horie.

Recently excavated glass

One of the main difficulties with recently excavated glass is that the exposure to a new environment can cause rapid and irreversible changes to take place (the deteriorated surface can dry out quickly, the crust may fall off or adhering soil may become impossible to remove). Methods of packing and storage should be designed to prevent – or minimize – these changes until conservation takes place.

Storage of damp or wet glass

It is difficult to prevent changes taking place under damp conditions. Leaching of materials from the glass may make the storage conditions increasingly

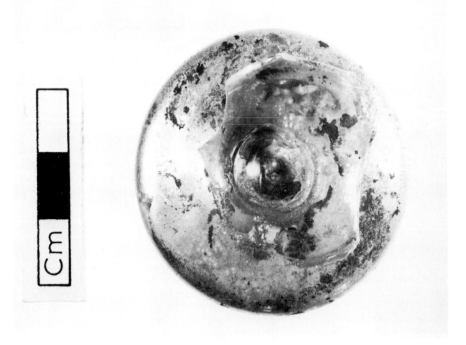

Figure 27.15 The base of a glass vessel with an iridescent surface. When handled thin iridescent flakes 'float' off the surface (Courtesy of Institute of Archaeology, University of London)

Figure 27.16 A fragment of dark-coloured glass showing patches of opaque whitish crust on the surface. A thick crust of this type may obscure the surface and colour of the glass totally (Courtesy of Institute of Archaeology, University of London)

Figure 27.17 Removal of the crust from this glass would result in loss of the original smooth surface and would reveal an unsightly pitting (already visible in the damaged areas on the right; (Courtesy of Institute of Archaeology, University of London)

alkaline, and this can be very damaging. Mould may grow on packing materials, and many biocides may be unsuitable because they are alkaline. Refrigeration slows the rate of chemical change and prevents mould growth. This can be a useful storage method but is not often feasible on a large scale. Hence, freshly excavated, damp glass should be stored *temporarily* in cool, dark conditions and conserved as soon as possible. It should not be unpacked for examination although, if necessary, the packaging can be checked to make sure it is still damp.

Storage of dry glass

Dry glass objects should be stored in boxes with shaped supportive padding. Sherds may be packed in horizontal layers between sheets of foamed plastic or pads of acid-free tissue paper. Normally, all glass may be housed in the sensitive store but all decisions about storage (and display) conditions should be taken with the advice of the conservator.

Indications of active deterioration on archaeological glass

Flaking, or shredding of the surface (often seen as very fine iridescent skins 'floating off') or a change from a glassy to a more or less opaque appearance indicate that the glass is fragile and highly deteriorated. It should not be handled, and immediate conservation should be arranged. Damp or wet glass which has been allowed to dry out in storage should also be sent for immediate treatment.

Metals

The condition of archaeological metal artefacts

A number of metals were used in antiquity, both pure and as alloys. Some were applied to others as a coating or decoration and many objects were made of combined metal and non-metal. Many metals are considerably changed by burial and corrode rapidly on excavation. The colour and texture of corrosion products may obscure both the nature of the metal and the shape of the artefact. In certain conditions such as waterlogging, metals may appear almost unaffected.

Non-metallic materials – such as enamel, niello (a black sulphide), glass (*millefiori*) and gemstones – were used to decorate metals. Some of these may be highly deteriorated. Enamel often remains only as a discoloured granular substance. They may be covered by the corrosion products of the metal.

Any organic feature such as a wooden handle, may have deteriorated completely. In some cases evidence of the feature or of associated material may remain as small traces, wholly or partly replaced by metal salts in the corrosion products of the metal (*Figure 27.18*). Such fragments of textile, compact or fibrous layers of leather, and slivers of wood are sometimes clearly recognizable. Often, however, this type of evidence is not detected or is lost if corroded objects are mishandled.

Figure 27.18 Traces of wood preserved in association with iron. The direction of the grain of the wood is clearly visible; the species may also be identified from traces of this kind. Injudicious cleaning could therefore result in considerable loss of evidence (Courtesy of Institute of Archaeology, University of London)

No attempt should be made to clean archaeological metal artefacts, however robust they may appear. Removal of corrosion products by picking or abrasion, polishing of any metal (particularly silver or gold), can be extremely damaging and will result in loss of evidence.

Details are given below of the main types of metal found in archaeological contexts and of how they appear when they are excavated. For a discussion of other metals, see the chapter by Horie.

Gold

If relatively pure, gold may appear to be in more or less perfect condition, but in this form it is fairly soft and the surface may be easily damaged. In some cases, what looks like a gold artefact is in fact gilded; the underlying metal may be very fragile and such objects should be handled with great care. Gold may be alloyed with other metals such as silver or copper in which case the corrosion products of the alloying metal may be visible. It may also be decorated, for example, with enamels or gemstones.

Silver

Silver may be fairly pure or alloyed with other metals, notably copper. It can be covered with black or mauve corrosion products or completely obscured by the green corrosion products of copper. It can be extremely fragile and the slightest pressure may cause it to crack or break. Silver can be decorated. It can be used as a thin decorative coating (for example, on copper alloys), or an inlay (for example, on iron).

Copper and its alloys

Copper is often alloyed with other metals, particularly tin to form bronze, and zinc to form brass. It is usually covered with green corrosion products which may be either compact (*Figure 27.19*) or powdery (*Figure 27.20*) and can incorporate soil particles (*Figure 27.21*). Bright green spots of 'bronze disease' may be apparent. It may be very fragile and cracks and fissures may not be immediately visible.

Objects should be examined carefully for traces of decoration. Small amounts of organic materials may be preserved in contact with copper alloys (*Figure 27.22*). These may be largely unchanged, being protected against micro-organisms by the copper, or the physical structure may be replaced and preserved by copper salts (*Figure 27.23*).

Iron

Iron objects may be covered with dark- or rust-coloured corrosion products which are often massive and incorporate soil, stones and other debris (*Figures 27.24* and *27.25*). The shape of the artefacts may be completely concealed as may other features such as pattern-welding, inlay, or associated organic materials such as bone handles, traces of wood, skin, or

Figure 27.19 Compact and stable corrosion products on a copper alloy object (Courtesy of Institute of Archaeology, University of London)

Figure 27.20 Active corrosion on a copper alloy, indicated by loose, powdery (bright green) products (Courtesy of Institute of Archaeology, University of London)

Figure 27.21 Patch of bright green powdery active 'bronze disease' on a copper alloy object. Such patches may vary in size and number, sometimes a 'rash' of small bright green spots may be seen (Courtesy of Institute of Archaeology, University of London)

Figure 27.22 The gilding on the brooch on the left is almost totally obscured by copper corrosion products. The brooch on the right was in similar condition before treatment (Courtesy of Institute of Archaeology, University of London)

Figure 27.23 Traces of textile preserved in association with a copper alloy object (Courtesy of Institute of Archaeology, University of London)

Figure 27.24 An iron shield boss covered in massive corrosion products incorporating soil (Courtesy of Institute of Archaeology, University of London)

textiles which may have been completely replaced by iron salts (*see Figures 27.18* and *27.30*). Iron may be very fragile, cracked and laminated and very often little actual metal remains, the shape being retained in the corrosion products. Visual examination provides only minimal information and the use of X-radiography is essential (*see Figure 27.1*).

Lead and its alloys

Lead may be used in more or less pure form or alloyed with tin to form pewter. It may be recognized by its considerable weight and its whitish or grey corrosion products (*Figure 27.26*). When heavily corroded, it may be cracked and very fragile. When apparently little-corroded, the surface may be

Figure 27.25 An iron object completely obscured by corrosion incorporating stones and other debris (Courtesy of Institute of Archaeology, University of London)

Figure 27.26 Lead alloy showing typical pitting and whitish corrosion products (Courtesy of Institute of Archaeology, University of London)

easily scratched and objects made of sheet lead may deform under their own weight.

General handling of metals
It is as well to assume that all archaeological metal work is fragile and that it needs particular care in handling. Moisture and salts may be introduced from the hands if the objects are touched. Clumsy handling, such as dropping or banging, may result in physical damage and renewed corrosion. As far as possible, important objects should be examined and handled in purpose-built containers.

Metals after long-term storage or display
Treatments, both past and recent, may have removed or inactivated potentially damaging corrosion products on archaeological metalwork. Some material may have been stripped of all corrosion. Copper alloys may appear coppery or brassy and may show pitted surfaces where the corrosion has

been removed (*Figure 27.27*); ironwork may appear thin, pitted and even 'lacy'. More recent treatments have aimed at conserving the corrosion products where they have preserved the shape or form of the object or have been otherwise informative. In this case, copper alloys may retain a greenish surface and iron may retain a layer of dark or brownish corrosion over the remains of the metal. On most objects, protective layers of wax or lacquer have been applied to the surface after treatment in order to exclude moisture. These may have collected dust or have been injudiciously applied in thick layers or with an incorporated tint.

The most important consideration when caring for such metalwork is to examine it for any signs of change which may indicate that active deterioration is taking place. However carefully the original treatment was undertaken, it may not have successfully removed or inactivated all harmful products. In addition, the protective coating or lacquer may have deteriorated or been scratched or punctured, thus allowing moisture and pollutants to reach the metal.

The effects of the museum environment on metals

Moisture
Different factors can be responsible for renewed corrosion of archaeological metalwork. In many cases, moisture reacts with the corrosion products formed during burial to cause further damaging changes. In general, therefore, if metal objects are kept in dry conditions (below 40 per cent relative humidity) deterioration will at least be slowed down.

A sudden and widespread outbreak of corrosion (for example, 'bronze disease') may indicate an unexpected, and possibly undetected, change in the normal climate of the museum or store. Lowering the central heating temperature as an economy measure may have unforseen effects on the climate and thus on metal objects.

Pollutants
Some metals should be protected from pollutants. Tarnishing on silver is caused by hydrogen sulphide, sulphur dioxide and other sulphur-containing compounds which occur in some textiles, paints, and rubber products. Corrosion on lead is caused by organic acids which may be given off by adhesives, woods, papers and cardboards. The advice of a conservator should be sought over the suitability of storage or display materials. Tests may be necessary before deciding which materials can be safely used.

Physical damage
Archaeological metal should be protected from physical damage. Well-designed and supportive packing methods provide good protection during

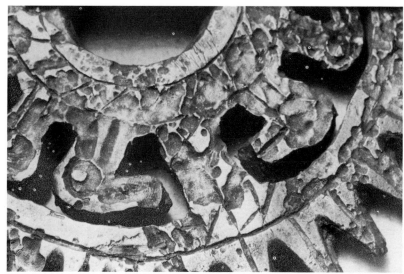

Figure 27.27 The shiny pitted surface which may result from the complete removal of the corrosion products from a copper alloy object (approximately ×2 (reduced by ⅘ in reproduction); (Courtesy of Institute of Archaeology, University of London)

storage. Soft metals (for example, gold and lead), brittle metals (for example, corroded silver) and generally fragile objects should be fully supported during display. Stresses caused by support at one or two points only can be very damaging. Metal items such as wire and nails should not be used in display. In contact with a metal antiquity, they may corrode readily themselves or cause local corrosion on the object.

Storage
Metal objects should be packed individually and stored in the sensitive store. In most instances silica gel should be used to maintain the relative humidity in the package to below 40 per cent. Where suitable, several small boxes containing artefacts of the same metal or alloy may be packed inside one large box.

Storage conditions for recently excavated metals

Recently excavated metals should be conserved as soon as possible. They must be stored carefully while awaiting treatment and in most cases they will need individually controlled conditions.

Gold, gilded objects, silver, copper alloys
These should be packed individually in polystyrene boxes grouped in larger Polythene boxes and stored in the sensitive store at a relative humidity of below 40 per cent. The material should be inspected regularly to make sure that conditions are properly maintained and to check the state of the artefacts. Copper alloy objects with decorative enamels or evidence of organic materials in their corrosion products should be kept damp and sent for immediate conservation.

Lead and its alloys
These should be stored in similar conditions but all sources of organic acids, such as cardboard, must be avoided.

Iron
Iron is more difficult to deal with. Such large quantities may be found that only a proportion can be conserved fully and the selection of artefacts for treatment must depend on thorough X-radiographic examination. Both before and after examination, iron objects need to be stored in conditions which as far as possible prevent further deterioration. They should be dried thoroughly and thereafter kept very dry (below 15 per cent RH) by storing in well-sealed Polythene containers with silica gel. The storage conditions should be monitored to make sure that the low relative humidity is maintained. Conservation of important artefacts should be undertaken as soon as possible (Appendix 27.2).

Metal with associated organics
Particular care should be taken of any metal object with an organic feature attached, or with evidence of organic remains preserved in its corrosion products. Such objects should be sent for immediate conservation.

Indications of active corrosion on archaeological metals (treated and untreated)

A powdery, loose or voluminous corrosion (which may appear in isolated spots), is likely to indicate that undesirable changes are taking place.

Gold
If it is alloyed with copper, the appearance of cracks or green copper corrosion products may indicate active corrosion. If it is alloyed or decorated with silver, a purple-brown staining is an indication of active corrosion. Gilded objects may show signs that the gilding is becoming detached due to active corrosion of the underlying metal.

Silver
On relatively pure silver, rapid tarnishing (producing a blackish or brownish colour) is particularly damaging. When alloyed with copper, spots of green corrosion products may appear and such alloys may become brittle.

Copper and its alloys.
Spots of bright green powdery corrosion indicate the presence of active and highly damaging 'bronze disease' (*Figure 27.28*; *see also Figure 27.21*). Black, mildew-like spots should also be reported to the conservator as they may indicate another form of active corrosion.

Iron
Patches or spots of bright rust-coloured products which may sometimes be seen as dampish 'pustules' indicate the changes sometimes referred to as 'weeping iron' (*Figure 27.29*). Cracks and laminae are also found in corroded archaeological iron.

Figure 27.28 A bright green patch of powdery 'bronze disease' showing clearly on a corroded copper alloy (Courtesy of Institute of Archaeology, University of London)

Figure 27.29 Damp rusty coloured 'pustules' typical of 'weeping iron' (approximately ×5; (Courtesy of Institute of Archaeology, University of London)

Lead
A whitish powdery deposit may indicate active corrosion.

Organic materials

The condition of archaeological organic materials
Most organic materials used in antiquity do not survive in the archaeological record. As they are particularly susceptible to deterioration during burial reasonably complete artefacts will be found only in areas or 'pockets' (microenvironments) where conditions for preservation are exceptional, as for example where conditions are extremely dry or where oxygen has been excluded by waterlogging.

On some sites, evidence or organic materials may be preserved only as small traces in the corrosion products of metal artefacts. In this case the substance is often wholly or partly replaced by the metal salts and is no longer really organic (*Figure 27.30*). Other organic materials survive because they contain appreciable amounts of inorganic material such as bone, or shell, or because they are resistant to biodeterioration, as is the case with amber and jet. Organic materials also survive in forms which hitherto may have been undetected, such as ancient organic adhesives or coatings on objects.

There are two main problems in caring for archaeological organic materials. Although the form of an artefact may have been almost perfectly preserved, the material will have lost the greater part of its mechanical strength and, on excavation, is likely to deteriorate more quickly than almost any other substance. Secondly, traces of organic materials on artefacts may not be recognized and may therefore fail to be recorded or sent for immediate conservation.

Figure 27.30 Traces of textile preserved in the corrosion products of an iron object. Although the form of the textile has been replaced by iron salts and no organic substance remains, extremely valuable evidence of this type of fibre and textile is retained (Courtesy of Institute of Archaeology, University of London)

Organic materials after long-term storage and display (dry organics)

Most of the archaeological organic material housed in museums is now in a dry state irrespective of the way it was originally preserved, and is likely to have lost much of its original strength. Artefacts from dry sites may be desiccated and consequently fragile. Previously wet objects which have been allowed to dry out are likely to be shrunken, brittle and distorted. Both these types will need care in handling and may need complete physical support before they can be safely lifted or carried.

Conserved objects from wet sites may display some of their normal characteristics, such as flexiblity in leather. However, most conservation treatments stabilize the object rather than increase its strength, so this material should also be handled carefully. Where treatments have failed the material is likely to be particularly fragile.

The effects of the museum environment on dry organics

Relative humidity

Deterioration may continue in the museum, particularly if the environment fluctuates. All organic materials contain moisture and during use and even after some deterioration they continue to take up and lose moisture in response to humidity changes. This leads to changes in dimension and so to stresses causing physical damage which is often seen as distortion and cracking. Repeated environmental changes are particularly damaging. It follows that one of the most important factors in the care of these materials is the maintenance of a constant level of relative humidity (45–60 per cent, preferably 50–60 per cent). Too low an RH may lead to further desiccation, too high an RH (above 68 per cent) can lead to mould and fungal growth.

Light

Light, particularly ultra-violet light, is very damaging to many organic substances and can cause considerable chemical breakdown. Although the effects on already very degraded and discoloured material may not be apparent, all organic materials should be protected from ultra-violet light. Moreover, textiles should be displayed at a suitably low light level, even where there is little remaining visible evidence of the use of dyes.

Insects, fungi, micro-organisms

In favourable conditions, insect and fungal pests may attack these materials. Insect frass or flight holes, whitish patches of mould, and strands (fungal hyphae) are danger signs. These are usually seen where the RH is above 68 per cent and conditions are somewhat dirty and poorly ventilated. Careful examination will be needed to establish whether the infestation is active or not. Whatever measures are taken by the conservator, improving the climate, the ventilation and the general cleanliness of the storage or display area will greatly decrease the chances of reinfestation. Specialist advice should be sought when dealing with an infestation of any size, particularly if it is affecting the structure of the building and furnishings as well as the artefacts.

Dust and dirt

Dust and dirt can be unsightly and can encourage further deterioration such as mould growth. Particles may adhere to consolidants on treated objects such as leather, and may become enmeshed in textile fibres where they can be particularly damaging. Repeated cleaning of dirty objects can in itself be harmful.

General care of dry organics

General care, therefore should include monitoring of the climate and where necessary, improvement of the conditions. It should also include careful and regular examination.

Storage of dry organics

Most dry organic materials should be stored in the sensitive store, a relative humidity of between 50 and 60 per cent being particularly suitable. They should be packed individually using acid-free tissue paper as padding. This will act as a buffer against slight humidity fluctuations. Some materials may need individually controlled packaging.

Care of individual dry organic materials

Wood

Wood from dry sites may be extremely desiccated, pale in colour and light in weight. Cracks may run along the grain but their presence across the grain, as also seen in charred wood, is a particular sign of weakness (*Figure 27.31*). Painted or decorated sur-

Figure 27.32 Pieces of treated waterlogged wood showing cracks and breaks typical of the brittle nature of such material (Courtesy of Institute of Archaeology, University of London)

Figure 27.31 Cracks across the grain of a piece of wood, indicating considerable deterioration and loss of strength (Courtesy of Institute of Archaeology, University of London)

faces may be flaking, powdery and dirty. They may have been treated at some earlier date with a coating which has subsequently become brittle or yellow. Some varnishes, such as those on Egyptian mummy cases, may be original and care must be taken to distinguish the 'old' from the 'new' before deciding on conservation treatment. Occasionally, dry material is consolidated at the time of excavation and may show the presence of, for example, paraffin wax.

Previously wet wood which has simply dried out is likely to be distorted and shrivelled severely with pronounced cracks or breaks across the grain. Depending on the original state of the timber, it may be relatively tough or extremely fragile. Treated waterlogged wood may appear substantial but is either light and fragile, or heavier but lacking in resilience (*Figure 27.32*). The surface, including valuable evidence such as tool-marks, may be readily damaged and is sometimes clogged with absorbed dirt which cannot be simply or safely removed.

The effect of fluctuating relative humidity may be particularly serious on wood since the resulting changes in dimensions are greater across the grain than along it (wood is anisotropic). Considerable warping, or cracking parallel to the grain can result; the effects can be worse in an artefact made of more than one piece of timber since the stresses set up will almost certainly run in different directions.

Danger signs are sudden warping, fresh cracks, insect or fungal attack, and surface deterioration such as paint flaking.

Bone, antler and ivory

Bone, antler and ivory are more widely preserved than other organic materials on archaeological sites. Excavated material may include human and animal skeletal remains as well as artefacts or parts of artefacts which may have been stained, painted or gilded and should be carefully examined for evidence of such decoration. It may be discoloured, desiccated, 'chalky' (*Figure 27.33*) and fragile or splitting as a result of drying out from a damp or wet state (*Figure 27.34*). Where attached to metal (particularly iron) it may be damaged by the disruptive action of the corroding metal. In cases where, for example, an object has been consolidated in the field, the consolidant may have failed to restrain subsequent warping and cracking as the material has dried slowly. Consolidants suitable for use on damp material may work well initially but may deteriorate or change with age. These materials are anisotropic and sensitive to changes in relative humidity; deterioration is often seen in the form of splits along the length of the bone or antler.

Ivory is particularly sensitive but it has a different physical structure and deterioration takes the form of splitting and lamination following the original circumference of the tusk (rather like onion rings; *Figure 27.35*). Even when highly degraded (or even fossilized) it can react in this way. Storage conditions for ivory should be particularly carefully controlled. Silica gel should be used to maintain a constant relative humidity of between 50 and 55 cent, together with acid-free tissue padding to minimize any fluctuations in RH. The main danger signs are fresh cracking or lamination and flaking of the surface.

Skin and leather

Skin and leather from dry contexts are often crumpled, shrunken and extremely brittle (*Figure 27.36*).

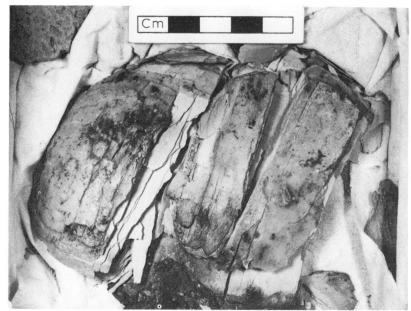

Figure 27.33 Highly deteriorated and 'chalky' ivory (Courtesy of Institute of Archaeology, University of London)

Figure 27.34 Splitting and flaking resulting from allowing a waterlogged bone to dry out (Courtesy of Institute of Archaeology, University of London)

They may show traces of decoration, such as paint. Fragments from a wet site may be dark, cracked and very hard or brittle (*Figure 27.35*). All such material will need careful handling and no attempt should be made to unroll or flatten artefacts in this state as they may crumble or shatter. Treated waterlogged material is usually dark in colour and should retain some flexibility. In some cases however the dressings or consolidants used may be 'sweating' or leaching out of the leather making the surface sticky and attractive

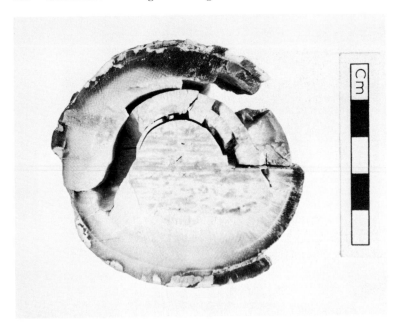

Figure 27.35 Concentric splitting typical of deteriorating ivory (Courtesy of Institute of Archaeology, University of London)

Figure 27.36 Cracking typical of leather weakened either by desiccation or by allowing it to dry out from a waterlogged state (Courtesy of Institute of Archaeology, University of London)

Figure 27.37 Leather from a waterlogged site; uncontrolled drying has resulted in distortion and rigidity (Courtesy of Institute of Archaeology, University of London)

to dust. Occasionally, the treatment has failed to stabilize the leather which may be becoming hard and cracked. Increased brittleness and the appearance of cracks, and patches of mould-growth (*Figure 27.38*) are signs are further deterioration.

Textiles
Archaeological textiles may vary from complete garments found on dry sites with their original colour well-preserved, to small, highly discoloured scraps from waterlogged sites. They may be folded crum-pled and brittle. No attempt should be made to unfold or spread them out, or to wash them; when wetted, degraded textiles of this kind can disintegrate.

Conserved textiles which have been provided with a backing should nevertheless be considered very fragile, and should be fully supported in storage or on display by, for example, lying flat or on a slightly sloping flat support. Garments should be padded out with acid-free tissue paper during storage to avoid folds and should be given the support of a purpose-made dummy figure for display.

Figure 27.38 White spots and patches on treated leather, indicative of mould growth (Courtesy of Institute of Archaeology, University of London)

Fluctuating relative humidity may be very damaging, causing the textile fibres to expand and contract. Dirt present in the textile may act as an abrasive when the fibres expand and contract against each other. At points of stress such as folds, the textile may be weakened considerably. They should be displayed and stored in dust-free conditions.

Light may be particularly damaging to textiles, especially cotton and linen, and to vegetable dyes. It is therefore necessary to exclude ultra-violet light and to display textiles at a low light level.

Powdering of fibres or breaking of threads during gentle handling indicates that the textile is in a very fragile state (*Figure 27.39*). Whitish patches or dark spots on the surface may indicate mould growth.

Recently excavated organic materials
Recently excavated organic material is likely to fall into two main categories: bone and antler, both of which may survive in several types of burial environment, and waterlogged organics. In many cases, unworked damp bone (and antler) can be allowed to dry slowly and be dealt with as dry material. Such material can be housed in the standard store. (Traces of organics preserved in the corrosion products of metals are considered under metals).

Waterlogged organic material

Although apparently well-preserved, waterlogged artefacts are often degraded considerably. They may be stained heavily, swollen, and soft or spongy in texture. The degraded structure is filled with water and if the water is allowed to evaporate the structure will collapse irreversibly. It is therefore extremely important to keep such material wet (*Figures 27.40 and 27.41 (a)-(c)*).

Waterlogged materials need special storage conditions and prompt conservation treatment. It is difficult to provide adequate facilities for large objects such as timbers. After consultation with all concerned, it may be better to record and sample them rather than lift and conserve them.

General care of waterlogged material
All waterlogged material must be kept thoroughly wet when being examined or photographed (photographic lights can cause considerable drying). A fine garden spray can be very useful. Once exposed to oxygen, micro-organisms may grow readily on the material and storage conditions should be designed to minimize this growth. Waterlogged objects should be handled carefully. Washing should not be undertaken without the advice of a conservator; the use of anything but the softest tools or fingers can damage the surface. Leaving an object under running water may be harmful, and in some cases washing may remove valuable evidence.

Storage
Small quantities can be stored in part of the sensitive store provided the containers are well sealed. Large quantities should be provided with a separate storage area.

Figure 27.39 Fine powder (visible in the centre of this plate) produced by handling the highly degraded textile fibres (Courtesy of Institute of Archaeology, University of London)

Figure 27.40 Pieces of waterlogged wood being stored in water. Although fragile, the structure and surface detail are well-preserved (Courtesy of Institute of Archaeology, University of London)

Containers

Small objects may be firmly sealed inside Polythene bags filled with water and immersed, in groups, in larger sealed boxes full of water. Larger objects can be housed in individually sealed boxes. Very large objects should be stored in tanks which may have to be purpose-built, although containers such as plastic dustbins can be useful. Objects can be sealed in bags and suspended in a tank from a horizontal bar, with an identifying label attached to the suspending cord to avoid 'fishing around'.

Labels

A label should be placed inside each package, and another outside. Spun-bonded polyethylene (Polythene) labels are suitable, using ball-point pens or spirit-based markers. To label individual timbers stainless steel embossing tape can be attached directly to the timber with stainless steel pins or wire bent into a staple shape. These labels withstand the effects of later treatment, including heat. It is important that all metals used should be rust-proof.

Prevention of micro-biological growth

To minimize growth of aerobic micro-organisms, oxygen should be excluded as far as possible. This can be done in two ways. First, objects can be closely

a

b

c

Figure 27.41 (a) Part of a large piece of waterlogged timber which had dried out slowly in inadequate storage conditions. The apparently flat area presented to the viewer is in fact two sides of a split along the grain, which can be seen more clearly in (b) The short score-mark seen on the upper left has been made with a thumbnail in order to indicate the softness of the wood. (b) View of the end of the same piece of timber showing position and extent of the split. (c) The same piece of timber after allowing it to dry freely for a further two weeks. The resulting collapse and distortion are extensive.

wrapped in thin Polythene sheet, enclosed in heavier grade sheet and kept wet. Large timbers can be stored, at least temporarily, by wrapping in thin Polythene, then wrapping in thoroughly wet foamed-plastic sheet and sealing the whole in heavy-grade Polythene. Second, objects can be sealed in bags or boxes that are completely filled with water, leaving little or no space for air. Cool, dark storage conditions also help to prevent algal and some microbiological growth. Tanks should be opaque and may be covered with black Polythene sheet; stacks of sealed boxes may also be covered with black sheet, but arrangements should always allow for easy inspection. Refrigeration also prevents micro-organism growth but, in general, objects should not be frozen.

Biocides can be used as a preventive measure but if material is needed for, for example, C-14 dating they should be avoided. Panacide (dichlorophen) can be added to produce a concentration of 0.20 per cent in the storage water, but the conservator should be consulted about selection and use of biocides. Large quantities of storage water containing biocide should be disposed of in accordance with Health and Safety regulations.

Wood

Wood may be difficult to store because of its size. It may appear misleadingly robust, and particular care should be taken to support long thin timbers along their length. Care should also be taken not to damage the surface.

Bone and antler

From 'dry' or damp sites bone or antler may be allowed to dry out slowly while partially enclosed in Polythene bags or boxes. It may be advisable to dry a sample bone in order to assess how well the material withstands this treatment. If it appears not to stand it well, then the material should be stored damp. Waterlogged material should be stored as outlined above.

Ivory

Ivory should not be allowed to dry out, but should be stored damp with foamed-plastic support, and sent for immediate conservation.

Leather

When handling waterlogged leather, care must be taken not to damage the grain surface which provides evidence of the animal source. Prolonged washing should be avoided as it may remove tannins and the remains of dyes. Complete objects such as shoes and purses should not be washed or handled more than is absolutely necessary as the stitching is likely to be very fragile.

Unlike most other organic materials, it is possible to freeze leather artefacts during storage as the fibrous structure of leather is not damaged appreciably by the formation of ice crystals. Objects should be wrapped in two Polythene bags from which the air has been excluded and then placed in a freezer. It is preferable to avoid the use of biocides as they tend to be alkaline and damaging to leather.

Textiles

Textiles should be handled as little as possible and particular care should be taken where seams or stitching remain. They should not be washed as evidence of dyes may be removed. They can be stored wet or frozen but fungicides should not be used in case they affect traces of dyes.

Other organic material

Materials such as amber, or jet should be kept damp or wet depending on the condition in the ground and sent for conservation treatments as soon as possible.

Composite objects

It is particularly difficult to decide on suitable storage for composite objects. Where the object is predominantly metal, it should be dealt with as a metal, where predominantly wood, as wood, and so on. Where suitable freezing may be used, but all such objects should be given priority conservation treatment.

Indications of active deterioration of waterlogged organics

It is important to inspect all stored waterlogged material carefully for signs of micro-organism growth (usually indicated by a foul smell and the presence of slime) and of drying out.

Acknowledgements

This paper was prepared with the advice of members of the Archaeology Section of the United Kingdom Institute for Conservation, amongst whom I would like to thank Louise Bacon, Michael Corfield, Janey Cronyn, Kate Foley, Velson Horie, Susanne Keene, Barry Knight, Sonia O'Connor, Wendy Robinson and Sylvia Turner. I am particularly grateful for being able to draw on the recent work on storage undertaken by members of the Section.

I would also like to thank my colleagues Sandra Davison, Stuart Laidlaw, David Scott and Kathryn Tubb and, especially, Nicholas Balaam for very useful comment, and help in preparation of the text and illustrations.

Further reading

Archaeological conservation

KEENE, S. (1980) (Ed.) *Conservation, Archaeology and Museums,* United Kingdom Institute for Conservation Occasional Paper No. 1

Conservation in the Field

LEIGH, D. (1972), *First Aid for Finds,* Rescue Publication No. 1 (3rd edn 1981)) Rescue, Hertford

ROBINSON, W. S. (1981), *First Aid for Marine Finds,* Handbooks in Maritime Archaeology No. 2, 1981, London, National Maritime Museum

Examination and Evidence

CORFIELD, M. (1982), 'Radiography of archaeological ironwork' in Clarke, R. W. and Blackshaw, S. M. (Eds.), *Conservation of Iron,* Maritime Monographs and Reports No. 53, 8–14

CORFIELD, M. AND FOLEY, K. (1982) (Eds.), *Microscopy in Archaeological Conservation,* United Kingdom Institute for Conservation Occasional Paper No. 2

JANAWAY, R. (1983), Textile fibre characteristics preserved by metal corrosion: the potential of S.E.M. studies, *The Conservator,* **7**, 48–52

KEEPAX, C. (1975), Scanning electron microscopy of wood replaced by iron corrosion products, *Journal of Archaeological Science,* **2**, 145–150

Records

BRADLEY, S. (1983), Conservation recording in the British Museum, *The Conservator,* **7**, 9–12

CORFIELD, M. (1983), Conservation records in the Wiltshire Library and Museum Service, *The Conservator,* **7**, 5–8

KEENE, S. (1983), Conservation records – editorial introduction, *The Conservator,* **7**, 4

Storage

ARCHAEOLOGY SECTION, UK INSTITUTE FOR CONSERVATION (1982), *Excavated Artefacts for Publication: UK Sites.* Archaeological Artefacts, Conservation Guidelines No. 1; *The Packaging and Storage of Freshly Excavated Artefacts from Archaeological Sites in the UK,* Guidelines No. 2 (forthcoming); *The Packaging and Storage of Waterlogged Materials from Excavations,* Guidelines No. 3 (forthcoming)

KEENE, S. (1977), An approach to the sampling and storage of waterlogged timbers from excavations, *The Conservator,* **1**, 8–11

KNIGHT, B. (1982), 'Why do some iron objects break up in store?' in Clarke, R. W. and Blackshaw, S. M. (Eds.) *Conservation of Iron,* Maritime Monographs and Reports No. 53, 50–55

SPRIGGS, J. (1980), The recovery and storage of materials from waterlogged deposits at York, *The Conservator,* **4**, 19–24

WHITE, A. J. AND PARTINGTON-OMAR, A. (1981), (Eds.), *Archaeological Storage,* Society of Museum Archaeologists and Yorkshire and Humberside Federation of Museums and Art Galleries

Monitoring and Control of the Storage/Display Environment

BOFF, R., DANIELS, V. D. AND WARD, S. E. (November 1981), Humidial Corporation humidity indicating card 6203–BB: A note on its use, *Conservation News,* **16**, 11

RAMER, B. L. (1981), Stabilising relative humidity variation within display cases: the role of silica gel and case design, *ICOM Committee for Conservation, 6th Triennial Meeting, Ottawa,* 81/18/6

RAMER, B. (November 1981), The use of colour-change relative humidity indicator cards, *Conservation News,* **16**, 10

THOMSON, G. (1978), *The Museum Environment,* Butterworths, London

WEINTRAUB, S. (1981), Studies on the behaviour of RH within an exhibition case. Part 1 Measuring the effectiveness of sorbents for use in an enclosed showcase, *ICOM Committee for Conservation, 6th Triennial Meeting, Ottawa,* 81/18/6

Testing Materials for Use in Display

BLACKSHAW, S. M. AND DANIELS, V. D. (1979), The Testing of Materials for use in Storage and Display in Museums, *The Conservator,* **3**, 16–19

DANIELS, V. AND WARD S. (1982), A rapid test for the detection of substances which will tarnish silver, *Studies in Conservation,* **27**, 58–60

ODDY, W. A. (1973), An unsuspected danger in display, *Museum J.* **73**, 27–28

ODDY, W. A. (1975), 'The Corrosion of metals on display, in Leigh, D. *et al* (Eds.), *Conservation in Archaeology and the Applied Arts,* International Institute for Conservation (IIC) Stockholm Congress, 1975, 235–237

General Conservation Literature

Conservation News. (Newsletter of the UK Institute for Conservation).

The Conservator. (The Journal of the UK Institute for Conservation).

Studies in Conservation. (The Journal of the International Institute for Conservation).

Appendix 27.1 Suppliers of packaging materials

This is not an exhaustive list and many of these materials can be obtained from a number of sources. They can be bought in large quantities from the addresses below and many can be obtained in small quantities from Frank W. Joel (see section on labels).

Plastic boxes

Polystyrene boxes	Transatlantic Plastics, Garden Estate, Ventnor, Isle of Wight (0983 852241)
	Supreme Plastics Ltd, Supreme House, Vale Road, London N4 1QB (01 802 4202)
Polythene boxes	Stewart Plastics, Purley Way, Croydon, Surrey CR9 4HS (01 686 2231)

Polythene bags

Self-sealing bags	Transatlantic Plastics (see above) Supreme Plastics (see above)

Foamed plastic sheet

Foamed polyethyene (Polythene): Plastozote (NB only the *white* grade is suitable)	Bakelite Xylonite Ltd, Mitcham Road, Croydon, Surrey CR9 3AL (01 684 3622)
Ethylene vinyl acetate foam (white grade): Evazote	Bakelite Xylonite (see above)
Polyether foam (white grade)	Pentonville Rubber Company, 48–52 Pentonville Road, London N1 9NF (01-837 0283)
Expanded polystyrene	Local hardware stores

Acid Free tissue paper

	L. Gimbert (Paper) Ltd, Unit 39, Meadow Mills, Water Street, Stockport SK1 2BX
	Local Stationers

Labels

Spun bonded polyethylene labels: Tyvek	Frank W. Joel Ltd, Oldmedow Road, Hardwick Industrial Estate, Kings Lynn, Norfolk PE 30 4HH (0553 60851)

Rust-free nails/staples etc

	J. and H. Rosenheim Glenford Works, Quay Road, Rutherglen, Glasgow
	Ships chandlers

String

Terylene blind cord	Local department stores
Polypropylene string	Local hardware stores

Silica gel

	W. R. Grace Ltd, Northdale House,

Silica gel—*cont.*

North Circular Road,
Park Royal,
London NW10 7UH
(01 965 0611)

Joseph Crosfield and Sons Ltd,
Applied Silicas Division,
PO Box 26,
Warrington,
Lancs WA5 1AB
(0925 31211)

Relative Humidity Indicator Cards

Mineral Derivatives Ltd,
St Christopher House,
217 Wellington Road South,
Stockport, Cheshire
SK2 6NY
(061 480 0447)

F. W. Joel (see above)

Biocides

Panacide (dichlorophen)	BDH Chemicals Ltd, Broome Road, Poole BN12 4NN (0202 745520)
Orthophenyl phenol (2-hydroxy biphenyl)	Picreator Enterprises Ltd, 44 Park View Gardens, London NW4 2PN (01 202 8972)

Note As manufacturers change the nature or content of their products from time to time, it is advisable to check with the conservator before ordering any packaging materials particularly if large quantities are needed.

Appendix 27.2 The Storage of Recently Excavated Iron

The storage of excavated iron poses a serious problem in that the reactions of the remaining metal and of the overlying corrosion products are different.

The method of storage given in the text (drying out and keeping at below 15 per cent RH) is a compromise but is the best which can be suggested at the time of writing (1983). Other methods being tested include wet storage (in an alkaline solution which should inhibit corrosion).

The results of current research will be published in the conservation literature, and any new recommendations which can be made about the storage of iron will be as widely publicised as possible. In the meantime, no arrangements for the storage of iron should be made without consulting a conservator.

28

Conservation and storage: archival paper

P. Michael Bottomley

Introduction

This paper deals with paper documents that become archives, that is, non-current records selected for permanent preservation. It will concentrate on the environment and equipment needed to promote the physical survival of such records. It will not discuss the repair of damaged documents as this should be left to competent and qualified conservators. Custodians of records should concentrate on passive conservation by providing the proper conditions: active conservation should be carried out by professional archive conservators. Amateur conservators often damage documents by ill-considered practices and treatments. Custodians who lack professional conservation staff, and who have records in need of repair, should contact their local record office in the first instance; most are listed by the Royal Commission on Historical Manuscripts (1982).

The first part of this paper describes the environmental conditions considered good for paper, the second considers harmful agents and how they may be countered, while the third looks at the equipment that is necessary or useful.

The ideal climate: temperature

Bad atmospheric conditions have done more damage to records than any other agent. The temperature should be low because many documents, especially those of the nineteenth and twentieth centuries, are not chemically inert. They may look healthy when stored initially, but over the years they can waste away as the organic dyes in the ink slowly oxidize, and the fibres of paper gradually break down, attacked by atmospheric acid. Such changes, like all chemical reactions, are accelerated by heat, and it has

been suggested that every ten-degree Fahrenheit rise in temperature can halve the life of paper (Briggs, 1980). Therefore, paper is preserved by keeping it cold. However, three pitfalls need to be avoided. First, a cold repository may cause discomfort to staff. Second, archives may be damaged by moving them from a very cold strongroom to a warm reading room and back again, unless they are given plenty of time to adjust to the changes. Third, a fall in the strong-room temperature tends to cause a rise in relative humidity, and a high relative humidity causes mould. The ideal temperature is thus a compromise between the need to keep archives as cool as possible, and the need to avoid the problems associated with cold strongrooms. A temperature between 13–18°C is considered correct, and there should be no large or sudden fluctuations.

Relative humidity (RH)

The RH of a document storage area is even more crucial than its temperature. If the air is too dry, paper becomes brittle and leather bindings may crack. If the air is too moist, documents may be damaged by fungi or bacteria. Paper documents should be stored at an RH of between 50 and 65 per cent. If the archive includes parchment or vellum documents, the RH should be kept between 55 and 65 per cent, since those materials are less tolerant of dry air than is paper.

Paper documents are damaged even more by fluctuations in RH than by fluctuations in temperature, because the documents themselves contain moisture, and their moisture content varies according to how moist or dry is the surrounding air. Paper, being mostly cellulose, readily absorbs moisture, and expands in the process. As it dries out, it contracts. Variations in RH therefore impose strains on the structure of paper, and the level of RH should not be allowed to move up or down by more than five per cent. The air itself, however, should be encouraged to move, since moving air discourages mould, and creates a more even distribution of heat and moisture within a room. The recommended rate of air circulation is six changes of air every hour. In addition, the air should be clean, with the maximum possible exclusion of dust particles greater than 2 μm, and with no less than 50 μg/m^3 of sulphur dioxide.

The enemies of paper:
Incorrect temperature and humidity

Controlling the temperature of a repository is usually a simple matter, but the RH, which is more important, is more difficult both to monitor and to regulate. If the air is too dry, the cheapest way to raise the RH is usually to lower the temperature. However, this course of action may not be acceptable, especially if the same heating system warms the staff as well as the records. In such a case, a humidifier is needed to put moisture into the atmosphere.

If the air is too moist, ways of lowering the RH need to be considered. The simplest method may be to raise the temperature, since each rise of 1°C will lower the RH by about 4 per cent, but this in turn presents problems. Heating is expensive; raising the temperature can shorten the life of paper; and unless the heat is distributed evenly throughout the strongroom, introducing more heat will simply drive moisture away from the heat source to cooler parts of the room. Atmospheric moisture moves to the coldest parts of a room (often the windows), and a concentration of heat in one area produces a concentration of humidity elsewhere. Unevenness of humidity can be reduced by using fans to keep the air circulating, but this involves more expense. It is better to use a dehumidifier which extracts water from moist air without an unacceptable rise in temperature. It does not force moisture to cooler parts of a store, and it uses much less energy than do room heaters.

Windows in strongrooms present problems. They cause fluctuations in temperature and RH, with areas near windows becoming hot and dry, especially in summer, and cold and moist, especially in winter. If there have to be windows, they should be double- or triple-glazed.

Light

Records can be damaged by light. Direct sunlight is particularly harmful, but ordinary daylight and electric light are also bad. The obvious effect of too much exposure to light is the fading of ink, but light can also degrade the paper itself. Windows should, therefore, be blocked up or – as a second best – fitted with blinds. Ultra-violet filters should be fitted to fluorescent lights. If original documents are exhibited, this should be done in accordance with BS 5454. Ultra-violet lamps are often used to decipher faded documents. However, they should be used only when absolutely necessary, and then only for short periods.

Atmospheric pollution

Polluted air may be harder both to diagnose and to rectify than incorrect temperature and humidity. Dust is bad for records, but it does at least show itself on flat surfaces. Sulphur dioxide, on the other hand, is more insidious, and more dangerous to paper. Cheap modern paper, made with mechanically ground wood-pulp contains lignin which readily absorbs sulphur dioxide, which becomes acid. The acid attacks the fibres of the paper, which becomes brittle and eventually disintegrates. This kind of attack is most severe against nineteenth and twentieth century paper, but even earlier, high-quality paper is at risk (Hudson and Milner, 1961). The danger is not just confined to repositories in large cities: it has been shown that a small town with practically no industry has an atmosphere which attacks paper.

The atmosphere can be tested for sulphur dioxide with strips of paper (the preparation of which is described in the *Society of Archivists' Repairers' News Sheet,* **16** February 1970) or custodians may prefer simply to assume that the air is polluted. Their options include the installation of an air-conditioning system which washes out sulphur dioxide from incoming air; or, more simply, windows (if any) should be closed, and records should be wrapped in acid-free paper or packed in acid-free boxes, or both. Such wrappings and boxes will gradually absorb atmospheric acid, and to prevent them from transmitting acidity to their contents, they may need to be discarded before they have obviously worn out. Containers and records can be tested with a pH meter or, less accurately but more easily, with pH indicator strips. Ideally paper should have a pH between 7 and 8.5 (that is, it should be neutral or slightly alkaline, to counter future acid attack). If the pH reading is below 5.5 remedial action is required, and expert advice should be sought.

Microbes, insects and people

Several life forms pose a threat to archives. At the microscopic level, fungi and bacteria need to be controlled by keeping the RH below 65 per cent. Documents that have been attacked by micro-organisms, and are not fragile, can be carefully cleaned out of doors with a soft brush, preferably on a warm summer day, and then may be stored in the correct climate. If they are seriously damaged, an expert conservator should be called in.

Insects can be controlled by putting 5 per cent DDT powder in corners and crevices. If they infest papers, fumigation is necessary, using paradichlorobenzine or whatever the conservator advises.

People can be a greater menace than both microorganisms and insects, and staff and the public must be made to treat records with great care. Handling should be minimized. Records subject to constant use should be made available in the form of transcripts, photocopies or microfilm.

Flooding

To protect archives from water the repository should be on a well-drained site and, of course, the building must be weather-proof. Basements are common but potentially hazardous places in which to store records. They are liable to flooding from outside when, for instance, drains become blocked or the water-table rises. Also, water may run down to the basement if there is a leak elsewhere in the building, or when a fire is put out with water. Many basements have water pipes running through them, which can be a hazard.

Should a flood occur, custodians need a contingency plan to deal with documents soaked by water (Gibson and Reay, 1980). Loose papers can be spread out to dry naturally but books take too long to dry out in this way and the pages may grow mould or become a soggy pulp. If ovens or fan-heaters are used to accelerate the drying of books, the outsides become parched while the insides remain wet. The best solution appears to be vacuum or freeze drying: each book is wrapped and frozen. To remove moisture the books are put in a vacuum chamber together with a large dish of silica gel (to absorb moisture) and a small dish of thymol (to discourage mould). A vacuum of about 745 mm Hg is maintained until the books are dry (which takes between about 80 and over 200 hours, depending on size). When the dry books reach room temperature, repair can begin. Custodians should therefore be prepared to acquire plastic bags in a hurry, and to have rapid access to freezers, for example, by keeping up-to-date information on the nearest cold-storage company in a convenient place. Once the wet books are frozen they will not deteriorate further, and the rest of the procedure is less urgent.

Fire

To protect archives from fire, the repository should be separate from other buildings, and the floors, doors and ceilings should have at least four hours' fire-resistance. Fire officers and building departments will advise on fire precautions, electrical safety, flame-retardant paints and ceiling tiles. Common-sense will suggest policies such as no gas appliances and no smoking near records. There should be a fire-alarm system based on smoke detectors (which tend to react to fires sooner than heat detectors), and a direct link to the fire brigade (which should be advised in advance of the special needs of the repository so that, for example, water is not used unnecessarily). An automatic extinguisher system is worth considering, especially to protect strong-rooms, which firemen might not be able to enter quickly. Gas extinguishers cause less damage to records than water or foam, and halon gas appears increasingly to be preferred to carbon dioxide. Halon is less dangerous to people, and requires less storage space. Carbon dioxide, on the other hand, is said to deal more effectively with deep-seated fires. The repository should also be equipped with hand-operated carbon dioxide or powder extinguishers for small fires.

Inherent enemies

A further group of enemies of documents consists of poor ingredients in the documents themselves. Most modern records are created with built-in self-destructive devices such as alum size or lignin which promote acid attack, and ink made with organic dye that fades. This problem is not confined to twentieth-century records. For example, Victorian tracing paper was treated with oil which hardens and darkens, rendering many architectural and engineering drawings indecipherable, and volumes of damp-press copy letters consist of tissue paper bearing a thin trace of watery ink that in thousands of cases is fading towards invisibility. In addition, many records eventually suffer from rust caused by staples, pins and paper-clips. Such items should, of course, be removed and custodians should consider, with the help of expert advice, how to deal with the other forms of archival self-destruction, deciding which of such records should be saved by proper (and expensive) treatment, and which should be 'preserved' by copying on to a more permanent medium.

Accommodation and equipment

Premises

The building, as has been noted, should be separate from other buildings, on well-drained ground, and record strong-rooms are best built of reinforced concrete insulated on the inside to prevent condensation.

Windows are good for staff but bad for records, and, in archive strongrooms, should be eschewed.

Shelves

It is cheaper to shelve a few large rooms than to install the same amount of shelving in a number of small rooms. Also, it is cheaper to erect stacks of shelving four meters or more high in a single-storey building than to divide the same amount of shelving between the different floors of a building. Shelves are usually about one meter long, and if they are made deep enough from front to back they can hold twice as many boxes, by double-banking. Double-banking the boxes can save some capital outlay because only about half as many uprights are needed to support a given number of boxes. The main saving, however, is in space because fewer gangways are needed. It is a useful step towards the kind of high-density storage that mobile shelving achieves. Triple-banking of records has been suggested as a way of saving even more space, but in such an arrangement the boxes at the back of each shelf are virtually inaccessible.

Mobile shelving is limited to a height of about 2 to 3 meters. It is expensive compared with static shelves and it does not allow air to circulate as freely as in static shelving. Only one gangway in a stack can be opened at a time, which may slow down the production of records. Also, any records which project beyond the end of their shelf are liable to be crushed. On the other hand, mobile shelving can hold almost twice as many records as static shelving of the same height and floor area, and it gives better protection against fire, water and polluted air because, apart from a single open gangway, the shelves form a compact block of records which is more resistant to damage than records which are more thinly distributed (in the same way that a bound volume is harder to damage than separate sheets of paper). Therefore, mobile shelving makes sense in strong-rooms with ceilings of normal height (2.5–3 m), where each square meter of floor space is costly, where the atmosphere may be polluted, and where documents are not often needed in such a hurry that simultaneous access to different parts of the strong-room is vital. Thus, mobile shelving is worth considering for archives in a repository in a city centre. With static shelving, a typical repository will run out of storage space almost twice as quickly.

If mobile shelving is chosen, there is the choice of power-operated, mechanically assisted systems or hand-operated ones. The choice depends on the funding available, on the weight of records to be moved and on the fitness of staff. Most people can move a couple of tons of records with a hand-operated system. About five tons can be moved without too much effort by mechanically assisted systems. Beyond that weight, a powered system is necessary. Whatever system is used, the tracks on which the racks run should not project above floor level. It is dangerous, and inconvenient, for staff to have to step over obstacles, especially when carrying heavy items or using kick-steps.

Shelving is normally constructed of either steel or wood. A common choice is steel shelving of the angle-post type made to BS 826; and this is preferable in many ways to wooden shelving. The latter is inflammable, it can rot, harbour insect pests, produce splinters and, because of its lignin content, it soaks up atmospheric acid. There is little different in cost. Whatever kind is used, the bottom shelf should be about 150 mm above floor level, to avoid immediate innundation and to allow air movement.

Non-standard storage

Outsize documents, especially maps and drawings, present problems. Maps should be stored flat if possible, not folded or rolled. Large, shallow drawers work well if repository staff are careful about producing and replacing the maps, if the pile of maps in each drawer is not too great, and if the map on top of each pile does not curl and get caught whenever the drawer is opened. If maps are consulted frequently, vertical storage may be better. This is said to cause distortion of scale, but in fact worse damage can be caused by pulling a map out of a heap of horizontally stored maps, and subsequently ramming it back again.

Outsize maps usually have to be rolled. Rolling causes some distortion, but this is minimal if they are rolled round the outside of a cylinder of large diameter. They should then be wrapped in acid-free paper, or buckram. Rolled maps should be shelved horizontally, supported for their full length, and not projecting into corridors.

Loose papers

If papers need to be clipped together, brass paper-clips should be used. If they are to be bundled, the bundles should be tied with unbleached cotton tape about 10 mm wide (string cuts into paper, and rubber bands decompose).

Boxes

Where possible, papers and books should be placed in boxes. Most record offices use boxes made of a single piece of container board of 2 mm caliper, having a pH value around 7, lined with kraft paper and stitched with brass or stainless steel staples. The lids should be made in the same way. Lids that are 50–75 mm deep are cheaper than full-depth lids, and can be removed and replaced more easily. Full-depth lids, on the other hand, strengthen the box and make it harder for dusty or polluted air to enter it. If the repository is sited in a place where the air is exceptionally clean, or if it has air-conditioning, the records may benefit from ventilation holes in the boxes. In most buildings, however, the air is not so pure, and ventilation holes are merely another hazard. Unboxed volumes should be packed vertically just tightly enough on the shelf to support each other. Very large volumes should be laid flat on their sides.

Labels indicating the contents of each box should be attached to the boxes rather than the lids, unless the boxes have permanently attached hinged lids. Boxes with detachable full-depth lids need labels on both boxes and lids to prevent them from being mismatched, resulting in boxes being misplaced. Labels should be attached firmly. Rolls of self-adhesive labels are not expensive and they can be typed to produce neat box labels at speed.

Monitoring the atmosphere

To maintain the correct atmosphere in record stores, regular monitoring and control are needed. Monitoring requires easily read thermometers with good, large divisions for each degree. Hygrometers are also necessary, and three types can be considered. First, electrical resistance hygrometers which tend to be temperamental, especially if the air is polluted, and need regular recalibration. Second, there are direct-reading dial hygrometers in which treated paper or bundles of hair absorb atmospheric moisture, and expand and contract as they become more or less moist. They too need regular recalibration. Third, wet- and dry-bulb thermometers indicate the rate at which water on the wet bulb evaporates. This last type appears in three forms. Static models are simply hung up in strongrooms, and can be unreliable because air movement accelerates evaporation so that readings are affected by draughts and by people moving about. Whirling hygrometers can be more accurate because rotating the thermometers is supposed to accelerate the air movement to a constant speed. This should eliminate the inaccuracy of static ones, but in fact the readings can vary, depending on who uses the instrument, and how vigorously. Thirdly, there are Assman-type hygrometers, which cost about five times as much as whirling ones. They have motor-driven fans to draw air over the bulbs at the correct speed.

The direct-reading dial type is very easy for repository staff to use, and although its calibration gradually drifts out of true, this seems better than the unpredictable fluctuations to which whirling hygrometers are subject. It makes sense, therefore, to install dial hygrometers in record stores, and to check their accuracy periodically against an Assman

hygrometer. The positioning of hygrometers needs a little thought: readings should not be taken in the main gangways, but also in parts of the strong-rooms where cold, stagnant air is suspected. Thermo-hydrographs should be considered if rapid fluctuations of temperature and humidity are suspected, or if stores are rarely visited by staff.

Controlling the atmosphere

The strong-room climate is best controlled by an air-conditioning system. If this is not possible, humidifiers or dehumidifiers need to be installed. Humidifiers are most likely to be needed in winter when central heating tends to dry out the air. The best kind appears to be a steam humidifier: other types are more complicated mechanically, and tend to cool the air. In the summer, dehumidifiers are more likely to be needed, and the refrigerant type is preferred by most record offices.

Conclusion

It is apparent that records, and especially modern papers, need carefully controlled conditions to ensure their long-term survival. Custodians should aim for the conditions specified in BS 5454 and, in addition to their routine consultations with fire protection, crime prevention and health and safety officers, they should liaise with archivists.

References

BRIGGS, J. R. (1980), 'Environmental Control for Modern Records', in Petherbridge, G. (Ed.), *Cambridge 1980: International Conference on the Conservation of Library and Archive Materials and the Graphic Arts,* Institute of Paper Conservation, London

GIBSON, J. A. AND REAY, D. (1980), Drying rare old books soaked by flood water, *Museums J.,* **80** (3), 147–148

HUDSON, F. L. AND MILNER, W. D. (1961), Atmospheric Sulphur and the Durability of Paper, *Journal of the Society of Archivists,* **2** (4), 166–167

THE ROYAL COMMISSION ON HISTORICAL MANUSCRIPTS (1982), *Record Repositories in the United Kingdom,* HMSO, London

Bibliography

BAYNES-COPE, A. D. (1981), *Caring for Books and Documents,* British Museum, London

BRITISH STANDARDS INSTITUTION (1973 and 1980), *Recommendations for repair and allied processes for the treatment of documents,* BS 4971, Parts 1 and 2, British Standards Institution, London

BRITISH STANDARDS INSTITUTION (1977), Recommendations for the storage and exhibition of documents, BS 5454, British Standards Institution, London

CUNHA, G. D. M. (1967), *Conservation of Library Materials,* Scarcrow Press, Methuen, New Jersey

PETHERBRIDGE, G. (1980) (Ed.), *Cambridge 1980: International conference on the conservation of library and archive materials and the graphic arts,* Institute of Paper Conservation, London

THOMSON, G. AND BULLOCK, L. (1980), *Simple control and measurement of relative humidity in museums,* Information Sheet No. 24, Museums Association, London

29

Conservation and storage: prints, drawings and water-colours

Jane McAusland

Introduction

Museums inevitably house quantities of paper-supported works of art such as drawings, prints and water-colours. To be aware of the conservation problems of preserving them, the curator needs to be familiar with, and vigilent over, mainly simple routine procedures and tasks.

A consequence of the law of conservation of organic matter is that once the life of an organism ends, its compromising matter reverts into primary compounds to be recycled. The primary compounds are carbon dioxide, water, oxygen, carbon and other chemically simple substances. As prints and drawings are always partially, if not completely, constructed from once-living material, recycling naturally beings to occur. Anyone involved in conserving these artefacts is contending with this law of nature.

It is necessary for the curator to bring practical judgement to bear upon the conservation of the collection. If problem areas can be pin-pointed and dealt with before serious problems arise, time, money, and labour will have been saved.

Heat, humidity, light, pollution, insects and man work to destroy paper artefacts and, where low budgets and small collections operate against the installation of air-conditioning, simple preventive operations may be carried out. To guard against light, curtains or blinds may be installed, while other light sources may be controlled by time switches. Fluctuations in relative humidity may be better controlled by leaving heating on for twenty-four hours rather than turning it off at night, while relatively cheap humidifiers and dehumidifiers may be installed to keep the level correct. It is relatively simple to make microclimates which act as buffers against fluctuations in RH in boxes, cases or drawers. Pollution may be minimized by housings of chemically stable materials, such as acid-free conservation boards.

Storage areas should be utilized to their best advantage, while taking into account the necessity for air movement, humidity control and dust and dirt eradication. Space should be allocated for carrying out practical tasks connected with arranging the collection. Good records must be kept of the condition and treatments carried out. A qualified conservator should be consulted when serious problems arise, and even beforehand. His expertise will help the curator to recognize where damage is occurring, or is likely to occur in the future. Only simple treatments should be carried out by the curator, and a conservator should deal with other operations. Plans against disasters such as floods, fire and theft should be made. Safe packing for transportation should be used, taking into account the likely changes in climate the works will encounter.

With thorough curatorial understanding of preventive conservation, and concern for collections of prints and drawings, they should survive for many years for the enjoyment and enlightenment of future generations.

Agents harmful to paper: the damage likely to be rendered

Light

The survival of many wonderful antique drawings has been aided by proper storage, either in bound volumes or mounted and boxed away from exposure to visible light and ultra-violet radiation.

All organic materials are damaged by photochemical degradation, (Brill, 1980), which implies oxidation by UV radiation and light. Cellulose is particularly vulnerable to these agents. All environmental factors (light, heat, humidity[1]) and pollution in the atmosphere and inherent in paper work together to produce either a good or a bad environment for the collection. Radiant heat from daylight or artificial light sources may change the balance in the immediate vicinity of the objects or in their storage areas, causing embrittlement. Ultra-violet rays will fade pigments and dyes or change them, while paper will start to deteriorate. This may not be apparent at first, but the poorer the quality of the paper, the sooner discolouration, an indication of this deterioration, will begin to appear.

There is more visible and UV radiation in daylight than in any other source. Tungsten incandescent lamps, and tungsten-halogen lamps give out more heat than fluorescent lamps, though some types of the latter give out a higher amount of UV light (Thomson, 1978b). 50 lux is the accepted light level for paper artefacts (Thomson, 1978b). The curator will also have to decide which type of illumination will display colours to their best advantage.

Preventive measures

(1). Use of UV filters in frames, on lamps, windows and show-cases.

(2). Careful choice of background colours in exhibition areas and the use of reflected light. Dark, light-absorbing backgrounds necessitate more highly illuminated areas and reducing this level to 50 lux makes for the gloomy exhibition of prints and drawings. Lighter walls surrounding exhibited works reflect the light, making for ease of viewing while keeping to the specified light level.

(3). Careful choice of light source colour. Warm rather than cool light sources are best for viewing.

(4). Rotation of the collection.

(5). Elimination of heat from light sources by means of fans and reflectors.

(6). Use of facsimile prints and drawings. This is not a popular solution, but maybe a last resort, especially when valuable works are involved.

(7). Time switches in rooms or on showcases. Blinds to cut down direct light. Night security lights of 10 lux.

Heat and humidity

Paper is hygroscopic because cellulose fibres readily absorb water vapour from the atmosphere, and it is therefore likely to be adversely affected by extremes of relative humidity as its moisture content adjusts to be in equilibrium with the relative humidity of its environment. Below 40 per cent RH the cellulose fibres of paper become dehydrated and embrittled, shrinking takes place causing buckling and distortion, tension builds up between pigments, gums and inks on the dehydrated paper, and flaking is likely. Above 60 per cent RH, the increased moisture content of the paper is likely to attract mould growth from spores in the atmosphere attracted by the moisture-activated impurities in the paper. Even without

mould growth, these impurities will be activated and cause the chemical destruction of the paper support of the print or drawing. Damage will certainly occur when the RH is below 30 per cent or above 70 per cent, while acute fluctuations are extremely damaging to prints and drawings, as they expand and contract, leading to physical breakdown.

Preventive measures

Both temperature and humidity must be controlled to obtain the optimal RH, that is, between 50 and 60 per cent. Ideally, air-conditioning should be installed and maintained to keep this balance. If this is too costly, a curator may nevertheless take various steps to guard the collection. The storage area should be carefully selected; there should be no direct sunlight, plenty of ventilation and no damp, and minimal atmospheric pollution and dust. Prints and drawings stored in Solander boxes[2] or drawers will automatically acquire microclimates of their own, leaving changes in the environmental RH of the rooms to fluctuate more widely. Further bolstering against RH fluctuation may be achieved by the use of moisture-absorbing agents such as silica gel which may be incorporated into the boxes in small bags.

Humidifiers and dehumidifiers may be necessary. On the whole, these are cheap to buy and run, and most small museums should be able to afford them.

Pollution

Paper may become chemically unstable through contact with materials that leach acids and other pollutants, or absorb impurities from the atmosphere. The purity of the materials of paper-making, and the lengths to which the manufacturers go to further purify them build a life-span into paper. For example, linen is very pure, and therefore has an advantage over wood-based paper. Although, with the right chemical treatments, the latter can be made as pure as linen, it needs much more processing at the pulping stage of paper-making to eliminate harmful residual bleaches, lignin and other acidic materials. Acid sizes are particularly damaging (McAusland and Stevens, 1979). As paper degrades, it changes and darkens in colour, becoming brown and brittle.

Some inks, pigments and dyes in works of art on paper may chemically break down its cellulose. Copper pigments and iron gall inks are the most common offenders. On the other hand, alkaline pigments such as pastels prolong the life of the paper.

It is clear, therefore, that all storage materials should be as pure as possible, chemically stable, and free from damaging agents, to protect not only the paper support, but also the pigments, inks and dyes that may be chemically altered by an unstable environment. Gums, pastes, and glues, in contact with or close to prints, drawings and water-colours should also be considered damaging pollutants; if impure, they may introduce more chemical instability.

Because paper is naturally highly hygroscopic, atmospheric hydrogen sulphide, nitrogen dioxide and other gases with water vapour, will be converted to sulphuric and nitric acids along with other damaging chemicals, and taken into the hollow paper fibres causing them to break down. Ozone is harmful to organic materials, including paper. Oils, fats, and minute suspended particles from the atmosphere settle on exposed prints and drawings and find their way into the crevices between the paper fibres.

Preventive measures

(1) With inherently unstable paper, the conservation treatment of de-acidification or alkaline buffering may be implemented. However, as many of the pigments and inks of prints and drawings may be pH-sensitive, it is *not* a recommended treatment for such works (Daniels, 1982). Also, a slight deposit is always apparent after this treatment and some de-acidificants may discolour the paper. Only in extreme cases should this treatment be used, and then only by a conservator who may also decide to rinse works to rid them of their pollutants.

(2). Mounts and storage boxes, drawers and other housings should be as acid-free as possible. A pH of 8 is ideal for these materials as it has a built-in margin against future absorbed pollutants.

(3). The air should be filtered by an air-conditioner. If one is not available, the rooms chosen for storage should be clean, and as pollution-free as possible.

Monitoring equipment

Acidity in paper may be tested with a pH meter, but complete accuracy is difficult to achieve as only the surface can be tested. Colour-change indicators as well as full pH testing may be used on storage materials. There are other tests for damaging agents such as ground wood, alum and rosin (Harding, 1972). The British Standard Institution[3] will test materials in the UK.

Moulds

Moulds are saphrophytic fungi and grow on any material that provides moisture and organic nutrients. Even finger-prints offer enough substrate for their growth. Paper and sizing solutions in paper, animal glue, adhesives, starch pastes and acquired dust particles are all attractive to moulds. However, the right conditions must prevail for moulds to thrive, moisture and heat being the necessary factors. Spores may lie dormant for years and become activated only when the RH rises above 70 per cent.

The most common mould of fungal attack on prints and drawings is known as 'foxing' and seen as brown spots of varying size and intensity. This type of damage is not only disfiguring but changes chemically the paper fibres in the vicinity of the spots, making the paper acidic and, therefore, weak. Little research has been done on this extensively damaging problem (books suffer badly too), but opinion generally holds that minerals inherent in the paper, especially iron and its salts, are attractive to fungi which release acids in reaction to these impurities (Meynell and Newcombe, 1978).

Preventive measures

(1). The RH should be kept between 50 and 60 per cent.

(2). Regular inspection of the collection should be carried out to look for signs of fungal attack.

(3). Any infected materials should be separated from the collection. Superfluous materials such as old mounts, which host contamination, must be removed. These will have a nostalgic, musty smell due to acidity and other pollution, and provides clear warning that all is not well with the collection.

(4). Fumigation should be carried out. This may be done by the curator if he has a thymol chamber[4], or by professional fumigators. However, no fumigation treatment has long-lasting properties. Treatment is effective for about a month, and as spores from moulds are ever-present fumigation seems pointless. However, where extreme contamination is occurring, fumigation is a sensible course of action, as the number of spores is reduced.

Insects and other pests

In the UK species of insect do considerable harm to prints and drawings. The larvae of furniture beetles (*Anobium punctatum*) eat the soft wood of frame backings and boxes, leaving frass in their wake along with a sticky deposit. They find paper even more attractive. This damage is evident in the common 'wormage' to be seen as holes in paper supports, upsetting the visual image of the work. Booklice (*Psocoptera*) feed on moulds. Silver fish (*Lepisma saccharina*) find the sizing agents in paper particularly attractive and can ruin the surface of a print or drawing over considerable areas by nibbling the size-coated fibres. Better quality papers and those with glazed surfaces appear to suffer most. Earwigs (*Dermaptera*) leave stains from their excrement, as do house files. In country areas, thrips (*Thysanoptera*) enter framed prints and drawings. No breeding appears to take place, but they die *in situ*, often leaving small brown stains.

The enormous damage that mice do to paper artefacts is well known. Besides chewing prints and drawings, their excrement can stain and irreversibly damage such works.

Although the pests listed above are the most common in the UK, the curator must be on the alert for unusual and immigrant species.

Preventive measures

(1). Drawers, shelves, boxes and storage areas should be regularly inspected and cleaned. A vacuum cleaner that can reach corners should be utilized.

(2). Appropriate insecticides should be put down[5]. Baits for mice should be strategically positioned. If infestation is severe, professional advice should be sought.

The curator's need to understand preventive conservation routines

Custodians and those who benefit from the aesthetic enjoyment or interest that prints and drawings intrinsically give are often most to blame for their damage, through ignorance, poor housekeeping, outmoded techniques and clumsy handling. They have a responsibility towards them and must understand that these delicate works may be damaged by inadequate storage facilities, inhospitable climatic conditions and unsuitable accommodation. It is the view of conservators that more damage has been done to works by inadequate and wrongly constructed housing, both framed and boxed, than by any other means. Dirty hands will stain, and sunlight will bleach colours and damage paper. A high RH will cause mould growth, a low RH will cause embrittlement. High incidence of acidity and other pollutants in the microenvironment of the print or drawing will cause chemical instability with the increased likelihood of its eventual destruction. Drawings and prints incorrectly stored in drawers may buckle and tear when drawn out.

The degree to which a collection is handled must be determined by the curator, and the housings and storage arrangements must be tailored to the demands made upon it.

Preventive measures

(1). Correct balance of heat and humidity: full air-conditioning; improvized microclimates.

(2). Well-planned storage areas.

(3). Protection from light: correct levels; blinds and curtains.

(4). Use of conservation techniques and materials for housing.

(5). Full instructions to users of collections; that is,

clean hands, correct handling, no smoking, no pens or inks.

(6). Good surfaces for viewing.

(7). Cleanliness.

(8). Use of facsimiles.

Examination analysis

Inspection

For the curator to make sound decisions regarding the priorities of the collection, it is first necessary to make a thorough inspection of each print or drawing for its individual conservation needs. If the collection is large, the curator must have an overall plan for the bulk of it, while listing other items for specialist treatment. Apart from his expertise, he should, with the help of a conservator, discover what signs indicate damage (Clapp, 1974).

Recording forms

It is important to keep a record of the condition of the works in the collection as well as all treatments that have been carried out. This is best organized to complement the general indexing system already in use. It may be necessary to develop a system of special forms for recording. The form should be as practical as possible, simple to complete, and be concise. If the museum has the use of a central computer system, the forms should comply with this amenity.

Photography

As a further aid to recording, good photographs should be taken. If colour slides are preferred, these should be reviewed for tonality every ten years, as all colour photographs are unstable, even in the dark. Good black-and-white prints on non-resin-coated paper should be chosen if colour is not a priority. Shots should be taken in flat and raking light. Photographs should be stored in containers that will not affect the silver emulsion. It would help curators to have a good copy stand and a single-lens reflex camera for immediate use (Stannard, 1979).

Unframing

Great damage can result from the clumsy removal of works of art on paper from their frames. The following steps should be taken carefully to reduce the chance of such damage.

It is wise to have a bench covered in felt, securely tacked or stuck down. The tools needed are a duster, a small vacuum cleaner, a selection of small pliers and pincers, a screwdriver (medium), a knife, a palette-knife, a scalpel and blotting paper. Prints and drawings are secured in their frames by many methods, so initially the framed 'package' should be closely examined. Obviously, until the backboard is removed, the interior cannot be revealed and has to be dealt with step by step. First, the frame should be dusted or vacuumed. Any paper, or paper tape, should be removed from the back with a knife, together with any important labels or other documentation. The latter may be removed by placing wet blotting paper over them which should release them after a short soaking. If this is not sufficient, or if the adhesive appears to be other than animal glue or starch paste, a professional conservator should be consulted. Any wires and their anchor screws should be removed.

After all the pins securing the backing board to the moulding of the frame are revealed, the frame should be held firmly with the side to be tackled 'pulled parallel to the body.' The top of the pin should be grasped firmly with pliers or pincers and gently pulled out. In early frames, the pins had no heads, but contemporary framing pins have small ones. Pins may be difficult to remove if they have rusted into their holes. A modern invention is the small diamond or 'U'-shaped pin, shot from a gun to secure the backing board to the moulding of the frame. These may be removed gently with a screwdriver. The frame should be turned so each side assumes a correct position in turn, until all the pins have been pulled. The backing board can then be lifted out. It may be necessary to repeat the vacuum treatment at this stage to remove debris caused by the operation. The interior of the frame should then be carefully scrutinized and the mounted print or drawing lifted out. It is sound practice to tilt the frame gently to allow the 'package' to drop back on to the supporting palm of the hand. Commonly, the contents will have been bound together with tape at the edges including the glass. If so, any tapes should be slit with a knife to separate the sections. At all times during the dismantling process, a keen eye should search for traces of pests such as silver-fish, beetles and their larvae.

After the work has been removed from the frame, the backing board may be returned and pinned into place for storage. Even if the board has to be replaced, it will support and protect the glass temporarily.

De-mounting

Deciding what should be discarded: the warning signs
Further close inspection should be carried out to determine how the work is attached to its mounting and whether any of the materials show signs of breakdown. Discolouration, especially the orange/brown bevel of a mount will indicate immediately the presence of an acid. This may not be in contact

with the front of the print or drawing, but more often than not the backing mount will be made of the same board and will be in full contact with the work. Adhesives may be discolouring the paper support of the print or drawing. Mould growth and insect attack will be obvious.

Many different practices, some good, but mostly bad, have been used to mount works of art on paper. The following are some common problems the curator will encounter, together with the suggested methods of dismantling on a clean flat surface.

Hinges
If, by good fortune, the work has been hinged simply with paper into its overlay mount, then these may be slit easily with a palet knife and the work lifted out.

Edge adhesion to backing board
To determine whether this is the method of attachment, the board should be very slightly flexed and the print or drawing will show slight cockling across the flex. If the original paper is thick it may be possible to insert a palet knife between this and the board releasing it. However, if there are any immediate problems the operation should be left to a conservator.

Spot adhesion to backing board
A certain amount of wrinkling will be apparent if the work is secured in this way. If the work is mounted on a paper this may be torn away, leaving a small amount on the adhered points. Only a skilled curator will be able to slice the work off the board under the adhered areas.

Adhered overmount
Extreme care should be exercised in determining whether overmounts are stuck to the original, or to the backing mount. It is always inadvisable for unskilled hands to attempt to remove overmounts adhered to the surface of prints or drawings.

Total adhesion to the backing board
The work may have been totally laid down on poor quality board, and the problems that arise will not only stem from the latter, because adhesives also play havoc with the mounted work. A good quality board with a layer of damaging adhesive will be a continuing problem as this can be an attractive layer for mould growth, or be itself chemically unstable and cause severe discolouration. Original artists' mounts, if they have to be detached, should be kept. Curators should *never* attempt to delaminate the original from its board or mount, but should consult an experienced conservator.

Dry-mountings

Dry-mounting has been in use since the 1930s, and the early tissues, being based on shellac, are completely insoluble. Even the use of soluble modern products is inadvisable. Yet this bad practice continues to be used by framers, and it is by no means uncommon to find beautiful prints and drawings hot-pressed onto boards. The curator should consult a conservator when this method has been used – the tell-tale signs being a shiny layer protruding beyond the edge of the print or drawing.

Textile stretcher and panel supports

An eighteenth- and nineteenth-century practice was to secure a print or drawing with starch paste or animal glue to an open textile stretcher of linen or cotton or a wooden panel (McAusland and Stevens, 1979). The former allowed dust and atmospheric pollution to penetrate the paper and, combined with the differences in expansion and contraction of the linen and paper, resulted in a break-up of the paper. Only a conservator should handle works mounted by this method as they are often extremely delicate and brittle.

When a print or drawing is totally adhered to a wooden panel, many problems will have arisen and damage to the work will continue. Discolouration and extreme brittleness will be apparent. Only when the medium of the work contains carbonate, as in pastel or gouache, will this have served to give it some protection. Conservators face enormous, sometimes insoluble, problems with prints or drawings mounted in this way. Curators should *never* attempt to remove them from the panels.

Adhesion to glass

If a print or drawing has been pressed against the glazing, gums or other thick pigments may have become stuck to it. Removal should *not* be attempted by the curator. If, at this stage, de-mounted prints and drawings are to be catalogued, any marking of them should be made only in pencil. Inks, and felt-tipped or ball-point pens should *never* be used.

Special problems

Old master drawings

Although old master drawings are created in many different media, those executed in iron gall inks are the most problematic. The ink is made from gall nuts, iron sulphate and gum arabic (Watrous, 1957). It is extremely acidic and therefore likely to attack the paper fibres and break them completely causing cracks and fissures. It is especially important to keep iron gall ink drawings in conditions of near 50 per cent RH and away from light, as both moisture and

UV radiation cause quick deterioration, accelerating the chemical instability of the ink. When originally executed, these drawings were dark black – their creators would scarcely recognize them today.

Prints

Unless executed on laid India paper (*Chine appliqué*), all prints should be free of backings unless they needed such support for conservation purposes. Their natural undulations should be understood and tolerated. Colour prints can fade in light as much as water-colours. Japanese prints are usually delicate and should never be subjected to light for any length of time.

Water-colours

Photo-oxidation is the greatest danger to water-colours. Many beautiful works have been ruined by the combination of light and atmospheric oxygen. If the colours are not uniformly affected, this will produce an imbalance in the design. Often, old mountings have partially obscured the edge, where the original freshness may be seen. Collections mounted in volumes have often fared best and the splitting-up of such books may ring the death knell for the water-colours. It is helpful to understand that inorganic pigments or dyes are much less susceptible to alteration by light than organic ones. However, vermilion may blacken, and verdigris, red lead, the chromates and lead white react with oxygen and other gases in the atmosphere, and darken. Other fugitive pigments and dyes include yellow lake, all the red lakes, cadmium yellow, gamboge, Van Dyke brown and indigo[6]. If storage areas are too dry, gums on water-colours dry out and crack further, and pigment may be lifted from the support surface.

Drawings: graphite, charcoal, conte crayon, inks and coloured chalks and crayons

The curator will have to note carefully which of the media of the drawings may be damaged by handling or by light. Loose particles of graphite, charcoal, chalk and crayon may offset or smudge, while inks and coloured crayons may fade in light. Deeper overlay mounts may be necessary to reduce the likelihood of contact with the glass or the mount when stored in Solander boxes. There is a lot to be said for the vertical storage of such works.

Pastels

The loose and delicate surface of a pastel drawing calls for extreme care in handling and storage. No modern fixative should be used on these works. The hygroscopic gums that bind the coarse pigment attract fungal growth. Apart from keeping these drawings in an RH of between 50 and 60 per cent, it is important to mount and frame them so as to achieve some air circulation. Unframed pastels should be stored horizontally in conservation boxes with a gap between the lid and the surface of the pastel sufficient to minimize any risk of offset. Pastels, like watercolours, and coloured chalks and crayons may fade in light.

Practical first-aid conservation procedures: recommended treatments

The curator should attempt very little practical conservation. Prints and drawings may be totally ruined by injudicious intervention. It is much more important that the curator understands the preventive conservation methods and practices that should be exercised on such collections. However, some small, but nevertheless important, tasks may be carried out without the help or guidance of a professional conservator.

Dry-cleaning

Accrued dust on the surface of the print or drawing when the medium is not itself loose may be dislodged with a very soft brush of sable or other equally soft hair. Some nylon brushes are fine enough for this purpose. Areas where more stubborn dust and dirt adhere to the surface (where the medium allows) may be removed with a plastic eraser[7]. Careful judgement must be exercised over this practice as a great deal of damage may be caused. The work should be placed on a large white blotter on a very even surface and it is important that the work does not slip. A small piece of blotting paper should rest beneath a small but heavy weight on an area of the work that balances the pull on the paper when the rubber is in action (*Figure 29.1*). Care must be taken not to raise the paper fibres during the operation. Dirt on a mount may be treated in the same way.

No attempt at surface cleaning should be made on soft European, long-fibred oriental, or Chinese papers. Surface cleaning should not be carried out if only partial cleaning is possible or if the works are delicate, that is, pencil, graphite, pastel or any other medium that is likely to lift off. Brittle papers may be further damaged by surface cleaning.

Mending edge tears

This first-aid action is a case of 'a stitch in time . . .', and a kit of the following equipment should be at hand. No torn print or drawing should be handled, and damage should be reported to the curator by researchers. A notice to this effect should be displayed in the print room.

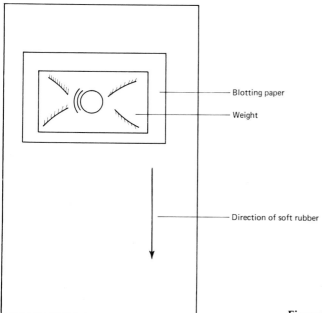

Blotting paper

Weight

Direction of soft rubber

Figure 29.1 Soft rubber cleaning of surface: weighted area

Equipment needed

Medium weight *kozo* paper.
Small scalpel with disposable blades (Swan Morton No. 15).
Pure starch paste (with preservative)[8].
White blotting paper.
Small flat pieces of plate glass.
Small paste brushes.
Scissors.
Small sable brush.
Wet cutting brush.
Melinex (20).
Silicone release paper.
Tweezers.
Burnisher.
Small heavy weight.

Method

A clean, smooth 'Formica' or glass table top should be utilized. First, examine the tear for dirt and dust, which may then be lightly brushed away with a small sable brush, then a plastic eraser (providing the paper is not too soft) may be drawn down and across each edge, from both the front and verso with extreme care so that no paper fibre is lost. A small piece of Melinex[9] may be inserted in the tear to facilitate this action (*Figure 29.2*).

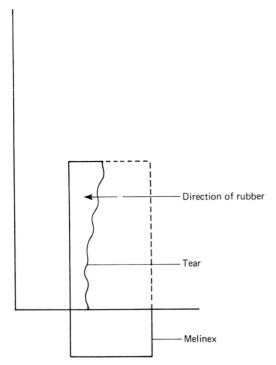

Figure 29.2 Cleaning a tear: insertion of Melinex

Direction of rubber

Tear

Melinex

Next, a piece of Japanese paper should be cut out with a scalpel, scissors or a wet brush. This latter method may be the best as the edge will be frayed and lie very flat, causing no ridge. This repair patch will be no larger than 1 mm on each side of the tear. The patch is laid out on a piece of glass and pasted. It is very important that the paste be as dry as possible to avoid any movement of water into the paper, which might result in staining. Any overlapping areas of the tear may be pasted together in the correct position. The remaining length of tear should be aligned correctly. Using tweezers, the patch should be lifted gently; the work is held firmly in place with the left hand, and the patch is then placed evenly along the tear, and gently patted to secure it. A piece of blotting paper is then placed beneath the tear, and a piece of silicone release paper above. The patch should then be gently burnished through this to secure adhesion. The silicone release paper should be discarded, then replaced with blotting paper topped with the glass and a weight. The sheet is then left for at least five minutes: the longer the better. Long tears may be dealt with in the same manner, but in stages, as they are difficult to manipulate. Abutting patches should be made.

Hinge removal

In order to stop bulking of old hinges on the verso of a drawing or print, some parts of these may be pulled away with tweezers. Great care must be taken not to 'thin' the original support. If this is likely, the hinges should await the attention of a professional, as should any self-adhesive tapes. If the work is backed, then more may be taken away as the original is not at risk.

Preventive conservation of prints and drawings

The way in which a collection may be mounted and stored depends ultimately on the demands that are to be made on it and the space available. However, a number of factors must be considered:

(1). Size of collection, amount of space available, organization of that space.
(2). Mounts and frames: use of conservation materials.
(3). Amount of use, and therefore handling, the collection will have.
(4). Security against fire, flood and theft.
(5). Aesthetic considerations, important historical evidence, and so on.
(6). Future increase in size of collection.

Allocation of available space

The size and shape of the storage area designated for the collection will determine how the store will be organized. First, a survey of the different sizes of prints and drawings, together with the sizes of likely additions (if possible) should be made. This survey should also embrace the number, size and shape of framed items. After this has been completed, the available space should be apportioned to the various types of item to be housed. The mount sizes needed for the collection should be determined. There is no uniform mount size in the UK, but the British Museum mount sizes are as follows: 22 × 26 inches (Royal); 27 × 20 inches (Imperial); 32 × 24 inches (Atlas); and 45 × 29.75 inches (Antiquarian or Double Elephant). Solander boxes should be purchased to match the sizes chosen. These must be sturdy and made of acid-free materials.

Following these decisions, an arrangement of shelves and boxed areas should be organized, taking into account the specifics of the collection housing. There are differing opinions as to whether prints and drawings should be stored horizontally or vertically. Having seen many badly rubbed and pressed works that have been stored horizontally, I favour the vertical method, but the boxes must be completely full, otherwise the mount will fall at an angle and damage is likely to occur. If double mounts are used it is probably best to use horizontal systems, housed in felt-lined boxed areas (Zegers, 1980).

Framed items may be stored vertically in boxed areas lined with felt to minimize scratching of glass or Perspex and damage to frames. Felt-covered separators should lie between each frame, otherwise drawers lined with felt may be used for framed-item storage. This method is considerably more expensive. All stored frames should be free of wires, rings and other projections.

Very large prints and drawings are a problem. If possible, they should be framed for full protection immediately they arrive at the museum, but if this cannot be done, they should be encapsulated (Library of Congress, 1980) and stored in plan chests. These chests have a hinged bar at the front and a protection bar across the top of the rear of the drawer to keep them from lifting up and becoming damaged. Drawers must be well-ventilated, as should boxed areas; holes in the backs will allow air circulation.

Various systems of sliding vertical racks are available commercially upon which framed works may be hung during storage. They have the advantage of providing easy visibility for the researcher, and from the conservation point of view any damage that has occurred can easily be seen. They have the further advantage of good air circulation. There are also systems for storing large paper artefacts in hanging chambers, bins or devices that pivot on a central column and support the works on arms extending from the centre.

An area should be selected for framing and unframing, with space to house all necessary equipment. If it is possible to clean this area thoroughly after use, it may also be used as the place where first-aid treatments are carried out. The lighting must be very good. There should be as many tables as possible for research purposes. A source of hot and cold water should be adjacent to the print room, and a notice displayed to draw attention to the need for absolutely clean hands.

Microclimates

To cope with extreme fluctuation in RH or high RH where there is no equipment for regulating this installed in the museum, the curator could improvise microclimates around the storage areas. It would be best to consult with a conservator before embarking on this course, but there are just a few points that should be understood first.

It is possible to install at little cost bags of silica gel in cabinets that will stabilize the environment and act as a buffer against adverse humidity levels. These cabinets must be air-tight and may be made of wood or metal, though the former is best because wood, in itself a bad conductor, is a buffer to start with. Gaps in cabinets should be sealed with a silicone sealant. As purchased, silica gel is a desiccant and should be brought up to the correct RH for the storage areas (around 50 per cent) by a conservator using controlled conditions. Bags may be made of muslin and closed with Velcro strips. They should lie on the shelves between, under or over the boxes, but do not need to cover the entire area. Dust is given off and therefore bags should not be put inside the boxes.

Mounts

Curators and conservators are not always able to determine whether all the materials of a print or drawing are chemically stable. More often they are not stable, and it may not be possible to put matters right by improving the environment because of lack of funds or equipment. However, placing these works in close proximity to a chemically stable environment will help. Conservation mounting and framing seem to be the best practical method of preventive conservation. The works can only be safeguarded by this practice. It is easy to organize, and many high-quality conservation materials are now available.

The type of mount chosen will depend on factors already mentioned. The curator must decide which of the different types best suits the requirements.

(1). A simple overlay mount (*Figure 29.3*) may be constructed in varying thickness to suit the collection.

(2). A double overlay mount with Melinex protection (*Figure 29.4*) is particularly useful if the collection is to be handled frequently. The Melinex makes for easy viewing and the overmount

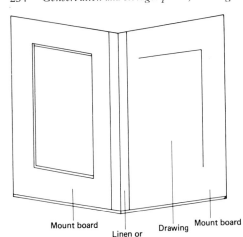

Mount board   Drawing   Mount board

Linen or
paper tape
with water-
soluble adhesive

Figure 29.3 Simple overlay mount

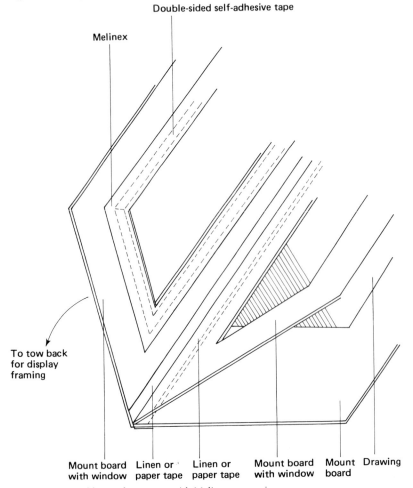

Double-sided self-adhesive tape

Melinex

To tow back
for display
framing

Mount board   Linen or   Linen or   Mount board   Mount   Drawing
with window   paper tape   paper tape   with window   board

Figure 29.4 Double-overlay mount with Melinex protection

protects the undermount from dirt thereby cutting long-term costs. The overmount may simply be folded back to show the clean undermount when the works are needed for exhibition. The disadvantages of this method are that it is bulky, more costly initially, and Melinex attracts dust.

(3). The inlaid Perspex double-sided mount (*Figure 29.5*) is useful for double-sided drawings

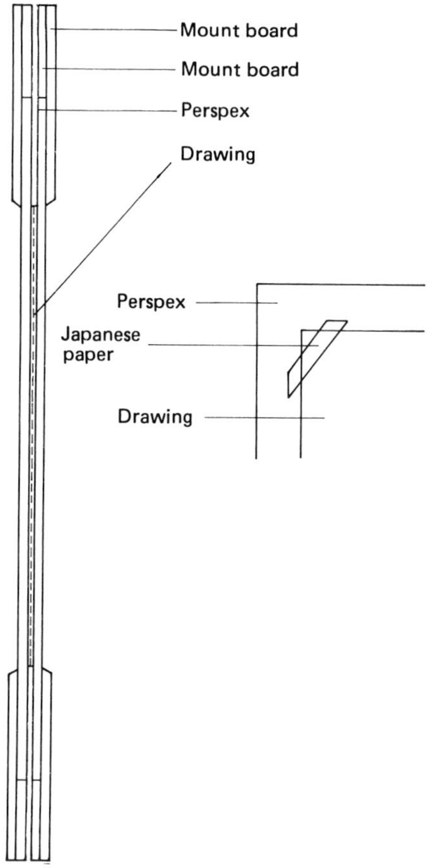

examples of various methods of hinging works to their mounts:

(1). A simple L hinge (*Figure 29.6*) is quite suitable for most small prints and drawings, as the entire image may be displayed. If the collection is housed horizontally, and not to be displayed in frames, the hinges should be on the left-hand side of the print

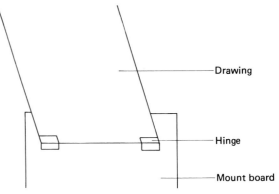

Figure 29.6 Simple L hinge

or drawing, to make for easy lifting by the researcher. On the other hand, vertically stored works and collections that are to be displayed should be hinged on the top. Two hinges at each corner (either left side or top) are required. More than two hinges will cause buckling. This method of hinging is a poor safeguard against theft. If the object is only just covered by the edges of the window, this method of hinging may allow it to become buckled and caught between the sides of the mount.

(2). A drop hinge with securing strip (*Figure 29.7*) is suitable and physically secure if it is not necessary to show the whole sheet of paper, that is, when there are large margins.

(3). Hinges supported through backing board (*Figure 29.8*) give firm hidden support when prints or drawings are very large and heavy.

Figure 29.5 Inlaid UV Perspex double-sided mount (the Japanese paper is adhered to the Perspex with PVA)

or works of great value. It is not suitable for works that have loose pigments or prints with platemarks or other natural undulations such as woodcuts. As long as conservation materials are used, mounts may be decorated to suit the aesthetic interpretation of the print or drawing or its historical background

Hinges

How the curator secures the print or drawing to its mount to protect it from damage or theft will depend on the above considerations. The following are

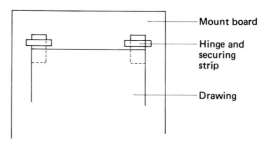

Figure 29.7 Drop hinge with securing strip

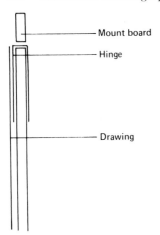

Figure 29.8 Hinges supported through backing board

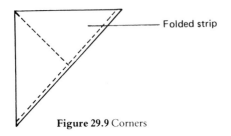

Figure 29.9 Corners

(4). Corners (*Figure 29.9*) make strong supports when the work should not have hinge attachments, or has large margins that lie under the overlay of the mount.

(5). Melinex strips (*Figure 29.10*) secured with PVA adhesive are a method of holding down works for display or storage.

Hinges should be made from either Japanese paper or thin, acid-free European paper. With the former it is possible to feather the edges by 'wet-cutting' and, therefore, to achieve a neat, flat hinge. The advantages of the latter are that it is slightly more firm and less likely to drop. The only suitable adhesive for hinging is pure starch paste. Carboxymethylcellulose is a little too wet. No commercially available paste or glue is sufficiently pure or reversible. All the available 'conservation' tapes are irreversible after a time and should not be used. Self-adhesive tape should *never* be considered.

Finally, when a drawing needs the greater support of a solid panel, a conservator – never a framer – should undertake this extremely delicate operation.

Inlays

An inlay is a piece of additional paper attached to the edge of a drawing on its verso, bevelled and adhered to the original to a depth of approximately 1 mm on all sides. Prints should never be inlayed as plate-marks and other natural undulations will be restricted or drummed out.

When a suitable paper for inlaying is being chosen it must be remembered that this additional edging will put a new stress on the original drawing, so it is important that a paper of similar weight is selected. If a lighter paper is attached, wrinkling will occur along the adhered edge of the inlay. However, it is possible to make an inlay with lens tissue[10] in order to display the work fully and control any inclination to curl or distort, although this would not be suitable for a collection that is handled a great deal, as the tissue is too fragile.

It is the current practice of some institutions to paste inlays down, both to the backing mount as well as to the overlay of the mount. From a security point of view this is helpful, but it obscures the verso for research purposes and also makes watermarks and other historical evidence unavailable.

Folders

If the curator is faced with extreme limitations of budget or a very large collection, a good simple method of storage is by means of folders. These should be made of strong, acid-free conservation card. Prints and drawings may be hinged to them as on a mount, or may be left free. Researchers should be warned of the likelihood of lifting the artefact on opening the folder.

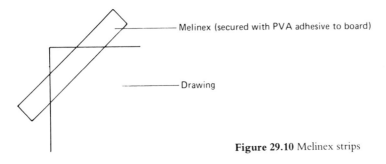

Figure 29.10 Melinex strips

Encapsulation

Full physical protection of prints and drawings may be achieved by encapsulation in Melinex (Mylar in North America) sheeting. Machines are available for welding this along the edges. A sewing machine may also be used. Double-sided tapes were once advocated, but the adhesive was found to migrate into the encapsulated area. Aesthetically, this method may not suit the collection (it is considered an archive treatment), but there might be occasions when it could be useful. As long as the relative humidity is correct at the time of encapsulation, this method provides a permanent microclimate for the object).

Framing

Permanent framing
Apart from its aesthetic appeal, the moulding of a frame is the support for the entire 'package', glazing mount and backing-board. It must be deep enough to house these integral parts, and sturdy enough to support them.

A glazing may be of glass or a polymethylmethacrylate sheet that cuts out a high proportion of UV light. The former is likely to shatter and is unsuitable for frames used for transportation. The latter attracts electricity and is not suitable for works that may be lifted by this property. It scratches easily, but it gives much better protection from UV light, and is much lighter in weight.

The backing-board both stabilizes the frame and protects the back of the mounted artefact. Hardboard or marine ply-wood are suitable for backing-boards but they should be coated with PVC varnish to hinder migration of impurities from the wood into the mount and eventually into the artefact.

A mounted print or drawing framed and sealed should be considered to be in a microclimate, and a certain amount of air movement is necessary to achieve a balanced RH. Self-adhesive tapes are not suitable for sealing the backing-board into the frame, because the adhesive will migrate, dry out and eventually lose its power. Further, they inhibit the movement of air into the frame. Pasted kraft paper or gummed brown tapes are the most suitable, although the latter may dry out and become loose.

Temporary framing
It may suit a collection better to have a system of framing that will enable the curator to rotate the collection on view with ease. A number of frames should be made to fit the mount sizes of the collection. These should have pivoting braces to secure the backing boards, which may be sealed with pasted or gummed tapes.

Collection marking and information recording: stamping, embossing and perforation

If information must be recorded on a print or drawing, it should be done in pencil only, and with light pressure. However, this practice should be avoided if possible, and information should normally be recorded on cards.

Items must be permanently identified as being part of the collection. There are various methods of marking items and others will no doubt shortly be available. The curator has the choice of ink stamps, embossed stamps, perforated marks and UV-sensitive stamps that are invisible without a UV light. It is important that marks should be impossible to remove without damaging the item, although such action can be skilfully concealed by an expert paper restorer. Ink stamps are conspicuous, but the ink must be chosen carefully. Pure black carbon printing-ink is the most stable, but inks should be tested before use to make sure that they are completely stable and able to withstand conservation treatments. Ink stamps should be carefully positioned.

Embossed stamps are aesthetically pleasing, but may be unsuitable as they press through the print or drawing. If the artefact has no margins it is impossible to use such a mark.

Perforated marks remove part of the paper and for this reason may be considered unsuitable. They are, of course, impossible to remove, but could be expertly repaired. Ultra-violet sensitive inks might appear to be a neat solution, but a thief would not necessarily be deterred by them.

Transportation

Before transportation, preventive conservation measures in the form of correct crating, handling, storage and labelling should be taken (Stolow, 1979).

Framed prints and drawings

The following steps should be taken in the case of framed prints and drawings.

(1). A condition report on each artefact should be made (if it does not already exist), and it should be checked carefully.
(2). Hinges, mounts and frames should be inspected.
(3). Glass should be criss-crossed with self-adhesive tape. It is better to send works framed with acrylic sheeting and a UV-absorbent filter as this will not shatter.

The following types of artefact should *not* be sent:

(1). Very brittle works.
(2). Works that are extremely sensitive to light.
(3). Pastels and drawings with unfixed surfaces should be handled separately and be sent by special courier.

Crates should be constructed to protect framed prints and drawings against vibration and shock, and should have a certain degree of temperature insulation and humidity-buffering capacity, such as that provided by silica gel. The design of the crate should accommodate the frames when held firmly in position and they should be protected further with corner padding. Ornate mouldings require specially designed packaging. For uniformly sized frames, slots to hold them vertically may be constructed, or a tray system may be utilized[11]. It is very important that the orientation of the crates be clearly marked on the outside, in more than one language if necessary. Wood is probably the best material to use for packing cases and crates.

Prints and drawings sent through the post

Whether these works are sent mounted or unmounted, they should be packed in the manner illustrated in *Figure 29.11*. It is very important that the recipient is informed precisely as to the packing arrangements, which should also be indicated on the outside of the package.

Rolled prints and drawings
Although rolling a print or drawing for transportation would seem the last resort as a great deal of damage can result from using this method, and it leaves the work curled, even if it has not suffered in other ways, contemporary screen prints seem ever to increase in size and it is often not practical to send these in any other way than rolled. Artists are also making even larger drawings which face the curator with the same problems. There are various ways to pack rolled works, but a safe method is illustrated in *Figure 29.12*.

There is a risk of condensation when Polythene sheeting is wrapped immediately next to the framed print or drawing, so it is advisable to separate any waterproofing from the object with a layer or two of tissue paper or other padding. This also applies to protective, 'bubbled' polythene.

Dealing with the conservator

When a curator has to resort to full conservation treatments he will have recourse to a conservator, and should discuss the proposed treatment with him. Each should respect and understand the other's priorities as a compromise may have to be made. Each will have a different, though allied, frame of reference. The curator will have historical knowledge to draw on while the conservator will have a knowledge of materials and their problems. It is necessary for the curator to have a broad understanding of conservation treatments and it is also necessary for the conservator to have an acquaintance with the history of art and in particularly with the art-history of the works concerned. Each is in a position to aid and further educate the other, and should act upon and respectfully understand the other's judgement.

Conservation treatments are often long and complicated and it is often impossible to predict how long they may take. Curators must give the conservator enough time to prepare material for exhibition. Timing should be discussed, and take into account mount-making, framing, transportation and mounting the display.

Disaster planning: fire, flood, theft

Fire
Fire detectors should be installed. These are inexpensive, but must be maintained properly with all other equipment for fire prevention. A carbon dioxide extinguishing system is the best for areas storing prints and drawings. Water sprinklers or hoses will damage these works, perhaps more than will the fire. All other fire precautions that must be practised in museums should be exercised.

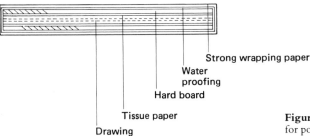

Strong wrapping paper
Water proofing
Hard board
Tissue paper
Drawing

Figure 29.11 Flat mounted or unmounted works packed for posting

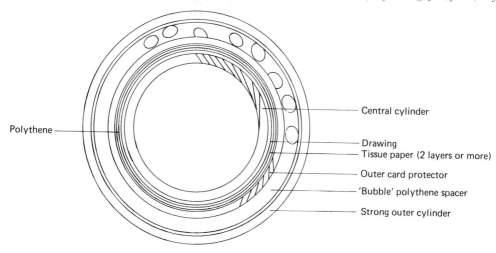

Polythene

Central cylinder

Drawing
Tissue paper (2 layers or more)
Outer card protector
'Bubble' polythene spacer
Strong outer cylinder

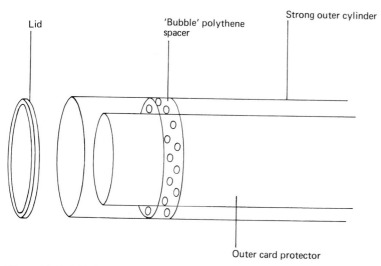

Lid

'Bubble' polythene
spacer

Strong outer cylinder

Outer card protector

Figure 29.12 Rolled prints and drawings packed for transportation (masking tape may be used to secure outer card and 'bubble' Polythene spacer

Flood

If flooding soaks a collection of prints and drawings there are several ways to tackle the problem, depending on the size of the collection and the nature of the flood. The works must be dried out quickly, though not so quickly as to cause distortion. If the collection is large and it is impossible to dry it completely, it may be frozen.

The curator will have to put in hand the drying of the collection, fungal treatment if immediate drying has not been possible, and first aid. Major conservation work will follow. Prints and drawings should be taken from their mounts. The equipment needed is

good white blotting paper and flat surfaces on which to lay out the works for air drying. If the quantity is too large to tackle wholly, the curator may resort to freezing, which should have been organized in advance. The works are then defrosted and dealt with in batches. On the other hand freeze-drying may be implemented (Grattan, 1982).

Theft

The marking of prints and drawings has been dealt with on pp. 257, but it may be necessary to further safeguard the collection. Many types of burglar alarms are available, and the police may be asked for guidance. Video systems, mirrors and good locks may be sensible methods of crime detection and prevention, while security checks may be operated. Where there is a high likelihood of theft, prints and drawings may have to be more securely housed in their mounts.

Notes

[1] Thomson, G. (1978), *The Museum Environment*, IIC and Butterworths, London, p. 65:

$$RH = \frac{\text{amount of water in a given quantity of air}}{\text{maximum amount of water which the air}} \times 100\%$$
$$\text{can hold at that temperature}$$

[2] Designed by Dr Solander of the British Museum between 1776–1782, these boxes consist of a case with hinged lid and side that fold out to a horizontal position when the box is opened so that the mounted original may easily be slid in and out.

[3] The British Standards Institution, 2 Park Street, London, W1

[4] Thymol chamber: a cabinet with low heating point where thymol dissolved in a solvent may be evaporated, destroying fungi and small insects.

[5] Insecticides: for guidance and information relating to the control of pests, contact Rentokil Limited, R and D division, Felcourt, East Grinstead, West Sussex RH19 2JY.

[6] Thomson, G. (1978a), *The Museum Environment*, IIC and Butterworths, p. 11. The table here lists light-fast categories for some common pigments, old and new.

[7] There are many erasers available but the one made by the West German company Staedtler called Mars-Plastic (No. 526 50) is very gentle and also comes in lengths of about 2 mm in diameter designed to fit a plastic holder; these are useful for controlled dirt removal over smaller areas.

[8] Pure Starch paste made up to the following formula:

90 g pure starch (arrowroot, wheat or rice),
10 g potato starch,
700 ml pure water,
100 ml saturated calcium hydroxide solution (2% in H_2O).

[9] Melinex – A polyester film which contains no plasticizers and does not embrittle with age. Brilliantly transparent, it comes in varying thicknesses, 0.5, 1, 2, 3, 4, 5, and 7 mm. Available from ICI.

[10] Lens cleaning tissue – available from Barcham Green and Co. Ltd, Hayle Mill, Maidstone, Kent ME15 6XQ.

[11] Stolow, N. (1979), *Conservation Standards for Works of Art in Transit and on Exhibition*, UNESCO, Paris, pp. 55–58. Good practical advice on case design and packing techniques. Well illustrated.

References

BRILL, T. B. (1980), *Light: Its Interaction with Art and Antiquities*, Plenum Press, New York, pp. 174–184

CLAPP, A. F. (1974), *Curatorial Care of Works of Art on Paper*, Intermuseum Conservation Association, Oberlin, p. 40

DANIELS, V. (1982), Colour changes of watercolour pigments during deacidification, *Science and Technology in the Service of Conservation*, Preprints of the Contributions to the Washington Congress of the IIC 1982, available from the IIC, 6 Buckingham Street, London EC2N 6BA

GRATTAN, D. W. (August 1982), A practical comparative study of several treatments for waterlogged wood, *Studies in Conservation*, **27**(3), *August 1982*, p. 133

HARDING, E. G. (1972), revised edn. 1980, *The Mounting of Prints and Drawings*, Museum Association Information Sheet No. 12, p. 1

LIBRARY OF CONGRESS (1980), *Polyester Film Encapsulation*, Publications on Conservation of Library Materials, Preservation Office Research Science, Library of Congress, Washington DC

McAUSLAND, P. AND STEVENS, P. (1979), Techniques of lining for the support of fragile works of art on paper, *The Paper Conservator*, **4**, 34

MEYNELL, G. G. AND NEWCOMBE, R. J. (1978), Foxing, a fungal infection of paper, *Nature*, **274**, 466–468; Foxed paper and its problems, *New Scientist*, 17 May 1979, p. 567

STANNARD, T. (1979), An introduction to the photographic recording of archive material during conservation, *The Paper Conservator*, **4**, 45–51

STOLOW, N. (1979), *Conservation Standard for Works of Art in Transit and on Exhibition*, UNESCO, Paris, 1979

THOMSON, G. (1978b), *The Museum Environment*, IIC and Butterworths, London, p. 15

WATROUS, J. (1957), *The Craft of Old-Master Drawings*, University of Wisconsin, pp. 69–74

ZEGERS, P. (1980), Mounting and Storage of the Graphic Arts Collection at the National Gallery of Canada, *Cambridge 1980: The Conservation of Library and Archive Materials and the Graphic Arts*, Institute of Paper Conservation and the Society of Archivists, pp. 135–140

Bibliography

Books on Conservation

BROMMELLE, N. AND SMITH, P. (1976), (Eds.), *Conservation and Restoration of Pictorial Are.* IIC and Butterworths, London. This volume consists substantially of papers presented at a congress in Lisbon of the International Institute for Conservation of Historic and Artistic Works in October 1972, entitled *Conservation of Paintings and the Graphic Arts.*

CLAPP, A. (1974), (2nd edn), *Curatorial Care of Works of Art on Paper*, Intermuseum Conservation Association, Oberlin, Ohio. This is the only comprehensive guide for curators which deals with this subject. Most of the advice is sound, although most of the 'do it yourself' information should be disregarded.

DOLLOFF, F. AND PERKINSON, R. (1972), *How to Care for Works of Art on Paper*, Museum of Fine Arts, Boston, Mass. This is a helpful small publication that every curator should acquire.

FLIEDER, F. (1969), *La Conservation des Documents Graphiques*, Eyrolles edition, Paris, 1969. In French and now somewhat out of date, Mme Flieder continues her researches in her laboratory in Paris and publishes regularly new information helpful to conservators of papers and books.

PLENDERLEITH, H. AND WERNER, A. (1971) (2nd edn), *The Conservation of Antiquities and Works of Art,* Oxford University Press, London. For long considered the best handbook covering the spectrum of objects conservation; however now Dr Plenderleith's book is out of date for art on paper conservation, in the light of all the mass of new research that has been done since it was first published. This second edition is not a great improvement on the first.

STOLOW, N. (1979), *Conservation Standards for Works of Art in Transit and on Exhibition,* UNESCO, Paris. Dr Stolow has consistently concerned himself with packaging works of art for transit and should be always the first person to turn to when faced with the problems that inevitably arise with travelling exhibitions and general transportation. Apart from the structure of packing cases he is also most concerned with changes in RH and fluctuations in temperature during transportation, by land, sea or air.

ZIGROSSER, C., AND GAEHDE, C. M. (1969), *A Guide to the Collecting and Care of Original Prints,* sponsored by the Print Council of America, Crown Publishers Inc., New York. Mrs Gaehde's section on the conservation of fine prints give sound useful information.

Reading list for students in Conservation of Historic and Artistic Works on Paper and on Photographs

BRILL, T. B. (1980), *Light: Its Interaction with Art and Antiquities,* Plenum Press, New York. The inspiration for this book came from lectures the author gave to students on the conservation course at Winterthur Museum, University of Delaware and is concerned with the nature of light, its properties, and its good and bad effects on materials.

CASH, M. S. (1980), (Ed.), AIC, Washington. Available from: the AIC, Kingle Mansion, 3545 Williamsburg Lane, Washington, D.C. 20008, USA. This is the only full bibliography available on the subject and is a most useful guide.

THOMSON, G. (1978), *The Museum Environment,* Butterworths in association with The International Institute for Conservation of Historic and Artistic Works, London. An invaluable guide for every curator.

Books concerned with Materials and Techniques

BIEGELEISEN, J. I., *The Complete Book on Silk Screen Printing Production,* Dover Publications, New York. A well-illustrated guide to the subject.

BRUNNER, F. (1962), *A Handbook of Graphic Reproduction Processes,* Arthur Niggli, Teufen, Switzerland. (to be reprinted in 1983). This volume is an invaluable aid to determining the different methods of graphic reproduction in English, German and French. Well illustrated.

CENNINI, C. (1953), *The Craftsman's Handbook,* Dover Publication Inc., New York. Translated by Daniel V. Thompson, from the Italian *Il Libro Dell' Arte* this early treatise is fascinating reading giving general information on the sixteenth-century craftsmen even mentioning an 'ideal' (fish) glue for paper mending.

COHN, M. B. (1977), *Wash and Gouache; A Study in the Development of the Materials of Watercolour,* Center for Conservation and Technical Studies, Cambridge, Mass. for the Fogg Art Museum and the Foundation of the American Institute for Conservation on the occasion of an exhibition of watercolours at the Fogg Art Museum. Although this publication was of more use during the exhibition at the Fogg Art Museum, nevertheless it stands in its own right as a fund of useful and interesting information on the subject.

GETTENS, R. AND STOUT, G. (1966), *Painting Materials: A Short Encyclopedia.* Dover Publications, Inc., 1966. Designed as a reference work for museum curators and conservators, it is therefore most helpful as a guide and aid to the mutual understanding of the terminology of conservation as well as techniques used by artists and craftsmen. An essential reference book.

HARLEY, R. (1970), (Reprinted 1982), *Artists' Pigments, 1600–1835.* IIC and Butterworths, London. The second edition of this work is more fully illustrated with some colour plates, it is better laid out and therefore easier to read. Another essential work to have at hand for general interest in this subject.

HIND, A. (1963), *A History of Engraving and Etching from the 15th Century to the Year 1914.* Dover Publications Inc., New York. The introduction to the book deals with processes and materials and proffers a short guide.

HIND, A. M. (1963), *An Introduction to a History of Woodcut,* Vols I and II. Reprint by Dover Publication Inc., New York. Arthur Hind was a Keeper of Prints and Drawings in the British Museum. These two volumes on the history of the woodcut covers Western woodcuts with a detailed survey of work done in the fifteenth century.

JONES, S. (1967), *Lithography for Artists,* University Press, Oxford. A short concise guide.

LUMSDEN, E. (1962), *The Art of Etching,* Dover Publications Inc., New York. The etcher, Prof Lumsden carefully and clearly explains each step in the creation of an etching from essential materials to completed proof. This is well illustrated.

MAYER, R. (1969), *A Dictionary of Art Terms and Techniques,* Thomas Y. Crowell Co., New York. This volume presents in succinct form the explanation of terms encountered in the study and practice of the visual arts and in their literature.

MAYER, R. (1970), *The Artist's Handbook of Materials and Techniques,* Viking Press, New York. Although of more use to the artist, this book gives a lot of interesting and helpful information on pigments. The conservation section should be omitted as the information is so scanty as to be positively dangerous.

WATROUS, J. (1967), *The Craft of Old Master Drawing,* University of Wisconsin Press, Madison, Wisconsin. A comprehensive and useful guide to the subject.

Some useful publications containing articles on conservation

The Abbey Newsletter: Bookbinding and Conservation. McCrady, E. (Ed.), c/o School of Library Service, 516 Butler Library, Columbia University, New York, NY 10027, USA.

AIC Newsletter. Published quarterly by the American Institute for Conservation of Historic and Artistic Works.

Conservation News. Quarterly newsletter of the United Kingdom Institute for Conservation.

The Conservator. Annual Journal of the United Kingdom Institute for Conservation. Available from the Publication Officer, UKIC, c/o Conservation Department, Tate Gallery, Millbank, London SW1P 4RG.

Journal of the American Institute for Conservation. Biannual journal of the American Institute for Conservation of Historic and Artistic Works, 3545 Williamsburg Lane, NW, Washington, DC 20008, USA.

Paper Conservation News. Quarterly Newsletter of the Institute of Paper Conservation.

The Paper Conservator. Annual Journal of the Institute of Paper Conservation, Leigh Lodge, Leigh, Worcester WR6 5L13

Restaurator. International Journal for the Preservation of Library and Archival Material. Christiansen, P. A. (Ed.). Published by Munksgaard International Publishers, 35 Norre Sogade, DK–1370 Copenhagen K. Denmark.

Studies in Conservation. Quarterly Journal of the International Institute for Conservation of Historic and Artistic Works, for the International Institute for Conservation of Historic and Artistic Works, London.

30

Conservation and storage: easel paintings

David Bomford

The structure of easel paintings

European easel paintings between the fourteenth and twentieth centuries display a huge range of styles and techniques, but all have comparable laminar structures. This allows a closely similar approach, in terms of classification, examination and treatment, to most easel paintings found in museum collections.

The main structural layer, the *support,* is most commonly of wood or of stretched fabric. A wide variety of wood types has been used for panel paintings, and often the species are indigenous to the geographical origin of the painting. At its simplest, a panel is made of a single piece of wood; at its most complex it may have many members, with wood-grain running in contrary directions, and secondary reinforcements such as battens or cradles. The peculiarly sensitive and unpredictable nature of wood panels necessitates precisely controlled conditions of storage and hanging. Canvas supports, usually made of linen stretched over a wooden frame, are less susceptible to environmental fluctuations but, at the same time, their lack of resilience makes them much more vulnerable to physical damage. This inherent weakness in old fabric paintings almost inevitably leads to the application of a secondary support of some kind, usually a lining. Other supports have been used for easel paintings: vellum, stone, copper, millboard and even glass, for example, may be encountered.

Usually, the support was prepared for painting by application of a *ground* or *priming,* although sometimes this layer is absent. The importance of the ground in the overall structure of a painting is often overlooked. Imperfectly prepared or deteriorating grounds can endanger an entire painting, with rather limited scope for treatment. The nature of grounds on canvas pictures is especially significant when the suitability of various lining processes is being consi-dered. Moreover, the influence of coloured or dark grounds in pictures that are worn or have become more transparent can be profoundly disturbing.

The *paint,* composed of coloured *pigments* dispersed in a *binding medium* (such as egg or a drying oil) may be a single layer, or many layers thick. There can be considerable complexity in terms of pigment mixtures and layer structure, and the possibility of added elements such as metal leaf in old pictures and collage in modern works may compound it. The state of preservation of the paint layers is often dependent more on the condition of the support and ground layers than on internal properties of pigments and media. Movement of supports and unsatisfactory adhesion to the ground are the most common causes of cracking and paint loss. Paint defects caused by pigment change or the drying mechanism of the medium are occasionally significant, but usually accepted as characteristic of the ageing of the picture.

When the paint was quite dry, it was usual to *varnish* the picture, to protect and make the colours properly visible. Traditional varnishes used to be natural resins in an appropriate solvent, sometimes combined with drying oils. All these resins discolour with time, some very badly. In addition, some oil varnishes become almost insoluble in normal cleaning solvents and therefore the cleaning of paintings is made more hazardous. Modern synthetic resin varnishes have largely replaced traditional types.

Each of the layers described above can have a marked effect on the appearance of a painting. In a deteriorating structure, it is not only their interaction with each other, but also *cleavage* between layers which becomes significant. It is customary when describing the condition of an easel painting and when proposing modes of treatment, to consider the layers one by one. This will be done in the following sections.

It is hardly necessary to point out that even the most routine methods of treatment applied to paintings by unskilled hands or in the wrong circumstances can have disastrous consequences. Examination of condition and treatment of defects should be carried out only by those properly trained in the conservation of easel paintings.

Conservation records

Ideally, every painting in a collection should have a detailed record of condition and treatment. Each time a painting is examined or treated, notes should be added to the records, together with photographs if necessary.

The nature of conservation records is a matter of convenience and personal preference. Some conservators favour a folder or loose-leaf system which allows expansion and flexibility of arrangement; a possible disadvantage of this is that, even with the most honourable intentions, photographs and reports may be extracted, borrowed and ultimately lost. An alternative system, somewhat more laborious but less likely to be abused, is to have blank volumes in which photographs and reports are mounted permanently.

A description of the condition of a painting in terms of its various layers forms the basis of any conservation record. Again, there are different approaches against which the needs of a particular collection must be balanced. It is wise to have some sort of printed examination report form to provide a formal framework around which an assessment of condition may be constructed. At its simplest, it would merely have sections corresponding to the principal layers of the painting in which features of those layers could be noted. At its most comprehensive, it might have boxes to be ticked for every possible variation in condition for every component of the picture. Detailed forms of this kind are recommended if an examination is to be made by someone other than an experienced conservator: if every section is completed correctly, then no vital feature is likely to be overlooked. As well as written records, a conservation dossier should have at least one photograph of the painting for identification, together with as many detailed technical photographs as is feasible. Where relevant, cross-reference should be made to material filed elsewhere such as colour transparencies, scientific examination reports, historical archives and so on.

If compilation of detailed conservation records is not possible, a card-index containing an essential summary of condition and treatment should be maintained. Even if full records are kept, a parallel card index summarizing the main points can be most useful for quick reference.

Wood supports

The warping of wood panels

The behaviour of panel painting is complex, not least because of the anisotropic nature of wood: although the properties of the various woods used for painting supports vary widely, generalization can be made. Wood has a cellular structure, the cells, for the most part, being formed like hollow straws parallel to the axis of the tree. The alternation of dense cells of summer wood and the lighter cells of spring wood as the tree grows outwards leads to the formation of annual growth rings and produces the visible grain in a piece of cut timber.

This cellular structure is hygroscopic and, in conditions of low or high relative humidity, will shrink or swell by an amount which varies directionally within the wood. In a log, swelling or shrinkage in a longitudinal direction (along the grain) is minimal, while in a transverse direction it is significant, the tangential change (along the arc of the growth rings) being about twice as great as the radial.

The manner in which a board was originally cut from a log is, therefore, significant in predicting its stability. A tangentially cut board, as it loses its natural moisture content, will have a tendency to shrink more at the outer face than the inner, and a warp will result. A radially cut board is more or less symmetrical, both faces will shrink by the same amount and there is no tendency to warp.

In the case of panel paintings, the situation is further complicated by the presence of an impervious layer of paint on one side and the possibility of panel constructions involving several boards. A paint layer effectively seals one face of the panel so that shrinkage and swelling caused by humidity changes occur only at the other face. Under conditions of high relative humidity (RH) one would expect the wood cells at the back to expand and therefore the painted side to be concave; under low RH, the painted side should be convex. This simple type of warping is reversible, simply by altering the humidity.

However, repeated cycles of expansion and contraction of the wood at the unprotected face can lead to permanent compression of the cells, which results in the characteristic convex warp seen in many panel paintings. With the aim of eliminating this warp, many misguided and damaging treatments have been carried out in the past.

Prevention and treatment of warping in panel paintings

Clearly, the most desirable factor in the conservation of panel paintings is precise environmental control since it is fluctuations in RH which lead to movement and, if violent enough, to the destabilization of the entire structure of the picture. No museum can control its climate with total precision, however, and so it becomes important that the natural movement of wood panels in conditions of varying humidity should not be restrained in any way, or else deformation and eventual splitting may result. Restraints such as attached bars of wood or metal, cradles, small mahogany buttons reinforcing old splits and even tightly fitting picture frames can all lead to permanent damage and should be removed if there is any indication of stress.

The theory of *cradling* appears sound, but frequently it creates more distortion than the warp it is designed to eliminate. In a traditional cradle, fixed bars are glued to the reverse of the panel, parallel to the wood-grain, and free-running cross-members pass through slots cut into them. In theory, the warp is controlled while natural movement across the grain is allowed, but in practice the cross-members usually become jammed as the panel tries to warp. In addition, the fixed bars act as individual restraints and many cradled panels exhibit the corrugated 'washboard' effect, which may be even more pronounced if the panel was thinned before cradling (as was often the case).

Cradling of panels is now considered an unnecessary and potentially harmful treatment and should be avoided. Existing cradles that still function properly can be left alone, but those that are thought to be acting as restraints should be removed in small sections by carefully sawing and chiselling the fixed members. Similarly, rigid bars of wood or metal fixed across the wood-grain should be removed if necessary. Frequently, such bars are tapered and dovetailed into grooves in the back of the panel and removal may be possible by sliding them laterally.

After removal of restraints, most panels assume a gentle convex warp, indicating the amount of stress that has been relieved. Many unrestrained panels also exhibit a convex warp due to development of permanent set. There is nothing inherently wrong with leaving a panel in a convex conformation – indeed, if the warp is visually acceptable it is the safest course. Once the panel has stabilized in the museum environment, it can be returned to its frame which should be adapted with slips of balsa wood within the rebate, shaped to the curvature of the panel. If the panel is structurally weak it can be held gently but firmly by shaped slips, just capping the front edges, against a rigid background on which are rubber or cork pads reflecting the correct curvature – a construction known as a 'tray'.

If a warp is considered unacceptable, then steps may be taken to eliminate it and maintain the panel in a flattened state. By exposing the back to high humidity (over, but not touching, moistened pads) for a period of some hours, the panel will flatten under its own weight. To prevent the warp recurring, a semi-rigid backing of balsa wood blocks may be applied using a wax-resin cement, while the panel is still in its humidified state. The overall restraint of the balsa backing, together with the trapped moisture, induces plastic deformation within the wood cells which allows the attainment of a new, flatter equilibrium state. This does not happen with the traditional cradle, because the wood dries out before plastic deformation occurs. A certain degree of permanent flattening may also be achieved simply by brushing a *moisture barrier* of wax-resin onto the back of the flattened humidified panel.

Occasionally a panel is encountered exhibiting a concave warp. This is a potentially dangerous state, and may be caused by a number of factors. Remedial treatment should be undertaken at once by an experienced conservator.

Other defects of panel paintings

More frequently, panel paintings may have to be treated for a number of other defects. Flaking or blistering of the ground and paint layers, caused by movement of the support and consequent breakdown of adhesion, is frequently encountered. Prominent craquelure, although perhaps arising from the same cause, is not in itself an indication of potential paint loss. Indeed, some of the most serious cleavages, often unnoticed and invariably difficult to treat, occur in apparently well-preserved parts with little or no cracking: this is so-called *blind cleavage*. Treatment of this and of straightforward flaking is described on p. 271.

Treatment of splits or loose joins in wood panels is carried out using standard cabinet makers' methods involving cash-clamps, G-clamps and woodworking adhesives. Purpose-built apparatus incorporating longitudinal and vertical clamping has been devised for gluing split and loose panel members, but since problems can vary so much in size and complexity many conservators prefer a simpler and more empirical approach. Often, the joining of panels forms only part of a more extended treatment of removals of restraints, flattening and reinforcement and it is important that the entire operation should be carefully planned in advance so that the correct sequence can be followed. Splits or joins should be glued simply edge-to-edge, if possible, without additional reinforcement of battens, buttons, 'butterfly' inlays, fabric and so on. Sometimes hardwood V-shaped inserts are let into the back of a split if reinforcement is necessary. Weak panels may be supported in a tray or by a balsa wood backing, as described already.

Panel paintings are often attacked by wood-boring insects. Where the insects are still found to be active, the pictures should be isolated and treated either by fumigation or by injecting with a suitable insecticide: the choice of insecticide is critical, since some oil-based liquids have a disastrous softening effect on paint films. Advice should be sought before treatment is attempted. The panel should be inspected at six-month intervals for evidence of continued activity: if existing holes are filled with wax, new ones will be easily detected.

Dry-rot, where it occurs, can also be treated with proprietary fungicides, but the same caution is necessary as with insecticides. Where wood panels are badly eaten or eroded, from whatever cause, they can be consolidated by impregnation with a wax–resin mixture or with a suitable wood-hardening compound. Wax–resin is an excellent consolidant, but it must be remembered that its water-repellant properties preclude the subsequent use of normal woodworking adhesives.

The most extreme form of treatment that can be applied to panel painting is *transfer,* in which the paint film, with or without the ground, is mounted on another support after removal of the original wood. It is only attempted when all other forms of treatment have proved ineffective. Circumstances in which it might be carried out are, for example, when the support is totally decayed, or when adhesion between the support, ground and paint layers has irreversibly broken down. Transfer is an extremely long and difficult operation with many hazardous stages: it should only be attempted by a very experienced conservator.

Finally, a word should be said about the *thinning* of panels – a sort of partial transfer in which the wood is drastically reduced in thickness before application of some secondary support. The practice is based on the belief, largely fallacious, that a thin veneer of wood is somehow less troublesome and easier to manipulate than a panel of normal thickness. Often, in fact, the reverse is true, and the potential for cracking and warping may actually be increased. As a general rule, the thinning of panels should be discouraged.

Canvas supports

Defects of canvas paintings

Many fabrics have been used for painting supports which are grouped under the traditional description of 'canvas'; linen, in a variety of different weaves (which may have a distinct effect on the appearance of a picture) has been most widely used, but cotton, hemp and even silk are sometimes found. The suitability of a fabric for use as a painting canvas depends on its ability to be stretched taut and to maintain tension. If tension is lost, the stability of the more brittle paint and ground layers is threatened.

Tension is maintained by the wooden *strainer* or *stretcher* upon which the fabric is mounted. A strainer has rigidly jointed corners and cannot be expanded,

whereas a stretcher has mitred or tongue-grooved corners which can be tapped-out by means of wooden *keys* or *wedges*. Other mechanisms for expansion can involve turn-bolts or springs and are preferred by some conservators: these can be perfectly satisfactory, but in view of their potential mechanical strength great care should be exercised when tightening, especially with fabrics whose fibres tend to *creep* or deform irreversibly.

Rigid strainers should be replaced if the opportunity arises, since retensioning of a canvas painting may be necessary in, for example, conditions of fluctuating relative humidity. Although they are not as unstable as wood panels in these circumstances, the behaviour of canvas paintings is, nevertheless, complex, because the response of fabrics to varying RH depends both on the tension within them and on coatings which have been applied to them. A stretched yarn behaves differently to an unstretched one, in which factors such as twist or crimp become significant. Moreover, a sized fabric behaves differently to an unsized one. Given the conditions usually present in canvas paintings (principally due to their traditional preparation with animal glue size) higher RH will generally result in slackening or sagging. Expansion of the stretcher to take up the slack should be carried out with caution, since a subsequent fall in RH may mean that the canvas becomes too taut. However, if a canvas is allowed to sag for too long it can deform permanently.

From the mid-fifteenth century when canvas supports were introduced into European painting, their advantage over wood was seen to be principally one of lightness relative to size. They were portable and could even, if necessary, be rolled up. If a large painting has to be rolled for transport today (and it is always best to avoid it if possible), certain elementary principles should be observed. A cylindrical roller of the largest possible diameter should be used, one end of the canvas attached to it with tape, and the painting rolled around it with the painted side *outwards* (paint will stretch more successfully than it will compress). In addition, tissue or non-stick film should be placed between each successive layer, and the whole assembly wrapped and taped around.

Although they have the advantage of portability, canvas paintings possess an inherent and ever-increasing lack of strength. This is largely due to materials used in the sizing and painting processes. Animal glues, both in the original size layer and from subsequent support treatments such as lining, encourage the growth of micro-organisms and moulds which attack and weaken the fabric; also drying oils not only embrittle the whole structure, but, through their own oxidation processes promote oxidation and degradation of the fibres.

The natural consequences of these processes is that

canvases are vulnerable to all kinds of physical impact and stress. Holes, tears and dents are commonplace. Canvas can be distorted by a label or patch stuck on the back, or by resting slackly against its stretcher. Repeated tapping-out can cause it to tear away from the tacks fastening it in place (a problem often worsened by rust from the tacks themselves) or to tear at the front edge of the stretcher. In association with the cracking of thick ground and paint layers, it can be distorted into a series of saucer-shapes known as *cupping*. Often, cupping is absent in an area where the back of the canvas has been protected by the stretcher; this is the *stretcher image* and is usually bounded by continuous straight cracks corresponding to the edges of the stretcher bars.

Methods of treatment, minor and major, have been devised appropriate to all the many ways in which canvas paintings can deteriorate. All are specific to particular circumstances, some are ill-advised under any circumstances. Treatment other than the major process of *lining* will be considered first.

Minor repairs to canvas paintings

Many of the defects of canvas paintings can be dealt with relatively simply, or avoided altogether by observing simple precautions. Clearly, all risks of impact or contact with sharp or rigid objects must be eliminated.

Stacking pictures in storerooms is a particular area of hazard: corners of other pictures or of frames must not be allowed to rest against a canvas. Parts of the structure of the picture itself can represent a danger. For example, untrimmed ends of picture wires can easily pierce a canvas; loose wedges and other foreign bodies can often fall between the bottom stretcher bar and the canvas, causing bulges on the surface of a painting. In the latter case, such bodies can be removed, with great care, by means of a flat palette-knife, and the problem avoided in future by securing the wedges with cord.

Dents or bulges can vary greatly in severity before the canvas is actually punctured. If caused by a blow on the reverse side, characteristic circular crack patterns in the paint and ground layers are often formed around the point of impact and there may be associated paint losses. It is possible to treat dents and bulges, and also localized wrinkles in a canvas, by careful damping of the reverse side of the area followed by tapping-out or flattening under weights on a flat surface. However, the utmost caution should be exercised, since some fabrics shrink excessively with moisture and throw off the paint.

Small holes in a canvas can be *patched* with thin material attached by a suitable adhesive. The danger with patching (as with attaching paper labels) is that the outlines of the patch (or labels) frequently become visible as distortions on the front of the pic-

ture. This is especially true if an aqueous adhesive is used. More satisfactory results can be obtained if a thermoplastic adhesive, such as wax-resin, is used and if the edges of the patch are *feathered,* or frayed, by removing some lateral threads. The repair is completed by filling and inpainting.

If the hole is larger, it can be filled by inserting a piece of canvas similar to the original, aligned correctly and held in place by patching. However, if the hole is more than a few centimetres across, lining is probably necessary. Tears, similarly, are usually too large to be satisfactorily treated by patching.

Sometimes the tacking edges of a canvas painting deteriorate, either at the tacks themselves or at the front edge of the stretcher, while the main picture area remains sound. In order to enable secure attachment to the stretcher, the edges may be reinforced by *striplining*; in this process, strips of new canvas are stuck behind the tacking margins (or in place of them if they are missing) and overlap the reverse of the main picture area by a centimetre or two. Various adhesives have been used. As with patching, there is a danger of the edges of the canvas strip showing as a ridge on the front of the painting, and so feathering and the use of a non-aqueous adhesive are advisable. Reattachment to the stretcher should be carried out with non-rusting tacks, either tinned or of copper.

Occasionally, under conditions of high humidity, canvas paintings are afflicted by mould which may feed off original size or lining materials. It may be treated by physical removal followed by spraying the reverse side with a suitable fungicide. Any mould on the paint surface may be removed by normal cleaning methods.

Lining and relining – traditional techniques

The usual cure for the maladies of paintings on canvas is *lining*. Very nearly all canvas pictures older than, say, the middle of the nineteenth century have been lined at least once and possibly several times. An old, unlined painting is something of a rarity and merits special consideration and treatment.

To *line* a painting is to reinforce it by attaching a second support to the back of the original canvas using a suitable adhesive. To *reline* a painting is to remove an existing lining and repeat the process. The purposes of lining are, traditionally, threefold:

(1). To strengthen a canvas support which may be weak, torn or incapable of being attached to its stretcher.
(2). To correct deformations of the support, ground and paint layers by application of heat, pressure or moisture, or combinations of those three.
(3). To ensure firm attachment of the paint and ground layers to the support by penetration and impregnation with the chosen adhesive.

The lining process was originally devised to achieve these three objectives in a single operation. Impregnation and lining of canvas paintings have been carried out using glue and drying oils since the seventeenth century. The use of beeswax and, later, beeswax-resin mixtures became widespread in the late nineteenth century and continues to the present day.

Traditionally, lining techniques are based on the use of fine linen for the secondary support and infusion with either a glue/flour paste or a hot-melt beeswax-resin adhesive; both types may have other additives designed to impart desirable properties. These remain standard techniques and, applied in the correct circumstances, produce excellent results. Indeed, without them, many paintings would not have survived. There are clear advantages and disadvantages in both techniques; it cannot be stressed too strongly that a painting can be ruined and even destroyed by injudicious application of an unsuitable method. Of all conservation procedures, lining is perhaps the most difficult to do well and requires great experience in a conservator.

Badly-cupped paintings, which will relax and flatten with moisture, may be successfully lined with aqueous, glue-based adhesives. However, certain canvases in combination with particular grounds shrink disastrously under the action of moisture and heat, throwing off the paint. Shrinking does not occur with non-aqueous beeswax-resin adhesives but, on the other hand, they are ineffective in treating cupping: some sort of pre-treatment with moisture is required if cupping is to be eliminated. (pp. 269–270).

The refractive index of lining adhesives is important, since it has a direct bearing on any possible darkening of a painting. Where ground and paint layers are poorly bound, or where the original canvas plays a visible role, infusion with certain adhesives can result in darkening and colour-change. In a general way, the reflective index of wax-resin is such that it is more likely to cause darkening than an aqueous adhesive. In most old pictures, painted in oil and repeatedly varnished, the change is not significant: however it is a factor that should always be considered.

One of the most common reasons for lining is the repair of tears or holes. It is obviously desirable that the chosen adhesive should be strong enough and stiff enough to maintain the edges of a tear in a flat state. Beeswax-resin adhesives are rather poor in this respect and tears may begin to curl and sag after a period of time. As well as using a different adhesive, the problem of badly torn paintings is often best dealt with by *marouflage,* in which the painting is mounted on a rigid panel, preferably of inert materials, or by *double lining*, in which a second lining confers additional stiffness. In double lining, different adhesives can be used for the two stages –

perhaps an aqueous adhesive followed by wax-resin.

The practical procedures involved in different lining methods are also of importance in deciding their suitability. Glue-paste lining is invariably done with hand-irons, which should be thermostatically controlled. Paintings of high impasto can present a problem and many are seen today with their texture crushed during previous hand-linings. Although there are ways in which the problem can be overcome, it is probably better to avoid hand-lining such paintings. Wax-resin linings may also be carried out with hand-irons, but they are particularly suited to *hot-table* methods. A hot-table, usually of polished metal, provides uniform control of heating and cooling over its whole surface. In combination with a membrane fastened to the edges of the table and a vacuum pump, paintings may be held under constant pressure during the entire lining process. Such methods are only suitable for thermoplastic lining adhesives and cannot be used for adhesives which involve evaporation of water or solvents.

Lining of paintings on the vacuum hot-table is usually carried out face-up, with the adhesive and lining canvas underneath. It is therefore a suitable method for paintings with impasto; even so, a combination of heat and the pressure of the membrane can soften and flatten paint texture. The lining of paintings face down on the hot-table should be discouraged for obvious reasons.

Although the introduction of the vacuum hot-table represented a major advance in lining techniques, possible limitations and disadvantages become apparent. The technique will not, by itself, eliminate cupping in paintings; neither will it permit the use of adhesives other than thermoplastic ones. Moreover, there is a possibility of unwelcome texture changes in paintings lined under vacuum pressure: sometimes the texture of the original canvas or the lining canvas may influence the paint surface by *weave emphasis* or *weave interference*. Such effects can be reduced by interposing a non-woven *interleaf* between the two canvases.

Marouflage can be carried out on a hot-table, provided that the panel is heat-conducting, as modern aluminium honeycomb constructions are. Otherwise hand-ironing is necessary, or use of a cold-setting adhesive.

The final criterion by which a lining should be judged is how it behaves subsequently. Here again, traditional techniques differ. Wax-resin linings are not affected by changes in RH; glue linings are, and may sag or contract if conditions alter. In order to combat this, they may have a moisture barrier of wax or wax-resin applied to the back of the lining canvas as a final stage. Wax-resin linings do not maintain tension wholly successfully and may slacken over a period of time: it has already been mentioned that repaired tears may curl and distort.

Lining is only a temporary measure, carried out in the full expectation that it will have to be repeated within 50–100 years. It therefore becomes vital that current treatment be *reversible* in the broadest sense. In the strictest sense, impregnation of a painting with any adhesive is fundamentally irreversible, but, in practical terms, reversibility implies only the possibility of physical removal of the old lining. The compatibility of adhesive within the original fabric with any future lining adhesive is important, however. Glue formulations tend to be compatible, both with the materials of the painting itself and with most other adhesives. Traditional beeswax-resin mixtures, on the whole, are not: it should always be borne in mind that once a canvas painting has been impregnated with wax-resin, treatment with other adhesives is inhibited.

Lining and related treatments – new directions

Until recent years, the choice of lining methods was limited, with minor variations, to one of the traditional techniques described above. Currently, investigation of alternative methods is a major area of research and any account must inevitably become out of date fairly rapidly; nevertheless certain trends may be identified.

Emphasis is moving away from impregnation techniques. The different objectives of the lining process – fixing of flaking paint, reinforcement of support and elimination of deformations – can be achieved in separate operations which do not necessarily require overall impregnation. Where possible, lining is avoided altogether.

Where lining is required merely as reinforcement, it is unnecessary and, indeed, undesirable to infuse the whole structure of a painting with adhesives, with possible consequences such as darkening and colour change. All that is required is a bond between the lining and the surface fibres on the reverse of the original canvas – a so-called *nap-bond*. This is very difficult to achieve using traditional adhesives, which penetrate and flow uncontrollably, and so a range of synthetic adhesives of more suitable properties has emerged.

A major advance has been the development of *heat-seal* adhesives, applied in solution (unlike conventional wax-resin mixtures which are applied molten) and heat-activated after drying. Heat-seal adhesives consist of, or contain, mixtures of resins of high and low molecular weight, which combine high viscosity with powerful adhesion. They will bond two pieces of fabric together without flowing into them. Formulations containing different grades of polyvinyl acetate (PVA) have been found especially suitable for the lining process.

By adding other components such as synthetic waxes, further useful properties such as increased flow and decreased heat-seal temperature can be incorporated. The versatile Beva adhesives, developed specifically for use in lining, are based on ethylene vinyl acetate copolymers and microcrystalline waxes. They can be used either as heat-seal adhesives or, by increasing the temperature, as impregnating adhesives with flow properties analagous to conventional hot-melts. Even when used for impregnation, the risk of darkening is less than with beeswax-resin mixtures, since the refractive indices of the components are lower.

The new generation of heat-activated adhesives can be used in conjunction with hand-irons, vacuum hot-tables or with the *vacuum envelope* technique, in which the canvases are held between two membranes stretched over a framework. The disadvantages of the rigid hot-table are overcome by this method, and heating and cooling can be more or less instantaneous.

Another development in lining adhesives is the use of water-based emulsions containing acrylic or vinyl resins. These are cold-setting and act by evaporation of water and solvent. Conventional vacuum hot-tables are unsuitable for the technique, and specially designed low pressure lining tables ('cold' tables) have been devised for it. These have metal surfaces with regularly spaced small perforations; a powerful down-draught of air not only holds the canvases in close contact but also carries away the evaporating water or solvents. With water-based emulsions such as these, the possible danger of shrinking in the picture canvas should always be considered.

The heat-seal and low pressure methods will not, in themselves, fix flaking painting or eliminate cupping. When necessary, these are carried out before the lining stage. Fixing of flaking paint is described on page 271. Cupping may be reduced by exposing the picture canvas to water and solvent vapours and pressing out the deformations with or without heat, after the canvas has relaxed. The necessary conditions are present in traditional glue-paste linings, which is why they are successful in this respect. Treatment of cupping as a separate stage before lining may be carried out by damping and hand-ironing (somewhat dangerous), by vapour treatment under warmth and pressure on the vacuum hot-table, or by repeated exposure to moisture and drying-out on the low pressure table. The most effective apparatus would appear to be a low-pressure table with heating and humidifying facilities, which at the time of writing, is still in the experimental stage.

As an adjunct to the treatment of distortions such as cupping, it is often necessary to place the picture canvas under tension, in order to encourage it to return to its former flat state. Various techniques combining vapour treatment and stretching have been devised, with or without additional pressure and heat, which are described by the general term *pre-stretching*. The subsequent lining may then be performed with the painting held in its pre-stretched condition.

As well as lining adhesives, lining fabrics have been the subject of research in recent years. Although fine linen remains the most widely used secondary support, other materials such as fibreglass, polyester fabrics and polyvinyl alcohol fabrics can have advantages in certain respects, such as permanence, stiffness, creep and so on. Fibreglass can result in a semi-transparent lining, if inscriptions on the back of the picture canvas are required to remain visible.

Lining, in the sense of permanent attachment of a secondary fabric, may sometimes be unnecessary, when the original canvas merely requires support. It can be enough to fasten a second canvas over the stretcher before stretching the picture canvas – this is so-called *loose lining* – in which the two canvases simply rest against each other. As a compromise between loose lining and full attachment, a recent development utilizes a fabric coated with a tacky silicone adhesive, which holds the picture canvas firmly, but which may be peeled off if, and when, this becomes necessary.

Other supports

Supports other than wood panel or canvas are sometimes encountered. Treatment of defects must necessarily be empirical, but a few specific problems may be mentioned.

The principal problem with supports of metal, stone, slate, marble and similar materials is one of poor adhesion between their smooth, unabsorbent surfaces and applied paint layers. Painters were well aware of the problem and would often etch or roughen surfaces to provide a key. However, flaking paint is the most common defect in such paintings, and may be treated by methods outlined below.

Copper, the most usual metal plate used for painting, is a reactive metal and this should be remembered when selecting adhesives for securing loose paint. Certain components of traditional wax-resin mixtures will react with copper, in time forming salts which will undermine and force off paint adjacent to treated areas. For this reason, wax-resin adhesives should never be used on copper pictures. Inert synthetic formulations are suitable and have been used with success.

Unsupported copper plates may be in danger of flexing, bending and creasing with consequent paint loss. A copper painting, once bent, is almost impossible to straighten satisfactorily. It is therefore important to remove this risk by backing it with a rigid panel of some kind. It should not be laid down with adhesives, but held against its backboard by capping the edges or with adhesive tape on the reverse side.

One other unusual support material should be mentioned, as it poses unique problems to the conservator of easel paintings. This is *vellum*, encountered only rarely, and perhaps difficult to distinguish from fabric – especially if it has been lined with canvas. The particular danger with vellum is that a combination of heat and moisture causes it to shrink markedly. Distortions and tears in a vellum picture may require treatment with controlled amounts of moisture, but it should be carried out only by an expert.

Ground, paint and varnish layers

Defects of paint and ground: treatment

Defects of paint layers arise from a number of causes. Inherent instability of materials, techniques of application, natural ageing processes, interaction with other layers and external influences, such as heat, light, humidity and physical damage, can all contribute to their deterioration.

A combination of processes is therefore operating, which manifests itself most clearly in the *craquelure* observed on the surface. Cracking of paint films is of two main types: *drying cracks,* initiated during the drying process, and *age* (or *mechanical*) *cracks* which occur after paint and ground have ceased to be flexible. On a microscopic scale, drying cracks tend to have rounded edges, since they are formed while the paint is still plastic, but their overall pattern is unpredictable. Whether or not they develop depends on the properties of both the paint and the ground or underlayer to which it was applied. Considerable shrinkage and cracking of a paint film can result from its own drying mechanism, especially when bituminous pigments are present which retard drying in particular areas. Also, if the ground or underlayer is still plastic, or its surface is glossy and rich in medium, then adhesive forces between layers are insufficient to counteract the contraction of the paint film. Many eighteenth- and nineteenth-century paintings show this phenomenon, resulting from the use of insufficiently aged or unsuitable commercially prepared grounds, and from the unwise use of certain paint formulations.

Whether or not drying cracks are present, most paintings of any period have a network of age cracks usually initiated by movement of the support. These are formed when the paint and ground have hardened and become brittle, and therefore penetrate both layers. Some tension remains in the paint and ground layers even when dried and this may result in the formation of concavities (*cupping*) between the age cracks. This tension can be strong enough to set up distortions throughout the entire structure of a picture and might lead ultimately to deformation of the support (in canvas paintings) or to cleavage from it. Cleavage is also caused by constant movement of the support weakening the bond between layers.

No treatment is required for craquelure as such: it is regarded as a normal ageing characteristic of a painting. If it is especially disfiguring (for example, drying cracks in dark areas which reveal a white ground) it may be inpainted using a fine brush.

However, associated cleavage leading to *blistering* and *flaking* must be treated before paint loss occurs – although, too often, loss of paint is the first indication that cleavage is present. It is important that paintings should be regularly inspected for signs of raised paint and blisters. Curators and conservators alike should resist the temptation to test raised paint with a thumbnail: a paint blister is very brittle and can shatter and be lost very easily.

Treatment of blistering and flaking is straightforward but requires much patience: it is a routine but vital operation in the maintenance of any picture collection. Canvas paintings, of course, may be treated by lining or relining and panel paintings by transfer, but for local areas on canvases, and for the vast majority of panel paintings, treatment is carried out using thermostatically-controlled heated spatulas.

The principle is to introduce adhesive into points of cleavage and to flatten and hold the paint in position until the adhesive sets. Traditional adhesives are hot-melts of the wax-resin type and weak animal glue solutions such as gelatine. More recently, synthetic adhesives have been widely used, as hot-melts, or in solution, or as water-based emulsions. The adhesive is usually introduced through a tissue *facing* which protects the surface of the paint and holds any loose flakes in place. Aqueous adhesives or those in solution may be brushed on; hot-melts can be picked up directly on the hot spatula. With practice, it is usually possible to persuade the adhesive to flow into blisters or under raised paint through the existing craquelure. If there is no craquelure – in cases of blind cleavage perhaps – it may be necessary to puncture the paint with a needle to allow the adhesive to penetrate. This can be done quite unobtrusively and there is no need for the excessive pricking sometimes encountered on old panel paintings.

As with lining, aqueous adhesives are more successful at dealing with cupped paint and ground, but the combination of heat and moisture can cause *blanching* of the varnish, which then has to be reformed using suitable solvents (see page 272). With an aqueous adhesive, ironing with a warm spatula is continued until it is set; with a hot-melt adhesive, setting is achieved by substituting a cold spatula for the hot one.

If a painting is found to be flaking and immediate treatment is not possible, then a *facing* of tissue should be applied to the affected area with a standard facing adhesive. This may be a starch paste, wax-resin based or synthetic; when dry, the tissue holds the paint firmly in place until remedial treatment can be carried out. Facing is a routine preliminary operation which precedes many conservation treatments: in support treatment, where there is a danger of paint becoming detached through movement, facing is essential.

Examples of inherent instability in paint and ground materials are the occasional chemical alterations undergone by a few pigments. The blue ultramarine may become a mottled grey colour under acid conditions; green copper resinate may become dark brown under alkaline conditions. Both processes may be accelerated by the use of unsuitable reagents during cleaning, and both are irreversible. Another pigment change identified in recent years is the discolouration of the blue smalt in oil media to a greenish-grey. In general, chemical interaction between pigments, such as the blackening of lead white by sulphides (not infrequently observed in water colours and murals) does not occur in oil and egg-tempera paintings.

The medium, too, sometimes undergoes optical changes. The most common example of this is the increased transparency of paint layers caused by a rise in the refractive index of drying oils as they age. *Pentimenti* and dark grounds that were not originally apparent, may, in time, show through.

Less predictable are the occasional cases of *blanching* in the paint film: two distinct types may be identified. The first is caused directly by exposure to moisture (flood-damaged paintings for example) but it is important to distinguish it from the far more common blanching of the varnish layers (see above). To a degree, it may be reversed by exposure to solvents and solvent vapours. The second type of blanching is more mysterious: it tends to occur with particular painters such as Claude or Cuyp, in passages such as landscapes and foliage. Whether it is caused by deterioration of pigment or medium or both has not yet been ascertained: it is reduced slightly by solvent treatment, but is largely irreversible.

The varnish layer: cleaning of paintings

An ideal picture varnish should be transparent, without colour and of a refractive index compatible with the dried paint film it is to protect; it should be tough and resist moisture and pollutants, and yet should also be readily removable in mild solvents. Most importantly, it should retain these properties for as long as it remains on the painting.

No varnish corresponding to this ideal has yet been produced. Traditional varnishes containing drying oils and hard resins discolour badly and become quite insoluble with time. Even the best of the natural resin varnishes, dammar and mastic – which have excellent handling properties and are still widely used – discolour appreciably and become less soluble. Most of the newer synthetic resins used for picture varnishes are reasonable in terms of reversibility and colour, but fall down on other considerations – surface appearance or handling, for example.

The relatively rapid deterioration of varnishes becomes evident in a number of ways. Discolouration, opacity and blanching all impair their optical properties. They can shrivel and contract and develop independent craquelures of their own, which attract dust and dirt. A thick varnish may also exert considerable traction forces as it ages and may actually endanger a weak paint film below.

For a variety of reasons paintings are cleaned. *Cleaning* implies removal of dirt, varnishes and other surface coatings, and also any non-original paint that may conceal damage or cover original paint. The technique of cleaning is simple, but much skill and experience is necessary to interpret and to deal with problems if they arise. Varnish removal is carried out with appropriate solvents on small cotton-wool swabs; as the swabs become saturated with dissolved residues they are changed.

Cleaning (in the sense of varnish removal) has been practised for centuries and has always been an inexact and empirical operation, relying on the skill of the restorer rather than on any precise application of scientific principles. Within reason, the choice of solvent was less critical than the dexterity of its user. More recently, it has been possible to quantify and classify materials used in cleaning and to relate them directly to the coatings that are being removed. This is done in terms of *solubility parameters* which have been calculated for a wide variety of solvents and resins. Solvent mixtures may be selected whose parameters fall within the range calculated for a particular resin. Equally importantly, solvents whose parameters correspond to the swelling region of the paint medium (and which therefore might endanger the paint film during cleaning) can be avoided.

A technique which is closely allied to varnish removal, either as a preliminary to it or as an alternative, is *reforming*. A refined version of a nineteenth-century practice known as the *Pettenkofer* method (after its inventor) in which varnishes were rejuvenated by suspending pictures over solvent vapours, it consists of spraying or brushing controlled amounts of selected solvents on to the picture surface. Where varnishes have become opaque or cracked or blanched, reforming will greatly improve their clarity, although it will have no effect on discolouration as such. It will also render varnishes more readily soluble in relatively mild solvents in any subsequent cleaning.

A form of varnish removal sometimes used is that of *frictioning* the surface. A small crystal of resin is rubbed on the existing varnish with the fingertips, causing it to break down into white powder which can be dusted off. This operation appears more alarming than it actually is. It is an extremely inefficient method of removing varnish, but it could be used if a paint film was soluble in normal cleaning solvents. It is more often used to even up an old, patchy varnish, followed by application of a new coating.

An occasional problem with some varnishes is *bloom,* a dull bluish cloudiness which appears intermittently. Its cause is uncertain, but humid conditions seem to encourage it. It can usually be removed with a damp cloth followed by polishing with a dry one. Application of a suitable wax polish will eliminate it, but the advantage of that must be balanced against the fact that wax coatings attract dirt appreciably more than varnishes alone.

Removal of surface dirt from paintings is carried out using water, or dilute solutions of appropriate soaps on cotton wool swabs. This is an operation that must be carried out with particular care, since both water and soap might have deleterious effects if allowed to penetrate the structure of the picture. If a painting has been varnished several times over an extended period, each time trapping a layer of dirt beneath the new coating, cleaning may require repeated alternation of solvents with aqueous agents.

Removal of overpaint and retouching during the cleaning process is often achieved with the same solvents used for varnish removal. This, of course, depends on differential solubility between later and original paint. Where the two cannot be separated by solvents or reagents, physical methods such as scraping with scalpels must be employed. Criteria for distinguishing original paint from later additions are well-established in the literature. If there is any doubt about the status of a particular passage, it must be left alone.

When cleaning is completed, a painting is given a thin brush-coat of a suitable picture varnish, in preparation for *filling* and *inpainting*.

Restoration of paintings: filling, inpainting and revarnishing

Where old damages have been revealed by cleaning, or new repairs are being carried out, the last stages of treatment are the filling of lacunae, inpainting (retouching) and the application of a final varnish.

There are many recipes for filling materials, some traditional, some synthetic. Most conservators have particular preferences, and as long as the filler satisfies certain basic conditions, the choice is not critical. Filling materials should be capable of being textured, in order to imitate the surface of the surrounding paint, either by carving or moulding in some way; they should not shrink or curl or fall out; and they should not become so hard that they cannot be removed without endangering adjacent paint (as some oil putties do). The success of a passage of inpainting depends largely on the skill with which the filling has been carried out. A check on the matching of texture may be made with the picture in raking light.

The criteria by which retouching paints should be judged are similar to those described above for an ideal varnish. Whether commercially prepared formulations are used or whether pure pigments are ground in a medium by the conservator himself, a retouching paint should retain its colour, not darken and should remain permanently removable in mild solvents. Oil paints are almost totally unsuitable for retouching, since they darken and become insoluble: even removal of excess oil with blotting paper (as some restorers do) does not render them suitable. Commercial artists' paints based on synthetic resins might be satisfactory, but the conservator may have no idea of the properties or permanence of the manufacturer's ingredients.

The most satisfactory inpainting materials appear to be pure pigments of known permanence, either ground in a range of synthetic resins of known and tested properties, or used as water-colours, or in pure egg-tempera. Suitable synthetic resins that are widely used are particular grades of polyvinyl acetate and acrylic copolymers of the Paraloid (Acryloid) range: their optical properties, permanence and reversibility appear to be excellent. Retouching using water-colour or egg-tempera is more difficult (especially in terms of colour-matching, since they change tone on varnishing) but, skilfully done, they can achieve unique luminosity and texture. It might appear that egg-tempera, which becomes insoluble in time, disobeys the principle of reversibility: but, provided it is applied over an isolating varnish that remains soluble, it can always be removed.

The degree and nature of any inpainting is a matter for consultation between curator and conservator. There are many possible compromises between leaving a hole in the fabric of a painting and 'complete' or 'deceptive' retouching. Any decision has to take into account the type of painting and the nature, size and position of the damage. But whatever that decision, it does not affect the basic ethics of restoration, which are that: materials should be reversible; no original paint that was intended to be seen should be covered; and a photographic record of the picture in its unretouched state should, if possible, be made.

The desirable properties in a final varnish have been discussed. Retouchings are usually varnished individually with a small brush before the last coating is applied by brush or spray. Variation in gloss and mattness can be achieved by incorporating additives such as synthetic waxes in the varnish formula-tion. Alternatively, gloss can be regulated by judicious manipulation of the spray gun, if that method of application is used.

Handling, storage and display

The importance of environmental control for easel paintings cannot be overstated and, while full air-conditioning is beyond the range of many museums, installation of blinds, humidifiers and so on can markedly improve conditions. Ideal values for temperature and RH are 20°C and 55 per cent respectively; a range of 10 per cent RH can be tolerated. Visible light and UV levels should also be controlled since photochemical changes do occur in easel painting materials, although phenomena such as fading are less pronounced than in water-colours or textiles, for example. A value of 200 lux at the picture surface is considered to be a reasonable compromise between the need to see the painting and the need to protect it.

If climate control is impossible, then serious consideration should be given to placing fragile paintings in a sealed case of some kind, either free-standing or fastened to the wall of the room. Conditions inside are more or less isolated from environmental changes outside, and a *microclimate* is established. Such cases can vary enormously in sophistication. The simplest are merely transparent boxes which serve to delay and suppress the transmittance of atmospheric fluctuations to the space around the painting. More elaborate designs have chambers incorporated within them, containing salts conditioned to maintain the air at a particular RH level.

Handling and storage of easel paintings is, above all, a matter of common sense. Accidents occur when staff have not been shown how to handle pictures, when economies are made in time and personnel and when space is limited. In most museums, storage areas are cramped and invariably become used for other purposes as well. If it is within the museum budget, a system of mesh screens to which pictures (with or without their frames) may be fixed on both sides, is ideal for storage. These may be fixed, in which case enough space must be left between them for access, or mounted close together on a series of parallel bearings so that a single screen can be pulled out of the stack; the latter system allows much more efficient use of available space.

Often, however, there is no alternative to stacking pictures against a wall, leaning them one against another. Clearly there are dangers involved, with paintings of different sizes, sharp corners, frame mouldings and so on. If possible, rigid boards should be placed between pictures so that they do not rest directly against each other, and a weight placed against the foot of the outermost picture to prevent it sliding forward. In a basement storage area, the possibility of damp, or even flooding, should not be discounted.

For pictures without frames, especially large modern ones, it is often sound practice to construct a temporary frame which will protect the edges and by which the picture may be carried.

The permanent framing and display of pictures are areas in which correct preparation and some forethought can have markedly beneficial effects on the paintings themselves. A frame should be deep enough to contain the thickness of the picture: if not, then the back should be built up until it is. A backboard of masonite or similar material can then be fixed to the frame, covering and protecting the back of the painting. For canvas pictures, this prevents dust and foreign bodies collecting behind the lower stretcher bar. For panel paintings it can act as a rudimentary buffer against atmospheric fluctuations.

The rebates of frames should be lined with material such as velvet ribbon so that varnish around the edges of a painting is not scuffed. For warped panels, shaped slips should be incorporated within the rebate (see page 265). The fastening of pictures into frames should be carried out using mirror plates screwed to the back of the frame and overlapping the back of the picture. Rubber pads may be placed between the plates and the picture to allow for movement in the support. The traditional practice of attaching pictures to their frames with bent nails should be discouraged. Spaces around the edges of the pictures should be packed with a relatively soft material like balsa wood.

Whether paintings should be glazed is usually a curatorial decision. It is undeniable that glass or perspex protects a picture surface from physical impact, dust and pollutants and, to a degree, from atmospheric changes, but against that must be weighed the undoubted aesthetic limitations imposed.

The problem of transporting pictures and of travelling exhibitions is discussed elsewhere, in terms of packing-case design and administrative considerations. Deciding whether a painting is fit to travel should be left to an experienced conservator, who will judge its present condition and any likely consequences. Some museums refuse on principle to lend any wood panels: although this is a commendably cautious attitude, it is probably better to consider each case on its merits. Indeed, many panel paintings will actually travel more successfully than some canvas paintings, in which constant vibration of the stretched fabric may play a major role in deterioration.

Perhaps the most vital aspect of maintaining any collection of easel paintings is regular inspection. Constant vigilance will detect many minor problems before they become major ones. A routine examination programme should be instituted and repeated periodically, although its frequency will obviously depend on the size of the collection.

Bibliography

The literature of paintings conservation is so extensive that no attempt has been made in the foregoing text to refer to specific papers. Neither is it feasible here to compile a complete bibliography of the subject, since some of the published work is repetitive or is now seen to be outdated.

The starting point for any literature survey of this subject is the massive annotated bibliography assembled by Joyce Plesters for *The Cleaning of Paintings* by Helmut Ruhemann (London, 1968). Everything of any importance published up to 1966 is listed, and the reader is referred there for works appearing before that date. The bibliography below only attempts to identify subsequent key publications and omission of a particular work does not necessarily imply unworthiness. Books of a general kind are listed first, followed by papers arranged by topic.

Abbreviations

SIC: Studies in Conservation
ICOM: ICOM Committee for Conservation, Triennial meetings (Year, location and paper number given in each case)
IIC: International Institute for Conservation, Preprints of International congresses (year and location given in each case).

Books

BROMMELLE, N. AND SMITH, P. (1976), (Ed.), *Conservation and Restoration of Pictorial Art,* Butterworths, London

EMILE-MALE, G. (1976), *The Restorer's Handbook of Easel Painting,* Van Nostrand Reinhold, Wokingham

FELLER, R. STOLOW, N. AND JONES, E. H. (1971), (2nd edn), *On Picture Varnishes and their Solvents,* Cse Western Reserve, Cleveland

GETTENS, R. J. AND STOUT, G. (1966), *Painting Materials: a Short Encyclopedia,* Dover, New York

KECK, C. (1967), *A Handbook on the Care of Paintings,* American Association for State and Local History, New York

MAYER, R. (1969), *A Dictionary of Art Terms and Techniques,* A. and C. Black, London

MAYER, R. (1973), (3rd edn), *The Artist's Handbook,* Faber, London

PLENDERLEITH, H. J. AND WERNER, A. E. A. (1971), (2nd edn), *The Conservation of Antiquities and Works of Art,* University Press, Oxford

RUHEMANN, H. (1968), *The Cleaning of Paintings,* Faber, London. Reprinted by Hacker Art Books, New York (1983)

STOUT, G. L. (1975), (2nd edn), *The Care of Pictures,* Dover, New York

THOMSON, G. (1978), *The Museum Environment,* Butterworths, London

TORRACA, G. (1975), *Solubility and solvents for conservation problems*, International Centre for the Study of the Preservation and the Restoration of Cultural Property, Rome

Wood supports

BEARDSLEY, B. (1978), A flexible balsa back for the stabilization of a Botticelli panel painting, *IIC, Oxford*, 153–156

BUCK, R. D. (1972), Some applications of rheology to the treatment of panel paintings, *SIC*, **17**, 1–11

CORNELIUS, F. DU PONT (1967), Movement of wood and canvas for paintings in response to high and low RH cycles, *SIC*, **12**, 76–80

HICKIN, N. (1970), Wood-destroying insects and works of art, *IIC, New York*, 75–80

HORNS, J. (1978), Induced strain in panel paintings undergoing conformational changes, *IIC, Oxford*, 123–130

JESSELL, B. AND PRICE, G. (1978), Some methods of repair and conservation of easel paintings on wooden supports, *IIC, Oxford*, 169–174

LENNON, T. (1978), The transfer of a sixteenth century panel painting: use of a lightweight paper honeycomb material as a support, *IIC, Oxford*, 185–190

MARTIN, M. AND REISMAN, S. N. (1978), The surface and structural treatment of a Payum portrait, *IIC, Oxford*, 191–198

MONCRIEFF, A. (1968), Review of recent literature on wood, *SIC*, **13**, 186–212

REIMOLD, F. (1972), Transferring an altarpiece by Konrad Witz, *IIC, Lisbon*, 815–830

SMITH, A., REEVE, A. AND ROY, A. (1981), Francesco del Cossa's S. Vincent Ferrer, *National Gallery Technical Bulletin*, **5**, 45–57

SPURLOCK, D. (1978), The application of balsa blocks as a stabilizing auxiliary for panel paintings, *IIC, Oxford*, 149–152

Canvas supports

BERGER, G. A. (1966), Weave interference in vacuum lining of pictures, *SIC*, **11**, 170–180

BERGER, G. A. (1970), A New Adhesive for the consolidation of Paintings, Drawings and textiles, *Bulletin of the American Group*, **11**(1), 36–38

BERGER, G. A. (1971), Application of heat-activated adhesives for the consolidation of paintings, *Bulletin of the American Group IIC*, **11**(2), 124–128

BERGER, G. A. (1972a), Testing adhesives for the consolidation of paintings, *SIC*, **17**, 173–194

BERGER, G. A. (1972b), Some effects of impregnating adhesives on paint films, *Bulletin of the American Group IIC*, **12**(2), 35–45

BERGER, G. A. (1972c), Formulating adhesives for the conservation of paintings, *IIC, Lisbon*, 613–630

BERGER, G. A. (1975), Heat-seal lining of a torn painting with Beva 371, *SIC*, **20**, 126–151

BERGER, G. A. (1976), Unconventional treatments for unconventional paintings, *SIC*, **21**, 115–128

BERGER, G. A (1978), Consolidation of delaminating paintings, *ICOM, Zagreb*, 78/2/1

BERGER, G. D. AND ZELIGER, H. I. (1975), Detrimental and irreversible effects of wax impregnation on easel paintings, *ICOM, Venice*, 75/11/2

BOMFORD, D. (1979), Moroni's 'Canon Ludovico di Terzi': an unlined sixteenth century painting, *National Gallery Technical Bulletin*, **3**, 34–42

BOMFORD, D. AND STANIFORTH, S. (1981), Wax-resin lining and colour change: an evaluation, *National Gallery Technical Bulletin*, **5**, 58–65

FIEUX, R. E. (1973), Teflon-coated fiberglass as a support for relining paintings, *Bulletin of the American Group IIC*, **14**(1), 73–74

FIEUX, R. E. (1978), Electrostatic hold: a new technique of lining, *ICOM, Zagreb*, 78/2/7

GREENWICH CONFERENCE ON COMPARATIVE LINING TECHNIQUES (1974), various papers, not formally published; similar material subsequently published elsewhere by some of the authors concerned. See also Percival-Prescott, W. W. (1974) and Percival-Prescott, W. W. and Lewis, G. M. (1974)

HACKE, B. (1978), A low-pressure apparatus for the treatment of paintings, *ICOM, Zagreb*, 78/2/12

HACKE, B. (1981), Low pressure, heat, moisture, stretching. Notes on further developments, *ICOM, Ottawa*, 81/2/8

HACKNEY, S. AND HEDLEY, G. A. (1982), Measurements of the ageing of linen canvas, *SIC*, **26**, 1–14

HEDLEY, G. A. (1975), Some empirical determinations of the strain distribution in stretched canvases, *ICOM, Venice*, 75/11/4

HEDLEY, G. A. (1975), The effect of beeswax/resin impregnation on the tensile properties of canvas, *ICOM, Venice*, 75/11/7

HEDLEY, G. A. (1981), The stiffness of lining fabrics: theoretical and practical considerations, *ICOM, Ottawa*, 81/2/2

HEDLEY, G. A. AND VILLIERS, C. (1982), Polyester sailcloth fabric: a high-stiffness lining support, *IIC, Washington*, 154–158

KECK, C. K. (1977), Lining adhesives: their history, uses and abuses, *Journal of the AIC*, **17**(1), 45–52

LEVENSON, R. (1978), A new method for strip-lining easel paintings, *ICOM, Zagreb*, 75/2/8

LEWIS, G. M. (1975), Preparatory treatment of paintings for lining *and* A vacuum envelope lining method, *ICOM, Venice*, 75/11/6

MAKES, F. (1981), Enzymatic consolidation of paintings, *ICOM, Ottawa*, 78/2/7

MAKES, F., AND HALLSTROM, B. (1972), Remarks on relining, Stockholm

MECKLENBURG, M. F. AND WEBSTER, J. E. (1977), Aluminium honeycomb supports: their fabrication and use in painting conservation, *SIC*, **22**, 177–189

MEHRA, V. R. (1975), Further developments in cold-lining, *ICOM, Venice*, 75/11/5

MEHRA, V. R. (1978), Cold-lining and the care of the paint layer in a triple-stretcher system *and* Answers to some questions and doubts about the cold-lining system, *ICOM, Zagreb*, 78/2/5

MEHRA, V. R. (1981), The cold lining of paintings, *The Conservator*, **5**, 12–14

PERCIVAL-PRESCOTT, W. W. (1974), The lining cycle, *Conference of Comparative Lining Techniques, Greenwich. See also* Greenwich Conference (1974)

PERCIVAL-PRESCOTT, W. W. (1975), Conservation of paintings: the Greenwich lining conference, *Museums J.*, **74**, 169–171

PERCIVAL-PRESCOTT, W. W. AND LEWIS, G. M. (1974) (Ed.),

Handbook of terms used in the lining of paintings, *Conference on comparative lining techniques, Greenwich*

RABIN, B. (1972), a poly(vinyl acetate) heat seal adhesive for lining, *IIC, Lisbon,* 631–635

VILLERS, C. (1981), Artists canvases: a history, *ICOM, Ottawa,* 81/2/1

WALES, C. (1968), Lining torn paintings on Aluminium Panel, *Bulletin of the American Group IIC,* **8**(2), 15–17

Paint and ground

BOISSONNAS, P. B. (1977), A treatment for blanching in paintings, *SIC,* **22,** 43

GOIST, D. C. (1977), Treatment of a flood-damaged oil painting, *Journal of the AIC,* **16**(2), 21–26

GREEN, J. AND SEDDON, J. (1981), A study of materials for filling losses in easel paintings, and their receptiveness to casting of textures, *ICOM, Ottawa,* 81/2/12

KECK, S. (1969), Mechanical alteration of the paint film, *SIC,* **14,** 9–30

KETNATH, A. (1978), The treatment of a fire-damaged picture painted on a masonite board, *SIC,* 168–173

LANK, H. (1972), The use of dimethyl formamide vapour in reforming blanched oil paintings, *IIC, Lisbon,* 809–814

PLESTERS, J. (1969), A preliminary note on the discolouration of smalt in oil media, *SIC,* **14,** 62–74

WATHERSTON, M. (1976), Treatment of cupped and cracked paint films using organic solvents and water, in Brommelle N. S. (Ed.) *Conservation and Restoration of Pictorial Art* Butterworths, London, pp. 110–125

WELSH, E. C. (1980), A consolidation treatment for powdery matte paint, *Preprints of the AIC 8th annual meeting,* San Francisco

WYLD, M, MILLS, L. AND PLESTERS, J. (1980), Some observations on blanching, with special reference to the paintings of Claude, *National Gallery Technical Bulletin,* **4,** 49–63

Varnishes and cleaning

DE WITTE, E. (1975), The influence of light on the gloss of matt varnishes, *ICOM, Venice,* 75/11/6

FELLER, R. L. (1972), Problems in the investigation of picture varnishes, *IIC, Lisbon,* 201–207

FELLER, R. L. (1975), Studies on the photochemical stability of thermoplastic resins, *ICOM, Venice,* 75/11/4

FELLER, R. L. (1976), The relative solvent power needed to remove various aged solvent-type coatings, in N. S. Brommelle (Ed.), *Conservation and Restoration of Pictorial Art,* Butterworths, London, 158–161

FELLER, R. L. AND BAILIE, C. W. (1972), Solubility of aged coatings based on dammar, mastic and resin AW2, *Bulletin of the American Group IIC,* **12**(2), 72–81

FELLER, R. L. AND CURRAN, M. (1970), Solubility and cross-linking characteristics of ethylene-vinylacetate copolymers, *Bulletin of the American Group IIC,* **11**(1), 42–45

FELLER, R. L. AND CURRAN, M. (1975), Changes in solubility and removability of varnish resins with age, *Bulletin of the AIC,* **15**(2), 17–26

HEDLEY, G. (1980), Solubility parameters and varnish removal: a survey, *The Conservator,* **4,** 12–18

HULMER, E. C. (1971), Notes on the formulation and application of acrylic coating, *Bulletin of the American Group IIC,* **11**(2), 132–139

LAFONTAINE, R. H. (1979a), Decreasing the yellowing rate of dammar varnish using antioxidants, *SIC,* **24,** 14–22

LAFONTAINE, R. H. (1979b), Effect of Irganox 565 on the removability of dammar films, *SIC,* 179–181

LAFONTAINE, R. H. (1981), Use of stabilizers in varnish formulations, *ICOM, Ottawa,* 81/2/5

LANK, H. (1972), Picture varnishes formulated with resin MS2A, *IIC, Lisbon,* 215–216

RAT, K. (1980), An examination of the value of the reforming technique in practice, *SIC,* **25,** 137–140

STOLOW, N. (1976), Solvent action in N. S. Brommelle (Ed.) *Conservation and Restoration of Pictorial Art* Butterworths, London, 153–157

WATHERSTON, M. (1972), Problems presented by colour field paintings *and* Cleaning of colour field paintings, *IIC, Lisbon,* 831–845

Storage, handling etc

CANNON-BROOKES, P. (1978), Museums and fine art transporters, *Museums Jl.,* **77,** 174–176

HOLDEN, C. (1979), Notes on the protection of modern art works during handling, packing and storage, *The Conservator,* **3,** 20–24

PERRY, R., AND BOOTH, P. (1978), Some notes on the framing of paintings, *The Conservator,* **2,** 41–44

SACK, S. P., AND STOLOW, N. (1978), A microclimate for a Fayum portrait, *SIC,* **23,** 47–56

STOLOW, N. (1977), The conservation of works of art and exhibitions, *Museums Jl.,* **77,** 61–62

31

Conservation and storage: decorative art

C. Velson Horie

Decorative art is a broad term, covering a wide range of objects in diverse subject disciplines, which may be classified in several ways. As conservation techniques are dictated primarily by the materials making up the object, these will form the main divisions of this chapter. They comprise stone, ceramics, glass, metals, wood, various organic materials, plastic and wax. Few items are composed solely of one material, or made in one piece, considerations that increase the complexity of preservation techniques.

Many objects were constructed for practical rather than ornamental purposes. The maintenance necessary to keep them usable by the standards of the day often involved considerable modification of the original. Once an object enters a museum collection its purpose is changed. It becomes the material evidence of history and can be used to interpret the past. 'Decorative Art' indicates the perception of these objects by museums: they are seen as decorative, and efforts are often focused on satisfying this criterion. The task of museum workers is, therefore, to enable the objects to appear visually attractive while not compromising their main function.

The aims of conservation

'Conservation' describes the efforts needed to ensure that the historical and material evidence of the object is not diminished. Various techniques have been developed to this end. First, a *record*, in as much detail as possible, reduces unnecessary examination and further handling. Second, objects must be *stored* somewhere, and, whether on display or in reserve collections, efforts must be made to reduce the possibility of damage by people, vermin, light, pollution and climate. Adequate standards of handling, security, packaging, and environmental control should be maintained. The above two activities should not

change the objects. Frequently, action on the objects themselves is necessary. Third, the minimum necessary may be termed '*first aid*'; and this is usually as much as a person untrained in conservation should so do. Fourth, many materials exposed to poor storage conditions need to be *stabilized* to stop further deterioration. This process may involve fumigation to kill insect pests, or lacquering to retard tarnishing. Fifth, deliberate changes to objects are made during *restoration*, the aim of which is to make an object appear in its original state. The amount of work can vary from the removal of surface grime to the remaking and refurbishing of entire objects.

Standards of care

Theoretical standards of environmental control and treatment (UKIC, 1981; AIC, 1979) are, in essence, quite straightforward. In practice, however, they are limited by the lack of competent personnel and resources. The basic skill for anyone working in museums is the ability to *handle* objects reliably, and to organize their safe storage. In view of the improvization frequently necessary in packing or displaying objects of decorative art, this should be carried out by someone with sympathy for, and knowledge of, the object and its fragility. Work with an object should preferably be carried out, or actively supervized, by a person familiar with the materials, techniques of manufacture and likely defects, of the object. Only this familiarity, gained through curatorial or conservation work, can alert the worker to incipient damage or weakness. The wrong form of first aid or environmental control may exacerbate, not help, a fault.

Treatment for stabilization or restoration should be carried out by a trained person, who will usually be a specialist conservator, although supervized laymen may be employed on less-exacting tasks[1]. The range of skills required means that objects from any one collection may go to many different conservators. Where a museum has a sufficiently qualified conservator, responsibility for the physical care of the collection and for the quality of remedial work will rest in his hands (Orraca, 1981). Unfortunately only the large museums can justify the cost of sufficient full-time specialists. In Britain, the Area Museums Services provide specialist conservation services which can be called upon by subscribing museums, but few of these can justify the services of a range of decorative art conservators. Many pieces in private hands are treated by restorers in private practice. It is, therefore, to those that the museum must often turn for conservation skills. A high proportion of these restorers are competent craftsmen, but only a few are trained or practised in the particular museum skills of conservation. Considerable care must therefore be taken when engaging an outside restorer for conservation work[2].

Storage and handling: general considerations (Fall, 1973)

The correct conditions for storing different materials are well-documented. However, considerable problems can arise when materials requiring markedly different storage conditions are part of the same object. The handling and movement of objects has received little study, with the result that uncertainty may arise in those without considerable experience. Guidelines follow, but the situation must be assessed for each object.

The requirements for each part and material in the object must be considered separately and a compromise achieved which causes least damage to the whole object. Some materials which are dealt with in other chapters must also be considered.

Inspection before touching

Inspect for strength. Most decorative art items are three-dimensional and have extended parts which are inherently more vulnerable than the main body of the object. With the passage of time, joins fixing individual pieces can loosen.

Inspect for surface delicacy. The finish on pieces of decorative art is important and should be protected from damage. Surface abrasion can remove paint or veneers; acids in finger-marks can cause long-term rusting or tarnishing on metals; fingers can leave permanent impressions in soft or sensitive surfaces such as lacquers.

Record the condition of the object. Any previously unrecorded defect or potential difficulty should be noted for future treatment.

Decide where the object will be carried and placed. There must be a clear, uncluttered route to a clear, uncluttered space where the object will be deposited. Any uncertainty or difficulty in carrying an object increases the risk of its being dropped or gripped incorrectly.

Provide carrying boxes or trays. It is usually unwise to carry a complicated or slippery object in one's hands. A suitable receptacle will prevent the object from rolling or sliding, and provide secure handholds.

Ensure that all surfaces are clean. Soiled objects must be cleaned, and cleaning may cause further damage. Although this is usually slight, it is occasionally irreparable. Hands should be washed; blankets or dust-sheets should be laundered and aired; padding must be replaced when dirty.

Consider wearing gloves. Damage caused by finger-marks can be immediate and easy to remove, for example, an impression on waxed furniture. However, finger-marks not visible at the time can later cause pitting corrosion in metals. The oils from fingers pick up dust and so cause future soiling. Clean, white, cotton gloves are useful, but can be hazardous if the surface is slippery or has filigree work that might catch in the gloves' threads. An alternative is the disposable plastic glove. Surgical gloves provide good tactile response while being slightly tacky.

Handling the object

Test the coherence of the object. Internal movements of the object should be tested before it is lifted clear of its support.

Support all moveable parts. All supports must be gently, but firmly, applied. A support need not harm the object if it is properly padded, and should not be so strong that it distorts the object. Examples are the framing-up of loose legs on a table, and a hand placed on the top of a lidded jar.

Lift near the centre of gravity. The most massive part of an object is usually the one to which all other parts are attached. It is normally safe to lift there, but care should be taken to support other heavy parts.

Practice the procedure first. If two or more people are involved, all should work as a team, with one person in charge and responsible for all procedures.

Packaging (Rosegrant, 1942; Wakefield, 1963; Holdon, 1979)

Never use cotton wool. The fibres can become trapped in filligree raised veneers etc., and cause visual distraction. On removing the fibres, the entwined surface may pull away, thus causing damage.

Do not use powdery materials. Some materials, for example cellulose wadding or vermiculite, gradually shed powder onto objects which must then be cleaned.

Polymer foams must be treated with caution. All foams are networks of polymer surrounding holes. These networks can trap and remove pieces of the surface in a similar fashion to cotton wool. In addition, some foams can cause corrosion in metals.

Use good quality tissue, never newspaper. For pottery, glass and stone ordinary tissue paper will suffice, but for metals and other sensitive materials acid-free tissue paper should be used.

Objects with particularly delicate surfaces can often be more easily handled and packed if stored in tie-up bags of a good quality close-weave cotton that has been well-washed and rinsed. Guns can also be stored in similar bags to prevent fingermarks on the metal and the removal of preservative oils.

Never wind packing around objects. They should rest on a bed of padding and be covered by a similar bed.

Ensure that the object cannot be lost in the packing material. If the object is likely to be overlooked during unpacking, it should be stored in a distinctive package, for example a plastic bag or box. Packaging should be scrupulously checked before being discarded.

Label the receptacle. This should list the contents of the box with notes on potential difficulties, for example 'Flask in three pieces'. The label should be amended if the contents changed. All old labels should be removed or thoroughly obscured.

Never stick labels onto objects. The correct way to label an object is by a neatly written number in an inconspicuous place or by a tie-on label. Stick-on labels should not be used. Some cannot be completely removed, while others may cause staining in porous materials or corrosion in metals.

Objects should not touch one another. When packed in the same box objects should be padded. Storage on open shelves is convenient, but can lead to overcrowding and consequent damage. Each object should be allocated a space defined by a tray or box containing the object. Objects should not be placed on top of, or inside, each other.

Objects should be protected from dust. Dust contains many deleterious agents such as abrasives, corrosive salts, tarry oils and black pigments. The best protection is complete encapsulation in a box. Failing that, the store can be dust-proofed and dust extraction provided. This will reduce the amount of dust, but curtaining with cloths will further limit deposition.

First aid

Breakage

Each fragment no matter how small, should be kept. If necessary use a dustpan and brush to collect all the pieces. A check should be made for the completeness of the fragmented object and all the pieces carefully packed to avoid chipping of edges.

Flood (Upton and Pearson, 1978)

If still wet, wash with clean water, taking care not to dislodge surface decoration, veneer, paint and so on. Remove all surface water. If metal or stone, dry evenly but speedily. Organic materials are more variable and if saturated with water, the best holding operation is to freeze the object. If not waterlogged, for example with woodwork, dry slowly. Mould formation can be reduced by circulating the air within the room or applying a mild fungicide.

Sticking

If for an urgent reason, parts of the object must be stuck together immediately, an appropriate adhesive that can be completely removed should be applied.

Washing

Washing is such a commonplace occupation that the need for care is often overlooked. No material with a porous or friable surface, and very few organic materials, should be washed unless absolutely necessary. Materials that might be washed are metals (except polished steel), hard stones, high-fired ceramics and glass. Washing will remove any water-based paints and can disturb oil-based paints, and even some enamels are liable to damage.

No surface touched by the object should be hard and unyielding such as metal or ceramic. Both the object to be washed and the water should be at room temperature. Any detergent should be of a non-ionic type, for example Synperonic[3] and be used in the smallest concentration e.g. 0.05%, with no foam covering the water surface. Only one object should be placed in the water at a time and precautions taken to prevent it floating around. The water should be replaced before it becomes visibly dirty. Objects should be rinsed a couple of times in clean water, the last rinse preferably being in purified water. Water should be dabbed off the surface to prevent water-staining. Drying should be thorough, and, for metals, speedy. Difficulties can arise in drying the inside of hollow vessels. Swilling out with white alcohol or acetone will remove the water and they will then evaporate fairly quickly[4].

The care of materials

The materials making up objects can be divided into three major groups; stone and vitreous materials, metals and organic materials. Though there are exceptions to every rule, the conditions required for the three categories are different. However, within each category the materials require more or less similar conditions. Before treating an object, information about it and its constituent materials must be sought. Discussion of material properties is here limited to dividing materials into logical groups. Further information should be sought in the references. Any person attempting a treatment must be conversant with the available information; irreparable damage can be caused by such seemingly innocuous action as washing with water.

Stone (Read, 1976; Hodges, 1976a; Thomson, 1971)

These materials can be divided into four categories by their method of formation; igneous (granite, obsidian), metamorphic (marble, slate), sedimentary (chalk, clay), and man-made (concrete, plaster). In general, the most robust are igneous while the least so are sedimentary. The man-made equivalents vary in similar fashion. Architectural stonework from buildings is usually in larger pieces and consequently heavy. These blocks can be easily damaged if they fall. Frequently, such stonework is of limestone or sandstone which has softened and decayed through weathering. The surfaces are, therefore, likely to be soft or friable and easily damaged by abrasion. For these reasons, adequate facilities for storage and movement must be provided, including sturdy shelving, hoists and loading bays (Hartley, 1981).

Stone can become impregnated with salts and the consequent efflorescence or sudden crumbling must be dealt with urgently. Some stonework was coloured by gilding or painting, and it is essential to check for remains of this before cleaning. Plasterwork saved from buildings will usually be crumbling with additional fracturing caused during removal. While plaster may be held together by fibrous material it will not support its own weight. Such pieces are best kept flat on a stout board, and handled as little as possible. Plaster should not be allowed to become wet. Water softens the surface considerably and also fixes dirt firmly into the pores. Stone used for furniture and decorative items is usually highly finished and thus easily marked by abrasion. The stones often chosen for these objects, such as marble, alabaster or soapstone, are soft and may be affected by water or acids in the atmosphere. Carvings may be coloured. Many large pieces of sculpture are made up of two or more pieces held together with iron dowels secured in place, frequently by plaster. If it becomes damp the iron will rust, causing staining and splitting around the dowel. The plaster becomes friable with time, so allowing the dowel to loosen. Both these deteriorations may allow pieces of the object to crack off. All joins should be inspected and strengthened with temporary supports where necessary. In general, therefore, stonework should be kept dry, though some plasterwork may be harmed by extreme desiccation.

A variety of stones are used in jewellery, sometimes carved and appearing either free-standing or inlaid. Some, like jade or ruby, are robust, while others are likely to suffer from bad storage or handling. *Table 31.1* indicates the general storage and

Material	Low relative humidity	Heat	Light exposure	Mishandling	Organic solvents	Absorbed oils	High RH
Alabaster				•		•	
Amber	•	•		•	•		
Calcedony						•	
Coral			•				
Corundum			•				
Dyed opal			•				
Fluorite		•	•				
Garnet		•					
Haematite		•					
Jet	•		•	•	•		•
Marcasite							
Opal	•	•	•	•		•	
Pearl	•	•	•				
Pitch (mounting)		•			•		
Quartz		•		•			
Lapis lazuli				•			
Rose Quartz			•				
Topaz			•				
Turquoise			•			•	

Table 31.1 Susceptibility of some stones to outside agencies

handling conditions for jewellery and carved stones, by isolating potential causes of damage (Sinkankas, 1981; Franks, 1982; Howie 1982).

Ceramics (Larney, 1975; Hodges, 1975, 1977b; Larson, 1980)

Ceramics are classified conveniently by the temperature of firing and, consequently, by the degree to which the materials making up the clay have fused together. At one extreme is the sun-dried mud brick which can disintegrate to mud. At the other are modern glass-like ceramics used for cooking surfaces. Ceramics were repaired in the past with the materials then available. Unfortunately, many of these subsequently failed and the pottery may be held together solely by rivets. Such objects should be handled with extreme care.

Most archaeological and ethnographical pottery was fired at relatively low temperatures (below 1000°C) as were many earthenware and terracotta items. These latter terms describe very similar ceramic materials, though they can refer to different types of objects; earthenware implying a practical use, whereas terracotta implies unglazed, decorative items. Earthenware is porous and some unfused components of the clay may still be water-sensitive and affected by changes in relative humidity. It is, therefore, wise to maintain uniform levels. Washing with water can also cause damage or staining. Many of the early or complicated earthenware objects were not well-constructed, with poor joins between handles and bodies, or various layers of sculpture. These require extra care when handling or supporting, to avoid stresses developing. Earthenware for domestic or architectural use was frequently covered with a glaze which, because of the low temperature of firing, does not bond properly to the body. Over time, and with exposure to water, knocks and so on, the glaze can craze, absorb dirt and, in extreme cases, fall off. A crazed glaze indicates that the ceramic is already weak. Some terracottas were finished with oil or water paint, the remains of which may be obscured under dirt, and so be overlooked.

When fired to higher temperatures of 1100–1500°C, the clay particles fuse together to form an impermeable body. The ceramic is less porous and stronger than earthenware, and so has more uses. However, highly fired material is glass-like and thus more brittle and sensitive to sudden changes in temperature than earthenware. Stoneware is the coarsest of these high-fired bodies. The glazes used on most western stonewares fit the body very well, and are unlikely to fall off. However, on Eastern stonewares, such as celadons, the glaze is more likely to become detached. Porcelain is prepared from purer ingredients and is made into much finer objects. It is fired to a temperature that creates a glass-like material in which the clay particles are imbedded. The methods of manufacture and firing, particularly of the early porcelains, often left the objects with residual stresses. Even slight knocks, such as putting down on a metal or ceramic surface, can, therefore, create cracks that release the stresses and so cause shattering. Porcelain should not be placed on cold surfaces or in warm water, as the temperature difference can cause additional stresses. After an initial firing, porcelain is usually decorated with glazes that are fused on by firing at a lower temperature. Some of these decorative glazes can be removed by abrasion or washing, the most delicate being gold. With the necessary precautions, high-fired ceramics can be stored in most environmental conditions.

Glass (Moncrieff, 1975; Hodges, 1976c; Wihr, 1977; Davison and Newton, to be published)

Glass is conveniently divided into categories by use; domestic and decorative, window, and enamels. All glass is fragile and can be easily chipped or broken by poor handling and sudden changes in temperature, even by the warmth of the hands. Broken glass provides a danger to anyone handling it, and care should be taken to label broken pieces.

Domestic and decorative glass can be further classified by its chemical and physical stability. Unfortunately, instabilities are very difficult to detect, except when deterioration is underway. The majority of glass objects are sufficiently robust to have withstood ordinary use throughout their lives. However, all glass slowly deteriorates by reacting with moisture in the air; the rate and extent of deterioration depending partly on the original manufacture of the object, and partly on its subsequent history. This deterioration increases the instability of the object. Chemical instability results from an imbalance in the ingredients used in manufacturing the glass. Gross errors in preparing glass melts have been made in the past, usually by those experimenting with novel glasses, for example early Venetian or early lead glass. Two related forms of deterioration can become apparent; weeping glass and crizzled glass (Brill 1975). If either condition is noticed, a competent conservator should be consulted immediately. Weeping glass results from the absorption of water from the atmosphere which dissolves the glass. It is recognizable by droplets of water on the glass surface or by its soapy feel. Extreme cases result in the objects being destroyed by this process. A less extreme form of deterioration occurs when soluble material moves out of the surface and is replaced by water. If the glass is dried by desiccation or heating, this water is removed, and the surface shrinks and cracks or falls off, producing crizzling. As a first aid measure, weeping glass should be kept in dry conditions with a relative humidity of 40–42 per cent, but not lower. Crizzling glass should be kept at about 55 per cent RH. Both these are short-term expedients until expert guidance can be obtained. In general, other glass can be stored safely at 45–55 per cent RH.

Physical instability (that is, increased susceptibility to cracking or chipping) can arise during manufacture or from surface deterioration by moisture. Residual stresses left in glass after annealing are particularly likely to occur in thick section glass or objects made from different types of glass, for example, cameos. Some objects have been made by partly fusing glass powders together, processes termed *pate de verre* or *pliqué à jour* when wire formers are used. Objects thus made are very fragile and liable to break without apparent reason. Reaction of water in the air with glass surfaces generates new stresses causing old glass objects to become increasingly fragile.

Glass can be decorated by firing on coloured enamels or gilding in a similar fashion to glazed ceramics, and is thus subject to similar forms of deterioration. Moreover, some glass objects were painted in water or oil colours, which look very similar to fused colours, but can be easily removed. Some glass is decorated with applied metals, usually silver. The bonding between the metal and glass is frequently insecure.

Washing glass in water at room temperature can be safely carried out, provided that precautions are taken, and that problem objects (described above) are not washed.

Window glass suffers from the same general faults in manufacture and subsequent deterioration as the glass described above, but being exposed to far greater extremes of temperature, light and moisture, it is likely to deteriorate faster than objects kept indoors. It can dissolve gradually when exposed to weathering over many years. Allied to the dissolution are increased strains and consequent brittleness of the glass. Considerable efforts must, therefore, be made to support and store sheets of glass adequately. Edges should be protected from chipping by a slightly loose frame of resilient material such as wood, and large sheets should be supported by backing panels which reduce the possibilities of bending and cracking. Leaded glass panels are more difficult to deal with. Even when new, the panels are flimsy constructions if not mounted in a window opening. The leaded panels are made from three components. The soldered lead network supports the fragments of glass which are secured in place by putty or mastic. Each of these components adds to the stability of the panel and deterioration of any one will weaken it. The putty, being a partly organic-based material, deteriorates first, becoming progressively hard, brittle and friable, and will eventually drop out. This allows the glass to move in the framework, reducing the rigidity of the structure.

The lead can deteriorate chemically or physically.

The corrosion of lead does not usually occur when the window is in place, but is often encouraged by the conditions in the store. The lead is soft and ductile and can be stretched considerably without breaking. In the window this can result in the panels slumping and bowing. However, the soldered joins between the canes are much more brittle and may crack rather than stretch under the strain. The glass fragments themselves suffer from several deterioration processes. Frequently the glass is corroded and covered with the crusts of corrosion products and dirt, and becomes cracked. In addition, the decorative techniques used, enamelling and silver staining, also suffer and, in extreme cases, can be simply brushed or washed off. Because of the flexibility of the leaded panels they must always be supported over the entire area when in store or being moved. If the panel becomes bent or bowed, it should be supported in this condition, and repaired only by a competent conservator. The same caution applies to the cleaning and mounting of panels for exhibitions.

Enamelling is the process of fusing glass onto metal. The glass, applied as a powder, fuses incompletely, and is thus less robust than glass prepared from a melt. As the glass cools to a solid on the metal backing, strains and weaknesses develop, due to the different shrinkage rates of metal and glass. These strains can result in the enamel cracking, or in the loss of adhesion between the glass and metal; both of which expose the clean metal under the enamel to corrosion, discolouration and further strains on the structure. For this reason, liquids should not be used on enamelled metal, as they may penetrate cracks and cause further damage. Enamels can be further decorated by fired on or painted materials in a similar fashion to ceramics and are subject to similar deterioration by knocking or abrasion.

Metal (Hodges 1976d)

Almost all metals that are stable in air have been used in the production of decorative art objects. Individual metals, like wrought iron, have been used alone. Some are alloyed (silver is usually mixed with copper), while others are used in combination (for example, gold-plated brass). Metals can deteriorate by chemical and physical means. However, both actions are also used in the formation and decoration of metals, and differentiating between deliberate, deleterious and adventitious changes can be difficult. A list of metals (in order of chemical stability) likely to be found in decorative art items would include magnesium, aluminium, titanium, zinc, iron, nickel, tin, lead, copper, mercury, silver, platinum and gold. However, their actual stability can vary considerably with the nature of the corrosion occurring on the metal. For example, aluminium, when exposed to air, forms a thin film of highly protective oxide, and is thus less likely to deteriorate than apparently more stable metals. By contrast, silver is fairly unreactive to oxygen, but when exposed to hydrogen sulphide, has a reactivity comparable to zinc's reactivity to oxidation. All except the most noble metals will react with air and corrode, causing, at best, discolouration and, at worst, disintegratpon. An important factor in the corrosion of metals is the presence of *moisture*, as little corrosion will occur in its absence. A major contribution to the conservation of metals can, therefore, be made by keeping them dry, below 45 per cent RH. Corrosion in most metals is initiated by an external activating influence, such as a pollutant, or alloyed or attached metals. Isolating the less-reactive metals from pollutants will reduce the corrosion which occurs, even in damp conditions. This can frequently be achieved by removing contaminants on the metal and storing it in plastic bags or boxes.

Table 31.2 summarises the main causes of corrosion in metals, and thus provides indications as to their most beneficial storage environment.

Corrosion products can be removed by chemical cleaning, but a complication arises with treatment which involves dissolving away the surface. Many surfaces were deliberately coloured or etched by corrosion processes during manufacture. It is, therefore, important that before any cleaning is started, the possibilities of deliberate colouring of the object be investigated and eliminated (see *Table 31.2*). Metal objects can be damaged physically by surface

damage, deformation of the structure, or breakage. All metals can be scratched or worn by harder materials. Even hard metals like platinum or titanium are affected by common materials such as glass or sand and considerable damage can be caused by the inexpert use of abrasives. Commercially available polishes contain abrasive and corrosive materials. Polishes are used to reduce the results of corrosion and scratches by removing and lowering the metal surface, along with any decoration in it. This partly destroys the object. Polishes should, therefore, be applied to metal objects as rarely as possible, and with great care.

Most metals have ductility and so can be bent or stretched. An extreme example of this is lead, which may slump or bend under its own weight, and ultimately crack. Support, often in the form of iron bars, was provided during manufacture for objects that might suffer from this problem, but it frequently proved inadequate over long periods. Such objects should be carefully framed to provide the necessary support, and adequate lifting gear provided to reduce the danger of knocking or dropping the easily distorted lead. Restoration must be left to a specialist lead conservator. Other metal objects suffer from dents or bending as a result of mishandling. Each metal reacts differently to these distortions. Some, like gold or pewter, stretch greatly when strained; others, like steel, stretch very little. Restoration should, therefore, be left to the conservator as damage can be caused by injudicious bending. All

Table 31.2 Corrosion behaviour of metals

Metal	Pollutants (Blackshaw and Daniels 1979; Daniel and Ward 1982	Surface effects deliberately created by corrosion	Corrosion from: High RH	Touching★	Metal possessing valuable, adventitious patinas
Aluminium†		●			
Aluminium† (impure)			●		
Copper alloys	★(organic acids)‡ (sulphur compounds)§	●		● (numismaticitem)	● (similar to artificial patinas)
Iron (cast)		●			
Iron (tinned)	★(organic acids)‡		●		● (brown–grey oxidation coating)
Magnesium alloys			●		
Pewter	★(organic acids)‡				● (brown–grey oxidation coating)
Silver	★(sulphur compounds)§	●		●	
Steel	★(organic acids)‡	●		●	
Zinc alloys★★			●		

★ Finger prints must be cleaned off immediately with a soft, clean cloth
† Common in pre-1950 objects
‡ Organic acids are given off in dangerous amounts by some woods (especially oak), cardboard and some adhesives
§ Sulphur containing compounds occur in the air, wool and packaging and display materials
★★ Typical materials are spelter and die castings

metals will break if subjected to sufficient bending, but some are more brittle than others. Cast metals (for example, cast iron and cast zinc alloys) are particularly susceptible to breaking under stress, and should be protected from being bent, dropped or crushed; items such as cast iron jewellery being particularly vulnerable. Solders and welds are formed by melting *in situ* and are also likely to be brittle.

Most metals are safe to handle, with one important exception. Mercury, being a liquid, will gradually evaporate, filling the surrounding air with its vapour, and the dangers of poisoning by inhaling this vapour have been recognized (Sax, 1979). When mercury is spilled it can flow into cracks and crevices and will remain as small droplets, slowly releasing its toxic vapour. Therefore, if mercury is stored in a museum, a mercury collector[5] should be available for immediate use whenever mercury is released.

Almost all metals can be coated with others. Some are used to protect the underlying metal (for example, galvanized iron or tin-plating cooking vessels) while others (for example, gold) are used for decoration and couterfeiting. These coatings can be abraded or cause chemical instability of one or other metal. Metals can be decorated with other materials, such as diamonds, enamels or paints. Each of these materials must be properly identified and treated accordingly.

Wood (Hodges, 1976e; Brommelle, et al, 1978)

Wood is very versatile, and has been used for many purposes from structural building timbers to delicate veneers. Being organic, its gross properties arise from the presence of the water-sensitive substances making up its structure. When moisture is absorbed the wood expands, and shrinks again as it dries. If either the expansion or shrinkage is excessive, permanent distortion can result. However, wood is not homogeneous, but has a structure (colloquially, grain) which varies from one type of wood to another and indeed varies in different parts of the same tree. It is the grain that provides not only attractiveness, but also problems in conservation. On absorbing moisture from the air, wood expands very little along the grain but considerably across it. If the grain is not straight and even, this inhomogeneous expansion or contraction gives rise to warping. After many damp/dry cycles, serious distortions can develop. If the wood is taken to extreme levels of dampness or desiccation it can split along lines of grain weakness. Distortions due to changes in humidity are properties of the wood structure, and occur whatever the age of the wood. Stabilizing humidity levels can, therefore, contribute markedly to the stability of the wooden objects. The optimum level of relative humidity will depend on the object's past history. For instance, if a piece of furniture was built and equilibrated in a relatively

damp environment, (RH of say 60–65 per cent), it is best to maintain this level in store, and it would be unwise to change the conditions greatly or suddenly. Equally, an object that has been kept in a very dry room should not be transferred suddenly to damper conditions. However, at low RH values, wood becomes more brittle and should not be stored below 45 per cent RH.

Other environmental factors affect wood. Light is probably the most important, causing colour changes and drying at high intensities. Other changes result from reaction with oxygen or pollutants in the air.

Various pests eat wood, which then remains weakened after the pest has been destroyed. When wet, wood will midlew or rot, and this can continue even at 68 per cent RH. For this reason, 65 per cent RH is the maximum humidity that can be safely maintained in museums. Except for dry-rot in buildings, fungus will be inactive below this level. A fungicide can be applied to rotten wood to prevent outbreaks recurring if conditions worsen. When badly rotted, wood becomes spongey and the surface cracks into cuboids when dry. If an object has active fungus growth a conservator should be consulted before it is dried. Efforts can then be made to reduce the cracking and subsequent surface loss on drying. Woodworm (Hickin 1972) destroys wood, and is particularly active in damp conditions. The larvae eat the wood, leaving wood dust (frass) behind. In extreme cases the wood can be reduced to a powder with only a thin skin of apparently sound surface wood. It should, thus, be treated gently, as there may be little strength left in it. The woodworm beetle normally emerges in June/July allowing small amounts of frass to drop out of the hole. The best method of woodworm control is fumigation or, if possible, vacuum fumigation by a specialist contractor. However, this provides no lasting protection, and reinfestation can occur immediately from other contaminated objects. Therefore, the entire store must be fumigated at the same time and all objects taken into that store must be free of infestation. A more common method of treatment is to apply a residual insecticide dissolved in a solvent. This soaks into the wood and kills the woodworm which eats the treated wood. The object must, therefore, be well soaked in the solution. This insecticide has a long life and provides semi-permanent protection against reinfestation. There are two major disadvantages with this method.

First, most wood is given a coating of paint, varnish or wax which is likely to be sensitive to the solvents carrying the insecticides and may be damaged. Second, the persistent insecticides are not only harmful to insects, but can also affect people, thus making the handling of treated specimens somewhat dangerous to uniformed staff and visitors.

Most wooden objects comprise many pieces joined together. Joins between pieces of wood can be effected by mechanical interlocking (mortice and tenon joints), by fixing (nails or dowels), or by adhering (glue). One of the most common forms of deterioration in these objects is the opening and loosening of joints between different pieces of wood, which is created by the movement of the component parts. Nails, screws and dowels can loosen gradually by the same distortion process. In addition, metal components may have corroded due to conditions and the corrosive materials in the wood, a common occurrence with oak. In corroding, the metals expand and cause seizing, splitting or degradation in the wood. Such damage may be increased by trying to move the corroded metal components. Glue and other types of adhesives are usually used in joining wood, even when other methods of mechanical keying or fixing have also been employed. An adhesive in good condition will prevent movement between attached pieces of wood. However, these adhesives may break down. Modern adhesives are much more resistant to failure than the traditional gelatine wood glue which sets into a jelly and becomes increasingly brittle as it dries and shrinks. In fairly high relative humidity it will absorb water and become flexible and resistant to cracking, but will wash out in water. Unfortunately, it is even more susceptible to mould growth than wood. When extremely dry, glue may crack through shrinkage or sudden shock, breaking the join and allowing the object to fall apart. The properties of both wood and glue suggest that the appropriate level of the storage of woodwork is around 55 per cent RH.

Wood is frequently covered with a coating for protection or decoration. If paint has been used, the strictures applying to paintings should be considered when dealing with an object, although the wood substrata of the object may affect the condition of the paint. For example, considerable shrinkage of the wood will cause the paint to fall off. When the grain is a significant feature of the object, it is usually given a transparent coating, sometimes coloured. Various coating materials have been used, shellac and wax being the most common. Each of these coatings reacts differently to water, solvents and abrasion; hence their treatment should first be assessed by a conservator. In order to provide a suitable base for gilding (and as a cheap substitute for wood carving) various compositions have been applied to wood frameworks and then moulded or carved. One of the more common of these is *gesso*, a paste of whiting and glue. With movements in the wood and *gesso*, caused by changes in relative humidity and deterioration of the adhesion and coherency properties of the glue, many *gesso* coatings are fragile and easily damaged. Similar changes arise in the handling and storage of other applied mouldings and appropriate pro-

tection must be provided. Wood may be inlaid with various other materials such as metal or stone. These are frequently held in place solely by the mechanical keying between the wood and the inlay. With movement of the wood, these inlays can be forced out of their grooves.

Other organic materials

A wide variety of materials obtained from plants and animals have been used for decorative art, from nut, amber and leather, to shell, ivory and butterfly wings. The environmental conditions required for sound storage approximate to those for wood; that is, constant humidity, the minimum of light, absence of pollution and protection from insect pests (Hickin, 1964). All organic materials are porous, and are therefore easily stained by water and oils. Such stains are difficult to remove or disguise and it is important to protect these materials from contamination. In general their deterioration is similar to that of wood. Dried leaves and flowers are fragile and become progressively more brittle with age. They should never be handled directly, but always on a support. Seeds and nuts have been used for jewellery and, because of their homogeneity, many have been intricately carved. These, and larger nuts like coconuts, are very similar to wood and are subject to the same dangers.

Leather and skin products were extremely important materials before the introduction of plastics and synthetic fibres, and were used for many of the purposes now the preserve of modern polymers (for example, shatter-proof mugs, flexible hinges, and waterproof upholstery). The term 'leather' applies strictly to tanned skin, but, due to the non-specialist's difficulty in distinguishing tanned from untanned skin, it will be used here to cover both categories. The complexities in dealing with actual objects, and the near impossibility of recommending treatment without examining them is exemplified by leather, one of the few materials ever surveyed in depth from the conservator's point of view. In his review on the conservation of leather, Waterer (1973) describes twenty-one major categories of leather, subdivides these, and discusses the choice of treatments applicable to each subdivision. Some of these varieties can be washed vigorously in saddle soap, while others should not even be flexed or touched by hand. Unfortunately, it can be very difficult (even for a specialist conservator) to decide which category a piece falls into, especially when the leather has deteriorated or is obscured by decoration. Each object should, therefore, be treated extremely carefully until its strengths and weaknesses have been clearly established.

Leather suffers from various forms of deterioration. These, although usually made manifest in a physical form, frequently result from chemical deterioration in the structure. Skin is a form of protein and can be dissolved by water, making a form of glue. This reaction can be reduced by tanning, a process designed to lessen the leather's susceptibility to water by chemically combining the protein, using widely varying materials applied in different ways. Untanned skin, such as parchment and some white and barely-tanned leathers, are extremely sensitive to water. Thus, exposure to water in the form of high humidity can cause severe distortion, while low humidity will cause shrinking and brittleness. All leather is gradually weakened by the reaction of its protein fibres with air. This makes leather far more prone to tearing or abrasion, even though its appearance is altered little during the degradation. Apparently sound, but old, leather objects should, therefore, be accorded more care than their modern equivalents. Leather, particularly of the nineteenth century, can suffer from complete disintegration, called red rot. This results from sulphur dioxide pollution and inadequacies of the tannage and cannot be reversed. The symptoms are a darkening to red, accompanied by a gradual powdering away of the leather. Treatment, if it is possible, should be left to a conservator. Leather, being flexible, will stretch and distort if unsupported, and if folded can develop creases that may be permanent. Care should be taken to ensure that leather is subjected to neither stress. Leather is frequently decorated with dyes, paints, or gilding, and sometimes with a surface lacquer. These objects suffer from the same problems of cracking, surface abrasion, and loss of decoration as other painted objects, and for similar reasons.

Other materials are often used with leather in the construction of objects, for example, wooden frameworks and metal fittings. Leather coverings can separate from the backing and are prone to accidental tearing. Such loose areas should be gently held in place by a tied-on bandage or soft cloth, until treatment can commence. When iron has been used, severe deterioration of both leather and metal can result, similar to that of oak with iron. The leather around iron nails may be blackened and disintegrating with the result that the leather is no longer securely held in place.

Hair has been used in jewellery, especially in mourning ware, and, as horsehair, in furnishing. The causes of deterioration are similar to those of wool. Hair used in jewellery, woven or plaited, can be encountered unexpectedly, and if broken or accidentally pulled, may unravel making restoration impossible.

Horn has properties similar to untanned skin, and was used to make spoons, spectacle frames and jewellery. It is water-sensitive, and, like leather, can weaken with time. Because of the oils in horn, applied paint tends to adhere poorly.

Bone was widely used for small carved and turned items. Although largely composed of minerals, it contains organic connective tissue which is sensitive to changes in humidity and may react by warping and splitting at extremes of humidity. Bone frequently contains fats and oils which gradually migrate to the surface. Bone objects may become grimy rapidly due to the fixing of dirt in the oil.

Ivory (V and A, 1971) has long been used for decorative items. Although similar to bone, its physical structure is different in that it is composed of layers. In most respects, therefore, ivory reacts similarly to bone, but it is far more prone to cracking and splitting between the layers. For this reason ivory must never be exposed to water, which can prompt the sudden release of the stresses between different layers. On ageing and handling, ivory acquires a yellow, then brown, patina. Neither this, nor the artificial imitations of the patina which may have been applied, should be cleaned off. Ivory, being a more precious material than bone, is frequently decorated by painting or inlay. Over long periods, especially when kept dry, ivory shrinks and distorts. The applied decorations will no longer fit the changed ivory and, thus may fall from, or be pushed off the surface. Similarly, ivory which has been used as an inlay may drop out when it shrinks. Care must, therefore, be taken when packing or unpacking objects containing ivory, to ensure that parts do not become lost.

Shell and pearl are similar to bone and ivory, being composed largely of minerals and containing a small but important proportion of organic binder. They thus react to relative humidity and other influences in similar ways. However, much of the beauty of pearl arises from the play of colours originating from the surface layers. These can be damaged by the drying out of the organic binder resulting in the surface becoming dulled. Therefore, such materials should never be subjected to the drying created by low humidity, heating or strong light. With extreme degradation, the surface layers will flake off.

A wide range of plastic modelling and moulding materials have been used over the centuries. Some, like wax or the oriental lacquer, are of great antiquity, while others (for example, compressed caesin or blood compositions) were developed during the industrial revolution. Early man-made polymers, like celluloid or bakelite, gave improved properties but have been largely superseded since the 1940s by a plethora of modern materials. A factor common to all is the binding materials, similar to the materials derived directly from plants and animals. For this reason they are also classified as organic materials.

The wax used in models and sculpture (Anderson, 1977) may be fairly pure beeswax, but it is more common to find it mixed with other plastic materials, fillers for bulk, and with reinforcing armatures or backing. The major danger to wax is heat, either ambient or local. Even slightly higher temperatures than normal, above 25°C, cause the wax to slump or distort. Wax mixtures can also become brittle with low temperature or time, and will be very fragile, especially when thin. Care should be taken to avoid sudden shocks of handling or temperature change. Light can fade the colourings used in the wax. A wax surface readily holds and imbibes dust, which should be kept away from the objects. Oriental lacquer is applied as a liquid or paste, but cures subsequently to an extremely hard and normally durable material. If poorly made, or subjected to extremes of temperature or humidity, the lacquer can crack or flake, particularly if its substrata has also moved in response to poor conditions. Lacquer was frequently wax polished in the past so causing soiling and difficulties in handling. Many different materials were used to decorate lacquerwork, either incorporated within the lacquer film or inlaid. Care should be taken that these materials are not harmed or do not drop out during storage. Occidental lacquers are much more sensitive to moisture and solvents.

Papier maché, prepared from paper, glue and fillers, is a strong material but is sensitive to water. For this reason, it was usually covered with a varnish which was then further decorated by paint or gilding. Over time, the movement of the components in response to handling and humidity changes gradually weakens the structure, making the item more fragile. Various proprietory compositions were developed for creating moulded items such as deguerrotype frames or imitation jet jewellery from organic binders, like blood or caesin, with various fillers for bulk and rigidity. Although some of these have proved to be stable, others have deteriorated. The usual defect is cracking, perhaps the result of the breakdown of the organic binder combined with the loss of oils and water used during manufacture. There is little that can be done at present to reverse this process. Causes of stress, for example changing humidity and temperature, may increase further deterioration. Similar difficulties are found with celluloid and bakelite. Celluloid is often fissured due to the slow, inevitable loss of plasticizer. The surface of bakelite often flakes due to the movement of water into the fillers of the composition. A wide range of polymers has been used in recent years for jewellery and decorative items, for example, acrylic, epoxy, and polyester. In general, these have proved to be relatively physically stable, but many discolour badly when exposed to light. They should not react adversely to the normal ranges of humidity, temperature and pollution encountered in museums. However, they are sensitive to organic solvents and even the vapour may cause surface damage.

Notes

[1] Unfortunately, the plethora of 'do-it-yourself' restoration books can tempt the inexperienced to try treatments beyond their competence.
[2] The recommended steps are as follows: a sufficiently competent person must first be found, probably by recommendation from an independent authority and from an examination of past work. The next stage is to prepare a written agreement with the restorer on the methods and limits of anticipated work. When the object is returned it should be accompanied by conservation reports prepared by the restorer, including:

(1). An examination of the object and diagnosis of its faults.
(2). A full account including explanatory diagrams/photographs of the conservation process.
(3). Recommendations for storage/display.
(4). Recommendations for future treatment.

Any restorer who is not prepared to provide these written reports is best avoided. The documentation will of course involve extra work over and above the care merited by the museum specimen and the museum must expect to pay a premium for special work.
[3] Available from F. W. Joel, Oldmeadow Road, Hardwick Industrial Estate, King's Lynn, Norfolk DE30 4HH.
[4] Precautions must be taken to ensure that the solvents do not affect the object and that safety regulations are followed.
[5] A useful product is 'Quicksolver' available from Jencons Ltd, Mark Road, Hemel Hempstead, Herts HP2 7DE.

References

AIC (1979), Code of ethics and standards of practice, American Institute for Conservation, *Museum News*, **58**(4), 27–34

ANDERSON, S. (1977), The care and cleaning of wax, *Museum Assistant Group Transactions*, **14**, 4–7

BLACKSHAW, S. M. AND DANIELS, V. D. (1979), The testing of materials for use in storage and display in museums, *The Conservator*, **3**, 16–19

BRILL, R. H. (1975), Crizzling, a problem of glass conservation, in Bromelle, N. S. *et al* (Eds), *Conservation in archaeology and the applied arts*, IIC, pp. 121–134

BROMELLE, N. S. *et al* (1978), Conservation of wood in painting and the applied arts, *IIC*

DAVISON, S. to be published, Conservation of Glass, Butterworths, London

FALL, F. K. (1973), *Art Objects,* McGilvery, La Jolla

FRANKS, J. W. (1982), Personal communication

HARTLEY, E. (1981), *Stonework,* (in Partington-Omar, A. and White, A. J., Eds), *Archaeological Storage*, Society of Museum Archaeologists, pp. 18–19

HICKIN, N. E. (1964), *Household Insect Pests*, Hutchinson, London

HICKIN, N. E. (1972), *The woodworm problem*, Hutchinson, London

HODGES, H. W. M. (1975), 'Problems and ethics in the restoration of pottery', in Brommelle, N. S. *et al* (Eds), *Conservation in archaeology and the applied arts*, IIC, pp. 37–38

HODGES, H. W. M. (1976a), *Artefacts,* Chapter 7, Baker, London

HODGES, H. W. M. (1976b), Chapter 1, Baker, London

HODGES, H. W. M. (1976c), *ibid,* Chapter 3, Baker, London

HODGES, H. W. M. (1976d) *ibid,* Chapter 4, 5, 6, Baker, London

HODGES, H. W. M. (1976e) *ibid,* Chapter 8, Baker, London

HOLDON, C. (1979), Notes on the protection of modern art works during handling, packing and storage. *The Conservator,* 3, 20–24

HOWIE, F. (1982), Personal communication

LARNEY, J. (1975), *Restoring Ceramics,* Barrie and Jenkins, London

LARSON, J. (1980), Conservation of Terracotta sculpture, *The Conservator,* 4, 38–45

MONCRIEFF, A. (1975), 'Glass', in Bromelle, N. S. *et al* (Eds), *Conservation in Archaeology and Applied Arts,* IIC

ORRACA, J. (1981), Shopping for a conservator, *Museum News,* 59(4), 60–66

READ, H. H. (1976), *Rutley's Elements of Mineralogy,* Murby, Hemel Hempstead

ROSEGRANT, R. G., (1942), Packing problems and procedures, *Technical Studies in Art and Archaeology,* 10, 138–156

SAX, N. I., (1979), *Dangerous Properties of Industrial Materials* Van Nostrand Reinhold, Wokingham, pp. 797–798

SINKAKAS, J. (1981), *Gemstone and Mineral Data Book,* Van Nostrand Reinhold, Wokingham

THOMSON, G. (1971), (Ed.), *Conservation of Stone,* IIC

UKIC (1981), *Guidelines for Conservation Practice,* United Kingdom Institute for Conservation. – A gloss on this document has been published: Ashley-Smith, J. The ethics of conservation, *The Conservator,* 6, 1–5

UPTON, M. S. AND PEARSON, C. (1978), *Disaster Planning and Emergency Treatments in Museums, Art Galleries, Libraries, Archives and Allied Institutions,* Institute for the Conservation of Cultural Material, Canberra

V AND A (1971), *The care of ivory,* Victoria and Albert Museum, Lonon

WAKEFILED, H. (1963), 'Methods of packing at the Victoria and Albert Museum', in Thomson G. (Ed.) Recent Advances in Conservation, Butterworths, London pp. 16–18

WARD, S. (1982), A rapid test for the detection of substances which will tarnish silver, *Studies in Conservation,* 27, 58–60

WATERER, J. W. (1973), *A guide to the Conservation and Restoration of Objects made Wholly or in Part of Leather,* Bell, London

WIHR, R. (1977), *Restuarieren von Keramic und Glass,* Callwey, Munich

32

Conservation and storage: biological collections

Geoffrey Stansfield

The conservation of biological collections differs from the conservation of objects of art and antiquity in a number of respects. First, animals and plants are usually collected live and the process of preparing them for the museum is termed preservation rather than conservation. This often involves several stages including collecting, narcotization, killing, fixing and preserving. In the natural sciences the term *conservation* is used normally when a specimen is in need of treatment after preservation and is due either to shortcomings in the preservation process or to damage caused by inappropriate conditions of storage and inadequate maintenance. Second, the preservation method employed often depends upon whether a specimen is destined to be used for exhibition or for research. In mounting a specimen for exhibition, much of its scientific value might be lost, due to the preservation method employed. Third, in many instances parts of the object are discarded, retaining only those parts which are easily preserved.

Collecting

Although there are circumstances in which biological specimens are collected by amateurs, in most cases it is preferable for specialists to undertake the collecting. Failing this, collectors should be provided with detailed instructions and training. Without such training, there is a danger that significant data will not be recorded, that appropriate techniques will not be used, and that significant specimens will escape attention.

As a general principle, material should be processed as soon as possible after collection. Biological decomposition begins to take place as soon as the animal or plant dies, and under warm conditions irreparable damage can take place within hours. If it is not possible to process the specimen immediately, interim steps should be taken to prevent deteriora-

tion until such time as a complete preservation can be undertaken. Such general measures include keeping the material as cool as possible, and taking precautions against damage by scavenging insects and animals which might regard the freshly collected specimens as sources of food.

General works of reference on collecting include the British Museum (Natural History) *Instructions for Collectors* Series, particularly Lincoln and Sheals (1979), Wagstaffe and Fidler (1955 and 1968), Knudsen (1975) and Steedman (1976).

Dry preservation

Preservation by drying may be used for whole organisms in the case of small animals and most plants. It may also be used for parts of organisms such as the shells of molluscs, the tests of echinoderms, the skins of mammals and birds and the bones of vertebrates. Drying may be carried out in air if the relative humidity is low enough but may be assisted by heat.

Wet preservation

Wet preservation is more appropriate for the complete preservation of vertebrates (including birds and fish, but not the large mammals), for soft-bodied invertebrates and for some immature animals. Wet preservation is most appropriate when the specimen is to be used for reference or research, and it is less suitable for material destined for exhibition, although there are some exceptions. Wet preservation is a complex process involving a number of steps which can include narcotization, killing, fixing and preservation. Many taxonomists have their own preferred methods and in many cases there is no universally agreed procedure.

Narcotization is a necessary stage in the preservation of many invertebrates where killing methods cause the animal to contract and to withdraw organs and appendages which carry characters which are essential for identification. Smaldon and Lee (1979) have produced an extensive list of alternative methods of narcotization for marine invertebrates.

Killing may be accomplished by depriving animals of oxygen or by the use of poisons. If poison is used, it is imperative that the curator is thoroughly familiar with health hazards and safety procedures.

Fixing is the process by which the protein constituents of tissue are stabilized. In some cases, specimens may be fixed and preserved in the same medium, while in others, two stages and two media are necessary.

Preservation A wide range of preservatives are in use, together with mixtures favoured for particular groups of specimens. The most common preservatives are formaldehyde, alcohol (in various forms) and phenoxetol. Formaldehyde in aqueous solution is one of the cheapest preservatives (the term formaldehyde is used here irrespective of the strength of solution, to avoid confusion which might arise through the use of the terms 'Formal' and 'Formol').

Formaldehyde is a colourless liquid readily obtainable as a 40 per cent aqueous solution. For use as a fixative and preservative it is usually diluted to between three and ten per cent. Although a good fixative, it is less favoured as a preservative because of its pungent and irritating odour and possible health hazards. It also has a tendency to become acidic with time, causing damage to calcareous material.

Ethyl alcohol diluted with water to a concentration of approximately 70 per cent by volume is one of the most widely used preservatives. In Britain, and many other countries, pure ethyl alcohol is very expensive owing to the high tax it carries. As an alternative to pure ethyl alcohol, industrial methylated spirit (IMS) is used. To purchase any quantity of IMS, a permit must be obtained from the Commissioners of Customs and Excise. Disadvantages of ethyl alcohol and IMS are that they are volatile and inflammable. If containers are not sealed they may need to be topped up periodically with preservative. It may also be necessary to take extra precautions against fire.

Propylene phenoxetol is a widely recommended post-fixation preservative. Its main advantages are that specimens stored in it retain their colour and remain pliable. It is non-flammable, transported as a concentrated solution, and is one of the least-expensive preservatives. Several authorities, including Steedman (1976), have recommended procedures for transferring material from alcohol to propylene phenoxentol.

Containers for spirit collections present a number of problems. Ideally, containers should be standardized, but as they are obtained from commercial sources suitable containers often go out of production. In general, flat-bottomed, glass tubes are most suitable for the smallest specimens, wide-mouthed glass jars for larger ones, and fibreglass tanks for the largest. Jars need to be well-sealed, particularly if alcohol is used. Evaporation may be reduced, however, if the temperature in the store is maintained at a low level. The 'Copenhagen' jars currently available in Britain present an inexpensive solution. Although there is a strong case for transferring specimens into standard jars, it is important to note that there are circumstances in which the jar itself can provide information about the origin of the specimen.

For the labelling of material stored in liquid preservatives, it is recommended that labels should be placed *inside* the containers but visible from the outside. Labels attached to the outsides of containers may become detached or may be eaten by insects. Label paper should be good-quality, non-sized, rag paper free from starch and mineral matter and with a high wet tensile strength. An alternative to paper is a spun-bonded, high-density polythene fibre which is manufactured under the trade name of Tyvek in Britain (*see* Pettit, 1975). Data should be written in waterproof ink or pencil. If there is any doubt, tests should be carried out to ensure that labels and ink are permanent.

Freeze drying

Described in simple terms, this is the process by which water is removed from frozen specimens by sublimation. That is, the water vapour passes directly from the solid phase (ice) to the gaseous phase without passing through the liquid phase. This has the advantage that shrinkage which often accompanies drying is reduced or eliminated. The application of freeze drying to the preservation of natural history specimens dates from the early 1960s, and follows experimental work carried out at the Smithsonian Institution in Washington (Merryman, 1960, 1961). Although the technique was originally used for the preservation of animals for exhibitions (and has been used successfully for quite large mammals), freeze-drying is most suitable for smaller animals. Its main potential lies in the preservation of soft-bodied animals for which the previous alternative was preservation in liquid. It should be noted, however, that when used to preserve specimens for exhibition, considerable skill is required to pose the animals in life-like attitudes and, for example, to replace the eyes in vertebrates.

For botanical specimens, freeze-drying has more

limited application. While it is excellent for many categories of fungi, it is less suitable for flowering plants which lose much of their texture and form and become very fragile. Freeze-drying has been used successfully for mosses, lichens and algae. The technique and its applications are fully described by Hower (1979).

The early equipment for freeze-drying was purpose-built, but a number of manufacturers have produced more or less standard pieces suitable for museum use. Larger units, however, remain custom-built. Considerable skill and experience are necessary to achieve consistently high-quality results.

Doubts have been expressed about the long-term preservation of freeze-dried specimens, and it is still too early to assess its use in the long term. It should be noted that freeze-dried specimens provide an attractive source of food for many animals (including carnivores) and care needs to be taken to prevent infestation by insect pests. More recently, concern has been expressed that freeze-drying equipment may be subject to explosions if azides are present in the specimens or have been used in preservation. The present consensus of opinion suggests that there is no danger from naturally occurring azides but that freeze-drying should not be used for specimens which have been preserved with azides.

Mammal collections

Mammal collections consist largely of mounted specimens, mounted heads, flat and round skins, articulated and disarticulated skeletons, specimens in liquid preservatives, specimens showing evidence of mammal feeding or damage, film and tape. Collecting methods are discussed in the standard works of reference cited below. It should be noted that the collecting of many mammal species is governed by wildlife conservation laws.

Mounting specimens for exhibition requires the services of a skilled taxidermist and the topic is outside the scope of this paper. However, the techniques are described in other works. It should be noted that mounting mammal specimens for exhibition may reduce the value of the specimen for scientific purposes, although there are many instances where mounts are of scientific importance. Most specimens intended for research and documentation are preserved by removing the skin from the carcasss, retaining only the dried skin, the skull, and some of the limb bones. In the case of the larger species, the skin has to be pickled or tanned after removing any remaining fat or flesh. For smaller species, the skin may be preserved by drying, often with the addition of a preservative as an extra precaution. The standard reference works are Anderson (1965); British

Museum (Natural History) 1968; and Nargorsen and Peterson (1980). The preparation of skeletons and skeletal material is discussed below.

There are no specific conservation problems peculiar to mammals but normal precautions must be taken against attack by insect pests in the case of skins. If the fat has not been completely removed during preservation, it will decompose, causing damage known as 'fat burn'. Skeletal material may be damaged if the relative humidity is too low.

The storage of mammals does not present particular problems. Mounted heads are best stored on vertical racks, skins in trays or drawers, and spirit collections in accordance with normal wet-storage procedures.

Bird collections

Bird collections consist largely of mounted specimens, skins, articulated and disarticulated skeletons, specimens stored in liquid preservatives, eggs, nests, specimens showing examples of feeding and damage, photographs, film and tape. Collecting procedures and mounting techniques are described in the literature cited below. Many species are covered by wildlife conservation laws and international agreements, including *The Protection of Birds Act 1954 and 1967, The Conservation of Wild Creatures and Wild Plants Act 1975, The Wildlife and Countryside Act 1981* and the *Convention on International Trade in Endangered Species*.

The mounting of skins for research and study is described by Harrison *et al* (1970). It is usual to leave the major part of the skull attached to the skin as well as the radius, ulna, tibia and tarsus. In most cases, the skin may be preserved by drying with the addition of a preservative as a precaution against deterioration. There are some exceptions, including water birds which must be treated with solvents to remove grease and fat. Egg-shells are usually preserved by drying after removing the contents through a drilled hole or holes (Prynne, 1963; Harrison *et al*, 1970). In the case of nests, material needs to be fumigated to destroy any life forms which might pose a threat to the collections. Storage of bird specimens in liquid preservatives should follow standard procedures for wet preservation, and skeletal material should follow normal osteological procedures.

The conservation problems affecting bird skins and skeletons are similar to those described for mammals. Bird eggs may be damaged by fungi or mould if the relative humidity is too high.

Amphibia, reptile and fish collections

Amphibia, reptile and fish collections largely consist of mounted specimens, skeletal material, specimens preserved in liquid preservatives, casts and photographs. Nearly all research and study collections are preserved in spirit. In cases where specimens were too large to preserve in their entirety casts have often been made. The traditional method of mounting specimens for exhibition has been to skin the animal and to preserve the skin. Because this technique has its limitations however, casting techniques using plaster and, more recently, fibreglass, have been preferred by many preparators. Mounting techniques are described by Migdalski (1960). McGonigal (1970) describes a technique for making fish mounts by vacuum-forming from a plaster mould. Gardner (1974) describes how casts can be made from living amphibia and reptiles. Mounted specimens of amphibia, reptiles and fish, particularly the fins, are susceptible to physical damage.

Collecting techniques are described in British Museum (Natural History) (1966) and in Wagstaffe and Fidler (1955). Collecting is governed by wildlife conservation laws.

Osteological collections

The preparation of osteological material merits special note. For larger vertebrates, the traditional method when collecting in the field at some distance from the museum has been to 'rough skin' the animal and remove the contents of the body cavities, allowing the specimen to dry before transportation. Once in the laboratory, the remaining flesh is removed after boiling in water. This method is still employed for large species although the drying stage can be omitted when the specimens are taken to the museum promptly; and the cleaning process can be speeded up by the use of enzymes. The bones may need to be subsequently degreased.

Smaller specimens are most conveniently cleaned by making use of a colony of dermestid beetles as described by Sommer and Anderson (1974). On no account should this process be undertaken in the vicinity of stored collections.

Insect collections

Insect collections consist largely of mounted specimens, specimens preserved in liquid preservatives, microscopical preparations and insect structures such as nests and galls, specimens showing evidence of insect attack, photographs and audio tapes.

There is a wide variety of collecting methods for insects many of which are peculiar to the particular insect. General reference works include Oldroyd (1970), British Museum (Natural History) (1974) and Walker and Crosby (1979). More specific methods are described in the publications of the Royal

Entomological Society. The collecting of some insects is subject to wildlife conservation laws.

Most small insects are prepared by drying. There are many conventions for mounting and the general principle is to mount the insect in such a way as to expose the diagnostic identification features. In some cases this entails dissection, (for example, genitalia) and mounting these separately but with the insect. Larger insects may need to have the contents of the body cavity removed and some insects may need to be degreased. In cases where the diagnostic features are within the body it may be necessary to clear the integument of the insect (as in the case of fleas).

Most insects are mounted on pins, pieces of card or other material which themselves are transfixed by pins. The pinned insects are then retained in trays, storage boxes or drawers. There are few standard storage systems, although the drawers manufactured by Stephenson Blake in Britain are used by many museums. These drawers are fitted with a layer of cork and with a glass lid. In the USA drawers are used in conjunction with small trays which fit within them to facilitate handling of the items and the addition of new material. Plastazoate is now being used by some curators as a substitute for cork.

The labelling of insects presents a problem because of their small size. For pinned insects it is usual to keep basic information with the insect in the form of one or more labels mounted on the pin. To identify insects from a particular collection or from a particular locality it is advantageous to have labels specially printed. Most labels are written by hand but some museums now use a typewriter with a very small typeface. There are also methods by which typewriting can be reduced photographically to produce small labels. Good quality paper, such as goatskin parchment, should be used.

Insect collections are particularly vulnerable to attack from pests including mites and the larvae of moth and beetle. For this reason it is usual to anchor a small quantity of insect repellant within the drawer or storage box. Insects are very fragile and some training is advisable in handling techniques. Conservation problems can arise with old pinned insects if the pins corrode, and it is recommended that stainless steel pins be used.

Mollusc collections

Mollusc collections consist largely of dried shells, whole animals in liquid preservative, specimens showing evidence of molluscan activity and feeding, and photographs. Molluscs present a problem common to many invertebrate groups in that collections largely consist of the dried exoskeletons which alone do not carry sufficient characters to permit identification. Collecting methods are described in Lincoln and Sheals (1979). A few species are governed by wildlife conservation laws.

Molluscs shells may be labelled by marking the shells (in the case of the largest species), by placing a label within the shell (gastropods) or by placing the shell with its label in a tray, box or tube. It is advisable to place very small specimens in tubes. Molluscs preserved in liquid preservatives should follow normal procedures.

Most mollusc shells are fragile and need to be handled carefully. Calcereous shells are susceptible to damage if they are stored in a acid environment (which might result from the use of unsuitable woods in the construction of storage cabinets). Chitinous shells dry out and distort in an atmosphere of too low relative humidity.

Other invertebrate collections

Other invertebrate collections include Protozoa, Arthropoda other than insects, Echinodermata and Coelenterata. Although these groups are very extensive in the wild, and may also be represented by extensive collections in museums, relatively few curators have specific responsibilities for these groups and there is very little in the way of established practices for them other than those described in the general works relating to invertebrates such as Wagstaffe and Fidler (1968) and Lincoln and Sheals (1979). Most procedures are covered by the general considerations pertaining to collections stored in liquid preservatives or general procedures for dried specimens and the maintenance of microscopic preparations.

Botanical collections

Botanical collections consist largely of dried specimens of plants, relatively small amounts of material in liquid preservatives, samples of wood, examples of economic use and photographs. Collectors should note that in Britain some plants are afforded special protection under wildlife conservation laws, and it is illegal to uproot plants (with the exception of some pest species) without the permission of the landowner.

Preservation is usually carried out by drying after the plant has been arranged to show its diagnostic features. In conditions of high relative humidity it may be advisable to use artificial heat to speed up the drying process. The usual conventions are to mount flowering plants on standard herbarium sheets (there is more than one standard size of sheet), and to store mosses, lichens and some fungi in tray, boxes or packets. Some marine algae and some fungi may be stored in liquid preservatives. Recently, some fungi have been preserved by freeze-drying which in many cases produces excellent results.

With few exceptions, preserved plants have little potential for exhibition, the exceptions being some fungi and samples of wood. Most botanical exhibits rely heavily on models. Some freeze-dried plants have been used but they are generally thought to be less than satisfactory. The standard reference works for the collection and management of botanical materials are Franks (1965), British Museum (Natural History) (1965b) and Savile (1973).

Labelling is accomplished either by adding a label to the herbarium sheet or to the packet or box in which the specimen is housed.

The main conservation problems arise through the danger of infestation by mites or insects, or through inappropriate storage and careless handling. Some herbaria treat their specimens with a poison such as mercuric chloride in solution as a matter of routine. Others feel that the health hazards posed by the use of such poisons are too great, and rely on periodic fumigation.

Some comments on the use of fumigants for natural history collections in general are set out below. Conservation problems also arise when the paper on which they are mounted deteriorates, necessitating replacement on a new sheet.

The storage of biological collections

As will have been noted, categories of natural history collections require special storage fittings. The general requirements are similar to those for most museum collections, namely stores which are secure from theft and accidental damage, and in which the temperature and humidity are maintained at levels appropriate to the collection. In addition, natural history collections are particularly susceptible to biological deterioration and the relative humidity needs to be maintained at a level which will prevent mould. Special precautions may have to be taken to prevent infestation with mites and insects. Provision may also have to be made for periodic fumigation.

In general, it will be found convenient to house similar collections together. As a general rule it is advisable, however, to store collections in liquid preservatives separately, particularly if alcohols are widely used. Because of existing inadequacies, some museums are now constructing purpose-built stores in which optimal conditions can be maintained. An example is the store at Tring in Hertfordshire which was built to house the British Museum (Natural History) ornithological collections.

Fumigation procedures

It is very difficult to give firm advice on fumigation procedures. In the past a wide variety of fumigants have been used, but in the face of health and safety laws and regulations, many traditional fumigants have been abandoned. In the USA, the use of fumigants is governed by *The Federal Insecticide, Fungicide and Rodenticide Act,* and the Association of Systematics Collections has published a book advising museums in the USA on Fumigants and procedures. Although the laws differ in Britain, many of the recommendations and procedures are relevant.

Health hazards in handling biological history collections

Health hazards in natural history museums arise from a number of sources. Live animals may be capable of inflicting injury, and should be handled with caution, particularly if the species is unknown. Gloves should be worn where appropriate. Recently killed vertebrates (and some invertebrates) present a risk of infection by dangerous pathogens. Detailed accounts of these dangers are described in McDiarmid (1966) and Irvin *et al* (1972). The dangers are greater in handling animals in poor condition or which have died through transmissible disease. (It should be remembered that a larger number of animals which find their way into museums have not died from natural causes). Some infectious organisms, such as anthrax, may persist for long periods after death. Vertebrates which have recently died may be carrying blood-sucking ectoparasites including fleas, flies, lice, ticks, and mites which are capable of biting and spreading infection. The following simple rules should be noted:

(1). Use plastic bags for collecting and handling dead specimens.
(2). Work in a well-ventilated room.
(3). Fumigate new specimens.
(4). Immerse whole bodies of animals in disinfectant where possible.
(5). Wear protective clothing including overalls, gloves, face masks and goggles where appropriate.
(6). Make sure that instruments and work surfaces are clean and sterilized.
(7). Maintain high standards of personal hygiene.

Other hazards may arise from the use of preservatives. In the past, arsenic trioxide was widely used to poison skins of vertebrates and mercuric chloride is still used in some herbia to poison new specimens. If such practices are followed, specimens should be handled with care, protective clothing worn, and the hands frequently washed. There are no generally accepted recommendations for the use of insecticides and fungicides in museums. Paradichlorobenzene, naphthalene, vapona, thymol and many other chemicals are widely used. In the absence of firm guidelines care should be taken to ensure that staff are not exposed to high concentrations of any of these substances or for any protracted period. It is a good principle for curators to forbid work in stores where insecticides are used.

A further hazard may arise from the use of plastics and resins in making moulds and casts. The manufacturer's instructions must be closely followed.

References

ANDERSON, R. M. (1965), *Methods of Collecting and Preserving Vertebrate Animals,* National Museum of Canada, Ottawa
BRITISH MUSEUM (NATURAL HISTORY) (1953), *Instructions for Collectors, No. 3 Reptiles, Amphibia and Fish,* British Museum (Natural History), London
BRITISH MUSEUM (NATURAL HISTORY) (1965a), *Instructions for Collectors, No. 3 Fishes,* British Museum (Natural History), London
BRITISH MUSEUM (NATURAL HISTORY) (1965b), *Instructions for Collectors, No. 10 Plants,* British Museum (Natural History), London
BRITISH MUSEUM (NATURAL HISTORY) (1968), *Instructions for Collectors, No. 1 Mammals,* British Museum (Natural History), London
BRITISH MUSEUM (NATURAL HISTORY) (1974), *Instructions for Collectors, No. 4a Insects,* British Museum (Natural History), London
EDWARDS, S. R. et al (1981) (Ed.) *Pest Control in Museums,* Association of Systematics Collections, Lawrence, Kansas
GARDNER, G. S. (1964), Casting lifelike models from living animals, *Curator,* **7**, 196–205
FRANKS, J. W. (1965), *A guide to Herbarium Practice,* Museums Association, London
HARRISON, C. J. O. et al (1970), *Instructions for Collectors, No. 2 birds* British Museum (Natural History), London
HOWER, R. O. (1979), *Freeze Drying Biological Specimens – a Laboratory Manual,* Smithsonian Institution Press, Washington DC
IRVIN, A. D. et al (1972), Possible health hazards associated with the collection and handling of post-mortem zoological material, *Mammal Review,* **2**, 43–54
KNUDSEN, J. W. (1975), *Collecting and Preserving Animals and Plants,* Harper and Row, London
LINCOLN, R. J. AND SHEALS, J. G. (1979), *Invertebrate Animals Collection and Preservation.* British Museum (Natural History), London and University Press, Cambridge
MCDIARMID, A. (1966), Safety precautions at post-mortem examinations *Mammal Society Bulletin,* **26**, 17–18
MCGONIGAL, S. (1970), Transparent fish casts for museum displays, *Museums Jl.,* **69**(4), 169–172
MIGDALSKI, E. C. (1960), *How to make Fish Mounts and Other Trophies,* Ronald Press, New York
NARGORSEN, D. W. AND PETERSON, R. L. (1980), *Mammal Collectors Manual,* Royal Ontario Museum, Toronto
OLDROYD, H. (1970), *Collecting, Preserving and Studying Insects,* Hutchinson, London

PETTIT, C. (1975), Label materials for wet-preserved biological specimens, *Museums Jl.,* **75**(4), 175–176

PRYNNE, M. (1963), *Egg Shells,* Barrie and Rockliff, London

SAVILE, D. B. O. (1973), *Collection and Care of Botanical Specimens,* Canada Department of Agriculture, Ottawa

SMALDON, G. AND LEE, E. W. (1979), *A Synopsis of Methods for the Narcotization of Marine Invertebrates,* Royal Scottish Museum, Edinburgh

STEEDMAN, H. F. (1976) (Ed.) *Zooplankton Fixation and Preservation,* UNESCO, Paris

WAGSTAFFE, R. AND FIDLER, J. H. (1955), *The Preservation of Natural History Specimens, Vol. 1 Invertebrates,* Witherby, London

WAGSTAFF, R. AND FIDLER, J. H. (1968), *The Preservation of Natural History Specimens, Vol. 2 Zoology/invertebrates, Botany, Geology* Witherby, London

WALKER, A. K. AND CROSBY, T. K. (1979), *The Preparation and Curation of Insects,* DSIR, Aukland, New Zealand

33

Conservation and storage: vertebrate material

George Y. McInnes

Vertebrate material, stored or displayed in museums, requires regular care and attention. Neglected or untreated specimens will soon deteriorate due to causes that may include improper preparation, poor environmental conditions and insect damage. The major categories of vertebrate materials dealt with here are; fresh or frozen material, mounted birds, bird study skins, mounted mammals, mammal study skins, fishes, reptiles and amphibians (cast and moulded), dry skeletal material, wet preserved material and birds eggs. No consideration is given here to fossil material or histological preparations.

Vertebrate specimens that have been properly prepared, mounted and stored should require only routine conservation or maintenance. There should be no need to call upon the services of a taxidermist or other zoological preparator provided the following requirements are met:

(1). Proper preparation and preservation.
(2). Good storage conditions.
(3). Proper handling procedures.
(4). Freedom from insect attack.
(5). Screening from ultra-violet light.
(6). Routine inspection and maintenance.

There are many specimens within museums that have been kept under these conditions for more than a hundred years and are still in excellent condition. Mounted specimens on display have a relatively limited life due to fading, while the study and reserve collections should last indefinitely.

Proper preparation and preservation are essential to the well-being of the specimen. It is important to ensure that any taxidermist or preparator engaged has a good reputation and is capable of carrying out the specified preparation.

Storage

Good storage conditions are important for the well-being of the specimens. The ideal environmental conditions for the storage and display of vertebrate specimens are a temperature of 15–18°C and relative humidity of between 55 and 60 per cent. All storage cabinets should be soundly constructed with sealed external joints and seams. The doors should be a close fit, complete with draught-excluding tape or felt to ensure dust free conditions and a dark interior. Each specimen must have adequate space and should not touch any adjacent specimen to prevent abrasion. Space should be made available for the incorporation of insect repellant such as flake napthalene or 'Vapona'. Specimens are best stored in a polythene bag; this reduces contact abrasion when they are taken in and out of storage.

Specimens should be handled carefully and with respect. All too often careless procedures or mishandling causes irreparable damage. Mounted specimens should be picked up and carried by the artificial base, and no attempt should be made to carry more than one small specimen in each hand. Bird study skins should be handled using the support stick, and mammal study skins by gripping gently round the torso. Under *no* circumstances should specimens be picked up by the head, neck, limbs or tail.

Insect attack

All specimens, except fish reptile and amphibian casts, are prone to attack by insects and mites. Moths, beetles, book lice and mites find the skin, fur, feathers or traces of flesh left in the skin an ideal food source. Signs of insect or mite attack are:

On birds

(1). Holes in the feathers.
(2). Chewed feather shafts causing part of the feather to fall out.
(3). Bald patches especially around the head and under the wing.
(4). Holes in the fleshy parts of the legs, feet and bill.

(5). Frass on the specimen base or in the Polythene bag.

(6). Old larval cases on base or feathers.

On mammals

(1). Loose or falling hairs.

(2). Bald patches on any part of the specimen.

(3). Frass on the specimen base, or in the polythene bag.

(4). Old larval cases on base or fur.

On fish

(1). Holes in the skin or between the rays of the fin.

(2). Frass on the specimen base.

Frass (insect droppings) varies in appearance from fine granular powder to small pellets, usually brownish in colour. As soon as any specimen has developed *any* of the above symptoms an entomologist or taxidermist should be consulted, as any delay could lead to irreparable damage to the entire collection. Some preventative measures can be taken against insect attack. It is vital that the storage cabinets and display units are insect-proof. An adequate supply of insect repellant should be placed in each storage cabinet or unit and renewed every six months. Remember that clean and tidy conditions discourage insect attack. It should be noted that high humidity (over 75 per cent) will encourage insect or mite attack.

The control and identification of insect attack is discussed more fully by Anon (undated); Edwards and Bell (1980); and Wagstaffe and Fidler (1968).

Effect of light

All mounted birds, mammals and fish on display have a limited life due to fading. Depending on the intensity of light, specimens may last from five to fifty years. The recommended rate is 50 lux or less (Thompson, 1974). The life of the specimen can be prolonged by using ultra-violet free light, and filters on the lights and on the glass fronts of display units are essential. Many specimens that have been on display for several years in natural or artificial light will have faded badly, and if they have been illuminated from one side only, the effects are more noticeable, the exposed side of the specimen facing the light being lighter than the side in shade. This is more easily seen with dark specimens such as otters or crows.

It is therefore imperative that any specimen not on display should be stored in darkened storage units. See Thompson (1974) for further details on museum lighting in relation to conservation. It is advisable that a routine inspection of all display and storage specimens be undertaken at least once every six months.

Fresh and frozen specimens

All fresh material, whether collected by staff or donated by a member of the public, should be recorded fully in the day book under the following eight headings:

(1). Accession number.

(2). Day-book number.

(3). Date received.

(4). Date found.

(5). Details of specimen (to include locality).

(6). Gift or purchase.

(7). Donor.

(8). Remarks – to include possible cause of death and what form of preparation is intended.

The appropriate day-book number should be attached to the specimen.

The curator should be aware of any current legislation concerning the specimens in his collection. *The Wildlife and Countryside Act 1981* should be studied and borne in mind when accepting specimens. *See* Anon (1982a, b) for summaries of this Act.

The specimen (with its day-book number attached) should be wrapped in a double layer of Polythene and placed in a deep freeze (set at between −18°C and −20°C) to await the attention of the preparator or taxidermist. The curator should be also aware of the hazards of handling post-mortem zoological material (*see*, for example, Irvin *et al*, 1972; Anon, 1978). In cases of doubt, qualified veterinary opinion should be sought.

Mounted birds

The most common problems arising with mounted birds are:

(1). Fading.

(2). Broken necks, legs, wings and tails.

(3). Dust.

(4). Grease marks on the chest, legs and bills (most common in ducks and geese).

(5). Insect attack.

Fading

Prevention rather than cure is the aim here, as once fading has occurred there is no treatment which can successfully restore the specimen to its original colour. All specimens not in use should remain in store. It is strongly recommended that ultra-violet free lights or filters should be used when specimens are on display. This will reduce fading to a minimum.

Breakage

This is usually caused by over-crowded storage conditions or improper handling. In most cases the specimen can be repaired by a qualified taxidermist.

Dust

Surface dust, if left untreated, may permeate the fur, feather or bone and become almost impossible to remedy. The use of Polythene bags, dust-proof storage cabinets and display units are essential in keeping specimens dust free. Light surface dust may be blown off using compressed air, or gently brushed off with a feather. Heavily soiled specimens require specialist attention.

Grease marks

These are due to improper preparation and degreasing. All specimens must be thoroughly degreased and cleaned before mounting. Failure to properly carry out this time-consuming procedure results in unsightly stains on the specimen. More importantly, grease stains are an attraction and food source for insects. Any specimen found to have been improperly prepared in this fashion should be isolated in a sealed Polythene bag, to await the attention of a taxidermist.

Insect predation

This may be recognized by the symptoms described above. If any specimen is suspect, place it in a Polythene bag and await the attention of a taxidermist.

Bird study skins

The case of bird study skins is similar to that of mounted specimens. One particular problem is that due to grease and age the twine attaching the labels to the specimen may deteriorate and break. If no support stick has been used in the preparation of the specimen, this is likely to occur. It is pointless to retie the label with new string or twine if the specimen has not been degreased and cleaned. Seek specialist advice and ensure that the label is kept with the specimen by placing both in a Polythene bag.

Ensure that all specimens in the collection are made up with support sticks. These not only reinforce the specimen but provide a firm anchorage for attaching the label. Bird skins should be stored in open-ended Polythene bags to prevent abrasion of feathers.

Mounted mammals

The most common conservation needs for mounted mammals are due to:

(1). Broken or damaged ears.
(2). Split lips or nose.
(3). Broken limbs and tail.
(4). Fading.
(5). Skin shrinkage causing splits or a 'drum-skin' effect.
(6). Dust.

Broken or damaged ears

This is usually caused by poor storage conditions or careless handling. Most specimens so affected can be repaired by a taxidermist.

Split lips or nose

This is most often seen when the specimen has been mounted with its mouth open. The medium used to model the lips, gums and the area between the skin and the jaws may shrink crack and detach from the skin or bone. Wax and paint may be used to seal and colour hair-line cracks and crevices. Large cracks or more serious damage requires the service of a taxidermist.

Broken limbs and tail

This problem arises commonly through poor conditions or mishandling and the services of a taxidermist are required.

Fading

Fading problems in mammals are basically similar to those encountered with birds. Although some specimens may be dyed to prolong their display life not all mammals, for example those with multi-coloured fur, are suitable for this treatment. A dye treatment should never be used on a taxonomically important specimen.

Skin shrinkage

This generally happens with older, larger specimens, stored or displayed under dry conditions. Due to high temperature and low humidity, the skin will dry out, shrink and come away from the depressions of the body. This shrinkage between the high spots of the manikin causes the 'drum skin' effect. If the problem is not dealt with as soon as possible, the shrinkage may be so great as to cause the skin to split. The main areas prone to this condition are the shoulders, the pelvis and under the legs. A taxidermist can make good this damage and offer advice on improving environmental conditions in which the specimen should be kept.

Dust

Lightly soiled specimens may be cleaned by blowing or using a feather duster. Heavily soiled specimens will require the services of a taxidermist. As always, prevention is better than cure.

Mammal study skins

Mammal study skins, whether flat, carded or round, tend to be more durable than bird study skins. Most of the older collections use flat skins for large mammals and round skins for smaller mammals up to fox size. More recent collections may contain a proportion of carded skins. Both carded and round skins have their advantages and disadvantages, but for the purposes of conservation both are treated in a similar fashion. It should be re-emphasized that the correct preparation of study skins is all-important. The skins must be cleaned, degreased and prepared properly.

The practice of using wire to support the tails of smaller mammals is to be discouraged. A sliver of bamboo cane tapered to the shape of the tail, is a more satisfactory method. Due to the more malleable nature of wire a tail with a wire insert is more likely to break the skin if knocked or bent than a tail with a bamboo insert, which tends to yield and return to its original position without damaging the skin. All mammal study skins should be stored in open-ended Polythene bags.

The more common conservation problems with mammal skins are:

(1). Broken limbs, tails and ears.
(2). Grease marks.
(3). Skull left in specimen after preparation.
(4). Insect attack.

Breakage

This is usually caused by improper handling or bad storage conditions and needs the services of a taxidermist.

Grease marks

The results of careless or improper cleaning and degreasing need special attention.

Skull left in skin

In many of the older collection the study skins were prepared in the field. To save time the skull was not detached from the skin but was roughly cleaned and preserved and kept in place. It is necessary to remove the skull as the identification of mammals is usually dependent on the examination of teeth and other skull characteristics. During this process the skin itself must not be damaged. This procedure should only be carried out by a qualified preparator.

Insect predation

Any specimen showing signs of insect damage must be removed from the collection and isolated in a sealed Polythene bag, and specialist advice sought immediately.

Mounted and cast fishes, reptiles and amphibians

Almost all fishes, reptiles and amphibians mounted or prepared for exhibition at the present day are cast and painted. The earlier method of skinning and mounting fish is now obsolete. It may be argued that a cast is not a real animal, but a model, but if the process of casting and painting is expertly carried out the end result is far superior to most mounted specimens. The advantages of this method are:

(1). There is no shrinkage or distortion.
(2). There are virtually no conservation requirements apart from dusting.
(3). The cast fish, reptile or amphibian, being fibreglass and resin, is stronger and more durable than a mounted specimen.
(4). The fins, tail, feet and claws are not liable to fray or break off.
(5). There is no danger of insect attack.

In short, once the specimen has been cast and painted, there should be no need for any future conservation. If permanent colours are used in the painting process this will keep fading to an absolute minimum.

Specimens prepared by the traditional method of skinning and mounting may require conservation treatment from time to time. The most common faults are:

(1). Shrinkage and distortion especially of the head around the eye socket.
(2). Discolouration due to grease.
(3). Broken fins, feet and claws.
(4). Fading.
(5). Insect attack.

Shrinkage and distortion

The head of a fish is extremely difficult to clean and degrease. The skull (being composed of bony or cartilagenous plates) tends to shrink and distort when drying even if cleaned and preserved thoroughly. Wax is often used to make good these defects. After some time, further shrinkage and distortion may take place when the only remedy is to remount or remodel the specimen. At this stage, expert help from a taxidermist is required. Reptiles and amphibians do not suffer this problem to the same extent.

Discolouration due to grease

This is caused by a failure to degrease the skin properly. The grease seeps to the outside of the skin, mixes with the paint, discolours the specimen and causes a dirty, yellowish, sticky stain. The specimen must be degreased and repainted by a taxidermist.

Broken fins, feet and claws

In fishes, the pectoral fin is the most likely to be damaged. If the fish is not mounted on a backboard the other fins may also be damaged. In many cases, the damage is minimal and may be repaired using tissue paper and varnish. Coat the back of the fins with varnish and place a piece of tissue paper over the damaged area and using more varnish stipple the tissue paper until it is saturated and forms the shape of the fin. After drying it can be painted if necessary. Major damage will require the services of a taxidermist as will the broken feet and claws of reptiles and amphibians.

Fading

This is usually caused by not allowing the original colour of the specimen to fade before painting. Eventually the original colour fades and a paler version remains. The specimen then requires repainting.

Insect attack

This is normally seen around the head and fins with the first evidence usually being frass and small holes. If the damage is not too serious the specimen may be repaired by the taxidermist.

Some earlier fish reptile and amphibian models were prepared by casting in plaster. This is not the best medium for casting fish as the specimens tend to be rather fragile and easily chipped. The repair of these specimens is a difficult task to be undertaken only by a skilled taxidermist. It is highly desirable that any such specimens, unless of scientific or historical importance, be replaced by a fibreglass and resin cast. Fish skins (or half skins) with all, or part, of the skull attached occur in some older taxonomic collections. Such specimens are fragile and prone to insect atttack.

Osteology material

Most specimens should require only minimal treatment. Dust may be gently washed off the bone and loose teeth may be stuck back in place using a contact adhesive. Any specimen that has been heavily soiled or is showing signs of grease will require treatment by a taxidermist or preparator.

Eggs

Generally, these do not require much conservation. Dust is the main problem together with breakages from careless handling. Nylon wool is preferred to cotton wool for the storage and display of eggs since it is more inert, will not snag as easily on the blow holes, and is less susceptible to damp or mould. Storage cabinets should be dust-proof and light-free. For further information on this subject see Wagstaffe and Fidler (1968).

Freeze-dried material

There are an increasing number of freeze-dried specimens in museum collections today. Although a very good method of preparation of mounted specimens, it must be emphasized that these specimens are more prone to insect attack. This is because the entire carcase, though dry, remains intact; hence it provides a more substantial food source than a conventional prepared specimen.

Study skins should not be prepared by freeze-drying for the above reason. Further disadvantages in the freeze-drying of study skins are that sex determination is rendered difficult in birds, in cases where dissection is required, and that since the skull is retained in the mammal specimen it is therefore inaccessible for identification purposes.

Spirit material

Apart from the occasional topping-up, spirit specimens should not require any further conservation treatment. It is only when the containers are damaged, or fluid escapes and the specimen allowed to dehydrate that problems arise. Contact a specialist if this occurs. Before the topping-up procedure is carried out ensure that there are adequate ventilation and drainage facilities. Both formalin and industrial methylated spirits are dangerous chemicals if not handled properly. The curator should make himself aware of the properties of these chemicals before use (*see* Clydesdale, 1982; Anon, 1981; and Fink *et al*, 1977, who discuss this matter more fully).

Acknowledgements

I would like to thank the Director, C. T. Fisher, Dr G. M. Reid and other staff of Merseyside County Museums for assistance and use of typing facilities. I would also like to thank my wife, Elizabeth, for her encouragement and assistance in writing this article.

References

ANON. (undated), *Control of Insect Pests in Museums,* Ministry of Agriculture, Fisheries and Food, Slough Laboratory, Berks

ANON. (1978), Taxidermist's guide to practical hygiene in the working environment, *Guild of Taxidermists Newsletter,* **1**, 10–15

ANON. (1981), Alcohols, *Curation Newsletter of the American Society of Icthyologists and Herpetologists,* **2**, 1–3

ANON. (1982a), Wildlife and Countryside Act, 1981. A summary of the main provisions, *Biology Curators Group Newsletter,* **3**(4), 199–202

ANON. (1982b), D.O.E., Wildlife and Countryside Act 1981, *Guild of Taxidermists Newsletter,* **9**, 5–7

CLYDESDALE, A., (1982), *Chemicals in conservation,* Conservation Bureau Scottish Development Agency, Scottish Society for Conservation and Restoration, Edinburgh

EDWARDS, S. R. AND BELL, R. M. (1980), *Pest Control in museums: A Status Report,* Association of Systematics Collections

FINK, W. L. *et al* (1977), *A Report on the Current Supplies and Practices used in Curation of Icthyological Collections,* American Society of Ichthyologists and Herpetologists, Smithsonian Institute, Washington

IRVIN, A. D., *et al* (1972), Possible health hazards associated with the collection and handling of post-mortem zoological material, *Mammal Review,* **2**(2), 43–54

THOMPSON, G. (1974), Conservation and museum lighting, *Museums Association Information Sheet,* **6**, 1–6

WAGSTAFFE, R. AND FIDLER, J. H., (1968), *The Preservation of Natural History Specimens,* H. F. and G. Witherby, London, pp. 66–69, 314–318

34

Conservation and storage: ethnographical material

Keith B. Priestman

Ethnographical collections are generally regarded as being the most susceptible of all to damage by destructive agencies. This is due largely to the fact that they usually incorporate a high proportion of organic material which is especially vulnerable to physical, chemical and biological hazards. Also the human factor, usually underestimated, is often the root-cause of accident or neglect.

All museum staff, especially those with curatorial responsibility, need to be aware of the agencies which threaten their collections. While the results of sudden physical damage are usually dramatic and readily observed, deterioration tends to be an insidious process and is often difficult to detect until it is well-advanced. In most cases it is irreversable and incurable in the strict sense. A specimen cannot 'recover' and thus damage is cumulative and inexorable. Deterioration is partly inherent, but its extent and rate of progress are largely governed by environmental factors. The key function of conservation, therefore, is to create and maintain a favourable environment for collections.

The environmental aspect of conservation is analagous to preventive medicine, in so far as prevention is better than cure. Where damage or disease is present, however, remedial measures are called for and the second major function of conservation comes into play, namely, the cleaning, consolidation and repair of specimens. This demands special skills and knowledge which can be provided only by the trained and experienced conservator. Conservation, however, should not be regarded solely as an esoteric activity restricted to specialists. It is a responsibility shared in some degree by all those involved in the handling, storage and display of specimens.

The requirements for the conservation of ethno-graphical material do not differ substantially from those necessary for dealing with other museum collections. Ethnography, however, embraces an exceptional diversity of cultures, creating characteristic problems both for curator and conservator. For Europeans, the unfamiliarity of non-European cultures can make their interpretation a far-from-simple matter. A proper understanding of the nature and purpose of a specimen can play an important part in its conservation; close co-operation between curator and conservator is therefore essential.

To provide the ideal environment for all types of museum material would be virtually impossible on grounds of cost alone. Moreover, the environmental requirements of composite objects conflict because of their different constituent materials. Specimen usage also implies an element of compromise: the handling of objects and their transfer or loan means that packaging has not only to protect specimens from direct physical damage but must also buffer the subtler, but equally serious, effects of sudden environmental change.

In order to take successful precautionary measures it is necessary both to recognize and understand the hazards represented by environmental factors. Broadly, these are: light (solar radiation and some artificial sources); temperature and humidity; atmospheric pollution; insect pests; rodents and micro-organisms. Light, temperature and humidity are the most significant of these, although in urban areas atmospheric pollution may also be a serious threat.

The diversity of objects represented by a typical ethnographic collection is difficult to classify, but they fall broadly into two categories: organic and inorganic. Each of these can be subdivided into groups whose contents are related materially and in their environmental requirements.

Organic objects

Textiles

All ethnographical textiles are highly susceptible to damage and decay. Animal fibres are proteinous, and insect pests, in particular the larvae of the common clothes moths, present a serious hazard. Both animal and vegetable fibres, however, are affected by light and in the presence of ultra-violet radiation or high illumination levels, photo-chemical reactions occur with dyestuffs, stains and other contaminants. These reactions produce not only fading of the dyes but degradation of the fibres. Textiles are absorbent, dirt retentive and often fragile; careless handling, therefore, is a serious threat due to the mechanical stresses it imposes on them. Humidity is also an important factor; dry conditions produce embrittlement whereas high moisture-levels encourage mould growths, and may accelerate photochemical reactions. The most appropriate environment is one with a relative humidity of 50 to 60 per cent. Ultra-violet radiation must be totally excluded, and lighting in storage and display areas should not exceed 50 lux. The light sources should be either fluorescent tubes of very low UV emission, with filter sleeves or tungsten lamps. If the latter are employed, care should be taken to ensure that the spot-light type of bulb is kept at a sufficient distance from specimens to avoid local intensification of light and heat. Bark cloth, although not of woven construction, is a fabric and should be kept in conditions similar to those provided for textiles. It is a cellulose material and though relatively strong when in good condition, is often found to be soiled and badly affected by folding marks which weaken the fabric and are very difficult to remove.

Collections may include pre-Columbian textiles from the Americas, which are, strictly, archaeological material and must be treated with the greatest care. They should always be kept in carefully controlled conditions and handled as little as possible. Cleaning, repair and mounting must be entrusted only to a specialist.

Fur, feathers, hair and skin

This group of material is proteinous and the major hazards are insect attack and light. Humidity is an important hazard to skin and leather because dryness will cause embrittlement and a relative humidity of above 65 per cent will result in the growth of moulds, especially where the ambient air is stagnant. Insect attack is extremely serious and is virtually impossible to remedy. Insecticides and deterrent substances are of preventive value although they are generally toxic in some degree to humans, and perhaps the best policy is regular inspection of collections and careful checking of new acquisitions. Some museums may be equipped to carry out small-scale fumigation, but the strictest precautions are necessary, and the gassing of storage areas calls for the services of specialist firms.

The natural pigments of fur, hair and feathers are readily damaged by light, and low intensity illumination (maximum 50 lux) free of UV emission is essential. Dirt and contaminants tend to encourage insect attack and should be removed by careful cleaning wherever possible. In the case of fur and feathers, cleaning techniques used by taxidermists can be of value, provided that specimens are in good condition. Ethnographical collections incorporate such a large proportion of animal and plant material that the advice of specialists of natural history can often be helpful, especially for identification.

Once again, the humidity level required is between 50 and 60 per cent.

Basketry, fibre, bark and wood

This group of materials is cellulosic and, except in the case of wood, the major problem is embrittlement and fragility. This is due in part to natural degradation but accelerative factors are exposure to light, low humidity and atmospheric pollutants. Basketry, fibre and bark are easily deformed and fractured when subjected to flexion and pressure; suitable storage arrangements are therefore very important. Where specimens are dyed or painted and incorporate fur, feathers or skin, the storage or display climate must be controlled to suit the more susceptible materials because the vulnerability of composite objects is gauged according to the most vulnerable part.

Wood is perhaps the most versatile and widely used material in primitive cultures. It has remarkable strength and durability in favourable conditions. It is, however, relatively easily damaged or destroyed by rot and insect attack. When seasoned, it is stable within a limited humidity range but, contrary to popular belief, seasoning does not enable it to withstand sudden or drastic change. It is anisotropic in that its response to changing humidity is unequal, movement taking place almost entirely across the grain rather than along it. The result is that the uncontrolled ambient humidity can produce serious warping and splitting in wooden objects, which cannot effectively be remedied. The recommended regime for materials in this group is a relative humidity of between 50 and 60 per cent, with a light level not exceeding 150 lux. In the case of dyed or painted specimens, the level of illumination must be reduced to a maximum of 50 lux with appropriate UV filtration.

Painted surfaces

Most ethnographical collections incorporate a considerable variety of painted decoration. Paint is basically a pigment in a binding medium which fixes it to a surface. Binding media include size, gum, drying oils, waxes, resins and sometimes egg yolk. Commercial paints are also occasionally found on ethnographic specimens. Pigments are mainly earths or ochres owing their colour to the presence of metallic ores such as those of iron, copper and manganese. Black is usually carbon in the form of soot or charcoal, and white is commonly calcium carbonate.

The most serious problem associated with painted decoration is the friability of the surface, which may powder almost at a touch. The presence of dirt and dust often complicates the situation and great care is necessary when cleaning is attempted. The application of some form of fixative is generally necessary but care should be taken to avoid synthetics whose long-term stability is questionable.

Much painted decoration was never intended to be particularly durable and was simply renewed when necessary. Specimens may often retain only traces of original colour which should be carefully preserved as evidence. In this category are the so-called patinas which encrust some objects and the remains of food which are sometimes found in bowls and other vessels. They constitute important evidence but may easily be damaged or entirely removed by incorrect treatment.

Where paint is bound with oil or tempera, careful cleaning with an aqueous medium is normally a safe procedure. Small-scale tests should always be carried out, however, to establish that paint will withstand such treatment.

The most suitable storage and display conditions depend mainly on the material to which the decoration is applied. Essential precautions, however, are careful handling, protection from dust and dirt and the control of illumination, which should be free of UV and not exceed 50–60 lux.

Ivory, bone, horn and shell

This group comprises animal products, some of which are composed partly or wholly of inorganic material. In this sense they form a transitional group between the two main categories.

Horn is entirely organic and proteinous. It is a tough, quite durable material but responds to changing humidity, and excessive heat or dryness may result in severe warping and distortion. Bone and ivory are hard substances, especially the latter; complex in structure and composed of both organic and mineral materials, they are also anisotropic and liable to warp or split in unfavourable conditions of temperature and humidity. Light, although not a vital factor in their preservation, should be free of UV radiation and not exceed an intensity of 150 lux.

Shell is composed of inorganic material and is often incorporated in ethnographical specimens. It is relatively strong and durable but is susceptible to attack by acidic pollutions. Light and humidity are not of first importance in its conservation, but it should be noted that the natural colourants present in many shells must be protected from light levels above about 50 lux. The relative humidity level for each of these materials is, again, between 50 and 60 per cent.

Inorganic objects

Pottery

With the exception of wares produced by the high civilizations of Asia, most ethnographical pottery is low-fired and relatively fragile. Burnished surfaces and paint decoration are easily damaged, and must be protected from careless handling and abrasion. The clarity and freshness of original colours is often obscured by dust and dirt, particularly in urban areas where aerosol contaminants may gradually degrade appearance, forming a layer of finely divided carbon plus tarry fractions, which is generally acidic and often difficult to remove from porous surfaces.

Protection from soiling, with careful storage, packing and handling are the main precautions for the conservation of pottery. In the case of broken or poorly repaired pots, reassembly should be affected with an adhesive which matches the hardness of the fabric. The use, for instance, of an epoxy resin glue on low-fired ware is pointless, when a cellulose nitrate or acetate adhesive may be quite strong enough. Friable pottery generally requires consolidation before reassembling, and where a portion of the original pot is missing it may be necessary to use a filling material. The fabrication of missing parts is primarily to strengthen an otherwise fragile object and not to create the illusion of an undamaged piece. It should be emphasized that there should be no conjecture in restoring missing parts; such restoration is only permissible where the exact form of the missing section is known.

Light is not a particularly significant factor where pottery is concerned, but humidity control is important where contained salts may crystallize and cause disruption of the body or surface damage. Traces of food can encourage mould growths in conditions of high humidity.

Stone

This is a generic term covering a vast range of rock and mineral substances, each with distinct physical and chemical characteristics.

There is a common misapprehension that all stone is extremely durable and resistant to decay. This is not the case, and many forms can be severely damaged by a number of agencies such as hydration, frost and the crystallization of contained salts. In urban areas, sulphation is the most characteristic form of chemical damage, although biochemical attack by micro-organisms also constitutes a hazard.

In the case of ethnographical material, stone artefacts are the main concern, rather than stone in an architectural context, although fragments of buildings or monuments may well be incorporated in collections. Objects commonly encountered include tools, weapons, small carvings, jewellery and sculpture. The harder forms of stone used for axes, adzes, clubs and querns present few problems. The main hazard is the risk of mechanical damage as these objects will fracture or chip quite easily if dropped or knocked against a hard surface: cutting edges, in particular, should be treated with great care.

When absorbed salts exist in porous stone, control of the ambient humidity within the range of 50 per cent to 60 per cent will reduce the possibility of damage. Fluctuations are especially dangerous, causing cyclical hydration and dehydration: this causes movement of salts within the stone, setting up great internal pressures which invariably produce surface damage and may even disrupt the object entirely. The tell-tale symptom is invariably a whitish surface crystallization, accompanied by flaking or powdering of the stone. When the specimen is in sufficiently sound condition, removal of soluble salts by soaking in changes of de-ionized water is desirable. Objects made from softer stones and shales must be handled with special care as mechanical damage is a particular hazard. Argillite carvings (America: North-West Coast) are typical of this category.

Light is not a significant factor in the conservation of stone but atmospheric pollution is a hazard; the presence of sulphur compounds being especially dangerous to stone composed of calcium salts, such as limestone and marble.

Metals

Almost without exception, metals need to be extracted from their ores by smelting and refining. The free metals so produced slowly revert to mineral form by combining with elements present in the ambient environment. This mineralization or corrosion is a complex electrochemical process for which moisture and oxygen are essential. Certain atmospheric pollutions, however, notably sulphur compounds, have a contributory effect.

Metals vary in their susceptibility to attack according to their position in the electrochemical series. Gold is virtually immune, whereas iron and steel are readily affected. The situation is further complicated when different metals are combined to produce an alloy. Alloys made by primitive methods tend not to be homogeneous and their susceptibility to corrosion is greater than in the case of uncombined metals.

In the museum environment, oxygen and moisture are the chief hazards. Control of humidity is, therefore, of great importance. Theoretically, if it were possible to keep metal objects permanently in conditions of low humidity (say 30 per cent RH or less), corroded examples would be stabilized and further corrosion reduced almost to zero. In practice, this is difficult to achieve, except perhaps by the use of dehumidifiers or low-level heating in a small store-room, or steel cabinet.

Weapons, as a group, are probably the greatest problem. Swords, spears, knives and arrows are all composite objects and very susceptible to corrosion, but dry conditions are inadvisable because of the presence of organic materials such as wood, bone, ivory and leather. The best solution is probably to treat all exposed metal with a commercial moisture barrier. These generally incorporate a corrosion inhibitor and leave a thin but tenacious waxy film on the surface which confers a satisfactory degree of protection. This treatment, combined with an RH of not more than 55 per cent will do much to solve the problem. In the case of weapons which are already badly affected by rust, chemical treatment should not be used. Rust solvents, generally based on phosphoric acid, attack the free metal producing an unpleasant, matt grey appearance. The use of light penetrating oil and careful mechanical cleaning with unhardened steel scrapers and steel wool is preferable. This method is far more controllable and the resultant surface has a satisfactory 'natural' appearance. Fine quality weapons and armour are often elaborately decorated with chasing and inlay in gold, and must be treated with particular care, especially when the surface of the metal has been chemically coloured.

In the case of non-ferrous metals, not all mineralization is unstable or destructive. Where copper and its alloys have acquired a smooth, green patination, this should be carefully preserved, and certainly never removed as it affords a natural protection against further corrosion. The appearance of bright green powdery spots, however, on an apparently stable patina is a sure indication of active corrosion and the need for immediate treatment, although simply removing the affected object to drier conditions will do much to reduce the rate of corrosion. Silver objects may also be disguised by an overall green patination, due to the presence of copper impurities.

Other metals found in ethnographical collections include brass, tin, lead and zinc. Since making contact with the products of modern technology, many races have adopted and 'recycled' material of different kinds, and though generally of low intrinsic value, will need the same care as items made from indigenous materials.

Storage

In many museums, the material on display represents only a small percentage of the whole collection and other specimens may remain in store for long periods. Thus, the proper control of the storage environment is essential.

There are other considerations such as the layout and location of the store, the system of storage employed, the accessibility of specimens and the efficient use of space. A store is not only a repository but also a working area used by curatorial staff and visiting specialists.

The basic requirements for the storage of ethnographical specimens are similar to those necessary for other types of material. Firstly, the store must be of adequate size. Insufficient space is itself a hazard and the overcrowding of specimens increases the risk of damage. Good access for the loading and movement of specimens is essential. It is probably true to say that material suffers as much damage in handling and transit as in any other way. Changing levels, with narrow staircases and doorways, can make the movement of specimens an awkward and hazardous procedure and where more than one floor level is involved, a lift is a valuable asset.

The store place must provide sufficient insulation to buffer the effects of exterior conditions. It need not be custom-built: indeed, older structures often satisfy this requirement better than modern ones. Lighting is not necessary in store-rooms unless staff are working in them. Windows and roof lights should be reduced to a minimum, in the interests of insulation: glass is a poor heat insulator and transmits a high proportion of damaging UV radiation. Where finances permit, air-conditioning is desirable, but in the absence of such environmental control, the major hazard is low humidity induced by heating systems. Careful control of heating can, therefore, do much to mitigate the problem. Conversely, in an unheated building where the relative humidity is high, the introduction of controlled heating will often bring down the RH to a safe level.

Given a store of adequate size with good access and an environmental regime within acceptable limits, the next consideration is the disposition of the stored material. This is dependent on the existing spatial arrangement and the system employed. Cultural classification may seem the most appropriate, but it precludes the effective grouping of specimens of similar function or material, which may be desirable, especially from a conservation viewpoint. Material and typological systems, on the other hand, make specimen retrieval less easy when cultural study is the primary concern. The choice of system thus ultimately depends upon circumstances and the preferences of the curator.

The arrangement of specimens requires careful planning to make optimum use of available space. The basis of most constructions is racking, either fixed or rolling. The latter is effective for security and protection, but is relatively expensive and requires space of the right proportions, being limited to about two metres in height. Fixed racking is satisfactory for most purposes but should not be higher than three metres or it can be a hazard to both specimens and staff. Passage-ways between racks should be wide enough to allow easy movement for people, specimens and equipment such as step-ladders. Shelves should not be overcrowded with specimens otherwise retrieval is hampered. Where many small objects are grouped together, storage boxes are necessary. These provide extra protection from light, mechanical damage and the effects of fluctuating humidity. Boxes should combine lightness with strength and be of a size which is convenient to handle. They may be filled with trays of various depths which are modules of the internal dimensions of the box. The box itself may also be a module of the main storage units, so that each rack or shelf carries the same number of boxes. Boxes should carry a card-holder at one end for a list of contents and perhaps a photograph.

There is, of course, little standardization of size among ethnographical specimens, except that which is based on function and human scale. Standardization of storage units, therefore, involves a compromise. Small objects present the least difficulty, whereas many of the middle range may be too large for a standard storage box. The largest items may either have storage boxes especially made for them or be wrapped in polythene sheet, which is also recommended as a means of protection for specimens stored on open shelves. It is obtainable in a variety of widths, and appropriate lengths can be cut and one end heat-sealed to form a bag. When a specimen is placed inside, the open end should not be sealed but simply folded and clipped. Being semi-transparent, polyethylene generally makes it possible to identify a specimen without removing it from its bag. It also provides extra buffering against variations in ambient humidity.

Cupboards and drawer units also form an important part of a storage system. Their design and dimensions depend upon the type of collection, but large cupboards with adjustable shelves are extremely useful for storing objects which will not fit into the average storage box.

Items of dress should be hung on padded clothes hangers and kept in wardrobe-type cupboards. Textiles should be kept either in shallow drawers, between sheets of acid-free tissue, or carefully rolled on cylinders of cardboard, well-padded with similar tissue. The diameter of the cylinder should be large enough to avoid undue flexion. When rolled up, textiles can be lightly tied with tapes and suspended on a rack in a store cupboard by a rod passed through the centre of the cylinder.

The inherent fragility of many ethnographical specimens is generally exacerbated by deterioration so that some items will hardly withstand handling: all such material requires some form of mount or support. This can be made from acid-free card, laminated foam card or even Perspex, which does not obscure the specimen. Objects may be attached by fine cord or tapes which pass through holes in the support. Care should be taken to avoid putting a strain on any part of the specimen. A handling support is a simple and effective means of protection.

Weapons of various kinds often form a significant part of ethnographical collections. Spears, swords, bows, arrows, knives and clubs are probably best stored in racks or in shallow cupboards. A similar but useful alternative is to sleeve weapons in polyethylene tubing and hang them by a tie and 'S' hook to chicken wire stretched on a batten frame. Arrows should preferably be arranged in shallow drawers, spaced out with notched strips of folded card or polystyrene; this keeps them in place and protects their flights.

Head-dresses and masks are often fragile and unwieldy and, wherever they are kept, may require specially constructed supports so that they are free-standing. Basketry and some items of skin and leather are easily deformed by pressure and should be padded out with acid-free tissue or a polystyrene 'former', cut to shape.

Many ethnographical pottery vessels incorporate no base ring and to hold such pieces securely, cork rings of the type used in chemistry laboratories may be employed. As a cheaper alternative, however, plaited straw rings serve almost as well, and even wedges cut from polystyrene are quite effective. Simple modifications which help to protect specimens and improve the efficiency of the storage system can be devised by curatorial staff at little expense.

Apart from museum staff and visiting specialists, few people have an opportunity of seeing stored collections. Yet display itself is a form of visible storage and it follows that if stores were arranged as 'compressed' displays, with glass cases rather than boxes or cupboards, supervised access could be allowed to parties of the public. Such systems have been introduced in America and Germany and may eventually become standard practice, especially where there are important collections and the ratio of stored to displayed material is high.

Whatever the system adopted, however, it is essential that those with professional responsibility for the care of collections should understand the significance of factors which affect the welfare of specimens. Techniques of treatment and practitional skills are the province of the conservator, but it is very necessary that the curator should be familiar with the principles of preventive conservation. Curator and conservator, after all, share much common ground and are guided by a common principle: that the object is of unique importance.

Bibliography

BOUSTEAD, W. (1968), *Conservation of Aboriginal Bark Paintings and Artefacts,* Kalori, Sydney, no. 35 pp. 46–48

EDWARDS, S. R. *et al* (1980) (Ed.), *Pest Control in Museums,* Assoc. of Systematic's Collections, USA

GOWERS, H. J. (1972), *Ethnographical Featherwork, Textile Conservation,* Butterworths, London pp. 228–234

GOWERS, H. J. (1975), The Conservation of Javanese shadow puppets, ICOM, 1 March 1975

GREENE, C. S. (1977), Storage techniques for the conservation of collections, *Oklahoma Museums Association Bulletin,* Oklahoma City 8, pp. 1–20

GREENE, C. S. (1978), Storage techniques for ethnology collections, *Curator,* New York

IDIENS, D. (1975), A survey of methods of storage of ethnographical collections, ICOM, 2 March 1975

JENKINS, J. (1970), 'Ethnic musical instruments. Identification – conservation, *ICOM Reports and papers on museums,* **6,** 40–42

LEEDEN, A. C. VAN DER (1972), *Ethnographical Textile Collections. Textile Conservation,* Butterworths, London pp. 225–227

LODEWIJKA, J. AND COURSIER, B. (1977), Conservation et restauration des collections du musée de l'IFAN à Dakar' *UNESCO,* Paris

SCHAFFER, E. (1974), Properties and preservation of ethnographical semi-tanned leather, *Studies in conservation,* London, **19**(2), 66–75

SCHAFFER, E. (1976), The preservation and restoration of Canadian ethnographic basketry, *Studies in conservation,* London, **21**(30), 129–133

SCHAFFER, E. (1978), Water soluble plastics in the preservation of artefacts made of cellulosic materials, ICOM, 7 March 1978

SCHMITZER, W. (1978), Conservation of leather objects in ethnographic museums, ICOM, 3 March 1978

THOMSON, G. (1978), *The Museum Environment,* Butterworths, London

UNESCO (1968 and 1975) *The Conservation of Cultural Property,* UNESCO, Paris

UNESCO (1981), *Appropriate Technologies in the Conservation of Cultural Property,* UNESCO, Paris

VANDYKE-LEE, D. J. (1975), A note on the cleaning of shell inlay on ethnographical specimens from Oceania, *Studies in conservation,* London, **20**(2), 114–117

VANDYKE-LEE, D. J. (1976), The conservation of Tandu, *Studies in conservation,* London, **21**(2), 74–78

VETTER, A. AND BAUER, W. P. (1978), Pest control in ethnographical museums by means of fumigation, ICOM, 6 March 1978

35

Conservation and storage: geological material

Francis M. P. Howie

Introduction

Geological material, whether rock, fossil or mineral is composed ultimately of one or more mineral species. A single, crystalline and generally inorganic phase constitutes what is usually defined as a mineral specimen. The mineral kingdom however encompasses a large variety of naturally occurring substances ranging from native metals to complex organic compounds (Hey, 1962). Rocks and fossils are, for the most part, composed of assemblages of minerals, which may be simple aggregates possessing integrity only through weak cohesive forces between particles or grains (as, for example, clays or lignite), or they may be complex intergrowths of crystalline and amorphous phases possessing great inherent strength, (as, for example, granite or mineralized fossil bone). Single minerals, as crystalline, cryptocrystalline or amorphous phases, do however make up a variety or rock types and fossils. Marble and quartzite are well-known examples of single phase or monomineralic rocks, and fossils replaced wholly by calcite or pyrite are abundant in sediments.

At the present time, more than 3500 minerals of terrestrial and extra-terrestrial origin are known. Of these it has been estimated by Waller (1980) that some 300 are unstable to varying degrees in museum and other collections. A small minority are extremely reactive and may rapidly deteriorate upon exposure to light and air. The majority are, however, metastable, being chiefly affected by variations in storage or exhibition environment over relatively long time periods. While the proportion of unstable to stable minerals is comparatively small, it should be borne in mind that, in terms of numbers of geological specimens, the proportion in many collections is very much larger. This is because a small number of unstable minerals occur commonly in a wide variety of fossils, rocks and mineral assemblages.

It is uncommon to find two or more unstable phases in close association within a single specimen, but where this does occur it is often the case that the phases require differing treatments or storage. In general, however, the problems encountered with the conservation and storage of geological material may be greatly minimized by taking simple measures for their safe handling and transport, and steps to moderate or exclude damaging environmental influences in their surroundings.

Published information on techniques used for preserving, conserving and storing geological material is comparatively scarce. The palaeontological field has perhaps been best covered by the useful bibliographies in Kummel and Raup (1965) (covering the period 1900–1955), by Rixon (1976) and a series of bibliographies published in *Der Praparator* (1974–1976). Bannister (1937) and Waller (1980) have provided comprehensive articles on conservation problems in mineralogy and the Appendix to this paper is largely based on these two authors' findings. Sharpe (1983) has produced a fairly comprehensive bibliography on museum geology. Further articles on these subject areas are published from time to time in *Curator, Studies in Conservation, The Geological Curator, Bulletin of the American Institute for Conservation, Mineralogical Record, Der Praparator, The Conservator* and *Museums Journal*.

The basic principles of, and approach towards, conserving geological specimens differ little from those adopted by practitioners in other disciplines. Although written for the antiquities and arts conservator, Plenderleith and Werner's (1971) standard reference work on conservation has much to offer those engaged in preserving geological material. However, as Feller (1974) has suggested, the long-term usefulness and advisability of many consolidative techniques should be questioned. In the past great numbers of geological specimens have been treated with an alarming range of natural and synthetic products in the name of preservation, many of which now cause considerable problems for the conservator attempting restabilization. There is considerable need for future research to be directed towards improving methods for the long-term preservation of unstable geological material both through a better understanding of its deterioration and through a more thorough assessment of contemporary conservation technology.

The general care of minerals

In general, physical methods for conserving minerals, other than those necessary to preserve the original form, either in the field, or during and after laboratory preparation or development, are not recommended. Applied resins and lacquers may react directly with a mineral and their removal for scientific examination is always attended by considerable risk to the specimen. Useful guidance on field collection, initial cleaning and processing is given by Croucher and Woolley (1982) and King (1982). Of great importance is the preservation of sometimes extremely delicate original assemblages and cleaning methods must allow for this.

Carrying by hand is usually the best way to transport highly delicate mineral specimens. However, many minerals will tarnish on contact with unprotected skin and everyday handling should in general be kept to a minimum. The transport of large or unwieldy specimens requires specialist assistance and methods applied to the movement of large, fragile antiquities may be appropriate (Stolow, 1981).

Minerals are classified and normally stored or exhibited primarily on a chemical basis commencing with the native elements and finishing with organic compounds. To some degree, this classification reflects the reactivity shown by unstable members of different groups but is not to be taken as a guide. Table 35.1 is organized on the generally accepted mineralogical classification as an aid to the curator looking for potential problem areas. Of the 300 or so unstable minerals known, the majority are comparatively rare and specific information on their physical, chemical and mineralogical properties may be found in Dana (1944) or by reference to *Mineralogical Abstracts*. Detailed data on their stability fields within collections is poorly known; Waller (1980) however has begun a review of this subject. Specific information is here provided on the behaviour of the more common unstable groups and species which has been published, and is presented in terms of differing environmental conditions as they affect stored and exhibited material.

Effects of light on mineral specimens

Some ninety minerals are known which are altered or decomposed by the action of light (*Table 35.1*). A minority, including varieties of some precious and semi-precious stones, suffer colour change only. Bannister (1937) describes varieties of topaz, sodalite, nepheline, fluorite, barytes, apatite and anhydrite which will fade if exposed to strong sunlight. With some of these, for example nepheline, the colour change is reversed when the specimens are replaced in the dark.

Although this problem was recognized by many early workers, little work on evaluating those wavelengths which may lead to colour change in specific mineral types has been undertaken. Observations made in modern mineral exhibitions suggest that low-level and UV-filtered artificial light may be used with care. In general, however, it is recommended that photosensitive minerals be stored in light-proof cabinets wherever possible. This should certainly apply to fine and important specimens.

More serious for the curator is the effect of light and (usually) oxygen on a large number of sulphides, sulphosalts, haildes, chromates and phosphates (*Table 35.1*). Many of those listed will decompose through dissociation or oxidation reactions, or both, which are photochemically initiated or sustained. Some will decompose instantaneously upon exposure to light, for example certain silver halides, others such as realgar, stibnite and vivianite may take days or months to degrade, depending to some extent upon crystal size. There is evidence from stored collections that certain minerals in this category may undergo oxidation in the absence of light. However, in general little is known about the photochemistry of many of these reactions and it is recommended that all light-sensitive minerals be stored in light-proof cabinets or boxes, preferably constructed from materials which are unlikely to emit acid vapours. Some organic compounds will react with sulphides and other minerals causing either surface contamination or, over the long term, degradation.

Vibration

Many minerals are highly sensitive to slight vibrations or jarring because of their extremely delicate crystalline nature. Examples are certain zeolites, native metals such as crystalline iron, and acicular or fibrous forms of common minerals such as halite. The individual crystals may adhere to a weak substrate or they may themselves be inherently brittle and fragile. Where the substrate or matrix can be strengthened the use of various consolidants, both of reversible and irreversible type, has been recommended. Waller (1980) suggests that weak, thin matrices can be adequately supported using polyester or epoxy resin bases provided these are applied to the matrix over a separator or film of readily removable adhesive. Where extremely fragile acicular crystals

Table 35.1 Effects on minerals of variations in environmental conditions: C, corrodes; Ch, colour change; D, decomposes; Dh, dehydrates; Dl, deliquesces; E, effloresces; Hl, hydrolyses; Hy, hydrates; O, oxidizes; T, tarnishes

High RH
Elements and alloys
Copper C
Iron C
Iron/nickel alloys C
Lead T
Nickel C
Sulphides and sulphosalts
Arsenopyrite O
Blende O
Bravoite O
Chalcocite O
Daubréelite O
Enargite O
Ferroselite O
Galena O
Gersdorffite O
Hessite O
Mackinawite O
Marcasite O
Oldhamite O
Plenargyrite O
Proustite O
Pyrite O
Pyrrhotine O
Realgar O
Smaltite O
Smythite O
Stannite O
Stibnite O
Volynskite O
Oxides and hydroxides
Opal Hy
Halides and oxyhalides
Albrittonite Dl
Antarcticite Dl
Bischofite Dl
Carobbiite Dl
Carnallite Dl
Chloraluminite Hl
Chlormanganokalite Dl

Low RH
Sulphides and sulphosalts
Daubréelite O
Oldhamite O
Halides and oxyhalides
Albrittonite E
Antarcticite E
Bischofite E
Carnallite E
Chloromanganokalite E
Chloromaganesite E
Douglasite E
Eriochalcite E
Erythrosiderite E
Kremersite E
Nickel-bischofite E
Borates
Boracite E
Borax E
Kernite E
Larderellite ?E
Probertite E
Carbonates
Gaylussite E
Hanksite E
Natron E
Pentahydrocalcite E
Spurrite E
Nitrates
Nitrocalcite E
Nitromagnesite E
Silicates and aluminosilicates
Chloropal Dh
Chrysocolla Dh
Clay minerals, e.g.:
Allophane Dh
Montmorillonite Dh
Sepiolite Dh
Vermiculite Dh
Zeolites, e.g:

Temperature change
Elements and alloys
Sulphur D
Halides and oxyhalides
Hydrohalite D, −5°C
Fluorite D
Borates
Tincalconite D, 60°C
Carbonates
Gaylussite D
Pirssonite D
Phosphates
Autunite Dh
Metaautunite Dh
Variscite Dh

High light levels
Oxides and hydroxides
Opal Ch
Corundum Ch
Halides and oxyhalides
Bideauxite Ch
Bromargyrite D
Calomel Ch
Chlorargyrite D
Eglestonite D
Embolite D
Huantajayite Ch
Iodyrite Ch
Iodembolite D
Kleinite D
Marshite D
Miersite D
Terlinguaite D
Silicates and aluminosilicates
Hackmanite Ch
Nepheline Ch
Serpentine Ch
Sodalite Ch
Topaz Ch
Phosphates
Turquoise Ch
Arsenates
Erythrite O
Symplesite O

Light and oxygen
Elements and alloys
Copper T
Lead T
Sulphides, sulphosats and sulphates
Acanthite T
Aguilarite T
Alabandite T
Alaskaite T
Andorite T
Antimonpearcite O
Aramayoite T
Argentite O
Argyrodite T
Arsenpolybasite O
Baumhauerite O
Berzelianite T
Canfieldite O
Chalcocite O
Chloanthite T
Cinnabar O
Daubreelite T
Daiphorite T
Dufrenoysite T
Fizelyite T
Freieslenbenite T
Hessite O
Hodrushite O
Hutchinsonite T
Jordanite T
Lengenbachite T
Linnaeite O
Lorandite T
Matildite T
Miagyrite O
Mckinstryite T
Naumannite T
Oldhamite O
Pavonite T
Pearceite T
Penroseite O
Plenargyrite O

Pollutants
Elements and alloys
Copper C
Iron C
Iron/nickel alloys C
Lead C
Nickel T
Silver C
Tin C
Carbonates
Calcite C

Mineral	Code
Chlorocalcite	Dl
Chloromagnesite	Dl
Douglasite	Dl
Eriochalcite	Dl
Halite	Dl
Huantajayite	Dl
Kremersite	Dl
Lawrencite	Dl
Molysite	Hl
Nantokite	Hl
Nickel-bischofite	Dl
Rinneite	Dl
Sal-ammoniac	Dl
Scacchite	Dl
Sylvine	Dl
Tachydrite	Dl
Borates	
Borax	Dl
Metakernite	Dl
Carbonates	
Cerrusite	Dl
Teschemacherite	Dl
Thermonatrite	Hl
Trona	Dl
Nitrates	
Nitratine	Dl
Nitre	Dl
Nitrobarite	Dl
Nitrocalcite	Dl
Nitromagnesite	Dl
Silicates and aluminosilicates	
Clay minerals (e.g.):	
Allophane	Hy
Montmorillonite	Hy
Sepiolite	Hy
Vermiculite	Hy
Zeolites (e.g.):	
Analcime	Hy
Chabazite	Hy
Laumonite	Hy
Natrolite	Hy
Vanadates and uranates	
Metatyuyamunite	Hy
Metavanuralite	Hy
Vanuralite	Hy
Vanuranilite	Hy

Mineral	Code
Analcime	Dh
Chabazite	Dh
Laumonite	EDh
Natrolite	Dh
Phosphates	
Autunite	Dh
Brushite	Dh
Metaautunite	Dh
Variscite	Dh
Vivianite	Hl
Vanadates and uranates	
Metavanuralite	E
Tyuyamunite	E
Arsenates	
Annabergite	E
Erythrite	?E
Symplesite	?E
Sulphates	
Bianchite	E
Bieberite	E
Bonattite	E
Boothite	E
Boussingaultite	E
Chalcanthite	E
Coquimbite	E
Cyanochroite	E
Epsomite	E
Ettringite	E
Goslarite	E
Gunningite	E
Halotrichite	E
Hexahydrite	E
Hydrocyanite	E
Jokokuite	E
Kainite	E
Kieserite	E
Mallardite	E
Melanterite	E
Mirabilite	E
Morenosite	E
Nickel-hexahydrite	E
Pentahydrite	E
Picromerite	E
Poitevinite	E
Rhomboclase	E
Sanderite	E
Starkeyite	E

Mineral	Code
Polybasite	T
Polydymite	O
Proustite	O
Pyrostilpnite	T
Rathite	T
Realgar	O
Samsonite	T
Sanjuinite	T
Smaltite	T
Smithite	Ch
Stephanite	T
Stibnite	O
Stromeyerite	T
Sylvanite	T
Trechmannite	O
Violarite	O
Volynskite	O
Vrbaite	O
Xanthoconite	T
Oxides and hydroxides	
Cuprite	T
Phosphates	
Anapaite	O
Graftonite	O
Hureaulite	O
Koninckite	O
Vivianite	O
Vanadates and uranates	
Tyuyamunite	Ch
Chromates	
Crocoite	D
Dietzite	D
Phoenicochroite	D
Organic compounds	
Amber	D
Copal	D

Table 35.1—*contd*

Table 35.1 Effects on minerals of variations in environmental conditions: C, corrodes; Ch, colour change; D. decomposes; Dh, dehydrates; Dl, deliquesces; E, effloresces; Hl, hydrolyses; Hy, hydrates; O, oxidizes; T, tarnishes

High RH		Low RH		Temperature change	High light levels	Light and oxygen	Pollutants
Sulphates		*Sulphates*					
Bieberite	Dl	Szmikite	E				
Bonattite	Hy	Szomolnokite	E				
Boussingaultite	Dl	Tschermigite	E				
Chalcanthite	Dl	Voltaite	E				
Chalcocyanite	Hy	Zinc-melanterite	E				
Coquimbite	Hy	*Organic compounds*					
Cyanochroite	Dl	Amber	Dh				
Goslarite	Dl	Retinite	Dh				
Gunningite	Hy	Copal	Dh				
Hanksite	Dl	Fusain	Dh				
Hexahydrite	Hy	Vitrain	Dh				
Hydrocyanite	Hy	Protein degradation					
Jokokute	Hy	products	Dh				
Kainite	Dl	Lignite	Dh				
Kierserite	Hy						
Leonite	Hy						
Mallardite	Dl						
Mascagnite	Dl						
Matteuccite	Dl						
Melanterite	Dl						
Mercallite	Dl						
Mirabilite	Dl						
Moorhousite	Hy						
Morenosite	Dl						
Nickel-hexahydrite	Hy						
Pentahydrite	Hy						
Pictromerite	Dl						
Poitevinite	Hy						
Retgersite	Hy						
Sanderite	Hy						
Starkeyite	Hy						
Szmikite	Hy						
Szomolnokite	Hy						
Thenardite	Hy						
Zinc-melanerite	Dl						
Organic compounds							
Amber (some)	Hy						
Retinite	Hy						
Copal	Hy						
Fusain	Hy						
Vitrain	Hy						
Protein degradation							

have been damaged or require direct support, the use of lacquers or synthetic polymers should not be considered except as a last resort. Where, for example, it is necessary to restore or repair a specimen for exhibition, the task should be referred to a specialist conservator, as any mistakes made in the application, or later attempted removal, of consolidants will lead to damage.

Fragile mineral specimens should, as a rule, be stored or exhibited in timber rather than metal-based cabinets or cupboards. Especially delicate or weak specimens may be further cushioned by setting on a slip or block of a stable expanded polythene foam with lint-free tissue or other non-fibrous material as a separator between the mineral and foam. Mineral specimens, like other categories of fragile geological material, should be stored in areas not subject to continuous or intermittent noise or vibration. Situations to avoid include proximity to air-conditioning and ventilation plants and major roads and railways. Special care should be taken to protect delicate material stored near building operations.

Effects of temperature

Contrary to popular belief, there are few minerals which are significantly altered by exposure to the temperature variations experienced in normal storage or exhibition environments. There are, however, many hydrated minerals which, if exposed to temperatures in excess of 30°C will melt in their own water of crystallization. There are also many minerals which contain aqueous inclusions which, if subjected to freezing and thawing, would undoubtedly crack. Of the few minerals which are damaged by rapid but slight temperature changes native sulphur crystals are the most sensitive and hand heat is enough to cause these to decrepitate. According to Waller (1980), some fluorites are damaged when washed in water which is not at room temperature or when transferred from a cold to a warm environment. It is recommended that minerals should be stored and exhibited at temperatures maintained between 10°C and 25°C with steps taken to prevent rapid fluctuations of more than ±10°C in this range. However, with moisture-sensitive materials (as described in the next section) it is necessary to further restrict temperature changes in enclosed cases to ±2°C to prevent gross changes in relative humidity.

Relative humidity

Of all the factors influencing the stability of minerals, variations in ambient relative humidity (RH) is considered to be potentially the most damaging. The changes brought about fall into four major categories:

(1). Corrosion – generally of native metals and alloys.
(2). Oxidation – decay of sulphide minerals.
(3). Dimensional instability – distortion of hydrated silcates.
(4). Deliquescence, efflorescence, hydrolysis and hydration.

The measurement and monitoring of RH in storage and exhibition areas requires the use of calibrated instrumentation and should be entrusted to a trained conservator or competent ventilation engineer. Thomson (1978) describes in detail both theoretical and practical approaches to this subject and his book is essential reading for those whose duties include the care and management of mineral collections.

Corrosion

Native metals such as copper, silver, lead and iron, and some meteoritic iron-nickel alloys are highly susceptible to humidity-enhanced corrosion. This may be limited to surface tarnishing or may be more serious through corrosion and etching reactions brought about by hygroscopic salts present on the surface or within interstices of the specimen. One of the most notable corrosion problems ever recorded was caused by the presence of lawrencite, a hygroscopic iron/nickel chloride, within the body of the Cranbourne Meteorite. In an attempt to enhance its stability this specimen was exhibited for many years at the British Museum (Natural History) under an atmosphere of dry nitrogen in a sealed exhibition case (Bannister, 1937).

Oxidation

It is now know that a significant number of sulphides, arsenides and sulphosalts will oxidize when exposed to high relative humidities at normal temperatures. The mechanisms involved in the oxidation of iron pyrites have been investigated by Howie (1977, 1979a), those of pyrite, chalcopyrite and pyrrhotite by Steger and Desjardins (1978) and those of galena, sphalerite and chalcocite by Steger and Desjardins (1980).

For many years it had been considered that thio bacteria were responsible for the oxidation of many museum sulphides, in particular pyrite, and treatments based upon bactericides were advocated by Broadhurst and Duffy (1970), and Booth and Sefton (1970). Howie (1978a) however, demonstrated that the complicity of thio bacteria in the oxidation of pyrite under museum conditions was most unlikely.

The oxidation reactions of pyrite, marcasite, chalcopyrite, galena, sphalerite, arsenopyrite, bravoite and pyrrhotite probably all proceed through purely chemical mechanisms initiated by high relative humidity. Above about 60 per cent RH, many of these minerals will react with oxygen and water to form hydrated metallic sulphates and free sulphuric acid. For pyrite it is now known that an important factor influencing rate of oxidation is crystal size, with microcrystalline pyrite being most susceptible to oxidation. This is undoubtedly an important consideration in the stability of other sulphides, arsenides and sulphosalts as well.

Pyrite oxidation can be prevented by storing specimens at RH levels below 55 per cent, and methods for restoring decayed pyritic material are detailed by Howie (1979a, b). These involve drying, removal of oxidation products by mechanical or chemical methods, neutralization and consolidation. The techniques involved require trained conservators and laboratory facilities.

Work by Thomson (1978), Stolow (1981), Kenjo (1981) and others has shown that optimum storage and exhibition microclimates may be achieved by using conditioned silica gel or other moisture buffering agents. The application of these techniques to the long-term preservation of unstable sulphides and other humidity-sensitive minerals is worthy of much wider consideration than has hitherto been accorded to it.

Dimensional stability
Certain hydrated alumino-silicate clay minerals, such as montmorillonite, have considerable capacity for moisture absorption and desorption, accompanied by significant swelling and subsequent shrinkage. This behaviour, which can be triggered off by changes in relative humidity, can cause extensive damage to specimens contained in shales. Swelling and shrinkage will cause shale delamination and shattering. Observations of stored shales suggest that below about 40 per cent RH rapid shrinkage can occur. An upper limit of 70 per cent RH is recommended, above which swelling may occur. Impregnation of particular types of shale using polyethylene glycol has been recommended by Oddy and Lane (1976) and polyvinyl acetate by Rixon (1976) and Waller (1980).

Other minerals affected by changes in RH are opal, chrysocolla, autunite and probably various types of amber. All develop shrinkage cracks through decrease in water content following lowering of ambient relative humidity. Critical humidity limits for these phenomena have not been determined.

Deliquescence, efflorescence, hydrolysis and hydration
A water-soluble mineral tends to draw moisture from the air, or deliquesce, when the ambient RH is higher than the water vapour pressure which would be exerted by a saturated solution of the same mineral at the same temperature. Deliquescence may occur with or without decomposition. The former occurs with some minerals containing multiple

cations or anions or both. The latter is in evidence either where crusts of original mineral reform on the initial mineral's surface or where crystal corrosion and etching has occurred.

Hydrolysis is a chemical reaction between the mineral phase and water vapour with the formation of products. This occurs with several halide materials. The products are generally basic salts and hydrogen chloride, the latter being potentially corrosive to many other minerals.

Efflorescence is the loss of water from a hydrated mineral caused by a decrease in ambient RH to a level below the water vapour pressure of the hydrate at that temperature. Such water loss usually results in a change in hydration state and hence in crystal structure. Specimens often decompose physically during efflorescence.

Hydration is the uptake of water from air to form a higher hydrate. The new hydrate generally appears as a crust on the original mineral.

The long-term preservation of minerals subject to these processes can only be accomplished by storage in sealed containers over suitable dessicants or materials pre-conditioned to hold RH levels within the known limits of stability. Detailed information on this aspect of mineral conservation is provided by Waller (1980).

Effects of atmospheric pollutants

The effects of the major atmospheric pollutants on mineral specimens has received little attention. It is wise to avoid exposing carbonates, oxides and hydroxides to atmospheres containing more than trace quantities of acid gases such as sulphur dioxide. The detection and activity of atmospheric pollutants in museum collections is discussed in considerable detail by Thomson (1978).

An often ignored aspect of storage and conservation is the potential danger of the build-up of corrosive vapours within exhibition or storage cases. This can be brought about by the presence of certain timbers such as oak and through the slow deterioration of a variety of natural and synthetic materials. Blackshaw and Daniels (1978) showed that metals such as silver and lead suffered considerable corrosion through the activity of many commonly used materials under accelerated ageing test conditions. Fitzhugh and Grettens (1971) and Howie (1978a) describe the damaging effect of organic acid vapours on calcareous material stored in cabinets containing oak components. Argyrakis (1981) provides a useful review of atmospheric pollutants and their activity in museum collections.

Fossils

Over the past century the conservation of fossil material in collections has tended to become synonymous with the use of a range of natural or synthetic resins, glues and waxes for the repair, impregnation and protective coating of specimens. However, during the past two decades, considerable advances have been made in understanding both the properties and long-term stability of many of the materials used in conservation, and there is now some knowledge about the factors governing the stability of certain categories of palaeontological material. It is perhaps in the wider field of technology that an increased awareness of the effects of processing palaeontological material, over both the long and short term, is required.

Processing fossil material

The active conservation of fossil specimens should begin at the time of collection or excavation. Damage caused by faulty procedure or through the use of unsuitable materials in the field can be extremely difficult to rectify later. The excavation of fragile fossil material from wet or loose sediments often necessitates the application of a consolidant or other supporting medium to exposed surfaces. The treatments used must be reversible during later processing without undue risk of damage to the specimen.

The excavation of unstable fossil material may present problems. For example, partly fossilized bone or tusk, lignitic or organic-rich fossil plant remains or specimens in paper shales often occur preserved in wet or waterlogged sediments. To prevent warping or even complete collapse it is essential to ensure that drying-out does not occur during excavation, transport or pre-treatment storage. Simple measures such as enclosure in field cocoons or wrapping in sealable plastic bags, with a fungicide to prevent mould growth, are often all that is required. On the other hand, pyritic material will inevitably deteriorate in a damp cocoon, and the sooner it is processed, the better.

A variety of techniques has been developed for safely collecting and transporting fossil material and these are described in Kummel and Raup (1965), Rixon (1976) and Croucher and Woolley (1982). Useful information on conservation-oriented excavation is provided by Dowman (1971), Leigh *et al* (1978) and Brothwell (1981). These publications, although written mainly for the field archaeologist, contain much of value to the palaeontological collector.

During specimen preparation or development one or other of a variety of processes or substances may be used which, without special precautions, could lead to damage or deterioration. Time and effort should be spent in protecting delicate material during mechanical preparation with percussive, rotary or vibratory equipment. Rixon (1976) describes the general use of a variety of shock-absorbing and supporting media, for specimens undergoing preparation, and Whybrow (1982) details, as a case study, the techniques used and precautions taken during the mechanical preparation of the delicate cranium of the holotype of *Archaeopteryx lithographica*.

With the increased use of chemical techniques for the development of fossil material there is greater risk of specimen damage during both the processing stage and in subsequent storage. Problems arise through a number of factors including the use of chemicals incompatible with the specimen, poorly applied or inadequate supporting resins and insufficient washing-out of applied chemicals. The importance of a thorough knowledge of the properties of the material to be treated, the substances to be used and the precautions required cannot be stressed enough. The use of any chemical process should be followed up by periodic examination of treated material in storage.

Storage and handling of fossils

The range of specimens in even a modest palaeontological collection can be extremely diverse. Handling and storing specimens as different as slide-mounted microfossils and multi-element fossil vertebrate skeletons present problems that require carefully considered solutions. Systematic or stratigraphic constraints usually dictate that collections be housed on a flexible basis with allowance made in storage areas and individual storage units for specimens of greatly differing size, fragility and stability. Doughty (1981) describes many of the shortcomings found in geological collections and has highlighted the poor state of conservation which results from inadequate storage. Rickards (1979) describes the basis for the development of the effective storage of fossil material and Owen *et al* (1981) detail the arrangements for storing the National Collection of fossils at the British Museum (Natural History). Useful guidance on the handling and storage of large and fragile vertebrate material is provided by Gentry (1979).

Delicate fossil material such as acid-developed specimens should be treated in the same way as fragile minerals and stored in shock-absorbent protective packing. The use of cotton wool for packing should be avoided at all costs as extensive damage and loss of material easily results.

Consolidation and repair

Fossils, whether large or small, robust or delicate can be damaged through neglect, mishandling, inherent instability or the deterioration of aged glues and consolidants. Repair and consolidation, except for the most basic type, should be entrusted to a conservator for a number of reasons. The type of consolidant required and its application may have to be varied depending upon, for example, permeability of the specimen; specific adhesives may be required for durable results with certain types of material; old consolidants and glues may, if not thoroughly removed, interfere with or inhibit retreatment with modern synthetic materials. In addition details of treatments should be recorded, and the records stored safely, for the guidance of future workers.

The amount of literature on this subject is extensive, and, for specific information on particular applications, reference should be made to standard texts such as Plenderleith and Werner (1971) and to conservation journals. Rixon (1976) and Howie (1979b) describe various methods developed for the repair, consolidation and restoration of several types of fossils, including old and salvaged specimens. Of importance to the storage and exhibition of treated material is the long-term stability of modern synthetic resins. Many of the standard conservation materials, for example polyvinyl acetate, polyvinyl butyral, and polybutyl-and polymethyl methactylate have been used in conservation for only a relatively short period. The limited data available from ageing tests and observations of behaviour under storage and exhibition conditions suggest that many polymers slowly degrade through exposure to ultraviolet radiation in the 250–500 nm band, and that high relative humidity and the presence of trace quantities of oxidizing agents in air can lead to accelerated scission, cross-linking and reduced resolubility (see also Grassie and Bejuki, 1966; Carlick (1976); von Fraunhofer and Boxall, 1976; and Howie (1984)). As a general rule the use of consolidants should be kept to a minimum, as with repair or restoration, undertaken only where necessary to support or impregnate material or render it transportable.

Relative humidity

Variations in relative humidity give rise to four main problems with the storage and exhibition of fossil material. At high RH pyritic fossils deteriorate. Low RH causes shrinkage of hygroscopic materials and warping or distortion occurs in certain types of shale, sub-fossil bone and enamel and in lignitic or partially carbonized fossil plant remains.

Pyritic fossil material
In fossils, pyrite occurs in a number of forms and its oxidation causes considerable damage, both through the destruction of bone or calcareous minerals present, and by destroying labels and containers. Howie (1979a) describes the occurrence of reactive and stable pyrite in fossil material, outlines the mechanisms proposed for the oxidation of reactive pyrite and shows that the use of conventional consolidants for specimen coatings gives little protection when the RH rises above about 60 per cent. The treatment

of decayed pyrite specimens is dealt with by Rixon (1976) and Howie (1979a, b), and because of the special technical facilities required, should be referred to conservation staff. The long-term prevention of pyrite oxidation should be achievable through control or modification of the storage environment. In older buildings the use of well-constructed timber cabinets generally provides a fair degree of protection, but in newer buildings, or where climate dictates, it may be necessary to have recourse to air-conditioning (Thomson, 1978; Owen, 1981). The use of moisture buffering agents, such as pre-conditioned silica gel in individual storage units or exhibition cases offers a low cost, low maintenance alternative; (Thomson, 1978; Howie, 1979a).

Hygroscopic shales
Many types of shale, most notably those containing montmorillonite will respond to decreases in relative humidity by delaminating and splitting, as with the notorious paper shales. Hard shales will, however, also degrade when exposed to low relative humidities by shrinking and shattering. Limiting conditions of humidity for their storage has not been determined. Conservation treatments suggested include: the use of water-soluble waxes where pyrite oxidation is not a problem, (Oddy and Lane, 1976); impregnation using polyvinyl acetate, (Rixon, 1976); and in suitable cases, removal of as much shale as possible, (Howie, 1979b).

Sub-fossil bone
Much sub-fossil bone contains collagen or its protein-rich breakdown products. Little research has been carried out into the deterioration of aged proteinaceous material. What data is available suggests that exposure to low humidities can cause temporary or permanent alterations in protein amino acids, (Karpowicz, 1981). The effects of lowering the RH around sub-fossil bone have been reported by Howie (1978b) and it is recommended that such material be stored at 45–55 per cent. The treatment for warped and split sub-fossil bone, detailed by Rixon (1976) and Howie (1979a, b), should be carried out by conservation staff.

Moisture-sensitive palaeobotanical material
Partially carbonized fossil plant material including leaves, wood, seeds and roots is perhaps the most difficult type of material to treat satisfactorily. When it contains pyrite, one successful method is storage immersed in an inert silicone fluid, (Howie, 1979a). When pyrite is not present, the use of polyethene glycols has sometimes been successful (Rixon, 1976). Palaeobotanists, however, do not generally work with immersed or coated material and the increasing use of scanning electron microscopy dictates that type specimens may be on stubs, thus precluding the

use of any coatings or liquids in their conservation. Collinson (1978) suggests the use of specially constructed desiccated units in which such specimens could be stored at an optimum relative humidity.

Acknowledgements

I thank Dr H. W. Ball and Dr L. R. M. Cocks, Keeper and Deputy Keeper respectively of the Palaeontology Department of the British Museum (Natural History), for reading the manuscript and making useful suggestions for its improvement. I also thank numerous colleagues in the Departments of Palaeontology and Mineralogy for advice and helpful discussion.

References

ARGYRAKIS, A. (1981), *Conservation Problems in Museums Displays,* The Area Museums Service for south-eastern England, Milton Keynes

BANNISTER, F. A. (1937), The preservation of minerals and meteorites, *Museums Jl.,* **36**(11), 465–76

BLACKSHAW, S. M. AND DANIELS, V. D. (1978), Selecting safe materials for use in the display and storage of antiquities *Preprint 5th Triennial Meeting ICOM Committee for Conservation, Zagreb,* 23 February 1978, pp. 1–9

BOOTH, G. H. AND SEFTON, G. V. (1970), Vapour phase inhibition of thiobacilli and ferrobacilli: a potential preservative for pyritic museum specimens, *Nature,* **226**, 185–6

BROADHURST, F. M. AND DUFFY, L. (1970), 'A plesiosaur in the Geology Department, University of Manchester, *Museums Jl.,* **70**(1), 30–1

BROTHWELL, D. R. (1981), *Digging up Bones,* British Museum (Natural History), London

CARLICK, D. J. (1976), Photodegradation, controlled, *Encyclopedia of Polymer Science and Technology, Supplement* **1**, 378–401, Interscience, New York

COLLINSON, M. E. (1978). *Palaecarpology and related Paeobotanical Studies of Sediments from Southern Britain,* PhD Thesis, Botany Department, Birbeck College, University of London

CROUCHER, R. AND WOOLLEY, A. W. (1982), *Fossils, Minerals and Rocks: Collection and Preservation,* British Museum (Natural History), London and University of Cambridge

DANA, J. D. (1944), *A System of Mineralogy,* Wiley, New York and London

DOWMAN, E. (1971), *Conservation in Field Archaeology,* Methuen, London

FELLER, R. L. (1974), Fundamentals of conservation science: induction time and the auto-oxidation of arganic compounds, *Bulletin of the American Institute of Conservation,* **14**, 142–51

FITZHUGH, F. W. AND GETTENS, R. J. (1971), Calclacite and other efflorescent salts on objects stored in wooden museum cases; in Brill, R. H. (Ed.), *Science and Archaeology,* Cambridge, Mass., pp. 91–102

GENTRY, A. W. (1979), 'Curation of fossil vertebrates' in Bassett, M. G. (Ed.) Curation of palaeontological collections, *Special Papers in Palaeontology* **22**, 87–95 The Palaeontological Association, London

GRASSIE, N. AND BEJUKI, N. W. (1966). Degradation, *Encyclopedia of Polymer Sicence and Technology,* **4**, 647–735, Interscience, New York

HEY, M. H. (1962), *Index of mineral species and varieties arranged chemically,* British Museum (Natural History) London

HOWIE, F. M. P (1977), Pyrite and conservation. Parts 1 and 2: historical aspects, *The Geological Curator,* **1**, 457–465, 497–512

HOWIE, F. M. P. (1978a), Storage environment and the conservation of geological material, *Conservator,* **2**, 13–19

HOWIE, F. M. P. (1978b), Storage and exhibition environment and the conservation of fossil material, *Preprint Museums Conservation Climate Conference ICCROM,* November 1978, Rome

HOWIE, F. M. P. (1979a), 'Museums climatology and the conservation of palaeontological material' in Bassett, M. G. (Ed.), Curation of palaeontological collections, *Special Papers in Palaeontology,* **22**, 103–25 The Palaeontological Association, London

HOWIE, F. M. P. (1979b), Physical conservation of fossils in existing collections, *The Geological Curator,* **2**(5), 269–280

HOWIE, F. M. P. (in press), 'Minerals used for conserving fossil specimens since 1930: a review', *Preprint 10th International Congress ICC, Paris,* Sept. 1984

KARPOWICZ, A. (1981), Ageing and deterioration of proteinaceous media, *Studies in Conservation,* **26**(4), 153–60

KENJO, T. (1981), A rapid-response humidity buffer composed of Nikka pellets and Japanese tissue, *Studies in Conservation,* **27**, 19–24

KING, R. J. (1982), Section one – the cleaning of minerals, *Journal of the Russell Society,* **1**(1), 42–53

KUMMEL, B. AND RAUP, D. (1965), *Handbook of Palaeontological Techniques* Freeman, San Francisco, London

LEIGH, D. (1978), First aid for finds: a practical guide for archaeologists, *Rescue,* Hertford

ODDY, W. A. AND LANE, H. (1976), The conservation of waterlogged shale, *Studies in Conservation,* **21**, 63–6

OWEN, H. G., PARSONS, E. AND PATERNOSTER, R. (1981), Rationalized storage of fossils in the British Museum (Natural History), *Curator,* **24**(2), 77–88

PLENDERLEITH, H. J. AND WERNER, A. E. A. (1971), *The Conservation of Antiquities and Works of Art,* University Press, Oxford

RICKARDS, R. B. (1979), The physical basis of paiaeontological curating, in Bassett, M. G. (Ed.) Curation of palaeontological collections, *Special Papers in Palaeontology,* **22** 75–86, The Palaeontological Association, London

RIXON, A. E. (1976), *Fossil Animal Remains: Their Preparation and Conservation,* Athlone Press, London

SHARPE, T. (1983), *Geology in Museums: a bibliography and index,* Geological series No 6, National Museum of Wales, Cardiff

STEGER, H. F. AND DESJARDINS, L. E. (1978), Oxidation of sulphide minerals, 4. Pyrite, chalcopyrite and pyrrhotite, *Chemical Geology,* **23**, 255–37

STEGER, F. H. AND DESJARDINS, L. E. (1980), Oxidation of sulphide minerals, 5, Galena, sphalerite and chalcocite, *Canadian Mineralogist,* **18**, 365–72

STOLOW, N. (1981), Procedures and conservation standards for museum collections in transit and on exhibition, *UNESCO,* Paris

THOMPSON, G. (1978), *The Museum Environment*, Butter-worths, IIC, London

VON FRAUNHOFER, J. A. AND BOXALL, J. (1976), *Protective Paint Coatings for Metals*, Portcullis Press, Redhill, Surrey

WALLER, R. (1980), The preservation of mineral specimens, *Preprint 8th Annual Meeting AIC*, pp. 166–28

WHYBROW, P. J. (1982), Preparation of the cranium of the holotype of *Archaeopteryx lithographica* from the collection of the British Museum (Natural History), *Neus Jahrbuch fur Geologie und Palaontologie, Monatshefte* **3**, 184–92

36

Conservation and storage: scientific instruments

Christopher J. Wheatley

With an increase in the popularity of museums has come a greater demand for conservation, and this paper will show some of the dangers of employing untrained staff for conservation work, particularly in the area of scientific instruments. Although some of the processes appear to be simple and straightforward, when carried out incorrectly they cause irreversible damage.

Scientific instruments and their materials of manufacture

The term 'scientific instrument' covers a wide range of museum objects. At its face value, it is an object that has been used for scientific purposes, but the term is normally limited to objects which have been used in precision measurement or in scientific observation.

The materials involved in their manufacture

Scientific instruments are used in a wide range of disciplines, and are fabricated from many different materials, such as metal, wood, ivory, stone, paper, textiles or leather. Brass has been a common material in the past, but metals are not always what they seem to be. Brass is a very specific alloy of copper and zinc and is yellow in colour. Not all yellow metals are made of copper and zinc; many can be one of a wide range of other yellow alloys. Many of these alloys contain copper alloyed with one or more of the following materials: lead, tin, nickle, phosphorous, and antimony. Some of these alloys are called brass, others bronze, and some have more specific names such as lead–bronze, or phosphorous–bronze. The only way to be certain of what alloy the instrument has been made, is for the metal to be analyzed.

Other metals commonly found in scientific instru-ments are silver alloys, steels, nickle alloys and lead. Organic materials such as wood, paper and textiles have been used almost as much as metals. Generally they were used as part of instruments only and details of their conservation can be found under specialist headings elsewhere in this manual. Another group of materials which have been used increasingly are the plastics which present new problems for the conservator. There has been very little research into this field, leaving many unanswered problems.

The examination of deterioration and its causes

Good conservation depends on knowing the process of deterioration. There are two categories of deterioration: the first is damage caused by mechanical means; the second involves a chemical reaction within the object.

Mechanical damage

Probably more damage to scientific instruments in museums occurs through bad handling than through any other cause. Many of them move mechanically and are therefore expected to respond as they did when first made. With the passage of time the materials become worn, brittle and weak, and it is courting disaster to expect an old instrument to respond as it did originally.

The temptation to exercise the instruments in a collection and to experiment with them unnecessarily, must be resisted. Research into the working properties of an instrument should always be carried out under laboratory conditions to reduce the risk of damage.

Display can be another area of high risk especially to objects which operate continuously, such as clocks. This presents a problem of ethics as well as conservation. The decision as to whether or not a timepiece should run on display must be taken by the curator and the conservator. One thing is certain: fragile objects which are allowed to run, if only for a short time, may be damaged considerably. Many more suffer invisible damage, shortening their life considerably.

Chemical damage

There are three main causes of chemical breakdown: humidity, light and pollution. Of these, humidity is the most dangerous, as it affects all materials.

In the presence of moisture, chemical and biological attack will take place. If the humidity is continually high, moisture forms on the surface of the object, and this will absorb pollution from the atmosphere. The pollutants then form a corrosive solution which causes metals to tarnish and corrode, and some organic materials to suffer chemical breakdown. Reactions of this type take place slowly while the object is on display or in store. Biological attack manifests itself in the form of mould growths and insect infestations. If these continue, the damage will be considerable, and ultimately affect all materials not normally considered vulnerable in this way. Mould growths and insects can give off waste products which are highly corrosive to materials such as glass lenses and metal fittings.

Examination for active deterioration

One of the most difficult problems is to decide at first sight whether the deterioration is active. When an object is in poor condition it is not always possible to be sure whether it has deteriorated recently, or whether the deterioration took place in the past and has since become dormant. The simplest and most effective way of deciding is by observation and comparison. This involves regular examination of the collection so that actively deteriorating objects can be identified quickly. At first this form of control will take time, but as the survey continues it becomes less time-consuming.

The handling of objects

The wearing of white cotton gloves when handling objects is of the utmost importance, since perspiration on the hands can be highly corrosive, particularly to metal objects.

Conservation

The most hazardous time in the life of an object is as it enters the conservation laboratory. At no other time in its life will it be subjected to such change. It may arrive for conservation as an old and dirty instrument, and leave fully restored, after a long and hazardous process.

Dismantling

An instrument is usually made of pieces, and in some cases they run into hundreds. Dismantling is therefore the first hazardous procedure. Pieces can be lost or mixed up so that on reassembly parts are missing or reassembled incorrectly. It is not difficult to prevent this from happening; all that is required is a simple record, and the labelling and tagging of each part. Screws should be kept either in their original holes or in a screw card: this is a card on which a drawing of the instrument is made, the screws being inserted in their correct places. Many screwdrivers on the market are unsuitable forsuch delicate work and conservators of scientific instruments often produce their own, and constantly adjust them to fit different screw heads.

Cleaning

If a museum object is considered to be a historic document which can supply information of its origin and life, it must be treated correctly. Even the layers of dirt on an old instrument can supply information. By careful cleaning, information on the types of lacquers formerly used, surface colourants, and surface texturing can be revealed. If automatic stripping is carried out this information will be lost and make the problems of authentication and restoration much greater.

Protective finishes

Clean metal is very susceptible to tarnish and corrosion, and so today, as in antiquity, the metal is coated to protect it. The coatings usually used for scientific instruments are *laquers*. There has been a trend in the last few years to use synthetic lacquers, which are based on plastic. Lacquer can be applied by brushing, but there is a danger of overlooking areas, which will cause problems when the unprotected metal becomes tarnished or corroded. On the removal of tarnish and corrosion, the metal will be found to be matt, and this is called etching. The reason for the matt finish is that tarnish and corrosion results from a reaction between the environment and the metal, thus forming a mixture of both. When this is removed, the metal from the surface is also taken away, leaving etched areas. The only way to remove etching is by grinding and polishing, which destroys the original surface. A better method of applying laquer is by spraying. This greatly reduces the possibility of missing sections. Spraying is difficult and requires specialist skill, but once it has been mastered it is a superior method.

Reassembly and restoration

Reassembly is the reversal of dismantling. It should present few problems if records have been kept throughout the conservation programme. On the other hand, probably the most difficult problem facing a conservator will be that of restoration, both ethically and practically.

One of the first things to consider is the replacement of missing screws. There is a great temptation to drill out the old screw thread and make a new thread to fit a modern screw, but the amount of necessary alteration is ethically unacceptable. The threads of an ancient screw are very similar to those of the present day, the only difference being their diameters and the number of threads per inch/mm. Most lathes have the ability to reproduce many of these screws in varying size and pitches, so there is no reason to alter the original instrument.

The restoration of scientific instruments can be divided into two categories:

(1). Restoration which involves the irreversible modification of an instrument such as the drilling of a new hole, or soldering.
(2). The replacement of missing parts which can be mechanically attached to the original such as a part made and held in place by screws, using the original holes.

The first of these needs a great deal of consideration, and should only be carried out if the advantages to be gained are considerable. The second is not so difficult, because if in the future it is decided that the restoration changes are no longer required, the piece can be unscrewed and discarded. It should be stated that all new parts should be marked as restoration, so that they are not confused with the original. This can easily be done by using a punch with the museum crest, denoting restoration, and a set of number punches to apply the date.

Storage and display

Storage

In general, stores for scientific instruments need not be different from those used for many other materials, the important features being tidyness and stability of the environment. Climatic conditions are responsible for a lot of the damage to objects in a museum. The biggest problem is varying humidity; this causes the expansion and contraction of most organic materials, and some will react faster than others, setting up stresses between them. In extreme cases, where there is a large block of material, and a rapid drop in humidity, a stress is set up between the inner core and the outer surface. As a result, the outer surface gives off moisture, causing shrinkage and splitting, because it can no longer contain the inner mass. This form of cracking can be prevented either by stabilizing the environment, or changing the humidity so slowly that the mass gives off moisture evenly. This can take a year or more.

Display

If the display area is considered to be an extension of the store, similar conditions should prevail in both areas, especially when moving objects from one to the other. However, displays change constantly in a modern museum, as new exhibitions are formed. With new displays comes the danger of introducing new materials which will cause deterioration to the objects. For example, many modern textiles and adhesives are based on petroleum products, and give off sulphur which is a major pollutant for museums. Silver is particularly at risk, as the black tarnish which forms so readily on the surface is caused by sulphur from the air.

To reduce this danger a simple test can be carried out on materials to be used both for display, and in store. It involves exposing three basic metals to the vapours of the materials to be tested: silver, copper and lead. This is done under conditions which will accelerate any reaction which is likely to occur.

Conclusion

Today there are many practices in the field of the conservation of scientific instruments which are in need of revision, and only by the conservator and the curator working together can progress be made. The curator should work with the collection and make an assessment of its condition; he should liaise with the conservator to improve conservation in this field.

Bibliography

BLACKSHAW, S. AND DANIELS, V. (1979), The Testing of Materials for use in Storage and Display in Museums, *The Conservator,* IIC, UKC, *3*

BROWN, F. (1977), *Corrosion and Metal Artifacts: a Dialogue between Conservators, Archaeologists and Corrosion Scientists,* Smithsonian Institute, Washington

FISHLOCK, D. (1962), *Metal Colouring,* Robert Draper, London

GLYDESDALE, A. (1982), *Chemicals in Conservation: a Guide to Possible Hazards and Safe Use,* Conservation Bureau SSCR

HUGHS, R. AND ROWE, M. (1982), *The Colouring of Bronze and Patination of Metal,* Crafts Council, London

MORGAN, W. (1969), *Outline of Paint Technology,* Charles Griffin and Co., London

SHREIR, L. L. (1978), *Corrosion, vol. 1 Metal/Environment Reactions,* 2nd edition, Newnes – Butterworths, London

TAYLOR, E. AND RICHEY, M. (1962), *The Geometrical Seaman,* Hollis and Carter, London

THOMSON, G. (1978), *The Museum Environment,* Butterworths, London

UNTRACHT, O. (1969), *Metal Techniques for Craftsmen,* Robert Hale, London

WATERS, D. (1958), *The Art of Navigation in England in the Elizabethan and Early Stuart Times,* Hollis and Carter, London

WRANGLEN, G. (1972), *An Introduction to Corrosion and the Protection of Metals,* Institute for Metallskydd, Stockholm

WYNTER, H. AND TURNER, A. (1975), *Scientific Instruments,* Studio Vista, London

37

Conservation and storage: technology

John Hallam

This paper cannot pretend to be an all-embracing guide to the restoration or operation of large technological exhibits, nor set out the ethics of such matters. Each museum authority (or private individual) must determine its own policy and practice in this respect, having sought first the advice of specialists if this is considered desirable.

In general, the paper refers to aspects of the management of technological exhibits removed from their working environment and received into museums. However, by describing some of the problems encountered by a wide variety of museums and related bodies, it is hoped that the non-specialist curator, faced with similar problems or the offer of a large exhibit, may be encouraged to explore the opportunities offered, and to seek advice in the knowledge that most problems have been encountered elsewhere.

Introduction

It is difficult to arrive at an acceptable definition of a large, working, technological exhibit, for opinion depends on a number of factors.

Technology may be defined as the application of science and the 'useful' arts to the apparatus, machines and processes used in the conversion of natural raw material into finished articles. A technological exhibit may, therefore, relate to such apparatus or processes and be extended to include the products. Thus, a technology exhibit may additionally be included within traditional museum disciplines such as archaeology, social history, transport or, on occasion, applied art.

The consideration of the physical *size* or *mass* of an exhibit is usually related to the ease with which that object can be handled. This may be determined by the limitations of a building structure or the handling

methods. In many cases, the principal objection to 'large' exhibits is that they are inconvenient, particularly for the small museum. The *museum*, in this context, is taken to include any private or public collection of artefacts assembled for preservation as evidence of man's material culture and environment.

Large or working technological exhibits are considered by many museum curators to pose particular problems of storage, conservation and display which are difficult to solve by non-specialist museums. Because of the difficulties, many public museums have preferred, until recent years, to leave the problems to a small number of specialized industrial museums or to the rapidly growing number of private ('independent') museums, Trusts, Preservation Societies and individual enthusiasts.

Before the Second World War, less than twenty public museums in Great Britain had significant collections of large industrial exhibits, and of these only three (The Science Museum, London, The Railway Museum, York, and the Municipal Museum of Science and Industry – now the Museum of Science and Engineering, Newcastle) were devoted exclusively to Industry and Technology. A great number of museums had large exhibits, often a small number of transport items or a local industry section, while others amassed technological material within a folk-life collection.

In the post-war years, public interest was awakened in industrial history and related subjects. By the early 1960s about fifty new 'technology' museums or collections had been formed. Many of these were the product of enterprising individuals or bodies who were openly critical of the lack of interest shown by the majority of the existing museums. R. H. Clark, an authority on traction engines who was later to become President of the Newcomen Society, could write in 1960 that:

'excepting South Kensington, Birmingham and New-castle-Upon-Tyne they all seem to regard machinery with abhorrence mainly, I think, because few of the staff and curators have had any technical training.'

This opinion was not without justification, for the number of qualified curators, conservators and technicians dealing with industrial collections outside these three museums barely exceeded three figures.

In 1959 the Council for British Archaeology had set up a Steering Committee for Industrial Archaeology and, in 1963, the Industrial Monuments Survey was sponsored jointly by the CBA and the Ministry of Public Buildings and Works (now the Department of the Environment). This official interest in the preservation of industrial monuments and, to a lesser extent, the associated machinery, was unable to attack the problem of the destruction of historic machinery which had survived in use for generations but which was rapidly becoming the casualty of modernization in many traditional industries.

From 1948 until 1963 the number of industrial museums doubled as both public and private interests became aware of this largely untapped, or neglected, area of our heritage. In the boom years in the late 1960s, and even into the 1970s, industrial and transport museums opened at an average rate of five per year, not including the phenomenon of railway preservation following the demise of the main-line steam locomotive in 1968.

It cannot be denied that the lack of agreed collecting policies and elements of over-enthusiasm have left a legacy of unbalanced coverage of technological history, with an excess of certain types of exhibit and considerable problems of storage and conservation.

Including transport museums and preserved railways, there are currently probably more than 750 separate locations offering access to large technological exhibits ranging from a single large item through the traditional museum displays to complete industrial environments, both original and recreated.

There is much obsolescent material remaining in current use together with a vast resource of privately owned items, particularly related to transport, agricultural machinery or forms of motive power. Much of this can be expected to become available to museums as it is recognized as being of historic, and often commercial, value. However, there is a growing awareness that the radical changes in industry have brought about a much higher discard rate for the artefacts of the 'second industrial' or 'electronic' revolution. Much of this material is being lost because it is not being identified as potential museum material. Indeed, R. H. Clark's remarks of 1960 could be repeated in this context. The curators, conservators and technicians now dealing with the nuts and bolts of an earlier age will need to learn new skills, for it is unlikely that sufficient private collectors will be motivated to preserve examples of today's technology.

Examination of the object

It is important that the curator, conservator and restoration engineer should have a thorough knowledge of the changing materials, design features and techniques of manufacture used in the construction of technological objects.

An object may be derived from any of a number of historical periods and will possess features dependent upon its origin and history. It may be made from one or more natural or manufactured materials including wood, metal, glass, ceramic, stone, leather, textiles or plastic. It is common to find organic and inorganic material in association, such as lubricants and fuels, water, minerals, the raw materials or products associated with use, or other products as a result of the object's interaction with its environment (including the products of deterioration).

Careful examination of the object, with systematic recording of information, will reveal much which is not apparent immediately. Dismantling of the object may be necessary before complete examination is possible. Chemical or non-destructive analysis may be required. During this period, the object is at greatest risk unless there is an agreed, systematic approach to the recording of all information and, *at the same time*, there is a continuing dialogue between curator and conservator. It is particularly important to establish this relationship when the work passes out of the hands of the museum to an outside agency.

Many objects received by the museum will have been repaired or altered deliberately during their working lives. This may have been as a result of wear or failure of an original, or replacement part, or as a conscious attempt at modification and improvement. In the case of exhibits which have been in the hands of private enthusiasts, this process may have extended to the almost complete fabrication of a replica (perhaps using modern material and methods) and with a minimum of original parts. This is particularly evident with transport exhibits. Vintage cars may not be all they seem and the gleaming showman's road locomotive may have once been a humble steam roller. On a lesser scale, it is not uncommon to find objects such as stationary engines or domestic and agricultural 'bygones' so over-restored that the maker would find it hard to recognize them. Not all brass was polished, nor were castings always fettled smooth and many coats of (synthetic) paint applied – except for show purposes or to special order.

The curator must be on his guard against accepting the materials and construction at face value. There may be some justification in continuing a process of modification or replacement of the parts of working exhibits, but this process may equally be required to be reversed. What is important is that at all stages of examination, conservation and restoration, existing evidence of original materials and methods of construction should be recognized and recorded before any further work is carried out on the object.

Materials and Construction

Even a cursory examination of the range of technological exhibits will reveal an almost limitless variety of materials used for construction. A convenient, but grossly over-simplified, classification could divide the use of materials into five historical periods.

The first, until the beginning of the sixteenth century, was based on wood as the principal material of construction. The craftsman (carpenter, boat-builder or millwright) selected the variety of timber according to its use. Wrought iron, obtained from primitive bloomeries in small quantities, was scarce and expensive and was used for fastenings and small machine parts in addition to clockwork.

The second period, up to the Industrial Revolution, saw the gradual replacement of wood by metal, particularly cast iron, together with early attempts at materials science and theory of machines. Even at the beginning of the eighteenth century wrought iron was still laboriously produced by small forges in quantities of a few tons per week. Steel was not generally available except in minute quantities.

The third period, the great age of coal, iron and steam popularly known as the Industrial Revolution, saw a hundred-fold increase in pig-iron production. By 1850, Britain was producing over two and a half million tons of pig-iron annually. This was used in the foundry for cast machine parts, such as cylinders, bedplates or beams of steam engines, gear wheels and sections of bridges, or it was converted to wrought iron to form rolled and hammered plates and bars used in forged or turned machine parts. Cast and wrought iron, together with lead, copper, tin and zinc (and the copper alloy series of bronzes and brasses) were the principal materials for the machines. The use of wood was becoming limited to non-mechanical uses, such as framing, carriage-building and specialized uses (lignum vitae bearings, horn-beam and apple wheel teeth, ash shafts and springs, and so on).

The 'age of steel' was heralded by Bessemer in 1856. By 1900 the widespread availability of reliable quality cheap steel had revolutionized the design of machines and structures. At this time other new materials, such as aluminium, were also being introduced into engineering.

The final period – 'the age of plastics' – has seen yet further advances in the use of synthetic materials either as a direct replacement for traditional material or because of new properties, for example a low coefficient of friction or the optical properties of acrylics.

In the last two historical periods (that is, roughly the past century from which most technological museum exhibits are derived) the materials scientist has been able to provide a wide range of new materials whose physical properties can be 'tailor-made' for a particular use. This has enabled the engineering designer and production engineer to introduce new methods of manufacture and reduce the size or weight of machines without reducing the factor of safety. Coupled with detailed studies in the problems of corrosion or the behaviour of materials under stress, this has led to the concept of a 'design life' for a machine or its component parts. Curators and conservators must take this into account when considering the long-term preservation (and particularly the operation) of a technological exhibit. Not only are there revenue implications in continued maintenance but the safety implications must be paramount.

Spectacular failures of working machinery have already occurred within the preservation movement and it can only be a matter of time before a machine fails in a museum as a result of unforseen and undetected deterioration, fatigue, stress cracking, crystallization of metals or inadequate restoration and maintenance. It is for this reason that thorough examination must be considered an essential preliminary to conservation, restoration or operation. Similarly, machinery must only be operated by qualified and experienced staff and must be subject to regular inspection, whether or not such inspection may be required by law.

Methods of Construction

The construction methods used in technological exhibits are too diverse to be described in this short survey. The whole range of techniques from crude handwork to high precision engineering will be encountered. Since the availability of new materials and the development of machine tools played such a key role in the design or development of any particular machine or technological artefact, it is not unreasonable to expect the artefact to display evidence of contemporary methods, together with later techniques used during maintenance, repair or modification. However, the varying rates of diffusion of techniques and availability of new methods and materials can give rise to the retention of outmoded or archaic features. Fortunately, there is a considerable body of information from extant drawings (such as the Watt Papers held by Birmingham Reference Library or the many technical and works records still held by long-established Companies) coupled with 'Engineer's Handbooks', design manuals and technical journals and treatises available in many libraries. It is therefore not an impossible task for the curator or restorer, aided by specialist colleagues from other institutions or preservation societies, to ensure the historical accuracy of a technological exhibit even to the extent of reconstructed parts and, for machinery after the introduction of standardization (from the 1850s), even to arrive at the correct screw threads.

Conservation or restoration?

Conservation may be regarded as the process of arresting or minimising deterioration in an object so that its existing features may be preserved for posterity. Restoration is generally taken to mean the deliberate return of an object to the original state or appearance when it was first made or to its condition at some other defined period within its history by the use of contemporary skills, methods and materials where available, or modern substitutes as necessary.

Available skills and techniques

There is an unfortunate tendency among owners of industrial, and particularly transport, objects for over-restoration. This may result from the deliberate grinding down of castings, use of filler and excessive coats of paint, or unintentionally from the use of modern machine tools and techniques which produce a standard of finish or dimensional accuracy incompatible with contemporary practice. Since most restorers have not been trained in contemporary techniques such as adze work, chipping surfaces, drawfiling, and so on, it is likely that this tendency will continue unless attention is given to the training of staff in these skills. However, it may be unreasonable to insist on the restoration of an exhibit to its original condition as first manufactured, particularly if the object has been modified or repaired during its working life. Such repairs or modifications, and even the 'wear and tear' are part of the historical evidence, and often part of the interest or attraction, of an object.

Raistrick, in describing the problems of the industrial archaeologist, aptly sums up the problems of the conservator and restorer:

> The engines, the machines, the processes of nineteenth and twentieth century industry are becoming so complex and involve so many different skills and professions that it is very difficult to define the legitimate place of the industrial archaeologist other than as that of the recorder of their existence and their overall appearance.

Yet curators and conservators are expected to preserve the material evidence of todays techniques, which relies so much on a rapid rate of obsolescence and throwaway parts rather than labour-intensive repair. It is unlikely, on economic grounds alone,

that museums will be able to provide the specialized parts, knowledge or technology to maintain an electronic washing machine or computer-assisted photo-composing machine. The techniques of restoration are rooted firmly on the electromechanical age which is already a generation or two past.

It will be interesting to see how technological museums deal with this new challenge. Perhaps the seemingly unattractive 'black-boxes' of modern technology will not engender the same demands for working exhibits as have the dinosaurs of the age of steam.

Some of the practical aspects of restoration of large or working mechanical objects are set out below. In general the final result must be the product of careful research and curatorial judgement, after continual dialogue between curator and conservator or restorer. It may be necessary to modify requirements on the grounds of necessity or expediency, particularly as restoration of obsolete mechanical or electrical objects is expensive of time. Whatever the decisions, the processes employed and decisions taken should be recorded meticulously so that future museum workers and the public may know what has been done.

Cleaning

Particular care must be taken during cleaning of technological exhibits. Valuable information may be gained by careful examination of the surface. This includes the layers of dirt, old oil or other material which is often found both outside and inside the object. This evidence of interaction with the environment should be recorded during cleaning and preparation, and samples kept if necessary. In particular, successive layers of paint should be identified and flakes kept for colour-matching.

The clean surfaces should be examined carefully before any further restoration is started. Evidence of manufacturing methods, such as hand or machine tool-marks may be found. Such evidence is easily overlooked unless both curator and conservator are constantly vigilant.

Conservators must recognize that toxic or hazardous materials may be found in association with the object, or may be produced during cleaning. Lead- or arsenic-based dusts from paint, mercury in electrical apparatus and asbestos in lagging materials are common examples. Biological hazards such as spores and fungi in dusts are less commonly recognized. Indiscriminate or uncontrolled use of organic solvents and mineral acids or the employment of blow-guns or shot-blasting plant frequently give rise to health and safety problems.

There are statutory regulations dealing with most hazards and advice is readily available from many sources such as the Health and Safety Executive, environmental health departments and individual manufacturers. Without exception it is the joint responsibility of the individual working conservator or restorer, together with curator and line management, to ensure a safe working environment.

Dismantling

Some machines may contain hundreds, if not thousands, of parts which may need to be assembled in a particular sequence. It is possible that the conservator or restorer may not be a specialist in the type of machine or object being worked on and it is common to find that all engineering records, drawings or operating details have been destroyed. It is therefore imperative that a systematic approach to the dismantling and restoration of any technological item be adopted.

The greatest danger to an object is when it is lying in pieces, possibly awaiting spare parts, with all the information on how the object was dismantled being entrusted to the fallible memory of an individual. Unfortunately this is not uncommon, particularly as many objects are dismantled in haste during urgent rescue operations. The stages of dismantling are essentially as follows:

(1). Before touching the item, all existing records should be obtained, or details recorded both by description, drawings and photographs. This should continue throughout the whole restoration process. If possible the method of operation of the exhibit, including individual peculiarities and safety aspects, should also be recorded.
(2). The object should be cleaned sufficiently for examination to establish whether parts are numbered or otherwise marked up. These marks should be recorded, together with any additional numbers applied by the museum. The method of numbering should be compatible with expected storage or process times and should not be readily removable. Wired-on tags, paints, special machinery markers, stamped, engraved, incised or simple 'pop' marks have all been used. Care must be taken to ensure that marks cannot be confused and that each part removed can be identified and replaced. The extent of marking-up must be jointly decided between curator and conservator, bearing in mind that the object may have been previously assembled incorrectly or marked in error. Major parts which appear identical and even nuts and bolts may not necessarily be interchangeable. This can apply to machinery made after engineering standards were introduced, as a result of original manufacturing tolerances, later wear or repairs.
(3). Separate parts or assemblies are set aside for careful examination and assessment. It may often

be found during dismantling that preliminary cost- or time- estimates for restoration may need to be revised drastically. If there is likely to be any major delay in restoration, it is advisable in many cases that the machine is built up again, after first applying suitable treatment against existing or expected deterioration.

Repairs and replacements

Having made a decision to restore an exhibit, it may be necessary for both curator and conservator to engage in extensive research to identify the correct method of restoration, particularly with regard to replacement of missing parts or the repair of earlier damage or modification.

For many exhibits, the manufacturers drawings or specifications are no longer extant. It is relatively straightforward to obtain advice and information on design methods, using contemporary journals, treatises and engineer's handbooks. There is a wealth of expertise within the larger or more specialized museums, together with learned societies such as the Newcomen Society or specialist clubs or associations.

Most restorers have built up a collection of spare parts and materials ranging from dozens of varieties of lubricating devices to magnetos. The introduction of metrication has begun to diminish the supply of imperial sizes in materials, with the exception of pipework which standardized on the British Standard. It is important for the restorer to be able to recognize and replicate screw threads and obsolete parts. With modern lathes the manufacture of, for example, Whitworth form screws with pre-Austerity sized heads, or indeed any other form of thread is not difficult.

There is little excuse for drilling out contemporary threads, and replacing with modern off-the-shelf parts. Still less is there an excuse for modern fastenings with 'Posidrive' heads or 'pop' rivets to be used.

In many cases, contemporary replacements may not be available for missing parts. Fabrication of parts may be necessary, particularly in the case of original castings. It may not be possible (or even desirable from the safety aspect) to use traditional materials such as wrought iron or hammered tinned iron sheet. Similarly, modern methods of construction, such as welding instead of riveting, may be necessary.

Many people would argue that the restorer is merely continuing the processes which an object would have been subjected to during its working life. This may be acceptable provided records are kept and the museum is totally honest about what the object may have become. All replacement parts should be identified permanently (for example, by a standardized punch mark) and significant original parts which have been removed must be retained.

In the case of a unique object of specfic technological or historic importance, or those objects which are substantially in original condition, it must be argued that such exhibits should not be operated nor subjected to ill-advised restoration. If it is necessary to demonstrate how such an item worked it is feasible to construct a 'replica' using modern materials. This is intrinsically safer and usually cheaper.

A case in point is that of an 1875 Hornsby portable steam engine owned by the Museum of Science and Engineering, Newcastle-Upon-Tyne. It was initially decided that the restoration of this exhibit would be limited to cleaning, setting up the motion, replacement of decayed timbers in the forecarriage and cosmetic repairs to the badly corroded base of the smokebox. Following dismantling (including removal of corroded fire-tubes) it was reported that it might be possible to put the engine back into steam if the tubes were replaced, minor repairs to blotched (pitted) tubeplates were carried out and the corroded longitudinal stays were replaced. Since none of this work would affect those parts of the original structure which were sound, it was decided to go ahead and the boiler was eventually inspected, hydraulically tested and passed to steam at 40 pounds pressure – half its original working pressure.

Because the engine would happily run for demonstration purposes at 5 lb per square inch steam pressure, the spring safety valve was reset to 20 lb so that the boiler would not be unnecessarily stressed. During the second operating season one of the original cylinder head bolts fractured due to crystallization of the wrought iron.

During preparation for one annual boiler inspection it was found that the foundation ring was excessively grooved at the corners. This would have necessitated extensive firebox repairs. In view of the fact that the foundation ring was the original one and was of Z-iron construction, it was decided that the firebox would not be repaired as this would significantly alter the original structure of what was probably the only boiler of this type still extant in substantially original condition. The decision was taken from a curatorial viewpoint. It is interesting to note however, that if the main requirement had been merely to show a working portable engine or to provide steam then a more modern example could have been purchased at half the cost of firebox repairs to the historic exhibit.

Modifications

It may be necessary to modify an exhibit on grounds of safety or to satisfy an operating requirement. For example, the replacement of town gas by natural gas requires modification of burners (and especially gas engines) because of the changed air–gas ratio for complete combustion of the chemically different fuel, together with other physical aspects such as the lower speed of propagation of flame.

More usually, modifications may be suggested on the grounds of expediency, often due to the cost of producing a replacement part by traditional methods. It may also be necessary to fit stops or devices to prevent unauthorized operation. In all cases the new part should be readily identifiable, even if the records should be lost. Even minor alterations, such as the resetting of steam engine valve-gear for running on light loads or on compressed air, require specialist knowledge. The research and development time involved may be great.

The decision to modify an exhibit must be carefully considered, and any modifications should be capable of being reversed.

Re-assembly and installation

Provided that correct records have been kept and procedures for dismantling and repair have been carried out, the reassembly and finishing of an exhibit should present few problems. With many exhibits, particularly complex or working machines, erection should not be rushed.

Before assembly of a large object is commenced the design of foundations or its eventual location should be settled, particularly with respect to floor loadings, suitability of foundations (especially in relation to vibration and noise), availability of services and access for maintenance.

During erection, each stage should be tested and adjustments carried out. Final testing should be carried out in the presence of the curator and restorer under the advice or instruction of any relevant responsible authority, for example, the H.M. Inspector of Factories or an Insurance Company Engineer/Surveyor. The question of adequate and suitable insurance must not be forgotten, together with necessary licenses or tax payable.

Paint and Polish

The principal function of an applied or chemically produced surface finish is to provide a permanent protective coating against deterioration of bare metals or organic materials exposed to attack by chemical or biological agents in the environment. The choice of finish is often dictated by the environment to which an object is exposed. For example, an iron surface could be painted with a drying oil containing inert filler or pigment, it could be covered with grease or tar, be vitreous-enamelled or deliberately subjected to controlled corrosion as in the browning of gun barrels. In some technological and scientific exhibits the choice of a coating may reflect an essential physical property, such as the use of varnish for electrical insulation.

Where an existing, but not necessarily contemporary, finish is sound, consideration must be given to conserving it, particularly if it exhibits a patina produced by age or use. It may be possible to match surface finishes if part of the surface has been damaged but it should be realized that modern synthetic finishes may not be compatible and will weather at a different rate. It is easy to match existing colours but with the exception of popular railway or transport colours available from specialist colourmen it may not be economic for museums to obtain the small quantities of specially prepared authentic paints required.

Museum-induced deterioration

In museums the most common cause of deterioration of original finishes, or wear on 'brightwork', is improper or over-enthusiastic cleaning and polishing. Highly polished metal surfaces are only achieved by deliberate abrasion. The rate of such damage can be assessed readily by observing the worn surfaces of nameplates on engines or the brass showing through tops of plated car radiators lovingly touched by a generation or two of visitors.

Large technological exhibits are frequently uncased and are therefore subject to mechanical and chemical damage during the daily housekeeping operations in the galleries. It is important that attendants or others entrusted with keeping exhibits clean should be instructed in correct methods. The use of wire wool or abrasive papers on bright steelwork – often the wearing surfaces of machines – is to be deprecated. Similarly, over-use of metal polish will contribute greatly to wear of surfaces and the residues left in inconvenient recesses will rapidly cause rot.

Consideration must be given to the application of lacquers, varnishes or transparent protective coatings to paint and brightwork in order to minimize mechanical damage caused by excessive polishing.

Other forms of museum-induced deterioration caused by improper storage or careless handling should be more readily identifiable and can be prevented by regular inspections, staff training and strict supervision.

Working exhibits

Museum curators are under increasing pressure from enthusiasts, educationalists and, perhaps to a lesser extent, the general public, to make exhibits more accessible, easier to understand or entertaining by demonstrating them. The demand is not confined to technological exhibits, for similar pressures are put, for instance, upon colleagues in costume or firearms collections. Similarly, it should not be thought that this is a new phenomenon. As a small boy, the writer can recall the Owens bottle machine clanking away in the basement of the Science Museum, which, incidentally, still retain the Lenoir gas-engine originally purchased in 1865 to drive workshop machinery in the South Kensington Museum. It is no longer demonstrated.

There used to be an inherent conservatism in the museum profession which to set it apart from private owners of historic machinery. This was, that the curator did not readily compromise the integrity of objects held in trust for future generations by exposing them to unnecessary wear and tear or risk from accidental damage or misuse. The vast increase in the number of technological museums, many of which have not pursued a well-defined collecting policy, has allowed certain classes of popular exhibit to be collected in excess of a strictly interpreted national plan to cover the whole range of technology. This is perhaps understandable, for every museum wants its Watt beam-engine or, if near the coast, its lighthouse optic. Having striven for popular acclaim, it is then difficult to refuse the next step of setting the exhibits in motion, especially as there may be several examples available. This should not be taken as advice to resist all demands for exhibits to operate but, in taking such a decision, the curator must explore the ethical and logistic arguments. Some of the important questions are set out below:

(1). Whether the exhibit is likely to suffer any biological, chemical or mechanical damage, including possible accident or misuse through being operated; coupled with the necessity to make modfications to meet new safety or operating requirements. For example, the platework of boilers and pressure vessels may not meet current safety standards, or a second means of feeding water to a mobile boiler may be mandatory.

(2) The likely extent and rate of deterioration, and whether such deterioration is justifiable or acceptable. Apart from the ethical considerations, this brings into question the concept of a museum deliberately acquiring an artefact with a view to its having a finite working life before being discarded, and also whether a continuing process of repair or replacement of original parts (which in some cases is only an extension of that object's past history and usage) is permissible. Most engines and some machines can be run on very light or frictional loads only to minimize wear.

(3) Whether the operation of an exhibit will expose museum staff or the public to any additional health hazard or risk of injury to person or property.

(4) The effect which working exhibits may have on the museum environment and upon other exhibits due to problems of noise, vibration, emis-

sion of heat, water vapour, exhaust fumes, dust or other pollutants.

(5) Statutory legislation related to the operation of certain classes of machine, industrial process or form of transport, including health and safety implications, use of qualified staff or other regulations.

(6) Whether the increased capital or revenue implications of providing and servicing working exhibits are cost-effective. Taking the case of occasional demonstration under its own power of steam-driven textile machinery re-erected within a museum gallery, it may be necessary to provide foundations, services, guards for exposed parts, a steam boiler, fuel, oil and supplies, a skilled stoker, engine driver and operatives plus increased requirements for technical resources. By provision of concealed electric motor drive, much of the capital cost will be eliminated, admittedly with the loss of 'atmosphere' and some public interest and educational potential. Provision of audio-visual aids would serve to maximize visitor enjoyment at minimal expenditure. This equation could be calculated for a wide range of exhibits, with different results each time.

(7). Whether the requirement for a working exhibit may be met without compromising an original artefact. In the case of unique exhibits it is possible to construct a model or replica with varying degrees of authenticity in order to demonstrate a technical feature or to provide an example of a significant machine where the original no longer exists. This source of working exhibits has become increasingly fashionable in recent years, although it is not a recent innovation. Extreme care (and absolute honesty) is necessary if museums are to extend the use of this powerful display technique and research tool. It may not be possible to use totally authentic materials or techniques due to modern safety standards, the non-availability of contemporary materials or the cost of labour-intensive methods of production such as one-off pattern making.

It should also be considered that in a very short timespan the replica is likely to become regarded as a genuine artefact – at least by the general public. One could, of course, extend these remarks to include many 'restored items' which will no doubt be acquired by museums. At the time of writing, I know of a perfectly good (and relatively rare) example of a Robey Tandem Steamroller, in excellent condition, which is being cut up to provide the parts for what will eventually be paraded as a Robey Steam Wagon of the same vintage. No doubt most Curators could add their own example.

(8). The possibility of preserving human skills related to the operation or maintenance of the exhibit. In this respect it is important for the museum to record existing skills. It may be impractical to ensure that skills no longer required in a fast-changing industrial society will be enshrined within the museum. On the simplest level, this may be possible. It can be argued that it takes comparatively little retraining for a person with a current driving licence to learn to drive a pre-war car or even a traction engine (but not a steam roller which requires a separate driving test!). However, the study of a book and a strong right arm for shovelling coal will not necessarily produce a locomotive driver competent to drive a passenger train. Much less, then, will the museum be able to preserve the special skills of the ring-spinner or ornamental turner when the present generation of practitioners dies out. The same might be said of traditional engineering skills in today's 'throw-away' society. In this respect the museum has a prime role in providing an insight into the history of an industrial society through direct experience, but this is outside the scope of this chapter.

Guarding of machines

Before putting any exhibit into motion the curator must determine whether he has done everything reasonably practical to protect visitor and staff from danger. It must be remembered that many technological exhibits are well below modern safety standards. The requirements of the Health and Safety at Work Act or other legislation does not distinguish between different grades of safety (although the Construction and Use Regulations for Motor Vehicles take the age of a vehicle into account). In the writer's experience, Officers of the Health and Safety Executive, Railway Inspectorate or other statutory bodies, are able to assist museums greatly in these matters.

It is rare to find a safety official who is obstructive without being able to advise on the best designs for unobtrusive guards and barriers. The curator will ignore such advice at his peril.

Code of operating practice

The safe operation of machinery is generally the subject of statutory legislation or local regulations. Museums with working exhibits should draw up an overall Code of Practice for the operation of working exhibits or for the conduct of public events. In addition, separate 'descriptions and working instructions' should be drawn up for individual exhibits. These should provide descriptions of the object, its methods of operation, routine maintenance instructions, together with details of regular inspections.

Operating staff, whether employee or volunteer, must be selected carefully and given thorough training, particularly in safety procedures. Ideally, a logbook should be provided in which the operator can record details of operation. The curator must be informed of any variation from normal (i.e. unusual) noises. The instructions (Standing Orders) must be clear, concise and leave no room for misinterpretation.

Public relations

One major disadvantage of providing working exhibits is that, from time to time, they may need to be withdrawn for maintenance or fail to work because of staff shortages, mechanical breakdown or interruption of supplies. The public relations aspect of this should not be undervalued. The visitor will judge the museum on the basis of a short visit and the failure to provide the advertised attractions will generate criticism.

This is a particular problem for smaller museums without adequate technical resources but is also met frequently in large museums. One solution is regular, preventive maintenance and the division of working exhibits into groups using different methods of 'motive power', so that a failure in one system need not affect all exhibits. It must be recognised that the displays involving working exhibits should allow for ease of maintenance, a point often forgotten until the whole display has to be dismantled in order to replace a minor part!

Storage

A major problem in the storage of museum collections relates to the wide variations in physical dimensions and mass of the objects, together with their environmental requirements. The essential difference between museum stores and commercial warehouses is simply that the latter is set up for the rapid turnover of a limited amount of stock, generally in a limited number of unit sizes. It is agreed generally that purpose-built stores are most efficient for convenience in use, security and on conservation grounds. Except in the case of large numbers of objects of similar size, it is difficult to devise a cost-effective storage system. Therefore, it is advisable for museums to divide the collection into different storage categories and to provide different types of facility for each store. A large object store is not simply a scaled-up version of a small store, for distinct advantages may accrue from the adoption of palletization and the provision of mechanical handling equipment. This can maximize access and facilitate the safe handling of exhibits, while reducing both staff costs and those for unit storage.

The principles of industrial storage are generally adaptable for museum use. Advice should be sought from independent specialists (such as the Institute of Purchasing and Supply, and the National Materials Handling Centre) rather than the individual manufacturers of equipment. It is the curator's responsibility to provide an accurate estimate of requirements for various types of storage. Proper specifications for parking bays, pallet loadings or capacities for pallet, fork-lift and stacker trucks are vital as overloading is dangerous and excess capacity is expensive.

In large exhibit stores the capital cost of installing heavy-duty, adjustable pallet racking together with a fork-lift truck to enable loads to be stored in several tiers must be balanced against the gain in available floor space and savings in staff costs or plant hire. The careful choice of module size and loadings will economize on equipment costs. It should be recognized, however, that without adequate records and the marking of parts, it is likely that even large parts may be mislaid during long-term storage through failure to recognize subsequently what they are.

Environmental conditions for storage

It is unlikely that the environment within a 'large exhibit' store will be satisfactory for all materials. Metal objects need to be kept in an atmosphere of low humidity. Condensate dripping from roofs or joists may fall on the uppermost surface of the objects, usually those most difficult to inspect. Highly polished surfaces (the brightwork or paintwork) on machines are likely to suffer from condensation problems because they may cause local chilling of the air below the dewpoint. Similarly, a microclimate may develop within a machine (or packing case) due to moisture being left in tanks and boilers or collecting in undrained cavities.

Wooden objects suffer from differential shrinkage cracks if kept in a dry (or varying humidity) atmosphere. Textiles, such as upholstery and leather, are also sensitive to low humidity. On the other hand, excessive moisture will cause fungus growth. With composite exhibits, it may be necessary to create a suitable microclimate within part of the exhibit, or to set apart an area within the store for more accurate, and costly, environmental control.

If 'waterproof' coverings are used, care must be taken to ensure that there is free circulation of air or that the environment within a closed container is desiccated. Once water enters a waterproof container it cannot easily escape. It is advisable that objects stored on the ground should be raised on battens to prevent damage by rising damp from concrete floors. The same advice applies particularly to large objects stored outside.

Preparation of exhibits for storage

The preparation of exhibits for storage requires expert advice. A 'first aid' approach is to protect bare metal by greases or protective barriers of which a number are available commercially (usually varnishes or waxes dissolved in volatile organic solvents). Oil paint or old sump oil applied liberally is considered reasonably effective and cheap, but the first has the objection of being difficult to remove, while the latter is messy and could cause problems due to free acids formed while the oil was in use. For this reason it is advisable to drain engine sumps or clean lubricated parts and replace with fresh oil.

Cooling systems, pump chambers and other parts containing water must be emptied thoroughly – including often-forgotten pockets in valve boxes and the like and the spaces opened to the free circulation of air. Boilers should be cleaned thoroughly of soot and ashes which form a corrosive paste when damp. Packing should be removed from the glands of steam engines. Wheeled exhibits should ideally be supported to relieve the weight on the bearings and springs. Hydraulic fluid, battery electrolyte and fuel should be drained and tanks flushed to prevent the formation of explosive mixtures. These few examples serve to highlight the necessity of obtaining advice on individual objects. Stored exhibits also need to be inspected regularly to detect corrosion or other deterioration.

Handling and transport of large exhibits

The availability of handling equipment with staff trained to use it is a distinct advantage in museum galleries, workshops and stores. The limit of safe handling of loads by manual means is low, particularly for technology exhibits (and some other items, for example, sculpture) which are frequently of high density, awkwardly shaped and without handholds.

The choice of equipment is dictated by finance, the limitations of the building and the skill of staff available. Simple devices such as sack barrows, piano bogies or rollers made from short lengths of scaffold pipe are available to most museums for loads of several tonnes. Jacks and machinery skates used in conjunction with temporary steel floorplates could extend the limit to some forty tonnes.

Many museums have found that a pedestrian-controlled hydraulic fork-lift truck of up to one tonne capacity with a fixed mast and accessory crane jib, to be ideal for general use within both galleries and stores. Small, multipurpose hydraulic cranes of up to a one and a half tonne capacity are now available, which can be dismantled for transit with a mobile base, floor mounting or fitted into a lorry chassis complete with swivelling gear. Pallet or low-lift stillage trucks can be adapted for use with showcases or carefully designed display plinths. Portable gantries with block and tackle are less useful and are not recommended for transporting suspended loads.

Many exhibits can be dismantled into sections which can be handled by the limited equipment described above. If the museum possesses a van, it is an advantage to have a tail-lift fitted to facilitate the loading of palletized or free-standing loads of up to one tonne.

It cannot be over-emphasized how valuable it is for a museum to possess the capacity to move its own exhibits, if only within its own premises. In the case of large industrial exhibits, it may be necessary to hire both equipment and expertise. The conditions of hire and responsibility for the use of a contractor's plant – with or without operators – should be examined carefully. It may be found that the hirer assumes responsibility for public or other liability. Operations by museum staff, hired contractors or volunteers outside the museum premises may also be the subject of restrictive agreements. It is common-sense to establish the limit of responsibility; the removal of items is sometimes undertaken with a sense of urgency, and these things can be forgotten.

Even with handling equipment, each removal job should be planned in advance as precipitate moves lead to damage of both objects and staff.

With respect to personnel factors, training should be given in the methods of safe operation of equipment and manual lifting methods; suitable protective clothing must be provided. In all cases, the control of people and equipment during the operation must be given to one experienced person.

Further reading

COSSONS, N. (1975), *B.P. Book of Industrial Archaeology*, David & Charles, Newton Abbott

RAISTRICK, A. (1975), *Industrial Archaeology*, Eyre Methuen, London

SINGER, HOLMYARD AND HALL (Eds.) (1954–78), *A History of Technology*, (7 Vols), University Press, Oxford

VARIOUS AUTHORS, Longman's *Industrial Archaeology* series (e.g. Civil Engineering, Railways, The Textile Industry, Metal Mining) from 1968

A few examples of individual technical histories with good bibliographies or references:

CLARK, R. H. (1960), *The Development of the English Traction Engine*, Goose & Son

CUMMINS, C. L. (1976), *Internal Fire*, Carnot Press

FREESE, S. W. (1957), *Windmills & Millwrighting*, University Press, Cambridge, (reprinted David & Charles, Newton Abbott)

ROLT, L. T. C. (1965), *Tools for the Job*, Batsford, Poole

SALAMAN, R. A. (1975), *Dictionary of Tools*, Allen & Unwin, London

38

Conservation and storage: textiles

Jean M. Glover

It is a sad fact that many objects classified as textiles have deteriorated more rapidly since their acquisition by museums than during their previous history. This deterioration has been due, most frequently, to mishandling and unfavourable environmental conditions, shortcomings in curatorial control which until comparatively recently, were attributable to ignorance of the factors which accelerate decay. Moreover, in certain quarters, textiles were not regarded as objects of artistic and historic value. In recent decades, a more enlightened approach has developed which, coupled with the emergence of textile conservation as a separate discipline, has contributed much to the preservation of material previously at risk.

Definition of a textile collection

A textile can be defined simply as 'a woven structure produced by the interlacing of two sets of threads' but in most museums, and within the context of this paper, the term is interpreted more broadly. It embraces most fabrics made from fibres and yarns, including those constructed by techniques other than weaving, costumes, and composite objects which combine textiles with materials such as wood, wax, paper, metals or leather.

Identification of fibres, yarns and fabrics

Despite the development of synthetic materials, it is with natural fibres – principally wool, silk, linen, and cotton – that most curators are primarily concerned, and which present the greatest problems of care and conservation.

Natural fibres have distinct characteristics which influence the properties and behaviour of fabrics made from them, and greatly assist their identification. Conversely, textiles composed of man-made fibres, for example, rayons, polyamides ('Nylon', 'Enkalon', 'Perlon'), polyesters ('Dacron', 'Tergal', 'Terylene', 'Trevira') and acrylics ('Acrilan', 'Courtelle', 'Dralon', 'Orlon') can be difficult to recognize, particularly if they have been made to resemble natural materials. The date of manufacture will be a guide, since, with the exception of rayon or artificial silk, man-made fibres began to appear in quantity only after the Second World War.

Every curator and conservator of a textile collection should have access to an optical microscope, giving magnification of ×40 upwards, for textile analysis. The basic techniques of fibre microscopy are easily learned, and, used in conjunction with a well-illustrated manual[1] enable all but the most degraded or uncommon fibres to be identified. A binocular stand-magnifier, giving ×10 magnification, is also an invaluable aid in the examination of yarn and fabric structures.

Caring for a textile collection

Preventive conservation, remedial conservation, and restoration

The care of museum textiles involves the curator in two forms of conservation – preventive (or passive) and remedial (or active).

Preventive conservation aims to delay deterioration by providing a favourable environment for every object. Remedial conservation, by removing destructive elements and introducing unobtrusive support for degraded material, aims to prolong the life of objects, and to present them in a form which enables their original purpose and qualities to be understood and appreciated.

Responsible remedial conservation requires that nothing which is an original part of, or a significant addition to, an object will be taken away, and that nothing will be added which could either deceive the observer or be confused with the original. It is a generally accepted principle that remedial conservation should also be reversible. It is usually possible, but not always practicable, to undo remedial conservation, as the removal of some forms of supplementary support from severely degraded textiles could result in their destruction.

Restoration allows for a measure of repair which, in the treatment of some objects, is a necessary aspect of preservation. However, the unpicking and replacement of worn or missing parts from textiles which have been preserved as historic documents is unethical, and unacceptable in the museum context.

Both forms of conservation should be the concern of the curator, although it is to be expected that, except in an emergency, his responsibilities will lie more directly with preventive than with remedial conservation, the latter being the province of the trained textile conservator. Nevertheless, the curator should co-operate closely with the conservator in caring for the collection. He should study the conservator's reports and recommendations, visit the conservation studio, and familiarize himself with the specialized vocabulary of textile conservation. As custodian of the collection, the curator is accountable for its safekeeping, and should understand how this can best be achieved.

Causes of deterioration in textiles

The importance of a controlled museum environment in which light, relative humidity, temperature and air pollution are kept within acceptable limits, has been stressed repeatedly as a means of preserving specimens and reducing the need for remedial conservation. Proper control is essential where textiles are stored and displayed, for natural fibres respond to the quality of their environment more readily than many other materials, and under unfavourable conditions will deteriorate with disturbing rapidity, and with consequent disfigurement and loss of strength.

Deterioration is generally due to a combination of factors, but foremost are the effects of light, dirt and mishandling, arising from unsatisfactory and often ill-considered methods of storage, display, and transportation. Nevertheless, damage caused by insects and micro-organisms cannot be disregarded, since even minor outbreaks can have a devastating effect on part of the collection.

In some instances, a remarkable improvement in the appearance of soiled and degraded textiles can be effected by remedial conservation. However, this is not always the case, and it subjects them to a further degree of stress and handling which, under more favourable circumstances, might have been avoided.

In a museum, the repeated treatment of conserved specimens should rarely be necessary. If a defective environment has contributed to their initial deterioration, it is essential that the defects be identified, and improvements made without delay. Until this has been done, conserved objects should be held in safe custody elsewhere.

Light

The visible and tangible effects on textiles of exposure to light are progressive loss of colour, strength and flexibility, a process which may be accelerated by a damp or overheated atmosphere, and intensified by the presence of certain dyes and finishing treatments.

Of common natural fibres, silk is the most readily affected by photodegradation, and wool the least, but all textiles suffer some degree of damage, and require protection from both ultra-violet and visible radiation (*Figure 38.1*).

The surest method of providing complete protection is to keep textiles in total darkness, but, as this is feasible only during periods of storage, every effort should be made to restrict the amount of light which falls on them at other times. The recommended *maximum* level of illumination for displayed textiles is 50 lux. The eye will adjust to this low level of illumination without fatigue or serious loss of visual acuity if the textile gallery is approached through gradually diminishing levels of illumination; exhibition lighting is positioned so as to avoid glare and deep shadows; backgrounds provide the right degree of contrast with displayed material.

In galleries designed for the exhibition of textiles, daylight should be excluded, since natural light is the strongest emitter of Uv radiation, and subject to seasonal and other variations which make the maintenance of a uniformly low level of illumination difficult. If, because the museum is housed in a historic building, or one of architectural interest, daylight cannot be excluded completely, a compromise can be achieved by the use of blinds or curtains, with a Uv absorbant at the windows, but greater care will be needed in positioning display-cases so that exhibits are shielded from all except supplementary lighting. To control the low-level artificial illumination of rare and particularly light-sensitive material visitor-operated time-switches can be provided, although in popular museums the switches tend to be depressed so frequently that the light is rarely extinguished during opening hours.

A further danger, which is increased where the volume of air inside an illuminated display-case has been reduced substantially by the quantity of material shown, is that of overheating, particularly when tungsten lighting is used. In a confined space this may be coupled with localized fading and tendering of fabric placed too close to the source of light. If, in

a

b

Figure 38.1 Destructive effects of light on silk and cotton, in an overheated show-case. (a) Front; (b) back. The magenta-coloured silk dress has faded and shattered, exposing the tendered white cotton lining and petticoat. Wax from the doll has melted, absorbed superficial dirt and impregnated the clothing

a standard display case, the lighting is concentrated above the exhibits, it should be separated from them by a translucent panel which serves the dual purpose of absorbing Uv and diffusing visible radiation.

Ultra-violet radiation should be eliminated from all parts of the museum where textiles are stored, studied, or displayed. Protection is provided by plastic Uv-absorbing material, in the form of varnish. for application to the inner surface of windows; as transparent, flexible sleeves, for fitting over fluorescent tubes; and as acrylic sheeting for augmenting window glass or for glazing framed textiles and small display cases (Thomson and Bullock 1978). Since the efficiency of these materials diminishes gradually, they should be checked. A reliable Uv monitor should be used at intervals and the material replaced as necessary.

Humidity and temperature

The property of natural fibres to absorb moisture, thereby swelling on wetting and contracting on drying, is utilized by conservators to straighten distorted textiles and to eliminate creases. However, these operations are controlled and infrequently applied. The permanent shrinkage of cellulosic fibres, under damp conditions, and the repeated expansion and contraction of all natural fibres with fluctuating relative humidity (RH) (Landi and Marko, 1980) is detrimental, and creates stresses which weaken the fabric. The problem is compounded in textiles which incorporate highly twisted yarns, or mixtures of fibres which have different absorption-rates. It is essential, therefore, to minimize movement by controlling relative humidity at a constant 55 per cent or allowing fluctuations of only between 50 and 60 per cent.

While the upper limits of safety must be emphasized, there are also lower limits. The flexibility of natural textile fibres is dependent on their retaining a certain percentage of moisture. If kept in an atmosphere which is too dry, they become dehydrated and embrittled, and for this reason, relative humidities below 40 per cent should be avoided.

The fading of dyes and degradation of fibres exposed to light is more rapid at high RH than at low, as is the leaching of fugitive dyes, for example from textiles which have been subject to periods of damp storage.

The unsatisfactory microclimate which is sometimes produced within a storage container or show-case can be a hazard. Closed storage containers should be ventilated, and not so densely packed that the circulation of air is inhibited. All stored and displayed textiles should be inspected at regular intervals for signs of biodeterioration and instruments should be used to record humidity and temperature, particularly in show-cases.

Biodeterioration (the degradation of textiles by micro-organisms and insects) is most likely to occur during periods of high RH. Mould-growth can be prevented if the relative humidity is kept below 65 to 70 per cent, but no conclusion has been reached regarding the activity of insect pests, which seem able to survive at relative humidities much higher and lower than these.

Since changes in RH are associated closely with changes in temperature the latter should also remain constant. The level is less important than its constancy, but 20°C is suggested as suitable.

Dirt and atmospheric pollution

Occasionally a dirty or stained textile holds more interest for the historian .than the same item when cleaned, but soiled textiles not only look, feel, and smell unpleasant, they are also at risk from the pollutants which have impregnated them; they act as a focus for destructive organisms and can, in extreme circumstances, be a health hazard. Usually it is preferable for soiled textiles to be cleaned, by a conservator, on entering the museum, but it is the curator's task to ensure that they remain clean and safe from further deterioration thereafter.

The more common forms of soiling result from the combustion of fossil fuels. The problem is currently less acute in Britain than before the passing of the *Clean Air Act 1956*, but is still sufficient to cause concern in industrial areas.

If allowed to accumulate on textiles, airborne dust and grit not only disfigure the surface, they work into the fabric and abrade the fibres. Ultra-fine particles of dirt penetrate the twists of yarn and convolutions of individual fibres, making cleaning a hazardous, and not wholly successful, operation. At the same time, cellulosic fibres, silk, and, to a lesser extent, wool, are rotted by sulphuric acid, which is produced in the fabric when sulphur dioxide vapour (SO_2) combines with oxygen and moisture. Nitrogen dioxide (NO_2) also attacks cotton, wool, and some dyes, but is less of an immediate problem.

The most satisfactory form of protection is afforded by a ducted air-cleaning system, although most museums in older premises rely on less sophisticated measures.

In museums without air-cleaning systems, storage cupboards and wardrobes should be well-made, preferably from seasoned timber, with doors which fit closely into a rebate. In heavily polluted areas, adhesive foam draught-excluder can be added, while overlapping curtains on runners inside wardrobes, and individual garment bags (both closely-woven and washable) will help protect hanging costumes from dust and excessive handling. To combat the restriction on the movement of air resulting from dust-proofing, cupboards and display-cases should be fitted with ventilators incorporating air-filters.

Where boxed storage is used, full-depth lids, combined with generous, loose wrappings of acid-free tissue paper, offer the best protection from atmospheric dirt. Polythene bags, whether sealed or not, *should be avoided*, because they attract, rather than repel, dust. Sealed bags are hazardous because of the risk of high RH and condensation within the packages, or the enclosure of destructive organisms.

Exhibition cases also should be dustproof. When new cases are constructed, a careful watch should be kept on textile material to ensure, first, that soiled air is not being drawn into the cases and filtered by the exhibits (*Figure 38.2*) and second, that the textiles and associated material are not being harmed by other pollutants. Even when all reasonable precautions have been taken, some dirt will enter show-cases in heavily polluted districts, so displays should be changed frequently and the exhibition of particularly rare or vulnerable material limited to short periods.

Although it is never advisable to display textiles in the open, the problem of caring effectively for large tapestries, carpets and upholstered furniture is unlikely to be resolved satisfactorily. Similar difficulties are encountered with military colours which, traditionally, are hung without protection, although some older colours have recently been preserved behind glass.

Pests: insects and micro-organisms

Insect damage among textiles is usually attributable to species of moths – most frequently the common clothes moth, and to the carpet beetle (Hueck, 1972; Gradidge *et al.*, 1967), the latter being more common in southern England. The materials most vulnerable to such attack are wool, hair, fur, feathers and skins. Nevertheless, evidence of moth infestation is found quite frequently on silk and cellulosic materials. In the museum, wool felt, popular with designers as a background fabric, is as much at risk as the collections, and if infested may become the source of widespread damage.

Favoured locations for the larvae of moths and beetles are the folds of hems and seams, pockets, undersides of collars, cuffs and hat bands, and the soiled fabric around armhole and crutch seams of garments, but infestation occurs almost anywhere on vulnerable objects (*Figure 38.3*).

Clothes moth larvae are about 1cm long, and are creamy-white in colour with dark heads. Their activities can be detected by irregularly shaped holes, and trails of superficial grazing on napped wool,

a

b

Figure 38.2 (a) Disfiguring effects of dirt on cotton and silk. The netted cotton dress has acted as a filter for dust-laden air entering through the floor of a defective display case. The satin trimming, being smoother than cotton, and of closer construction than netting, has resisted heavy soiling. (b) Remedial conservation; dress after cleaning

accompanied by silky deposits, cocoons and accumulations of granular excreta, resembling sand.

Carpet beetle larvae usually make clean holes which tend to be dispersed over a much broader area of cloth. They deposit no silken trail, but moult several times during the larval stage, leaving transparent cast skins as evidence.

Control of insect pests begins with good housekeeping and constant vigilance; by the removal of all potential sources of infestation; by regular cleaning of the museum premises; and by *immediate*, thorough, examination of *all* newly-acquired material (not only textiles).[2] It should be followed by fumigation and cleaning whenever possible, and a period of several months' isolation from the rest of the collection, and by inspection at frequent intervals of stores and displays incorporating high-risk material. If live insect larvae are found, they should be destroyed immediately and the infested articles isolated.

Micro-organic deterioration of textiles, by colonies of mould or bacteria, occurs as a result of high RH (above 65 to 70 per cent), caused usually either by a poorly controlled environment or by the siting of stores in unsuitable premises. The materials most rapidly affected are those made from cellulosic fibres – for example, cotton, linen, hemp, jute and viscose rayon – but if the damp conditions persist, and particularly if the temperature rises, all fibres and their dyes will deteriorate, sometimes within a matter of days. The onset of trouble is usually detectable by an unpleasant musty odour, but in severe cases, colonies of mould will appear on damp fabric, and gradually destroy its structure (*Figure 38.4*).

Damp and decayed textiles should be dried thoroughly, but not too rapidly, in a current of warm air, or with a dehumidifier, then wrapped securely in acid-free paper, incorporating thymo-impregnated paper as a fumigant, and isolated. Emergency treatment other than drying should be undertaken by a qualified textile conservator and carried out in a room well away from undamaged specimens.

The control of biodeterioration is receiving urgent consideration by organizations concerned with the preservation of textiles and other organic materials (Group for Costume and Textile Staff in Museums, 1982). Increased knowledge of chemicals, and of their effect on people, has, since the passing of the *Health and Safety at Work Act 1974*, resulted in the withdrawal of many insecticides and moth deterrents. Less toxic substitutes are being sought. Curators needing up-to-date information on pest control are, therefore, advised to consult the specialist manufacturers, suppliers and contractors.

Handling

A point which is often overlooked is that even before entering the museum most textiles will have lost a proportion of their former strength. Historic textiles

a

b

Figure 38.3 (a) Effects of long term neglect: heavy soiling; leaching of dyes; destruction by moths, micro-organisms and rats; overall creasing. Coat from a volunteer field officer's uniform, *c.* 1804–1808. Part of a small museum collection, stored in a cellar for the duration of the 1939–1945 war, and forgotten. The complete uniform was rediscovered in 1974. (b) Destruction of wool cloth by clothes moths. Left side of breeches from volunteer officer's uniform, *c.* 1804–1808

are thus particularly at risk from handling which may subject them to further stress (*Figure 38.5*).

Most damage arising from mishandling can be prevented by forethought. An intuitive sense of strengths and weaknesses may develop with experience, but since fragility is not always apparent, *all* textiles should be regarded as potentially fragile objects requiring continual underlaid support and a steady, gentle hand. They should never be moved without the aid of a tray, box or roller, nor stored or displayed so that they are stretched taut, or so that the full weight of the object is borne by only a few threads; nor should they be crushed, folded or subjected to rough or excessive manipulation. As a precaution, all those likely to handle textiles (including exhibition designers, ancillary and voluntary workers) should be shown how to do so safely. However, handling is essentially a task which should be undertaken, or supervised, by the conservator or curator.

Anything which is abrasive, sharp, or otherwise potentially disfiguring, should be kept away from textiles. For this reason, it is advisable to remove watches and personal jewellery, and to prohibit smoking, eating, drinking and the use of ink, ballpoint pens and artists' colours in the workrooms and stores. Pencils should be used for recording details of textile design, cut and construction.

Tables on which specimens are to be laid for examination, should be smooth-surfaced, easily-cleaned, and entirely free from projections which could catch threads or elongate existing tears. Until unsuitable furniture can be replaced, it must be covered. It is useful to have available several clean sheets or large pieces of calico for this purpose, which can also be used to cover the floor during the examination or conservation of large items.

Identification labels of the type illustrated in *Figure 38.6*, which incorporate two sharp prongs, should *never be used*, nor should numbers be inscribed directly onto specimens. They should be written with indelible, waterproof ink on white tape, which can be sewn neatly and securely to the object, in a position which is easily located, but which can be hidden from view when the object is displayed.

Figure 38.4 Degradation of linen by micro-organisms, during a period of damp storage. Lining and underside of embroidery, worked with laid metal threads on linen

Inherent weaknesses

The structure of some textiles, particular combinations of materials, and processes used during dyeing and finishing, can accelerate deterioration. Silk damask, for example, first shows signs of weakness by splitting along the outlines of the woven design, while nineteenth-century challis, a plain-woven fabric with a fine silk warp and thicker wool weft, begins to disintegrate when the silk threads weaken and can no longer support the heavier weft.

Tapestries have several characteristics which make them vulnerable. Their structure almost always dictates that they should be hung from a warp edge, so that the weight is borne by the weaker weft threads, which form the design. Frequently, in the upper part of a tapestry, these threads are almost entirely of silk, which is more susceptible than wool to tendering by light, yet is required to take more strain. As the silk deteriorates, splits will often appear near the top of the tapestry where, being above eye level, they are less easily detected. If splits pass unnoticed until a tapestry is moved, extensive damage may occur.

Therefore, regular, thorough scrutiny is advisable, coupled with professional advice when repairs become necessary. One of the techniques of tapestry weaving creates deliberate slits in the weft, which should be distinguishable from accidental tears. These are usually sewn up when the weaving is finished, but where old thread has rotted and the stitching broken, the slits reopen, weakening the general structure. They should be repaired as soon as they are noticed (Finch, 1980).

Another cause of deterioration, evident in Gothic tapestries of the sixteenth century, but also in embroideries of the same and later periods, is the rotting, by oxidation, of dark-coloured threads – usually black or brown wool and silk – which have been mordanted with iron salts during dyeing. These tendered threads fall away long before other colours, often leaving only traces on the underside, or stitch holes, to indicate their former position.

A contributory factor in the deterioration of some woven silks is the effect of 'weighting', a process whereby light-weight silks are impregnated with a

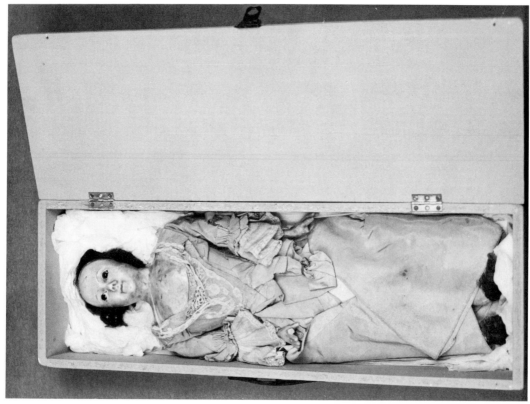

Figure 38.5 Mishandling during packing for transport. A mid-eighteenth century doll, photographed on arrival at the conservation studio, the wax shoulder-plate and right fore-finger having been broken in transit, by pressure of the box lid on compacted tissue paper

solution of iron salts or of stannic chloride, a tin salt, which improves the draping quality, and acts as a mordant for dyes. Excessive weighting damages the silk fibres, causing treated fabrics to crack along sharp creases, and to shatter uncontrollably. Degradation is accelerated in silks exposed to light and heat, or stained by perspiration. Although the use of this treatment persisted well into the twentieth century, the fabrics most commonly affected date from the late-Victorian and Edwardian periods, when tin-weighted silk was much used for women's clothing, especially bodice linings, petticoats, and trimmings.

Concealed hazards

Pins, and sometimes nails, which could tear the fabric, may be encountered. Unless they are of the early, separate-headed variety and thereby likely to be an original feature of a garment or accessory, pins should be removed, taking care (especially if they are corroded) to ease them out gently. They will mostly be evidence of previous exhibition-mounting, dressmakers' pins or crude forms of temporary repair (*Figure 38.6*).

Stretcher-frames of the type used for easel-paintings are a hazard if used as mounts for embroidered pictures and samplers. They hold the fabric unnaturally taut, offer no support in the centre, and no protection from atmospheric pollution. Some light-weight stretchers have weak, glued joints, which fracture when handled, with consequent damage to the textile. Seen from the outside of a glazed frame, stretcher-mounted textiles usually show a firm outline which may be cleaner than the centre where dirt has penetrated. Since they are inclined to split along the unsupported inner edge of the stretcher they should be detached and remounted, by a textile conservator, on a fabric-covered board.

Some stored costumes are a potential hazard, both to themselves and to others, because of pronged or hooked metal fastenings, and abrasive trimmings, especially if these are combined with flimsy or

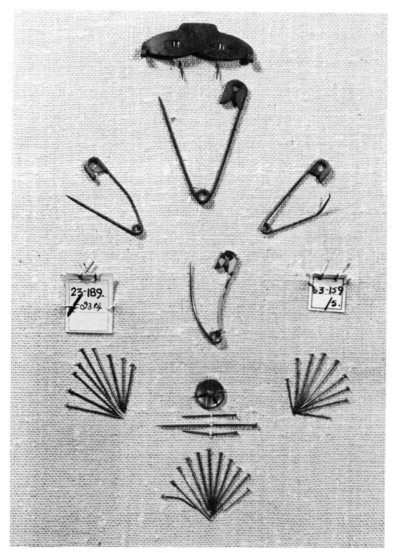

Figure 38.6 A selection of potentially dangerous items recovered from textiles during conservation treatment. None of the pins is an original feature of the object concerned

degraded fabrics. They should be enclosed separately, with their fastenings closed, in ventilated garment bags (not Polythene), or enshrouded in washed muslin, or packed carefully with plenty of tissue paper if horizontal or boxed storage is used. Other costumes, especially if they are close-fitting and made from silk, may be at risk because their cut, and the way in which they were worn, has created areas of stress and consequent weakness. They should be handled with utmost care and never be shown on live models.

Storage of textiles

Essential requirements for the safe storage of textiles are sufficient space for the collection, absence of light, a controlled environment, protection from airborne dirt, and freedom from pests. Added to these should be ease of access.

Materials needed for packing and support should include a plentiful supply of white, acid-free tissue paper, cardboard tubes of various lengths and diameters, custom-made cardboard boxes, plain wooden coat-hangers (including some of shorter length, and others with extra-long hooks), polyester wadding, muslin, calico, and rolls of white cotton tape in several breadths. Acid-free board should be specified for tubes and boxes, but, as an added precaution, it is advisable to cover rollers and to line boxes with acid-free paper before use. The use of self-adhesive tape which can be damaging if it comes in direct contact with textiles should be avoided.

Coat-hangers should be strong and generously padded, particular attention being paid to thick cushioning of the upper edge and ends. In the past, resilient polyurethane foam has been used as padding, but it is *no longer recommended* because it degrades and needs replacing within five to ten years. In the event of fire, it is also a dangerously toxic hazard. Polyester wadding (as sold for interlining quilted garments), covered with muslin and either tissue paper or washable cotton slip-covers, is suggested as an alternative. Coat-hangers made from plastic or wire should be avoided, as they are thin, sharp and cannot provide effective support.

For the purposes of storage, it is convenient to classify textiles as either 'flat' or 'shaped' since these characteristics usually influence the ways in which objects are handled.

Flat textiles

In this category are included (regardless of size) all textiles which lie or hang against a flat surface, such as flags, banners, military colours, tapestries, curtains, table and bed linen, cushion covers, and unframed embroideries. Also included are lace, shawls, handkerchieves and ribbons, fragments of excavated textiles, and samples of dress and furnishing fabrics.

Flat textiles of moderate size should be stored flat, separated from each other and from contact with the container, and protected from dust by sheets of acid-free paper. They may be placed in separate folders made from acid-free board, or in individual trays, or in shallow boxes, provided that the containers are not overpacked, thereby causing pressure on the lower layers, impeding ventilation, and encouraging excessive handling. Small and irregularly-shaped pieces will be safer if they are sewn neatly (never glued or stapled) to carefully-made individual woven supports, which leave part of the underside of the mounted textile visible, and from which the specimens need not be removed if they are required for exhibition (*Figure 38.7*). A fine needle, fine soft thread, such as silk, and only sufficient stitching to

Figure 38.7 Rolling a flat textile for storage. A strip of Coptic textile, mounted on woven linen for support, being prepared for rolled storage.

secure the textile safely, should be used, passing the needle between, (never through) the woven threads.

Larger flat textiles, and long narrow strips, which are too large to be stored flat, should be rolled, right side outermost, and interleaved with acid-free tissue, onto hollow cylinders of relatively broad diameter (*Figure 38.7*). They should never be folded. Keeping the topside of the textile outermost, during rolling, enables a lined textile to remain smooth, as the lining takes up the wrinkles which develop when two or more combined layers of fabric are rolled together.

If textiles incorporating metal threads, or raised surface decoration *have* to be rolled, a cylinder of a greater diameter than usual should be used, and a thick layer of polyester wadding laid between the interleaved sheets of tissue paper. The wadding will absorb variations in thickness, and reduce uneven pressure within the roll.

Tapestries should be rolled so that the more prominent and stronger warp ends pass around the roller. Usually this requires that the textile be rolled from side to side. A tapestry should never be rolled for storage or transportation with the ridges parallel to the length of the roller, as this puts great strain on the weaker weft threads.

All rolled textiles should be secured with broad tapes fastened over soft pads, or held with 'Velcro', a nylon contact fastener; they should never be bound with cords. Unless the store is air-conditioned, the rolls should then be wrapped in acid-free paper, or washed calico (not Polythene) to exclude dust but permit the unimpeded movement of air. Alternatively, large rolls can be provided with cylindrical draw-string bags made from calico or closely-woven canvas. The rolls should be identified clearly on the outside, ideally with a photograph or drawing, as well as the reference number. Pressure on the rolled textiles should be relieved by supporting the ends of the cylinders, or by passing rods through them into some form of rack.

Shaped textiles

In this category of textiles, costumes are dominant. Because of their cut and construction they require proportionately more storage space than flat textiles and even greater care in packing if they are not to suffer the effects of tension and pressure. The choice of storage method for full-length garments lies between horizontal and vertical support. Factors such as size, scope and condition of the collection, its relative importance, space and finance may influence the curator's choice, but a combination of storage methods is usually an appropriate solution. Horizontal storage is preferred for costumes which could be damaged by hanging, for example, those which are are heavily ornamented, bias-cut, knitted or in a weakened condition.

Boxes are a convenient method of storing dresses made from soft, light-weight fabrics (with only one dress in each) and children's clothing, but are less satisfactory for heavy and bulky items, particularly those made from stiff silks. The boxes should be lined with acid-free tissue paper, and each garment packed (with minimal folding) to fit the box. Sleeves, the legs of breeches, bodices, puffed trimmings and ribbon loops should be filled with *lightly crushed* (not compacted) tissue paper, to preserve their shape, and every pleat and fold softened with a roll of tissue. (Several sheets rolled independently, or pressed into rough 'concertina' folds, are more effective than the same number of sheets rolled together). Any space around the garment should also be filled with lightly-crushed tissue paper, to minimize movement within the box.

Sharp creases and pressure on folded textiles must be avoided, as creases will eventually become permanent, and if the fabric is brittle, will crack under pressure (*Figure 38.8*). All degraded textiles are subject to this type of damage, but it is most common among silks, and cotton fabrics which have been exposed to heavily polluted air. When sharp creases are a necessary feature of objects, such as parasols and fans, pressure should be reduced by storing them partly open (not fully stretched), and with the fabric supported, where practicable (*Figure 38.9*).

Tray-drawers are ideal for horizontal storage of costumes, for they give overall support and easy access, provided that they are wide enough (approximately 1.5 metres) to allow for a full-length garment to lie without cross-wise folds, and that only one item is laid in each tray.

Costumes to be hung need padded hangers, but standard coat-hangers may have to be adapted, or special supports made for some garments, to provide adequate support across the shoulders and at the neckline. They must not be too long since if the ends of a hanger protrude too far into the sleeves of a garment, they can cause damage, even when padded. Coats and dresses which have high collars need hangers with extra-long hooks, but in an emergency a short hook can be suspended from the garment rail with string. A supplementary 'collar' of folded tissue paper slipped over the hook will prevent contact of the metal with the garment.

The garment rail should be fixed as high above the wardrobe floor as can be reached easily, to allow long dresses to hang freely. Trains should be raised by tapes sewn to the underside, and tied around the stems of the hangers. Dresses with wide necklines need loops of tape, sewn like shoulder-straps to the front and back bodice linings, to hold them securely on their hangers. Skirts require similar long loops, sewn to the front and back of the waist band. Heavy, one-piece dresses can be relieved of strain by attaching broad tapes (like braces) to the inside of the

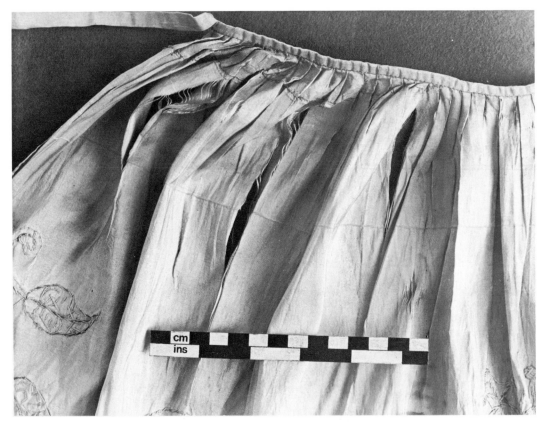

Figure 38.8 Pressure-induced creases and tears in eighteenth-century silk. Part of the pleated waistline of an embroidered silk apron seen from the underside. Additional well-defined vertical and horizontal creases show how the apron has been folded and compressed during long-term storage

waist seam, so that the weight of the skirt is borne by the hanger, and not by the bodice.

Wardrobes should not be so full that garments are compressed. Nevertheless, crushed tissue paper should be used to preserve the shape of sleeves and puffed trimmings. Whatever the size of the collection, it is advisable to separate women's from men's clothing, since the latter, being usually heavier and more robust, could abrade more fragile items.

Undergarments, children's clothing and baby linen can be stored in one of the ways described, and accessories by the method most appropriate to their shape and size, although some, such as hats, bonnets and caps may also need specially devised supports, which can double as exhibition mounts (*Figure 38.10*).

The mounting of textiles for exhibition

Ideally, the curator, textile conservator and exhibition designer should collaborate in the planning, designing and mounting of the exhibition. All possi-

ble causes of deterioration should be considered, and measures taken to eliminate them, while the conservator's opinions should be sought, especially with regard to the exhibition of fragile or rare material.

Sufficient preparation time should be allowed for any remedial conservation, and each item should be mounted in the way which is least liable to cause distortion, stress and damage. The use of pins, wire staples, self-adhesive tape and other forms of makeshift support should be forbidden.

Flat textiles

Whenever possible, flat textiles should be displayed against a horizontal or slightly inclined surface. This support may be a simple board or a three-dimensional structure. If it is made from hardboard, the smooth side should be outermost; if of wood or blockboard, it should be sanded smooth, particularly at the edges and corners.

The support should be covered with fabric whose fibre, texture and colour are in sympathy with the textile, and to which it can be sewn for exhibition (*Figure 38.11*). If a lightweight fabric is chosen, a

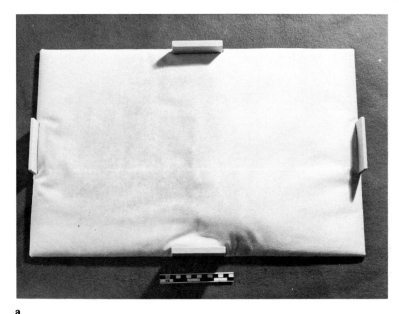

a

b

Figure 38.9 (a) Padded storage board for a fan. The padding increases in depth from left to right, so that both guards and all the sticks receive equal support. Blocks at the edges act as handles and allow for several boards to be stacked, without pressure on the fans. (b) Board with conserved fan of Maltese lace and inlaid mother-of pearl

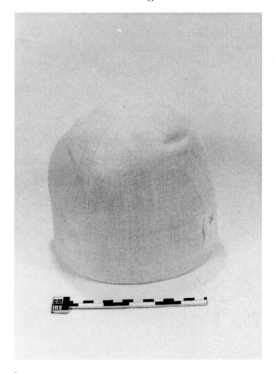

a

b

Figure 38.10 (a) Resilient support for a man's embroidered cap. The soft dome and firm base are covered with washed linen whch has been shaped to fit the lining of the cap.
(b) Cap, after remedial conservation, mounted for exhibition or storage

thicker soft underlay, such as cotton flannelette may also be needed. It is inadvisable to use felt or other wool fabric for this hidden underlay because of the danger of attracting moths. If a coloured background is required, only fast-dyed fabric should be used, so that there is no risk of the dye staining the textile. Dyes can be tested by wetting scraps of fabric and pressing them between pieces of white absorbant paper for several hours.

When covering a board for use as an exhibition mount, the fabric should be stretched taut over the surface, and fastened securely to the underside only. The woven threads should lie parallel to the edges of the board, and between 10 and 20 cm of extra fabric should be allowed on each side for turning under. Polyvinyl acetate emulsion is a suitable adhesive for securing the fabric to the board. It can be augmented with wire staples if the board is large, heavy, and intended to support a substantial weight of textile. However, they must not penetrate the upper surface and neither adhesive nor staples should come into contact with the exhibit. The textile, also aligned with the edges of the prepared board, should be secured *temporarily* with fine stainless steel pins

before being sewn to the board-covering. A fine curved needle should be used for the stitching, with fine softly-spun thread. Monofilament nylon ('invisible thread') is not suitable.

Frames for textiles should be made in the same way as for pictures, but with an extra deep rebate, to accommodate a wooden fillet, or sub-frame, placed between the mounted textile and the glass, or acrylic sheet. The fillet should be thick enough to prevent contact between the underside of the 'glass' and the surface of the textile, but for semi-three-dimensional subjects such as stump-work and thickly padded embroidery, a shallow box-frame may be more suitable. In either instance, the back should be sealed with adhesive paper to exclude dust when the mounted textile has been secured in its frame.

It is not usually advisable to display historic textiles by draping them, because of the distortion and creasing which occurs, but it is sometimes necessary when furnishings or costume accessories are shown in the manner in which they would have been used. They should be given as much support as possible, their folds softened unobtrusively with polyster wadding, and they should not be left on view for so

Figure 38.11 Military colour, *c.* 1856, mounted in preparation for exhibition in a glazed frame. A board, covered with fabric drawn taut across the surface, and secured to the underside, is used as a support for the colour, which is sewn to the board covering along the edges and main seams. Pieces of appropriately coloured fabric, laid behind holes in the silk, give an illusion of completeness

long that the prominent exposed surfaces become more noticeably soiled, tendered or faded than the rest of the textiles.

Tapestries, and other textiles which are used as wall-hangings, should always be lined to protect them from the dust and grime which usually accumulates on the underside. They should hang from a continuous length of 'Velcro' nylon contact fastener to distribute the weight evenly across the full width of the textile. This method of hanging is secure, yet allows the textile to be pressed into position, adjusted or removed, with equal ease.

An alternative method depends on the provision of a sleeve, made from strong linen or webbing, which should be stitched to the underside, just below the top edge of the textile, and through which a rod or batten can be slotted, this being supported at each end by brackets or suspended by chains or cords.

Banners and military colours, which are intended to be seen from both sides, are not usually lined, but may need less obtrusive forms of protection and support, to withstand being hung. This work should be carried out by a qualified textile conservator. Col-

ours should always hang smoothly from horizontal poles or pikes, never in diagonal folds from angled staves.

Shaped textiles

Exhibitions of historic costumes are popular with the visiting public, but clothes, which are intended to be seen in the round, and in movement, lose some of their character and appeal when separated from their original wearers. Both skill and imagination are needed in their presentation, if they are to succeed in static exhibition.

Ideally, costumes should be displayed three-dimensionally. Outer garments, in particular, should be provided with a 'body' of the correct size and proportions, shaped to portray the fashionable silhouette and deportment of the period represented. A costume which is stretched onto an unsuitable figure will not only look incongruous, it could be severely damaged. For the same reasons, historic costumes should never be worn.

Costume display dummies can be specially commissioned – an attractive proposition – but one which is beyond the means of most museums. The choice lies, more usually, between mass-produced dummies and those constructed in the museum. Whichever type is used, it is essential that the dummy should be made to fit the garment, and not *vice versa*, with sufficient soft padding inserted between the shell of a rigid dummy and its outer covering to provide a resilient support for the costume (*Figures 38.12* and *38.13*).

Museum-made dummies are generally better-suited to the display of female than male attire, because the majority are based on a torso only, the absence of legs being concealed by petticoats and a long skirt. A variation on the museum-made torso is the adapted home-dressmaker's dummy, which can be reduced in girth, if necessary, before being padded and covered with stockinette.

Except when fairly recent fashions are being shown, modern shop-display dummies, in adult women's sizes, have only limited usefulness in the museum, for unless they are subjected to ruthless alteration, proportions and measurements rarely suit costumes of previous generations. Boys' and youths' figures, from certain ranges, can be more useful and are adaptable for either male or female clothing.

In addition to bodies, costumes need the support of appropriate foundation garments and underclothing, to enable them to hang correctly, and if the collection cannot supply genuine examples, reproductions should be made. In the same context, if part of an outfit, or an essential accessory is missing, without which the costume would appear incomplete, a reproduction should be made, using, as a guide, another costume of the same date, contemporary portraits and other primary sources, aided by one of the well-researched books on costume construction. It is advisable to understate colour, in reproductions, and if necessary to dye the fabric specially, to a slightly duller tone than the original, if combining new fabric with old. The presence of reproductions should always be stated on the exhibition label.

Generally, the exhibition of costumes against a flat surface should be avoided because of creasing and the strain imposed on heavy garments. Exceptions might be accessories and light-weight cotton garments such as underwear, children's and babies' clothing, which can be mounted on boards, using similar techniques to those suggested for flat textiles, provided that all folds are padded lightly, and sufficient stitching is used to provide firm but unobtrusive support (*Figure 38.14*).

Finally, costumes need accessories to bring them to life. Unless the collection is very small it should be possible to find suitable items, but they must be chosen carefully, with reference to contemporary illustrations, to ensure that they are correct, not only in period, but also for the occasion on which the costume would have been worn.

Caring for a textile collection: remedial conservation

Staff involvement with conservation: curator and conservator

Until comparatively recently it was the custom for curators or technicians to carry out collection maintenance, or to entrust the care of textiles to an accomplished needle-woman, but such practices led to unintentional damage through the use of unsuitable methods and materials.

The number of qualified textile conservators is still relatively small, but ideally, every museum which houses a notable textile collection should employ at least one, whose job is to advise on all aspects of textile care and, in consultation with the curator, to carry out remedial conservation. Where financial or other restraints preclude such an appointment, advice and practical help must be sought from external conservation agencies and reputable free-lance textile conservators. At present the distribution of these resources is poor, and even in the better-served areas rarely satisfies the demand from potential clients. Nevertheless, textiles which require remedial treatment should be stored carefully until they can receive expert attention.

Internal conservation resources

The textile conservation studio-workshop-laboratory

If specialist conservation is to be carried out in the museum, it is preferable to appoint the conservator before planning the studio in detail.

It is difficult to generalize about space requirements for textile conservation, but approximately fifty square metres would be the minimum for small-scale work. Essentially, the furnished area must bee sufficient to enable the largest items in the collection to be extended fully and to be handled safety and easily. One large room, or two (for wet and dry work), connected by a wide archway to allow for the unhindered movement of large objects and textiles supported on boards, is preferable to a series of smaller rooms. If carpets, tapestries, or flags are collected, planning will need to be on a grander scale than for costumes, and if the collection is large, provision should be made for expansion of the conservation facilities, as the work-force is increased.

Ideally, the conservation studio should be in a clean area near the textile store, and separated from the public part of the museum. It must comply in every way with legislation imposed by the *Health and*

Figure 38.12 Volunteer field officer's uniform,
c. 1804–1808, after conservation and mounting for
exhibition. The difficulty of obtaining a
suitably-proportioned male dummy for this uniform
(shown before conservation in *Figure 38.3*) led to the use of
the flocked foam-covered figure illustrated, which has
undergone extensive 'surgery' and adaptation. The gaiters
and boots are reproductions, copied by the conservator
from contemporary illustrations

Safety at Work Act 1974, and the requirements of fire prevention officers. It should be easily accessible, well-lit by natural and artificial light, comfortably warm, and have good general ventilation augmented by apparatus for efficient fume and vapour extraction. An unlimited supply of hot, cold, and de-ionized water, good drainage and a generous allocation of power-points (which should bee of the water-proof type in 'wet' areas) are also essential.

The basic equipment need not be elaborate, but should be of the best quality. It should include at least one stainless-steel sink, approximately 200×50

Figure 38.13 Group of dresses mounted on identical cast polyurethane torsos, each with 71 cm (28 in) chest and 43 cm (17 in) waist. Padding and underclothing have been added, with also reproductions of a corset and silk petticoat for the open robe, *c.* 1775–1785. (left)

× 20 cm with adjacent workbenches; several large tables (or adjustable trestle supports with loose tops) having water-repellent surfaces, and dimensions which allow them to be used either singly or in groups; enclosed storage for conservation materials and work in progress; a steel cabinet for small quantities of chemicals; and for each conservator an adjustable chair, an adjustable magnifying lamp and a small mobile cabinet or trolley, for personal tools and small equipment. A wide selection of portable equipment will also be required as well as reference books, a microscope, a binocular magnifier, a washing table and possibly a vacuum hot-table.

Since requirements vary it is advisable to study published descriptions of conservation laboratories, and where possible, to visit several established workshops[3] before purchasing the equipment.

Briefing the conservator
While the ultimate responsibility for consigning an object to remedial conservation rests with the cura-

tor, ideally, he will be guided in his decision by the textile conservator, following a thorough examination of the object, and an assessment of its condition.

The conservator needs information about the object, and about the conditions to which it will be returned. She should have access to associated documentation, particularly if previous conservation treatment is recorded, and her attention should be drawn to features of special interest, which, if they are to be preserved and remain accessible for study, might influence her choice of cleaning medium, or method of supporting the textile. It is not a textile conservator's usual practice to unpick original stitching, but when it is unavoidable that details of construction are disturbed or partly obscured, the conservator will also appreciate guidance from the curator concerning the permitted extent of the treatment.

During the initial examination, the conservator will note the type and degree of soiling, the nature and position of damage, and the extent to which the textile as a whole has deteriorated. Using all this

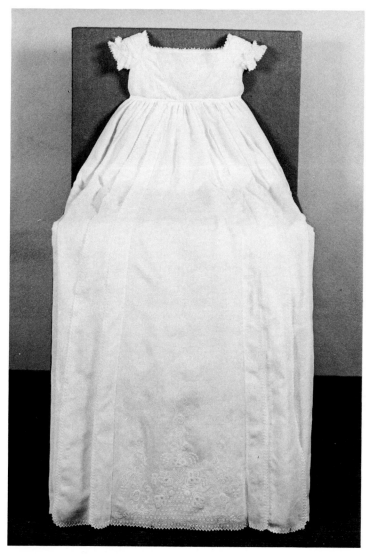

Figure 38.14 Baby's long gown of fine cotton, lightly padded and mounted for exhibition on a felt-covered inclined and stepped support

information, she will devise a programme of treatment for the curator to discuss, before the work is put in hand.

External conservation resources

Area Museum Services
The principal external conservation resources used by museums in the UK are provided by the Area Museum Services (or Councils), whose role is to assist museums (other than the national institutions) in maintaining satisfactory standards of conservation and presentation of their collections.[4]

In some regions, textile conservation is carried out for the Area Museum Services on an agency basis at independent conservation centres by conservators working in the larger museums, and by private conservators.

Independent conservation agencies
At present, the Textile Conservation Centre at Hampton Court Palace is the only independent conservation agency specializing in textiles, which employs a staff of professional conservators. The Centre accepts commissions from museums, historic

houses, churches and other sources, and is one of the few workshops, in the UK, which can handle large tapestries.

Private conservators

Among the textile conservators who practise privately are many who are also employed in museums, or are respected former museum conservators of long experience who are accustomed to working to very exacting standards. It is advisable, nevertheless, for curators to be cautious, and to consult their Area Museum Service, before sending work to a conservator who lacks appropriate professional qualifications or a well-founded reputation for high-class work.

Volunteers and textile conservation

From time to time, museums receive offers of voluntary assistance with textile conservation, from individuals, or local branches of national organizations, which specialize in the repair of church furnishings and material from historic houses. The prospect of supplementary help may be welcomed, for some museums, and organizations such as the National Trust have used volunteers with considerable success.

While it is generally inadvisable to involve volunteers with remedial conservation, small groups can assist with less specialized aspects of textile care, which emphasize the need for prevention of damage, rather than cure. For example, they can make curtains to exclude light from stores and dust from wardrobes; cover coat hangers and sew garment bags; or devise supports for fans, millinery and footwear. It is essential, however, that volunteers should be instructed and supervised by a responsible and suitably qualified member of the museum staff; that the limits of their duties should be clearly defined; and that the museum security and safety measures should be strictly observed. If this takes up more of the professional's time than can be justified, the museum may benefit little from the project.

Acknowledgements

The author is grateful to the following authorities for permission to publish photographs of items from their collections:

Cheshire Military Museum, Chester.
Manx Museum, Library and Art Gallery, Douglas.
Abbey House Museum, Kirkstall, Leeds.
Merseyside County Museums, Liverpool.
Gallery of English Costume, Manchester.
Borough of Trafford Library Service, Manchester.
The Trustees of St Patrick's College Museums, Maynooth.
The Trustees of the Rachel Kay-Shuttleworth Collections, Gawthorpe Hall, Padiham.
The Castle Museum, York.

Remedial conservation was carried out in the Textile Conservation Department of the North Western Museum and Art Gallery Service, by Jean Glover, Vivian Lochhead, and Nanette Muir.

Photographs were taken by T. G. Caunce, and are reproduced by courtesy of the North Western Museum and Art Gallery Service, Blackburn.

Notes

1. The Textile Institute (1970) (6th edn.), *The Identification of Textile Materials*, The Textile Institute, Manchester. Readers who require instruction in the use of the microscope, and in fibre microscopy are advised to enquire about tuition at the nearest College of Technology.

2. It is essential that specimens are scrutinized *before* being put aside for cataloguing or conservation. Infested textiles should *never* be despatched to an external conservation agency without prior warning and the consent of the agency staff.

3. Institutions in Great Britain with studios/laboratories equipped to carry out remedial conservation of textiles:

Birmingham Birmingham Museum and Art Gallery.
Blackburn North Western Museum and Art Gallery Service.
Bristol Blaise Castle House Museum.
Cardiff Welsh Folk Museum, St Fagans.
East Molesey The Textile Conservation Centre, Hampton Court Palace.
Edinburgh Royal Scottish Museum.
Edinburgh The Scottish Museums Council.
Glasgow The Burrell Collection.
Leeds Aberford Conservation Centre.
London Museum of London.
London The National Maritime Museum.
London The Victoria and Albert Museum.
Manchester Gallery of English Costume.
York Castle Howard Textile Conservation Centre.

4. An explanatory booklet, *Area Museum Councils* (1978) (revised 1982), North Western Museum and Art Gallery Service, can be obtained on application to the nearest Area Museum Service headquarters.

References

ARNOLD, J. (1964) (reprinted 1972) *Patterns of Fashion 1: Englishwomen's dresses and their construction c. 1660–1860*, Macmillan, London
ARNOLD, J. (1965) (reprinted 1972), *Patterns of Fashion 2: Englishwomen's dresses and their construction c. 1860–1940*, Macmillan, London
ARNOLD, J. (1973), *A Handbook of Costume*, Macmillan, London

BUCK, A. M. (1958), *Handbook for Museums Curators – Costume*, The Museums Association, London

FINCH, K. (1980), 'Some notes on the care of tapestries' *Museums J.* **80**(1), 40–41

GLOVER, J. M. (1973), *Textiles: their Care and Protection in Museums*, IS No. 18, The Museums Association, London

GRADIDGE, J. M. G. *et al* (1967) *Clothes moths and carpet beetles: their life-history, habits and control*, British Museum (Natural History), London

GROUP FOR COSTUME AND TEXTILE STAFF IN MUSEUMS (1982), *Pest Problems and their Control in Costume and Textile Collections*, Museum of London Symposium, November 1982

HUECK, H. J. (1972), Textile pests and their control, in LEENE, J. E. (Ed.), *Textile conservation*, Butterworths, London, pp. 76–97

LANDI, S. AND MARKO, K. (1980), The maintenance *in situ* of architecturally related textiles, in BROMMELLE, N. S., THOMSON G. AND SMITH, P. (Eds.), *Conservation within Historic Buildings, IIC*, pp. 151–154

THOMSON, G. and BULLOCK, L. (1978) (3rd edn.), *Conservation and Museum Lighting*, IS No. 6, *Museum Association*

WAUGH, N. (1954) (reprinted 1972), *Corsets and Crinolines*, Batsford, London

WAUGH, N. (1964), *The cut of men's clothes*, Faber, London

WAUGH, N. (1968), *The cut of women's clothes*, Faber, London

Bibliography

Among the publications listed, are some which describe remedial conservation procedures. For reasons of their own and others' safety, as well as that of museum objects, readers are advised not to practise these procedures unless they have had previous practical experience of conserving textiles, and of handling chemicals.

Many of the publications also contain useful bibliographies.

Technical analysis of textiles

General

LEENE, J. E. (1972), (Ed.), *Textile Conservation*, Butterworths, London. *See* in particular 'Textiles', pp. 4–22. A standard textbook, concerned with both preventive and remedial conservation.

Identification of fibres

CATLING, D. (1981), 'Guidance for the inexperienced microscopist, *The Conservator*, **5**, 15–19

The Textile Institute (1970) (6th edn), *The Identification of Textile Materials*, The Textile Institute, Manchester

Identification of textile techniques

BEUTLICH, T. (1967), *The Technique of Woven Tapestry*, Batsford, London

BROOKE, M. L. (1923), *Lace in the Making*, Routledge, London – very clear line illustrations and text

BURNHAM, D. K. (1980), *Warp and Weft: a Textile Terminology*, Royal Ontario Museum, Toronto

CLARKE, L. J. (1968), *The Craftsman in Textiles*, Bell, London

COLLINGWOOD, P. (1968), *The Techniques of Rug Weaving*, Faber, London

COLLINGWOOD, P. (1977), *The Techniques of Sprang*, Faber, London

D'HARCOURT, R. (1968), *Textiles of Ancient Peru and their Techniques*, University of Washington, Seattle

DILLMONT, T. DE (1891) (numerous edns), *Encyclopedia of Needlework*, Dollfus-Mieg et Cie., Société Anonyme, (DMC) France – detailed illustrated explanation of the techniques of plain sewing, mending, embroidery, knitting, crochet, tatting, macramé, netting, lace-making and making trimmings for furnishings

EARNSHAW, P. (1980), *The Identification of Lace*, Shire Publications, Aylesbury, Bucks

EMERY, I. (1966), *The Primary Structures of Fabrics – an Illustrated Classification*, The Textile Museum, Washington DC – very clear text, profusely illustrated; essential reading

HALLS, Z. (1964) (2nd edn 1973), *Machine-made Lace in Nottingham*, City of Nottingham Museums and Libraries Committee

HALSEY, M. AND YOUNGMARK, L. (1975), *Foundations of Weaving*, David and Charles, Newton Abbot

LEADBETTER, E. (1976), *Handspinning*, Studio Vista, London

PICTON, J. AND MACK, J. (1979), *African textiles*, The British Museum, London

SEAGROATT, M. (undated) (2nd edn c. 1977), *Coptic Weaves*, Merseyside County Museums, Liverpool

STRAUB, M. (1977), *Hand weaving and cloth design*, Pelham Books, London

SUTTON, A., COLLINGWOOD, P. AND ST AUBYN HUBBARD, G. (1982), *The Craft of the Weaver: a Practical Guide to Spinning, Dyeing and Weaving*, BBC Publications, London

SUTTON, A. AND HOLTON, P. (1975), *Tablet Weaving*, Batsford, London

TABER, B. AND ANDERSON, M. (1975), *Backstrap Weaving*, Pitman, London

TATTERSALL, C. E. C. (1920) (4th impression, 1961), *Notes on Carpet Knotting and Weaving*, Victoria and Albert Museum, (HMSO), London

WEIR, S. (1970), *Spinning and Weaving in Palestine*, The British Museum, London

Miscellaneous (1937–1975), *CIBA Review*, Chemical Industry of Basel, Switzerland – a series of monographs by experts on all aspects of textile history and technology. Out of print, but sets exist in reference libraries

Introduction to conservation

ASHLEY-SMITH, J. (1978), Why conserve collections, *Museum Professionals' Group Transactions*, **15**

CONSTABLE, W. G. (1954), Curators and conservation, *Studies in Conservation*, **1** (1954), 97

The museum environment

General

LEENE, J. E. (1972) (Ed.), *Textile Conservation*, Butterworths, London

PLENDERLEITH, H. J. AND WERNER, A. E. A. (2nd edn, 1971), *The Conservation of Antiquities and Works of Art*, University Press, Oxford, pp. 1–18.

THOMSON, G. (1968) (Ed.), *London conference on museum climatology*, The International Institute for Conservation (IIC), London

THOMSON, G. (1978), *The museum environment*, Butterworths, London – a standard textbook for curators and conservators, concerned with the damaging effects and control, in museums, of light, humidity and air pollution. Substantial bibliography.

Light

BROMMELLE, N. S. AND HARRIS, J. B. (1961–1962), Museum Lighting Parts 1–4, *Museums J.*, **61** (3), 169–176; **61** (4), 259–267; **62** (3), 176–186; **62** (4), 337–346

BEEK, H. C. A. VAN AND HEERTJES, P. M. (1966), Fading by light of organic dyes on textiles and other materials, *Studies in Conservation*, **11** (1966), 123

CRAWFORD, B. H. (1960), Colour rendition and museum lighting, *Studies in Conservation*, **5,** 41

DUFF, D. G., SINCLAIR, R. S. AND STIRLING, D. (1977), Light-induced colour changes of natural dyes, *Studies in Conservation*, **22**, 161

PADFIELD, T. AND LANDI, S. (1966), The light-fastness of natural dyes, *Studies in Conservation*, **11**, 181

THOMSON, G. (1961), A new look at colour-rendering, level of illumination, and protection from ultra-violet radiation in museum lighting, *Studies in Conservation*, **6**, 49

THOMSON, G. (1967), Annual exposure to light within museums, *Studies in Conservation*, **12**, 26

THOMSON, G. AND BULLOCK, L. (1978) (3rd edn), *Conservation and Museum Lighting*, IS No.6, Museums Association

Humidity, heating and ventilation

PADFIELD, T. (1966), The control of relative humidity and air pollution in show cases and picture frames, *Studies in Conservation*, **11**, 8

THOMSON, G. (1964), Relative humidity – variation with temperature in a case containing wood, *Studies in Conservation*, **9**, 153

THOMSON, G. AND BULLOCK, L. (1980), *Simple Control and Measurement of Relative Humidity in Museums*, IS No.24, Museum Association

WERNER, A. E. A. (1957), Heating and Ventilation, *Museums, J.*, **57**, 159

Air pollution

BEECHER, R. (1970), Apparatus for keeping a showcase free of dust, *Museums J.*, **70** (2), 69

HARVEY, J. (1973), Air conditioning for museums, *Museums J.*, **73**(1), 11

Textile pests and their control

GRADIDGE, J. M. G. *et al.* (1967), *Clothes Moths and Carpet Beetles: their Life History, Habits and Control*, British Museum (Natural History), London

HUECK, H. J. (1972), Textile pests and their control' in LEENE, J. E. (1972) (Ed.), *Textile conservation*, Butterworths, London, pp. 76–97

VIGO, T. L. (1980), 'Protection of textiles from biodeterioration' in PERTEGATO, F. (1982) (Ed.), *Conservation and Restoration of Textiles,* International conference, Como, 1980, CISST Lombardy Section, Milan, pp. 18–26

Handling: movement, storage and exhibition of textiles

BLYTHE, A. R. (1974), Anti-static treatment of 'Perspex' for use in picture frames, *Studies in Conservation*, **19**, 102 – applicable also to framed textiles

BUCK, A. M. (1958), *Handbook for Museum Curators – Costume*, The Museums Association, London

FINCH, K. AND PUTNAM, G. (1977), *Caring for Textiles,* Barrie and Jenkins, London – a practical handbook of particular value to curators without specialized knowledge of textiles

GINSBURG, M. (1973), The mounting and display of fashion and dress, *Museums J.*, **73**(2), 50

GLOVER, J. M. (1973), *Textiles: their care and protection in museums*, IS No. 18, Museums Association

BUCK, A. (1972), 'Storage and display' in LEENE, J. E. (Ed.), *Textile conservation*, Butterworths, London, pp. 113–127

PERTEGATO, F. (1982) (Ed.), *Conservation and Restoration of Textiles*, CISST Lombardy Section, Milan

> pp. 32–37: EKSTRAND, G. 'Display: problems and methods' – costumes at the Royal Armory, Stockholm
> pp. 27–31: FLURY-LEMBERG, M. 'Examples of storage and display of historical textiles' – textiles at the Abegg-Stiftung, Bern
> pp.215–218: GRÖNWOLDT, R. 'Textile display and textile exhibitions at the Württembergische Landesmuseum, Stuttgart
> pp. 38–35: HARRIS, K. J. 'Some recent advances in the storage and display of costumes in the United States'

PRICE, M. AND MARKO, K. (1976), The storage of museum textiles in Switzerland, West Germany and Holland, *Museums J.*, **76**(1), 25

PUGH, F. (1978), *Packing and Handling Works of Art*, Arts Council of Great Britain, London – primarily concerned with pictures, sculpture etc., but applicable also to framed textiles, bulky costumes, and three-dimensional textile objects

The textile conservation studio/workshop/laboratory

LANDI, S. B. (1972), 'The equipment of a textile conservation workroom' in LEENE, J. E. (Ed.), *Textile Conservation*, Butterworths, London, pp. 128–136

LANDI, S. (1977), A textile conservation workshop at Osterley, *The Conservator*, **1** (1977), 28–30

MEREDITH, C. (1974), Design of conservation and general laboratories, *Museum Professionals' Group Transactions*, **13**, 10

PERTEGATO, F. (1982) (Ed.), *Conservation and Restoration of Textiles,* CISST Lombardy Section, Milan

> pp. 129–136: BAER, N. S. *et al*, 'Considerations in the development of textile conservation laboratories'
> pp. 116–121: THURMAN, C. C. M., 'Setting up a workshop: technical equipment'

THURMAN, C. C. M. (1978), The department of textiles at the Art Institute of Chicago, *Museum*, **30**, 122

UNITED KINGDOM INSTITUTE FOR CONSERVATION (1982), *Conservation News*, **17** and **18** UKIC

Health and safety in laboratories and textile stores

HER MAJESTY'S GOVERNMENT (1974), *Health and Safety at Work etc. Act 1974*, Chapter 37, HMSO, London

CLYDESDALE, A. (1982), *Chemicals in Conservation: a Guide to Possible Hazards and Safe Use*. Conservation Bureau, Scottish Development Agency and Scottish Society for Conservation and Restoration, Edinburgh – also includes chemicals used as fumigants and pest deterrants

MUSEUM PROFESSIONALS' GROUP (1974), *Transactions*, **13**:

> CLAYTON, R., 'Ventilation'
>
> GATES, R. J., 'The Health and Safety at Work etc. Act 1974, in relation to museums'
>
> GLOVER, J. R., 'Working with toxic hazards'
>
> MASON, I., 'Hazard awareness in lifting and handling'
>
> RIDEOUT, R. W., 'The law relating to industrial safety in the UK, based on the Health and Safety at Work Act, 1974'

PASCOE, M. (1980), Toxic hazards from solvents in conservation, *The Conservator*, **4**

ROBERTS, M. P. C. AND MONEY, J. (1977), A mobile fume extractor, *The Conservator*, – of limited value in textile conservation

Conservation resources

AREA MUSEUM SERVICES (1978) (Revised edn in preparation, available 1983), *Area Museum Councils*, North Western Museum and Art Gallery Service, Blackburn

CRAFTS COUNCIL (1979) (with later supplements), *Conservation Source-book*, Crafts Council, London

UNITED KINGDOM INSTITUTE FOR CONSERVATION (1974), *Conservation in Museums and Galleries: a Survey of Facilities in the United Kingdom'*, UKIC, London

Ethics in conservation

AMERICAN INSTITUTE OF CONSERVATION (1980), Code of ethics and standards of practice, *American Institute of Conservation Directory* 1980, pp. 9–22

PEASE, M. *et al* (1963), The Murray Pease report *Studies in Conservation*, **9**, 116 – AIC standards of practice and professional relations for conservators

MUSEUM PROFESSIONALS' GROUP (1981), Towards a code of ethics in museums, *MPG Transactions*, **16**

UNITED KINGDOM INSTITUTE FOR CONSERVATION (1981), *Guidance for conservation practice*, UKIC Occasional Paper, UKIC, London

Periodicals concerned with textiles and/or textile conservation

Studies in Conservation (1952 onwards), Quarterly journal of The International Institute for Conservation of Historic and Artistic Works (IIC), 6 Buckingham Street, London WC2N 6BA

AATA Abstracts (Art and archaeology technical abstracts), Biannual, IIC, London

The Conservator (1977 onwards), Annual journal of the United Kingdom Institute for Conservation (UKIC), c/o The Tate Gallery, Millbank, London SW1P 4RG

Conservation News (November 1976 onwards), Triannual newsletter of UKIC

SSCR News, Occasional newsletter of the Scottish Society for Conservation and Restoration (SSCR), c/o Kelvingrove Art Gallery and Museum, Glasgow, G3 8AG

AIC Bulletin, Journal of the American Institute for Conservation

CCI Journal (1976 onwards), Journal of the Canadian Conservation Institute, Ottawa

Textile Museum Journal, Annual Journal of The Textile Museum, 2320 S Street, Northwest, Washington, DC 2008

Textile History, Biannual journal containing scholarly articles on textile and costume history and conservation, Butterworth Scientific Ltd – Journals Division, for the Pasold Research Fund Ltd, Guildford

Museums Journal, Quarterly journal of the Museums Association, 34 Bloomsbury Way, London WC1A 2SF

Museum, Quarterly review of the United Nations Educational, Scientific and Cultural Organisation UNESCO, Paris

39

Conservation and storage: coins and medals

Roger Bland and Hannah P. Lane

Since it is seldom possible for a museum to display more than a small fraction of its total collection of coins, the following relates to the storage of that part of a museum's collection which is not on exhibition. It should be stressed at the outset that wherever possible the coins should be arranged as a single sequence, according to their geographical and historical series, rather than in any other way. However, there are certain groups of coins which should be kept apart from the main series (for example, hoards) where the main interest lies not in the coins themselves, but in the fact that they were found in a particular place under known circumstances. Another class of material that could profitably be housed separately is a special collection of particular historic or local interest.

Methods of housing collections

There are three main methods of housing a collection of coins, all of which have advantages and disadvantages. Obviously, the collection should be readily accessible and easy to consult, but this can sometimes conflict with the needs of security and with the necessity of keeping the coins in stable conditions where they will not deteriorate.

Envelopes

The simplest method of storage is to keep the coins in special envelopes of brown manilla or good quality white paper about 70 mm square, and then to file them in stiff cardboard or wooden boxes. This will work well for a small collection of perhaps a hundred or so pieces. Its advantages are that it is easy and cheap to obtain and that details about each coin, such

as its accession or registration number together with a brief identification and description, can be written on the outside of each envelope. It is also one of the safest ways of housing coins from the point of view of conservation, although care should be taken that the materials of which the envelopes are made do not contain harmful substances. Manilla envelopes can also cause silver coins to become tarnished, but this can be avoided by wrapping the coins in anti-tarnish tissue. The main drawback of this method of storage is that subsequent examination is a laborious process, since each one must first be removed and then returned to the envelope. Moreover, it is difficult to keep a secure check on coins stored in this way.

Albums

Another method, which is also best suited to small collections, is to keep the coins in transparent plastic pages or sheets. These pages can be kept in loose-leaf albums and are often used by private collectors. Alternatively, the coins could be placed in plastic sheets, similar to those used for transparencies, which are suspended in filing cabinet drawers. This technique has been successfully used by the Museum of London. With this method, both sides of the coin can be seen quickly and easily, and it also provides a reasonable degree of security for the collection. However, in order to provide essential details about the objects without obscuring one or other side of them, it is necessary to interleave the coin sheets with pages of text. It can also be quite difficult to remove the coins from their plastic pages if they need to be examined closely, weighed, or photographed. It should be noted that plastic sheets should not be used for objects made of iron, zinc, lead, or aluminium, or their alloys, as they are liable to be damaged by the plastic.

Cabinets

For housing coin collections of any size the traditional method, the coin cabinet, is still the best. This is usually made of wood, and equipped with a series of shallow drawers or 'trays', each one of which contains a larger number of separate circular *piercings* or holes, for individual coins (see *Figure 39.1*). The size of the piercings vary according to the size of the coins. Where it is necessary to keep items of widely differing diameters together, as, for example, medals, it is best to use completely blank trays which can be filled with square cardboard boxes, one for each object. These boxes can be obtained in a range of sizes. In such a cabinet, large numbers of coins can be stored economically and easily consulted.

The requirements of security can be met by ensuring that every piercing or box in a coin tray is filled – if not by an actual coin – then either by a heading ticket of coloured card which will indicate the appropriate series and sub-division of the series, or by a coloured blank security disc which will leave space for new coins to be incorporated in the tray.

For essential information about the coins, such as their registration numbers and description, small round tickets of white card can be used, and these can be placed under the coins. If it is necessary to remove a coin from the main series in order to exhibit it, or to have it photographed, a special coloured ticket bearing information to this effect can be substituted for the coin in its piercing (see *Figure 39.1*). In this way it should be possible to see at a glance that no coins are missing from the tray; if the tray has an empty piercing or one with only a white ticket on it, then it will immediately be clear that something is wrong. Plastic and steel can also be used for making cabinets. Polystyrene is a suitable inert plastic, which can be used to house all types of coins in perfect safety. However, although these cabinets are now quite widely available, they are seldom as pleasing to handle as a well-made wooden cabinet.

Photographic record

Because of their small size and the relatively high value of some of them, coins are liable to be stolen.

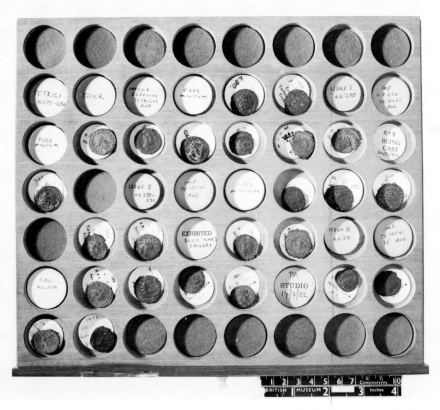

Figure 39.1 A typical coin tray, showing the use of blank security discs, coloured heading tickets, and tickets used to denote coins that have been removed from the trays either to have plaster casts made (third row) or to be put on exhibition (fifth row) or to be photographed (sixth row) (Courtesy of the British Museum)

For this reason it is important to have a complete photographic record of the collection. Not only will this be invaluable if any coins are stolen, but it will also prove to be of great use to students and researchers. It is not, however, necessary to photograph each coin individually: groups of 50 to 75 pieces should be adequate.

The conservation aspects of coin storage

Most of the metal objects in museums, particularly those from excavations, are at risk unless stored and displayed in a suitable environment. The rate of corrosion of coins is dependent on many factors, including temperature, humidity, handling damage and atmospheric pollutants, as well as the possible harmful effects of certain storage and display conditions.

Temperature

Temperature has three main effects on metals. The higher the temperature, the faster the rate of chemical deterioration. Temperature fluctuations cause physical damage due to different rates of expansion and contraction between dissimilar alloys, corrosion products or protective coatings. The level of relative humidity is affected by temperature changes. Because they are simpler in construction than nearly any other group of metal objects, coins can be considered less prone to chemical attack. Therefore, the control of temperature is not as important as it is for some other antiquities but fluctuations must be avoided, particularly for excavated coins. The recommended temperature is approximately 18°C.

Humidity

The atmospheric corrosion processes of metals require the presence of moisture and oxygen, and the lower the moisture level in the surrounding atmosphere, the slower the rate of decay, until a point is reached where it stops completely. The relative humidity (RH) level at which no corrosion occurs is usually so low that work becomes uncomfortable. Moreover, it is too expensive to maintain to be practical.

Because they are small, relatively flat and of a single composition, even archaeological coins are usually more stable than other metal objects. Corrosion layers can form a protective barrier against the ingress of moisture; alternatively, if coins are corroding actively, they can be stabilized by appropriate conservation treatments. Coins that have not recently been excavated are often protected by a patina and, provided that this layer is not damaged, RH levels of up to 55 per cent are permissible. For actively corroding objects that cannot be stabilized, including bright polished steel coin dies and some copper and iron archaeological coins, the level should be reduced to 40–45 per cent. Such vulnerable items may have to be stored under separate controlled conditions provided by de-humidifying equipment or silica gel.

Lead is a very stable metal, and forms a surface layer of oxide which gives protection, unless damaged by rough handling or by certain air pollutants. The rate of corrosion of lead is reduced by lowering RH levels, though not as successfully as with iron and copper, but removing pollutants is a more important consideration, as is the case with zinc and aluminium.

Mechanical damage

All coins and medals can be damaged by careless handling. If they are stored loose in trays or drawers, every movement is liable to cause rubbing of the surface and knocking of the edges. Metal containers have a serious effect, but so do wood and plastic over a period of time. Hence, coins should be kept in such a way as to prevent movement. Placing coins on absorbent material or in envelopes can resolve this problem, provided the materials are inert to metals.

Grit or any other hard substance will scratch the surface, decreasing the value and damaging any form of protective layer. Storage drawers must be kept clean and the objects themselves should be handled with care, by the edge wherever possible, and with clean hands. However, metal tweezers are unsuitable for this purpose, as they can scratch the surfaces of the coins.

Pollution

The deterioration of metal antiquities can be greatly accelerated by the presence of small amounts of certain gases and vapours. Although having fresh air circulating around the objects will dilute and remove vapours given off by the surrounding materials, in order to eliminate dust, to keep a steady temperature and humidity, and to maintain the requirements of security, it is usual to enclose the object within as small a space as possible. Although this will greatly reduce the ingress of pollutants from outside the atmosphere, if the materials of the enclosed storage or display containers give off harmful vapours, which react with metallic surfaces, these will build up to levels that cause corrosion within such confined spaces. The most vulnerable metals are bright silver and copper alloys, which quickly tarnish to a brown or black surface, and lead, which reacts to produce the disfiguring white powder of basic lead carbonate.

Many materials used in the storage and display of antiquities give off small amounts of harmful gases and vapours which react with metallic surfaces (see Blackshaw and Daniels, 1978). The most common is hydrogen sulphide (H_2S), which is naturally present in the atmosphere from rotting vegetation at a level which will cause the tarnishing of copper, and more particularly, silver; but it may also be given off by some protein materials such as wood, parchment, leather and various adhesives and dyes. Elemental sulphur vapour produces the same effect as hydrogen sulphide; this can be found either as a gap filler, or it can be present in the objects themselves, such as sulphur casts or vulcanized rubber. All woods contain organic acids that can be given off and may cause the corrosion of metals.

All materials used in the storage of metals should be tested for their suitability (Blackshaw and Daniels, 1979), and only those that give negative corrosion results should be used. However, it is rarely possible to eliminate completely such pollutants and yet keep the coins available for study and handling. Unfortunately, unsuitable materials may have to be used, but if this is the case, the corrosive effects should be reduced to an absolute minimum.

Absorbing materials, such as silica gel for moisture and acetic acid (Blackshaw and Daniels, 1978), can be used to trap harmful vapours before they reach the metals. The main disadvantage is that there is no easy means whereby the absorbers can be monitored to establish when they have become exhausted (except for the coloured silica gel used to control moisture content), nor do the conditions in the general storage areas or galleries reflect those within the enclosed case or tray where the coins are kept. Quite apart from the fact that they can present a health hazard to staff, corrosion inhibitors are not an effective way of protecting coins from atmospheric pollutants.

Storage materials

Wood

Wood has three major advantages over other materials. First, since it is relatively soft, it does not wear away the surfaces of metal easily, although lead can be vulnerable. Second, because wood is absorbent, it acts as a buffer against fluctuations of external atmospheric humidity, thus maintaining a steady level within the case, except during prolonged spells of high RH. The main disadvantages of using wood is that it contains organic acids, especially free acetic acid, which cause metal corrosion at a concentration as low as 1300 mg/m^3. Other organic acids cause corrosion at varying degrees. Lead is most affected, while copper reacts to form green verdigris (copper acetate). Finally, the use of fine woods is aesthetically pleasing, both for coin cabinets and for exhibition cases.

All woods, whether seasoned or not, must be considered a potential cause of corrosion of base metals; freshly cut oak and sweet chestnut being the worst, elm being in the middle range, and Norway spruce being the least harmful. Maximum evolution of organic acids occurs after wood is rendered down into sawdust. In many woods, the acid content increases with time and does not decrease as it dries, as was formerly thought to be the case. Most wooden storage and display cases made today are of composite construction. The wood consists of layers, blocks, chips or sawdust, held together by an adhesive, sometimes with a surface veneer of the wood required. The resulting vapours are a mixture of all the woods and adhesives present, which can vary with each batch as the constituents are liable to be varied by the manufacturers without notice. Sundeala board (a form of chip board) will tarnish silver within a few months, but is one of the safest stiff materials on which to pin small items for vertical or sloping displays. In general, the wood used in exhibition cases has a relatively small surface area and the acids have to diffuse to the surface before they affect the metal. Since soft woods are more permeable than hard ones, they are generally unsuitable for the storage of metal items, and, hence, tropical hardwoods are more satisfactory.

Cardboard and paper

Cardboard and paper are made from wood with the addition of adhesives, surface finishes and dyes, and, therefore, should be considered as being potentially damaging. The small discs used in coin storage, either as labels on which the coins rest, or as spacers between series, have been showed to be particularly corrosive to lead, and should not be used. All paper should be tested for use with metals, since even some so-called 'acid-free papers' have been found to cause corrosion.

Adhesives, paints, lacquers and varnishes

Many of these substances can give off harmful vapours, and, before use, should be tested for their effect on the metals of which coins are made. Polysulphide adhesives give off harmful hydrogen sulphide. Nitrocellulose adhesives and lacquers are a possible source of nitrogen oxide, but in the long use of these materials there have been no recorded cases of damage arising from their application, presumably due to the inclusion of stabilizers in the manufactured products. The oils in air-drying paints evolve formic acid vapour as they become dry. The absorption of moisture from the atmosphere can cause reactions that result in the release of acid from the acetic-type solvents in other types of paints and varnishes. The different dyes in paints can produce different effects on metals even when used in the same paint base, so each colour should be tested, as well as each type of paint or lacquer.

Metal

Metal does not give off corrosive vapours and, if used in the form of protective foil, it will be impermeable to pollutants. However, it is a hard substance that may abrade other metals. If a coin is in contact with a metal surface, and moisture is present, an electrochemical cell could be established, causing corrosion of the baser metal. Unlike wood, metal cannot absorb moisture and cannot act as a buffer against fluctuations in humidity. If metal trays are lined with a non-corrosive plastic or filter paper then metal storage cases are preferable to wood, since the damage done to coins through corrosion from organic acid vapours is likely to be more harmful than that resulting from a high RH level, especially as regards non-archaeological material. However, for archaeological materials, especially copper and iron alloys, high humidity tends to be more damaging, due to the chlorides that the coins contain as a result of being buried, and to the general loss of a polished metal surface. Lead should always be stored in lined metal containers, or plastic ones which cannot evolve organic acids. The same general comments apply to metal pins used to mount coins for display; these should be made of stainless steel, and preferably be plastic-sleeved.

Fabrics

Fabrics used in display are the most sensitive of all storage materials as coins often rest directly on them, thus forming an ideal microclimate of trapped and concentrated vapours at the back of the coin, with the textile forming a reservoir of retained moisture and so accelerating corrosion. All fabrics should, therefore be tested against the appropriate metal before use (Blackshaw and Daniels, 1979). Felt is corrosive towards silver, but may be satisfactory for lead. Plain terylene and nylon are relatively safe, but any fabric that has been treated to impart non-crease properties is liable to give off hydrogen sulphide.

Plastics

For coin storage, plastic cabinets have several advantages. They can be soft enough not to cause wear, yet strong enough to support trays of coins and medals. They also put less strain on floor loading than other materials. Cabinets made of plastic are now produced in a range of sizes by several manufacturers, but as the materials of composition vary in their reaction to metals, they should all be tested. As in the case of fabrics, different manufacturers use different additives; so each individual batch should be tested, even when the basic chemical type is known and approved.

Small individual plastic envelopes can create a microclimate within the enclosure. Some moisture will always be present either in the coin, or in the entrapped air, or will enter through the plastic, and create an excessively high level of humidity, even to the point of forming condensation. This will tarnish freshly minted coins in a short time and eventually will instigate corrosion. Therefore, completely sealed plastic wallets and fluctuations in temperature should equally be avoided.

The conservation of coins

The principal metals used for coins have been gold, silver and copper, together with their alloys. Lead has been used in India, and tin in certain periods in Europe. Since the eighteenth century other metals have been introduced, such as platinum, zinc, iron, aluminium and cupro-nickel which is now widely used as a substitute for silver. Medals are made of similar materials, with a higher proportion of pieces being made of lead. The range of metals and their alloys produces a wide variety of corrosion products, and these are further complicated by the varied conditions through which the coins have passed during their history. The processes of corrosion are described in Plenderleith and Werner (1971).

It is important to try to identify the main metal(s) of the coin and which of these metals, if an alloy, is primarily responsible for the corrosion products, as the selection of the wrong treatment could damage the object. This is particularly true when wet methods of conservation are used. Often it is a minor constituent that causes the most corrosion; for example, in a silver alloy with copper, it will be the copper that corrodes, and a small amount of copper can give rise to enough corrosion to obscure completely the surface of a coin. Therefore, for the removal of copper corrosion, a treatment should be selected which has a minimal effect on silver as well as on the remaining copper, and which does not redeposit copper on the surface to give a false appearance. The same applies to groups of coins that are to be treated together.

The conservation of coins is labour-intensive and so usually has to be limited to selected items, especially in the treatment of large hoards. Many coins, particularly those that have not been buried, have acquired a patina, or fine layer of tarnish, which does not obscure their types and legend. It is often considered to be an improvement to the appearance of a coin provided that it is stable, and should not be removed. The patina can act as a protective layer against further corrosion, although all corrosion layers slowly increase in thickness due to pollutants in the atmosphere. Bright metal reacts quickly to normal pollutants, and with the present difficulties of finding a completely impermeable lacquer, or perfect storage conditions, many curators prefer to retain the patina rather than clean the coin, unless the design is obscured. Three categories of coins are usually selected for cleaning.

(1). Items required for display or illustration, in which case every detail needs to be seen.

(2). Any coin whose design is sufficiently obscured to prevent identification. Discussion between the curator and conservator may confine the amount of cleaning required to part of the coin, or only a selection from a large hoard. Corroded coins must be examined with particular care, as some of them, particularly Roman coins, may have plated surfaces. This plating may be hidden within the corrosion layers, and would be lost if all the corrosion were removed. Similarly, the design of the coin may be preserved only within the corrosion layers, so that the corrosion must not be removed.

(3). In certain cases after excavation, the corrosion contains active salts that are causing decay to continue, while in others external atmospheric pollutants cause continuous tarnishing. In these cases urgent action is required. Coin details are relatively shallow and can soon be irretrievably lost. Corrosion slowly formed in the ground tends to be compact and will reproduce the surface design, whereas that which is caused by unsuitable storage tends to be much more porous and does not contain surface details. Thus, the copper carbonate found on coins that have recently been excavated can form a delicate patina, but the powdery green of 'bronze disease', which may occur during storage, destroys the original design and leaves only a pitted metal surface. Conservation may be required, depending on what stage the corrosion has reached, but transfer to correct storage conditions is essential. Various treatments can successfully stabilize the active salts and these are described fully in Plenderleith and Werner (1971) and MacDowall (1978).

The detailed conservation of coins is a highly skilled process and should be carried out by an experienced conservator in consultation with the numismatist (Grierson, 1975). Many of the chemicals used are toxic and must only be used in a laboratory with proper fume extraction. The fine details of coins can be easily lost or irretrievably altered by incorrect conservation, so that a knowledge of coins together with a knowledge of conservation and appropriate equipment is essential. Details of the deterioration and conservation of metals are given by Plenderleith and Werner (1971), and the specialized techniques of coin conservation by McDowall (1978). Full records of all treatments must be kept so that future assessments can be carried out on the relative success or failure of the treatments used.

Acknowledgements

This chapter is founded on the work of MacDowall (1978) which itself owes much to the experience and expertise of K. A. Howes, Senior Conservation Officer at the British Museum. The writers would also like to express their thanks to W. A. Oddy, Head of the Conservation Division at the British Museum, for reading through the draft and making a number of helpful suggestions.

References

BLACKSHAW, S. M. AND DANIELS, V. D. (1978), Selecting safe materials for use in display and storage of antiquities, *ICOM 1978 Conference,* 23 February 1978, pp. 1–9

BLACKSHAW, S. M. AND DANIELS, V. D. (1979), The testing of materials for use in storage and display in museums, *The Conservator,* **3**, 16–19

GRIERSON, P. (1975), *Numismatics,* Oxford

MACDOWALL, D. W. (1978), *Coin Collections: Their Preservation, Classification and Presentation,* UNESCO, Paris

PLENDERLEITH, H. J. AND WERNER, A. E. A. (1971), (2nd edn, 1st edn 1956), *The Conservation of Antiquities and Works of Art,* University Press, Oxford

40

Conservation and storage: photographic materials

Anne E. Fleming

The very title of this paper, embracing as it does both cinematographic film and still photographs under the general heading of 'photographic materials', is in itself a distillation of the multiplicity of problems confronting those curators concerned with the conservation of either type of photographic image.

While the motives for archiving both film and photographs are very similar, whether as works of art, historical records or social evidence, the techniques required for handling, storing and conserving the two mediums are not identical and should be viewed as two distinct, specialist fields, although there are a considerable number of overlapping areas.

Recognizing this, the present paper can do no more than outline the main procedures necessary to protect film and photographic collections, and wherever possible direct curators to publications which provide more detailed information. Nor will it be possible to discuss the conservation of photographs made by processes that were in use before negatives and prints were made on gelatin-chloride or gelatin-bromide materials, since the care of photographic images produced by nineteenth-century processes such as Daguerrotype, Calotype, Ambrotype, Collodion Wet Plate, Tintype, Albumen Paper and Platinum Prints, require detailed individual consideration beyond the scope of this article.

The fundamental conservation problem is the same for both film and photographs, since it is in the nature of the photographic process which presupposes that multiple copies can and will be struck from a single negative and that it will be used and re-used. Even where the only existing original is a positive print of some sort, the same assumption is made.

The curator of any collection of photographic material will, therefore, inevitably be approached by individuals and companies wanting copies of the material for which he is responsible. Clearly, the curator must try to provide access to the material since this is part of the purpose of any archival collection. However, because the medium is both fragile and chemically unstable there is an inherent conflict between a policy of access and a policy of conservation. Any frequently-used negative will show signs of wear, and the quality of image it is possible to reproduce from it will gradually deteriorate. Where the original is a positive print, excessive handling or, in the case of motion picture film, projection, will likewise cause damage to the image.

Therefore, the curator's first duty is to ensure that original negatives and master prints are used and handled as little as possible and that they are stored in conditions that will at least promote, if not ensure, their long-term survival. If conservation is to be combined with access this means producing dupe negatives and positives from which users of the collection can work. Not only does this necessitate spending considerable sums of money on a duplicating programme, but it also means doubling, and sometimes tripling, the amount of storage space needed to house the collection. As Eugene Ostroff (1976), the Curator of Photography at the Smithstonian Institute has written:

> A long range financial obligation is incurred when photographs are collected; they require storage space, equipment and staff.

This statement is even more true of cine film because of its greater bulk.

The curator who embarks on a policy of duplication is immediately faced with the problem of where to begin. A systematic approach is clearly desirable but the choice of system must depend on the type of collection which should be given priority. Apart from considerations of subject content and artistic value, the base materials on which the collection is held are also relevant. Nitrate-based film or photographs should probably go to the head of the program because they are inherently unstable and doomed to destruction sooner or later. In this case, copying is not merely an adjunct to conservation, done to provide access and protect the originals, it is the *only* means of ensuring the survival of the image. Glass plates are another obvious priority area, since despite their stability their extreme fragility makes frequent handling particularly undesirable.

Demands for access may also affect the structure of the duplicating program. While in an ideal world such demands should not be allowed to interfere with an established schedule of copying, the curator of a collection in constant use will probably have to adopt a more pragmatic approach, identifying those negatives which are most in demand and making these a priority area for duplication. An institution with restricted funds for copying may even be able to turn demands for access to financial advantage by making the production of an archival negative or print at the applicant's expense one of the conditions for use of the material. Each curator, therefore, must tailor his duplicating program to the nature of his collection.

Having relieved the strain on original negatives and prints by producing working copies the curator must then ensure that the originals are stored adequately. Different base materials require different handling and storage conditions and these are perhaps best explained by a consideration of the basic structure of photographic materials.

Both cinematographic film and photographs are comprised of multi-layered materials. They consist of a base-support and a very thin adhesive substratum upon which an emulsion layer is coated for the optical recording of the image and, in the case of motion pictures, of sound as well. Black and white film and photographs have only one emulsion layer consisting of light-sensitive silver halides in gelatin, whereas modern colour materials have three such layers for each of the basic substrative colours (yellow, magenta and cyan) and one or more filter layers. Since most older collections are black and white, these will be considered first.

Tables 40.1 and *40.2* show the principal materials for concern in black and white photography.

Gelatin

Since the substratum of gelatin is common to all forms of photographic materials considered here, it

Table 40.1 Cinematographic film

Film base	Gauge (mm)	Substratum	Emulsion layer
Nitrate Acetate Polyester	35 35–16, 9.5–8mm 16–8	Gelatin	Silver halides

Table 40.2 Photographs

Film base	Substratum	Emulsion layer
Nitrate Acetate Polyester Glass Paper	Gelatin	Silver halides

is worth stating its basic properties before discussing the various bases and how it interacts with them.

Gelatin is a highly purified animal protein, (animal albumen) that is very stable as long as it is kept dry. If it becomes moist however, it will swell, spread and become sticky, thereby endangering the image. The hazard is increased by warmth. As an organic substance, it is also an excellent nutrient for bacteria and fungi and promotes their growth at high levels of relative humidity (RH). These can penetrate the emulsion layer and attack the image. To prevent this, RH levels should never exceed 60 per cent whatever the photographic base.

It is also attacked by strong acids and acidic gases that may be present in the environment or produced by deterioration of the film base and it is therefore at its most vulnerable when in contact with the inherently unstable base nitro-cellulose, or nitrate film.

Nitrate-based materials

Nitrate-based film, whether cinematographic or still, deteriorates even under favourable storage conditions and in any considerable quantity, constitutes a fire hazard.

This hazard is proportionately greater for cinematographic film because of its greater bulk. While safety-based material has always been used for 16 mm and 8 mm film from the introduction of these gauges, professional 35 mm cinematographic film was produced on nitro-cellulose (nitrate) up to 1951. Photographic sheet negatives were also produced on nitrate-based material for much of this period although acetate-based stock was phased in during the 1930s and early 1940s for certain kinds of photography.

How long any piece of nitrate film can survive is dependent on the purity of the original film stock, how well it was processed and how it has subsequently been stored, for while deterioration can be retarded it cannot be prevented. In the process of deterioration, nitrate film gives off harmful gases, in particular nitrogen dioxide (NO_2). These combine with the moisture in the gelatin to form nitric acid or nitrous acid and these bleach the silver (or colour) image in the emulsion and accelerate the decomposition of the base, (Bowser and Kuiper, 1980).

The following visible signs of nitrate decomposition occur in the order shown below:

(1). The silver image becomes faded and there is a brownish-yellow discolouration of the emulsion. (In colour film the colours fade and a loss of balance between the colours occurs).
(2). The emulsion becomes sticky.
(3). The emulsion softens and becomes blistered, bubbles rising as it separates from the base, and a pungent odour is given off.
(4). Cinematographic film congeals into a solid mass, or a group of single photographic negatives may weld together.
(5). The base disintegrates into a brownish powder giving off an acrid smell.

Only in the first and second stages is rescue possible by immediate treatment and copying.

Decomposition is speeded up by storage at high temperatures particularly when accompanied by high RH. While awaiting copying, nitrate film materials should therefore be stored at around 4°C with the RH controlled at about 50 per cent. Every endeavour should be made to keep climatic conditions constant since if they are allowed to fluctuate the emulsion can become detached from the base.

At high temperatures nitrate film can self-ignite. Most nitrate materials in existence today are of an age where the ignition point may be as low as 38–40°C. It burns with the force of an explosion and, since a nitrate fire cannot be extinguished, great care must be exercised by all personnel handling nitrate-based material, particularly cinematographic film.

Ventilation of storage areas is crucial since the gases produced must be allowed to escape. Cine film, even in an unsealed can, gives off larger quantities of gas because of its bulk. The cans must be opened regularly and the films wound through to disperse accumulated gas and slow the rate of deterioration. Similarly, large photographic negatives stored in enclosed packages are at high risk since the damaging gases can escape only slowly and the archivist would be well-advised to make such packages a starting point in checking his nitrate holdings.

Since the gases given off by deteriorating nitrate are powerful oxidizing agents, they have a damaging effect on any other photographic materials stored in proximity to them. Acetate-based negatives stored in contact with nitrate materials will exhibit a yellowing and fading of the silver image and a softening of the gelatin. It is therefore essential to identify any nitrate elements in a collection and ensure that they are segregated as soon as possible.

Identification of nitrate film may in itself be a problem. Any 35 mm negatives produced before 1951 are suspect, although acetate-based stock was also in use for both film and photographs for a considerable time before that. Cinematographic film often has the word 'nitrate' or 'safety' printed along both edges outside the perforations, and sheet negatives may also be identified in the same way along one edge near the code match. However, not all stock manufacturers used these forms of identification. If in doubt there are two standard tests which may be used to determine the presence of nitrate.

(1). Cut a very small segment from the edge of the photograph or film negative and drop it into a test tube containing trichlorethylene and shake it to immerse it completely. If it floats, it is safety film. If it sinks, it is nitrate (Eastman Kodak Co., 1957).
(2). One frame of cinematographic film or a thin strip from the edge of a photographic negative may be submitted to a colouring test. The frame or strip should be taken to a spot well away from any combustible materials, placed upright on a flat, non-inflammable surface and lit at the top using a long match or taper. If it ignites easily and burns rapidly, it is nitrate. If it is difficult to ignite and either keeps going out or burns very slowly then it is safety film.

Clearly it is also desirable to check the stage of deterioration of any nitrate item in a collection, since a nitrate-based film or photograph apparently in good condition may reach a point where copying is impossible only six months later.

For cinematograph film the most common method is the Alizarin Red heat test (Ashmore *et al.*, 1957). A film punching approximately 6 mm in diameter is dropped into a test tube closed by a glass stopper, around which is wrapped a piece of filter paper impregnated with Alizarin Red indicator dye and moistened with a mixture of glycerine and water. The tube is then heated in an air bath to 134°C and the time take for acid vapours to develop is revealed by the bleaching of the lower edge of the paper. A range of times from 60 minutes down to 10 minutes may be obtained. If the Alizarin Red test paper reacts in 30–60 minutes, the film may be stored and retested in a year's time; if it reacts in 10–30 minutes, retesting is recommended within six months; under 10 minutes the film should be copied and destroyed.

This test is unsuitable for single photograph negatives since it involves taking punchings from the film which would damage the image. 'Kodak' therefore recommend the following test for photographic negatives (Eastman Kodak Co., 1979). Cut a small strip from the clear margin of the negative, fold it to check for brittleness then soak the strip in water for a minute. Scrape the gelatin from the surface and place it on a sheet of white paper so that the degree of discolouration can be observed. The discolouration will range from faintly yellowish through to amber, and the darker the colour the more advanced the deterioration. Extreme brittleness also indicates an advanced stage of deterioration.

Acetate-based film

Before the First World War the first 'safety base' was produced. This was cellulose diacetate and, although it proved inadequate as a professional motion picture film base because of poor geometrical stability, tensile strength and flexibility, it was used from 1922 onwards as a base for 16 mm amateur film. The search for a safety base with improved physical and chemical properties led next to the production in 1931 of a basetype made from mixed cellulose esters, and although this was an improvement on diacetate it was still not tough enough to withstand 35 mm theatrical use. Research therefore continued and in the early 1940s cellulose triacetate was developed. In its earliest form its application was limited because it proved only of limited solubility in conventional solvents, but by 1948 a slightly less esterified form of cellulose triacetate (high acetyl) was manufactured. This overcame the solubility problem and it rapidly became the prefered base for theatrical production and exhibition as well as for photographic sheet negatives.

Acetate-based film is comparatively stable under good storage conditions. These depend on a balance between temperature and RH, but of the two humidity is the more critical. Prolonged dry storage conditions cause the acetate base to shrink and become brittle and the gelatin may also begin to flake away from the base. High RH on the other hand, promotes the growth of fungi, and, under such conditions, the plasticizer in the base tend to form crystals. Moreover, the gelatin layer becomes soft and its capacity to absorb moisture can result in linear expansion as well as distortion of the image (Sargent, 1974). Sudden swift temperature fluctuations may also encourage the detachment of the emulsion from the base. The most damaging conditions of all are temperatures above 24°C coupled with RH exceeding 60 per cent. Ideally RH should be held between 40–50 per cent with temperatures between 10–12°C, but higher or lower temperatures can be tolerated as long as humidity is controlled.

Polyester-based film

Polymers of the polyester type have been introduced to replace acetate base in a number of film stocks. The chemical name for this material is polyethylene terephtholate. Super 8 mm and 16 mm magnetic tracks are now routinely produced on this base and it is gradually replacing acetate as a support for both amateur and professional photographic sheet negatives.

Accelerated ageing tests indicate that polyester is equal to, or better than, acetate. It has great tensile strength, high dimensional stability and greater resistance to extremes of temperature. Unfortunately its use has not yet been extended to the intermediate fine-grain stocks which are normally used to produce the archival record of cinematographic film productions, because of unresolved problems in binding the emulsion firmly to the polyester base.

Glass-based photographic material

Glass, (an inert transparent material), is an ideal support for negative emulsions, but it is also bulky, heavy and extremely fragile. While it is no longer used for most photography, except for certain technical applications where dimensional stability is very important, many earlier photographs exist as glass negatives. Handling must be kept to a minimum and temperature and humidity held at levels similar to those for acetate film.

Paper-based gelatin prints

The paper used for early paper prints was produced from linen and cotton rags, but as the demand for paper increased it became difficult for manufacturers of photographic material to find rags of sufficient purity since dyes and other additives were being used in the making of cloth. The purity of the base is important since it affects the keeping properties of the emulsion coated on it. This problem led to the development of paper made from purified wood pulp and today's paper bases are made from high alpha cellulose wood-fibre containing additives to provide wet strength and water and chemical resistance.

More recently, resin-coated (RC) paper has been developed. The paper base is coated on both sides with synthetic resins and the gelatin and emulsion layers are coated on top. RC paper is water-resistant, washes more thoroughly and has a shorter drying and fixing time than ordinary paper base. Its use for archival prints should, however, be avoided since it is a recent development and its keeping properties are not fully understood. In an article on print conservation, Alice Swann (1981) noted that RC paper had 'already shown oxidation problems, and should be expected to suffer worse emulsion difficulties than conventional papers'.

Relative humidity, as with other types of photographic base, is the crucial environmental factor. The different layers expand and contract with fluctuations in humidity, with the paper base being affected least and the emulsion and supercoat layers reacting most. This causes the print to curl with the image inside the curve when RH levels are low and the reverse when humidity is high. If the RH can be held fairly constant, around 40 per cent, this problem is greatly lessened. Temperature is much less crucial, but for long-term archival storage, temperatures of between 10 and 16°C are recommended, although a temperature as high as 20°C can be tolerated if humidity is controlled.

Deterioration of the black–and–white silver image

The photographic silver image is extremely susceptible to chemical change, since the silver of photographic images is very finely divided, occurring in very small particles and clusters of fine filaments. Therefore, it has a very large surface area in relation to its mass, making it far more vulnerable to chemical reaction than bulk silver. The two major chemical reactions in the silver image are oxidization and the formation of silver sulphide both caused by a combination of atmospheric pollutants in the environment and residual processing chemicals in the image itself. Both chemical reactions are accelerated by heat, particularly in the presence of high humidity.

The main visible sign of oxidization is the appearance of spots on the image. In cinematographic film these appear first in the outer layers of the reel while on photographs they are likely to appear first as yellowing of the highlights, spreading to the mid-tones or areas of middle silver density as oxidization increases.

Oxidizing factors include pollutants in the air such as hydrogen sulphide, ammonia, sulphur dioxide, ozone and nitrogen oxides. Where there is a wide variety of industrial processes producing such pollutants, for example, areas of dense population, it is desirable to introduce an air-filtering system into the archival storage area. It should also be noted that no photograph or film should be stored near an electrostatic copying machine since this gives off ozone (Collings and Young, 1977).

Other oxidizing agents include peroxides given off by deteriorating paper and cardboard storage materials, paint fumes, some plastics and bleached woods. Wooden storage cabinets and shelving should therefore be avoided and if they are already in use should be replaced by metal ones as soon as possible. Deteriorating paper or cardboard storage materials should also be replaced with clean acid-free papers or polyester sleeves which are chemically inert. If polyester or mylar sleeves are used to store gelatin prints however, it is essential that humidity is controlled since at high RH the gelatin will swell, become sticky and adhere to the smooth waterproof polyester surface with disastrous results.

The formation of silver sulphide on photographic images is closely connected to oxidization since it occurs whenever oxidized silver contacts a source of active sulphide. Silver sulphide is the layer of tarnish which appears on all silver ware, and on photographic prints it is usually first seen along the edges where oxidization has occurred. The image turns brownish yellow, begins to fade and may in time disappear completely.

Although active sulphur is present in polluted air and in some storage materials, the major source is unfortunately frequently contained in the film or photograph itself.

Residual traces of sulphur-containing chemicals, sodium thiosulphate or ammonium thiosulphate used in fixing the image and silver compounds formed by the fixing reaction are often left behind after poor processing and washing. These residual chemicals and silver compounds react with the silver of the image to form silver sulphide. Paper prints are particularly susceptible to this problem because the fibrous construction of the paper base does not wash free of residual chemicals as easily as the comparatively impenetrable film bases. Collections containing many news photographs are certain to contain many examples of yellowing and fading due to residual chemicals since such prints are likely to have had quick and poor processing.

The problem is compounded by the fact that it is impossible to tell simply by inspection which prints contain harmful residual chemicals, since a print in apparently good condition may much later begin to stain and fade.

Two tests are commonly recommended to determine whether residual silver thiosulphate complex or thiosulphate itself are present in a print. These are 'Kodak Hypo Test Solution ST–1' and 'Kodak Hypo Test Solution HT–2 (Eastman Kodak Co., 1979). Unfortunately, these tests are not suitable for archival prints since they involve dropping the solutions onto the margin or highlight area of a print to see whether a stain is formed. If a stain is produced residual chemicals are present, but as this stain is permanent the print itself has been irretrievably damaged.

In a collection where there are many prints whose processing is suspect, it may be best to treat the prints against residual chemicals by reprocessing. This involves refixing and treating with a washing aid such as Kodak Hypo Clearing Agent followed by immersion in hypo eliminating agent and finally rewashing very thoroughly. Unfortunately reprocessing of older prints in this way may present some problems, since the wet strength of some early paper bases is very poor and these prints will require very gentle and careful handling if they are to survive the treatment.

Colour materials

The deterioration of colour in film and photographs is a chemical process in which the colour dyes of all three layers are destroyed. Discolouration or fading does not usually take place uniformly since the different pigments react differently to destructive agents in the atmosphere which may destroy the colour balance in a remarkably short space of time under adverse conditions. The process of deterioration in colour film and photographs is therefore more complex than for silver-based monochrome prints, and there are many areas of uncertainty in its archival preservation. It is, however, clear that high temperatures and high RH greatly increase the rate of fading and that storage at low temperatures with correspondingly low RH will lengthen the life of any colour film. The International Federation of Film Archives recommends storage of archival cinematographic film at −5°C with RH between 20–30 per cent; the film being preconditioned to the required level of humidity and placed in a sealed container before going into the cold store. Moreover, they stress that the temperature must not rise much above −5°C while in store since it has been observed that between −2 and +2°C the adhesive substratum between the base and emulsion deteriorates, causing detachment of the emulsion layer. Clearly, few archives can afford to operate such strict controls and most institutions are forced to compromise, storing their colour materials, whether film or photographs, at +2°C to +5°C with the RH between 15–30 per cent for acetate and 25–30 per cent for polyester-based materials.

It has also been found that the slower the film used to make a colour film or photograph, the better its resistance to fading. Therefore, new archival prints and negatives should be produced using the slowest film available.

Due to the inherent instability of the dyes used in colour film and photographs and the difficulties in maintaining the storage conditions required to prevent fading, it has been traditionally held that the best method of ensuring archival permanence is to produce three colour separations on black-and-white stock. This is probably still the best long-term solution and it should certainly be considered for any important item in a collection. However, this method produces other problems for the archivist. It automatically increases the cost of storage since three reels of film or three photographic negatives must be stored instead of one, and the greatest care must be taken to ensure that all three separation masters are stored in identical conditions to prevent varying amounts of expansion, shrinkage or curl between the different copies, which would make the exact registration essential to reconstituting the full colour image impossible.

Thus, there is no simple solution to the conservation and storage of colour film and this is an area in which a great deal of work remains to be done.

In conclusion, it must be stressed that the chemical reactions described above, whether one is dealing with black-and-white or colour images, are greatly slowed if temperature and humidity are controlled. These are the two most crucial environmental factors in the storage of film and photographs whether from the point of view of the base, the gelatin substratum or the image-bearing emulsion layer. Thus, their control must be a major priority for any archive storing photographic material.

Acknowledgements

I should like to thank the following for help and advice given during the preparation of this paper: Jane Carmichael, Department of Photographs, Imperial War Museum; Michelle Snapes, Head of Stills Library, National Film Archive and David Walsh, Department of Film, Imperial War Museum.

References

ASHMORE, S. A., ELLIS, L. AND HUTCHINSON, A. L. (1957), *Surveillance of Cinematograph Record Film During Storage,* British Government Chemical Research and Development Establishment and the Department of the Government Chemist Report no. 2/R/48. (Reproduced in summarized form in Eastman Kodak Co Data Book.)

BOWSER, E. AND KUIPER, J. (1980) (Ed.), *A Handbook for Film Archives,* FIAF Secretariat, Brussels – based on the experiences of members of the International Federation of Film Archives (FIAF)

COLLINGS, T. J. AND YOUNG, F. J. (1977), *The Care of Photographic Collections,* Area Museums Service for S. E. England, Milton Keynes

EASTMAN KODAK CO. (March, 1957), *Storage and Preservation of Motion Picture Film,* Kodak Data Book, Eastman Kodak Co., Rochester, NY

EASTMAN KODAK CO. (1979), *Preservation of Photographs,* Kodak Publication No. F. 30 Eastman Kodak, Rochester, NY

OSTROFF, E. (1976), *Conserving and Restoring Photographic Collections,* American Association of Museums, Washington DC – an updated and revised version of 4 technical reports first published in the May, September, November and December 1974 issues of *Museum News*

SARGENT, R. M. (1974), *Preserving the Moving Image,* Corporation for Public Broadcasting and the National Endowment for the Arts, USA

SWANN, A. (1981), *The Care and Conservation of Photographic Materials,* Crafts Council, London

41

Classical antiquities – forgeries and reproductions

Donald M. Bailey

There has been, since the Renaissance, a greater demand for the artefacts of Greece and Rome than finds of actual antiquities could supply. Engraved gems and cameos, in particular, were highly prized by collectors, and many of the finest 'Greek' and 'Roman' gems in museum collections today are products of the sixteenth to nineteenth centuries. Indeed, although the antiquity of many an ancient gem is easily determined with a little experience, and while many non-ancient gems are readily recognized, there is a whole middle ground, mostly of engraved gems and cameos of the highest quality, where even the most expert student of the subject can have no certainty, but can only guess. Gems and cameos both ancient and more recent come occasionally onto the market, but there can be few artisans these days skilful enough to produce forgeries of really fine gems. However, more and more interest is being shown of late by collectors, and good forgeries might well start to be made again.

Gold jewellery is another fruitful field for forgers as it can command a high price; gold normally bears no sign of ageing, and style is the main visual criterion for accepting or condemning a particular piece. However, it is worth while examining the composition of the gold, as the metal used in most Greek and Roman jewellery is almost pure, while most modern gold is considerably alloyed with base metals. Non-destructive methods of analysis are now extremely accurate. A forger could, however, use broken pieces of ancient jewellery as his raw material. It has been argued that poor workmanship is a bad sign, but there is just as much badly-made jewellery of the classical period as there are other low quality artefacts from antiquity. Over the past twenty years or so, a large quantity of 'Etruscan' jewellery has emanated from Italy. It is often on a much larger scale than is ancient jewellery, and sometimes exhibits low-grade granulation work. For really fine modern gra-

nulation (but not the finest dust-like globules on some Etruscan pieces) one has to go back to the products of the Castellani family, working in Italy in the middle years of the nineteenth century. They made unequivocal modern jewellery copying ancient forms, but as dealers in antiquities they often repaired and made good ancient but broken articles before selling them.

Sculpture in marble and other stones has always attracted collectors, landowners with country houses to embellish, and museums, and forgers have readily produced statues and busts for this lucrative trade. The only portrait of Caesar and the best portrait of Nero in the collections of the British Museum were both probably made as early as the seventeenth century. As most collectors preferred complete pieces, the restorers' workshops in eighteenth-century Rome were adept at completing even the most truncated ancient fragment, so one gets, for example, the torso of a Roman marble copy of Myron's bronze Discobolus, transfigured into a rather contorted Diomedes stealing the Palladium by the addition of all four limbs, a head and a small figure of Minerva, all modern. To determine what is ancient, what is broken and replaced, what is ancient but alien and what is restoration is not always easy, and analysis of the marbles of such a pastiche is often helpful, as is the use of ultra-violet light to distinguish patching and recent overworking. In more recent times, the master forger Dossena (1878–1937) made superb examples of Greek archaic statuary which convinced many scholars, and there are pieces of sculpture whose antiquity is still not proven to everyone's satisfaction: the Boston Throne, for example.

At the lower end of the market, peasants with a little imagination, less skill and a sharp knife have, throughout the Mediterranean, carved small pieces of limestone into extraordinarily inept human figures and sold them to travellers as antiquities. From the

368

so-called Baphomets of the mid-eighteenth century, to the 'Siculan' figures of the 1860s (examples of both groups are in the British Museum), to the works of modern Turkish Cypriots and inhabitants of Tunisia, these figures, bearing a family likeness imposed by the material and the ignorance of the makers, are legion and they may well be brought to museums for identification.

There is always a market for fine bronze and brass figures of Greek, Etruscan and Roman origin, both small and large, and forgers have not failed to make good its deficiencies. Most forgeries tend to be of small-scale objects, as the casting of life-size sculpture is a formidable task, particularly in these days of high technology. But heads 'broken' from statues are not beyond the modern forger. The difficulty with copper alloys is to build up a convincing series of corrosion products in the induced patination, which many of the forgeries affect. It is not easy, perhaps impossible, to reproduce the copper alloy/red cuprite/green malachite sequence, with natural adhesion between the layers, of a well-patinated ancient bronze. However, ancient bronzes sometimes lack these features, depending upon the conditions of burial: Roman objects from the mud of the Walbrook in London, for instance, can appear no different from the day they were lost. Thus, the lack of a patination is no firm objection to the antiquity of an object.

Some collectors in the past have cleaned all such corrosion products from the bronzes. Richard Payne Knight, despite deploring the restoration of marble sculpture, had something very odd done to the bronzes in his superb collection, bequeathed to the British Museum in 1824. The majority appear to have been stripped of their patination and given a polished brown surface. The compositions of ancient bronzes and brasses are now being actively analyzed, and the examination of a small drilling is often conclusive in determining whether an object is likely to have been made in antiquity.

Until fairly recently, when the work of Schumann, Bimson and Noble showed the materials and processes involved, the production of a convincing Greek vase was not really possible. Science and archaeology are in their debt but so, unfortunately, is the forger. But to suggest that such technical information should not be published, as has been done, is to argue against the very real contributions of the scientist to the study of the past, and these results just cannot be hidden. Although fired-on ceramic colourings of different compositions have been used in the past, these normally produced results which were unlike Greek black glaze. The only way to make a realistic vase was to fire the pot and paint it afterwards, and such colouring matter can be removed with solvents. Many a vase made in this fashion has found its way into museums and pri-

vate collections. Nowadays, such is the accuracy with which forgers can emulate Greek glazing techniques that it is only lapses in painting styles and the shaping of the pots which indicate their falsity. One has to fall back on subjective art-historical criteria. Fortunately, most forgers do give themselves away in this manner, but there must be highly skilled practitioners against whom the only weapons are clay analysis and thermoluminescence examination (and even here it is said that irradiation methods can circumvent the latter). Most good forgeries of Greek vases are made in Italy, and some in France; some are sold openly as reproductions. Samian ware, which employed the same production techniques as Greek black glaze, except for a reduction-firing phase, is also being produced. Other aspects of vase falsifying to watch for include the extensive replacement of missing portions combined with complete over-painting to give the effect of an unbroken vessel, the scratching away of the glaze of undecorated vases to produce 'red-figured' scenes, and the cutting of inscriptions to add interest to ancient plain pots.

In the 1870s the cemeteries of the Greek city of Tanagra in Boeotia were discovered, the tombs of which often contained exquisite terracotta statuettes, many of these attractive figures of draped women. These, together with terracottas from Myrina in Asia Minor, discovered a few years later, were much prized by collectors and connoisseurs. When the supply dried up as the cemeteries were worked out, enterprising forgers continued to supply the market. Not only Tanagra ladies were made, but many complex mythological groups, alleged to be from Asia Minor, were produced, often in a romantic prettified style owing more to nineteenth-century concepts of decorative art than to anything conceived of by Hellenistic Greeks. Although giving the impression of being mould-produced objects, many of these figures and groups were hand-modelled one-off pieces; they commanded very high prices indeed in the sale-rooms of Europe. They were eventually exposed by the savant Salomon Reinach (who himself was deceived decades later by the forgeries of Glozel). The output of the more spectacular of these groups was probably not very great, but examples survive in the collections of museums, and others may well be brought into museums from time to time. Other terracotta forgeries include the large-scale Etruscan warriors in the Metropolitan Museum of Art in New York, made by the Riccardi family at Orvieto during and immediately after the First World War. Comparable to these is the Penelli Sarcophagus in the British Museum, sold to that institution in 1873 by Alessandro Castellani, and made a few years prior to that by the Penelli brothers. The difficulties of firing such a large object are such that, like the New York Etruscan Warriors, it was probably modelled, broken up, the fragments fired in small kilns, and then was pieced together.

Probably one of the most forgery-beset fields of small antiquities is that of pottery lamps. At least as early as the beginning of the eighteenth century false lamps have been made for hapless collectors. Between 1739 and 1754 Cardinal Passeri published his lamp collection in three sumptuous volumes: a very large proportion of these are false. Since then false lamps have been made in large numbers, principally in Italy in the nineteenth century, but now everywhere the tourist treads in Mediterranean lands, forgeries or reproductions of lamps are offered him. In Turkey, Egypt, Petra, Cyprus and Cathage false lamps are for sale to the unwary, and these are brought back to Britain. Unlike the eighteenth- and nineteenth-century examples, most of these are of appallingly bad workmanship, much worse than the poorest of Roman products.

Ancient glass, in the main the product of illicit tomb-robbings, is possibly the most frequent class of classical artefact to be seen in sale-room catalogues in recent years, and is very popular with collectors. Even here, where the supply seems adequate to meet the demand, forgeries are found. In most cases, because of the difficulties of producing glass vessels both ancient in shape and in physical appearance, the majority of forgeries are easy to recognize, but there are some convincing specimens which are hard to detect.

The curator must also be aware of the presence of reproductions, not made to deceive, but sold legitimately as souvenirs. These can be very fine pieces of work, although the majority of souvenirs are trashy objects with only a superficial resemblance to the originals they purport to copy. But decorative bronzes made in the eighteenth and early-nineteenth centuries for neo-classical interiors are often of high class workmanship and are often difficult to recognize as not ancient. In the second half of the nineteenth century and the early part of the twentieth, there were many foundries in Naples making very close copies of ancient artefacts in bronze, and also in marble and terracotta. Such firms as de Angelis, Sommer and Chiurazzi were very prolific, and it is fortunate that many issued illustrated catalogues from which their products can nowadays be recognized. Once such souvenirs change hands or are even thrown away and found again, their origin is forgotten and they are brought to museums for identification or are sold as ancient in sale-rooms. For example, about twenty years ago a bronze was found buried deep in the earth and was described in a national newspaper by an unwary museum curator as one of the finest bronzes from Roman Britain yet found. The response was immediate: several readers wrote to say that they had one just like it, as a garden ornament in one case. The bronze turned out to be a copy of the so-called Narcissus found at Pompeii in 1862, examples of which were made in various sizes by Naples foundries.

Forgeries have been made in every culture where collecting the products of the past becomes fashionable or is regarded as an investment. The range of classical forgeries is much wider than has been described briefly above, and embraces such things as wall-paintings, mosaics, sarcophagi, Minoan objects, and, recently, those popular and pricey objects, marble Cycladic idols. Scientific analysis of the composition of the substances of which an object is made is becoming more and more useful, but forgers are constantly seeking to counteract this work, using the very results of the scientists to aid them. Thus, present day forgeries can be among the most difficult to detect, much more so than counterfeit objects of the past. Museums must beware of out-and-out forgeries, fine quality reproductions and highly restored objects. With most of the objects discussed here, years of experience, working with and constantly handling the material is the main defence, and this expertise is not easily acquired by the curator of a small museum with a non-specialized collection; it is here that national Museums may be of use to provincial institutions.

Bibliography

General

KURZ, O. , (1948), *Fakes*, London
PAUL, E. (1962), *Die Falsche Gottin*, Leipzig
PAUL, E. (1981), *Gefälschte Antike*, Leipzig

Particular

BAILEY, D. M. (1974), Taormina Forgeries in the British Museum, ΚΩΚΑΛΟΣ **XX**, 172–183
VON BOTHMER, D. AND NOBLE, J. V. (1961), *An Inquiry into the Forgery of the Etruscan Terracotta Warriors*, New York
LUSETTI, W. (1955), *Alceo Dossena, Scultore*, Rome

Reproductions

CHIURAZZI, J. ET FILS – DE ANGELIS, S. ET FILS(1914), *Fonderie Artistiche Riunite, Bronzes, Marbres, Argenterie*, Naples
SOMMER, G. (1984), *Fonderie Artistique en Bronze, Atelier de Sculpture en Marbre*, Naples

42

Coins: fakes and forgeries

John P. C. Kent

The recognition of the very competent coin forgeries which have been produced in modern times will generally be beyond the powers of curators without specialist training and interest. There remain, however, many forgeries that can be detected with greater facility, and curators with access to a well-arranged general collection should not despair of becoming competent judges of authenticity.

General principles

Most coins are (relatively) mass-produced objects, and even if individually rare, will conform to the norms of *style, form* (fabric), *metrology* and *technique* of their series. The detection of forgeries is, therefore, essentially a matter of comparison, and objects of undoubted authenticity provide the essential base of reference. Forgeries are of two kinds: those made contemporaneously with the genuine prototypes, and designed to enter circulation; and those made in order to deceive collectors. The two categories are mainly, but not totally, mutually exclusive. For instance, certain false silver half-crowns made early in this century for currency bore dates never found on authentic pieces and some have been sold in recent years to collectors as genuine rarities. Such contemporary forgeries for currency have an evidential value related to that of the prototypes, and are 'false' in a different sense of the second category, to which the ensuing remarks will be largely restricted.

How forgeries are made

The identification of the way in which a piece has been made will often suffice, on its own, to condemn a fake. Most coins have been produced by striking a prepared blank between two engraved dies. These have been produced by freehand engraving or by the use of a master punch or (earlier) punches. The resulting design, however crude, possesses a characteristic *style,* that a modern engraver working with modern tools finds difficult to reproduce. Most coins down to the later seventeenth century were either struck by hammer-blows upon the upper die, or by machinery that has become entirely obsolete; these methods produced coins of characteristic *fabric* (outline, thickness, edge, flatness), which are almost impossible to recreate in modern workshops. Since, on the whole, style betrays his hand more readily than fabric, the forger has sometimes sought to reproduce designs onto dies by some facsimile process, such as spark-erosion.

Metrology – correct weight and dimension – is the characteristic most easily achieved by the forger, and one can only be surprised and gratified at how often he has failed to pay attention to these details. With the development of non-destructive techniques of analysis, metrology now has a new dimension – metallic composition. The coinage alloys of antiquity were often of some complexity, and their composition is now known to have varied in a systematic way. It requires unusual knowledge and skill to reproduce the correct alloy. This can be achieved to some extent by melting down genuine contemporary pieces, but this renders much forgery unprofitable, and is not without its own pitfalls.

Many false coins are *cast* rather than struck. Style remains, of course, that of the original, and certain details can, if desired, be altered on the mould before use; but the other characteristics invariably suffer, to an extent dependent on the skill of the forger. Casting in a two-piece mould, despite its relative simplicity, is employed surprisingly often, no doubt on account of its technical simplicity. It relies, often with success, on the collector's unfamiliarity with authentic material. More refined methods can, however, give a dangerously convincing finish to the cast. In recent times, the flow of metal in stationary moulds has been accelerated by electro-magnetic and vacuum processes, or by centrifugal action in rotating moulds.

Forgeries can be made by electrotyping, though it usually happens that the electrotypes themselves were originally made for study or exhibition, and have subsequently fallen into dishonest hands. The abuse of authentic coins is also to be guarded against. Examples include the numerous 'double-headed' pennies, and rarities such as the 1933 penny. A variety of tools and skills, which should not be underestimated, have been employed to achieve these results.

Probabilities

It would obviously be wrong for the curator to assume that everything unusual that is brought to him is false. On the other hand, he would be unwise to lend too credulous an ear to the circumstantial tales which may be told in justification of the piece almost, if not quite, too good to be true. Many a fake has been accepted because it 'had a provenance' or because the person showing it 'could not have known enough to make up such a story, unless it were true'.

Always reserve judgement until the suspect object can be examined unhurriedly and dispassionately, and away from the urgent representations of the owner or would-be vendor. Under no circumstances, write a 'certificate of authenticity' for a specific piece. Even if the object *is* genuine, the authentication may eventually be attached to a fake of similar type. When it is necessary, a formula such as 'the object (coin and so on) I have examined is, *in my opinion,* authentic', should satisfy the genuine enquirer; always write the identification itself on a separate sheet of paper, such as the envelope in which the coin is placed.

Some forgeries and their characteristics

Casts

The product of the two-piece mould is generally recognizable by its blurred appearance; details are much less distinct than the apparent state of wear warrants. For instance, the enclosed portions of letters such as ABP and R may be largely filled in. Lines in the design may show unaccountable weaknesses or breaks, while the extremities of details are often deformed or missing. The design does not meet the

field at a sharp angle, but at a curve. Pock-marks on the surface are due to air-bubbles; sometimes the surface has been tooled over to remove these, but there remains a scraped and soapy finish. The edge of a cast sometimes shows traces of a raised line, marking the junction between the two halves of the mould. Generally, however, this line will have been tooled off, leaving a smooth and vertical edge unusual in an authentic early coin. Large ancient coins sometimes split at the edge in striking; look out for such 'splits' that appear on each face, but that do not go right through the flan, or are incorrectly positioned with regard to each other – sure signs of a cast copy. Such casts may show every sign of age. Not only were they made by counterfeiters in antiquity, but they have been produced for unwary collectors at least from the seventeenth century down to the present day. Casts of this character are not necessarily of rare coins. Early casts often appear to be very small; this is due to shrinkage of the mould.

Pressure-cast pieces are all recent, and are generally of silver or gold coins. They can be difficult to recognize, but may sometimes be distinguished by a tendency for the relief of the lettering and outer border to fail to match that of the centre of the design. The surface, too, may appear lifeless and slightly soft. These fakes are usually very clean and 'new' in appearance; any toning will have been artificially induced, and will have a shallow and chemical look.

A cast, when balanced on the finger and tapped with a coin, will not 'ring' in the same way as a struck piece. Absence of a 'ring', however, may also result from cracks or degradation of metal structure, and is not of itself proof of falseness. It should be remarked here that numerous replicas produced and sold by museums, or made privately, or as advertising material, make excellent bases for cast forgeries, whatever they themselves be made of.

Struck forgeries

Some of the best-struck forgeries were produced more than a century ago. They are, therefore, well known and well-published – but also widely disseminated. The products of Becker (mainly Greek and Roman) and Emery (mainly medieval and Tudor) are still dangerous because of the skill of the forgers in reproducing the styles and fabrics of their chosen periods. Older struck pieces often copied the engraved plates of books rather than originals, and have a correspondingly unconvincing style and finish. Modern strikings may be made by machinery exerting greater pressure than was available in earlier times, and such forgeries often show greater and more even definition, particularly at the circumference, and higher relief, than the genuine article. Almost all large ancient and medieval coins show traces of double-striking – evidence of the 'jumping' of the upper die under repeated blows. The total absence of this feature gives grounds for suspicion.

Curators are recommended not to attempt the authentication of modern gold coins; the recognition of such forgeries is a very difficult and technical process that should be referred to specialists.

Electrotypes

These are formed by two thin shells of copper, appropriately coloured on the surface, backed and joined together by another metal, often lead. Electrotypes may therefore show signs of a junction running round the edge, though this can easily be plated over. Look on the edge for the small impressed letters BM or RR, showing the piece to have been produced long ago as a British Museum replica. Electrotypes never 'ring' and due to their composition their weights are almost always wrong.

Alterations to authentic coins

The purpose is usually to make a rare coin out of a common one, or to 'improve' the design or inscription of a poor specimen. In the case of altered dates, two techniques are used. The appropriate digit may be altered by the skilful use of the engraver's tool; or it may be completely cut away from the surface and replaced by the required figure which has been moulded from some other source. The new digit will generally lack the sharp outline of a genuine figure, and under high magnification, traces of the solder with which it has been fixed may appear. 'Double-headed' coins, or other incompatible combinations of head and tail, are sometimes produced by grinding away one face up to the rim, and inserting in the hollow thus created the required portion cut from some other piece. The join should be sought just inside the raised rim of one face, where there will generally be found a slight deformation of the beaded border. Such a composite piece will, of course, not 'ring' correctly.

A suggested procedure

If one is asked to authenticate a coin, it is useful to give some thought to the possible motivation and technique of a potential forger. If the piece appears to be a rare (or documentarily impossible) variant of a common coin – for example, the 1933 penny – then alteration of an authentic object should be suspected. Great rarities in the classical series, particularly if they are Greek, often turn out to be electrotype copies. Try to decide how a piece has been made, and if it looks 'new'. Ring it, examine its edge and surface, look at the definition of the detail of the lettering and design, and compare it, if possible, with material already in the collection, as well as with catalogue illustrations. Weigh it, and see if the weight is plausible.

Do not be discouraged by the failure of a piece to appear in a standard work. Unrecorded varieties and even types are constantly turning up, and the forger is more likely to reproduce a known rarity than to attempt a novelty. But if in real doubt, it is better to refer the enquiry to a specialist rather than to accept – or condemn – a piece on unsure grounds.

Bibliography

BOON, G. C. (1974), 'Counterfeit coins in Roman Britain' in Casey, J. and Reece, R. (Eds.), *Coins and the Archaeologist* pp. 95–171

HILL, G. F. (1924–1925), *Becker the Counterfeiter*, London

KLAWANS, Z. H. (1977), *Imitations and Inventions of Roman coins*, Santa Monica

LAWRENCE, L. A. (1904), Forgery in relation to numismatics, British Numismatic Journal 2, 397–410

NEWMAN, E. V. G. (1976 onwards) (Ed.), International Bureau for the Suppression of Counterfeit Coins, *Bulletin on Counterfeits*, London

PAGAN, H. E. (1971), Mr Emery's mint, *British Numismatic Journal*, **40**, 139–170

SECTION THREE

VISITOR SERVICES

Section Editors

Douglas A. Bassett
and
David R. Prince

43

Introduction

Douglas A. Bassett and David R. Prince

Museums have been booming in popularity both in Britain and elsewhere in an unprecedented fashion since the early 1960s. It has been estimated, for example, that during the mid 1970s as many as twenty-five million people visited museums in Britain as a whole. A recent English Tourist Board survey indicated that over 24 per cent of the adult population of England visited museums in 1981 – an estimated total of over ten million people.

Some of the reasons advanced for this trend have been the influence of television, the growth of tourism and the revolution in teaching methods in schools. Others have included the considerable upsurge in the concern for the conservation of both the natural and the man-made heritage, and the very definite growth of a general feeling of nostalgia.

The museum visitor

As far as the nature of the museum public is concerned, few generalizations are possible because it differs from country to country, from region to region and even from museum to museum. It is possible to state, however, that almost any museum public is extremely heterogeneous in its make-up, that it is composed of people from a wide range of age-levels and with varying economic, ethnic, social and educational backgrounds. However, it is clear from recent research that visitors are drawn largely from the upper and middle social classes (see, for example, English Tourist Board, 1982). Moreover, the range is qualitative as well as quantitative in that the visitors have widely varying levels of literacy, numeracy and graphicacy (or visual-spacial understanding) (see, for example, Boardman, 1983) and that they include representatives of the four main types of personality which correspond to the four major modes of mental activity (thinking, feeling, sensation and intuition) and to four distinct modes of perception. Individuals are also motivated to visit museums for different reasons. The Director of the National Museum of Ethnology at Leiden in the Netherlands, for example, distinguished three *motives* amongst visitors, each of which he considered made particular demands on the way in which the museum displays its material. He isolated the aesthetic, the romantic (or escapist) and the intellectual (or the wish to satisfy a thirst for knowledge).

In spite of the diversity of the museum public, it is helpful to try and group them so that, if possible, various 'models' of visitor behaviour can be constructed. A quotation from Paul Perrot's chapter in *The Smithsonian Experience* (1977) provides a useful starting point and underlines the fact that the major services provided by museums are based on the collections:

> Collections are the essential raison d'etre of museums. They are the source from which the museum's unique role in the cultural fabric of society emanates. They are the basis of its contribution to scholarship, the instruments of its educational role, and the cause of its public enlightenment. (p. 76)

Such a grouping identifies three groups of people which, although not mutually exclusive, are readily distinguishable:

(1). The person involved in the advancement of knowledge in a particular discipline – the scholar or research worker (and it may be appropriate to include the professional man and 'the collector' in this category).
(2). The person involved in the formal education system – the pupil and the teacher; at primary, secondary and tertiary level.
(3). The person with little, if any, systematic knowledge of a particular subject – a member of the so called 'public'.

These subdivisions are virtually identical to those proposed – apparently for the first time – by Francis Bather in his Presidential Address to The Museums Association in 1903. Bather considered the main functions of a museum to be 'Investigation, Instruction and Inspiration', appealing respectively to the 'Specialist, the Student and Man in the Street'.

Services for all three groups are described and discussed in this section and elsewhere in the *Manual*.

Museum schools and educational services

P. Graham Carter's paper on Educational Services within the museum begins with a short introductory section on the history and current situation of such services in Britain, and from this isolates a number of important considerations elaborated throughout the remaining parts of the paper. The benefits of museum education services are discussed in detail from the viewpoint of the recipients of such benefits, including students, teachers, local education authorities and the museum itself. A second section deals with the planning involved in establishing a museum educational service in relation to staff, accommodation, objects and equipment. Various categories of museum services are discussed from an initial understanding of intramural and extramural services, and their sub-groups of direct services to students and teachers, and indirect services to the general public and schools, through, for example, publications. A further distinction between formal and informal services is elaborated. An indication of the range of services available is made through an understanding of the role and function of, for example, lecture theatres, gallery tours, workrooms and teachers' notes. Of the extramural services, loan services and mobile services are discussed in detail as are field trips, and informal educational activities relating to clubs and holiday activities.

Adult education receives independent assessment and its relationship to Friends Organizations is discussed. The problems of establishing and maintaining an educational service in a small museum are elaborated in detail, as are the steps required to establish such a museums service and the relationship between, for example, the museum and the local authority and various educational institutions. In the concluding section, the wider role of the educational staff is discussed, particularly in the way they can contribute to the development of exhibitions, publications, and to the general interpretive work of the museum, be it large or small.

Stephen Locke's paper picks up some of the points made by P. Graham Carter in an understanding of the relations between educational and curatorial and administrative staff needed to fulfil the museum's central functions. Running throughout the paper is the understanding that such functions can only be fulfilled satisfactorily if staff from a variety of subject specialisms contribute to the fulfilment of the museum's overall policy objectives. Taken on a section basis, the paper discusses the administrative function of museums, the educational function, the use of collections, the overall security of both buildings and objects, environmental control within museums, and accessioning procedures. Other topics discussed include loans, transport, insurance, and health and safety at work. Particular emphasis is given to financial control and the use of secretarial and clerical support, together with personnel matters and display policy, the last area clearly overlapping with those ideas discussed in the section on Exhibitions.

The range of services

Many, if not most, museums do provide a wide range of services, both indoor and outdoor. These include: temporary and permanent exhibitions, publications, advice and information from experts, guided tours and gallery talks, activities for children, evening lectures, films and audio-visual programmes and extension (or extra-mural) programmes (including expeditions and guided walks), refreshments as well as other facilities and social events. In addition, many museums also provide a specifically educational service to both school and college students. Before discussing the main services it is as well to point out that all support services, including toilets, catering facilities and cloakrooms should be of a high standard as they reflect – just as much as the formal services – on the museums, overall image.

The three major services (provided in one way or another by every museum) are: the preparation and mounting of exhibitions; the publication of books, catalogues, and various ephemera; and the giving of advice and information. Each of these is considered in separate papers in this Section of the *Manual* and are introduced separately a little later in this introduction.

In most museums the Departmental structure was initially based entirely on subject matter. During the three decades 1950 to 1980, however, a period described by one commentator as the 'didactic period' in the history of museum development, 'a movement of evangelical fervour for the recognition of the educational purpose of museums burst forth in the early 1950s and one after the other, museums large and small vied with each other in setting up Schools Services' and, to a lesser extent, Educational Departments. In the last decade or so there has been a tendency to create separate Public Service Departments (*see*, for example, the final section in W. T. Stearn's *The Natural History Museum at South Kensington* (1981), which outlines the background to the creation of such a department in the British Museum (Natural History).

Visitor services relative to other museum activities

Visitor services cannot, however, be seen in isolation: they are part of a hierarchy of other activities and their position in it is determined by a particular museum's philosophy.

In the British Museum (Natural History), for example, the allocation of money for the Institution's two main functions – taxonomic research and public education – is broadly 80 per cent for the scientific work and 20 per cent for exhibition and education.

In the recent review of the national museums and galleries of Scotland, for example (*A Heritage for Scotland, Scotland's National Museums and Galleries, the Next 25 years,* Williams 1981), each of the six institutions investigated regarded acquisition, conservation, research and security of collections as primary functions. Presenting and interpreting collections for the public was ranked as a lesser activity. And in their report on *Conservation,* the then Standing Commission on Museums and Galleries considered that in a time of cut-back 'conservation of objects should have a clear priority'.

The problems of determining the relative importance of particular museum functions is discussed in the chapter entitled 'The present dichotomy' in Ian Finlays (1977) book *Priceless Heritage.*

Museum subjects (or perspectives)

Such services have to be provided in a diversity of subjects which cover a wide spectra of the humanities, the arts and the sciences. There are, inevitably, a number of different groupings. The then Standing Commission on Museums and Galleries, for example, in preparing its *Framework for a System for Museums* (1979), set up panels of experts to advise on the following groups of collections:

(1) Fine and Decorative Arts.
(2) Natural History and Geology.
(3) Archaeology.
(4) Ethnology and Social History.
(5) Science, Technology and Industrial Archaeology.

George Henri Rivière, on the other hand, in his plan for the Museum of Negro Civilization at Dakar (Unesco Working Paper, 1975), envisaged a fusion of seven disciplines (or, as he preferred to call them, approaches) – anthropological, ecological, technoeconomical, sociological, idealogical, aesthetic and historical. The problems of presentation or interpretation (as indeed of housing, curation and conservation) differ from one group of subjects to another, in part because of the differing size and the differing nature of the materials of the various subjects and because the disciplines themselves vary in their nature.

One striking difference is neatly summed up in the following words by Benjamin Ives Gilman (1918):

> Objects of art were made to be looked at, and looked at they are accordingly. Objects of science were not made to be looked at, and looked at they are, nevertheless. The scientific collection, as the less natural type of exhibition, calls for an independent name. But in default of any convenient term, we shall doubtless use the phrase 'museum science' in spite of its contradiction, and 'museum of art' in spite of its redundancy'

A fundamental distinction exists between the problems of communication in art museums and those in museums of history and natural science. The following quotation from *On Understanding Art Museums* (Lee, 1975) underlines the fact that the problems in the one are only tangentially applicable to those in the other:

> In a science museum, for example, the laws governing planetary revolutions, the genetic structure of cells, or the development of lower vertebrates may not be self-evident, which is to say visually intelligible, without the support of written texts. For the sake of argument I shall assume that the development of artistic structures is much more, possibly almost wholly intelligible with a minimum of peripheral documentation.
>
> From this position I deduce a distinction between the kind of knowledge, usually historical, which is supplied by verbal sources and comprehended by the conscious, rational mind, and the kind of knowledge which grows from artistic experience, conveyed through the senses when confronting a work of art as a work of art. Such knowledge, irreducible to verbal formulae and not easily communicated by one individual to another, is largely nonrational; for the work of art may generate emotional responses from the preconscious and unconscious areas of psychic life.

One of the fullest discussions of this difference is still that of Gilman's *Museum ideals* (1918).

Types of museums

Museums, and the services they offer, vary considerably in size and nature from the 'conventional' civic or national museum in city centres (some of which have been described as 'monolithic') to open-air museums, with re-erected buildings, museums on sites of archaeological importance, industrial buildings or complexes adapted as museums and historic houses. Inevitably different kinds and different sizes and ages of buildings – from the monolithic to the re-erected cottage – create different problems of orientation and crowd management and the provision of other ancillary services.

Access to museums and to their collections

There are generally two aspects to this question. First, the accessibility of a museum (or museums) to the population of an area (*see,* for example, the recent report on the national museums of Scotland in which concern is expressed that the museums concerned should develop 'outreach programmes from the whole of Scotland). Second, the accessibility of the materials in a particular museum to the visitor. It is this second aspect which is considered briefly here.

The problem of access to museums and to their collections is a wide-ranging one and much discussed: it has, for example, been the subject of a recommendation at the Unesco General Conference on 14th December 1960 – a recommendation 'concerning the most effective means of rendering museums accessible to everyone'. It was also a matter under constant review throughout the recent enquiry into the national museums of Scotland.

Some aspects of the problem of access to the collections are indicated in the first paragraph (par. 55) of the section on Public Access in the Rayner Scrutiny (see Burrett, 1982) of the two major Departmental Museums (the Victoria & Albert Museum and the Science Museum):

> The whole concept underlying a great national museum requires that it should aim to make itself and its object available to the public as fully as possible. Such an aim admits of no absolute satisfaction. Moreover, as in other areas, a balance has to be struck. The balance no doubt indicates clearly enough that in principle a museum should open its doors during periods of maximum public demand eg on Saturdays, Sundays and major holidays; and should maximise its opening hours at other times. But at some point the cost of opening according to a particular weekly pattern has, for the greater good of the museum (and therefore of the public) to be balanced against other powerful priorities.

The wider problems of access – both physical access and intellectual and prefaced by an interesting anecdote about 'the Museum Brat Syndrome' and including a summary of early efforts made by the Museum increased access – is given by Duncan F. Cameron in 'Museums and public access: the Glenbow approach' (1982).

Major services

Each of the three major services is introduced separately and a brief introduction is also provided to the relationships of museums and education.

Exhibitions

For the vast majority of visitors, exhibitions represent the primary and traditional means by which the museum reaches and serves – at whatever level and by whatever means – its public. Their formulation, development and presentation are, therefore, of fundamental concern to the museum, and rank – alongside conservation, education and research – as primary museum functions. There can be no doubt that in recent years the adoption of new approaches to exhibition design has transformed the appearance of many museums; although the essential criterion of displaying objects of cultural and natural worth within a sympathetic environment has continued to remain at the centre of this philosophy.

The five papers in the first part of this Section all concentrate on the role and function of exhibitions from the viewpoint of the educational psychologist, the designer and the evaluator. The central theme underpinning all the contributions is that successful exhibition design is a team affair, drawing on the skills and professional experience of specialists in many fields, including subject, design, education and – as a means of focusing and developing these elements – evaluation. Although each exhibition is, by definition, unique, all share characteristics that are available for analysis and comment. The papers in this section focus, therefore, on overall themes rather than specific subjects, with the understanding that it is the way in which each subject is handled within the theme – the way in which the museum adapts, develops and interprets its unique material – that determines success, and failure.

The first paper (by Alt and Griggs) examines the nature of a museum visit from the viewpoint of the visitor, and proposes a radical approach to exhibition design based on an understanding of visitor behaviour and perception. This is contrasted sharply with approaches based on recognizing the overtly identifiable characteristics of the exhibition material, and the strategies of communication employed.

The authors discuss two opposing psychological perspectives used to examine behaviour and learning, and demonstrate how such perspectives have influenced exhibition design – albeit largely unknown to those originating the designs themselves. In so-doing, the notion of the visitor as merely a passive onlooker – absorbing and appreciating material placed before him in previously defined systems outside his control – is replaced by a model of the visitor as an active, selecting, rationalizing individual seeking to impose sense and meaning on the exhibition; meanings couched necessarily in his own terms and stemming from past experience and prior understanding, as well as present circumstance. Having established this base, the paper explores a psychology of the museum visitor, and from this considers areas of behaviour, intention and expectation that an exhibition should seek to fulfil in an attempt to aid the visitor towards the construction of a worthwhile experience. This contrasts sharply with the view that exhibitions should be designed to meet goals and objectives defined and articulated in terms, and in ways, comprehensive only to the museum staff and based solely on *their* understanding of the nature and value of the objects on display.

Two examples from the authors' own experience are used to demonstrate how interest and expectation influence a visitor over and above those factors inherent in the exhibition itself. The crucial role that perception plays in imposing meaning on objects and events is used to demonstrate that any understanding or comprehension of the content of an exhibition comes from the visitor, and is not, in itself, a characteristic of the exhibition. This notion is carried forward in the papers on exhibition evaluation (by Griggs and Prince), where the idea that learning takes place through the organization of new material by previously known and understood frames of reference is used to complement and extend the views expressed here.

The paper concludes by suggesting that curators have adhered to an erroneous and out-dated model of visitors and that this has led to the construction of exhibitions that are difficult to understand and are – in some cases – wholly inappropriate to the visitor and to the act of visiting a museum.

The second and third papers examine the nature, characteristics and development of museum exhibitions. The second (by Velarde) describes a number of types of exhibition based on their physical properties and informative characteristics, and relates these to varying modes of presentation. The paper discusses, in some depth, the input made by designers from divese subject specialisms and the role played by them – and the other staff of the museum – in realizing an exhibition programme. This is developed through an understanding of the role and production of the design brief and the translation of this brief into workable design solutions.

Further sections discuss the physical maintenance of an exhibition and the methods of publicity involved in bringing the completed work to the attention of its intended audience, together with an assessment of the advantages and disadvantages of in-house and freelance design. The conclusion stresses the essential professionalism inherent in such design, and reinforces the important relationship between the designer and curator in the creation and maintenance of an exhibition scheme.

The third paper (by Belcher) focuses on the museum exhibition as a medium of communication and develops this through the designation and implementation of an exhibitions policy as an integral part of the museum's overall policy towards its collections. The nature of the communication strategy is detailed, and its relationship with the general exhibitions policy stated clearly. The factors determining the generation of this policy are made clear, includ-

ing the characteristics of the collection, available space, staff and resources, and the role and input of the curatorial, educational and design staffs. The importance of the visitor is described in detail, particularly in relation to the realization of the exhibition policy and communications strategy through specifically formulated design solutions and the information gained from visitor surveys and evaluations. The paper goes on to examine the implementation of such solutions through the selection and deployment of available resources, and the definition of the design problem. The use of critical path and network analyses is cited as important methodological aids. Vistor orientation – as a pre-condition of effective communication – is stressed.

Griggs' paper discusses a number of important considerations inherent in the evaluation of exhibitions, and sets out to examine the nature of differing evaluations within the museum, and how they are implemented. The paper explores the constraints imposed upon evaluation, and distinguishes clearly between informal and formal evaluation and, through a discussion of 'what', 'when', 'how', and 'why' to evaluate, isolates three central constructs within the overall evaluative strategy – front-end, formative and summative evaluation – and goes on to examine the first two in detail; the third becoming the focus of the following paper (by Prince).

Running throughout Griggs' paper is the understanding that evaluation – at whatever stage in the overall strategy – is a specialized field requiring a certain set of skills, and that these skills are best applied throughout the formulation of an exhibition and not – as is often the case – simply at the end of the scheme and on the completed project. The importance of front-end evaluation to the original concept of the exhibition is stressed through a concentration on the assessment of plans, ideas and theories. Formative evaluation – taking place during the process of exhibition development, and characterized by the assessment of mock-up displays on their intended audience – is seen as an important tool in the validation (or otherwise) of the initial design solution.

The paper describes a number of techniques currently available for evaluation at both levels, and is supported by examples from the author's own experience. The paper concludes by describing the strengths and weaknesses of each type of evaluation, and reinforces the importance of both to exhibition design.

Prince's paper concentrates on summative evaluation – evaluation undertaken on a completed project – and begins by stressing the crucial role played by objectives in the evaluation process, and the way in which such objectives can be defined, organized and translated into workable indexes for evaluation. The paper stresses that such objectives form the basis of the evaluative strategy, and that this in turn governs the choice of techniques used in, for example, visitor surveys, and for the analysis itself. The most commonly applied strategy – that of evaluating the exhibition in terms of its communicational effectiveness – is discussed in detail, as are the various techniques stemming from this approach, and an alternative method is described. Various procedures for gaining information about, and from, visitor samples are examined, and criticisms given. Throughout the paper, the essential role that evaluation can play in the design and implementation of exhibitions is stressed. It is seen as a part of – and not simply an adjunct to – the design process.

Enquiries

As public institutions, museums have traditionally fulfilled the role of responding to enquiries from diverse sources, including those of the general public. Although more general enquiries can perhaps be pre-empted by publications and special exhibitions relating to contemporary or popular themes, the museum's role in responding to enquiries of a more specific nature from individuals is discussed in the paper by David T-D Clarke. Beginning with a definition of 'the Golden Rule' for museum enquiries, relating to responding to enquiries and indicates some of the more general inquiries received by museums. These are grouped into general administrative enquiries relating to the functioning of the museum itself, enquiries relating to the museum's collections, for example, those concerned with specimens, acquisitions, and research, requests for factual information, and an important, growing, area, that of requests from private collectors for information relating to the repair and conservation of objects.

In a section overlapping with the ideas presented by P. Graham Carter, in his paper on Museum Education, Clarke discusses requests from students and teachers with respect to the collections. A further section is devoted to the establishment of an enquiries service, and guidelines are given for its effective administration. Conditions for the acceptance of various objects are discussed, and enquiries involving external museum work are elaborated. The paper also discusses the important area of enquiries made from one institution of another, and the whole process of passing on information from one museum to another. The paper concludes by giving an example of archetypal enquiry form.

Publications

Iain Bain's paper, by drawing heavily on his work at the Tate Gallery, London, discusses the role, development and function of museum publishing and shops. From an examination of the roles fulfilled by these activities in relation to the overriding concerns of the museum or gallery, the paper explores five separate areas of publishing and isolates the various target groups to which each is primarily aimed. The relationships between publications and the exhibition policy and scheme of the museum is elaborated and linked with the practical aspects of decision making in, for example, the determination of print runs, costs, price to the visitor and so on. Various types of publication, from exhibition catalogues, through leaflets, guides and posters, to diaries, calendars and the production and sales of colour transparencies are discussed in detail and related to the demands of both the museum staff and the visiting public.

Through an examination of the staffing of the Tate's publishing department, inferences can be drawn for the workings of most museum-based operations, and the relationship between them and, for example, the work of outside agencies. Pricing strategies for the various initiatives developed by museums are discussed in detail, as are the considerations involved in the distribution of the published material.

Museum shops are given separate consideration and discussed in terms of their role as part of the overall service offered to visitors. The siting, arrangement and display of books, replicas and other items are discussed, as is the relationship between the shop and the other activities and departments of the museum. The security of saleable stock is afforded special consideration.

Museums and education

Most museums are committed in one way or another – whether implicitly or explicitly – to education. The term is either included or implied in virtually every widely used definition of a museum. There are, however, problems with the use, or the connotation, of the word. This is reflected in the fact that usually when the relationships of museums to education are discussed in conference or seminar, the discussions turn to the definitions of the two terms or concepts.

The term 'education' would appear to have at least three senses, which can be categorized (as Benjamin Ives Gilman suggested long ago in his book *Museum Ideals: of Purpose and Method* (1918)) into three – the loose, the broad and the narrow.

The *loose sense* was defined by John Stuart Mill in 1867 in the following words 'Whatever helps to shape the human being and to make the individual what he is, or hinder him from being what he is not – is part of education'. The *broad sense* includes every exercise or activity which is valued, not for its direct results, but by its indirect effects upon the capacity of the person who is engaged therein. It is the sense implied in D. A. Allan's cryptic epigram: 'museums *and* education? museums *are* education', and also in the often quoted definition from John Amos Comenius' *The Great Didactic* (1628) (*see* Limiti, 1983).

The *narrow sense,* and the one most commonly understood, covers more than influence, more even than formative influence: it means intentional formative influence. Education in this sense is equated with what happens in schools, colleges and universities, and therefore with pedagogy – and it exists as a function of teaching.

Education in this sense is, in the words of R. M. Hutchins, taken as the deliberate, organized attempt to help people to become intelligent, it takes 'actual, visible form in educational systems'. (*The Learning Society,* 1968).

Much of what has been written on education in museums deals with the word in this third sense, often to the exclusion of the other two. See, for example, the article 'Thirty years of museums education: Some deflections by Gerard van der Hoek (1982).

A museum, however, is not a conventional educational institution in the important respect that there is no obligation for the museum visitor to *learn.* Yet because the museum can present the actual object, it has an opportunity to provide a unique educational experience without necessarily employing traditional educational methods. It thus provides 'the perfect open-ended learning situation'. Put in another way, the major educational function of a museum lies within the somewhat indefinite margins of general or liberal education, as distinguished from professional and vocational training.

While acknowledging a responsibility to 'educate', museum authorities are not very clear on what their educational role is, or should be. See, for example, the selected views given in *Communicating with the Museum Visitor* (Royal Ontario Museum, 1976, p. 17).

In this context, one of the reasons given for the increasing number of visitors to museums is the so-called revolution in education. It is also important to emphasize the fact that the concentration of interest on the educational process over the last two decades has resulted in a revolutionary avowal of the obvious – namely that there are elemental factors in education – what is taught (knowledge, wisdom), the teacher and the taught. Educational systems have long centred on knowledge and the teacher. What is now happening is a very belated result of the combined inspiration of Rousseau, Pestalozzi, Froebel and others – simply to shift the centre of gravity from knowledge to the learner, recognizing that it is the learner and his characteristics which alone provide the key in any effort to make something organic of education. It is also probably true that this change in formal education has influenced the relationship between the museum communicator and the visitor.

Any current discussion of the meaning of the word education in a museum context implies the use of the term *interpretation*.

Most modern commentaries attribute the first formal definition of the word 'interpretation' to the American, Freeman Tilden who, in his book, *Interpreting our Heritage: Principles and Practice for Visitor Services in Parks, Museums and Historic Places* (University of North Carolina Press, 1957 (and 1967)), defined or described interpretation as: 'an educational activity which aims to reveal meanings and relationships through the use of original objects by first hand experience, and by illustrative media, rather than simply to communicate factual information.'

His definition (or purpose) was later summarized by Shulz (1962) in the mnemonic: 'through interpretation, understanding; through understanding, appreciation; through appreciation, conservation'.

The concept is developed further, in Don Aldridge's *Principles of Countryside Interpretation and Interpretive Planning* (1975), the first British 'text book' on interpretive services and in the activities of the Society for the Interpretation of Britain's Heritage, which was established in 1975. See also *Understanding our Surroundings: a Manual of Urban Interpretation* (1979), prepared by Arthur Percival for the Civic Trust.

Tilden maintained that he and his colleagues were clearly engaged in a new group education based upon a systematic kind of preservation and use of national cultural resources. 'The scope of this activity has no counterpart in old nations or other times'.

Tilden maintained that his work was based on six principles:

(1). Any interpretation that does not somehow relate what is being displayed or described to something within the personality or experience of the visitor will be sterile.
(2). Information, as such, is not interpretation. Interpretation is revelation based upon information. But they are entirely different things. However, all interpretation includes information.
(3). Interpretation is an art, which combines many arts, whether the materials presented are scientific, historical or architectural. Any art is in some degree teachable.
(4). The chief aim of interpretation is not instruction, but provocation.
(5). Interpretation should aim to present a whole rather than a part, and must address itself to the whole man rather than any phase.
(6). Interpretation addressed to children (say, up to the age of twelve) should not be a dilution of the presentation to adults, but should follow a fundamentally different approach. To be at its best it will require a separate program.

For a discussion of these principles and their application to thematic displays in a countryside setting *see* Prince (1981), and for an explanation and discussion of their implications *see* Prince (1982 and 1983).

The terms 'interpretation' and 'interpreter' used in this sense do, however, seem to be much older. They were certainly in use in American museums in the first decades of the century – as is evident in Gilman's book *Museum Ideals,* and in some museums in Britain in the 1920s, 1930s, and 1940s. Sir Frederick Rees, in honouring one of the British pioneers, stated in the citation to Dr. F. J. North's Honorary Degree of Doctor of Science: 'For him a museum is essentially an interpreter's house' (*see* Bassett, 1973).

The definition of the word or concept of 'museum' also varies. The widest is probably that given by ICOM in 1974:

> a non-profit making, permanent institution in the service of society and of its development, and open to the public, which acquires, conserves, researches, communicates and exhibits for purposes of study, education and enjoyment, material evidence of man and his environment.

The concept is considered to cover botanical gardens, zoological parks and nature reserves.

A useful survey of such institutions is given in *Environmental Awareness. A Survey of Types of Facilities used for Environmental Education and Interpretation in Europe* (Strasbourg, Council of Europe, 1978).

Sir John Forsdyke's description (1949) of a national museum as 'all things (the inside) to all men (the outside) – the content of the museum and its public services' is therefore very appropriate. Sir John went further in discussing the universality of material in a national museum by stating that this 'involves the obligation of universality of use: every kind of service to every kind of person, or rather for every kind of interest, for the interests vary from time to time in one and the same person'.

Bibliograpic notes

The various themes in this Section are discussed in varying ways and at varying length in a number of well-known general volumes on museums and museum work. Of these, the following four by eminent American museum curators are of particular interest:

(1) *The Sacred Grove. Essays on Museums* (1970) by Dillon Ripley (distinguishehed ornithologist, former Director of the Peabody Museum of Natural History and the present Secretary of the Smithsonian Institution), in which the underlying theme is the need to recognize the largely unexploited potential which museums have for education, for enjoyment and for increasing awareness.

(2) *Mostly about Museums* (1959): selections from the papers of Albert Eide Parr, distinguished marine biologist, Director of the American Museum of Natural History from 1952 to 1959 and first recipient of the Award for Distinguished Service to Museums inaugurated by the Council of the American Association of Museums in 1980. The section: 'The museum and the people' (pp. 31–44) is of particular relevance.

(3) *Museum Ideals: of Purpose and Method* (1918) by Benjamin Ives Gilman (one of the pioneers of museology in North America and for many years Secretary of the Museum of Fine Art, Boston), which, although over sixty years old, contains much relevant material.

(4) *Museums in Motion* by Edward P. Alexander (1979) and published in manual format, which examines the history and major functions of museums and assesses the state of the profession today. It has been described as one of the most vaulable books to appear in the last decade and one reviewer suggests that 'Beginners should not find themselves "re-inventing the wheel" if they avail themselves of excellent resources like this'.

Equally, the following work by an equally eminent British curator is also of particular interest: *Priceless Heritage: The Future of Museums* (1977) by Ian Finlay, one-time Keeper of the Department of Art and Ethnography and late Director of the Royal Scottish Museum, Edinburgh, which, in part because it addresses the museum profession and invites debate, has been described as 'the best museum buy in books in a few years'. The chapters 'Museums and the schools', 'The present dichotomy', and 'The museum image', are of particular interest.

One very useful composite volume is *On Understanding Art Museums* (1975) edited by Sherman E. Lee in which eight specialists, including museum directors, art scholars, an artist and a psychiatrist examine the aims, tasks, problems, and future of art museums. The chapters on 'Education and scholarship in the American Museum' and 'The Art Museum and the pressures of society', are particularly relevant in the present context. Another, *Communicating with the Museum Visitor. Guidelines for Planning* (1976), prepared by the Communications Design Team of the Royal Ontario Museum, is also of particular relevance as one of the widest ranging discussions on the subject and designed 'to explore problems rather than present solutions'.

In addition there is: (a) the issue of *Curator* (XIV/1) for 1971 which includes several papers commenting on the role and function of the museum in society today – and particularly the introductory statement by Thomas D. Nicholson entitled 'A question of function'; (b) the seven papers read before the Royal Society of Arts in 1949 and published as *Museums in Modern Life* (1949); and (c) the slightly more specialized volume *Natural History Museums and the Community* (edited by K. Engstrom and A. G. Johnels) based on the symposium held in Stockholm in 1969 to mark the occasion of the 150th Anniversary of the Swedish Museum of Natural History.

Similar general volumes concerned with museums and education are described in the bibliography essay by Douglas A. Bassett.

References

ALDRIDGE, D. (1975), *Principles of Countryside Interpretation and Interpretive Planning: Guide to Countryside Interpretation: Part I*, HMSO, Edinburgh

ALEXANDER, E. P. (1979), *Museums in Motion: An Introduction to the History and Functions of Museums*, American Association for State and Local History, Nashville

ALLAN, D. A. (1949), Museums and education, in *Museums in Modern Life* Royal Society of Arts, London

AMERICAN ASSEMBLY (1975), *On Understanding Art Museums*, American Assembly, Washington, DC

BASSETT, D. A. (1973), Extra-mural work of the Departments of National Museum of Wales: 1 – Geology, *Amgueddfa*, **15**, 20–36

BATHER, F. A. (1903), (Presidential Address to the Museums Association at Aberdeen in September, 1903), *Museums J.*, **3**, 71–94 and 110–132

BOARDMAN, D. (1983), *Graphicity and Geography Today*, Groon Helen, London

BURRETT, F. G. (1982) *Rayner Scrutiny of the Departmental Museums: Science Museum and Victoria and Albert Museum* (Cyclostyled Report)

CAMERON, D. F. (1982), Museums and public access: the Glenbow approach, *The Int. J. Mus. Management and Curatorship*, **1**(2), 177–196

COUNCIL OF EUROPE (1978), *Environmental Awareness. A Survey of Types of Facilities used for Environmental Education and Interpretation in Europe*, Strasbourg

DEPARTMENT OF EDUCATION AND SCIENCE (1982), *Rayner Scrutiny of the Departmental Museums: Science Museum and Victoria and Albert Museum*, HMSO, London

ENGLISH TOURIST BOARD (1982) *Visitors to Museums Survey 1982. Report by English Tourist Board Market Research Department and NOP Market Research Limited*, London List No. 32824 (Cyclostyled)

ENGSTROM, K., JOHNELS, A. G. (Eds.) (1973) *Natural History Museums and the community. Symposium held in October 1969 at the Swedish Museum of Natural History (Naturhistoriska riksmuseet) in Stockholm*, Universitetsforlaget, Oslo, Bergen, Tromso

FINLAY, I. (1977), *Priceless Heritage: the Future of Museums*, Faber & Faber, London

FOSDYKE, J. (1949), The functions of a national museum, in *Museums in Modern Life*, Royal Society of Arts, London

GILMAN, B. I. (1918), *Museum Ideals: of purpose and method*, Harvard University Press, Cambridge, Mass

HOEK, G. VAN DER (1982), Thirty years of museum education: some reflections, *The Int. J. Mus. Management and Curatorship*, **1**(4), 374–376

HUDSON, K. (1977), *Museums for the 1980s – a survey of world trends*, MacMillan, London

HUTCHINS, R. M. (1968), *The Learning Society*, Pall Mall Press, London

LEE, S. E. (Ed.) (1975), *On Understanding Art Museums*, The American Assembly, Columbia University. Mentor/Prentice Hall International, New Jersey

LIMITI, G. (1983), Profiles: John Amos Comenius, *Prospects, Quarterly Review of Education*, **13**(1), 117–121

NICHOLSON, T. D. (1971) A question of function, *Curator*, **14**(1), 7–10

PARR, A. E. (1959) *Most about Museums: From the papers of A. E. Parr*, American Museum of Natural History, New York

PERCIVAL, A. (1978) *Understanding our surroundings: a manual of urban interpretation* Civic Trust, London

PRINCE, D. R. (1981), *Countryside Interpretation in the North York Moors National Park: A Socio-Psychological Study* (Unpublished PhD Thesis, University of Hull)

PRINCE, D. R. (1982), *Countryside interpretation: a cognitive evaluation, Museums J.*, **82**(3), 165–170

PRINCE, D. R. (1983), Behavioural consistency and visitor attraction, *Int. J. Mus. Management and Curatorship*, **2**(3), 235–247

RIPLEY, D. (1975), *The Sacred Grove. Essays on Museums* Gollancz, London; Simon & Schuster, New York (1969)

RIVIERE, G. H. (1975), *The Museum of Negro Civilization at Dakar*, UNESCO, Paris

ROYAL ONTARIO MUSEUM, COMMUNICATIONS DESIGN TEAM (1976) *Communicating with the Museum Visitor. Guidelines for Planning*, Toronto

SHULZ, P. (1962), Interpreting park values, *Park Practice Guidelines*, **3**, 12–16

SMITHSONIAN INSTITUTION (1977), *The Smithsonian Experience: Science – History – the Arts . . . the Treasures of the Nation*, Smithsonian Institution

STANDING COMMISSION ON MUSEUMS AND GALLERIES (1979), *A Framework for a System of Museums*, HMSO, London, (The Drew Report)

STANDING COMMISSION ON MUSEUMS AND GALLERIES (1980), *Report by a Working Party on Conservation 1980*, HMSO, London

STEARN, W. T. (1981), *A History of the British Museum (Natural History) 1753–1980*, Heinemann/British Museum (Natural History), London

TILDEN, F. (1957), *Interpreting Our Heritage*, University of North Carolina Press, Chapel Hill

UNESCO (1960), *General Conference*, UNESCO, Paris

(WILLIAMS, A. J.) (1981), *A Heritage for Scotland – Scotland's National Museums and Galleries: the next 25 Years*, HMSO, Glasgow

44

Psychology and the museum visitor

Michael B. Alt and Steven A. Griggs

It does not require much thought to realize that to be successful an exhibition must simultaneously meet the needs of the museum and its visitors. Simple and self-evident though this is, it is surprising just how infrequently exhibitions are mounted with more than a perfunctory consideration of what these sentiments might imply. Usually, the tacit needs of the museum (and its visitors) rest with a curator who probably has strong views about what *he* wants to display but who has little knowledge about the interests and capacities of the majority of people who will visit the exhibition once it has been opened. For example, often there is a great deal of soul-searching about the specimens that should be included at the expense of others in the collections but little thought is given to ways of organizing the chosen materials so that it is understandable to the visitors. And even if an honest and sincere attempt has been made to organize the material into digestible segments or episodes, making use of current knowledge concerning the principles of instructional design, this is usually done on an implied assumption that the visitor will *want* to follow the course displayed before him; or failing that, the exhibition will somehow or other *make* him want to follow it in the way the curator intended. This is a point we shall pick up later.

In this chapter, we shall be addressing ourselves to a basic question of what it means to be a museum visitor, and in doing so we shall also be exploring particular aspects of the *psychology* of the visitor. At the same time we shall discuss how an exhibition might be designed to match the psychology of the visitor. We should note at the outset, however, that in making this proposal, we are putting forward a *radical* notion of exhibition design. In fact, we are suggesting a reversal of the typical process of such design whereby exhibition themes, their organization and the particular objects and information to be displayed are determined on an *a priori* basis. This

applies equally to didactic exhibitions with a clear educational intent and to more traditional exhibitions where the educational intent, in so far as there is any serious intent at all, is rather diffuse and difficult to infer. In fact, one of the major differences between these two approaches to exhibition design is that in the former case, the educational objectives and intent are made clear at the outset whereas in the latter case, they are never made manifest at all. There are, of course, other differences, not the least being that in serious didactic exhibits an effort is made to organize the material in such a way that the so-called *motivated*[1] lay visitor will be able to follow the intellectual ideas represented in the exhibition. But herein lies the problem mentioned earlier, namely the assumptions either that visitors are predisposed to 'learn' in the rather narrow sense delineated by didactic exhibitions, or that didactic exhibitions have the power to dispose visitors to learn once in the exhibition even if they visited the exhibition without any such prior intention. To understand why such a view is prevalent in exhibition design, it is necessary to understand the 'models of man' that have influenced psychology and education in general and, by association, exhibition design in particular.

Models of man

The view that the museum visitor is by nature a passive being whose behaviour can be manipulated by 'well-designed' exhibits, is a particular brand of a very general and influential conceptualization of human thought that has dominated psychology and education for over half a century. Essentially, the view holds that man's actions are *determined* by forces over which he *himself* has no control. There are very many brands of this conception of man. Since Darwin, we have seen the rise of the organismic view of man. More recently with the advent of so-called intelligent machines (computers) we have seen man depicted as a computer.

This view is set in opposition to Cartesian dualism. Descarte, the founder of modern rationalism, saw man as a rational extensionless soul set above and outside nature. He thought that if we used our capacity for rational thought we should become 'masters and possessors of nature'. Descarte divided the world into three realms: God, Mind and Nature. Nature was the realm of matter in motion governed by laws which made its states necessarily so. Mind was the realm of man and each soul or self had a *free will* independent of the laws of nature.

The supernatural side of the rationalist position had caused psychologists to fight shy of the study of 'mind' altogether for most of this century; although more recently the notion of 'man' as an agent with a free-will or mind has been incorporated within a modern empirical psychology without any overtones of Cartesian spiritualism. Nevertheless, the deterministic view has been the dominant force since J. B. Watson first published his now classic book *Behaviourism* in 1924; and *behaviourism* has had a strong influence on studies of museum visitors and the recommendations for exhibition design that have stemmed from them. For example, the work of Robinson and Melton (see Chapter 47) concentrated solely on observing the behaviour of museum visitors in response to environmental stimuli in art galleries (pictures) in the view that by appropriately organizing the environment, visitors would make the required and predictable responses, that is, to look at the pictures in a certain order.

The deterministic view also implicitly underpins the basis of didactic exhibitions. Here, the assumption seems to be that by organizing exhibition material in a certain way, a drive to learn will be set in operation and the visitor will learn in the way the exhibition designers intended, thereby reducing this drive. Indeed, didactic exhibitions often begin with the drawing up of a set of *behavioural objectives* which state quite explicitly what the visitor is expected to learn. If the visitor does not learn what was intended (as measured by such things as pencil and paper tests of knowledge), the inevitable conclusion must be reached that the exhibits were badly designed. In other words, no admission that the visitor might not have intended or wanted to learn is permissible. His behaviour is assumed to be *determined* completely by the exhibits. To avoid this rather ludicrous conclusion, museum professionals sometimes pre-empt the logical force of the above argument by putting forward a let-out clause to the effect that the testing procedure was not sensitive enough to reveal changes in behaviour or learning, or that there were other (unstated) aims the tests failed to take into account.

It should now be apparent that all the theories of exhibit effectiveness that have arisen in the literature on visitor behaviour, have attributed to the visitor an essentially passive nature and the mark of them is to treat visitor behaviour as a natural and determined phenomenon. Apart from any random factors (giving rise to probabilistic laws) the visitor accordingly behaves predictably in given conditions and can be manipulated by engineering appropriate conditions (that is, effective exhibits). Thus the individual has no *free will* to govern his own behaviour. Exhibit learning, the routes taken through exhibitions, exhibit interest, and so on, are determined by the design of the exhibition, quite independent of the psychology of the museum visitor.

Some designers of traditional exhibits appear to accept that visitors do have their own (free) will since they seem to operate on the basis that visitors will amble through an exhibition hall stopping at artefacts that happen to take their fancy rather like people browsing in a curiosity shop or bookstall. (We say this because traditional exhibits appear to have no intellectual organization other than the sort of categorical systems that one finds in a bookshop). More probably, however, this is a fortuitous outcome of the curators' misplaced belief that the organization of artefacts most appropriate to themselves (for example biological classification, chronological sequencing and so on) is the most appropriate organization to promote an understanding among an uninformed public.

The purpose of this brief discourse is to raise for discussion the important question of what 'model of man' is appropriate to uphold when designing a museum exhibition. It will come as no surprise that, philosophically there is no simple answer to the question of the extent to which man's actions are determined. Nevertheless, it is also true to say that in recent years psychology has rediscovered 'mind' and humans are increasingly being credited as active, hypothesis-testing individuals who exert a considerable amount of control over their behaviour in many circumstances and in many situations. We believe that it is particularly appropriate to uphold such a view of 'man the museum visitor' but leave it to the reader to make up his own mind whether he believes he would have any control over the exhibits he would look at in an exhibition, or whether he would behave like some kind of helpless puppet jerked into life by them.

Having made our position on this issue clear, it is also necessary to remove any misconceptions we might have raised along the way. First, in accepting that visitors have 'free will', we are not at the same time, suggesting that traditional exhibits are in any significant sense (for the visitor's point of view) superior to didactic exhibits. Indeed, by any criteria one might apply, it seems to us that designers of traditional exhibits make no serious attempt to communicate with the visitors. The same cannot be said of didactic exhibits. In our experience, designers of didactic exhibits are painstakingly conscientious in their attempts to make exhibitions understandable and interesting. We believe that the intention to create a worthwhile museum experience, where the visitor will enjoy himself and be illuminated rather than be intimidated, is laudable and well-meaning; but the goals currently set by designers of educational exhibits are unattainable because they have misunderstood what it means to be a museum visitor.

In addition, we are not suggesting that museums should abandon any attempts to 'educate' their visitors but that they should lower their sights in the light of a fuller understanding of what it is possible to achieve in the museum setting given the nature of their visitors. It is wrong to think of the museum as a sort of informal school and to apply, uncritically, a curriculum model developed in a different context. These are themes we shall return to later but we note in passing that it is possible to salvage the current approach to didactic exhibits by supposing an active museum visitor whose intentions in visiting an exhibit coincide with the intentions of the designers. However, this so severely limits the potential audience that we believe a more radical alternative is necessary.

Finally, we raise for discussion a side issue which might be illuminating in the light of these remarks. We have often heard it mentioned that the so-called didactic approach, while it might be appropriate for science museums, is not so for art galleries. The 'aesthetic' experience which it is felt characterizes art galleries is so far removed from the 'behavioural objectives' approach to learning about science that characterizes didactic exhibitions, that it is easy to reject the latter's relevance to art galleries. We hope that our considerations have convinced the reader that the approach is not appropriate for either; and we shall put forward an alternative framework of relevance to both.

Psychology of the museum visitor

It does not seem unreasonable that designers of educational exhibits should turn to the psychological and educational literature for direction and advice on the learning process; and, in turn, apply the knowledge accumulated in these fields to their own sphere. Unfortunately, it is our belief that many of the theories of learning developed by academic psychologists are almost totally irrelevant to the design of educational exhibits. A great many of the experimental studies of learning have taken place in 'stressful' situations. Typically, in animal studies, for

example, organisms are deprived of food or threatened with electric shocks until they make the required response. Notwithstanding the rather dismal model of learning generally represented by this approach, it is *fundamentally* inappropriate as a charactization of how we might learn in a museum. In a museum there should be no coercion to force the visitor to learn and there is no necessary compulsion on the part of the visitor to learn. Within reason, the visitor can do as he pleases; and if we wish to help him construct a worthwhile experience it is incumbent upon us as designers to attempt an understanding of *his* intentions and expectations rather than impose a rather moribund view of how learning takes place in the hope that we can manipulate his behaviour to achieve *our* goals and *our* intentions.

In line with this, the notion of motivation so cherished by psychologists and educators has little more than a superficial relevance to museum design. Motivation, as understood by many experimental psychologists, is *operationally* defined in animal studies, for example, by the number of hours of food deprivation, or in studies of human learning by an assumed desire to succeed on various tests of knowledge after a learning task. Clearly these notions of motivation have little bearing on how a casual visitor views exhibits.

So rather than invoke a quasi-scientific concept of motivation, it is probably more reasonable to use everyday notions such as expectation, purpose, intention and the visitor's own good reasons as a basis for understanding the psychology of the museum visitor. In so doing, we also hope that some of the resistance to the idea that psychology has anything to offer designers of exhibitions will be dispelled.

After this brief preamble we can now turn to the major theme of this section, namely to explore and explain just what sorts of expectations, purposes and intentions a visitor might have in visiting a museum. In so doing, we shall be suggesting some of the ways these considerations can be applied to the design of an exhibition. Obviously, it is beyond the scope of the present chapter to provide a detailed account of the psychology of the museum visitor or the implications this has for exhibit design and what follows is, of necessity, a rather brief account. However, some suggestions for further reading are given at the end of the chapter.

The notion of a 'model' figures prominently throughout this chapter. We have already talked about the 'models of man' that psychologists have used to understand and explain human behaviour and we shall also be talking about the sorts of 'models of the world' that individuals construct in order for them to make sense of the environments in which they find themselves. This is not a new idea – the notion crops up in a variety of ways and in a variety of different guises throughout the whole of psychology.

When we talk about someone having a 'model of the world' what is meant is that he or she will have some internal representation of the world which is used to guide, anticipate and interpret behaviour. With particular reference to a museum visit, we can see that part of a person's model of the world will incorporate a set of experiences, expectations, rules of behaviour and so on of a 'museum visit'. This will be true no less for the first-time visitor than for the experienced museum-goer, the difference between them being one of quality. The former's expectations are based upon received knowledge whereas the latter will have first-hand 'real' experience. To illustrate what we have in mind, we can compare, anecdotally, the behaviour of two imaginary visitors – the window-shopper and the scholar. The window-shopper wanders from one exhibit to the next in leisurely fashion, sometimes pausing briefly in front of an exhibit but most often glancing at it in passing. He or she is likely to visit the whole museum in the space of an hour or two. The scholar, on the other hand, arrives armed with note book and pencil. He or she goes more or less directly to a particular set of exhibits and examines them in detail, reading all the labels, and taking notes where necessary. These two imaginary visitors are behaving quite differently. If we asked them, we would find their expectations concerning their visit to the museum were quite different. Note however, that we would not necessarily find that we could generalize from this one instance as to how they would both behave in other museums. Supposing the above descriptions arose from visiting an art gallery and our scholar was an art historian while our window-shopper was a motorbike mechanic by profession. Now consider how they might behave in a motorbike museum – very likely their roles would be reversed. What this tells us is that any given visitor will have certain experiences and expectations concerning museums and how to use them, but that these will interact with his or her interests and past experiences.

Another point about the 'models of the world' people construct is that they are not static representations but are modified through experience. Thus, a visitor's expectations and experiences concerning 'a museum visit' will be altered, if necessary, during the course of a visit. For example, someone who thinks all museums are dull, dusty places might have to revise this attitude following a visit to a modern museum which encourages visitor participation and interaction with exhibits and which attempts to incorporate a range of media in the displays.

As well as a notion of 'a museum visit' a visitor will also bring with him or her self a variety of more general past experiences, interests, expectations and presuppositions. Most museums pay little heed to this fact, assuming that people who visit must, by definition, be interested in the subject matter. In fact, people visit museums for a whole range of reasons and not always because they have a particular interest in the subject matter. Some visitors will be interested in only certain topics found in the museum.

Two examples from our own work illustrate how the visitor's interests and expectations influence a visit.

Example 1

To test the idea that prior interest in the subject matter would determine how interesting visitors rated exhibitions on those topics, we asked one group of visitors to rate its interest in the topics when it first arrived at the museum. A second group of visitors was asked to rate how interesting it found these exhibitions after the visit. The results revealed that almost without exception, interesting exhibitions were those on topics for which visitors had a high prior interest (Griggs and Alt, 1982).

Example 2

Dinosaurs, without doubt, occupy a rather special place in our culture. Stop any schoolboy and ask him what he knows about dinosaurs and you will probably uncover a wealth of knowledge. Not surprisingly, many people visit natural history museums to see the remains of these prehistoric beasts. They bring with them a vast range of fact and fiction, fantasy and myth. The current dinosaur exhibition at the British Museum (Natural History), *Dinosaurs and Their Living Relatives,* provides an explanation of how biologists work out relationships between plant and animal groups and then uses this knowledge to show how we can work out how dinosaurs are related to groups of animals alive today. After the exhibition had been opened, information from a number of sources suggested that many visitors experienced difficulty with it. One of the reasons behind this was that at no point did the exhibition touch upon what most visitors wanted to find out about dinosaurs; were they all large and ferocious meat-eaters?, and so on. These expectations were getting in the way of the points that the exhibition was trying to get over. The exhibition now begins with a video programme which among other things tries to fulfil visitors' expectations as well as correcting some of the common misconceptions about dinosaurs.

Current research from the psychology of perception indicates that the perceptual processes, whether they be in the modes of sight, sound or touch, are largely under the control of the perceiver. Thus perception entails an active exploration of the environment by the perceiver. This can be demonstrated with reference to ambiguous figures. *Figure 44.1* can be seen either as a beautiful young woman or as an old hag; and *Figure 44.2* can be seen as a cube with the surface identified by the small cir-cle seen as either the face or the rear of the cube. For present purposes, the important thing to note is that while the pattern on the retina remains unaltered. It is possible to *see* different objects. Perception does not just happen but is guided by our model of the world; that is, we anticipate and construct hypotheses, we 'see what we want to see'. We have all experienced a mouth-watering sensation when coming across a picture of a delicious spread of food in a magazine, yet were we to look at the same picture shortly after enjoying a gourmet meal, the chances are that the sensation experienced would be different. Again, the picture has not changed, what has altered is our act of construing (or perceiving). To use the jargon of psychology, perception is not driven by the object but driven by the perceiver. Another related aspect of the act of perceiving is our tendency to 'pigeonhole' objects. By this means, objects and events are organized by the perceiver into meaningful categories according to one's view of the world. A piano is first and foremost a musical instrument to most people whereas it is more likely to be seen as a heavy piece of furniture to the removal man. Similarly, to someone with a sweet tooth a bee may be perceived primarily as a 'honey-maker' whereas to someone who has been stung, the same bee may be perceived as a dangerous pest. We should note also that to the professional taxonomist the bee is perceived as a particular species of hymenoptera iden-

Figure 44.1 After Boring, E. (1930), A new ambiguous figure, *American J.*, **42**, 444

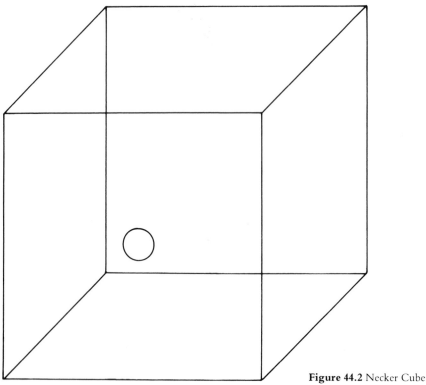

Figure 44.2 Necker Cube

tified as such by its morphological characteristics. These considerations have important implications as to how objects are displayed in an exhibition. For example, the trained zoologist looking at an unfamiliar animal will be able to perceive whether or not the animal is a mammal, whether it is a herbivore or a carnivore, a tree- or ground-dweller and so on. To the layman, the same animal may possibly remain as little more than a curiosity or freak of nature. Perhaps a more familar example is from the field of art where it is all too commonplace for the lay public to perceive an 'important' example of abstract expressionism as a valueless piece of daubing. Curators do little encourage non-trivial responses to objects in their collections by failing to appreciate the nature of past experience and knowledge in the act of perceiving. Contrary to museum folk-lore, objects do not speak for themselves and visitors need a framework or context within which to view them. Without such a framework, visitors will make their own sense of the objects they perceive and often this can have unfortunate consequences for the institution responsible.

The information available in any given situation is immensely rich and perhaps nowhere is this more true than in the museum. Hundreds if not thousands of objects are on display. There is always more to see than anyone sees. The museum visitor will pay attention to some aspects of the environment while ignoring others. The decision to stop at one particular display rather than another is a complex one, but it is a decision made by the visitor (albeit an unconscious one much of the time) rather than reflecting some intrinsic property of the exhibit. (This is, of course, a logical consequence of perception as a process of interpretation and construing rather than the passive registering of stimuli in the 'real-world'.) The problem for the visitor is how to concentrate on the thing he or she is interested in while ignoring everything else, at least for the time being. We seem to be better at coping with competing messages when they are both visual than when they are auditory. For example, we can simply turn our backs on a scene but there is no analogous course of action with sound. Sound-tracks on films, for example, distract the visitor's attention from other exhibits. Perhaps the hardest state of affairs is when he or she is listening to one sound-track and a second, different sound-track is also audible. Rather than getting the best of both worlds, most visitors will quickly experience frustration and give up.

Although any one visitor cannot be expected to attend to everything in a gallery, he or she will find it easier to attend to more information if some means of organizing the information can be discovered. As we have seen, perception involves organization and interpretation. Consider the following two sequences of the same nine numbers:

(a) 4 7 3 2 8 6 9 1 5
(b) 1 2 3 4 5 6 7 8 9

Which is easier to recall – (a) or (b)?

Here is another example with sequences of letters:

(a) DOCRSH?NYAE UIA T
(b) CAN YOU READ THIS?

The point is that we can increase our span of attention by organizing the information into meaningful units.

As the visitor wanders around he or she will recognize certain objects, will recall items and events and will store interesting details in his or her memory. Facts are not remembered as isolated entitites, instead we tend to remember meanings and themes. Think of the last novel you read. If necessary, you could probably provide a reasonable outline of the plot and the main characters. You would probably find it harder to say what happened in any particular chapter and you would find it impossible to recall what took place on page forty-eight. It is also very rare for us to remember themes and meanings outside of a more general framework. This is because things are stored in memory by organizing them into our existing representation of the world. New information is integrated with existing knowledge, and where necessary, modifies it. Recall is also an active process whereby we recall not only what actually happened but very often we fill in any gaps and draw new inferences.

During his or her wanderings around a museum the visitor will be exploring the environment. He or she will be curious and will seek out new and unusual objects and experiences. At the same time, he or she will seek reassurance from the safety of familiarity. This is not surprising given that our ability to interpret the novel rests firmly in our ability to integrate it with the familiar. There is no doubt that novelty is important. Consider the impact of using television monitors and various audio-visual devices in museums during the 1960s, and the reaction of visitors today to computer-based exhibits. Visitors flock to these displays almost regardless of their content. Everyone has heard of the impact these machines are supposed to be having on our everyday lives but for most people the visual display unit and keyboard represent their first opportunity of personally experiencing a computer.

While too little novelty will quickly lead to boredom, if too much novelty is provided it becomes difficult for us to find an appropriate frame of reference or model of the world. In a study by Falk *et al.* (1978) the effects of novelty on school children during a field-trip were investigated. They discovered that children in a totally new environment learnt less than children who were more familiar with the setting because their attention was distracted from the purpose of the trip as they tried to adjust to the novelty.

From the point of view of the museum professional perhaps the most important aspect of a visitor's behaviour concerns which galleries are visited and which exhibits are stopped at or simply ignored. If we could explain *why* some exhibits succeed in attracting the visitor's attention whereas others are overlooked, the task of the exhibit producer would become clearer. Unfortunately, while a great deal of time and effort has been spent on showing which exhibits attract and hold visitor's attention, no attempt has been made to explain why some exhibits have a high attraction while others have a low attraction. When museum professionals have addressed this problem it is invariably couched in terms of the exhibit (for example interactive versus non-interactive, the choice of medium and so on). The answer lies not in the exhibit but in the way the visitor perceives the exhibit. An understanding of how people respond to exhibits requires an understanding of people not exhibits. We have already indicated in general terms how people go about interpreting their environment and the same principles apply to the perception of exhibits. We have also indicated how a visitor's interests and experiences will influence his or her behaviour. When it comes to analysing how the visitor decides whether or not to stop at any given display (albeit an unconscious decision much of the time), we have to consider the perceived cost-reward values. The resources of any visitor are limited (particularly his or her time). Thus, a decision to stop is based upon weighing up how much effort is required by the visitor for any given return. If an exhibit deals with something of interest to the visitor, he or she may decide to invest more time, but if it tells him or her nothing new then he or she will probably not decide to stop. Likewise, the subject matter may appeal to the visitor but the sheer amount of reading required may be perceived as too much. Only by reacting and understanding the way visitors perceive or construe exhibits and how cost-reward values are quantified, can we begin to understand how the visitor reacts to any given exhibit.

A final consideration of some importance to the visitor is fatigue. As the visit wears on, so he or she will experience fatigue. This will not be restricted to physical tiredness through having walked past so many displays; the visitor will also experience mental fatigue or *ennui*. This phenomenon was first described by Melton (1972). Unfortunately from the museum professionals point of view, mental fatigue does not set in only after an hour or more into the visit but appears immediately and can be quite pronounced even in visits as short as five minutes. Although this has been known for nearly 50 years, one could be forgiven for believing it to be a very recent finding!

Conclusion

It is impossible in the space of a single chapter to provide an adequate account of the relevance of psychological theory and practice to exhibit design. Psychology has much to contribute both to a greater understanding of what it is to be a museum visitor and to the design of exhibits. We have chosen to concentrate largely on the first of these issues in this chapter somewhat to the neglect of the latter. We justify this decision on the ground that much has already been written concerning the application of educational principles to exhibit design. We believe, however, that the wholesale application of principles derived from a curriculum model developed in a different context *may* be inappropriate. We also believe that most museum professionals at worst lack any real understanding of what it is to be a museum visitor, or least pay homage to an inappropriate and out-dated model. We have tried to outline what we consider to be a more appropriate model of a visitor and to suggest the implications of such a model for exhibit design. Space prevents us from providing a more detailed exposition. Instead, we suggest below some further reading to cover the main areas we have covered here as well as some of the areas we have not been able to touch upon.

Notes

[1] 'Motivation' is a much-abused concept in education, generally, and consequently in museum education. It is discussed in greater detail later in the chapter.

References

GRIGGS, S. A. AND ALT, M. B. (1982), Visitors to the British Museum (Natural History) in 1980 and 1981, *Museums J.*, **82**(3), 149–156

FALK, J. H., MARTIN, W. W. AND BALLING, J. D. (1978) The novel field-trip phenomenon: adjustment to novel settings interferes with task of learning, *Journal of Research in Science Teaching*, **15**(2), 127–134

MELTON, A. W. (1972), Visitor behaviour in museums: some early research in environmental design, *Human Factors*, **14**(5), 393–403

WATSON, J. B. (1924), Behaviourism, Norton, New York

Further reading

Models of Man

We owe much of our ideas to Harré, R. and Secord, P. F. (1972), *The Explanation of Social Behaviour*, Basil Blackwell, Oxford, and Neisser, U. (1976), *Cognition and Reality*, W. H. Freeman, San Francisco.

Harré and Secord is possibly a little difficult for the lay reader, but they provide a very detailed critique of the mechanistic model of man. Neisser's book is the more readable and he also provides an account of many of the basic psychological processes we have touched on (perception, memory, attention and so on).

Psychology of the visitor

As well as Neisser's book, Richard Gregory has written some interesting and readable books on perception, for example Gregory, R. (1972), (2nd edn.), *Eye and Brain,* Weidenfeld and Nicolson, London. An early but still pertinent collection of readings on the psychology of communication is Miller, G. (1968), *The Psychology of Communication,* Penguin Books, Harmondsworth.

Very little research has been carried out into how *visitors* construe exhibits. Some of our own work has been in this direction, for example: Alt, M. B. and Shaw, K. M. (1984) *Characteristics of Ideal Exhibits,* British Journal of Psychology, **75**, 25–36.

Educational principles and exhibit design

A great many books have been written on the topics of designing educational materials (for example, Gagne, R. M. and Briggs, L. J. (1974), *Principles of Instructional Design,* Holt, Rinehart and Winston, New York. However we have tried to argue that the relevance of much of this work can be questioned. A very good account of the relevance of educational principles to exhibit designs about which we have very few reservations is the chapter by Brian Lewis (1982), 'Psychological and educational aspects of exhibition design' in *The Design of Educational Exhibits,* (compiled by Miles, R. S.), George Allen and Unwin, London.

Interested readers are also referred to Brian Lewis's article in *Museums Journal* in which he provides a critique of museums as educational environments (Lewis, B. (1980), The museum as an educational facility, *Museums J.,* **80**(3), 151–155). On the ques-

tion of the educational function of museums, we have much sympathy with the views expressed by Kurylo, L. (Summer, 1976), On the need for a theory of museum learning, *Canadian Museums Association Gazette,* pp. 21–24.

Other areas of interest

As well as the relevance of educational principles to exhibit design, there are a number of other areas we have not touched on. These include ergonomics, the choice of media, the use of computers in the museum setting and the problems of providing orientation.

There are a number of basic texts on ergonomics such as Murrell, K. F. H. (1965), *Ergonomics: Man in his Working Environment,* Chapman and Hall, London, and Shackel, B. (1974) (Ed.) *Applied Ergonomics Handbook,* IPC Science and Technology Press, Guildford, Surrey. Some basic ergonomic data relevant to exhibit design may be found in Gosling, D. (1982), (chapters 7 and 8), in Miles R. S. (Ed.), *The Design of Educational Exhibits,* George Allen and Unwin, London.

One might be forgiven for expecting psychology to have something to say about the choice of appropriate media. Unfortunately, this is such a methodologically difficult area in which to carry out research that it is impossible to provide sound criteria for reaching a decision. This is not to say that there are no advantages and disadvantages associated with each medium which allow common-sense decisions to be made. Some of these are discussed by Gosling (see previous reference, Chapter 9).

An introduction to the use of computers for educational purposes can be found in Rushby, N. J. (1979), *An Introduction to Educational Computing,* Croom Helm, London, who also provides a bibliography.

Visitors to museums may require help in finding their way round both the physical and the conceptual environment. Suggestions for how this might be achieved may be found in Griggs, S. A. 'Orientating visitors within a thematic display', *The International Journal of Museum Management and Curatorship,* (1983).

45

Exhibition design

Giles Velarde

Had the museum curator been alive to commerce earlier, design and designers would have been brought into museums at least a quarter of a century before they were. It was, after all, in the world of commerce that the exhibition started. In the market place, the need to sell goods gave rise to the need to display them to advantage. In the museum the need to display objects to advantage is, in very simple terms, the essence of museum exhibition design.

Unknown to most curatorial staff, nearly all the display techniques now used in museums were being developed by exhibition designers working for commerce. At the same time others working mainly in the field of conferences and propaganda were developing the devices now commonplace in information and educational technology. These fields have merged within the single discipline of museum exhibition design.

Now that the bridge between mammon and museum has been built, it is in everyone's interests to maintain it. The obvious advantages include sponsorship for the museum and up-market advertising for industry. It is, however, worth remembering that no industrialist would consider any involvement with a museum exhibition unless highly professional designs were involved.

Intentions

Before starting any design project in any specialization it is essential to decide exactly what needs to be done. A specialist can help with this decision and, particularly when working with an in-house designer, it is best to make this decision together; thus guaranteeing not only mutual enthusiasm for the project but also increasing its likelihood of success.

Exhibitions have, like any other medium of expression, their own particular set of advantages

394

and disadvantages. The danger is that the curator, keen to express his ideals in glamorous, three-dimensional terms, will select the wrong subject to expose in this way. When examining what is a good subject, it is well to remember what museums are for. The curation and preservation of objects is fundamental; therefore any exhibition which has little to do with objects and is simply narrative has little hope of success unless objects can be made or found to form the basis of the story. After twenty years' barrage with the flat image it is likely that the museum visitor is craving to see something real and round. Not only to see it, but to touch it and walk around it. We are tactile three-dimensional creatures. It cannot be satisfactory to sit in the man-made twilight of television and then to make the brave step outside and through the door of a museum to see yet more of the same thing. It is essential to think in terms of giving the visitor something he cannot get at home, at school or from a library or shop; and to decide what the public should learn, feel, enjoy or believe when it leaves the exhibition.

There are many reasons for mounting an exhibition. Ideally the curatorial and design staff who form the production team should have these reasons in common. It is not possible to get a good exhibition out of tortured, mistrustful relationships. However, assuming that such harmony of intentions exists, the defined, well-articulated and mutually agreed list of intentions is an excellent platform upon which to build.

Unfortunately, at least as many effects of an exhibition can be unintended as are intended. Some are laudable; to please and excite, to give three-dimensional assistance to the process of education, to inform a specific age or social group. Some are circumstantial necessities: to draw publicity, attention or money to influence events or people. Some, especially when intended are inexcusable: to pander to fellow-professionals, to build a memorial, to isolate the learner from the learned: in other words to show off, to bore, to confuse or to irritate. Every exhibition may do a combination of these things, assuming of course that it receives any attention at all. What visitors do and how they behave in response to varied types of display is vital knowledge for all curators and designers. Unfortunately, most information sought on the subject seems to relate to the educational value of museums.

In essence, however, museums are places of what might be termed 'higher entertainment'. They are the places to which those who delight in knowledge resort. They are the havens for those who love to rootle among the clues to man's immortality. They are the repositories of tangible reality where the actual paint that Van Gogh used can be seen, the thigh that Rodin smoothed can be touched or the ring that Henry V wore can be seen. There is no way that factors like that can be quantified in statistics, and banal though they may sound when set down here it is nothing to their banality when tabulated nebulously under 'pleasure'.

The designer, of necessity, must be open to all sources of information about his potential audience. It is of great value for the objective designer to observe for himself public reaction to his work. For one employed in a museum there is the unique opportunity to mingle, unrecognized, with the visitors, hear their comments and watch their movements. If he notes down these observations, and when and where they were made, all to the good. But he is entirely the wrong person to approach the visitor, ask him questions, declare himself and thus get involved in an inevitably subjective, and possible offensive, confrontation. At this point the importance of the professional evaluator is manifest and there can be no doubt that recent work in Canada, the USA and London is of immense value and significance. But can anyone, either designer, evaluator or psychologist, appreciate – by observations or questioning – the intensity of the relationship between the visitor and the object? Can a visitor put into words his possibly vague reasons for being in a museum? And, if asked the question 'why did you visit this museum?' will probably respond with an answer which he knows will either please or embarrass the bright-eyed young questioner he sees before him. Like every other means of improving the work of designers and curators, professional evaluation can only be used satisfactorily with a clear eye to its limitations, and should not be regarded as the complete solution.

Types of exhibition

Consideration of the visitor is basic when discussing design, and this consideration leads logically into an assessment of the types of exhibition that can be mounted. These broad, differing types are inevitably a permutation of two factors. First, their *physical properties*: permanent, temporary, portable and mobile, all of which are separate descriptions (though 'temporary' may well be applied to both portable and mobile). Second, the exhibition's *informative characteristics*: thematic, systematic, object-oriented, interactive and responsive. Some, or all of the latter can appear in the same exhibition. A definition of all these general terms is necessary as they are an important part of the language of museum exhibition production.

Permanent speaks for itself, or it should, but it really ought to be taken to mean 'for as long as curatorial policy upholds the need for the exhibition'. This, therefore, means over twenty years in a national museum and perhaps seven to ten years in a small provincial museum. It is almost inevitable that, assisted with central government funds, the permanent exhibition in a national museum will be built to far higher standards of finish, if not design, than its provincial counterpart. But it will inevitably date. Furthermore, since it is more likely to be built by in-house designers than freelance, it has earned the former the reputation of conservativism and the latter a name for trendiness and poor attention to detail, neither necessarily deserved. 'Permanent' should mean built to last, using well-seasoned timbers and well-tried methods of construction and finish. It would be unwise, for instance, to build these structures using materials such as chipboard and hardboard, or clad them with finishes of unknown durability using untried adhesives and non-fast colours. Clearly, the information presented in these displays should be thoroughly researched, since errors are more difficult to rectify in permanent finishes and, when left uncorrected, stand as irritating memorials.

Temporary. In many museums a temporary exhibition, to be accurate, frequently means semi-permanent. It may be planned for three to six months but its popularity, or lack of funds to replace it, may result in it remaining for many years. By its ephemeral nature, a temporary exhibition has a freedom not allowed to the permanent. It is an abuse of this freedom to constrict people into tight aisles, deprive them of fresh air and make them struggle to read text and labels, but it seems, quite wrongly, to be permissible when the exhibition is only standing for a short period. This is patently bad design and can only be got away with because there is not sufficient time for a body of complaint to develop. 'Temporary' should only apply to the durability of the materials used in construction, and to the loan of valuable exhibits.

Portable quite definitely means only one thing: an exhibition which can be dismantled, carried to another place and re-erected. The main considerations for such exhibitions are evident: strong, light construction; compatibility of services, voltages and so on; and construction from easily cleaned and repaired materials. They should be designed with repackaging as an integral feature. Problems arise when exhibitions of this kind are considered in conjunction with valuable or fragile exhibits, neither of which lend themselves to constant handling. It is also necessary to keep the maintenance of such exhibitions to a minimum, since museums have differing facilities for such work. Some have none at all.

Mobile again means precisely that. It is an exhibition which has its own wheels or, in some cases, keel. In the UK the use of such a design is more common among commercial organizations or government information services, for there is in fact a very wide distribution of museums among the population. However in countries like Canada, where the population is more widely spread, there are many communities hundreds of miles from a museum, and this has led to the creation of a successful and continuing program to take the museum to the public. Caravans, trains and even fishing boats have been most effectively used. There are rare occasions when this is the logical solution in this country, but before embarking on such a scheme it would be as well to consult organizations which have been involved in the production of such exhibitions.

An exhibition's informative qualities, not being practical, are more difficult to define. Many words in specialist use take on a meaning peculiar to the user and the words 'thematic', 'systematic' and so on – used in the beginning of this section – apply only to broad types of exhibition, although in a single exhibition many different types of display can be found. Work is currently being done on categorizing these display types, so it is dangerous to embark on definitions which may eventually be proved wrong. Nevertheless, for the sake of this work an attempt must be made.

Thematic means with a theme, the theme being the original concept. The objects are found or made to support the story line. It is narrative oriented (*Figure 45.1*).

Systematic means that it is evolved around a specific system of classification. Cases are laid out according to a classical order, or in order of the age of the objects. In broad terms, the collection exists, is classified and then the exhibition is laid out systematically around it. It is therefore largely object-oriented (*Figure 45.2*).

Object-oriented is, however, a term often associated with one, or a collection of, fine objects not laid out in any system; it is simply the preferred order. The objects are the reasons for the display (*Figure 45.3*).

Interactive is probably the most misused word in the vernacular. It means a slightly different thing to almost every user. Does an interactive display interact with a neighbouring display or the visitor in front of it? Is it interacting or responding? Is it interactive or simply active? Those displays which depend for their effect on the visitor's contribution, whether electronic or mechanical, should be termed *interactive* (*Figure 45.4*). Those which are simply changing or oscillating constantly should be termed *active*. Those which automatically respond to the arrival of the visitor should be termed *responsive* (*Figure 45.5*). Therfore, those which respond to the visitor's arrival and depend on his presence are *responsive–interactive*.

Presentation

The museum designer must not be considered simply as an arranger, decorator or man of taste. In fact he will hate to be so considered, commonplace

Figure 45.1 Story of the Earth (James Gardner 1972)

Figure 45.2 British fossils (Geological Museum, 1980)

Figure 45.3 Appollo module (Science Museum, 1979)

though it is to think of the designer in those terms, or even as a man of fashion. A museum designer is an *information designer* or nothing. It is the information that, in today's museum, is considered by the visitor to be integral with the object. Museums that make no effort to inform are rewarded by poor attendance, despite the public's rising interest, and awareness of, cultural matters. In a *narrative-oriented* exhibition it is the glamour of the story which attracts the public: for instance, the temporary bicentenary exhibition at the Maritime Museum in 1976 or the permanent 'Story of the Earth'[1] exhibition at the Geological Museum, opened in 1972. The construction of those

narratives is crucial to the story told in three-dimensional form and the presentation of the story's words is the basic design problem. The effective designer must be involved, not only in the deployment of these words, but also in their quantity, meaning and use. It is no good, for instance, choosing big, easy-to-read and eye-catching type for headings that cannot be understood. In fact the designer is, if sufficiently detached, an excellent arbiter of what is comprehensible to the ordinary visitor. If his knowledge of the subject is too specialized he ceases to be of value in this way and professional advice should be sought. There are indices of readability[2],

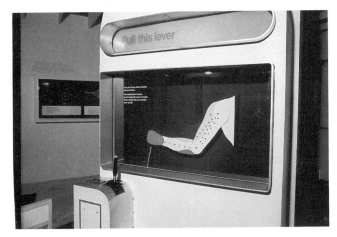

Figure 45.4 Human biology (British Museum, Natural History, 1976)

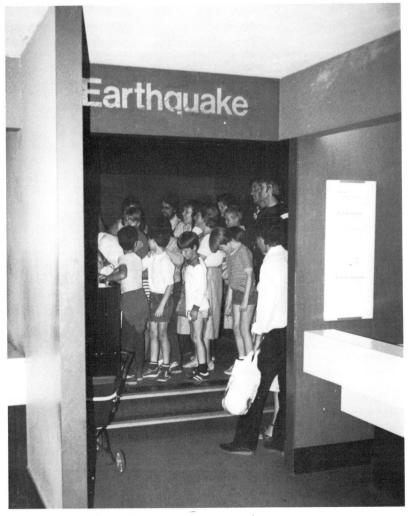

Figure 45.5 Earthquake simulation operated by pressure pad below final step and under target (Geological Museum, 1981)

and tests and theories of comprehension, all of which are of value. None, however, seems completely satisfactory in this field where attitudes vary almost regionally. The good information designer and the involved curator should, if they are to form an effective production team be sensitive to these problems.

Types of designer

Consideration of the extent of involvement of the designer inevitably leads to a discussion of what type of designer is or should be involved in museum work. In such a recent discipline it is inevitable that practitioners should come from a variety of backgrounds. Interior designers, through invitation or demand, have moved into the field. Exhibition designers with either commercial or information backgrounds, have taken the short step across to museums, while the most prolific of all groups – graphic designers – have taken the major number of jobs that have become available in the past ten years (unpublished GDIM Survey). Obviously, none of these fields is immediately perfect and the need for museum exhibition design to be treated as a separate specialist discipline is only now being recognized. Even though it is not possible to commission or employ a designer who has the precise academic qualifications for museum work, there are – and always will be – designers who qualify through experience and demonstrable expertise. It is the selection of such a person that is clearly in need of consideration. It is vital for the curator/designer relationship to be that of equals: professional to professional. It is hopeless for the curator to see the designer as the expresser of his own ideas and fancies. He should employ someone whose work, or pictures of whose work, he has seen, understood and respected: someone who can execute the curator's policies in the designer's style. If the curator's policy leads more in one direction than another, then the designer should be selected with a similar leaning. It should be someone with an interior design background if it is the development of the museum as a tourist attraction with increased public facilities; someone with a graphic design background if the museum's three-dimensional form is essentially unchangeable and the information presentation is paramount. If the curatorial policy is to start afresh with new exhibitions and galleries, then it is best to employ a designer with a background in exhibitions. This last type of designer is also likely to, and indeed should, along with the graphic designer, have a strong informational bias and if not actually a graphic designer will certainly appreciate the need to use such a designer in the production team.

The word 'team' has, until now, been avoided deliberately. Among the museum fraternity the numbers of establishments who can even think of employing teams of people is minimal. To many, even one full-time designer is out of the question. There is no doubt, however, that team production – where complementary talents are assembled in concerted effort – is an ideal to be striven for. A small museum occasionally acquires lump sums, or can find sponsors for a once-only exhibition on popular or industrially connected subjects, so that small museums would be well-advised to hire a design team on a freelance basis for the production of that one exhibition. There are many design practices in existence offering varying levels of capability, but frequently the quality, or lack of it, is as much to do with the relationship between the commissioner and the commissioned as it is to do with the abilities of the members of the practice. The curator in the position of needing such expertise should spend part of his new-found budget travelling from one newly-constructed exhibition to another until he finds one that he understands and with which he is in sympathy. He should then hire the design practice responsible for it, not before talking to both the curator and the designer to sound out any possible future difficulties.

Larger museums can, of course, afford to employ teams and it is the make-up of these teams, together with the attitude of the employer towards the teams which will determine their success. There can be no set rule, but a team of four designers will undoubtedly need managing by a fifth member, preferably a specialist design manager. The other four might well be two exhibition designers, a graphic designer and an information designer – a newly emerging specialism. There is a good case for employing a scriptwriter/editor in a museum where words are given a high priority; museums with a very strong natural science orientation for example. Perhaps that editor could assume the management, if not the leadership, of the team. The leader should be the most experienced person, and from any discipline within the team, provided he can articulate the ideals of the group. Every circumstance will make a different demand and these generalizations must be taken only as a very loose guide.

To refer back to the question 'in-house or freelance?', a big museum should have its own design team and place its confidence in it. That team's capabilities will be eroded if directors are constantly going to freelance practices for their more glamorous enterprises. A small museum is best advised to go freelance, but an in-house design post at a clearly defined level would be of great value, and act as a starting-point for a young designer.

The brief

Whether in-house or freelance, the essential link between the curator and the designer is the brief.

This is a word easily used, but as easily misunderstood, being often confused with a script or a specification. A good brief *is* brief; it is the essential basic information together with a synopsis of the curator's requirements. The essential information is generally statistical; place, size, cost and so on, together with the curator's requirements of subject, purpose and duration. The best brief is evolved and written by the curator and the designer, but it is important that what is written does not take the form of a detailed specification. The ideal brief stimulates the designer. It is a catalyst. The bad brief depresses the designer. The quality of the brief will inevitably be reflected in the eventual design. There is a tendency for curators to instruct designers; to leave nothing to their initiative and to provide so many, often outdated or impractical ideas of their own that there is no room for the designer's creativity to be fully exploited. Such curators should employ draughtsmen.

Assuming that the designer is well-chosen and capable, his creative input is of considerable value. This creative factor is rarely understood. It tends to be airily described as 'artistic' or assumed to be the ability to draw, choose materials or colours. Design is in fact the creative process allied to technical knowledge. The most easily-understood expression of this alliance is the architect. The optimum effect of briefing a designer well is for that designer to find the perfect means of expressing the ideals in the brief. He must then convince the curator with drawings, models or words and then use his technical abilities to communicate that perfect solution through drawings and specifications to the craftsmen, technicians and contractors who will execute the finished exhibition.

The contractual side of the process or exhibition production is potentially less hazardous than the relationships between curators and designers. Nevertheless, the lack of business expertise of many curators can leave them at a considerable disadvantage when working with commercial organizations. It is as well to be aware of these shortcomings and to involve the museum's administrators closely in any contractual arrangements. It is well to inform such administrators at an early stage of the general intentions and to describe what is to be done in the hope of gaining their interest in, and sympathy for, the ideals. If, in fact, all contracts are placed at an informed administrative level, it leaves the curator and in-house designer free to maintain their necessarily amicable relationships with the various producers while any contractual or financial conflicts are ironed out by executives elsewhere. It is also advisable, where possible, to place contracts precisely where they are needed. Involvement with one company and many subcontractors means the museum will pay the main contractor's handling charges on top of the subcontractor's actual costs, while simultaneously losing control of the work done by the subcontractors. If the museum wants all the supervisory chores taken off its hands, then it can pay that price, but it should remember that if the main contractor goes bankrupt it will lose everything. The subcontracts might well be for models and special effects, photographic or screen-printed treatments, and audiovisual devices. If contracted by the museum, it will have total control of their production and also will be in a position to monitor any unforeseen developments. Obviously, basic contractual items such as electrical wiring or lighting, or decorative work can be precisely specified and therefore subcontracted by the main contractor if he does not hold these services, but anything which involves other designers or craftsmen with development work is best contracted and supervised by the commissioner of the exhibition. As stated earlier, an intrinsic part of the brief is the cost, and any competent designer must be able to stay within, or close to, that stated.

Publicity

There are two areas which are given very little consideration by the commissioners of exhibitions but which are, in fact, very important. The first is the publicity associated with the exhibition. This ranges from a curator's fond hope that the press might notice what he has done, to the employment of a full publicity machine drumming up an audience with which the exhibition and staff are completely unable to cope. It is not up to the designer to go out and publicise his exhibition (though if he is freelance and the exhibition is good, he will welcome the publicity). The essence is balance; good exhibitions do acquire their own audiences with very little bought publicity, but it is a slow process. A campaign of press releases, interviews, television coverage or posters which can generate media hysteria over evocative subjects such as 'gold' can produce an audience far in excess of the exhibition's capacity to cope. The publicist should be involved at the design stage of the exhibition to assess the possible traffic of visitors, and their ease and spread of movement resulting from the positioning and readability of the captions and labels. He can then at least attempt the depth of publicity coverage which will attract the right number of the right type of visitors. Unhappily, when this is not done the public is subjected to horrendous conditions never experienced or reported by journalists on press day. Simply because the public do not complain, nothing is done. It can, and should be. It is up to the curator and the designer to consider the problem with professional publicists and evaluators. On the other hand, a delightful but empty exhibition is as great – if not as offensive – a disaster. It cannot be emphasized enough that the employment of professionals (in any field) while initially costing often hard-earned money, does generally pay off in the long term; if not necessarily in countable cash, certainly in the knowledge that the enterprise which costs so much is not just there as a monument to curatorial and design expertise, but is of positive service and benefit to the community.

Maintenance

The second generally ill-considered area is that of maintenance. While this certainly applies to temporary exhibitions, especially when electronic, mechanical or live exhibits are concerned it is a problem most associated with permanent constructions. Where galleries are fabricated on conventional, showcase-and-panel lines, the only maintenance to be considered is that involved with the deterioration of the structure, decorative finishes and lighting, together with the regular cleaning (these comments are restricted to the exhibition, not to the exhibits or objects on display – they are a curatorial problem). In most exhibitions built today there is at least one audio-visual system involving a minimum of three projectors. There may well be other devices which will need regular attention from either their manufacturer, his agent, or staff especially employed by the museum. Again it is a question of balance. Many manufacturers will enter into service or maintenance contracts, but how quickly they can get to the ailing device is one thing and how much this service will cost when a large number of units is involved is worth taking into account when compared with the value and cost of in-house maintenance technicians. In the process of design, the designer, confronted by the too small space and too long script, will be anxious to direct the bulk of the space towards the public. So often this is done at the expense of access for service personnel. Good design will consider maintenance at the earliest planning stages and the far-sighted curator will ensure that this is so. At the same time, the curator must consider the long-term maintenance needs at the earliest point in costing. He will also balance his exhibition program with the need to employ further maintenance and cleaning staff as new areas and galleries open to the public. Obviously if he cannot foresee the staff being available he must balance his exhibition policy accordingly. A poorly-maintained exhibition with non-working display devices is worse than no exhibition at all.

Summary

Everything said in this paper has been in the form of advice and generalizations, hopefully informative but in no sense didactic. Even when care has been taken to be explicit about the exact meaning of the words used, there has been only the most superficial treatment of the subject.

Design and creativity, while in no sense dependent on fashion, are undoubtedly influenced by it. Materials and techniques are continually evolving and developing. What is considered to be fundamental today may be trivial tomorrow. The concern of this section has been to help the curator and design worker together to a pre-stated, common good. It has been concerned to show that the designer, recently arrived on the museum scene, is a professional and, when treated and respected as such by the curator, is an integral part of the expression of the best museological ideals. Designers by and larger are advocates of the theory that form follows function. If the function is clearly defined and its demands met then the form which follows from the designer will generally be satisfactory. Design is not an exclusive world wherein the visually oriented lurk, hiding their fiendish and exotic ideas from the curator lest he balk at their expression; it is a specialist field. It is unlikely that even with the aid of visuals or models, the curator will ever be able to visualize clearly what the designer intends. A large element of trust is therefore involved. The importance to the curator of knowing the designer's capabilities cannot be overstressed. The expression of confidence in the designer should encourage him to produce his best and not surprise the curator with outlandish displays or costly and unnecessary gimmicks. The ultimate aim of both must be the improvement of the visitor's mind and the enhancement of his life.

Notes

[1] These exhibitions are not quoted as examples of success or failure, but as examples of type.
[2] See References.

References

BORMUTH, J. R. (1966), Readability: a new approach, *Reading Research Quarterly*, **1**, 79–132
DALE, E. AND CHALL, J. S. (1948), A formula for predicting readability, *Educational Research Bulletin*, **27**, 11–20, 37–54
FLESCH, R. (1948), A new readability yardstick, *J. Applied Psychology*, **32**(3), 221–233
FLESCH, R. (1949), *The Art of Readable Writing*, Harper and Brothers, New York
FLESCH, R. (1950), Measuring the level of abstraction, *J. Applied Psychology*, **34**, 384–390
FLESCH, R. (1951), *How to Test Readability*, Harper and Brothers, New York
FRY, E. (1968), A readability formula that saves time, *J. of Reading*, **11**, 513–516

GILLILAND, J. (1972), *Readability, University of London Press,* London

HUNT, J. D. AND BROWN, P. J. (1971), Who can read our writing?, *J. Environmental Education,* **2**(4), 27–29

KLARE, G. R. (1963), *The Measurement of Readability,* Iowa State University Press, Iowa

MCLAUGHLIN, H. (1969), Smog grading – a new readability formula, *J. of Reading,* **22**, 639–646

TINKER, M. A. (1963), *Legibility of Print,* Iowa State University Press, Iowa

46

Communicating through museum exhibitions

Michael Belcher

The concept of the museum as a medium of communication is not new. It has long been recognized that a major role of the museum is to facilitate an encounter between object and observer. This experience, for the majority of museum visitors, occurs mainly through the museum's exhibitions and, for many, the reason why museums and art galleries exist at all is to enable them to see objects. However, effective communication by the museum with its public must go beyond the exhibition galleries. Indeed, it should include every point at which contact with the public is made.

This paper will consider the museum's communication policy. It will also discuss those factors which determine the formulation of a specific exhibition policy, and examine briefly how this might be implemented.

Museum policy

Many museums had, at their inception, clearly stated aims and objectives. However, few have revised them periodically, or defined clearly their function, particularly in relation to the public. Miers (1928) lamented the fact that, given policy and resources, 'the duty of a museum to the public had yet to be defined'.

On the same theme, American museums were criticized by Theodore Low (1942), when he said

> . . . of all the institutions, both public and private, which have flourished in this country, few, if any, have wandered so aimlessly toward undefined goals as have the museums.

Today, there is generally a greater awareness of the need for each museum to consider how it relates to its public, and the type of service it should provide. However, few museums have undertaken the type of study which the Royal Ontario Museum (1976) pioneered, entitled *Communicating with the Museum Visitor,* which provides a comprehensive analysis of its communications strategy.

By determining the role of the institution in contemporary society, museums should come to understand better their motivation and function. Industry has, for many years, recognized the benefits of setting targets and implementing some form of total resource management in order to obtain specific priority objectives. Museums should consciously do likewise.

The formulation of an overall policy is the obvious starting point. However, unless a museum is clear about its aims and objectives and unless the policy is known, understood and supported by the entire museum staff it is unlikely to be effective.

The policy must consider all the purposes to which the total resources of the museum are to be put. It must keep the provision of resources under review and make the necessary changes in order that the objectives can be achieved. It must state priorities and assign these the necessary proportion of the resources available. Within this overall policy, consideration should be given to the museum's function as communicator.

It must be recognized that all museums are different. Each needs to examine those factors which affect its role – for example, location, size, extent and quality of the collections, expertise and quality of staff, the basis of funding and the proximity of other institutions and their respective functions and resources.

Communications strategy and planning

The Communications Strategy will eminate from, and be an integral part of, the museum's overall policy. Answers must be sought to such basic questions as:

(1) To what extent should the museum educate?
(2) To what extent should it entertain?
(3) What is the audience the museum is wanting to attract?
(4) What is to be the nature of the inter-action of museum and its immediate and remote audience?

Answers to the foregoing questions will help determine the overall image which the museum wishes to project and the work it will undertake. Experience of visiting museums has furnished the public with the knowledge that museums can be colourless and depressing, unintelligible and aloof – but that they can also sparkle, kindle excitement and generate a sense of wonder, satisfaction and fulfilment. They can also be empty and deserted – or teem with noisy, excited children. They can be part of the community – or stand apart.

Responsibility for the formulation and implementation of a communications plan should be clearly identified. All senior staff and interested junior staff should want to contribute to any debate, the outcome of which could have far-reaching implications.

Once a policy has been agreed, the implementation of that policy through a comprehensive plan will need to be co-ordinated and managed. It might be that in larger museums a committee should be formed to oversee communications. But irrespective of size, all museums should charge one person with the necessary expertise, commitment, personality and management skills, for the responsibility of implementing the communications plan, giving the individual the necessary exeuctive power and the resources to proceed effectively.

The communications plan will need to be comprehensive, and should provide guidance without unnecessary constraint. Within the overall policy of the institution, it will need to clarify the museum's approach to education. It should provide guidance on the nature of information to be conveyed and the means of communicating it.

The respective roles to be played by 'permanent', 'temporary' and 'travelling' exhibitions and the content and nature of these will need to be determined carefully. Other related activities such as lectures, demonstrations and schools work also need to be defined. The total range of media available to the museum will also need to be considered. The traditional media of leaflets, guides and catalogues must be evaluated along with the products of recent technological advances – slide tape presentations, video, microcomputers and so on. Care should be taken to select the most appropriate medium for any communications task.

Exhibition policy

It has already been stated that the museum exists primarily to facilitate an encounter between object and observer. For the majority of museum visitors this is brought about in the museum exhibition. Any policy for exhibitions should be part of the overall museum policy, and how that policy for exhibitions is to be implemented, will be incorporated in the communications plan.

Specific factors which determine Exhibition Policy

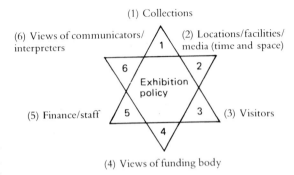

Collections

The objects in the museum's collections have traditionally formed the basis for the communication. Indeed, Cameron (1968) was of the opinion that the museum as a communications system:

> depends on the non-verbal language of objects and observable phenomena.

The selection of objects in order to illustrate an idea which is to be communicated to the visitor, must be done with care and exactness. But what is important is the idea – the message to be conveyed. Displaying the wrong objects, or the right objects but in wrong relationships to one another, will only serve to confuse. Displaying too many objects of a similar type zill bore all but the specialist.

The collections therefore form one of the resources to be used in relation to exhibitions. Omissions and weaknesses can be overcome through adequate finance or loans. The richness and uniqueness of the material available to a museum will be a factor in deciding how comprehensive the exhibition can be, and whether, within its own resources, change can be implemented.

The need for change must be recognized if visitors

are to be encouraged to revisit the museum. While certain objects will justify permanent display, others will not, and these should be identified and used, perhaps, in temporary exhibitions.

Location, facilities, media – time and space

The need for an overview of museum and exhibition facilities on a regional basis has already been stressed. This must extend to the increasing number of related developments which include nature and town trails, site interpretive centres, historic houses, parks, gardens and zoos, industrial sites and craft centres. Each museum will need to determine its role as provider of exhibitions in relation to its location, and the other facilities available within the region. As both time and space are limited, the usage of both needs to be maximized. One of the most difficult decisions to be taken is how to utilize a given space, and the proportion of changing exhibitions to more permanent exhibitions needs careful consideration. This will vary from one museum to another and within the same museum over time, depending on circumstance.

It is not difficult to think of certain regional art galleries which, for short periods each year, give over the majority of their gallery space to important temporary exhibitions. Nor is it difficult to think of museums which provide little more than a single display-case for such work. The potential of special and temporary loan exhibitions in providing the visitor with a constant source of material which might otherwise not be seen, has long been recognized. Special exhibitions are mainly regarded as those originating from material already in the museum's collection, but prepared especially for some topical feature or particular purpose.

Temporary exhibitions might be prepared by a museum, drawing mainly on the museum's 'reserve' collections, but also borrowing material from other sources. Once prepared and shown in one location, it may well be circulated to other institutions in order to further justify its creation and possibly also help offset production costs by imposing an appropriate hire charge on host museums. The subjects chosen for special and temporary exhibition programmes will therefore need to be selected with care, paying particular attention not only to the interests of visitors, but also to those of the exhibitors. These may be museum staff with particular research interests, but they may also be local groups. An art gallery must, for example, formulate a policy in respect of the work produced by local contemporary artists, while each museum and gallery will want to consider the role it can play as part of the social environment. The timing and duration of exhibitions are complex issues. It is dangerous to generalize when so much will depend on the size and topic of the exhibition,

the type of museum and its visitor pattern. A national museum might well be able to maintain fairly constant visitor attendance at a 'temporary' exhibition even after several years, whereas a small local museum, especially outside the tourist season, might reach exhaustion point – when all those likely to visit the exhibition have done so – in only a fortnight. The typical attendance pattern is that attendance is high at the beginning and at the end of any exhibition period.

Another factor influencing the longevity of an exhibition is its durability. Exhibition materials and equipment need to be specified with a particular 'life' in mind. Unless adequate maintenance facilities are available, a museum should not undertake an exhibition which, for example, incorporates extensive electronic and mechanical equipment. Similarly, the ability of the museum to provide adequate security should be given careful consideration and will have a direct influence on what exhibitions can be mounted.

Visitors

Recently, some museums have been keen to discover something about their visitors and a number of studies and surveys[1] have been undertaken. Most agree that the visitors consist of a heterogeneous group with numerous variables. These include age and sex; intelligence and knowledge; social and economic grouping, and particularly important, motivation. Motivated visitors derive more benefit from displays than those who casually visit the museum or wander aimlessly around the galleries.

The various studies which have been made of visitor characteristics and behaviour, notably by Melton (1935), Goins and Griffenhagen (1957), Shettel *et al.* (1968), de Borhegyi and Hanson (1968) and Screven (1974) provide much detailed information which should be considered in relation to exhibition design and planning. However, care must be exercised in the interpretation and application of the data. For example, it is known that the average time a visitor spends before a display is between 20 and 45 seconds (Neal, 1965; Shettel *et al.*, 1968). Coles (1982) reports that people walking around a large exhibition of paintings spend on average 5 seconds in front of a picture. However Alt (1982) quite rightly makes the point that the concept of an average time may not be very useful, since it does not necessarily describe many people. Of more use is the fact that visitors to museums seldom come alone. This clearly has implications for the designers of exhibitions and supporting facilities. Observations too, which establish whether certain exhibits attract visitors or not can also be helpful, as can information on circulation patterns. The salutary observation of Gardner and Heller (1960) that 'an exhibition does not in fact exist until it is crowded with people'; should not be forgotten.

In addition to studies of the behaviour of visitors, the opinions of visitors are of prime importance in assessing the effectiveness of the museum. Borun (1977) recognizes the need for regular channels of feedback for visitor response, 'so that the museum becomes a flexible, self-correcting institution in touch with the needs and desires of its public'.

The expectations of visitors should also be considered. Generally, visitors returning to a museum will expect to see new things, as well as renewing their acquaintance with established favourites.

Most visitors not only expect high standards of presentation, but also the use of modern techniques. The substance of an exhibition must also be sufficient to justify the visit. All too frequently visitors have been motivated by advertisements to visit an exhibition, only to find it consisted of so little material that they have come away feeling dissatisfied and, in some way, cheated. Visitors who leave the museum in this mind will do nothing to promote it. One of the most effective ways of advertising a museum remains the personal contact between visitors and other groups.

Views of funding body

Inevitably the body funding an organization, or charged with responsibility for it, will have a view on how the resources should be deployed. Trustees, governors, local authority representatives and industrial sponsors will all need to be satisfied with the exhibition policy pursued, as will organizations such as the Arts Council and Regional Arts Association if financial support from these bodies is to be sought successfully.

The museum also has an obligation to its public, and although representatives of the public are frequently elected to committees charged with the oversight of museums, those elected do not necessarily reflect the views of the public in general or of the museum audience. In this context, the specialist advice and opinion of the professional museum staff is invaluable. However, it must be remembered that it was this very group of professionals who, in the early development of museums, were responsible for isolating them. The prudent professional will take note of both the wishes of his governing or funding body and the public, and then use his professional judgement to determine the exhibition policy to pursue.

Finance/Staff

Adequate finance is a prerequisite of any effective exhibition program. Pearson (1981) makes the point that public art galleries have suffered in the past from the idea that exhibitions can be run on the cheap. The same can be said of museums. Money buys staff – and staff need money in order to function effectively. Materials, equipment, transport charges and insurance all have to be paid for, even if the manpower is available.

What can be achieved in any one exhibition will inevitably depend, not only on the total resources available, but also on the manner in which these resources are deployed. Money spent, for example, on creating a suitable environment in which objects can be viewed, can so heighten the experience of the visitor to the exhibition that it is money invested wisely. The most memorable exhibitions tend to be those in which special consideration has been given to the environment in which objects are seen.

Where funds are restricted, it may be that exhibitions are smaller, less well-produced and less frequent. Financial considerations may also determine whether the items displayed are two- or three-dimensional and whether the exhibition environment can be changed to relate to each successive display. A consequence of limited finance and the ensuing restrictions on exhibitions could be a falling off in visitor interest.

In the pursuit of professional standards, and the need for the museum to be respected by the public for its professional approach, it is necessary that not only is sufficient finance available, but also the right type of expertise. This will vary according to the scale of operation. However, suitable scientific or academic expertise must be available in respect of the exhibition content. Professional advice on conservation and design must also be sought, and educational and editorial expertise is clearly advantageous.

Where professional staff are not available, one solution could be to hire exhibitions produced by others. Pearson (1981) makes the distinction between art galleries and exhibition spaces, regarding the former as active and the latter as passive. It is not enough for a gallery merely to receive exhibitions from others. It needs to initiate its own policy, and implement it through the exhibition programs and other organized events. It needs to fulfil a social role, stimulate and educate, and have an active relationship with an involved public.

The successful museum or gallery will carefully initiate and select exhibitions which complement and extend its activities. It will look to those bodies which prepare and circulate exhibitions – the Arts Council, the Area Museum Services and commercial and industrial organizations and make a selection from that offered. It will also be aware of the grants available for the production of exhibitions, and the criteria which have to be met in order to qualify. In particular, it will be opportunist and take advantage of the benefits to be derived in participating in festivals and other promotions as well as national events.

Consideration will also need to be given to charging admission to exhibitions, and to the purchase by visitors of supplementary information in the form of catalogues, leaflets or souvenirs such as postcards and badges. The issues raised by the principle of charging for access to information have been well-rehearsed, and the extent to which charging will create a barrier to the museum communicating with its public and to what extent it will aid it, must be the central question to resolve.

Views of Communicators/Interpreters

Few should have a greater input into the formulation and implementation of the exhibition policy than the communicators and interpreters themselves. The subject specialists, designers and educationalists should form the nucleus of this group.

It will be the communicators/interpreters who advise on what the specific objectives of a particular exhibition will be, and how and by what means they can be attained. The qualities which distinguish good communicators from the mediocre are difficult to define, but they are those which enable the attention of the intended audience to be gained, held and then satisfied. So much, therefore, will depend on the skills, experience and preferences of those charged with the task of communicating. Communicating through exhibitions is not an exact science.

Exhibitions, although designed for a purpose, nevertheless remain a plastic art form. As such, they can be fashioned by their creators to illicit certain responses from visitors, and can impart the personality of the main contributors – be they designers or curators.

Policy implementation

The implementation of the exhibition policy needs to be considered on three levels; first, the practical organization of staff and the deployment of resources; second, the formulation of the design problem; and finally, its solution.

The practical organization of staff and the deployment of resources

It cannot be over-emphasized that the production of successful exhibitions is a group activity, with each member contributing specialized knowledge and skills. In implementing the policy, each individual will need to liaise closely with colleagues at all stages.

Briefly, in a medium-sized museum, responsibilities might be undertaken in the following way. The Director should initiate the project, seek the necessary approval and authorize the resources in accordance with the agreed policy. The curator's role is to provide the specialist information, contribute to the writing of the design 'brief', and identify the material

from which the final selection of what to display in the exhibition will be made. The designer should assist in the preparation of the brief and will provide design solutions. Once approved, the design solutions will be translated into specifications and working drawings by the designer, who will normally supervise the contractual arrangements and production stages of the project. The conservation staff will prepare the material for exhibition and advise on the environmental conditions of the display. The overseeing of all aspects of security, both for the exhibition in preparation and once it is complete, will be the responsibility of the security officer.

Education staff should also contribute to the brief and provide advice on aspects of educational technology and psychology. It may also be that, in the absence of a professional editor, the education specialist will assist in writing and editing the exhibition text. The production and maintenance staff with responsibility for producing and maintaining the exhibition, will also be able to provide practical advice at the design stage on their aspects of the project.

A further activity for all concerned with the project, perhaps aided by subject specialists and samples of the intended audience, will be evaluating the proposals. Taking the industrial models of research and development, test marketing and market research and applying these to the museum situation, evaluation will be seen as a continuous process. It should be undertaken as the project is taking shape (formative evaluation) and once it is in existence (summative evaluation). Only through this can the museum be the flexible, self-evaluating and self-correcting institution described by Borun (1977). It is important that everyone concerned with the exhibition should be involved right from the start, consulting and discussing as necessary, before ideas are fixed.

In order to maximize the efficiency and production capacity of staff, effective organization and management techniques will need to be introduced with a system to determine, control and monitor the complexities of exhibition production. Possibly the most helpful techniques are critical path analysis and network systems, which assist the planner in providing visual data on the major stages of a project. Howell (1971) has produced a detailed network system for the planning, designing, construction and installation of exhibits, within which he identified the individual activities that are involved in the complete exhibition project and showed how each activity is dependent on others. At its simplest, critical path analysis can be little more than a bar chart, listing activities and indicating the duration of the activity on a time scale, together with the critical points at which one activity has a bearing on another. It may also indicate the individuals or groups responsible for undertaking a particular activity.

For these techniques to be valid, estimates of the

time taken to complete a particular activity must be obtained from those competent to make such estimates, and ideally those responsible for the work. Once target completion dates are fixed, the system must incorporate suitable contingency factors and should be updated as new information becomes available. Its benefit is as a planning tool; to help those responsible for a project to consider all its aspects and to show all participants the importance of the part they play.

Formulation of the Design Problem

The definition of the problem should be given in the design brief. This should identify a particular need and state simply what is required and why. It should not state how it is to be done, for that constitutes the solution. Much has been written on the design problem in terms of stated objectives (Shettle, 1968; Nicol, 1969; Screven, 1974). It is generally agreed that the following are required:

(1) The need for an exhibition should first be identified.
(2) The aims and objectives of each display within the exhibition need to be clearly stated, that is, what it is intended that the exhibit will achieve.
(3) Where possible, these should be stated in measurable terms.
(4) The purpose of exhibits is to bring about some change in the visitor and to do this, the characteristics of the intended audience must be identified.

Every element of an exhibit – whether it be specimen or artefact, label or caption, model or diorama, audio-visual presentation or interactive device, must be related to a stated objective of the exhibit. Each will compete for the visitor's attention, but all components should have a considered purpose. The changes that the exhibit is intended to bring about may be either affective or cognitive – changing attitudes or feelings or levels of knowledge through exposure to, or interaction with, the exhibit.

In addition to defining the problem in terms of aims and objectives, information is also required on those factors which will have an effect on the solution – the constraints. These will include such practical considerations as a budget, time schedule, location, and may extend to such matters as security and conservation. If specialists not in the museum staff are to be employed, terms of contract will also have to be specified and agreed by all parties at the outset.

Providing a solution to the Exhibition Design Problem

Design may be defined as arranging elements to some purpose, or to solve a stated problem. Exhibitions have rightly been regarded as an art form providing the opportunity for self-expression and argu-

ment, and capitalizing on the effects which space, form, light, colour and sound have on the senses. They are also purposeful, in that an exhibition exists to communicate with the visitor in order to bring about change. This can be an increase in knowledge, greater awareness and understanding of concepts or facts previously unknown. Or it can also be an emotional change – elation, enjoyment or sadness – brought about through an aesthetic experience.

In attempting to provide a solution to the design problem, the designer will adopt a methodical approach and formulate his proposals in the light of previous experience and current research. While accepting that no two problems are identical, and that exhibition design is, as Gardner and Heller (1960) said 'an empirical process', there are, nevertheless, certain theories and practices which have application and relate to each element associated with an exhibition. At the centre of these is the information which exists on the behaviour of visitors both psychological and ergonomical.

Of paramount importance is the scientific data available on the conservation of the specimens. This determines the environmental conditions in which the specimens may be displayed. Light, heat, relative humidity and other atmospheric factors must be carefully determined and monitored if the object is to be displayed safely.

Finally, there exists a body of knowledge relating to exhibition components and their application. The media and materials of exhibitions – dynamic models, audio-visual presentations, photographs, lighting, labels and backgrounds – have been evaluated, as have their strengths, weaknesses and suitability of purpose.

It is, then, primarily the designer's task to draw on this body of knowledge and to consult colleagues as necessary; to propose, test and modify solutions in response to the design brief. This brief will suggest whether the character of the overall solution to the problem will be aesthetic (enabling the visitor to experience the beauty of the objects); romantic or evocative (providing an escape from every-day life) or didactic (informing the visitor and satisfying his intellectual curiosity). It may also be a combination of these.

Orientation

One aspect of exhibitions which is often neglected is the need to prepare visitors for what they are about to experience. Orientation relates both to the physical location as well as the subject matter (conceptual orientation). Cohen (1974), in a survey of orientation in twelve selected institutions in the USA, defines orientation as 'the logical relationship of one situation to another already familiar' which is in accordance with the accepted educational principle of progressing from the known to the unknown.

Orientation can be a gradual process, with each stage capable of standing on its own, yet building up to provide a complete coverage. It might commence through advertisements providing advanced awareness of an exhibition and progress through extensive press, radio and television *exposés* of the subject concerned. Detailed information leaflets might follow, and information packs perhaps comprising background information, exhibition content and plan, and worksheets, which are invaluable for school parties in preparing for a visit, and ensuring that the time spent in the exhibition is used to the best advantage. To this end, at the entrance to each exhibition, a plan and a guide as to how the exhibition may be best seen is clearly important.

Signposting is an aspect of orientation neglected by virtually every museum in the country. Despite the references made to them in the early reports of Miers (1928) Markham (1938) and many since museums, to their detriment, are still not generally signposted from the centres of towns, from bus- and railway-stations or from major and other roads. Adequate signing should be provided for both pedestrian and motorist – signing which would aid direction as well as serve as advertisement. Buildings too, need to be clearly indentifiable, with the entrance marked and hours of opening stated. Inside museums, particularly large ones, there is also a need for a plan and guide to the exhibits plus a comprehensive signing system to enable visitors to find their way around.

Summary

Communicating through museum exhibitions is a highly complex process. Although much is known, there remain many gaps in our knowledge. This is compounded by the fact that the circumstances of every exhibition, as it exists in time and space, are different.

This paper has stressed the need for museums to face up to the problem – to consider and formulate a policy on communicating with the visitor and on exhibitions per se. The very process of examining where each museum stands on this, one of the most important of issues, will generate in every institution the impetus to improve existing facilities and to progress. This can only be to the benefit of both museums and visitors.

Notes

[1] *See:* Elliot, P. and Loomis, R. J. (1975), *Studies of Visitor Behaviour in Museums and Exhibitions: An Annotated Bibliography of Sources Primarily in the English Language,* Office of Museum Programs, Smithsonian Institution, Washington DC. This work lists 204 published books and papers, plus a number of unpublished dissertations and reports.

References

ALT, M. (1982), in *Research in Illustration*, 1981 Conference at Brighton Polytechnic, Proceedings, **11**, p. 140.

DE BORHEGYI, S. F. E. AND HANSON, I. A. (1968) (Eds.), The Museum Visitor, *Publications in Museology*, **3**, Milwaukee Public Museum, Milwaukee

BORUN, M. (1977), *Measuring the Immeasurable – Pilot Study of Museum Effectiveness,* Franklin Institute Philadelphia

CAMERON, D. F. (1968), A viewpoint: The museum as a communications system and implications for museum education, *Curator*, **XI**(1), 33–40

COHEN, M. S. (1974), *The State of the Art of Museum Visitor Orientation*, Smithsonian Institution, Washington DC

COLES, P. (1982), Eye movements and picture perception, in *Research in illustration*, 1981 Conference Proceedings **11**, Brighton Polytechnic, pp. 123–142

GARDNER, J. AND HELLER, C. (1960), *Exhibition and display*, Batsford, London

GOINS, A. AND GRIFFENHAGEN, G. (1957), Psychological studies of museum visitors and exhibits at the US National Museum, *The Museologist*, **64**, 1–6

HOWELL, D. B. (1971), A network system for the planning, designing, construction, and installation of exhibits. *Curator*, **XIV**(2), 100–108

LOW, T. (1942), in *The Museum as a Social Instrument*, The Metropolitan Museum of Art, New York

MARKHAM, F. (1938), *The Museums and Art Galleries of the British Isles*, Carnegie United Kingdom Trust, Dunfermline

MELTON, A. W. (1935), Problems of installation in museums of art, *Publications of the American Association of Museums*, New Series No. 14, Washington DC. (This article originally appeared in *Museum News*)

MELTON, A. W. (1972), Visitor behaviour in museums: some early research in environmental design, *Human Factors*, **14**(5), 393–403

MIERS, H. (1928), *A Report on the Public Museums of the British Isles*, Edinburgh

NEAL, A. (1965), Function of display: Regional Museums, *Curator*, **VIII**(3), 228–234

NICOL, E. H. (1969), *The Development of Validated Museum Exhibits,* US Department of Health, Education and Welfare, Office of Education, Bureau of Research, Washington DC and Children's Museum, Boston

PEARSON, N. (1981), *Art Galleries and Exhibition Spaces in Wales,* Welsh Arts Council, Cardiff

ROYAL ONTARIO MUSEUM (1976), *Communicating with the Museum Visitor*, Royal Ontario Museum, Ottawa

SCREVEN, C. G. (1974), *The Measurement and Facilitation of Learning in the Museum Environment: An Experimental Analysis*, Smithsonian Institution, Washington DC

SHETTEL, H. H. *et al.* (1968), *Strategies for Determining Exhibit Effectiveness*, Project No. V-011; Contract No. OE-6-10.213, American Institute for Research, Pittsburgh

Bibliography

ALT, M. B. (1977), Evaluating didactic exhibits: a critical look at Shettel's work, *Curator*, **20**(3), 241–257. A thorough analysis of Shettel's paper, from which he concludes that by ignoring the fact that visitors to museums are different in make-up and intention, Shettal does not come to grips with evaluating the educational effectiveness of didactic exhibits.

ALT, M. B. (1980), Four years of visitor surveys at the British Museum (Natural History) 1976–1979, *Museums J.*, **80**(1), 10–19. A review of the annual surveys of visitors carried out in September each year. Visitors profiles, expectations, interests and their most memorable exhibits are given in 20 detailed tables.

ARNELL, U. HAMMER, I. AND NYLOF, G. (1976), *Going to Exhibitions* Riksutstalingar/Swedish Travelling Exhibitions, Stockholm. A critical appraisal of the work of Swedish Travelling Exhibitions and the effect of the exhibitions on knowledge and attitudes.

BAYER, H. (1961), Aspects of design of exhibitions and museums, *Curator*, **IV**(3), 257–287. Selected exhibition elements and characteristics are traced back to their nineteenth- and twentieth-century origins.

BEDEKAR, V. H. (1978), *So you want Good Museum Exhibitions*, Department of Museology, Faculty of Fine Arts, MS University of Barona. A manual on exhibition preparation and design intended for trainees for the museum profession.

BERNADO, J. R. (1972), *Museum Environs for Communications: A Study of Environmental Parameters in the Design of Museum Experiences*, unpublished PhD dissertation, Columbia University. Considers those elements of the environment which a designer can manipulate to influence desired behavioural responses in museum audiences.

BORUN, M. (1975), *Museum Effectiveness Study – a Bibliographic Review*, The Franklin Institute, Philadelphia.

BRAWNE, M. (1965), *The New Museum: Architecture and Display*, Architectural Press, London. Illustrated international survey of new museums and their displays.

BRAWNE, M. (1982), *The museum interior – Temporary and Permanent Display Techniques*, Thames and Hudson, London.

BUTLER, P. M. (1970), *Temporary Exhibitions*, Museums Association, London. Suggestions of sources and checklist.

BRIGHTON POLYTECHNIC (1981), *Research in Illustration*, Conference Proceedings, Parts I and II, Brighton Polytechnic, Brighton. Proceedings of the conference held on 26/27 March 1981 – possibly the first to be held in the UK on research in illustration. The aim of the conference was to explore potential areas of investigation in relation to illustration.

CANNON-BROOKES, P. (1971), The loan of works of art for exhibition, *Museums J.*, **71**(3), 105–107. A discussion of draft conditions of loan, for the protection of object, lender and borrower.

CARMEL, J. H. (1962), *Exhibition Techniques – Travelling and Temporary*, Reinhold, New York. A comprehensive, well-illustrated manual related to all aspects of the design and preparation of temporary exhibitions.

CORDINGLY, D. (1975), Methods of lettering for museums, Museums Association, London. A guide to production methods.

COUNTRYSIDE COMMISSION (1978), *Interpretation in Visitor Centres*, Countryside Commission, Cheltenham. A study of the visitors and displays at seventeen centres in the UK.

EAST, M. (1952), *Display for Learning: Making and Using Visual Materials*, Holt, Rinehart and Winston, London. A brief introduction to the theory of display for learning, followed by specific examples, mainly for use in schools, or small units without professional assistance.

ELLIOT, P. AND LOOMIS, R. J. *Studies of visitor behaviour in museums and exhibitions.* Smithsonian Institution, Washington DC. An annotated bibliography.

FAZZINI, D. (1972), *The Museum as a Learning Environment: A Self Motivating, Recycling, Learning System for the Museum Visitor*, unpublished PhD dissertation, University of Wisconsin, Milwaukee. Meticulous study of a recycling system applied to the museum environment.

FOLLIS, J. AND HAMMER, D. (1979), *Architectural Signing and Graphics*, Architectural Press, London. A comprehensive, well-illustrated study of contemporary sign design practice.

GARDNER, J. AND HELLER, C. (1960), *Exhibition and Display*, Batsford, London. A comprehensive treatment of the subject. Although photographs are now dated, illustrations and text are very relevant today.

GATACRE, E. V. (1976), The limits of professional design, *Museums J.*, **76**(3), 93–99. A paper read at the Museums Association Annual Conference, 1976. Contemporary designers are taken to task for responding to fashion, and doubts are expressed on current museum design developments.

GLEADOW, E. T. (1975), *Organising Exhibitions*, Arts Council of Great Britain. A manual which outlines the methods used to organize temporary exhibitions of works of art.

GREEN, M. (1977), The museum designer: an examination of the present to anticipate the future, *Conference Proceedings for 2001. The Museum and the Canadian Public*, Canadian Museums Association. A brief paper expressing concern regarding commercial design as applied to museums, and stressing the need for the development of a museum's own communications technology.

JOHNSTONE, C. (1980), Art museums in the communications age: a summary, *Museums J.*, **80**(2), 72–77. Summaries of papers presented at a one-day conference in February 1980 on how art galleries should interpret their collections to the general public, including: Grote, D. A. 'Art and Information'; Macdonald-Ross, M. 'Research and development for museum exhibits'; Luckett, H. 'An experiment in interpretive design – "Landscapes" at Southampton Art Gallery'; Johnstone, C. 'A guide to interpretive techniques'.

KNEZ, E. L. AND WRIGHT, A. G. (1970), The museum as a communications system: an assessment of Cameron's viewpoint, *Curator*, **XIII**(3), 204–212. An alternative viewpoint: that Cameron's 'subsidiary media' (labels, photographics etc) are really primary and that objects are not the medium.

LEWIS, B. N. (1980), The museum as an educational facility, *Museums J.*, **80**(3), 151–155. A critical appraisal of museums as educators.

MALIK, M. (1963), Principles of automation in museum exhibitions, *Curator*, **VI**(3), 247–268. Account of the 'Interkamera' project which introduced automation to the museum exhibition. Brief technical details given.

MANCHESTER POLYTECHNIC LIBRARY (1980), *Exhibition Design. Bibliographic Series* No. 11, Manchester Polytechnic, Manchester. Annotated bibliography of 152 items.

MILES, R. S. AND ALT, M. B. (1979), British Museum (Natural History): a new approach to the visiting public, *Museums J.,* **78**(3), 158–162. Article based on a paper read at the Museums Association Annual Conference 1978, in which the new approach and its use of educational technology and evaluation studies is outlined.

MILES, R. S. et al (1982), *The design of educational exhibits,* George Allen and Unwin, Hemel Hempstead.

MORRIS, R. G. M. AND ALT, M. B. (1978), An experiment to help design a map for a larger museum. *Museums J.,* **77**(4), 179–181. Results of an experiment to test and compare axonometric and plan drawings of a museum map to aid visitor orientation. Both were found to be inadequate and neither better than the other.

NEAL, A. (1963), Gallery and case exhibit design, *Curator,* **VI**(1), 77–96. A brief introduction of the ergonomic factors related to exhibitions and various design proposals for cases and case layouts.

NEAL, A. (1965), Function of display: Regional museums, *Curator,* **VIII**(3), 228–234. Address given to the Utah Museums Conference, 1965 in which the need is stressed for regional museums to cover the local story first.

PEARSON, N. (1981), *Art Galleries and Exhibition Spaces in Wales,* Welsh Arts Council, Cardiff. A report commissioned by the Welsh Arts Council to survey existing galleries and exhibition spaces in Wales, and to reappraise their activities and potential.

ROBINSON, P. V. (1960), *An Experimental Study of Exhibit Arrangement and Viewing Method to Determine their Effect upon Learning of Factual Material,* unpublished DEd dissertation, University of Southern California. A comprehensive review of related literate and in depth account of experiments undertaken to determine the effect of selected exhibit installations on learning.

ROYAL ONTARIO MUSEUM (1976), *Communicating with the Museum Visitor,* Royal Ontario Museum, Toronto. A most comprehensive guide to planning, bringing together the findings of previous researchers and presenting them in an accessible form. Extensive bibliographies and appendices. A major work, essential to all concerned with museum and exhibition design.

SOBOL, M. G. (1980), Do the 'blockbusters' change the audience?, *Museums J.,* **80**(1), 25–27. A brief analysis of visitor profiles in relation to major temporary exhibitions at Dallas Museum of Fine Arts.

SORSBY, B. D. AND HORNE, S. D. (1980), The readability of museum labels, *Museums J.,* **80**(3), 157–159. A comparison between newspaper reading habits of the general population and those of visitors of Merseyside County museums in 1975, leading to the conclusion that at least two-thirds of museum labels will not gain the full attention of the majority of visitors.

SPENCER, H. (1969), *The Visible Word,* Lund Humphries, London. A brief survey of the major research undertaken in word legibility.

SPENCER, H. AND REYNOLDS, L. (1977), *Directional signing and labelling in libraries and museums: a review of current theory and practice,* Readability of Print Unit, Royal College of Art, London. A study of current practice and a review of relevant research findings. Twenty-seven libraries and eighteen museums were examined in detail.

STANSFIELD, G. (1981), *Effective Interpretive Exhibitions,* Countryside Commission, Cheltenham. A review of the research into the effectiveness of communication achieved through exhibitions and the printed word, with particular emphasis on results and conclusions which, it is considered, have wider application.

SVEDBERG, E. (1949), 'Museum display' in *Museums in Modern Life,* Royal Society of Arts, London. Much of the post-war museum design movement is identifiable with the concepts put forward in this paper.

SZEMERE, A. (1978) (Ed.), *The Problem of Contents, Didactics and Aesthetics of Modern Museum Exhibitions,* Institute of Conservation and Methodology of Museums, Budapest. Papers read at the International Museum Seminar (July 1977).

THOM, V. M. (1980), Evaluating countryside interpretation: a critical look at the current situation, *Museums J.,* **79**(4), 179–185. A review of recent studies on aspects of visitor centre operation.

THOMSON, G. AND BULLOCK, L. (1978), (3rd edn.) *Conservation and Museum Lighting,* Museum Association, London. Identification of dangers and recommendations for protection, including product guide.

TYLER, B. AND DICKENSON, V. (1977), *A Handbook for the Travelling Exhibitionist,* Canadian Museums Association. A brief check-list for those preparing travelling exhibitions. Amusing cartoon illustrations.

WEINER, G. (1963), Why Johnny can't read labels, *Curator,* **VI**(2), 143–156. An examination of label content, legibility and form.

WILLIAMS, L. A. (1960), Labels: writing, design and preparation, *Curator,* **III**(1), 26–42. A step-by-step account of label production.

WITTEBORG, L. P. (1958), Design standards in museum exhibits, *Curator,* **1**(1), 29–41. A brief history of exhibition design.

WITTLIN, A. S. (1971), Hazards of Communication by exhibits, *Curator,* **14**(2), 138–150.

47

Evaluating exhibitions

Steven A. Griggs

During the last fifteen to twenty years there has been a considerable upsurge of interest in exhibition evaluation in North America which is now beginning to filter through to Great Britain. While most of us may feel we know what evaluation entails in some general sense, one only has to look at the literature to appreciate that many of the studies reported are methodologically unsound. Loomis (1973) has made a similar point in relation to visitor surveys. The lesson to be learnt from this is that exhibition evaluation is just as complex as anything else done in a museum, be it taxidermy, exhibit design, the cataloguing of collections, or whatever, and that it requires a certain set of skills.

The aims of this paper are twofold. First, to examine in some detail what exhibition evaluation entails. This is done by asking a number of questions – 'What is evaluation?', 'Why evaluate?', and so on. Second, to discuss how such evaluation studies are carried out. A distinction is made between 'front-end', 'formative', and 'summative' evaluation. The first two are then elaborated in some detail. The last is taken up as the theme of the following paper.

What exhibition evaluation entails

What is evaluation?

The process of evaluation is usually defined in terms of determining the 'success' or 'worth' of the object or event under consideration. In fact we can distinguish at least four components of this process.

(1) *The identification of certain qualities or attributes.* For exhibitions, these tend to be the ability of an exhibit to attract and hold the visitor's attention (attracting and holding power), and sometimes, the ability to communicate an intended message.

(2) *Obtaining scores as to the degree to which an exhibi-tion possesses these qualities.* For example, designing an observational research program to yield data relevant to computations of holding power and attracting power.

(3) *Eliciting expressions of liking or preference for the thing being evaluated.* Components (2) and (3) tend to be muddled in the evaluation literature but they are not the same thing. For example, a given display may score highly on the quality 'awe-inspiring', but if one believes exhibits should aim to educate and inform rather than simply generate feelings of awe, one is unlikely to be impressed with the display. Too often it is falsely assumed that the mere possession of certain properties necessarily entails that people will prefer that display as against one which lacks those qualities.

(4) *'Evaluation' of the results.* Having identified the qualities and measured them, and having obtained people's preferences, there remains the task of 'evaluating' the results: has the exhibit passed or failed? To do this we need some sort of yardstick against which to make a decision. Usually, these are generated once the results are known. There is no reason why such yardsticks should not be set out prior to any measurement, indeed this can lead to a more objective aporoach. (This point is elaborated below.)

These four components probably characterize any evaluation study. The way studies differ is not so much in terms of whether certain elements are omitted but more in terms of the rigorousness with which the components are applied. For the sake of convenience we can distinguish between 'formal' and 'informal' evaluation. Both have merits and disadvantages and they both have a place in the development of exhibits.

The term 'informal' is used to refer to uncontrolled, non-rigorous evaluation. It includes the use of anecdotal evidence, intuition, experience, prejudice, and so on. Informal evaluation is quick, on the spot and requires little in the way of effort or resources. Its major disadvantage lies in its unreliability. A typical scenario for this approach to evaluation would be a designer thinking about various options and rejecting some in favour of others. He uses his own experience, training, intuition and bias to reach a decision. A second designer in the same position would probably use the same procedures to come to a different solution. Such evaluation tends to occur at an early stage in the process of developing exhibits.

'Formal' evaluation refers to the systematic, rigorous evaluation carried out by someone with the relevant skills and training. It requires more in the way of effort and resources since it needs detailed planning and takes time to put into effect. However, its major advantage is that it produces reliable data on which informed decisions can be taken and thus tries to avoid, and if necessary, overcome, prejudice. Formal evaluation tends to occur at the end of the development process. One of the central arguments of this paper is that formal evaluation should occur at all stages of developing exhibits.

Why evaluate?

In most cases within the museum world, evaluation does not take place other than informally. Where it occurs it does so for a variety of reasons. In fact, there are certain climates in which it is probably better *not* to evaluate. If the system is rigid and inflexible to change, then evaluation findings which entail making modifications are simply going to be ignored. Indeed, the findings might well be suppressed in order to avoid embarrassment.

One reason underlying some evaluation studies is 'paying lip-service', in other words, evaluating because it is felt to be the thing to be seen doing. Again, this type of evaluation is best avoided.

One of the most often-cited reasons for evaluation is to provide *feedback* to this process of developing exhibits. While this in itself is a laudable objective, adherence to such a model as the sole reason for evaluation is extremely naive. The model tends to overlook stage (3): the elicitation of preference or likes and dislikes. Thus a person may evaluate an exhibition unfavourably even though it has been shown to be successful in achieving its stated aims. The reverse can also be true. This is particularly important when the person who comes to this conclusion is in a position of power or authority. As such their personal preference is likely to outweigh most other considerations. This is because evaluation is by nature *political*.

A frequently cited *raison d'etre* of evaluation is accountability (either cost, head-counts, or some other index). However, it needs to be pointed out that it is rare for public opinion to be the only determinant of policy-making. The opinions of so-called experts and peer groups are usually more telling.

It should be clear from all this that the question of why one is evaluating needs to be considered carefully by everyone concerned. This point is worth making because often those people who want to evaluate just do not realize what it entails. Without ample consideration of this question, the naive evaluator may well spend a great deal of effort, time and money only to be disappointed at the end of the day. A more detailed account of the politics of evaluation may be found in Alt and Lewis (1982).

When to evaluate?

'Informal' evaluation tends to take place at the early stages of exhibit development when the options are fairly open. 'Formal' evaluation, if it occurs at all, usually takes place once the exhibits have been built and displayed in the gallery. Exhibit developers should (and probably do) carry out 'informal' evaluation all the time. They should be continually asking themselves questions such as 'Is this the most appropriate method of displaying this material?', 'Have I reached this decision simply through my own prejudice, or are there good reasons to support my conclusions?' Similarly, 'formal' evaluation should also occur at all stages. In fact, experience shows the earlier the better. For convenience, the process can be divided into three stages, but it must be emphasized that the three overlap and complement one another[1].

(1) *Front end evaluation* which takes place prior to any exhibit development.
(2) *Formative evaluation* which takes place during the process of developing exhibits.
(3) *Summative evaluation* which takes place once the exhibition has been built.

A detailed comparison of these three types of evaluation is set out in the second part of this article.

What is evaluated?

At first glance, the answer to this question seems obvious: the exhibits. However, it is not quite so straightforward. Front-end evaluation occurs prior to any exhibit development and is thus the evaluation of plans, ideas and concepts; formative evaluation is carried out using mock-up exhibits and is thus evaluation of intended exhibits: summative evaluation is carried out once the exhibits have been built and installed in the galleries. As such, only summative evaluation can truly be said to be the evaluation of exhibits.

There is another reason why the answer to this question may not be quite so obvious. The request

'Here is an exhibit, please evaluate it' is, as it stands, fairly meaningless, and one to which the reply should be, 'Evaluate with respect to what?'

In terms of the four components set out above, the first need is to determine the qualities/attributes of interest *before* beginning to measure them. At the simplest level this may be no more than attracting and holding power (how many and for how long). In those cases where the interest lies in the extent to which a display educates, the need is to define quite precisely what the information is to be learnt, and how this information will affect visitors. In other words, what would a visitor be expected to know or do after experiencing the exhibit which she did not know or could not do beforehand. The usual approach here is to try and define certain aims and objectives. This approach owes its existence to the work on curriculum development and educational evaluation and has subsequently been applied to exhibition evaluation[2].

Unfortunately, by concentrating on defining objectives and measuring how well these have been achieved, exhibition evaluators have tended to ignore the third stage of evaluation identified earlier. The emphasis has tended to be on finding out whether a given exhibit succeeds in getting visitors to behave in some predetermined way rather than looking to see if the exhibit matches up to the interests and needs of visitors, whatever these may be[3].

At a more pragmatic level, attempts to gauge visitors' reactions are often ham-strung by the phenomenon referred to by psychologists as the 'halo effect'. This refers to the fact that when visitors are invited to comment on an exhibit they always find plenty of good things to say about it but are generally loathe to criticize displays since this might also be seen as a criticism of the institution, the evaluator and so on. The need here is to be sensitive to this possibility and act accordingly. For example, by asking visitors to choose between a number of options, or to place a number of options into an order of preference.

Having defined and measured the relevant qualities and having gauged visitors' interests and preferences, the findings are evaluated against some notional yardstick. Occasionally, where one is trying out a number of possible solutions for an exhibit the different options form their own yardsticks: given three options, A, B and C, which one is most successful in meeting the stated aims and satisfying visitors' preferences? Even here difficulties might arise. For example, assuming that an appropriate questionnaire has been administered, the results of which reveal that exhibit A does better than B and C, should option A be used? An examination of the total scores on the questionnaire might show that A results in 9 out of 20 questions correctly answered,

while B and C both result in 5 out of 20. Now, although A is the most successful of the three chosen options, it has to be considered if a mark of 9 out of 20 warrants the acceptance of option A as the final choice. If the answer is no, the result must be a return to the drawing board to generate new options to test. However, it is a luxury to have both the time and the money to construct a number of such options. The usual state of affairs is the one-off exhibit. In such cases, questions must be asked. For example, are some of the stated objectives more important than others? If the exhibit provides a key concept for understanding the rest of the exhibition, what percentage of visitors would be expected or hoped to stop at the display[4].

Questions such as these should be asked *and* answered prior to gathering the data. Exhibit developers are often resistant to providing such yardsticks in advance, and for obvious reasons – very often the criteria can only be 'shots in the dark'. However, they may be only too pleased to develop criteria after the study has been carried out and the results known. Of course, the problem here is the tendency to develop criteria to meet the findings rather than the other way round! Thus, it is important that the criteria of success or failure are formulated in advance of the evaluation. These do not have to be too precise but one should have some notion of what constitutes a success, a marginal success, a marginal failure and so on. For example: 'objective 1 to be obtained by 40 to 60 per cent of the sample.'

Experience shows that people tend to start off by setting their aims too high. The real answer here is to try it out a few times and learn from experience. A useful starting point may be to divide one's objectives into two classes: important and less important.

Finally, a word of warning. Even though the ostensible reason is to evaluate exhibits (or mock-ups, or ideas) some people may feel threatened by this activity because they see it as evaluating *them,* their policies, skills and so on. A sensitive approach is vital in situations where people are less keen to learn the results of the evaluation, let alone implement any necessary changes.

How to evaluate

The number of available techniques is virtually unlimited and it is certainly beyond the scope of the present article to attempt an exhaustive summary. Some useful guidelines may be found in the chapter by Alt (1982a). Observation of the literature suggests that the most common methods tend to fall into one or more of three categories (Alt and Morris, 1979):

(1) Large-scale sample surveys.
(2) Behavioural observations.
(3) Pen and paper tests.

The first of these, the large-scale sample surveys, are most often used to find out who visits museums, why they visit and what they get from the visit[5]. This type of approach is useful when quantitative information is called for. The utility value of such surveys lies in the fact that they provide information for directing work and as such should be carried out as front-end evaluation.

Behavioural studies involve observing visitor behaviour in the galleries. The pioneering studies in this area as far as museums are concerned were carried out in the 1920s and 1930s by Robinson (for example, Robinson, 1928) and Melton (1935, 1972). They tracked visitors around galleries noting their route, the displays stopped at, and the time taken. During the 1960s and 1970s a number of similar studies were carried out (for example, Weiss and Boutourline, 1963; Parsons, 1965; Lakota, 1975).

The basic 'theory' of exhibit effectiveness to emerge from these behavioural studies (if, indeed, it can be called a theory) is that to be effective an exhibit must achieve two things:

(1) It must attract the visitor's attention and make him stop; this gives rise to a measure of attractiveness defined as the proportion of the total sample who stop at any one display.
(2) Having gained the visitor's attention it must then hold it long enough for the message to get across. This gives rise to a measure of holding power defined as the length of time a visitor spends at any one display[6].

The pen and paper tests are usually educationally based, their aim being to discover how much learning has taken place. This approach owes its existence to the work on curriculum development which gained momentum in America during the 1960s. The most common approach is to determine to what extent some pre-set educational objectives are achieved by a sample of visitors following exposure to the relevant exhibits.

Studies of this type, when carried out on casual visitors, reveal that, as a whole, *very little* is learned from exhibits. Despite this finding, adherents of this approach have argued that a third index of exhibit effectiveness needs to be added to the list given above:

(3) An effective exhibit not only attracts and holds the visitor's attention, it will also succeed in communicating its intended message.

This approach to exhibit evaluation is disappointing in several ways, not the least of which is the implicit model of what it is to be a visitor. Visitors are assumed to be passive and mechanistic, and to be moulded to the needs of the exhibits, rather than accepting them as active, purposive agents with pre-

ferences and interests and then finding ways of designing exhibits to meet these interests.

Furthermore, despite the quantity of such work reported in the literature, almost no attempt has been made to test hypotheses concerning why one exhibit is more effective than another. Thus, the whole bulk of this research serves to indicate which exhibits are and which are not successful. What it fails to reveal is why.

Carrying out exhibition evaluation

Summative evaluation

The usual position is that when evaluation forms part of a museum's program only summative evaluation takes place. While not wishing to devalue the importance of summative evaluation, this state of affairs can lead to serious problems.

Evaluation, by its very nature, seeks to find ways of changing, improving or criticizing exhibitions. However, usually it is very expensive and time-consuming to modify exhibitions even in minor ways once they have been built and installed in the gallery. It can also be politically sensitive since if such changes are agreed there must also be agreement that the exhibition has failed in some way. Perhaps most importantly from the point of view of exhibit developers, it is psychologically difficult to change their ideas at this stage. A large, permanent exhibition may have a gestation period of two or three years. During this time a number of people would have invested a great deal in the exhibition and would have become very attached to their ideas and designs (it is not uncommon to hear such people talk about 'my exhibition'). To be told at the end of all this that they have been wasting their time is not very helpful and, understandably, most people in this situation look for all sorts of reasons to justify their original ideas.

This is not to say there is no place for summative evaluation in museums. On the contrary, there are at least two *very* important reasons for carrying out such work. First, when all is said and done and an exhibition is finished and set up in the gallery, the *only* way to get definitive answers to questions like 'Does it work', 'Can it be improved?', 'Do people like it?', is to carry out summative evaluation.

The second reason for summative evaluation is that it can provide information for future work. In this sense it is more like orthodox research by allowing the construction of theories of visitor—exhibit relationships which can then be built into the process of designing exhibits. It is just this aspect of exhibition evaluation which is so sadly lacking[7].

The remainder of this paper concentrates on formative and front-end evaluation. A more detailed account of summative studies is to be found in the next paper.

Formative evaluation

The most effective way of using evaluation techniques in order to maximise the benefit for exhibit developers is to carry them out during the process of development. Such evaluation is referred to as 'Formative evaluation'. The usual methodology is to construct cheap mock-ups of proposed exhibits and try these out on a sample of visitors.

The main goal of formative evaluation is to assess the extent to which a particular set of mock-ups communicate their intended message. This statement requires clarification because it can mean different things to different people. Adherents of the educational evaluation model would impose a rather strong interpretation on this statement. By 'communicate' they would mean 'teach', and the concern would be to discover how much visitors 'learn' from such displays. For example, Screven (1975) has said (italics mine):

> There is a large body of useful educational and psychological research, principles and methodology which can help you to properly 'evaluate' the communication (*teaching*) effectiveness of your exhibitions and improve their effectiveness.

A strict definition of learning requires a *permanent* change in a visitor's behaviour, that is, after seeing an exhibit he or she is able to do something which he or she could not previously do and this change is a permanent one. Unfortunately, most studies have failed to find even transient changes let alone permanent ones. A somewhat weaker interpretation of this statement is to argue that an exhibit communicates its message if a visitor, on seeing the display, can *comprehend* the information without any misunderstanding or misconception about its content and intention. With this weaker interpretation there is no need to call upon the notion of learning as a permanent change in behaviour. As with any other communication setting, if you can understand what I am trying to say, if I am expressing myself clearly, then communication can be said to have taken place. What you choose to do with that information is then up to you. Assuming that I told you something you did not already know some learning might take place, again it is up to you. You may decide the information is not worthy of your attention and promptly forget it. This does not mean that communication has failed.

So, rather than trying to gauge some quantity of learning, formative evaluation can be much more productively employed in the identification of errors, confusions and misconceptions which in themselves represent a breakdown of communica-

tion. This does not only relate to a display's content, it also includes the way things are said. Thus, the quantity of material involved, the clarity of instructions, the consistency in the use of terms, the readability of texts are all included under the notion of communicating the message. (See Linn, 1976 and In press, who also questions the wisdom of evaluating exhibitions in terms of visitor learning).

From the point of view of the exhibit developers, formative evaluation needs to provide answers both quickly and cheaply. Thus, it is no use carrying out elegant but elaborate studies which require several weeks before results are known. Information must also be provided as cheaply as possible because all programs work to a fixed budget and while formative evaluation can provide valuable information, it should not be seen to absorb too much of the initial budget.

These two constraints have consequences for the approach finally adopted. Generally speaking, formative evaluation is *not* 'hypothesis-testing' in the usual sense, nor is it concerned with generalizing the findings to a larger population of exhibits or visitors (this being one of the aims of summative evaluation). Rather, it is concerned with obtaining *specific information* about *specific mocked-up exhibits,* in order to introduce any necessary modifications, and ultimately to produce a set of successful mock-ups which can be constructed as finalized exhibits[8]. The real question to be addressed is how is it possible to collect this specific information from a small sample of visitors? From a practical point of view, perhaps the most useful way of tackling this problem is to approach it from more than one angle.

An illustration of such a procedure carried out at the British Museum (Natural History) is useful here (Griggs, 1982). The first section of the Hall of Human Biology entitled 'Living Cells' was redeveloped recently. The proposed exhibits were subjected to formative evaluation. A total of 3o visitors were selected to take part in the study. The visitors were approached by the interviewer on a random basis[9].

When visitors agreed to participate in the survey they were taken to the room housing the mock-ups and allowed to have a good look at them. They were then taken to one side, out of sight of the mock-ups. The interviewer explained that the mocked-up exhibits attempted to tell a story. The visitors were then asked to provide their version of the story. A tape-recording was taken of what was said and transcripts made at a later stage.

Having completed telling their version of the story, they were asked a number of specific points in the form of a questionnaire. This was administered to them as they were seated in full view of the exhibits. Each exhibit was considered in turn. Interviewees were first asked to interpret each exhibit by explaining in their own words what they thought it was about. Whereas previously, respondents were having to recall what they had seen, now they simply had to interpret what they saw in front of them.

The questionnaire also asked interviewees whether they found anything confusing about each exhibit. Their responses afforded the identification of stretches of text which were unclear, and other such problems. Finally, it presented a series of questions specific to each mock-up. These often arose from a preliminary survey of museum staff and tackled particular problem areas. For example, respondents might be asked to interpret a particular analogy.

Thus, the study involved a multiple-approach procedure which attempted to cover various aspects of the mocked-up exhibits.

The transcribed story-lines produced from our sample of visitors were subjected to a form of content analysis. Basically, this involves *systematically* noting down which parts of the intended story-line are mentioned by each visitor. This revealed that the main topic areas were mentioned by the majority of visitors. In other words, the mock-ups did seem to be successfully communicating their main points.

The evaluation turned next to an analysis of the questionnaires. This exercise produced some surprising results. Certain of the mock-ups were interpreted by the majority of visitors to be saying something totally at odds with the intended message! For example, one of the mock-ups was intended to illustrate the structure of the two sex cells and how these structures are specially adapted to perform particular functions. Most people overlooked this aspect of the exhibit and stated that it was supposed to illustrate the moment of fertilization. This confusion arose for two reasons. First, the exhibit was poorly positioned. It was part of a series of exhibits beginning with an introduction to the two types of sex cells and where they are produced, through how the sperm cells enter the woman's body and their journey to the ovum. The exhibit in question was placed at the end of this sequence rather than at the beginning since the exhibition developers felt that one could only appreciate the structural adaptations once one knew the functions. However, the logical interpretation of the exhibit in this position is that given by most people: the moment of fertilization. This interpretation was reinforced by the graphics which suggested that the two cells were indeed 'meeting'. The problem was easily resolved by repositioning the exhibit and carrying out minor modifications to text and graphics.

Thus, by approaching the evaluation study from two ends (an unstructured interview in which visitors tried to recall the story, and a questionnaire) it was possible to conclude that the mock-ups were largely successful in communicating their information. However, specific problems were isolated where further work was required before an exhibit could be finalized.

The key advantage of formative evaluation is that any errors can be isolated at an early stage so that the necessary modifications can be introduced with a minimum of disruption. However, there are a number of disadvantages associated with this approach.

To begin with, such studies provide essentially negative information. That is to say, they can reveal what probably will not work but in most cases can go no further than provide only general guidelines as to what might succeed in its place. For example, assuming that as the result of interviewing a number of visitors, a particular piece of text is found to be difficult. Peoples' responses to the questions reveal it is both too long and uses too many technical words. It is, therefore, decided to rewrite the text to make it shorter and more plain. The immediate problem is that some of the technical words can only be translated into plain English by substituting lengthy descriptions. What can be done? The evaluation has revealed the problem but it has not said how to solve it. The only recourse is to evaluate the rewritten text and trust that the experience gained from the first attempt is sufficient to overcome the difficulties, and furthermore than no new problems have been introduced.

One of the difficulties of summative evaluation may also crop up with formative studies since even here exhibit developers may already have invested a lot of energy in their ideas and so resistance to change can still be present. Furthermore, formative evaluation can not help in providing basic information concerning what people already know about a topic, or what misconceptions they might bring with them[10]. It is fairly obvious that an exhibition needs to be pitched at the appropriate conceptual level for its intended audience. In most cases, this is arrived at by guess-work and assumption and, not surprisingly, the assumptions are often inappropriate; it often fails. This difficulty is fairly easily overcome by carrying out front-end evaluation.

Front-end evaluation

Front-end evaluation aims to identify and eliminate errors *before* they arise. It can be visualized as the evaluation of unrealized plans. Excluding visitor surveys, such work is rarely carried out in the museum world, yet if done properly, it helps to avoid many subsequent problems.

Front-end evaluation can be used to find out, for example, what people know, the misconceptions they hold, and where their interests lie. Its main disadvantage lies in identifying problems. At such an early stage in the development process it can be difficult to focus on specifics since these have not yet been generated.

As with all other approaches to evaluation, front-end work can be 'formal' or 'informal'. An example of the latter would be a group of exhibition developers participating in lengthy discussions, the aim being to generate as many ideas as possible. Each idea is then considered on its merits and faults, many are discarded but a few may survive to form the basis of an exhibition.

An example of 'formal' front-end evaluation is market research to discover what visitors know about the topics of a planned exhibition, any misconceptions held, and equally important, what they are interested in. It does not have to be restricted to sample surveys, however. Front-end evaluation also entails the application of existing knowledge and bodies of research to new problem areas. Thus, much psychological research is relevant to the design of exhibitions whether these be general statements about the way people handle quantities of information (see Wittlin, 1971) or specific facts pertinent to, for example, the choice of colour for figure-ground displays on a Visual Display Unit.

Similarly, information from earlier evaluations can be fed forward to proposed solutions to new problems. An example from the work in the British Museum (Natural History) illustrates how this can be effected. On a number of different occasions, employing very different exhibits, the same finding has arisen, namely, that whenever an exhibit tried to explain a general principle by using a single, specific example, it was found that most visitors would interpret the display as an illustration of that particular example. In other words, when a single example was used, visitors had difficulty going from the concrete illustration to the abstract generalization. The difficulty was removed simply by using a number of different examples of the general concept. Given that this has occurred on a number of occasions with different displays, generalization about new displays can be made with confidence.

When carrying out front-end evaluation the first problems, as with any other sort of evaluation study, is to identify and define the target audience. This may be everyone who comes to the museum. In other cases, if an exhibition is aimed at a particular section of the population of visitors, the target audience needs to be defined clearly. In practice, this means setting out to identify members of the target group. In other words, what questions could we ask visitors to the museum, the answer(s) to which would allow them to be categorized as either members or non-members of the target audience.

For example, an exhibition on British natural history at the British Museum (Natural History) was aimed primarily at 'amateur natural historians'. Thus, while it was to be accessible to any visitor, the target audience was defined as:

those people who have a more than passing interest in natural history and who have some degree of commitment to its study.

At the same time, however, the exhibition was not intended for specialists who have a professional interest in the field or amateurs with an equivalent competence.

Having identified the target audience in theoretical terms, the next step was to translate this description into an *operational definition*. The key phrase in the above definition was 'some degree of commitment to its study'. What was needed was some measure of commitment. To this end, the following set of criteria were developed:

(1) Would you call yourself an amateur naturalist?
(2) Which of these statements, if any, apply to you?
   (a) I belong to a natural history or some equivalent society (ornithology club, etc).
   (b) I try to get out into the country at least once a month to pursue my interest in natural history, and I usually manage to do so.
   (c) I have some equipment necessary to pursue my interest in natural history (for example, binoculars, microscope, and so on).
   (d) I read at least 2 or 3 books a year on natural history subjects of special interest to me.
   (e) I regularly read magazines and newspapers on natural history subjects.

A visitor was required to respond 'Yes' to at least two of these five statements to be included as a member of the target audience. A final question was asked to check the visitor's profession to rule out those people with a professional interest in the field of natural history. Note that such things as 'watching natural history programs on television' were not used since this by itself does not indicate a *commitment*.

Having defined the relevant target audience and decided upon how to identify members of the group, the next stage was to approach the audience and collect the necessary information. The sort of technique adopted depends on the aims of the study, the availability of the target audience and the sorts of decisions that will be made on the basis of the data.

Some front-end work was carried out for the exhibition of British natural history. In this case, the aim of the survey was to find out if there was a consensus among the target audience as to what they wanted from the exhibition. Initial discussions with scientists in the Museum had centered round the notion of a taxonomic display of specimens. However, given that the target audience was *not* comprised of specialists it was felt that such an arrangement might not be particularly appreciated by the committed naturalist. Given that when 'in the field' the live specimens are seen in context, it was felt that an exhibition organized by habitat would provide a more functional tool for the target audience. Thus, a major aim of the survey was to collect information on this specific matter.

It was also known from other work that the size of the intended audience would be relatively small. Given this, it was decided that a small number of in-depth interviews eliciting qualitative information would be preferable to a large number of short questionnaires. To this end, a total of 14 visitors were each interviewed for between 30 to 45 minutes. No attempt was made to select a random sample of visitors, instead likely candidates were actively sought out, using the above criteria.

None of the visitors interviewed thought the exhibition should present just the specimens in a taxonomic display. Several visitors emphasized that they did *not* want to see 'butterflies pinned up in ranks'. It could be argued that 14 visitors was not a large enough sample on which to make any conclusions, but this is not necessarily the case. The aim was to look for a consensus. Although visitors were not selected for interview randomly, there was no control over the population of visitors available, and each visitor's selction was independent of every other visitor. Thus, the likelihood of selecting 14 consecutive visitors all of whom state a similar point of view would be low if this did not represent a consensus of opinion. The survey also yielded other useful information as to what members of the target group expected to find in such an exhibition.

The survey was carried out at an early enough stage so that the information it gave rise to could be brought to bear before making any major commitment of resources.

Conclusion

The second half of this paper has concentrated on some of the issues surrounding the process of carrying out evaluation studies. In doing so, it has focused on a small number of examples from my own work. In the case of front-end evaluation this is because very few museums carry out such work let alone publish the results. A small number of formative evaluation studies have been published in the museum literature and the interested reader is referred to the selected bibliography given at the end of this article.

The major conclusion of this paper is that three types of evaluation can be distinguished on the basis of when it takes place and what forms the focus of the enquiry. Each type of evaluation has strengths and weaknesses, but if used in conjunction with one another, the advantages of one often overcome the disadvantages of the others.

Acknowledgements

A great many of the ideas and arguments presented in this paper owe their existence to my colleague Mick Alt. I am indebted to him for the many discussions we have had concerning exhibition evaluation and design. I would also like to thank Dr Roger Miles for his comments on the paper, along with his encouragement and support for my work in general. While both of them have provided much of the input to this article, any mistakes are, of course, my own.

Notes

[1] The terms 'front-end', 'formative' and 'summative' are derived from the curriculum development literature (*see,* for example, Scriven, 1967). Their usage here is simply for convenience and should not be taken to imply any adherence to the curriculum development model of evaluation.

[2] The major proponents of *educational* evaluation of exhibits have been Screven (1974, 1975a, 1975b, 1976a, 1976b, 1978) and Shettel (1968, 1973, 1976, 1978). Their approach is that exhibit design and evaluation should proceed according to a set of predetermined 'objectives' similar to the type of instructional objectives developed in mainstream education (*see* Bloom *et al,* 1956; Mager, 1962; Popham, 1975). For a critique of the educational evaluation approach to museum exhibits see Alt (1977). MacDonald-Ross (1973) has provided a critical review of the use of so-called behavioural objectives.

[3] For example, an exhibit may be designed to meet a set of educational objectives but still 'fail' because it deals with a subject-matter of very little *interest* to most visitors. The converse is also true (and more common!) Attention needs to be turned to discovering just what attributes of exhibits visitors use to distinguish between an exhibit they will stop at and one that they will glance at and walk by. Recent work at the British Museum (Natural History) has been doing just that (Alt and Shaw, 1984). This work reveals that visitors' perceptions of exhibits can sometimes be rather different to those of the exhibit developers.

[4] This sort of approach, whereby one sets up a number of criteria prior to testing materials is sometimes referred to as criterion-reference testing (see Popham, 1975, especially pp. 126–168).

[5] The number of published visitor surveys is extremely large, in fact so large that Loomis (1973) has pleaded that no more be carried out. For those people interested in how to design and carry out a good visitor survey, *see* Abbey and Cameron (1959; 1960) and Alt (1980).

[6] While it is self-evident that attracting power is a valid measure of effectiveness (an exhibit can only be effective if visitors stop at it), the heavy reliance by museum researchers on holding power as a valid measure of effectiveness is tenuous. This is true even if one uses a measure of holding power ratio (Screven, 1976a, b) whereby power is expressed as a ratio of actual time spent to required time. No account is taken as to whether visitors are willing to invest the necessary time; instead it is assumed that 'effective' exhibits can manipulate visitors so as to generate the required holding time. This

assumption flies in the face of all published research which indicates that, on average, visitors spend less than a minute at individual displays (*see*, for example, Melton, 1936. Unpublished data recorded by the British Museum (Natural History) confirms this finding).

[7] The comments here should not be taken to imply a devaluation of summative evaluation. However, I believe that in the long term the only way forward is by means of summative *research* rather than summative *evaluation*. However, until people drop their obsession with recording attracting and holding power and similar measures, and start addressing the question of *why* some exhibits are more effective than others, the rate of progress will be slow. It is suggested that the general lack of any utility value of most summative evaluation studies (i.e. providing useful and meaningful guidelines for designers) is a direct consequence of this obsession. Summative research (as opposed to summative evaluation) must be theory-based (i.e. predictive) in order that hypotheses may be tested and generalizable results obtained. For an example of the approach espoused here see Alt (1982b).

[8] It may seem strange to suggest that no attempt is made to generalize the findings of formative evaluation to a larger audience of visitors, and in fact, this is not entirely the case. Obviously, any decisions taken at this stage need to have significance for all visitors who stop at a finished display. However, such generalizations must be based on certain assumptions. The usual procedure with formative evaluation is to show the mock-ups to a small number of visitors and then get their reactions to them using, for example, a questionnaire. This means that the small group of visitors take on a special status, and furthermore they are aware of this special status. Out of all the people coming to the museum, they have been picked out to provide their views and have had their attention drawn to the mock-ups. This is very different to the casual visitors wandering through the galleries who will probably walk past as many exhibits as they stop at, and when they do stop, they are probably unlikely to scrutinize the display as critically as the 'special' visitor.

Given the difference between the casual visitor and the 'special' visitor, what assumptions must be made in order to generalize findings from 'special' visitors to causual ones? The argument runs like this. If the 'special' visitor finds it difficult to understand what a display is trying to do, despite giving all her attention to it, then it is extremely unlikely that a casual visitor, who is perhaps less prepared to devote such an effort to understanding the display, will do any better. Indeed, the casual visitor will probably get less out of it. So, if any failures in communication occur with 'special' visitors, it can be fairly certain that they will also occur with casual visitors and thus action can be taken to reduce the rate of failure. Unfortunately, the reverse position is more difficult. If a display succeeds in communicating to the 'special' visitor it can not be assumed that it would succeed with a casual visitor. We can say that for those casual visitors who are prepared to devote the same degree of time and effort as the 'special' visitor, the display will probably succeed, but otherwise it is not known. This is not a particularly satisfactory conclusion, but it is the best that can be offered at this time. If definite answers to this question

are required, summative evaluation must be undertaken.

[9] The reason for selecting visitors at random is two-fold. First, to try to select a sample of visitors that is representative of the general population of all visitors. However, when small samples are used (in this case 30 visitors) it can only be hoped to approximate the population in terms of major characteristics (for example, sex and age). In such cases, the more important reason for selecting people at random is to avoid interviewer bias. That is the tendency of interviewers to approach visitors who *appear* to be co-operative, intelligent and so on, while avoiding those individuals who *appear* to be unco-operative.

[10] In fact, there are some experimental designs which can cope with these problems but they are more complex and require more time and effort. For example, one could compare the results of a group of visitors who see the mock-ups with the results of a second, matched group of visitors who have not seen the displays. The assumption is that any difference between the two groups must be due to exposure to the displays. The difficulty with this design is to obtain properly matched groups on relevant variables.

Another approach is to 'test' visitors both before and after exposure to the mock-ups. The difficulty with this is that a pre-test will almost certainly sensitize the visitors to search out relevant information from the displays which they might otherwise have ignored (see Yalow *et al.*, 1980).

References

ABBEY, D. S. AND CAMERON, D. F. (1959), The Museum Visitor: 1: survey design, *Reports from Information Services, 1,* Royal Ontario Museum, Toronto

ABBEY, D. S. AND CAMERON, D. F. (1960), The Museum Visitor: 2: survey results, *Reports from Information Services, 2,* Royal Ontario Museum, Toronto

ALT, M. B. (1977), Evaluating didactic exhibits: a critical look at Shettel's work, *Curator*, **20**(3), 241–258

ALT, M. B. (1980), Four years of visitor surveys at the British Museum (Natural History), 1976–1979, *Museums J*, **80**(1), 10–19

ALT, M. B. (1982a), 'Designing and carrying out the evaluation study', in Miles, R. S. (Ed.), *The Design of Educational Exhibits,* George Allen and Unwin, London, Ch. 18

ALT, M. B. (1982b), *A Cognitive Approach to Understanding the Behaviour of Museum Visitors,* PhD thesis, Institute of Education, University of London

ALT, M. B. AND LEWIS, B. N. (1982), 'Evaluation: its nature, limitations and danger; in Miles R. S. (Ed.), *The Design of Educational Exhibits,* George Allen and Unwin, London, Ch. 15

ALT, M. B. AND MORRIS, R. G. M. (1979), The Human Biology Exhibition at the Natural History Museum, *Bulletin of the British Psychological Society*, **32**, 273–278

ALT, M. B. AND SHAW, K. M. (1984), Characteristics of Ideal Exhibits, *The British Journal of Psychology*, **75**(1), 25–36

BLOOM, B. S., ENGELHART, M. D., FURST, E. J., HILL, W. H. AND KRATHWOHL, D. R. (1956), *Taxonomy of Educational Objectives: Handbook 1: Cognitive Domain,* David McKay, New York

GRIGGS, S. A. (1982), Formative evaluation of exhibits at the British Museum (Natural History), *Curator,* 24(3), 189–201

LAKOTA, R. A. (1975), *The National Museum of Natural History as a Behavioural Environment, Part 1: An Environmental Analysis of Behavioural Performance,* Office of Museum Programs, Smithsonian Institute, Washington DC

LINN, M. C. (1976), Exhibit evaluation – informed decision making, *Curator,* 19(4), 291–320

LINN, M. C. (In press), Evaluation in the museum setting: focus on expectations, *Educational Evaluation of Policy Analysis*

LOOMIS, R. J. (1973), Please! Not another visitor survey!, *Museum News,* 52(2), 21–26

MACDONALD-ROSS, M. (1973), Behavioural objectives: a critical review, *Instructional Science,* 2, 1–52

MAGER, R. F. (1962), *Preparing instructional objectives,* Fearson, Belmont, California

MELTON, A. W. (1935), 'Problems of installation in museums of art', No. 14 in *Publications of the American Association* of Museums, New Series, American Association of Museums, Washington DC

MELTON, A. W. (1936), Distribution of attention in galleries in a museum of science and industry, *Museum News,* 13(3), 5–8

MELTON, A. W. (1972), Visitor behaviour in museums: some early research in environmental design, *Human Factors,* 14(5), 393–403

PARSONS, L. A. (1965), Systematic testing of display techniques for an anthropological exhibit, *Curator,* 8(2), 167–189

POPHAM, W. J. (1975), *Educational Evaluation* Prentice-Hall, New Jersey

ROBINSON, E. S. (1928), 'The behaviour of the museum visitor; No. 5 in *Publication of the American Association of Museums, New Series,* American Association of Museums, Washington DC

SCREVEN, C. G. (1974), Learning and exhibits: instructional design, *Museum News,* 52(5), 67–75

SCREVEN, C. G. (1975), The effectiveness of guidance devices on the visitor learning, *Curator,* 18(3), 219–243

SCREVEN, C. G. (1976a), Exhibit evaluation: a goal-referenced approach, *Curator,* 19(4), 271–290

SCREVEN, C. G. (1976b), *Evaluating the Impact of Museum Exhibits,* Paper present at the International Meeting of the ICOM Committee of Natural History Museums and the National Museums of Canada, Ottawa, Ontario

SCREVEN, C. G. (1978), *Improving Exhibits through Formative Evaluation,* Third International Congress of Maritime Museums

SCRIVEN, M. (1967), 'The methodology of evaluation', in Stake, R. E. (Ed.), *Curriculum evaluation,* American Educational Research Association Monograph Series on Evaluation, No. 1, Rand McNally, Chicago

SHETTEL, H. H. (1968), An evaluation of existing criteria for judging the quality of science exhibits, *Curator,* 11(2), 137–153

SHETTEL, H. H. (1973), Exhibits: art form or educational medium?, *Museum News,* 52(1), 32–41

SHETTEL, H. H. (1976), *An evaluation of visitor response to "Man in his environment",* Paper presented at ICOM meeting, Ottawa, Canada

SHETTEL, H. H. (1978), A critical look at a critical look: a response to Alt's critique of Shettel's work, *Curator,* 21(4), 329–345

WEISS, R. S. AND BOUTOURLINE, S. (1963), 'The communication value of exhibits, *Museum News,* 42(3), 23–27

WITTLIN, A. S. (1971), Hazards of communication by exhibits, *Curator,* 14(2), 138–150

YALOW, E. S., STROSSEN, R. J., JENNINGS, D. L. AND LINN, M. C. (1980), Improving museums through evaluation, *Curator,* 23(4), 275–286

Selected bibliography

Evaluation Theory

(1) The dominant approach to exhibit evaluation has been that based on educational evaluation models. References to the main proponents of this approach have already been given (*see* note 2). A very good account of the museum as a learning environment can be found in Lewis, B. N. (1980), The museum as an educational facility, *Museums J.,* 80(3), 151–155, and in Chase, R. A. (1975), Museums as learning environments, *Museum News,* 42(1), 37–43. A more pertinent question is the extent that people learn from a casual museum visit when no attempt is made to evoke learning. This has been addressed by Boggs, D. L. (1977), Visitor Learning at the Ohio Historical Centre, *Curator,* 20(3), 205–214.

(2) Other approaches to exhibit evaluation include:
  (a) Criterion-referenced testing (*see* Popham, 1975)
  (b) Informed decision making (Linn, M. C. (1976), Exhibit evaluation: informed decision making, *Curator,* 19(4), 291–302).
  (c) Naturalistic evaluation (Otto, J. (1979), Learning about "Neat Stuff": one approach to evaluation, *Museum News,* 58(2), 38–45; Wolf, R. L. (1980), A naturalistic view of evaluation, *Museum News,* 58(6), 39–45).

(3) A useful set of general readings can be found in de Borhegyi, S. F. and Hanson, I. A. (Eds.) (1968), *The Museum Visitor: Selected Essays and Surveys of Visitor Reaction to Exhibits in the Milwaukee Public Museum,* Milwaukee Public Museum.

(4) The politics of evaluation is discussed in Alt, M. B. and Lewis, B. N. (1982), 'Evaluation, its nature, limitations and danger', in Miles, R. S. (Ed.), *The Design of Educational Exhibits,* George Allen and Unwin, London, Ch. 15; and in Anderson, S. B., Ball, S., Murphy, R. T. and associates (1974), *Encyclopedia of Educational Evaluation, Concepts and Techniques for Evaluating Education and Training programs,* Jossey-Bass, San Francisco.

Evaluation Studies

The majority of published studies fall into the category of summative evaluation and as such are the topics of the following article. With the exception of visitor surveys (*see* note 5), no front-end studies have been reported. In fact, the number of truly formative evaluations is also very small:

EASON, L. P. AND LINN, M. C. (1976), Evaluation of the effectiveness of participatory exhibits, *Curator,* 19(1), 45–62

FRIEDMAN, A. J., EASON, L. P. AND SNEIDER, C. I. (1979), Star games: a participatory astronomy exhibit, *Planetarium*, **8**(3), 3–7

GRIGGS, S. A. (1982), Formative evaluation of exhibits at the British Museum (Natural History), *Curator*, **24**(3), 189–201

NICOL, E. M. (1969), The development of validated museum exhibits, *Final Report USOE Project 5-0245*, US Office of Education, Washington DC

A number of bibliographies of exhibition evaluation have been put together. Two of the more comprehensive of these are:

ELLIOT, P. AND LOOMIS, R. J. (1975), *Studies of Visitor Behaviour in Museums and Exhibitions: An Annotated Bibliography of Sources Primarily in the English language*, Smithsonian Institution, Washington DC

SCREVEN, C. G. (1979), A bibliography on visitor education research, *Museum News*, March/April, 56–59, 86, 88

48

Approaches to summative evaluation

David R. Prince

This paper develops a number of the ideas presented in the previous contribution by focusing on the methodologies and techniques currently available for the application of summative evaluation: essentially, evaluation undertaken on completed exhibitions. A consideration of the more important objectives of this type of evaluation helps to define it by drawing attention to its intended role in museums:

(1) To provide definitive data about the functioning of completed exhibitions in relation to their stated aims (educational or otherwise) and their intended audience.
(2) To isolate and identify problem areas that may hamper the effective communication of information carried by an exhibition.
(3) To provide a core of reliable data around which remedial action may be justifiably taken.
(4) To provide data directly applicable to the future design of related exhibitions (feedforward information).
(5) To provide data of a general nature related to the functioning of the museum itself, as part of the strategy developed for exhibition evaluation.
(6) To provide data to substantiate (or otherwise) the recommendations made by front-end and formative evaluation; that is, to aid in the evaluation of the evaluation process itself.

Although such information – perhaps idealized in the above form – is highly important to the organization and maintenance of an exhibition scheme within the overall policies of the museum towards its visitors, it is surprising that little evaluation has been undertaken at, or by, museums. The emphasis continues to be placed on design and implementation, often by non-specialist staff[1]. Clearly, the role of evaluation *as part of* an exhibition program has not been sufficiently appreciated (perhaps through a lack of knowledge, finance or incentive) with the result that the evaluations that do occur tend to be on a qualitative level and undertaken in an *ad hoc* way, while others, through the lack of a clearly defined research perspective, operate within a theoretical vacuum.

This paper establishes a number of guidelines for undertaking summative evaluation and, by examining the current situation in museums and the techniques developed by other, but related, institutions, places such evaluation firmly at the centre of exhibition planning.

Objectives

Of primary importance to any evaluation are the exhibition criteria that the evaluation sets out to analyze. These predetermine to a considerable degree the eventual evaluative strategy developed and help shape the nature and effectiveness of the information obtained. In essence, this demands that the evaluation is geared to assess the success of the exhibition in meeting its objectives. These are (or should be) established during the initial planning stage, but may be refined occasionally during formative evaluation when the displays themselves are modified. At the summative stage they are used as the central criteria against which the evaluation is made and are thus not available for modification or change. Thus, a lack of clearly defined objectives effectively places an exhibition outside the possibility of summative evaluation unless post-dated (and hence spurious) objectives are assigned to it. Moreover, it emphasizes the importance of keeping the evaluation process firmly in mind when formulating the overall exhibition scheme.

Therefore, objectives used as the basis for summative evaluation are gleaned from the reasons inherent in establishing the exhibition in the first instance and are thus rooted in the general perspective on exhibitions devised by the museum and develop from the overal policy objectives for the museum itself, institutionalized in, for example, policies related to the type of material collected and exhibited. In this way, the collections themselves, and the way they are used, help to define the nature of the exhibition and indirectly lay the foundations for evaluation[2].

Hence, for most evaluative purposes, objectives are best viewed as being organized hierarchially from the most general and all-embracing to the most specific and analyzable. Concentrating for the moment on exhibitions designed primarily to communicate knowledge (didactic exhibitions), it is possible to isolate five levels (or stages) in the life of an exhibition scheme where evaluation objectives may fruitfully be applied in order to generate data of summative quality (*Figure 48.1*).

In the system outlined, summative evaluation may be applied to a number of levels depending on the type of question posed for the evaluation. Detailed questions related to the transference of knowledge, for example, would occur in Level 5, while general background data on the types of visitors to the exhibition would be gleaned from Level 3. Similarly, questions related to the communicational characteristics of the displays themselves (for example, attracting and holding power, visitor preference) would appear in Level 4.

Equally important is the concept that each level's objectives are defined in relation to those immediately preceeding it, and that they in turn influence the framing of those of the subsequent level. In this way, the results of the evaluation can have an influence not only on the specific level assigned to them, but also on the preceding levels in the system. Clearly, the emphasis here is on pairing exhibition and evaluation objectives at each level and these, by definition, vary from one institution to another and within the same institution over time.

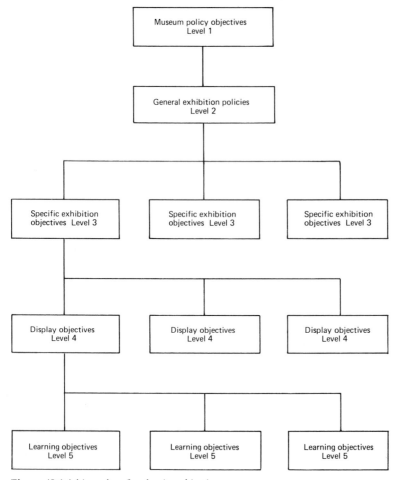

Figure 48.1 A hierarchy of evaluation objectives

However, a number of core features can be isolated for each level that are generally applicable to most types of exhibition, and hence to most of the demands currently made on summative evaluation. These are: visitor evaluations (loosely, surveys) (Level 3); display and display-based evaluations (Level 4); and learning/educational assessments (Level 5). Clearly, these categories are not mutually exclusive (for example, a learning evaluation must be active in all three levels), but they do provide a useful framework for discussion.

This form of objective hierarchy has long been known to be of value to exhibition evaluation. In a paper devoted entirely to this issue, Putney and Wager (1973) isolate three levels of objectives, ranging from policy objectives (general aims), through selection objectives (for media and location), to evaluation objectives. They note (p. 44) that:

> For evaluation to be most useful, it is important to have a hierarchy of objectives in which objectives at each level are consistent with broad policy objectives but are increasingly more numerous and specific. Thus, if evaluation permits us to achieve increased effectiveness at the most specific level, we can infer that effectiveness has been increased at the more general levels; including the level of policy objectives

The framing of objectives

Although the construction of a suitable framework around which to construct objectives presents few problems, the formulation of the objectives themselves is far from easy. A number of factors have to be taken into account, among the most important being:

(1) The nature and characteristics of the exhibition scheme.
(2) The intended function and scope of the exhibition.
(3) The relationship between the exhibition and the others of the museum.
(4) The nature and characteristics of the intended (target) audience.
(5) The type and quality of information required from the evaluation.
(6) The methods of data collection, preparation, analysis and presentation to be employed.
(7) The depth and scope of action to be taken on the conclusions and recommendations of the evaluation.
(8) The peculiar characteristics of the test site that may influence the data through, for example, rapid changes over time.

Clearly, some of these are more directly applicable to the creation of a valid evaluative strategy, but they should be borne in mind at this stage in order to avoid the construction of erroneous objectives.

Strategies

By far the most common form of formal evaluation undertaken on exhibitions has been aimed at assessing the teaching effectiveness of displays and display units, often through the use of recall questions involving verbal answers and/or photograph or object recognition. Cameron (1967, 1968a, b), Shettel (1968, 1973). Shettel and Reilly (1965) and Screven (1969, 1974a,b, 1976) have been particularly active in developing such evaluative techniques, and are at pains to stress that objectives should be stated as clearly as possible. Defining objectives in purely *educational* terms allows an educational definition of 'objective'. Mager (1962), in an influential statement on the role of instructional objectives, defines a learning objective as:

> an *intent* communicated by a statement describing the proposed change in the learner – a statement of what the learner is to be like when he has successfully completed the learning experience. It is a description of a pattern of behaviour (performance) we want the learner to be able to demonstrate (p. 3) . . . that will be accepted as evidence that the learner has achieved the objective (p. 13).

The emphasis is clearly placed on the construction of objectives in *behavioural* terms; objectives that are available for evaluation either by external observation or, more usually, by direct questioning through interviews accompanied by a battery of test items carried by a questionnaire[3].

Against such a background, objectives are assigned *performance criteria,* for example 'name', 'list', 'identity', and may be contrasted with the more general aims of, for example, 'knowing', 'discovering', 'understanding'. For example, a curator wishes to convey knowledge about the tracks produced by a number of woodland animals. The overriding aim of the exhibition is (say) 'to increase the visitors' awareness of the tracks produced, in the understanding that this will lead to a greater appreciation of woodland life'. A specific learning objective for evaluation purposes from this perspective might be:

> given eight colour photographs in two blocks of four, each containing the tracks of one of the animals on display, the visitor will identify correctly three out of four tracks

Such an objective not only specifies the kind of behaviour involved (identifying), but also the conditions under which the behaviour is to occur ('given eight colour photographs in two blocks of four'), together with the acceptable level of performance ('three out of four tracks in each block') against which the evaluation can be made. As importantly, the objective generates a series of constraints on the evaluative strategy developed, and reflects directly on the achievement of the original aim.

Such objectives can then be assigned to individual

displays, groups of displays, or to the exhibition as a whole, and thus form the basis for defining summative evaluation as (Moses *et al.*, 1977, p. 12).

> the systematic examination of . . . activities where objectives are rigorously specified and performance in meeting these objectives is rigorously measured.

That is, an activity aiming to produce (Warwick and Lininger, 1975, p. 52):

> an overall appraisal of a programme indicating the relationship between the major outcomes and the intended goals.

This type of definition underpins many of the evaluative techniques used to study didactic exhibitions, for example those by Shettel (1973) on the communication of scientific and technological information. The most common evaluative strategy generated by this approach is that of straightforward visitor interviewing (to gain profile information and to establish an acceptable visitor sample) accompanied by direct questioning and the recall of factual knowledge. In most cases, the results of a test sample exposed to the media are compared with those of a control group of non-users (*see*, for example, Parsons, 1965; Cameron, 1968b; Eason and Linn, 1976; DART, 1978), although occasionally only one group is used (Wagar, 1972; Boggs, 1977; Prince, 1982). Learning is said to have occurred from the exhibition if the members of the test group score significantly higher than those of the control group (as identified by tests of association and significance on the groups), and the displays are defined as successful (or not) following this criterion. As a direct extension, the museum itself may be defined – and evaluated – in terms of its ability to function as a 'communications system'.

Critique

Used in isolation, this approach – by concentrating on the supposedly measureable outcomes of the relationship between the visitor and the exhibition – carries with it a number of problems. First, it underestimates the complex and subtle nature of human learning and behaviour based on that learning, particularly the role that past experience plays in shaping present perception, and learning resulting from that perception (see Neisser, 1967; Ausubel, 1968; Blumenthal, 1977; Wickelgren, 1979). Second, by concentrating attention on a selected, 'observable' aspect of cognitive functioning (simply, knowledge recall) it seeks to assess learning by focusing on the characteristics of the exhibition without making sufficient reference to the characteristics of the visitor. Where such reference is made it is usually through the use of easily-identifiable sociological components

(age, sex, occupation); acceptable enough if that is the aim of the study, but not so for a learning assessment which must, by definition, seek to examine psychological components. Third, by using direct questioning, it brings into play problems involving the successful transference of meaning through language – although Borun (1977) has been active in developing non-verbal test measures designed to lessen this problem.

As a direct consequence, little data is gathered on the associated psychological factors that influence learning; the most immediate being *motivation*, reflected in *pre-visit intention* (Alt, 1977), and on-site factors, for example, *expressed interest* and *preference* for media, media combinations, overall strategy of communication and subject theme, and general *attitudinal orientation* towards the museum as a whole and to the exhibition in particular. Moreover, the equally important roles that aesthetic response, mood and feeling play in influencing behaviour generally (Tuan, 1974; Appleton, 1975) and hence, by implication, that within a museum, are largely undervalued.

Thus, this approach places too great an emphasis on the overtly teaching role of exhibitions and defines 'education' in too narrow a way, through making insufficient reference to other, non-measureable effects of exhibitions. This problem is acute when the approach is applied to art galleries.

However, this perspective has had a considerable influence on the way exhibitions are approached in summative evaluation, almost to the point where learning assessments based on visitor interviews accompanied by test questions are viewed by some as the only way of effectively evaluating exhibitions. As Screven (1974b, p. 68) suggests:

> so far as its teaching function is concerned, the exhibit's descriptive physical components have no instructional worth in themselves. This instructional worth can be evaluated only by the effect of the exhibit on its viewers.[4]

Be that as it may, the criticisms noted earlier suggest that the results of such studies should be treated with some caution, particularly as learning implies a permanent change in the cognition of the learner, and many of the studies simply examine immediate post-visit response on a group basis[5]. As Griggs noted in the previous paper, a move away from viewing such studies as measures of learning and towards indexes of *comprehension* – where the emphasis is placed on evaluating the exhibition in terms of whether it is understandable – may render them less susceptable to this type of criticism. However, didactic exhibitions are teaching devices, and hence an evaluation in learning terms remains a goal to be striven for.

Visitor surveys

Leaving aside this issue for the moment, one of the benefits of such group-based evaluations is that they demand that visitor samples are selected carefully from the general visitor pool so that the results can be freed from sampling (evaluation-imposed) bias. Thus, the core of the methods applied here can be taken directly as background data for an analysis of the visiting public; an analysis at Level 3 of the hierarchy.

Three types of information will be useful at this stage. First, total visitor counts – to the museum in general and the exhibition in particular. Second, profile data of visitor-type, based on sociological criteria and employing standardized techniques of categorization that allow the data to be freed from the confines of the site, and hence comparable with those from other institutions as well as national figures. Third, specific profile data enabling the identification of the target audience as distinct from that visiting the museum generally.

It is not proposed to discuss the methods of gathering data for the first two to any extent since they are well-documented elsewhere[6], save to note that the detail of the answer required of the visitor, and the way in which the responses are pre- and post-coded, depends to a large extent on the aim of the survey and the method of data preparation employed[7]. The selection of a suitable sample from the total visitor flow is a crucial aspect, and one that has a direct bearing on the validity of the results obtained[8]. The main considerations are that the value of this type of survey depends as much on the framing of questions and the categorization of answers as it does on the selection of a valid sample population, and that the background to the survey must be borne in mind when drawing conclusions and making recommendations. All too often observations are made on specific points that go far beyond the support provided by the results of a particular research programme.

The identification of the *target audience* should follow the acquisition of the profile data since it extends the knowledge gained about the visitor. The characteristics of this audience should have been defined at the exhibition's initial planning stage and translated into accessible indexes as part of formative evaluation. At the summative stage, questions are so framed as to elicit responses to reinforce this *operational definition,* and a visitor defined as being part of this audience (or not) depending on the way in which his responses fit the accepted criteria established during formative evaluation. Moreover, some indication as to this audience's representation should have been established at that stage. For example, if an exhibition is aimed primarily at 'amateur natural historians', what proportion of the total visitor pool is an acceptable measure that it has achieved this general aim? – 40 per cent? 60 per cent? The figures need not be too precise at the outset, but without them the conclusions that can be drawn are limited, and since summative evaluation is concerned with the effect of the exhibition on its intended audience, then clearly this finding is of some importance. Having thus isolated this group, it is possible to proceed with a number of detailed questions aimed at drawing a closer understanding of how the visitor has interacted with the exhibition he has just seen or, indeed, may still be viewing.

Preference and interest

Visitor preference, and its associated expressed interest, are important variables available for analysis, partly because the indications brought out at the formative stage can be assessed, and partly because a body of educational psychology suggests strongly that learning is facilitated by interest through its association with intrinsic motivation[9], an hypothesis that should have been borne in mind when undertaking front-end analysis on the proposed exhibition scheme. Two different, though not mutually exclusive, aspects can be assigned to the study of visitor preference: *what* is preferred and *why* it is preferred, and *what* is most interesting and *why*. Although both are equally important, most of the exhibition-based studies have concentrated on the 'what' aspect (see Mahaffey, 1970; Washburn and Wagar, 1972; Dick *et al,* 1975; DART, 1978; Hammitt, 1978; Griggs and Alt, 1982; Prince 1982) and have tended to rely on supporting literature – occasionally drawing on material from perception and mass communication studies – to infer why. Considerable scope exists, therefore, to investigate this latter aspect on site, an investigation perhaps best approached through unstructured, open-ended, conversation-based interviews associated with *naturalistic evaluation* (see Wolf and Tymitz, 1977; 1978a,b, 1979a,b) – a method rooted in the participant-observation technique of social enquiry (see Campbell, 1970; Friedrichs and Ludtke, 1975). The formative stage may provide a useful starting point, its recommendations helping to guide the evaluator towards imposing a loose structure during summative evaluation. A further point is that visitors have occasionally been asked to identify the exhibit they found the most interesting as a basis for detailed questions about that exhibit (Alt, 1980; Prince, 1982).

Methods

Given this background, two major techniques have been employed consistently to assess visitor preference:

observation and *interviewing,* either separately or, more commonly, in conjunction. In terms of the former, two approaches present themselves. First, a count of the total number of visitors stopping at each display within a given time span – the higher the count, the greater the preference. Second, the tracking of a selected sample of visitors through the exhibition noting the time spent at each display – the greater the time, the greater the preference. Time-lapse photography and the use of remote-controlled cameras present the possibility of unobtrusive observation in both methods (see Coker and Coker, 1973).

Although these strategies undoubtedly provide useful data – most commonly interpreted through behavioural maps[10] and important in studies of visitor orientation (Winkel *et al,* 1975) and the assessment of the *attracting* and *holding power* of the displays themselves (Lakota, 1976) – their value to summative evaluation is limited on two counts. First, no assessment of *why* the visitor has stopped can be made and, second, no analysis of what aspects of the display have proved initially attractive can be undertaken. For summative evaluation to provide feedforward information, both aspects are important.

The only realistic method of gaining such data is to engage the visitor in conversation or interview. If this is to be done as part of a larger survey – and it is necessary if the results are to be validated – then the latter may be a more appropriate method. Although questions probing the visitors' motives and preference for theme, media and strategy of communication can be asked, there are clear dangers in making sweeping judgements based on the results due to the respondent reacting in a way he feels appropriate to the occasion, and the consideration that the questions themselves may instigate patterns of analysis and evaluation not previously contemplated by the visitor – a problem also encountered when assessing attitudes (see Shaw and Wright, 1967; Diab, 1969; Warren and Jahoda, 1973).

However, since this is the most appropriate method, the evaluation must ensure that the questions themselves are as free from internal bias as possible – a pilot survey is necessary to test both questions and interviewers – and that bias in recording the visitors' comments is reduced to a minimum[11]. Since it is probable that visitors unskilled in criticizing exhibitions (the majority) are only likely to comment briefly on the major components, this last problem may not be too severe. However, the over-zealous interviewer, prompting answers from visitors, must be warned of the potential danger[12].

A further consideration is that such information, by its very nature, is not available for statistical analysis, except at the most fundamental levels. Although no bad thing in itself, it must be realized

when drawing conclusions from the observations. In general, the techniques of eliciting value judgements from visitors are in their infancy and must be handled sympathetically in the knowledge that they are a potentially fruitful source of information[13].

Attitudes

Data about the exhibition on this level may be termed loosely 'public reaction', and a realistic extension of such work is to assess the general attitudinal orientation of visitors towards the museum as a whole. A number of techniques are available, including those designed to elicit agreement (or disagreement) to a series of opinion or value statements (a rating-scale technique developed by Likert, 1932, and refined subsequently by, amongst others, Cook and Sellitz, 1964 and Upshaw, 1968), the evocation of social judgements (Sherif *et al,* 1965), and the use of semantic differential scales to assess meaning (Osgood, 1964). (For a review *see* Dawes, 1972, and Lemon, 1973). In the last case, attitudes are assessed by plotting the position of responses on a number of paired word-scales, for example 'entertaining – boring', 'interesting – dull', 'enjoyable – unenjoyable'. The true value of this type of survey comes in assessing general attitudes rather than in eliciting opinions on specific issues, and it may provide valuable information as background for a more detailed study of display preference. Comparing the views of various subgroups within the visitors (as identified by the profile and target audience data) may indicate differences of value in more effectively tailoring an exhibition to meet their needs.

Non-user surveys

To gain a wider understanding of the way in which the museum, as a social institution, is perceived by the public, a potentially fruitful area of research lies in non-user surveys. Although this is removed somewhat from exhibition evaluation, it can provide important data for the future planning of exhibition schemes by concentrating on the expectations of non-visitors in relation to the image of the museum and the type of material exhibited[14]. With the recent moves towards linking museums with other tourist attractions within a given area[15], and the political initiatives involved in gaining commercial sponsorship, this type of research is all the more needed. However, few guidelines exist at present, since this is an area of enquiry not commonly undertaken either by museums or social research generally (for an early review see Pearson, 1978), although the results obtained can be revealing (Prince, 1983). Particular problems exist in establishing a reliable sampling frame and in the basic practicalities of handling such non-specific information. Moreover, it can be argued that the first task of museum evaluation is to look to its users in relation to their experience, rather than to non-users in relation to theirs.

Communicational effectiveness

Returning, then, to the main concern of the paper: the estimation of the quality of experience gained from an exhibition and, in particular, the assessment of the exhibition as a communications medium. Of the techniques noted earlier most, by trying to evaluate teaching effectiveness through the recall of isolated facts, are open to criticism because they take too narrow a view of learning (and, indeed, the role of the museum) and assume (wrongly) that the storage and recall of such information is a valid estimation of real learning change. Grappling with this problem is difficult, not least for a museum which has little or no experience of handling such evaluations. However, the work of Lee and Uzzell (1980a) on the assessment of the educational effectiveness of farm open days for the Countryside Commission for Scotland, may provide a useful starting point for such an evaluation.

Taking a cognitive psychological perspective towards the work, a perspective which, simply, suggests that learning occurs when new material is assimilated into an organizing *schema* – this schema being the total collection of past learnings and experiences associated with, in their case, farming, for a museum, the topic of the exhibition – they suggest that learning is best assessed in terms of whether or not the visitors' schemas have been modified (or extended) in some way[16]. To facilitate this, two discrete samples of visitors are questioned, one before exposure to the exhibition and one after, with a view to probing the central *constructs* organized by the visitors in both samples. If substantial changes have taken place – as identified by significance tests on the two groups (and if the groups themselves do not differ statistically in basic, profile information) – then it can be assumed that a learning change has taken place as a result of exposure to the exhibition.

In the survey by Lee and Uzzell, these constructs were assessed through a technique similar in style to that of the semantic-differential noted earlier, although in this case the issue was to assess how *accurate* a description of a type of farm or farming method was, the visitors being asked to record their answers on a scale from 1 (not at all accurate) to 7 (very accurate). If the two visiting samples recorded different patterns – and the group exposed to the exhibition was similar in orientation to the information contained in the exhibition – then a favourable learning change was said to have occurred. As an extension to this work, a battery of recall, test questions was used on a self-selected sample in a similar way to that previously described.

This approach, although only sketched briefly here, offers a number of advantages over the use of isolated, recall questions.

(1) It is based on a coherent body of psychological theory that can suggest not only *how* to evaluate, but also *why* the recorded changes have occurred.
(2) It is a more realistic method of assessing learning which, as a process, is not concerned simply with the retention of isolated facts.
(3) It concentrates on the whole experience gained from an exhibition in terms of its ability to alter and reinforce preconceived ideas, and is thus more attuned to behaviour generally exhibited in museums.
(4) By not isolating specific items of information for analysis (objects, media, strategy) it is a more flexible, and powerful, analytical tool and can indicate the effectiveness of the exhibition as a whole, and not just part of it.
(5) By its very nature, it concentrates attention towards an analysis of the visitor rather than systems within the exhibition, and is thus a direct extention of the theory on which it is based.

A potential disadvantage lies in the sophisticated way in which the responses have to be treated in order to make the data amenable to the detailed assessment of the results. However, this should not be viewed as a problem and, if necessary, the museum can seek the advice of outside specialists.

Placing this discussion on a more pragmatic level may help to isolate the main points. Say, for example, that a small, thematic exhibition, containing 15 discrete display units of various sizes and complexity, has been organized to explore the theme of life in an Iron Age community. The focal point, the most significant finds from a recently-excavated Celtic burial, occupies the six central units, and is supported by ancilliary material from the museum's collections and others on loan from a neighbouring museum (four units). In addition, a number of interpretive aids, including photographs of the excavation process and accompanying text (two units), slides (one unit), a three-dimensional model of the site (one unit) and a scale reconstruction of the burial chamber (one unit) are used to elaborate aspects of the central theme and to highlight features of the newly discovered material. The target audience has been defined as the interested layman (this definition having been translated into an operational one) with the result that some previous knowledge has been assumed in the level of presentation, particularly with regard to the selection of supporting material. A sequential information flow has been chosen as the most appropriate for interpretive purposes, and the displays have been designed and arranged accordingly.

The recall approach would tend to isolate facts from the text to act as the basic test material, and would include photograph recognition based on the artefacts in the exhibition. As a result, the presentation would be evaluated in terms of how well it had communicated this information, and the visitor said to have learned from it if he can recall it in line with pre-set criteria. It would be assumed subsequently that his understanding of the central theme had been enhanced accordingly.

Similarly, questions posed about visitor preference would seek to establish which display units had proved attractive and why. A behavioural mapping technique could be established to isolate the most popular units and to observe the pattern of movement around the gallery.

However, the approach suggested by Lee and Uzzell (1980a) would involve taking a broader view of the exhibition by focusing on Iron Age *life* and *community* as constructs, and would seek to establish whether the visitors' understanding of them had been modified as a result of exposure to the exhibition. The scales placed before both pre- and post-visit samples would be the same and might include the following:

1 $\longrightarrow$ 2 $\longrightarrow$ 3 $\longrightarrow$ 4 $\longrightarrow$ 5 $\longrightarrow$ 6 $\longrightarrow$ 7

not at all not very   fairly   very
accurate accurate   accurate accurate

How accurate are the following statements:

(1) Iron Age people lived in isolated communities.
(2) Most Iron Age people were buried in burial mounds.
(3) Most Iron Age people lived in hill forts.
(4) Iron Age people got most of their food from farming.

Clearly, the content of the statements would depend upon whether reference was made to the information in the exhibition, and the above serve only to show the style of presentation. However, they differ considerably from the type of question posed in recall-based evaluation, where the emphasis might be placed on the age of a specific find, the name of a warrior king, the size and style of burial chamber. Such statements also reveal a great deal of information about the knowledge brought to the museum, not about specifics, but about a more general impression of the Iron Age: an important point when considering the amount of educationally redundant (previously known) information carried by the exhibition, and useful as feedforward data for the planning of related exhibitions. Moreover, by comparing the results recorded by various subsamples

within the visitors, important considerations may emerge that help the identification of future target audiences.

A fundamental difference between this and the recall-approach is that the central variable in the evaluation is the *visitor* and not the particular characteristics of the exhibition material or style of presentation, although these may be inferred from the results. This fits in well with the overall strategy behind this evaluative technique, and may eventually prove valuable in constructing a more appropriate model of visitors and visitor behaviour – an essential factor in the development of a valid evaluative methodology.

Moreover, it is possible that this technique can be broadened to include the evaluation of exhibitions not amenable to the recall approach; that is, beyond those dealing with specific types of information on a didactic basis. It may be possible, for example, to develop a series of constructs for examining art exhibitions – perhaps by concentrating on schools and styles – and exhibitions where the communication of factual knowledge is not the primary consideration. However, there are major problems here, not least those concerned with translating a theoretical understanding of mood, feeling and aesthetic response into workable research criteria.

Conclusion

This paper, by drawing attention to the published material and techniques available for summative evaluation, has stressed that the results obtained by any survey or user-analysis are governed ultimately by the objectives of the study and the type of material support available for research and analysis. It has suggested that survey objectives are best viewed as being organized hierarchically from the most general and all-embracing to the most specific, and has suggested that the observations must be placed in the context of the level from which they originate. The framing of objectives in a workable form was seen as an important part of the evaluation process – the objectives then becoming the criteria against which visitor behaviour is evaluated. Of this behaviour, learning was singled out for detailed discussion; the methods based on recall test questions and the assessment of schema changes were compared, and the suggestion was made that the latter was more acceptable. The assessment of visitor interest, preference and motivation was viewed as an essential prerequisite of summative evaluation, and care was taken to describe the isolation of a suitable target audience as part of a wider visitor survey. The role of summative evaluation was seen as extending beyond the confines of the museum into non-user surveys and attitude measurement. Various techniques were described in relation to their potential to evaluate exhibitions at a summative level.

Notes

[1] Much of the 'evaluation' currently in print (especially from British sources) is highly informal and based either on descriptions (often by interested parties) or on reviews sketching their more basic components and occasionally drawing attention to their supposed educational/communicational outcomes. The *Museums Journal* (The Museums Association, London) carries a number of such reviews per issue.

[2] Although this is generally the case, not all exhibitions are organized around collections. The Hall of Human Biology at the British Museum (Natural History) – described by Miles and Tout (1978) and reviewed by Duggan (1978) – is a good example. Here only one object is used – a human skull and spinal column – and even this did not come from the Museum's collections, but from a teaching hospital (Griggs personal communication). This does not, however, devalue the central premise since in this case the approach to learning and design used lay the foundation for the evaluation, rather than the specific characteristics of the collection. The essential point is that the evaluation has a core of theory and practice upon which to work.

[3] For a general criticism of this approach, see Macdonald–Ross (1973).

[4] Most of the standard educational assessment techniques that are quick and easy to administer have been used in this context. Straightforward yes/no, agree/disagree formats are common, as are multiple choice questions. It should be noted that the questions need not require verbal answers; some studies have asked for a choice of objects (or representations of those objects) from a field of similar objects or representations. For a general review, *see* Stansfield (1981).

[5] For a detailed criticism of this approach, *see* Alt (1977).

[6] The only viable tool for collecting on-site, profile data is the questionnaire. A number of guidelines exist for their construction (see Payne, 1951; Oppenheim, 1966; Blalock, 1970; Davidson, 1970a, b; Saarinen, 1971; Countryside Recreation Research Advisory Group (CRRAG), 1973). A reading of those contained in other papers may also prove useful, bearing in mind that the final document must be tailored to the peculiar characteristics of the test site (see Abbey and Cameron, 1959; Cruickshank, 1972; Doughty, 1968; Mason, 1974, Digby, 1974; McWilliams, and Hopwood, 1973; Mass Observation (UK) Ltd, 1978; Alt, 1980). For a brief discussion on the automated ways of achieving total visitor counts *see* Bayfield and Pickrell (1971), Bayfield and Moyes (1972), and Coker and Coker (1972).

[7] The most important questions here are:

(1) The scope of the profile survey – is it part of a larger, more wide-ranging one, or is this the sole aim?
(2) What method of data preparation (simply, manual or computer-assisted) is to be employed?

Since the actual interview time will be limited (most visitors will be unwilling to give more than 15 minutes of their time) the number of questions devoted to the collection of profile data will be influenced by the overall objectives of the study. Hence, deciding on the value of this data to the final evaluation will influence the number of questions – of increasing specificity – devoted to it. The method of data handling is also crucial to the type, and depth, of questions asked, and revolves round whether or not a non-manual means of analysis is available. There can be no doubt that the true potential of such a survey can only be realized through an in-depth statistical analysis employing methods of statistical association and significance on selected, grouped variables, but that this requires a sophisticated level of data handling beyond the scope of the museum without the advantage of a computer-based statistical package capable of handling non-parametric (counted) data – especially if the number of responses is large. Indeed, the depth of information this produces is beyond the normal requirements of a museum which has not yet undertaken a visitor survey beyond the level of simple visitor counts. In such a case, the placing of simple percentage points alongside the variables may be all that is required. If this is being attempted, it is important that the categories assigned to the variables are directly comparable not only with national figures, but also with similar studies elsewhere. Not to do so severely limits the scope of the final analysis.

[8] Two aspects are central here:

(1) The definition of the visiting *population*.
(2) The method employed to extract a representative *sample*.

The definition of (1) depends on the aims of the study and may involve just adults (what age ?), children, school parties, types of visiting group and so on. A straightforward definition may be 'all adult visitors (16 and over) who have entered the museum on the day of interview', but the actual one used depends on what the evaluation is trying to demonstrate. Sampling methods to select from this population for the type of survey being considered fall into one of three major classes:

(1) Quota sampling.
(2) Self selection.
(3) Random sampling.

(1) Individuals are selected on the basis of some predetermined variable or set of variables (cf. opinion polls). This is difficult to achieve if the distribution of these variables is not previously known (as in the case with most museums), and it carries the disadvantage that statistical tests of assocation and significance (of which probably the most useful for general purposes is chi-square – χ^2 – see Everitt, 1977) are not amenable to this type of sampling frame.

(2) Questionnaires are left for the visitor to collect and (usually) return later. It has the major disadvantage of an unrepresented response (which effectively rules it out for use with profile data), but it may be useful in isolating 'interested' visitors for subsequent, in-depth study.

(3) Strictly determined by the use of random numbers or other non-biased sampling procedure (*see* Warwick and Lininger, 1975). Difficult to achieve if entrances and exists are many and/or difficult to observe. A useful compromise is to select 'every alternate person', but it

should be noted that this tends to over-sample at slack times and under-sample at peak times. The more common method of interviewing every '*n*th' person may present problems due to the irregularity of arrivals and departures at the museum.

The actual method adopted is influenced by the particular characteristics of the site, and the reader is referred to Philips (1971), Atkinson, (1973), Pillay, (1973), Weisberg and Bowen (1977) and Youngman (1979) for an extended discussion of sampling theory, practice and methods of correlation.

[9] For a general discussion on the role played by temporary motivational states in the learning process, see Logan (1969), Bruner (1973), Bourne *et al.* (1979), Estes (1976), and Chapter 44 by Alt and Griggs.

[10] A simple behavioural map consists of a plan of the exhibition area with all the major features (entrances, exits, display units, sales points) clearly located. The results of the survey (be they total counts or visitor tracking) are marked on at the survey points (perhaps at each display unit) together with some indication of visitor flow, usually achieved by arrows. The results indicate the most popular displays and the route taken to them. Subsequent analysis should seek to establish *why* these findings were recorded. For an example of this technique, as used in visitor centres, see DART (1978), and for a brief guide to its implementation, see Lee and Uzell (1980b).

[11] For a brief, readable review of the techniques available for checking test validity and reliability, see Pidgeon and Yates (1968).

[12] The type of questions asked are obviously geared towards the peculiar characteristics of the test exhibition but, as a general rule, the aim is to progress from the general to the specific and, for ease of recording, to have as many pre-coded categories as possible in the test sheets. To try to take down a visitor's comment verbatim is both difficult and time-consuming and may lead to substantial errors.

[13] An important development in assessing visitor response within an interpretive, rather than a judgemental, framework is provided by the work of Wolf and Tymitz at the Smithsonian Institution (1977, 1978a, b). By advocating a technique involving extended, face-to-face conversation, the aim is to achieve a holistic interpretation of the visitor's total experience, rather than to the parts of it that may be exposed during a structured questionnaire-interview. The technique is therefore more flexible and can accommodate spontaneous changes in mood and feeling – important when probing attitudes and values, and where the object of the exhibition is not didactic.

[14] For example, Sobol (1980), in a study of 'blockbuster' exhibitions in attracting audiences to museums, found that one that captured the imagination of the public was more effective in drawing visitors than one of a more specialized nature, and that the resulting visitor profiles were more socially representative. Although this may be understood intuitively by a number of museum workers, the type of material exhibited, and the publicity involved in bringing it to the attention of a wider audience, remain problems for investigation.

[15] For a description of how such a project can be undertaken, see the DART (1979) project on the

'Defense of the Realm', where an attempt was made to integrate the on-site attractions of the Portsmouth area with the local museums around the theme of maritime defence.

[16] For a more detailed discussion, see Chapter 44 by Alt and Griggs.

References

ABBEY, D. S. AND CAMERON, D. F. (1959), *The Museum Visitor 1 – Survey Design*, Royal Ontario Museum, Toronto

ALT, M. B. (1977), Evaluating didactic exhibits: a critical look at Shettel's work, *Curator*, **20**(3), 241–258

ALT, M. B. (1980), Four years of visitor surveys at the British Museum (Natural History) 1976–79, *Museums J.*, **80**(1), 10–19

APPLETON, J. H. (1975), *The Experience of Landscape*, John Wiley, London

ATKINSON, J. (1973), 'Questionnaire surveys: practical guidance in fieldwork techniques' in *The Use of Site Surveys in Countryside Recreation Planning and Management*, Countryside Recreation Research Advisory Group (CRRAG) 1973, Countryside Commission, London, pp. 5–7

AUSUBEL, D. P. (1968), *Educational Psychology: a Cognitive View*, Holt, Rinehart and Winston, New York

BAYFIELD, N. G. AND MOYES, S. M. (1972), Simple automatic people counters, *Recreation News Supplement*, **6**, 18–20

BAYFIELD, N. G. AND PICKRELL, B. G. (1971), The construction of a photoflux people counter, *Recreation News Supplement* **5**, 9–12

BLALOCK, H. M. JR (1970), *An Introduction to Social Research*, Prentice-Hall, Englewood Cliffs, New Jersey

BLUMENTHAL, A. L. (1977), *The Process of Cognition*, Prentice-Hall, Englewood Cliffs, New Jersey

BOGGS, D. L. (1977), Visitor learning at the Ohio Historial Centre, *Curator*, **20**(3), 205–217

BORUN, M. (1977), 'Exhibit evaluation: an introduction' in *The Visitor and the Museum*, the 1977 Program Planning Committee of the American Association of Museums, Seattle, Washington

BOURNE, L. E., DOMINOWSKI, R. L. AND LOFTUS, E. F. (1979), *Cognitive Processes*, Prentice-Hall, Englewood Cliffs, New Jersey

BRUNER, J. S. (1973), *Beyond the Information Given: Studies in the Psychology of Knowing*, W. W. Norton, New York

CAMERON, D. F. (1967), How do we know that our visitors think?, *Museums News*, **45**(7), 31–33

CAMERON, D. F. (1968a), A viewpoint: the museum as a communicational system and implication for museum education, *Curator*, **11**(1), 33–40

CAMERON, D. F. (1968b), Measuring effectiveness: the evaluation viewpoint, *Museum News*, **46**(5), 43–45

CAMPBELL, F. L. (1970), Participant observation in outdoor recreation, *J. of Leisure Research*, **2**(4), 226–236

COKER, A. M. AND COKER, P. D. (1972), Some practical details of the use of pressure sensitive counters, *Recreation News Supplement*, **7**, 14–17

COKER, A. M. AND COKER, P. D. (1973), A simple method of time lapse photography for use in recreation studies, *Recreation News Supplement*, **8** 31–38

COOK, A. W. AND SELLITZ, C. (1964), 'A multiple indicator approach to attitude measurement' in Warren, N. and

Jahoda, M. (Eds.), *Attitudes,* Penguin, Harmondsworth, pp. 364–394

COUNTRYSIDE RECREATION RESEARCH ADVISORY GROUP (CRRAG) (1973), *The Use of Site Surveys in Countryside Recreation Planning and Management,* Countryside Commission, London

CRUIKSHANK, G. (1972), Jewry Wall Museum, Leicester: trial by questionnaire, *Museums J.,* **72**(2), 65–67

DART (1978), Dartington Amenity Research Trust and the Department of Psychology, the University of Surrey, *Interpretation in Visitor Centres: a Survey of the Effectiveness of Interpretive Services Provided in Visitor Centres,* Countryside Commission, Cheltenham

DART (1979), Dartington Amenity Research Trust *Defence of the Realm,* Southern Tourist Board/Portsmouth City Council, Portsmouth

DAVIDSON, J. (1970a), *Outdoor Recreation Surveys: the Design of Questionnaires for Site Surveys,* Countryside Commission, London

DAVIDSON, J. (1970b), *Outdoor Recreation Information: Suggested Standard Classifications for use in Questionnaire Surveys,* Countryside Commission, London

DAWES, R. M. (1972), *Fundamentals of Attitude Measurement,* John Wiley, New York

DIAB, L. N. (1968), 'Measurement of social attitudes: problems and prospects' in Sherif, C. W. and Sherif, M. (Eds.), *Attitude, Ego-involvement and Change,* John Wiley, New York, pp. 140–158

DICK, R. E., MYKLESTAD, E. AND WAGAR, J. A. (1975), *Audience attention as a basis for evaluating interpretive presentation* USDA Forest Service Research Paper PNW-198 US Dept. of Agriculture (Forest Service)

DIGBY, P. W. (1974), *Visitors to Three London Museums,* London Office of Population, Censuses and Surveys, Social Survey Division, HMSO, London

DOUGHTY, P. S. (1968), The public of the Ulster Museum: a statistical survey, *Museum Journal,* **68**(1), 19–25 and **68**(2), 47–53

DUGGAN, A. J. (1978), The shape of things to come? Reflections on a visit to the Hall of Human Biology, South Kensington, *Museums J.,* **78**(1), 5–6

EASON, L. P. AND LINN, M. C. (1976), Evaluating the effectiveness of participatory exhibits, *Curator,* **19**(1), 45–62

ESTES, W. K. (1976) (Ed.), *Handbook of Learning and Cognitive Processes – Volume 3: Approaches to Human Learning and Motivation,* Lawrence Erilbaum, New York

EVERITT, B. S. (1977), *The Analysis of Contingency Tables,* Chapman and Hall, London

FRIEDRICHS, J. AND LUDTKE, H. (1975), *Participant Observation: Theory and Practice,* Saxon House/Lexington, Farnborough, Hants

GRIGGS, S. AND ALT, M. (1982), Visitors to the British Museum (Natural History) in 1980 and 1981, *Museums J.,* **82**(3), 149–158

HAMMITT, W. E. (1978), A visual performance approach to measuring interpretive effectiveness, *J. of Interpretation,* **3**(2), 33–37

LAKOTA, R. A. (1976), 'Techniques to improve exhibit effectiveness', in *Communicating with the Museum Visitor,* Royal Ontario Museum, Toronto, pp. 245–279

LEE, T. R. AND UZZELL, D. L. (1980a), *The Educational Effectiveness of the Farm Open Day,* Countryside Commission for Scotland, Perth

LEE, T. R. AND UZZELL, D. L. (1980b), *Forestry Commission Visitor Centres: an Evaluation Package,* Dept. of Psychology, University of Surrey

LEMON, N. (1973), *Attitudes and their Measurement,* Halsted Press/John Wiley, New York

LIKERT, R. (1932), A technique for the measurement of attitude, *Archives of Psychology,* No. 140, New York

LOGAN, F. A. (1969), *Fundamentals of Learning and Motivation,* William C. Brown, Dubuque, Iowa

MACDONALD-ROSS, M. (1973), Behavioural objectives: a critical review, *Instructional Science,* **2**, 1–52

MAGER, R. F. (1962), *Preparing Instructional Objectives,* Lear Siegler/Fearon, San Francisco, California

MAHAFFEY, B. D. (1970), Effectiveness and preference for selected interpretive media, *Environmental Education,* **1**(4), 125–128

MASON, T. (1974), The visitors to Manchester Museum: a questionnaire survey, *Museums J.,* **73**(4), 153–157

MASS OBSERVATION (UK) LTD (1978), *National Trust Visitors Survey: Part 1 – Report of Principle Findings; Part II – Appendix of Tables and Comments on Properties,* Mass Observation (UK) Ltd, London

MCWILLIAMS, B. AND HOPWOOD, J. (1973), The public of Norwich Castle Museum: 1971–72, *Museums J.,* **72**(4), 153–156

MILES, R. F. AND TOUT, A. F. (1978), Human biology and the New Exhibition Scheme in the British Museum (Natural History), *Curator,* **21**(1), 36–50

MOSES, EPSTEIN, WISEMAN INC. (1977), *Assessing the Impact of Interpretive Programmes,* prepared for the Division of Interpretation and Visitor Services, National Park Services, Washington DC (unpublished) Contract: PX-001-07-0702

NEISSER, U. (1967), *Cognitive Psychology,* Appleton-Centurt-Crofts, New York

OPPENHEIM, A. N. (1966), *Questionnaire Design and Attitude Measurement,* Basic Books, New York

OSGOOD, C. E. (1964), Semantic differential technique in the Comparative Study of Cultures, *American Anthropology,* **66**(3), 171–200

PARSONS, L. A. (1965), Systematic testing of display techniques for an anthropological exhibit, *Curator,* **8**(2), 167–189

PAYNE, S. L. (1951), *The Art of Asking Questions,* Princeton University Press, Princeton, New Jersey

PEARSON, L. F. (1978), *Non-work Time: A Review of the Literature,* Research Memorandum No. 65, Centre for Urban and Regional Studies, the University of Birmingham, Birmingham

PHILIPS, D. L. (1971), *Knowledge from What?: Theories and Methods in Social Research,* Rand/McNally, Chicago, 111

PIDGEON, D. AND YATES, A. (1968), *An Introduction to Educational Measurement,* Routledge and Kegan Paul, London

PILLAY, C. (1973), Questionnaire surveys: some sampling problems discussed and illustrated, in CRRAG (1973) (above), pp. 1–4

PRINCE, D. R. (1982), Countryside interpretation: A cognitive evaluation, *Museums J.,* **82**(3), 165–170

PRINCE, D. R. (1983), Behavioural consistency and visitor attraction, *Int. J. Museum Management and Curatorship,* **2**, 235–247

PUTNEY, A. D. AND WAGAR, J. A. (1973), Objectives and evaluation in interpretive planning, *J. of Environmental Education,* **5**(1), 43–44

SAARINEN, T. F. (1971), Research approaches and questionnaire design, in Sewell, W. R. D. and Burton, I. (Eds.), *Perceptions and Attitudes in Resource Management,* Policy Research and Coordination Branch, Department of Energy, Mines and Resources, Ottawa, pp. 13–19

SCREVEN, C. G. (1969), The museum as a responsive learning environment, *Museum News, 47*(10), 7–10

SCREVEN, C. G. (1974a), Learning and exhibits: instructional design, *Museum News, 52*(5), 67–76

SCREVEN, C. G. (1974b), *The Measurement and Facilitation of Learning in the Museum Environment: An Experimental Analysis,* Smithsonian Institution Press, Washington DC

SCREVEN, C. G. (1976), Exhibit evaluation: a goal-referenced approach, *Curator, 19*(5), 271–290

SHAW, M. E. AND WRIGHT, J. M. (1967), *Scales for the Measurement of Attitudes,* McGraw-Hill, New York

SHERIF, C. W., SHERIF, M. AND NEBERGAL, R. E. (1965), *Attitude and Attitude Change: The Social Judgement-involvement Approach,* W. B. Saunders, Philadelphia

SHETTEL, H. H. *et al* (1968), *Strategies for Determining Exhibit Effectiveness,* American Institute for Research, Pittsburgh (AIR-e95-4/68-FR)

SHETTEL, H. H. (1973), Exhibits: art form or educational medium?, *Museum News, 52*(1), 32–41

SHETTEL, H. H. AND REILLEY, P. C. (1965), *An Evaluation of the Existing Criteria for Judging the Quality of Science Exhibits,* American Institute for Research, Pittsburgh

SOBOL, M. G. (1980), Do blockbusters' change the audience?, *Museums J., 80*(1), 25–27

STANSFIELD, G. (1981), *Effective Interpretive Exhibits,* Countryside Commission, Cheltenham

TUAN, TI-FU (1974), Topophilia: *A Study of Environmental Perception, Attitudes and Values,* Prentice-Hall, Englewood Cliffs, New Jersey

UPSHAW, H. S. (1968), 'Attitude measurement' in Blalock, H. M. Jr and Blalock, A. B. (Eds.), *Methodology in Social Research,* McGraw-Hill, New York, pp. 60–111

WAGAR, J. J. (1972), *The Recording Quizboard: A Device for Evaluating Interpretive Services,* USDA Forest Research Paper PNW-139, Washington DC

WARREN, N. AND JAHODA, M. (1973) (Eds.) *Attitudes,* Penguin, Harmondsworth

WARWICK, D. P. AND LININGER, C. A. (1975), *The Sample Survey: Theory and Practice,* McGraw-Hill, New York

WASHBURN, R. F. AND WAGAR, J. A. (1972), Evaluating visitor response to exhibit content, *Curator, 15*(3), 248–254

WEISBERG, H. F. AND BOWEN, B. D. (1977), *An Introduction to Survey Research and Data Analysis,* W. H. Freeman, San Francisco

WICKELGREN, W. A. (1979), *Cognitive Psychology,* Prentice-Hall, Englewood Cliffs, New Jersey

WINKEL, G. H., OLSEN, R., WHEELER, F. AND COHEN, H. (1975), *The Museum Visitor and Orientational Media: An Experimental Comparison of Different Approaches at the Smithsonian Institution National Museum of History and Technology,* Smithsonian Institution, Washington DC

WOLF, R. L. AND TYMITZ, B. L. (1977), *Things to Consider when Evaluating,* Indiana Centre for Evaluation, Indiana University, Bloomington

WOLF, R. L. AND TYMITZ, B. L. (1978a), *A Preliminary Guide for Conducting Naturalistic Evaluation in Studying Museum Environments,* Smithsonian Institution, Washington DC

WOLF, R. L. AND TYMITZ, B. L. (1978b), *Whatever Happened to the Giant Wombat?: An Investigation of the Impact of the Ice Age Mammals and the Emergence of Man Exhibit,* National Museum of Natural History, Smithsonian Institution, Smithsonian Institution, Washington DC

WOLF, R. L. AND TYMITZ, B. L. (1979a), *The Pause that Refreshes: A Study of Visitor Reactions to the Discovery Corners in the National Museum of History and Technology,* Smithsonian Institution, Washington DC

WOLF, R. L. AND TYMITZ, B. L. (1979b), *Do Giraffes ever Sit?: A Study of Visitor Perceptions at the National Zoological Park, Smithsonian Institution,* Smithsonian Institution, Washington DC

YOUNGMAN, M. B. (1979), *Analysing Social and Educational Research Data,* McGraw-Hill (UK), London

49

Educational services

P. Graham Carter

After a century of spasmodic growth, the development of museum education in the UK has now reached a plateau. This is not an indication that development is complete, as the majority of museums in Britain do not yet employ qualified full-time educational staff, but it is rather an indication of the current economic situation, in which limited progress in some areas is more than offset by cuts of varying severity in others. Unfortunately, this brake on development comes at a time when museum education should be expanding to meet new depands. Changing patterns of employment and leisure, expansion of the school curriculum, television programs which stimulate interest in both natural and cultural heritage and increased awareness within museums of the need to provide services for the local community, all provide opportunities for initiatives in museum-related educational activities.

History

In 1883 the Rev. Henry H. Higgins M.A. wrote to the Liverpool School Board on behalf of the Museum Sub-Committee offering to distribute useful duplicate specimens among the various elementary schools to help them establish school museums. So began the development of formal museum education in Britain. As a former Schools Inspector, Higgins was well-placed to influence educational opinion, but he did not visualize the development of a loan service. Mr Hewitt, Science Inspector for Liverpool Schools Board did, however, propose the formation of such a collection of selected objects to illustrate special lessons for elementary schools, and in 1884 the Circulating Schools Museum came into being. Sheffield Museum launched a similar service in 1891.

School visits to museums began in 1894/5, coinciding with the opening of Haslemere Education Museum. The impetus for such visits was provided by changes in the day-school code; 'Visits paid during school hours under proper guidance to museums, art galleries and other Institutions of educational value approved by the Department may be reckoned as attendances, provided that not more than twenty attendances may be claimed for any one schollar in the same school year and that the general arrangements for such visits are submitted for the approval of the Inspector'. This enlightened statement preceded by some sixty years the post-war move to push back the walls of the primary classroom.

Between 1901 and 1940, Leeds Museum introduced a Schools Service, and in 1902 Manchester Museum employed a special teacher to work with children. The Horniman Museum appointed a guide/lecturer in 1904 for three half-day sessions each week, one session being reserved for teachers. The Horniman also introduced worksheets on three themes in 1908 for distribution to visiting children. Newport (1912), Manchester (1915) and Norwich (1916) were the next museums to introduce schools services and in 1920 Lord Sudeley achieved the appointment of guide/lecturers in national museums.

During the 1930s, the number of school services almost doubled, from eight to fifteen. Leicester Museum appointed Ruth Weston as Schools Museum Officer in 1931. This was the first full-time education appointment, and the second followed in 1936 when a full-time schools museum officer was appointed by Derbyshire County Education Committee. Other new services included Reading (1930), Geffrye, Horniman and Letchworth (1935) and Luton (1936).

The period of the Second World War was marked by the establishment of the museum education survice in Glasgow, and it was to provide a pattern for many which followed. Not only were qualified staff appointed, but a department was established within the museum having equipped classrooms and lecture facilities and offering a wide and varied programme of activities based on the collections within the museum and art gallery.

The growth of such services continued steadily in post-war years where it was marked by increasing co-operation between the education officers of various museums. The Group for Educational Activities in Museums (later the Group for Education in Museums) was formed following a meeting of the Children's Subject Section of the International Council of Museums in London in 1948.

In 1963, the Rosse Report was published. This survey of provincial museums and galleries gave unequivocal support to museum education, when it stated that 'It seems to us impossible to over estimate the importance to future generations of teaching children the use and significance of museum objects and we urge that those authorities which have not yet developed, or assisted museums in the area to develop a schools museum service, to do so without delay, and especially to provide a loan service in all rural areas'. This report identified expenditure by Borough or County Education Committees on financing museum schools services as 'relevant expenditure' for the purpose of the general grant made by Her Majesty's Government to Local Authorities for education. The report stimulated development of museum education services and led a number of local authorities to set up loan services independent of museums. Among these were Nottinghamshire, East Sussex and Yorkshire.

In the same year the Group for Educational Services in Museums registered a list of 34 services, and by 1967 the number had grown to 48. As they developed, so the demands placed on the services increased sharply and soon exceeded the point when each group could be met by a museum education officer. New methods were required to meet this rising demand and many services began to concentrate on the production of resource packs for use by teachers both on site and in the classroom. Many ran in-service courses for teachers wishing to bring groups to the museums. At the same time there was a growth in informal activities for family groups, adults, pensioners and others. In 1967, the Museum Association published the Handbook on Museum Schools Services written by the Group for Educational Services in Museums. This aimed to provide a general guide for museum officers including those studying for the Museums Association diploma and for committee members and officers of local authorities who may be concerned in establishing or administering schools museums services. It was also addressed to teachers who may wish to avail themselves of such services.

The end of the 1960s and beginning of the 1970s was a period of marked growth in educational support services. Not only did such educational services continue to expand, but teachers' centres were established and there was a rapid growth of interest in environmental studies leading to the establishment of both urban and rural interpretive centres. In the museum world in general, the main growth was in the independent sector. The first museum education appointments in independent museums were made in the early 1970s, as were the first educational appointments to the Department of the Environment's Ancient Monuments Division, and the National Trust. The 1970s also marked the publication of an increased number of papers and reports related to museum education. In 1971 the Department of Education and Science published a survey on 'Museum in Education'. In the Introduction to this report, Her Majesty's Inspectorate wrote:

> Awestruck was the term used in an American report on 'Museums and Education' to describe the feelings of contributors when they contemplated the fantastic potential of museums as places for education. The same expression could be used about collections in Britain. To conserve is a museum's first priority, to educate and entertain is a close second. To conserve for future generations whilst ignoring the present generation would be absurd. However, the use made of these enormous resources is uneven – admirable in some museums, in others it is less well organised to meet the demands of today.

The report highlighted problems of accommodation for museum education services, the need for development in the field of adult and informal education, the value of the participatory approach to education in museums, and the importance of teacher training.

Further support for the development of museum educational services to meet the needs of the national education system came in the Wright report on provincial museums and galleries (1973). In a general statement, this report said that 'the increasing demands of education, national trends towards more leisure and greater mobility, the growth in cultural television programmes and the increase in tourism are putting pressure on the resources of museums to an extent that calls for a fresh initiative'. Turning more specifically to education, the report recommended that 'local education authorities should be involved to a greater extent in the planning of museum education services', that these should be run by the museum and that 'museums should' be enabled to provide properly equipped accommodation specifically for educational use, including in appropriate cases suitable accommodation for an educational loans service.' Much of the impact of the Wright Report was, however, lost in the turmoil of local government reorganization. While the general feeling within the museum profession was that such education should be linked to general education in the new authorities, many museum services found themselves grouped under leisure activities. This, this reorganization brought many museum education services into direct contact with the staff of country parks, visitor centres and urban study centres. In the course of reorganization, some new museum education services were founded, for example those in Tyne and Wear and Southampton.

During this period, the report of the Schools Council's Working Party on Museums was published under the title 'Pterodactyls and Old Lace'. This considered ways in which services provided by museums, both local and national, could be more effectively exploited by teachers. The working party was also charged with preparing 'a publication containing a clear statement of the philosophy of the educational use of museums'. In this it largely failed.

Following recommendations in the 1971 report of the Museums Association, the DES organized a series of in-service training courses in the educational use of museums. Initially, these were held in London and concentrated on the education services of the national museums, but since 1978 some have been held in the provinces in conjunction with the DOE and have dealt with the educational use of ancient monuments, historic houses and museums.

The initiative of the DES, and later that of the DOE, are only two examples of the increase in opportunities for the in-service training of museum educators which characterized the 1970s. In the first half of the decade, the Museum Association introduced an educational option on its Diploma course with the first examinations being held in 1974. Annual Conferences of the Group for Educational Services in Museums continued, but the trend was away from a conference format towards that of an in-service training course, and this pattern is now firmly established. In 1975, the Group organized an international conference in London on the theme of 'Museums as an influence on the quality of life'. One interesting by-product of this conference was the establishment of regional discussion groups in the UK. This regional structure has persisted, and several of the regional groups now have firm links with Area Museum Councils. Some Area Councils have established regional education panels to discuss policy, run courses, provide advice and carry out development projects.

The present situation

There are, in 1983, 362 professional posts in education within 154 museums, 15 per cent of which are entitled 'teacher', or 'lecturer' and 55 per cent include the word 'officer' or 'organizer' in the title and could be considered to be outside the line management system of their museum. The trend, however, is towards the use of the title of 'keeper of education and display' or of 'education and interpretation' and reflects the growing acceptance of education as both a central museum function, and as a function of museum display.

At the beginning of the 1980s, museum education suffered from the decline in school roles, the difficult economic situation and the general retrenchment within education generally. It is interesting to note that quotes from the Rosse Report which were used in the 1960s to stimulate the growth of museum educational services are now being used in an effort to protect the same service from cuts.

Benefits of museum educational services

Students

The main beneficiary of museum educational services must always be the student – of whatever age and ability – and such benefits are both many and varied. Some are related to the personal development of the individual, while others have a more direct relevance to the curriculum.

A dominant trend within education in the past two decades has been the increased participation by the student in the learning process. This is characterized in the sciences, for example, by the experimental approach – intended to give the learner first-hand experience – and in history by the increasing use of first-hand evidence. Yet by the very nature of classroom teaching, much of this experience is still second-hand. Drawings, photographs, slides and film are used to provide representations of objects and activities. It is here that museums have the greatest contribution to make as they can provide direct encounters with original objects. This process is a forceful communicator, and can be strengthened greatly if more than one physical sense is employed.

Benefits to the student in terms of personal development are manifold. Encounters with objects can, for example, enhance greatly the ability to observe, many educational activities in museums are directed towards helping people to look constructively and creatively at objects. Other benefits are aesthetic. Students are given an opportunity to experience beauty which may not be bountiful in their home environment. Museums also present opportunities for encounters with excellence; outstanding examples of work in fine and decorative art, craft, science and technology, which may help them to redefine standards in an age of mass production. They also provide encounters with the objects of past generations, thus carrying the cumulative tradition and culture of a people from one generation to the next.

Teachers

Museum education services can offer substantial benefits to the class-room teacher. Teaching based on objects requires particular skills which are developed to a high degree by museum education staff. Class-room teachers can take advantage of these skills either by arranging for museum staff to meet their pupils, or by learning the skills themselves through preliminary vists and in-service training courses. Moreover, most primary school teachers cannot be expected to have detailed, specialist knowledge of the full range of the material and may lack both the time and the facilities to carry out the necessary background research relevant to the collections. Museum educators acquire this specialist knowledge as a matter of course, and can make it readily available to school teachers. Co-operation between museum and class-room teachers before the visit can lead to a well-planned course of study for students which integrates their museum experience with work in the class-room. Such co-operation can also ensure that the standard museum educational services are tailored to meet the needs of the group. In many cases education departments can provide resource materials for use both during the visit and in the class-room.

Local education authorities

For Local Education Authorities, investment in museum services is a sound one. In the course of their careers, most students undertake a number of out-of-school visits. In many cases these are to destinations without specialist education staff and their education value is very often questionable. The presence of qualified and experienced education staff in local museums increases greatly the effectiveness of such visits and in the course of an academic year a single education officer can advise a large number of school parties. The per capitum cost of such visits is therefore very small and the improved quality of the visit more than compensates for this expenditure.

The museum

It is becoming increasingly important that museums demonstrate that they provide a general service for the community in which they are situated. Provision of education staff is one of the most straightforward ways of achieving this. This is true particularly if the education department provides services for the whole community, rather than simply to school groups.

Planning museum education services

In the planning or reassessment of the educational potential of a museum, the shape of the service will be influenced by a number of factors including: the size and resources of the museum; the level of commitment to education of the director and management committee; the nature of the collections; available space; proposed staffing levels; predicted demand; the nature of the catchment area, be it urban or rural; the nature of the museum; national, local authority or independent; and the attitude of the Local Education Authority.

Important as they are, they must not be allowed to distort or overwhelm the education requirements of the service in terms of staffing, accommodation and the nature of services provided.

Staff

In choosing members of the professional staff (or officers) the following guidelines should apply: that they should be graduates in a discipline relevant to an aspect of the museum's collection; have a professional teaching qualification; have spent at least three years in class-room teaching; have experience of working with children outside the class-room; and be skilled in the use of audio-visual aids. They should also have sympathy with, and enthusiasm for, the objectives of the museum. They must have a confident and relaxed manner and be capable of dealing with people of all ages, including students, teachers, local authority committee members, and the general public.

The position of the education officer within the management structure must be determined at an early stage. It is important both to the department and to the museum that the senior education appointment should be at keeper level and should be regarded as part of the line management. This not only facilitates inter-departmental co-operation but also ensures that the museum derives maximum benefit from education staff.

Such staff should also be afforded the same facilities for continued personal and professional development as are extended to other members of the museum management team, and should be given the same opportunities for extra-mural activities and professional contacts.

It is essential that the professional staff in the education department should receive adequate administrative and technical support. The minimum necessary is the provision of adequate administrative assistance. Where a museum education service has a large collection of objects under its care, for example, where a loan service is run or a large teaching collections is maintained, adequate technical assistance will be required. Technicians will need to prepare, clean and service the artefacts, models and replicas, and audio-visual equipment used by the department. Such staff should be qualified and trained to agreed museum standards.

Accommodation

If it is to function efficiently, the department must be provided with adequate accommodation. The nature of the accommodation will obviously vary according to the type of service offered. One requirement is for adequate office space, preferably located within convenient reach of the museum entrance so that staff may, if required, meet incoming parties without undue delay.

A second requirement is for adequate teaching space. The aim is clearly not to take children from a school class-room and simply seat them in a museum class-room; nevertheless, there are many activities which cannot be undertaken satisfactorily in the public galleries.

Where only one room is provided this must be as large as possible and must be treated as flexible space. It should also house original objects similar to those in the museum collection and should be provided with adequate, safe storage facilities. Blackouts and adequate audio-visual equipment and aids are essential. The room should be within easy reach of the galleries and, if possible, adjacent to toilets. Associated with the workroom should be adequate storage for the coats and bags of visiting groups and access to the education space should be easy, with ramps and wide doors to permit its use by physically handicapped groups.

Where two rooms are available, one of these should be equipped as a lecture room while the other retained as flexible space. Whether the seating in the lecture room is tiered or on the flat, care should be taken in the planning of this space to make sure that it is easily adaptable for use with film, concert, drama, or dance performances.

If a third room is available an art-and-craft workshop can be created. Such a room should be equipped with adequate work benches, power points and sinks and the floor well-sealed for easy cleaning. The equipment will vary according to the nature of the collections and the interests of the officers within the department, and may include potters' wheels, and a kiln, sewing machines and irons, art materials, woodworking tools, and microscopes.

Objects and equipment

There is a constant debate about the nature and the quality of objects which should be made available for educational use. There are several principles which should be borne in mind, including:

(1) Wherever possible, original objects should be used. A major purpose of bringing children to the museum is to provide direct contact with such material.
(2) Materials should be of a high quality.
(3) They should be selected by the education staff in consultation with curatorial staff and conservators.
(4) The use of replicas in museum education services is a controversial subject. One school of thought is that nothing but original objects explained fully should be used. Proponents of these arguments stress that museums are accepted by the public as homes of genuine articles only and that the use of replicas in any form may undermine this basic trust between the public and museums. This is probably the majority view. Others feel that, although very much second best, replicas have their uses. Well made replicas, clearly identified, may be used in particular where the most important purpose of the educational activity is demonstration of a process rather than examination of an object.
(5) Scale and working models both have a part to play in the museum. They can be used to represent items too large to be included in the collection or too small to be seen clearly with the naked eye. They also have a value in demonstrating the principles by which machines work.
(6) Printed and audio-visual material should be used only as supports, and not as surrogates for the originals.

It follows, therefore, that the education department will require an acquisition budget and an annual allowance for restoration and conservation work similar to that made available to other curatorial departments.

Categories of service

When planning a new service or reviewing an existing one, decisions taken will be affected by the outside influences noted earlier. The strength of resources in terms of staffing and facilities will also affect the nature and quality of the service. The cumulative effect of these influences should be an education service which is uniquely adapted to fill the requirements of the museum and the catchment area which it serves.

In order to ensure that such a service does not develop haphazardly, it is necessary to review alternative approaches periodically and to assess what contribution the service can be making under each of several headings. It is convenient to consider these choices in contrasting pairs but it must be stressed that in many cases they are not mutually exclusive.

The questions to be asked are: Will the service offered be intra-mural or extra-mural; be direct or indirect; serve the pupil or the teacher; serve schools and colleges or a wider audience; be formal or informal? In brief, intra-mural services concentrate on groups and individuals visiting the museum; extra-mural services reach out into the community. Direct services rely on personal contact; indirect services minimize this contact and rely heavily on the production of resource materials.

Services directed at the pupil ensure that the education officer retains control over the quality of each pupil's experience; while services directed at the teacher aim to help him/her more effectively with their own groups in the museum. Provision of activities and facilities for school groups only represents a traditional approach. Increasingly, museum education staff are seeking to reach adults and family groups as well. The formal approach is again traditional, involving a carefully planned presentation (lecture, gallery tour and so on) to an identifiable audience. Informal activities encompass children's clubs, holiday activities, society meetings and special events.

Most services are a mixture of these approaches, each of which has its own strengths and weaknesses.

Intra-mural services

Direct services to pupils
The advantage of this approach is that of immediate impact. Staff become skilled in bridging the gap between the cultural setting of the objects and that of the student, and direct contact with the pupil can have a freshness and immediacy which no other approach can equal. Whatever the method used, be it lecture, gallery tour, workshop session, art and craft or drama, the education officer is on hand to guide, question, encourage and support the student. The stimulation received by pupils from such a visit will carry over into class-room follow-up work.

There are, however, problems with this approach. Firstly, unless the programme is carefully planned, a museum teacher can be involved in repeating the same programme to successive groups of children frequently and for long periods. Such repetition can destroy spontaneity and lead to boredom and frustration.'Second, the approach places a strict limit on the number of pupils who can benefit. With careful programming the numbers handled can be large, but where demand is overwhelming reliance on the direct approach alone will mean that some students will receive no assistance with their visit and will have to cope alone. It is probably only in museums serving communities which place only limited pressure on museum resources that the direct teaching approach can be used in isolation.

Direct service for teachers
Recognizing these limitations, education staff have recently been placing greater emphasis on contact with teachers. The object is to familiarize them with the collections and to help to develop teaching methods which are appropriate to museum visits. This approach has a number of advantages. First, compared with direct student contact it is extremely cost-effective. A morning's work with 30 teachers is enhancing the quality of a museum visit for between 900 and 1000 children in the first year, and many more hundreds thereafter. Moreover, if the class teacher is directly involved in the visit itself it is much easier for him/her to organize suitable follow-up work.

Contact between museum educators and teachers should begin while the teachers are still in training. This can ensure that new teachers understand the educational value of museums and have had practice in the use of such sites. Contact can be maintained through in-service training. Perhaps the most important contact is, however, with the individual teacher making a preliminary visit before bringing a school group. Discussion with museum staff at this stage can make the group visit much more productive.

Indirect service
Provision of an indirect service by means of, for example, publications, has one major disadvantage: it deprives both pupils and teachers of direct contact with museum staff. However, the advantage of such a service should not be overlooked. Whether this is the only service offered or whether it is used to support direct services, once developed and tested, pupils' and teachers' publications are readily available.

Every teacher or student who visits the museum can be provided with them and they may be used when the museum education officer is engaged elsewhere. Publications can be designed to meet the needs of a particular age range and, in certain cases, can be closely linked to the school curriculum. Well-planned children's publications will not only stimulate careful, accurate observation and recording, but can also guide children to think constructively about what they are seeing. Publications aimed at the teacher can provide background information and suggestions for work during a visit and in the class-room. Provision of publications-based services is essential in museums with a limited number of education staff facing heavy demands. The alternative is to take a deliberate decision to make museum education services available to only a very limited number of potential visitors.

Formal and informal services

Over the past 100 years, formal services have been the main point of emphasis for museums, and this is likely to remain so for the foreseeable future, particularly where there has been funding from the Local Education Authority. However, it is now becoming increasingly desirable that education staff should be involved in a much wider programme of informal activities. The trend toward increased leisure, high level of unemployment, and early retirement, as well as an increased interest in first-hand participation rather than second-hand observation, combine to create a potentially large market for information about educational activities based on museum collections.

Extra-mural activities

There are certain circumstances under which an education department may concentrate on the provision of extra-mural activities as a first priority, e.g., a museum serving a diffuse population in rural areas where public transport is unsatisfactory. Alternatively, a museum may opt for the provision of extra-mural services where it has very large collections and comparatively limited display space. The main problem with the provision of such services is that they require the appointment of additional technical, clerical and transport staff and can place heavy demands on available storage space. The most common argument advanced against them is that of expense. While this may be true in terms of the museum's budget alone, it is an argument which is difficult to sustain when overall costs are considered. It may cost 25 times as much to bring one class to a museum for a day as it does to transport one museum loan unit to a school where it can stay for several weeks and may be used by hundreds of children.

Whatever the advantages and disadvantages of the different types of service, most museum education departments will offer a mixed programme. A museum with a large demand and a limited number of education staff may concentrate on the provision of resources and then offer direct teaching services to a few visitors. A county museum service may offer direct services in a number of branch museums scattered throughout its area and support this with a loan service for those schools lacking ready access to museum collections. All the elements will combine to ensure that there are almost as many types of museum education service as there are museums with education staff.

Range of services

The range of services offered is great and it is difficult to give a comprehensive coverage. However, it may be helpful to select a few examples and to consider possibilities.

Lecture theatres

The lecture theatre, for so long the heart of museum education services, still has an important part to play. Some institutions have developed its use to a very high degree. The Science Museum, for example, offers lectures at several levels and with different objectives. It provides a request lecture service for groups from age 10 upwards, which is used extensively by secondary schools. The service provides talks in a theatre fully equipped to project slides, films or closed circuit television programmes on to a large screen and many working demonstrations are readily available. It has also an extensive array of demonstration apparatus to illustrate both historical achievements and some of the latest developments in science and technology. In addition, the Museum offers joint industrial lectures given by outside speakers, often research workers. These are addressed to A-level students and are related to the industrial applications of topics related to the examination syllabus. The same theatre is used for public lectures giving short introductory talks at lunch-time and full-scale lectures and demonstrations on Saturdays. Special lectures on popular subjects for family groups are devised for the Christmas and Easter holidays.

Gallery tours

Another traditional element, gallery tours, can be very difficult to organize effectively, particularly in galleries which are crowded with other visitors. However, many believe that a guided tour led by an informed and sensitive teacher can be of great assistance in helping to bridge the gap between the culture of the pupil and that of the exhibit. For students of school age, tours linked to practical activities are usually more successful. Thus, a tour of an art gallery may be linked to a session in which children attempt to re-create with costume and acting some of the pictures in the collections, while a tour of a spinning and weaving collection may be preceded by an opportunity for children to spin wool by hand.

Workrooms

An increasing number of museums now have a room away from the distraction of the public gallery in which an introduction to a specific topic is given. This is where material can be handled or, if for safety and conservation reasons it cannot be handled, may at least be looked at in the round and without the intervention of the display case. Usually, the specimens are similar to those in the galleries and are often put into context with the aid of slides, films, and sound cassettes. The aim of a visit is not to transpose the children from a school class-room to a museum class-room. Work sessions undertaken at the museum must always have a dimension which cannot be provided at the school. In addition to close contact with objects, there is an increasing use of simulation and role-play as a means of bringing collections to life. At Clarke Hall in Wakefield, for example, the seventeenth century house is used as an educational resource where the staff play the role of the inhabitants of the house in 1680 and involve the children in a variety of activities related to life at the time.

Publications

Publications for pupils and teachers are many and varied. The main aim of *worksheets* is to focus attention on objects in the collection, and to help visitors to understand the exhibits. The best are designed to suit the particular requirements of specific age or ability groups. All focus on the objects and direct the thoughts of the reader purposefully. They are counter-productive when they concentrate on labels rather than objects and act as competitive, time-based treasure hunts.

Workbooks are more extensive and may contain a mixture of information and activities for students to do. They provide a record of the student's time in the museum and suggest follow-up work to be done at home or school. *Teachers' notes* are designed to provide adequate background material for non-specialists so that a visit may be incorporated into the general pattern of class-room work. The preparation a teacher gives in the class-room before a visit to the museum is vital to the attitudes and expectations of the visiting class. A visit which is reinforced by discussion with an enthusiastic class-room teacher back at school and incorporated into their scheme of work will be one which lives in the mind.

Extra-mural activities

Loan service
This is the most traditional and longest established of the extra-mural activities. The services vary greatly in their nature and range from those with a very limited number of loans to those offering large collections accommodating secondary information. It is thus difficult to select a typical example. The service offered by Manchester Museum does, however, demonstrate most aspects. Its loan collection comprises some 2000 objects, replicas, photographs, books, slide sets and slide tape units which are available on monthly loan to schools in Manchester and the surrounding area. The service was initiated in 1960 with financial support from the Local Education Authority. The collection is card-indexed and objects are booked out to schools in advance. Curatorial staff who co-operated in the development of the loan collection had to be convinced that they were not risking the objects when allowing them to go to schools. They also needed reassurance that items would be boxed securely with due respect for conservation requirements and that they would be returned rapidly if required by the museum.

Mobile services
At the time of writing, nine authorities in Britain operate mobile services. Of these only the Merseyside County Council operates a service exclusively for schools. The others provide mobile museums for the public either at special events or in places remote from the base museum. The service operated by Merseyside County Museums and the Walker Art Gallery has the specific aim of improving the educational provision in an area of social disadvantage, but its organizers believe that the same methods could be used more widely. With the support of the Urban Aid Scheme, Merseyside provides a travelling gallery supported by education officers. The project team, comprising the leader and three assistants, is supported by a designer and two attendants/drivers. Within the mobile gallery, displays are created on specific topics. At each site, or school visited, children are given an introductory talk supported by a short slide presentation. They then explore the exhibition and complete worksheets. After the visit, they return to the class-room for a follow-up session led by a member of the project team. Here, objects are used to expand the themes of the exhibition and provide a springboard from which the class teacher can develop project work. The teachers are then invited to bring their groups to the museum for a support session provided by the education service. In its first two years of operation, the mobile gallery visited two-thirds of the inner city schools and requests for return visits now outstrip the Department's ability to provide them.

Field trips
Many departments run field excursions as a part of their normal programme. As well as biological and geographical excursions related to the collections, destinations for such visits include archaeological and industrial archaeological sites.

Informal educational activities

As important as the formal activities for students are the informal programmes. The great strength of such activities is that they cater for the individual enthusiast visiting the museum on a purely voluntary basis. Informal activities for children generally are of two kinds: museum clubs and holiday activity programmes.

Clubs

The majority of children's clubs in museums operate throughout term-time on Saturdays and may also meet during the week in school holidays. The most common element in the program is probably art and craft work related to the collections. The degree of direction in the work of such clubs varies greatly. Children are sometimes encouraged to select an object of particular interest and to find out more about it or to portray it through the medium of painting, modelling or embroidery. In other situations the organizer will select a theme on which all children will work. This is particularly common in museums which have a strong programme of temporary exhibitions. In clubs without a membership scheme, it is often difficult to provide continually developing activities but if a regular membership exists it is possible to identify and develop the interests of the individual child. Whichever method is adopted, clubs can provide exciting experiences for their members, a valuable service to the local community and excellent public relations for the museum.

Holiday activities

One of the most exciting and creative of educational activities is to be found in the holiday programs organized by many museums throughout the country. These activities have two major advantages. Firstly, attendance is voluntary and all those who participate are usually enthusiasts – although there are cases of unenthusiastic children being plunged into unsuitable activities by over-enthusiastic parents. Second, educators have contact with the children over a much longer period than is normally possible with school groups. Many holiday activity programmes last for a day, and some for a week. Over such periods it is easier to identify a child's strengths and weaknesses and to help him/her develop particular skills. Holiday programmes are as varied as the museums and staff who operate them and are usually restricted only by financial considerations, and limitations on space and available manpower. The range of activities is great. For example, a military museum has organized classes on military modelling both for beginners and advanced students as well as arranging war games; a maritime museum has organized maritime days involving a study of the exhibits, rope and knot work, the cooking of ship's biscuits, learning the hornpipe and singing sea shanties; historic houses have organized Elizabethan and Edwardian Christmases where children in costume sing carols, listen to period stories, make appropriate toys and gifts and decorate the house for Christmas for the benefit of other visitors; natural history museums have arranged weeks not only of biological fieldwork and recording, but also in practical conservation activities. In other locations, children have engaged in role play in a variety of settings, visited archaeological sites, learned various crafts and skills, participated in concerts, made musical instruments and cooked food from various periods in history.

One interesting expansion of the holiday activity concept has been the growth of family group activities. A small number of museum now deliberately plan weekend and holiday courses in which all members of the family can participate. Although few in number, the idea of grandparents, parents and children joining together to make music, learn dances, study art, paint, join field trips and learn medieval cooking is attractive, and should be encouraged. There are increasing indications that families are seeking more and more active pastimes and this is an area with a considerable growth potential.

Adult education

Another such growth area is the field of adult education. High levels of unemployment, early retirement and the increase of available leisure-time create exciting opportunities for museum education departments to use the collections to capture the enthusiasm, and develop the individual interest, of members of the local community.

Although the number of adult education opportunities in museums is limited at present, the range available is considerable. Some have organized university extra-mural courses. For example, the Geological Museum in London has evening classes sponsored by the University of London and staffed by members of the Institute of Geological Science.

Other, more local museums have offered evening classes for the study of local or natural history. In common with children's holiday activities, many of these initiatives last less than a calendar year. Some run for a term only and others for a matter of days. Once again the variety is large. Museums have offered courses on Egyptology, archaeology, natural history, embroidery, spinning, dyeing, weaving, folk dancing and the making and playing of musical instruments.

Another way of developing adult participation is to offer educational facilities within the museum as a base for local clubs and societies. If the museum serves as the local environmental records centre, there is a strong case for using its facilities for meetings of clubs such as the Royal Society for the Protection of Birds, the County Naturalists' Trust, the local history society and so on. In all such cases, in addition to normal club meetings, it is possible to develop educational activities based on the collections and records. Such activities can increase greatly the levels of knowledge and skill of club members and enable them to make a more positive contribution to the historical and biological conservation of the region.

Some museums may be keen to develop adult educational opportunities but may lack the staffing resources necessary to undertake them successfully. Such museums should seek support from elsewhere in the local community. The two most obvious sources are the adult education institutes of the local education authority and the Workers' Educational Association. In some areas, both institutions have proved extremely willing to co-operate in such developments. The museum derives three major benefits from such co-operation. First, the institutes and the Association both have networks through which courses at the museum may be publicized. Second, either the Association or the institutes will normally handle booking and administration, thus relieving the museum of this administrative burden. Third, when courses are organized through either adult education institutes or the WEA, these organizations will pay lecturers to run the courses. Museums interested in pursuing this development should begin by contacting the Principal of the local adult education institute or the Local University Extension Department.

A major problem in considering adult classes is often the difficulty of evening opening. In many museums, simply opening the front door puts the whole collection at risk, due to the absence of secure closing methods for individual galleries. Employment of a full evening shift of security staff so that a single evening class may operate is an expensive option, particularly where staff are paid at overtime rates. In museums where development of evening classes is rated as a priority activity, it may be worth considering whether building work could produce a building in which one section may be quickly and securely isolated, thus reducing both staffing and security problems.

Friends organizations

Some museums are hesitant over the creation of a Friends' organization. In some curatorial minds, it may raise the spectre of over-enthusiastic amateurs running riot through collections demanding great professional expertise, and – at the most extreme – trying to dictate to the management how the museum should be run. There is also concern over the amount of professional staff time which can be absorbed in the management of organization. However, most museums consider a Friends' organization as primarily an informal, adult education activity. If this approach is adopted, then education staff can be involved in the organization of a programme for them based on the collections. As well as inviting the group to participate in adult education classes organized for the general public (perhaps with some priority booking) the education department can also lay on special activities for the Friends' organization alone. These could examine the museum as an institution and help to develop a clear view of its objectives, and of the work of its departments. Such an understanding will form a sound basis for the development of other activities in which Friends can participate. Moreover, Friends' programmes are excellent public relations activities for the museum and can be a source of attractive press stories.

Education services in small museums

So far, this paper has concentrated on museums which either already have well-established education departments or are seeking to found them. However, the majority of museums in the United Kingdom do not employ education staff. In some museums this indicates a serious neglect on the part of the curator or management committee.

There are, however, many other museums which are too small and insufficiently financed to be able to afford professional education staff. Some, however, have curators wishing to develop educational services. In order to provide sound services at minimal cost it will be necessary for these curators to seek outside support, almost certainly from the Local Education Authority (LEA). An understanding of the structure of the education system in the UK will enable them to direct their requests towards the most appropriate targets. Administration at the national level (DES, SED and DENI) is of little relevance to the curator of a small museum. These Departments are involved with the implementation of broad policy objectives and in overseeing general standards. They are rarely involved at the local level. However, there is one branch of the national system which can be of great assistance to the museum curator via Her Majesty's Inspectorate. Although employed to report on standards and trends in education, inspectors fulfil a much wider function in that they generally hold a district responsibility. In this capacity they travel widely within an area to participate in curriculum development, in-service training and discussions of educational policy. Through this they come to know many creative individuals and organizations, and can be an invaluable source of advice to the curator. In addition to district responsibilities, inspectors also have a specialist subject area responsibility. Of particular curatorial interest is the fact that the Inspectorate has a committee of which one member assumes special responsibility for museums. Appropriate inspectors can be contacted through the National Education Department. It is from the county, metropolitan district or borough level of educational organizations that the curator is likely to obtain the most support. The first request for advice and assistance should be directed to the Chief Education Officer who will probably delegate responsibility for any response to a more junior member of staff. This delegation may be to an assistant education officer with responsibility for resources or perhaps the support services. But it is much more likely to be passed to a member of the local authority inspectorate or advisory team. LEA advisors usually have responsibility for a particular age range or area of the curriculum. The curator may be well-advised to ask a team of advisors to visit the museum for initial discussion.

The level of aid requested will depend on the precise needs of the museum, the resources of the LEA and the nerve of the curator. The curator may, for example, begin by requesting the advisors to outline the nature of the service which they feel should be based on the museum; recommend a local teacher who may be prepared to assist in the development and testing of materials; establish a working party of teachers based at a local teachers' centre or curriculum development centre to produce a wide range of materials for use in the museum; allow the local curriculum development centre to print and distribute the materials.

The curator could also request secondment of teachers to the museum financed by the LEA, ask the authority to consider the possibility of redeploying teachers to the museum staff; ask the authority to fund the creation of a permanent post for a museum education officer, and to assist with materials and equipment for the embryonic education service.

Whatever course of action is chosen, the curator should ensure that the service provided can be maintained. Thus, if a curriculum development team is brought together by the LEA for a limited period to develop and test educational materials, the museum must be prepared to ensure that those materials stay in print and available to schools once the development project has ended.

Local advisors and members of HM Inspectorate are not the only sources of aid in educational development. Principals of the local adult educational institutes and WEA should be consulted on any proposed developments in their own fields of expertise. Local colleges of higher education, university departments, and schools of education may also be prepared to co-operate in the production, development and testing of materials designed for

both pupils and teachers. Assistance with lay-out, graphics or illustration of materials may also be obtained from local colleges of art. Such students must be given a clear brief. They must know the design limits and deadlines. There is little point in students developing full colour artwork for educational materials if the museum has only a limited printing budget.

As long as unemployment remains at its current high level, money for educational development may be available from the Manpower Services Commission's Community Programme: numerous precedents exist. The criteria for acceptability for these programmes vary from time to time but, in general, any application should meet the following requirements: the project should be for community or environmental benefit; it should not be for financial profit; staff should not be appointed to take the place of full-time permanent posts.

Applications from most small museums, whether they be local authority or charitable trust bodies, would match these requirements. A curator may decide to enlist the aid of a team comprising one or more teachers a secretary and a designer. The programme of work must be planned carefully to make completion possible within one year; although when one project has terminated sponsorship of a second scheme may be proposed. Although some experienced professional manpower is available under community programmes, it must be remembered that the majority of teachers available through this scheme will have had little or no class-room experience and will require guidance not only from the curator but also, if possible, from an experienced member of the education profession.

Although essential to the activities of education departments in many American museums, it is not proposed that unqualified volunteers should be used to develop services in small museums in the UK. The critical word here is 'unqualified'. Curators who can find no other way of launching a service may find the use of qualified volunteers very productive. There are, within any community, a number of trained experienced teachers who are not currently engaged in schools.

However, educational work in museums differs greatly from that of the class-room, and it is essential that such volunteers should not be left to work alone but should receive the constant and enthusiastic support of the curatorial staff. Only in this way can the museum director ensure that the objects from the collection are not put at risk and that the information conveyed by the education volunteers is correct.

Each curator should also consider whether there are any special circumstances relating to his or her own museum which may make grants available from other sources. An inner city museum wishing to develop community education programmes may receive funding through an Urban Aid Grant. Similarly, an ethnology museum which uses its collecion to provide services for ethnic minorities may be able to attract funding from a multi-cultural education project.

Another source of assistance which should not be neglected is the Area Museums Service. Some services are able to provide detailed educational advice on a consultancy basis and this is usually grant aidable. In addition to advice, services may also assist with the practical side of an educational development by giving grant aid for new equipment, facilities, and publications.

The Group for Education in Museums (GEM) will also be very pleased to help curators seeking to establish or extend educational services. The committee of GEM will always nominate a group member willing to give advice on development of the service, or to review educational materials. They will also arrange for newly appointed staff to visit well established services and to make contact with their closest colleagues. The Group is the official specialist organization for museum educators. Officers change from time to time, but name and address of the current secretary may be obtained from the Museum Association.

With help available from such a variety of sources, and at so many different levels, it should be possible for every museum – no matter how small – to make a sound educational service available to schools and teachers.

The wider role of educational staff

The curator who employs professionally qualified and experienced education staff and then confines them to working solely with school groups is under-using the considerable potential of some of the museum's most skilled manpower. Museum educators may have training in the teaching of reading and the development of language, the psychology of learning and child development. They will have considerable experience of analysing complex concepts and presenting them in a simple way to an audience with little background in any particular subject. They may be, in fact, the only professional communicators in the museum. Even where design staff are employed, the skills of designers and teachers are complementary. This background of qualification and experience, together with a period of time working with objects and children in museums, places the museum educator in a unique position in terms of developing interpretive programmes for the museum as a whole. Education staff should work with curatorial and design staff in the development of new displays, temporary exhibitions, publications and special events, as well as participation in the initial discussions and planning. The education staff should have a particular contribution to make in the analysis of concepts to be transmitted by the display and in the production of storylines. Museum educators should be amongst the more fluent of the speakers on the museum staff and may be asked to participate in programmes of outside lectures. This enables the museum to highlight a different aspect of its activities each time in lectures to a particular audience.

Getting the message across

There is little point in opening the doors of a museum if no one knows when it is open and what it has to offer. Similarly there is little point in developing the museum education service and then neglecting to tell the heads of surrounding schools the nature of the service that you can offer. While general publicity must remain the province of the director, the publicity and public relations value of the education service must not be under-estimated.

Marketing is, of course, a much wider subject than simply publicity and public relations. It is concerned not only with informing potential users about the museum but also with making it acceptable to its public. The musuem should be presented as a product which the general public wants, or at least thinks it wants.

An outward-looking approach by curatorial staff and the employment of educational staff in a wider role as outlined above should result, over a period of several years, in the creation of an eminently marketable project.

It is vital that the museum is presented regularly to the potential user. Here publicity is essential. To ensure efficiency and co-ordination, it is necessary to establish a routine procedure to ensure that publicity takes place. Where the museum operates a well-organized publicity campaign, education should work through that framework. Where this is not the case, the education service must handle its own publicity. In fact, there will always be elements of the education service which must be presented to the public by the education department, rather than by the museum as a whole.

Press releases should be a regular feature of departmental publicity. Stories should be selected with care and releases should be brief. Pre-event publicity is invaluable, but post-event press releases accompanied by photographs will probably be well received by the local press.

LEA's should also be kept well informed of educational activities. The analysis of attendances will reveal those education authorities making use of the service and also, perhaps more importantly, those which are not. The method of publicizing activities in schools is a matter for discussion with the local authority advisors. Some will arrange for the mailing of material explaining the museum services, while others would prefer to insert details in the local education authority's own news sheet.

The publication of adult education initiatives can be achieved through the adult education institute's own programmes if courses are to be arranged on a co-operative basis. Simple, printed posters may be used in the vicinity of the museum, and displayed in libraries, community centres, public notice boards, and shops within the catchment area.

The key to all publicity and public relations activity is to keep the name of the product constantly before the potential purchaser.

Dealing with the media

It is often possible to build up an excellent relationship with local papers. Such an association can be mutually beneficial. The newspaper articles will engender interest in your activities, many of which will, in turn, provide excellent and offer slightly offbeat articles for the papers. Remember that editorial coverage of museum education is as valuable as advertising, but less costly.

In addition to local papers, there are several national periodicals, both specialist and general, that may be worth a contact. Editorials in *The Times Educational Supplement, Teacher,* or the various publications of the Historical Association or Institute of Biology, for example, will be read by large numbers of teachers. Many such magazines and journals invite freelance contributions.

Contact with local radio and television studios can succeed at several levels. Despatch of press releases may bring the news reporters or cameras to record an item for transmission, and this is generally the simplest form of contact. However, it is possible to build a much closer relationship, particularly with local radio stations. In some instances, museum education staff have written and presented whole series on local radio relevant to their own collections. The radio station involved may then assist with the publication of support material for schools and may also be willing to make tapes of the programmes available to schools on loan.

In addition to establishing contact with local television and radio, it is essential that museum educa-

tors take careful note of proposed educational transmissions by the major national networks. Without adequate forward planning, a television schools' programme of series on 'The Egyptians', 'The Indians', etc, can result in severe pressure on the resources of the museum's education department. The Group for Education in Museums is establishing closer liaison with the networks to improve the pre-planning of support services for schools following series relevant to museums near them.

Contact with the media can be time-consuming. However, the consolation is that, if carefully planned in advance, it is usually time very well spent.

In this section, I have tried to cover the basics of museum education. For those who wish to pursue the story in greater detail, the bibliographic essay which follows will prove valuable.

Bibliography

Athene, The Journal of the British Society for Education through Art (established 1939)
CBA Newsletter and Calendar, London Council for British Archaeology
THE COUNCIL FOR MUSEUMS AND GALLERIES IN SCOTLAND, SCOTTISH EDUCATION DEPARTMENT, (1981), *A Directory of Museum Education in Scotland,* HMSO, Edinburgh, which includes brief notes on planning the visit
DEPARTMENT OF MUSEUM STUDIES, Bibliography for Museum Students, The University of Leicester
Journal of Art and Design for Education, **1**(1) 1982 (Published for the National Society for Art Education)
Journal of Education in Museums, The Group for Educational Services in Museums, London
McCABE, G. (1972), *Education through Museums: A Bibliography,* Group for Educational Services in Museums, London
MOORE, D. (1982), Thirty years of museum education: some reflections, *The International J. of Museum Management and Curatorship,* **1**(1), 213–230. A very useful and recent overview. *See* also 'Thirty years of museum education: some reflections' by Gerard van der Hoek in the same *Journal;* **1**(4), 374–376
ROYAL ONTARIO MUSEUM (1979), *Hands On: Setting up a Discovery Room in Your Museum or School,* Royal Ontario Museum, Toronto
SHARPE, T. AND ROWE, S. R. (1982), Family Expeditions – the Museum Outdoors, *Museums J.,* **82**(3), 143–147

50

Museums and education: a brief bibliographic essay

Douglas A. Bassett

Introduction

The growth of educational activities in museums, and particularly the growth of the schools service movement, has been described as one of the outstanding developments in the techniques of the museum profession in the last forty or so years.

The initiative in forming schools museum services and in providing educational services in general in museums appears to have come in large measure from the institutions themselves and not from the educationalists. The growth has not, therefore, followed a set pattern as decreed, for example, by a Ministry of Education, but has evolved according to local resources and to meet local needs.

There is no comprehensive history of the growth of education in museums either in Britain or elsewhere, nor indeed is there a truly comprehensive bibliography. There is, however, an extensive literature. For the purposes of this brief, selective essay references are deliberately subdivided differently from most other bibliographies in order to give some indication of the growth of education in museums, to draw attention to the long standing commitment of certain institutions to education and to try and provide links between museum education and education generally:

(1) Literature on the developments in specific museums.
(2) Surveys of educational services at a particular time or period.
(3) Publications produced as the result of symposia or as a result of the activities of corporate bodies.
(4) Publications concerned primarily with education through the medium of one subject or discipline.
(5) General works on education which are of relevance to museum workers.

Each of these groups is illustrated separately.

Literature on the developments in specific museums

A representative selection from this group – outlining developments in individual museums or local education authority areas – includes, in chronological order:

Leicester Art Gallery and Museum (1934), *Leicester Museum and the Schools: an Illustrated account of the activities of the Museum in Relation to Leicester Schools.* A brief description of the work of a Department which was created in 1924 when a resident guide lecturer was appointed. In the second edition, in 1943, the subtitle referred to the work of the School Service Department.

Winstanley, B. R. (1940), The Derbyshire School Museum Service. *Museums J.*, **39**, 472–478. In September 1936, The Carnegie United Kingdom Trust offered to assist one or two experimental circulating museum schemes in country areas and invited county authorities to submit proposals. The first of these grants was given to the Derbyshire Education Committee to cover an experimental period of three years, ending in August 1939. The experiment is described briefly by the organizer.

Swanton, E. W. (1947), *A Country Museum. The Rise and Progress of Sir Jonathan Hutchinson's Educational Museum at Haslemere,* Educational Museum, Haslemere. An outline, by the first curator, of the story of the work and growth of this 'strongly individualistic' Museum started at Haslemere in 1888. (*See also* Hutchinson, M. and Jewell, A. L. (1973), The museum that started in a barn, *Natural Science in Schools, Journal of the School Natural Science Society,* **11**(1), 12–15

Harrison, M. (1950), *Museum Adventure. The Story of the Geffrye Museum,* University of London Press, London. The story of working with children at Shoreditch – 'one approach, in one small museum, in one area of London' – by the Curator, including a section on 'How the children come', four sections on 'what the children do' and one on 'An assessment of the work'. The service for organized visits from schools was established in 1935. (*See also: Introducing the Educational Work of the Geffrye Museum,* London County Council, 1964).

Glasgow Art Gallery and Museums (1951), (Foreword by Honeyman, T. J.) *Educational Experiment: 1941–1951,* Corporation of the City of Glasgow. A description of an experiment initiated during the 'holidays at home' scheme of 1940 and carried out in the schools and museums of Glasgow. The sections of the description are on the early years; looking for space; building a team; the class visit; the Saturday morning class; the annual art competition; exhibitions; adult education; the loan section; training in citizenship; some conclusions. The appendices include: a list of the Schools Museum Service publications and of the staff (which included six trained teachers) of the Museum's Education Department; details of specimen lessons for primary schools, for secondary schools and for adults; and an extract from the summary of records (e.g. that 199 476 children attended the Art Gallery for instruction during the period 1941–1951).

Dilwyn John, D. D. (1955), *The Museum Schools Service. The First Five years,* National Museum of Wales, Cardiff. An outline of the work of the first national service to schools which was inaugurated shortly after the *Education Act 1944,* financed on a voluntary basis by all but one of the Local Education Authorities in Wales and administered by the National Museum of Wales. *See also:* Ministry of Education (1954), *A Survey of the Schools Service of the National Museum of Wales,* and Edwards, V. (1969), Twenty years' service to schools [in Wales], *Amgueddfa, Bulletin of the National Museum of Wales,* **2**, Summer/Autumn 27–35. Saunders, J. R. (1956), Development of educational services, 1869–1956. *Eighty seventh Annual Report of The American Museum of Natural History,* 11–30. The article contains a useful 'chronolgy of highspots'.

Surveys of educational services at a particular time or period

A selection of surveys or reviews of the general situation by individuals at a certain stage or over a period includes the following, again in chronological order:

Weston, R. (1939), American museums and the child, *Museums J.,* **39**(2), 93–115, a Supplement. A report by the Education Officer at Leicester City Museum and Art Gallery of a study tour of museums in the USA and Canada sponsored by the Carnegie United Kingdom Trust. Miss Weston returned to organize a loan scheme based on American practice which was to become a model for future services.

Allan, D. A. (1949), Museums and education, in *Museums in modern life. Seven papers read before the Royal Society of Arts in March, April and May 1949,* pp. 86–106, with a folding map [Reprinted from the *J. of The Royal Society of Arts*]. Douglas Allan, Director of the Royal Scottish Museum, assesses the role of education in museums and reviews current developments.

Walden, T. A. (1967), 'The alternatives: a survey of methods of providing educational services in museums in Great Britain', *Museums J.,* **67**, 141–148. The author surveys the educational activities of some of the museums in this country, considers the alternatives they offer and comments upon them.

Winstanley, B. R. (1967), *Children and Museums,* Basil Blackwell, Oxford. The work contains sections on: children and museums (children on their own in museums); schools to museums (organized group visits); museums to schools (school museum loan services); teachers and museums (How to make best use of museums where there are no schools services); and museums and other places. The Appendices include an inventory of public school museum services in the British Isles (1966) and an annotated bibliography of reference books and material subdivided according to the subject matter of the chapters in the book.

Moore, D. (1982), Thirty years of museum education: some reflections. *International J., of Museum Management and Curatorship,* **1**, 213–230. A review, in three sections: What is museum education?: Evaluation; and Conclusions. In the third section the author, who was an officer of the Museum Schools Service at the National Museum of Wales for over twenty years, suggests that the 1950s saw 'the introduction as it were of a Trojan horse full of teachers into a museum world which had become for the most part inward-looking and static'; the 1960s were marked by the rise of the designer, and the 1970s, in which 'a golden age seemed to have dawned', was not to fulfil its promise. *See also:* Hoek, G. Vander (1982), 'Thirty years of museum education: some reflections', *Int. J. Museum Management and Curatorship,* **1**, 374–376.

The educational potential of museums was clearly expressed in two very widely quoted works. The first was:

Markham, S. F. (1938), *A Report on the Museums and Art Galleries of the British Isles (other than the National Museums)* T. and A. Constable Ltd, Edinburgh, a report to the Carnegie United Kingdom Trustees. The work includes chapters on: School visits; Loans to schools and school museums; and Adult education – each containing details of the services available at the time.

The following quotation, taken from the chapter on Loans to schools and school museums, draws attention to the work of the Victoria and Albert Museum which although the oldest such service otherwise receives comparatively little attention in published sources.

> The situation now is that the museum movement is asking itself, if the children cannot be brought into the museum, can the museum be brought into the schools? It is over eighty years ago since the first collection was loaned by a museum to a school, for in 1855 the Victoria and Albert Museum began the circulation of exhibits to certain schools of art and to museums attached to such schools, and in 1880 the system was extended to other museums and galleries. In 1908 the loan collections were separated from the main collections. Since then the service has been continually improved and extended, and received great commendation in the Report of the Royal Commission in 1929. Some conception of the present scope may be derived from a few recent statistics – in 1957 loans comprised 41 015 works of art, 15 427 lantern slides, and 300 books. They were issued to 413 secondary schools, 224 art schools, 94 local museums, and 96 other institutions.

The second work dealing with the educational potential of museums was: Wittlin, A. S. (1949), *The Museum, its history and its tasks in education.* International Library of Sociology and Social Reconstruction, Routledge and Kegan Paul, London. Alma Wittlin's essay, in which one-fifth of its 297 pages is devoted to museums and education, was written for two reasons: first, the conviction that the unsettled conditions in contemporary society would not find a balance until general education, both as to its content and to its method, had been radically revised and adjusted to existing reality; and second, the belief that the method of communicating information and experience by the visual means of the exhibition and the appeal of the three-dimensional object held special potentialities for the fulfilment and furtherance of educational requirements.

Publications produced by corporate bodies

A selection of the landmarks in the development of co-operative work includes the following, arranged under the title of the body responsible:

British Association for the Advancement of Science

The Association was one of the first to establish a Committee on the relationship of museums and education. It was formed, under the chairmanship of Professor J. A. Green (Sheffield University), at the Birmingham Meeting in 1913 with the following terms of reference: 'To examine, inquire into, and report on the character, work, and maintenance of Museums, with a view to their organisation and development as institutions for Education and Research; and especially to inquire into the requirements of schools'.

The final report (1920), Museums in relation to education, *Report of the British Association,* 267–280, – which included a brief report on 'The Manchester Scheme' – almost immediately followed the *Education Act 1918* and the *Libraries Act 1919* which profoundly modified the position of museums in relation to education. The Act of 1918, for example, made it possible for local education committees to seek the assistance of museums in the furtherance of local schemes of educational development.

The Museums Association

In 1889 the first circular issued by the Museums Association suggested as a working subject for discussion, 'The preparation of small educational loan collections for circulation to schools', and the first Presidential Address, delivered only a few months later, referred to exhibition cases which had been circulated by the Liverpool Museum since 1884 to sixty voluntary and board schools.

In the intervening years much attention has been paid to education in museums, both at the Annual Conferences and in the Association's Journal. In 1967, for example, the increasing awareness of the potential role of museums in education both in schools and among adults was reflected in the pages of the Journal, in the theme of the Annual Conference and in the issue of the handbook, (1967), *Museum Schools Service,* prepared by the Group for Educational Services in Museums and edited by Francis W. Cheetham.

In 1970 the Council of the Association established a Working Party 'to examine the role of museums in education in the United Kingdom and to recommend a policy for the future'. The resulting pamphlet, *Museums in Education* (Museums Association Report No. 1) containing twelve recommendations (three general, two relating to informal and seven to formal education), was published in 1971.

The Working Party was established in response to three significant events – the survey carried out by a Working Party of the Schools Council on museums as a source of curriculum material; the establishment, by the Department of Education and Science, of a Committee under the Chairmanship of Sir Lionel Russell, to examine the present non-vocational adult education; and the survey carried out by Her Majesty's Inspectorate, under the guidance of Mr W. W. Taylor, HMI, on the educational services provided by national museums and selected provincial museums with the object of making recommendations to local authorities. The results of the first and third of these are mentioned later.

In November 1977 a new Working Party was established, 'to review the role of Museums in education bearing in mind the 1970/71 Policy Statement in order to provide further guidelines for the profession and other interested Bodies'. The resulting Report – 'Working Party – Museums in education', with nineteen recommendations – was published in *Museums J., 81*, 236–239, in 1982.

Group for Education in Museums (GEM)

An organized museum education group was established in this country in 1949. It became the 'Group for Children's Activities in Museums' in 1952; the 'Group for Educational Services in Museums' (GESM) in 1969; and 'Group for Education in Museums' (GEM) in 1981. The Group has produced a number of important publications including:

Education through Museums, a bibliography compiled by McCabe, G. I. (1972). The 235 references are arranged in four groups – books, booklets and reports; articles on particular museums; articles (general); and reports (general). They range in date of publication from 1902 onwards. An Addendum, issued in 1975, includes forty-eight additional references, including seven unpublished theses.

Museums as an Influence on the Quality of Life. Proceedings of an International Conference held in Britain 6–11 April 1975. Five of the papers presented at the Conference are included in the Proceedings. They are: 'Museums and museum education within a changing society, (Roy Strong, Victoria and Albert Museum); 'Museums in our education tomorrow' (Hugh Jenkins, Minister for the Arts); 'Museums as an influence on the quality of life' (Luis Monreal, Secretary-General of ICOM); 'Five years on – the future of museum education' (Geoffrey McCabe, County Museum Curator, Shropshire); and, 'The museum and its public' (Geoffrey Lewis, Merseyside County Museums).

Museums and the Handicapped, Leicestershire Museums, Art Galleries and Records Service, Leicester, 1976. Papers read at a seminar organized by the Group and the Departments of Museum Studies and Adult Education at Leicester in September 1975.

Policy Statement for the Group for Educational Services in Museums (1978). This cyclostyled document contains the objects of the Group, as laid down in the Constitution. They are: 'to promote and co-ordinate interest in and information about, educational work in Museums and Art Galleries, by pooling and exchanging ideas and information concerning the work already being done in and by museums in this country and abroad; and by extending among educationalists and teachers an appreciation of how museums can help them and their students'; and there are sections on: status; pattern of services; museums and the community; professional liaison; salaries; training and courses; general co-operation; and publicity, publication and information.

In September 1980 the Group issued the first part of the *Journal of Education in Museums* in which there are a number of papers outlining the history of the 'movement'. For example: 'History of museum education in the United Kingdom'; 'Museum education 1948–1963'; 'The past twenty years'; and 'Museum education in 1980'.

The fourth number of the Journal (August 1983) contains a series of short articles on education in museums in thirteen different countries. The number was issued to mark the meeting of ICOM 83 in London. Unfortunately, bibliographic references are very sparse.

Council of Museums and Galleries in Scotland

In October 1968 the Council for Museums and Galleries in Scotland set up a committee to report on the educational services provided by museums and galleries in Scotland, and in what way their services could be expanded and improved. The report, *Report on Museums and Education* (1970), was presented to the Scottish Education Department and to education authorities and museum authorities in Scotland for consideration and action. Its appendices include a brief account of some prominent schools museum services in the UK and elsewhere, and a selective bibliography of publications concerning museum school services in this and other countries and of education in museums in general.

In 1981 the Council, in co-operation with the Scottish Education Department, published *A Directory: Museum education in Scotland,* HMSO, Edinburgh. The first part of the Directory examines the general role of museum education and explains how to plan a visit – 'the simple routine necessary to make the occasion a success'. The second, and by far the larger part, is a directory of museums (arranged by Region) and the educational sources they provide. The third is a very selective bibliography of books and monographs with very brief annotations, intended to give 'an introduction to museum education in its broadest sense but with particular emphasis on the use of museums by schools'.

The February 1981 issue of *OmniGatherum (News from The Council for Museums and Galleries in Scotland)* was issued to coincide with the publication of the directory and had an educational theme.

Museums and Galleries Commission

Publications by the Commission (originally the Standing Commission on Museums and Galleries) which contain assessments of educational services in museums include:

Survey of provincial museums and galleries, HMSO, London, (1963). The main body of the survey contains a brief but succinct section on educational activities in which the Commission strongly recommends the extension of museum schools services all over the country; and an appendix, compiled by Barbara R. Winstanley, on school museum services in the British Isles. The Appendix contains a historical sketch, a list of services and a distribution map.

Universities and museums. Report on the universities in relation to their own and other museums, HMSO, London, (1968). The report was the outcome of a full survey which included the services performed by local museums for university teaching and research. The appendices, which make up thirty of the forty-five pages, contain brief descriptions of the collections in the various university museums.

Report on university museums, HMSO, London, (1977). This report is concerned solely with those university museums open to the public with collections which in terms of scope, quality and size transcend the needs of departmental teaching collections.

The Commission also issues a four-yearly report which, although comprehensive to the extent that it covers all museums and galleries in Britain, is biased somewhat towards the national museums. The most recent report covers the period from mid-1973 to 31 December 1977 and contains a section on 'Education and interpretation'. The section starts thus:

> We have already emphasised the important role of museums in education generally in both our Ninth Report and in our *Report on University Museums.* The steady expansion of educational services in recent years in the national and non-national museums is described in the appendices. It is important, however, to strike the right balance in the allocation of the limited resources of museums between education and their other responsibilities and to define where a museum's obligations to education and those of local education authorities begin.

Schools Council

A Working Party was set up jointly by the Schools Council and the ICOM Committee for Education in Museums in the UK in 1967 in order to consider ways 'in which the services provided by museums, both national and local, could be more effectively exploited by teachers and to prepare a publication containing a clear statement of the philosophy of the educational use of museums'. The resulting report was, *Pterodactyls and Old Lace: Museums in Education,* Evans/Methuen for the Schools Council, London, (1972).

Two short films *What I See* and *Insight* were made in the Art Gallery and Museum at Lincoln, sponsored by the Working Party as experimental exercises in visual perception.

The Supplement in 1970 to *Dialogue, the Schools Council Newsletter,* entitled 'School and innovation 1870–1970', provides a short but useful survey of a century's change in education.

Department of Education and Science

A group of HM Inspectors visited a number of museums in the UK in 1969 to examine the contribution of museums to education and to suggest how available resources might be better used. Their conclusions were recorded in *Museums in education,* Education Survey 12, HMSO, London, (1971). Five loan services were described in some detail.

Among its many Bibliographies and Reading Lists the Department of Education and Science issues one on *Museums and Education* Booklist 1983). The August 1982 version contains items divided into official publications and general publications.

United Nations Educational, Scientific and Cultural Organisation (UNESCO)

UNESCO arranged two international seminars on *The Role of Museums in Education* at Brooklyn in 1952 and at Athens in 1954. The titles of both seminars were identical but they differed considerably in a number of respects. The place chosen for them dictated in each case the examples examined and the methods used. The papers read at the two symposia are published in special issues of the quarterly UNESCO Journal: *Museum* (1953), **6**(4), 213–281 (introduced by Douglas A. Allan); and *Museum* (1955), **8**(4), 201–265 (introduced by Grace L. McCann Morele).

Other special issues of *Museum* dealing with education in museums are: *Museum* (1968), **21**(1), 1–86 – devoted to a seminar for South-east Asia at New Delhi in 1966, with papers introduced by Renée Marcousé; and *Museum* (1979), **21**(3), the Special Issue for the International Year of the Child, entitled

'Museums and children', with sections on: theoretical aspects (3 papers); case studies (4 papers); and album (6 papers); with an introduction by Georges Henri Rivière, the Director of ICOM.

In UNESCO's Department of Education series Educational studies and documents, No. 17: *Museum Techniques in Fundamental Education'*, was issued as one of the contributions to the first International Campaign for Museums organized by ICOM in 1956. The volume is in two parts: general considerations (including a chapter on the relevance of museum techniques to three program areas: arts and crafts, technical assistance problems, and health programmes); and the Mysore experiments. No. 38 in the same series is concerned with the *UNESCO Regional Seminar on the Educational Role of Museums* held at Rio de Janeiro in 1958.

In the series 'Museums and monuments', the fifteenth volume – *Museums, Imagination and Education* (1973) – contains twelve papers on international themes including one on collaboration between museum and school, which contains brief notes on the major UNESCO and ICOM seminars on education up to the UNESCO International Symposium at Paris in 1968, and a brief annotated bibliography of the growth of the idea of the museum as educator.

In the ninth volume in the same series (*The Organisation of Museums: Practical Advice*, Paris, 1959) there is a section (pp. 81–92) on Education in museums, by Molly Harrison.

In the series 'Monographs on education', the tenth volume, published during the International Year of the Child, 1979, is *Museums and Children*, edited by Ulla Keding Olofsson. An 'assemblage' of studies of educational work in fourteen countries is contributed by specialists, with an introduction by the editor. Mrs Olofsson provides a critical panorama of the work of museums in relation to teaching practice throughout the world. Each of the other contributors considers and discusses the themes most relevant to his or her country. The chapter on the UK and Northern Ireland is by Victoria Airey. Her contribution includes sections on: contents and methods; programmes – activities offered; how the museum's special potentials as education instruments are used; the role of museum staff and school teachers in educational activities at museums; information; and problems and future plans.

The selective bibliography for the volume as a whole is prepared by the UNESCO-ICOM Documentation Centre at Paris in collaboration with Stella Westerlund. The volume is illustrated by Gerard Teichert.

Details of the foreign language editions of some of these publications are given in Section 069 of *Bibliography of publications issued by UNESCO or under its auspices for the twenty-five years 1946–1971*, UNESCO, Paris, (1973).

International Council of Museums (ICOM)

The educational role of museums has been one of the major points of the program of ICOM since its inception in 1946. Two well-known early publications are *Museums and Young People,* Paris, (1952) and *Museums and teachers,* Paris, (1956).

The 1952 publication contained three reports, a foreword by Georges Henri Rivière and a thoughtful introduction by Peter Floud, Keeper of Circulation at the Victoria and Albert Museum and Chairman of the ICOM International Committee for Children's Museums and Museum Activities for Young People, in which he exposes several recurring misconceptions about museum programs for children based on his own experience at the Victoria and Albert Museum. The reports were: 'Museums and young people in continental Europe' by Germaine Cart; 'Museums and young people in Great Britain and the British Commonwealth' by Molly Harrison; and 'Children in the museums of the Americas' by Charles Russell.

A third important publication sponsored by ICOM is Zetterberg, H. L. (1968), *Museums and Adult Education,* Evelyn, Adams and Mackay, London; and a fourth is Transactions International Council of Museums Meeting on the role of Museums in Education and Cultural Action, Moscow and Leningrad, 14–21 May 1968, and Bath, 1969.

Since 1969 ICOM has issued an annual publication – initially called *Annual – Museums, Education and Cultural Action,* and more recently, *ICOM Education.* The first issue was devoted almost entirely to a factual bibliography for national Working Parties, with lists of their publications and reports from 1964 to 1969. A selective bibliography for the years 1970–1976 is given in No. 7 (57–60, 1975/76) and bibliographies for 1976–1978 and 1979–1981 in No. 8 (41–42, 1977/78) and No. 9 (42–45, 1978/79).

The Smithsonian Institution, Washington

In August 1966 the Smithsonian Institution held a conference on Museums and Education at the University of Vermont. The three principal objectives of the conference were: (a) to survey the present relations between museums and education: (b) to explore possible methods of involving museums more directly and more fruitfully in the educational process at all levels; and (c) to formulate proposals for research and development activities relating to museums and education. In a broad sense the purpose of the conference was, 'to learn, or at least begin to learn, ways of making more effective educational use of the more than five thousand Museums that exist in the United States'.

The proceedings were issued as Larrabee, E. (1968) (Ed.), *Museums and Education,* Smithsonian Institution, Washington DC.

In his anthology and summary, Eric Larrabee demonstrates the difficulty of coming to grips with specific educational needs through the medium of the museum, revealing the inherent complexity of the subject and the remoteness of direct visual learning from the formal school system.

The sections of the volume are on: dimensions and approach; the existing situations; reasons for concern; methods of presentation and analysis; kinds of museums – youth, art, history, science; and a look at the future (the implication of technology for museum education). There is also a remarkable chronological bibliography of museum visitor surveys of about 150 items covering the period 1897–1968.

In January 1970 the Smithsonian Institution, supported by the National Science Foundation, organized another conference at the Belmont Conference Center. A summary report of the Conference is provided in Goldman, K. T. (1970), (Ed.), *Opportunities for Extending Museum Contributions to Pre-college Science Education.* Katherine Goldman is co-ordinator of studies in museum education of the US National Museum. The report is issued as one of the informal publications of the Smithsonian Institution.

The contents are subdivided into three sections – museums as educational facilities: general considerations, (including 10 contributions); particular educational programs in operation and cooperation (20 contributions); and, possibilities for future uses of the museum as an educational resource (5 contributions). The conference proceedings are summarized by Alma S. Wittlin, and Philip C. Ritterbush provides an excellent and wide-ranging annotated bibliography of 98 items. The references are divided into two main sections – 'Of interest to education' and 'Of interest for museum libraries'. The first section is subdivided into three: a shelf of references on museums; education in museums – selected writings; and from the literature on research on education, potentially or actually applicable in museums. The second section is also subdivided into three: some useful writings on education; extending the museum into the school; and exploration bearing upon the museum potentials for education.

The Smithsonian has also issued a series of cyclostyled publications outlining studies of visitor reactions and perceptions. They include: Wolf, R. L. and Tymitz, B. L. (1978), *Whatever Happened to the Giant Wombat: an Investigation of the Impact of the Ice Age Mammals and Emergence of Man. Exhibit. National Museum of Natural History, Smithsonian Institution;* Wolf, R. L., Munley, M. E. and Tymitz, B. L. (1979), *The Pause that Refreshes: A Study of Visitor Reactions to the Discovery Corners in the National Museum of History and Technology, Smithsonian Institu-*tion; and Wolf, R. L. and Tymitz, B. L. (1979), *'East side, West side, Straight down the Middle,: A Study of Visitor Perceptions of 'Our Changing Land', The Bicentennial Exhibit, National Museum of Natural History, Smithsonian Institution.*

Royal Ontario Museum (ROM), Toronto

Two of the Royal Ontario Museum's publications are relevant:

Communicating with the Museum Visitor. Guidelines for Planning, prepared by the Communications Design Team (April 1976), which, among other things, has an appendix on types of learning.

Hands on. Setting up a Discovery Room in your Museum or School, (1979), The experience gained by the Royal Ontario Museum in providing a variety of opportunities for its visitors to use all their senses in learning within a museum context, coupled with the desire to share with the visitor some of the sense of discovery which museum staff members constantly experience in working with the museum collections, has been consolidated through the operation of its proto-type discovery Room. During the first year and a half of its existence, over 100 000 visitors used its facilities, and the discovery room has been evaluated by the Urban Design Consultants, under contract. An account of the objectives of this evaluation, the methodology used, the immediate results and the analysis of the data gained, takes over two-thirds of the volume. The range of materials used is drawn mostly from the natural history and ethnographical collections.

Department of Museum Studies, University of Leicester

Relevant publications of the Department include:

Bibliography for Museum Studies Students (1980), (2nd, revised edn. 1981). Under the section 'Museum education services', the items are grouped into: (a) general; (b) history of museum education services; (c) children and museums; (d) adult education; and (e) special education.

Museum Education Option Learning Goals and Bibliography for Museum Studies Students (1983). The 30-page bibliography – of 801 items – is one of the most elaborate yet compiled and certainly the most elaborately subdivided. The list is divided into four sections which have the following headings and sub-headings:

(1) Education in the museum context, with sections on: the historical and philosophical context; and on the professional context.

(2) The management of collections in the museum education services context, with sections on: the nature, the use, the acquisition and disposal, the documentation and the storage of collections; and on research of collections.
(3) The management of museum education services, with sections on: structure; personnel; buildings and rooms; equipment and materials; and finance.
(4) Theory and practice of museum education services, with sections on: theory and principles of communication and interpretation (including four sub-sections: theories of communication, educational theories, theories of museum education, and evaluation); Traditional knowledge areas (art, history, science, archaeology); mobile mueums and travelling exhibitions; children's museums; historic houses; historic sites and monuments; the clientele (including six subsections: working with the community, adult education, schools services, loan services, special education, and holiday activities); the media; educational innovation (drama, music, dance); servicing the visitor (general, design); and books for children in the museum.

Other Leicester publications which include some reference to educational studies are the archeology-(1983), history-(1982), and natural history-option learning goals booklets (1982).

Finally in this section, references should be made to *Musée et enseignement* in the series 'Memoires et documents scolaires' (n.s. no. 8, 1957), issued by the **Institut Pedagogique National** in Paris, which is considered as one of the first reports from the Continent on museum education research and *Wir besuchen ein Museum: Handreichungen zur Bildung und Erziehung im Museum für Leiter von Gruppen*, edited by Kurt Patzwall and Willi Ehrlich, Berlin (Volk and Wirsen Voltseigener Verlag), 1976 – a valuable compendium, gathered by the editors and their colleagues in museum and teaching posts, of interest for comparison with work in other non-communist countries.

Publications concerned with education through one subject

Many museums specialize in one discipline and are subdivided or classified accordingly. For example, in Alexander, E. P. (1979), *Museums in Motion. An Introduction to the History and Functions of Museums,* American Association for State and Local History, Nashville, museums are grouped into four classes – art; natural history; science and technology; and history. Botanical Gardens and zoos are considered as a separate class. In *Framework for a system for museums: Report by a Working Party 1978,* HMSO, London, on the other hand, the Standing Commission subdivides collections into: (i) fine and decorative arts; (ii) natu-

ral history and geology; (iii) archaeology; (iv) ethnology and social history; and (v) science, technology and industrial archaeology.

These terms mean different things to different people, as illustrated by William T. O'Dea in his contribution to the second UNESCO seminar *The Role of Museums in Education* at Athens in 1954 (O'Dea, W. T. (1955), Science museums and education, *Museum,* **8**, 242–245). The term 'science museum' embraces a number of institutions of very different character. Museums of the history of science, such as those in Leyden or Oxford, are intended in the main for the specialist visitor and are part of a University complex. Other museums of very much broader scope, such as those of London, Munich and Stockholm, show comparable exhibits, but are a relatively small part of the whole display. Industry is their chief concern in terms of exhibition area, but for convenience they are referred to by the same comprehensive title of 'science muxeum'. Yet another variant is to be found in Paris, where most of the historical material is exhibited in the oldest established science museum of all, the **Conservatoire National des Arts** et Métiers. The **Palais de la Decouverte**, specializing in the interpretation of modern thought in the world of science and industry, is the institution within the complex of the University of Paris.'

In this essay the papers dealing with education through the medium of particular disciplines are divided as follows:

The biological sciences (commonly referred to as natural history)

The number of papers on education through the medium of biological materials in museums is usually small. For example, eight references only are given in the section on natural history in *Natural history option learning goals and bibliography for Museum Studies Students,* University of Leicester, and of these three were issued before the Second World War!There are, in addition, three papers on education in Engström, K. and Johnels, A. G. (1973) (Eds.), *Natural History and the Community. Symposium held in October 1969 at the Swedish Museum of Natural History [Naturhistoriska Riksmuseet] in Stockholm,* one each on the British Museum (Natural History), the Swedish Museum of Natural History and one on the role of the natural history museum in university education. There are also short but useful papers such as one by Peter N. Haase in the special issue of *Museum* devoted to 'Museums and children' Haase, P. N. (1979), Educational activities within the framework of the Zoological Museum of Copenhagen, *Museum,* **31**, 197–199. Of the 300 000 visitors at Copenhagen approximately one half are children and for this reason 'former museum guards, or custodians, . . .

have been replaced by biology students, which has been especially important from the educational standpoint'. And finally, there are some papers in the *Newsletter* of the International Committee **5** (1979) which includes the transactions of a session held during the International Year of the Child.

There are obvious and strong links between the biological and the geological sciences with field work and with environmental studies generally. Useful references include: Greenwood, E. F. and Osler, A. (1967), Museums and fieldwork, *School Science Review*, **49**, 56–63 – a description of two courses offered by the City of Liverpool Museums and based on the Ainsdale Sand Dunes National Nature Reserve; Walden, T. (1965), Museums and field studies, in *The Countryside in 1970, Second Conference, Keele; (1976), Environmental Awareness. A Survey of Types of Facilities used for Environmental Education and Interpretation in Europe*, Council of Europe – being the result of a survey carried out under the auspices of the European Committee for the Conservation of Nature and Natural Resources; Stansfield, G. (1969), Museums and environmental education, *Museums Assistants Group Transactions*, **8**, 3–6; Whiting, J. (1979), The role of natural history museums in environmental education, *ICOM Natural History Museums Newsletter*, **5**, [20–27]; Sharpe, T. and Howe, S. R. (1982), Family expeditions – the museum outdoors, *Museums Journal*, **82**, 143–147; and Lord, G. and Paterson, J. (Eds.) (1983), *Interpretation of the Environment. A Bibliography*, The Carnegie U.K. Trust, Dunfermline, Fife.

Another major theme common to biology and geology is the theory of evolution. The problems of presenting what has been described as a metaphysical research programme is considered in the following three papers: Deadman, J. A. and Kelly, P. J. (1978), What do secondary schoolboys understand about evolution and heredity before they are taught the topics, *Journal of Biological Education*, **12**(1), 7–15; Brumby, M. (1979), Problems in learning the concept of natural selection, *Journal of Biological Education*, **13**(2), 119–122; and Dobzhansky, Th. (1973), Nothing in biology makes sense except in the light of evolution, *American Biology Teacher*, **35**, 125–129.

The geological sciences

A number of papers on education through geology are included in *Geology Teaching (Journal of The Association of Teachers of Geology)*. Volume **3**(2) nor June 1978 is devoted almost entirely to the theme of museums: educational services in geology, with papers on the services provided by the Geological Museum, the National Museum of Wales and a 'Catalogue of Museum Education Services in Geology'. Twenty-four papers on 'education' (from Britain, Germany, Canada and the USA) are listed in

Sharpe, T. (1983), *Geology in Museums: A Bibliography*, National Museum of Wales, Cardiff. The range of material offerred on loan to schools by one of the larger services is clearly illustrated in *Catalogue of Loan Material in Geology* (1972), (5th edn.), National Museum of Wales: Schools Service, Cardiff: handling boxes (unmounted specimens, and notes); exhibition cases; model cases; framed charts; illustration boxes; filmstrip containers; slide packs; etc.

Experimental work on the identification of minerals, rocks and fossils was carried out by D. Emlyn Evans in an 'activites' room (or 'do it yourself' laboratory) at the National Museum of Wales and in association with the Schools Council 5/13 project. This is described in two papers – Evans, D. E. (1972), Investigating Minerals and Evans, D. E. (1973), Investigating and identifying rocks, *Amgueddfa, Bulletin of the National Museum of Wales*, **10**, 9–21 and **14**, 16–27 respectively. The same investigator also experimented with the use of new media (particularly polystyrene) in the making of models (topographical, crystallographic, mineralogical and geological) by children and described his results in the paper – Evans, D. D. (1971), Involving the student in the study of the materials and the concepts of geology (with particular reference to an experiment at the National Museum of Wales), *Geology (Journal of the Association of Teachers of Geology)*, **3**, 54–64. The concepts included: the unit cell, glaciation, vulcanicity, faulting, folding and sea-floor spreading. *See also*, Bassett, D. A. (1971), Geology in education today. [Presidential Address to The Association of Teachers of Geology. 1970] *Geology Teaching*, **3**, 65–80.

The physical sciences (or 'Science')

Most 'science' museums and most publications dealing with 'science' museums confine their attention to the physical sciences and their application in technology. Differentiating the scientific aspect from the technological one in the published literature on science museums is commonly very difficult. The volume *Science Museums in Developing Countries*, by Frank Greenaway (with additional chapters by Torsten Althin, W. T. O'Dea and W. Stephen Thomas), ICOM, (1962), includes the chapters: 'How do science museums teach adults?'; 'How do science museums teach children?'; and 'Science museums are international'. The Appendices include: 'Some analyses of objects in science museums – by relevance and by form'.

Other general works include: Byung-Hoon Lee (1970), *A Study of Science Museums with Special Reference to their Educational Programs*, a special publication of the Office of Museum Programs of the Smithsonian Institution; two papers in Larrabee, E. (Ed.), *Museums and Education*: 'The role of science museums', by an 'outstander', Frank Oppenheimer and 'Gawk or think', by Michael V. Butler, Associate Curator of Physics at the Cranbrook Institute of Science. The latter starts by stating the readily identifiable results of education in science: (1) the knowledge of the facts, (2) skill in observing, and (3) the ability to reason (inductively) from observation.

Among the individual papers, the following are of particular interest:

Omand, P. N. (1974), The Ontario Science Centre, *Museum*, **26**, 76–85

Danilov, V. J. (1975), Science museums as education centers, *Curator*, **18**, 87–108;

Author? (1980), 'Science education and museums' in the 'Talking points' series in the *Journal of Education in Museums*, No. 1, 22, 23

Hills, R. L. (1968), The Manchester Museum of Science and Technology; an experiment in education, *Museums J.*, **68**, 16–18).

Miles, R. and Lewis, B. (1983), Science museums on the move, *New Scientist*, **98**, 379–381

Brooks, J. A. M. and Vernon, P. E. (1956), A study of children's interests and comprehension at a science museum *British Journal of Psychology*, **47**, 175–182

Van Rennes, E. C. (1978), Educational techniques in a science museum [The Cranbrook Institute of Science, Michigan, USA], *Curator*, **21**, 289–302

Whitman, J. (1978), More than buttons, buzzers and bells, *Museum News*, **51**(1), 43–50

John Whitman's article starts with the statement: 'If the Louvre, the Prado and the Museum of Modern Art have been the swans of the modern world, science museums have been the ugly ducklings'. He distinguishes between 'process-oriented' science museums and 'object-oriented' museums and his article includes excerpts from interviews with four museum directors on how they conceive the educational role of their institutions.

History

Papers and books dealing with teaching through the medium of history commonly include material of an archaeological, and ethnographical nature. General historical references include:

Fairley, J. A. (1977), *History Teaching through Museums*, Longman Education Today Series, Harlow. The work contains sections on: the educational purpose of visiting the museum or historical site; types of museums and historical sites; organizing the visit; work directives; compiling a work directive; Schools Museum Services; project work and the London Museum; examples of study guide and work directive material; and a bibliography.

National Museum of Canada (1976), *The History Museum as an Effective Educational Institution*, National Museum of Canada, Ottawa. (National Museum of Man Mercury Series, Communications Division Paper 4). Includes a bibliography.

Heslin, J. J. (1968), Does the museum of history teach history?, in Larrabee, E. (Ed.), *Museums and Education*, Smithsonian Institution Press, Washington DC, pp. 153–165

Barrand, J. (1969), Museums and the teaching of history, *Teaching History*, **1**(2), 65–71

See also: Ballard, M. (Ed.) (1970), *New Movements in the Study and Teaching of History*, Temple Smith, London

Archaeology

Archaeological references include:

Moore, D. (1978), 'Beyond the written word: history from pictures and artefacts'. in Jones G. and Ward, L. (Eds.), *New History, Old Problems; Studies in History Teaching*, University College of Swansea, Faculty of Education, pp. 59–77

Grinsell, L. V. (1960), Children and archaeology, *Museums J.*, **60**, 5–12

Taylor, A. P. (1973), Children and artefacts – a replacement for textbook learning, *Curator*, **16**, 25–29

Parsons, D. (1968), Discovery learning in archaeology, *Adult Education*, **41**, 241–249

Webster, G. (1959), Archaeology in adult education, *Adult Education*, **32**, 166–178

See also Burkitt, M. C. (1949), The place of archaeology in our national education, *Advancement of Science*, **6**, 249–256; Corbishley, E. (1979), *Archaeological Resources Handbook for Teachers*, Council for British Archaeology – a mimeographed volume based on collaborative work by members of the CBA Schools Committee. The use of museums and historical sites, in Burston, W. H. (Ed.), *Handbook for History Teachers*, Methuen Educational, London, 1972; and items in *Bulletin of Archaeology* for schools issued by the Council for British Archaeology on behalf of its Schools Committee. The first issue, for example, contains an introduction to the work of the CBA Schools Committee, a note about the workshop on archaeology in the Primary School held at Verulaniam Museum and a report of a week's archaeologicl project carried out by a junior class in Cambridgeshire.

Ethnography and anthropology

Ethnographical and anthropological references are scarce. They include:

Freese, H. H. (1957), The living museum: educational work in the National Museum of Ethnology [Rijksmuseum voor Volkenkunde], Leyden, *Museum*, **10**, 297–299

van Wengen, G. (1968), The development of educational methods in an ethnological museum, in *Role of Museums in Education and Cultural Action,* ICOM, pp. 233–234

Wilson, P. (1978), The Ulster Folk and Transport Museum, *Teaching History,* **22**, 12–14

See also: Hands on. Setting up a Discovery Room in your Museum or School, Royal Ontario Museum (1978); and *Anthropology and the Public: the Role of Museums,* Leiden, Brill, 1960, *Medelingen van Het Rijsmuseum voor Volke-Kunde* No. 14.

Art

There is a more extensive literature on the use of works of art in education than on any other subject. Among the most regularly quoted works are:

Marcousé, R. (1961), *The Listening Eye. Teaching in an Art Museum,* HMSO for the Victoria and Albert Museum, London. In 1951, the Ministry of Education asked Mrs Marcousé to experiment at the Victoria and Albert Museum on methods of teaching children and adolescents in museums. This publication describes some of the work carried out.

Newsom, B. Y. (1970), *The Metropolitan Museum as an Educational Institution,* New York, Newsom, B. Y. and Silver, A. Z. (1978), (Eds.), *The Art Museum as Educator. A Collection of Studies as Guides to Practice and Policy,* published for the Council on Museums and Education in the Visual Arts by the University of California Press. Berkeley. This is almost certainly the most comprehensive production of its kind. It provides not only a rationale of the work but a detailed account of every institution in the USA offering facilities. The book contains conclusions, judgements and statistical evaluations. It contains two short preliminary articles on: 'Issues in Art Museum education: a brief history' and 'Art Museums and education'; and major sections on: the art museum and its general public; the art museum and the young, their teachers and their schools; and the art museum and its college, university, and professional audience.

The sections contains chapters on: teachers training and classroom material; the artist and the museum; training for museum education; and co-operation among museum professionals. The last-mentioned chapter contains a description of Washington DC's Museum Education Roundtable (MER), founded in 1969 and incorporated in 1971. There is a bibliography for each chapter.

In addition to the art museums and art galleries – naturally the great majority of the institutions discussed – included, there are descriptions of the Discovery Room at the National Museum of Natural History (Washington), the 'Anticosti Neighbourhood Museum' and the Exploratorium, Los Angeles.

Two expansive Appendices contain basic information about the institutions including the programmes survey in the study. *See also:* Marcousé, R. (1974), *Using Objects. Visual Learning and Visual Awareness in the Museum and Classroom,* Schools Council, Art and Craft Education 8–13 Project, Van Nostrand Reinhold Co.; and Read, H. (1948), *Education through Art,* Pantheon Books – this is an analysis of the artistic activity of children, illustrated by many reproductions of children's drawings, and shows how these drawings can be used to determine the psychological disposition of the individual child.

General works on education

Among the volumes of general educational interest the three volumes by Jerome S. Bruner, Professor of Psychology at Harvard University, and published by the University, are of particular relevance:

The process of education (1965) which is a report on a conference of some thirty-five scientists, scholars and educationalists convened in 1959 to discuss how education in science might be improved in the primary and secondary schools. Bruner does not give any bibliographic references but refers the reader to the collection of readings by Robert Ulrich in *Three thousand years of educational wisdom* (Cambridge, Mass., 1959). *On knowing: essays for the left hand* (1962), which concentrates on three themes: the shape of experience (including an essay on 'Art as a mode of knowing'); the quest for clarity; and the idea of action. The author clearly states his indebtedness to the work of Jean Piaget in Geneva and L. S. Vygotsky in Moscow. *Toward a theory of instruction* (1966), a series of seven essays which consider a dual theme: how children learn and how they can be helped to learn – how they can be brought to the fullest realisation of their capacities.

A good cross-section of the extensive literature on education published during the sixties and early seventies is given in a twenty-page special book review section in *Encounter* for October, 1972. It includes references, for example, to the five volumes published in America and re-issued as Penguin Education Specials. Among these is *The lives of children,* by George Dennison (Random House, New York, 1969), the journal of the lives of twenty-three children involved in an eighteen-month experiment at a small private museum in Lower East Side, New York. In the estimation of another well-known writer on educational matters in the USA, John Holt, the book is by far the most perceptive and important document on education of the era: 'Virtually every page of it contains more truth than can be found in most writings on educational psychology'.

American equivalents of the *Encounter* series are published in the *New York Review of Books* for June

1970, May 1973 and for November and December 1975. More extensive lists of the voluminous American literature are produced by The Library of Contemporary Education (Riverside, New Jersey); and the general context in which this material is produced is provided in *The making of a counter culture*, by Theodore Roszak (Doubleday, 1969) and Paul Goodman's *Growing up absurd* (Random House, 1960).

The opinions of 212 teachers on the problems of the classroom drawn from a cross-section of schools throughout England, both primary and secondary, are given in, *Teachers talking. Aims, methods, attitudes to change* (Allan, 1973).

Of the many official reports of the sixties and seventies in this country, the clearest guide is *Crowther to Warnick. How fourteen reports tried to change children's lives*, by Rick Rogers (Heinemann Educational Books, London, in association with The International Year of the Child, 1980).

Works concerned with basic problems in the teaching of art include:
The companion volumes by E. H. Gombrich – *Art and illusion. A study of the psychology of pictorial representation*. The A. W. Mellon Lectures in the Fine Arts, 1956 (Phaidon Press, London, 1960); *The sense of order. A study in the psychology of decorative art*. The Wrightman Lectures delivered under the auspices of the New York University Institute of Fine Arts (Phaidon Press, London, 1979).

Three other volumes of wider scope are:
Art, perception and reality, by E. H. Gombrich, Julian Hochberg and Max Black (Johns Hopkins University Press, Baltimore, 1972). The book consists of three essays all concerned with the problem of understanding pictures. The problem is viewed from different stances – those of a philosopher (Black), a psychologist (Hochberg) and an art historian-cum-psychologist (Gombrich). *Illusion in nature and art* (Duckworth, London, 1973), edited by the neuropsychologist R. L. Gregory and E. H. Gombrich, with contributions by the psychologist Colin Blakemore, the zoologist H. E. Hinton, the psychologist Jan B. Deregowski and the President of the Institute of Contemporary Arts, Roland Penrose. *Art and visual perception: a psychology of the creative eye*, by Rudolf Arnheim (University of California Press, 1974), intended for the general reader but of interest to the educator because of its practical consequences for the function of art in education and, more broadly, for visual training in all fields of learning.

A work which is concerned largely with the teaching of biology is: *The anatomy of judgement: an investigation into the processes of perception and reasoning*, by M. L. Johnson Abercrombie (Hutchinson, 1960)

which develops ideas first published by the author in three papers in the *School Science Review* – 'Biology and training in observation' (1942), 'The scientific value of Higher School Certificate Zoology' (1946) and 'Biology and training in scientific method' (1948).

And among the papers dealing with the problems of 'time' – of particular relevance to the teaching of history – the following two are noted:
'The growth of the concept of time', by K. Lovell and A. Slater, *Journal of Child Psychology and Psychiatry*, **1**, 1960, 179–190; 'Children's concepts of time and history', by G. Jahoda, *Educational Review*, **15**, 1963, 87–104.

The full historical context of the controversies and debates on educational philosohy and method is neatly summarised in 'Educational disputes. On the polemical use of "traditions"', by Jacques Barzun in *Encounter* for November 1973. The tradition is traced from Plato to Comenius and Rousseau through two of Rousseau's disciples – Pestalozzi and Froebel (founder of the *Kindergarten*) – to the physician and philosopher, Maria Montessori.

Among the many books on these and other pioneers, three are noted:
A teacher's guide to reading Piaget, by Molly Brearley and Elizabeth Hitchfield (Routledge and Kegan Paul, 1966); *Neill of Summerhill. The permanent rebel*, by Jonathan Croall (Routledge, 1983); *Maria Montessori. A biography*, by Rita Kramer (G. P. Purman's Sons, 1976). *See also* John Amos Comenius (Profile), by Giuliana Limiti, *Prospects. Quarterly Review of Education*, **13**(1), 1983, 117–121.

Useful reference works include: Wallis, E. (1983) *Where to Look Things Up: A–Z of Sources on All Major Educational Topics*. 3rd ed. Advisory Centre for Education. A reference guide to sources of information on education in Britain. Lists major educational topics and organisations with information on relevant terminology, campaigns, official reports, etc. (1983) *The Education Factbook: An A–Z Guide to Education and Training in Britain*. Macmillan. *British Education Index*. British Library, London. Formerly compiled by the Institute of Education in England but now centrally computed by the BSD of the British Library; indexes articles in education in some fifty British periodicals. It is published four times a year by the Library and is intended to complement the American *Education Index*.

Acknowledgements
Acknowledgement is due to the staff of the curatorial departments and the Museum Schools Service at the National Museum of Wales, and to Donald Moore of the National Library of Wales.

51

Museum publishing and shops

Iain Bain

The need to publish progress reports, collection and exhibition catalogues, and at least a modicum of colour postcards, has been long-established in the minds of museum directors and curators; but the thought that this and other sometimes more popular material might be sold in larger quantities by looking to the outside world is relatively recent. For many years, sales facilities in the museums and galleries of this country were of the most rudimentary kind, and it was probably not until the 1950s that the serious development of the commercial possibilities began to be considered. The lead was taken in America where the Museum Store Association was established in 1950. Twenty-eight years later, and with somewhat broader concerns, the Group for Museum Publishing and Shop Management was set up in Britain, and there are now clear signs that the museum profession as a whole has come to regard such activities as necessary and respectable. How necessary, and how respectable they may be considered does of course vary greatly and very much depends on the constitution of the individual museum and its original source of funds. Here we have a particular difficulty for anyone attempting to present a summary of basic principles that can be applied to a commercial enterprise: the infinitely varying size, organization and purpose of our museums. So what follows has to be very much a personal view, based on the activities in publishing, wholesaling and retailing in a national art gallery. Although the circumstances may be very far removed from those of some readers, they should nevertheless find enough generally applicable matter to be useful in their own deliberations.

The Tate Gallery's publications department laid the foundations for its independence in the 1930s when the Trustees made use of a private bequest to publish a series of postcards. For some time larger projects such as permanent collection catalogues and trustee reports continued to be published with the assistance of Her Majesty's Stationery Office, but the success of other activities based on a separately run account, in which profits coild be retained, eventually enabled the department to achieve complete freedom. Now, in the current financial year 1983–1984, receipts are running at an annual rate of £13 million. While the responsibility for the publishing of important, substantial, but often financially unprofitable books remains, the flexible availability of surplus cash for broadening the activity of the department has been extremely useful – in a way that would not have been possible under the Gallery's annual budget system where surpluses have to be given up to 'appropriations in aid'. The department has, of course, contributed quite largely to other Gallery interests, in cash or in kind, – some £57 000 in the financial year 1981–1982, and it is certainly the hope of such assistance that encourages the support of better-developed commercial activity. But while in some museums such help may be the sole source of salvation, it would be foolish to ignore the fact that much of what is published and sold by an institution is vital to the sustaining of contact with the visitors long after they have left the building. It must be good sense to re-invest a large part of any surplus in new and replacement stock.

The department's publishing activity can be divided into five separate areas:

(1) Information relating to the permanent collections – as guides to material displayed, and as scholarly catalogues of the complete collection.
(2) Temporary exhibition catalogues and broadsheets.
(3) Colour reproductions – presented as 35 mm transparencies, postcards, prints and posters.
(4) General trade books related to the collections.
(5) Stationery and gifts, such as calendars, diaries, address books and puzzles.

There are a certain number of basic information leaflets, relating for instance to forthcoming exhibitions, which are available free in the entrance hall and these are generally produced by the information department through HMSO; anything that is to be sold is the responsibility of the publications department.

The first three categories all include material that may well have to be published as a service to the visitor, without hope of commercial return: neither the scholar specialist, not the need for a balanced representation of the collection can be ignored. To support the display of any public collection, there must be a provision of basic guides, and to produce anything reasonably substantial at a favourable price requires a large edition; this in turn has to be sold over a relatively long period. If the collection described is one that is frequently reorganized – as the Modern Collection at the Tate now has to be – then satisfactory conditions for viable publishing are almost impossible to achieve. A very successful *Room-by-Room Guide* had to be discontinued for this reason. This forty page booklet, which sold at 40–50 pence, besides being a useful summary guide to each room in the Gallery, was also ideal for those many visitors looking for a tangible reminder of their visit. The room content summaries are now to be transferred to wall cards which can be more readily adjusted as the need arises. There are, nevertheless, two other publications serving this purpose, though at a higher price and in more general terms: a *Companion Guide* of 152 pages with 250 colour illustrations currently selling at £3.95, and *Looking at Pictures in the Tate Gallery*, of 72 pages with 45 colour plates selling at £1.95. The *Companion Guide* was expressly written to cover the principal areas of the collections without relating them to specific rooms: it serves as a good, general guide to British and modern foreign art and as such achieves a reasonable trade sale. About 12 000 copies are sold in a year, which is about half the former sales of the *Room-by-Room Guide*. In this context it is important to remember that every additional title can affect the sales of established material: the *Companion Guide* sales were reduced when the cheaper booklet was available.

At the time of the opening of the Gallery's new extension, the opportunity was taken to publish a 15 pence, eight-page broadsheet which gave a concise account of the building's development since its foundation; this was accompanied by short articles on the workings of the Gallery's various departments – all answering the questions most frequently asked at the information desk and heard among conducted parties. Sales were not as brisk as had been expected and this may have been the fault of the tabloid format, or perhaps may have been due to some feeling that the kind of information provided should have been available at no charge.

It is the temporary exhibitions which generate the largest proportion of the Gallery's publishing output, and it is the degree of popularity of the subjects of these shows that most influences the department's success or otherwise. Apart from making possible larger printings of catalogues, attendances at really popular exhibitions markedly improve general sales in the Gallery shop. Up to the present time, it has been broadly accepted that the service of scholarship is a priority in exhibition publishing, and that every exhibit should be illustrated with generous limits on the extent of the text. Where large attendances are expected it is possible to support this principle as edition sizes can be sufficient to achieve a reasonable selling price. It is the less popular shows which provide the greatest financial problems and the constant hope is that their number will be few enough for their losses to be covered by the more popular shows. Wherever possible the catalogues are designed to present the introductory text generously, so that the ephemeral feeling sometimes conveyed by massed catalogue entries is counter-balanced: the purpose here is to encourage the book-trade sales that can be so useful when exhibitions have ended; to this same end the exhibition dates are not prominently displayed on title-pages, but rather are placed with other bibliographical details on the title versos. An interesting fact to emerge from a survey of ten years' exhibition publishing is that in a number of unexpected cases post-exhibition sales have been the greater than those made during the exhibition itself.

Edition sizes are usually calculated on a basis of 5 to 15 per cent of the expected attendance, depending on the subject matter – modern art generally, but not always, attracting smaller sales. An additional allowance has to be made for possible trade sales which can vary from 1000 to 5 000 copies or more. The pricing of catalogues at the exhibition desk seldom exceeds 1½ times cost. With a popular show, swift sales direct to the public over a relatively short period can justify such a policy. But it has to be made plain to the visitor that these are special prices, and that the full trade figures which allow the bookseller the accepted 35 per cent discount apply after the exhibition ends.

As costs continue to increase, it may soon become necessary to give serious consideration to the publishing of briefer, more general, texts accompanied by a good selection of large illustrations which would satisfy the majority of exhibition visitors, and to look for alternative methods of presenting the essential scholarship – perhaps publishing on demand as xerox from microfiche, which would avoid the locking up of considerable amounts of capital. As it is, for some years past, simple summary broadsheets have been published at 20 to 40p, to serve those visitors unable to afford the £4 to £9 catalogue prices that are now becoming commonplace. There is no doubt that these broadsheet sales have diminished the success of the main catalogues.

If there is a shortage of working capital, and an anxiousness to produce a more elaborate catalogue than usual, it is tempting to consider the current interest of a number of trade publishers. However, not many of the proposals they make show a true advantage to the museum and they should be examined with very great care. They naturally find it difficult to accommodate the almost inevitably short production times associated with exhibitions and generally what is found to be on offer is a production, design and distribution facility, with, hopefully, reduced unit costs but no risk capital, beyond what they put into copies for their own sales to the trade. If the museum is attempting to establish a list and to be recognized in the trade as a regular publisher, the involvement of other houses can be counter-productive in the long term. Co-operation with other publishers may sometimes be easier to effect with books devoted to some aspect of the permanent collections, where a clear advantage can be seen in fitting a title to a compatible existing list.

The publishing of single images from the collections, in colour either as slide, postcard or large reproduction print, contributes about 30 per cent of the Tate's retail turnover, and at a very much better margin than achieved by book sales. So the choice of a substantial number of commercially successful subjects is particularly important. For the slides and postcards there is a good deal of curatorial involvement in the choice – the needs of scholars and teachers make it necessary to be sure that the various aspects of the collections are properly represented. There are approximately 520 postcards and 750 slides available currently, though of course the list, however, large, will never suit every visitor to the Gallery. Sales would only be moderately reduced if the number of titles was to be cut down to as few as the 100 most popular subjects – as was recently shown at the National Gallery during a temporary reduction of display space. Some sections of the list may show an unexpected bias towards one or other artist – the simple result of taking advantage of the availability of colour separations made for past special exhibitions. Sales can be very much affected by the position of the originals in the gallery: numbers can drop dramatically if a picture is removed to store; and the fact that a subject is popular in the Gallery shop does not necessarily mean that it will sell well in the outside trade where the buyer cannot be inspired by the sight of the original.

The same can be said of the series of large colour reproductions published by the Gallery. There are at present just over one hundred subjects available and here commercial considerations affect the choice rather more vigorously. The very high cost of framing has reduced the volume of sales over the past two years, and any new subjects introduced will have to be of dimensions smaller than the current average of about 18×24 inches (45.7×60.9 cm). While a print may currently sell for £3 to £6, its framing could amount to as much as £25 to £35. However, the sale of exhibition and general gallery posters, which incorporate text matter and sell at £2.90, has increased. While fashion is no doubt part of the reason, there may well be something in the thought that here the buyer feel less constrained to buy a formal frame and feels easier about pinning the 'ephemeral' poster direct to the wall.

The annual production of a calendar and desk diary has been a regular part of the publishing program for some years. There is always some degree of speculation here, and the correct choice of subjects particularly for the covers, is crucial. In some years, costs may barely have been covered, but both products are considered to be a very important means of keeping the Gallery's name prominently displayed over a long period. Calendars have to be ready in proof from a full year in advance: trade orders for the 1985 edition are taken by representatives in January 1984. Diaries are produced to a similar schedule and can be sold to the first tourists arriving in the Easter holidays for use in the following year. The Tate calendar is produced in collaboration with a trade specialist printer/publisher whose representatives sell about 15 000 copies to the trade; a further 5–7,000, are sold in the Gallery. 3500 copies of the Diary are given a special cover for sale by Harrods; 4000 of the remaining copies of the 11500 edition are sold in the Gallery, and a similar quantity goes to the trade at large. There are a number of other stationery items such as address books, note books, sketch books, playing cards and jigsaws that can be adorned with colour reproductions, and it is worth seeing if the separations can be applied to several uses. For example, those prepared for the illustration of the complete catalogue of large colour prints, were redeployed in the production of sets of colour gift tags which sold very successfully in packets of ten; jigsaw puzzles have been produced from separations used for both postcards and large prints. It is worth visiting gift shops and fairs on a regular basis, to keep an eye on ideas for new products. The art museum has fewer opportunities for product development than its fellows in other fields. The production of replicas, for instance, is limited to small sculpture, of which there may be nothing suitable, whereas the museums of antiquities or the applied arts can often have an embarrassment of riches. Not that the production of replicas has ever been easy. Neither here nor in America has it been a simple matter to get regular supplies of consistent quality from manufacturers who, almost without exception, have limited production facilities.

The fact that the publications department controls

copyright permissions and the hire of transparencies enables it to keep watch on commercial applications from the trade, and sometimes useful collaborative schemes can be developed; certainly the securing of adequate fees is of great importance: if for example the Gallery is deprived of the opportunity of publishing an image on its own account, it is only reasonable to negotiate a return that compensates for the loss. Sometimes payment can be made in kind which can be sold in the Gallery shop, thus taking greater return than could be had from a straighforward fee. Although many works in the collection are now out of copyright, the commercial potential in them is retained by controlling access. Any transparencies made have their own copyright and with very few exceptions these are produced by the Gallery; and all transparencies, even if made by outside photographers, carry the Tate copyright notice as part of the exposed film.

The department's staff averages just over twenty full-time employees; they are not members of the Civil Service but are paid at equivalent rates. There is a storekeeper and two packers, a copyright controller, a clerk/receptionist with responsibility for the black-and-white photograph library and sales, a shop supervisor and six salespersons, a shop manager/stock controller, a deputy manager with responsibility for accounts and general administration, a computer clerk and a cashier. The general manager, his assistant/secretary and a designer are directly responsible for the publishing activity. There is no full-time editor, although if there was adequate office accommodation there could be a case for employing one. At present this essential responsibility is taken on by the relevant curator on the main gallery staff. Freelance help is occasionally used for general or copy editing and for proof-reading. Design is handled in the house – primarily to maintain some consistency of style and quality, but also because the very tight schedules, and the fact that copy is frequently received piecemeal up to the eleventh hour, preclude the use of the less-accessible freelance. But whatever the individual circumstances, it is vital that there should be no compromise on design quality and that money should be spent on professional skills. In the case of art galleries it is important to hire persons experienced in the fitting of picture reproductions to text – paintings cannot be cropped to make a comfortable fit in a grid – in the manner so often suffered by photographs. On the subject of cover designs, it is astonishing to see how often designers have been allowed to forget that an exhibition catalogue will usually have to compete for space and attention in the bookshops after the show is over – without spine lettering a book is lost on a crowded shelf.

The relationship between quality and cost demands a nicety of judgement not easy to achieve.

It is always possible to find a supplier who will be prepared to deliver at a lower price, but to judge the loss of quality and service that may result is a difficult business. It is certainly important to work with suppliers who are fully sympathetic to one's purpose – the commitment of the people involved is, in the long run, more important than the ultimate in sophisticated equipment.

The origination of colour and monochrome illustration is a constant preoccupation in most museum publishing operations and it is important that one member of the staff should have a grasp of the basic technicalities. It is also important to work with a specialist supplier since even when new, very few colour transparencies are absolutely true to their originals; they deteriorate quite severely in the second and third years of their life, and the process can be hastened by careless handling. It follows that before separation work begins, transparencies should be checked against the originals, by the printer, and under controlled lighting conditions. The degree to which the appearance of colour can be affected by a changing light source or surroundings is astonishing, and only by eliminating these influences can each stage of colour proofing be checked with confidence. The Gallery has devised its own mobile lamp and light box for this purpose. All transparencies should contain standard grey scales and colour patches from which the printer can obtain much essential information relating to colour bias and tonal range.

Black-and-white half-tone reproduction has its own problems and these are particularly marked when dealing with paintings that contain much detail in both shadow and highlight. It should always be made plain that extra handwork is expected of the printer – the camera alone cannot cope with the full tonal range and if highlight detail is retained in a relatively short exposure then shadow detail will need opening up with subsequent hand-retouching.

The printing of fine art standard colour presents particular problems when multiple subjects are combined together on one sheet, and here colour postcards are a typical example. While one can control ink supply on the press from side to side across the sheet, the supply from front to back cannot be adjusted and indeed is not always consistent. This means that if, for instance, a subject heavily weighted in the magenta printing is in line with one that is predominantly light blue, then the latter can be severely affected. The ideal would be to print all postcards in a single line across the sheet with no subjects following behind, but more often than not economics force the publisher into the printing of as many as 32 or more cards on a sheet, in four rows of eight: the compromise that results is usually all too evident. In colour work demanding any degree of care, it is important to encourage the inclusion of control strips on both proof and machine plates, which can be of great assistance to both printer and customer in judging colour balance and dot sharpness. Sometimes this will mean having to specify a slightly larger sheet of paper or board, and the extra cost encourages the less careful to dispense with this useful aid.

The pricing of museum publications often produces a conflict between the desire to make things available in this museum at the lowest possible price and the necessity to give full trade discounts if any reasonable distribution is to be achieved beyond the museum. The special circumstances of exhibition publishing have already been referred to; any other product for which capital has to be locked up for some time before reasonable returns have been achieved will certainly need a mark-up of more than 1½ times cost. In general trade publishing the factor will be at least ×4, if not ×4½ or ×5, to allow for distribution and trade discount, royalties and general overheads, before a modest profit can be found. If the museum has good attendance figures, then the likely proportion and speed of direct sales to the public at full price in its own shop, can be taken into account when deciding on a satisfactory multiplication factor. At the end of the day it is a satisfactory overall gross profit that has to be achieved. It is not a good sign if this falls below 42 per cent of turnover at the Tate. If there is an opportunity for negotiating bulk sales, say of a large proportion of an edition to an overseas publisher, it may be necessary simply to view the transaction as a means of increasing quantities – though little or no profit comes through, the unit costs overall are reduced and thus margins on UK sales are improved.

Distribution to the retail trade has to be arranged with the help of a sales team, either directly engaged freelances, or in association with a regular publisher running a compatible list. If the museum has a large enough department, and is able to handle invoicing and despatch, then it is a simple matter of recorded orders sent in by the representatives on which they are paid a percentage of 10 to 12 per cent. In these circumstances single copy orders bring home most forcibly the cost of distribution. At the Gallery it has been policy for some time to charge postage on orders below a certain value. If the resources for handling orders are too slender, then it may be possible to secure the full service from a specialist distribution house, or from a publisher with capacity who is looking for a means of absorbing overhead.

The use of direct selling techniques has been much discussed in museum circles during the past few years. There have been great success stories in America, but they are few and related only to the largest museums. It is tempting to consider putting together glossy mail-order catalogues, but too seldom is it realized what a specialized business this is. It is little help to look in the cupboard for something to sell –

the products have to be devised for the medium, and they have to be sufficiently highly priced to cover the remarkably high cost of securing orders. The trade in America is at present shrinking, two museums have discontinued their annual catalogues, and a firm in this country which produced museum-based catalogues has recently ceased to trade. If a museum product appears to lend itself particularly well to this type of selling then it is probably more sensible to approach a firm already producing a general catalogue.

The sale of museum publications to fellow institutions can be encouraged by establishing some kind of standing order system, although there can be a very high overhead in the supervision of such a scheme. The Tate's sales are very much reduced by the Library Exchange Scheme, which secures free copies from other institutions in return for our own material. In this way the publications department provides a valuable subsidy to support the library.

For the future it is clear that if ever a greater degree of collaboration between museums and galleries can be established – in the shape of some kind of central marketing and order fulfilment – there would be much to be gained. Whether or not we can overcome the problems raised by the very great diversity in the structure of their businesses remains to be seen.

For many museums and galleries the retail shop has now assumed a considerable degree of importance and particularly so for those with an independent publishing operation and larger numbers of visitors, for it is from the shop that a great proportion of the working capital can be raised. At the Tate two-thirds to three-quarters of turnover is achieved through retail sales. In 1973 the move from a post-card desk and two small book and print stalls in the entrance halls, to 1800 square feet of specially fitted gallery space near the entrance, doubled sales overnight, underlining the simple maxim 'you sell what you show'. To provide space where visitors can linger and browse is crucial. Too often one finds museum sales areas in corridors, or neglected hallways or cloakrooms, poorly lit. The area should be easy to find and wherever possible with its own access to the street. For many visitors the shop visit is left to the end of the day, and if, as at the Tate, access to the shop has to be denied after 5.30 p.m. in order to be sure that everyone is past the tills in time to be clear of the main door closing at 6 p.m. then a good many can be dissapointed. It is possible that at busy times as much as one thousand pounds' worth of potential sales could be lost in a week.

The planning and stocking of any shop needs considerable thought, and professional advice is essential. In a museum, of course, there are other considerations beyond the purely commercial. There will always be considerable temptation, if not pressure, to stock important material germane to the collections but of relatively limited appeal, and often at prices that allow below-average discounts. To be sure that such stock does not take up a disproportionate amount of space it is vital to prepare regular analyses of sales. Fifty per cent of the turnover in the Tate shop comes from the sale of books – forty per cent of which will be from other publishing houses. The average gross profit is reduced to about 21 per cent, even though the trade average is 35 per cent. The lower figure is brought about by a combination of two principal factors, the low margin limited appeal material referred to earlier, and stock losses which run at a fraction over the national average of 2½ per cent. The business to be successful needs gross profits to run at about 42 per cent, so it is easy to see the importance of postcard sales (10 per cent of turnover at ×3½ mark up) and colour reproductions (20 per cent of turnover at ×4 mark up), and the fact that they must have prime selling space.

Museums and galleries with collections that provide an opportunity to produce high-priced replicas of small sculpture, artefacts and jewellery have good opportunities for creating good profits – but such products need good display and appropriate shop facilities: it is particularly difficult to sell such materials in supermarket conditions. The turmoil of a busy till queue is no help to the quiet contemplation and discreet encouragement needed for high-price transactions. In an art gallery there are opportunities for dealing in more expensive, limited-edition original prints but only in the right conditions. The Tate shop does not have these, though when, for example, it was possible to set up a separate sales point associated with an exhibition showing many modern prints, several thousands of pounds worth were sold in a few weeks. The smaller museum may well be able to take advantage of less busy sales areas to sell high-price goods, provided that they can be elegantly displayed and lit.

For selecting stock it is important to seek as much information and advice as possible. Visits to other shops in the trade at large and in museums provide a useful guide to what is available, in demand and fashionable. Suggestions and enquiries from customers and staff are most valuable, and although publishers' and manufacturers' representatives can consume much time, if their visits are planned their information can be very helpful.

In display, apart from good lighting, presentation, and signing, prominence should be given to the museum's basic publications, new books and other products, and to material relating to current exhibitions. To have a reasonable number of sale or remainder items available is always helpful, though too large a display can rebound on the sales of full-price stock. The sale of souvenirs such as key-rings and book-marks can be a difficulty for businesses registered as educational charities. Such items are not sold at the Tate as the Inspector of taxes would view them as non-educational. It is in fact possible to set up a holding company as a charity, from which a subsidiary trading company stems. This, by paying over all its profits to the parent body at the end of the financial year, can avoid tax. The holding company then reinjects those profits or part of them as working capital for the trading company's following year.

It is important to take particular care in the recruiting of staff who should be trained in the basics of good creative selling. For many visitors they are the sole personal contact with the museum and bad impressions can do untold damage to the institution's reputation. Uniforms, or at least simple forms of identification, are not popular with staff at present, but they are certainly helpful to customers. Part-time volunteer staff are used a good deal in the smaller museums of America, but the understandable want of commitment can sometimes provoke endless difficulties.

Shop losses are a perennial problem. Though it is difficult to believe – and unpleasant to have to consider – the statistics in the UK and America show that more losses are due to staff pilferage than to customers. It is therefore particularly important that till and counting systems are as tightly controlled as possible – avoid putting temptation in the way of staff by running a slack system. Shop layout may well be at fault in the temptation of customers. As ever, professional advice should be taken – not from a book, but from a specialist on the spot. This should be done in conjunction with shopfitters if plans for a new layout are being considered.

While there is a considerable trade literature on publishing and merchandizing, there is virtually nothing available that has been written specifically for the museum world. At present the best source of help and inspiration comes from the British and American specialist groups. The bulletins and meetings provide the best possible means of discussing the problems and potential of our business. More information may be obtained from the following:

Museum Store Assocation
260 Cherry Lane,
Doylestown, PA 18901, USA.

Group for Museum Publishing and Shop Management
c/o Honorary Secretary,
Ashmolean Museum,
Oxford

Further Reading

BABBIDGE, I. (1972), *Beginning in Bookselling: A Handbook of Bookshop Practice,* Andre Deutsch, London
BARSOOK, B. (1982), A code of ethics for museum stores, *Museum News,* **60**(3), 50–52

BLACKER, G. (1971), Design standards for printed matter, *Kalori*, **42**, 110–116

BLUME, H. (1981), *Charity Trading Handbook*, pp. 75–98, Charity Trading Advisory Group, London

BOOKSELLERS ASSOCIATION, (1977), *Opening a Bookshop – Some of Your Questions Answered*, Booksellers Association, London

CANNON-BROOKES, P. (1980), The evolution of the art exhibition catalogue and its future, *Museumleven*, **7–8**, 139–144

CHANDLER, J. G. (1974), The press release and the small to medium-sized museum, *Museum News*, **58**(1), 73–74

FARLAND, E. (1967), Quality posters – the meaning of original posters, *Museum News*, **46**(4), 33–37

FERGUSON, M. D. (1978), Do-it-yourself design, *Museum News*, **56**(4), 38–41

FRITZ THYSSEN STIFTUNG (FOUNDATION) (1970), The promotion of learned museum catalogues, *Museums Journal*, **70**(1), 3–6

GERMANN, S. (1979), Practically speaking, *History News*, **34**(9), 265–267

GORE, G. (1978), Phototypesetting: getting the most for your money, *History News*, **33**(1), 9–24

GROVE, K. (1975), Museum cookbooks: for fun and profit, *Museum News*, **53**(9), 53–59

HILL, M. (1967), Catalogues, guides and gimmicks: three aspects of gallery publications, *Museum Assistants' Group Newsletter*, **8**, 8–13

HODRIPP, S. (1978), *The Shopper's Guide to Museums Stores*, Ash & Grant, London

JONES, L. S. (1975), Where to publish? Where to index?, *Museum News*, **53**(5–6) 30–31

KJORLIEN, R. (1974), Out of print, *Museum News*, **52**(5), 60–62

KRAHEL, D. H. (1971), Why a museum store, *Curator*, **14**, 200–204

LING, J. (1978), Museum publications, *Kalori*, **54**, 73–76

LONG, M. AND SORRELL, D. (Eds.) (1978), *Museum Shops – A Powerful Force in Education*, Area Museum Service for the Midlands

MCHUGH, B. (1979), Display and sales in gallery and museum shops, *Kalori*, **56**, 30–33

MOORE, E. (1975), The rocky road to publication, *Museum News*, **53**(5), 21–24

MUNRO, G. (1977), Museum shops for the outside, *Museums, J.*, **76**, 143–145

MUSEUMS ASSOCIATION (1978), Museum shops, *Museums Association*, IS22, London

MUSEUM CATALOGUES – OUTSIDE LONDON, *The Burlington Magazine*, **112**(808), 427–431

NEWCOMB, K. K. (1977), *The Handbook for the Museum Store*, Museum Publications, Virginia

PUTNAM, J. B. (1975), An offer you should not refuse, *Museum News*, **53**(5), 42–43

RUSHTON, B. H. (1968), Producing and selling slides, *Museum News*, **46**(5), 27–32

SEKERS, D. (1976), The educational potential of museum shops, *Museums J.*, **76**, 146–147

SER, T. L. (1971), Museum sales shops and the IRS, *Museum News*, **49**(10), 20–23

THOMAS, L. (1967), The small store – quality service to the community, *Museum News*, **46**(4), 37–39

TIETZ, R. M. (1981), Museum publications, *SAMAB*, **14**(6), 227–238

VARIOUS AUTHORS (1974), A shopper's guide, *Museum News*, **53**(4), 37–39

WILLIAMS, M. (1969), A museum sales system for the future, *Museum News*, **48**(4), 22

SEE ALSO Newsletters of the *Group for Museum Publishing and Shop Management*

52

Museum publications and museum publishing: a brief introduction – with a note on museum libraries

Douglas A. Bassett

The volume of material published by museums and museum bodies in any one year is considerable. It is estimated, for example, that the world's art museums are publishing at the rate of three volumes a day. The *Worldwide Art Catalogue Bulletin* (Worldwide Books Inc.) lists 962 to 1075 annual publications, while the editor estimates that no more than two-thirds of the total number of museums is included in these figures. Again, 22,000 publications in print are listed in *World Museum Publications 1982, A Directory of Art and Cultural Museums, Their Publications and Audio Visual Materials* (R. R. Bowker Co., 1982).

This development is in part a reflection of the rapid growth of museums, and of visitors to museums, and in part of the ease of publication and the change in the aesthetic environment captured so neatly in André Malraux's basic metaphor 'le musée imaginaire'. It is also almost certainly linked in part with the rapid developments in museum shops and the resulting growth of sales of museum publications. These developments are clearly reflected in the *Newsletter* of the 'Group for Museum Publishing and Shop Management'. The Group, created in 1978 and affiliated to the Museums Association in 1980, was conceived as a professional organisation of museum personnel, 'to provide a forum for discussion and exchange of ideas and information between members of the museum profession involved in any part of publishing, shop management, or related activity'.

The obligation to publish has always been one of the duties that has been readily accepted by most major, and many minor, museums. (*See*, for example, *That noble cabinet. A history of the British Museum* by Edward Miller (Andre Deutsch, London, 1973, pp. 107, 263)). The nature and organisation of this role has, however, changed quite considerably over the last quarter century. The changes in the British Museum – 'the first national, public and secular museum' and the Victoria & Albert Museum, 'the museum of the art of living', are indicative.

Until the late 1950s the publishing role of the British Museum was undertaken, on an *ad hoc* basis, by the various Departments. It was then centralised in a section specifically created for the purpose (which also undertook the responsibility for the Museum bookshop). Since 1973 this role has been undertaken by a company, British Museum Publications Limited, totally owned by the Trustees, but wholly separate from government finance and the staffing limitations of the Museum.

Since the formation of the Company, the annual turnover has risen from £156,000 per annum to £1,102,000 in 1979/80 and the expenditure on book production in the three years 1978 to 1981 has averaged £367,000 per annum.

Many of these are works of great importance in terms of scholarship and research but can in no way be regarded as viable books in any commercial sense. *The Catalogue of Medieval lead-glazed earthenware tiles in the Department of Medieval and Later Antiquities, British Museum* by Elizabeth Eames (in two volumes – 1980) and *The Sutton Hoo ship-burial* by Rupert Bruce-Mitford and others (in three volumes – 1975, 1978, 1983) are examples. The two parts of the third volume of the Sutton Hoo series, for example, contain 1,000 pages and cost £100 a set.

An additional and separate imprint, Colonnade Books, was launched to publish books which are not official British Museum publications, and not necessarily written by the staff of the Museum, but which are intended as contributions to the enjoyment, study and understanding of art, archaeology and history. Examples include: *Ruins. Their preservation and display*, by M. W. Thompson, (1981); *Iron-age farm. The Butser experiment*, by Peter J. Reynolds (1979); *The Bible and recent archaeology*, by Kathleen M. Kenyon (1981).

Several of the books oriented towards the general public have been licenced for editions in the United States, and seven had been selected by British book clubs in the period up to 1981. Books have also been published in association with outside publishers when their specialist knowledge and marketing experience make it appropriate to do so.

Until comparatively recently the Victoria & Albert Museum published its books through both Her Majesty's Stationery Office and commercial publishers. Although these links continue, in the last few years the V & A has published the majority of its books independently. This has been due to restructuring both at HMSO and at the V & A. The V & A has thus built up a stock of titles in anticipation of establishing a Publishing Company following the Museum's change of status in 1983 from a Departmental Museum to a Trustee Museum. All the books in the current catalogue of the V & A ([32pp.], distributed by A. Zwemmer Ltd., London) 'have been, or will be, published by the Victoria and Albert Museum'.

The role of publication

The relationship of publication to the research and curatorial roles of museums is clearly reflected in the Report by a working part of the Ancient Monuments Board for England, Committee for Rescue Archaeology, *Principles of publication in rescue archaeology* (Department of the Environment, 1975), 16pp.). In the Introduction it states: 'Archaeologists and those who employ or sponsor them in undertaking excavations have an obligation to publish their work: they also have the responsibility of seeing that the significant excavated material and the full original records of the work are preserved for reference by future scholars. The two aspects of publication and preservation of the records are inter-related.' The authors continue: 'It has long been a cardinal principle that archaeologists should publish their work in full in a permanent form, available to anyone who wishes to read it in a good library or to purchase it.'

The same emphasis is given in the chapter on 'Community and communications' in Professor John Ziman's *Public knowledge. An essay concerning the social dimension of science* (Cambridge University Press, 1968, pp. 102 et seq.). The main thrust of his thesis about the nature of science is that the 'literature' of the subject is quite as important as the research work that it embodies. To paraphrase and adapt his words slightly: A scholarly investigation or a piece of research work is by no means completed when the last specimen has been collected or described and the correlations and comparisons made. The form in which it is presented to the scholarly community – the 'paper' or the 'monograph' in which it is first reported, the subsequent criticisms and citations from other authors and the eventual place that it occupies in the minds of a subsequent generation – these are all quite as much part of its life as the germ of the idea from which it originated.

In spite of the obvious importance of publication to museum work, comparatively little has, however, been written about it and few debates initiated.

One exception is: 'Do museums of science and technology have a publications policy? A review of the current situation,' by G. L. E. Turner. pp. 3–9 in *Museum publications in science, technology and medicine. Papers from a joint meeting held at the National Railway Museum, York, 27 April 1981*. Group for Scientific, Technological and Medical Collections. Group for Museum Publishing and Shop Management. Ashmolean Museum, Oxford/Science Museum, London, 1982. *See also: A national museums policy for the 80s; Preliminary statement of intent and brief to the Federal Cultural Policy Review Committee*. National Museums of Canada, Ottawa, 1981; and *Towards a policy*, edited by P. J. Boylan. Leicestershire Museums, Art Galleries and Records Service, 1981.

The different kinds of museum publications

General reviews of museum publications are almost non-existent. One of the very few exceptions is the two-part essay on museum publications in Great Britain in *British Book News* by Anthony P. Harvey, which attempts to demonstrate the range of subjects in such publications. The first part (November 1967) deals with the scientific literature and the second (December 1967) that of fine and applied art. The emphasis in both parts is on the publications of the provincial museums, as opposed to the nationals, and on the material in print at that time. Harvey confines himself to the publications of specific museums and does not include the publications of museum bodies or societies. In the current review, the phrase 'museum publications' is interpreted to include both museum and museum association or society publications; and consideration is given to publications other than those issued in the United Kingdom and not of necessity in print at present.

Books published by museums and museum bodies can be sub-divided in a number of different ways: – (i) according to the museum that issues them (as in *The bibliography of museum and art gallery publications and audio-visual aids in Great Britain and Ireland 1979/ 80*, edited by Michael Roulstone (Chadwyck-Healey, Cambridge, 1980) or in *World museum publications 1982* (R. R. Bowker Co., 1982); (ii) according to subject matter (as in the usual book catalogue and also as in most of the catalogues of books in print issued by the larger museums); (iii) according to the audience for which the book is designed; (iv) whether they are examples of 'primary', 'secondary' or 'tertiary' literature as classified in the various guides to literature; or (v) according to the following readily recognisable categories:

(a) those that are concerned specifically with collections and exhibitions and that are, therefore, distinctive to or readily associated with museums, galleries and libraries. Prominent among these are the handlists, handbooks or catalogues to permanent collections and to temporary exhibitions, and illustrated guides to the museums and galleries.

(i) Handlists, Handbooks and Catalogues to permanent collections

Denis Farr, in the Chapter 'Research: Fine Art Collections', cites a number of examples of Handlists, Summary Catalogues and Catalogues Raisonnés (also called 'Classed catalogues' and 'Classified catalogues' by Librarians) to collections in the major galleries in this country and overseas. Two other examples not quoted by Farr are: The 'monumental' *Van de Velde drawings. A catalogue of drawings in the National Maritime Museum made by the Elder and Younger Willem Van de Velde* (1961); and *National Gallery of Scotland. Shorter Catalogue*, by Colin Thompson and Hugh Brigstocke (2nd revised edition, 1978). This Shorter Catalogue, first published in 1970, with a Supplement in 1976, is designed to make available all the information that is likely to be needed by the great majority of visitors. The revised edition contains a complete list of the collection and concise details of 408 principal works, and of the works on extended loan.

Selected examples of equivalent publications describing museum collections and archaeological and scientific materials of this and of other countries are: *Catalogue of the Prehistoric metalwork in the Merseyside County Museums*, by Susan M. Nicholson. Smithsonian Institution Press, Washington 1981; *National Maritime Museum Catalogue of ship models to 1815*. Part I. *Ships of the Western Tradition to 1815*, by A. H. White. HMSO, for the National Maritime Museum, 1980; *Type specimens of invertebrates (excluding insects) held at the Royal Scottish Museum*, by G. Smaldon, D. Heppell and K. R. Watt. Royal Scottish Museum, 1977; *Collections and collectors in North West England (Botany, Geology, Zoology)*. Volume 1 (Main List), Volume 2 (indices). By E. G. Hancock and C. W. Pettit. Manchester Museum Computer Produced Publication, No. 1, 1979. [Initial edition limited to 60 copies.]

Many other examples are cited in the lists of current publications issued by the British Museum (*British Museum Publications. Complete Book List 1983*, 40pp.), the British Museum (Natural History) (*British Museum (Natural History). Book Catalogue 1984*, 58pp.), The Smithsonian Institution (*Smithsonian Institution Press. New Publications. Books in Print*, 44pp.), The Victoria & Albert Museum (*Government Publications. Sectional List* 55. Victoria & Albert Museum/HMSO, 20pp. and the catalogue mentioned earlier). There are, in addition, some references to very early catalogues in the chapter on a 'brief world survey' by G. D. Lewis in this *Manual*.

(ii) Handlists, Handbooks and Catalogues to temporary exhibitions

Exhibition catalogues occupy an important place among art publications. They range in subject matter from the thematic to the chronological, and may cover an artist, a group of artists, a period in history, or a specific theme. Curators intend that both museum exhibits and their catalogues will bring out a new aspect of the main theme of the exhibition or bring to public attention a subject or artist that they feel has been neglected. Because they cover material not easily available elsewhere, catalogues are of value to the researcher.

One peculiarity of museum catalogues which is often forgotten, whether of collections or of exhibitions, is the disparate audience to which they are expected to appeal.

Denis Farr cites examples of various kinds of temporary exhibitions in the Chapter 'Research: fine art collections'. These include thematic and period exhibitions as well as major commemorative exhibitions. (*See also*: Publishing with museums, by Naomi B. Pascal. *Scholarly Publishing. A journal for authors and publishers*, **10**(2), January 1979, 147–153 – which, in spite of its wide-ranging title is concerned almost exclusively with the problems of collection and exhibition catalogues; and 'The museum catalogue – a disappearing art form', by Robert Anderson, in the joint publication *Museum publications in science, technology and medicine*. Ashmolean Museum, Oxford/Science Museum, London, 1982 mentioned earlier). *See also*: 'Selected recent exhibition catalogues' by Beth Houghton and Krysztof Z. Cieizkowski in *Arts Libraries Journal*, 3(4), 1978, 44–46.

Dianne M. Nelson, of the Boston Museum of Fine Arts Library, in an article in *Special Libraries* (Methods of citation analysis in the fine arts, **68**(11), 1977, p. 394), points out the value of museum catalogues as source material for research workers. Analysing the bibliographic references of eight books on Chinese bronzes and eight books on Chinese art in general, the author concludes that, 'collection catalogs, in the area of early Chinese art, are vital to research and should be acquired and preserved with care in the library'. She points out that the descriptive analysis, the inscriptions and the illustrations are also valuable.

The number of temporary exhibitions in the natural sciences and in archaeology is not anything like as great as those in the fine arts, and exhibition catalogues are accordingly much fewer in number. They are also different in nature.

Well-known examples include: *Nature stored, nature studied. Collections, conservation and allied research at the Natural History Museum.* British Museum (Natural History), London 1981. Although its *raison d'être* was to accompany a temporary exhibition of the same title, the booklet stands in its own right as a brief account of the structure and function of the Natural History Museum. *The story of the earth*, HMSO for the Geological Museum (Institute of Geological Sciences, London), a companion volume to one of the most spectacular (and expensive) natural science exhibitions of the 1970s, was first published in 1972, with a second edition in 1981. *The Vikings*, by James Graham-Campbell and Dafydd Kidd, published for the Trustees of the British Museum by British Museum Publications Limited on the occasion of the exhibition of The Vikings at the Museum in 1980. The publication was one of the Museum publications selected by a British and an American book club and, as a result, sold over 146,000 paperback copies and over 43,000 hardback editions.

(iii) Illustrated guides to museums and galleries

These vary considerably in size and shape and range from the single sheet folding leaflet to booklets or books. Examples include: those produced by the Natural History Museum, ranging from *Miniguide to the Natural History Museum* (one sheet) to *The Souvenir Guide*, Centenary Edition (1981), to *The British Museum (Natural History)* by Peter Whitehead and Colin Keates (128 pp. with numerous colour plates) issued in association with Scala/Philip Wilson in 1981, and the guide for young visitors (1979); and those by the National Gallery ranging from ' – *a quick visit to the National Gallery . . . for those people with restricted time, we suggest this tour taking in 16 masterpieces'* – (large folding sheet) to *The National Gallery Children's Book: 100 Great Paintings*, by Dillon Gordon and *The National Gallery Children's Book*, by Anthea Peppin with Illustrations by Pauline Bayres (1983).

Other examples include: *Young visitor's Ironbridge*. Ironbridge Gorge Museum Trust, 1974; *British Museum guide*. British Museum Publications Ltd., London, 1976; *The National Maritime Museum*, edited by Basil Greenhill. Scala/Philip Wilson, London, 1982; *100 things to see in the Victoria & Albert Museum*, London, HMSO, 1962.

Some of the guides are issued in a number of languages: for example, the BM(NH) *Souvenir Guide* (1981) is issued in French, German, Italian and Spanish and the *British Museum Guide and Map* (1981) in Japanese as well.

Most guides have to serve both as means of orientation and instruction and also as Souvenirs or Keepsakes (a token that the visit has actually taken place) as is indicated in some of the titles.

Written self-study guides to art exhibitions are discussed in, 'Self-study guides for the Adult Art Museum visitor' by Patricia Marra in *Museum Studies Journal*, **1**(1), Spring 1983, 37, 43–45. Self-study guides for school-age students are considered in the same issue of the Journal by Lois Swan Jones and Robert Wott. Other educational guides are referred to in the bibliographical essay on museums and education in Chapter 50 of this *Manual*.

Some of the problems preparing information sheets in museums, based on experience at the Berlin State Museums (Preussischer Kulturbesitz), are discussed in 'Some observations on information sheets in museums' by Andreas Grote in *International Journal of Museum Management and Curatorship*, **1**, 1982, 149–156.

(b) Publications 'common' to other institutions

Museums publish a very wide range of material other than catalogues and guides. These include annual reports, annual and special lectures, bibliographies, directories, facsimiles, festschrifts, floras and faunas, glossaries, inventories, journals (serials or periodicals) monographs, occasional publications, questionnaires, picture books, resource (study) packs, site descriptions, technical bulletins, trail leaflets, transactions (or reports) of symposia, as well as ephemera (or 'the small change' of publishing) which include postcards and posters; and, finally, records and casettes.

Representative examples of some of these categories, which are clearly not mutually exclusive, are:

(i) Annual reports

Most museums and many other bodies are required – either by Act of Parliament or Charter – to prepare an annual report for the Governing Body and usually to publish it as well. These vary in frequency of publication, in size and in coverage, but most contain a statement of accounts, some details of the development of the museum or gallery, of purchases, donations, exhibitions, publications, number of visitors, members of the Governing Body and also, commonly, of members of the museum staff.

Because of the 'austerity' of the conventional annual report, some museums issue complementary publications. The Tate Gallery, for example, issues an illustrated catalogue of acquisitions (e.g. 1976–78, 1979). The British Museum introduced the *British Museum Quarterly* in 1926 (and later added the subtitle, *A journal dealing with recent acquisitions and research concerning the Museum's collections*) and when, in 1973, the Library Departments of the British Museum became the Reference Division of the British Library, replaced it by *The British Museum Yearbook* (which retains the dual role of providing short notes on recent acquisitions and longer items resulting from retrospective research on the collections – and still aimed at the regular museum visitor), each annual volume containing contributions grouped around a common theme.

Because of the problems of presenting all the relevant material in one publication, the British Museum (Natural History), for example, issues a published report every three years and much more detailed cyclostyled departmental reports for restricted distribution every year.

Some annual reports are not confined to a review of a year's activities; they include historical reviews and discussion of particular topics without reference to any one particular year. A. E. Parr, for example, in his Director's Reports in the Annual Reports of the American Museum of Natural History, invariably prefaced the Review of a particular year with a more general survey. Some of these are extensive and extremely valuable. For example, his three assessments – in 1953, 1954 and 1955 – of the Museum's work over half a century, each attempt to compensate for the usual neglect of systematic research in public awareness. The three reports are: 'Filling the gaps of knowledge, I. The anthropological sciences (including physical anthropology, ethnology and archaeology, II. 'living nature', III. 'the geological sciences' – each review being over 40 pages in length.

The Secretary's Reports in *The Smithsonian Year* are equally discursive and their titles are often indicative. In 1974, 'A decade of increase and diffusion'; in 1975, 'Limits to growth'; in 1976, the Bicentennial Year, 'The attic refurbished'; in 1977, 'The years ahead'; and in 1978, 'To knit the ravelled sleeve . . .'

(ii) Periodicals (journals or serials)

Periodical publications fall fairly readily into two groups; the 'scholarly' research journals and the interpretive or 'popular' ones. British examples of the former include the *Bulletin of the British Museum (Natural History)* with separate series for Botany, Entomology, Geology, History, Mineralogy (now incorporated into the Geology series) and Zoology, all initiated between 1949 and 1953. Papers in the various series of this Bulletin are primarily the result of research carried out on the unique and ever-growing collections of the Museum, both by the scientific staff of the Museum and by specialists from elsewhere who make use of the Museum's resources. Parts are published at irregular intervals as they become ready, each is complete in itself, available separately and separately priced. (Volumes contain

about 400 pages and are not necessarily completed within one calendar year.) There are, in addition, a series of Supplements.

Some academic journals, which are not officially published by a museum, are edited and their preparation and publication managed by members of museum staff. Some of these journals are, therefore, associated in people's minds with particular museums. A well-known example is: *The Journal for the Society for the Bibliography of Natural History*, initiated in 1936 and renamed *Archives of Natural History* in 1981. The Society was formed under the Natural History Museum's auspices in 1936 and has received much support from the Museum ever since. The relations of the two bodies, in biological terms, have not been simply commercial but symbiotic. Another is: *Folk Life. Journal of the Society for Folk Life Studies* (later *A Journal of Ethnological Studies*), initiated in 1963, is closely associated with the National Museum of Wales (Welsh Folk Museum). It was the successor of *Gwerin* (Basil Blackwell, Oxford), largely a personal venture initiated by Dr. Iorwerth C. Peate.

British examples of the latter, the interpretive serial, include: the *Natural History Magazine*, issued by the British Museum (Natural History) from 1927 to 1936; *Amgueddfa, Bulletin of the National Museum of Wales*, issued three times a year from Spring 1969 to Autumn 1976; *The Victoria and Albert Museum Bulletin*, issued quarterly from 1965 to 1968; the *Leeds Art Calendar* (Leeds City Art Gallery) issued twice a year; and *Scottish Art Review*, initiated in 1944, published by the Glasgow Art Gallery and Museums Association (i.e. the Friends) and now issued irregularly.

The general purpose of such periodicals is stated by Sir Sidney F. Harmer, Director of the British Museum (Natural History), in his introduction to the first issue of the *Natural History Magazine*: 'The study of natural history has many fascinating aspects, but the subjects are often so complex and their elucidation is often so overwhelmed with technical terms unintelligible to the layman that their interest remains unknown except to the specialist. It is hoped that the *Natural History Magazine* will make some of these obscure places plain and show that the result of study of Nature by its professional devotees are capable of being explained in such a way as to convince the public of their absorbing interest.'

Two examples of recently inaugurated serials are:
(1) *The Ashmolean*, launched on the threshold of the Museum's 300th anniversary – and at 'a time to wonder about the past and to worry, perhaps, about the future'. Each issue contains, as its core, three or four short articles on museum topics and also features on Oxford as well as on the Ashmolean.
(2) The series of essays, *The V & A Album*, published every year before Christmas by Temple-

gate Publishing Ltd. in association with the Friends of the Victoria & Albert Museum and initiated in 1982. The Foreword of the first issue describes the contributions as 'scholarship worn lightly' and expresses the hope that the series will become as well loved an institution as *The Book of Beauty* of the 1840s or the *Saturday Book* in the post-war era.

All of these 'popular' journals and magazines are seen by the museums concerned as expressions of their 'outreach'.

American examples of the first category include: *Curator, Quarterly publication of the American Museum of Natural History* and *Syllogeus*.

The rationale for creating the journal *Curator*, which has an editorial board drawn from science, art and historical museums, was described by the first editor in the first number in the following words: 'Museum men and women have things to say and contributions to make to the common fund of museology in all its phases. These by-products of dedication to museum techniques deserve the dignity and the value of a publication which will make them available to colleagues now too scattered and too numerous for informal or easy communication.' During the 25th Anniversary year in 1983, six numbers of *the Journal* were issued, a total of 450 pages. The special commemorative number contains a cumulative index of the material in the journal from its inception. (*See 'Twenty five years of Curator'*, by T. D. Nicholson. *Curator*, **25**(4), 1982).

Syllogeus, now at No. 44, is a publication of the National Museums of Canada, designed to permit the rapid dissemination of information pertaining to those disciplines and educational functions for which the Museum is responsible. In the interests of making information available quickly, normal publishing procedures have been abbreviated. The serial appears at irregular intervals and is published in English and French.

American examples of the second category include *Natural History* and *Smithsonian*:

Natural History, also issued by the American Museum of Natural History, is designed to provide a medium for papers and articles on natural history generally. Initiated at the turn of the century as *The American Museum Journal*, it was devoted to natural history, exploration, and the development of public education through the museum. The title was changed in 1919 to: *Natural History. The Journal of the American Museum of Natural History*, with the words 'For the people: for education: for science' boldly printed on the outside back cover. Even by the mid 1970s this journal was a $3 million operation which yielded an annual profit to the Museum of $185,000. The circulation at that time was around 300,000 and the print run is now just over 500,000 (460,000 of

which are distributed to the Museums Associates). (*See* 'Some thoughts on reaching eighty', by A. Ternes. *Natural History*, **89**(4), 7–15.)

Smithsonian – issued by the Associates of The Smithsonian Institution to the 2,000,000 members and described as 'the fundamental benefit of Associate membership'. In 1981 the magazine printed 2,172 pages, of which 1,047 were pages of advertisements. *The best of Smithsonian*, an anthology of articles from the first decade of the magazine, was issued in 1981 by Smithsonian Exposition Books (designed to carry out the Institution's mandate for the 'increase and diffusion of knowledge' to the general public. The first title in this particular series was, *The Smithsonian experience. Science – History – The Arts. The treasures of the Nation*, issued in the bicentennial year (and now available in paperback).

Among the other journals issued by museum associations the best known are, in alphabetical order: the monthly magazine *History News*, issued by the American Association for State and Local History (AASLH) at Nashville, Tennessee since 1940; the quarterly *Icom News*, issued by the International Council at Paris since 1948; the quarterly *Musées et Collections Publiques de France*, issued by Association Générale des Conservateurs des Collections Publiques de France at Paris since 1932; the quarterly UNESCO magazine *Museum*, issued from Paris since 1948; the quarterly *Museums Journal*, issued by the Museums Association at London since 1901; and the quarterly *Neue Museum Kunde*, issued by Rat für Museumswesen beim Ministerium für Kultur der Deutschen Demokratischen Republik since 1958.

Two recent journals devoted entirely to museum matters are: the quarterly *International Journal of Museum Management and Curatorship*, issued by Butterworths & Co. (Publishers) Ltd., London since 1982 and the *Museum Studies Journal*, issued by the Center for Museum Studies of the John F. Kennedy University, New York since 1983.

(iii) Bibliography and bibliographies

Bibliographic studies are usually subdivided into systematic or enumerative and analytical or critical (or descriptive). Examples of both types are produced by museum staff. The basic idea of an enumerative bibliography is the listing of the salient details about a particular group of books which have some kind of coordinating factor. Examples include:
A search for environmental ethics. An initial bibliography. Compiled by Mary Anglemyer, Eleonar R. Seagraves and Catherine Remaistre. With an Introduction by S. Dillon Ripley. Sponsored by the Rachel Carson Council Inc., 1980.
Geology in museums: a bibliography and index, compiled by T. Sharpe. National Museum of Wales, Cardiff

1983. This bibliography is in two parts: a list arranged alphabetically by author with the bibliographic citation and key words; and a keyword (or subject) index, also arranged alphabetically, which cites author, date and full keyword listing for each entry. It was suggested, in the Foreword to this publication, that used in conjunction with the Association of Systematics Collections publication *Museum collections and computers* (by L. Savasen and A. M. Neuner, 1983), the *Bibliography and Index* will provide geological curators with a comprehensive background to museological literature.

There are, in addition – and in both categories – bibliographies and carto-bibliographies. Examples include:

A compendium of the biographical literature on deceased entomologists, by P. Gilbert. British Museum (Natural History), London, 1977.

A sourcebook of geological, geomorphological and soil maps for Wales and the Welsh Borders (1800–1966), by D. A. Bassett. National Museum of Wales, Cardiff, 1967.

The importance of bibliographic study for the major museums, and in particular as part of their research role as well as reference to analytical bibliographies, is given in a number of papers in *History in the service of systematics. Papers from the Conference to celebrate the Centenary of the British Museum (Natural History) 13–16, April 1981* – which is Special Publication No. 1 of the Society for the Bibliography of Natural History (1981). In his contribution to this symposium, W. T. Stearn defines bibliography as the description or knowledge of books in regard to their authors, subject, editions and history. 'Thus in biological terms bibliography resembles some species complexes with such overlapping diversity that they can be regarded as a sample polymorphic species or as an essemblage of several closely allied and subtly distinguishable species or as a hybrid swarm derived from intercrossing in the past'.

The function of a bibliography of any type, enumerative or descriptive, can never be fully realised unless the method chosen to display the material is really adequate. To quote the words of Pollard: 'If we take anything at all for granted on the part of our readers we may assume a knowledge of the alphabet'. And, after listing a number of other positive advantages, he cites one limitation – 'simply that it gives little or no help to the reader'.

See also: *Contributions to the history of North American Natural History. Papers from the First North American Conference of the Society for the Bibliography of Natural History held at The Academy of Natural Sciences, Philadelphia, 21–23 October 1981*, edited by Alwyne Wheeler, Special Publication of the Society for the Bibliography of Natural History, No. 2, 1983.

A very useful series of bibliographies, in book form, is issued by the American Association for State and Local History (Nashville, Tennessee). The series, edited by Frederick L. Rath Jr. and Mervityn Rogers O'Connell, include: *Historic preservation* (1975), *Conservation of collections* (1977), *Interpretation* (1978), *Documentation of collections* (1979), *Administration* (1980). Each volume has a section headed 'Basic Reference Shelf' and another on 'Historical organisations' which is a select directory of national (U.S.) and foreign and international organisations which includes brief notes on many of the museum associations publishing in English.

Another useful series is the cyclostyled bibliographies of the Department of Museum Studies, University of Leicester (*see* the Bibliographic Essay on Education in Museums for individual references).

(iv) Directories

Alphabetical lists of names and addresses – of individuals, of associations and of commercial firms – appear under many titles – either in Calendars (see, for example, the Calendar of British Universities) or Registers, Yearbooks, Lists and Indexes. Such 'directories' also appear in many guises. Some of the more important and better-known are published annually. For example, *The Museums Yearbook* of the Museums Association. Others appear irregularly. For example, *Museums Directory of the US and Canada* (American Association of Museums, 1961); and others are one-off publications: for example:– *A directory of natural history and related societies in Britain and Ireland*, compiled and edited by Audrey Meenan. British Museum (Natural History), London, 1983.

Two other examples are: *A directory of agricultural machinery and implement makers in Wales*, by Elfyn Scourfield. National Museum of Wales, Cardiff, 1979; *British taxidermists: a historical directory*, edited by S. Herriot. Leicester Museums and Art Gallery, 1968.

(v) Monographs

Representative selections of the kind of scholarly monographs that are produced by major museums are given in the following three publications: (a) *The Smithsonian Institution*, Paul H. Oehser. Praeger Publishers, New York, Washington, London, 1970 – a selection of approximately 100 works selected for their monographic character and which have attained some reputation and importance, and as typical specimens of the Smithsonian's programmes; (b) *Filling the gaps in knowledge, Parts 1, 2* and *3*. The American Museum of Natural History, 84th, 85th and 86th Annual Reports, New York, 1954; and (c) *Catalogue of early works. Monographs, Catalogues of the Collections and Reports on Scientific Expeditions still in print in limited supplies*. British Museum (Natural History), 1982.

Preparation and publication

'Since museum directors and curators read volu-
minously and have written at least an unpublished
thesis or dissertation, they tend to be reluctant to
admit that they don't know everything there is to
know about books.'

Ethel Moore: 'The rocky road
to publication.' *Museum News*,
February 1975, p. 21.

In a few of the largest museums, the publication procedures are similar to those at major commercial
publishers, but for the most part the museum curator
has to teach himself the principles of publishing. One
of the very few general texts published by a museum
body is: *Researching, writing and publishing local history*, by Thomas E. Felt, American Association for
State and Local History, Nashville, Tennessee, 1976.

A number of guides to research writing and publishing are analysed by Barbara Currier Bell in 'Maps
for learning' (*Scholarly Publishing*, **14**(1), October
1982, 61–78). Three types of guide – descriptive, critical and 'training' – are recognised, and nine of the
most useful examples are considered in detail. All
nine have two general and related failings: they lag
behind the development of new or newly important
fields in their disciplines and they do not adequately
cover computerised research techniques. The most
useful guide is judged to be *The modern researcher* (3rd
edn., 1977, Harcourt Brace Jovanovich, New York),
by two well-known and respected historians – Jacques Barzun and Henry F. Graff – and the only British publication mentioned is the first in the series of
the *Use of . . . literature* guides issued by Butterworths. All six (Economics, Biology, Earth Science,
Mathematics, Chemistry, Physics) are, however,
cited in the classified list of guides provided. In
choosing the overall list of the guides for the article,
all publications with a strong American emphasis
were excluded.

Four other manuals are considered by Naomi B.
Pascal in 'Four more enchiridia' (*Scholarly Publishing*,
10(4), July 1979, 351–358).

Two other works, by Jacques Barzun, which are
regularly cited are: *On writing, editing and publishing.
Essays explicative and hortatory*, University of Chicago
Press, Chicago and London, 1971; and *Simple &
direct. A rhetoric for writers*, Harper & Row, New
York, 1975. An equivalent British publication is: *The
reader over your shoulder. A handbook for writers of
English prose*, by Robert Graves and Alan Hodge,
Jonathan Cape, London, 1943 (1963). In the first part
the authors outline the principles of clear statement
and, in the second, apply the principles to selected
items from the writings of authors known for the
quality of their writing. Among the journals, one is
of particular relevance: *Scholarly Publishing. A journal

for authors and publishers*, published quarterly since
1969 by the University of Toronto Press.

All the major publishing houses issue one or more
guidebooks for the use of writers, authors or printers. The Oxford University Press, for example,
issue: *The Oxford Dictionary for writers and editors*,
compiled by Oxford English Dictionary Department, 1981 – a thoroughly revised and extensively
rewritten successor to eleven editions of the *Authors'
and Printers' Dictionary*, first published in 1905, and
commonly known as 'Collins' after its first editor, F.
Howard Collins. The policy of the book continues to
be a presentation of the house style of the Oxford
University Press, and the reader is therefore strongly
recommended to use it in conjunction with *Hart's
Rules for Compositors and Readers at the University
Press, Oxford* (38th edn., completely revised, 1978).
In addition, there are: *A dictionary of modern English
usage*, by H. W. Fowler, 2nd edn. revised by Sir
Ernest Gowers, 1965, and *The Concise Oxford Dic-
tionary of current English*, edited by H. W. Fowler and
F. G. Fowler, 6th edn., edited by J. B. Sykes, 1976.

Some of the Cambridge equivalents are: *First principles of typography*, by Stanley Morison; *Making an
index*, by G. V. Carey; *Notes and references*, by P. G.
Burbidge; and *Punctuation*, by G. V. Carey. The
University of Chicago's equivalent is: *A manual of
style* 12th edn., 1970.

Similarly, many of the major learned societies and
associations issue guidebooks. For example, the
*MHRA Stylebook. Notes for authors, editors and writers
of dissertations*, edited by A. S. Maney and R. L.
Smallwood, in consultation with the Committee of
the Association. Modern Humanities Research Association, London, 3rd edn., 1981. There are sections
on: Preparing the typescript; Spelling; Abbreviations; Punctuation; Capitalization; Italics; Dates,
Numbers and Currency; Quotations and Quotation
Marks; Footnotes; References; Presentation of
Theses and Dissertations; Glossary – with a guide to
examples of Proof Corrections and an Index. *See
also*, the equivalent but slightly smaller publication
issued by the Royal Society, *General notes on the preparation of scientific papers*, 1974.

Relevant volumes in the British Standards Institution Series include: *Recommendations for proof correction
and copy preparation* BS1219, 1958; *Table of symbols for
printers' and authors' proof corrections* BS1219C, 1958,
Bibliographical references BS1629, 1950; *Letter symbols, signs and abbreviations* BS1991, 1967. *See also:
Indexing for editors*, by R. F. Hunnisett, an Assistant
Keeper of Public Records, British Records Association, Archives and the User No. 2, 1972; and two
books by Eric Partridge, *The gentle art of lexicography
as pursued and experienced by an addict*, Andre Deutsch,
London, 1963 and *You have a point there. A guide to
punctuation and its allies*, Hamish Hamilton, London, 1953.

And finally a very helpful reference work is, *Har-*

rod's *Librarians glossary of terms used in librarianship, documentation and the book crafts and reference book*, 5th edn., revised and updated by Ray Prytherch, Advisory Editor, Leonard Montague Harrod, A Graften Book, Gower Publishing Co., 1984, originally published in 1938.

Turning to the problems of printing and publishing the material, the following volumes and articles chosen from among the many publications issued cover a range of problems: *The culture and commerce of publishing*, by Lewis A. Coser, Charles Kadushin and Walter W. Powell, Basic Books, New York, 1982; *Bookmaking: the illustrated guide to design and production*, by Lee Marshall, 1965, reprint, R. R. Bowker Co., New York, 1972, which covers every step in the process of designing and producing a book, including creative and practical details on designing, layout, costs and paper and definition of terms, illustrated with examples and diagrams. *See also*: the section on 'The art of the Book' (Printing, Book Illustration, etc.) in the various issues of HMSO Sectional List 55, The Victoria & Albert Museum).

Among other volumes are: *Photo composition at the Alden Press, Oxford*, by Hugh Williamson, The Bodley Head Ltd., London, 1981; *Microform publishing*, by P. Ashby and R. Campbell, Butterworths, London, 1979.

Finally, a series of papers in the *Newsletter* of the Group for Museum Publishing and Shop Management which are concerned with museum publishing and museum book sales: Victoria & Albert Museum/ Pitman Publishing Series, by Nicky Bird, No. 4, 1980; Museum co-publishing, by R. S. Cross, No. 2, 1979; Fitzwilliam Museum Enterprises Limited, by J. M. Huskinson, No. 3, 1980; Selling postcards at the National Railway Museum, by P. W. B. Semmers, No. 4, 1980; The small museum's publishing function, by J. W. H. Silvester, Nos. 2 and 3, 1979 and 1980.

A short note on museum libraries

Museum libraries differ considerably in size and importance. Each one is, however, of importance to the staff of the institution it serves (for purposes of research, curation and education) and also in many instances to the scholars and the public generally. Yet it is probably true that few people outside the museum service are aware of the existence of such libraries let alone the extent of their holdings.

The libraries of the major London museums are of international importance. The special role of the libraries in two of these is given in a double feature in the *Library Association Record* (June, 1977) – 'The National Art Library [at the V & A]', by Vera Kaden, pp. 310–311 and 'Tate development responds to increased demands', by Anthony C. Symons and Beth Houghton, pp. 311–313.

The policy of the Library at the V & A 'has always been to maintain a comprehensive coverage of fine, decorative and applied arts of all ages and countries'. The Library is also a Museum Department with the responsibility of collecting fine examples of book illumination, calligraphy, book-binding, book illustration and printing.

The history of the British Museum Library and its evolution into the British Library is provided in *That noble cabinet* by Edward Miller (1973) and the growth of the Science Library at the Science Museum is given in some detail in David Follett's *The rise of the Science Museum under Henry Lyons* (Science Museum, 1978), see particularly pp. 127–133.

Among the many publications issued by the library staff of museums, the following are representative:

Creasy, John S. *Museum Procedure*: *Library*, Institute of Agricultural History and Museum of English Rural Life, Reading.

British Library. *Librarian's guide to The British Library*, Reference Division services, a guide to the services and expertise available within(??) the British Library Reference Division.

Science Museum. *Classification for works on pure and applied science in The Science Museum Library*, HMSO 3rd edition, 1936.

Serial publications in the British Museum (Natural History) Library. Third edition, 1980, in three volumes, 1436 pp. This list contains the titles of serial publications held in the General Library, in the libraries of the Departments of Botany, Entomology, Mineralogy, Palaeontology (including Anthropology), Zoology and in the Zoological Museum, Tring. It includes all the titles received up to the end of June 1979, totalling some 20,000 entries.

List of acquisitions [to the Library], Victoria & Albert Museum. Issued a number of times each year since 1978.

The National Art Slide Library at the Victoria & Albert Museum, *Art Libraries Journal*, ii(1977), no. 4, 31–36

A useful 'handbook' for small libraries is provided by the Museum of Anthropology, University of Missouri, *Libraries for small museums*, by Marcia Collins and Linda Anderson, 1977. Miscellaneous Publication in Anthropology No. 4, 50 pp.

In addition to books many museum libraries have extensive collections of archival material. Three papers in the *Art Libraries Journal* for Winter 1978, under the general title 'Art and archives', are representative: 'Manuscripts and archives at the V. & A.', Irene Whalley, pp. 33–35; 'The Furniture and Interior Design Information Centre [V. & A.]', Clive Wainwright, pp. 36–38; 'The National Archive of 20th Century British Art and Artists at the Tate Gallery', Sarah Fox-Pitt (Head of Department, Tate Gallery Library & Archives), pp. 37–42.

53

Enquiries

David T.-D. Clarke

Most museum visitors are in essence enquirers, for curiosity is the human impulse from which springs the whole concept of museums. Conversely, curiosity should be the hallmark of every museum worker; a curiosity not confined to the collections themselves, but broadening into every aspect of the job.

These two elements, internal and external, are closely interrelated. Before considering them, however, it is necessary to promulgate one golden rule.

The Golden Rule

To the ennquirer, his query is of paramount importance, and not to be satisfied is a rebuff. There is, thus, for all enquiries, one golden rule – be as helpful as possible. At the end of a long day, and with other pressing needs, every museum worker knows how difficult this can be. Even so, it is worth remembering how often such enquiries may prove to be the most rewarding. A model summary has been given by Rachel Young (1972):

> In assisting enquirers . . . museum officers perform a valuable educational function, stimulating interest as well as providing information: in return the museum may expect to acquire knowledge, material, useful friends and much public goodwill

Good museum presentation will both satisfy and stimulate enquiries. In the front line are displays, intelligently and imaginatively conceived, and with legible and informative labels. To continue the metaphor, the entire support service in terms of general information, handbooks, catalogues, talks, guided visits, in fact the whole area of *communication* is an essential prerequisite. Monthly information leaflets, even annual reports have their part to play.

As a result of these, many visitor's queries may find a ready answer, but equally many may not. The range of such questions will be very wide, and the enquiries will be made in person, by telephone or by letter. The first step, is to sort them out properly, and refer them to the appropriate officer as promptly as possible. For this purpose, all staff need to be properly informed of their respective duties, especially those at the 'receiving end,' for example, the attendant and clerical staff. The degree of information will vary with the size of the institution, but written instructions will reduce mistakes and create confidence. The potential value of a list of 'who does what' should not be overlooked. This done, consideration may be given to the form such enquiries are likely to take.

General enquiries

These may seem so self-evident as not to warrant a mention, but they will be the most frequent and it is surprising how much the image of a museum may depend upon the giving of a satisfactory answer. It may not be directly the museum's job, but a handy train time-table, a knowledge of where the buses go from, and where overnight accommodation can be obtained or information retrieved may put the finishing touch to an agreeable visit.

Under this head the telephone warrants special mention, since its anonymity and ability to intrude upon personal privacy render it particularly liable to provoke aggressive instincts. All staff at all levels should be trained to answer the telephone in an informative and friendly manner. 'Barchester museum, good morning' or 'Good morning this is John Smith speaking' are useful examples: they save repetition, and if, as sometimes happens, there is indignation at the other end of the line, it helps to defuse it. People *do* talk about these things, and the bread returns on the waters, even after many years.

476

Administrative enquiries

A substantial proportion of the enquiries in most museums is concerned with requests for administrative information – times of opening, dates of exhibitions, numbers of visitors, service costs and the like. For the intending visitor, a printed sheet giving opening times, brief descriptions of what services are offered, the location of car parks, access for the disabled and toilet facilities, is a useful beginning and can also serve as general publicity.

Many organizations tend to present their queries in the form of questionnaires, which can be relied on to be set out in such a way that there is insufficient space for the answers, or to be so ordered that direct copying from the previous one is impossible. It is, therefore, imperative to have statistics readily available and up-to-date so that prompt and accurate answers can be given.

Staff should also be aware of the needs of auditors, simply satisfied if records are properly kept, and indexes adequately maintained.

The complexities of modern life are such that enquiries will also come from staff as to their entitlements and responsibilities: the good curator should not only anticipate them in terms of clear directives and guidelines, but also ensure that the appropriate literature is available to answer individual problems. It is a truism that little worries irritate more than big ones – an unpaid allowance rankles, and the employees may be too shy to ask about it. This area is an excellent one in which to build up a constructive relationship with trade union representatives: many crises can be avoided if they are dealt with promptly.

Specimens

The most obvious queries will be those which arise in connection with the museum's collections. They may vary from a desire to know more about a particular object on display, or a request to view a previous donation, to information on the wheareabouts of similar material.

For all of these the maintenance of good internal records and organized and accessible storage are the essential pre-requisites of a prompt and satisfactory answer. If this be a counsel of perfection, nevertheless the overall situation is improving, and it is our proper duty to ensure it. Attention should, however, be paid to the possible confidentiality of location records.

Acquisitions

Under this heading come offers of gifts or possible purchases, and requests for loans. For each of these it is imperative to have clear policy statements with proper delegation of decision making, and a routine to ensure the recording of appropriate data.

In the case of potential acquisitions, an interview, if not already provided, is imperative. With rising commercial values, the owner of such a piece is, alas, far less inclined to be influenced by the desire to present it rather than sell it to a piblic collection, and may well take fright lest he be deprived of a substantial income. It is, therefore, best to suggest that, if a sale is contemplated, one or more independent valuations are sought, und that these are suitably communicated to the owner, bearing in mind that *buying* and *selling* prices are different, and hence to suggest a point in between as being of mutual advantage.

If, however, the owner wishes to make a oift, no time should be lost in providing a written acknowlegement, with such publicity as may be appropriate or acceptable.

Research enquiries

These are relatively easy, since the researcher will usually know what information is required, and, again, good indexes, storage and filing systems should make individual requests relatively easy to solve. However, a few caveats are necessary. It is desirable to have a place where researchers can study, preferably under supervision, and where the objects or data can be brought to them. Regrettably, not all researchers are equally dedicated – the utmost care is necessary at all times to ensure that a record is kept of their address, and objects produced are properly noted (with a list, if necessary) and checked off in the presence of the enquirer before he leaves. Special care should be taken with small objects, such as might be eligible for substitution. This may sound hard, but it can be confimed by experience.

Conversely, no object in a display should be so fixed that it cannot be moved to satisfy a genuine researcher if necessary. It is also worth while remembering that no one has a monopoly of knowledge, and in appropriate cases a researcher should be encouraged to look at material which may have been wrongly classified in the past. Many useful discoveries have been made in drawers marked 'miscellaneous'.

Enquiries for factual information

The first essential for dealing with factual enquiries is access to a good reference library, and since no library can be fully comprehensive, 'we may not know, but we do know who does,' is an excellent precept. Nor is it difficult to achieve, since an active interest in the work of colleagues in other museums and related fields of study can usually produce an answer. Care should be taken, however, to ensure that names and addresses are not given to enquirers until it has previously been ascertained that the individuals are prepared to help.

Conservation

The growing interest in private collections of all kinds also generates enquiries relating to the repair or conservation of objects collected. In museums where conservation staff are available such enquiries can readily be referred to them, or to the conservators employed by an Area Museum Service. It should, however, hardly need emphasizing that, as with medical treatment, each problem needs to be assessed on its merits, and only the simplest tasks should be attempted by non-specialists; anything difficult should be entrusted to properly qualified personnel. Since this may require reference to commercial sources, attention is drawn to the ethical problems.

Some collectors may even seek advice as to what to collect, thus posing further ethical difficulties, which are discussed elsewhere in this manual.

Requests from students

Modern educational practices encourage personal fact-finding and staff will be familiar with letters beginning, 'Please can you tell me about . . .' usually a comprehensive subject like Roman Britain or John Constable. With these, the key is to try to relate them to the museum's collections or publications, and perhaps to provide a brief bibliography with the suggestion that the enquirer makes use of local library or school library services to obtain the relevant reading matter. As many of these enquiries come from educational establishments, this work should have been done by the appropriate teaching staff, but frequently it is not, and as the guardians of the nation's heritage, whether or not supported by public funds, museum staff have a clear duty to obey the golden rule. Children grow up to become taxpayers and ratepayers, and a polite letter, pinned on the classroom wall, may ensure that they are lifelong Friends of museums.

Requests from teachers

General educational enquiries will normally be the province of the museum's education staff who will have their own resources in terms of loan material, literature and visual aids. Whether or not such services are available, it is useful to provide a room where teachers can study, and, if the museum's col-

lections justify it, a small reference collection can prove useful. This provision also applies to older students, who may have a clear idea of what they require, but do not need to obtain other than general information on their chosen subject.

Lectures

Most curators will receive requests for talks and lectures to local groups: Rotary Clubs, Women's Institutes and specialist societies are typical examples. Most of them will meet in the evenings, but the advantage to the museum in terms of explaining its purpose to a sympathetic audience, and even the possibility of locating a potential acquisition, is so great that every effort should be made to fulfil the request. It is useful to develop a small range of subjects, since such organizations are not always certain what they want, and they can then be given a choice. As regards fees, it is well to establish a standard practice in consultation with the museum's governing body, and even if no fees are offered, a donation to the museum's purchase fund can usually be arranged.

Requests for talks on television and radio are increasing, particularly with the growth of local radio and other television channels, and they undoubtedly represent a future growth area. The potential advantages to the museum movement are immense, and every opportunity should be taken not only to accept such requests, but actively to seek them. Possible resistance from governing bodies may arise over the allocation of fees or outdated ideas of professional anonymity, but a previously agreed policy should remove most of the implied difficulties: ethical ones are discussed elsewhere.

Objects for identification

Very many enquiries will be concerned with objects. The motivation of the enquirer will range from a simple desire to know what it is, through to the hope that the object has some financial value. The distinctions are rarely, if ever, clear cut, and the curator may be confronted with items culled from every aspect of natural and human history, and in every sort of condition. The range and demand is so great that some system s necessary, and this is normally treated as an enquiry service.

Method

There can be no doubt that the best approach is to see the enquirer personally. This is what is expected, and offers the best method of assessing the enquirer's goodwill. Individual interviews are, however, time-consuming, even if some arbitrary time limit is imposed. Sometimes too, there may be a need to consult works of reference or other persons with specialized knowledge. There is also the risk that information given verbally is misunderstood, even subsequently distorted, and, hence, a written answer may be preferable.

In some museums it may be possible to provide a duty officer, or to stipulate certain times when enquiries can be brought in. In others, enquirers may be asked to leave the object, to which a written answer will be supplied by a defined date. If the latter course is adopted, documentation is essential, and the main headings of an enquiry form are set out in *Table 52.1*. For many museums a duplicate copy will suffice, but in large institutions it may be necessary to have more than one copy for departmental or administrative purposes.

Proper provision should also be made for the *immediate* photography of interesting objects which the owner may wish to retain, and other relevant details recorded in such a way that they could later, if necessary, be related to the object in question or included in general records of such data held by the museum or other bodies. Accurate map references of the find, details of previous ownership, artists signatures, hallmarks, and similar related facts should not be overlooked.

Table 53.1 Basic details for an enquiry form (optional items in brackets)

Name and address of enquirer (Mr. Mrs., Miss, Ms., etc., postcode, telephone number)	Date received By
(Name and address of owner if different from above)	
Brief description of objects, number of items, condition if damaged	Recorded by
Where found or how obtained	
Type of information required	
(Record of transit to department(s) if appropriate)	
Report (By)	
Receipt to be given to enquirer and presented on retrieval	Serial number
Conditions of acceptance (Opinion only, no valuations, responsibility, possible disposal)	
Signed by enquirer	Date

Problems

It is obvious that no museum, however competent its staff, can be expected to identify every enquiry with accuracy. Various courses are, therefore, open. In practice, it is usually fairly easy to be able to decide whether an object may warrant further investigation or whether it does not; though the middle ground is occasionally difficult to determine. It would be wrong to trouble specialist colleagues with trivia, just as the failure to identify a masterpiece could have obvious repercussions on the reputation of the museum. As stated above, the curator should try to build up a list of colleagues or local people who might be able to help.

There can be no definite rules, but a catholicity of interest when visiting other museums can prove of inestimable help.

Operating an enquiry service

The following rules should apply:

(1) The system must be efficient and reliable, ensuring that objects are not confused, are kept safely and are available for collection on time.
(2) If the object is damaged a note of this should be made in the presence of the enquirer.
(3) The provision of replies should always be properly delegated to a responsible officer.
(4) Written reports should be brief, but courteous and informative.
(5) It must be made clear in writing that the report is an opinion only, not a guarantee of authenticity or otherwise. Some museums also emphasize the right of an officer to refuse to give information, though this is an ethical matter which is discussed in Chapter 11.
(6) Some detachable form of receipt, recording the enquirer's acceptance of relevant conditions is essential, and no enquiry should be returned without the presentation of this receipt.
(7) If enquiries tend to be relatively repetitive, a duplicated sheet may be useful, and can provide more detail than might otherwise be practicable.

Conditions of acceptance

The following are important:

Valuations
It must be stipulated that valuations will not be given. Apart from being the proper province of professional valuers, museum staff have not the necessary experience, nor is the practice conducive to the museum's image as a trustee. Some museums will provide a list of local licensed valuers and/or dealers, but the ethical problems are obvious, and the practice is perhaps best avoided.

Authentication

The enquiry form should state clearly that the report is an opinion only, and *not* an authentication of the object. Nevertheless, there is no satisfactory means of ensuring that the form is not subsequently used to enhance the sale value of the object. Worse, it might even be associated with a similar object which did not fully correspond with the written report. In such circumstances, the legal position is by no means clear, and for the present the situation can only be regarded on trust. It seems unwise, therefore, for opinions to be signed, and some code reference is to be preferred, if one is needed.

Responsibility for loss or damage

While it has been the practice to print a disclaimer on an enquiry receipt, it is no longer likely that this could be sustained in law, and it is, therefore, desirable to arrange insurance coverage.

Disposal of uncollected items

In larger museums this is normally covered by specific legislation and by the *Local Government Act 1982* in respect of local authority museums. In other cases the curator should consult the legal advisers to the governing body.

Enquiries involving external work

Some enquiries will evoke a need for a visit outside the museum by a member of staff. Advice on an object which cannot be moved or the discovery of a potentially interesting site are typical examples. Decisions in this respect are difficult and can easily become the prey of underemployed auditors. Each case will need to be judged on its merits, and the main guidelines will need to be whether the information so gained is likely to be of advantage to the museum. In practice, this apparently simple yard-stick is not as simple as it appears, for though the object of the enquiry may be relatively trivial, the opportunity to talk to individuals may elicit information which can prove very helpful.

The author, leaving a house after inspecting some relative trivia, found a superb bronze age axe acting as a door-stop, while an Anglo-Saxon vase was observed by a colleague maintaining a complement of geraniums in a cottage window. No line save common sense can be drawn, but certainly any total prohibition should be resisted.

General administrative problems

Priorities

It must be recognized that in some museums there is a strong feeling that internal work, by a relatively limited staff, on and with the collections, is of paramount importance, and enquiries other than those of a specialized nature, are a distraction from the primary objective. It is not the purpose of this paper to argue this issue, and it can be appreciated that a museum of national repute will tend to attract enquiries far beyond its resources to give them individual attention. While it must be for each museum to establish its own policy, nevertheless there would appear to be a duty – at least in museums supported by public funds – for some degree of response. As education and leisure continue to develop, it is evident that this pressure will increase, and further thought will need to be given to the best ways of dealing with it.

Charging for enquiries

Proposals for charging for enquiries are a hardy annual. In essence, if the philosophy of answering enquiries in order to obtain information for the museum and to render a service is accepted, charging can be clearly shown to be potentially counter-productive. To charge someone for bringing in a specimen which he might subsequently desire to donate would be embarrassing, to say the least. A gentle reminder and a handy donation box would seem to be the best source of revenue in this area. If a charge were made for an identification which subsequently proved to be incorrect and caused financial loss to the enquirer, it might be agreed that the payment to the museum would lend support to any claim for compensation.

Our own enquiries of others

It is relevant to give some consideration to the other side of the coin: enquiries made of others by museum staff. As a profession we should all be prepared to help our colleagues, whether it be by the provision of statistics or with detailed knowledge of our own subject. It is, therefore, incumbent upon us to ensure that the information required is clearly set out, and especially if the ubiquitous questionnaire is employed, there is sufficient space of the answers and the inclusion of any limiting factors. As a simple example, bald statements of annual expenditure can be of little relevance unless distinctions are made between capital and revenue expenditure. The former will be largely determined by the size and age of the appropriate premises. Subject-based enquiries should be as specific as possible, since it is much easier to provide answers if it is known exactly what is required.

Passing on information

Thus far, enquiries have been considered in the passive sense, i.e. those directed to the museum. There is, however, an active element which is frequently overlooked. It is best defined as the stimulation of research by the communication of information gained from enquiries to potentially interested sources. For example, there is a clear responsibility to communicate new information to such organizations as biological data banks, sites and monuments records and the annual surveys of bodies concerned with particular fields of study. Similarly, a museum known to have a major, specialized holding in a particular subject area should be informed if relevant information is acquired elsewhere.

It is the proper responsibility of museum staff to be aware of the activities of kindred organizations in their chosen discipline, and to make suitable provision for them to be informed. This can only be achieved by consultation and personal co-operation, but it should not be difficult to determine, and once determined to adhere to it.

Conclusion

Few, if any of us, could honestly admit that there has never been an occasion when, just as we were starting for lunch or finishing a show-case, we have not harboured un-Christian thoughts towards the person at the other end of a ringing telephone.

As the most memorable form of instruction, therefore, two parables may form a fitting conclusion. Both are true. A certain curator, hastening to retrieve a Bronze Age founder's hoard, just discovered on a housing estate, was approached in the entrance hall by a person holding a grubby paper bag. Resisting the temptation to refer the enquirer to the desk, he opened the bag. It was the Snettisham torc.

Three minutes before the author's museum was due to close, a man entered the office with four Charles I half-crowns.

'They look like a hoard', I said. 'Was this all you found?'

'How did you know?' he said. 'I didn't bring the other hundred.'

The hoard is now in the museum.

Acknowledgements

This paper is principally indebted to the Museums Association's Information Sheet No. 11, 'Museum enquiries' by Rachel M. R. Young (1972), which it condenses, but could not presume to supersede.

The author is grateful to Dr D. A. Bassett, Director of the National Museum of Wales, for his constructive comments. Thanks also to the many museums who have, over the years, provided information as to their enquiry services, and to all our enquirers, knowledgeable, knowledge-seeking or nutty, who, through their faith in museums, broaden our experience.

References

YOUNG, R. M. R. (1972), *Museum Enquiries,* Museums Association Information Sheet 11, Museums Association, London

Bibliography

CAMERON, D. F. (1982), Museums and public access: The Glenbow approach, *The International J. of Museum Management and Curatorship,* **1**(3), 177–196

GIBBS-SMITH, C. H. (1975), *The Arranging of Lectures,* Museums Association Information Sheet 8, Museums Association, London

GRIGGS, S. A. AND ALT, M. B. (1982), Visitors to the British Museum (Natural History) in 1980 and 1981, *Museums J.,* **82**(3), 149–159

MUSEUMS ASSOCIATION (1975), *Reproduction Fees, Photography etc: Guidelines for Museums,* Museums Association Information Sheet 20, Museums Association, London

MUSEUMS ASSOCIATION (1979), *Careers in Museums,* Museum Association Information Sheet, Museums Association, London

PARK, E. (1977), 'Why do we want your grandfather's teeth? in *The Smithsonian Experience,* Smithsonian Institution Washington, DC

ROYAL ONTARIO MUSEUM (1976), 'Arrival and orientation' in *Communicating with the Museum Visit. Guidelines for Planning,* Royal Ontario Museum, Toronto

SHARPE, T. AND ROLFE, W. D. (1979), 'Geological Enquiries', *Museums J.,* **79**(1), 61–62

54

Relations between educational, curatorial and administrative staff

Stephen Locke

Effective museum work draws equally on a person's capacity to use individual talents and flair, and an ability to work with others as a team. The importance attached to a curator's ability to make a special personal contribution, usually enhanced by regarding the curator as individually responsible for collections and allocating to him substantial responsibility in this regard at a relatively early state in his career – can militate against achieving integrated team-work when this is required. If this is a problem, it can be exacerbated when curatorial staff work closely in association with staff who serve the museum in different capacities and who frequently have different, or non-academic, backgrounds and experience. The curator is properly considered the central figure in the museum, his direct association with the collections – the *raison d'etre* of the museum – gives him a particular status and it is a small step from agreeing that the care of the collection is crucially important, to regarding the interest of the curator as paramount.

Usually in the past and commonly still today, the curator has undertaken a broad range of tasks encompassing all or many of the activities needed to operate a museum. We can distinguish clearly between a conservator, responsible for much of the physical care of collections, and the curator, identified with all the primary functions of a museum. The growth and increasing sophistication of museums has required in many cases the development of ancillary specialized skills such as education and administration, which can be seen by curators as eroding the comprehensiveness of their function.

While considering the relationship of curatorial, educational and administrative staff, it is worth remembering that there are numerous circumstances where a curator is still personally responsible for all these elements of museum work. Furthermore it should not be assumed from these prefatory

remarks that friction between curatorial, educational and administrative staff is frequent. Where a good relationship exists, there is obviously no problem, but it is to problems that attention must be addressed and hence the emphasis of this article is on potential sources of conflict.

The administrative function in museums

Administration and administrators impinge on curators in a number of ways in typical museums. The entire museum will usually be enveloped within the overall administration of the governing body. This is most clearly the case in local authority, national and university museums, where the museum is automatically subject to a comprehensive range of administrative procedures, where indeed it is part of, 'the administration'. Substantial elements of such administrations will apply regardless of the museum function, such matters as personnel and financial procedures applicable uniformly throughout an entire nation-wide system of government. In this, the most common situation, administrators will be applying procedures which have as their essence a demand for uniformity in as wide a range of circumstances as possible. This approach can run directly contrary to the curatorial attitude. Not only is curatorial practice frequently inconsistent from one museum to another, but the prime motivation of much curatorial activity is to emphasize the special character and importance of the collection and the curator's work. Although differences in motivation need not prevent the smooth integration of different tasks within the museum, the outlook of administrative and curatorial staff can be expected to broadly conform to the nature of their respective tasks and a degree of mutual antagonism is therefore possible.

Such a problem at a personal level is exacerbated when both parties are operating within a giant administrative framework which has been created to gain advantage from uniformity rather than to provide for unconformity. Local authority and university museums are additionally subject to a more restricted administrative framework consisting of procedures and rules which reflect local traditions and needs, which apply generally to numerous departments of which the museum may be the smallest. Moreover, administrative staff in such circumstances frequently possess, and take advantage of, a greater opportunity for mobility in their career, which is seen in terms of obtaining responsibility for a larger and more complex administrative field, regardless of function. Administrators can thus come to be regarded by curators as in some ways less committed to the fundamental purpose of the museum.

In 'independent' museums administration is likely to be solely orientated towards fulfilling the function of the museum. This can lead to a very positive attitude by both parties vested in a common purpose, but even so, important conflicts of interest can arise from the special pressures on these museums. These arise chiefly from the overriding importance of generating sufficient income (which stresses the importance of marketing the museum, and responding to the needs of those outside the museum) which is often a primary objective of the governing body vested in the administrative arm of the organization.

Finally, administration affects museums as it is practised within the museum itself. At this level the administrator is clearly identified by all staff and is personally accountable for his activities. But it follows that most of this activity will be conditioned by a much wider and powerful system imposed on the museum, with which any purely departmental procedures must conform.

The educational function in museums

Education is capable of the widest definition, but however defined would be regarded by most as a central function, and by many as *the* function, of museums. In the context of this article, education staff are considered to be those with a specific duty to directly teach, or help others to teach, through the medium of the museum, and have not themselves any significant duty to physically care for collections. It is, however, still the rule rather than the exception in many museums, that the curator has an important educational role, as defined above, in addition to caring for his collections. University and similar institutional museums have, of course, a primary responsibility to teach, in many cases to a very well-defined and often very restricted category of student. In some cases, such museums have sought to become

both more accessible and more attractive to a wider range of people, although a strongly didactic approach to their exhibitions and other services still predominates.

Where educational staff have been introduced, the educational role of the curator is likely to diminish, partly because another member of staff with the specific brief to undertake this role and the ability to concentrate solely on it naturally attracts more of the appropriate tasks to himself, and partly because the introduction of education staff is often the result of a management policy to codify and concentrate duties among staff. As with administrative duties therefore, this process can diminish a curator's role, and it is at least arguable that if this occurs its implications can be more serious than the loss of an administrative role. In the first place, it is more likely to happen. The disparity in outlook between curator and education officer is likely to be less than between either of these and an administrator. Indeed, while education officers frequently enter museums from formal teaching backgrounds, many are recruited through the curatorial mainstream. The curator and the education officer see themselves as allies, mutually enhancing the museum in a very visible and attractive way. The curator may be delighted to be relieved of the responsibility for direct contact with educational parties with which he feels technically ill-equipped to deal. Increasing demarcation between education and curatorship follows all the more easily in an ethos of mutual esteem. There are of course advantages; the curator can have more time to concentrate on the care and study of his collection, the education officer should be a more effective teacher or teacher's guide, but there are possible losses also. The overall amount of educational activity can actually be reduced, particularly if a number of curatorial staff are relieved of educational duties which perhaps a single education officer cannot entirely replace. Moreover, even if a curator is not a good teacher in a technical sense, there can be a loss by reducing his interaction with an important section of the public: the students are denied an opportunity of direct contact with a specialist, and the curator loses an important source of influence and motivation. This is not to suggest that education officers are less than wholly useful in a museum, but it should be recognized that they and curators can do much to prevent the diminishment of any aspect of education in the museum.

As with administrators, but to a far lesser extent, education officers in museums can be part of, and subject to, a sphere of influence wider than the museum itself, which can affect their relationship with other staff. In a university, the museum may be seen as a small adjunct to the overall teaching resources, and onerous demands may be made on both curators and collections by specialist academic staff. It is not uncommon to find in local authority museums education staff who form part of the Local Education Authority (LEA). They may be based in district council museums where they expand the use of that museum for educational purposes and in addition perhaps administer a country-wide loan service. In any event, their defined region of interest may transcend the boundaries of the host museum's authority. In addition, their salaries and conditions of service may frequently be related to the Burnham scale and teachers' conditions of service, which can be better than National Joint Council provisions. Education officers may have responsibilities to senior advisors in the LEA and follow policies and priorities in relation to their work which are not determined by the museum. Her Majesty's Inspectorate of Education may also have a more direct role than they do in relation to the other activities of the museum.

On the whole, however, these influences are far more likely to be regarded as aligned to the purposes and motivation of the museums as a whole than administrative procedures are thought to be. Indeed, independence of thought is perhaps jealously guarded and nurtured (it is to be hoped) in the educational sphere more even than among curators. If the administrator represents convention and good order, then the education officer can represent the radical and iconoclastic element in the museum.

It is now possible to note some areas of activity where curatorial, administrative and education staff often have a common interest and where opportunities for effective liason exist alongside possibilities of friction.

The use of collections

Curators have a primary obligation to safeguard the collections in their care and frequently refer to their duty to preserve 'in perpetuity', 'for posterity'. This can lead to conflict with people who want to use the collections now and the curator's view of his duty towards the user of the future. In its most general form this factor can express itself in a wish to minimize any physical movement of or access to collections – almost any degree of fluctuation in the physical environment of collections is potentially harmful when measured against the infinite requirements of 'posterity'. Conflict can even arise between staff of museums as they seek to exploit the full potential of collections from their own particular point of view. Typical areas of stress involve: the research worker in relation to the scientific use of specimens; the education officer in relation to the active educational use of specimens; and the designer in relation to the presentation of specimens.

National, university and a number of provincial museums, have extensive collections which provide primary material for research, or were originally created as research collections, and may have staff actively undertaking such research in addition to outside researchers. In the fields of natural science and archaeology particularly, such research can require not only the very protected and close examination of specimens, but in rarer cases the physical alteration or even destruction of material. A variety of scientific procedures for examination and analysis can subject objects to manipulation, heat, radiation and intense light. In cases where the researcher is also the curator, it is particularly important that this dilemma is generally appreciated. Some kind of formal scrutiny of requests to examine important collections in a potentially damaging way, which could well embrace requests for loans outside the museum, is highly desirable, and in appropriate circumstances could utilize the advice of independent authorities.

The educational use of collections is a more frequently encountered and discussed problem in provincial museums. The museum educationalist is particularly concerned to add a unique dimension to interpretation and may eschew the photograph, graphic or video, in favour of the actual specimen to which he will seek to have the most intimate access possible. The obvious conflict inherent in this is exacerbated by the uncontrolled circumstances (for example, a large party of excitable children) which often prevail when this contact between people and objects takes place.

While the potential risks to material through display may seem less extreme, the vastly greater proportion of material involved and the duration of its display mean that in gross terms, this is the most important area of concern. The risks themselves are generally well known – excess light, variations in and levels of temperature and humidity, atmospheric pollution, emanations of vapour from display materials, physical exposure in open displays, reduced security and so on – and are increasingly guarded against, but few of these hazards can be eliminated entirely and most of them will persist indefinitely in permanent displays. Arrangements which reduce the risks are very likely to run counter to the requirement for a display to communicate effectively with the visitor.

All these situations exemplify the fundamental tension between the curator's perception of the need to preserve and the demands of the users of collections. While good curatorial practice can minimize risks, the conflict is surely in essence irreconcilable. Collection management involves a perpetual balance between the claims of the user now and in the future. An onerous responsibility devolves on senior management to consider this in relation to their own museum, perhaps in conjunction with wider circles of opinion, and ensure that the relevant staff have a common understanding of the museum's policy.

Overall security

Administrative staff are frequently responsible for security procedures, including such matters as key control, general staff access, public access and the instructions given to warding staff. The importance of fundamental 'human' security, (restricting keys, locking more doors more frequently, vetting visitors to non-public areas and so on) as opposed to reliance on technological security aids (burglar alarms) is very frequently underestimated in museums. The administrator, or security officer (who may be the same person, or colleagues in the same section), often has the difficult task of imposing regulations which are seen by curators as irksome, petty and distasteful. They reduce his own mobility, impugn his trustworthiness (usually correctly when it comes to caring for keys properly) and offend his esteemed scholarly visitors. The control of warding staff who have to interpret and 'police' regulations can provide further opportunities for conflict.

The overall attitude of warding and education staff to public and in particular children's behaviour is important to the educational use of the museum. General attitudes to what is permissible behaviour by young people can vary widely among teachers, education officers and museum attendants. The constraints of the museum itself (method of display and so on) and the priority it consciously or unconsciously accords to different cetegories of visitor, the type of activity encouraged by the education staff, and the attitude of the visitors to the museum, can all make a common approach to discipline by the museum staff responsible for such matters, exceedingly difficult to attain. It is not unusual to find that the museum has not clearly determined how responsiblity for discipline of school parties should be allocated between the education staff, staff accompanying the party, and the warding staff. This is an obvious cause of friction and difficulty but can be removed easily by proper management.

Environmental control of the museum

Museums have become more aware of the need to regulate temperature and the related factor of relative humidity, and lighting, to reduce deterioration of museum objects, so there is a need for far more control of the day-to-day operation of heating and lighting equipment. Here there are boundless opportunities for conflict. At the outset, different demands exist; those of good conservation practice (usually lower temperatures, lower lighting levels), economy

(the same), and those of static warding and other staff (higher temperatures) and the public (variable). Imposed on this, particularly in the many museums lacking centralized systems, is the day-to-day operation of equipment. If security discipline is frequently casual, control of heating and lighting can be chaotic. Frequently anybody can and does switch equipment on and off and alters controls. This can even include local authority technical departments arriving at rigidly defined dates (for example May 1st and October 1st) and simply turning off, or on, the heating plant. This is enormously difficult to control except by physically denying access except to authorized personnel, itself a cumbersome and complex task. Standing instructions and memoranda frequently suffice only for a matter of days. One can say that this is a far from trivial matter which management must make an effort to solve in an appropriate way. The interests of no one party can be regarded as paramount and certainly the matter is one of those genuinely requiring discussion and advice from all types of staff. As it is, the administration is usually, by default if not by policy, ultimately responsible for the day-to-day control of heating, ventilation and lighting systems, and they cannot be blamed if they do this in the absence of a clear brief as to the objectives of this control.

Accessioning procedures

The administrator, either directly or through control of clerical staff, is frequently responsible for some element of the accessioning procedure. At the least this is likely to involve responsibility for typing records, but more sophisticated tasks can also be the duty of the administrator. In this field there usually will be a clearly understood and defined procedure, and problems are more likely to arise because of the actual implementation of the system by either party, for instance the priority given to the work by clerical staff, the quality of their work, or, on the other hand, the difficulty of processing information presented badly by curatorial staff.

Loans, transport and insurance

Similarly, these are all fields where the administrator is likely to be responsible for initiating or at least channelling action. In some cases, especially local authorities, there may be overall rules relating to hire of transport or the allocation of insurance which may inhibit the flexibility of the administrator and may indeed make it difficult to reach the proper standard demanded by the curator. An administrator can have an important role in advising the authority that such rules may be preventing the museum achieving a proper standard and seeking to change them and interpret them as flexibly as possible. At the same time, curators can be lax in foreseeing eventualities and consequently unreasonably annoyed when their last-minute demands for transport or insurance cannot easily be met.

Health and safety at work

The *Health and Safety at Work Act 1974,* imposes an absolute requirement on everybody at work to operate an effective system for monitoring and improving health and safety. In fact it creates a legal requirement to devise just such a system of overall awareness and common purpose as is so frequently lacking in such fields as museum security and control of the museum environment. We must assume therefore that in health and safety matters a proper policy will exist. The administrator may well be a key person, combining the role of safety officer, or working closely with the safety officer. He is likely to be specifically responsible for the maintenance of hazard books, for instance, and the correct processing of action arising from the use of hazard notices. Because of his common role as supervisor of the warding and handyman staff and in relation to general housekeeping of the museum, he will usually be the clearing house for health and safety matters at a more informal level. And for these reasons also, he of course has an important direct influence on the standard of health and safety achieved. The requirements of health and safety can conflict with people's personal, ingrained attitudes and behaviour and since, contrary to widespread belief, the act does not lay down a host of standards applicable to everyday situations, the opportunities for conflicting interpretations of what is reasonably healthy and safe, are great.

General housekeeping

This omnibus category includes much of what has already been mentioned, but it is worth emphasizing that the administration will generally be responsible for (indeed is perhaps at fault if not) the daily comings and goings in the museum. Collection and delivery of goods, entry by workmen to spaces otherwise under curatorial control, the maintenance of the building, are all matters which can have the utmost importance in the museum context. It is widely agreed that the most substantial proportion of deterioration of museum objects is due to bad housekeeping, and some of this can be due to administrators not being sufficiently aware of potential dangers to collections. Consequently, access to vulnerable material is permitted to people not aware of the dangers, and maintenance and building processes are

allowed which are incompatible with conservation. Conflict can arise when routine programs of maintenance, financed from the museum's budget but controlled by an outside technical service or architect's department, are imposed. Such a situation can lead to expenditure which is not aligned to the museum's view of its own priorities. Again the capable administrator can be a creative force in identifying this situation and seeking beneficial flexibility within the system.

Financial control

Any museum with more than one member of staff spending money needs some centralized control of day-to-day expenditure. The types of control vary widely. On the one hand the administrator may be specifically responsible for making out all orders for goods and services and subsequently arranging financial transactions, and in this way directly controlling day-to-day expenditure. Alternatively, the curator (or other spending officer) may have considerable freedom to spend money within an agreed budget. In this case the administrator will have a crucial role in advising spending officers of the budgetary position, and to be able to do so, all financial information must ultimately pass through his hands. This is in fact almost invariably the case. But in the same way as the bringer of bad news is frequently blamed for the content, it is all too easy for the administrator to be identified personally with the harsh realities and consequences of financial restrictions. In the many independent museums which lack the overall financial support of a public authority, the control of cash flow will be a very important factor. In many such museums, expenditure must be related to annual cycles of cash flow (for example seasonally varying income from admissions) and the necessity to eliminate or reduce loan charges is paramount. This not only calls for effective specific control procedures, but a good all-round understanding by all staff of the financial position of their museum. It is quite common for the financial officer of an independent museum to be an honorary official, serving the institution voluntarily in his spare time. This can increase the problems of communication and add to the problem if a volunteer is controlling an aspect of a paid official's work.

Secretarial and clerical services

Museum clerical and secretarial staff, serving a wide range of curatorial, education and technical staff, are usually supervised by the administrator, who is responsible for 'the office'. At an ordinary human level, opportunities for conflict obviously exist, and the administrator may have considerable sympathy for his clerical and secretarial staff when they complain of egotistical, irascible, careless and tardy curatorial and education staff. Staff outside the office who expect perfect typing from illegible, highly technical manuscripts, who have no idea what is involved in despatching a large mailing of franked post of assorted weights, whose manner to the switchboard is obstreperous, cannot expect to receive an ideal service from the office and usually won't. Blissfully unaware of his own tactlessness, he blames the administration for yet further obstuctions to the grand curatorial purpose.

Personnel matters

The administrator will usually be responsible for the administration of personnel matters such as holiday entitlements, sickness provision, travel and subsistence payments and some aspect of the routine salary payment to members of staff. Invariably the entitlement to such provisions will be clearly defined in the appropriate conditions of employment and the administrator will probably only need to make the simplest and most obvious interpretations as to the applicability of regulations. Nevertheless, he can be associated with very personal matters and sometimes with decisions that are not liked by the other member of staff, and this can make overall relationships more difficult.

Exhibition policy

Museums differ in how they determine the content, appearance and function of display and exhibitions. In some the curator has still the paramount influence, determining not only the content and scope of the display, but its general style of appearance and also perhaps details of decor. In others, a more corporate approach is taken and a greater variety of staff involved in discussions about many facets of the display. It has long been urged that education officers have a most important role to play here. In many museums, the education officer's particular customers are a very substantial proportion, sometimes the majority, of visitors and furthermore, customers that the education officer has usually closely accompanied around the museum. Education officers indeed often have a greater knowledge of public reaction to the museum than any other member of staff. The same can be true of warding staff, whose channel of communication can often be the administrator. Both these groups of people can also have a sharp awareness of the ability of the public to grasp various concepts and the misunderstanding and misinterpretations which occur as a result. Education officers are

likely to have formal knowledge of this factor. Both education and administrative staff will have an important interest in many practical aspects of display and exhibitions, as they have their own responsibilities for helping people use the displays, and for the security and cleanliness of public areas. Even when the museum management does not feel it appropriate to accept some of the major and radical suggestions about display policy which can emanate from education officers and administrators, both these groups can make a very useful contribution to the more detailed working out of any exhibition.

Some conclusions

It is perhaps necessary to repeat that we should not expect commonly to encounter within museums this catalogue of potential problems, even though it is incomplete. The problems are primarily addressed from the point of view of the impact of the administrator upon the curator, for although it is true that curators can be responsible for much inefficiency and ineffectiveness, it is also true that they do represent the central function of the museum. The administrator should serve the curator, to the extent that the curatorial function is paramount. But curators and good curatorship do not necessarily march hand in hand and there will be occasions when curatorship can be greatly enhanced by effective administration. It has been known for curators not to accept this fact. And for curators, in almost every case, we can read education, and indeed technical, staff. In summary, some common factors can be identified and suggestions made for the reduction of conflict.

(1) Administrators frequently work within a large-scale administrative framework which emphasizes consistency and routine. Aspects of this system can militate against good curatorship and in this case a united effort by the museum as a whole should endeavour to alleviate this problem.
(2) Administrators frequently find themselves working in just those areas which seem broadly within most people's knowledge and to be susceptible to plain common sense. At the same time these areas are those that affect everybody in the museum closely and personally. Since, on closer examination, it often needs more than plain common sense to regulate the day-to-day operation of a museum, it is important that management, as a priority, ensures that there are good policies, properly defined and fully understood by all affected, for the operation of museum housekeeping, security, environmental control, clerical and financial procedures, health and safety and related matters. There is no field in which participation at all stages of formulating and implementing policies so genuinely involves all staff.

(3) There is a tradition of independence of thought among curators and a tendency to resist the application of disciplined analysis of their function. Combined with the acknowledged primacy of the curatorial function, this can lead to a degree of arrogance among some curators which makes their relationship with any staff difficult, and which only they can ameliorate.

(4) Relative to curatorship, administration tends to be held in low regard generally and administrative posts in museums lowly graded. In these circumstances it is questionable whether museums can demand the quality of administration they require. There is a need to enhance the regard and quality of museum administration.

(5) Where education officers work in museums it is important that the fundamental educational role of the curator is not diminished. Education officers should regard curators as one of the resources of the museum and seek to engage them appropriately in the specifically educational work of the museum.

(6) Education officers particularly, and administrators also, can make a valuable contribution to general display policy and as they have important responsibilities in relation to displays, their views on certain practical details shoild be sought as a matter of course.

SECTION FOUR

MANAGEMENT AND ADMINISTRATION

Section Editor

John M. A. Thompson

55

Introduction

John M. A. Thompson

The series of papers which comprise this section cover important areas which demand the time and attention of senior staff in museums and which require a range of new knowledge and skills which have until recently been outside the scope of the traditional curriculum of training for museum work. The usual career progression of the majority of museum professionals is such that the major part of the new responsibilities and duties of curators and senior staff lie in areas covered by this section.

One of the dilemmas to be faced by the senior museum professional is that museum services are now provided against a background of increased demand from a more informed public which coincides with a period of constraint in public expenditure. At the same time, there is a growing awareness by the governing bodies that museums have inherited special problems arising from the care of collections and the maintenance and adaptations of the building in which they are housed which require higher levels of both capital and revenue expenditure. In spite of these difficulties, considerable progress has been made in improving existing museum facilities to a more acceptable standard and in establishing new museums to fill gaps caused by the inadequate coverage of certain subjects or as a result of geographical factors through which certain areas have been without museum provision in the past. That this has been achieved at a time of general recession in western Europe, and in many other countries, is recognition of the importance of museums to both cultural and economic development.

With higher levels of expenditure on museums, public authorities have encouraged new forms of management to ensure that the available funds are being used wisely to meet recognized needs. Techniques such as management by objectives, and planned program budgeting carefully adapted to museum requirements, are now widely practiced with gener-ally beneficial results. The clear definition of museum objectives and the recognition and acceptance of these by staff and committees alike is now as important as a statement of collecting policy and, if properly communicated to staff, can lead to a renewed sense of purpose and direction. The various management systems are aimed at deploying resources – whether financial, human or material – in most economic way to meet these objectives. Because priorities are likely to alter as policies change, management systems are designed so that the necessary adjustments can be made as and when required, within the resources then allocated.

The high costs of museum projects often require additional resources over and above the traditional funding through rates, taxes, or admission charges, in order to meet the costs involved. These have included substantial funds available under the special programs of government to assist the unemployed, and to improve the quality of life in inner city areas, as well as the European Regional Development Funds and, in a different form, sponsorship of specific projects by commerce and industry.

Atkinson's paper surveys the various types of financial assistance available to museums, and describes the advantages of the opportunities now available. In many of the new museums, where a mixture of financial resources are applied and where the majority of income is derived from paying visitors, there is an associated need for flexible management and entrepreneurial flair which assumes a degree of autonomy from direct central or local government control. The Association of Independent Museums now offers a portfolio of information and advice designed to assist this new type of museum in starting and development. The move towards greater independence and autonomy has also come from the established national museums and was recognized in the *National Heritage Bill 1983* whereby the former departmental museums, the Victoria and Albert Museum, and the Science Museum, have established boards of trustees with wide discretionary powers. The duties and responsibilities of trustees are described in the papers by Bowness and Fenton, the latter illustrating the way one body of trustees has adapted to changing circumstances by establishing special subgroups to deal with particular aspects of the work of the institution and continues to exercise a large degree of day-to-day involvement, perhaps greater than that described by Bowness.

The changes that have occurred in museums controlled by local government, particularly since the reorganization in 1972 are considered in the paper by Cheetham which emphasizes the need for formal co-operation between museums, especially within a county or region, to make the best use of available resources and to ensure that museum provision is evenly distributed across the country. There is clearly no consensus as to the most beneficial relationship between museums and the governing bodies other than that which can most readily provide a framework for the healthy development of museums and their services to the public.

The complexity of the tasks facing heads of museum services is illustrated in the managerial skills required in the adaptation of provision of new buildings and Hebditch's paper outlines the respective responsibilities of architect and client, and emphasizes the need for a clear definition of the purposes of museums in order that the new, or adapted, building can enhance and define the museum function. In a related paper, Sudbury outlines the new responsibilities of all staff, especially heads of services arising from recent legislation under the *Health and Safety at Work Act 1974*.

As well as becoming effective managers, heads of museums have to administer their services in accordance with the various standing orders and financial regulations of the authority, and through committees or subcommittees. Staff should understand the discipline of working within an annual cycle of committee meetings, where specialist officers and elected members, often from different backgrounds and disciplines, will have to consider jointly aspects of museum policy including staffing arrangements, financial matters, and building developments. It follows that the establishment of good working relations with other officers of the authority is an essential feature of effective management and the need for clear communication both written and verbal in the preparation and presentation of reports is necessary to enable decisions to be taken in a way which is sensitive to the needs of museums.

In the final analysis, the true source of professional strength lies in the people employed in museums. In order to make the best use of personnel resources, Diamond's paper emphasizes the importance of the staff structure as a way of meeting the needs of the organization, and illustrates how these are changing with an emphasis on new aspects in recent years including commercial development, the control and management of volunteers, and the need for greater financial control. A planned training program to meet the recognized needs of the institution, and as a way of developing the potential of staff at each stage in their careers, is one of the most important responsibilities of heads of museums and senior staff, if museums are to develop a common sense of purpose to meet the challenges of a changing society.

Bibliography

ELCOCK, H. (1982), *Local Government Politicians, Professionals and the Public in Local Authorities,* with a chapter by Wheaton, M. Methuen, London and New York

HAMBLETON, R. (1979), *Policy Planning in Local Government,* Hutchinson, London

REDCLIFFE-MAUD LORD AND WOOD, B. (1974), *English Local Government Reformed,* University Press, Oxford

HMSO (1972), *The New Local Authorities: Management and Structure. The Report of the Bains Committee,* HMSO, London

MUSEUMS AND GALLERIES COMMISSION (1982), *County-wide Consultative Committees for Museums,* HMSO, London

HM GOVERNMENT (1982), *The National Heritage Bill,* HMSO, London

56

Financial management

Frank Atkinson

This is not an essay on financial techniques. There are plenty of books available on this broad subject. Yet management techniques which may assist a museum's operation or development must be applied to certain sources of finance.

The variety of methods of funding a museum or art gallery may in the first instance be linked to the generally-accepted technique of dividing one's operation into *revenue,* (that is, day-to-day running) expenditure, and *capital* (that is, once-off) funding.

Revenue funding and expenditure

Revenue expenditure is without doubt the most regular and serious contender for attention. Future expansion and development may be desired but, if the operation is failing on a day-to-day or seasonal basis, then future development is better postponed unless it is seen as the only means of recouping the losses.

There are three chief sources of funds to match revenue expenditure: earned income (from, for example, admission charges and shop sales), annual grants (for example, local government annual estimates), and sponsorship.

Earned income

This leads, in terms of museums and galleries, into the ethical question of charging admission and will be dealt with later. However, from a purely economic point of view, it broadens into the field of marketing. The product has to be of a type which an audience desires, at the price which that audience will bear. If it is too esoteric, badly presented, or over-priced, then no amount of agonizing about 'ethics' will produce adequate finance.

At this point the precise economics of levying an admission charge must be considered, obvious though they may seem. For example, placing a ticket-seller at a doorway or gate is by no means the end of the cost. Wages, plus on-costs (national insurance, etc.), must be taken into account, and the other, less obvious, items examined, such as capital charges (repayments on borrowed capital), if any, incurred by establishing the charging point. There will also be associated costs such as rates, heating, lighting and cleaning. All this could well equal the wages payment. So is it worth while making an admission-charge in the first place? How much of the receipts will remain after all these items have been set against them?

Leaving the pros and cons of levying such a charge until later, let us take up the less controversial, though nonetheless complex, topic of running a museum shop. Is it to be entirely a major profit-earner or is it to proselytize for the museum? Whichever may be the case (or probably a mid-way position), one must not overlook the concealed costs of the operation. There may be an appreciable input of time and effort by a senior member of the staff – not only in establishing the shop but in the continuing purchasing policy. Accounting work by the office staff, plus rates, heating, lighting and cleaning and the easily-forgotten capital charges, must all be considered. Whether or not the museum has a cash-flow problem (and it must be accepted that a strictly local government museum may not), there is clearly a need for well-defined criteria and careful thought before deciding to open a museum shop.

One other technique for earning revenue receipts is worth mentioning – that of 'facility fees'. Probably more museums could earn in this way if greater thought was given to it. Charges can be made (and will be willingly paid) for special photographs which might be used for illustrating calendars, television films, books, and so on. Special television filming facilities can be made available under certain conditions, although a careful distinction has to be made between educational or children's programs and costume drama – not so much because the former is perhaps looked upon as 'more worthy', as that the latter has a vastly greater budget at its disposal. The *Museums Association Information Sheet on Reproduction Fees* (1975, No. 20, Museums Association, London) can be helpful here, but in the end the curator may well find himself in a bargaining situation, so it will be necessary to ensure that the auditor accepts this in advance.

Annual Revenue Grants. These should be regarded with some care, unless there is dependable long-term commitment. Look at them carefully: what will happen if the grant is suddenly cut or severely reduced? Can the museum withstand this, and if so by what means? On the other hand, is the museum giving good value for such a grant? Is its operation encouraging the grant-giver to continue with this generosity or indeed increase the grant? There may be justification, for example, for a revenue grant for something specific but ongoing, such as conservation or cataloguing. Equally, it may be thought that a particular visitor-oriented operation should be funded by way of the visitor. The Area Museums Service type of grant can, if properly planned, help along the lines suggested here.

Other grants may be specific, such as the purchase grants administered by the Science Museum or the Victoria and Albert. By careful control and planning these can effectively be seen as a means of upgrading the museum's purchase fund, even though each such grant is of course specific to the item being purchased.

The Manpower Services Commission has aided museums (as it has similar) operations, but is becoming increasingly concerned to aid only developments and specific finite operations, rather than ongoing commitments. This trend should be carefully monitored.

Sponsorship
This is supposedly a potential, major source of revenue funding, although general museum experience does not support this. Small sums (ranging from say £50 to £1000) may be available for popular museum activities, but few museums are likely to move into the multi-thousand-pound situation commanded by prominent sports with their television potential.

Major exhibitions in London have been funded by Sunday newspapers; leaflets and 'trails' have been funded by oil companies and one-day events may be supported by local breweries and the like, but apart from the first, these tend to be specific and relatively limited. It is true that cigarette companies and *The Illustrated London News* have supported the publicity

potential of the 'Museum of the Year Award', for several years, but nowhere is the kind of sponsorship that supports and maintains the major sports.

Nevertheless, this source of revenue funding cannot be entirely discounted, and serious thought must be given to the needs of the sponsor. Why should he provide the funds? What is in it for him? Will the publicity justify the expense? Equally importantly, is the event under consideration unique, or will he be expected to repeat the sponsorship next year? Sponsorship must not be confused with charity-giving, which will be dealt with later. The former is a strictly commercial operation to be funded out of the sponsor's advertising budget. Is the museum prepared to have the sponsor's advertising banner on its building and their logo on its printed material? Is it acceptable to have the exhibition linked with the product?

As to accounting for this expenditure, the sponsor will probably be satisfied with an approximation of cash spent, but with a certainty in terms of advertising material, whereas the Treasurer or Auditor will, of course, be concerned that expenditure and receipts match, if the sponsorship takes the form of a cash payment.

Capital funding

The word 'capital', in the sense used here, generally means 'accumulated wealth used in producing more'. Capital funds are therefore, in practical terms, used to pay for the erection of a building or some other singular operation such as fitting out a store or constructing an exhibition.

A museum's capital funds may be received in the form of a specific grant, or may be borrowed and repaid (together with interest) over a period of time which is related to the purpose for which they have been borrowed. Such loans are best left to financial experts. Arranging the best borrowing rates and – if the museum is not local government – the provision of collateral security, is complex. The chief point to note is that such loans are expensive and bear upon the operation for many years to come. If, by so borrowing, the museum is able to carry out some work which will generate a similar or greater income, then all is well. But the burden upon the revenue estimates should otherwise be seriously considered.

There may be an alternative, for times and techniques change. Thus, while it was once common practice for local government to cover, say, the purchase of a museum van by a fairly short-term loan, this would probably now be financed by a hire/maintenance agreement.

A similar 'grey area' can be seen in the grants made to museums through the Science Museum and the Victoria and Albert. These are generally matched by the recipient museum out of a revenue purchase fund, but could equally logically be treated as additions to the capital stock of the museum.

On the other hand most substantial grants are seen clearly as of a capital nature. Such may be grants from the Countryside Commission (for such projects as car parks or tree-planting) or from the national Tourist Board for some addition to the 'tourist potential' of a region.

The recent introduction of capital grants through the area councils, from the newly constituted Museums and Galleries Commission may be seen as a welcome, if small, addition to the stock-in-trade of the ambitious museum director. These grants tend, as do many national grants, to be 50 per cent of the approved expenditure on a specific project. They may not be exceeded, though they may be underspent. At a time of fluctuating rates of inflation, it may be advisable to ascertain whether a promised grant is a specific figure or whether it is 'inflation-proofed'.

Another recently introduced source of grand-aid is that obtained through the Department of the Environment, from the European Regional Development Fund (ERDF). A few, relatively major, grants have so far been made to museums, for sums around £100 000 to £200 000, in connection with 'the regional infra-structure'. These grants, needless to say, are not easy to negotiate (probably up to a year should be allowed for this procedure) and are for 30 per cent of the total estimated expenditure). Thus, 70 per cent of the total still has to be found, and this may be borrowed, begged or obtained as another grant. But it is important to note that the ERDF grant (in common with all nationally funded grants) may not be matched against another national grant.

In applying for any national or European grant the administrative processes should not be undertaken lightly. Not only is it necessary to have the full authority of one's committee or board, it is often equally necessary to have planning consent and building regulations consent in advance of making the application, as well as a certainty of being able to provide the other 50 per cent (or appropriate percentage). Good estimating is another prerequisite.

A moment ago the word 'begged' was used as suggesting an alternative means of 'topping-up' one's funds. This of course refers to the very real possibility of funds being raised by application to a trust, or by an appeal to industry, commerce and individuals. Some indication of the kinds of activities supported by various trust will be found in the *Directory of Grant-Making Trusts*.[3]. This of course needs to be read with great care and an application should not be made until one is conversant with the requirements of the selected trust. It can often prove helpful to write to the secretary of the trust in advance of making the formal application, and indeed visiting him, in order to discuss the problem.

The establishment of a development trust by the museum itself as a means of raising substantial funds is dealt with later. But it will not remove every problem! As with all capital developments, the task is not ended when that capital project has been completed. For beyond all this another spectre haunts which may not be immediately apparent. It was pointed out above, that 'capital' means 'accumulated wealth used in producing more'. So is your capitally funded construction work going to earn further funds? In museum terms it is more likely to cost an additional sum. What is the nature of this newly committed annual expenditure? It will include, inevitably, loan charges, rates, heating, lighting and cleaning. Probably it will also result in additional manpower costs. Are these included in future revenue estimates? And has allowance been made for any income which may be generated by this new operation?

In short, capital developments are not to be undertaken lightly. On the other hand, any organization which does not expand or diversify will eventually ossify. The choice may, therefore, be between a painful rebirth or a lingering death.

Admission charges

A good museum is not cheap to run. How are these costs to be recouped? Some may be avoided by the use of volunteers, and activities which would not otherwise have been undertaken may be supported by the temporary use of additional labour provided by the Manpower Services Commission. While the former may be a reasonably satisfactory and long-term measure, the latter must be viewed with caution. What happens if such a source of 'funding' ceases: if national policies are changed or regional emphases modified?

Many museums in Britain are funded by their Local Authority and, although rarely generous, such a source has seemed reasonably secure until recent years. Now financial restrictions and accounting 'realities' have revealed the danger of assuming that local authority funding is an inalienable 'right'. At the same time, the number of privately-funded museums has grown to a remarkable degree, culminating in the establishment of the Association of Independent Museums (AIM). So, is charging admission fees to museums the answer to these rising costs and falling revenues? The existing pressures should be examined before discussing the ethics of free admission.

It will be helpful to identify the two chief areas of expenditure required to run a museum. These must be *preservation* and *presentation*. The former covers such operations as collecting, cataloguing and conserving, while the latter will include display and interpretation. Even in an ideal world these two functions ought to be examined separately and justification for any public support decided according to their varied merits. It may, for example, be agreed that preservation is serving a communal need, being carried out for the benefit – in cultural terms – of the whole community. Presentation on the other hand benefits the individual (family group/tourist/schoolchild).

If this argument is upheld, then the community should support the (reasonable) costs or preservation as a matter of social responsibility, whereas the costs of presentation could be covered by admission charges to the individuals concerned. Even within this framework subsidies are still entirely possible, as for example, reduced (or free) rates for school parties and special rates to benefit local families/individuals, by reducing charges out of the tourist season. It is also possible to help the less well-off members of the community by, for example, offering reduced transport charges if the museum is sited away from the main centre of population.

On the other hand those who stand for free education and free public library services, will not readily accept this argument when it is differentially applied to museums. If visiting a museum is part of one's education, then surely it must be free to all. Yet nominal charges are frequently made for 'further education' and generally for the more specialized activities of libraries such as the loan of records and tapes, or the reservation of unusual or popular books. Perhaps a more positive approach is to make the museum so exciting and stimulating that a small charge is acceptable.

In conclusion, if pragmatism rather than passion is applied to the discussion, it may seem reasonable to anticipate that the preservation activities of the museum will be funded by the community as a whole, while the cost of maintaining a satisfactory presentation will be borne by the individuals who choose to view this, though subsidies can be selectively applied here, if so desired. In other words, instead of arguing about the 'ethics of admission charges', perhaps we should be considering the nature and degree of social benefit: what percentage of any such benefit should be subsidized, or what type of visitor should be specifically aided – or encouraged. It then follows that many institutions could reasonably consider raising a proportion of their funds directly from their visitors.

Before leaving the question of admission charges it may be helpful to stress the value of *marketing* as a discipline for museum curators. It is not good enough to dismiss this as irrelevant, nor intelligent to decry it. For however much we may deplore some of the jargon such as 'maximizing one's resources', the principles of good marketing are worthy of consid-

eration. In the words of this subject, most museums are *product-oriented* rather than *market-oriented*: they try to interest their public in what they have to offer, rather than producing something designed to satisfy a particular 'market' or group of people. They suffer accordingly. Is it not possible to go just a little further in deciding what type of visitor museums would like to entice, and then setting targets more towards this end?

As a footnote to the foregoing, and because not all museum curators are aware of the realities of commercial thought, mention may be made of the 'breakeven' graph. A diagrammatic example is illustrated in *Figure 56.1*, applied to a theoretical museum operation.

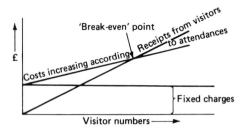

Figure 56.1 A 'breakeven' graph

Fixed charges are such things as telephone charges, rates, staff costs; *varying costs* include, for example, cleaning and additional security necessitated by increased numbers of visitors. In reality this 'varying costs' line is rarely straight, but advances in steps occasioned by, for example, additional attendant staff. The 'receipts' line will change its angle according to the actual level of admission charges.

Breakeven point is the position achieved when receipts equal outgoings. Beyond that point lie profits or, in museum terms, the possibility of having additional funds to apply to more and better activities, including those of conservation.

Fund-raising

If charging for admission is a means of matching revenue expenditure then fund-raising permits greater capital expenditure.

As indicated above, sponsorship is not the same as capital fund-raising: it is generally intended for support of a popular activity such as a one-day event. It is a direct charge upon the publicity budget of the commercial operator, and must therefore have some commercial content, whether this lies solely in the name of the event, or in associated advertising such as banners, logos and the like.

A development trust, however, is a long-term

attempt to encourage industry, commerce and individuals to support the overall capital development of the museum. It may anticipate obtaining grants from the charity budgets of industrial and commercial concerns, or it may go further and encourage such organizations to feel directly involved in the active growth of this meritorious activity.

Commercial organizations exist to provide the advice necessary to establish a development trust and, if so desired, to direct its operation. Alternatively an 'appeals director' may be appointed. In either case neither the museum committee nor its curator should think that their responsibilities in this matter have ceased. Active involvement by the museum staff is imperative if a lively program of fund-raising is to be achieved. Indeed, it is often the enthusiasm and obvious dedication of the staff which convinces those businesses and commerce that here is something worthy of support.

Finally, one cannot stress too greatly the need for a professional approach to this matter. For while it will be instructive to examine the brochure of successful fund-raising schemes and to identify the names of their trustees and appeals committees, it must be remembered that what generally makes them successful is their activities about which little is written: that which 'goes on behind the scenes'. Add to this a close application to routine work on a large scale and it will be seen that fund-raising should not be lightly undertaken.

Bibliography

BESTERMAN, T. AND BOTT, V. (1982), To pay or not to pay, *Museums J.*, **82**(2), 118–119

CHARITIES AID FOUNDATION *Directory of Grant-Making Trusts* (published annually).

WARE, M. (1982), *Fund-Raising*, (AIM Guideline 4), Publishing Association of Independent Museums

57

The management of premises

Max Hebditch

With the possible exception of religious observance, in no other activity is architecture so important as a means of communication as in museums and galleries. The curator ignores an understanding of the practice and aesthetics of architecture at his peril, not least because the artefact created for the expression of his museum purposes is in itself often part of the evidence for the historical continuum that he is presenting.

It follows, therefore, that museum buildings have evolved in response to changes in the liturgy of museum communications and the way in which museums see themselves as custodians of truth. This is perhaps most clearly seen in contrasting the attitudes expressed in the architecture of the great museums of the nineteenth century and those constructed today. The former saw themselves, in a world untrammelled by other forms of immediate communication, as educative institutions in which the needs of the scholar and the generally curious were met in one totally displayed collection wrapped in an appropriate architectural envelope. The British Museum (Natural History) is a particularly fine example.

The effect of nineteenth century policy was to make available to the many what had previously been the preserve of the few, whose privileges ranged from the possession of works of art to the time to undertake scientific research. This century has added other roles to museums, mainly in response to egalitarian thought. First, the range of the significant has been extended to include many more classes of material; second, the private possession of 'significant' material has come to be regarded as antisocial. Their most obvious manifestation in architectural terms is that new museums have to be constructed with vast stores for material, which would formerly have been either ignored or privately owned. Sadly, however, there is a danger that

architectural effort will still be concentrated mainly on the traditional gallery functions, rather than on the new obligations that museums have assumed.

Most curatorial staff will be faced with an examination of the architectural needs of an existing museum, often itself of some antiquity. In this context, a number of questions must be asked at regular intervals: is the fabric being maintained properly; is the best use of the available space being made; can the policies being pursued by the museum be fulfilled in this building, and, if so, for how long?

More rarely, the curator will have the opportunity to create new museum premises. It should be pointed out that no distinction need be drawn here between museums in buildings and so-called open-air museums, site museums or interpretative centres, although for convenience this article will call all of them museums, and treat them as if they were a single building. All pose problems requiring architectural solutions. New ventures will fall into three main categories:

(1) The re-use of premises originally designed for an entirely different purpose.
(2) The use of premises of historical interest, often related to the museum's own purpose.
(3) The commissioning of totally new premises.

To take the use of existing premises first; if no other use for a given site has been found, then it is probably not suitable for a museum. The exceptions to this rule mey be where those premises are subject to the constraints imposed by planning requirements, by listing or scheduling under the Historic Buildings or Ancient Monuments legislation, or where the overriding economic situation of the area makes any development unattractive. In general, though, the ease with which buildings can be made weatherproof and structurally sound, converted for new purposes, maintained at reasonable cost and made accessible for the public, will determine the suitability of the site for museum purposes. If an assessment of these points is favourable then the site could almost certainly be equally well used as offices, warehouses or a factory.

If a new building and site is on offer (at the present time this is often as an element of 'planning gain' in a much larger commercial development) then an equally keen examination is required. In particular, examine how far the realization of the value of the previous museum site or buildings is to be made available to the new building. Even if all the financial benefit accrues to the museum, will the new site afford the same number of visitors, for instance?

Any assessment, whether of the use of existing premises, of the possibilities of using other existing buildings, or of commissioning totally new structures must take account of the functions that are to be undertaken.

This process is described as 'programming' (Hume *et al*, 1979): a discipline which is applicable to many types of projects and which in large schemes may require specialists in this field alone as well as curators, architects, engineers and others. Programming exercises should do three things:

(1) Provide those who want the work done ('the client') with the aims of the project, the resources required and a system of control over their realization.
(2) Develop systems for transmitting information and instructions between the client, the architect, the contractors and other parties involved.
(3) Assist all involved in taking the correct decisions at the correct time in the light of the fullest information.

The stages into which programming falls are conveniently summarized in *Figure 57.1*. This process is not only applicable to commissioning new projects, but also to examining existing premises. As any museum is a dynamic organization, the programming assessment should also take account of for how long the proposed project will meet the needs which brought it into being.

The use of existing premises

No assessment of existing accommodation or plan for conversion to museum use of other premises can commence without forming some view of what the museum wants from it. This must reflect the priorities that the museum attaches to its various activities in the light of known and expected financial, staffing and collection resources. It is no good creating a space for a conservation laboratory if there is no possibility of staff to run it. The activities of a museum will need to be defined in the light of the individual

circumstances affecting each museum, particularly taking into consideration relevant administrative factors bearing upon each activity. Such factors will include: numbers and movements of people (both staff and museum users); numbers and movements of objects and related data; overall staff organization; the extent of exhibition production and other capabilities; conservation and other needs.

All the museum's activities and administrative requirements need to be formulated into a plan for the organization of the appropriate spaces within the existing museum or converted building. It is, of course, the basis of any museum operation that there should be a relationship with the public. Any thinking about space must aim to facilitate that relationship, whether with the casual visitor or the specialist. The reception of visitors is thus the kernel of the operation. Around this are grouped the resources of objects, information and expertise to which the visitor requires access. Around that are the various support services that are required to make a useful relationship between the user and the museum's resources. *Figure 57.2* indicates the various elements with some of the spaces needed for each.

Reception

The most essential requirement is an obvious front door and an entrance hall in which the visitor can orientate himself. The entrance in older buildings is usually more apparent than in modern buildings. The entrance hall should include space for waiting, sitting and the assembly of parties of visitors, with clear access to other reception areas. These may include toilets, public telephone, refreshment facilities, educational facilities, lecture theatres and shops. If provided, and if important as a source of income, the exit from the museum can be arranged through the shop. To service these public reception areas there must be non-public offices providing information facilities, ticket issuing arrangements and cloakrooms. It would not be unreasonable that these spaces plus the necessary corridors for communication within the building should take up perhaps 25 per cent of the space in a museum.

The museum's resources

It is usual to start an examination of the spaces needed by reference to the exhibition galleries. There are a number of dangers in this. First, it leads to the presupposition that the museum is designed around the exhibition. Second, it is assumed that other spaces are less important. Third, that what is inappropriate for public view (such as ducting and services) can be pushed into the 'less important' spaces. More usefully, the study should begin with an examination of spaces in which to accommodate

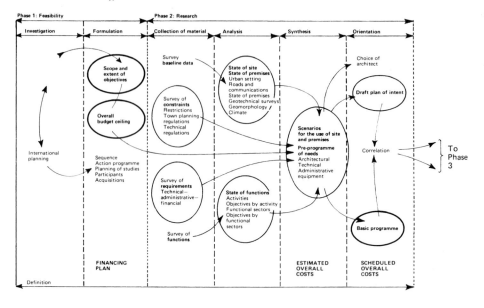

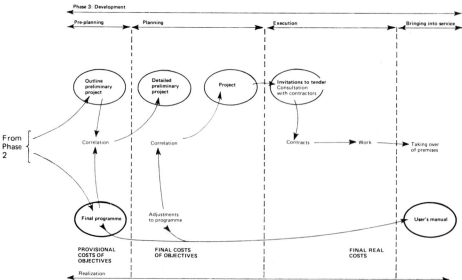

Figure 57.1 Stages in programming. Reproduced from Pecquet, C. and O'Bryne, P. 'Programming – a tool at the service of the curator . . .' in Hume *et al* (1979)

the main study collections. In this it will be necessary on central urban museum sites to balance what needs to be kept centrally, and what can be accommodated in out-of-town locations. It is well worth examining the approach of libraries to this problem (Thompson, 1977).

Related to the storage of collections are a number of other important areas. These comprise the archives in which paper, photographic, sound, video

and other records related to the collections are stored. These may be either recently generated, such as material related to archaeological excavations, or original records, such as business records linked to objects in the collection.

The use of both classes of data, objects and records, demands the provision of adequate study areas for use by visitors. Unhappily, many museums still do not provide the facilities to be expected in any

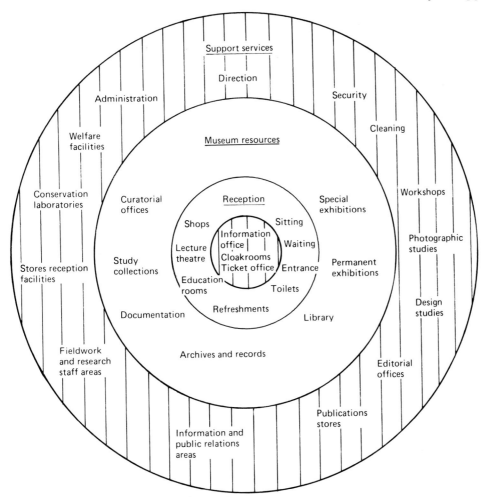

Figure 57.2 Relationship of functional elements in a museum plan (non-public areas cross-hatched)

reference library. This space, or one closely related to it should also accommodate the indexes to the material held, ideally in a way which permits consultation directly by the user rather than through the curatorial staff.

Other spaces which accommodate the resources the museum has available will include the main exhibition galleries, special exhibition galleries, the library and the offices of the curatorial staff; it is often forgotten that curators are supposed to be accessible to the public. The total spaces allocated to museum resources in a general museum might be as follows:

storage collections, storage areas, archives	25%
permanent and special exhibitions	30%
	55%

The individual percentages allocated to collections and exhibitions will vary according to the scale of collections and their importance.

Support services

In order to maintain and make available the museum's resources, space must be allocated to a range of support functions. General museum services include direction, administration, security, maintenance workshops, cleaning equipment stores, materials stores, mess rooms and welfare facilities. In support of the collections space must be found for conservation laboratories and studios, the reception (and decontamination if necessary) of incoming material and facilities for staff involved in fieldwork, research and collecting activities. In support of the presentation of the collections must be workshops, photographic facilities, design studios, offices for editorial staff, publications storage, information and public relations activities. Total spaces might comprise:

General museum services	3%
Collections support facilities	7%
Presentation support facilities	10%
	20%

Again, the relative proportions of each element may vary substantially depending on, for instance, the extent of a museum's involvement in research and collecting programmes in the field.

It is, of course, a prerequisite that any building for museum use should be structurally sound. The checking of this is a matter for a professional architect or a building surveyor. However, it is not difficult for the curator on a preliminary inspection to form some assessment of the soundness of walls, roofs, windows, floors and so on by applying the ordinary skills he or she would apply to buying a house. Similarly, one can make initial enquiries about planning proposals for the area which may affect an existing or proposed museum.

However, museums are often so desperate for accommodation that critical faculties are sometimes dimmed. Two points should be borne in mind. First, do not get so carried away with the potential of a site or building that the realities of siting or the cost of restoring a dilapidated structure are ignored. Second, remember the requirements of good access, plenty of storage space, good floor loadings, ample display space and so on, may be lacking – precisely the reason it may have been turned down by another user.

For the requirements of each museum space the reader is referred to the bibliography. However, there are some points which should be referred to a professional adviser. The environment required for museum objects is well-understood and the specifications for temperature, humidity, lighting and dust can all be provided. It is necessary to decide in each instance the extent to which the ideals can be achieved in relation to available finance and the importance of the material. However, impress upon the professional adviser that air-conditioning, if specified, is for the comfort of the collections, not the staff and public. Buildings must also be free of pests and any materials to be used should be unattractive to pests.

Floor loadings and ceiling heights must also be adequate to accommodate the proposed study collections or exhibitions. A height of 3.66 m and a loading of 4 kN/m^2 are the recommended minimum for flexible galleries, but many classes of material would probably require a higher floor loading. Adequate and flexible lighting systems must be provided.

There must also be sufficient hoists and lifts to enable the collections to be handled properly from arrival in the museum, to store and to display. Buildings must also be capable for being made secure, and safe both for the staff and visiting public.

Above all, in areas where collections, archives and other records are to be stored or exhibited, the services for the building must be arranged in such a way that the risk of damage from water, fuel oil and other materials is reduced to the minimum and all necessary servicing is undertaken wherever possible from outside these areas. The objective is to ensure that if any part of the system fails, the collections are not placed at risk from leaks, or from a person trying to put the matter right.

In considering the use of an existing building, or proposed alterations to enable another building to be used for museum purposes, or in new works in an existing building (including exhibitions), there are numerous acts and regulations which have to be observed. Here are some:

(1) *Health and Safety at Work Act 1974.* This places upon everyone, but heads of museums and senior staff in particular, a responsibility to ensure that both those who work in a museum and those who have any reason to visit it can do so safely. Failure to do so is a criminal offence. Particular attention should be paid to machinery. Related to this are the *Factories Act 1961* and *Office Shops and Railways Premises Act 1965* and other regulations. There are also numerous codes of practice relating to everything from safety to control of noise from intruder alarms.

(2) Planning regulations. Certain sorts of work, and all those involving changes in the use of premises, require planning consent. There are also the special consents required in relation to the use of historic buildings and ancient monuments under their own legislation.

(3) Building regulations. Virtually nothing can be done to a building that does not require the local authority to give building regulations approval. This includes the construction of exhibitions. Related to this are the various regulations governing prevention of fire, which are extremely rigorous and severely limit the choice of fabrics and other materials used in exhibitions.

In all these matters the curator will require professional advice from an architect and also advice from the chief fire officer, the building inspector and possibly a professional safety consultant. It is always wise to establish close contact with the fire department, not only at the initial planning stage but with regard to any future plans. It is also very necessary to bear in mind the needs of handicapped visitors, not just the obvious ones of those in wheelchairs, but the needs of the infirm and hard of hearing as well.

Finally, the commissioning of almost any new works in a public authority museum requires set procedures for tendering to be followed where contracts are above a certain figure. Independent museums should also adopt standing orders to govern this aspect of museum work since if in receipt of public funds they are also open to public scrutiny.

Museums are often located in historic buildings. Apart from the additional planning requirements already referred to, the curator has certain professional responsibilities to observe. The building is itself an artefact, as important as any other item in the collections. If considering the use of a historic building, it is necessary to ensure that any proposals respect the historical and architectural significance of the building. These 'curatorial' qualities in a building are not always so obvious to architects, who may be influenced either by aesthetic considerations alone, or worse, by spurious olde-worldiness of the 'wealth of exposed beams' kind. But both architectural and historical considerations can fall foul of building regulations in general, and fire regulations in particular. Enclosing staircases, the installation of escape routes and sprinklers are well-known problems, but discussion with appropriate inspectors at a very early stage can sometimes lead to relaxations or other solutions which minimize the damage to the building's qualities. In general, however, historic buildings should not be entrusted to architects without their having the fullest possible briefing as to the significance of the building.

Any building needs maintenance requiring both organization and money. In most public authorities the organization will be in the hands of an architect or surveyor in charge of the authority's property. It is essential that adequate funds are provided for the purpose, if expense of a major nature is not to arise at some future date to rectify a serious defect. In looking at maintenance, it is necessary to consider a number of elements and make financial provision accordingly. First, there are the charges for the consumption of energy. This will include gas, oil, electricity and water. In some instances, where these commodities are being used in conjunction with sophisticated ventilation and heating systems in the building, it will be necessary to employ engineering staff to operate them. Alternatively, where a museum shares a system with other users, a percentage of the personnel costs in running the system may be passed on. Second, there are the costs involved in providing maintenance contracts for fixed plant and equipment. These will include lifts, hoists, fire and burglar alarms and television monitors. Third, there will be cleaning contracts for windows, and possibly also for offices and public areas. Fourth, there will be structural maintenance. The arrangement of a planned cycle of repainting and washing of the fabric is straightforward. The cycle will include internal and external work and indicate the frequency required for key areas such as external paintwork, and gallery walls. The frequent repainting of areas such as toilets and the immediate rectification of damage is essential if vandalism is to be minimized. Other maintenance items, such as the replacement of carpets or the resurfacing of car parks, will be in much longer cycles. In addition, the standard maintenance programme must include provision for unforeseen problems, such as damage to the building and, since museums are dynamic institutions, minor building works to accommodate the museum's changing needs. The costs of energy and maintenance can be high, perhaps 20 per cent of the total expenditure of a museum, excluding rent or debt charges. Do not forget, also, that although museums operated by charities will be partially exempt (often to the extent of 50 per cent) they will nevertheless incur some liability for local authority rates.

Commissioning new buildings

From time to time it does happen that museums are able to commission new buildings or to make major works of adaptation to existing premises. The importance of sound programming has already been stressed. The disciplines imposed by that process are important to realizing the full potential of existing or proposed assets.

The main consultant with whom the curator will deal in this process is the architect and the relationship between these two people, or groups of people, is very important. However, although the curator may see himself as the client, this is not always the case. The commissioning authority and ultimate paymaster may often be the museum's controlling authority. It is thus very important that the curator's precise position in the relationship between the commissioning authority and architect is closely defined. Other consultants likely to be appointed, with whom the relationship will be less direct, are structural engineers, quantity surveyors, electrical engineers and mechanical service engineers.

There are two aspects to the design of new premises. These will be reflected in:

(1) Documents prepared by the curatorial and programming side, shown bold in *Figure 56.1*, which assumes the construction of a medium-sized museum.
(2) Documents prepared by the architect (Bell, 1972).

Table 57.1 lists the type of contents that might be in each category.

Such a scheme is not often realized in practice and too often the documents prepared in the right-hand column by the architect have to include the curatorial report on the left.

Table 57.1 Requirements when designing new premises

Curator/programmer	Architects
Scope and extent of objectives/budget ceiling	Choice of architect
Curatorial objectives	
Area requirements	
Plant requirements	
Activities to be undertaken	
Administrative arrangements	
Financial constraints	
Pre-program and scenarios for use Site and premises	*Feasibility studies*
Selection of site/building	Site factors
Setting and communications; nature of users; state of site; land acquisition requirements	Geology
	Structural problems posed
Planning constraints	Services available
Specific technical requirements in performance of building and environmental controls	Preliminary visual interpretation of the various options
Specific analysis of space requirements and their relationship	Town and country planning consideration
General purposes	Building costs – preliminary assessment
Alternative options for realizing them	
General cost estimates	
Basic program	*Outline proposal* leading to planning application etc.
Detailed specifications and analysis of costs in light of preferred option	Planning of main elements in the light of the preferred option
• Preliminary time-tabling of operation	Sketch designs
• Schedule of specific requirements	Firm estimate of building costs
• Financing and costing of the project	
Final programme	*Scheme design*
Remaining instructions, costings, operational requirements to enable project to proceed	Development of the outline proposal
Detailed timetable	Detailed investigation of specific elements and design of services, etc
	Detailed design
	Working drawings
	Production
	Tenders and execution of contract
Users manual	
Almost invariably forgotten!	

Security

The security of premises and the collections and data they contain is of vital importance (Robertson *et al*, 1981). It is not proposed here to go into detail on the measures to be adopted; the references in the bibliography contain ample guidance. The main threats are known: fire (or explosion) and theft. The object of any museum system designed to deal with a threat is:

(1) Detect something is wrong.
(2) Communicate that information rapidly and reliably.
(3) Take effective action.

The quicker this is done the better; the growth of damage from fire, for instance, is exponential. The average damage done in non-domestic fires in 1 minute is £5000; by 5 minutes it is £50000. The time taken for an intruder to penetrate various types of barrier is known; the reaction time must be within these limits.

However, as well as the known threats, natural disasters such as flooding should not be ignored. While in the UK it is unlikely that the problems caused by earthquakes, volcanoes, and tropical storms will be experienced, flooding is a real hazard to some museums. Obviously, steps should be taken to minimize the risks. Paper and archives (and specimens boxed in cardboard) should be above flood level. But a disaster plan should also be prepared so that even if the unlikely does happen, steps can be taken immediately to minimize the damage. The plan must identify the chain of command in an emergency, the addresses and telephone numbers of key staff that may need to be called in, the relative importance of items in the collections when removing them from hazard, the location of special supplies of new packaging materials and so on, the instructions for relocating the materials and the procedures to be followed rectifying damage.

A brief summary can only examine the main points of which the curator should be aware in the care and use of museum buildings. But it is not possible to leave the subject without reiterating the importance of architecture in the total experience of using a museum. The quality of that experience will be a vital factor in determining whether the visitor finds his use of the museum's resources enjoyable and enlightening or a disappointment and an irritation.

Acknowledgements

The author is indebted to Ray Collins, Chief Administrative Officer at the Museum of London, and Bernard Thorp, of Powell Moya and Partners (architects) for reading the text and making a number of helpful suggestions. Responsibility for the views expressed remains with the author.

Bibliography

The following list is selective. For a fuller list see the recommended bibliography of the Department of Museum Studies, University of Leicester.

Facilities needed in museums

DANILOV, V. J. (1977), *Starting a Science Centre? A Planning Guide for Contemporary Science and Technology Museums.* Poses certain questions about the type of building and space required and gives areas of selected examples in the USA.

GRETTON, R. (1966), Museum Architecture – a primer, *Museum News*, **44**, 13–17. A brief statement of the qualities needed in museum architecture. Includes some basic facts about siting and proportions of floor area required for each function.

HARRISON, R. O. (1967), The Technical requirements of small museums, *Canadian Museum Association Technical Paper 1*, Canadian Museum Association, Ottawa. Useful basic study of what is needed. Museum functions, their space requirements and their special relationships are shown at the level appropriate for anyone planning a very small museum.

HUME, T. A. *et al* (1963), The planning of museums and art galleries, *Museums J.*, **63**, 4–87. Still a useful basic account by a number of authors; a number of projects are described, *some* of which were built!

THOMPSON, W. G. (1977), (2nd edn.), *The Planning and Design of Library Buildings,* Although geared to library needs, it has much relevant information. There is no comparable museum study.

Development of museum facilities

BELL, J. A. H. (1972), Museum and gallery building, *Museums Association Information Sheet 14,* Museums Association, London. Basic information on what is put in the architects brief.

HUME, T. A. *et al,* (1979), Programming for museums, *Museum,* **31** (UNESCO), 71–144. A number of authors consider the theoretical base for organizing museum development and give a number of case studies.

Environmental requirements of museums

HARRIS, J. B. *et al,* (1980), Lighting of art galleries and museums, *Chartered Institute of Building Services Report 14,* Chartered Institute of Building Services, London

THOMSON, G. (1977), Museum climatology, IIC Report, IIC

THOMSON, G. (1978a), Conservation and museum lighting, *Museums Association Information Sheet 6,* Museums Association, London

THOMSON, G. (1978b), *The Museum Environment,* Butterworths, London

Maintenance

LEWIS, R. H. (1976), *Manual for Museums.* Although geared to the needs of the US National Parks service, it contains much useful advice.

Security

CORNING MUSEUM OF GLASS (1972), *The Museum under water*

ROBERTSON, I. G. *et al* (1981), Museum security, *Museums Association Information Sheet 25,* Museums Association, London

TILLOTSON, R. G. (1977), *Museum Security*, ICOM, A main survey by ICOM. Does not provide detailed advice.

TILLOTSON, R. G. (1977), *Prevention et Sécurité dans les musées.* (Direction of the Museums of France). Provides detailed instructions appropriate to French needs.

TILLOTSON, R. G. (1982), Building services for museums and art galleries, *Chartered Institute for Building Services Symposium,* Chartered Institute for Building Services, London. Provides background information on museum security.

UPTON, M. S. AND PEARSON, (1978), *Disaster Planning and Emergency Treatments in Museums* (Canberra). Australian experience and recommendations in the light of natural disasters.

The quality of architecture

BRAWNE, M. (1965), *The New Museum*

HUDSON, K. (1981), *Museums for the 1980s,* UNESCO, Paris

58

Personnel management

Michael Diamond

It is only in the last twenty years or so that people have begun to talk about personnel management at all in museums. Before that time many museums were so small that they were staffed on the whole by a handful of enthusiasts working as a small team, often on close personal terms. Formal qualifications were the exception rather than the rule, and the character of the museum often depended upon the personal enthusiasms of the staff rather than on any real conception of public service, or of basic management practices.

Many museum services still operate quite satisfactorily on this basis, but during the last twenty years many institutions have grown, aided by a period of increasing public expenditure in the 1960s and 1970s, and with this growth has come a new range of management problems. Rapidly developing collections and the growth of 'professionalism' has led to an increasing emphasis on the employment of specialist, properly-trained curators, conservators and technicians. At the same time, there has developed a heightened awareness of the educational potential of the collections, leading to the employment of specialist staff for education services and exhibition programs. Design and publicity departments have emerged during the same period, in order to ensure that the highest possible standards of presentation are applied.

If there are new factors for museum management, one has always been present: that most museums operate within much larger organizations, the structures and practices of which have been designed for purposes very different from those of museums. Central and local government are the obvious examples, where a welter of regulations and procedures for financial and personnel management have to be followed, regardless of their value to the museum service concerned. Museums set up by large companies often encounter similar problems. In all such

cases, the museum service forms such a small part of the whole, that any attempt to make special arrangements more appropriate to the real needs of the service is almost certainly fraught with difficulties.

The position of the growing number of Charitable Trust museums appears quite different, but essentially similar effects apply. They are usually independent bodies, and are therefore not constrained by the plethora of regulations applied by governments or major industries. Nevertheless, the pressure to devote large manpower resources to fund-raising and/or the management of volunteer labour is equally constraining.

The constitutional context within which a museum operates is therefore crucial to any discussion of its management. There are so many such contexts, however, that this paper cannot cover them all. Indeed, museums, as such, regardless of their constitutional context, are far too varied to allow detailed treatment. A large, multi-disciplinary museum obviously has quite different needs from a small, single-discipline Charitable Trust museum.

This paper cannot cover all the management situations that arise from such a complex set of variables, but can attempt to identify a range of common problems, pointing to possible approaches to the solution of those problems, by drawing on the experience of a wide range of museums in the UK.

Day-to-day problems

The most important single factor for personnel management in museums is that museum professionals are highly specialist individuals, either academically or in skill. Their commitment to their own discipline is often matched by a corresponding indifference to that of their colleagues, and, therefore, the management problem of establishing a coherent, balanced organization is often considerable. All too often friction over competition for limited resources takes the place of creative achievement.

Further tension can often develop between curatorial staff and 'support' sections such as administration, display, museums education, publicity and security. The development of strong commercial sections adds further stress in some cases.

Theoretically, the creation of specialist 'support' sections should make life simpler for the curator by removing whole areas of activity from his field of responsibility. In practice, of course, it often has the reverse effect and new problems of communication are created. These new sections may be separate, but they still depend on the collections and expertise of the curator. Furthermore, in creating a separate section the institution implies that it attaches growing importance to that area of activity and new work will be created, most of it requiring *curatorial* support.

Three processes can help to reduce tensions in these areas of activity. First, it should be possible to create a better understanding between the parties through debate which focuses on the nature of the processes which engage them. A proper forum for the discussion of display, education or publicity policies should establish a clearer relationship, where each understands the part he plays, what he can and cannot expect of the other, and what is expected of the whole exercise. Second, there needs to be developed a fuller understanding of the role of individual sections in the strategies and policies of the institution as a whole. Here the senior staff, including the director, should give a clear lead on broad strategic issues and on specific major policy areas. Clear statements at either of these levels should do much to remove many of the uncertainties and inconsistencies which have crept into museum organizations in recent years. These uncertainties lie at the root of many of the morale problems which develop at times of economic stringency, when competition for funds is at its most acute.

The third avenue to explore for solutions to problems of competitive stress is that of personalities. This is not the place for an introduction to management psychology, but a little delicate probing can often produce a fairly simple cause for a major problem, in the personal circumstances of one of the protagonists.

Relationships between sections of the organization is one of two major problem areas for personnel management in museums. The other is the relationship between specialist and management responsibilities in an individual. The traditional career pattern in local authority museums generally involve promotion to positions involving broader responsibilities, and with them additional management functions which have to be fulfilled in time formerly devoted to specialist duties. This has always been a

source of frustration to people with highly specialized training and deep commitment to their subject.

The real issue here is the effective use of limited specialist resources. Of course a senior officer must accept senior management responsibilities, but this need not and should not be associated with the quantity of routine paperwork that tends to go with it, and more attention does need to be given to the distinction between managerial and administrative duties.

Staff structure

It is through the staff structure that the relationship between the individuals in the organization is set out, and their responsibilities defined. Furthermore, the staff structure reflects the objectives of the institution through the balance it expresses between functions. To quote Bains (1972):

> Its objective is to influence and create an environment in which the authority can recruit and develop the employees it needs to achieve its objectives.

The relationship between the structure and the nature of the institution is vividly illustrated by a comparison between a typical, multi-disciplinary local authority arrangement, and one from a single-discipline Charitable Trust museum. The local authority has the traditional weighting in favour of curatorial activities (*Figure 58.1*), whereas the Charitable Trust attaches far more importance to fund-raising, not so much as an objective in itself, but as a recognition of the facts of economic life (*Figure 58.2*). Charitable Trust museums have had to develop the potential of commercial, volunteer and grant-aid resources to survive,1 but in the process they have drawn attention to new possibilities for many publicly-owned institutions. Some, as a result, now have extensive commercial, volunteer and grant-aid operations which have significantly altered the shape of their staffing structures. Things do change. Our perception of the potential of our heritage, the public's expectations of us, and the collections themselves on occasion, can be transformed to the point where existing structures no longer meet the demands made on them. Having determined the structure, it should be capable of change.

Many structures did indeed change quite significantly at the time of local government reorganization in 1974 (1975 in Scotland). As local authority boundaries changed, so too did the responsibilities of many museum services. In some areas a significant geographical factor was added to the existing functional ones, as responsibility for a number of widely-spread branches was added to the brief of a single existing service. In some cases this has been dealt with by giving responsibility for a branch museum

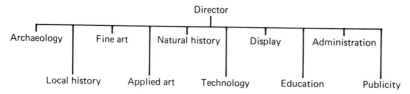

Figure 58.1 Local authority staff structure

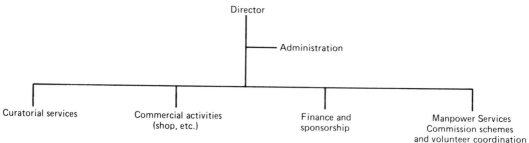

Figure 58.2 Charitable trust staff structure

to the most appropriate curatorial department (*Figure 58.3*). In others, a structure based on buildings rather than functions has been adopted (*Figure 58.4*).

Here, co-ordination can be a major problem, most obviously where specialists in one discipline exist in more than one museum. Clearly a choice has to be made between a structure based on functions, and one based on buildings, and arrangements will have to be made to minimize the weaknesses of either option. A choice will in any case have to be made when determining what might be described as the philosophy of the structure. This issue was brought into sharp focus by the Bains Report (1972) in England and Wales and the Paterson Report (1973) in Scotland. The central proposal of both reports was that the 'corporate management process' should be applied to local government. Bains observed that local government in the 1960s consisted essentially of a 'vertical' structure of separate service departments, each responding to the demands made of it as it saw fit. There was duplication, there were large gaps in provision, one department would be found working against the interests of another, there was little consistency in staff structure and salaries, and little sense

of forward planning. In short, there was no comprehensive co-ordination of policy making or implementation; no 'corporate' identity.

The Bains solution at Authority level was to create a new management structure above the chief officer tier, and give that structure the job of co-ordinating and directing the development and implementation of policy. This process was reflected in restructures within individual departments, and a typical post-Bains museum situation might appear as in *Figure 58.5*.

Here a departmental management team of three would be responsible for the development, co-ordination and implementation of policy for eleven separate sections.

Authorities which have embraced the Bains philosophy have often managed to improve co-ordination and to increase the amount of time devoted to policy issues. But the philosophy does create its own problems. Vast quantities of paper tend to be generated to support this corporate activity (though this is often offset by a reduction in the quantity of paper flowing 'vertically'), and many hours are spent in management team meetings at one level or another; these meetings, moreover, often

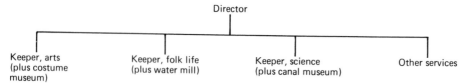

Figure 58.3 Responsibility for geographically dispersed branches given to the most appropriate curatorial department

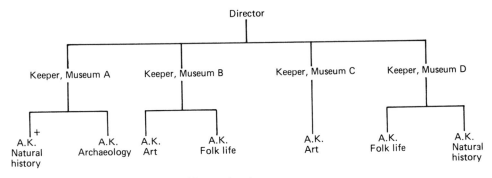

Figure 58.4 Staff structure based on buildings rather than functions

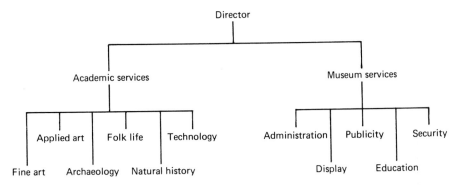

Figure 58.5 Typical museum staff structure, post-Bains

spend much time on detail rather than on the policy issues for which they were intended.

There is, therefore, a fundamental choice to be made between a 'vertical' (or line-management) structure and a 'horizontal' (or corporate) one. The choice itself, however, is arguably less important than an understanding of the strengths and weaknesses of the two options. If this understanding is there, then arrangements can be made to minimize the weaknesses of the structure adopted, and make provision for the strengths of the one rejected. Thus a vertical system would include arrangements for horizontal debate on matters affecting two or more sections, and a horizontal system would take care not to spend time on unnecessary communication and programming at the expense of attention to real, operational issues. Whatever the choice, it must always be understood that no amount of abstract management philosophy can obscure the fact that the structure is only a means to an end – that of providing a framework within which the staff of the service can work effectively towards the achievement of its objectives.

It must be repeated in this context that the structure finally adopted is all too frequently required to conform to that of the constitutional parent body, be

it central or local government, or a major company. Such a situation presents both opportunities and difficulties; it is up to the senior management of the museum service to see to it that the value of the former outweighs the constraints of the latter.

Some examples may help to illustrate the points being made. First, while local authorities have been under enormous pressure in recent years to reduce their 'revenue', (or current) spending there has often been less difficulty with 'special', or (one-off) projects. They have also been heavily involved in new central government spending programs, such as those of the Manpower Services Commission or the Inner City Partnerships. Some local authority museum services have been very successful in offsetting revenue cuts with new finance from these other sources. Second, structural constraints imposed from above need not necessarily limit the flexibility of the service itself. Thus a 'vertical' structure does not preclude the establishment of a working-party to examine a major, across-the-board policy issue, such as how to continue producing academic (and possibly loss-making) publications in the face of a directive to make all trading activities self-financing. Such exercises can often produce the additional advantage of bringing competing sections of the organization together to solve common problems. No abstract structure can do this on its own, particularly in a museum service, where so much depends on the personalities and abilities of individuals. Whatever structure is adopted, it must be sufficiently flexible to take account of these rather special factors.

Staff training

Staff training is as closely related to an institution's performance as any other aspect of personnel management. Just as the staff structure and its management arrangements should be designed to meet the needs of the institution's overall objective, so the training program should be designed to meet the needs of the individual posts within that structure.

At this point the job description becomes important, since it is in this document that the objectives of the post are, or should be, made clear. It will also make clear the qualifications required of the post-holder on appointment (such as a relevant degree), and those he will be expected to acquire in post (such as the Museums Diploma)

Thus far nothing has been suggested which is not already fairly general practice in British museums, though many still view the Museums Diploma as an 'optional extra'. The usual reasons advanced for ignoring the diploma are that it teaches nothing that cannot be picked up as part of the individual's working experience, or that it teaches things that are irrelevant to the needs of the curator.

In fact the diploma has to cater for such a variety of professional situations that its usefulness to individuals is bound to vary. It could indeed be argued that the level of specialism at which many staff in major national institutions operate makes much of the syllabus irrelevant. Equally, large local authority establishments do present opportunities for 'picking up' much of the course information through day-to-day experience. However, this still leaves many hundreds of curators with real training needs, and constant cries from all quarters for museum curatorship to be recognized as a genuine profession. Without a generally-accepted professional qualification, such appeals cannot be answered.

The organization of the Museums Diploma has undergone considerable changes in recent years, and the details of the current arrangements are dealt with elsewhere. It is sufficient to say in the present context that while its wide-ranging program is often difficult to match with the specific requirements of an individual curator, it has become the major post-graduate qualification in vast numbers of museums, is the model for training programs in many parts of the world, and surely provides the best basis available for the recognition of museum staff as a 'profession'. The diploma is a post-graduate qualification,

originally for curators, but widened in recent years to include museum educationalists, designers and conservators.

Non-curatorial departments will, of course, have their own basic specialist qualifications; thus a display officer would have a degree in fine art from a polytechnic school of art, where he would have specialized in graphic or three-dimensional design. An education officer would have a teaching degree, and an administrator, at least at a senior level, might well have a degree in economics or business studies. At this point, however, we find that full-time higher education qualifications are shading into in-service training, as many very able administrators have worked through from day-release polytechnic or CFE courses for ONC and HNC qualifications to the Diploma in Public Administration.

Thus some senior staff may have acquired their 'basic' qualifications on an in-service basis in junior posts, rather than in full-time higher education. But the principle of in-service training extends across the whole range of museum activities, and well beyond the scope of the Museum's Diploma.

First, all staff are subject to certain legal requirements, and must be made aware of the legal framework within which their institution operates. This will vary somewhat according to the museum's constitution, that is, whether it is a national of local authority museum, privately owned or a charitable trust. Whatever its constitution, there will be a document which sets it out, and usually further papers setting out administrative rules and procedures. In local government, the standing orders of the individual local authority are supplemented by financial regulations and the *National Scheme of Conditions of Service* ('Purple Book' in England and Wales, 'Blue Book' in Scotland). All professional staff should be familiar with these documents and senior administrators should be able to advise colleagues on their contents to a high level of detail.

Legal issues may crop up in many guises. How much physical force, for example, may be used in restraining a thief or vandal? Which hygiene regulations cover the preparation of sandwiches for a Friends' function? How do you deal with conflicting claims of ownership of a loan item, when the original lender dies? Some of these issues are best dealt with on an *ad hoc* basis by reference to the museum's legal advisers; others should be covered by short training courses given by appropriate specialist bodies; others may be covered quite adequately by making available appropriate publications.

The main legal obligations of museum employees are set out in the *Code of Conduct for Museum Curators* and need not be repeated here. Clearly, it is essential for all staff to receive proper training in the provisions and implications of the appropriate legislation, and such training is now often available through local authority personnel departments. Those without access to local or central government training facilities can usually make arrangements with local polytechnics, universities, colleges of further education or the private sector, if necessary through their Area Museum Service

Even when these basic training requirements have been met, substantial further needs may arise. The first group of these may be described as 'specialist' professional needs, often arising from professional developments elsewhere which create a requirement for some updating. Technical advances in storage, security and conservation are classic examples. Short courses, of one to three days, are arranged by a variety of bodies, including federations, area councils, the Museums Association, specialist professional groups and the Association of Independent Museums.

Some of these courses will also be of value in tackling the second group of training requirements, best described as 'staff development'. In this case a comparison is made between the performance of the person in post and job description of that post, as a result of which training needs are identified which will help to narrow any gaps which appear between objectives and achievement. Few organizations operate any very formal procedures for such an assessment, and indeed it is usually a fairly simple matter for an officer to agree with his superior where any training needs may lie. Sometimes, however (the Civil Service is a case in point), formal annual assessments take place which include the examination of training needs.

Some of these needs will be 'specialist' professional ones. Thus the trainee paintings conservator attending a course on recent advances in techniques relating to the transfer of panel paintings may be developing a whole new range of skills as well as updating himself on technical advances in his craft.

However, a whole new area of training has developed over the last twenty years which is concerned with the acquisition of administrative and management skills. Courses in report writing, receptionist skills, interview techniques, or critical path analysis are provided, or can be arranged through, local authority personnel departments, and generally last one to three days.

Senior staff may require more advanced courses of a week or more covering such things as leadership psychology, decision taking, work programming and performance measurement. Until recently these have been conditioned by a specific management technique, such as 'management by objectives', or 'planned program budgeting', but it is more usual for such techniques to be taught as useful tools rather than complete management philosophies. Courses are again available through local authorities, although a significant recent development has been

the program put together by the Association of Independent Museums. In these courses the quite different financial situation of private and trust museums is reflected in the time devoted to marketing and fundraising techniques. Local authority courses are clearly not designed for this kind of institution, but it is particularly interesting to note that up to half the delegates to AIM's longer courses are from local authorities, reflecting the increasing awareness of commercial possibilities in all quarters. One problem which affects most of these longer courses (and some, such as ones offered by INLOGOV, run for six weeks), is that of cost. Small museums, in particular, are frequently priced out of the market, with the result that their training opportunities are limited.

One further training area, and one which is critical for any museum, is that of induction training for security staff. Every new arrival should be fully briefed on the geography of the building, patrol patterns, emergency fire, theft and bomb procedures, fire fighting and legal issues relevant to his work. In many cases, training may also be needed in the handling of exhibits, packing, and the use of display equipment. Precise arrangements will vary according to the size and character of the museum. Small institutions usually find it possible to handle the general induction on a one-to-one basis with the supervisor. Larger ones will need to make more formal arrangements. The important thing is that a sound basic grounding must be given immediately on arrival, and that constant supervision is provided for a period of some weeks. A written manual should be provided for all security staff, covering all basic aspects of their work.

Specific training on fire fighting and first aid is usually organised by local authority personnel departments. Detailed training for security staff is arranged by many of the Area Councils, leading if required to the Attendant's Certificate and Senior Attendant's Certificate of the Museums Association.

However, it is often difficult to release security staff for courses lasting several days. Such courses are often infrequent in any case, and most training is therefore carried out 'in-house'. Most of it happens on an *ad hoc* basis, involving security supervisors and curatorial staff, and it must be said that it is still not taken very seriously by many museum managements, which is remarkable when it is considered how much of the handling, packing, moving and displaying of collections is actually done by security staff. In many institutions the syllabus for the Association's Attendants Certificate could be taught by existing staff, but it rarely is.

One further training need, and one of increasing importance, is created by the development of the use of volunteer and temporary staff, the latter often employed under Manpower Services Commission

(MSC) schemes. Volunteers work irregular hours, and MSC staff work on short-term contracts. Both present security and supervision problems, and care must be taken to ensure that their numbers do not exceed the capacity of the permanent staff to handle these problems. They will usually have a very specific brief, and should receive training designed to meet that brief. This may be quite informal, but must cover the basic essentials of security and fire procedures, what they can and cannot do, and, in the case of curatorial helpers, how to handle collections and how to operate documentary systems.

Frequent references have been made to a number of agencies specialising in various fields of training. It must be emphasized, however, that the pattern of training provision varies greatly across the country. Universities, polytechnics, colleges of further education, area services, federations, specialist professional groups and local authorities are all providers of training opportunities, and to these may be added the larger private sector companies and business management organizations. But the strength and character of provision does vary, and museum personnel officers will need to research the local situation carefully if they are to construct coherent training programmes.

They would also do well to examine the potential within their own organizations. The gradual demise of the apprenticeship system is now affecting many museums, where the older craftsmen, often possessing time-honoured skills no longer taught on formal courses, are reaching retirement age. The problem of passing on their skills is a very real one, but with due forethought trainees, or early replacements, can be arranged so as to meet it, at least in part. It must also be said that in-house training is sometimes, for financial reasons, the only possible training in the less well-endowed museums, such as some of the charitable trusts.

In summary, two things must be said of training as a whole. First, it is not a panacea. The business of management is to make the most of people's strengths, and minimize the effect of their weaknesses. Training can help to do this, but it cannot convert a weakness into a strength. Second, it must serve a clearly identified purpose, and that identification should arise from the comparison of a job specification with the performance of the individual doing the job. Training, like everything else, should be designed to meet a genuine need.

Appointments and conditions of employment

During the last ten years or so the law relating to terms and conditions of employment, health and safety, and trades unions has become very complex. It has therefore become necessary, for legal as well as management reasons, to prepare comprehensive statements on all these matters for every employee.

The current position with regard to such statements is set out in the *Code of Conduct for Museum Curators*.

This documentation is necessary not only to meet legal requirements, but also to avoid unnecessary misunderstandings when disputes arise. Most useful in the operational context, however, is one further document, the 'job specification'. It is here that the fullest description of the post is set out, including formal reporting relationships, responsibilities, decision making, a list of duties, qualifications, experience and salary. Clearly this document should be formulated in the context of the staff structure as a whole, and of related job specifications in particular. It should be as clear and specific as possible in order to avoid unnecessary dispute, and this can be difficult in the museum context where the success of a project often depends upon a flexible approach to responsibilities on the part of staff.

It is particularly difficult to quantify the responsibilities of museum personnel, and this has led to continual problems with regard to the establishment of a proper pay structure across the country as a whole. Generally the national museums, where Civil Service scales apply, have developed significantly higher salaries than the local authority establishments, but there are also variations between authorities, with the larger ones often offering better rewards than the smaller ones. The Museums Association does recommend a minimum scale of AP4 (local government) or equivalent for holders of its diploma, but this is difficult to enforce and only affects the bottom end of the problem. Attempts to persuade unions such as NALGO to exert pressure have failed, and individual directors are effectively left to fight their own battles up and down the country. It is hard, in these circumstances, to see how things can be changed, but it is clear that the quantifications of responsibilities set out in job specifications can only be helpful.

Precise specifications are also important when new appointments are being made. It is surprising how many appointments are made without any clear view of what is being asked of the candidates concerned, and even when there is a clear view many posts are filled by candidates who meet only a limited number of the requirements. Dealing with new appointments is itself a skilled business, and one with significant consequences when one realizes how long one may have to live with the result. Specialist short courses are now generally available, and are well worth the investment for senior staff.

Industrial Relations

Few museims experience serious industrial relations problems, probably because their small scale encourages a level of personal contact which defuses problems arising from poor communications. Personality clashes can, however, lead to difficulties anywhere, and it will be a continual management responsibility to watch for such problems and deal with them before they get out of hand. Some aspects of industrial relations are enshrined in law; the *Health and Safety at Work Act,* for example, requires employers to appoint safety representatives at each place of work if employees ask for them. Safety committees must also be set up at the employees' request.

Other formal machinery arises from the need for good communication between management and employees. Most large organizations now have a system of joint consultative committees (JCCs) where management meets with union representatives on a regular basis. In local government JCCs generally operate at departmental and authority level, with further committees at regional and national level for issues transcending local significance. In the museum context, the important factor in establishing such structures is to ensure that they meet a real need for the transmission of information and the resolution of problems which could not otherwise be dealt with.

It has to be said that most of the industrial relations difficulties that do occur can be put down to personality clashes exacerbated by the very unusual conditions of curatorial life. The values of the curator are often a mystery to the security officer and the clerical assistant, and when lack of understanding is added to impatience on either side, then trouble often ensues. There is undoubtedly room in most museums for informal seminar-type arrangements to reduce friction of this kind.

Summary

The situation just outlined in many ways mirrors the position in which museums as a whole find themselves. Misunderstanding of the role of museums by those responsible for funding them, and misunderstanding by museum staff of the perspective of the 'world outside' are at the root of many of our problems. Better communication between the parties concerned may provide part of the answer to improving our lot. Internally, the management challenge is to adapt the conditions imposed in such a way as to make the best possible use of the considerable abilities our profession possesses.

References

BAINS REPORT (1972), *The New Authorities,* HMSO, London
PATERSON REPORT (1973), *The New Scottish Local Authorities: Organisation and Management Structures,* HMSO, Edinburgh

Bibliography

BOOT, E. L., COWLING, A. G. AND STANSWORTH, M. J. K. (1977), *Behavioural Sciences for Managers,* Edward Arnold, London
HANDY, C. B. (1976), *Understanding Organizations,* Penguin, London
OLDCORN, R. (1982), *Management: A Fresh Approach,* Pan Breakthrough Books, London
STEWART, R. (1967), *The Reality of Management,* Pan, London
VROOM, V. H. AND DECI, E. L. (1970), *Management and Motivation,* Penguin, London

59

Relations between museums and employing authorities and governing bodies: national museums, with special reference to museums with boards of trustees

Alan Bowness

The British national museums, like many other state institutions in this country, are totally dependent on government funds and yet not directly under political control. This is the peculiarly British solution to an international problem, most obvious perhaps in organizations such as the Arts Council and the BBC, but the so-called Trustee museums were very early examples of it.

The works of art in the nation's possession need to belong to somebody, rather than to something, and a board of independent Trustees is as good an answer as any. The Tate Gallery is, essentially, an offshoot of the National Gallery, and the Tate's ten Trustees first assumed ownership of the Tate collection when the Gallery became independent in 1955. The British Museum has twenty-four trustees, some of them co-opted, or nominated by Her Majesty the Queen, or from such distinguished bodies as the Royal Society, the Royal Academy, the British Academy and the Society of Antiquaries. Nevertheless the majority are, like all the National Gallery and Tate Trustees, appointed by the Prime Minister, as First Lord of the Treasury. They are, to date, not political appointments as such – successive prime ministers have always chosen those best-qualified and best-suited to serve with counsel and advice. Four of the Tate's Trustees must be practising artists.

The British Museum Trustees also own the building, which is not the case for the National Gallery or the Tate, where the building is Crown Property, maintained by the Property Services Agency of the Department of the Environment (which also looks after the British Museum on behalf of the Trustees). This is an arrangement with both advantages and disadvantages. The museum can hand over all matters concerning the building to a body of professionals, and not have to worry about the problems that arise. On the other hand, things can easily get beyond the control of the museum staff, and frustrations arise because the Director is not always master of his own gallery.

It should be stressed that the Trustees' responsibility is essentially to the collection: they are the temporary owners, and must ensure that all is well with its preservation and exhibition. Loans need their approval, and the Trustees have the independence to withstand pressure that can be exerted by government in the case of some European countries, when prestigious loans are requested for naked political (or national) purposes. Trustees are also very much concerned with the additions that are made to the collection. At the Tate and National Galleries only the Director can propose work for acquisition; at the British Museum, the Keepers act for the Director. In every case, smaller items excepted, the last word rests with the Trustees.

The staff in the Trustee museums are not strictly civil servants, since they are employed by the Trustees and not by the Crown, but their terms of employment are in every other respect identical with those of civil servants – in conditions of service, salaries and wages, and the staffing grades within the museum which are either civil service grades (in the finance and administrative departments) or linked

514

grades (for curatorial staff). Directors of the National collections are, for example, Under-Secretaries in civil service parlance; executive officers and clerical officers abound.

The Director's position is an unusual one: in the case of the Tate Gallery, he is appointed by the Prime Minister on the recommendation of the Trustees, with the civil service establishment represented on the Selection Board. As far as the running of the Gallery is concerned, he is, like the head of a civil service department, held responsible for the funds voted annually by Parliament, and he is subject to government accounting procedures. The Trustees hold a watching brief – they clearly must have confidence in their Director, and *in extremis* have the power to act if all is not well. They are not directly concerned with the day-to-day running of the Tate, and are not expected to monitor the spending of the vote, although, of course, they have a close interest in the grant-in-aid.

The Government vote, including the Grant-in-Aid for acquisitions for the collection, is fixed annually by Parliament. The actual sums, within the cash limit for the Arts Vote, are decided by the Minister for the Arts. His department, the Office of Arts and Libraries, has enjoyed a degree of independence, but is attached to the Lord President's Office. The directors of the national museums negotiate with the senior officers of the Office of Arts and Libraries for their annual votes, presenting estimates based on present practice, making bids for extra money for this or that development. The particular difficulty of this situation is that by far the greater part of the vote is required for salaries and wages, and these are fixed nationally, according to civil service pay awards. So the director of a national collection can suddenly find himself having to find money for a nationally agreed increase in pay, over which neither he nor the Office of Arts and Libraries staff had the slightest control. It is a little like the mysterious sums that are needed for the maintenance of the buildings, for here government funds are transferred from the Arts Vote to the Property Services Agency with no direct reference to the museum directors whatever. As so often happens, however, such practices can work to the museum's advantage, when funds that are unexpectedly not required on one project can suddenly be made available elsewhere.

The system, such as it is, is in fact a generally benevolent one. Practices have arisen out of need on a pragmatic basis, and nothing is ever so rigid as to preclude the possibility of change. Comparison with the national museums of continental Europe which are more directly controlled by Government through art ministries, or with the great independent museums of the USA, where financial survival is now precarious, is more often than not to British advantage.

60

Administration of a national museum through a board of trustees

Alexander Fenton

The National Museum of Antiquities of Scotland was founded by the Society of Antiquaries of Scotland in January 1781. The collections and the library were transferred to the nation in July 1851. Details of the beginnings and development of the Museum were recently published in the bicentenary volume of the Society of Antiquaries of Scotland (Stevenson, 1981, pp. 31–85, 142–211).

The present phase of the museum's existence began in 1954, when a Board of Trustees was set up under the *National Museum of Antiquities of Scotland Act 1954* (2 & 3 Eliz. 2. Ch. 14) following recommendations contained in the *Report of Committee on The National Museum of Antiquities of Scotland*. The full board numbers 23 at present, though it has been recommended that there should be a reduction to 12 (Williams Report, 1981, p. 51). The implementation of any such change will require legislation.

Every museum has aspects of administration which are peculiar to itself. It is therefore necessary to relate the composition of the National Museum's Trustees to the nature of the Museum.

The Museum deals solely with Scottish archaeological and historical material and to that extent is more purely 'national' than any other British museum. The Museum of London, concentrating as it does on the city of London, is its nearest equivalent. The collections (and library) cover over 8000 years in time from prehistory to the present day, in three departments: Prehistoric to viking; medieval; town and country. The last includes a branch, the Scottish Agricultural Museum, formally opened on 24 May 1982. There are also conservation and research laboratories, an Artefact Research Unit, and various stores at varying distances from home base. The scatter of units in itself creates an administrative problem.

The Trustees consist of twelve members appointed by the Secretary of State (including the

chairman); four representatives of the older Scottish universities; five representatives of the Society of Antiquaries of Scotland (including the president, *ex officio*); and two holders of Scottish chairs of archaeology, *ex officio*). They reflect a strong archaeological interest, and members are also chosen to give geographical coverage of Scotland, as befits the national nature of the Museum.

The Trustees undertake the general management and control of the National Museum, while Government responsibility for the Museum lies with the Scottish Education Department, following a transfer from the Scottish Home and Health Department on 1 June 1965. Under the authority of the Secretary of State for Scotland, the board may accept gifts or bequests of money or objects or other property; exchange, sell or otherwise dispose of any object not required for the purpose of the Museum, and apply any money received from this or from any other source for the acquisition of objects appropriate to the collections; lend objects to any gallery or museum or exhibition under the control of a public authority or university in Great Britain (or any such approved for this provision by the Secretary of State), subject to the object's safety and insurance requirements; and destroy objects if they have become infested by destructive organisms or have deteriorated so far as to become useless for Museum purposes. The Board's duties, therefore, relate very closely to the collections, and to the deployment of the annual purchase grant.

The Director of the Museum is also Secretary to the Board, which operates through two main committees, labelled 'Finance and Staff,' and 'Technical and Library'. Each meets twice a year. There is also the Emergency Committee, usually consulted by telephone or by letter to handle urgent matters between meetings. There are currently six subcommittees, meeting irregularly as required, which cover matters such as staffing, laboratories, publicity and display, educational services and publications, library, and museum development. These report back to the appropriate main committee, which in turn reports to the full Board at its twice-yearly meetings. By means of annual reviews of work submitted by staff members through the Director to the Board, Trustees are kept in close touch with the ongoing activities of each department; these reviews appear in digested form in the Museum's *Annual Reports*.

Though the Museum is responsible for the administration of its own funds, paid by the Treasury into the Museum's account at the Paymaster General's Office, annual estimates are subject to scrutiny by the Scottish Education Department who have overall responsibility for expenditure falling within the classification 'Education and the Arts'. In the current economic climate, this is a fairly academic exercise, since cash limits are set by the Government before work on the estimates begins. Expenditure on salaries and the general administration of the Museum must therefore be manoeuvred within the given figure. The cash limit also takes account of receipts (from the Museum bookstall and other services) and includes a purchase grant for the acquisition of objects.

As far as staffing is concerned, any changes involving new posts, promotions or regrading must be approved by the Manpower and Organisation division of the Scottish Office, as well as by the Board, before being implemented, and the Scottish Education Department must be kept informed because of their financial interest. Once approved, new posts of non-graduate level are recruited directly by the Museum, though draft advertisements and job descriptions must be referred to the Personnel Management Division of the Scottish Office before publication, and a Scottish Office representative is usually invited to chair the Selection Board. Posts of graduate level are recruited for the Museum by the Civil Service Commission. Personnel Management Division approve, on behalf of the Secretary of State for Scotland, the appointment of all successful candidates.

Bibliography

Annual Reports of The National Museum of Antiquities of Scotland, (1955 onwards), HMSO, London

BELL, A. S. (1981) (Ed.), *The Scottish Antiquarian Tradition. Essays to mark the Bicentenary of the Society of Antiquaries of Scotland and its Museum, 1780–1980,* Edinburgh

BRYCE, T. AND TATE, J. (1980) (Ed.), The laboratories of the National Museum of Anitquities of Scotland, (NMAS), *Proceedings of One-day Conference with the Laboratories' Honorary Scientific Advisers*

FENTON, A. (Ed.) (1979), The past and the present. The role of the National Museum of Antiquities of Scotland (NMAS), *Proceedings of a One-day Conference held Jointly with the Society of Antiquaries of Scotland,* February 1979

National Museum of Antiquities of Scotland Act 1954 (2 & 3 Eliz. 2. Ch. 14)

PHILIP REPORT (August 1952), *Report of Committee on The National Museum of Antiquities of Scotland,* HMSO, Cmnd. 8604, London

STEVENSON, R. B. K. (1981), The Museum, its Beginnings and its Development, in Bell, A. S., op cit, 31–85, 142–211

WILLIAMS REPORT (1981), *A Heritage for Scotland. Scotland's National Museums and Galleries. The Next 25 Years,* HMSO, London

61

Relations between museums and employing authorities and governing bodies: local authority museums with special reference to county museums

Francis Cheetham

A large number of museums in Britain are governed by local authorities, and in addition many independent museums receive substantial financial support from local authorities. Since local government reorganization of 1974, following the *Local Government Act 1972,* all the local authorities in England and Wales, with the exception of the smallest (the parish town and community councils), have the powers to run museums. These powers are concurrent, meaning in effect that the museum authorities in England and Wales comprise all the metropolitan counties (such as Merseyside), all the metropolitan districts (such as Sheffield), all the non-metropolitan or shire counties (such as Norfolk) and all the non-metropolitan districts (such as Nottingham). The nomenclature of the reorganized English and Welsh local authorities is somewhat confusing in its use of county and district, for a shire county has very different powers from a metropolitan county and a metropolitan district from a non-metropolitan district, although all possess museum powers. This difference is reflected in part by the national associations of local authorities. The metropolitan counties and districts are represented by the Association of Metropolitan Authorities (AMA), the shire counties by the Association of County Councils (ACC) and the non-metropolitan districts by the Association of District Councils (ADC). In Scotland, the local authorities (regions and districts) are, generally speaking, geographically much larger than those in England and Wales. Following the Local Government and Planning (Scotland) Act 1982, only the districts now have museum powers, but a number of districts in each area are encouraged to share management decisions and resources 'in order to provide a comprehensive service at minimum cost' (Scottish Education Department, 1982). While the present concurrent museum powers in England and Wales enable a large number of local authorities to run museums, the *Local Government Act 1972* reduced the number of local authorities and took away museum powers from parish and town councils.

Local authorities in Britain are structured in such a way that every service is responsible to a committee, which is made up of elected councillors. There may be in addition co-opted members who are not councillors, for example, representatives from a university or a museum friends organization – although these must always be in a minority. In the new, and usually larger, local authorities which emerged in 1974, museums have often become merged with larger services such as 'amenities', 'leisure' or 'recreation', although this merging may have been more influenced by the Bains Report (1972) than by the size of the authority. The result of this has been uneven, museums sometimes benefitting financially by being grouped with other 'recreational' activities, while at other times the linking has lead to neglect, when the museums are considered a minority interest. However, since the new local authorities are generally larger than their predecessors, this has led to more museums working together in one department, under a single Director of Museums and Art Galleries Services. Even so, in a small number of authorities, for example, the Metropolitan Districts of Sheffield and Leeds, and the Metropolitan County of Merseyside, the division of directorship between local museums and art galleries has been perpetuated.

County councils were created in 1888 and only acquired museum powers under the Public Libraries Act in 1919. However, only a few counties ran museums or museum services between then and 1974, for example Derbyshire and County Durham. The new metropolitan and shire counties have, since 1944, become much more involved in museum provision which is currently estimated at more than one-third of the local authority total. County councils are now responsible for approximately 40 per cent of all local authority museum expenditure (Boylan, 1982). The metropolitan county of Merseyside has, for example, by mutual agreement with the City of Liverpool taken on the responsibility for the museums and galleries formerly run by that city, and similarly the shire county of Leicestershire is now responsible for the museums formerly run by the City of Leicester. The biggest growth of museum activity is in the new shire counties, and a noteworthy development has been in the creation of rural life museums such as the Acton Scott Farm Museum in Shropshire and the Gressenhall Rural Life Museum in Norfolk. Beamish – the North of England Open Air Museum – is uniquely funded by four counties, which are all represented on the management committee. Experience has shown, however, that joint arrangements between neighbouring local authorities are difficult to achieve no matter how desirable they may be.

Concurrent museum powers between districts and counties are at the nub of the difficulties experienced by many local authority musuems. Fragmentation of responsibility, parochialism and lack of co-operation are among the biggest problems facing museums, not only in Britain. In the Netherlands, for example, the Ministry of Cultural Affairs, Recreation and Social Welfare has found it necessary to encourage the appointment of 'museum consultants' in all eleven provinces to persuade small museums to work together. The problems of museums received scant attention in the English and Scottish local government reorganizations, doubtless because they are perceived to be a relatively minor activity in the whole range of local authority services. However the promotion of co-operation between museums was recognized in the Drew Report (1979) with its support for the existing Area Museum Services and its concept of new 'countywide consultative committees' based on the administrative counties.

The recently published *Report on Countywide Consultative Committees* (Museums and Galleries Commission, 1982) makes clear that for co-operation to be really effective it must not be 'a talking shop which lacked both powers and pence'. The Report shows there is substantial co-operation in a few counties like Leicestershire, Norfolk, Oxfordshire and Tyne and Wear but little in the majority.

The Report examines the degree of museum co-operation within the present administrative counties and gives a précis of each. It is clear that a number of different developments have taken place. Leicestershire has a straightforward County Council Museum Service with none of the districts exercising museum powers. Merseyside administers the former Liverpool City museums and art galleries but the five districts choose to exercise their museum function. In Oxfordshire all six local authority museums form part of the County Museum Service, Abingdon, Banbury and Wantage, being managed on behalf of the districts and town councils, who retain ownership of their collections and provide premises and attendants. In 1974 a countywide museum service was established in Norfolk, based on the delegation of museum powers by all seven district councils and the county council to a Joint Committee on which all are represented. Many counties, like Hampshire, have a county museum service and several district museums which are administered independently. In the words of the Report (pp. 31, 32):

> Efforts (in Hampshire) to promote wider co-operation, for example in the provision of exhibitions and particularly technical services, have so far proved unavailing

In the great majority of counties, the districts and the county councils run their museums separately with little co-operation on an administrative level, although there may be some professional co-operation on an informal basis. The position stated in the Report for the majority of counties is 'no county-wide consultative committee', and if it is borne in mind that this is merely the first step in achieving museum co-operation the results are most disappointing. Indeed the report diplomatically states 'Unfortunately the giving of the function concurrently to Counties and Districts has not always led to the degree of mutual help and adequate coverage presumably contemplated – but not spelt out – by the legislators in 1972' (p. 7). There is, in fact, no evidence to support the idea that the legislators gave any thought at all to the problems of local authority museums in 1972. The Area Museums Service for South-East England whose policy is to actively encourage co-operation within counties, is, however, confident that some gradual improvement is taking place in its own area.

The structure of the Norfolk Museums Service, based on a unique voluntary agreement, is outlined below. An understanding of this structure may help those in other parts of the country who are still striving to achieve better co-operation and make the best use of limited resources.

On 1st April 1974, the Norfolk Museums Service emerged from a joint agreement made for an initial and renewable ten-year period by all seven district councils and the new County Council. The Norfolk

Museums Service was subsequently (in 1983) responsible for running 15 museums and an archaeological unit.

The Joint Committee of the Norfolk Museum Service is composed of representatives both from the County Council and from each of the seven district councils. The County Council has twelve members. Each district council has one member with the exception of King's Lynn and Yarmouth, which, because of their existing museum collections and buildings have two members, and Norwich which has four members. In addition, there is provision for up to six co-opted members. Perhaps the most common fear expressed by district councils is that the County is taking away their museums and depriving them of any effective voice over their future. This fear has been met by the district council representation already mentioned on the Joint Committee, as well as by the acceptance that both the museum buildings and the museum collections remain in the ownership of the district council, with the existing buildings and collections simply being 'on loan' to the Joint Committee. Where the district council wishes to have reasonable access to its museum buildings for use outside normal museum hours the district council will take on the financial responsibility for the maintenance of the fabric of the buildings. All alterations or improvements to the fabric required for museum purposes, are, however, borne by the County. If a district council does not wish to have such access, the cost of maintenance will be undertaken by the County through the Joint Committee. Yarmouth District has decided not to meet this cost since it does not wish to retain access. With the exception of these maintenance costs, which are covered by a voluntary arrangement made by the District and the Joint Committee, the total costs of the service, which of course is county-wide, is met by the County Council, which levies its precept over the whole county. The estimated gross revenue expenditure for 1984–1985 is £1,212,960. In addition, Norwich City estimates to spend in 1983 £46,400 on the maintenance of the fabric of its four museum buildings. The staff of the Norfolk Museums Services comprises 53 full-time plus 6 part-time professional staff and 24 full-time plus 22 part-time manual and attendant staff. All the staff in every part of the service are on the payroll of the County Council and the Director of the Norfolk Museums Service is a Chief Officer of the County. While the Chairman of the Joint Committee is a county councillor, it has been agreed that the Deputy Chairman should be drawn from one of the district councils. Being a joint committee it cannot be a sub-committee, but it does in fact report its decisions to the County Libraries and Recreation Committee.

The practical results of this joint arrangement are many. There is a more efficient use of resources; for example the conservation laboratory, and the display/design department in Norwich Castle Museum give support to all the 15 local authority museums throughout Norfolk. In addition, the central administration of the Service in the Castle Museum is sympathetic to the special needs of museums and the chief officer and his deputy are museum professionals. A close relationship has been established between the county education department and the county library service, which results in, for example, small museum exhibitions being placed in branch libraries in the rural areas and in publicity about the Norfolk Museums Service's educational and recreational work being circulated to every school in Norfolk. The collecting of museum material within the county is carried out in a much more rational and less parochial manner, problems being resolved by the staff themselves, usually without too much difficulty. Storage of the collections, a perennial problem for all museums, can also be tackled more broadly and less expensively on a county-wide basis. With the increased responsibility of dealing with the whole county it was possible to regrade the senior staff thereby making it easier to attract staff of high quality. Relationships with other bodies are easier in that there is a single voice speaking for museum interests in Norfolk. Conversely the Area Museums Service does not have to deal with each individual museum separately. Indeed, it would make the work of the Area Museums Service much easier overall if it simply had to deal with a few county-wide organizations instead of literally hundreds of museums. So far as the general public is concerned, who are not the slightest bit interested in which authority is responsible for a museum as long as the service is good, the joint arrangement has been well-received. Associations of Friends of Museums have flourished with no less than six different associations in Norfolk now supporting their own local museum. Three new museum friends organizations have been established since 1974, one has been resurrected, and the Friends of the Norwich Museums now have a membership of over 1,300.

It may be objected that what works in Norfolk will not work elsewhere. Such a response is unconvincing and presents a pessimistic view of the possibilities within each county, for the basic structure can be adapted to almost any situation. It may be that there are very special problems in a few counties. For example, the *Report on Countywide Consultative Committees* makes special mention of Derbyshire. An alternative for the north of that County which is not suggested in the Report and which apparently has not been officially considered could be a museum service administered by the Peak District National Park on which the constituent authorities – both county and district are already represented. But the arrangements could still be on the Norfolk model, in this case the National Park being used as the administrative structure instead of the county.

With greater resources, which one hopes may eventually become available, a county-wide service opens up more imaginative possibilities for small touring exhibitions on local themes. It also opens up the possibility of 'museum-mobiles' for village schools and other rural institutions, in the shape of converted trailers fitted out as mini-museums which can be left in the playground of a village school for a week at a time. Many of the problems of small weak museums and the uncoordinated, sometimes conflicting activities of neighbouring museums can be corrected by a county-wide service. The future of our museums in the provinces most definitely lies in voluntary co-operative agreements between districts and county councils.

References

BAINS REPORT (1972), *The New Authorities*, HMSO, London
BOYLAN, P. (July 1982), Italian spotlight on museums, *County Councils Gazette* **75**(4), pp. 128, 129
THE DREW REPORT (1979), A Framework for a System of Museums, HMSO, London
MUSEUMS AND GALLERIES COMMISSION (1982), *Report on Countywide Consultative Committees*
SCOTTISH EDUCATION DEPARTMENT (1982), *Museums and Galleries, Scottish Education Department Circular (JUA/12/3), 17th November*

62

Health and safety at work

Patrick V. Sudbury

This paper aims to help the curator towards a broader understanding of his duties and responsibilities with regard to health and safety at work. It is suggested that the curator should know the sources of information, how to apply the administrative and management devices such as the safety policy statement and the safety audit that can help in identifying and reducing risks, and when to seek expert advice.

Sources of information

Thousands of publications deal with health, safety, and welfare at work. Although the working curator may not have the time to read many of them, their value lies in providing the curator with sufficient knowledge to brief an expert quickly, and to understand the advice received. For details of references given herein see Appendix 62.1.

Out of all the publications available, two can be singled out for essential reading. The first is the Trades Union Congress *Guide to Health and Safety at Work*. This provides a straightforward introduction to the law and the main hazards at work. Although it is intended primarily for safety representatives appointed by trade unions, it is a helpful introduction to the subject. The second is the *Publications Catalogue* produced by the Health and Safety Commission and Executive. This contains over 10 000 entries to relevant acts, regulations, codes of practice, notices and forms published by HMSO, and to the booklets and guidance notes produced by the Health and Safety Executive (HSE). Even this extensive catalogue is not exhaustive, and the index to the privately produced *Barbour Health and Safety Microfiche Library* contains a list of other relevant publications and organizations (Appendix 62.1).

Having obtained these catalogues, choosing relevant publications from them may prove difficult,

due to the diverse activities undertaken in, and by, museums. As buildings and places of public resort, museums are likely to be subject to a range of public health acts, fire precautions acts and, possibly, local licensing acts, shop acts, and the *Occupier's Liability Act*. As places of work, they may be subject to the *Offices, Shops and Railway Act,* the agricultural acts and are subject to the *Health and Safety at Work Act* (HASAWA). As depositories for collection, they may be subject to regulations regarding, for example, the storage of flammable liquids, firearms, radioactive or poisonous substances and drugs with the understanding that the improper storage of such items could be construed as an offence under the HASAWA.

The selection will, therefore, depend on the curator's role within the institution, and the nature of the institution in which he works. The most pragmatic approach is through the HSE Guidance Notes which deal with specific topics and contain references to relevant codes of practice, regulations and acts. Having established the core material, the curator should still be wary of applying such knowledge until consultation with a relevant expert has taken place.

Sources of advice

The curator should never pretend to be a health and safety expert and must know when to seek expert advice. Amateurism in health and safety can not only waste large sums of money for negligible effect; it can also be lethal.

Advice concerning buildings and public access and safety is most likely to be found in the building surveyor's department or the fire department of the local council. For workshops, laboratories, offices, stores, equipment and machinery, the inspectors of the HSE or of insurance companies will give guidance. For dangerous materials and substances, the HSE Fire Prevention Information and Publication Centre and the Fire Protection Association may give advice or suggest that further information be sought from analysts or experts on environmental hygiene. Sources of advice are given in Appendix 62.2.

Before seeking guidance from the relevant safety advisor the curator should be quite clear that the experts will assess the risk and suggest how to eliminate it. This may involve the destruction of, for example, historic interiors or part of a collection. The curator must, therefore, be prepared to explain that the complete elimination of risk is not acceptable and that a compromise needs to be found. Such a compromise will make the work of the safety expert more difficult and the explanation will, therefore, require constructive thinking and it will be helpful if the curator understands fully the safety officer's problems. Good preparation and careful briefing is, therefore, essential to obtain the desired result.

One source of advice and information that should not be overlooked is the experience of the museum's profession. In common with other places of work, museums should have prepared their safety policies and guidelines for safety. Specialist groups and area services have, in some cases, organized meetings and prepared publications with health and safety as their theme. If the problem is of a specialist nature, and has the kind of sensitivity just mentioned, it may be helpful to write to an organization that may have already encountered a similar problem.

The legal framework

In Britain, hundreds of items of legislation concerned specifically with health, safety and welfare have been approved by Parliament. Because museums can occupy buildings, manage land and water, employ people, admit the public, contain almost anything and engage in various activities, there are few items of that legislation that are not relevant to some museum at some time.

The construction and operation of a museum building as a place of public resort may be subject to a range of legislation including the *Public Health Act 1936*, the *Fire Precautions Act 1971*, as amended and widened by the *Health and Safety at Work Act 1974*, and the *Cinematograph (Safety) Regulations 1955* and also local acts. This Legislation is concerned mainly to ensure that, in an emergency, anyone within the building has a safe means of escape to the open air at ground level. The legislation has implications in the construction of displays, the provision of emergency lighting, the tendency of museum storage to spill over into escape routes and, above all, for security.

The work areas of a museum may be subject to the Factories Act 1961, the *Offices, Shops and Railway Premises Act 1963* (OSRPA), or the *Health and Safety at Work Act 1974* (HASAWA) and a host of subordinate regulations. Together, these relate to installed plant and machinery, cleanliness, lighting, heating, ventilation, fire escapes, washing and toilet facilities, as well as with general duties (under HASAWA) to care for the health, safety and welfare of those who may be affected by acts or omissions at work.

Site or farm museums may well use a range of agricultural machinery and pesticides. They may then be subject to the *Agriculture (Poisonous Substances) Act 1952* and the *Agriculture (Safety, Health and Welfare Provisions) Act 1956*. Similarly, museums with several branches and their own transport will be concerned with the regulations covering the operation of vehicles, the working hours of drivers, and the transport of goods under the road traffic and transport acts.

Museums store materials and machinery, both as support to their laboratory, workshop and maintenance operations, and also as part of their collections. They may routinely use radiography, air compressors and a range of solvents, as well as operating a range of engines and machinery on display. The *Radioactive Substances Act 1960*, the *Ionising Radiation (sealed sources) and (unsealed) radioactive substances Regulations 1968 and 1969*, the *Petroleum (Consolidation) Act 1928*, the *Highly Flammable Liquids and Liquified Petroleum Gas Regulations 1972*, the *Explosives Acts 1875 and 1923*, the *Boiler Explosions Act 1882 and 1890*, the *Celluloid and Cinematograph Film Act 1922* are just examples of the kind of acts, with such modifications as were introduced under HASAWA 1974 that can have supporting regulations of direct relevance to museums.

The Factories Act (1961), OSRPA (1963) and HASAWA (1974) are all likely to apply to some part of every museum operation. The curator would do well to read all three as background and to then use the publications' catalogue to obtain such acts, regulations, codes of practice and guidance notes as may be required to deal with routine operations and special problems as they arise.

The curator's duties

The legislation of direct, personal concern to the curator and, indeed, to everyone working in museums is HASAWA (1974). The Robens Committee on Health and Safety at Work, reporting in 1972, noted that the greatest single cause of accidents at work is apathy. Accidents do not just happen; they are caused. They arise out of ignorance, indifference, carelessness, bad luck or a combination of these things. Few accidents have a single cause and just one right action among many wrong ones may save serious injury or death.

HAWAWA (1974) seeks to overcome apathy by making everyone at work personally responsible for safety. The act believes this by first making the employer responsible for the health and safety of his employees and those who might be affected by acts and omissions at work. Secondly, the act requires the employer to prepare a statement of safety policy which should delegate those responsibilities to his employees at all levels: directors, managers, supervisors and operatives alike. Finally, the act imposes a general duty of care and co-operation in safety matters on everyone at work. Failure to discharge that duty in a reasonable manner (for example, by contravening safety rules or an agreed safety policy) is, in the last resort, an offence punishable by law.

Thus, although legislation refers mainly to 'the employer', the employer must discharge these responsibilities through his work force. The curator will, therefore, on his employer's behalf, be responsible for safety aspects of the staff, accommodation, collection and equipment under his control. The curator cannot, and must not, regard health, safety and welfare as an administrative matter that interferes with his curatorial work. He is legally liable if he does not perform adequately his health and safety duties.

The Health and Safety at Work Act (1974)

The aims of this act and its relationship to earlier legislation are set out in Section 1 of the act. The duties of employers, employees and suppliers of goods are outlined in Sections 2 and 9. Sections 10 and 54 are mainly concerned with provisions for inspection and enforcement. Sections 55 to 85 and Schedules 1 to 10, while concluding the act, deal mainly with changes to existing bodies and legislation. Thus, Sections 1 to 9 are of most importance, and of most immediate relevance, to the curator.

Section 1 states the aims of the act in terms of securing the health and safety of people at work, preventing risk to the health and safety of the general public arising from work activities, controlling and acquisition, possession and use of dangerous substances and controlling atmospheric pollution that might be damaging to health. It then explains the relationship of the act to earlier safety legislation and the fact that existing legislation remains in force beside the provision of the new act.

The act seeks to achieve its aims by making *everyone* at work responsible for safety and the devices for achieving this are contained in Section 2. This section begins by stating the general duties of an employer to ensure the health, safety and welfare of his employees and gives five examples of the ways this duty should be discharged. They include the maintenance of safe plant and systems of work, proper arrangements for dealing with dangerous substances, the provision of adequate information, instruction, training and supervision, safe access and exit, and the maintenance of a good working environment and welfare facilities.

Section 2 further requires the employer to prepare a written statement of his safety policy and the organization and arrangements for carrying out that policy. This policy is crucial to the curator because it should place specific responsibilities on people at all levels within an organization and should make arrangements for ensuring that those responsibilities are discharged. Thus, although duties under the act are those of 'employer', it is the staff who are required to discharge that responsibility in respect of the employer's accommodation, collections and equipment under their control. The duty falls inescapably on the staff both by virtue of their employment and as citizens subject to the law of the land. A detailed safety policy statement is thus essential for the curator because it should establish clear guidelines for the practical achievement of health and safety within his area of control. It should be regularly and routinely revised and brought to the attention of every member of staff (Appendix 62.3).

Section 2 also makes provision for the appointment, or election, of safety representatives from among employees and requires employers to consult such representatives. These in no way diminish the duty or authority of the employer and his staff or organize for safety, nor are they a substitute for proper communication on safety matters. Their role is supplementary and advisory. However, they can be of enormous help in ensuring effective co-operation on health and safety matters and in checking the effectiveness of the safety policy at all levels within an organization.

The development and monitoring of a safety policy should be carried out routinely through the mechanism of a safety audit. This should provide a clear checklist of the persons to be protected, of potential dangers and the way those dangers are controlled and of the need for additional monitoring and the revision of existing safety policies (Appendix 62.4).

Sections 3 of the act sets out the duty of every employer or self-employed person to minimize risks to health and safety of those not in his employment. This section is of particular importance to museums in that the public is invited to enter them. As places of public resort they are already covered by a wide range of legislation contained in public health acts, local acts and the *Fire Precautions Act 1971*. However, the 1974 act places an additional responsibility on museums to ensure that visitors are not affected by work activities within the museum that may arise, say, from maintenance work in the public galleries during opening hours.

Section 4 of the act explains employers' duties under the act to those who are not their employees but may use their premises. These would include contractors working within the museum and any volunteer groups carrying out work on the museum's behalf. It can also be applied where a firm has a concession, say for catering, within museum premises.

Section 5 deals with atmospheric pollution and the emission of noxious or offensive substances. This section may apply to a taxidermy laboratory or to workshops using plastics or resins for model making where fumes are extracted to the open air.

Section 6 deals in some length with the duties of designers, manufacturers, importers or articles used at work and their responsibilities for ensuring that they are safe, for testing them and for providing information about their method of use and any risks involved. Museums need to ensure that not only equipment, articles and substances that they obtain for their own use have been adequately checked for dangers, and that relevant information has been obtained from the supplier, but also that any items that they may sell or lend are similarly safe and free from risks to health.

Sections 7, 8 and 9 make clear the duty of every employee to take reasonable care of the health and safety of himself and other persons, to co-operate in any requirements place upon him under the statutory provisions (for example, the safety policy) and not to interfere with or misuse anything provided in the interest of health, safety and welfare. It also states that the employer may not levy any charge on an employee in respect of anything done under the statutory provisions.

Conclusion

This article has dealt with sources of information and advice and with the legal framework of health, safety and welfare legislation within which the curator has to do his job. The subject has been dealt with in an abstract, theoretical and general way. Reality is very different. Day-to-day safety is often a matter of small things. A walk round the premises with a safety officer, notebook in hand, will probably do more for health and safety than a thousand hours' reading. It is the everyday things that often injure and kill. The faulty ladder, the tear in the carpet, the unlocked door to the roof, the box in the gangway . . .

Like many other matters, safety implies constant vigilance over trivial things. The law, the safety policies, the consultation and the safety audits will all help to make that vigilance part of the daily routine. However, at the end of the day it is the care that each and every person shows that will make museums safe and healthy. The attitude, training and knowledge of the curator will play an important part in determining that level of care.

Appendix 62.1 – Sources of Information

Publications

Health and Safety at Work, Trades Union Congress Guide
Publications Catalogue, Health and Safety Executive, HMSO
Barbour Health and Safety Index, Barbour Index
Guidance Notes, Booklets etc., Health and Safety Executive, HMSO
The Factories Act 1961, HMSO
The Offices, Shops and Railway Premises Act 1963, HMSO
The Health and Safety at Work, etc. Act 1974, HMSO
Other acts, regulations, notices, forms, codes of practice, HMSO, London
British standards, codes of practice, British Standards Institution

Addresses

Trades Union Congress
Congress House,
Great Russell Street,
London WC1B 3LS

Health and Safety Executive
Public Enquiry Point,
Baynards House,
1 Chepstow Place,
Westbourne Grove,
London W2 4TF
01–229–3456

HMSO
The Government Bookshop,
PO Box 569,
London SE1 9NH
01–928–6977 or through regional offices or agent booksellers.

British Standards Institution
Newton House,
101 Pentonville Road,
London N1 9ND
01 837–8801 (orders only).

Appendix 62.2 – Sources of Advice

Local authority and national museums
Most local authorities and government departments have full-time safety officers who should be the first point of contact on health and safety matters. Specialist advice may be obtained from building surveyors, the fire brigade, environmental health and analyst departments.

Private museums
Safety officers in large local organizations may be prepared to offer advice on an occasional basis. Advice from safety officers in industry may be particularly helpful to some specialist museums.

Health and Safety Executive
Address and telephone number of regional officers are in the local telephone directories. Relatively few inspectors have to cover a large area. Must be involved if there is a serious accident.

Museum colleagues
Contact curators who may have a similar role to your own. Perhaps obtain a copy of their safety policy.

Museum Professional groups and area Museums Service
Reports of meetings and special publications may be relevant.

Appendix 62.3 – The Safety Policy Statement

The requirement for a safety policy
Every employer of five or more persons is required to prepare and, as often as may be appropriate, revise a written statement of his general policy with respect to the health and safety at work of his employees and the organization and arrangements for the time being in force for carrying out that policy, and to bring the statement and any revision of it to the notice of all of his employees.

General statement of intent
This will generally reflect the employer's intention to achieve the aims of HASAWA Section 1(1) by ensuring that the general duties outlined in HASAWA Section 2(2) are carried out.

Personal Responsibilities
This part of the policy will generally begin with Section 7 of HASAWA, which states the general duties of employees. It should then state the health and safety duties and responsibilities attached to each post within the organization

Consultation
The policy will generally refer to HASAWA Section 2(4), 2(5), 2(6), and 2(7) and to the *Safety Representatives and Safety Committees Regulations 1976*. It will then describe the consultation arrangements currently in force and perhaps give the objectives, functions and membership of the Joint Consultative Committee

Resources
The policy will generally make clear how resources are made available to meet health and safety needs and that they do not come from a bottomless pit.

Arrangements for safety
This section may follow through the general duties outlined in HASAWA Sections 2–9 with a description of the arrangements for ensuring that they are performed. Alternatively, it may incorporate existing procedures within an organization detailing the arrangements for say:

— common hazards and housekeeping
— maintenance of premises
— control of processes and work activities
— maintenance of records of work
— emergency procedures
— accident reporting and investigation
— provision of protective clothing
— introduction of new machinery, substances and processes
— safety inspections and audits
— communications with staff, contractors and public
— safety training plan

Rules, regulations and codes of practice
This would be a listing of relevant documents with a note of which staff should be familiar with their content.

Appendix 62.4 – The Safety Audit

Subject	Points to Check
Persons to be protected	
(a) Employees	How many, which work places, what duties, how much travel, special risks.
(b) Non-employees	How many volunteers, visitors on premises, contractors on premises, persons passing premises, special risks.

Subject	Points to Check	Subject	Points to Check
(c) Users of products	Customers of shops and cafes, recipients of loans, reproductions etc.	(f) Work systems	Staff responsibilities, standing orders, regulations, time-tabling, monitoring, working conditions.

Identification and control of dangers

(a) Premises	Emergency evacuation, fire precautions, first aid, electrical safety, lifts, access to roofs, toilets and messrooms, house-keeping.	(g) Products and waste	Disposal of workshop or laboratory waste, taxidermy post-mortem materials, sewage, items sold or lent.

Monitoring and revision

(b) Articles and substances	Poisons, fire hazards, gas cylinder, pesticides, laboratory materials, collection materials.	(a) Safety inspections	Regular inspection of all premises. Checking of duties at all management levels. Are systems for introducing new equipment, substance processes effective? First aid, welfare and emergency procedures adequate.
(c) Operations and processes	Workshop and laboratory activities, construction of displays, glass handling, electrical work, movement of objects, use of synthetic materials, model making, gardening, forestry, farming, excavation field-work, cafe, sales, warehousing.	(b) Accident, near miss and health records	Are accidents being reported and investigated. To whom are they notified? Are health records monitored? To who are they notified?
(d) Environment	Heating, ventilation, lighting, noise, vibration dust, fumes, radiation, cleaning, plant maintenance.	(c) Safety representatives and workforce consultation	Which trade unions represent the workforce. Who represents non-unionists? Are workforce aware of consultation procedure. Is it effective?
(e) Jobs and work methods	Staff qualifications, training, supervision, working hours, workloads. Has training plan been implemented?	(d) Formal audit and review	Senior management reviews. Health and Safety Executive involvement. Changes to safety policy.

Appendix I

General Legal Notes

David J. Chapman

A number of articles throughout this manual have made reference to legal considerations, including those by Geoffrey D. Lewis, Anthony J. Duggan, Patrick V. Sudbury, Max Hebditch and Francis Cheatham.

At the present time, legal problems seem to be arising in an ever-increasing way. Regarding the museum service, they may be looked at in two ways. First, those matters which should not concern curators and their staff, apart, of course, from preliminary discussions, such as conveyancing and leasing problems; second, the more practical issues such as employment, health and safety at work, and compliance with bye-laws which can, of course, affect curators and their staff at any time.

The first piece of general advice concerning the practical matters referred to above, was stated succinctly by Patrick V. Sudbury in his paper on health and safety at work: so far as possible, use common-sense and experience. Furthermore, there are certain instances where these qualities may not be enough. These may be divided into two categories: first, those instances which affect the public at large; and second, those which principally affect members·of staff.

So far as the first is concerned, without stating the obvious, it is always worth bearing in mind that museums and galleries are public places that occupy, in many cases, prominent buildings where the public has ready access. Furthermore, in one way or another, the public pays for the use of museums either through the rates or through admission charges. Consequently, they expect a high standard of safety and general facilities. If, at any time, possibly through accident, an incident occurs, then obviously this would be publicized and the staff – rightly or wrongly – will most probably come in for a certain amount of public criticism. In consequence, when considering such buildings, possibly a higher

standard is demanded by the public than is expected in a great many buildings which they might enter in their normal lives. Although obvious, every effort should be made to prevent any unfortunate incident occurring in the museum. If anyone, therefore, is at *any* time in *any* doubt as to the standards of safety of the amenities provided they should consult such officials as the County Safety Officer, the Chief Fire Officer or the Planning Officer or the Environmental Health Officer to obtain early advice and guidance.

Turning to those matters which relate particularly to staff, they are, of course, covered under the Health and Safety at Work provisions and the employment laws but in this latter field it is particularly advisable to take great care. Over the past 10 years there has been a considerable amount of legislation relating to employment and these are constantly being amended. It is strongly recommended that anyone in any doubt seeks advice either from a lawyer or from the personnel department. This relates particularly to issues which may affect discipline, dismissal or redundancy matters.

In this respect, two cases in which I have been involved personally in recent years may be cited to highlight the complexities of employment law.

Case 1

A small department which happened to be related to the museum service decided to take on a trainee in certain specialist work. The training period was advertised as being for four years. After an appointment had been made and a trainee had been in post for about 18 months, the position was reviewed. It was then decided that the trainee post was not necessary and in order to save expense should be deleted from the establishment. As the trainee had been in post for less than 2 years no redundancy payment was payable. This fact in itself somewhat clouded the

528

issue and caused some of the difficulties that followed. The matter was discussed fully by the appropriate committee on several occasions and *after* the decision had been made to dismiss her, the trainee was informed. The matter went to the Industrial Tribunal on the basis that she had been unfairly made redundant and although a formal decision was not recorded, the authority was placed in such a position that a monetary settlement had to be made. Because the trainee had been undergoing her apprenticeship and living some distance from her place of employment she had not been kept fully informed of the situation. The authority could be excused for failing to do so, but legally they were under an obligation to consult her, or her union, *before* she was dismissed and this was where the authority was at fault.

Case 2

Another, larger, local authority-based undertaking had for some time employed outside security staff, both male and female. After prolonged efforts to achieve this, central government approval was given to the authority to employ security guards themselves, but this was initially limited to male staff only. An advertisement was placed in the press and although the advertisement in itself did not show discrimination between male and female, only males were interviewed as of course central government approval had been limited to men only. A lady who was employed by a private firm on the authority's site and who was aware of the position, complained to the director that the *Sex Discrimination Act 1975* was being contravened because only men were being interviewed. The director was not too sympathetic at the interview and she alleged that he told her rather brusquely to leave. When, some months later, central government approval had been received and women were interviewed, the lady in question applied for a job. She was not interviewed or given a job. She took the authority to the Industrial Tribunal on the following basis:

(a) That an advert had gone in the press for security guards but women had not been considered.
(b) That when women were considered at a latter date the director had discriminated against her by not giving her a job, seemingly because of what happened at the interview with him.

She was successful at the Industrial Tribunal and was awarded damages on both accounts.

Although both these cases are rather isolated instances, they illustrate clearly the pitfalls which can await the unwary.

As indicated earlier, employment law can be a difficult field. The whole subject has been discussed, of course, in other papers as well. From my own experience, the best general guides are those published by the Local Authorities Conditions of Service Advisory Board (LACSAB). This board has produced several booklets on various topics of employment law. The current editions are coloured green and can be obtained either from the Local Provisional Council or the Secretary of LACSAB at 41 Belgrave Square, London SW1X 8NZ.

The following lists the main, current British legislation relating to the provisions of museums, art galleries and similar institutions.

National Museums

England & Wales
  National Gallery Act 1856
  Imperial War Museum Acts 1920 and 1955
  National Maritime Museum Act 1934
  Education Act 1944
  Wellington Museum Act 1947
  National Gallery & Tate Gallery Act 1954
  Commonwealth Institute Act 1958
  British Museum Act 1963
  Museum of London Acts 1965 & 1973

Scotland
  National Galleries of Scotland Acts 1906 & 1959
  National Museum of Antiquities of Scotland Act 1954

Northern Ireland
  Museums Order (Northern Ireland) 1981

Local Authority Museums

London
  London Government Act 1963
  Public Libraries & Museums Act 1964

England & Wales
  Local Government Act 1972
  Public Libraries & Museums Act 1964

Scotland
  Local Government (Scotland) Act 1973
  Public Libraries (Scotland) Acts 1887 & 1955
  Education (Scotland) Act 1980

Northern Ireland
  Local Government (Boundaries) Act (Northern Ireland) 1971
  Museums (Northern Ireland) Order 1981

Independent Museums

  Literary and Scientific Institutions Act 1854
  National Trust Act 1907
  Charities Act 1960
  Companies Acts 1948–1980

Appendix II

Code of Conduct for Museum Curators

Rules and Guidelines

The following *Code of Conduct for Museum Curators* was accepted by the Museums Association at its Annual Conference in September 1983, and is based on a submission by the Museums Association's *Working Party on Ethics* under the Chairmanship of Dr Antony J. Duggan.

It is the intention of the Museums Association to update the Code regularly. As a statement of rules and guidelines the code is not intended to provide a definitive interpretation of the law.

The words 'he' and 'his' should also be read as 'she' and 'her' throughout the document

Part I: Rules and Guidelines for Professional Conduct

1. Management and Care of Collections

1.1 **Rule.** It is a curator's duty to take all possible steps to ensure that a written acquisition policy is adopted by the governing body of his museum. Thereafter it is his duty to recommend revisions of that policy at regular intervals. He must ensure that the policy, as formally adopted and revised by the governing body, is implemented, and ensure that his colleagues are fully acquainted with it.

Guideline. An appropriate and detailed acquisition policy is recognised as essential to the orderly management of a museum. It implies the acceptance of responsibility for the curation and physical accommodation of collections as defined in the policy for as long as they are held. It is clearly improper to expand an acquisition policy unless the institution is able to provide high standards of curatorial care for the collections which it already has and intends to acquire. Many instances of neglect have resulted from uncontrolled collecting and many museum stores contain unclassified residues that are the legacy of passive collecting.

Where modification of an acquisition policy would lead to expansion, it should be recommended to the governing body only after a full assessment of the immediate and long-term implications.

Some curators hesitate to recommend the adoption of an acquisition policy, believing that it would constrain the exercise of their professional discretion. Others design a policy so loosely phrased and lacking in detail that there is no possible restriction of their freedom to collect. Neither attitude is acceptable.

A curator cannot oblige a governing body to adopt an acquisition policy but he must be seen to do all in his power to encourage it.

Where the museum is involved in fieldwork, it is not unethical for surplus material to be collected in excess of the museum's requirements. Such material should only be collected with due regard to the conservation requirements in the area and with the intention of exchanging with, or donating the excess material to, related institutions.

1.2 **Rule.** It is a curator's primary responsibility to do all in his power fully to protect all items in his care against physical deterioration whether on display, in store, subject to research or conservation procedures or on loan elsewhere.

Safeguards against fire, theft and other hazards must be established in consultation with appropriate specialists and be frequently reviewed. A curator must apprise the governing body of the recommendations made to him and enforce all safeguards subsequently adopted.

Guideline. All items within a curator's custody, including items left as enquiries by the public, should be kept in conditions that are as near as possible to the optimum for their physical preservation.

A curator should be aware of the actions needed for the proper conservation of objects within his care. He has professional responsibility for the integrity of the collections and shares with conserva-

530

tors a corporate responsibility for treatment methods, records and the nature and extent of restorations. Damage to museum objects must be recorded as must the cause and the steps taken to prevent repetition.

The interchange of items between museums depends on the confidence of those lending, their insurers and indemnifiers. It is essential to obey loan conditions explicitly and declare immediately any change of circumstances that makes this impossible.

Careless or deliberate disclosure of information regarding safeguards against theft of details of transportation can put not only the items but persons at risk.

Every effort must be made to comply with accepted national and international standards for safeguarding museum objects under all circumstances, whether on display, in storage or in transit.

1.3 Rule. All items within a curator's care must be recorded, including the circumstances and conditions of acceptance and such other information as is necessary to complement the object, in an appropriate, secure and permanent form capable of easy retrieval.

Guideline. A curator is accountable for all objects in his charge and proper documentation is essential for audit as well as management purposes. It creates the link between the object and its associated data which is fundamental to the value of the object. (Detailed guidance is available from the Museum Documentation Assocation in the form of publications and advice.) Guidance concerning the audit value and security of documentation is available in the Museums Association Information Sheet No 25, *Museum Security*.

1.4 Rule. There must always be a strong presumption against the disposal of specimens to which a museum has assumed formal title. Any form of disposal, whether by donation, exchange, sale or destruction requires the exercise of a high order of curatorial judgement and should be recommended to a curator's governing body only after full expert and legal advice has been taken.

Guideline. Guidance on the disposal of collections is contained in section 5 of the Museums Association's *Code of Practice for Museum Authorities*. A curator is expected to bring that *Code* and any qualifying conditions relating to objects in the collection to the attention of the governing body should a matter of disposal be raised. Subject to legal considerations, the long-term loan of objects to other museums may be a satisfactory way of dealing with items which are under consideration for disposal. The recipient curator must take care that the provisions of such loan or transfer of material between museums are in accordance with the *Code* and conditions. However, cases may exist where the donor clearly agrees to dispose of the object when a better example is acquired.

1.5 Rule. A curator may not delegate curatorial functions to persons who lack the appropriate knowledge and skill.

Guideline. Although volunteer assistants and holders of temporary posts are valuable to museums, a curator must maintain control of essential curatorial functions. In particular, the possession and filling in of accession registers, acquisition, the implementation of disposal decisions of the governing body, conservation and security must be undertaken only by a curator or under his direct supervision.

1.6 Rule. A curator must never discourage legitimate research into the collections under his care by those qualified to perform it.

Guideline. It is improper for a curator to regard the museum collections in his care as his own or to assume exclusive rights of research and publication. From time to time there may be circumstances wherein, for security or other reasons, access to the collections must be restricted. Such circumstances should nevertheless be regarded as exceptional and the curator should take all possible steps to overcome them.

1.7 Rule. All research undertaken in the museum should relate to the institution's collections or objectives.

Guideline. A curator should generate research on the collections in his charge and take all reasonable steps to ensure its completion and publication. His skills and experience, and those of his colleagues, should be made available to the profession and the public whenever they can be of service.

Museum staff, having direct access to the collections for which they are responsible, are best placed to study them in depth, and thus should be prepared to take advantage of the privilege and opportunity to make a positive contribution to knowledge in their chosen discipline.

However, no curator should allow research by museum staff to occupy so much time as to jeopardise proper administration or other curatorial duties.

The unpublished results of a curator's research should be protected from plagiarism during the reasonable term of completion, but in principle the results are public property. The same applies to research notes after any realistic chance of their publication has passed.

1.8 Rule. A curator has a clear duty to consult professional colleagues outside his own institution when his expertise and that of his immediate colleagues are insufficient to ensure the welfare of items in the collection under his care.

Guideline. Few museums are likely to contain all the expertise necessary for complete identification of their collections and for decisions regarding matters such as conservation and security. Relevant advice should be sought from national institutions, Area Museum Councils, specialist curatorial groups or neighbouring museums and universities.

1.9   **Rule.** The practice of maintaining live populations of vertebrate animals in museums has been well-established for many years. The health and well-being of any such creatures must be a foremost ethical consideration. The breeding of certain kinds of animal must be in accordance with regulations laid down by breeding societies.

It is essential that a veterinary surgeon be available for advice and for regular inspection of the animals and their living conditions.

The museum must prepare a safety code for the protection of staff and visitors which has been approved by an expert in the veterinary field, and all museum staff, both curatorial and otherwise, must follow it in detail.

Guideline. The introduction of living animals into the museum environment extends the range of curatorial responsibility very considerably, and the curator must ensure that all the necessary facilities are installed before such a policy is embarked upon. Curators are urged to keep living animals in a part of the museum separate from other displays. Stress can be caused to animals through the behaviour of visitors, and the barriers between one and other must be effective and secure at all times. The governing body of the musum and the staff must realise that if a notifiable disease of man or animals breaks out among the stock, this could lead to the immediate closure of the museum without notice.

A further burden is placed on the staff of museums which keep live animals, because the responsibilities of care are continuous and staff must be on hand to look after them even when the museum is closed.

2.   Management and Care of Environmental Records

2.1   **Rule.** Where the collection and organisation of records concerning the local historic, cultural or natural environment is specified in the policy of his museum, a curator must ensure their accuracy in so far as he is able, and provide reasonable access to such records to any bona fide enquirer.

Guideline. A curator may find himself in difficulty regarding his decisions about public access to local records. The underlying principle must be that the information is publicly available, and decisions must be taken as to the bona fides of the applicant. A curator has a clear responsibility to withhold information if he has reasonable cause to believe that its release would result in the abuse of significant sites or sensi-

tive material (*see Code of Practice for Museum Authorities,* Section 4).

A curator must take care not to become identified with any public pressure group or lobbying faction, by making his information available to all parties in dispute. An enquiry may come from a group whose interests may be opposed to those of his museum, such as a request from a development company regarding the whereabouts of archaeological sites. In this instance the developer has the right to know, at least in general terms, of the possible existence of sites so that he can make commercial judgements regarding his proposals to build (*see* Boylan, P. J., 1982, *Museums Journal,* **82** (1) 21–23.)

However, in making a recommendation on proposals affecting a site, a curator's view may conflict with those of interested parties, including another department of his governing body, or he may be required by the governing body to divulge information which, in the exercise of his professional judgement, he would prefer to withhold. He can only resist as far as is reasonable, and make known to the governing body the possible consequences of its decision.

2.2   **Rule.** Wherever possible, a curator must make clear to the appropriate authorities the impact of any planning proposal or other activity which would result in the loss or destruction of material pertaining to the historic, cultural or natural heritage.

Guideline. The responsibilities imposed by this rule may be impracticable unless the museum's range of staff specialisation is adequate. A curator should make a reasonable attempt to monitor and advise on planning proposals and other activities of the authority.

3.   Accessibility of Data

3.1   **Rule.** It is a curator's responsibility to safeguard the confidentiality of senstive data contained in the records which he maintains. Sensitive data consists of information to which uncontrolled access might put at risk rare, unique or vulnerable material and of personal details and statements the disclosure of which could lead to legal action. A curator may disclose such information only to enquirers whose reputations, interests and intentions he has established beyond reasonable doubt to be consistent with the needs of conservation.

Guideline. Information contained in the data associated with the museum's objects, or in environmental records, or in records of private collectors' or other institutions' material can be of a highly sensitive nature. A rare plant in a herbarium, for instance, with all locality data accessible to the casual enquirer, could direct an irresponsible collector to a vulnerable and important site of botanical significance. Similarly, records of a temporary exhibition where valuable material had been lent to the museum for display, could jeopardise the security of the objects concerned.

A curator should always be aware of the sensitive nature of such information and ensure that effective, and preferably built-in controls exist between data and enquirer. Objects with sensitive associated data could be accompanied by a card directing the enquirer to the curator for locality details. Files containing confidential information on private collections should be securely kept. Information records whether written or on computer can never be regarded as wholly secure. If the museum has computerised records, sensitive information should not be entered into the computer but signposted in the computer entry and maintained in a manual form to which the curator alone has access.

4.   Personal Activities

4.1   Rule. The acquiring, collecting and owning of objects by a curator for his own private collection is not in itself unethical and can enhance professional knowledge and judgement. However, serious dangers are implicit when a curator collects for himself privately objects similar to those which he and others collect for his museum. In particular, no curator should compete with his institution either in the acquisition of objects or in any personal collecting activity. Extreme care must be taken to ensure that no conflict of interest arises.

On his appointment, a curator with a private collection must provide his governing body with a description of it, and a statement of his collecting policy. Thereafter, any agreement between a curator and his governing body on matters concerning his private collection must be scrupulously kept.

Staff members who collect for the musum on expeditions, however funded, shall only engage in private collecting on such expeditions if
(a)   the collecting is incidental and the time involved is reasonable under the circumstances; and
(b)   the pertinent laws and regulations are observed.

Guideline. The problems posed by personal collecting are sensitive and difficult. Attitudes of museum professionals and their institutions vary widely on this topic. Some institutions see personal collecting in the same subject area as that of the museum itself, to be evidence of connoisseurship. Other institutions might require the employee not to collect in any field where a conflict of interest arises. Such personal collecting by curators is an activity not to be encouraged.

It is highly desirable that a curator and his governing body should reach an agreement on this matter which leaves no room for misunderstanding. In any event, the main criteria governing a curator's actions should be: that the curator, who occupies a position of trust, is seen at all times to discharge the responsibilities which that trust implies; and that there is no competition between his collecting aspirations and those of his institution. Where the balance between these two aspirations is determined by the same individual, then, in the interests of complete integrity, the curator is advised to eschew the practice of personal collecting.

If he does collect, a curator should always indicate to his governing body the extent and policy of his personal collecting. For the protection of his professional integrity it would be prudent for him to declare any subsequent personal acquisitions. If requested by his governing body, he is advised to allow it first option to acquire such material at his costs of acquisition. Objects acquired prior to the staff member's employment in a museum and objects acquired by bequest or genuine personal gift may properly be excluded from such arrangements. It is advisable that documentation of private collections be of professional standard, in the interests of scholarship and for the protection of the owner.

What has been said here refers to relations between a curator and his own institution. Curators should, however, be aware that they are part of a wider community concerned with the preservation of part of the national and international heritage. Whereas it is impracticable to draw up a written code concerning private collecting which extends beyond the curator's relations with his own institution, a curator should be mindful that accession to a museum collection offers the best opportunity for an object to become a lasting part of the national and international heritage for the benefit of scholarship and public education and enjoyment.

4.2   Rule. On no account may a curator solicit a personal gift or bequest from a member of the public.

Guideline. A curator would be unwise to accept any gift of a collectable object as a result of contacts made in the course of his duties. If acceptance of a gift is unavoidable he should apply the same criteria as those described in connection with personal collecting.

Behaviour regarding other kinds of gifts or favours is dealt with in various laws and the codes of practice for public employees.

4.3   Rule. Dealing (buying and selling for profit) in material which is collected by a curator's institution is an unacceptable practice.

4.4   Rule. A curator must be fully aware that to undertake identification and authentication outside his duties for personal gain with the intention of establishing the market value of an object, is fraught with danger. If it is to be done, a curator must declare such intention beforehand to his governing body, and be at pains to observe the highest standards of academic objectivity.

Guideline. In some countries professional rules totally prohibit curators from undertaking identification, authentication or valuation for personal advantage or gain. Dealing in any material that is likely to be of interest to other museums is best avoided if a curator is to maintain an unimpeachable image. Curators should be aware that these practices are vulnerable to abuse. Specifically, a curator should never become involved in identification or authentication for a commercial body if he is aware that the objects may later be sold to his museum or to a Friends organisation of the same, or to any museum or fund which he advises in a professional capacity.

In common with other professional persons, a curator could face legal proceedings for compensation if advice is given negligently. Further, due care should be taken to qualify any statement when providing an opinion on, or an identification of, an object submitted by a member of the public. An object identified by a curator and subsequently sold could be the subject of proceedings under the Trade Descriptions Act, and the curator called to give evidence on behalf of the vendor. It is advised that valuations should not be given in any circumstances.

4.5 **Rule.** A curator is not normally qualified to undertake valuations and must therefore be aware of any implications of using his position for direct or indirect personal profit. In the course of his duties, a curator will, from time to time, be required to have regard to the financial value of objects. In such circumstances he must always pay attention to the possible implications arising therefrom.

4.6 **Rule.** When the conditions of a curator's contract of employment so require, he must obtain the express consent of his governing body before undertaking private work from which personal financial gain may accrue, such as publication, authorship, lecturing, consultantship and contributions to the media.

Even when consent has been obtained, such activities should not be allowed to interfere with the discharge of his official duties and responsibilities.

Guideline. Curators who do not work under the constraints implied by this rule are nevertheless advised to inform their governing bodies of such activities.

5. Responsibilities and Services to the Public

5.1 **Rule.** The acquisition of museum items from members of the public must be conducted with scrupulous fairness to the seller or donor.

Guideline. It is difficult to establish what constitutes fair trading with the public. In the case of a professional dealer or auction house, the principles are those of normal fair trading, but in the case of unqualified members of the public it would be improper to take advantage of their unawareness of the nature or the financial value of the objects offered. Where an object is of considerable financial value, the curator should advise the owner to approach an independent valuer before entering into negotiations with the museum. These considerations would not apply where the object is acquired by bequest or legacy. When an object is offered as a gift from a member of the public, a curator should not proceed without apprising the donor of the scale of the proposed donation.

5.2 **Rule.** Although circumstances exist wherein a curator may refuse to identify an object, as a general rule he is expected to do so when, in the course of his employment, he is asked by a member of the public. A curator must not withhold significant facts about the object or deliberately mislead the enquirer. If a curator's knowledge of the object is incomplete, this should also be stated.

Guideline. This rule is subject to the policy of the museum. Not all museums offer an identification service and the procedure to be adopted is at the discretion of the governing body. A curator should be objective about his own capabilities and when in doubt should refer the matter to a more knowledgeable colleague. Alternatively, the enquirer may be referred elsewhere for specialist advice. It is important for a curator to be aware that no stigma attaches to the objective and honest realisation of the limitations of his own expertise, but rather that this is a merit worthy of respect. The professionally unacceptable stance is for a curator to pretend an authority he does not in fact possess.

5.3 **Rule.** Notwithstanding the lack of official government ratification of the UNESCO *Convention on the Means of Prohibiting and Preventing the Illicit Import, Export and Transfer of Ownership of Cultural Property,* 1970, a curator must not identify, accept on loan or acquire by any means, an object which he has good reason to believe was acquired by its current owner in contravention of the terms of that *Convention,* or by any other illegal means.

Guideline. This rule is subject to the policy of the museum's governing body, which should be discouraged from acquiring or dealing in material obtained contrary to the terms of the UNESCO *Convention.* Where the governing body has endorsed the Museums Association's *Code of Practice for Museum Authorities* and abides by the principles of the *Convention,* a curator may seek its agreement to disclose details to the proper authorities of cases where the *Convention* has been contravened. Until the *Convention* has been ratified by the United Kingdom Government, a curator has no right to withhold the object from its owner (*see* Museums Association Information Sheet No 25, *Museums Security*). In any case of this nature, a curator should exercise extreme tact in all communications with the member of public or institution presenting the object, since he or they may well be unaware of having infringed any national law or international convention.

5.4 **Rule.** A curator must not reveal information imparted to him in confidence during the course of his professional duties. (*See also* par 3.1).

Guideline. Professional confidentiality is a mainstay of all walks of life. Information given in confidence to a curator in the course of his professional duties should not be divulged except: (a) when the information is demanded by law; (b) when an overriding duty to society requires that it be revealed; (c) when the information has already been published or publicised by others; (d) after consent has been freely given by the person who provided the information; (e) when disclosure of the information is desirable for the good of the informant.

5.5 **Rule.** Museum objects on public display, with all forms of accompanying information, should present a clear, accurate and balanced exposition and must never deliberately mislead. These principles apply also to books and information published or otherwise disseminated by the museum.

Guideline. The American Assocation of Museums in its *Museum Ethics* states 'Museums may address a wide variety of social, political, artistic or scientific issues. Any can be appropriate, if approached objectively and without prejudice.

'The museum professional must use his best efforts to ensure that exhibits are honest and objective expressions . . . Exhibits must provide with candour and tact an honest and meaningful view of the subject. Sensitive areas such as ethic and social history are of most critical concern.

'The research and preparation of an exhibition will often lead the professional to develop a point of view or interpretive sense of the material. He must clearly understand the point where sound professional judgement ends and personal bias begins. He must be confident that the resultant presentation is the product of objective judgement.'

Museum displays are a medium of mass communication, and a curator therefore has a responsibility to present an exposition which is at all times accurate and, over a period of time, balanced in content. A curator should ensure that his museum displays never provide a propaganda vehicle for his own views or those of any political, social, economic or governing group, lobby or faction. This does not preclude displays which state a point of view which reflects only one side of an issue or argument, so long as this is clearly stated to be the case. Ideally, the other point of view should be given equivalent exposure either in the same or in some future display. These principles apply equally to any other medium of information through which a curator may communicate with the public, such as publications, lectures and interviews.

5.6 **Rule.** Material sold in the museum shop should be of a standard and nature relevant to and compatible with the aims and objectives of the museum service. The curator must ensure that the standard of book-keeping meets the requirements of his governing body's internal auditors or, in the case of shops run as private limited companies, with the requirements of the Companies Acts. He should also ensure that the activities of the shop fall within the provisions of the Trade Descriptions Act. All replicas of museum objects must be marked in a permanent manner.

Guideline. The curator should always bear in mind that the shop is an adjunct to his museum service. Commercial considerations such as revenue and promotion should not be allowed to take precedence over the service function.

No line should be offered for sale without relevant curatorial consultation. It is appropriate to sell original works by local artists, craftsmen and artisans. There should be the strongest presumption against the sale of historic artefacts or natural objects that relate to areas in which the museum is concerned and thus may be confused in the public mind with material in the collections. Additionally, goods offered for sale should not conflict with public awareness of the need to conserve the natural and historic heritage.

Any curator with responsibility for running a shop should seek advice from a body such as the Group for Museum Publishing and Shop Management.

If museums delegate their shop trading activities to a commercial enterprise or set up a trading company to run the shop, it is important that the overall direction and supervision by the curator of all the shop's activities is enshrined and guaranteed in a formal agreement between the museum and the commercial concern.

5.7 **Rule.** The curation of human remains and material of ritual significance is a sensitive undertaking and a curator must be aware of the possible impact of such activity on humanistic feelings or religious beliefs. He must therefore take all reasonable steps to avoid giving rise to public outrage or offence in his management of such material.

5.8 **Rule.** In cases where his professional advice is sought, a curator must ensure that such advice is consistent with museological principles and as far as possible in the best interests of the enquirer.

6.   Relationship with Commercial Organisations

6.1   **Rule.** It will often be a legitimate part of a curator's duty to work with commercial organisations, whether they be vendors, suppliers, auctioneers or dealers, in respect of possible acquisitions, potential sponsors, or the media (press, radio, television). However, in all such dealings, a curator must never accept from such sources a personal gift in whatever form which might subsequently be interpreted, whether rightly or wrongly, as an inducement to trade with one organisation to the exclusion of others. Equally, in the course of his duties, should a curator be asked to advise a member of the public on an appropriate commercial organisation to be approached, the utmost care must be taken to ensure that no personal prejudice could subsequently be inferred from such advice.

Guideline. Paragraph 9882 of the *Civil Service Pay and Conditions of Service Code* has the following to say on the acceptance of gifts and rewards: 'The behaviour of officers as regards the acceptance of gifts, hospitality, etc should be governed by the following general guidance. The conduct of a civil servant should not foster the suspicion of a conflict of interest. Officers should therefore always have in mind the need not to give the impression to any member of the public or organisation with whom they deal, or to their colleagues, that they may be influenced by any gift or consideration to show favour or disfavour to any person or organisation whilst acting in an official capacity. An officer must not, either directly or indirectly, accept any gift, reward or benefit from any member of the public or organisation with whom he has been brought into contact by reason of his official duties. The only exceptions to this rule are as follows:

(a) isolated gifts of a trivial character or inexpensive seasonal gifts (such as calendars);
(b) conventional hospitality, provided it is normal and reasonable in the circumstances. In considering what is normal and reasonable, regard should be had:
  i.   to the degree of narrow personal involvement. There is of course no objection to the acceptance of, for example, an invitation to the annual dinner of a large trade association or similar body with which a department is much in day-to-day contact; or of working lunches (provided the frequency is reasonable) in the course of official visits;

  ii.   to the usual conventions of returning hospitality, at least to some degree. The isolated acceptance of, for example, a meal would not offend the rule whereas acceptance of frequent or regular invitations to lunch or dinner on a wholly one-sided basis even on a small scale might give rise to a breach of the standard required.'

When in doubt, a curator should consult a senior officer or the chairman of his governing body, whose decision should be recorded.

6.2   **Rule.** In the area of industrial sponsorship, there will be an agreed relationship between the museum and the sponsor, and a curator must ensure that the standards and objectives of the museum are not compromised by such a relationship.

Guideline. Commercial sponsorship may of itself involve ethical problems in respect of the products or political connections of the intending sponsor. Although there clearly has to a trade-off between sponsor and museum, so that the former obtains promotional benefits in return for the financial support given to the museum care must be taken that an acceptable balance is struck. Displays, catalogues and promotional material may otherwise appear to be merely the vehicle for the sponsor's own promotion. (*See also* para 5.5)

6.3   **Rule.** When providing information for the media, a curator must ensure that it is factually accurate and, wherever possible, enhances the reputation of the museum (*See also* para 5.5.)

Guideline. Contact with the media will involve the provision of information and personal comment. The media are trained to approach news from a personal standpoint and this needs to be understood both by staff and governing bodies. For example, a new acquisition is more likely to be reported as 'Mr X, Curator says that this is an interesting object', rather than 'the museum has acquired . . .' Since publicity is important, curators must be prepared for it.

The same applies if a personal interview is sought. Ethical problems may arise, if, for example, a curator is invited to take part in a discussion on a topical issue such as conservation of the environment. Again, it is best to seek approval from the governing body, but the curator must realise that personal opinions will not be divorced, by the listening or viewing public, from the position he holds, and that he must, therefore, speak with objectivity.

7.   Relationship with Professional Colleagues

7.1   **Rule.** A curator's relationship with professional colleagues should always be courteous, both in public and private. Differences of professional opinion should not be expressed in a personalised fashion.

Guideline. Particular care must be taken to avoid any dispute coming to the public notice so as to bring discredit on the persons concerned and the profession at large. Where a point of professional principle cannot be resolved by individuals, the arbitration of the President of the Museums Association or his nominee should be sought.

7.2 **Rule.** When acquisition policies and collecting areas overlap, the curators concerned should draft a mutually satisfactory agreement. This should then be referred to the governing bodies concerned for approval, either as a substantive change or as an appendix to their acquisition policies. Where conflict with other museums over the acquisition of an object is likely, curators must take all possible steps to ensure that the issue is amicably resolved.

Guideline. Disputes over acquisition policies and collecting areas should not be allowed to continue indefinitely. Positive steps should be taken by the curators concerned to resolve the conflict with the minimum of publicity. On no account should disputes be carried into the public arena in such a way as to place an owner or landowner in the invidious position of an arbitrator.

7.3 **Rule.** In the course of his duties, a curator forms working relationships with numerous other people, both professional and otherwise, within and outside the museum in which he is employed. A curator is expected to conduct these relationships with courtesy and fair-mindedness and to render his professional services to others efficiently and at a high standard.

Guideline. As in 7.1, this rule is a counsel of perfection. Courtesy should be accorded to relationships with all other professionals and members of the public. Notwithstanding, the curator may properly object to practices which may have a damaging effect on his institution or the profession.

8. Responsibility to Governing Body

8.1 **Rule.** A curator should ensure that all his activities and those of the institution for which he is responsible are consistent with the provisions of the *Code of Practice for Museum Authorities*. He should never act in a way that could reasonably be judged to conflict with the aims and objectives of the *Code of Practice*.

Appendix to the Code:

The Contractual Relationship between a Curator and his Governing Body

1. Preamble

This section of the Code is concerned with the obligations and responsibilities placed upon the curator resulting from the circumstances of his formal employment. Both the law and various kinds of code of practice are discussed, but, because curators are employed by many different types of organisation, the legal and contractual conditions that apply to

staff do vary between national museums, local authority museums, independent charitable trust museums, regimental museums and university museums; and there is also considerable diversity within some of these groups. Where possible the relevance to these different groups, of the provisions under discussion, will be outlined.

No attempt has been made to provide a synthesis of labour-related legislation as it affects the employment of staff in museums. What is offered is an abstract of the law and related codes as they affect the competent discharge of the curator's ethical and professional duties to his employer as required of the curator by statute and contractual code.

Although most of this section of the Code treats the curator as employee, curators in middle and senior management positions take on certain additional duties in the discharge of which they act, in effect, on behalf of the employer.

Curators should familiarise themselves with the particular procedures that operate in their own employing authorities. They should also be aware of the powers and responsibilities that are delegated from employer to employee in respect of disciplinary procedures, complaints, and procedures contained in the job description.

Finally, the term 'curator' is used in the sense of any member of staff employed in a professional capacity in a museum; 'museum' to include museums and art galleries; 'national museum' to denote all museums funded exclusively by Central Government either directly from a Department, or indirectly via a Board of Trustees.

2. Legal Obligations Placed upon a Curator through his Employment

2.1 Legal obligations on a curator acting on behalf of his employer

2.1.1 Curatorial staff in middle and senior management position will normally under the terms of their contracts be responsible, on behalf of the employer, for the appointment, welfare and discipline of museum staff and may also be involved in dismissal proceedings. It is important, therefore, that in fulfilling this role, the curator is aware of the enacted legislation and codes of practice (*see* 3.1) which protect the interests of the employee and employer in all kinds of museum.

2.1.2 The Employment Protection (Consolidation) Act 1978 brought together in a coherent form the employment-related legislation enacted since 1964. Broadly speaking the provisions of the 1978 Act and the Employment Act 1980 are designed to protect the rights and interests of the employee, and also set out the rules and terms of reference of industrial tribunals.

Contracts of Employment

The actual contract between an employer and employee is frequently an oral one: when at interview the successful candidate is offered employment and accepts, this forms a verbal contract which is binding on both parties within the provision of the Act. The contract itself is *not* required by law to be in writing. However the Act does require that the particulars of terms of employment must be confirmed to him within 13 weeks from the date the employee starts his job. There is no prescribed title for the written statement of terms of employment, but it must contain specified particulars including date of appointment to post, details of continuous service, hours of work, scale of remuneration, terms and conditions relating to holiday, sick-leave, pension, notice and disciplinary and grievance procedure and 'job title'. This last should be some form of words describing succinctly 'the nature of the work he is employed to do in accordance with his contract and the capacity and place in which he is employed'. A detailed job description may be provided as a supplement to the written statement of terms of employment.

The written statement need not be fully comprehensive, and may, therefore, refer the employee to another document (*See* 3.2.)

2.1.3 The Health and Safety at Work Act etc, 1974 was intended to supersede, in a new approach, the old legislation which sought to protect the physical welfare of employees at their place of work.

Despite the fact that under the new legislation the burden for safety responsibility is shared between employer and employee, Section 2 of the Act states clearly that 'It shall be the duty of every employer to ensure, so far as is reasonably practicable, the health, safety and welfare at work of all his employees'. It further specifies that the employer must take all reasonable steps to ensure the provision and maintenance of plant and systems that are safe, and to organise the use, handling, storage and transport of substances in such a way that they present no risk to health. The employer is also expected to provide relevant instruction in safety procedures and to draw up a safety policy statement. The Health and Safety Executive is responsible for ensuring that the employer complies with these regulations, and will prosecute for non-compliance.

2.2   Legal obligations on the curator as employee

2.2.1 There are two main areas of legislation that affect curatorial staff in museum employment. The first of these (2.2.2 and 2.2.3) seeks to protect the public interest in the activities of 'public bodies' and consequently proscribes certain activities of those employed therein. This relates to all curators in publicly-funded museums and possibly to charitable trust independent museums. The second area of legislation (2.2.4) relates to the responsibility of all members of curatorial staff for their own and each others physical welfare in all museums.

2.2.2 The Prevention of Corruption Acts 1889–1916. The Public Bodies Corrupt Practices Act, 1889 was enacted to prevent and punish corruption and bribery of and by members, officers, or servants of Corporations, Councils, Boards, Commissions or other Public Bodies. The Act makes it an offence for any person to offer, give, solicit or receive any reward or inducement to influence any kind of transaction in which a public body is involved.

The Prevention of Corruption Act 1906 makes it an offence for an 'agent' corruptly to accept any gift or consideration as an inducement or reward either (i) for doing or refraining from doing anything in his official capacity, or (ii) for showing favour or disfavour to any person in his official capacity.

The Prevention of Corruption Act, 1916 effectively shifted the burden of proof from the Crown to the accused. In effect under the 1916 Act if an 'agent' is proved to have received a gift or reward from a person or organisation holding or seeking to obtain a contract from a public body, he will be deemed to have acted corruptly unless he can prove to the contrary.

Although, without question, all curators employed in national and local authority museums come within the ambit of the Prevention of Corruption Acts 1889–1916, the position of curators in charitable trust and university museums in relation to the Acts is not clear. However, it is worth mentioning that an 'agent' in the 1906 Act is defined as: 'any person serving under the Crown, or under any corporation or any municipal, borough, county or district Council, or any board of guardians'.

Subsequent case law, notably a case that went to appeal in 1977 (*See All England Law Reports,* 1977, DPP v. Holly and DPP v. Manners, House of Lords, 27/1/77, established that under the Prevention of Corruption Acts 1889–1916 the expression 'public body' is not restricted to local authorities but also refers to any body which has public or statutory duties to perform, and which performs those duties for the benefits of the public and not for private profit. This could therefore be taken to include museums run by charitable trusts, although no case law relates specifically to this interpretation.

2.2.3 Local Government Act 1972. Part VII of the 1972 Act deals with staff employed by local authorities. Section 117 makes it obligatory for any officer to notify his employer of any direct or indirect pecuniary interest which he or his spouse may have in a contract negotiated with his employing authority.

The second part of this section makes it an offence for a local government officer to accept any fee or reward (other than his proper remuneration) when acting 'under colour of his office or employment'. In Scotland the relevant Statute is the Local Government (Scotland) Act 1973.

2.2.4 Health and Safety at Work Act etc, 1974 places responsibility for safety firmly with the employee (as well as employer *see* 2.1.3) in sections 7, 8 and 20 of the Act. In particular section 7 states that: 'It shall be the duty of every employee while at work (a) to take reasonable care for the health and safety of himself and other persons who may be affected by his acts or omissions at work; and (b) as regards any duty or requirement imposed on his employer or any other person by or under any of the relevant statutory provisions, to co-operate with him so far as is necessary to enable that duty or requirement to be complied with'.

Section 8 states, in addition, that: 'No person shall intentionally or recklessly interfere with or misuse anything provided in the interests of health, safety or welfare in pursuance of any of the relevant statutory provisions'.

These provisions apply to all curatorial staff in all museums, without exception. The employee's individual responsibility under the Act runs parallel with the employer's responsibility to supervise the implementation of the provision of its safety policy. Enforcement is the responsibility of the Health and Safety Executive which can prosecute for non-compliance. A curator should be aware of the extent and limit of his liability as delegated by the employer under his contract of employment.

3. Codes of Practice Related to Employment

3.1 Codes of Practice drawn up by statutory bodies

The following bodies have been charged with statutory responsibility for producing and maintaining codes of practice under the relevant legislation: Advisory, Conciliation and Arbitration Service (industrial relations practice); Equal Opportunities Commission; Commission for Racial Equality; and the Health and Safety Commission.

Although these bodies exist under statute, their powers are limited. Their responsibility is to amplify and supplement the provisions of the relevant legislation by drafting codes of practice in each of their designated areas of responsibility. The Secretary of State must approve a final draft code they produce before laying it before both Houses of Parliament for final approval. Once approved, the Code of Practice, though supplementary to the relevant legislation does not have the full force of law behind it. So,

failure to observe any provision of the Code will not render the curator liable to proceedings. However he should be aware that in any proceedings before an industrial tribunal the Code is admissible in evidence and any provision of it which is relevant to the proceedings must be taken into account by the Tribunal when determining the case.

The provisions of these codes of practice would be generally applicable to all grades of curatorial staff in all kinds of museum.

3.2 Conditions of Service Codes of Practice drawn up between employer and employee

3.2.1 The two largest employers of museum staff, the Civil Service and Local Authorities, have drawn up exhaustive codes of practice in full consultation with union representation of the employees in each of these two public sectors. Some of the independent charitable trust museums have developed close links with their local authority, and their staff have, in consequence, been contracted under the local authorities' scheme of conditions of service.

The two codes of practice referred hereto provide an exhaustive exposition of all the details of terms and conditions together with aspects of conduct. They form part of the contractual conditions of service since they are referred to in the written statement (*See* 2.1.2). However, it should be remembered that paragraph 61 of the Industrial Relations Code of Practice, drafted by ACAS (*See* 3.1) reads:

'Where (the written statement) refers the employee to another document, the Act requires that he must have reasonable opportunities of reading that document in the course of his employment or that it must be made reasonably accessible to him in some other way. He should be told clearly, in the written statement, where he can see the document.'

This arrangement would also permit the museum employer to refer the curatorial employee to a museums' professional code of conduct (or sections thereof) which would, *per se*, become part of the contractual conditions of service, providing it is not a breach of any of the provisions of the Act. It would, however, be good industrial relations practice to consult the relevant union representatives of the employee to obtain their agreement to the implementation of such a move.

3.2.2 **Civil Service Pay and Conditions of Service Code (formerly 'Estacode').** Civil Servants working directly under the Crown do not have contracts of employment since they would be unable to institute legal proceedings against their employer, the Crown. However, the *Civil Service Pay and Conditions of Service Code* sets out the conditions under which civil servants are employed. Curators working in national museums funded and administered directly by a central government department, for example, staff in the Victoria and Albert and Science Museums (under the DES), and Royal Scottish Museum (Scottish Education Department) conform to this Civil Service rule. Other national museums such as the British Museum, National Portrait Gallery, Ulster Museum, and the National Museum of Antiquities of Scotland are each run 'at arm's length' from central government (which funds them) by a board of trustees, who are the employers. Because of this, curatorial staff in the latter category do have contracts of employment which require them to abide by the *Civil Service Pay and Conditions of Service Code.*

In that document, considerable emphasis is placed upon the special fiduciary nature of the civil servants' role with respect to the public. Paragraph 9870 outlines the general principles which should govern the civil servants' conduct both at work and in private:

' a civil servant must not subordinate his duty to his private interests'

a civil servants' private activities . . . must not be as might bring discredit on the service'

'the civil servant must not only be honest in fact, but also he must not lay himself open to suspicion of dishonesty'.

With reference to accepting gifts, rewards and hospitality, the Code states in paragraph 9882:
'The conduct of a civil servant should not foster the suspicion of a conflict of interest. Officers should therefore always have in mind the need not to give the impression to any member of the public or organisation with whom they deal, or to their colleagues, that they may be influenced, or have in fact been influenced, by any gift or consideration to show favour or disfavour to any person or organisation whilst acting in an official capacity. An officer must not, either directly or indirectly, accept any gift, reward or benefit from any member of the public or organisation with whom he has been brought into contact by reason of his official duties.'

This is followed by certain exceptions such as the acceptance of small, isolated gifts, and reasonable hospitality. Paragraph 9883 advises a civil servant who has doubts about the propriety of accepting a gift (by him or a member of his family) to consult an appropriate officer. In this section reference is also made to the Prevention of Corruption Acts 1906 and 1916.

3.2.3 Scheme of Conditions of Service of the National Joint Council for Local Authorities' Administrative, Professional, Technical and Clerical Services (known as the 'Purple Book', except for Scotland where the 'Blue Book' applies).
Curatorial staff employed in museums funded and administered by metropolitan, county or district councils, together with some of the indepen-

dent museums (*See* 3.2.1) are employed under contractual conditions of service laid down in the 'Purple Book' or 'Blue Book' relating to regional or district councils or island authorities in Scotland.

Purple Book Section 7, paragraphs 70–74 and Blue Book Part VII, section 70, paragraphs (a)–(d) relate specifically to official conduct:
Purple Book para 70(a)

'The public is entitled to demand of a local government officer conduct of the highest standard and public confidence in his integrity would be shaken were the least suspicion, however ill-founded, to arise that he could in any way be influenced by improper motives.'
Purple Book para 70(b)

'. . . he should not subordinate his duty to his private interests or put himself in a position where his duty and his private interests conflict.'
Purple Book para 71

This paragraph makes it clear that above the grade of AP5, the curator is, in effect, the servant of his employing authority 24 hours per day and that 'he shall not engage in any other business or take up any other additional appointment without the express consent of the Council.'
Purple Book para 72
Blue Book para (a)

This paragraph forbids an officer from divulging to the public 'the proceedings of any committee meeting, etc, nor the contents of any document relating to the authority unless required by law or expressly authorised to do so.'
Purple Book para 70(c)
Blue Book para (b)

This paragraph ensures that an officer can remain at arm's length from the political activities of his employing authority. 'An officer should never be called upon to advise any political group of the authority either as to the work of the group or as to the work of the authority, neither shall the officer be required to attend any meeting of any political group.'
Purple Book para 73
Blue Book para (c)

This paragraph requires an officer to declare a pecuniary interest he may have in a contract involving the authority (*See* 2.2.3).
Purple Book para 74
Blue Book para (d)

Paragraph 74 forbids the employer or employee to supply a person outside the service of the authority with information concerning an officer's private affairs, except with his consent.

Index